A TEXTBOOK OF BUSINESS AND INDUSTRIAL LAWS

(For the students of B.Com. and B.Com.(Hons) courses of University of Delhi and other equivalent examinations of all other Indian Universities)

P.P.S. GOGNA

S. CHAND & COMPANY LTD.

(An ISO 9001 : 2000 Company)

RAM NAGAR, NEW DELHI - 110 055

S. CHAND & COMPANY LTD.

(An ISO 9001 : 2000 Company)

Head Office: 7361, RAM NAGAR, NEW DELHI - 110 055

Phone: 23672080-81-82, 9899107446, 9911310888

Fax: 91-11-23677446

Shop at: **schandgroup.com**; e-mail: **info@schandgroup.com**

Branches :

AHMEDABAD : 1st Floor, Heritage, Near Gujarat Vidhyapeeth, Ashram Road, **Ahmedabad** - 380 014, Ph: 27541965, 27542369, ahmedabad@schandgroup.com

BANGALORE : No. 6, Ahuja Chambers, 1st Cross, Kumara Krupa Road, **Bangalore** - 560 001, Ph: 22268048, 22354008, bangalore@schandgroup.com

BHOPAL : 238-A, M.P. Nagar, Zone 1, **Bhopal** - 462 011, Ph: 4274723. bhopal@schandgroup.com

CHANDIGARH : S.C.O. 2419-20, First Floor, Sector - 22-C (Near Aroma Hotel), **Chandigarh** -160 022, Ph: 2725443, 2725446, chandigarh@schandgroup.com

CHENNAI : 152, Anna Salai, **Chennai** - 600 002, Ph: 28460026, 28460027, chennai@schandgroup.com

COIMBATORE : Plot No. 5, Rajalakshmi Nagar, Peelamedu, **Coimbatore** -641 004, (M) 09444228242, coimbatore@schandgroup.com

CUTTACK : 1st Floor, Bhartia Tower, Badambadi, **Cuttack** - 753 009, Ph: 2332580; 2332581, cuttack@schandgroup.com

DEHRADUN : 1st Floor, 20, New Road, Near Dwarka Store, **Dehradun** - 248 001, Ph: 2711101, 2710861, dehradun@schandgroup.com

GUWAHATI : Pan Bazar, **Guwahati** - 781 001, Ph: 2738811, 2735640 guwahati@schandgroup.com

HYDERABAD : Padma Plaza, H.No. 3-4-630, Opp. Ratna College, Narayanaguda, **Hyderabad** - 500 029, Ph: 24651135, 24744815, hyderabad@schandgroup.com

JAIPUR : A-14, Janta Store Shopping Complex, University Marg, Bapu Nagar, **Jaipur** - 302 015, Ph: 2719126, jaipur@schandgroup.com

JALANDHAR : Mai Hiran Gate, **Jalandhar** - 144 008, Ph: 2401630, 5000630, jalandhar@schandgroup.com

JAMMU : 67/B, B-Block, Gandhi Nagar, **Jammu** - 180 004, (M) 09878651464

KOCHI : Kachapilly Square, Mullassery Canal Road, Ernakulam, **Kochi** - 682 011, Ph: 2378207, cochin@schandgroup.com

KOLKATA : 285/J, Bipin Bihari Ganguli Street, **Kolkata** - 700 012, Ph: 22367459, 22373914, kolkata@schandgroup.com

LUCKNOW : Mahabeer Market, 25 Gwynne Road, Aminabad, **Lucknow** - 226 018, Ph: 2626801, 2284815, lucknow@schandgroup.com

MUMBAI : Blackie House, 103/5, Walchand Hirachand Marg, Opp. G.P.O., **Mumbai** - 400 001, Ph: 22690881, 22610885, mumbai@schandgroup.com

NAGPUR : Karnal Bag, Model Mill Chowk, Umrer Road, **Nagpur** - 440 032, Ph: 2723901, 2777666 nagpur@schandgroup.com

PATNA : 104, Citicentre Ashok, Govind Mitra Road, **Patna** - 800 004, Ph: 2300489, 2302100, patna@schandgroup.com

PUNE : 291/1, Ganesh Gayatri Complex, 1st Floor, Somwarpeth, Near Jain Mandir, **Pune** - 411 011, Ph: 64017298, pune@schandgroup.com

RAIPUR : Kailash Residency, Plot No. 4B, Bottle House Road, Shankar Nagar, **Raipur** - 492 007, Ph: 09981200834, raipur@schandgroup.com

RANCHI : Flat No. 104, Sri Draupadi Smriti Apartments, East of Jaipal Singh Stadium, Neel Ratan Street, Upper Bazar, **Ranchi** - 834 001, Ph: 2208761, ranchi@schandgroup.com

VISAKHAPATNAM : Plot No. 7, 1st Floor, Allipuram Extension, Opp. Radhakrishna Towers, Seethammadhara North Extn., **Visakhapatnam** - 530 013, (M) 09347580841, visakhapatnam@schandgroup.com

First Edition 2007
Revised Edition 2010

ISBN: 81-219-2830-3 **Code :** 07A 431

PRINTED IN INDIA

By Rajendra Ravindra Printers Pvt. Ltd., 7361, Ram Nagar, New Delhi -110 055 and published by S. Chand & Company Ltd., 7361, Ram Nagar, New Delhi -110 055.

PREFACE TO THE SECOND EDITION

I feel happy in presenting the second revised edition of **A Textbook of Business and Industrial Laws**. The warm welcome which the previous edition of this book has earned, has been a matter of great satisfaction for me. The general response to the previous edition was very encouraging and I personally feel that my work has been amply rewarded.

I express my deep sense of gratitude to the large number of readers who have used this book and in particular to those who have sent helpful suggestions from time to time. Keeping in view the suggestions of my professional colleagues and the requirements of the students, IMPORTANT LEGAL PROVISIONS discussed in each chapter and the PRACTICAL PROBLEMS have been added at the end of each chapter to make the book complete and useful for the students. All these additions included in the book make it a complete, comprehensive and unique book for the students preparing for the Business & Industrial Law Paper of B.Com. Examination.

The payment of Bonus Act, 1965 has been recently amended by the Payment of Bonus (Amendment) Act, 2007 (45 of 2007). The changes brought in by this Amendment Act of 2007, have been duly incorporated at appropriate place in the Book. Section 2(13) defining the expression 'employee' has been amended and the ceiling of monthly salary of an employee for eligibility for bonus has been enhanced from Rs. 3,500/- p.m. to Rs. 10,000/- p.m. and by omitting clause VI of Section 32, the Act has been made applicable to employees employed through contractors on building operations. It is earnestly hoped that the revised edition of the book will continue to earn the appreciation of the teachers and students alike.

Although every care has been taken to check mistakes and misprints, yet it is difficult to claim perfection. Any errors, omissions and suggestions, for the improvement of the book, brought to my notice, will be thankfully acknowledged and incorporated in the next edition.

P.P.S. Gogna
M : 9810556778

PREFACE TO THE FIRST EDITION

I feel happy in presenting the book entitled, **A Textbook of Business and Industrial Laws** to the students of B.Com. & B.Com (Hons.) courses of Delhi University. The book has been written keeping in view the new syllabus prescribed for the courses. The object of the book is to present the subject matter in the most concise, to the point, lucid and illustrative manner.

While writing this book, an attempt has been made to present, as far as possible, within the compass of this volume, the fundamental principles of Business and Industrial Laws. To make the book more useful, it has been written in an easy and illustrative style. All along the approach to the subject matter, every care has been taken to arrange the matter in a systematic way with full detail and examples.

All the judicial and statutory developments taken place so far have been taken into account while preparing the present volume. The two important Acts namely, the Negotiable Instruments Act, 1881, and the Payment of Wages Act, 1936 have been recently amended by the Negotiable Instruments (Amendments and Miscellaneous) Provisions Act, 2002, and the Payment of Wages (Amendment) Act, 2005, respectively. The changes brought in by these Amending Acts have been duly incorporated at appropriate places. In the Negotiable Instruments Act, among other changes, the punishment of imprisonment for an offence of dishonour of cheques due to insufficient funds has been enhanced from one year to two years. In the Payment of Wages Act, the wage ceiling for the applicability of the Act has been enhanced from Rs. 1,600 per month to Rs. 6,500 per month. It is earnestly hoped that the book will meet the requirements of the students and earn the appreciation of the teachers and students alike.

Although every care has been taken to check mistakes and misprints, yet it is difficult to claim perfection. Any error, omissions and suggestions, for the improvement of this volume brought to my notice, will thankfully be acknowledged and incorporated in the next edition.

P.P.S. Gogna

SYLLABUS
UNIVERSITY OF DELHI
B.COM - PART I
PAPER - III
BUSINESS AND INDUSTRIAL LAWS

Duration : 3 hrs | Max. Marks : 75
Lectures : 75

1. THE INDIAN CONTRACT ACT, 1872

Contract - Meaning and Essentials, Kinds, Offer and Acceptance, Contractual Capacity, Free Consent, Consideration, Void Agreements, Quasi Contracts, Modes of Discharge of Contract and Remedies for Breach of Contract, Contract of indemnity and Guarantee, Law of Agency; its creation, Personal Liability of Agent, Sub Agent and Substituted Agent, Termination of Agency. 25 Lectures

2. THE SALE OF GOODS ACT, 1930

Meaning of Contract of Sale, Difference Between Sale and Agreement to Sell, Conditions and Warranties, transfer of Property in Goods, Unpaid Seller and his Rights. 10 Lectures

3. THE INDIAN PARTNERSHIP ACT, 1932

Meaning and test of Partnership; Implied Authority of a Partner, Position of a Minor in Partnership, Consequences of Non-registration of a Partnership, Firm Expansion, Death and Insolvency of a Partner, Dissolution of a firm by Court, Public Notice. 9 Lectures.

4. THE NEGOTIABLE INSTRUMENTS ACT, 1881

Meaning and Characteristics of a Promissory Note, Bill of Exchange and Cheque, Holder and Holder in Due Course, Negotiation and Assignment; Crossing of Cheque : Kinds and Effects, Bouncing of Cheques (Section 138). 6 Lectures

5. THE PAYMENT OF WAGES ACT, 1936

Definitions : Employed Person, Employer, Factory, Industrial or Other Establishment, Wages, Responsibility for Payment of Wages (Section 3), Fixation of Wage Period (Section 4), Time of Payment of Wages (Section 5), Moder of Payment of Wages (Section 6), Deductions from Wages (Sections 7 to 13) 10 Lectures

6. THE PAYMENT OF BONUS ACT, 1965

Definitions : Allocable Surplus, Available Surplus, Accounting Year, appropriate Government, Employer, Employee, Salary or Wages, Eligibility for Bonus, Disqualification for Bonus, Payment of Minimum and Maximum Bonus, Calculation of Number of Working Days, Adjustment of Customary or Interim Bonus Against Bonus Payable, Deduction of Certain Amounts from Bonus Payable under the Act, Time Limit for Payment of Bonus, Recovery of Bonus from Employer. 10 Lectures

7. THE PAYMENT OF GRATUITY ACT, 1972

Applicability of the Act, Employee, Employer, Continuous Service, Payment of Gratuity, Forfeiture of Gratuity, Duty to Pay Gratuity, Recovery of Gratuity, Penalities.

5 Lectures.

Suggested Reading : M.C. Shukla, Mercantile Laws, S. Chand & Company Ltd., Delhi

SYLLABUS

UNIVERSITY OF DELHI
B.Com (Hons.) - Part I
PAPER - V

BUSINESS LAW

Duration : 3 hrs | Max. Marks : 75
Lectures : 75

Objective : The objective of the course is to impart basic knowledge of the important business laws alongwith relevant case law.

Course Contents :

1. The Indian Contract Act, 1872 — **35 Lectures**

(a) Contract : Meaning, Characteristics and Kinds — 3 Lectures

(b) Essentials of a Valid Contract : Offer and Acceptance, Consideration, Contractual Capacity, Free Consent, Legality of Objects — 7 Lectures

(c) Void Agreements — 2 Lectures

(d) Discharge of contract : Modes of Discharge including Breach and its Remedies — 4 Lectures

(e) Contingent Contracts — 2 Lectures

(f) Quasi Contracts — 2 Lectures

(g) Contract of Indemnity and Guarantee — 5 Lectures

(h) Contract of Bailment — 5 Lectures

(i) Contract of Agency — 5 Lectures

2. The Sale of Goods Act, 1930 — **10 Lectures**

(a) Contract of Sale : Meaning and Difference Between Sale and Agreement to Sell — 2 Lectures

(b) Conditions and Warranties — 2 Lectures

(c) Transfer of Ownership in goods including Sale by Non-Owners — 2 Lectures

(d) Performance of Contract of Sale — 2 Lectures

(e) Unpaid Seller : Meaning and Rights of an Unpaid Seller against the Goods and the Buyer — 2 Lectures

3. The Negotiable Instruments Act, 1881 — **10 Lectures**

Kinds and Characteristics of Negotiable Instruments, Holders and Holder-in-due Course, Privileges of Holders-in Due course, Negotiation and Endorsement, Crossing of Cheques, Types of Crossing, Bouncing of Cheques.

4. The Information Technology Act, 2000	**20 Lectures**
(a) Definitions	3 Lectures
(b) Digital Signature	1 Lecture
(c) Electronic Governance	2 Lectures
(d) Attribution, Acknowledgement and Dispatch of Electronic Records	2 Lectures
(e) Regulation of Certifying Authorities	3 Lectures
(f) Digital Signature Certificates	2 Lectures
(g) Duties of Subscribers	1 Lecture
(h) Penalties and Adjudication	1 Lecture
(i) Cyber Appellate Tribunal	3 Lectures
(j) Offences	2 Lectures

4. The Information Technology Act, 2000	**20 Lectures**
(a) Definitions	3 Lectures
(b) Digital Signature	1 Lecture
(c) Electronic Governance	2 Lectures
(d) Attribution, Acknowledgement and Dispatch of Electronic Records	2 Lectures
(e) Regulation of Certifying Authorities	4 Lectures
(f) Digital Signature Certificates	2 Lectures
(g) Duties of Subscribers	1 Lecture
(h) Penalties and Adjudication	1 Lecture
(i) Cyber Appellate Tribunal	2 Lectures
(j) Offences	2 Lectures

CONTENTS

Part IV : THE NEGOTIABLE INSTRUMENTS ACT, 1881

Part V : THE PAYMENT OF BONUS ACT, 1965

Part VI : THE PAYMENT OF WAGES ACT, 1936

Part VII : THE PAYMENT OF GRATUITY ACT, 1972

Part VIII : THE INFORMATION TECHNOLOGY ACT, 2000

The Indian Contract Act, 1872

- Nature and Kinds of Contracts
- Offer and Acceptance
- Consideration
- Capacity of Contract
- Free Consent
- Legality of Object and Consideration
- Void Agreements
- Illegal Agreements
- Contingent Contracts
- Quasi Contracts
- Performance of Contracts
- Discharge of Contracts
- Damages for Breach of Contract
- Indemnity and Guarantee
- Bailment and Pledge
- Natue and Kinds of Agency
- Relations of Principal with his Agent
- Relation of Principal with Third Parties
- Termination of Agency

1
CHAPTER

NATURE AND KINDS OF CONTRACTS

1. Introduction
2. Law of Contract creates jus in personam.
3. Definition of Contract.
4. Essential Elements of a Valid Contract.
5. Classification of Contracts.
6. Classification of Contracts According to their Enforceability or Legal Validity.
7. Classification of Contracts According to their Formation.
8. Classification of Contracts According to their Performance.

1.1. INTRODUCTION

The Law of Contract deals with the law relating to the general principles of contract. It is the most important part of Mercantile Law. It affects every person in one way or the other, as all of us enter into some kind of contract everyday. When a person lends a book to a friend, takes a seat in a bus, goes to a cinema to see a movie, deposits his luggage in a railway cloak room etc., he enters into a contract, though he may not be aware of this fact. Such contracts create certain legal rights and obligations. Without the Law of Contract, it would have been difficult to determine and enforce the rights and obligations of the persons. For business community, the Law of Contract is of great significance as all the business transactions are based on the contracts. The Law of Contract determines the circumstances under which a promise or an agreement shall be legally binding on the person making it. It also provides the remedies which are available in a Court of Law against a person who fails to fulfil his obligations.

In India, the law relating to contracts is contained in the INDIAN CONTRACT ACT, 1872. The Act came into force on the first day of September 1872, and it applies to the whole of India except the State of Jammu and Kashmir.[1] The Act does not deal with all the branches of law of contracts. The contracts relating to Partnership, Sale of Goods and Negotiable Instruments are outside the scope of the Indian Contract Act. There are separate Acts which deal with these contracts, *i.e.* The Indian Partnership Act, Sale of Goods Act and Negotiable Instruments Act. The Indian Contract Act consists of the following two parts:

1. General principles of the Law of Contract.
2. Special kinds of contracts.

The general principles of the Law of Contract are contained in Sections 1 to 75 of the Indian Contract Act. These principles apply to all kinds of contracts irrespective of their

1. Under Article 370 of the Indian Constitution, Jammu and Kashmir enjoys a special status.

nature. Special contracts are contained in Sections 124 to 238 of the Indian Contract Act. These special contracts are Indemnity, Guarantee, Bailment, Pledge and Agency.

It may be noted that the Indian Contract Act does not affect any usage or customs of a trade. However, both the parties, to a contract, may agree otherwise *i.e.*, they may agree that certain trade custom shall not apply in their contract.

1.2. LAW OF CONTRACT CREATES JUS IN PERSONAM

The term *jus in personam* means a right against or in respect of a specific person. Under the Law of Contract, the right is available only against particular persons.

Example 1.1. *A* owes Rs. 50,000 to *B*. Here *B* has a right to recover this amount from *A*. This right of *B* to recover the amount from *A* is a *jus in personam*.

Thus, law of contract creates *jus in personam and not jus in rem*. A *jus in rem* means a right against or in respect of a thing.

Example 1.2. *A* is the owner of house. Here, *A* had a right to have quiet possession of the house against every member of the society. Likewise, every member of the society is under an obligation not to disturb *A*'s possession. This right of *A* is a *jus in rem*.

1.3. DEFINITION OF CONTRACT

A contract may be defined as an agreement between two or more persons which can be enfored in a court of law. Some of the eminent jurists have defined the contract as under:

1. "Every agreement and promise enforceable at law ia a contract." —**Pollock**
2. "A contract is an agreement between two or more person which is intended to be enforceable at law and is constituted by the acceptance by one party of an offer made to him by the other party to do or abstain from doing some act." — **Halsbury**
3. "A contract is an agreement creating and defining obligations between the parties" — **Salmond**

The term contract is defined in Section 2(h) of the Indian Contract Act, which reads as under:

"An agreement enforceable by law is a contracts."

The analysis of this definition shows that a contract must have the following two elements:

1. An agreement, and 2. The agreement must be enforceable by law.

An agreement is enforceable if it gives rise to legal obligations (*i.e.,* if the parties are bound to do or not to do something). Thus, a contract is a combination of an agreement and its enforceability. In other words:

Contract = An agreement + Enforceability.

The term agreement is defined in Section 2(e) of the Indian Contract Act, which reads as under:

"Every promise and every set of promises forming the consideration for each other, is an agreement."

The term promise is defined in Section 2(b) of the Indian Contract Act, which reads as under:

"A proposal when accepted, becomes a promise."

We can easily conclude from both the above two mentioned provisions that an agreement is an accepted proposal (offer). Thus, every agreement consists of an offer from one party and its acceptance by the other. In other words:

Agreement = Offer + Acceptance.

It is important to note that every agreement is not a contract. When an agreement creates some legal obligations and is enforceable by law, it is regarded as a contract. The conditions of enforceability are laid down in Section 10 of the Indian Contract Act, which reads as under:

"All agreements are contracts if they are made by the free consent of parties competent to contract, for a lawful consideration and with a lawful object and are not hereby expressly declared to be void."

The analysis of this definition shows that an agreement becomes a contract only if the following conditions are satisfied:

1. The agreement must be made by the free consent of the parties.
2. The agreement must be made by the parties who are competent to contract.
3. The agreement must be made for a lawful consideration and with a lawful object.
4. The agreement must not be expressly declared to be void.

All these conditions will be discussed in detail in separate chapters.

Note. In our discussion on the Law of contracts from chapters 1 to 19, unless otherwise stated, the Sections mentioned are those of the Indian Contract Act, 1872.

1.4. ESSENTIAL ELEMENTS OF A VALID CONTRACT

In order to become a contract, an agreement must have the following essential elements:

1. *There must be an offer and its acceptance*
2. *There must be mutual consent of the parties*
3. *There must be legal obligations*
4. *There must be free consent of the parties*
5. *The parties must be competent to contract*
6. *There must be lawful consideration*
7. *There must be lawful object*
8. *The agreement must not be declared to be void*
9. *The agreement must be certain*
10. *The performance must not be impossible*

1. ***There must be an offer and its acceptance:*** In an agreement there must be at least two parties, one of them making the offer and the other accepting it. In other words, there must be an offer by one party and its acceptance by the other. The offer when accepted becomes agreement.

2. ***There must be mutual consent of the parties:*** The parties to an agreement must have the mutual consent *i.e.* they must agree upon the same thing and in the same sense. This means that there must be *consensus ad idem* (*i.e.*, meeting of minds).

Example 1.3. A owned two horses, one black and the other white. He offered to sell one horse to *B*. While making the offer, *A* had the black horse in mind. But *B* accepted the offer, thinking that it was made for white horse. In this case, there is no *consensus ad idem*, as the parties did not agree upon the same thing in the same sense. Thus, no agreement came into existence.

3. ***There must be legal obligations:*** An agreement must create legal obligations (*i.e.*, an obligation which is enforceable by law). An obligation is the legal duty to do or abstain from doing a definite act or acts. Moreover, the parties must have the intention to create legal obligations. If the parties do not intend to create legal obligations, there is no contract between them. In commercial or business transactions, the usual presumption is that the parties intended to create legal obligations. It may be noted that an agreement which gives rise to a moral or social obligation is not a contract.

Example 1.4. *A* invited *B* to a dinner. *B* accepted the invitation. It is a social agreement. If *A* fails to serve dinner to *B*, he (*B*) cannot go to Courts of Law for enforcing the agreement. Similarly, if *B* fails to attend the dinner, *A* cannot go to Courts of Law for enforcing the agreement.

4. *There must be free consent of the parties:* The contract must have been made with free consent of the parties. It may be noted that the consent is not free, when it is obtained by coercion, undue influence, fraud, misrepresentation of facts etc. If the consent of the parties is not free, then no valid contract comes into existence.

Example 1.5. *A* threatened to shoot *B*'s son unless *B* signs a promissory note for Rs. 20,000 in favour of *A*. *B* signed the promissory note under the threat. In this case, *B*'s consent is not free as it is obtained under pressure, therefore the promissory note is not valid.

Example 1.6. *A*, by misrepresentation, leads, *B* erroneously to believe that 5 tonnes of indigo were made annually at *A*'s factory. Upon this representation, *B* bought the factory. The actual production was found to be only 2 tonnes. In this case, *B*'s consent is not free as it is obtained by misrepresentation.

5. *The parties must be competent to contract:* The parties to an agreement must be competent to contract. In other words, they must be capable of entering into a contract. It may be noted that minors, or persons of unsound mind are not competent to contract. If the parties are not competent to contract then no valid contract comes into existence.

Example 1.7. *A*, a minor, borrowed Rs. 500 from *B* and agreed to repay it within two months. This is not a valid contract as *A* is not competent to contract.

6. *There must be lawful consideration:* The agreement must be supported by a lawful consideration. The lawful consideration is that which is not fraudulent, forbidden by law, immoral or opposed to public policy etc. If the consideration is not lawful, then no valid contract comes into existence.

Example 1.8 *A* promised to obtain an employment for *B* in a government department, and *B* promised to pay Rs. 10,000 to *A*. In this case, the agreement is not valid as the consideration for it is unlawful.

7. *There must be lawful object:* The object of the agreement must be lawful. It may be noted that a lawful object is that which is neither fraudulent, forbidden by law, immoral nor opposed to any public policy etc. If the object is not lawful, then no valid contract comes into existence.

Example 1.9 *A*, *B* and *C* entered into an agreement for the division of gain, among them, which is to be acquired by them by fraud. In this case, the agreement is not valid as its object is unlawful.

8. *The agreement must not be declared to be void:* The agreements must not have been expressly declared to be void by any law in force in the country. If certain agreements are expressly declared to be void by the law of the country, then such agreements if entered into, shall not be enforceable by Courts of Law.

Example 1.10. *A* agreed to pay Rs. 500 to *B* if he (*B*) does not marry throughout his life. *B* promised not to marry at all. In this case the agreement is not valid because agreements in restraint of marriage are expressly declared to be void (*i.e.*, not enforceable by law).

9. *The agreement must be certain:* The meaning of the agreement must be certain. In other words, an agreement whose meaning is not certain, is not valid.

Example 1.11 *A* agreed to sell to *B* "a hundred tonnes of oil". Here it is not clear what kind of oil is intended to be sold. In this case, the agreement is not valid as it is not certain.

Example 1.12. *A* agreed to sell his white horse for Rs. 2,500 or Rs. 3,000 to *B*. There is nothing to show which of the two prices was to be given. In this case the agreement is not valid as it is uncertain.

10. *The performance must not be impossible:* The performance of an agreement must be possible. An agreement to do an impossible act is not valid.

Example 1.13. *A* agreed with *B* to discover treasure by magic. In consideration, *B* agreed to pay Rs. 500 to *A*. In this case, the performance of the agreement is impossible, therefore it is not a valid agreement.

Note: All the above points will be discussed in detail in separate chapters.

1.5. CLASSIFICATION OF CONTRACTS

All the contracts may be broadly classified into following three main categories:

1. According to enforceability *i.e.,* legal validity.
2. According to formation *i.e.,* mode of creation.
3. According to performance.

1.6. CLASSIFICATION OF CONTRACTS ACCORDING TO THEIR ENFORCEABILITY OR LEGAL VALIDITY

1. ***Valid contracts***
2. ***Void contracts***
3. ***Voidable contracts***
4. ***Unenforceable contracts***

The contracts may be classified into the following types according to their enforceability or legal validity:

1. *Valid contracts:* We know that a contract is an agreement which is enforceable by law. The conditions of enforceability are laid down in Section 10 of the Indian Contract Act. And A valid contract is that which satisfies all the conditions of enforceability.

2. *Void contracts:* A void contract is that which is not enforceable by law. As a matter of fact, a void contract is not at all a contract, as it is without any legal effect. The term void contract, is defined in Section 2(*j*) of the Indian Contract Act, which reads as under:

"A contract which ceases to be enforceable by law becomes void when it ceases to be enforceable."

Thus, when a valid and enforceable contract subsequently becomes legally unenforceable due to some reasons, it is called a void contract. It may be noted that a void contract cannot be originally entered into. It is rather illogical to talk of a void contract originally entered into.

Example 1.14. *A* promised to marry *B*. Later on *B* died. In this case, the contract becomes void on the death of *B*.

Example 1.15. On 1st June, *A* agreed to sell his car to *B* for Rs. 30,000. It was agreed that the car was to be delivered on 15th June after making full payment. But on 10th June, the car was destroyed in an accidental fire. In this case, the contract between *A* and *B* becomes void on the destruction of the car.

Note: The comparison between a void agreement and a void contract will be discussed in chapter 7.

3. *Voidable contracts:* We know that "free consent" is an essential element of a valid contract. If the consent of a party is not free then such party, (*i.e.,* whose consent is obtained by force etc.), may avoid the contract (*i.e.,* may put an end to the contract). Such contract is voidable at the option of the party whose consent is not free. The term 'voidable contract' is defined in Section 2(*i*) of the Indian Contract Act, which reads as under:

"An agreement which is enforceable by law at the option of one or more of the parties thereon, but not at the option of the other or others, is a voidable contracts."

Thus, a contract, which can be put to an end at the option of one party to the contract, is called a voidable contract. It may be noted that a voidable contract continues to be valid and binding till it is avoided by the party entitled to do so. It may also be noted that the party entitled to avoid the contract may or may not do so. If he so desires, he may elect to be bound by it.

Example 1.16. *A*, intending to deceive *B*, falsely represented that two hundred automobile parts are manufactured every week in his factory, and thereby induced *B* to buy the factory. Believing the statement to be true, *B* bought the factory. The contract is voidable at the option of *B*. In this case *B*'s consent is not free because it is obtained by fraud. And *B* may put an end to this contract if he so decides.

Example 1.17. *A* agreed to sell his horse to *B* for Rs. 20,000. The consent of *A* was obtained by use of force. The contract is voidable at the option of *A*, and he (*A*) may put an end to this contract if he so decides.

Note: The consent is not free when it is obtained by fraud, misrepresentation, coercion, force etc. These points will be discussed later in separate chapter 5.

4. *Unenforceable contracts:* The unenforceable contracts are those which cannot be enforced in a Court of Law because of some technical defects. In certain cases, there are special provisions of law which require some formalities to be fulfilled, *e.g.*, there are special provisions which provide that a contract must be in writing, or it must be registered, or it must be properly stamped or it must be attested etc. If such formalities are not properly observed, the contract cannot be enforced in a Court of Law. Otherwise, such a contract is perfectly valid and has all the requirements of a valid contract. Some of such contracts can be enforced if the technical defect is removed *e.g.*, where a document requires to be stamped and it is understamped (*i.e.*, the stamp affixed is of less value), the contract as such is unenforceable. But if the required stamp is now affixed, the document becomes enforceable.

1.7. CLASSIFICATION OF CONTRACTS ACCORDING TO THEIR FORMATION OR MODE OF CREATION

1. *Express contracts*
2. *Implied contracts*
3. *Quasi-contracts*

The contracts may be classified into the following types according to their formation or mode of creation:

1. *Express contracts:* An express contract is that which is made in writing or by the words of mouth. [Section 9]

Example 1.18. *A* wrote a letter to *B*, "I am prepared to sell my car for Rs. 50,000. *B* also accepted the offer by a letter. This is an express contract.

2. *Implied contracts:* An implied contract is that which is not made in words. Such contracts come into existence on account of act or conduct of the parties. In a continuing course of dealing, the acts or conduct of the parties may give rise to implied contracts.

Example 1.19. *A* went to a restaurant, and took a cup of tea. In this case, there is an implied contract that he will pay for the cup of tea.

Example 1.20. A fire broke out in *A*'s farm. He believed that he was entitled to the free services of 'Upton Fire Brigade'. He, therefore, called it to put out the fire. The Fire Brigade put out the fire. *A*'s farm was not actually within the free services zone of the Fire Brigade. The Fire Brigade therefore claimed compensation from *A* for the services. It was held that *A* was liable to pay for the services rendered by the Fire Brigade as the services were rendered on an implied promise to pay. [*Upton Rural District Council v. Powell* (1942) All. ER 220]

3. *Quasi-contracts:* As a matter of fact, quasi-contracts are not contracts as there is no intension of the parties to enter into a contract. In fact, it is an obligation which the law creates in the absence of any agreement. A quasi-contract is based upon the equitable principle that a person shall not be allowed to enrich himself at the expense of another.

Example 1.21. *A* supplied *B*, a lunatic, with necessaries suitable to his conditions in life. In this case, *A* is entitled to be reimbursed from *B*'s property.

Example 1.22. *A*, a tradesman, left certain goods at *B*'s house by mistake. *B* treated the goods as his own. In this case, *B* is bound to pay for the goods.

1.8. CLASSIFICATION OF CONTRACTS ACCORDING TO THEIR PERFORMANCE

1. *Unilateral contracts*
2. *Bilateral contracts*
3. *Executed contracts*
4. *Executory contracts*

The contracts may be classified into the following types according to their performance:

1. *Unilateral contracts:* A unilateral contract is a one-sided contract in which only one party has to perform his obligation. In such contracts, promise on one side is exchanged for an act on the other side. It may be noted that after the formation of a unilateral contract, only one party remains liable to perform his obligation because the other party has already performed his obligation by doing some act. The unilateral contracts are also known as contracts with executed consideration.

Example 1.23. *A* promised to pay Rs. 100 to anyone who finds his lost dog. *B* found the dog and returned it to *A*. It is a unilateral contract which comes into existence when the dog is found. Now, only *A* has to perform his obligation by paying Rs. 100 to *B*, because *B* had already performed his part of obligation by finding the dog. Here *A*'s promise to pay was for *B*'s act of finding the dog.

2. *Bilateral contracts:* A bilateral contract is a two-sided contract in which both the parties have to perform their respective obligations, *i.e.*, at the time of formation of a contract the obligations of both the parties are outstanding. In such contracts, promise on one side is exchanged for a promise on the other. The bilateral contracts are also known as contracts with executoryconsi deration.

Example 1.24. *A* promised to paint a picture for *B*, and *B* promised to pay Rs. 100 to *A*. It is a bilateral contract as there is exchange of promises, and obligations of both the parties are outstanding at the time of formation of the contract.

3. *Executed contracts:* When a contract has been completely performed, it is termed as executed contract, *i.e.*, it is a contract where, under the terms of a contract, nothing remains to be done by either party.

Example 1.25. *A* agreed to sell his horse to *B* for Rs. 1,000. *B* paid the price and *A* delivered the horse. It is an executed contract as both the parties have performed their respective obligations.

*4. **Executory contracts:*** Executory contract is that where under the terms of a contract something remains to be done by the parties. In other words, where one or both the parties to the contract have still to perform their obligations in future, the contract is termed as executory contract.

Example 1.26. *A* agreed to sell his car to *B* for Rs. 30,000. Car was to be delivered by *A* on 15th of next month, and price was to be paid by *B* on 25th of that month. It is an executory contract, as both the parties have to perform their respective obligation in future.

Suppose *A* delivered the car to *B* on due date *i.e.*, on 15th. The contract is still executory, because *B* is still under obligation to pay the price on 25th of the month. In such cases, the contract as a whole is an executory one, though it may be said that it is partly executed and partly executory.

Note: A contract comes into existence immediately from the time it is made, and not from the time when its performance is due. Thus, an executory contract is perfectly valid even if both the parties agree to perform their respective duties at a later stage.

LEGAL PROVISIONS (SECTIONS) DISCUSSED IN THE CHAPTER

Important legal provision (sections) of the Indian contract Act, 1872, discussed in this chapter are reproduced hereunder for rady reference:

1. *Section 2 (a): Proposal*
"When one person signifies to another his willingness to do or to abstain from doing anything, with a view to obtaining the assent of that ohter to such act or abstinence, he is said to make a proposal"
2. *Section 2 (b): Promise*
"When the proson to whom the proposal is made signifies his assent thereto, his proposal is said to be accepted. A proposal when accepted become a promise".
3. *Section 2 (c): Promisor and Promisee*
The person making the proposal is called the 'promisor', and the person accetping the proposal is called the 'promisee'.
4. *Section 2 (e): Agreement*
Every promise and every set of promisers, forming the consideration for each other, is an agreement.
5. *Section 2 (g): Void Agreement*
An agreement not enforceable by law is said to be void.
6. *Section 2 (h): Contract*
An agreement enforcable by law in contract.
7. *Section 2 (i): Voidable Contract*
An agreement which is enforceable by law at the option of one or more of the parties thereto, but not at the option of the other or others, in a a voidable contract.
8. *Section 2 (j): Void Contract*
A contract which ceases to be enforcable by law becomes void when it ceases to be enforceable.
9. *Section 9: Promises, Express and Implied*
In so far as the proposal or acceptance of promise is made in words, the promise is said to be express. In so far as such proposal or acceptance is made ohterwise than in words, the promise is said to be implied.
10. *Section 10: What Agreements are Contracts (Conditions of Enforceability of Agreement)*
All agreements are contracts if they are made by the free consent of the parties competent to contract, for a lawful consideration and with lawful object, and are not expreassly declared to be void.

TEST QUESTIONS

1. Define the term contract. What are the essentials of a valid contract?
2. "An agreement enforceable by law is a contract."—explain the statement illustrating the essential elements of a valid contract.
3. "All contracts are agreements but all agreements are not contracts."—Comment.
4. Explain the test to be applied in determining whether an agreement is enforceable at law.
5. How would you classify the contracts—
(*a*) according to their enforceability (*b*) according to their formation *i.e.*, mode of creation
(*c*) according to their performance?
6. Define the distinguish the following classes of contracts:
(*a*) void and voidable contracts (*b*) express and implied contracts
(*c*) unilateral and bilateral contracts (*d*) executed and executory contracts.
7. Write notes on the following:
(*a*) Valid contracts (*b*) Unenforceable contracts
(*c*) Quasi-contracts (*d*) Illegal agreements.

MULTIPLE CHOICE QUESTIONS

1. The Indian Contract Act, 1872 applies to the
(*a*) whole of India including Jammu & Kashmir
(*b*) whole of India excluding Jammu & Kashmir
(*c*) states notified by the government every year
(*d*) northern and eastern Indian states.

2. A *jus in personam* means a right against
   (*a*) a specific person (*b*) the public at large
   (*c*) a specific thing (*d*) none of these.
3. Which of the following statement is true
   (*a*) an agreement enforceable by law is a contract
   (*b*) an agreement is an accepted proposal
   (*c*) both (*a*) and (*b*) (*d*) none of these.
4. A void contract is one which is
   (*a*) enforceable at the option of one party (*b*) enforceable at the option of both the parties
   (*c*) enforceable at the direction of court (*d*) not enforceable in a court of law.
5. A voidable contract is one which
   (*a*) can be enforced at the option of aggrieved party
   (*b*) can be enforced at the option of both the parties
   (*c*) cannot be enforced in a court of law (*d*) courts prohibit.
6. Implied contract, even if not in writing or express words, is perfectly valid if other conditions are satisfied
   (*a*) True, as an aimplied contract has the same effect as an express contract
   (*b*) False, as the Contract Act recognises only express contracts.

ANSWERS

1. (*b*)	2. (*a*)	3. (*c*)	4. (*d*)	5. (*a*)	6. (*a*)

OBJECTIVE TYPE QUESTIONS WITH REASONING

State with reasons whether the following statements are correct or incorrect.

1. Every agreement is necessarily regarded as contract.
2. Social agreements are enforceable in courts.
3. All kinds of agreements created between the parties form part of contract.
4. All contracts are agreements but all agreements are not contracts.
5. The legal effect of void agreement and void contract is the same.
6. A void agreement is *void ab initio* but a void contract is not *void ab initio*.
7. A contract in which one or both the parties have still to perform their obligations in future, is invalid and cannot be enforced in law.

ANSWERS

1. ***Incorrect.*** Only those agreements are contracts which create some legal obligations and are enforceable in the Courts of Law.
2. ***Incorrect.*** Social agreements do not give rise to any legal obligations and thus are not enforceable.
3. ***Incorrect.*** Only the legal obligations form part of contract and are enforceable in law. The social obligations do not form part of a contract.
4. ***Correct.*** Only those agreements are contracts which are enforceable in law.
5. ***Correct.*** Both of them do not create any legal obligations and are not enforceable in law.
6. ***Correct.*** In case of a void contract, initially a valid contract is created which subsequently becomes unenforceable due to some reasons.
7. ***Incorrect.*** Such a contract is known as an executory contract and is perfectly valid.

PRACTICAL PROBLEMS

1. *A* had two cars, one golden and the other silver and offered to sell the silver car to *B* for Rs. 70,000. *B* accepted the offer believing that it was made for golden car. Is there a valid contract between *A* and *B*.

   Hint : No. There is no valid contract as there is no *consensus ad idem i.e.,* meeting of minds.

2. *A* invited *B* to dinner at his house on a particular day and *B* accepted the invitation. On the agreed day, *B* reached at *A's* house for dinner but found the house locked. *B* contacted *A* on mobile phone and *A* informed that he could not entertain *B* for dinner as he had gone out of station for some urgent work. *B* left the place and had his dinner in some hotel for Rs. 500. *B* wants to recover this amount from *A*. Advise him.

   Hint : There is no valid contract between *A* and *B* as mere social or moral obligations do not give rise to an enforceable contract. *B* cannot recover this amount from *A*.

3. *A* invited *B* to a cinema hall to see a movie with him and *B* accepted the offer. On the appointed day *A* purchased a ticket for *B* also and waited for him at the cinema hall, but *B* did not turn up. *A* wants to take legal action against *B*. 'Advise him'.

   Hint : In this case, no valid contract comes into existence between *A* and *B*. Such invitations are of social nature and social obligations do not give rise to an enforceable contract.

4. *A* agreed to sell to *B* " a hundred tones of oil" and *B* agreed to buy the same. Is this a valid contract?

   Hint : No. It is not a valid contract as it is not certain. It is not clear what kind of oil is intended to be sold.

5. *A* promises his son *B* to give him monthly allowance of Rs. 2,000 for three years. After making payments for one year, *A* stops making further payments. Is *A* bound to make payments for the remaining two years?

   Hint : No. In this case, no valid contract arises between *A* and *B*. In such type of family arrangements, there is no intention to create legal relationship.

OFFER AND ACCEPTANCE

2.1. INTRODUCTION

It is an established principle that an agreement arises only when an offer is made by one person and is accepted by the other person, to whom it is made. Thus, an offer is the starting point in the making of an agreement. However, an offer in itself does not create any legal relationship. The legal relationship results only when an offer is accepted. The acceptance of an offer is, therefore, necessary to create legal relationship. In this chapter, we shall discuss in detail about the 'offer', and 'acceptance' as well as essentials and legal rules for a valid offer and acceptance.

2.2. DEFINITION OF OFFER

An offer is the proposal by one party to another to enter into a legally binding agreement with him. The term 'offer' or 'proposal' is defined in Section 2(a) of the Indian Contract Act, which reads as under:

"When one person signifies to another his willingness to do or abstain from doing anything, with a view to obtaining the assent of that other to such act or abstinence, he is said to make a proposal."

The analysis of this legal definition shows that an offer consists of the following two parts:

(*a*) Expression of one person's willingness to do or to abstain from doing something.

(*b*) Such expression should be made with a view to obtain the assent of the other person to the proposed act or abstinence.

Example 2.1. *A*, with a view to obtain the assent of *B*, says to him, "will you purchase my motorcycle for Rs. 10,000". In this case, *A* is making an offer to *B* as he signifies to *B* his willingness to sell his motorcycle to him for Rs. 10,000. And *A* is doing so with a view to obtain *B*'s assent to purchase the motorcycle.

It may be noted that every proposal made by a person is not legally regarded as an offer. A legal offer must consist of the above-mentioned two points. These two points have been elaborated with suitable examples in the following discussion.

The person making the offer is known as 'offeror', 'proposer' or 'promisor'. And the person to whom the offer is made is known as 'offeree' or 'promisee'.

2.3. ESSENTIALS AND LEGAL RULES FOR A VALID OFFER

1. *The offer must be communicated to the other party*
2. *The offer must be made with a view to obtain the contest of the offeree.*
3. *The offer must have its terms definite and clear.*
4. *The offer must be capable of creating legal relationship.*
5. *The offer must express the final willingness of the offeror.*
6. *The offer must be distinguished from an answer to a question.*
7. *The offer must be distinguished from an invitation in receive offer.*
8. *The offer must be distinguished from mere statement of intention.*
9. *The offer be made to the world at large.*
10. *The offer may be positive or negative.*
11. *The offer may be express or implied.*

The legal definition of an offer, discussed in the last article, reveals the essential elements of an offer. An offer is legally valid only if it satisfies all the requirements of its definition. The essential elements are discussed in points 1 to 5, in the following discussion, and the rest are the legal rules for a valid offer.

1. *The offer must be communicated to the other party:* It is an important and essential element of a valid offer. The first part of the definition, mentioned above, emphasises this requirement. According to this, the willingness to make offer should be 'signified' (*i.e.*, indicated or declared). In other words, the offer is completed only when it has been communicated to the offeree. It may be noted that until the offer is communicated, it cannot be accepted. Thus, an offer accepted without its knowledge, does not confer any legal rights on the acceptor.

Example 2.2. *A*'s nephew had absconded from his home. He sent his servant to trace his missing nephew. When the servant had left, *A* then announced that anybody who discovered the missing boy, would be given a reward of Rs. 500. The servant discovered the missing boy without knowing of the reward. When the servant came to know about the reward, he brought an action against *A* to recover the same. But his action failed. It was held that the servant was not entitled to the reward because he did not know about the offer when he discovered the missing boy.

[*Lalman Shukla v. Gauri Datt* (1913) All LJ 489]

2. *The offer must be made with a view to obtain the consent of the offeree:* The second part of the definition emphasises the requirement that an offer must be made with a view to obtain the consent of the offeree to the proposed act or abstinence. Thus, when a person is making an offer it means that he is making it with a view to obtain the consent of the offeree. As soon as the offeree accepts it, the offeror is bound by it.

Example 2.3. *A*, jokingly, said that he was willing to sell his horse for Rs. 2,000. *B* knowing that *A* was not seriously making the offer, said that he has accepted the offer. In this case, *A*'s offer is not the real offer as he did not make it with a view to obtain the consent of *B*. Moreover, he was not willing to be bound by the same.

3. *The offer must have its terms definite and clear:* The terms of an offer must be definite, clear and certain. If the terms of the offer are vague and uncertain, no contract will come into existence. The reason for the same is that when the offer is vague, loose or uncertain, it cannot be said what exactly the parties intended to do.

Example 2.4. *A* offered to sell to *B* his Atlas cycle for Rs. 500 or Rs. 1,000. There is nothing to show which of the two prices was to be given. This offer cannot be accepted as it is not clear. Thus, no contract will result from this offer.

Example 2.5. *A* offered to sell to *B*, "a hundred tonnes of oil". The offer is uncertain as there is nothing to show what kind of oil is intended to be sold.

Example 2.6. *A* promised to buy the horse from *B* if it proved lucky. This is a vague and loose offer. Thus, it cannot give rise to any contract.

4. *The offer must be capable of creating legal relationship:* An offer must be such that when accepted it will result in a valid contract. A mere social invitation cannot be regarded as an offer, because if such an invitation is accepted it will not give rise to any legal relationship.

Example 2.7. *A* invited *B* to a dinner and *B* accepted the invitation. It is a mere social invitation. And *A* will not be liable if he fails to provide dinner to *B*.

It is important to note that there is no provision in the Indian Contract Act that an offer or acceptance should be made with the intension of creating legal relationship. But in English Law, it is the accepted principle that for a valid contract there must be common intension of the parties to enter into legal relations. "It is not every loose conversation that is to be turned into a contract, although the parties may seem to agree."

[*Castigan-Cases on Contract 32, 3rd Edn*]

Example 2.8. *A* was working in Ceylon. During the holidays, he and his wife *B* went to England to enjoy the leave. When *A* was to return to Ceylon, his wife was advised to remain in England, due to ill health. And *A* agreed to send his wife $30 per month for maintenance expenses. For sometime he sent the amount, but afterwards differences arose between them, and he stopped payment. The amount of maintenance fell in arrears, and *B* brought a legal action against *A* to recover the amount of arrears. In this case, wife's (*B*'s) action to recover the arrears failed and it was held that such type of family arrangements are not contracts because the parties did not intend that they shall be attended by legal consequences. [*Balfour v. Balfour* (1919) 2 KB 571]

5. *The offer must express the final willingness of the offeror:* The terms of the offer should be such that they contain final willingness of the offeror. Sometimes, a party does not express his final willingness. But proposes certain terms on which he is willing to negotiate. In such cases, he is not making an offer because he is not expressing his final willingness to enter into a contract.

Example 2.9. *A* offered to purchase a lodge from *B* for Rs. 95,000. *A* wrote to *B*'s agent, asking whether his offer has been accepted, and also stated that he was prepared to accept any higher price if found reasonable. *B*'s agent replied "we won't accept less than Rs. 100,000". *A* accepted this offer. But *B* refused to sell the lodge for Rs. 100,000. *A* brought a legal action against *B* for specific performance that *B* should sell the lodge for Rs. 1,00,000. In this case *A*'s action failed. Here *B* did not make any offer to sell the lodge for Rs 100,000, because he did not express his final willingness to sell. He simply proposed this price on which he was willing to negotiate. The negotiation did not result into a contract, as he did not agree to sell for Rs. 100,000 as asked by *A*.

[*Based on McPherson v. Appana*, AIR 1951 SC. 184 .
See also Badri Prasad v. State of M.P., AIR 1970 SC 706]

6. *The offer must be distinguished from an answer to a question:* The terms of an offer should be clear so that there is no confusion whether it is a valid offer or an answer to a question. An answer to a question cannot be taken as an offer.

Example 2.10. *A* sent a telegram to *B* writing "Will you sell us Bumper Hall Pen (Plot of land)? Telegraph lowest cash price". *B* replied by telegram "lowest price for Bumper Hall Pen £900". *A* sent a telegram stating therein "I agree to purchase Bumper Hall Pen for £900 asked by you. Please send us your title deeds." *B* refused to sell the plot of land at that price. *A* brought legal action against *B*. It was held that *B* did not make any offer to sell at that price, he simply answered the question asked by *A*. The court observed that *A* asked the following two questions in his first telegram.

(*a*) willingness to sell, and (*b*) lowest price.

B only answered the second question, and reserved his answer to his willingness to sell. Therefore, he had made no offer. [*Harvey v. Facie* (1893) AC 522; *See also* AIR 1951 SC 184]

7. *The offer must be distinguished from an invitation to receive offer:* The terms of an offer should be clear so that there is no confusion whether it is a valid offer or an invitation to receive offer. Sometimes, a party does not make an offer but simply proposes certain terms and invites the other party to make an offer on proposed terms. When a person advertises that he has got a stock of books to sell or houses to let out, there is no offer to be bound by any contract. In fact, such advertisements are 'offer to receive offer' and not an offer to sell in itself. Similarly, a shopkeeper's catalogue of price is not an offer. It is only an invitation to receive offer from his customers. Display of goods in a shop, with price chits attached, is not an offer even if there is self-service system in a shop. The buyer cannot compel the seller to sell the goods at those prices.

Example 2.11. Goods were displayed in *A*'s shop with price chits attached to the articles. *B*, a customers entered the shop and picked up a bottle of medicine from the shelves. This will not amount to acceptance of an offer to sell. It is merely an offer by the customer to buy, and there will be no acceptance of the offer until the price is accepted by *A*, the shopkeeper.

[*Pharmaceutical Society of Great Britan v Boots Cash Chemist Ltd.* (1952) 2 Q.B. 795]

Example 2.12. *A* advertised stating "Cocks and hens 25s each". *B* accepted it and agreed to buy cocks and hens for 25s each. It was held that such classified advertisements are merely an invitation to receive offer and not offer to sell. [*Partodge v. Critterden (1968) ALL ER 421*]

Example 2.13. In *Harvey v. Facie* discussed in Example 2.10, the first telegram of *A* was a mere invitation to receive an offer to sell. It was not an offer in itself. Last telegram of *A* was an offer to buy. But it was not accepted by *B*, thus there was no valid contract.

8. *The offer must be distinguished from mere statement of intention:* The terms of an offer should be clear so that there is no confusion whether it is a valid offer or a mere statement of intention. Sometimes, a person declares that he has the intention to do something, this does not amount to an offer. Such statements merely indicate the intentions that an offer will be made in future or an offer will be invited in future.

Example 2.14. *A*, an auctioneer, announced that specified goods will be sold by auction on a particular day. This statement is not an offer to hold the auction. It is merely a statement of an intention to hold auction. *A* will not be liable if he does not hold the auction on specified day.

[*Harris v. Nickerson* (1973) LR 8 Q.B. 286]

9. *The offer may be made to the world at large:* It means that it is not necessary that an offer should be made to a specific person. An offer may be *specific* as well as a *general* one. A specific offer is one which is made to an ascertained person. And a general offer is one which is not made to a specific person, but to the public at large. This point will be discussed in detail in Art. 2.4.

10. *The offer may be positive or negative:* An offer may be to do something or not to do something. An offer to do something, is a positive offer. And an offer not to do something is a negative offer. [Section 2(o)]

11. *The offer may be express or implied:* An offer may be express as well as implied. An offer which is expressed by words, written or spoken, is called an express offer. The offer which is expressed by conduct, is called an implied offer. [Section 9]

Example 2.15. Following are the examples of an express offer:

(*a*) *A* says to *B*. "Will you purchase my white horse for Rs. 2000?"

(*b*) *A* writes to *B* in a letter, "I want to sell my car for Rs. 40,000."

(*c*) *A* advertises in a newspaper that, "I will pay Rs. 500 to any one who traces my missing son."

Example 2.16. Following are the examples of an implied offer:

(*a*) A transport company runs buses on a particular route. There is an implied offer from the transport company to carry passengers on the route who are prepared to pay the specified fare. The acceptance of the offer is complete as soon as the passengers board the bus. A passenger who enters the bus also impliedly promises to pay the prescribed fare.

(b) Similarly, in a self-service restaurant there is an implied promise to pay for consuming the eatables.

Similarly, a bid at an auction is an implied offer to buy. Also where a customer of a bank did not object to the charge of a compound rate of interest in accordance with the usual course of business, it was held that he impliedly contracted to pay the compound interest. [*Haridas Ranchordas v. Mercantile Bank of India,* (1920) 47 IA 17]

2.4. SPECIFIC OFFER AND GENERAL OFFER

A specific offer is one which is made to an ascertained *i.e.,* definite person. It can be accepted only by the person to whom it is made.

A general offer is one which is not made to any specific person, but to the public at large. It can be accepted by any person who having the knowledge of the offer, comes forward and acts accordingly.

It may be noted that in case of a general offer, the contract is not made with the entire world. But it is made only with the person, who having the knowledge of the offer, comes forward and acts according to the conditions of the offer.

Example 2.17. A young boy absconded from his father's house. The father offered a reward in a pamphlet stating that anybody who traces the missing boy and brings him home will be given Rs. 500. One Mr. Har Bhajan Lal, who knew about the reward, saw the boy at Dharamsala Railway Station and took him to the police station. Har Bhajan Lal sent a telegram to the boy's father that he had found his son. In this case, it was decided that an offer through hand bill (pamphlet) was an offer to the whole world and could be accepted by anyone who fulfilled the conditions of the offer. Here as Mr. Har Bhajan Lal, by tracing the missing boy, had substantially performed the conditions of the offer, therefore it was held that he was entitled to receive the amount of reward.

[*Harbhajan Lal v. Harcharan Lal,* AIR 1925 All 539]

Another authority on this point is of *Carlill v. Carbolic Smoke Bal. Co.* (1893) 1 Q. B. 256 which was followed in Har Bhajan Lal's case mentioned above. This being the important case, is illustrated in detail in the following example.

Example 2.18. Carbolic Smoke Ball Co. advertised in the newspaper that anyone who would take, according to the printed directions, the 'smoke balls' manufactured by it would not contract the increasing epidemic influenza or colds. The reward of £100 was offered by the company to anyone who contracted influenza or cold after having used the smoke balls according to the printed directions. It was also added that £1,000 are deposited with the Alliance Bank showing the sincerity of the company. One Mrs. Carlill used the smoke balls according to the printed directions. But she subsequently suffered from influenza. In this case, it was decided that she was entitled to recover the reward.

To avoid the liability in this case, the Smoke Ball Company forwarded the following contentions:

(a) that there was no intention on the part of the company to enter into a legal relation as the advertisement was merely a puff.

(b) that the offer was not made to any particular person.

(c) that Mrs. Carlill had not communicated her intention to accept.

With regard to the first argument, it was said by His Lordship that as the advertisement said that £1,000 were deposited in the bank, therefore it cannot be said that "£100 would be paid" was intended to be a mere puff.

With regard to the second argument, it was decided that an offer need not be made to a specific person. But it can also be made to the world at large. In such cases, the contract is made only with the person who comes forward and performs the conditions of the offer.

With regard to the third argument, it was decided that in cases like this, communication of acceptance is not necessary. Performance of the conditions is the sufficient acceptance.

It may be noted here that where the general offer is of a continuing nature as in the *Smoke Ball's* case, it can be accepted by any number of persons until it is retracted. But where the offer needs the finding of a missing thing or some information as in the case of *Har Bhajan Lal's* case, it is closed as soon as the first information is received by the offeror.

2.5. ACCEPTANCE OF AN OFFER

In the preceding discussion, we have noted that an offer is the starting point for making an agreement. But, it may be noted that an offer in itself does not create any legal relationship. The legal relationship results only when an offer is accepted. Thus, acceptance of an offer is necessary to create legal relationship.

2.6. DEFINITION OF ACCEPTANCE

An acceptance is the manifestation by the offeree of his willingness to be bound by the terms of the offer. The term acceptance is defined in section 2(b) of the Indian Contract Act, which reads as under,

> *"When the person to whom the proposal is made signifies his assent thereto, the proposal is said to be accepted. A proposal when accepted becomes a promise."*

The analysis of this legal definition shows that an acceptance is the consent given to the offer (proposal), and a binding contract between the offeror and the offeree comes into existence on the acceptance of the proposal.

Example 2.19. A offers to sell his car to *B* for Rs. 90,000. *B* accepts this and agrees to buy *A*'s car for Rs. 90,000. In this case, a binding contract comes into existence between *A* and *B*.

2.7. ESSENTIALS AND LEGAL RULES FOR A VALID ACCEPTANCE

1. *The acceptance must be communicated*
2. *The acceptance must be communicated to the offeror himself*
3. *The acceptance must be communicated by a person who has the authority to accept*
4. *The acceptance must be absolute and unqualified*
5. *The acceptance must be in the prescribed manner*
6. *The acceptance must be given in some usual and reasonable manner*
7. *The acceptance must be given within the time prescribed or within a reasonable time*
8. *The acceptance must be given before the lapse of offer*
9. *The acceptance must show an intention that acceptor is willing to fulfil the terms of the offer*
10. *The acceptance cannot be presumed from silence*
11. *The acceptance may be express or implied*

The legal definition of an acceptance, discussed in the last article, reveals the essential elements of an acceptance. An acceptance is valid only if satisfies all the requirements of its definition. The essential elements are discussed in points 1 to 4, in the following discussion, and the rest are legal rules for a valid acceptance.

1. ***The acceptance must be communicated:*** It is an important and essential element of a valid acceptance. The definition of acceptance as given in section 2(*b*) emphasises this requirement. According to this, the consent to the offer should be signified (*i.e.*, indicated or declared). In other words, the acceptance is completed only when it has been communicated to the offeror. It may be noted that until the acceptance is communicated, it does not create any legal relations.

Example 2.20. *A* offers to buy *B*'s plot of land for Rs. 10 lakhs. *B* discusses the proposal with C, his own lawyer, and agrees to sell the plot for Rs. 10 lakhs. But *B* does not communicate the acceptance to *A*. In this case, no contract comes into existence between *A* and *B*.

Example 2.21 *A* agreed to supply coal to a Railway Company. Agents of both parties met, and a draft agreement was drawn. Agreement was approved by *A*, and then sent to manager of the Railway Company for his acceptance. The manager approved the draft and put it in the drawer of his table, and the agreement remained there without final approval being signified. In this case, no valid contract is concluded between the parties as the acceptance was not communicated.

[*Brogden v. Metropolitan Railway* (1877) 2 AC 666]

2. *The acceptance must be communicated to the offeror himself:* A valid contract arises only if the acceptance is communicated to the offeror himself. If acceptance is communicated to the person, other than the offeror, it will not create any legal relationship. In fact, such communication is no communication at all.

Example 2.22. *A* offered to purchase *B*'s horse and wrote a letter saying, "If I hear no more about the horse. I shall consider the horse mine at £35". To this letter no reply was sent, but *B* instructed *C*, an auctioneer, not to sell the horse as it was already sold to *A*. By mistake, *C* put up the horse for auction and sold it. *A* filed a suit against *C* on the ground that under the contract the horse had become his property and *C* is liable for conversion of his property. But his action failed. In this case *A* in his own mind accepted the offer. But he had not communicated his acceptance to *B*.

[*Felthouse v. Bindley,* (1863) 7 LT 835]

However, if the offer is made by an agent on behalf of his principal, then the acceptance may be communicated, either to the principal or his agent.

3. *The acceptance must be communicated by a person who has the authority to accept:* A valid contract arises only if acceptance is communicated by a person who has the authority to accept. If it is communicated by any unauthorised person, it will not create any legal relationship.

Example 2.23. *A* applied for the post of a headmaster in a school. He was selected by the appointing authorities. But the decision of his appointment was not communicated to him. One of the members of the appointing committee informed him of his appointment. But this member was not authorised to communicate the decision. He communicated the decision in his individual capacity. Subsequently, the appointing authority cancelled his selection. *A* brought a legal action for breach of contract. His action was rejected by the court, and it was observed, that "there must be notice of acceptance from the contracting party in some way. Information from an unauthorised person is as insufficient as over hearing from behind the door". [*Powell v. Lee,* (1908) 24 TLR 606]

However, the communication of acceptance can be dispensed with in cases of unilateral contracts, such as Smoke Ball's and Har Bhajan Lal's cases.

4. *The acceptance must be absolute and unqualified:* It is another important essential element, of a valid acceptance. A valid contract arises only if the acceptance in absolute and unqualified. It means that the acceptance should be in *toto* (*i.e.,* of all the terms of the offer), and without any condition.

Thus, an acceptance with a variation is no acceptance. It is simply a counter offer. A counter offer puts an end to the original offer, and it cannot be revived by subsequent acceptance.

Example 2.24. *A* offered to sell his house for Rs. 70,000 to *B*. *B* wrote a letter stating that he was prepared to buy it for Rs. 60,000. This is a counter offer, and not acceptance. Now, if *B* accepts the original offer to buy the house for Rs. 70,000, *A* will not be bound to sell the house, because *B*'s counter offer has put an end to the original offer. [*Nihal Chand v. Amarnath,* AIR 1926 Lah. 645]

If the offer is accepted with some condition then also the acceptance is invalid and without any legal effect.

Example 2.25. *A* offered to purchase certain goods from *B* at a specified rate. *B* accepted the offer but on the condition that some advance should be paid. There is no valid contract between the parties as the acceptance is conditional and also no amount of advance is specified.

[*Moolji Jaitho and Co. v. Seth Kirodhimal,* AIR 1961 Kerala 21]

5. *The acceptance must be in the prescribed manner:* It is the legal rule of the acceptance that it must be accepted in the prescribed manner. If the offer is not accepted in the prescribed manner, then the offeror may reject the acceptance within reasonable time. It may, however, be noted that, if the offeror does not reject the acceptance within a reasonable time then he becomes bound by acceptance.

6. *The acceptance must be given in some usual and reasonable manner:* It is another important legal rule of an acceptance that where no mode is prescribed, acceptance must be given in some usual and reasonable manner. In such cases, the mail course is considered, a very reasonable manner. [*Dunlop v. Higgins,* (1848) 1 HLC 381]

7. *The acceptance must be given within the time prescribed or within a reasonable time:* Sometimes, the time limit is fixed within which an acceptance is to be given. In such cases, the acceptance must be given within the fixed time limit. In case, no time is prescribed, the acceptance should be given within a reasonable time. The term 'reasonable time' depends upon the facts and circumstances of each case.

Example 2.26. *A* applied for shares in a company in June. The allotment (acceptance) of shares was made in late November. *A* refused to take shares. It was held that the allotment of shares was not within a reasonable time, therefore *A* was not bound by the allotment.

[*Ramsgate Victoria Hotel Co.* v. *Monteflore,* (1866) LR 1 Ex. 109]

8. *The acceptance must be given before the lapse of offer:* A valid contract can arise only when the acceptance is given before the offer has elapsed or withdrawn. An acceptance which is made after the withdrawal of the offer is invalid, and does not create any legal relationship.

9. *The acceptance must show an intention that acceptor is willing to fulfil the terms of the offer:* A valid contract can arise only when the acceptance is given with the intention of fulfilling the terms of the contract. An acceptance which is made jokingly and without any intention of entering into a contract, is invalid and does not create any legal relationship.

10. *The acceptance cannot be presumed from silence:* Sometimes, the acceptor does not convey his decision to the offer or/and keeps silent. In such a case, his silence does not amount to acceptance. Similarly, the offeror does not have the legal rights to say that if no answer is received within a certain time, the offer shall be deemed to have been accepted. He (the offeror) cannot impose a condition that offeree's silence will be regarded as equivalent to acceptance. [*Felthouse* v. *Bindley,* (1863) 7 LT 835]

Example 2.27. *A* offered his car to *B* for Rs. 95,000, and wrote that if he did not hear from him (*B*) within a week, he would assume that he has accepted the offer. No reply was given by *B*. In this case, no valid contract is concluded between *A* and *B*.

11. *The acceptance may be express or implied:* An acceptance, which is expressed by words, written or spoken, is called an express acceptance. The acceptance which is expressed by conduct, is called an implied acceptance. [*Section 9*]

Example 2.28. At an auction sale of a car, *A* is the highest bidder. The auctioneer accepts the bid (*i.e.,* offer) by striking the hammer on the table. It is an implied acceptance. Here, auctioneer's conduct of striking the hammer on the table shows that the auctioneer has accepted the highest bid.

2.8. COMMUNICATION OF OFFER AND ACCEPTANCE

1. *Communication of offer*
2. *Completion of communication of offer*
3. *Communication of acceptance*
4. *Completion of communication of acceptance*
5. *Conclusion of the contract*

We have already discussed that an offer and an acceptance of offer are complete only when they are communicated. Now we shall discuss, how the communication of offer and acceptance is made, and when such communication is complete. The communication of offer and acceptance may be studied under the following sub-heads:

1. *Communication of offer:* An offer has no legal effect unless it is communicated to the other party. An offer can be communicated by any act or omission of the offeror by which he intends to communicate it. It may also be communicated by any act or omission of the offeror which has the effect of communicating it (Section 3). In simple words, the offer can be communicated in any way which has the effect of laying before the offeree, the offeror's willingness to do or abstain from doing something. Thus, an offer can be communicated by words, spoken or written, or by conduct.

2. *Completion of communication of offer:* The communication of an offer is complete when it comes to the knowledge of the person to whom it is made (Section 4). As a matter of fact, an offer cannot be accepted unless and until it is brought to the knowledge of the offeree. When the communication of an offer is complete, the offeror becomes bound by it (*i.e.*, if it is accepted by the offeree, then the offeror cannot retract it). It may be noted that an offer, accepted without its complete knowledge, does not create any legal relations.

Example 2.29. *A*'s nephew ran away from his house. *A* sent his servant in search of the boy. When the servant had left, *A* offered to pay Rs. 500 to anybody who discovers the boy. The servant came to know of the offer only when he had already traced the boy. The servant brought an action against *A* to recover the amount of the award. His action failed as he had no knowledge of the offer when he traced the boy. [*Lalman Shukla* v. *Gauri Datt*, (1913) 11 All L.J. 489]

When an offer is made by post, its communication will be complete when the letter containing the offer reaches the offeree. The term 'reaching of letter' means, when the message of letter reaches and comes to the knowledge of the offeree.

Example 2.30. *A* offers by letter, to sell his house to *B* at a certain price. The letter is posted on 25th December. It reaches *B* on 27th December. Here, the communication of the offer is complete when *B* receives the letters (*i.e.*, on 27th December).

3. *Communication of acceptance:* An acceptance of an offer has no legal effect unless it is communicated to the other party. Like, an offer, the acceptance can be communicated by any act or omission of the acceptor by which he intends to communicate it, or by any act or omission which has the effect of communicating it (Section 3). In simple words, the acceptance can be communicated in any way which has the effect of informing the offeror, about the offeree's consent. Thus, an acceptance can be communicated by words, spoken or written, or by conduct.

4. *Completion of communication of acceptance:* The communication of an acceptance is complete at different times for the offeror and the acceptor. For the offeror, the communication of an acceptance is complete when it is put in a course of transmission to him. Thus, the offeror becomes bound by the acceptance as soon as the letter of acceptance is posted by the acceptor. And for the acceptor, the communication of an acceptance is complete when it comes to the knowledge of the offeror (Section 4, second para). Thus, the acceptor becomes bound by his acceptance only when it comes to the knowledge of the offeror.

Example 2.31. *A* offers to sell his house to *B* for Rs. 15 lakhs by a letter dated 25th December. The letter reaches *B* on 27th December. *B* accpts the offer by a letter posted on 28th December. This letter of acceptance reaches *A* on 30th December. Here, for *A*, the communication of acceptance is complete when the letter of acceptance is posted *i.e.*, on 28th December. And for *B*, the communication of acceptance is complete when the letter of acceptance is received by *A i.e.*, on 30th December.

5. *Conclusion of the contract:* Sometimes, the contracting parties are face to face, and negotiate in the presence of each other. In such cases, a contract comes into existence as soon as the acceptor gives his acceptance (*e.g.*, says "*Yes*") to the offer made by the offeror. But when the parties are at distance, and are contracting through post or by messengers, then the contract comes into existence as soon as the communication of offer and acceptance is complete as per the rules mentioned above.

2.9. CONTRACT THROUGH POST

We have already studied that an offer and an acceptance are complete when they are properly communicated. A valid contract is concluded when a properly communicated offer is accepted, and the acceptance is completed by communication. When an offer and acceptance are made by post, then the offeror becomes bound when a properly addressed letter of acceptance is posted to him. Thus, the contract is concluded immediately after the letter of acceptance is posted.* It is to be noted that the contract is complete even if the letter of acceptance is lost in post. However, it is necessary that the letter of acceptance must be properly addressed, stamped and posted. Though, the offeror becomes bound when the letter of acceptance is posted to him, but the acceptor becomes bound only when his letter of acceptance is received by the offeror. The gap of time, between the posting and the delivery of acceptance, can be utilised by the acceptor for revoking his acceptance by a speedier communication which will overtake the acceptance letter.

Example 2.32. *A*, a resident of Chandigarh, posted an offer on 1st March to *B* of Delhi to sell some specific property for Rs. 70,000. The offer was received by *B* on 4th March. Next day *i.e.,* on 5th March, *B* posted his letter of acceptance which reached *A* on 9th March. In this case, the contract is complete, for *A*, on 5th March (*i.e.,* when the letter of acceptance is posted). Thus, *A* becomes bound on 5th March. But *B* becomes bound on 9th March *i.e.,* when his acceptance is received by *A*.

Note: 1. The English Law is different on this point. The difference is in the position of the acceptor. In English Law, when a letter of acceptance is posted, both the offeror and the acceptor become bound. But in India, the acceptor is not bound merely by posting his acceptance. He becomes bound only when his letter of acceptance is received by the offeror (*i.e.,* when the acceptance comes to the knowledge of the offeror).

2. Where the offer and acceptance are made by letters, the contract is complete at the place where the letter of acceptance is posted.

[*Bhagwandas Goverdhandas Kedia v. Girdharilal Parshotam. Das* AIR 1966 S.C. 543]

2.10. CONTRACT OVER TELEPHONE OR TELEX

A contract by telephone is treated on similar principles as a contract in each other's presence. In fact, when a contract is made by telephone or telex, the parties are in direct communication and no contract will arise until the offeror actually receives the notification of acceptance. Thus, the contract will be complete only when the acceptance is received by the offeror, and not when it is transmitted by the acceptor.

Example 2.33. *A* made an offer to *B* over telephone. *B* accepted the offer, but during his reply the line went dead, and the acceptance was not heard by *A*. In this case, there is no contract at that moment. If *B* wishes to make a contract, he must wait till the line is clear, and then again convey his acceptance so that *A* can hear.

Note: Where the offer and acceptance are made over telephone or telex, the contract is complete at the place where the acceptance is received. [*Bhagwandas's case*]

2.11. REVOCATION OF OFFER AND ACCEPTANCE

The term 'revocation' means the 'taking back' or 'withdrawal'. Both an offer as well as an acceptance may be revoked. By valid revocation, the parties become free, and no longer remain bound by the terms of the offer or acceptance as the case may be. In fact, the offer or the acceptance comes to an end by valid revocation. The legal position in this regard is discussed in the following pages.

* However, the current feeling is that even in reference to postal communication, the principle of consensus (*i.e.,* meeting of mind) should be followed and there should be no contract till the acceptance is received (*Holwell Securities v. Hughes* (1973) 1 WLR 757)]

2.12. REVOCATION OF AN OFFER

An offer may be revoked at any time before the communication of its acceptance is complete for the offeror, but not afterwards (Section 5). We know that for the offeror, the communication of acceptance is complete when it is put in a course of transmission so as to be out of the power of the acceptor. It means that *an offer may be revoked at any time before the letter of acceptance is posted by the acceptor.* The revocation is effective when it reaches the offeree before he (offeree) mails his acceptance. Thus, an offeror may cancel his offer by a speedier mode of communication which will reach before the acceptor posts his acceptance.

Example 2.34. *A* offers, by letter, to sell his house to *B*, *B* accepts the offer by a letter. *A* may revoke his offer at any time before *B* posts his letter of acceptance and not afterwards.

Example 2.35. *A* offered, by a letter, to sell his car to *B* for Rs. 1,00,000. The letter was posted on 15th March which reached *B* on 17th March. *B* accepted the offer and posted his letter of acceptance on 20th March. Here, *A* became bound by the offer on 20th March. In this case, the offer could have been revoked by *A* at any time before 20th March.

Thus, the communication of revocation of offer should reach the acceptor before he posts his letter of acceptance.

The rules relating to revocation of offer may be summed up as under:

1. It can be revoked at any time before its acceptance is complete as against the offeror.
2. Its revocation takes effect only when the revocation is communicated to the offeree.
3. In case, where the offeror keeps his offer open for a certain period, he can revoke it before the expiry of that period only if in the meantime, it has not been accepted.

2.13. REVOCATION OF AN ACCEPTANCE

An acceptance may be revoked at any time before the communication of the acceptance is complete for the acceptor, but not afterwards (Section 5). We know that for the acceptor, the communication of acceptance is complete when it comes to the knowledge of the offeror. It means that *an acceptance may be revoked at any time before the letter of acceptance reaches the offeror.* The revocation is effective when it reaches the offeror before he (offeror) receives the acceptance. Thus, an acceptor may cancel his acceptance by a speedier mode of communication which will reach earlier than the acceptance itself.

Example 2.36. *A* offers, by a letter, to sell his house to *B*. *B* accepts the offer by a letter. *B* may revoke his acceptance at any time before his letter of acceptance reaches *A*, and not afterwards.

Example 2.37. *A* offered, by a letter, to sell his car to *B* for Rs. 100,000. The letter was posted on 15th March which reached *B* on 17th March. *B* accepted the offer and posted his letter of acceptance on 20th March which reached *A* on 22nd March. Here, *B* becomes, bound by his acceptance on 22nd March. In this case, the acceptance could be revoked at any time before 22nd March.

Thus, the communication of revocation of acceptance should reach the offeror earlier than the acceptance itself. But sometimes, both the communications (*i.e.*, acceptance and revocation) reach together. In such cases, which one of the two is opened first decides the issue. Where the acceptance is revoked by a telegram, a person is more likely to open the telegram first. Therefore, the acceptance will be treated as revoked. It is to be noted that there is no clear provision in Section 5 of the Indian Contract Act. The only illustration, appended to the section, seems to show that in such a case, the acceptance will be deemed to have been revoked.

Example 2.38. *A* offers, by letter sent by post, to sell his house to *B*. *B* accepts the offer by a letter. *B* may revoke his acceptance at any time before or at the moment when the letter communicating it reaches *A*, but not afterwards.

The use of the words "before or at the moment", shows that the acceptance is deemed to be revoked when the 'acceptance' and 'revocation' reach together.

2.14. COMMUNICATION OF REVOCATION

The revocation of an offer or acceptance is effective if it is communicated. The communication of revocation is complete at different times for the person who makes it, and also for the person to whom it is made. For the person who makes the revocation, the communication of revocation is complete when it is put into a course of transmission to the person to whom it is made. And for the person to whom the revocation is made, the communication of revocation is complete when it comes to his knowledge (Section 4).

Example 2.39. *A* offers, by a letter, to sell his house to *B* at a certain price. *B* accepts *A*'s offer by a letter sent by post. If *A* revokes his offer by telegram, revocation of offer is complete for *A* when the telegram is sent. And for *B*, it is complete when *B* receives the telegram.

If *B* revokes his acceptance by telegram, the revocation of acceptance is complete for *B* when the telegram is despatched. And for *A* it is complete when *A* receives the telegram.

Example 2.40. *A* offered, by a letter, to sell his car to *B* for Rs. 95,000. The letter was posted on 10th January which reached *B* on 13th January. *A* revoked his offer by telegram on 14th January which reached *B* on 15th January. For *A* the revocation is complete when the telegram is despatched *i.e.,* on 14th January. But for *B*, it is complete when *B* receives the telegram *i.e.,* on 15th January. Here if *B* despatches his acceptance by telegram on 13th itself then *A* will be bound by his offer because revocation of offer is effective only if it is made before the acceptor despatches his acceptance.

Example 2.41. *A* of Bombay, offered, by a letter, to sell some specific property to *B* of Delhi for Rs. ten lakhs. The letter of offer was posted on 1st April, which reached *B* on 5th April. *B* posted his letter of acceptance on 7th April, which reached *A* on 11th April.

How would the contract be affected if

(*i*) *A* posts a letter of revocation of offer on 6th April which reaches *B* on 10th April.

(*ii*) *B* despatches a telegram cancelling his acceptance which reaches *A* on 10th April.

The effect on the contract is as under:

(*i*) The offeror becomes bound as soon as the letter of acceptance is posted. And for the offeree, the revocation of an offer is complete only when it comes to the knowledge of the offeree. In this case, the letter of acceptance was posted by the acceptor on 7th April, while the letter of revocation of offer was received by him (acceptor) on 10th April. The contract between *A* and *B* is not revoked because the offeror became bound by his offer on 7th and the revocation was effective from 10th.

(*ii*) Acceptance can be revoked at any time before it is complete for the acceptor (*i.e.,* before it reaches the offeror). In this case, the letter of acceptance is received by *A* on 11th April, while the telegram of revocation of acceptance reaches *A* on 10th April. The revocation is effective on 10th. Thus, there was no contract between *A* and *B*.

2.15. LAPSE OF OFFER

1. ***By communication of notice of revocation***
2. ***By lapse of time***
3. ***By failure to accept condition precedent***
4. ***By the death or insanity of the offeror***
5. ***By counter-offer by the offeree***
6. ***By not accepting the offer, according to the prescribed or usual mode***
7. ***By rejection of offer by the offeree***
8. ***By change in law***

An offer should be accepted before it lapses (*i.e.,* comes to an end). An offer may come to an end in any of the following ways stated in section 6 of the Indian Contract Act:

1. *By communication of notice of revocation:* An offer may come to an end by communication of notice of revocation by the offeror. It may be noted that an offer can be revoked only before its acceptance is complete for the offeror. In other words, an offeror can revoke his offer at any time before he becomes bound by it. Thus, the communication of revocation of offer should reach the offeree before the acceptance is communicated. A notice of revocation will take effect only when it is brought to the knowledge of the offeree. It may be noted that notice of revocation must come from offeror or his duty authorised agent.

Example 2.42. *A* made a bid at an auction sale of a property. *A*'s bid was the highest bid. But before the bid was knocked down, *A* discovered that the property was subject to mortgage, and he retracted his bid. Even so the auctioneer knocked down the property to *A*. It was held that *A* is not bound with the auction sale. *A*'s bid was an offer and he was entitled to withdraw the same before it was accepted by knocking down the property. Here, A's retraction of bid is the notice of revocation of the offer which was given before acceptance (*i.e.*, before knocking down the property).

2. *By lapse of time:* Sometimes, the time is fixed for the acceptance of the offer, and it is not accepted within the fixed time. In such cases, the offer comes to an end automatically on the expiry of fixed time.

Example 2.43. *A* offered on Thursday to sell wool to *B*. Three days time was given to *B* for acceptance. *B* accepted the offer on Monday, but by that time *A* had already sold the wool after waiting for the allowed period of three days. It was held that the offer had lapsed, and *A* was not bound by the acceptance. [*Head* v. *Diggon* (1828) 2 M & R 97]

Where no time for acceptance is prescribed, the offer has to be accepted within reasonable time. The offer lapses if it is not accepted within that time. The term 'reasonable time' will depend upon the facts and circumstances of each case.

Example 2.44. *A* applied for shares of a company in June. The allotment (acceptance) was made in November. It was held that the offer to take shares had lapsed as the reasonable time had passed since the making of the offer, and *A* was not bound to take shares.

[*Ramsgate Victoria Hotel Co.* v. *Montefoir,* (1866) LR & Ex. Ch. 109]

3. *By failure to accept condition precedent:* Sometimes, the offer requires that some condition must be fulfilled before the acceptance of the offer. In such cases, the offer lapses, if it is accepted without fulfilling the condition.

Example 2.45. *A* offered to sell his cycle to *B* for Rs. 400 subject to the condition that *B* should pay advance of Rs. 100 before certain date. *B* accepted the offer but did not send the advance of Rs. 100. In this case, the offer stands lapsed as the advance is not paid.

4. *By the death or insanity of the offeror:* Sometimes, the offeror dies or becomes insane. In such cases, the offer comes to an end if the fact of his death or insanity comes to the knowledge of the acceptor before he makes his acceptance. But if the offer is accepted in ignorance of the fact of death or insanity of the offeror, the acceptance is valid. This will result in a valid contract, and legal representatives of the deceased offeror shall be bound by the contract. It is to be noted that there is no provision in the Indian Contract Act about the effect of the death of an offeree, if he dies before acceptance. But it is an established rule, that the offer comes to an end by operation of law, because death automatically bring about the termination of the offer. As an offer can be accepted only by an offeree and not by any other person, therefore it cannot be accepted by his executors also.

In addition to the modes stated in section 6, an offer is also revoked in the following cases:

5. *By counter-offer by the offeree:* Sometimes, a counter-offer is made by the offeree. In such cases, the original offer automatically comes to an end, as the counter-offer amounts to rejections of the original offer.

Example 2.46. *A* offered to sell a farm to *B* for Rs. 100,000. But, *B* offered to buy it for Rs. 95,000. *A* refused to sell for Rs. 95,000. Subsequently, *B* offered to purchase the farm for Rs. 100,000. It was held that no contract came into existence as *B*, by offering Rs. 95,000, had rejected the original offer. In fact, the counter-offer to an offer amounts to the rejection of the original offer. [Based on *Hyde* v. *Wrench,* (1840) 3 Beav. 334]

6. ***By not accepting the offer, according to the prescribed or usual mode:*** Sometimes, some manner of acceptance is prescribed in the offer. In such cases, the offeror can revoke the offer if it is not accepted according to the prescribed manner. It may be noted that within a reasonable time offeror should give notice to the offeree that the offer should be accepted in the prescribed manner, and not otherwise.

7. ***By rejection of offer by the offeree:*** Sometimes, the offeree rejects the offer. In such cases, the offer comes to an end. Once the offeree rejects the offer, he cannot revive the offer by subsequently attempting to accept it. The rejection of offer may be express or implied. Express rejection is that where the offeree rejects the offer by words, written or spoken. Implied rejection is that where offeree's conduct shows that he is not accepting the offer, *e.g.*, where the offeree makes a counter-offer, or where he gives conditional acceptance.

8. ***By change in law:*** Sometimes, there is a change in law which makes the offer illegal or incapable or performance. In such cases also, the offer comes to an end.

2.16. TENDER AND ITS ACCEPTANCE

The term 'tender' may be defined as an offer to supply certain goods or execute certain work at a specified cost. Sometimes, a person requires certain goods or services from time to time. In such cases, he may invite tenders for the supply of specific goods or services. The tenders are usually invited by an advertisement in newspapers. An advertisement inviting tender is not an offer. But merely an invitation to receive offer. On the basis of such advertisement, many persons send their tender for the supply of required goods or services, and specify the rates to be charged for the same. Thereafter, the person inviting tender may accept (*i.e.*, approve) the one which suits him. On such approval, the tender is converted into a 'standing offer' or 'open offer' *i.e.*, an offer for the continuous supply of certain goods or services at a certain rate over a definite period of time. The approval of the tender amounts to an intimation to the person sending the tender that his offer will be considered to remain open during the specified period of time. A binding contract arises only when the tender is accepted by placing an order according to the terms thereof, with the person submittng the tender. Moreover, each separate order constitutes a separate contract.

[*Chatturbhuj Vithaldas* v. *Moreshwar Parshram*, AIR 1954 SC 236]

The following points are important to note in connection with the contracts through tenders:

1. Where, the tender is in the form of a definite or single offer, a binding contract comes into existence as soon as the tender is accepted *e.g.*, where the tenderer agrees to supply 100 cement bags at the rate of Rs. 100 per bag. Its acceptance will result into a binding contract.
2. Where the person inviting tender agrees to purchase all the goods required by him from the tenderer, whenever he requires goods during the period of tender, he must place the order with the tenderer. However, he will not be bound to make any order if there is no requirement during the period of tender.

2.17. CROSS OFFERS

Sometimes, two persons make identifiable offers to each other in ignorance of each other's offer. In such cases, the offers are called 'cross offers'. It may be noted that one's offer cannot be treated as acceptance of other's offer. The reason for the same is that one is not made with reference to the other. And thus, no binding contract will come into existence.

[*Tinn* v. *Hoffman & Co.* (1873) 29 LJ 272]

Example 2.47. *A*, by a letter, offered to sell his motorcycle to *B* for Rs. 10,000. Without knowing about *A*'s offer, *B* also, by a letter, offered to buy *A*'s same motorcycle for Rs. 10,000. Both the offers crossed each other in post. In this case, the offers are cross offers, and thus, no binding contract will come into existence.

2.18. AGREEMENT TO MAKE A CONTRACT IN FUTURE OR AGREEMENT TO AGREE IN FUTURE

Sometimes, the parties enter into an agreement to make a contract on the terms to be settled in future. In such cases, no binding contract comes into existence. And thus, in future date, the parties are not bound to enter into a contract as previously agreed. The reason for the same is that unless all the terms of the contract have been finalised and agreed by the contracting parties, no contract comes into existence.

Thus, an agreement to agree in future is not a valid contract and cannot be enforced in a Court of Law.

Example 2.48. *A*, an actress, and *B*, the owner of a theatre, entered into an agreement that for a particular play to be shown in London on some future date, she (*A*) would be given a role at a salary to be agreed in future. On the future date of the play, *A* was not given any role, and she filed a suit against *B* for the breach of contract. It was held that there was no binding contract between *A* and *B*, and thus he (*B*) is not guilty of breach of contract. [*Loftus* v. *Roberts*, (1902) 18 TLR 532].

2.19. STANDARDISED FORMS OF CONTRACTS CONTAINED IN PRINTED DOCUMENTS AS IN TICKETS ETC.

Nowadays, many contracts are contained in printed forms, which are the standardised forms of contract of various organisations such as life insurance corporation, railways, shipping companies, banks, hotels etc. As a matter of fact, it is difficult for such big organisations to draw out a separate contract with every individual. Therefore, they have printed forms of contract. It may be noted that certain individuals such as drycleaners, cycle stand owners etc. are also having their printed forms of contract. Such printed forms are the standardised forms of contract, which contain large number of terms and conditions, which usually limit or exclude their liability under the contract. The person signing such forms becomes bound by the terms and conditions even if he never acquainted himself with its terms. However, the special terms and conditions contained in the printed form must be brought to the notice of the offeree (the person with whom the contract is made).

Example 2.49. *A* deposited his bag at the cloak room at a railway station and received a ticket. On the face of the ticket, the words 'see back' were printed. And on the back of the ticket there was a condition that "the company will not be responsible for any package exceeding the value of £10", A notice to the same effect was also hung up in the cloak room. *A*'s bag was lost from the cloak room. And he claimed the actual value of the bag which was more than £10. The railway company, relied upon the condition. *A* contended that he knew that something was printed on the ticket, but he did not see what it was. It was held that *A* was bound by the condition on the back of the ticket even if he did not read it. And, thus, the company was liable for £10 only

[*Parker* v. *South Easterns Rail Co.*, (1877) 2 CPD 418]

Note: The standardised forms of contracts have been described as **'Compulsory Contracts'** as they are a kind of imposition on the offeree, or **'Contracts of Adhesion'** which means that the individual has no choice, but to accept. He does not negotiate, but merely adheres.

2.21. LEGAL RULES RELATING TO STANDARDISED CONTRACTS

The printed forms of contracts are governed by established legal rules. And if these rules are not observed, the party, delivering the printed forms of contract, will be liable even if its liability was excluded by special terms and conditions. These rules may be discussed under the following heads:

1. ***The printed terms and conditions must be brought to the notice of the offeree:*** It is the duty of the person, delivering a printed form of contracts, to bring all the terms and conditions

> 1. *The printed terms and conditions must be brought to the notice of the offeree*
> 2. *The terms and conditions must be brought to the notice of the offeree before or, at the time of making of contract*
> 3. *The terms and conditions must not be misrepresented to the offeree*
> 4. *The terms and conditions must not be unreasonable*
> 5. *The terms and conditions must not exclude party's liability for failure to perform his fundamental obligations*
> 6. *The document containing the terms and conditions must be a contractual document and not merely a receipt or voucher*

to the notice of the concerned party, *i.e.*, offeree. This can be done by expressly communicating the terms to the offeree; or by giving a reasonable notice of the existence of these terms, *i.e.*, by printing them in such a clear way that his attention is drawn towards them *e.g.*, by printing the words 'see back', or 'for conditions see back' on the face of the printed form or ticket. If this is not done, the offeree accepting the printed contract, will not be bound by the terms and conditions contained in it.

Example 2.50. *A* bought a steamer ticket for travelling from Dublin to Whitehaven. On the face of the ticket, the only words printed were 'Dublin to Whitehaven'. On the back of the ticket, there were printed certain conditions one of which excluded the liability of the shipping company "for loss, injury or delay to the passenger or his luggage". However, *A* did not see the back of the ticket, nor was there any indication on its face about the conditions on the back. *A*'s luggage was lost due to the negligence of the servants of the shipping company. It was held that *A* was entitled to recover, from the shipping company, the damages suffered due to loss of his luggage. In this case, there was no indication on the face of the ticket to invite *A*'s attention to the special terms printed on the back of the ticket. [*Henderson* v. *Stevenson*, (1875) 32 LT 709]

However, if the terms and conditions have been brought to the notice of the offeree, he will be bound by them even if he is illiterate or does not known the language in which terms and conditions are printed. Once he knew of the existence of these terms, it is then his duty to get them explained.

2. *The terms and conditions must be brought to the notice of the offeree before or, at the time of making of contract:* It is another duty of the person delivering a printed form of contract to bring the terms and conditions to the notice of the offeree before or at the time of making the contract. A subsequent notice will amount to the modifications of the original contract which will not bind the other party unless he gives his consent to the same.

Example 2.51. A delivered certain goods to a transport company for carriage. The transport company issued a ticket which did not contain any condition. Subsequently, the company issued a circular to the consignors limiting its liability for the goods damaged or lost in transit. *A*'s good were damaged during transit. He filed a suit against the transport company for the recovery of damages. It was held that *A* was not bound by the circular issued subsequent to the making of the contract. And thus, the transport company was held liable for damages.

[*Raipur Transport Co.* v. *Ghanshyam*, (1956) A. Nag. 145]

3. *The terms and conditions must not be misrepresented to the offeree:* It is also the duty of the person delivering the printed form of contract not to make any misrepresentation about the terms and conditions contained in it. If the offeree accepts such terms and conditions on the basis of misrepresentations made by a person delivering the contract, then he will not be bound by the same.

Example 2.52. *A* delivered her white 'wedding dress' to *B*, a dry cleaner, for cleaning. On being asked by *B* to sign a receipt, she enquired why she was to sign it. *B* told her that she was to take responsibility for any damage to 'beads and sequins' (*i.e.*, ornamental work) only. She then signed the receipt without reading it. In fact, the receipt contained a condition excluding liability for all the damage to the dress howsoever caused. When the dress was returned, there were stains on it. *A* filed a suit against *B* for damages. *B* pleaded that he had excluded his liability for any loss. It was held that *B* was liable for damages as *A* was made to sign the receipt by misrepresentation.

[*Curtis* v. *Chemical Cleaning and Dyeing Co.,* (1951) 1 K.B. 805]

4. *The terms and conditions must not be unreasonable:* The terms and conditions contained in the printed form of contract must not be unreasonable. A term is unreasonable if it is against the public policy, or if it would defeat the very purpose of the contract.

Example 2.53. *A* delivered some clothes to a laundry for cleaning, and a receipt was given to her. The laundry receipt contained a condition on its reverse that in case of loss, the customer would be entitled to claim only 15% of the market price or value of the article. *A*'s new sari was lost due to negligence of laundry owner. It was held that *A* was not bound by the condition as it was unreasonable. Because it was imposed without caring for the public interest. And thus, laundry owner was held liable to compensate *A* for the loss of the sari.

[*Lilly White* v. *Mannuswami,* AIR 1966 Madras. 13]

5. *The terms and conditions must not exclude party's liability for failure to perform his fundamental obligations:* Party's liability for failure to perform fundamental obligations cannot be excluded by such terms and conditions contained in printed forms of contracts.

Example 2.54. *A* deposited his luggage at the parcel office of a railway station and agreed to pay the ordinary rates. The railway company gave him a ticket which contained a condition that the railway company will not be liable for misdelivery or loss of any article exceeding £5 in value unless special charges of the same were paid. *B,* a stranger, demanded the luggage from the railway company pretending himself to be *A*'s friend. And the railway company allowed him to take away the luggage. Subsequently, *A* claimed the luggage from the railway company. The railway company contended that it had excluded its liability for misdelivery of articles. It was held that the railway company was liable as it had failed to perform its fundamental obligation to take care of the deposited articles in allowing an unauthorised person to take away the goods.

[*Alexendar* v. *Railway Executive,* (1951) 2 KB 882]

6. *The document containing the terms and conditions must be a contractual document and not merely a receipt or voucher:* If the document is merely a receipt or voucher, the party receiving it will not be bound by its terms and conditions. In such cases, extra care will have to be taken to communicate the terms of voucher etc, *e.g.,* to use red ink to draw one's attention towards the conditions.

Example 2.55. *A* went to a beach and hired a deck chair from the District Council. He paid the hire charges of the chair. He was given a ticket by the attendant, which he put in his pocket without reading. While he was sitting on the chair, it broke and injured him. The ticket contained a condition that "The District Council will not be liable for any accident or damage arising from hire of chairs." *A* filed a suit against the District Council for the recovery for damages. The District Council relied upon the condition contained in the ticket. It was held that the District Council was liable for damages. The court observed that the ticket was no more than a 'receipt', and was quite different from a railway ticket which contains the terms upon which a railway company agrees to carry passengers. In this case, the purpose of the ticket was to give a receipt for the hire charges paid by a person. [*Chapelton v. Barry Urban District Council* (1940) 1 K.B. 532]

LEGAL PROVISIONS (SECTIONS) DISCUSSED IN THE CHAPTER

Important legal provisions (Sections) of the Indian Contract Act, 1872, discussed in this chapter, are reproduced hereunder for ready reference:

1. ***Section 2 (a): Proposal (Offer)***
   When one person signifies to anotber his willingness to do or to abstain form doing anything, with a view to obtaining the assent of that other to such act or abstinence, he is said to make a proposal.
2. ***Section 2 (b): Acceptance***
   When the person to whom the proposal in made signifies his assent thereato, the proposal is said to be accepted.

3. ***Section 3: Comunication, Acceptance and Revocation of Proposals***

The communication of proposals, the acceptance of proposals, and the revocation of proposals and acceptances, respectively, are deemed to be made by any act or omission of the party proposing, accepting or revoking, by which he intends to communicate such proposal, acceptance or revocation, or which has the effect of communicating it.

4. ***Section 4: Communncation When Complete***

The communication of a proposal is complete when it comes ot the knowledge of the person to whom it is made. The communication of an acceptance is complete,—

as against the proposer, when it is put in a course of transmission to him so as to be out of the power of the acceptor;

as against the acceptor, when it comes to the knowledge of the proposer.

The communication of a revocation is complete—

as against the person who makes it, when it is put into a course of transmission to the person to whom it is made, so as to be out of the power of the person who makes it;

as against of the person to whom it is made, when it comes to his knowledge.

5. ***Section 5: Revocation of Proposal and Acceptance***

A proposal may be revoked at any time before the communication of its acceptance is complete as against the proposer, but not afterwards.

An acceptance maybe revoked at any time before the communcation of the acceptance is complete as against the acceptor, but not afterwards.

6. ***Section 6: Revocation How Made***

A proposal is revoked—

(1) by the communication of notice of revocation by the proposer to the other party;

(2) by the laspe of the time prescribed in such proposal for its acceptance, or, if no time is so prescribed, by the lapse of a reasonable time, without communication of the acceptance;

(3) by the failure of the acceptor to fulfil a condition precedent to acceptance; or

(4) by the death or insanity of the proposer, if the fact of his death or insanity comes to hte knowledge of the acceptor before acceptance

7. ***Section 7: Acceptance must be absolute***

In order to convert a proposal into a promise, the acceptance must–

(1) be absolute and unqualified;

(2) be expressed in some usual and reasonalbe manner, unless the proposal prescribes the manner in which it is to be accepted. If the proposal prescribes a manner in which it is to be acceptd, and the acceptance is not made in such manner, the proposer may, within a reasonable time after the acceptance is communicated to him, insist that his proposal shall be accepted in the prescribed manner, and not otherwise; but, if he fails to do so, he accepts the acceptance.

8. ***Section 8: Acceptance by Performing Condition or by Receiving Considerations***

Performance of the conditions of a proposal or the acceptance of any consideration for a reciprocal promise which may be offered with a proposal, is an acceptance of the proposal.

TEST QUESTIONS

1. Define the term 'offer'. Explain the essentials and legal rules for a valid offer giving suitable examples. When does an offer lapse?
2. Distinguish between the followings:
   (*a*) Offer and invitation to offer. (*b*) Offer and mere statement of intention.
   (*c*) Offer and an answer to a question.
3. Elucidate—"The communication of a proposal is complete when it comes to the knowledge of the person to whom it is made."
4. Define the term 'acceptance'. Explain the essentials and legal rules for a valid acceptance giving suitable examples.
5. "An acceptance to be effective must be communicated to the offeror." Comment with exceptions, if any.
6. Describe the mode by which an acceptance can be given. Is there any time limit within which the acceptance is to be given?

7. Discuss briefly the legal provisions relating to the communication of offer, acceptance and revocation. When an offer and acceptance may be revoked?
8. When is communication of proposal, acceptance and revocation complete? How and on what grounds does a proposal stand revoked?
9. How and on what grounds the offer and acceptance can be revoked? Is there any time limit after which a revocation of offer and acceptance cannot be made?
10. Discuss the law relating to standardised form of contracts.
11. Write short notes on the following:
    (*a*) Contracts by post.
    (*b*) Contracts over telephone.
    (*c*) Counter offer.
    (*d*) Lapse of offer.
    (*e*) Carlill v. Carbolic Smoke Ball Co.
    (*f*) Cross offers.

MULITIPLE CHOICE TYPE QUESTIONS

1. An offer accepted without knowledge does not confer any legal rights on the acceptor.
   (*a*) True, as the offer cannot be accepted without its knowledge.
   (*b*) False, as there is no such legal provision/decision in this regard.
2. Which of the following is not the legal requirements of a valid offer?
   (*a*) It must be communicated to the offeree.
   (*b*) It must be made with a view to obtain offeree's assent.
   (*c*) It must express offerer's final willingness.
   (*d*) It must be made to a specific person and not to public at large.
3. A general offer made to the public at large is valid, and a binding contract is made with a person who having the knowledge of the offer
   (*a*) comes forward and acts accordingly.
   (*b*) acts accordingly, and his act is ratified by the offeror
4. On the acceptance of an offer by an offeree,
   (*a*) only the acceptor becomes bound by accepting the offer
   (*b*) only the offeror becomes bound as his terms are accepted.
   (*c*) both the acceptor and offeree becomes bound by the contract.
   (*d*) none of these.
5. Which of the following is not the legal requirements of a valid acceptance?
   (*a*) It must be communicated.
   (*b*) It must be absolute and unconditional.
   (*c*) It must be presumed from silence if not communicated within specified time.
   (*d*) It must be accepted by a person who has the authority to accept.
6. *A*, by a letter dated. 25th Dec. 1998, offers to sell his house to *B* for Rs. 10 lakhs. The letter reaches *B* on 27th Dec. 1998, who posts his acceptance on 28th Dec. 1998 which reaches *A* on 30th Dec. 1998. Here, the communication of offer is complete on
   (*a*) 25th Dec. 1998.
   (*b*) 27th Dec. 1998.
   (*c*) 28th Dec. 1998.
   (*d*) 30th Dec. 1998.
7. In the above question No. 6, the communication of acceptance is complete against *A* on 28th Dec. 1998, and against *B* on
   (*a*) 25th Dec. 1998.
   (*b*) 27th Dec. 1998.
   (*c*) 28th Dec. 1998.
   (*d*) 30th Dec. 1998.
8. *A*, by a letter dated. 15th March, offers to sell his car to *B*, who posts his acceptance on 20th March. Here.
   (*a*) *A* can revoke his offer before he receives the letter of acceptance.
   (*b*) *A* cannot revoke his offer as he becomes bound by the acceptance on 20th March.
9. In the above question No. 8,
   (*a*) *B* can revoke his acceptance at any time till his letter reaches A.
   (*b*) *B* cannot revoke his acceptance as he becomes bound by posting his acceptance letter.

10. *A*, by a letter, offers to sell his T.V. to *B* for Rs. 10,000. Without knowing *A*'s offer, *B*, by a letter, offers to buy the same T.V. from *A* for Rs. 10,000. Here,
    (*a*) a binding contract comes into existence as *B*'s letter is equivalent to acceptance of *A*'s offer.
    (*b*) no binding contract comes into existence as *B*'s letter is merely a cross offer.

ANSWERS

1. (*a*)	**2.** (*d*)	**3.** (*a*)	**4.** (*c*)	**5.** (*c*)	**6.** (*b*)
7. (*d*)	**8.** (*b*)	**9.** (*a*)	**10.** (*b*)		

OBJECTIVE TYPE QUESTIONS WITH REASONING

State with reasons whether the following statements are correct or incorrect.

1. An advertisement for holding an auction sale amounts to an offer.
2. A general offer may be accepted by any one.
3. An acceptance can be made even without the knowledge of the offer.
4. If only a part of offer is accepted, then a valid contract comes into existence only in respect of that part.
5. The communication of offer is complete when the letter of offer is posted though it has not reached the person to whom the offer is made.
6. If the properly addressed letter of acceptance is duly stamped and posted to the offeror, the offeror is bound by the same, even if the letter is lost in post.
7. If an offer is accepted in ignorance of the fact of death or insanity of the offeror, the acceptance is valid and binding.
8. An acceptance once made cannot be revoked in any case.
9. An advertisement inviting tender is not an offer.
10. Under the English Law, when a letter of acceptance is posted, both the acceptor and the offeror become bound by the same.

ANSWERS

1. *Incorrect.* It is only a statement of intention to hold auction.
2. *Correct.* A general offer can be accepted by any person who has the knowledge about the offer.
3. *Incorrect.* An offer can be validly accepted only if the acceptor has the knowledge of the offer.
4. *Incorrect.* In such a case, acceptance is invalid and without any legal effect.
5. *Incorrect.* In contracts through post, the communication of offer is complete when the letter of offer reaches the offeror and comes to his knowledge.
6. *Correct.* It is the law on the point. The offeror becomes bound by acceptance as soon as it is put in a course of transmission to him.
7. *Correct.* It is the legal position on the point.
8. *Incorrect.* An acceptance can be revoked at any time before the communication of acceptance is complete as against the offeror.
9. *Correct.* It is merely an invitation to receive offer.
10. *Correct.* It is the legal position under the English Law.

PRACTICAL PROBLEMS

1. *A*'s brother absconded from home. He sent his servant in search of his brother. When the servant had left, *A* by handbills, offered to pay Rs. 50,000 to anyone who discovered his brother. The servant came to know about the reward only when he had already discovered *A*'s brother. The servant, however, brought an action against *A* to recover the reward. Will be succeed ? Give reasons.

   Hint : The servant will not succeed in recovering the reward. The reason for the same is that the acceptance of an offer without its knowledge does not confer any legal rights on the acceptor.

2. *A* has three cars and says to *B*, "I shall sell my car to you, will you buy it? " *B* say, "yes, I shall buy it." Is it a binding contract ? Give reasons.

   Hint : No. It is not a binding contract. The reason for the same is that the terms of the agreement are not certain. It is not clear as to which car *A* intends to sell to *B* and what is the price at which he wants to sell.

3. *A* sent a telegram to *B* writing, "will you sell me your 'ROSE' farm house? Telegraph lowest cash price." *B* replied by telegram, " lowest cash price for the ROSE farm house Rs. 3 crores". *A* sent another telegram stating, " I agree to buy the ROSE farm house for Rs. 3 crores asked by you, please send the title deeds." However, *B* refused to sell the farm house and *A* brought legal action against *B*. Will be succeed? Give reasons.

   Hint : No, *A* will not succeed. The reason for the same is that *B* did not offer to sell the farm house at Rs. 3 crores, he simply answered the question asked by *A*.

4. *A* entered *B*'s shop where goods were displayed with price list attached. *A* picked up a show-piece with price tag of Rs. 500 and placed Rs. 500 on the counter. But *B* refused to sell the same to *A*. Is *B* justified ? Give reasons.

   Hint : Yes, *B* is justified in refusing to sell the show-piece. In such cases, price labels amounts to 'invitation to offer' only and not the offer to sell. Picking up the show-piece and placing Rs. 500 at counter is merely an offer to buy by *A* which may or may not be accepted.

5. A gave an advertisement in Hindustan Times that he would sell his car and furniture by auction on 10th August, 2007 at his residence at New Delhi. *B* from Chandigardh reached Delhi on the appointed date and time, but *A* had already cancelled the auction. *B* seeks your legal guidance. Advise him.

   Hint : In this case, *B* will not succeed in his legal action. Such an advertisements is only an invitation to receive offer' and not an offer in itself.

6. On Ist January, 2007, *A* by a letter offered to sell his property to *B* for Rs. 10 lakhs which stated that offer will be kept open until 10th January, 2007. On 5th January, 2007 B visited *A*'s office and while sitting at reception, *B* heared that *A* was finalizing the deal of the same property with another person C and entered into an agreement to sell the property to *C*. Next day *i.e.* on 6th January, 2007, *B* accepted the offer and delivered the letter of acceptance to *A*. Is *B*'s acceptance valid? Give reasons.

   Hint : Yes, *B*'s acceptance is valid as it has been made before revocation of the offer by *A*. The overhearing by *B* does not amount to revocation of offer made to him.

7. *A* offered to sell his car to *B* for Rs. 95,000 and wrote that if he did not hear from him *B* within a week, he would presume that *B* had accepted the offer. No reply was given by *B*. Is there a binding contract ? Give reasons.

   Hint : No binding contract is concluded between *A* and *B*. The acceptance cannot be presumed from silence.

8. *A* offers to sell his Laptop to *B* for Rs. 30,000. *B* offers to buy the same for Rs. 25,000 and *A* refuses to sell at this price. Subsequently *B* offers to buy the Laptop at Rs. 30,000, the price originally asked by *A*, but *A'* again refuses to sell the Laptop. Is there a binding contract? Give reasons.

   Hint : No binding contract is concluded between *A* and *B* as by offeree Rs. 25,000 *B* had rejected the original offer. *A* counter offer by the offeree amounts to rejection of original offer.

9. *A* makes an offer to *B* by a telegram stating, " I will sell my plot of land for Rs. 25 lakhs if you give me your Honda City Car." *B* accepted the offer to buy the plot but did not accept the condition to sell the car. Is the acceptance valid ?

   Hint : No. it is not a valid acceptance. The offer should be accepted as a whole.

10. *A* offers, by a letters, to sell his house to *B* at a certain price on 15th December which reaches *B* on 17th December. *B* accepts the offer by a letter posted on 18th December. But the next day *B* revokes his acceptances by a telegram which reaches *A* before his letter of acceptance. *A* sues *B* on the ground that revocation is not valid. Will he succeed ?

    Hint : No, *A* will not succeed. In this case, the revocation of acceptance is valid because an acceptor can revoke his acceptance at any time before the letter of acceptance reaches the offeror.

CONSIDERATION

3.1. INTRODUCTION

The consideration is one of the essential elements of a valid contract. We have discussed, in the last chapter, that a mere promise is not enforceable. As a matter of fact, an enforceable agreement must be supported by consideration also. Section 25 of the Indian Contract Act specifically states that "an agreement made without consideration is void". Thus, the general rule is that an agreement is void if there is no consideration to it. However, certain exceptions to this rule are also provided in Section 25 itself, which will be discussed in Article. 3.4.

It may be noted that a valid contract arises only when three things, namely, the offer, the acceptance, and the consideration concur. We have studied that mutual assent takes place by offer and acceptance. But to have the mutual assent, there must be something which is to be assented and agreed upon to each other. That 'something' is the consideration. In this chapter, we shall discuss the legal provisions relating to consideration.

3.2. DEFINITION OF CONSIDERATION

The term 'consideration' may be defined as the price of the promise. This term is used in the sense of *quid pro quo* (*i.e.*, something in return). It means that when a party to an agreement promises to do something, he must get *something* in return. This 'something' which a party gets in return is the consideration. Some of the eminent jurists have defined the consideration as under:

1. "Consideration is the price for which the promise of other is bought, and promise thus given for value is enforceable." [*Pollock on Contract*, 13th end. p. 133]
2. "Consideration is the price of a promise, a return or *quid pro quo*, something of value received by the promisor as inducement of the promise." [*Fazaladdin* v. *Panchanan Das*, AIR 1957 Cal. 92]
3. "Consideration means something which is of some value in the eyes of law. It may be some benefit to the plaintiff or some detriment to the defendant." [Justice Patterson, in *Thomas v. Thomas*, (1842) 2 Q.B. 859]
4. "A valuable consideration in the sense of the law, may consist either in some

right, interest, profit or benefit according to the one party, or some forbearance, detriment, loss or responsibility given, suffered or undertaken by the other."

[Justice Lush in *Currie*, v. *Misa*, (1875) LR 10, EX. 153 at P. 162]

The term 'consideration' is defined in section 2(*d*) of the Indian Contract Act, which reads as under:

"When at the desire of the promisor, the promisee or any other person has done or abstained from doing, or does or abstains from doing, or promises to do or abstain from doing something, such act or abstinence or promise is called a consideration for the promise."

The analysis of this definition shows that following are the essential parts of consideration:

1. The consideration is an act (*i.e.*, doing of something), or an abstinence (*i.e.*, abstaining from doing something). It means that consideration is an act 'to do' or 'not to do' something.
2. Such act or abstinence should be done at the desire of the promisor.
3. Such act or abstinence may be done by the promisee or any other person.
4. Such act or abstinence is either already executed, or is in the process of execution or may be still executory. It means that the consideration may be past, present or future.

The meaning and essentials of consideration become clear from the following examples.

The detailed discussion on the above points is given in the next article of Essentials and Legal Rules for a Valid Consideration.

Example 3.1. *A* agrees to sell his car to *B* for Rs. 1,40,000. In this case, *B*'s promise to pay the sum of Rs. 1,40,000 is the consideration for *A*'s promise to sell the car. And *A*'s promise to sell the car is the consideration for *B*'s promise to pay the sum of Rs. 1,40,000.

Example 3.2. *A* owed Rs. 10,000 to *B*. *A* failed to pay the amount on due date, and *B* filed a suit against him for the recovery of this amount. Afterward, A's friend *C* requested *B* to withdraw the suit. He also promised that if *B* withdrew the suit then he will pay the amount due to *B* from *A*. In consideration of this promise, *B* withdrew the suit. This is a valid agreement and *B* can recover the amount from *C*.

3.3. ESSENTIALS AND LEGAL RULES FOR A VALID CONSIDERATION

1. ***The consideration must move (i.e., must be done or promised to be done) at the desire of the promisor***
2. ***The consideration must be lawful***
3. ***The consideration must be real and not illusory***
4. ***The consideration must be of some value in the eyes of law***
5. ***The consideration must not be the performance of existing duties***
6. ***The consideration need not be adequate***
7. ***The consideration may be furnished by the promisee or any other person***
8. ***The consideration may be either positive or negative***
9. ***The consideration may be forbearance to sue***
10. ***The consideration may be past, present or future***

The legal definition of consideration discussed in the last article, reveals the essential elements of consideration. The consideration is legally valid only if it satisfies all the requirements of its definition. The essential elements are discussed in points 1 to 5 in the following discussion, and the rest are the legal rules for a valid consideration.

1. *The consideration must move (i.e., must be done or promised to be done) at the desire of the promisor:* This essential element has been emphasised in Section 2(*d*) of the Indian Contract Act which says that an act or abstinence, which forms consideration for the promise, must be done or promised to be done according to the desire of the promisor.

In simple words, an act shall not be a good consideration for a promise unless it is done at the desire of the promisor.

Example 3.3. On the order of the collector of a town, *A* built certain shops in the Bazaar at his own expenses. These shops were occupied by *B*. In consideration of *A* having spent money in construction, *B* promised to pay some money to *A*. *A* sued *B* to recover the money as promised. The agreement between *A* and *B* to pay the money was held void being without consideration. *A*'s action to recover the money was rejected. In this case, the shops were not built at the desire of the promisor (*B*), but at the desire of the collector. [*Durga Parsas* v. *Baldeo* (1880) 3 All 221]

2. *The consideration must be lawful:* This essential element has been emphasised in Section 23 of the Indian Contract Act which says that "every agreement of which the consideration is unlawful, is void". It means that an agreement must be supported by lawful consideration.

Section 23 also gives certain instances of unlawful consideration. It states that consideration should not:

(*a*) be forbidden by law; (*b*) defeat the provisions of any law; (*c*) imply injury to the person or property of another person; and (*d*) be immoral or opposed to public policy.

Note: These points will be explained in a separate chapter 6 on 'Legality of Object and Consideration.'

Example 3.4. A promised to obtain for *B* an employment in the public service, and *B* promised to pay Rs. 70,000 to *A*. The agreement is void as the consideration for it is unlawful.

Example 3.5. *A* promised to pay Rs. 500 to *B* if he (*B*) beats *C*. The agreement is void as the consideration involves an injury to *C*, which is unlawful.

3. *The consideration must be real and not illusory:* It is one of the essential elements of consideration that it must be real and not illusory. It is important to note that though there is no provision in the Indian Contract Act, but it is an established principle that the consideration must be real.

Example 3.6. *A* promised to pay Rs. 500 to *B* if he (*B*) bring a star from the sky to earth. Here, consideration for *A*'s promise to pay Rs. 500 to *B* is "to bring a star from the sky". The contract is void as the consideration is illusory. This promise is also physically impossible to perform.

More discussion and examples on impossibility of performance are given in a chapter 11 on Performance of Contract.

4. *The consideration must be of some value in the eyes of law:* We know that consideration is an act, abstinence or promise on the part of the promisee or any other person, which has been done at the desire of promisor. It may be noted that such an act, or abstinence must be of some value in the eyes of law. The Supreme Court of India has laid down that "consideration shall be something which not only the parties regard, but the law can also regard as having some value."

[*Chidambara* v. *P.S. Renga*, AIR 1965 SC 193].

Thus, a worthless act will not be a sufficient consideration even if the act is done at the desire of the promisor.

Example 3.7. *A* promised to give his new car to *B* provided *B* will fetch it from the garage. Here, *B*'s act of fetching the car satisfies the words of definitions as it is done at the desire of the promisor. But it does not catch the spirit of the definition, and cannot be regarded as valuable consideration.

5. *The consideration must not be the performance of existing duties:* The term 'existing duties' includes legal obligations or contractual obligations.

(*a*) ***The consideration must not be the performance of legal obligations:*** A person may be bound to do something by law. The consideration must be something more than that what the promisee is already bound to do by law. The performance of legal duty is not a consideration for the promise.

Example 3.8. *A* promised to pay Rs. 500 to *B* (a Police Officer) for investigating a crime, which *B* was already bound to investigate by law. Here *A*'s promise to pay the amount is without valid consideration as *B* is already under a legal obligation to investigate the crime.

It may be noted that where a person agree to do something more than what he is legally bound to do, this will serve as a good consideration for the promise.

Example 3.9. *A*'s wife was caught in fire in a burning building. *A* offered reward to anyone who would rescue his wife, dead or alive. *B*, a fireman, at a great risk to his life and health, rescued *A*'s wife. He was allowed to receive the amount of reward because the court found that as a fireman of the city, he was not legally bound to risk his life in this rescue operation.

(*b*) ***The consideration must not be the performance of contractual obligations:*** The performance of legal obligation is no consideration for a promise. Similarly, the performance of contractual obligations is also not a consideration for the promise.

Example 3.10. *A* engaged *B*, an advocate, in a certain suit. *B* accepted a *vakalatnama* from *A* to act for him (*A*) on receiving his usual fee. Subsequently, *A* promised to pay to *B* certain sum of money as a special reward, if the suit was decided in his (*A*'s) favour. Here *A*'s promise was held to be without valid conideration. *B* having accepted the 'vakalatnama' was already bound to render his best services as an advocate. [*R. Chintaman* v. *Kalu Raju* (1877) 2 Bombay 362]

Thus, we see that where there is a pre-existing obligation between the promisor and promisee, a fresh promise to perform the existing obligations will be void for want of valid consideration. In fact, performance of existing obligations is no consideration for a promise.

6. *The consideration need not be adequate:* This legal rule for a valid consideration is contained in the Explanation II of Section 25 of the Indian Contract Act. According to this rule, an inadequate consideration does not render a contract void. The law simply requires that contract should be supported by consideration. So long as consideration exists and it is of some value, courts are not required to consider its adequacy. The adequacy of the consideration is for the parties to consider at the time of making the agreement, not for the court when it is sought to be enforced. [*Bolton* v. *Madden* 1873 LR 9 Q.B. 55]

Example 3.11. *A* agreed to sell a watch worth Rs. 500 for Rs. 20. *A*'s consent to the agreement was freely given. The consideration, though inadequate, will not affect the validity of the contract.

However, the inadequacy of the consideration can be considered in order to know whether the consent of the promisor was free or not. [Section 25 Explanation II].

Example 3.12. *A* agreed to sell his horse worth Rs. 1,000 for Rs. 10 only. *A* said that his consent to the agreement was not freely given. In this case, the inadequacy of the consideration is a fact, which the court should take into account in considering whether or not *A*'s consent was freely given.

7. *The consideration may be furnished by the promisee or any other person:* This legal rule for a valid consideration is clear from Section 2(*d*) of the Indian Contract Act. According to this section, the act which forms a consideration may be done by "the promisee or any other person". It means that so long as there is a consideration for a promise, it is immaterial who has furnished it. In other words, consideration may be furnished by the promisee, or by any other person *i.e.*, even by a stranger.

Example 3.13. *A* an old lady, by a deed of gift, transferred certain landed property to *B*, her daughter. By the terms of the gift deed, *B* was required to pay certain sum of money to *C* (sister of *A*), annually. On the same day, *B* executed an Iqrarnama (agreement) in favour of *C* promising to pay the stipulated amount. Later on, *B* refused to pay the amount to *C* on the plea that no consideration had moved from *C* to *B*. *C* sued *B* to recover the amount. It was held that *C* is entitled to recover the amount as the consideration was validly furnished by *A*, the old lady.

[*Chinnaya* v. *Ramaya*, (1882) 4 Madras 137]

Note: Under the English Law, the consideration must move from the promisee and the promisee alone.

8. *The consideration may be either positive or negative:* According to Section 2(*d*) of the Indian Contract Act, the consideration may be a promise to do something or abstain from doing something. Thus, a consideration may be an act 'to do' or 'not to do' something, *i.e.*, it may be positive or negative.

Example 3.14. *B* requested *A* to sell and deliver to him certain goods on credit. *A* agreed to do so provided *C* will guarantee the payment of the price of the goods which *A* sells on credit to *B*. *C* guaranteed the payment of price. Here, the selling of goods by *A* to *B* is the consideration for *C*'s promise to guarantee the payment. This is a positive consideration as *C* promises to do some act *i.e.*, to guarantee the payment.

Example 3.15. *A* was a tenant in *B*'s house. The tenancy was for two years. After the expiry of two years, *A* did not vacate the house, and requested *B* not to file a suit for six months. *A* promised that after the expiry of six months he will himself vacate the house. *B* agreed not to file a suit for six months. Here the consideration is negative as *B*'s agreement not to file a suit is the consideration for *A*'s promise to vacate the house within six months.

9. *The consideration may be forbearance to sue:* The term 'forbearance to sue' means that the plaintiff has a right of action against the defendant or any other person, and on a promise by the defendant, he (plaintiff) refrains from bringing the legal action. The forbearance to sue is regarded as a valid consideration.

Example 3.16. *A* sold and delivered the goods to *B* on credit. *C* afterwards requested *A* not to file a suit against *B* for the recovery of the price of the goods for a year. And *C* promised that if he (*A*) agreed not to file the suit for a year, then *C* will pay the price if *B* failed to pay. *A* agreed not to file a suit against *B* for a year. Here, *A*'s forbearance to sue is the valid consideration for *C*'s promise.

Example 3.17. *A*, the wife of *B*, was ready to sue *B* for maintenance allowance. *B* promised to pay *A* monthly allowance provided she (*A*) did not file a suit against *B*. A agreed to forbear to sue. This contract is a valid one and supported by valid consideration. In this case, wife's (*A*) forbearance to sue amounts to consideration for husband's (*B*) promise for the payment of maintenance allowance. [*Based on Debi Radha Rani* v. *Ram Das* AIR, 1941 Patna 282.]

On the basis of the above principle, a compromise of a valid disputed claim, and composition with the creditors is also a good consideration, and such a compromise is enforceable in the eyes of law.

10. *The consideration may be past, present or future:* This legal rule for a valid consideration is emphasised in Section 2(*d*) of Indian Contract Act, the relevant portion reads as under:

> *".... The promisee or any other person has done or abstained from doing, or does or abstains from doing, or promises to do or abstain from doing something.... ."*

Here the words "has done or abstained from doing" refers to past consideration. The words "does or abstains from doing" refers to present consideration, and the words "promises to do or abstain from doing" refers to future consideration.

The above-mentioned three types of consideration are illustrated hereunder:

(a) Past consideration: The words "has done or abstained from doing" means that consideration is an act which has already been done at the desire of the promisor. In other words, when the present promise is based on the consideration already taken place (*i.e.*, before the date of the promise), it is termed as past consideration. The past consideration is also adequately covered by the provision in Section 25(2) of the Indian Contract Act.

Example 3.18. *A* found *B*'s purse and gave it to him. *B* promised to give *A* Rs. 50 as a reward. Here, for *B*'s promise, the act of *A* in finding *B*'s purse is the past consideration.

Note: Under the English Law, the past consideration is not regarded as good consideration, though certain exceptions have been admitted, *e.g.*, past act at request, promise to pay a time-barred debt and a negotiable instrument issued for a past consideration.

(b) ***Present consideration:*** The words "does or abstains from doing" mean that consideration is an act which a promisee or any other person does in present (*i.e.*, simultaneously with the promise) at the desire of the promisor. In other words, when the promisor receives consideration simultaneously with his promise, it is termed as present consideration. Thus, when the consideration and promise go together then consideration is regarded as present consideration.

Example 3.19. *A* promised to sell his horse to *B* for Rs. 1,500. *B* paid the amount to *A* at the time of making the contract. Here, the money received by *A* is the present consideration for his promise to sell the horse to *B*.

(c) ***Future consideration:*** The words "promises to do or to abtain from doing" means that consideration is an act which a promisee or any other person promises to do at some future time (i.e., after making the promise). In other words, when the consideration for a promise is rendered in future it is termed as future or executory consideration.

Example 3.20 *A* agreed to sell certain goods to *B* after a week at agreed price. *B* agreed to pay the price after fifteen days. Here, as the amounts and 'property in the goods' (*i.e.*, legal possession of goods) are to be transferred in future, therefore the consideration is future for both the parties.

3.4. LEGALITY OF AGREEMENT WITHOUT CONSIDERATION

1. *Natural love and affection*
2. *Past voluntary services*
3. *Promise to pay time-barred debt*
4. *Gift actually made*
5. *Consideration is not required for the creation of an agency*

The general rule is that an agreement made without consideration is void. This rule is contained in Section 25 of the Indian Contract Act, which reads as under:

"An agreement made without consideration is void....".

However, there are certain exceptions to this general rule which are provided in Section 25 itself. Following are the exceptional circumstances under which the agreement is valid and enforceable even if it is made without consideration:

1. *Natural love and affection:* This exception is contained in Section 25(1) of the Indian Contract Act. According to this exception, an agreement in writing which is registered and is based on natural love and affection between near relatives is valid and enforceable even if there is no consideration. The following conditions must be satisfied for the application of this exception:

(*a*) The agreement must be in writing and registered.

(*b*) The agreement must be based on natural love and affection.

(*c*) The agreement must be between the parties who are in near relation to each other.

Example 3.21. *A*, for natural love and affection, promised to give Rs. 1,000 to his son *B*. *A* put his promise to *B* in writing and registered it. This is valid contract.

The expression 'near relations' will include parties related by blood or marriage. And the expression 'natural love and affection' will mean the love and affection between the parties nearly related. But it may be noted that nearness of relationship does not always mean natural loue and affection between the parties.

Example 3.22. *A* promised to pay his wife *B*, a fixed sum of money every month for her separate residence and maintenance. This agreement was written and registered one. In this agreement, certain quarrels and disagreements were also mentioned between *A* and his wife *B*. It was held that agreement was not enforceable because it was not made on account of natural love and affection. The court could find no trace of love and affection between the parties whose quarrels had compelled them to separate.

[*Raj Lukhy Dabee* v. *Bhootnath Mukherjee* (1900) 4 Cal. W N 488]

2. ***Past voluntary services:*** This exception is contained in Section 25(2) of the Indian Contract Act. According to this exception, a promise to pay for past voluntary services is binding even though it is without consideration. The following conditions must be satisfied for the application of this exception:

(*a*) The services should have been rendered voluntarily.

(*b*) The services should have been done for the promisor.

Example 3.23. *A* found *B*'s cycle and gave it to him. *B* promised to give *A* Rs. 100 as reward. This is a valid contract.

This exception also covers the situation where the promisee has done something for the promisor which otherwise was the legal duty of the promisor.

Example 3.24. *A* supported *B*'s infant son. *B* promised to pay *A*'s expenses in doing so. This is a valid contract. Here, *A* has done that act which *B* was legally bound to do.

3. ***Promise to pay time-barred debt:*** This exception is contained in Section 25(3) of the Indian Contract Act. According to this exception, a promise to pay a time-barred debt is enforceable if such promise is in writing and duly signed. The following conditions must be satisfied for the application of this exception:

(*a*) The promise to pay must be definite and express.

(*b*) The promise must be in writing.

(*c*) The promise must be signed by the promisor or his authorised agent.

(*d*) The debt must be time-barred, *i.e.*, the limitation period for the recovery of the debt, must have expired.

Example 3.25. *A* owed Rs. 1000 to *B*. This debt was barred by Limitation Act *i.e.*, the limitation period for the recovery of debt has already expired. *A* signed a written promise to pay Rs. 500 to *B* on account of this debt. This is a valid contract.

4. ***Gift actually made:*** This exception is contained in Explanation 1 of Section 25 of the Indian Contract Act. According to this exception, the gift actually made is valid even though it is made without consideration. Thus, the absence of consideration shall not affect the validity of any gift actually made.

5. ***Consideration is not required for the creation of an agency:*** This exception is contained in Section 185 of the Indian Contract Act. According to this exception, a contract of agency made without consideration is valid. Thus, when a person is appointed as an agent, his appointment is valid even if there is no consideration. Generally, an agent is remunerated by way of commission for services rendered, however, no consideration is immediately necessary at the time of appointment.

3.5. PRIVITY OF CONSIDERATION OR STRANGER TO CONSIDERATION

The term 'privity of consideration' means stranger to the consideration, or consideration given by any other person other than the promisee. The validity of privity of consideration is covered in Section 2(*d*) of the Indian Contract Act which states that the act which is to constitute consideration may be done by the "promisee or any other person". Thus, it is not necessary that the consideration should be furnished by the promisee only. A promise is enforceable so long as there is some consideration for it, and it is immaterial whether it is furnished by the promisee or other person even a stranger.

Example 3.26. *A* owed some money to *B*. In satisfaction of *A*'s debt, *C* a friend of *A*, transferred his property to *B*. And *B* accepted the property in satisfaction of the amount due to him from *A*. This transfer of property was held to he valid and binding on *C*. The consideration in the present case was the discharge of *A*'s obligation. [*Dawson's Bank* v. *May*, 1939 ALJ 844 PC]

The case of *Chinnaya* v *Ramaya* discussed in Example 3.13 is also relevant on this point

Note: Under the English Law, the consideration furnished by a stranger is not a good consideration.

3.6. PRIVITY OF CONTRACT OR STRANGER TO CONTRACT

The term 'privity of contract' means stranger to a contract. As per the doctrine of privity of contract, a person, who is not a party to the contract, cannot sue for carrying out the promise made by the parties to the contract. In other words, a contract cannot be enforced by a person who is not a party to the contract. The basis of the doctrine is that a contract is always a private relationship between the parties who make it. And no other person can acquire rights or incur liabilities under it.

Though there is no provision in the Indian Contract Act that a stranger to a contract cannot sue, yet it has become an established practice and is validly applicable in India.

Example 3.27. 'Dunlop & Co.' a tyre company, sold certain tyres to *D*, a wholesaler and secured an agreement from *D* not to sell the tyres to other trader below the Dunlop's list price. *A* further condition was also imposed that any retailer to whom *D* re-supplied the tyres should also promise *D* not to sell the tyres to the public below Dunlop's list price. *D* sold the tyres to 'Selfridge & Co' who agreed not to sell the tyres to the public below the Dunlop's list price. But 'Selfridge & Co.' sold the tyres below the Dunlop's list price. 'Dunlop & Co'. sued 'Selfridge & Co.' for damages for breach of the contract. 'Dunlop & Co.'s action to recover damages from 'Selfridge & Co. failed as 'Dunlop & Co.' was a stranger to contract between *D* and 'Selfaridge & Co.'

[*Dunlop Pneumatic Tyre Co.* v. *Selfridge & Co.*, (1915) A.C. 847]

Example 3.28. '*A*' borrowed Rs. 40,000 from *B*. As security for the loan, *A* executed a mortage of his property in favour of *B*. Later on, *A* sold his property to *C* for Rs. 44,000. Out of this amount of Rs. 44,000, *A* received Rs. 4,000 from *C* and allowed him to retain the balance of Rs. 40,000 in order to redeem the mortage by paying the amount to *B*. *B* sued *C* for the recovery of the mortgage money, but he could not succeed as he was not a party to the sale agreement between *A* and *C*.

[*Jamna Das* v. *Ram Autar* PC (1911) 39 I.A. 7]

3.7. EXCEPTIONS TO THE RULE OF PRIVITY OF CONTRACT

1. *Trust or charge*
2. *Marriage settlement, partition or other family arrangements*
3. *Acknowledgement of payment*
4. *Agreements relating to the land*
5. *Contracts through an agent*
6. *Holder in due course of a negotiable instrument*

In the following exceptional circumstances, a person who is not a party to the contract can enforce the contract.

1. *Trust or charge:* Sometimes under contract, a benefit is given to a person who is not a party to the contract. This benefit can be given by creating a trust or charge in favour of such person. In such cases, the beneficiary under the trust or charge may enforce the contract even though he is not a party to it. It may, however, be noted that a stranger must be clearly designated as a beneficiary, and the trust or charge in his favour must also be of some specific property.

Example 3.29. *A* had a minor son *S*, and *B* had a minor daughter *D*. In consideration of *S*'s marriage with *D*, *A* agreed with *B* that he would pay to *D* Rs. 500 per month in perpetuity for the betel leaf expenses called *Kharcha-i-Pandan*. *A* also charged certain properties with the payment, with authority to *D* to enforce it. After sometime, *D* and *S* separate on account of quarrel, and *D* filed suit against *A* for the recovery of arrears of the allowance. It was held that *D* was entitled to recover the amount of arrears although she was not a party to the contract. The court observed that as *A* also charged certain specific properties in favour of *D* for the payment of allowance, therefore *D* was the only person beneficiary entitled under it.

[*Khwaja Mohd. Khan* v. *Hussaini Begum* (1910) 32 All 410]

Example 3.30. *A* transferred certain properties to *B* to be held by him in trust for the benefit of *C*. In this case, *C* although not a party to the trust, can sue for the benefits available to him under the trust.

2. *Marriage settlement, partition or other family arrangements:* Sometimes, an agreement is made in connection with marriage, partition or other family arrangements, and a provision is made for the benefit of some person. In such cases, a person, for whose benefit the provision is made in such family arrangements, can enforce the agreement even if he is not a party to it. It may, however, be noted that provision must be made for the benefit of the person who wants to enforce such marriage arrangements.

Example 3.31. The father of a minor girl, *A*, entered into an agreement for her marriage with *B*. Afterwards, *B* refused to marry *A*. On attaining majority, *A* filed a suit against *B* for damages for breach of the promise of marriage. It was held that *A* could recover the damages although she was not a party to the agreement between her father and *B*.

[*Rose Fernandez* v. *Joseph Gonsalves* ILR (1924) 48 Bom. 673; AIR 1925 Bom. 97]

Example 3.32. On a partition of joint properties, two brothers agreed to invest, in equal shares, a certain sum of money for the maintenance of their mother. It was held that she was entitled to require her sons to make the investments for her maintenance although she was not a party to the parition of the property. [*Shuppa Ammal* v. *Subramaniyam* ILR (1910) 33 Madras 238]

3. *Acknowledgement of payment:* Sometimes, one of the parties to a contract acknowledges the payment to a third party or otherwise contitutes himself as an agent of the third party. In such cases, the party incurs a binding obligation towards the third party who can enforce it.

Example. 3.33. *A* sold his house to *B* for Rs. ten lakhs. The sale price was left in the hands of *B* for payment to C who was *A*'s creditor. *B* made part payment to C and agreed to pay the balance later on. In this case, C was allowed to recover the balance from *B*.

[*Based on Devaraja Urs* v. *Krishniah*, AIR 1952 Mysore 109]

Example 3.34. *A* received some money from *B* to be paid over to C. *A* admitted to C that he had received money from *B* for making payment to him (C). In this case, C can successfully recover the money from *A*.

4. *Agreements relating to the land:* In certain cases, the owner of land is entitled to certain rights and obligations created by an agreement affecting the land. When any person purchases such land with the notice of rights and obligations of the owner, then he shall be bound by those rights and obligations although he was not a party to the agreement.

Example 3.35. Certain persons were the owners of land adjoining a stream. A 'Catchment Board' agreed with the land owners to improve the banks of the stream and to maintain them in a good condition. The land owners paid the costs to the 'Board'. Subsequently, one of the land owners sold his land to *A*, who further sold it to *B*. Due to the negligence of the 'Board', the banks of the stream were not properly maintained. Consequently, the banks of the stream burst and the land adjoining the stream was flooded. *A* and *B* filed a suit against the 'Board' for breach of contract of maintaining the banks. Their action was allowed though the agreement for maintaining the banks was between the original land owners and the 'Board'. [*Smith & Snipes Hall Farm Ltd.* v. *River Douglas Catchment Board* (1949) 2 K.B. 500]

5. *Contracts through an agent:* A principal can enforce the contracts which are entered into by his agent though he was not a party to the contract. It may, however, be noted that the agent must act within the scope of his authority, and also in the name of his principal.

6. *Holder in due course of a negotiable instrument* : A 'holder in due course' of a negotiable instrument is a holder who has obtained the negotiable instrument in good faith and for valuable consideration. He may sue the prior parties to the negotiable instrument. The special privileges and rights of a holder in due course will be discussed in detail in chapter 35.

LEGAL PROVISIONS (SECTIONS) DISCUSSED IN THE CHAPTER

Important legal provisions (sections) of the Indian Contract Act, 1872, discussed in this chapter, are reproduced hereunder.

1. *Section 2 (d): Consideration*

   When, at the desire of the promisor, the promisee or any other person has done or abstined form doing, or does or abstans form doing, or promises to do or abstains form doing someting, such act or abstinence or promise is called a consideration for the promise.

2. ***Section 25: Agreement without consideration, void unless it is in writing and registered or is a promise to compensate for something done or is a promise to pay a debt barred by limitation law.***

   An agreement made without consideration is void, unless–

   (1) It is expressed in writing and registered under the law for the time being in force for the registration of documents, and is made on account of natural love and affection between parties standing in a near relation to each other; or unless

   (2) it is a promise to compensate, wholly or in part, a person who has already voluntarily done something for the promisor, or something which the promisor was legally compellable to do; or unless.

   (3) It is a promise, made in writing and signed by the person to be charged therwith, or by his agent generally or specially authorized in that behalf, to pay wholly or in part a debt of which the creditor might have enforced payment but for the law for the limitation of suits.

   In any of these cases, such an agreement is contract.

   Explanation 1.—Noting in this section shall affect the validity, as between the donor and donee, of any gift actually made.

   Explanation 2.—An Agreement to which the consent of the promisor is freely given is not void merely because the consideration is inadequate; but the inadequacy of the consideration may be taken into account by the Court in determining the question whether the consent of the promisor was freely given.

TEST QUESTIONS

1. Define 'consideration'. Why is it treated as an essential part of a contract? State the legal rules regarding consideration.
2. Define 'consideration'. "A contract without consideration is void." Are there any exceptions to this rule? If so, explain.
3. Define consideration. Distinguish it from motive. Is the existence of consideration essential for the validity of the contract?
4. Explain consideration as an element of a valid contract, and discuss the effects of
   (*a*) total absence of consideration (*b*) inadequacy of consideration
   (*c*) past consideration.
5. "Insufficiency of consideration is immaterial, but an agreement without consideration is void."- Comment.
6. Are the following good consideration for the validity of the contract, if so, explain with suitable examples.
   (*a*) Future consideration
   (*b*) Forbearance to sue
   (*c*) Performance of existing legal or contractual obligations
   (*d*) Compromise of disputed claims.
7. "No consideration no contract"—critically examine.
8. In what cases a contract without consideration is not void?
9. "A contract not supported by consideration is unenforceable." Dsicuss.
10. A stranger to a contract cannot sue, but a stranger to a consideration can sue.
11. "The legal effects of a contract are confined to the contracting parties."—Comment.
12. "Consideration may be past, present or future."—explain with examples.

13. "Inadequacy of consideration is of itself no ground for rescinding a contract. But it may be an evidence of undue influence."—Explain.
14. "Consideration is something in return. But it is not necessary that this something in return should be equal in value with something given."—Comment.

MULTIPLE CHOICE QUESTIONS

1. As a general rule, an agreement made without consideration is
   (*a*) void (*b*) voidable
   (*c*) valid (*d*) unlawful.
2. All agreements made without consideration are void
   (*a*) True, as there is no exception to this rule.
   (*b*) False, as there are certain exceptions also.
3. *A* agrees to sell his car worth Rs. 100,000 to *B* for Rs. 20,000 only, and *A*'s consent was obtained by coercion. Here, the agreement is
   (*a*) void (*b*) valid
   (*c*) voidable (*d*) unlawful.
4. An agreement made with free consent to which the consideration is lawful but inadequate, is
   (a) void (*b*) valid
   (*c*) voidable (*d*) unlawful.
5. If the consideration to an agreement is furnished by a stranger and not by the promisee himself, the agreement will be void.
   (*a*) True, as the consideration must be furnished by the promisee.
   (*b*) False, as the law requires that there must be some consideration, who furnished it is immaterial.
6. A person who is not a party to the contract can enforce the contract on the same principle that consideration furnished by a stranger is valid.
   (*a*) True, as the rule is that a stranger to a contract can sue.
   (*b*) False, as the rule is that a stranger to a contract canot sue.
7. For the enforcement of a promise to pay a time-barred debt without consideration, which of the following conditions is not required?
   (*a*) It must be in writing (*b*) It must be definite and express
   (*c*) It must be signed by the promisor (*d*) It must be registered in Court of Law.

ANSWERS

1. (*a*) 2. (*b*) 3. (*c*) 4. (*b*) 5. (*b*) 6. (*b*)
7. (*d*)

OBJECTIVE TYPE QUESTIONS WITH REASONING

State with reasons whether the following statements are correct or incorrect.

1. Consideration may move even from a person who is not a party to the contract.
2. Inadequacy of the consideration cannot be taken into account by the court in determining whether the consent was freely given.
3. The consideration must be something more than that what the promisee is already bound to do by law.
4. Consideration may be present or future but not past.
5. No consideration is required for the creation of an agency.
6. A stranger to consideration can enforce the contract.
7. A stranger to the contract cannot enforce it.

ANSWERS

1. *Correct.* The law on the point is that the consideration may move from the promisee or any other person.
2. *Incorrect.* The law provides that the inadequacy of the consideration can be considered by the courts to know whether the consent of the party was free or not [Section 25, Explanation II].
3. *Correct.* The performance of existing legal obligations only, is not a consideration for the promise.
4. *Incorrect.* The law recognises the past, present and future consideration as good consideration. Thus, the consideration may be past, present or future.
5. *Correct.* It is the law on the point that a contract of agency made without consideration is valid.
6. *Correct.* Consideration may be furnished by promisee or any other person [Section 2(*d*)]. Thus, a stranger to consideration can enforce the contract.
7. *Correct.* It is the law on the point. The basis of this rule is that a contract is a private relationship between the parties who make it.

PRACTICAL PROBLEMS

1. *A* promises to pay Rs. 50,000 to *B* if he beats *C*. Is this a valid contract ?

   Hint : No. The agreement is void as the consideration involves an injury to C, which is unlawful.
2. *A* agreed to sell his Honda city car worth Rs. 4 lakhs to *B* for Rs. 50,000 only. *A*'s consent to the agreement was freely given. Is it a valid consideration?

   Hint : Yes, it is a valid consideration. The legal rule in this regard is that the inadequacy of the consideration does not affect the validity of the agreement.
3. *A*'s son was missing. *A*'s servant *B* found the missing boy and brought him back. *A* then promised to pay Rs. 10,000 to *B* as a reward for the services rendered. Later on, *A* refuses to pay the money to *B* and *B* sues *A* in a court of Law. Will he succeed ?

   Hint : Yes, *B* will succeed as past consideration is regarded as valid consideration.
4. *A* contracted to indemnify the publishers of a weekly magazine against the consequences of any libel which they will publish in their magazine defaming *B*. The publishers published a defamatory statement against *B* and were forced to pay damages to *B* for the same. The publishers sued *A* to recover the compensation as per the agreed terms. Will they succeed ?

   Hint : No. The agreement between *A* and the publishers is void as in this case the consideration and object of the agreement is unlawful.
5. *A* promises to give his new car to *B* provided he fetches it from garage. Is this a valid consideration ?

   Hint : No. Consideration must be of some value in the eyes of law. *A* worthless act will not be a sufficient consideration even if it is done at the desire of the promisor.
6. *A*'s wife *B* was ready to sue *A* for maintenance allowance. *A* promised to pay monthly allowance to *B* provided she did not file a suit against *A*. *B* agreed not to file a suit against *A*. Is the contract supported by valid consideration ?

   Hint : Yes. In this case, *B*'s forbearance to sue amounts to valid consideration for *A*'s promise to pay monthly allowance.
7. *A*, for natural love and affection, promised to give Rs. 50,000 to his son *B*. This agreement was made in writing and was also registered. However, *A* refused to pay the agreed amount and *B* sued the father (*A*). *A* contended that he is not bound to pay as the agreement is void being without consideration. Advise *A*.

Hint : *A* is not justified in denying the validity of the agreement. An agreement without consideration is enforceable if it is in writing and registered and is based on natural love and affection between the parties who are near relatives.

8. *A*, an old lady, by a gift deed, transferred certain landed property to her daughter *B*. By the term of gift deed, *B* was required to pay certain sum of money to *A*'s sister *C*, annually. On the same day *B* executed an agreement in favour of *C* promising to pay the stipulated amount. Later on, *B* refused to pay the amount on the plea that no consideration has moved from C to B and C sued B to recover the amount. Will she succeed ? Give reasons.

Hint : Yes. The consideration may be furnished by the promise or any other person. In this case, the consideration was validity furnished by *A*, an old lady.

9. The father of a minor girl, *A*, entered into an agreement for her marriage with *B*. Afterwards, *B* refused to marry *A*. On attaining majority, *A* filed a suit against *B* for damages for breath of promises to marry. *B* contended that *A* cannot enforce the contract as she was not a party to the agreement between him and *A*'s father. Is *B*'s contention valid ? Give reasons.

Hint : No, B's consent is not valid. The marriage agreement or other family arrangements where a provision is made for the benefit of some person can be enforced by the beneficiary even if he is not a party to the same.

10. *A* agrees to marry *B*'s contention is valid daughter in consideration of dowry of Rs. 10 lakhs to be paid by *B*. Is it an enforceable agreement ?

Hint : No. In this case, the consideration is unlawful.

4

CHAPTER

CAPACITY OF CONTRACT

1. Introduction.
2. Persons not Competent to Contract.
3. Minors.
4. Nature of Minor's Agreements.
5. Effects of Minor's Agreements.
6. Doctrine of Restitution.
7. Minor's Liability for Necessaries.
8. Persons of Unsound Mind.
9. Agreements by Persons of Unsound Mind.
10. Persons Disqualified by Law.

4.1. INTRODUCTION

We have already discussed that an agreement grows into a contract only when it is enforceable by law.* One of the essential conditions for the enforceability of an agreement, is that the concerned parties must be competent to enter into an agreement. Section 10 of the Indian Contract Act specifically requires that the parties must be competent to contract. Thus, an agreement is valid and enforceable only if the parties to it are competent to enter into contract. The 'capacity to contract' means the competence (*i.e.*, capability) of the parties to enter into a valid contract. The term 'capacity to contract' is defined in Section 11 of the Indian Contract Act, which reads as under:

"Every person is competent to contract who is of the age of the majority according to the law to which he is subject, and who is of sound mind, and is not disqualified from contracting by any law to which he is subject."

The analysis of this section shows that a person who is major, of sound mind, and is not disqualified from contracting by law, is competent to enter into a valid contract.

4.2. PERSONS NOT COMPETENT TO CONTRACT

As per the statement of Section 11 of the Indian Contract Act, the following persons are not competent to contract, *i.e.*, they are incapable of entering into a valid contract.

1. Minors. 2. Persons of unsound mind. 3. Persons disqualified by law.

4.3. MINORS

A minor is a person who has not attained the age of majority. For the purposes of entering into contract, the 'age of majority' is eighteen years. Thus, a minor is a person who is below the age of eighteen years. The term 'minor' is explained in Section 3 of the Indian Majority Act, 1875, which reads as under :

"A minor is a person who has not completed eighteen years of age."

Note : In the following two cases, a person becomes major on completing the age of 21 years:

(*a*) Where a guardian of a minor's person or property has been appointed under the Guardians and Wards Act, 1890; and

* Section 2(*b*) of the Indian Contract Act.

(b) Where the superintendence of minor's property is assumed by a Court of Wards.

The age of majority is to be determined according to the law to which the minor is subject. In England, for all purposes, a minor is a person who is under the age of eighteen years.

4.4 NATURE OF MINOR'S AGREEMENTS

As a matter of fact, Sections 10 and 11 of the Indian Contract Act deal with the competence of the parties. According to Section 10, the parties must be competent to contract. And according to Section 11, every person is competent to contract if he is not a minor. From these two provisions, it is clear that a minor is not competent to contract. It is important to note here that the Indian Contract Act does not make it clear whether minor's agreement would be void or voidable at his (*i.e., minor's*) option. However, this controversy was finally resolved in 1903 by the Privy Council in *Mohoribibi* v. *Dharmodas Ghose,* (1903) 30 Calcutta 539, in which it was held that minor's agreement is absolutely void. It was observed that the question whether a contract is void or voidable presupposes the existence of a contract within the meaning of the Act. And a contract cannot arise in case of an infant (*i.e.,* minor). Thus, from this it is clear that minor's agreement is *void ab initio* (*i.e.,* not existent from the very beginning), and is therefore absolutely void and devoid of any consequences.

In certain exceptional circumstances, minor's agreements are considered valid and enforceable. For example where agreement is for the benefit of the minor, or is for the supply of 'necessaries' to the minor. Such cases are discussed in detail in the following discussion.

4.5. EFFECTS OF MINOR'S AGREEMENTS

1. *Void ab initio*
2. *No estoppel against minor*
3. *No liability in contract or in tort arising out of contract*
4. *No ratification*
5. *Restoration of property or money*
6. *Beneficial contract*
7. *Minor's property liable for necessaries*
8. *The minor as a partner*
9. *The minor as an agent*
10. *The minor as an insolvent*
11. *The minor can execute a negotiable instrument:*
12. *The liability of minor's parents of guardians*

The law relating to minor's agreement and effects thereof may be discussed under the following heads:

1. *Void ab initio:* We have already discussed that an agreement with a minor is *void ab initio, i.e.,* absolutely void. In other words, an agreement with a minor does not create any legal rights and obligations between the concerned parties. And thus, cannot be enforced in a Court of Law.

Example 4.1. *A* a minor, mortgaged his house in favour of *B*, a money-lender, to secure a loan of Rs. 20,000. A part of this amount (Rs. 10,500) was actually advanced to *A* by *B*. Subsequently, *A* sued for the cancellation of the mortgage on the plea that he was minor when he executed the mortgage. In this case, the mortgage was held void, and was thus cancelled. Further *B*'s request for the repayment of the amount advanced to *A* as part of consideration for the mortgage was also not accepted. Privy Council held that as the minor's contract was absolutely void, therefore, there was no question of refunding money in these circumstances. [*Mohoribibi's case,* (1903) 30 Colcutta 539]

2. *No estoppel against minor:* The term 'estoppel' may be defined as prevention of a claim or assertion by law. In other words, when someone makes another person to believe that a particular thing or fact is true, then later on he cannot be allowed to deny the truth of that thing. [*Section 115 of the Indian Evidence Act, 1872*]

Example 4.2. *A* intentionally and falsely made *B* to believe that certain land belonged to him, and induced *B* to purchase the land. But in fact, the land did not belong to *A*. However, subsequently *A* became the owner of the land. He then sought to set aside the sale on the ground that at the time of sale, he was not the owner of the land. In this case, *A* will not be allowed to defend his case on the ground that he was not the owner of the land at the time of sale.

It is important to note that there is no such estoppel against the minor. In other words, when a minor fraudulently enters into a contract, representing that he is a major, but in reality he is not, then later on he can plead his minotiry as a defence and cannot be estopped (*i.e.*, prevented) from doing so.

Example 4.3. *A*, a minor borrowed Rs. 500 from *B*, by fraudulently representing himself to be a major. *A* refused to repay the money to *B* as per agreement. *B* sued *A* for the recovery of money. Here, *A* can take the defence that he was minor at the time of entering into contract and hence the contract is *void ab initio*. In this case, *A* will get the benefit of his minorty. He can't be prevented from taking the defence of his minorty.

As regards the repayment of money received by the minor by fraudulently representing his age, the discussion on 'doctrine of restitution' discussed later in this chapter is relevant on the point.

3. *No liability in contract or in tort arising out of contract* : The term 'tort' may be defined as any wrong for which a civil suit can be brought (except for breach of contract or breach of trust). We have already discussed that a minor's agreement is absolutely void. Moreover, he is not liable either for breach of contract or for damages on account of tort of deceit (fraud). If a minor enters into an agreement by misrepresenting his age, he cannot be sued either in contract or in tort for deceit (*i.e.*, fraud). Because if the injured party is allowed to sue, it would be an indirect way of enforcing the void agreement. It may, however, be noted that the minor is not liable for tort, only where the tort is directly connected with the contract.

If the wrongful act (*i.e.*, tort) of minor is independent of the contract, then the minor is liable for damages in tort.

Example 4.4. *A*, a minor hired a mare from *B* for the purpose of riding. He was given strict instructions 'not to jump or lark with the mare'. *A* lent the mare to his friend *C*, who killed the mare by making it to jump. *B* brought an action against *A* for damages in tort. *A* was held liable to pay damages. Here, *A*'s wrongful act of unauthorised lending the mare, to a friend, is independent of the contract. [*Burnard* v. *Haggis*, (1863) 14 C.B. NS 45]

4. *No ratification* : Then term 'ratification' may be defined as the act of confirming or approving. The doctrine of 'no ratification' implies that an agreement made by a minor (during his period of minorty), cannot be confirmed by him on attaining majority. This is so because minor's agreement is *void ab initio* (*i.e.*, void from the very beginning) and, therefore, cannot be made valid by ratification. However, if the minor wants to carry out the agreement, a fresh agreement should be made on attaining majority. It may be noted that a new agreement will also require fresh consideration. The consideration which was given under the earlier agreement (during minority) cannot be taken as consideration for the new agreement (during majority). [*Nazir Ahmed* v. *Jiwanda*, AIR 1938 Lahore 159]

Example 4.5. *A* a minor borrowed Rs. 5,000 from *B*, a money-lender. A executed a promissory note in favour of *B* for the repayment of this amount. On attaining majority, *A* executed a fresh promissory note in favour of *B* for the repayment of the amount, borrowed earlier. The second promissory note was also void because there was no fresh consideration for it. *B* could not recover the amount on the basis of the second promissory note. Here, *A*'s act of executing a fresh promissory note will not ratify his agreement made during his period of minority.

[*Indran Ramaswami* v. *Anthiappa Chettiar*, (1906) MLJ 422]

5. *Restoration of property or money :* Sometimes, the minor receives some property or money by falsely representing his age. In such cases, the minor can be asked to restore such property or money so long as the same is traceable in his possession. This point will be discussed in detail in Article 4.6 on 'Doctrine of Restitution'.

6. *Beneficial contract :* A minor can be a beneficiary or a promisee. In other words, if a contract is beneficial to a minor, it can be enforced by him. However, there is no provision in the Indian Contract Act according to which the contract for minor's benefit is enforceable. It is only on the basis of judicial decisions that contracts for minor's benefit are held to be valid. No doubt, the law declared by Privy Council in the famous *Mohoribibi's* cases that minor's agreement is absolutely void has been generally followed. But, it has been confined to cases only where a minor is charged with obligations, and the other contracting party seeks to enforce those obligations against the minor. In majority of the cases, where the contracts are for the benefit of the minor, they are held to be valid and enforceable. Accordingly, a minor is allowed to enforce a contract which is of some benefit to him and under which he is required to bear no obligation. This is so, because these days the minors are appearing in public more frequently than ever before. Therefore, it will be unjust in the circumstances to deprive a minor of a benefit which he may be legally entitled to get under a contract.

Example 4.6. *A*, a minor, advanced certain sum of money to *B*. *B* executed a mortgage of his immovable property in favour of *A*, as a security of money advanced by him. In this case, the mortgage can be enforced by *A* as the transaction is for his benefit.

[*Raghava Chariar* v. *Srinivasa* (1916) 40 Madras 308]

In the above case, the question involved was whether a mortgage executed in favour of a minor, who has advanced the whole of the mortgage money, is enforceable by him or by any other person on his behalf. Full bench of the Madras High Court held that the transaction is enforceable by or on behalf of the minor.

Thus, a minor is capable of purchasing immovable property. If the seller refuses to hand over the property to the minor, then he may sue to recover the possession of the property. Similarly, a minor may also enforce a promissory note executed in his favour. It may be noted that the law does not regard a minor as incapable of accepting a benefit. A contract of marriage is held for the benefit of the minor, and thus can be enforced against the other contracting party by or at the instance of the minor.

Example 4.7. *A*, the father of a minor girl *B*, entered into a contract with *C*, where *C* promised to marry *B*. Subsequently, *C* refused to marry *B* and she brought a suit against *C* for damage for breach of contract. It was held that contract was for the benefit of *B*, and therefore she was entitled to recover damages from *C*. [*Rose Fernandez* v. *Joseph Gonsalves*, (1924) 48 Bombay 673]

It may, however, be noted that while the contract of marriage could be enforced against the other contracting party at the instance of the minor, but such contract cannot be enforced against the minor. [*Khimji Kuverji* v. *Lalji Karamsey*, (1941) Bombay 211]

The contracts of apprenticeship are also for the benefit of the minor and are enforceable. However, a contract of personal services does not stand on the same footing as the contract of apprenticeship or a contract of marriage of a minor.

Example 4.8. *A*, a minor, was allowed the role of an actress in a particular film by *B*, a film producer. This agreement was made with *A*'a father. Subsequently, *B* allotted that role to another artist and terminated the agreement with *A*'s father. It was held that the agreement was not enforceable. The court observed that "the contract of personal service do not stand on the same footing as the contract of apprenticeship or a contract of marriage of a minor."

[*Raj Rani* v. *Prem Adib*, AIR 1949 Bombay 215]

7. *Minor's property liable for necessaries:* Sometimes, a person supplies necessaries to a minor. In such cases, the supplier of necessaries can claim reimbursement from the property of minor.

Example 4.9. *A* supplied *B*, a minor, with necessaries suitable to his condition in life. In this case, *A* is entitled to be reimbursed from *B*'s property.

This point will be discussed in detail in Art. 4.7 on "Minor's Liability for Necessaries."

8. *The minor as a partner:* The partnership of partners results from their agreement. A minor, being incompetent to enter into a contract, cannot be a partner in the firm. However, he may be admitted only to the benefits of the firm with the consent of all other partners [Section 30(1) of the Indian Partnership Act, 1932]. For detail see 'The Partnership Act' portion of the book.

9. *The minor as an agent:* An agent is merely a connecting link between his principal and third person. Therefore, a minor can be appointed as an agent. But he will not be personally liable for his acts as an agent [Section 184]. It may however, be noted that the principal will be liable to the third persons for the acts of the minor agent which he does in the ordinary course of dealings.

10. *The minor as an insolvent:* A minor cannot be declared as an insolvent. This is so because all agreements with a minor are absolutely void. Moreover, the minor is not personally liable for any debt incurred during the period of his minority.

11. *The minor can execute a negotiable instrument:*

The minor is competent to draw, negotiate endorse the negotiable instruments. It may, however, be noted that the minor will not incur any personal liability under such instruments. But, the negotiable instruments executed in favour of the minor can be enforced by him.

12. *The liability of minor's parents of guardians:* As a matter of fact, the minor's contracts do not impose any liability on his parents or guardians even if the contracts are for 'necessaries'. The parents or guardians of the minor may pay money borrowed by him just out of moral obligations. But there is no legal obligation to make such payments. It may, however, be noted that the parents or guardians can be held liable when the minor child is acting as an agent of his parents or guardians.

4.6. DOCTRINE OF RESTITUTION

The term 'restitution' may be defined as the act of restoring back to the rightful owner that which has been taken away or lost. Thus, the doctrine of restitution implies that when a person obtains property or goods by false representation, he can be compelled to restore it to the person from whom he has received it. *This doctrine also applies to minors.* However, the minor can be compelled to restore the property or goods only so long as the same is traceable in his possession. It may be noted that earlier there was some controversy on the point whether the doctrine of restitution is applicable to money or not. And whether the minor can also be compelled to restore back the money which he obtained by misrepresenting his age. Now this controversy has been resolved by Section 33 of the Specific Relief Act, 1963. According to this section, the doctrine of restitution applies to money also. And the minor may also be required to restore the money received under the contract. Where a minor successfully defends any suit on the ground that the contract is void because of his being minor, the court may require him to restore to benefits obtained by him under the contract. It may, however, be noted that the minor can be asked to restore the benefits only to the extent to which he or his property has been benefited. Thus, when the minor receives the benefits of money, he may be compelled to restore the same. This is based on the principle that he, who seeks equity, must do equity.

Example 4.10. *A*, a minor sold certain properties to *B* and received Rs. 10,000 as part of the purchase money. Subsequently, *A* applied to the court that the sale should be cancelled as he was minor at the time of sale. And he should be allowed to recover the possession of the property from *B*. He was allowed to recover the possession of property sold by him only subject to the condition that he should restore the part of purchase money received from *B*.

[*Based on Jagar Nath's case, also see Mohd. Syedoe* v. *Yeoh Gark*, AIR 1916 PC 242]

However, the court has the discretion to required a minor to restore the benefits received by him.

4.7. MINOR'S LIABILITY FOR NECESSARIES

The liability of incompetent persons for necessaries is contained in Section 68 of the Indian Contract Act, which reads as under:

"If a person, incapable of entering into a contract or anyone whom he is legally bound to support, is supplied by another person with necessaries suited to his condition in life, the person who has furnished such supplies is entitled to be reimbursed from the property of such incapable person."

The analysis of this section shows that if a person supplies necessaries to a person who is incapable of entering into a contract or to anyone whom such incapable person is legally bound to support, then he can claim reimbursement from the property of such incapable person. It may, however, be noted that the liability of minor is not personal (*i.e.*, he is not personally liable). It is only the property of minor which is liable for meeting the liability for necessaries supplied to him.

Example 4.11. *A* supplied the wife and children of *B*, a lunatic, with necessaries suitable to their condition in life. In this case, *A* is entitled to be reimbursed from *B*'s property.

Example 4.12. *A* supplied *B*, a minor with necessaries suitable to his condition in life. In this case, *A* is entitled to be reimbursed from *B*'s property.

As a matter of fact, the minor's property is liable for necessaries if the following two conditions are satisfied:

(*a*) The contract must be for goods reasonably necessary for minor's support in his life.

(*b*) The minor must not have already a sufficient supply of these necessaries.

Example 4.13. *A*, a minor, was amply supplied with proper clothes according to his position. He bought a number of new dresses, including eleven fancy waist-coast from *B*. *B* could not recover the price as it was held that these were not necessaries. [*Nash* v. *Inman*, (1908) K.B. 1]

It is to be noted that, there is no definition of the term 'necessaries' in the Indian Contract Act. The term 'necessary' is a relative fact which is to be determined with reference to facts and circumstances of a particular case. It is not limited only to such things, without which an individual cannot exist, *e.g.*, food, clothing, lodging etc. But it also includes all such things which are provided to a minor according to his position and status in a particular class of society. It includes both the 'necessary goods' and the 'necessary services' rendered to a minor. However, the supplier of such necessaries has to prove that the minor actually needed the goods, and they are suitable to the conditions in life of the minor. The term 'necessaries' is defined in Section 2 of the English Sales of Goods Act 1893, which reads as under:

"The 'necessaries' are the goods suitable to the life of infant or other person, and to his actual requirement at the time of sale and delivery."

The above definition is also relevant for our discussion on the subject. The analysis of this definition shows the term 'necessaries' includes the goods:

(*a*) suitable to the position and status of a minor; and

(*b*) which were actually required by the minor at the time of supply.

We have already discussed that 'necessaries' will be determined keeping in view the facts and circumstances of each individual case. The judicial decisions should also be kept in view while determining the meaning of necessaries. However, the following cases have already been decided by the courts in connection with 'necessaries', and thus the following are included in necessaries:

1. The funds supplied to a minor for the marriage of a female minor in the family are held necessaries. And the moneylender may get himself reimbursed from the property of a minor. [*Tikki Lal* v. *Kamal Chand,* AIR 1940 Nagpur 327]
2. The expenses incurred for performing funeral obsequies (funeral ceremonies) of father of a minor are held necessaries.
[*Bochu Singh* v. *Baldeo Prased,* AIR 1933 Oudh 132]
3. The costs incurred in successfully defending a litigation in which the minor's property or liberty is threatened are the 'necessaries'.
[*Sham Charan* v. *Ch. Debya Singh* (1894) 21 Calcutta 872]
4. The money advanced to save minor's property from sale in exection, is 'necessaries'. [*Kedar Nath* v. *Ajudhia Prasad* (1883) Punjab 165]
5. Certain serivices rendered to a minor have been held to be necessaries, *e.g.*, education, training for trade, medical care legal advice etc.
[*Chappel* v. *Cooper,* (1844) 13 M & W 252]

A watch may be considered necessary for an undergraduate student in his college. Similarly, an ear-ring may also be considered a necessary for a girl at the time or her marriage. The courts have observed that the articles, which are purely ornamental, are not considered as necessaries as they cannot be requisite for anyone. However, there may be exceptional cases in which things purely ornamental may also be considered to be necessary.
[*Ryder* v. *Wombwell,* (1868) 38 LJ Ex. 8]

4.8. PERSONS OF UNSOUND MIND

1. *Idiot*
2. *Lunatics*
3. *Drunken or intoxicated persons*

A person of unsound mind is one who is not of sound mind. The term 'sound mind' for the purpose of contracting, is defined in Section 12 of the Indian Contract Act, which reads as under:

"A person is said to be of sound mind for the purpose of making a contract if, at the time when he makes it, he is capable of understanding it and of forming a rational judgment as to its effects upon his interest."

The analysis of this section shows that a person of sound mind is one who satisfies the following two conditions:

1. He should be capable of understanding the nature and contents of the contract; and
2. He should be capable of forming a rational judgement about the effects of the contract on his interest.

Thus, a person who does not satisfy these conditions, is of unsound mind and is incapable of entering into a valid agreement. The agreement made by persons of unsound mind (like that of minors), are also absolutely void. The reason for the same is that a valid agreement requires the assent of two sound minds. But a person of unsound mind does not have the capacity of proper thinking which the law recognises as a sound mind. Section 11 of the Indian Contract Act also specifically declares that persons of unsound mind are incompetent to enter into an agreement. The following persons are also considered to be the persons of unsound mind.

1. ***Idiot:*** An idiot is a person who has completely lost his mental faculties of thinking. Such a person is completely incapable of forming a rational judgment. An agreement with an idiot is completely void.

Example 4.14. *A* entered into an agreement to sell his property worth about Rs. 25,000 to *B* for Rs. 7,000. *B* brought an action for the recovery of the property. It was proved by *A*'s mother that he was a congenital idiot. The sale was held to be void.

[Based on *Inder Singh* v. *Parmeshwardhari Singh,* AIR 1957 Pat 491]

2. ***Lunatics:*** A lunatic is a person whose mental faculties of thinking are deranged (disordered) due to some mental strains or some other reasons. However, the mental powers of such a person may not be completely lost. He suffers from intermittent intervals of sanity or insanity. Thus, the term 'lunacy' denotes periodical insanity with lucid intervals (*i.e.,* the period in which a person is in his senses). Whereas, the 'idiocy' is permanent feature. But a lunatic can enter into a valid agreement during lucid intervals (*i.e.,* during the period when he is of sound mind). Except the agreements made during lucid intervals, all the agreements with a lunatic (like that of minor are absolutely void. However, the agreements for necessaries are valid. The validity of the agreements for necessaries, is the same as in the case of minors. Thus, a lunatic is not personally liable for 'necessaries' supplied to him. Only the property of a lunatic is liable.

Example 4.15. *A* supplied *B*, lunatic, with necessaries suitable to his condition in life. *A* is entitled to be reimbursed from *B*'s property.

Example 4.16. *A* supplied the minor son of *B*, a lunatic, with the necessaries suitable to his condition in life. *A* is entitled to be reimbursed from *B*'s property.

3. ***Drunken or intoxicated persons:*** A drunken or intoxicated person is one who is so drunk or intoxicated that he is incapable of understanding the terms of agreement, and to form a rational judgment as to the effects of the term of the agreement. Such persons fall in the same category as that of persons of unsound mind. An agreement made during such drunken or intoxicated position is absolutely void.

Note. Under the English Law, a person of unsound mind is competent to enter into an agreement. However, he may put an end to the contract, if he satisfies the court that he was incapable of understanding the agreement while the other party knew of it. In other words, in England the agreement made by persons of unsound mind are not absolutely void. But they are voidable at the option of the person of unsound mind.

4.9. AGREEMENT BY PERSONS OF UNSOUND MIND

We have already discussed that an agreement made by a person of unsound mind is absolutely void. However, a person of unsound mind may enter into a valid agreement when he is of sound mind. This provision is contained in Second para of Section 12 of the Indian Contract Act, which reads as under:

"A person who is usually of unsound mind, but occasionally of sound mind may make a contract when he is of sound mind. A person who is usually of sound mind, but occasionally of unsound mind may not make a contract when he is of unsound mind."

The analysis of this section shows that a person can enter into a valid and enforceable agreement if he is of sound mind at the time of the agreement.

Example 4.17. *A*, a patient, was in a lunatic asylum. It was noticed that at intervals, he was of sound mind. During such intervals, *A* borrowed Rs. 5,000 from *B* and executed a promissory note in favour of *B* for the repayment of the loan. This promissory note is valid and *A* is liable to repay the loan taken from *B*. However, if the promissory note is executed by *A* during the period when he is of unsound mind, then it will be void, and *B* cannot recover the loan on the basis of the promissory note.

It may, however, be noted that an idiot cannot enter into a valid agreement. His incapacity is permanent, and at no time he is of sound mind.

4.10. PERSONS DISQUALIFIED BY LAW

1. *Alien enemies*
2. *Foreign sovereigns, diplomatic staff, and accredited representatives of foreign states*
3. *Insolvents*
4. *Convicts*
5. *Corporations and companies*

The following persons, who are disqualified by the law to which they are subject, are not competent to enter into a contract.

1. ***Alien enemies:*** An 'alien' is a person who is a foreigner to the land. He may be either an 'alien friend' or an 'alien enemy'. If the sovereign or state of the alien is at peace with the country of his stay, he is an alien friend. And if a war is declared between the two countries, he is termed as an alien enemy. An alien friend, living in India, is competent to contract with any Indian citizens. On the declaration of the war between the country of an alien and the union of India, he becomes an alien enemy, and the contracts with him are governed by the following rules:

(*a*) Contracts during the war, and

(*b*) Contracts made before the declaration of war.

It may be noted that during the war, an alien enemy cannot enter into a contract with an Indian citizen. He is also disqualified from suing in an Indian court. He can do so only if he obtains the prior approval from the central government. Thus, any contract made by an alien enemy, during the continuance of the war and without a licence from the central government, is unenforceable.

The contracts made before the declaration of the war are either terminated or suspended (*i.e.*, their performance is stayed) during the continuance of war. The stayed or suspended contracts may be performed after the war is over. However, the government can impose such restrictions on the performance of stayed contracts as it deems necessary in the interest of the nation. But if the government thinks that performance of such contracts is against the national interest, then they will be terminated.

2. ***Foreign sovereigns, diplomatic staff, and accredited representatives of foreign states:*** Such persons can enter into valid contracts and can enforce them in Indian courts. However, a suit cannot be filed again them, in the Indian courts, without the prior sanction of the central government.

3. ***Insolvents:*** When a person is declared as an insolvent, his property vests in the Receiver or 'Official Assignee'. And the insolvent is deprived of his power to deal with the property. Therefore, he cannot enter into a contract relating to his property. However, this disqualification of an insolvent is removed when the court passes an order of discharge.

4. ***Convicts:*** A convict cannot enter into a contract while he is undergoing imprisonment. But when he is pardoned or the sentence expires, he becomes capable of entering into a contract. Thus, the incapacity is only during the period of sentence. It may be noted that in calculating the limitation period to enforce his rights, the period of sentence is not taken into account.

5. ***Corporations and companies:*** A corporation or a company is an artificial person created by law. It has a separate legal entity independent of its members. It exists in the eyes of law though it has no physical shape or form. Therefore, it can enter into a contract through human agents. A statutory corporation comes into existence by a Special Act of Legislature. And a company is formed by registration under the Companies Act 1956. The contractual capacity of the corporation is expressly defined by the Special Act under which it is created. Whereas, the contractual capacity of a company, registered under the Companies Act 1956, is regulated by the terms of its 'Memorandum of Association' and

the provisions of the Companies Act. Thus, a contract entered into by the corporation or company will be valid only if it is within the powers conferred by the 'Special Act' or 'Memorandum of Association' as the case may be. Any act done in excess of powers is *ultra virus* and void.

A corporation or company, being an artificial person, and having a separate legal entity, can hold property; can purchase or sell property; and can sue or be sued in the Courts of Law. But it cannot enter into contracts which are strictly of personal nature.

LEGAL PROVISIONS (SECTIONS) DISCUSSED IN THE CHAPTER

Important legal provisions (sections) of the Indian Contract Act, 1872, discussed in this chapter, are reproduced hereunder;

1. ***Section 10: What Agreements are Contracts-Competence of Parties Emphasised***

   All agreements are contracts if they are made by the free consent of parties ***competent of contract,*** for a lawful consideration and with a lawful object, and are not hereby expressly declared to be void.

2. ***Section 11: Who are competent to contract***

   Every person is competent to contract who is of the age of majority according to the law to which he is subject, and who is of sound mind and is not disqualified form contracting by any law to which he is subject.

3. ***Section 12: What is Sound Mind for the Purposes of Contacting***

   A person is said to be of sound mind for the purpose of making a contract, if, at the time when he makes it, he is capable of understanding it and of forming a rational judgment as to its effect upon his interests.

   A person who is usually of unsound mind, but occasionally of unsound mind, may make a contract when he is of sound mind.

   A person who is usally of sound mind, but occasionally of unsound mind, may not make a contract when he is of unsound mind.

4. ***Section 68: Claim for Necessaries Supplied to Person Incapable of Contracting***

   If a person, incapalbe of entering into a contract or any one whom he is legally bound to support, is supplied by another person with necessaries suited to his condition in life, the person who has furnished such supplies is entitled to be s reimbursed form the property of such incapable person.

TEST QUESTIONS

1. Define the term 'capacity to contract'. State the law relating to the competence of the parties giving suitable examples.
2. Explain the meaning of 'capacity to contract'. To what extent can a minor under the Indian Contract Act be held liable for necessaries supplied to him?
3. Minor's agreements are absolutely void. Is there any agreement with a minor which can be enforced in a Court of Law? If so, discuss with examples.
4. What protection is given to a minor by the Indian Contract Act? In what circumstances, an infant is bound by his/her contract for necessities?
5. "A minor is allowed to enforce a contract which is of some benefit to him and under which he is required to bear no obligation." Comment.
6. Certain persons, other that minors, are also not competent to contract. What are those ? Discuss in brief the effects of agreement with such persons.
7. "A person who is usually of unsound mind, but occasionally of sound mind may make a contract when he is of sound mind." Explain.
8. Discuss the following doctrines with special reference to minors:

   (*a*) Doctrine of Restitution. (*b*) Doctrine of Ratification.
9. State the effects of the agreement made with the following persons. Is there any difference between the Indian Law and English Law on the point? If so, what?

   (*a*) Lunatics (*b*) Drunken or intoxicated persons.

10. Dicuss the contractual capacity of the followings:

(*a*) Aliens (*b*) Insolvents

(*c*) Convicts (*d*) Corporations and companies.

MULTIPLE CHOICE QUESTIONS

1. Which of the following persons are not competent to contract ?

(*a*) minors (*b*) persons of unsound mind

(*c*) persons disqualified by law (*d*) all of these.

2. For the purposes of entering into a contract, a minor is a person who has not completed the age of

(*a*) 16 years (*b*) 18 years

(*c*) 20 years (*d*) 21 years.

3. As a general rule minor's agreements are

(*a*) void ab initio (*b*) voidable

(*c*) valid (*d*) unlawful.

4. The leading case, on the point that minor's agreement is void *ab initio,* is

(*a*) Carlill *v.* Carbotic Smoke Ball Co. (*b*) Mohoribibi *v.* Dharmadas Ghose

(*c*) Nash *v.* Inman (*d*) None of these.

5. A contract with the minor, which is beneficial for him, is

(*a*) void ab initio (*b*) voidable

(*c*) valid (*d*) illegal.

6. Can a minor be held personally liable for the 'necessaries' supplied to him?

(*a*) Yes, under section 68 minor is personally liable

(*b*) No, under section 68, only minor's property is liable.

7. Which of the following persons do not fall under the category of persons of unsound mind?

(*a*) idiot (*b*) lunatics

(*c*) drunken persons (*d*) alien.

8. An agreement made by a person of unsound mind is void. Which of the following provisions in the Indian Contract Act, states that such a person can enter into a valid contract if he is of sound mind at the time of agreement?

(*a*) Section 10 (*b*) Section 11

(*c*) Section 12 (*d*) Section 13.

ANSWERS

1. (*d*)	**2.** (*b*)	**3.** (*a*)	**4.** (*b*)	**5.** (*c*)	**6.** (*b*)
7. (*d*)	**8.** (*c*)				

OBJECTIVE TYPE QUESTIONS WITH REASONING

State with reasons whether the following statements are correct or incorrect

1. For the purpose of entering into contract, a minor is a person who has not completed twenty one years of age.

2. The general rule is that minor's agreements are voidable.

3. An agreement made by a minor during his minority can be ratified (*i.e.,* confirmed) by him on attaining the age of majority.

4. A contract to take a loan by a boy of sixteen years of age from a money lender of 50 years old, is a valid contract.

5. If a minor obtains some property or goods by misrepresenting his age, he can be asked to restore it to the person from whom he has received it.

6. A promissory note duly executed in favour of minor is void
7. A minor can be beneficiary or a promisee.
8. A minor is personally liable for the necessaries supplied to him.
9. A minor cannot become a full fledged partner in a partnership firm.
10. A minor cannot be appointed as an agent, as he is not competent to contract.
11. A person who is usually of sound mind, but occasionally of unsound mind is unable to make the contract.

ANSWERS

1. ***Incorrect.*** For this purpose, a minor is a person who has not completed eighteen years of age.
2. ***Incorrect.*** The established law is that minor's agreements are ***void ab initio*** *i.e.,* non existent from the very beginning. However, there are certain exceptions also.
3. ***Incorrect.*** Minor's agreement is *void ab intio,* and cannot be made valid by ratification.
4. ***Incorrect.*** Minor's agreements are void.
5. ***Correct.*** It is based upon the doctrine of restitution. However, the minor can be asked to restore the property or goods only so long as the same is traceable in his possession.
6. ***Incorrect.*** It has been recognised by the courts that contracts for minor's benefit are valid and enforceable by the minor.
7. ***Correct.*** A contract which is beneficial to a minor is valid and can be enforced by him. Thus, a minor can be a payee or promisee in a contract.
8. ***Incorrect.*** The minor is not personally liable. It is only the property of minor which is liable for meeting the liability for necessaries supplied to him.
9. ***Correct.*** Minor being incompetent to contract, he cannot be a partner in the firm. However, he may be admitted only to the benefits of the firm [Section 30 (1) of the Indian Partnership Act, 1932].
10. ***Incorrect.*** An agent is merely a connecting link between his principal and third party. Therefore a minor can validly be appointed as an agent. However, he will not be personally liable for the acts as an agent. [Section 184]
11. ***Incorrect.*** Such a person can enter into a valid contract during the period when he is of sound mind.

PRACTICAL PROBLEMS

1. *A*, a minor borrowed Rs. 5,000 from *B* and executed a promissory note in his favour. On attaining majority, *A* executed a fresh promissory note in *B*'s favour for the repayment of money borrowed earlier. Can *B* recover money from *A* ? Give reasons.

   Hint : No. The second promissory note is also void as there was no fresh consideration for it. Also, ratification of contract, made during minority, is not allowed on attaining age of majority.
2. *A*, a minor, obtained a loan from *B*, by falsely representing his age. On due date, *A* refused to repay it and *B* brought an action for breach of contract, but his action failed. *B* seeks your advice to recover damages from *A* on account of tort of deceit (*i.e.* fraud). Advise him.

   Hint : *B* will not succeed in recovering damages on account of tort of deceit. *A* minor cannot be made liable to pay damaged by changing the form of action.
3. *A*, a minor borrowed Rs. 10,000 from *B*. After attaining majority, *A* requested *B* for another loan of Rs. 15,000 which he gave. Now, *A* gave a combined promissory-note for Rs. 25,000 to *B*. Can *B* recover loan amount of Rs. 25,000 on the basis of this promissory note?

   Hint : Yes. This is not the case of ratification. In this case the promissory-note of Rs. 25,000 will be treated as a fresh contract based on fresh consideration.
4. *A*, a minor, borrowed Rs. 10,000 from *B*, a money-lender for performing the funeral ceremonies of his (A's) farther who had died in an accident. Can *B* recover the money ?

Hint : Yes. Expenses incurred for performing funeral ceremonies are regarded as 'necessaries'. However, *B* is entitled to be reimbursed from *A*'s property only as a minor is not personally liable.

5. *A*' a minor, borrowed Rs. 50,000 from *B* as an education loan to complete his education. Does *B* has any remedy to recover the money?

   Hint : Yes, *B* can recover the same out of *A*'s property as expenses for certain services such as education, training for trade, sports training, medical care, legal advice etc. fall in the category of necessaries.

6. *A*, a minor of 16 years, suffered a severe leg injury during a cricket match. He engaged *B*, a qualified doctor for the treatment. Can *B* claim any thing for the services rendered to *A*.

   Hint : Yes, medical care falls under the category of 'necessaries' and *A*'s property, if any, can be held liable for the payment of services rendered by *B*.

FREE CONSENT

1. Introduction.
2. Definition of Free Consent.
3. Elements which Affect the Consent of the Parties.
4. Coercion.
5. Essentials and Legal Rules for a Valid Coercion.
6. Effects of Coercion.
7. Undue Influence.
8. Essentials and Legal Rules for a Valid Undue Influence.
9. Effects of Undue Influence.
10. Presumption of Domination of Will.
11. Presumption of Undue Influence.
12. Burden of Proof of Undue Influence.
13. Comparison Between Coercion and Undue Influence.
14. Fraud.
15. Essentials and Legal Rules for a Fraud.
16. Acts which Constitute Fraud.
17. Silence as Fraud.
18. Effects of Fraud.
19. Remedies Available on Account of Fraud.
20. Circumstances of Losing the Right of Rescission.
21. Misrepresentation.
22. Essentials and Legal Rules for Misrepresentation.
23. Acts which Constitute Misrepresentation.
24. Effects of Misrepresentation.

5.1. INTRODUCTION

We have already discussed that when two parties enter into a contract they should given their consent. The consent of the parties means that there is perfect identity of mind of both the parties, *i.e.*, there is no misunderstanding between the parties regarding the subject-matter of the contract. The term 'consent' is defined in Section 13 of the Indian Contract Act, which reads as under:

"Two or more persons are said to consent when they agree upon the same thing in the same sense."

The analysis of this section shows that the 'consent' means that the parties should have the identity of mind, *i.e.*, the parties must understand the subject-matter of the contract in the same sense. In English Law, this is called *consensus ad idem* (*i.e.*, meeting of the minds). For the creation of contract, there must be *consensus ad idem.* When the parties enter into an agreement, concerning a particular person or a thing, but each has a different person or thing in mind, then there is no consent of the parties and no contract comes into existence between them.

Example 5.1. *A* had two scooters, one of green colour and the other of white. *A* offered to sell his green scooter to *B* for Rs. 8,000. *B* accepted the offer believing it to be for the white scooter. In this case, no contract arise between *A* and *B* as there is no consent of the parties.

Thus, the complete absence of consent prevents the existence of any contract. Salmond describes it as ***error in consensus.*** Error in consensus is the misunderstanding and prevents the existence of *consensus ad idem,* which is the essential element of a contract.

The consent of both the parties entering into contract must also be free. It is the essential requirement of a valid contract. A contract which is regular in all other respects, may still fail because of the fact that there was no real consent to it by one or both of the parties. Section 10 of the Indian Contract Act specifically states that a contract is valid and enforceable if it is made with the free consent of the parties.

5.2. DEFINITION OF FREE CONSENT

The term 'free consent' may be defined as the consent which is obtained by the free will of the parties, and neither party was forced or induced to give his consent. If the consent is there but it is not free or real, then the contract will be voidable at the option of the party whose consent is not free. The term 'free consent' is defined in Section 14 of the Indian Contract Act, which reads as under:

"Consent is said to be free when it is not caused by–

(1) *coercion, as defined in Section 15, or*

(2) *undue influence, as defined in Section 16, or*

(3) *fraud, as defined in Section 17, or*

(4) *misrepresentation, as defined in Section 18, or*

(5) *mistake, subject to the provisions of Section 20, 21 and 22.*

Consent is said to be so caused when it would not have been given but for the existence of such coercion, undue influence, fraud, misrepresentation or mistake."

The analysis of this section shows that when consent of either party is obtained by one of the above-mentioned elements, it will not be free. When the consent is there but it is not free, Salmond describes it as ***error in causa.*** These points will be discussed in detail in the following discussion.

5.3. ELEMENTS WHICH AFFECT THE CONSENT OF THE PARTIES

According to Section 14, discussed in the last article, the following elements affect the consent of the parties:

1. Coercion.
2. Undue Influence.
3. Fraud.
4. Misrepresentation.
5. Mistake.

The consent obtained by any of the above elements is not free consent. It may be noted that in the first four elements mention above (*i.e.,* coercion, undue influence, fraud and misrepresentation), the consent is there but it is not free. But in the last element (*i.e.,* mistake), there is not consent at all because there is not identity of minds. The effect of 'no free consent' and 'no consent at all' on the contract may be stated as under:

(*a*) When the consent is not free, then the contract is voidable at the option of the party whose consent is not free. A voidable contract is enforceable at the option of the party whose consent was not free.

(*b*) When there is no consent, then the contract is *void ab initio* (*i.e.,* from the very beginning). In fact, no contract will come into existence in such a case. A void contract being *void ab initio,* is not enforceable at the option of either party.

Thus, there is lot of difference between 'no free consent' and 'no consent at all.' In the following cases, there is complete absence of consent (*a*) when there is error as to the nature of the contract itself, (*b*) when there is error as to the identity of the parties, (*c*) when there is error as to the subject-mater of contract.

5.4. COERICION

The term 'coercion' means forcibly compelling a person to enter into a contract. In such cases, the consent of the party is obtained by use of force or under a threat. An agreement, in which consent is caused by coercion, is voidable at the option of the party whose consent was so obtained. The term 'coercion' is defined in Section 15 of the Indian Contract Act, which reads as under:

"Coercion is the committing or threatening to commit, any act forbidden by the Indian Penal Code, or the unlawful detaining or threatening to detain, any property, to the prejudice of any person whatever, with the intention of causing any person to enter into an agreement."

The analysis of this section shows that, the coercion implies a committing or threatening to commit some act which is contrary to law. The consent is said to be caused by coercion when it is obtained by either of the following techniques:

1. Committing or threatening to commit any act forbidden by Indian Penal Code (IPC).

2. Unlawful detaining or threatening to detain any property.

Example 5.2. *A* threatens to kill *B* if he does not agree to sell his car to *A* for Rs. 10,000. Fearing death, *B* enters into an agreement with *A* for the sale of his car for Rs. 10,000 only. This agreement is voidable at the option of *B* as the consent to it is obtained by threatening to kill a person, which is forbidden by the Indian Penal Code.

The above two types of acts which amount to coercion are discussed in detail in the next article.

5.5. ESSENTIALS AND LEGAL RULES FOR A VALID COERCION

The legal definition of coercion, discussed in the last article, reveals the essential elements of coercion. The coercion is legally valid if it satisfies the requirements of its definition. The essential elements of coercion are discussed in points 1 to 4 in the following discussion, and the rest are the legal rules for a valid coercion. Points 1 to 3 are different parts of the main essential elements. These are discussed separately for the sake of clarity and easy understanding. If the consent is obtained by *any of* these three acts, the consent is said to be obtained by coercion:

> **1.** ***The coercion must be the committing of any act forbidden by the Indian Penal Code***
>
> **2.** ***The coercion must be the threatening to commit any act forbidden by the Indian Penal Code***
>
> **3.** ***The coercion must be the unlawful detaining or threatening to detain any property***

4. *The acts of coercion must be done with the intention of causing the other party to enter into a contract*
5. *The Indian Penal Code may or may not be in force where the coercion is committed*
6. *The acts of coercion may be initiated by any person*
7. *The coercion may be by way of threat to commit suicide*
8. *The coercion may not be by way of threat to file a to suit*

1. ***The coercion must be the committing of any act forbidden by the Indian Penal Code:*** It is an important and essential element of coercion. When the consent of a person is obtained by committing any act which is forbidden by the Indian Penal Code, the cosent is said to be obtained by coercion.

Example 5.3. *A* took *B* into unlawful confinement and asked him (*B*) that he would not be released until he executed a gift deed of his property in *A*'s favour. This gift deed will be voidable as it has been executed by committing an act forbidden by Indian Penal Code. 'Unlawful Confinement' is forbidden by Indian Penal Code.

2. ***The coercion must be the threatening to commit any act forbidden by the Indian Penal Code:*** It is another part of the main essential element of coercion. When the consent of a person is obtained by threat of committing any act which is forbidden by the Indian Penal Code, the consent is also said to be obtained by coercion, *e.g.*, consent obtained at the pistol point, or by threatening to cause death or by intimidation.

Example 5.4. *A* threatened to kill *B* if he (*B*) did not execute a bond of Rs. 5,000 in his (*A*'s) favour. *B* executed a bound for Rs. 5,000 in *A*'s favour. This bond will be voidable as the consent to it is obtained by threatening to kill a person (*B* in the present case), which is forbidden by Indian Penal Code.

3. ***The coercion must be the unlawful detaining or threatening to detain any property:*** In case the consent of the party is obtained by unlawful detaining or threatening to detain any property, the consent is said to be obtained by coercion.

Example 5.5. An agent refused to hand over the account books of the business, at the end of his term of office, to the new agent unless the principal freed him from the liability in respect of his agency. The principal executed a release deed under which the agent was freed from liability. It was held that the release deed was voidable at the option of the principal as he was made to execute the release deed under coercion. In this case, the consent was obtained by unlawfully detaining the property (*i.e.*, account books) of the principal.

[*Muthia* v. *Muthu Karuppa*, (1927) 50 Madras 786]

The threat of unlawfully detaining any property also amounts to coercion.

4. ***The acts of coercion must be done with the intention of causing the other party to enter into a contract:*** It is also an essential element of coercion. Threats, which amount to coercion, must be done with the intention of causing the other party to enter into a contract. In other words, the acts amounting to coercion must be done with the intention of obtaining the consent of the party, and inducing him to enter into a contract. If the act of coercion is done without any intention of obtaining the consent of the other party, it will not amount to coercion.

Example 5.6. *A* gave a threat to *B* that he (*A*) would take into possession all the land belonging to *B*, and will not vacate it at any cost, *B* may do whatever he wants. Here, *A*'s threat is to detain *B*'s property by unlawful means. In this case, *A*'s threat is not coercion as it is not done with the intention of inducing *B* to enter into contract.

5. ***The Indian Penal Code may or may not be in force where the coercion is committed:*** This legal rule for coercion is emphasised in the Explanation to Section 15 of the Indian Contract Act. According to this explanation, it is immaterial whether the Indian Penal Code is or is not in force in the place where the act amounting to coercion is committed.

Example 5.7. *A* on board in English ship on the high seas, caused *B* to enter into an agreement by an act amounting to criminal intinmidation under the Indian Penal Code. *B*, afterwards, sued *A* for breach of contract at Calcutta. *A* had employed coercion, although his act was not an offence by the Law of England, and although Section 506 of the Indian Penal Code was not in force at the time when, or at the place where the act was done.

6. *The acts of coercion may be initiated by any person:* It is also a legal rule for coercion. According to his rule, the threat amounting to coercion need not necessarily be initiated from a party to the contract. It may be initiated by any person, even by a stranger. Similarly, it may be directed against any person including a stranger.

Example 5.8. *A* threatened to shoot *B*'s son unless *B* signed a promissory note for Rs. 10,000 in favour of *A*. *B* signed the promissory note under the threat. Here, *B*s consent is obtained by coercion. The promissory note is voidable. In this case, the threat amounting to coercion is directed against a person who is not a party to the contract.

7. *The coercion may be by way of threat to commit suicide:* Sometime, by threat to commit suicide, a person obtains the consent of the other. In such cases also, the consent is said to be obtained by coercion.

Example 5.9. *A* person, by giving a threat of suicide, induced his wife and son to execute a release deed in favour of his brother, in respect of certain properties which they claimed as their own. The wife and son executed a release deed under the threat. It was held that the threat of suicide amounted to coercion within Section 15 of the Indian Contract Act. And the release deed was, therefore, voidable. It was further observed that threat to commit suicide is coercion even though it is not punishable under the Indian Penal Code. The court made the following observations in support of this decision:

"The term 'any act forbidden by the Indian Penal Code' is wider than the term 'punishable by the Indian Penal Code'. Simply because a man escapes punishment, it does not follow that the act is not forbidden by Indian Penal Code. For example, a lunatic or a minor may not be punished, this does not show that their criminal acts are not forbidden by the Indian Penal Code." [*Chikham Amiraj* v. *Chikham Seshamma,* (1912) 16 IC 344]

Thus, the threat to commit suicide being forbidden by Indian Penal Code, amounts to coercion within the meaning of Section 15 of the Indian Contract Act.

8. *The coercion may not be by way of threat to file a to suit:* The threat to file a civil or criminal suit cannot be said to be coercion because it is not forbidden under the Indian Penal Code. However, threat to file a suit on false charge amounts to coercion, since such an act is forbidden by the Indian Penal Code.

[*Gobardhan Das* v. *Jai Kishan Das,* (1900) 22 Allahabad 224]

5.6. EFFECTS OF COERCION

The effect of coercion is that is makes the contract voidable at the option of the party whose consent is obtained by coercion, *i.e.*, such party can put an end to the contract if he so chooses [Section 19]. Moreover, the party is also entitled to take back the money or the goods etc., paid or delivered under the contract [Section 72].

Example 5.10. A transport company refused to deliver certain goods to the consignee unless he paid some illegal charges for transporting the goods. The consignee paid the illegal charges in order to obtain the goods. He is entitled to recover the charges which were illegal.

---

*(*a*) Holland has defined undue influence as "undue influence is the unconscientious use of power over another person, such power being obtained by virtue of a present or previously existing dominating control, arising out of relationship between the parties."

(*b*) Lord Halsbury has defined it as "undue influence is the unconscientions use, by one person, of power possessed by him over another in order to induce the other party to enter into a contract".

It may, however, be noted that the burden of proving, that the consent was obtained by coercion, shall lie upon the party who wants to set aside the contract on the plea of coercion. Moreover, such party has to prove that he would not have entered into a contract had the coercion not been employed.

Note : In England, the term used for 'coercion' is 'duress'. The term 'coercion' in India covers much wider field than 'duress' in England. The term duress means threat by one person to another or his wife, parents or child, with a view to get his consent to the contract. In other words, under 'duress' the consent is obtained by the threat of bodily harm to another person or his wife, parents or children. But it does not include unlawful detaining or threatening to detain property (*i.e.*, threats to property are not duress). The other point of distinction is that coercion may be initiated by any person and employed against any person, even a stranger. But the 'duress' must be initiated by the party to the contract or his agent, and it must be employed against the other party or his children, parents or wife.

5.7. UNDUE INFLUENCE

The term 'undue influence' means the unfair use of one's superior power in order to obtain the consent of a person who is in a weaker position. Sometimes, the parties to an agreement are so related to each other that one of them is in a position to dominate the will of the other. The party who occupies the superior position may obtain the consent of the other by unfair use of his power. When a party enters into a contract under any kind of mental pressure, unfair influence or persuasion by the superior party, the undue influence is said to be employed. The contract will be voidable at the option of the party whose consent was obtained by undue influence. The term 'undue influence',* is defined in Section 16(1) of the Indian Contract act, which reads as under:

"A contract is said to be induced by 'undue influence' where the relations subsisting between the parties are such that one of the parties is in a position to dominate the will of the other, and uses that position to obtain an unfair advantage over the other."

The analysis of this section shows that the following are the three essential parts of undue influence:

1. The subsisting relations between the parties are such that one of the parties is in a position to dominate the will of the other.
2. The dominant party uses his superior position to obtain an unfair advantage over the other.
3. By the use of such dominant position, the dominant party obtains the unfair advantage over the other.

These parts will be discussed in detail in the next article.

Example 5.11. *A*, a spiritual adviser (guru), induced *B*, his devotee, to gift to him the whole of his property to secure benefit to his (devotee's) soul in the next world. The consent to gift was held to be obtained by undue influence. It was observed by the court that "would any reasonable man in full possession of his senses and not under unusual influence of some kind or the other do such a thing?" [*Mannu Singh* v. *Umadat Pandey,* (1890) 30 Allahabad 523]

Example 5.12. *A*, an illiterate elderly woman, was possessing certain property. *B*, her nephew, was managing the affairs of his aunt (*A*). *A* gifted whole of her propertyes to *B*. It was held that *B*, who managed the affairs of his aunt, was in a position to dominate his aunt's will. Therefore, the gift deed was set aside on the ground of undue influence.

It may be noted that undue influence here does not mean the excessive influence. It means, something wrongful which compels a person in a weaker position to do something which he otherwise would not have done, if he had been left free to do the things. Thus, undue influence is a kind of '***mental coercion***' as opposed to physical coercion as defined in Section 15.

As a matter of fact, undue influence is the domination of a weak mind by a strong mind. It destroys the free mind of a person and constrains him to do which is against his will. Moreover, he would not have done if left to his own judgment and volition.

5.8. ESSENTIALS AND LEGAL RULES FOR A VALID UNDUE INFLUENCE

1. *One party must be in a position to dominate the will of the other*
2. *The dominant party must use his superior position to obtain an unfair advantage over the weaker party*
3. *The dominant party must have obtained an unfair advantage over the weaker party*

The legal definition of undue influence, discussed in the last article, reveals the essential elements of undue influence. An undue influence is valid if it satisfies the requirements of its legal definition.

1. *One party must be in a position to dominate the will of the other:* It is an important and essential element of undue influence. The party is said to be able to dominate the will of the other, where the parties are not on equal footing or there is active trust or confidence between the parties. In *Smith v. Kay* (1859) 7 HLC 750, Lord Kingsdown observed that "The principle applies to every case where influence is acquired and abused, where confidence is reposed and betrayed."

Example 5.13. *A*, a lady gifted all her property to *B*, a medical practitioner, who was attending on her. When she recovered from illness, she disputed the validity of the gift deed. The undue influence was held to the employed. In this case, *B* was in a position to dominate the will of *A*.

[*Sunder Kumari* v. *Kishore*, 5 W.R. 246]

In the following circumstances, one party is presumed to be in a position to dominate the will of the other:

1. Where one party holds a real or apparent authority over the other.
2. Where on party stands in a fiduciary relation to the other.
3. Where one party makes a contract with another in a mental distress.

All these points are contained in Section 16(2) of the Indian Contract Act, and will be discussed in detail in Art. 5.10

2. *The dominant party must use his superior position to obtain an unfair advantage over the weaker party:* We have discussed above the cases in which a party is said to dominate the will of the other. Another essential element of undue influence is that the dominant party must use his superior position to obtain an unfair advantage over the other.

Example 5.14. *A*, was suffering from number of ailments, and *B* was his family doctor. *B* induced *A* to agree to pay *B* an unreasonable sum for his professional services. Here, *B* has employed undue influence over *A*. In this case, *B* used his superior position to obtain unfair advantage over *A*.

3. *The dominant party must have obtained an unfair advantage over the weaker party:* In case the dominant party uses his superior position and obtains an unfair advantage over the weaker party, the undue influence is said to be employed.

Example 5.15. *A*, has advanced money to his son *B*, during his minority. Upon *B*'s attaining majority, *A* obtained, by misuse of parental influence, a bond from *B* for a greater amount than a sum due in respect of the advance. Here, *A* has employed undue influence. *A* has obtained undue advantage to himself.

5.9. EFFECTS OF UNDUE INFLUENCE

The effect of undue influence is that it makes the contract voidable at the option of the party whose consent is obtained by undue influence, *i.e.*, such party can put an end to the contract if he so chooses. [Section 19 A].

Example 5.16. *A*, a money-lender, advanced Rs. 10,000 to *B*, an agriculturist. By undue influence, *A* induced *B* to execute a bound for Rs. 20,000 with an interst at 6 per cent per month. The bond is voidable at the option of *B*. And the court may set the bond aside, ordering *B* to repay Rs. 100 with such interst as it may seem just.

5.10. PRESUMPTION OF DOMINATION OF WILL

1. *Where one party holds a real or apparent authority over the other*
2. *Where one party stands in a fiduciary relations to the other*
3. *Where one party makes a contract with the other who is in mental distress*

We have discussed, in the last article, that an undue influence arises where one party is in a position to dominate the will of the other. In the following circumstances one party is presumed to be in a position to dominate the will of the other:

1. *Where one party holds a real or apparent authority over the other* [Section 16(2)(a)]: When a person holds an authority over the other, he is definitely in a position to dominate the will of the person over whom the authority is held. The authority may be real or apparent. The 'real authority' means that person has a real power over the other. The 'apparent authority' would include the cases in which a person has no real authority, but is able to approach the other with the show or colour of authority. Instances of the cases which are included in this category are relations between master and servant, income tax officer in relation to an assessee, a magistrate or a police officer in relation to an accused person.

Example 5.17. *A* sold his cycle to his servant *B* for Rs. 800. Subsequently, *B* refused to take the cycle on the ground that the cycle was overvalued. Here, *A* being the master, holds a real authority over *B*, and is in a position to dominate his (*B*'s) will. In such cases, the undue influence can be easily employed. This contract of sale is, therefore, voidable at the option of *B*.

2. *Where one party stands in a fiduciary relations to the other* [Section 16(2)(a)]: The relations of trust and confidence are known as fiduciary relations. A party who is trusted by the other, or in whom the confidence is reposed by the other, may easily use his superior position to dominate the will of the other. This is so because the relationship of trust and confidence gives a very good oportunity to the person, in whom trust or confidence is held, to exploit it for his personal benefits. If the consent is obtained by exploiting the trust or confidence, the consent is said to be obtained by undue influence. This category is very wide. The following types of relations are judicially held to be of trust and confidence:

(*a*) Solicitor and client.
(*b*) Doctor and patient.
(*c*) Spiritual adviser and devotee.
(*d*) Parents and child.
(*e*) Guardian and ward.
(*f*) Trustee and beneficiary.
(*g*) Woman and her confidential managing agents.

These cases usually raise the presumption of undue influence.

Example 5.18. *A*, a solicitor, sold certain properties to one of his clients, *B*. Subsequently, *B* sought to rescind (cancel) the sale of the property on the ground that the property was considerably over-valued. The court held that relationship of solicitor and client is of trust and confidence, and undue influence could easily be employed by the party in influential position.

[*Moody* v. *Cox*, (1917) 2 Ch. 71]

3. ***Where one party makes a contract with the other who is in mental distress*** **[Section 16(2)(*b*)]:** sometimes, a person makes a contract with a person, whose mental capacity is temporarily or permanently affected by reason of age, illness, or mental or bodily distress. In such cases, he is in a position to dominate the will of such persons. A person is said to be in distress when his mental capacity is temporarily or permanently affected due to any of the above causes. A person in distress can be easily induced to give his consent to a contract which may be unfavourable to him. Such contract will be voidable on the ground of undue influence.

Example 5.19. *A*, an illiterate old man of about 90 years, physically infirm and mentally in distress, was not in a position to look after his daily affairs and manage his cultivation. His nearest relative *B*, looked after his daily needs, and managed his cultivation. Under the influence of *B*, *A* executed a gift deed of his properties. The court held that *A* was in distress by reasons of old age and physical and mental illness. And *B* was in a position to dominate his will. And thus, the gift deed was voidable. [*Sher Singh* v. *Pirthi Singh*, AIR 1975 Allahabad 259]

Example 5.20. *A*, a poor Hindu widow was in great need of money to established her right to maintenance. She was persuaded by *B*, a money-lender, to agree to 100 per cent rate of interest. The court held that this is a clear instance of undue influence being exerted upon a person in distress, and the court reduced the interest rate to 24 per cent.

[*Rani Annapurni* v. *Swaminath*, (1910) 34 Madras 7]

But, it may be noted that, the money borrowed at a high rate, in the ordinary course of business, cannot be said to be borrowed under mental distress.

Example 5.21. *A* was facing criminal prosecution at the instance of *B*, his father. *A* borrowed on very high rates, a sum of money to defend himself. The court held that he was not in such mental distress as would enable a moneylender to dominate his will.

[*Raghunath Prasad v. Sarju Prabad*, AIR 1924 PC 60]

Thus, the mere urgent need of money on the part of the borrower is not, in itself, a sufficient evidence of mental distress.

5.11. PRESUMPTION OF UNDUE INFLUENCE

1. ***Unconscionable transaction***
2. ***Contracts with pardanashin woman***

We have discussed above that in three cases namely (*a*) when one party is holding real or apparent authority over the other, (*b*) where there is fiduciary relationship between the parties, (*c*) where the contracts are made with the persons in mental distress, it is presumed that one party is in a position to dominate the will of the other. It is to be noted that there are also certain cases in which it is presumed that the contract is induced by undue influence. The effect of this presumption is that once it is shown that one party was in a position to dominate the will of the other, it will be understood that the superior party must have used his position to obtain an unfair advantage over the other. In such cases, the superior party has to show that the consent of the other party was freely obtained. Following are the two circumstances which indicate the presumption of undue influence:

1. ***Unconscionable transaction*** **[Section 16(3)]***:* Sometimes, the parties are not on equal footing, *i.e.*, one is stronger (influential) and the other weaker. The stronger party may make an unreasonable use of his superiority (influence) over the weaker party, and enter into a contract which, on the face of it, is of great advantage to himself (stronger party). Such transaction is said to be unconscionable. In other words, where one of the parties, to a contract, is in a position to dominate the will of the other and the contract is apparently unconscionable, *i.e.*, unfair, the transaction is unconscionable. In such cases, the law presumes that the consent must have been obtained by undue influence. The burden is shifted to the stronger party to prove that the consent of the other party is freely given.

Following are some of the judicially decided cases in which the transaction was held to be unconscionable, and the presumption of undue influence was raised.

Example 5.22. *A*, an old and illiterate woman incapable of any business, conferred on *B* her confidential managing agent, without any valuable consideration, an important monetary benefit under the guise of a trust. It was held that all the fact of the case show that there was active undue influence. [*Wazid Khan* v. *Raja Ewaz Ali Khan,* (1891) 18 1 A 144]

Example 5.23. *A*, a spendthrift, and a drunkard youth of 18 years, borrowed from *B*, a money-lender, Rs. 900 on a bond bearing compound interest at 2 per cent per month with monthly rents. The court held that the transaction was unconscionable as the rate of interest was so exorbitant.

[*Kirpa Ram* v. *Sami-ud-din,* (1903) 25 Allahabad 284]

Example 5.24. *A*, a poor framer, being unable to pay back a loan, sold his land to *B*, his creditor. The property was worth three times the value of the amount due. The transaction was held to be unconscionable and the relief was granted to the farmer by setting aside the sale.

[*Bhambat* v. *Yeshwantrao,* (1900) 25 Bombay 126]

However, it may be noted that in such cases parties must not be on equal footing (*i.e.*, one of the parties must be in a position to dominate the will of the other). As between the parties on equal footing, mere unconscionableness of the bargain does not create the presumption of undue influence. Thus, the unconscionableness of the bargain is not the first thing to be considered. The first thing to be considered is the relation of the parties.

[*Raghunath Prasad* v. *Sarju Prasad,* AIR 1924 PC 60]

2. *Contracts with pardanashin woman:* The term 'pardanashin woman' is not defined either in the Indian Contract Act or in any other Act. However, the accepted definition is that a pardanashin woman is one who observes complete seclusion because of customs of particular community to which she belongs. In other words, a woman who is totally secluded from social intercourse is known as a pardanashin woman.

The contracts with the pardanashin woman are presumed to have been induced by undue influence. The law provides a special protection to a pardanashin woman. Once it is shown that a contract is made with a pardanashin woman, the law presumes undue influence. The burden lies on the superior party to shown that no undue influence was used, and that the contract was fully explained to her and that she freely consented.

It is important to note that a person who deals with a pardanashin woman has to prove the following points in order to show that the contract was not induced by undue influence :

(*a*) That the nature and effect of the transaction was explained to her, and was also understood by her;

(*b*) That she had an independent advice in the matter;

(*c*) That her consent to the contract was freely obtained;

(*d*) That she carried out the transaction deliberately and of her own free will.

5.12. BURDEN OF PROOF OF UNDUE INFLUENCE

When a contract is challenged in a Court of Law on the ground of undue influence, then it is the duty of the weaker party to prove that his consent was obtained by undue influence. He has to establish the following two points:

1. The superior party was in a position to dominate his will, and
2. The superior party actually used his influence to obtain his consent to the contract.

In other words, the weaker party has to prove that the superior party was in a position to dominate his will. It may be noted that mere proof of nearness of relations is not sufficient for the court to assume that one person was in a position to dominate the will of the other. The dominating will of the stronger party must be proved. Moreover, the weaker party has also to prove that the superior party actually used his influence to obtain the consent of the weaker party. It may also be noted that mere dominating will of the party is not sufficient for the court to assume that undue influence has been employed. It must also be proved by the weaker party that the dominating party has actually used his position to obtain an unfair advantage over him (the weaker party).

Thus, the burden of proving undue influence is on the plaintiff (*i.e.*, who files a suit in a Court of Law). The suit is, generally, filed by the weaker party to avoid *i.e.*, rescind the contract.

In those cases where there is presumption of undue influence (*i.e.*, it is presumed that the consent of the party is obtained, by undue influence), the burden of proving undue influence is shifted from the weaker party to the stronger party. In other words, it is then for the stronger party to prove that the consent of the weaker party was freely given, and the contract is not induced by any undue influence.

5.13. COMPARISON BETWEEN COERCION AND UNDUE INFLUENCE

The following tabe gives the comparison between coercion and undue influence.

S.No. *Coercion*	*Undue Influence*
1. The consent of one of the parties is not free.	The consent of one of the parties is also not free.
2. The contract is voidable at the option of the party whose consent was obtained by coercion.	The contract is also voidable at the option of the party whose consent was obtianed by undue influence.
3. Relationship between the parties is immaterial.	Some kind of relationship must exist between the parties. The relationship should be such which shows that one party is in a position to dominate the will of the other.
4. The coercion may be initiated by any person, even by a stranger to the contract. It may also be employed against any person including a stranger.	The undue influence is employed by a party who is in a position to dominate the will of the other.
5. The consent of a party is obtained by committing or threatening to commit an act forbidden by the Indian Penal Code, or by unlawful detaining or threatening to detain any property.	The consent of a weaker party is obtained by dominating his will, and by taking an unfair advantage of one's superior position.
6. The force used is of physical nature.	The force used is of moral nature, *i.e.*, force used in the shape of moral pressure.

5.14. FRAUD

The term 'fraud' may be defined as an intentional, deliberate or wilful misstatement of facts, which are material for the formation of a contract. The most important requirement of a fraud is that the misstatement of facts must be made by one party *with an intention to deceive* the other. The contract is voidable at the option of the party whose consent is obtained by fraud (in the same way as was in case of coercion and undue influence). The term 'fraud' is defined in Section 17 of the Indian Contract Act, which reads as under:

"Fraud means and includes any of the following acts committed by a party to a contract or with his connivance or by his agent, with intent to deceive another party thereto or his agent, or to induce him to enter into the contract:

(1) *the suggestion, as to a fact, of that which is not true, by one who does not believe it to be true;*

(2) *the active concealment of a fact by one having knowledge or belief of the fact;*

(3) *a promise made without any intention of performing it;*

(4) *any other act fitted to deceive;*

(5) *any such act or omission as the law specially declares to be fraudulent."*

The analysis of this section shows that the intention of the party, making the fraudulent statement, must be to deceive the other party to the contract or to induce him to enter into a contract. This section further makes it clear that any act which falls in the above-mentioned five categories, amounts to fraud. These acts which constitute fraud will be discussed in detail in Art. 5.16

Example 5.25. The prospectus of a company contained a statement that the company had been authorised by Special Act of the Parliament to use steam or mechanical power for running the trains. In fact, the authority to use the steam was subject to the approval of the 'Board of Trade'. But this fact was not mentioned in the prospectus. The Board of Trade did not approve the use of steam, and consequently the company was wound up. The sharecholders of the company filed a suit against the directors, for fraud. But the court held that they were not liable for fraud. The directors were not guilty of fraud, as they honestly believed that once the Parliament had authorised the use of steam, the consent of the Board of Trade practically concluded.

[*Derry* v. *Peck*, (1889) 14 App. Cas. 337]

In the above case, LORD HERSCHEL observed that:

"Fraud is proved when it is shown that false representation has been made

(*a*) *knowingly, or*

(*b*) *without belief in its truth, or*

(*c*) *recklessly careless whether it be true or false."*

Thus, the intentional misstatment is the essence of fraud. A person making a false statement is not guilty of fraud, if he honestly believes that the statement given by him is true.

5.15. ESSENTIALS AND LEGAL RULES FOR A FRAUD

1. *The fraudulent act must be committd with an intention to deceive*
2. *The fraudulent act must be committeed with knowledge of its falsity*
3. *The fraudulent act must have been committed by a party to the contract*
4. *The fraudulent act must have been committed upon the party to the contract or his agent*
5. *The fraudulent act must have actually deceived the other party*
6. *Mere silence is not fraud*

The legal definition of fraud discussed in the last article, reveals the essential elements of fraud. A fraud is said to be committed if it satisfies the requirements of its definition. The essential elements of frauds are discussed in points 1 to 5 in the following discussion, and the rest are the legal rules for a fraud. The other party can complain about fraud only if its essential elements are statisfied.

1. *The fraudulent act must be committd with an intention to deceive:* It is an important and essential element of a fraud. The act, which constitutes fraud, must be committed by a party, to a contract, with the intention to deceive the other party. This essential element has been emphasised in Section 17 of the Indian Contract Act. It provides that fraud means and includes any act committed by a party, to a contract, with the intention to deceive another party or to induce him to enter into the contract. Thus, there must be intention to decive the other party, or the intention to induce him to enter into a contract.

Example 5.26. *A* fraudulently informed *B* that *A*'s estate was free from any encumbrance. *B* believing it to be true, bought the estate. Actually the estate was mortgaged. Here, *A* is guilty of the fraud, as he, with the intention to deceive *B*, induced him (*B*) to buy the estate.

Example 5.27. *A*, intending to deceive *B*, falsely represented that five tonnes of ice was manufactured daily in his factory. And thereby, induced *B* to buy the factor. In fact, the production was 3.5 tonnes per day. The contract is voidable at the option of *B*, as his consent is obtained by fraud.

2. *The fraudulent act must be committeed with knowledge of its falsity:* It is also an essential element of fraud that the party committing the fraudulent act must be aware that his act is false. In other words, the fraudulent act must have been made with the knowledge of its falsity (*i.e.*, without belief in its truth). A person making a false statement is not guilty of fraud if he honestly believes in its truthfulness. *Derry* v. *Peek* illustrates this point. This case has already been explained in Example 5.25.

3. *The fraudulent act must have been committed by a party to the contract:* This essential element has been emphasised in Section 17 of the Indian Contract Act, according to which, the fraud must have been committed only by the party to the contract or his authorised agent. It may be noted that a fraud committed by a stranger (*i.e.*, by a person who is not a party to the contract), does not affect the validity of the contract.

Example 5.28. *A* was induced to buy shares in a company, on account of a false statement made by *B*. *B* was neither a director nor representative of the company. But was a mere stranger. *A* wanted to set aside the contract on the ground of fraud. It was held that he could not set aside the contract because the false statement was not made by the company or its authorised agents.

4. *The fraudulent act must have been committed upon the party to the contract or his agent:* It is also an essential element of fraud, that it must have been committed upon the party to the contract. If it is committed on a stranger, then it will not amount to fraud, and a contract shall not be voidable on account of fraud.

5. *The fraudulent act must have actually deceived the other party:* The party, induced by fraud must have relied upon the fraudulent statement and must have been actually deceived. In other words, fraud must have induced the other party to enter into a contract. This essential element has been emphasised in the Explanation to Section 19 of the Indian Contract Act, which provides that a contract is not voidable if the party is not actually deceived by the fraud. *i.e.*, such a fraud is not effective.

Example 5.29. *A* had a defective connon. In order to conceal the defect, he put a metal plug on it. He sold the cannon to *B*, who accepted it without examining. When *B* used the cannon, it burst. *B* refused to pay the balance price on the ground that *A* was guilty of fraud. It was held that *B* was liable to pay the price, as he was not actually deceived by the fraud because he would have bought it even if no deceptive plug was inserted. [*Horsefall* v. *Thomos*, (1862) 1 H&C 90]

6. *Mere silence is not fraud:* It is a legal rule according to which mere silence does not amount to fraud. As a matter of fact, a contracting party is under no obligation to disclose the whole truth to the other party, or to give him the whole information in his possession affecting the subject-mater of the contract. This legal rule is contained in the Explanation to Section 17 of the Indian Contract Act, which reads as under:

"Mere silence as to facts likely to affect the willingness of a person to enter into a contract, is no fraud."

Thus, mere silence is not fraud.

Example 5.30. *A* sold, by auction, to *B*, a horse which *A* knew to be unsound. *A* said nothing to *B* about the horse's unsoundness. This is not fraud by *A*.

Example 5.31. *A* and *B*, being traders, entered into a contract. *A* had private information of a change in prices which would affect *B*'s willingness to proceed with the contract. *A* is not bound to inform *B*. If he does not inform, it will not amount to fraud.

5.16. ACTS WHICH CONSTITUTE FRAUD

1. *False statement of fact*
2. *Active concealment of a fact*
3. *A promise made without any intention of performing it*
4. *Any other act fitted to deceive*
5. *Such acts or omission as the law specially declares to be fraudulent*

Section 17 of the Indian Contract Act provides five categories of acts which constitute fraud. These are discussed in detail in the following pages. Any act committed with an intention to decieve amounts to fraud if if falls in anyone of these five categories.

1. *False statement of fact:* According to Section 17(1) of the Indian Contract Act, a false statement is considered as a fraud when

(*a*) there is a statement, which is false, and

(*b*) the statement relates to the facts, and

(*c*) the statement is made by a person who knows that it is not true, *i.e.*, the statement must be made with the knowledge of its falsehood.

Example 5.32. *A* said to *B* that his car of 1980 Model is in an excellent condition, though he knew that this is not true. *B* purchased the car believing the statement to be true. It is a fraud by *A* as he intentionally made the untrue statement of fact and induced *B* to enter into a contract. The contract is voidable at *B*'s option.

The false statement must relate to the facts. A mere option, a statement of expression or intention, commendatory or puffing expression is not regarded as statement of fact, and hence will not amount to fraud.

Example 5.33. *A* while selling his horse to *B*, said that the horse cost him Rs. 1,000. Actually he paid Rs. 800 for it. *B* bought the horse for Rs. 1000 believing the statement to be true. Here, *A* will be guilty of fraud, as he knowingly made the false statement of facts.

Note: In the above illustration, if *A* says to *B* that the horse is lucky and worth Rs. 1,000. And *B* buys the horse for Rs. 1,000 believing the statement to be true. Afterwards, *B* learns that *A* had purchases it for Rs. 800. Here, *A* will not be guilty of fraud because the statement made by him is mere statement of opinion and not of fact.

2. *Active concealment of a fact:* According to Section 17(2) of the Indian Contract Act, an active concealment is considered as a fraud when

(*a*) there is a concealment of fact, and

(*b*) the concealment is active (*i.e.*, all efforts are made to conceal fact), and

(*c*) the concealment is made by a party who has the knowledge of it.

Example 5.34. *A* was legally entitled to succeed to an estate at the death of his relative *B*. *B* died. *C*, a third person knowing the death of *B*, prevented the information from reaching *A*. And *C* induced *A* to sell him his interest in the estate. The sale is voidable at the option of *A*. In this case, there is active concealment of fact by *C* as he prevents the information of material fact from reaching *A*.

Example 5.35. *A*, a horse dealer, sold a horse to *B*. *A* knew that the horse had a cracked hoof which he filled up in such a way as to prevent its detection. The defect was, subsequently, discovered by *A*. It was held that agreement could be set aside by *B* as his consent was obtained by fraud. In the present case, there is active concealment of fact by *A* as he adopted the means, *i.e.*, filled up the cracked hoof and prevented the information from reaching *B*.

3. *A promise made without any intention of performing it:* According to Section 17(3), a promise made without any inention of performing it is considered as a fraud if it is made with the intention of deceiving the other party.

Example 5.36. A man and a woman went through the ceremonies of marriage. The husband had no intention to regard it as a real marriage. It was held that the consent of the wife was obtained by fraud as the man had no intention of performing the promise.

[*Shireen Mall* v. *John James Taylor,* AIR 1952 Punj. 227]

Example 5.37. *A* purchased certain goods from *B*. He had no intention to pay the price. It is a fraud on the part of *A* as he made the promise without the intention of performing it.

4. *Any other act fitted to deceive:* According to Section 17(4) of the Act, any other act fitted to deceive is also fraud if done with the intention of deceiving the other party. The expression 'act fitted to deceive' means any act which is done with the obvious intention of committing fraud. This is a general clause and includes all cases which do not fall in any one of the other categories specified in Section 17(1), 17(2) and 17(3). Thus, this clause covers all tricks and unfair ways which are used by cunning and clever people to cheat others.

Example 5.38. *A* persuaded his illiterate wife *B* to sign certain documents telling her that he was going to mortgage her two pieces of land to secure his indebtendness. But actually he mortgaged four pieces of land belonging to her. This was held to be an act done with the intention of deceiving her. [*Ningawa* v. *B.S. Hire Kurabar,* (1968) SCR 797]

5. *Such acts or omission as the law specially declares to be fraudulent:* This category includes the acts or omissions which the law specially declares to be fraudulent *e.g.,* the Insolvency Acts, and Companies Act declares certain kinds of transfer to be fraudulent. The Tansfer of Property Act also declares that any transfer of immovable property with the intention of defrauding the creditor, is taken as a fraud.

5.17. SILENCE AS FRAUD

1. *Duty to speak*
2. *Where silence is equivalent to speech*
3. *Half truths*
4. *Change of circumstances*

We have already discussed that a mere silence is not fraud. However, there are certain exceptions to this rule in which the mere silence amounts to fraud. Two statutory exceptions are contained in the Explanation to Section 17, itself, which provides that the silence amounts to fraud in the following two cases, namely:

(*a*) Where there is a duty of the person keeping silent to speak and

(*b*) Where the silence is equivalent to speech.

1. *Duty to speak:* Mere silence amounts to fraud when the person keeping silent, is under a duty to speak. The duty to speak arises, where one party reposes trust and confidence in the other.

Example 5.39. *A* sold by auction, to his son *B*, his old car which *A* knew to have defective engine. *A* said nothing to *B* about the defects in the car engine. This amounts to fraud as the relation between the father and the son makes it father's duty to tell his son about the condition of the car engine.

It is to be noted that in contracts of absolute *good faith,* there is a duty to disclose all material facts which are in the knowledge of one party. All the contracts of insurance are the contracts of absolute *good faith,* as the insurance company has to depend on the disclosures made by the assured. It becomes the duty of the assured to disclosed all the material facts affecting the risk covered. Thus, where there is duty to speak, the silence amounts to fraud.

2. *Where silence is equivalent to speech:* Sometimes, the silence is equivalent to speech. In such cases, the silence of a person amounts to fraud *e.g.*, where a person keeps silent, knowing that his silence is going to be deceptive, he is guilty of fraud.

Example 5.40. *A*, a buyer, saw the horse of *B*, a seller. *A*'s first impression was that the horse was sound. He asked *B* to confirm the soundness of the horse. *B* kept silent. This is a fraud, because *B*'s silence is equivalent to speech.

The above two are the statutory exceptions to the rule that mere silence is not fraud, which are contained in the Explanation to Section 17. In the following two more cases the silence, as to material fact, is considered as fraud.

3. *Half truths:* The silence may amount to fraud when a person discloses only the half truth and then keeps silent. A person may become guilty of fraud by non-disclosure also if he voluntarily discloses something and then stops half the ways. A person may keep silent. But if he speaks, he is duty bound to disclose the whole truth.

Example 5.41. The prospectus of a company contained the statements that the company had paid dividends every year between 1921 and 1927. These statements were true. But the fact was that in each of these years, the company had incurred substantial losses and the dividends were paid only out of the secret reserves. No disclosure was made of these losses. It was held that the prospectus was false and the director who knew that it was false, was held guilty of fraud.

[*R.* v. *Kylsant,* (1932) 1 K.B. 442]

4. *Change of circumstances :* Sometimes, a statement is true when made. But when it is actually acted upon by the other party, it may become false due to the change of circumstances. In such cases, it is the duty of the person, who made the statement, to communication the change of circumstances.

Example 5.42. The prospectus of a company contained a statement that certain person are the directors of the company. This statement was true when made. One the basis of this statement, certain persons applied for the allotment of shares. But before the allotment took place, some directors retired from the company. This change was not communicated to the applicants of share. It was held that they were entitled to avoid the allortment.

[*Rajagopala Iyer* v. *South Indian Rubber Works,* (1942) 2 ML 228]

5.18. EFFECTS OF FRAUD

The effect of fraud is that it makes the contract voidable at the option of the party whose consent was obtained by fraud. And such party may put an end to the contract if he so chooses [Section 19].

Example 5.43. *A*, intending to deceive *B*, falsely stated that his scooter runs 35 kilometrs in one litre of petrel. And thereby induced *B* to buy the scooter. But actually the scooter runs 24 kilometres in one litre. The contract is voidable at the option of *B*.

It may, however, be noted that in the following two circumstances, the contract is not voidable on account of fraud:

1. Where the silence amounts to fraud, the contract is not voidable, if the other party had the means of discovering the truth with ordinary diligence [Section 19 (exception)]. Thus, a party cannot complain of fraudulent silence if he had the means of discovering the truth with ordinary means.
2. Where the fraud does not induce the other party to enter into a contract, the contract is not voidable [Section 19, explanation]. Thus, if the consent is given independently in spite of fraud, the contract is not voidable.

5.19. REMEDIES AVAILABLE ON ACCOUNT OF FRAUD

The aggrieved party, *i.e.*, the party whose consent was obtained by fraud, has the following two remedies (or rights):

1. He may rescind (*i.e.,* revoke or put an end to) the contract.
2. He may affirm (*i.e.,* accept) the contract.

1. *Right to resind the contract:* Since the contract is voidable at the option of the party whose consent was obtained by fraud, the aggrieved party can rescind the contract. But in those cases where silence amounts to fraud, the aggrieved party cannot rescind the contract, if he had the means of discovering the truth by ordinary diligence. Moreover, he can also not rescind the contract if the fraud has not been relied upon by him *i.e.,* the consent is given irrespective of the fraud.

2. *Right to affirm the contract :* If the aggrieved party thinks proper, he may accept the contract and insist upon its performance. He may compel the other party to put him in the position in which he would have been if the fraud had not been committed.

[*Section 19, second para*]

Example 5.45. *A* fraudulently informed *B* that his house was free from encumbrances. *B,* believing the statement to be true, bought the house. But actually the house was subjected to mortgage. In this case, *B* may either rescind the contract or may insist on its being carried out after *A* agrees to pay the mortgage money.

The aggrieved party can exercise his option either to rescind the contract or to affirm it, only once. Later on, he has no option to change his stand for the fraud. Once the option is exercised, both the parties are bound by it.

5.20. CIRCUMSTANCES OF LOSING THE RIGHT OF RESCISSION

1. *By lapse of time*
2. *By affirmation*
3. *When the third party acquires right in the subject-matter*

Aggrieved party's right of rescission is lost in the following circumstances:

1. *By lapse of time:* After the fraud is discovered by the aggrieved party, the contract must be rescinded within a reasonable time. But if the contract is not rescinded withim the reasonable time, this right is lost. The 'reasonable time' is an important factor which depends upon the facts and circumstances of each case.

Example 5.46. A person purchased certain shares in a company on the basis of misleading prospectus. After five months, he wanted to set aside the sale. The court held that the unexplained delay of five months is unreasonable for obtaining the relief.

[*In re. Jagannath Prasad,* AIR 1938 Allahabad 1931]

2. *By affirmation:* Sometimes, after becoming aware of the right to rescind, the aggrieved party affirms the contract. In such cases, he loses the right to rescind the contract. The affirmation may be express or implied.

Example 5.47. *A* fraudulently sold his VCR to *B.* Afterwards, *B* came to know about the fraud. Instead of rescinding the contract, *B* further sold the VCR to *C.* In this case *B*'s right to rescind the contract with *A* is lost.

3. *When the third party acquires right in the subject-matter:* Sometimes, the third party acquires the right in the subject-matter of the contract, in good faith, without any knowledge of fraud between the other two parties. And the third party pays the due consideration for acquiring the rights. In such cases, the aggrieved party loses the right to rescind the contract.

Example 5.48. *A* fraud, obtained certain goods from *B.* And sold the same to *C* who purchased them in good faith. In this case *B*'s right to rescind the contract with *A* is lost, as the third party (*i.e., C*) has acquired interest in the subject-matter in good faith.

[*Phillips* v. *Brooks Ltd.,* (1919) 2 KB 243]

5.21. MISREPRESENTATION

The term 'misrepresentation' may be defined as an innocent misstatement of facts which are material for the contract. In other words, misrepresentation is a false representation which is made innocently (*i.e.*, without any intention to deceive the other party). A 'representation' means a statement of facts made by one party to the other with a view to induce the other party to enter into the contract. The representation must relate to some fact, which is material to the contract. A false representation made by a person may be either:

1. Innocent or unintentional, *i.e.*, without any intention of deceiving the party, or
2. Intentional or wilful or deliberate, *i.e.*, with the inention of deceiving the party.

The former in called the '*misrepresentation*', and the latter, '*fraud*'. It is thus, clear that the intention of making the false statement distinguishes between fraud and misrepresentation. Thus, the most important requirement of misrepresentation is that the false statement of facts is made by a party *without any intention to deceive* the other party. The contract is voidable at the option of the party whose consent is obtained by misrepresentation. The term 'misrepresentation' is defined in Section 18 of the Indian Contract Act, which reads as under:

"Misrepresentation means and includes: —

(1) *the positive assertion; in a manner not warranted by the information of person making it, of that which is not true, though he believes it to be true.*

(2) *any breach of duty which without an intent to deceive, gains an advantage to the person committing it, or anyone claiming under him, by misleading another to his prejudice or to the prejudice of anyone claiming under him.*

(3) *causing however innocently, a party to an agreement to make a mistake as to the substance of the thing which is the subject of the agreement."*

The analysis of this section shows that, a misrepresentation is an innocent misstatement of facts. It includes (*a*) a positive false statement made without any basis for information, (*b*) a breach of duty which brings advantage to the person committing it, and (*c*) inducement of mistake about the subject-matter. These acts which constitute misrepresentation will be discussed in detail in Art. 5.23.

5.22. ESSENTIALS AND LEGAL RULES FOR MISREPRESENTATION

1. ***The misrepresentation must be of material facts***
2. ***The misrepresentation must be false, but the person making it honestly believes it to be true***
3. ***The misrepresentation must induce the other party to enter into contract***
4. ***The misrepresentation must have been addressed by one party to the party misled***
5. ***Change of circumstances, may amount to misrepresentation***

The legal definition of misrepresentation discussed in the last article, reveals the essential elements of misrepresentation. A misrepresentation is said to be made, if it satisfies the essentials of its definition. The essential elements of misrepresentation are discussed in points 1 to 4 in the following discussion, and the rest are legal rules for misrepresentation. The other party can complain about misrepresentation only if its essential elements are satisfied.

1. *The misrepresentation must be of material facts:* It is an important and essential element of misrepresentation that the false statement must be of material facts. A mere expression of one's opinion is not a statement of facts. It is to be noted that there is a lot of difference when the seller states that his property is worth one lakh of rupees, and when he states that he paid one lakh of rupees for the property. The first is the opinion which the buyer may adopt if he so wishes. And the second is a statement of fact, which if false, makes the contract voidable.[1]

1. *Lindsay Petroleum Co. v. Hurd* (1874) LR 5 PC 221.

Example 5.49. *A* agreed to purchase from *B* certain lands for the purpose of sheep farming. However, *A* had agreed to purchase the land relying upon *B*'s statement that he estimated that the land would carry two thousand sheep. But neither *B* nor any other person had, at any time, carried on sheep farming on the land in question. When *B* claimed the balance of purchase price, *A* wanted to set aside the contract on the ground of misrepresentation that the capacity of the land was much less than stated by *B*. It was held that *B*'s statement was merely an opinion which according to him was true. Therefore, the contract was not set aside.

[*Smith* v. *Land & Housing Corpn.*, (1884) Ch. D. 7]

However, in certain cases commendatory expression may also amount to misrepresentation if it is false to the knowledge of the person making it.

Example 5.50. *A* sold his hotel to *B*. At the time of sale, *A* stated that a part of the hotel is occupied by a tenant who is most desirable. In fact, the rent from the tenant could only be obtained under pressure, and was currently much in arrear. This statement was held to be a misrepresentation, and *B* was allowed to set aside the contract. [Based on *Brown* v. *Raphael* (1958) Ch. 636]

2. *The misrepresentation must be false, but the person making it honestly believes it to be true:* The statement of facts which amounts to misrepresentation must be a false statement. But the person making it should believe it to be true.

Example 5.51. *A* believed the engine of his motor cycle to be in an excellent condition. At the time of sale of this motor cycle, *A* without getting it checked in a workshop, told *B* that the motor cycle was in excellent condition. On this statement, *B* bought the motor cycle, whose engine proved to be defective. Here, *A*'s statement is misrepresentation as the statement turns out to be false.

3. *The misrepresentation must induce the other party to enter into contract :* The person making false representation must have the intention to induce the other party. Moreover, the second party must enter into a contact believing the representation to be true.

Example 5.52. *A*, the owner of an apple orchard, believed that all the apple trees in his orchard were the fruit bearing trees. However, he had no sufficient ground for his belief. He stated this fact to *B*, and thereby induced him to purchase the orchard. Believing this representation to be true, *B* purchased the orchard. Later on, it was found that only 60 per cent trees are fruit bearing. In this case, the contract is voidable as *A* induced *B* to purchase the orchard who purchased the same relying upon the statement.

4. *The misrepresentation must have been addressed by one party to the party misled:* The false statement which amounts to misrepresentation must have been addressed by the person making it to the party who is misled by it. If it is not addressed to the party who is misled, then it is not misrepresentation and the contract is not voidable at his option.

Example 5.53. The promoters of a company were sued by *A* who had purchased certain shares on the faith of a false statement contained in a prospectus issued by them. *A* was not a person to whom the shares had been allotted on the first allotment of the company. He had merely purchased the shares from the first allottees. It was held that the prospectus was addressed to the first applicants for shares. It could not be supposed to extend to others than the first applicants.

[*Peek* v. *Gurney* (1873) LR 6 HL 377]

5. *Change of circumstances, may amount to misrepresentation:* Sometimes, a representation of fact is made, and the circumstances change before the conclusion of the contract. In such cases, the change of circumstances which affect the facts already represented, must be brought to the knowledge of the other party. If the change is not brought to the knowledge of the other party, then the contract can be set aside on the ground of misrepresentation.

Example 5.54. *A*, a medical practitioner, wanted to sell his medical practice to *B*. *A* stated to *B* that his practice was worth £ 2000 per annum, and he had a sufficient number of patients on this panel. This fact was true when *A* represented it to *B*. The negotiations lasted for five months, and then the contract was signed. During this period, *B* became ill and could not attend to his practice. This resulted in a serious loss of practice. These facts were not disclosed to *B*. The court emphasised that the change of circumstances should have been brought to the notice of the purchaser. And it was held that *B* was entitled to set aside the contract. [*With* v. *O. Flanagan*, (1936) 1 All ER 727]

5.23. ACTS WHICH CONSTITUTE MISREPRESENTATION

1. *Positive unwarranted statement*
2. *Breach of duty*
3. *Inducing mistake about subject-matter*

Section 18 of the Indian Contract Act provides three categories of act which constitute misrepresentation. These are discussed in detail in the following pages. Any act amounts to misrepresentation if it falls in any one of these three categories.

1. ***Positive unwarranted statement:*** The term 'unwarranted statement' means a statement made on the basis of information received from untrustworthy source. In other words, a statement made without any reasonable basis, is unwarranted statement. When a person makes a positive statement that a fact is true when his information does not warrant it to be so, though he believes it to be true, this act amounts to misrepresentation. Thus, a false statement made without any trustworthy source of information amounts to misrepresentation.

Example 5.55. A believed his horse to be sound although he had no sufficient ground for his belief. *A* while selling his horse to *B*, stated the horse to be sound. On the basis of this statement, *B* bought the horse. Later on, *B* found the horse to be unsound. In this case, the positive statement made by *A* is a misrepresentation.

Example 5.56. *A* told *B* that *C* would be the director of a company. *A* had obtained this information not directly from *C*, but from another person, *D*. The information proved to be false. In this case, it was held that *A*'s statement was unwarranted because it was a second had information derived from third person. [*Banarsi Debi* v. *New India Assurance Co.*, AIR 1959 SC 40]

2. ***Breach of duty:*** Sometimes, a person commits a breach of duty, which brings advantage to him and loss to the other prty. It will be termed as misrepresentation, if it has been done without any intention of deceiving the other party. This clause covers all those cases where one party is under a legal duty to disclose all material facts to the other party, but does not disclose the same. Such cases of misrepresentation are often termed by the courts as cases of '*constructive fraud*'.

Example 5.57. *A* having no time to read the contents of a deed, signed it as he was given the impression by *B* that it contained nothing but formal matters already settled between them. The deed, however, contained a release in favour of *B*. In this case, *A* was allowed to set aside the deed. Here, although *B* was under no obligation, legally or morally, to communicate the contents of the deed to *A*. But as *A* placed confidence in *B*, it became the duty of *B* to state all the contents of the document. [*Oriental Banking Corpn.* v. *John Flemming*, (1879) 3 Bombay 242]

3. ***Inducing mistake about subject-matter :*** As a matter of fact, the subject-matter of every agreement must clearly be understood by all the parties concerned. If one of the parties, leads the other, even innocently, to commit a mistake regarding the nature of quality of the subject-matter, it is considered a misrepresentation. The cases of concealment or suppression of material facts will also fall under this category. Because by concealment or suppression of the material facts by one party, the other party is induced to commit a mistake regarding the subject-matter.

Example 5.58. In the negotiations for a marriage contract, the relatives speaking for the girl failed to disclose the she was suffering from epileptic fits. The engagement was held to be voidable by reason of misrepresentation. In this case, the non-disclosure of very material facts was held to be misrepresentation. [*Hazi Ahmed* v. *Abdul Gani Khan*, AIR 1937 Nagpur 270].

5.24. EFFECTS OF MISREPRESENTATION

The effect of misrepresentation is that it makes the contract voidable the option of the party whose consent is so obtained. And such party may put an end to the contract if he so chooses. [Section 19].

Example 5.59. *A*, by misrepresentation, lead *B* erroneously to believe that five hundred T.V. sets where manufactured per month in his factory. Upon this representation, *B* bought the factory. The actual production was found to be only four hundred sets per month. Here, *B*'s consent is caused by misrepresentation, and thus, the contract is voidable at his option.

It may, however, be noted that in the following two circumstances the contract is not voidable on account of misrepresentation.

1. *Where the other party had the means of discovering the truth with ordinary diligence* [Section 19 (exception)]. The party cannot complain of misrepresentation if he had the means of discovering the truth with ordinary means.

Example 5.60. *A* bought certain quantity of rice from *B*. *A* was living very near to the place where the rice was lying. Subsequently, it was found that rice was of inferior quality. *A* wanted to set aside the contract on the ground that there was misrepresentation about the quality of rice. But it was held that the contract could not be set aside on the ground of misrepresentation because *A* lived very near to the place where the goods (rice) where lying and he could have easily discovered the truth with ordinary diligence.

[*Shashi Mohan P. Chaudhari* v. *Nobo Kristo Poddar*, (1874) 5 Calcutta 801]

However, where the truth cannot be discovered with ordinary diligence, the party guilty of misrepresentation cannot rely upon the above defence.

2. *Where the misrepresentation does not induce the other party to enter into contract, the contract is not voidable* [Section 19 (explanation)]. If the consent is given independently in spite of misrepresentation, the contract is not voidable.

Example 5.61. The prospectus of a company contained a statement that *A* was a director of the company. *B*, who never heard about *A*, bought shares in the company on the faith of the prospectus. As a matter of fact, *A* was not actually on the Board of Directors of the company. *A* wanted to set aside the contract on the ground of misstatement in the prospectus and claimed damages. It was held that *B* could not do so, because the untrue statement was immaterial to him as he never heard of *A*, and the untrue statement had not induced *B* to buy the shares.

[*Smith* v. *Chadwick*, (1884) App. Cas. 187]

5.25. REMEDIES AVAILABLE ON ACCOUNT OF MISREPRESENTATION

The aggrieved party, *i.e.*, the party whose consent was obtained by misrepresentation has the following two remedies (or rights):

1. He may rescind (*i.e.*, accept or put an end to) the contract.
2. He may affirm (*i.e.*, accept) the contract.

1. *Right to rescind the contract* : Since the contract is voidable at the option of the party whose consent was obtained by misrepresentation, the aggrieved party can rescind the contract. But the aggrieved party cannot rescind the contract if he had the means of discovering the truth with ordinary diligence. Moreover, he can also not rescind the contract if the misrepresentation has not been relied upon by him, *i.e.*, the consent is given irrespective of the misrepresentation.

2. *Right to affirm the contract:* If the aggrieved party thinks proper, he may accept the contract and insist upon its performance. He may compel the other party to put him in the position in which he would have been if the representation made had been true. This right is contained in second para of Section 19, which has already been stated under this right in case of fraud.

The aggrieved party can exercise his option either to rescind the contract or to affirm it only once. Later on, he has no option to change his stand for the misrepresentation. Once his option is exercised, both the parties are bound by it.

5.26. CIRCUMSTANCES OF LOSING THE RIGHT OF RESCISSION

1. *By lapse of time*
2. *By affirmation*
3. *When the third party acquires right in the subject-matter*

Aggrieved party's right of rescission is lost in the following circumstances:

1. ***By lapse of time:*** After the misrepresentation is discovered by the aggrieved party, the contract must be rescined within a reasonable time. But if the contract is not rescinded within the reasonable time, this right is lost. The 'reasonable time' is an important factor which depends upon the facts and circumstances of each case.

2. ***By affirmation :*** Sometimes, after becoming aware of the right to rescind, the aggrieved party affirms the contract. In such cases, he loses the right to rescind the contract. The affirmation may be express or implied.

Example 5.62. *A*, by misrepresentation, sold his plot of land to *B*. Later on, *B* came to know about the misrepresentation. However, instead or rescinding the contract, *B* constructed a house on the plot. In this case, *B*'s right to rescind the contract is lost.

3. ***When the third party acquires right in the subject-matter:*** Sometimes, the third party acquires the right in the subject-matter of the contract in good faith, without any knowledge of the misrepresentation between the parties. And the third party pays the due consideration for acquiring the rights. In such cases, the aggrieved party loses the right to rescind the contract.

Example 5.63. *A*, by misrepresentation, obtained a watch from *B*. And sold the same to *C* who purchased it in good faith and paid the due consideration. In this case, *B*'s right to rescind the contract with *A* is lost, as the third party (*i.e.*, *C*) has acquired interest in the subject-matter in good faith.

5.27. COMPARISON BETWEEN FRAUD AND MISREPRESENTATION

The following table gives comparison between fraud and misrepresentation:

S. No.	*Fraud*	*Misrepresentation*
1.	The consent of one of the parties is not free.	The consent of one of the parties is also not free.
2.	There is false representation by one party.	There is also false representation by one party.
3.	The contract is voidable at the option of the party whose consent was obtained by fraud.	The contract is also voidable at the option of the party whose consent was obtained by misrepresentation.
4.	The fraud is *intentional or wilful wrong*. The person making the false statement does not believe it to be true.	The misrepresentation is an *innocent wrong*. The person making the false statement believes it to be true.
5.	There is intention to deceive the party	There is no intention to deceive the party.
6.	Where the silence amounts to fraud, the contract is not voidable if the deceived party had the means of discovering the truth. However, in case of active fraud, the contract is voidable even if the deceived party had the means of dis covering the truth.	The contract is also not voidable if the deceived party had the means of discovering the truth.
7.	The aggrieved party can rescind the contract. Moreover, he can also claim damages from the other party.	The aggrieved party can rescind the contract. But he cannot claim damages from the other party.
8.	The fraud also amounts to tort.	The misrepresentation does not amount to tort.

5.28. MISTAKE

The term 'mistake' may be defined as incorrect belief about something. It is in fact an erroneous (or incorrect) belief which leads one party to misunderstand the other. It, generally, takes place where the concerned parties are not fully aware of the terms of the agreement, and they take the terms in a different sense.

5.29. TYPES OF MISTAKE

The following types of mistakes are important from the subject point of view:

1. Mistake of fact.
2. Mistake of law.

5.30. MISTAKE OF FACT

The mistake of fact may be classified into the following two types:

1. Bilateral mistake.
2. Unilateral mistake.

5.31. BILATERAL MISTAKE

The term 'bilateral mistake' may be defined as a mistake in which both the parties to an agreement are confused about the facts which are essential to the agreement. A bilateral mistake may be *common mistake* or *mutual mistake.* The common mistake takes place when both the parties to an agreement are confused about some fundamental fact, and make the same mistake. The mutual mistake takes place when both the parties to an agreement make a different mistake. In such cases, both the parties misunderstood each other. A bilateral mistake of fact renders the agreement void.

5.32. ESSENTIALS OF A BILATERAL MISTAKE

1. ***The mistake must be of both the parties***
2. ***The mistake of fact must be about the essential fact of the agreement***
3. ***The mistake must be about existing fact***

Following are the essential elements of a mistake which must be fulfilled to render the agreement void on account of bilateral mistake:

1. ***The mistake must be of both the parties:*** It is an important and essential requirement of a bilateral mistake of fact. An agreement will be rendered void when *both* the parties to an agreement are under a mistake of material fact. [Section 20].

Example 5.64. *A* agreed to sell to *B* a specific cargo of goods supposed to be on its way from England to Bombay. Later on it was found hat the day before the bargain, the ship carrying the cargo had sunk and the goods lost. Neither party was aware of these facts. In this case, the agreement is void as both the parties to an agreement are under a mistake of fact.

2. ***The mistake of fact must be about the essential fact of the agreement:*** It is also an important essential element of a bilateral mistake of fact. An agreement will be rendered void only if there is mistake about the fact, which is essential to the agreement. It may be noted that only mutual mistake of fact, which goes to the root of the agreement and frustrates its object, renders the agreement void.

Example 5.65. *A* agreed to buy a horse from *B*. At the time of bargain, the horse was dead, though neither party was aware of this fact. The agreement is void. In this case, the fact that the horse was dead, is essential to the agreement.

3. ***The mistake must be about existing fact:*** It is another essential element of a bilateral mistake of fact. An agreement will be rendered void when the mistake is about the existing fact and not about the future event[2] Thus, where the agreement is frustrated by subsequent event, it may fall under Section 56 of the Indian Contract Act (according to this Section the agreement become void when the performance become impossible).[3] But it cannot be declared *void ab initio* under Section 20 of the Indian Contract Act[4] (*i.e.,* on the ground of mistake).

2. A 1948 Cal 257 (261).
3. Impossibility of performance will be discussed in a separate Chapter 12 on 'Discharge of Contract'.
4. *Chandumal Jhaleria v. Clive Mills,* AIR 1943 Calcutta 257.

Example 5.66. *A* agreed to sell a piece of land to *B*. Actually, this piece of land was already acquired by the government. But neither of the parties was aware of this fact. This agreement is void as both the parties are under a mistake of fact essential to the agreement. In this case, the fact that the government has already acquired the land, is material to the agreement. And this fact was existing when the parties entered into agreement. Now suppose, that the government acquires the land subsequent to the agreement between the parties. In such a case, the agreement will not be void on the ground of mistake. But it will be void on the ground that its performance has become impossible.

5.33. TYPES OF BILATERAL MISTAKE

The following types of bilateral mistake, which render the agreement void, are important from the subject point of view.

1. Mistake about subject-matter. 2. Mistake about possibility of performance.

5.34. MISTAKE ABOUT SUBJECT-MATTER

1. ***Mistake about the existence of the subject-matter***
2. ***Mistake about the title of the subject-matter***
3. ***Mistake about the substance of the subject-matter***
4. ***Mistake about the quality of the subject-matter***
5. ***Mistake about the quantity of the subject-mater***
6. ***Mistake about the price of the subject-matter***
7. ***Different subject-matter in the minds of both the parties***

The identity and nature of subject-matter of an agreement is an essential fact to every agreement. The bilateral mistake about the subject-matter renders the agreement void. Following are the mistakes about subject-matter:

1. *Mistake about the existence of the subject-matter:* Sometimes, the subject-matter of the agreement ceased to exist before the agreement was made, and both the parties are not aware of this fact. In such cases, the agreement is void. In other words, when both the parties believe the subject-matter of the agreement to be in existence at the time of the agreement, which in fact is not in existence, then the agreement is void.

Example 5.67. *A* being entitled to an estate during the life of *B*, agreed to sell his interest to *C*. But at the time of agreement, *B* was dead. Both the parties were ignorant of this fact. The agreement is void. In this case, both the parties were mistaken about the existence of the subject-matter (*i.e., A*'s interest in the estate).

Example 5.68. *A* agreed to sell to *B* certain goods supposed to be on their way from Bombay to England. Unknown to both the parties, the goods having been damaged on the way, had already been disposed of by the shipping company. The agreement is void as both the parties were mistaken about the existence of the subject-matter (*i.e.,* goods).

2. *Mistake about the title of the subject-matter:* No agreement will come into existence where the seller does not have the right to sell, and the parties mistakenly believed that he has the right.

Example 5.69. *A* agreed to sell to *B* all his rights in a land including the right to mine minerals. Subsequently, it was found that *A*'s rights did not include the right to mine the minerals. This fact was not known to both the parties at the time of the agreement. The agreement was held to be void because without this right to mine, the land was worthless for *B*, whose only object was to work the mines. [*Ramchandra* v. *B. Ganesh Chandra*, 39 IC 78]

3. *Mistake about the substance of the subject-matter:* The term 'substance of the subject-matter' means an essential and integral element of the subject-matter. When both the parties are mistaken about the existence of some fact or facts which form an essential and integral element of the subject-matter, then the agreement is void.

Example 5.70. *A*, the owner of a forest, granted a licence to *B* to cut, process and manufacture all sisal growing in the forest. *B* in return undertook to manufacture and deliver to *A*, 50 tonnes sisal fibre per month. But it was found that the leaf potential of the sisal area was not sufficient to manufacture 50 tonnes of sisal fibre per month. As such, *B* could not perform the contract. *A* filed a suit against *B* for the breach of the contract. The agreement was held to be void. And the court observed that "having regard to the nature of the contract, it was the very basis of the contract that the sisal area should be capable of producing an average of 50 tonnes a month throughout the term of the licence, and the mistake was about the matter of fact essential to the agreement."

[*Sheikh Bros.* v. *Ochener*, (1957) AC 136 (PC)]

But if the mistaken fact is not essential to the agreement, it will not be void.

4. *Mistake about the quality of the subject-matter:* A mistake about the quality of the subject-matter may not render the agreement void. But if the bilateral mistake is about the quality of the subject-matter which makes the subject-matter different from that as was believed to be, the agreement will be void.

Example 5.71. *A* offered to purchase a race horse from *B*, a horse dealer. *B* accepted the offer believing it to be for a cart horse. In this case, the agreement is void as both the parties are mistaken about the quality of the subject-matter. Here, the mistake as to quality makes the subject-matter altogether different from the thing as it was believed to be.

5. *Mistake about the quantity of the subject-mater:* Sometimes, both the parties are under a mistake about the quantity of the subject-matter. In such cases, the agreement is void because the parties are mistaken about the essential fact (*i.e.*, quantity of the subject-matter) of the agreement.

Example 5.72. *A* agreed to buy 200 sewing cotton reels each containing 400 metres of thread. But unknown to both the parties, the length of the thread per reel was much less than 400 metres. The agreement was void as there was mistake of both the parties about the quantity of the subject-mater. [*Earnest beck & Co.* v. *K.S. Owski & Co.*, (1924) AC 43]

6. *Mistake about the price of the subject-matter:* Sometimes, both the parties are under a mistake about the price of the subject-matter. In such cases, the agreement is void because the parties are mistaken about the essential fact (*i.e.*, price of the subject-matter) of the agreement.

Example 5.73. *A* agred to let out his house to *B* for a monthly rent of Rs. 450. But in the written agreement the figure of rent was put as 540 by mistake. The agreement was held to be void. [*Garrad* v. *Frankel* (1862) 54 ER 961]

7. *Different subject-matter in the minds of both the parties:* Sometimes, both the parties have different subject-matter in their minds. In such cases, the agreement will be void because there will be no true consent of the parties.

Example 5.74. *A* bought from *B* certain goods which were to arrive from Bombay through a ship named 'Peerless'. Two ships with the name 'Peerless' sailed from Bombay, one in October and the other in December. *A* had the first ship in his mind, and *B* had the second in his mind. The agreement was held to be void as there was no true consent of the parties. [*Raffles* v. *Wichelhans Exch.*, (1864) H & C 906]

5.35. MISTAKE ABOUT POSSIBILITY OF PERFORMANCE

Sometimes, both the parties believe that the agreement is capable of being performed, but in fact it is not possible to perform. In such cases, the agreement is void as both the parties are mistaken about the possibility of performance of the agreement. In other words, where the agreement is impossible to perform but the fact of impossibility is unknown to both the parties, the agreement is void.

Example 5.75. *A* hired a room from *B* for watching the coronation procession of King Edward VII. Unknown to both the parties, the procession had already been cancelled. This agreement was held to be void. In this case, the performance of the agreement was impossible as the purpose for which the room was hired had been defeated. And both the parties were mistaken about the fact of impossibility of performance. [*Griffith* v. *Brymer* (1903) 19 TLR 534]

The agreement for an impossible act will also be void even if the parties were aware of the fact of the impossibility. This rule is contained in First para of Section 56 of the Indian Contract Act, which reads as under:

"An agreement to do an act impossible in self is void."

Example 5.76. *A* agreed with *B* to convert a brass plate into a gold plate by magic. *B* agreed to pay Rs. 1,000 to *A* for this act. This agreement is void as it is for an impossible act.

Note: This point will be discussed in detail in Chapter 12 on 'Discharge of Contract'.

5.36. EFFECTS OF BILATERAL MISTAKE

The effect of bilateral mistake is that the agreement is void and cannot be enforced at the option of either party to be agreement. Section 20 of the Indian Contract Act states the effect of bilateral mistake, which reads as under:

"Where both the parties to an agreement are under a mistake as to a matter of fact essential to the agreement, the agreement is void."

The analysis of this section shows that, the bilateral mistake of essential facts renders the agreement void.

Example 5.77. *A* agreed to sell certain goods supposed at the time of contract on their way from Singapore to Madras. Unknown to both the parties, the goods having been damaged had already been sold by the shipping company. In this case, the agreement is void as both the parties are mistaken about the existence of subject-matter.[Based on *Couturier* v. *Hastie,* (1856) 5 HLC 673]

5.37. UNILATERAL MISTAKE

The term 'unilateral mistake' may be defined as a mistake in which only one of the parties to an agreement is confused about the facts which are essential to the agreement. Generally, a unilateral mistake does not render the agreement void *i.e.,* it does not affect the validity of the agreement. Where the agreement is otherwise valid, the mistake of only one of the parties cannot affect its validity. However, there are certain cases in which a unilateral mistake renders an agreement void. These are the cases in which a unilateral mistake has the effect of defeating the true consent of the parties. These will be discussed in Art. 5.39.

5.38. ESSENTIALS OF A UNILATERAL MISTAKE

1. *The mistake of fact must be about the essential fact of the agreement*
2. *The mistake of fact must defeat the true consent of the parties*

Following are the essential elements of a unilateral mistake which must be fulfilled to render an agreement void:

1. ***The mistake of fact must be about the essential fact of the agreement:*** An agreement will be rendered void only if the unilateral mistake is about some fact, which is essential to the agreement. The nature of the agreement, and the identity of the parties is an essential fact. And a unilateral mistake about these facts renders the agreement void.

Example 5.78. *A*, an old man was unable to manage his cultivation and other affairs. He appointed *B* to look after his cultivation and other affairs. *B* asked *A* to grant him a lease of his land. *A* agreed to it and placed his thumb-impression on a deed produced before him by *B*, which was in fact a gift deed. The deed was held to be void. In this case, *A* was mistaken about the nature of the document.

[*Raja Singh* v. *Chaichoo Singh*, AIR 1940 Patna 201]

2. *The mistake of fact must defeat the true consent of the parties:* An agreement will be rendered void only if the unilateral mistake has the effect of defeating the true consent of the parties. A unilateral mistake defeats the true consent of the parties when it prevents the parties from coming to an agreement upon the same thing in the same sense. It may be noted that the agreement will be void, where the unilateral mistake is so fundamental as goes to the root of the agreement. All such cases where it can be shown that a mistake was caused by fraud or misrepresentation on the part of one party, will fall under this category of unilateral mistake.

Example 5.79. A lady named Ann Robinson, was convicted for allowing disorderly conduct in her restaurant. Subsequently, she assumed a false name Ann Potter, and hired a house of Mrs. Sowler. On becoming aware of the true identity of Ann Potter, Mrs. Sowler wanted to set aside the lease of house. It was held that the lease was void because Mrs. Sowler was mistaken about the identity of the Ann Potter. In this case, the true consent of Mrs. Sowler was defated.

[*Sowler* v. *Potter,* (1940) 1 KB 271]

5.39. TYPES OF UNILATERAL MISTAKE

1. *Mistake about the identity of the parties to an agreement*
2. *Mistake about the nature of the agreement*

The following types of unilateral mistake, which render the agreement void, are important from the subject point of view:

1. *Mistake about the identity of the parties to an agreement:* The identity of both the parties entering into an agreement is very essential. The mistake about identity occurs when one of the parties represents himself to be some person other than he really is, or where party enters into an agreement with some person believing him to be some other person *e.g.,* where *A* intends to enter into an agreement only with *B*, but enters into an agreement with *C* believing him to be *B*. In this case there is a mistake about the identity of the contracting party, and the agreement will be void if *A* intended to contract with *B* only. It may be noted that the mistake about the identity of the contracting party will render the agreement void *only* if (*a*) the identity of the party is of material importance to the agreement, and (*b*) the fraudulent party knows that he is not intended to be a party to the agreement.

Example 5.80. *A* received orders, in writing, from a fraudulent man called 'Blenkarn'. The order papers had a printed heading, 'Blenkarn and Co. 37 Wood Street'. There was a well-known and respectable firm named 'Blenkiron and Co.', in the same street. *A* believing that the order have come from the genuine firm, sent a large quantity of handkerchiefs. The fraudulent Blenkarn received the goods and disposed them of to *B*, who acted in *good faith*. It was held that there was no contract between *A* and Blenkarn because *A* intended to contract with 'Blenkiron and Co.' and no with 'Blenkarn'. *A* knew nothing about 'Blenkarn' and never intended to deal with him.

[*Cundy* v. *Lindsay,* (1878) 3 AC 459]

But is may be noted that where the name assumed by the fraudulent person is fictitious (*i.e.,* the person of assumed name is not in existence), there will be no mistake of identity. There can be a mistake of identity only when a person bearing a particular identity exists within the knowledge of the person who intends to deal with the person of that particular identity only.

Example 5.81. *A*, a fraudulent man, adopted the name of 'H & Co.'. The firm with the name of 'H & Co.' was not in existence. It was only a fictitious name adopted by *A*, who placed an order with *B* for the supply of some goods. On the basis of this order, *B* supplied the goods to *A*, who further sold the goods to *C* who acted in a *good faith. B* sued *C* for the value of the goods. It was held that the contract between *B* and 'H & Co.' was not void because *B* contracted to sell the goods to the writer of the letter. Here, *A* and 'H & Co.' being the same person, *B* had not made any mistake as to the identity of the contracting party. The contract between *B* and 'H & Co' was voidable for fraud and it could not be revoked after C had acquired the goods in *good faith*.

[*King's Nortan Metal Co.* v. *Edridge Merrett & Co.,* Court of Appeae (1897) 14 TLR 98]

However, if it could have been shown in the above example that there was a separate entity called 'H & Co.' and another entity called *A*, then the case might have been covered within the decision in *Cundy* v. *Lindsay,* discussed in the previous Example 5.80.

Thus, a unilateral mistake renders an agreement void where the identity of the person contracted with is important, and the seller wants to contract with the person of the particular identity. It may, however, be noted where the identity, of the contracting party, is immaterial and a person is prepared to enter into an agreement with anyone in his presence, the mistake about the identity of the person will not make the agreement void.

2. *Mistake about the nature of the agreement:* Sometimes a deed (*i.e.,* document) of one nature is executed under the mistaken impression that it is of a different nature. In such cases, it is wholly void and inoperative, as there is a mistake about the nature of the agreement, *e.g.,* a gift deed is signed under the impression that it is only a power of attorney, the deed is void. Generally, the mistake of this kind is brought about by the fraud or misrepresentation of one party, *e.g.,* where a party is under a duty to disclose the true nature of the document to the other, and thereby induces him to sign the same under the belief that he is signing some other document of a different nature. In such cases, there is no consent as required by Section 13 of the Indian Contract Act, and the agreement is void.

Example 5.82. *A* place a document before *B*, an old man. *A* falsely told *B* that it was an ordinary guarantee, and induced him to sign the document. *B* signed the document on the belief that it was a mere guarantee. In fact, the document was a bill of exchange which was later on endorsed by *B* to *C*. *C* filed a suit against *A*, on the basis of the bill of exchange. It was held that *A* was not liable for the bill, as he never intended to sign the bill of exchange. He was deceived not merely for the legal effect, but also for the very nature of the document.

[*Foster* v. *Mackinnon,* (1869) LR 4 CP 704]

5.40. EFFECTS OF UNILATERAL MISTAKE

The effect of unilateral mistake is that, generally the agreement is not void on account of such mistake. Section 22 of the Indian Contract Act states the effect of a unilateral mistake, which reads as under:

"A contract is not voidable merely because it was caused by one of the parties to it being under a mistake as to the matter of fact."

The analysis of this section shows that, a unilateral mistake does not affect the validity of the agreement. However, where the unilateral mistake defeats the true consent of the parties, as discussed above, the agreement will be void.

5.41. MISTAKE OF LAW

The mistake of law may be of the following two kinds:

1. Mistake of the law of the land (Indian Law).
2. Mistake of foreign law.

The mistake of law of the land, does not render the agreement void. This is based on the well established rule of law namely, *ignorantia juris non excusat* (*i.e.,* ignorance of law is no excuse). Everyone is presumed to have the knowledge of the law of the land. He cannot get any relief on the ground that he had done a particular act in the ignorance of the law. Thus, the mistake of the Indian Law does not affect the validity of the agreement. This provision is contained in Section 21 of the Indian Contract Act, which reads as under:

"A contract is not voidable because it was caused by a mistake as to any law in force in India."

In simple words, the mistake of the law of the land is no ground for revoking the contract.

Example 5.83. *A* and *B* entered into a contract on the erroneous belief that a particular debt was barred by the Indian Law of Limitation, (the law which provides the time limit for the enforcement of rights). This contract connot be set aside on the ground of mistake of law, because each of them is supposed to know the law of the land.

Example 5.84. *A*, a widow was entitled to certain occupancy rights. She remarried and believed that she has lost her occupancy rights by reason of her second marriage. Under this mistake, she agreed to take the lease of the same land from *B*, her Zamindar, at increased rate of rent. Here both *A* and *B* honestly believed that *A* had lost her occupancy rights by reason of remarriage. But legally she had not lost her occupancy rights. On becoming aware of this fact, *A* wanted to revoke the new lease agreement with *B*. It was held that she cannot revoke the new lease agreement because there was a mistake of law. [*Sahiban Bibi* v. *Madho Lal*, (1906) 4 All LJ 475]

But it may be noted that the mistake of the foreign law has the same effect as a mistake of fact. Therefore, it renders the agreement void. This provision is contained in the second part of Section 21 of the Indian Contract Act, which reads as under:

"A mistake as to a law not in force in India has the same effect as a mistake of fact."

In simple words, a mistake of foreign law is a valid ground for revoking the agreement. Thus, a mutual mistake of foreign law renders the agreement void.

LEGAL PROVISIONS (SECTIONS) DISCUSSED IN THE CHAPTER

Important legal provisions (sections) of the Indian Contract Act, 1872, discussed in this chapter, are reproduced hereunder.

1. *Section 13: Consent Defined*

   Two or more persons are said to consent when they agree upon the same thing in the same semse.

2. *Section 14: Free Consent Defined*

   Consent is said to be free when it is not caused by

   (1) Coercion, as defined in section 15, or
   (2) undue influence, as defined in section 16, or
   (3) fraud, as defined in section 17, or
   (4) misrepresentation, as defined in section 18, or
   (5) mistake, subject to the provisions of sections 20, 21 and 22,

   Consent is said to be so caused when it would not have been given but for the existence of such coercion, undue influence, fraud, misrpresentation or mistake.

3. *Section 15: Coercion Defined*

   Coercion' is the committing, or threatening to comuit, any act forbidden by the Indian Penal Code (45 of 1860) or the unalwful detaining, or threatening to detain, any property, to the prejudice of any person whatever, with the intention of causing any person to enter into an agreement.

   Explanation.– It is immaterial whether the Indian Penal Code (45 of 1860) is or is not in force in the place where coercion is employed.

4. *Section 16 (1): Undue Influence Defined*

   A contract is said to be induced by 'undue influence' where the relations subsisting between the parties are such that one of the parties is in a position to dominate the will of the other and uses that position to obtain an unfair advantage over the other.

5. *Section 16 (2): Domination of Will*

   In particular and without prejudice to the generality of the foregoing principle, a person is deemed to be in a position to dominate the will of another—

   (*a*) where he holds a real or apparent authority over the other, or where he stands in a fiduciary relation to the other; or

   (*b*) where he makes a contract with a person whose mental capacity is temporarily or permanently affectd by reason of age, illness, or mental or bodily distress.

6. *Section 16 (3): Burden of Proof of Undme Influence*

Where a person who is in a position to dominate the will of another, enters into a contract with him, and the transaction appears, on the face of it or on the evidence adduced, to be unconscionable, the burden of proving that such contract was not induced by undue influence shall be upon the person in a position to dominate the will of the other.

7. *Section 17: Fraud Defined*

Fraud means and includes any of the following acts committed by a party to acontract or with his connivance, or by his agent, with intent to deceive another party thereto or his agent, or to induce him to enter into the contract:

(1) the suggestion, as a fact, of that which is not true by one who does not believe it to be true;

(2) the active concealment of a fact by one having knowledge or belief of the fact;

(3) a promise made without any intention of performing it;

(4) any other act fitted to deveive;

(5) any such act or omission as the law specially declares to be fraudulent.

8. *Section 17, Explanation: Mere Silence as Frand*

Mere silence as to facts likely to affect the willingness of a person to enter into a contract is not fraud, unless the circumstances of the case are such that, regard being had to them, it is the duty of the person keeping silence to speak or unless his silence, is, in itself equivalent to speech.

9. *Section 18: Misrepresentation Defined*

Misrepresentation means and inclndes:

(1) the positive assertion, in a manner not warranted by the inforamation of the person making it of that which is not true, though he believes it to be true;

(2) any breach of duty which, without an intent to deceive, gains an advantage of the person committing it, or any one claiming under him, by misleading another to his prejudice, or to the prejudice of any one claiming under him;

(3) causing, however innocently, a party to an agreement, to make a mistake as to the substance of the thing which is the subject of the agreement.

10. *Section 19: Agreements without Free Consent are Voidable*

When consent to an agreement is canused by coerain, fraud or misrepresentation, the agreement is a contract voidable at the option of the party whose consent was so caussed.

A party to a contract, whose consent was caused by fraud or misrepresentation may, if he thinks fit insist that the contract shall be performed, and that he shall be put in the positiion in which he would have been if the representation made had been true.

Exception.—If such consent was caused by misrepresentation or by silence, fraudulent within the meaning of section 17, the contract, nevertheless, is not voidable, if the party whose consent was so caused had the means of discovering the truth with ordinary diligence.

Explanation.—A fraud or misrepresentation which did not cause the consent to a contract of the party on whom such fraud was practised, or to whom such misrepresentation was made, does nto render a contract voidable.

11. *Section 19-A: Contract Induced by Undue Influence is Voidable*

When consent to an agreement is caused by unadue ifluence, the agreement is a contract voidable at the potion of the party whose consent was so obtained.

Any such contract may be set aside either absolutely or, if the party who was entititled to avoid it has received any benefit thereunder, upon such terms and conditions as the court may seem just.

12. *Section 20: Agreement Void when both Parties under Mistake of Fact*

Where both the parties to an agreement are under a mistake as to a matter of fact essential to the agreement, the agreement is void

Explanation–An erroneous opinion as to the value of the thing which forms the subject-matter of the agreement, is not to be deemed a mistake as to a matter of fact.

13. *Section 21: Effect of Mistakes as to Law.*

A contract is not voidable because it was cuased by a mistake as to any law in force in India; but a mistake as to a law not in force in India has the same effect as amistake of fact.

14. *Section 22. Contract Caused by Mistake of One Party as to Matter of Fact*

A contract is not voidable merely because it was caused by one of the parties to it being under a mistake as to a matter of fact.

TEST QUESTIONS

1. Define consent. When is consent said to be free? How a contract is affected if the consent of one of the parties is not free?
2. "A contract which is regular in all other respects may still fail if there is no *consensus ad idem*"— explain the statement with suitable examples.
3. Define the term 'coercion' as used in the Indian Contract Act. What are the essentials and legal rules for a valid coercion ? What is the effect of coercion on the validity of the contract?
4. "A threat to commit an act forbidden by the Indian Penal Code amounts to coercion"— explain and illustrate this statement. Does a threat to commit suicide amount to coercion? If yes, how would you justify that a threat to commit suicide is forbidden by Indian Penal Code?
5. Define the term 'undue influence' as used in the Indian Contract Act. What are the essentials and legal rules for a valid undue influence? What is the effect of undue influence on the validity of a contract?
6. Under what circumstances a contract is said to be induced by undue influence? State the comparison between coercion and undue influence.
7. Define the term fraud as used in the Indian Contract Act. What are the essentials and legal rules for a fraud? What is the effect of fraud on the validity of a contract?
8. State the acts which constitute fraud. Does mere silence amount to fraud? If yes, state the cases in which the silence amounts to fraud.
9. "Mere silence may amount to fraud"—comment.
10. Define the term misrepresentation as used in the Indian Contract Act. What are the essentials and legal rules for a misrepresentation? What is the effect of misrepresentation on the validity of a contract?
11. Explain clearly the meaning of 'fraud' as defined in the Indian Contract Act. In what way does fraud differ from misrepresentation?
12. State the acts which constitute misrepresentation. What is the comparison between fraud and misrepresentation?
13. "A deceit which does not deceive is no fraud"—critically examine this statement giving suitable examples.
14. What remedies are available to the aggrieved party whose consent is obtained by fraud or misrepresentation ? State the circumstances in which party's right to rescind the contract is lost.
15. What do you understand by bilateral mistake of fact ? What are the essentials of a bilateral mistake which affects the validity of contract? How does the bilateral mistake affect the validity of the contract?
16. What do you understand by unilateral mistake of fact ? What are the essentials of a unilateral mistake which affect the validity of contract? How does a unilateral mistake affect the validity of the contract?
17. State the circumstances under which a contract can be affected on the ground of mistake of fact, and what is its effect?
18. How does the following mistakes affect the validity of the contract? Give examples in support of your answer.
    (*a*) Mistake about subject-matter.
    (*b*) Mistake about possibility of performance.
    (*c*) Mistake about the identity of parties.
19. Write notes on the following:
    (*a*) *consensus ad idem*
    (*b*) *error in causa*
    (*c*) Half truth as fraud
    (*d*) *Derry v. Peek*
    (*e*) Ignorance of law is no excuse

MULTIPLE CHOICE QUESTIONS

1. Which of the following elements does not affect the free consent of the parties?
   (*a*) coercion (*b*) fraud
   (*c*) incompetency (*d*) undue influence.
2. When the consent of a party is obtained by coercion, undue influence, fraud or misrepresentation, the contract is
   (*a*) void (*b*) voidable
   (*c*) valid (*d*) illegal.
3. *A* threatens to kill *B* if he does not agree to sell his scooter to him for Rs. 1,000 only. Here *B*s consent is obtained by
   (*a*) undue influence (*b*) fraud
   (*c*) coercion (*d*) none of these.
4. The consent is said to be obtained by coercion if it is obtained by threatening to commit any act forbidden by Indian Penal Code (IPC). If the IPC is not in force where the coercion is committed, then the contract is
   (*a*) valid (*b*) voidable
   (*c*) void (*d*) illegal.
5. When the consent to an agreement is obtained by coercion, the agreement is voidable at the option of
   (*a*) either party to the agreement (*b*) a party whore consent was so obtained
   (*c*) a party who obtained the consent (*d*) none of these.
6. Where one party is in a position to dominate the will of another and uses his superior position to obtain the consent of a weaker party, the consent is said to be obtained by
   (*a*) coercion (*b*) undue influence
   (*c*) duress (*d*) misrepresentation.
7. The consent obtained by threatening to commit suicide amounts to consent by
   (*a*) coercion (*b*) undue influence
   (*c*) fraud (*d*) none of these.
8. Which of the following is not an essential element of fraud ?
   (*a*) It must be committed with an intention to deceive
   (*b*) It must be committed with the knowledge of its falsity.
   (*c*) It must be committed by a party of contract.
   (*d*) It must fall in a category mentioned in Section 16.
9. Where the consent of a party is obtained by fraud, the contract is
   (*a*) valid (*b*) void
   (*c*) voidable (*d*) illegal.
10. Which of the following acts does not fall under the categories of fraud?
    (*a*) Intentional false statement of facts. (*b*) Active concealment of facts.
    (*c*) Innocent false statement. (*d*) Promise made without intention to perform.
11. A false statement of fact, made without any intention to deceive the other party, falls under the category of
    (*a*) Fraud (*b*) Misrepresentation
    (*c*) Coercion (*d*) Under Influence.
12. Where the consent of a party is obtained by misrepresentation, the contract is
    (*a*) valid (*b*) void
    (*c*) voidable (*d*) illegal.
13. Which of the following statement is false?
    (*a*) A contract is not voidable if fraud or misrepresentation does not induce the other party to enter into a contract.
    (*b*) A party cannot complain of fraudulent silence or misrepresentation if he had the means of discovering the truth with ordinary means.

(c) In case of fraud or misrepresentation, aggrieved party can either rescind or affirm the contract.

(d) A party who affirms the contract, can also change his option afterwards if he so decides.

14. The aggrieved party can rescind the contract on account of fraud. Can he also claim damages from the other party?

(a) Yes (b) No.

15. The aggrieved party can rescind the contract on account of misrepresentation. Can he also claim damages from the other party?

(a) Yes (b) No.

16. Where the consent of both the parties is given by mistake, the contract is

(a) void (b) valid

(c) voidable (d) illegal.

17. As per Section 20, the contract is void on account of bilateral mistake of fact. But as per Section 22, if there is mistake of only one party, then and contract is

(a) void (b) valid

(c) voidable (d) illegal.

18. A contract made by mistake about the Indian Law, is

(a) void (b) valid

(c) voidable (d) illegal.

19. A contract made by mistake about some foreign law, is

(a) void (b) valid

(c) voidable (d) illegal.

20. A mistake as to a law not in force in India has the same effect as:

(a) mistake of fact (b) mistake of Indian law

(c) fraud (d) misrepresentation.

ANSWERS

1. (c)	**2.** (b)	**3.** (c)	**4.** (b)	**5.** (b)	**6.** (b)
7. (a)	**8.** (d)	**9.** (c)	**10.** (c)	**11.** (b)	**12.** (c)
13. (d)	**14.** (a)	**15.** (b)	**16.** (a)	**17.** (b)	**18.** (b)
19. (a)	**20.** (a).				

OBJECTIVE TYPE QUESTIONS WITH REASONING

State with reasons whether the following statements are correct or incorrect.

1. When there is a no consent, no contract comes into excitence.

2. In case of error in consensus, there is no contract between the parties.

3. An agreement, in which the consent is caused by coercion, is voidable at the option of either party.

4. The threat to commit suicide amounts to coercion under Section 15 of the Indian Contract Act, 1872.

5. There is a presumption of domination of will in the relationship of solicitor and client and parents and child.

6. A contract induced by fraud is voidable at the option of either party.

7. A deceit which does not deceive is no fraud.

8. Silence as to the material facts always amount to fraud.

9. Misrepresentation is a false statement which the person making it does not believe it to be true.

10. A party connot complain of misrepresentation if he had the means of discovering the truth with ordinary diligence.
11. Where both the parties to an agreement are under a mistake as to a matter of fact essential to the agreement, then the agreement is voidable.
12. An agreement is void on account of bilateral mistake if the mistake is about the fact which is essential to the agreement.
13. A contract to purchase a black horse which was dead at the time of bargain, is voidable.
14. A mistake of the law of the land (*i.e.,* Indian law) is no ground for avoiding a conract.

ANSWERS

1. ***Correct.*** In case of no consent there is no consensus *ad idem* (*i.e.,* meetings of mind), and thus no contract comes into existence.
2. ***Correct.*** Error in consensus is the misunderstanding and prevents the existence of consensus *ad idem*, which is essential element for the formation of contract.
3. ***Incorrect.*** Such an agreement is voidable at the option of the party whose consent was obtained by coercion.
4. ***Correct.*** It has been decided by the courts that the threat to commits suicide is forbidden by the Indian Penal Code. Hence, it amounts to coercion within the meaning of Section 15.
5. ***Correct.*** The relations between these persons are fiduciary relations.
6. ***Incorrect.*** Such a contract is voidable at the option of the party whose consent is obtained by fraud.
7. ***Correct.*** An essential requirement of fraud is that there must be an intention to deceive and the other party must have been deceived by the same. If a party is not deceivd, then his consent cannot be said to be caused by fraud.
8. ***Incorrect.*** The general rule is that the silence as to material facts does not amount to fraud.
9. ***Incorrect.*** Misrepresentation is the false statement which the person making it honestly believes it to be true.
10. ***Correct.*** It is statutory exception to the rule that a contract induced by misrepresentation is voidable [Section 19 (exception)]
11. ***Incorrect.*** In such a case, the agreement is void [Section 20]. In fact, in such cases the element of consent is missing, and thus the contract is void.
12. ***Correct.*** Only a bilateral mistake of fact which goes to the root of the agreement and frustrates its object, renders the agreement void.
13. ***Incorrect.*** Such a contract is void. In this case, there is a bilateral mistake about the existence of the subject-matter of contract.
14. ***Correct.*** Every one is presumed to have the knowledge of the law of the land. The rule of law is that ignorance of law is no excuse.

PRACTICAL PROBLEMS

1. *A* threatens to kill *B* if he does not agree to sell his car to *A* for Rs. 40,000. Fearing death, *B* enters into an agreement with *A* for the sale of his car for Rs. 40,000 only. Can *B* avoid the contract ? Give reasons.

   Hint : Yes. *B*'s consent is obtained by coercion, he can avoid the contract on this ground.
2. *A* gave severe beating to *B* and caused him grievous hurt by dislocating his teeth. After this, *A* made *B* to agree to sign a promissory note for Rs. 50,000 in his fovour, which *B* signed. Is the promissory note valid ? What option is available to *B* ?

   Hint : The promissory note is voidable at *B*'s option as his consent is obtained by coercion. He can avoid the contract on this ground.

3. *A*'s son had forged *B*'s signature on a promissory note. *B* threatened *A* to prosecute his son for forgery if he *A* does not execute a promissory note for Rs. 10,000 in *B*'s favour. Accordingly, *A* executed the promissory note. Is this a valid promissory note ? Give reasons.

   Hint : No. *A*'s consent is obtained by undue influence and this promissory note for Rs. 10,000 is voidable at *A*'s option. In this case *B* was in a position to dominate the will of *A* and he influence *A*'s consent.

4. *A* met with an accident and was hospitalized in a private nursing home. *B*, a senior doctor at the nursing home, agreed to treat him provided he signs a promissory note for Rs. 100,000 in his favour, which *A* signed. Does the promissory note entitle the doctor to recover Rs. 100,000 from *A*? Give reasons.

   Hint : No. The doctor has obtained the promissory note by employing undue influence on *A*. The promissory note is voidable at *A*'s option. The doctor is entitled to the reasonable fee only and not the full amount of promissory note.

5. *A* applied to a banker for a loan at a time when there was stringency in the money market. The banker declined to make the loan except at an unusually high rate of interest. *A* accepted the loan on these terms. Whether the contract is induced by undue influence ? Decide.

   Hint : No. This is a transaction in the ordinary course of business and the contract cannot be said to be induced by undue influence. Here, the banker cannot be said to be in a position to dominate the will of the borrower (*A*). The borrower had the option to borrow money from other sources.

6. *A* frandulently informed *B* that *A* had a Honda city car in excellent condition and he wanted to sell it. *B*, at his own, passed on this information to *C*, a third person. Relying upon this information and without questioning *A* about the car, *C* bought the car. Later on, it was discovered that the car was in a deteriorated condition. Whether the contract is induced by frand ? Decide.

   Hint : No, the contract is not induced by fraud. A contract is said to be induced by fraud when frand is committed by a party to the contract and upon a party to the contract or his agent. Here the fraud by *A* was committed upon *B*, a stranger and not upon *C*.

7. *A*, sold, by auction, to *B* a horse which *A* knew to be unsound. But *A* said nothing to *B* about the unsoundness of the horse. Is the contract induced by fraud ?

   Hint : No, the contract is not induced by fraud. Mere silence as to facts likely to affect the willingness of a person to enter into contrail, is not fraud.

8. *A*, a medical practitoner, wanted to sell his medical practice to *B*. He stated to *B* that his practice was worth Rs. 80,000 per month and he had a sufficient number of patients on his panel. This fact was true when *A* represented it to *B*. The negotiations lasted for five months and then the contract was signed. During this period, *A* become ill and could not attend to his practice. This resulted in serious loss of practice, but this fact was not disclosed to *B*. *B* wanted to avoid the contract on the ground of misrepresentation. Will he succeed ? Give reasons.

   Hint : Yes. *B* will succeed in his action. Here the change of circumstances was material to the contract and should have been brought to the notice of the purchaser (*i.e. B*).

9. A lady named Ann Robinsion was convicted for allowing disorderly conduct in her restaurant. Subsequently, she assumed a false name Ann Potter and hired a house of Mrs. Sowler. On becoming aware about true identity of Ann Potter, Mrs. Sowler wanted to set aside the lease of the house. Will she succeed ? Give reasons.

   Hint : Yes. Mrs. Sowler will succeed in her action. Here, the lease is void because Mrs. Sowler was mistaken about the identity of Ann Potter and her consent was defeated *i.e.* not free.

10. *A* and *B* entered into a contract on the erroneous belief that a debt of Rs. 50,000 which *A* owed to *B* is barred by the Indian Law of limitation and *B* would not recover the same. Subsequently, it was discovered that the debt was not barred by the limitation law. *B* wanted to recover the debt from *A* taking the plea that the contract on erroneous belief was voidable and he is not bound by the same. Will he succeed ? Give reasons.

    Hint : No. *B* will not succeed in his action. Here, the parties are under a mistake of Indian Law and such mistake does not render the agreement voidable. The contract between *A* and *B* is perfectly valid and both the parties are bound by the same.

LEGALITY OF OBJECT AND CONSIDERATION

1. Introduction.
2. Definition of Legality of Object and Consideration.
3. Cases of Unlawful Object and Consideration.
4. Doctrine of Public Policy.
5. Heads of Public Policy.

6.1. INTRODUCTION

In the preceding chapters, we have discussed the various essentials of a valid contract. The last requirement for a valid contract is that the parties must contract for a lawful object. This requirement is emphasised in Section 10 and last para of Section 23 of the Indian Contract Act, which respectively read as under:

"All agreements are contracts if they are made for lawful consideration and with lawful object."

"Every agreement of which the object or consideration is unlawful, is void."

The analysis of these sections reveals that a contract is valid and enforceable only if it is made for a lawful consideration and with lawful object. And if the consideration or object of an agreement is unlawful, such an agreement is void. It may be noted that Section 23 covers the illegality of object of the contract as well as the illegality of the consideration. The 'object' means the purpose for which the agreement is entered into *e.g.*, where money is borrowed for the purpose of the marriage of a minor, the consideration for the contract is a loan, and the object is the marriage of a minor. In this chapter, we shall discuss which considerations and objects are unlawful, and the legal provisions relating to them.

6.2. DEFINITION OF LEGALITY OF OBJECT AND CONSIDERATION

The term 'legality' may be defined as conformity to law. Therefore, the legality of object and consideration for a contract means that it must be lawful. Section 23 defines the unlawful object or a consideration in negative way, *i.e.*, it provides that the object or consideration of an agreement is lawful unless it falls within the purview of the cases mentioned in the section itself. This section deals with the cases in which the object or consideration of an agreement is lawful, and reads as under :

"The consideration or object of an agreement is lawful, unless, it is forbidden by law; or
is of such a nature that, if permitted, it would defeat the provision of any law; or
is fraudulent; or
involve or implies injury to the person or property of another;
or the court regards it as immoral, or opposed to public policy.
In each of these cases, the consideration or object of an agreement is said to be unlawful.
Every agreement of which the object or consideration is unlawful is void."

The analysis of this section shows that the object or consideration of an agreement is unlawful in the following cases:

(*a*) where it is forbidden by law.
(*b*) where it defeats the provisions of any law.
(*c*) where it is fraudulent.
(*d*) where it is injurious to another person or his property.
(*e*) where it is immoral.
(*f*) where it is opposed to public policy.

These cases will be discussed in detail in the next article.

Note: Unlawful consideration has already been discussed in chapter 3 on 'consideration'. However, in this chapter it is also discussed along with the unlawful object.

6.3. CASES OF UNLAWFUL OBJECT AND CONSIDERATION

1. ***Where it is forbidden by law***
2. ***Where it defeats the provision of any law***
3. ***Where it is fraudulent***
4. ***Where it is injurious to another person or his property***
5. ***Where it is regarded as immoral***
6. ***Where it is opposed to public policy***

The cases in which the object and consideration of an agreement is considered unlawful are as under:

1. *Where it is forbidden by law:* Sometimes, the object or consideration of an agreement is forbidden by law. In such cases, the object or consideration is unlawful. The agreement, with such an object or consideration, is unlawful and void. As a matter of fact, an act is forbidden by law, when it is punishable by criminal law of the country, or when it is prohibited by special Legislation or by the regulations made by a competent authority under power derived from the legislature. The term 'law' means the law for the time being in force in India, and includes the personal laws (*i.e.*, Hindu Law and Muslim Law).

Example 6.1. *A*, a Hindu already married and his wife alive, entered into a marriage agreement with C, another lady. This is a void agreement because the second marriage is forbidden by Hindu Law. In this case, the object of the marriage is unlawful.

Example 6.2. *A* agreed to pay Rs. 600 to *B* if he steale *C*'s cycle. This agreement is void as the consideration is unlawful. The theft is forbidden by law.

Example 6.3. *A* agreed to obtain an employment for *B* in the Income Tax Department. *B* promised to pay Rs. 5 lakhs to *A*. This agreement is void as the consideration for it is unlawful.

Example 6.4. *A* sold liquor without licence, to *B*. The sale is void as the sale of liquor without licence is forbidden by law. [*K.M. Kamath* v. *K.R. Baliga & Co.*, AIR 1959 SC 781]

2. *Where it defeats the provision of any law:* Sometimes, the object or consideration of an agreement is not directly forbidden by the law. But it is of such a nature that, if permitted, it would defeat the provision of any law. In such cases, the object or consideration is unlawful. The agreement with such an object or consideration is unlawful, and void. Here also the term 'law' means the law for the time being in force in India and includes Hindu Law and Muslim Law.

Example 6.5. *A*, an accused, was required, under the Criminal Procedure Code, to furnish a surety for the sum of Rs. 5,000 for his good behaviour. *A* deposited the required amount with *B*, and requested him to become surety. After the period of suretyship was over, *A* filed a suit against *B* for the recovery of the amount. The court held that the agreement between *A* and *B* was void, and the money is irrecoverable. It was observed that the intention of the law requiring a surety is that a person shall become surety at his own risk. In this case, this purpose is defeated by an agreement between *A* and *B*. [*Fateh Singh* v. *Sanwal Singh*, (1878) 1 Allahabad 751]

Example 6.6. *A*'s estate was to be auctioned for arrears of revenue under the provisions of an Act of the Legislature. According to the Act, the defaulter was prohibited from purchasing his own estate. *B* on understanding with *A*, purchased the estate in auction, and agreed to return the same to *A* after receiving the price paid by him (*B*). The agreement between *A* and *B* is void as the defaulter will be able to purchase back the estate. It would defeat the object of the law.

3. *Where it is fraudulent* : Sometimes, the object or consideration of an agreement is fraudulent. In such cases, the object or the consideration is unlawful. The agreement based on such an object or consideration is unlawful, and void. Thus, if the two parties agree to practise a fraud on third party, then the agreement between the first two parties is unlawful and void.

Example 6.7. *A* an agent of a landlord agreed for some money, without the knowledge of his principal, to obtain for *B* a lease of land belonging to his principal. The agreement between *A* and *B* is void. In this case, *A* practises a fraud, by concealment, on his principal.

Example 6.8. *A, B* and *C* entered into an agreement to carry on some fraudulent business, and to divide the gains of the business in equal proportions. In this case, the agreement is void because its object in unlawful.

4. *Where it is injurious to another person or his property:* Sometimes, the object or consideration of an agreement is to injure third person or his property. In such cases, the object or consideration is unlawful. The agreement with such an object or consideration is unlawful, and void. Thus, an agreement to commit a crime or any wrong action for which a civil suit can be brought, is unlawful and void.

Example 6.9. *A* agrees to pay Rs. 15,000 to *B* if he kills *C*. The agreement is void.

Example 6.10. *A* requested an editor of a newspaper to publish a defamatory article against *B*, and promised to pay Rs. 5,000 for this work. The agreement is void as it involves injury to *B*, and the editor cannot recover the amount from *A*.

5. *Where it is regarded as immoral:* Sometimes, the object or consideration of an agreement is such that it is regarded as immoral. In such cases, the object or the consideration is unlawful. The agreement with such an object or consideration is unlawful, and void. The term 'immoral' depends upon the standard of 'morality' prevailing at a particular place and time. But certain acts have been regarded as immoral since time immemorial, *e.g.*, interference with marital relations.

Example 6.11. *A*, a bachelor gave money to *B*, a married woman, to obtain a divorce from her husband. *A* agreed to marry her as soon as she obtained a divorce. It was held that *A* was not entitled to recover back the amount as the agreement was void, its object being immoral.

[*Baivijli* v. *Hamda Nagar,* (1885) 10 Bombay 152]

Similarly, an agreement to marry a married woman after the death of her husband, is void. Dealings with prostitutes have also been regarded as immoral. Thus, where the object of an agreement is to enable a prostitute to carry on her profession, the agreement is immoral, and is void.

Example 6.12. *A*, a landlord, knowingly let out his house to *B*, a prostitute, for carrying on her profession in the house. The agreement is void and the landlord cannot recover the rent. However, if the landlord did not know the purpose, he may recover the rent.

[*Gangamma* v. *Kupamal,* AIR 1939 Madras 139]

Example 6.13. *A* agreed, for some money, to give her daughter for concubinage to *B*. The agreement is void because it is immoral.

6. *Where it is opposed to public policy:* Sometime, the object or consideration of an agreement is opposed to public policy. In such cases, the object or consideration is unlawful. The agreement based on such an object or consideration is unlawful, and void. An agreement is said to be opposed to public policy when it is against public interest, *i.e.*, when it is harmful to the public welfare. The 'public policy' is that principle of law which holds that no person can lawfully act in such a way which has a tendency to be injurious to the public, or which is against the public good or public welfare. The term 'public policy' is not capable of exact definition. This is a wider term, and it is difficult to determine its limits with any degree of exactness. However, there are certain well settled categories of public policy, and the courts generally rely on them and apply them in varying situations. These categories will be discussed in Art. 6.4 and 6.5.

6.4. DOCTRINE OF PUBLIC POLICY

We know that public policy is that principle of law which holds that no person can lawfully act in such a way which has a tendency to be injurious to the public or which is against the public good or public welfare. It is known as the doctrine of public policy. An agreement which is against the general public, is said to be an agreement opposed to public policy. And such an agreement is unlawful, and void. It may be noted that the doctrine of public policy has been criticised by various judges and jurists. The reason for the same is that there is no exact definition of the term public policy. According to some jurists the term 'public policy' is a vague and unsatisfactory term, which makes the doctrine flexible, and this flexibility of the doctrine of public policy is potentially dangerous. It is also observed that the doctrine could provide a judge with an excuse for invalidating any contract which he violently disliked. The following judicial observations are worthnoting in connection with the **criticism** of the doctrine:

1. *"The doctrine of public policy is a very unruly horse, and when once you get astride it you never know where it will carry you"*.[1]
2. *"Public policy is always an unsafe and treacherous ground for legal decisions."*[2]
3. *"The categories of public policy are closed, and that no court can invent a new head of public policy."*[3]

It is to be noted that in spite of this criticism, the doctrine of public policy does exist. However, this doctrine should only be invoked in clear cases in which the harm to public is substantially, incontestable.[4] There are well settled categories of public policy, and the courts generally rely on them and apply them in varying situation. But the view that the categories of public policy are closed, appears to be too rigid, and is not applicable in India. Section 23 of the Indian Contract Act provides that the courts are authorised to decide the question of public interest and public policy. The court may, therefore, mould the settled categories of public policy to suit the new conditions in the changing world. The following judicial observations are worth noting in connection with the **prevailing position** of the doctrine :

1. *"In a modern progressive society with fast changing social values and concepts, new heads of public policy need be evolved whenever necessary."*[5]
2. *"The law relating to public policy cannot remain immutable. It must change with the passage of time. The wind of change blows upon it."*[6]

Thus, the doctrine of public policy should be invoked keeping in view the public good and public interest. Wherever necessary, the court can rely upon this doctrine it considers it in the interest of public welfare. The courts can invent a new head of public policy if the circumstances of the case of public good so requires.

---

1. Burrough J. in *Richardson* v. *Mellish,* (1824) 2 Bing 229 at p. 252.
2. Lord Davey in *Janson* v. *Drieftein consolidated Mines Ltd.,* (1902) AC 484.
3. Load Halsbury in *Janson's* case, (1902) AC 484.
4. Lord Atkin in *Fender v. St. John Mildmay* (1938) AC 1.
5. *Ratanchand Hirachand v. Asker Nawaz Jang,* AIR 1976 AP 112.
6. Dankwerts L.J. in *Nagle v. Fielden* (1966) 2 Q.B. 633.

6.5. HEADS OF PUBLIC POLICY

1. *Trading with an enemy*
2. *Trafficking in public offices*
3. *Interference with administration of justice*
4. *Marriage brokerage contracts*
5. *Agreements tending to create interest opposed to duty*
6. *Agreements in restraint of parental rights*
7. *Agreemen restricting personal liberty*
8. *Agreement to commit a crime*

The following are some of the commonly accepted heads of public policy. On these grounds, the agreements are declared void as being opposed to public policy.

1. *Trading with an enemy:* Trading with an enemy is regarded as opposed to public policy. Thus, an agreement made with an alien enemy is unlawful on the ground of public policy, and is void. In such cases, the agreements made with an alien enemy, before the outbreak of war between India and his (alien's) country, are either suspended or dissolved according to the intention of the parties, It may be noted that the suspended agreements may be performed after the end of the war.

2. *Trafficking in public offices:* The agreements which affect the normal working of government offices are void as they are opposed to public policy, *e.g.*, appointment decisions in consideration of money are void. Similarly, the agreement for the procurement of a public recognition such as Param Veer Chakra or any other title, for monetary or other consideration, are void. This is based on the principle that an agreement by which it is intended to induce a government officer to act corruptly is contrary to public policy.

Example 6.14. *A* paid a certain sum of money to *B*, a public servant, inducing him to retire from service. This was done for the purpose of paving a way for *A* to be appointed in place of *B*. It was held that the agreement was void. [*Venkataramananya* v. *J.M. Lobo*, AIR 153 Madras 506]

Similarly, an agreement with voters to procure their votes for monetary consideration, an agreement with a person for procuring a seat in a college for monetary consideration, are void on the ground of public policy.

3. *Interference with administration of justice:* An agreement is opposed to public policy if its object is to interfere with the administration of justice. It may take any of the following forms.

(*a*) ***Interference with the course of justice:*** It is an established principle that an agreement which obstructs the ordinary process of justice is unlawful, and is void.

Example 6.15. *A*, a moneylender, filed a recovery suit against *B*. *A* induced his friend *C* to given false evidence against *B*. And *A* agreed to give Rs. 500 to *C* for this work. In this case the agreement is void as it interferes with the course of justice. Such agreements are opposed to public policy.

Similarly, an agreement for using improper influence of any kind with the judge, is unlawful as it interfers with the administration of justice.

(*b*) ***Stifling prosecution:*** The public interest requires that criminals should be prosecuted and punished. An agreement not to prosecute an offender, or to withdraw a pending prosecution is an agreement for stifling prosecution, and is void. No Court of Law can give effect to an agreement which attempts to take the administration of law out of the hands of the judges and put it in other hands.

Example 6.16. *A* had instituted prosecution against *B* for robbery. *A* promised to drop the prosecution, and *B* promised to restore the value of the robbed articles. In this case, the agreement is void as its object it to stifle prosecution.

(c) ***Maintenance and champerty :*** The term 'maintenance' may be defined as the instigation of litigation by a person who has no legal interest of his own. Sometimes, a stranger who has no legal interest in the suit, promises to give assistance (monetary or otherwise) to another person to enable him to bring or defend legal proceedings. In such cases, the agreement between the stranger and such person is known as maintenance agreement. Here, the motive is to stir up litigation. The term 'champerty' may be defined as a bargain in which a stranger promises to give assistance (monetary or otherwise) to another person in recovering the property. And also promises to share the profits obtained by legal action. Such an agreement is known as 'champertous agreement'. The purpose of the agreement is to share the proceeds of the litigation.

It may be noted that in India the maintenance and champertous agreements are not absolutely void. If an agreement is fair and is made with the *bona fide* object of assisting a person, it will be valid. Similarly, a fair agreement to supply funds to a person to carry on a suit in consideration of having a fair share of property, if recovered, is not opposed to public policy. But much depends upon the quantum of share which the person giving assistance has stipulated to get in the fruits of the action.

Example 6.17. *A* agreed to supply funds to *B* to enable him to file a suit for the recovery of his property. And *B* promised to give him 3/4th share in the property, if recovered. The agreement was held to be champertous, and void. [*Nuthahi Venkataswami* v. *Katta Nagi,* AIR 1962 AP 457]

However, the agreements to pay 1/3rd, 1/4th and 1/8th shares have been held to be valid. An agreement to pay the lawyer according to the results of the case is against public policy.

Note. Under English Law, both the above-mentioned types of agreements are illegal and unenforceable.

4. ***Marriage brokerage contracts:*** An agreement to procure the marriage of a person in consideration of a sum of money is called a 'marriage brokerage contract'. Such agreements being opposed to public policy are void.

Example 6.18. *A* promised with *B* to procure a wife for him. And *B* agreed to pay a certain sum of money to *A* for the procurement for the wife. In this case, the agreement is void as it is opposed to public policy.

Similarly an agreement to pay money to the parents of a minor to induce them to give the minor in marriage, is void.

Example 6.19. *A*, a father of a girl, promised to give a certain sum of money to *B*, a father of a minor boy. And *B* agreed to marry his minor son with *A*'s daughter. In this case, the agreement is void as it is opposed to public policy.[Based on *Kalavanguta* v. *Laxmi Narain,* (1909) 32 Madras 185]

5. ***Agreements tending to create interest opposed to duty :*** The public policy requires that a person must perform his duties honestly. If a person enters into an agreement by which he is bound to do something which is against his public duty, the agreement is void on the ground of public policy *e.g.,* an agreement by a person in the government service for the purchase of property which is prohibited by law, an agreement by an agent to enable him to make secret profits, and agreement by an editor of a newspaper not to publish reports about the conduct of a particular person, shall be void being opposed to public policy.

Example 6.20. *A* directs his agent *B* to buy for him a certain car from *C*. *B* buys the car from *C* for himself and further sells the same to *A* at a higher price. On discovering that *B* has bought the car at a lower price, *A* may compell his agent to return the secret profit to him (*A*).

6. ***Agreements in restraint of parental rights:*** The father and the mother are the natural guardians of a minor child. This right of guardianship cannot be bartered away by any agreement. Thus, an agreement which is inconsistent with the duties arising out of such guardianship is void as being opposed to public policy.

Example. 6.21: *A,* for a sum of Rs. 500, agreed to place his daughter at the disposal of *B,* to be married as he likes. The agreement is void as it interferes with *A's* parental duty to select a husband in the best interest of the girl. [*Atmaram* v. *Bankumal, (1930) Lahore 561*]

Similarly, an agreement in which a father agreed to transfer guardianship of his two minor children in favour of a lady, was held to be void.

[*Agiddu Narayanish* v. *Mrs. Annie Besant* (1907) 38 Madras 807].

7. ***Agreemen restricting personal liberty:*** An agreement which restricts the personal liberty of an individual is void as being opposed to public policy.

Example 6.22. *A,* a servant borrowed some money from his employer, *B.* And *A* agreed that he would not leave *B's* job, borrow money, dispose of his property, or move from his house without *B's* written consent to this effect. It was held that the agreement was void as it unduly restricted the liberty of *A.* [*Harwood* v. *Miller's Timber & Trading Co.,* (1917) JKB 305]

8. ***Agreement to commit a crime:*** An agreement to commit a crime is void being opposed to public policy. Thus, an agreement to indemnify a person against consequences of his criminal act is void as opposed to public policy.

Example 6.23. *A* promises to indemnify *B* in consideration of his killing *C.* This agreement is void being opposed to public policy.

Besides the above-mentioned heads of public policy, there are three more heads of public policy which have been specified in the Indian Contract Act itself. These may be grouped under the following heads:

(*a*) Agreements in restraint of marriage.

(*b*) Agreements in restraint of legal proceedings.

(*c*) Agreements in restraint of trade.

All these three agreements will be discussed in detail in the next chapter on 'Void Agreement.'

LEGAL PROVISIONS (SECTIONS) DISCUSSED IN THE CHAPTER

Important legal provisions (sections) of the Indian Contract Act, 1872, discussed in this chapter, are reprodnced hereunder:

1. ***Section 23: What Consideration and Objects are Lawful and what not***

The consideration or object of an agreement in lawful unless:

It is a forbidden by law; or

is of such a nature that, if permitted, it would defeat the providsions of any law; or is fraudulent; or

involves or implies, injury to the person or property of another; or

the Court regards it as immoral, or opposed to public policy.

In each of these cases, the consideration or object of an agreement is said to be unlwful. Every agreement of which the object or consideration is unlawful is void.

2. ***Section 26, 27, 28 and 30: Agreements Void Being Fobidden by law***

These sections will be repoduced at the end of next chapter on void Agreements.

TEST QUESTIONS

1. What do you understand by the legality of object and consideration? State the cases in which the object and consideration is unlawful.
2. "All agreements are contracts if they are made for lawful consideration and with lawful object." Explain with suitable examples.

3. "Every agreement of which the object or consideration is unlawful, is void", exaplain and state the cases in which the object and consideration is unlawful.
4. Explain the doctrine of public policy. What are the heads of public policy ? Do you agree with the view that the heads of public policy are not closed ?
5. "The doctrine of public policy is a very unruly horse, and when once you get astride it, you never know where it will carry you." Critically examine the statement.
6. "The law relating to public policy cannot remain immutable. It must change with the passage of time. The wind of change blows upon it." Explain.

MULTIPLE CHOICE QUESTIONS

1. An agreement the object or consideration of which is unlawful, is
   (*a*) void (*b*) valid
   (*c*) voidable (*d*) contingent.
2. The consideration or object of an agreement is considered unlawful, if it is
   (*a*) forbidden by law (*b*) fraudulent
   (*c*) immoral (*d*) all of these.
3. *A* agrees to pay Rs. 5 lakhs to *B* if he (*B*) procures an employment for *A* in Income Tax Department. This agreement is
   (*a*) void (*b*) valid
   (*c*) voidable (*d*) contingent.
4. *A* agrees to pay Rs. 50,000 to *B* if he kills *C*. The agreement is
   (*a*) void (*b*) valid
   (*c*) voidable (*d*) contingent.
5. An agreement is void if it is opposed to public policy. Which of the following is not covered by heads of public policy ?
   (*a*) Trading with an enemy (*b*) Trafficking in public offices
   (*c*) Marriage brokerage contracts (*d*) Contracts to do impossible acts.

ANSWERS

1. (*a*) 2. (*d*) 3. (*a*) 4. (*a*) 5. (*d*)

OBJECTIVE TYPE QUESTIONS WITH REASONING

State with reasons whether the following statements are correct or incorrect.

1. The object or consideration of an agreement is unlawful where it is forbidden by law.
2. Every agreement of which the object or consideration is unlawful is voidable.
3. *A*, a Hindu already married and his wife alive, entered into a marriage agreement with *B*, another lady. This agreement is void.
4. *A* and *B* entered into an agreement to carry on trading in smuggled goods and to divide the gains of business in equal proportion. This agreement is valid.
5. An agreement to marry a married woman after the death of her husband, is void.
6. An agreement to procure the marriage of a person in consideration of a sum of money is void.
7. A marriage agreement in contemplation of divorce is valid.
8. An agreement with voters to procure their votes for monetary consideration, is void.
9. An agreement with a person for procuring a seat in a medical college for monetary consideration, is void.

ANSWERS

1. ***Correct.*** Section 23 of the Indian Contract Act clearly states so.
2. ***Incorrect.*** Such an agreement is void [Section 23].

3. *Correct.* The second marriage is forbidden by Hindu law. In this case, the object of marriage is unlawful.
4. *Incorrect.* Such an agreement is void. In this case, the object of the agreement is unlawful as smuggling is forbidden by law.
5. *Correct.* The object of such an agreement is immoral and thus unlawful.
6. *Correct.* Such an agreement is opposed to public policy, thus unlawful and void.
7. *Incorrect.* Such an agreement is immoral and opposed to public policy, thus unlawful and void.
8. *Correct.* Such an agreement is unlawful on the ground of being opposed to public policy, and is void.
9. *Correct.* Such an agreement is unlawful on the ground of being opposed to public policy, and is void.

PRACTICAL PROBLEMS

1. At the time of marriage, *A*, a Mohammedan, entered into an agreement with his wife, *B* that she may live with her parents. Is this a valid agreement ?
   Hint : No. it is not a valid agreement. This agreement is void being unlawful as it defeats the provisions of Mohammedan Law. As per Mohammedan Law, the parties contracting a marriage cannot enter into a separation deed in which the husband allows his wife to live with her parents.
2. *A*, a bachelor, gave Rs. 50,000 to *B*, a married woman to obtain a divorce from her husband and agreed to marry her as soon as she obtained the divorce. *B* did not divorce her husband and *A* sued *B* for recovery of the money already paid to her. Will he succeed? Give reasons.
   Hint : No, *A* will not succeed in his action. Here, the agreement between *A* and *B* is void, its object being immoral.
3. *A* paid Rs. 10 lakhs to *B* and agreed to obtain a seat for *A*'s son in a Medical College. Can this agreement be enforced in a court of Law ? Give reasons.
   Hint : No, it cannot be enforced in a court of Law. Here, the agreement is void, as it is opposed to public policy.
4. *A* promised with *B* to procure a wife for him and *B* agreed to pay Rs. 70,000 to *A* for the procurement of a wife for him. Can this agreement be enforced in a court of Law ? Give reasons.
   Hint : No, it cannot be enforced in a court of law. Here, the agreement is void as it is opposed to public policy.
5. *A*, an accused was required, under the criminal Procedure code, to furnish a surety for the sum of Rs. 50,000 for his good behavior. *A* entered into an agreement with *B* that *A* would deposit the required amount with *B* and in consideration *B* would become surety in the court. Is this agreement enforceable? Give reasons.
   Hint : No, this agreement is not enforceable. Here, the agreement is void as it defeats the provision of criminals law. The intention of the law requiring a surety is that a person shall become surety at his own risk.

VOID AGREEMENTS

1. Introduction.
2. Types of Void Agreements.
3. Agreements in Restraint of Marriage.
4. Agreements in Restraint of Trade.
5. Exceptions in the Agreements of Trade.
6. Agreements in Restraint of Legal Proceedings.
7. Exceptions in the Agreements of Legal Proceedings.
8. Uncertain Agreements.
9. Wagering Agreements.
10. Essentials of Wagering Agreements.
11. Effects of Wagering Agreements.
12. Exceptions in the Wagering Agreements.
13. Important Transactions of Wagering Nature.
14. Contract of insurance.
15. Comparison Between a Wagering Agreement and a Contract of Insurance.
16. Agreements for Impossible Acts.
17. Comparison Between a Void Agreements and a Void Contract.
18. Comparison Between a Void Agreement and a Voidable Contract.

7.1 INTRODUCTION

A void agreements is one which is without any legal effects. The term 'void agreement' is defined in Section 2(g) of The Indian Contract Act, which reads as under:

"An agreement not enforceable by law is said to be void".

Thus, an agreement which the Courts of Law will not enforce is a void agreement. A void agreement does not create any legal rights and obligations. It is *void ab initio* (*i.e.*, void from the very beginning) and without any legal effect. It is, therefore, clear that all agreements are not enforceable by the Courts of Law. The courts will enforce only those agreements which fulfil the conditions of enforceability as laid down in[1] Section 10 of the Indian Contract Act. If the conditions laid down in Section 10 are not satisfied, the agreement will be void. Certain types of agreements have been specifically declared to be void by the Indian Contract Act itself. In this chapter we shall discuss the various types of void agreement.

7.2 TYPES OF VOID AGREEMENTS

Following are the various types of void agreements. These are contained in section 11, 20, 23 to 30 and 56 of the Indian Contract Act, and have been expressly declared to be void by the Act itself.

1. Agreements by persons who are not competent to contact. (Section 11)
2. Agreements under a mutual mistake of fact material to the agreement. (Section 20)
3. Agreement with unlawful consideration or object. (Section 23)

1. These have already been discussed in Chapter 2.

4. Agreements, the consideration or object of which is unlawful in part. (Section 24)
5. Agreements without consideration. (Section 25)
6. Agreements in restraint of marriage. (Section 26)
7. Agreements in restraint of trade. (Section 27)
8. Agreements in Restraint of legal proceedings. (Section 28)
9. Agreements the meaning of which is uncertain. (Section 29)
10. Wagering agreements. (Section 30)
11. Agreements to do impossible acts. (Section 56)

The above first five types of void agreements have already been discussed in earlier chapters. In this chapter, we shall discuss the remaining types, and the legal provisions relating to them.

7.3. AGREEMENTS IN RESTRAINT OF MARRIAGE

Every person has the freedom to marry. The law regards the marriage as the right of every person. It is the policy of law to discourage agreements which restrain the freedom of marriage. 'An agreement in restraint of marriage' is the agreement which restrains a person from marrying. Such an agreement is void. This provision is contained in Section 26 of the Indian Contract Act, which reads as under:

"Every agreements in restraint of marriage of any person other than a minor is void".

Thus, an agreement which prevents a person from marrying, is void. It may be noted that the restraint may be complete or partial, the agreement is void in both the cases. A complete restraint is that which prevents a person from marrying altogether, And the partial restraint is that which prevents a person from marrying a particular person, or a person of particular class or which prevents from marrying for a fixed period. However, a restraint is valid in case of minors.

Example 7.1. *A* agreed to marry *B* and none else. He Further agreed to pay Rs. 1000 to *B* if he (*A*) married someone else, But *A* married *C*. *B* brought an action against *A* for the recovery of the agreed sum on the ground that he (*A*) married someone else. It was held that the agreement was void as it was in restraint of marriage. *B* could not recover the amount as the void agreements is not enforceable in Courts of Law. [*Lowe* v. *Peers, (1918) 98 ER. 160*]

It may, however, be noted that a penalty upon remarriage may not be regarded as a restraint of marriage.

Example 7.2. A husband and his wife entered into an agreements that upon the husband marrying a second wife, the first wife would get the right to divorce him. It was held that the agreement was not void as the husband was not restrained from marrying. Simply a penalty was imposed if the married the second time. [*Badu* v. *Badarnessa (1919) CLJ 230*]

Similarly, an agreement that upon remarrying, the widow would lose the right to maintenance was not held void.[2]

Note: The English Law is different on this point. Under the English Law, a partial restraint is valid. Only an absolute restraint is void. Thus, in England an agreement restraining marriage with a particular person of with a person or particular community, is valid.

7.4. AGREEMENTS IN RESTRAINT OF TRADE

As a matter of fact, every person has the freedom of legal trade, commerce or profession. The law regards the legal trade, commerce or profession as the fundamental right of every person. And this fundamental right is protected by the Constitution of India. 'An agreements in restraint of trade' is the agreement which restrains a person from

2. *Latafatunissa* v. *Shaharbanu*, AIR 1932 Oudh 108.

exercising a lawful trade, occupation or profession of any kind. Such an agreements is void. This provision is contained in Section 27 of the Indian Contract Act, which reads as under:

"Every agreement by which anyone is restrained from exercising a lawful profession, trade or business of any kind, is to that extent void".

Thus, an agreement, which prevents a person from carrying on any lawful business, is void. In this case also, the restraint may be partial or complete. The agreement is void in both the cases. A complete restraint is that which prevents a person from carrying on any kind of business at all. And the partial restraint is that which prevents a person from carrying a business within a particular locality, or for a particular time, or which prevents him from carrying on a particular kind of business. Thus it makes no difference that the restraint is general or partial, unqualified or qualified.

Example. 7.3. *A* and *B* were rival shopkeepers in a locality in Calcutta. *A* agreed to pay a sum of money to *B* if he (*B*) would close his business in that locality. *B* closed his business in that locality, but *A* refused to pay the agreed amount of money. It was held that the agreement was void, and the money could not be recovered, as void agreements are not enforceable by law.

[*Madhub Chander* V. *Raj Coomar* (1874) XIV Bengal Law Reports 76]

In the above case, though the restraint was partial, the agreement was held to be void.

Similarly an agreement that one party would sell beef for 14 days in a month[3], and and agreement to close a mill for 3 months in a year,[4] have been held to be void.

It is to be noted that where an agreement in restraint of trade is divisible, the valid portion will be enforced. However, where it is not divisible, the whole agreement will be void. This is clear from the words 'to that extent void' used in the langauge of Section 27. The words 'to that extent' means that only void portion is unenforceable.

Example 7.4. *A*, a businessman sold the goodwill of his trade to *B*. Both of them agreed that *A* will not practise the same trade for 3 years, and also that *A* will not carry on any business competing in any way with the business of *B*. Here, the agreement being divisible, the first part was held to be valid as necessary to protect the interest of the purchaser of goodwill. The second part was held to be void as it prevented *A* form carrying on any business.

7.5 EXCEPTIONS IN THE AGREEMENTS OF TRADE

1. *Exceptions under Indian Contract Act*
2. *Exceptions under Partnership Act*
3. *Exceptions under judicial decisions*

The general rule is that all the agreements, in restraint of trade, are void. In other words, any restraint in the agreement of trade, makes it void. However, following restraints, which are exceptions to the general rule, are considered as valid in the agreement of trade, and do not affect the validity of agreements.

1. ***Exceptions under Indian Contract Act:*** This exception is applicable in the sale of business along with its goodwill only. It is contained in Section 27 of the Indian Contract Act. According to this section, when the goodwill of a business is sold, the seller may be restrained from carrying on a similar business within specified local limits. Thus, an agreement which restrains the seller of the goodwill, from carrying on similar business, is valid. However, the restraint should be reasonable and applicable within specified local limits. The object of this restraint is to protect the interest of the purchaser of the goodwill. If this restriction is not imposed on the liberty of the seller of goodwill, he may set up a similar business next day and attract all the customers. However, for the application of this exception, following conditions must be satisfied.

3. *Mohamad* v *Ona Md. Ebrahim*, AIR 1922 Upper Burma 9.
4. *Khem Chand Manek Chand* v. *Dayaldas B. Mal*, AIR 1942, sindh 114.

(*a*) The restriction should specify the local limits, *i.e.*, the seller can be restrained within certain territorial or geographical limits.

(*b*) The restriction must be reasonable. The reasonableness will depend upon many factors *e.g*, the area in which the goodwill is effectively enjoyed, the price paid for the goodwill etc.

(*c*) The restriction should apply only for such period for which the business sold is actually carried on by the buyer, or by any person who derived his title to the goodwill from the buyer.

(*d*) The restriction should be from carrying on a similar business only.

(*e*) There should be reasonable goodwill to be sold.

2. *Exceptions under Partnership Act :* Following are the four provisions in the Indian Partnership Act, 1932 which provide that agreements in restraint of trade are valid if the restrictions imposed are reasonable:

(*a*) ***Restraining a continuing partner from carrying on any business:*** This restraint is contained in Section 11(2) of the Indian Partnership Act. According to this Section, a continuing partner of the firm may be restrained from carrying *any* business other than the business of the firm. Thus, an agreement which restrains a continuing partner from carrying on any business, other than the business of the firm, is valid. It means that during the continuance of the firm, the partners should carry on the joint business of the firm only.

Example 7.5. *A*, *B* and *C* were the three partners in a firm carrying on the business of importing salt from foreign countries and reselling the same. The partnership agreement provided that a continuing partner shall not carry on any personal business so long as he is a partner. *A* was given the charge of importing the salt. While importing salt for the firm, he was also importing sugar for himself and selling the same on his personal accounts. The restriction imposed in the agreement is valid. And thus, *A* may be restrained from carrying on the sugar business.

Note. Where a partner carries on any personal business in breach of this kind of agreement, the other printers may apply to the court for the dissolution of the firm on the ground of persistent breach of agreement. [*Dean* v. *Macdowell, 8 Ch.D. 345*]

(*b*) ***Restraining on outgoing partner from carrying on a similar business:*** This restraint is contained in Section 36(2) of the Indian Partnership Act. According to this Section, an outgoing partner of the firm may be restrained from carrying on the business which is similar to the business of the firm. Thus, an agreement which restrains the outgoing partner from carrying on the business which is similar to the firm business, is valid. However, the restriction must be reasonable and should specify the local limits or the period for which it will remain in force.

Example 7.6. *A*, *B* and *C* were the three partners in a firm carrying on spare parts business in Delhi. The partnership agreement provided that any partner, on ceasing to be a partner, will not carry on any business similar to that of the firm. The agreement also provided that the outgoing partner will not carry on such business for one year within the city of Delhi. A retired from the firm and after six months set up his own spare parts business in the same locality. The restriction imposed in the agreement is valid. And thus, *A* may be restrained from carrying on this business.

(*c*) ***Restraint in anticipation of dissolution:*** This restraint is contained in Section 54 of the Indian Partnership Act. According to this Section, upon dissolution or in anticipation of dissolution of the firm, the partners may enter into an agreement which restrains each other partner from carrying on a business *similar* to that of a firm. However, such restraint should be reasonable, and specify the local limits or period for which it will remain in force. This restraint is necessary for the protection of the interest of a partner or any other person, who has purchased the business of the firm.

Example 7.7. *A* and *B* were two partners carrying on shoe making business. Some differences arose between them and they agreed to dissolve the firm. As per the terms of the agreement, *A* agreed to purchase *B*'s share in the firm. The agreement also provided that *B* shall not carry on the similar business for two years within the same locality. This is a valid agreement. And if *B* starts a similar business in breach of the agreement, he may be restrained from doing so.

(*d*) ***Restraint when goodwill is sold:*** This restraint is contained in Section 55(3) of the Indian Partnership Act. According to this Section, when the goodwill of a firm is sold, a partner may be retained from carrying on a similar business within specified local limits or within specified period. Thus, upon the sale of goodwill of a firm, an agreement which restrians a partner from carrying on a similar business, is valid. However, the restriction must be reasonable and specify the local limits or the period for which it will remain in force.

Example 7.8. *A* and *B* were two partners carrying on the business of manufacturing and selling rubber goods in Bombay. *A* sold his share in the business to the other partner and agreed not to carry on a similar business for three years within the city of Bombay. But *A* started his own business in breach of the agreement. It was held that the restriction was valid. And thus, *A* was restrained from carrying on the business. [*Krishnarao* v. *Shankar,* (1954) 56 Bombay LR 973].

3. *Exceptions under judicial decisions:* Following are the important restraints which have been recognised by the courts as the exceptions to the general rule:

(*a*) ***Restraints upon employees:*** A service agreement may validly contain some provisions which prevent an employee from working elsewhere during the period covered by the agreement. This means that, during the period of such agreement, the concerned employee may be restrained from taking part in any business which is in direct competition with the business of his employer.

Example 7.9. *A* agreed to become assistant for 3 years to *B* who was a doctor. It was agreed that during the term of the agreement, *A* was not to practise on his own account in the same locality. *A* left the service within a year, and began to practise there on his own account. It was held that the agreement preventing *A* from practising was valid. Accordingly *A* was prevented from practising during the period of his employment.[*Charlesworth* v. *Donald, ILR (1898) 23 Bombay 103*].

Example 7.10. *A* was appointed in a company for period of 5 years. One of the conditions of that agreement was that during this period, he shall not serve anywhere else even if he left service earlier. It was held that the agreement was not void. *A* was accordingly restrained from serving anywhere else during the period of agreement.

[*Niranjan Shankar* v. *Century Spinning & Mfg. Co.* IR 1967 SC 1098].

However, such an agreement must be reasonable, *i.e.,* the restriction imposed must be reasonable. The reasonableness of the restriction depends upon the facts and circumstances of each case. For example, where a person joined service for 20 years and agree not to work elsewhere during the period 20 yeses, the agreement was held to be void as the term being unreasonable.

Similarly, a restraint on an employee not to engage in a similar business, or not to accept similar employment *after* the termination of service, is void, For example an agreement which restrains an employee from taking service or engaging in any similar business for a period of five years after the termination of service, is void being unreasonable.

[*Brahamputra Tea Co.* v. *Scarth* (1885) 11 Calcutta 545].

(*b*) ***Restraints in trade combinations:*** It is the normal practice for traders or manufacturers who are in the same line of business to form associations and carry on their trade in an organised way. The primary object of such associations is to regulate and promote business and not to restrain it. Such combinations are often desirable in the interest of trade itself and also for the promotion of public interest. They help in eliminating ruinous competition and bring about fixed prices and standardised goods. Thus, an agreement between manufactureres or traders not to sell their goods below a certain price, to pool profits and to divide business profits in certain proportion, does not amount to restraint of trade, and is perfectly valid. Similarly, regulations as to the opening and closing of business in the market, licensing of traders, supervision and control of dealers and the mode of dealing are also not illegal.

[*Municipal Committee, Khurai* v. *Kaluram Hiralar*, AIR 1944 Nagpur 73].

Example 7.11. Certain ice manufacturers entered into an agreement relating to manufacturing and sale of ice by them. The minimum sale price was fixed, and it was agreed to put all the profits in a common pool and then divide that total profits in certain proportions. It was held that the agreement was not void as the main object was to regulate the business and not to restrain it.

[*S.B. Fraser & Co.* v. *Bombay Ice Mfg. Co.*, (1904) 29 ILR Bombay 107].

But where the regulatory agreement is in the nature of a restraint, the courts would not allow such an agreement.

Example 7.12. Certain traders of Brahmin Community entered into an agreement that they shall carry on their business within the members of their caste only. The agreement is void as it is in the nature of a restraint. [*Vaithelinga* v *Saminanda*, ILR (1872) Madras 44]

Similarly, if such agreements tend to create monopolies. They will be against public policy, and void[5].

(*c*) ***Restraints in sole or exclusive dealing agreements:*** This is also a common practice that a producer or manufacturer likes to sell his goods through a sole agent or distributor. And the latter agrees not to deal in similar goods of any other producer or manufacturer. For example, a producer may agree to sell all his output to one agent or distributor, who in turn, agrees not to buy his requirements from any other producer. Such agreements are held to be valid by the courts.

Example 7.13. *A* agreed to sell all the mica produced by him to *B* only and not to sell it to any other firm, nor to keep any stock. It was held that the agreement was valid.

[*Subha Naidu* v. *Haj Badsha*, ILR (1902) 26 Madras 168].

Example 7.14. *A*, a trader of Calcutta bought certain goods from *B*, a manufacturer of Madras. It was agreed between them that *A* can sell these goods in Calcutta market only and not in Madras market. This agreement is valid.

It may, however, be noted that if after meeting the complete requirement of a buyer, a manufacturer still has surplus to sell. He cannot be restrained from selling the surplus product to others.[6] And also an agreement which binds the seller for an unreasonable period of time or by which the buyer intends to monopolies the commodity so that he may resell at his own price, may not be held valid by the courts.

Example 7.15. *A*, a comb seller, entered into an agreement with all the manufacturers of combs in the city of Patna. According to this agreement the manufacturers undertook during their life time to sell all their products to *A* and subsequently to his heirs. They further agreed not to sell the combs to any one else. The agreement was held to be void.

---

5. *Australia* v. *Adclaid S.S. Co* (1913) A.C. 724.
6. *Har Bilas v. Mahodeo pd.* AIR 1931 Allahabad 539.
7. *Halsbury's Law of England Vol.* 9 Page 352.

7.6 AGREEMENTS IN RESTRAINT OF LEGAL PROCEEDINGS

1. *Restrictions from enforcing legal rights*
2. *Agreement which cuts short the limitation period*
3. *An agreement which extinguishes the rights of a party*
4. *An agreement which discharges a party form liability*

As a matter of fact, every person has a freedom to enforce his legal rights. Moreover, justice also requires that one should be free to go to 'Courts of Law for the enforcement of his legal rights. An agreement which interferes with the course of justice is void on account of its being opposed to public policy. It is a well known rule of English Law[7] that "an agreement purporting to oust the jurisdiction of the courts is illegal and void on ground of public policy". This rule of English Law has been incoporated in Section 28 of the Indian Contract Act. This section has been amended in 1996 by the **Indian Contract (Amendment) Act, 1996** and the amended section reads as under:

"Every agreement,—

(*a*) *by which any party thereto is restricted absolutely from enforcing his rights under or in respect of any contract, by the usual legal proceedings in the ordinary tribunals, or which limits the time within which he may thus enforce his rights; or*

(*b*) *which extinguishes the rights of any party thereto , or discharges any party thereto from any liability, under or in respect of any contract on the expiry of a specified period so as to restrict any party from enforcing his rights, is void to that extent".*

The analysis of this section reveals that following are the four kinds of agreements which are in restraint of legal proceedings, and are therefore, void:

(*a*) An agreement which restricts absolutely the parties from enforcing their legal rights.

(*b*) An agreement which cuts short the period of limitation prescribed by the law of limitation.

(*c*) An agreement which extinguishes the rights of a party.

(*d*) An agreement which discharges a party from his liability.

The agreements in points (*c*) and (*d*) above are included in this category by the Amendment Act of 1996. All the above points are illustrated as below:

1. *Restrictions from enforcing legal rights:* An agreement which restrains a person form enforcing his legal rights, is void. It may be noted that the restriction must be absolute. In other words, a person must be wholly restrained from enforcing his legal remedies in the Courts of Law.

Example 7.16. *A* borrowed Rs. 5,000 from *B*, a money lender. It was agreed between the parties that *A* would repay the loan within one year. And if the amount was not repaid, *B* would not take any legal action against him. This agreement is void as it prevents *B* from enforcing his legal rights.

But a partial restraint is valid, *i.e.*, the partial restraint does not make the agreement void.

Example 7.17. *A* was a tradesman in Calcutta. *B*, carried on business in Delhi. *B*, by his agent in Calcutta, bought goods from *A* and requested him to deliver them to the Railway Company . Accordingly, *A* delivered the goods to the Railway Company in Calcutta. In case of failure to pay the price, *A* had the option to file a suit against *B* either in Calcutta or in Delhi, The parties, however, entered into an agreement that *A* can enforce his rights in Delhi only, and not in Calcutta. This agreement is valid as it puts a partial restraint only.

The right to appeal does not come within the purview of this section. Thus, a party to a suit may agree not to appeal against the decision of the court.[8]

8. *Anant Das* v. *Ashburner & Co.*, (1876) 1 Allahabad 267.

2. ***Agreement which cuts short the limitation period:*** An agreement which reduces the limitation period than that prescribed by the Law of Limitation, is void *e.g.*, according to the Indian Limitation Act an action for breach of contract may be brought within three years from the date of breach. If an agreement provides that no action should be brought after two years, is void as it curtails the period of limitation.

Example 7.18. *A* sold and delivered his car to *B*. *B* agreed to pay the price within 6 months of the sale. It was agreed between the parties that if *B* failed to pay the price within this period, *A* must take action for recovery of the price within two years, otherwise he (*B*) would not be liable. It is a void agreement as it cuts short the limitation period for taking the legal action.

3. ***An agreement which extinguishes the rights of a party:*** An agreement which extinguishes the rights of a party, is void. By entering into an agreement, the parties acquire certain rights under the agreement. Any agreement, which states that such rights would be extinguished after the expiry of a specified period, is void.

Example 7.19. *A* sold his flat to *B* for Rs. 15 lacs. *B* paid the entire money to *A* and the possession of the flat was to be given to *B* within three months. In this case, *B* has acquired a right to take possession of the flat. It was agreed between the parties that if *B* failed to take possession within this period, then after the expiry of three months his right to take possession would be lost. It is a void agreement as it extinguishes *B's* right to take possession of the flat.

4. ***An agreement which discharges a party form liability:*** An agreement which discharges a party from liability, is void, By entering into an agreement, the parties also become liable to perform certain obligations. Any agreement, which states that a party would be discharged from his liability after the expiry of a specified period, is void.

Example 7.20. In the above example, *A* is under obligation, *i.e.*, liable to hand over the possession of the flat to *B* within three months. Suppose, they enter into an agreement which states that after the expiry of three months, *A* will not be liable to hand over the possession of the flat to *B*. It is a void agreement as it discharges *A* from his liability to hand over the possession of the flat to *B*.

7.7. EXCEPTIONS IN THE AGREEMENTS OF LEGAL PROCEEDINGS

1. *Restraints for referring the future disputes to arbitration*
2. *Restraints for referring the existing disputes to arbitration*

The general rule is that all the agreements in restraint of legal proceedings are void. In other words, an absolute restraint in the agreement of legal proceedings makes it void. However, following restraints, which are exceptions to the general rule, are considered as valid in the agreements of legal proceedings, and do not affect the validity of the agreements:

1. ***Restraints for referring the future disputes to arbitration:*** Sometimes, the concerned parties agree that any future dispute, which may arise between them shall be referred to arbitration. Such an agreement is not void. [Section 28, Exception I].

Example 7.21. *A*, a trader, entered into an agreement with *B*, a manufacturer of clocks, agreeing to purchase 500 clocks per month at the rate of Rs. 150 per clock. It was agreed that *A* will purchase this quantity for one years. The parties also agreed that any dispute which may arise about the payment of the price or quality of the clocks shall be referred to arbitration and not to Court of Law. This is a valid agreement.

It may, however, be noted that the right to proceed against arbitrations award cannot be excluded by the agreement *e.g.*, the party has the right to go to Court of law, and have the arbitration award set aside. This right cannot be excluded by the agreement.

2. *Restraints for referring the existing disputes to arbitration:* Sometimes, the parties agree in writing that any existing dispute between them shall be referred to arbitration. Such an agreement is also not void. [Section 28, Exception II]

Example 7.22. *A* agreed to sell his typewriter to *B* for Rs. 5000 And *B* agreed to pay the price on delivery. According to the agreement, the typewriter was to be delivered on 31 - 12 - 98. On this date, a dispute arose about the quality of the typewriter, and *B* refused to pay the price and take the typewriter. They agreed in writing that this despute shall be referred to arbitration, and not to Court of Law. This is a valid agreement.

It may also be noted here that the right to proceed against arbitration's award cannot be excluded by the agreement. Thus, an agreement will be void if it provides that the parties will be bound by the arbitration award alone, whether just or unjust.

7.8. UNCERTAIN AGREEMENTS

An uncertain agreement is one, the terms of which are uncertain or vague. Such an agreement is void and without any legal effect. This provision is contained in Section 29 of the Indian Contract Act which reads as under:

"Agreements, the meaning of which is not certain or capable of being made certain, are void".

In simple words, an agreement with uncertain meaning is void. Thus, where the parties have failed to express their intention in clear terms, the law cannot enforce their agreements.

Example 7.23. *A* agreed to purchase a horse from *B* for Rs. 2000. He also agreed to pay Rs. 100 more if the horse proved lucky. It was held that the agreement was void. It was observed that the court had no machinery to determine what luck, bad or good, the horse had brought to the buyer.

[*Guthina* v. *Lynn* (1831) 2. B. Ad. 232]

Example 7.24. *A* agreed to sell his cycle to *B* for a price which *B* may be able to pay. The agreement is void as it is not certain about the price to be paid by *B*.

Example 7.25. *A* agreed to sell his radio to *B* for Rs. 500, or Rs. 800. The agreement is void as there is no certainty about the price. It is not clear whether the price is Rs. 500, or Rs, 800.

Example 7.26. *A* agreed to sell to *B* 100 tones of oil. The agreement is void as it is not certain about the quality and kind of oil.

But sometimes, the meaning of the agreement is capable of being made certain. In such cases, the agreement is not void, *e.g.*, where the price is left to be fixed by third party, there is no uncertainty about the price as it can be made certain by the third party.

Example 7.27: *A* agreed to sell to *B*, 100 tins of coconut oil at the price to be fixed by C. This is a valid agreement.

Similarly, if the agreement is totally silent about the price, it will be valid because in that case Section 2 of the Sale of Goods Act will apply, and the reasonable price shall be payable.[9]

In the following examples also there is no uncertainty about the meaning and terms of the agreement.

Example 7.28. *A* agreed to sell to *B* all the production of his factory situated in Okhla. This is a valid agreement as there is no uncertainty about the product to be sold.

Example 7.29. *A*, a dealer of 'crompton' fans only, agreed to sell to *B* 200 pieces of fans @ Rs. 1000 each. This agreement is valid, as the nature of *A's* trade is an indication that the agreement is for the sale of 'crompton' brand of fans.

7.9. WAGERING AGREEMENTS

The term 'wagering agreement' or 'wager ' may be defined as an agreement in which one person agrees to pay certain amount of money (*i.e.*, stake money) to the other person on the happening or non-happening of a specified uncertain event. The wagering

9. *Law of Contract*, 25 [23rd Edn. By Guest, 1972].

agreements are void. This provision is contained in Section 30 of the Indian Contract Act, which reads as under:

"Agreements by way of wager and void".

Thus, a wagering agreement is void. It is to be noted that the term 'wagering agreement' or 'wager' has not been defined in the Indian Contract Act. However, this term has been interpretted by various courts. And its meaning becomes clear from the following judicial observations:

(1) *"Sir William Anson's definition of 'wager' as a promise to give money or money's worth upon the determination or ascertainment of an uncertain event brings out the concept of wager declared void by Section 30 of Indian Contract Act".*[10]

(2) *"A wagering agreement is one by which two persons, professing to hold opposite views touching the issue of a future uncertain event, mutually agree that, dependent on the determination of that event, one shall pay or hand over to him a sum of money or other stake..... It is essential in a wagering agreement that each party may under it either win or lose. Whether he will win or lose being dependent on the issue of the event and, therefore remaining uncertain until that issue is known, If either of the parties may win but cannot lose, it is not a wagering agreement".*[11]

Thus, a wager may be defined as an agreement to pay money or money's worth on the happening or non-happening of a specified uncertain event. It is a game of chance in which winning or losing is wholly dependent on specified uncertain event, *i.e.*, it is an agreement of betting. It may be noted that the contracting parties should not have any interest in the contract other than the amount which they will win or lose.

Example 7.30. *A* and *B* enter into an agreement that if it rains on Monday, *A* will pay Rs. 100 to *B*. And if it does not rain on Monday, *B* will pay Rs. 100 to *A*. This is a wagering agreement.

7.10. ESSENTIALS OF WAGERING AGREEMENTS

1. ***The agreement must be dependent upon uncertain event***
2. ***There must be mutual chances of gain or loss***
3. ***The parties must not have any other interest in the event***
4. ***The parties must not have any control over the event***

Following are the essentials of a wagering agreement :

1. *The agreement must be dependent upon uncertain event:* It is an important element of a wagering agreement that it must be dependent upon a uncertain event, *i.e.*, the agreement must be conditional on the determination of an uncertain event. In other words, the performance of the agreement must depend upon the happening or non-happening of an uncertain event. Generally, the wager contemplates a future event. However, it may also relate to an event which has already happened in the past. But in such cases, the parties must not be aware of the results of the event or the time of its happening.[12]

Example 7.31. *A* cricket match between India and Australia is to start on 15th Dec. 2002 in Bomay. *A* and *B* enter into an agreement that if India wins *A* will pay Rs. 500 to *B*, and if Australia wins, *B* will pay Rs. 500 to *A*. This is a wagering agreement and is void. If India wins the match, *B* cannot recover the amount. Now suppose that the test match has already been concluded. But *A* and *B* are not aware of the result of the match. They enter into an agreement that *A* will pay Rs. 500 to *B* if India had won the match, and *B* will pay Rs. 500 to *A* if Australia had won the match. It is also a wagering agreement.

10. *Suba rao j. in Gherulal* v. *Mahadeo,* (1959) 2 SCR 342.
11. *Howkins j. in Carlil* v. *Carbolic Smoke Ball Co.,* (1892) 2 QB. 484.
12. *Ansons Principles of the Law of The Law of Contract,* 22nd Edn by A.G. Guest 1964 p. 301.

2. *There must be mutual chances of gain or loss:* It is another essential element of the wagering agreement that each party to the agreement must stand to win or lose. In other words, upon the conclusion of the agreement, one party has to win while the other to lose.

Example 3.32. A hockey match is going to be held between India and Pakistan. *A* agrees to pay Rs. 1,000 to *B* if India wins the match. And *B* agrees to Pay Rs. 1,000 to *A* if Pakistan wins. This is a wagering agreement. In this case each party has the chances to win or lose. And the gain of one party, will be the loss of the other.

It may be noted that if in an agreement, one party may win and cannot lose, or he may lose and cannot win then the agreement is not the wagering agreement.

Example 7.33. Carbolic Smoke Ball Co. adversited in the newspaper that anyone who would take, according to the printed directions, the smoke balls manufactured by it would not contract the increasing epidemic influenza or cold. The reward of £100 was offered by the company to any one who contracted influenza or cold. One Mrs Carlill used the somke balls according to the printed directions. But subsequently, she suffered from influenza. It was held that she was entitled to recover the award. In this case the transaction was not a wager. Because, the company had no chance of winning, neither Mrs. Carlill any chance of losing.

[*Carlill* v. *Carbolic Somke Bill Co.*, (1892) 2 QB 484]

3. *The parties must not have any other interest in the event:* It is also an important essential element of a wagering agreement. Neither party should have any interest in the happening or non-happening of the event other than the sum or stake he will win or lose. If either party has some other interest, the transaction will not be a wager.

Example 7.34. *A* is the owner of a house. He insures his house against the loss by fire with *B* & Co., an insurance company. According to the terms of the insurance policy, *A* has to pay Rs. 5,000 per annum as the premium. And in case the house is destroyed in fire, the insurance company will pay actual amount of loss suffered by him. This is not a wagering agreement, as *A* has interest in his own house which he wants to protect by insuring it. Moreover, on the happening of the event (*i.e.*, fire) *A* will not gain anything. He will merely be indemnified for the loss suffered by him on the happening of the event. It is contract of insurance, and is valid.

4. *The parties must not have any control over the event:* It is also an essential element of a wagering agreement. Neither party should have any control over the happening of the event one way or the other. If either party has the event in his own hands, the transaction will not be a wager.

Example 7.35. *A* and *B* enter into an agreement. *A* agrees to pay Rs. 1000 to *B* if he (*B*) does not marry *C*. And *B* agrees to pay Rs. 1000 to *A* if he (*B*) marries C. It is not a wagering agreement as *B* has the event under his control.

5. *The promise must be to pay money or money's worth:* The parties must agree to pay money or money's worth on the happening or non-happening of the uncertain event.

7.11. EFFECTS OF WAGERING AGREEMENTS

The effects of wagering agreements may be discussed under the following two heads:

1. *Effects on main transaction:* A wagering agreement is void, and cannot be enforced in a Court of Law. This provision is contained in Section 30 of the Indian Contract. Act, which expressly states that agreements by way of wager are void. Thus, the winner in wager cannot recover the stake money from the other party to the agreement. It is important to note that event a new promise to pay the stake money (already won) upon a wager, is also void, Moreover, the money deposited with a third person (stakeholder) to enable him to pay to the winner cannot be recovered by the winner. But the depositor may recover it back from the stakeholder if it has not been paid to the winner. However, where the money has already been paid to the winner, it cannot be recorded back from him.

Example 7.36. *A* agreed to pay Rs. 500 to *B* if *X* won election. And *B* agreed to pay Rs. 500 to *A* if *X* did not win. Both of them deposited this amount with *C*, a stakeholder, to enable him to pay to the winner. It is a wagering agreement, and cannot be enforced in a Court of Law. If *X* wins the election, *B*, the winner, cannot recover from *C* the amount deposited by *A*. However, *A* can recover his money back from *C* if it has not been paid to *B*. But if *C* pays the money to *B*, the money cannot be recovered back from him.

Though a wagering agreement is void and unenforceable, but it is not forbidden by law.[13] In other words the wagering agreements are void but not unlawful (illegal). However, in Gujarat and Old Bombay States, the wagering agreements have been declared to be illegal.[14]

2 ***Effects on callateral transactions:*** A'collateral transaction' means an incidental or a parallel transition. For example, where *A* bets with *B* and loses; and obtains a loan from *C* in order to pay to *B*. In this case the transaction between *A* and *B* is the main transaction, and the transaction between *A* and *C* is the collateral transaction.

The transactions collateral to the main transaction are not void. And thus, these transactions are valid and enforceable.

Example 7.37. *A* took a bet of Rs. 500 with *B* that a certain car would win in the certain car rally. *A* borrowed Rs. 500 from his friend *C* for the purpose of this bet. *A* lost the bet and paid Rs. 500 to *B*. In this case, the agreement between *A* and *C* is collateral to the wagering agreement, therefore it is not void. *A* is liable to repay the amount of loan to *C*.

Example 7.38. *A* instructed his agent *B* to enter into a wagering agreement on his behalf. Accordingly, *B* entered into a wagering agreement with *C*. But *B* lost on this agreement out of his own pocket. In this case, the wagering agreement is between *A* (the principal) and *C*. But payment by *B*, the agent, on behalf of his principal *A* is a collateral one. Therefore, *B* can recover from *A* the amount paid by him (*B*).[15]

Note : In Gujarat and old Bombay the collateral transaction are also void because in these States the wagering agreements are declared as illegal. In England, the wagering agreements are unlawful, therefore collateral transactions are also void there.

7.12. EXCEPTIONS IN THE WAGERING AGREEMENTS

1. *Horse racing competition*
2. *Skill competition*

The general rule is that all the wagering agreements are void. However, in the following two exceptional cases the wagering agreements are valid and binding.

1. ***Horse racing competition:*** Horse racing is permitted by some local laws, and the State Government may authorise the horse racing competitions. Sometimes, a person makes a subscription or contribution towards any prize or sum of money which is to be awarded to the winner of any horse race. Such a subscriptions or contribution towards prize, etc, of the value of Rs. 500 or upward, shall not be unlawful. An agreement to subscribe or contribute towards such prize or sum of money is also valid and enforceable.

Example 7.39. The Race Course Authority was permitted to conduct the horse race competitions. *A* agreed with the Race Course Authority to contribute Rs. 1000 towards the money which was to be paid to the winner of the horse race to be held on a particular day. This is not a wagering agreement.

It may, however, be noted that betting on horse race is a wagering agreement.

13. *Gherulal Parekh* v. *Mahadeo Das* AIR 1959 SC 781.
14. Avoiding wagers (Amendment) Act 1861.
15. AIR 1954 SC 500, AIR 1960 Kerala 122; However in such cases, The agent can recover the amounts from his principal only on the proof of actual payment. He cannot recover on the ground that he has become liable to pay to third parties (AIR 1951 Nagpur 392).

Example: 7.40. *A* bet with *B* that a particular horse would win the race to be held on a particular day. This is a wagering agreement.

2. ***Skill competition:*** Sometimes, skill plays a substantial part for the successful solution of certain competitions, *e.g.*, crosswords competitions, picture puzzles, athletic competitions, etc. And the prizes are awarded according to the merits of the solution. Such prize competitions which are games of skill, are not wagers. Thus, literary competitions which involve the application of skill, and in which an effort is made to select the best and most skillful competitor, are not wagers, But where prizes depend upon a chance, that is a lottery (*i.e.*, a game of chance), and therefore a wager.

Example 7.41: A crossword puzzle was given in a newspaper. It was stated in the newspaper that whose solution of the crossword puzzle would correspond (*i.e.* agree) with the solution kept with the editor, he would be given the first prize, This is a game of chance and therefore a lottery. And thus, is a wagering transaction.[*State of Bombay* v. *R.M.D. Chamarbangwala*, AIR 1957 SC 699].

Note: According to the Prize Competition Act 1955, the prize competitions involving games of skill are not wagers. But if the amount of prize exceeds Rs. 1000 they will be regarded as gambling and void.

7.13. IMPORTANT TRANSACTIONS OF WAGERING NATURE

1. *Lotteries*
2. *Settlement of difference in prices*
3. *Speculative transactions*

There are certain important transactions which may come within the purview of wager, and are void. These may be discussed under the following heads:

1. ***Lotteries:*** The term 'lottery' may be defined as the distribution of prizes by lot or chance. In other words, a lottery is a game of chance in which the event, either of gain or loss of the absolute right to prize, is wholly dependent on the drawing of lots.[16] It necessarily involves an agreement by way of wager between the persons taking part therein. Thus, the winning in the lottery is not possible to be recoverable through Court of Law.[17] Moreover, an agreement to buy a lottery ticket is a wagering agreement and is void.[18] It may be noted that the government may give sanction for conducting lotteries. But the sanction of the government does not change the nature of the lotteries, *i.e.*, it remains a wager. The only effect of the sanction is that the persons conducting the lotteries will not be liable to punishment.[19]

Sometimes, theres is no invitation to the public, but the transaction is limited to a certain number of subscribers each of whom gets his money's worth . In such cases, the transaction is not a lottery, though there is an element of chance in it.[20]

Example 7.42. Twenty-two persons were conducting a transaction. According to the terms and conditions of the transaction, each person was to contribute Rs. 10 for first week. At the end of the week, the prizes were drawn and the winner gets gramophone and drops out of transaction. The remaining members contribute for the next week. Again the prizes were drawn at the week-end. The new winner gets the gramophone and drops out of the transaction. The similar contributions and drawings continued for 20 week, and the subscribers keep on getting the gramophone and dropping out. It was held that it was not a lottery, and thus not punishable under Section 294-

16. *Maung San* v. *I.T.A Club*, 38 IC 566.
17. 1970 Ker LT 358; 1970 Ker. LJ 193.
18. AIR 1917 Bombay 138.
19. *Dorabfi* v. *Lance* 1942 Bombay 676; The persons conducting lotteries without sanction of the government are punishable under Section 294 A of the Indian Penal Code.
20. *Durga* v. *Kedaria*, 149 IC 489.

A of Indian Penal Code. In this case, each person got his money's worth though some got less and some more by lot. Moreover, the transaction was conducted between definite number of persons and there was no invitation to public to join. Thus, the transaction was not a lottery and did not amount to wager. [AIR 1934 Madras 136]

2. *Settlement of difference in prices:* Sometimes, the parties enter into an agreement for the purchase and sale of goods without any intention of delivering the goods. In fact, the parties agree to settle the difference between the contract price and the market price of the goods on a specified day. Such type of transactions are of wagering nature and therefore void.

Example 7.43. *A* agrees to purchase 100 bags of rice from *B* at the rate of Rs. 100 per bag. *B* agrees to deliver the bags to *A* at the rate of Rs. 100 per bag. As per agreement, the bags are to be delivered after three months. However, the intention of both the parties is not to actually deliver the bags but to settle the difference between the contract price of Rs. 100 per bag and the market price after three months. Now suppose, after three months the market price of one bag is Rs. 125. Then as per the agreement *A* will pay Rs. 2500 (Rs. 25 per bag) being the difference between the contract price and market price. This is a wagering transaction ,therefore void.

It may be noted that in order to constitute a wagering transaction, the intention of both the parties must be to settle the differences, *i.e*,. there must be common intention to wager. In other words, neither party should intend to perform the contract itself, but only to pay difference.

3. *Speculative transactions:* Sometimes, a person enters into an agreement with another person to purchase some goods. And thereafter, he agrees to sell the same quantity of goods either to the same seller or to someone else so as to secure the profits or to ascertain the loss. Such transactions are known as speculative transactions. A speculative transaction is not necessarily a wagering agreement. It will be a wager only when at the time of entering into the agreement, the parties agree that the delivery of the goods shall not be made under any circumstances. In other words, a speculative transaction will be a wager only when the intention of the parties is not to perform the contract, but to settle the difference between the price at the time of the agreement and at the time of settlement.[21]

7.14. CONTRACT OF INSURANCE

The term 'contract of insurance' may be defined as the contract whereby a person (*i.e.*, an insurer or insurance company) in consideration of a certain sum of money, undertakes to make good the loss of the other arising on the happening of uncertain specified event *e.g.*, death, fire, accident, etc. In other words, it is the contract where a person, in consideration of certain sum of money, agrees to bear the risk regarding the property or life of another person in which such other person has insurable interest. The term 'insurable interest' means a pecuniary (*i.e.*, monetary) interest in the subject- matter of insurance which the insured person wants to protect against some uncertain event. Thus, it is the 'risk of loss' to which the insured person is likely to be exposed on the happening of the event insured against *e.g.*, a person has an insurable interest in his own life, and he can enter into a valid contract to insure his life. Similarly, a person has an insurable interest in his house, he can insure it against the loss of fire. At the first sight, the contract of insurance appears to be a wagering agreement, as the insured person has to receive some money on the happening of an uncertain event (*e.g.*, accident, fire, death, etc) Though it resembles to a wagering agreement, but precisely it is not a wagering agreement. It is perfectly valid and recognised by law.

---

21. AIR 1961 Rajasthan 52.

7.15. COMPARISON BETWEEN A WAGERING AGREEMENT AND A CONTRACT OF INSURANCE

The following table gives the comparison between a wagering agreement and a contract of insurance:

S.No. *Wagering Agreement*	*Contract of Insurance*
1. The parties have no interest in the happening or non-happening of the event except the money or stake that a party will win or lose. In other words, the parties have no other interest to be protected by the agreement.	The parties (insured person) has an 'insurable interest' in the contract. In other words, the contract is entered into to protect the insurable interest.
2. The amount is fixed which is to be paid to the winner on the conclusion of the uncertain event.	The amount which is to be paid to the insured person is not fixed. Only the actual loss suffered by him is to be compensated. However, in case of life insurance, the amount of loss may be treated as fixed. Because on the death of the insured person, the amount of policy is taken the amount of loss as it is not possible to value one's life.
3. It is not a contract of indemnity because the amount to be paid to the winner is not paid as a compensation for loss.	It is a contract of indemnity because, the underlying idea of the contract is to indemnify the insured person, *i.e.,*, to compensate him for the loss suffered by him. However, the life insurance contracts are not the contracts of indemnity.
4. It is void and without any legal effect. Moreover, it cannot be enforced by the Courts of Law.	It is a valid and can be enforced in Court of Law. Moreover, the contracts of insurance are beneficial to the general public and, therefore, encouraged.

7.16. AGREEMENTS FOR IMPOSSIBLE ACTS

Sometimes, the parties enter into an agreement for some act which is not possible to do. Such type of agreements are void. This provision is contained is Section 56 of the Indian Contract Act, which reads as under:

"An agreement to do an act impossible in itself is void".

Thus, an agreement to do an impossible act is void.

Example 7.44: *A* agreed with *B* to discover a treasure by magic. *B* agreed to pay Rs. 1000 to *A* for this act. The agreement is void on the ground of impossibility.

Example 7.45: *A* agreed with *B* to draw two parallel lines in such as way that they will cross each other. *B* agreed to pay Rs. 100 to *A* for this act. This agreement is void on the around of impossibility.

Note. The agreements to do impossible acts will be discussed in detail in Chapter 12.

7.17. COMPARISON BETWEEN A VOID AGREEMENT AND A VOID CONTRACT

A void contract is one which is also without any legal effects. The term 'void contract' is defined in Section 2(j) of the Indian Contract Act, which reads as under:

"A contract which ceases to be enforceable by law become void when it ceases to be enforceable".

Thus, a void contract is one which ceases to be enforceable by the Court of Law. It may be noted that contract should be valid and legally enforceable at the time when it was made. But later on, if it becomes legally unenforceable due to some reasons, it is called a void contract. The following table givens the comparison between a void agreement and a void contract:

S.No.	*Void Agreement*	*Void Contract*
1.	It is without any legal effect and cannot be enforced in a Court of Law.	It is also without any legal effect and can not be enforced in a Court of Law.
2.	It is *void ab initio* (*i.e.*, void form the very beginning). And no contract comes into existance at all.	It is not *void ab initio*. Initially, a valid contract comes into existence but, it becomes void and unenforceable later on.

Note. The legal effect of void agreements and void contract is the same. Both cannot be enforced in a Court of Law. Thus to avoid confusion, void contract may be called as void agreements.

7.18. COMPARISON BETWEEN A VOID AGREEMENT AND A VOIDABLE CONTRACT

A voidable contract is one which is enforceable at the option of one party but not at the option of the other. The term 'voidable contract' is defined in Section 2(*i*) of the Indian Contract Act, which reads as under:

"An agreement which is enforceable by law at the option of one or more of the parties thereon, but not at the option of the other or others, is a voidable contract".

Thus, a contract which can be put to an end at the potion of one party to the contract, is called a voidable contract. When the consent of one party is obtained by fraud, misrepresentation, etc., the contract is voidable at the potion of the party whose consent was so obtained. He may avoid (*i.e.*, put an end to) the contract. It may be noted that a voidable contract remains valid and binding till it is avoided by the party entitled to do so . The following table gives the comparison between a void agreement and voidable contract :

S.No	*Void Agreement*	*Voidable Contract*
1.	It is *void ab initio* (*i.e.*, void from the very beginning). Thus, it has no legal effect and is not enforceable at all.	It is not *void ab initio*. It becomes void and unenforceable only when the aggrieved party (*i.e.*, whose consent is obtained by fraud, misrepresentation, etc.) chooses to avoid it.
2.	In this case, no conract comes into existance	In this case, a valid contract comes into existence. And it remains valid till it is avoided by the party who is entitled to do so.
3.	In this case, even a third party cannot acquire any title to the goods obtained under a void agreement. This is so because a void agreement has no legal effect.	In this case, a third party acquires a valid title to the goods obtained under a voidable contract. However, the goods must have been obtained before the contract is avoided. And the third party must have bought the goods for value and without any knowledge of voidable contract.
4.	In this case, if one party fails to perform his obligation, the other party is not entitled to any compensation from him. This is so because, a void agreement has no legal effect.	In this case, if a party rightfully avoids (*i.e.*, puts an end to) the contract, he can claim compensation from the other party for loss or damages suffered by him on account of non-performance of the contract.

LEGAL PROVISIONS (SECTIONS) DISCUSSED IN THE CHAPTER

Important legal provisions (sections) of the Indian contract Act, 1872, discussed in this chapter, are reproduced hereunder:

1. ***Section 2 (g): Void Agreement.***

   An agreement not enforceable by law is said to be void.

2. ***Section 26: Agreement in Restraint of Marriage is Void***

   Every agreement in restraint of the marriage of any person, other than minor, is void

3. ***Section 27: Agreement in Restraint of Trade is Void***

   Every agreement by which any one is restrained form exercising a lawful profession, trade or business of any kind, is to that extent void.

   Exception 1.—Saving of agreement not to carry on business of which goodwill is sold.—One who sells the godwill of a business may agree with the buyer to refrain from carrying on a similar business, within specified local limits, so long as the buyer, or any person deriving title to the goodwill from him, carries on a like business therin, provided that such limits appear to the Court reasonable, regard being had to the nature of the business.

4. ***Section 28: Agreements in Restraint of legal Proceedings, void***

   Every agreement

   (a) by which any party thereto is restricted absolutely from enforcing his rights under or in respect of any contract, by the usual legal proceedings in the ordinary tribunals, or which limits the time within which he may thus enforce his rights; or

   (b) which extinguishes the rights of any party thereto, or discharges any party thereto, form any liablitity, under or in respect of any contract on the expiry of a specified period so as to restrict any party form enforcing his rights, is void to that extent.

   Exception 1.—Saving of contract to refer to arbitration dispute that may arise.—This section shall not render illegal a contract, by which two or more persons agree that any dispute which may arise between them in respect of any subject or class of subjects shall be referred to arbitration, and that only the amount awarded in such arbitration shall be recoverable in respect of the dispute so referred.

   Exception 2.— Saving of contract to refer questions that have already arisen.—Nor shall this section render illegal any contract in writing, by which two or more persons agree to refer to arbitration any questions between them which has already arisen, or affect any provision of any law in force for the time being as to references to arbitration.

5. ***Section 29: Agreement Void for Uncertainty***

   Agreements, the meaing of which is not certrain or capable of being made certain, are void

6. ***Section 30: Agreements by Way of Wager, Void***

   Agreements by way of wager are void, and no suit shall be brought for recovering anything alleged to be won on any wager, or entrusted to any person to abide the result of any game or other uncertain event on which any wager is made.

   Exception in favour of certian prizes for horse-racing.—This section shall not be deemed to render unlawful a subscription or contribution, or agreement to subscribe or contribute, made or entered into for or toward any plate, prize or sum of money, of the value or amount of five hundred rupees or upwards, to be rewarded to the winner or winners of any horse-race.

7. ***Section 56: Agreement to do Impossible Act, Void***

   An agreement to do an act impossible in itself, is void.

TEST QUESTIONS

1. What do you understand by void agreement? What are the various agreements which have been expressly declared to be void by the Indian Contract Act?
2. "Agreement in restraint of trade is void" — Comment and state exceptions, if any.
3. "Liberty to trade is not an asset which the law will permit a person to barter except in special circumstances within well-recognised limitations"— comment.
4. "Agreement in restraint of legal proceedings is void"—Comment and state the exception, if any.

5. What do you understand by a wagering agreements? What are the essentials of a wagering agreement? Discuss the effects of wagering agreement.
6. What is wager? Discuss its legality.
7. "A wagering agreement is void and unenforceable, but it is not forbidden by law"—critically examine the statement with suitable examples.
8. "The law does not compel the impossible"—comment.
9. State the comparison between the following:
   (*a*) Wagering agreement and contract of insurance.
   (*b*) Void agreement and void contract.
   (*c*) Void agreement and voidable contract.
10. Write notes on the following :
   (*a*) Agreement in restraint of marriage. (*b*) Agreement in restraint of trade.
   (*c*) Uncertain agreements. (*d*) Contract of insurance.

MULTIPLE CHOICE QUESTIONS

1. A void agreement is one which is
   (*a*) not enforceable by law. (*b*) enforceable at the option of both party.
   (*c*) enforceable at the option of both party. (*d*) enforceable with permission of courts.
2. An agreement in restraint of marriage, *i.e.*, which prevents a person from marrying, is
   (*a*) valid (*b*) voidable
   (*c*) void (*d*) contingent.
3. An agreement which puts a partial restraint on marriage, *i.e.* which prevents a person from marrying a particular person, is valid.
   (*a*) True, as partial restraint is recognized by law.
   (*b*) False, as both restraints, complete or partial, makes the agreement void,
4. An agreement in restraint of marriage is valid in case of following persons.
   (*a*) Minors (*b*) Educated
   (*c*) Married (*d*) None of these.
5. An agreement, which prevents a person form carrying a lawful business, is
   (*a*) valid (*b*) void
   (*c*) voidable (*d*) contingent.
6. An agreement in restraint of trade is void only if the restraint imposed is
   (*a*) complete (*b*) partial
   (*c*) conditional (*d*) any of these.
7. All agreements in restraint of trade are void and there are no exception to this.
   (*a*) True, the Indian Contract Act provides so.
   (*b*) False, the Indian Contract Act and Partnership Act contains exceptions.
8. An agreement in restraint of legal proceedings is void. It does not cover an agreement which
   (*a*) restricts absolutely the parties from enforcing their legal rights.
   (*b*) cuts short the period of limitation.
   (*c*) discharges a party from liability or extinguishes the rights of a party.
   (*d*) provides for a reference to arbitration instead of court of law.
9. A agrees to sell his car to *B* at a price which *B* may be able to pay. This agreement is
   (*a*) void (*b*) valid
   (*c*) voidable (*d*) contingent
10. An agreement to pay money or money's worth on the happening or non-happening of a specified uncertain event, is a

(*a*) wagering agreement (*b*) contingent contract
(*c*) quasi contract (*d*) uncertain agreement.

ANSWERS

1. (*a*)	**2.** (*c*)	**3.** (*b*)	**4.** (*a*)	**5.** (*b*)	**6.** (*d*)
7. (*b*)	**8.** (*d*)	**9.** (*a*)	**10.** (*a*)		

OBJECTIVE TYPE QUESTIONS WITH REASONING

State with reasons whether the following statement are correct or incorrect

1. An agreement which does not restrain a person form marrying altogather but simply restrains him form marrying a particular person or form marraing for a fixed period, in valid.
2. An agreement in restraint of trade is void only if the restraint imposed is complete *i.e.*, total.
3. An agreement among partners which restrains an outgoing partner form carrying on a business similar to that of the firm, is void.
4. A restraint on an employee not to engage in a similar business or not to accept similar employment after the termination or completion of employment is void.
5. A person joined service of 20 years and agreed not to work elsewhere during the period of service. The agreement is valid.
6. An agreement which restricts absolutely the parties from enforcing their legal right, is void.
7. An agreement not to file an appeal against the decision of the court is void as being an agreement in restraint of legal proceedings under Section 28.
8. An agreement to refer an existing dispute to arbitration is valid.
9. An agreement the meaning of which is not certain or capable of being certain is not void.
10. An 'agreement to agree in future' is void.
11. An 'agreement to sell' which is totally silent about the price, is void as being uncertain.
12. In England, transactions collateral to wagering agreements are also void.

ANSWERS

1. *Incorrect.* The law on the point is that whether the restraint is complete or partial, the agreement in restraint of marriage in void in both the cases.
2. *Incorrect.* The law on the point is that whether the restraint is complete or partial, the agreement in restraint of trade is void in both the cases.
3. *Correct.* It is the statutory exception to the general rule that an agreement in restraint of trade is void. [section 36 (2), Indian Partnership Act]
4. *Correct.* Such a restraint is not covered under judicially recoginised exception to the rule that an agreement in restraint of trade is void.
5. *Incorrect.* Such a term is unreasonable and is not covered under the judicially recognised exceptions of service agreements.
6. *Correct.* Agreements in restraint of legal proceedings have been specifically declared to be void under Section 28 of the Indian Contact Act.
7. *Incorrect.* It has been judicially held that the right to appeal does not come within the purview of section 28 [See *Anant Das* v. *Ashburnes & Co*, (1876) I Allahabad 267]
8. *Correct.* It is the statutory exception to the general rule that an agreement in restraint of legal proceedings in void [Section 28, Exception II]
9. *Incorrect.* Uncertain agreement have been specifically declared to be void by Section 29 of the Indian contract Act.
10. *Correct.* In is an uncertain agreement. In this case, there is no certainty whether the parties will agree under the future circumstances.

11. *Incorrect*. Such an agreement is valid. In this case Section 2 of the Sale of Goods Act will apply and the reasonable price shall be payable.
12. *Correct*. In England, the wagering agreement are unlawful. And a transaction collateral to an unlawful agreement is also unlawful and void.

PRACTICAL PROBLEMS

1. *A* agreed to marry *B* and none else, and further agreed to pay Rs. 50,000 to *B* if he married someone else. But, *A* married another girl *C* and *B* sued *A* for the recovery of Rs. 50,00 as per the terms of the agreement. Will she succeed? Give reasons.

   Hint: No, *B* will not succeed in her action. Here, the agreement between *A* and *B* being in restraint of marriage, is void under section 26 of the Indian contract Act.
2. *A* and *B*, two rival shopkeepers in a locality in Delhi, entered into an agreement that if *A* would close his shop in that locality then *B* would pay Rs. 100,000 to him. Accordingly, *A* closed his business in that locality. *B* failed to pay the agreed amount and *A* sued *B* for recovery of the same. Will he succeed? Give reasons.

   Hint: No, *A* will not succeed in his action. Here, the agreement between *A* and *B*, being in restraint of trade, is void under section 27 of the Indian Contract Act.
3. *A* agreed to purchase a horse from *B* for Rs. 5000 and also agreed to pay Rs. 1000 to *B* if the horse proved lucky. Is it a valid agreement? Give reasons.

   Hint: No, it is not a valid agreement. Here, the agreement, being uncertain, is void under section 29 of the Indian contract Act. There is no machinery to determine what luck, good or bad , the horse would bring for the buyer.
4. *A* took a bet of Rs. 5,000 with *B* that a certain car would win the Delhi Car Rally. *A* and *B* are both residents of Delhi. *A* borrowed Rs. 5,000 from his friend *C* for this purpose. *A* lost the bet and paid Rs 5000 to *B*. Can *C* recover the loan amount form *A*? Give reasons. What would have been the difference had the transaction took place in Mumbai between the parties residing there?

   Hint : Yes, *C* can recover the loan amount form *A*. The transaction between *A* and *C* is a collateral transaction which is valid though the main transaction between *A* and *B* is void, being a wager. Had the transaction took place in Mumbai, *C* could not have recovered the loan as in Mumbai the wager transactions are illegal and a transaction collateral to it is also void on the ground of illegality.
5. *A* took a bet of Rs.1,000 with *B* that a certain horse would win the race. *A* borrowed Rs.1,000 from his friend *C* for the purpose of this bet and entered into an agreement with him (*C*) that *A* would return Rs.2,000 if he (*A*) won the bet, but if he lost, nothing would be returned. *A* won the bet. Can *C* recover Rs.2,000 from *A* as per the agreement?

   Hint: No, *C* cannot recover any amount form *A*. Here, both the agreement *i.e.* between *A* and *B*, and between *A* and *C* are of wagering nature and void under section 30 of the India contract Act.
6. *A* and *B* enter into an agreement by which *A* agrees to pay Rs. 5,000 to *B* if he does not marry *C*, and if *B* marries *C* then he (*B*) will pay Rs. 5,000 to *A*. Is it a wagering agreement? Give reasons.

   Hint: No, it is not a wagering agreements. One of the essential of a wagering agreement is that neither party should have any control over the happeing of the event one way or the other. In this case, *B* has the event under his control.
7. *A* agreed to sell his car to *B* for Rs. 40,000 or Rs. 50,000. Can this agreement be enforced in a court of law? Give reasons.

   Hint: No, it cannot be enforced in a court of law? This agreement in void as there is no certainly about the price *i.e.*, whether the price is Rs. 40,000 or Rs.50,000.

ILLEGAL AGREEMENTS

8.1. INTRODUCTION

In the previous chapter, we have discussed certain agreements which are void and cannot be enforced in a Court of Law. However, they are not illegal, *i.e.,* they are not forbidden by law. There are certain agreements, which are directly forbidden by law and are, therefore, void. Such agreements are known as illegal agreements. In this chapter, we shall discuss the legal position of such agreements.

8.2. DEFINITION OF ILLEGAL AGREEMENTS

The term 'illegal agreement' may be defined as the agreement which is expressly or impliedly forbidden by law *e.g.,* by Indian Penal Code, or by some other special legislation, etc. Thus, an agreement to commit a murder, or to publish a libel (a defamatory statement) is an illegal agreement. Moreover, the agreements, which are immoral or opposed to public policy, are also illegal.

The illegal agreements are void and do not confer any rights and obligations on the parties concerned. As a result of this, they are not enforceable in a Court of Law.

Note: An illegal act is one which the law directly forbids. But an act is not illegal in the strict sense simply because it is not recognised by the law as capable of giving rise to rights.[1]

Example 8.1. *A* promised to give Rs. 1000 to *B* if he (*B*) would steal C's car and deliver it to *A*. It is an illegal agreement as the theft is forbidden by law.

Example 8.2. *A, B* and *C* entered into an agreement to carry on the business of smuggling, and agreed to divide the profits in equal shares. It is an illegal agreement as the smuggling is forbidden by law.

Example 8.3. *A* agreed with *B*, a prostitute, to give her certain ornaments on hire. *A* knew that *B* had to use these ornaments in the furtherance of her trade. *B* failed to pay the hire charges, and *A* filed a suit for the recovery of the same. It was held that the agreement was illegal and void. And thus, *A* could not recover anything from *B*.[Based on *Uphill* v. *Wright* (1911) 1 K.B. 506]

8.3. EFFECTS OF ILLEGAL AGREEMENTS

The effects of illegal agreements may be discussed under the following two heads:

1. ***Effects on main transaction:*** We have already discussed that an illegal agreement is void *ab-initio* (*i.e.,* void from the very beginning) and without any legal effects. As a matter of fact, the illegal agreement is non-existent, and the law will not permit the

1. Venkataramaiyas' Law Lexicon Vol. 1; 1971 edn.

parties to enforce any right under it. This is so because the law treats the illegal agreement as if it had not been made at all. Therefore, no remedy is available to either party. Thus, nothing can be recovered under the illegal agreement. And if something has been paid by any party, that party cannot get it back from the other party.

Example 8.4. *A* let out his premises to *B*, a known prostitute, for the purpose of her trade. *B* refused to pay the rent of the premises. *A* filed a suit against *B* for the recovery of the rent. It was held that the agreement was illegal and void. And thus, *A* could not recover the rent from *B*.

[*Girardy* v. *Richardson*, (1793) 1 Esp. 13]

It may be noted that in case of illegal agreements, the courts are neutral, *i.e.*, the courts refuse to help either party. In this connection, the following observation of the Supreme Court[2] is worthnoting:

"The court will help neither party. Let the estate lie where it falls".

Thus, no party has any right of action on an illegal agreement.

Example 8.5. *A* entered into an agreement with *B* to sell certain stolen goods to him at a certain price. *B* paid the price to *A*. But *A* refused to deliver the goods. In this case, the agreement is illegal and void. And *B* cannot file a suit against *A* for the non-delivery of the goods. Similarly, if the seller delivers the goods and the buyer fails to pay the price, the seller cannot recover the price from the buyer.

Thus, the plaintiff (*i.e.*, the person who files the suit) who founds his cause of action upon an illegal agreement, will not get any assistance from the court. And the defendant (*i.e.*, the person against whom the suit is filed) may retain the benefit, if any, received under the illegal agreement. It appears that as a result of court's refusal to help the plaintiff, the defendant who is equally guilty, stands to win. However, this does not mean that the courts help the defendant. As a matter of fact, the defendant gets the advantage of court's neutrality, *i.e.*, court's refusal to help either party. It may be noted that the court refuse to help only when both the parties are equally guilty.

The general principle of law that no suit can be filed in respect of an illegal agreement, is based on the following two maxims:

(*a*) ***Ex turpi causa non oritur actio:*** This means that from an illegal cause, no action arises. Thus, the courts refuse to help either party. Moreover, the law discourages people from entering into an illegal agreement which arise from an illegal cause.

(*b*) ***In pari delicto potior est conditio defendentis:*** This means that in case of equal guilt, the defendant is in a better position. Thus the party, who has paid some money against an illegal agreement, cannot get it back. In other words, the defendant can keep whatever has been received by him against the illegal agreement. This is because of the fact, that the courts do not help either party.

2. ***Effects on collateral transactions:*** A collateral transaction is one which is incidental or subsidiary to the main transaction *e.g.*, the loan taken for the purpose of carrying an illegal business such as smuggling. The collateral transaction, to an illegal agreement, also becomes illegal. And thus, a collateral transaction is void and cannot be enforced in a Court of Law. It may be noted that even if the collateral transaction is lawful in itself, it will be treated as illegal and void.

Example 8.6. *A* and *B* entered into a partnership agreement for the purpose of carrying on smuggling business. They borrowed money from *C*, a money-lender, for their business. In this case, the main transaction, *i.e.*, the partnership for smuggling business, is illegal. And thus, the loan taken for the same is also illegal and void. *C* cannot get back his money.

2. *Surasaibalini* v. *P. Majumdar*, AIR 1965 SC 1364.

Example 8.7. *A*, the father of a minor girl, borrowed some money from *B* for the purpose of the marriage of his minor girl. It was held that *B* was not entitled to recover the money, the marriage of the minor being illegal under the Child Marriage Restraint Act.

[*C. Shrinivas* v. *R.K. Mohan Rao*, AIR 1952 Madras 579]

8.4. EXCEPTIONS IN ILLEGAL AGREEMENTS

1. *Where the contract is still executory*
2. *Where the recovery is possible without relying on the illegal agreement*
3. *Where the parties are not 'in pari delicto' i.e., not equally guilty*
4. *Where the illegality is servable*

The general rule is that nothing can be recovered under an illegal agreement. However, in the following circumstances, which are exceptions to the general rule, the money paid or property transferred can be recovered back:

1. *Where the contract is still executory:* Sometimes, the purpose of the illegal agreement is still executory, *i.e.*, it has not been carried out. In such cases, the money paid or goods delivered for the illegal purpose may be recovered back.[3] This is based on the principle that a person is allowed to repent in case the contract is still executory.

It may however, be noted that the party entitled to recover the money or goods must also withdraw from the transaction before the illegal purpose is completed. If he waits till the illegal purpose is carried out, or if he seeks to enforce the illegal transaction, he cannot get any relief in either case. Thus, the party entitled to recover must take effective steps for withdrawal from the transaction. But sometimes, the illegal purpose has been frustrated by the failure of the other contracting party to fulfil his part of the illegal contract or due to some other circumstances beyond his control. In such case, the courts may not allow him to recover the money or property.

Example 8.8. In breach of the provisions of Exchange Control Act 1947, *A* entered into an agreement with *B*. By this agreement, *B* agreed to pay £150 worth of Italy currency to enable *A*'s wife and daughter to travel in Italy. *A* deposited his share certificate with *B*, A security for the same. *B* failed to pay the agreed money, and *A* sued *B* for the recovery of his share certificate. In this case, *A* did not succeed in his suit. It was held that there was no withdrawal on *A*'s part. The contract had merely been frustrated by *B*'s failure to supply the money.

[*Bigos's case* (1951) All ER 92].

Note: Sometimes, money is paid to a person to induce him to commit a crime. In such cases, whether or not it can be recovered before he does anything to commit the crime, will depend upon the degree of criminality. For example, where the money is paid to another to commit the murder, may not be recovered.

2. *Where the recovery is possible without relying on the illegal agreement:* Sometime, a party can maintain his action without relying upon the illegal agreement. In such cases, the money or goods transferred under an illegal agreement can be recovered back if the party can frame a cause of action entirely independent of the illegal agreement.

Example 8.9. *A* knowingly let out his house to *B*, a prostitute, at a monthly rent of Rs. 1000. This is an illegal agreement and, *A* cannot recover the rent from *B*. But he can file a suit against her for the eviction and getting the possession of the house in his capacity as the owner. Moreover, for this action, he is not required to disclose the illegality. [*Sita Ram* v. *Radha Rai*, AIR 1968 SC 534].

3. *Where the parties are not 'in pari delicto' i.e., not equally guilty*: Sometimes, the concerned parties are not equally guilty, *i.e.*, one party is more guilty than the other. In such cases, the less guilty party may be able to recover the money paid or property transferred under the illegal agreement. In the following situations the parties may not be equally guilty, and the plaintiff is considered as less guilty:

(*a*) Where the agreement is of such a kind which has been made illegal by the

3. *Anand Prakash Om Prakash* v. *Oswal Trading Agency, AIR 1979 Delhi 24.*

statute (*i.e.,* Act of Parliament) in the interest of a particular class. And the plaintiff belongs to that class.

(*b*) Where the plaintiff is induced to enter into the agreement by fraud or strong pressure.

(*c*) Where a person is under a fiduciary duty to the plaintiff. The plaintiff may be allowed to recover the money or property transferred.

Example 8.10. *A* got 5 insurance policies for his family members with an insurance company. But subsequently, *A* decided not to continue the policies and thus, the premium fell in arrears. Therefore, *B*, an agent of the company, fraudulently represented to *C*, a woman who had no insurable interest in the lives insured, that if she cleared the arrears of premium and thereafter paid the premium regularly, then she would be entitled to the policies money. Accordingly, *C* paid the arrears and the premium on the policies. In fact, the policies were illegal as *C* had no insurable interest in the policies. When *C* came to know that the policies were illegal, she filed a suit against the insurance company for the recovery of the premium which she had paid. It was held that, she was entitled to recover the amount paid. In this case, fraud was practised by the agent of the insurance company, as such *C* was not equally guilty.

[*Hughs* v. *Liverpool Victoria Society,* (1916) 2 K.B. 482]

Example 8.11. For the protection of Africans in Uganda, an Act was passed which prohibited any transfer of property to the non-Africans. In violation of the law, certain land was given to a non-African under a lease. The African party brought an action for the recovery of rent and possession. The other party pleaded illegality. It was held that the African party was entitled to recover the rent and possession of the land, as the law was made for the protection of Africans.

[*Mistri Amar Singh* v. *Kulubya,* (1963) 3 All ER 499; (1964) AC 142 PC].

4. *Where the illegality is servable:* Sometimes, the agreement consists of two parts, one legal and the other illegal. And the legal part is separable from the illegal one. In such cases, the court may enforce the legal part of the agreement. But if the legal and illegal parts cannot be separated, the whole agreement is unenforceable. Thus, the following conditions must be satisfied for the severability and enforcement of legal part:

(*a*) The illegal portion must be capable of being easily separated from the remainder of the agreement.

(*b*) The illegal consideration must not form the whole or the main consideration for the agreement.

(*c*) The severance will not be allowed where it will entirely alter the scope and intention of the agreement.

Sometimes, the persons reciprocally promise, firstly to do certain things which are legal, and secondly to do certain other things which are illegal. In such cases, the first set of agreement can be enforced, whereas the second cannot [Section 57].

Example 8.12. *A* and *B* agreed that *A* would sell a house for Rs. 10 lakh. But if *B* used it as a gambling house, he would pay Rs. 15 lakh to *A* as the price of the house. In this case, the first set of promise, (*i.e.,* to sell the house and pay Rs. 10 lakh for it) is legal and enforceable. And the second set of promise (*i.e.,* promise under which, *B* is allowed to use the house as a gambling house), is illegal and cannot be enforced. The object of second set of promise is unlawful.

Similarly, where there are alternative promises, one of which is legal and the other illegal, the legal promise alone can be enforced [Section 58].

Example 8.13. *A* and *B* entered into an agreement that *A* would pay 1000 to *B*. And in its consideration, *B* would afterwards deliver to *A* either 10 bags of rice or 10 kg of smuggled opium. In this case, the agreement to deliver the rice is legal and enforceable. But the agreement to deliver opium is illegal and cannot be enforced.

8.5. COMPARISON BETWEEN AN ILLEGAL AGREEMENT AND A VOID AGREEMENT

We have already discussed that both the illegal and the void agreements are *void ab initio*, and have no legal effects. But the illegal agreements have wider impact than void agreement as they are also actually forbidden by law. Whereas, the void agreements may or may not be forbidden by law. It is thus concluded that:

"All illegal agreements are void, but all void agreements are not illegal".

The following table gives the comparison between an illegal agreement and a void agreement.

S. No.	*Illegal Agreement*	*Void Agreement*
1.	It is *void ab initio* and has no legal effect as between the immediate parties.	It is also *void ab initio* and has no legal effect as between the immediate parties.
2.	It has a wider impact as it also has further effects. A collateral transaction to an illegal agreement is also illegal, and thus void.	It has no further effects. A collateral trans action to a void agreement is not void and it can be enforced in a Court of Law.

TEST QUESTIONS

1. What do you understand by an illegal agreement? What are the effects of illegal agreements on main transactions, and on collateral transactions?
2. "No action is allowed on an illegal agreement"—explain and state the exceptions to this rule.
3. In case of equal guilt the position of the defendant is better than that of the plaintiff"—explain.
4. State the comparison between illegal agreements and void agreement.
5. "All illegal agreements are void, but all void agreement are not illegal"—Comment.

MULTIPLE CHOICE QUESTIONS

1. An agreement to do an illegal act *e.g.*, to share the earnings of a smuggling business, is
   (*a*) valid (*b*) void
   (*c*) voidable (*d*) contingent.
2. An illegal agreement is void. However, a collateral transaction to an illegal agreement *e.g.* money borrowed to carry on an illegal business, is
   (*a*) void (*b*) valid
   (*c*) voidable (*d*) uncertain
3. Where an agreement consists of two parts one legal and the other illegal, and the legal part is separable from the illegal one, such legal part is
   (*a*) void (*b*) valid
   (*c*) voidable (*d*) illegal
4. *A* knowingly let out his house to *B*, a prostitute. *A* cannot recover the rent as it is an illegal agreement and void. Can he file a suit for eviction and recovery of possession?
   (*a*) Yes, as his right as owner is enforceable
   (*b*) No, as he knowingly let out the house

ANSWERS

1. (*b*) **2.** (*a*) **3.** (*b*) **4.** (*a*)

OBJECTIVE TYPE QUESTIONS WITH REASONING

State with reasons whether the following statements are correct or incorrect.

1. An illegal agreement is void but not forbidden by law.
2. An illegal contract is fatal to the main contract, but not to collateral transactions.
3. Collateral transactions to an illegal agreement also become tainted with illegality.
4. *In pari delicto potiorest conditio defendentis i.e.,* in case of equal guilt, the defendant is in a better position.
5. In case of reciprocal promises, firstly to do certain things which are legal, and secondly to do certain other things which are illegal, both the first and the second set of promises are void agreements as illegality affects both.
6. *A* and *B* agree that *B* shall sell his house to *B* for Rs. 10 lacs. But if he (*A*) uses it as a gambling house then he shall pay the price of Rs. 15 lacs. Due to illegality, no part of the agreement is valid.
7. In case of alternative promises, one branch of which is legal and the other illegal, the legal branch can be enforced inspite of illegality of the other illegal alternate promise.
8. A promise to take either rice or smuggled opium for a consideration of rupees one thousand is wholly void.
9. Where the legal and illegal parts of an agreement cannot be separated, the whole agreement is illegal and unenforceable.
10. Where there are several objects of an agreement with a single consideration, the agreement is void if any of the objects is unlawful.

ANSWERS

1. ***Incorrect.*** An illegal agreement is also directly forbidden by law.
2. ***Incorrect.*** The transactions collateral to the main contract are also illegal, and thus void.
3. ***Correct.*** It is the law on the point that collateral transactions to an illegal agreement are also affected by the illegality, and thus void.
4. ***Correct.*** In case of illegal agreements, the courts do not help either party. The defendant is in a better position as he can keep whatever has been received by him under an illegal agreement.
5. ***Incorrect.*** In such cases, the first set of promises is a valid contract and only the second is a void agreement due to illegality [Section 57].
6. ***Incorrect.*** The first set of reciprocal promises, namely to sell the house and to pay Rs. 10 lacs for it, is valid and enforceable. But, the second set of promises under which *B* may use it as a gambling house, is illegal and void.
7. ***Correct.*** It is the legal position on the point that in such cases the legal branch alone is valid and enforceable [Section 58].
8. ***Incorrect.*** In such cases, the legal branch is valid and enforceable. Here, the promise to take rice for rupees one thousand is valid, but the alternate promise to take smuggled opium is illegal and void.
9. ***Correct.*** It is the legal position on the point [Section 24].
10. ***Correct.*** In such a case, there being *single consideration* for several object of the agreement, the lawful object cannot be separated from the unlawful one. Thus, the whole agreement is illegal and void [Section 24].

PRACTICAL PROBLEMS

1. *A* agreed with *B*, a prostitute, to give her certain ornaments on hire knowing that she (*B*) had to use these ornaments in furtherance of her trade. *B* failed to pay the hire charges and *A* sued her for recovery of the same. Will *A* succeed in his action? Give reasons.

Hint: No, *A* will not succeed in his action. In this case, the agreement is illegal and thus void.

2. *A* entered into an agreement with *B* that if *B* would kill *C*, he would give Rs. 5,0000 to *B*. Accordingly *B* killed *C*. *A* borrowed Rs. 50,000 from *D*, who know the purpose, for making the payment to *B*. Afterwards, *A* refused to return the money to *D* on due date and *D* sued *A* for recovery of the same. Will *D* succeed? Give reasons.

   Hint: No, *D* will not succeed in his action. In this case, the main agreement between *A* and *B* being illegal, the collateral transaction between *A* and *D* is also illegal and thus void.

3. *A* agreed to sell his house to *B* for Rs. 25 lakhs, but if *B* used it as a gambling house then the price would be Rs. 40 lakhs. Is it an enforceable agreement? Give reasons.

   Hint: This agreement consists of two parts one legal and the other legal and both are separable. The first set of promise *i.e.* to sell the house for Rs. 25 lakhs is legal and enforceable. The second set of promise i.e. to allow the house to be used as gambling house, is illegal and cannot be enforced.

4. *A* knowingly let out his house to *B*, a prostitute, at a monthly rent of Rs. 10,000. *B* failed to pay the monthly rent and *A* filed a suit for recovery of the rent, but his action failed on the ground of illegality. Can *A* recover the possession of the house by filing case of eviction? Give reasons

   Hint: Yes, *A* is entitled to the possession by filing a suit for eviction. *A* can file such a suit in his capacity as the owner, and for such a suit he is not required to disclose the illegality.

9
CHAPTER

CONTINGENT CONTRACTS

9.1. INTRODUCTION

We know that the performance of an absolute contract becomes due immediately after making the contract. But sometimes, the performance of a contract is not immediately due, and it becomes so only after the happening or non-happening of some contingency (*i.e.,* some uncertain event). Such contracts are known as contingent contracts. The contracts of insurance,[1] contracts of indemnity and guarantee are the common examples of contingent contracts. In this chapter we shall discuss the legal definition of contingent contracts, and the rules regarding their enforcement and other legal provisions.

9.2. DEFINITION OF A CONTINGENT CONTRACT

The term 'contingent contract', in simple words, may be defined as a conditional contract. This term in legal words, is defined in Section 31 of the Indian Contract Act, which reads as under:

"A contingent contract is a contract to do or not to do something if some event, collateral to such contract, does or does not happen."

The analysis of this section shows that a contingent contract is a contract which is dependent on the happening or non-happening of some event. The performance of a contingent contract becomes due only upon the happening or non-happening of some future uncertain event. In simple words, it is a conditional contract.

1. A contract of insurance, which provides that fixed amount of money shall be paid on the happening of the event, *e.g.,* fire, accident etc., is a contingent contract. But a contract of insurance which provides for the payment according to the loss suffered by the insured person, is a contract of indemnity.

Example 9.1. *A* contracts to pay Rs. 10,000 to *B* if his (*B*'s) house is burnt. This is a contingent contract as its performance is dependent upon an uncertain event (*i.e.*, burning of *B*'s house).

Example 9.2. On 1st January, *A* agrees with *B* that if he (*A*) gets a new car by 13th January, he will sell his old car to him for Rs. 40,000. It is a contingent contract as the performance of *A*'s promise depends upon his getting a new car.

9.3. ESSENTIALS AND LEGAL RULES FOR A VALID CONTINGENT CONTRACT

1. *There must be a valid contract*
2. *The performance of the contract must be conditional*
3. *The event must be uncertain*
4. *The event must be collateral to the contract*
5. *The event may be an act of the party*
6. *The event should not be the discretion of the promisor*

The legal definition of the term contingent contract, discussed in the last article, reveals certain essential elements of a contingent contract. *A* valid contingent contract must satisfy these essential requirements. The essential elements are discussed in points 1 to 4 in the following discussion, and the rest are its legal rules:

1. *There must be a valid contract:* It is the first essential requirement of a valid contingent contract that there must be a valid contract between the parties. In other words, a contract to do or not to do something must be legally valid, *i.e.*, it must fulfil the basic requirements of a valid contract.

2. *The performance of the contract must be conditional:* It is an important requirement of a valid contingent contract that its performance must be conditional. In other words, the performance of a contingent contract must depend upon the happening or non-happening of some future event.

Example 9.3. *A* promises to pay Rs. 500 to *B* if it rains on first of the next month. It is a contingent contract as its performance depends upon future event (*i.e.*, rain).

3. *The event must be uncertain:* It is also an important requirement of a valid contingent contract. The future event, upon which the performance of a contract depends, must be an uncertain event. If the event is certain, *i.e.*, the event is bound to happen, then the contract is not a contingent contract.

Example 9.4. *A* agreed to sell his agricultural land to *B* after obtaining the necessary permission from the collector. As a matter of course, the permission was generally granted on the fulfilment of certain formalities. It was held that the contract was not a contingent contract as the granting of permission by the collector was almost a certainity.

[*Pahunch Lal* v. *Man Singh AIR*, 1971 Allahabad 444].

4. *The event must be collateral to the contract:* It is another important requirement of a valid contingent contract. The uncertain event, upon which the performance of the contract is dependent, must not form a part of the consideration of the contract. In other words, the event must be independent or ancillary to the contract.

Example 9.5. *A* agreed to purchase *B*'s horse for Rs. 2000, if the horse proved lucky. It is not a contingent contract as the event (*i.e.*, luck of the horse) is directly connected with the contract. In this case, the contract is void for uncertainity.

Similarly, a contract for the sale of goods to be delivered on arrival is an absolute contract and not a contingent contract. The delivery of the goods on arrival is a part of the main contract of sale of goods, not a condition upon which the contract is dependent.

[*Ranchhodas* v. *Nathmal Hirachand*, (1949) 51 Bombay L.R. 491].

5. *The event may be an act of the party:* The event upon which the performance of the contract depends, may also be an 'act of the party'. In other words, for the purpose of a contingent contract, the word 'event' also includes the 'act of the party'. Thus, a contract which is dependent upon some 'act of the party' is also a contingent contract. It is important to note that the 'act' may be of the either party to the contract or of a third party.

Example 9.6. *A* agreed to pay Rs. 2000 to *B* if he (*B*) married *C*. It is a contingent contract. In this case, *B*'s act of marrying *C* is an uncertain event because he may or may not marry. Now suppose that there is already an agreement between *B* and *C* whereby *B* has agreed to marry *C*. And in consideration of this agreement, *A* agrees to pay Rs. 2000 to *B*. This is not a contingent contract because its performance does not depend upon an uncertain event. As *B* has already agreed to marry *C*, and thus his marriage with *C* cannot be said to be an uncertain event. In fact, this is an absolute contract, because each party has given a promise to the other party and one's promise is consideration for the other.

6. *The event should not be the discretion of the promisor:* We have already discussed that an event, upon which the contingent contract is dependent, also includes an 'act of the party'. However, the 'mere will or 'discretion' of the promisor is not an event for the purpose of a contingent contract. Thus, if the performance of a contract depends upon the sweet will or discretion of the promisor, the contract is not a contingent contract. Such a contract is void on the ground of uncertainty.

Example 9.7. *A* promise to pay Rs. 500 to *B* if he (*A*) likes to pay. It is not a contingent contract as its performance depends upon the sweet will of the promisor (*A*). In this case, the contract is void on the ground of uncertainity.

Similarly, if a promisor says that for a certain service he will pay whatever he thinks right or reasonable. It is not a valid contract as the performance of the promise depends upon the pleasure and discretion of the promisor.[2] However, a contract dependent on the act of a third person is valid even if it is dependent on the will of the third party.[3] For example, a promise to pay the amount which shall be determined by a third party shall be valid.

9.4. RULES REGARDING ENFORCEMENT OF CONTINGENT CONTRACTS

The contingent contracts are perfectly valid, though they can be enforced in a Court of Law only upon the happening or non-happening of the uncertain event, as the case may be. The rules regarding the enforcement of contingent contracts are contained in Section 32 to 36 of the Indian Contract Act, which may be discussed under the following heads:

1. Contingent contracts dependent on the 'happening' of future uncertain event. (Section 32).
2. Contingent contracts dependent on the 'non-happening' of future uncertain event. (Section 33).
3. Contingent contracts dependent on the 'happening' of specified uncertain event 'within fixed time.' (Section 35)
4. Contingent contracts dependent on the 'non-happening' of specified uncertain event 'within fixed time'. (Section 35).
5. Contingent contracts dependent on impossible event. (Section 36).

These are discussed in the following pages.

9.5. CONTINGENT CONTRACTS DEPENDENT ON THE 'HAPPENING' OF FUTURE UNCERTAIN EVENT

Sometimes, a contingent contract is dependent on the 'happening' of a future uncertain event. In such cases, the contract can be enforced only when that uncertain event has happened [Section 32].

---

2. *Robert* v. *Smith* (1859) 4 H & N. 315.
3. *Sardar Arjun Singh* v. *Sahu* 1950 A 32.

Example 9.8. *A* offered to sell his horse to *B* for Rs. 4,000. Subsequently, *A* entered into a contract with C to sell the same horse to him for Rs. 3500 if *B* refused to buy it. The contract between *A* and C is contingent and can be enforced by law only when *B* refuses to buy the horse from *A*.

It may however, be noted that if the event becomes impossible, then such contract becomes void and thus cannot be enforced by law.

Example 9.9. *A* contracted to pay Rs. 1000 to *B* when he (*B*) married C. But C dies before the marriage. In this case the contract becomes void as *B*'s marriage with C has become impossible.

9.6. CONTINGENT CONTRACTS DEPENDENT ON THE 'NON-HAPPENING' OF FUTURE UNCERTAIN EVENT

Sometimes, a contingent contract is dependent on the 'non-happening' of future uncertain event. In such cases, the contract can be enforced only when the happening of that event becomes impossible as then that event cannot happen. And then the contract becomes enforceable as its performance was dependent on the non-happening of that event [Section 33].

Example 9.10. *A* agreed to pay *B* Rs. 500 if a certain ship did not return. The ship was sunk. It is a contingent contract and can be enforced by law when the ship sinks. Because when the ship sinks the event becomes impossible as the ship can never return.

It may, however, be noted that if the event happens or does not become impossible, then such contracts become void and cannot be enforced by law, *e.g.*, suppose in the above example, the ship returns, then the contract becomes void.

9.7. CONTINGENT CONTRACTS DEPENDENT ON THE 'HAPPENING' OF SPECIFIED UNCERTAIN EVENT WITHIN FIXED TIME

Sometimes, a contingent contract is dependent on the 'happening' of a specified uncertain event within fixed time. In such cases, the contract can be enforced if that event happens within the fixed time.

Example 9.11. *A* agreed to pay Rs. 1000 to *B* if a certain ship returned within a year. It is a contingent contract and can be enforced by law if the ship returns within a year.

Example 9.12. *A* entered into a contract with *B* to buy his house if C died within one year. It is a contingent contract and can be enforced by law if C dies within one year.

It may, however be noted that, a contingent contract dependent on the happening of specified uncertain event within fixed time, becomes void in the following cases [Section 35]:

(*a*) If the event does not happen within the specified time; or

(*b*) If before the expiry of that time, the event becomes impossible.

Example 9.13. *A* agrees to sell his old 'Crown T.V.' to *B* for Rs. 8,000 if he gets a new 'Sony T.V.' from Singapore within 6 months. It is a contingent contract and becomes void if *A* does not get a new 'Sony' television within 6 months.

9.8. CONTINGENT CONTRACTS DEPENDENT ON THE 'NON-HAPPENING' OF SPECIFIED UNCERTAIN EVENT WITHIN FIXED TIME

Sometimes, a contingent contract is dependent on the 'non-happening' of a specified uncertain event within fixed time. In such cases, the contract can be enforced if that event does not happen within fixed time, or if it becomes certain, that such event will not happen [Section 35, second para]. Thus, a contingent contract dependent on the non-happening of a specified event within a fixed time, can be enforced in the following cases:

(*a*) If that event does not happen within the fixed time; or

(*b*) If before the expiry of that time it becomes certain that the event will not happen.

Example 9.14. *A* agrees to pay Rs. 2000 to *B* if a certain ship does not return within a year. It is a contingent contract and can be enforced if the ship does not return within a year. The contract can also be enforced if the ship is burnt or sunk within a year. Because, then it becomes certain that the event will not happen (*i.e.*, the ship will not return).

9.9. CONTINGENT CONTRACTS DEPENDENT ON IMPOSSIBLE EVENT

Sometimes, a contingent contract is dependent on the happening of impossible events. In such cases, the contract is void and cannot be enforced by law. The contract is void because it can never be enforced as the impossible event will never happen. It may be noted that such a contract will be void whether the imposibility of the event is known or not to the parties at the time of making the contract [Section 36].

Example 9.15. *A* agreed to pay Rs. 500 to *B* if he proved that two straight lines can enclose a space. This is a void agreement as two straight lines can never enclose a space.

Example 9.16. *A* agreed to pay Rs. 1000 to *B* if he (*B*) would marry *A*'s daughter *C*. But *C* was dead at the time of the agreement. This is a void agreement as *B*'s marriage with *C* can never take place.

9.10. EVENT BECOMING IMPOSSIBLE WHICH IS A FUTURE CONDUCT OF LIVING PERSON

We have already discussed that the word 'event' also includes the 'act of the party'. And thus, the 'future conduct of a living person' is an event for the purpose of contingent contracts. Such an event shall be considered impossible if such person does anything by which it becomes impossible to perform the contract within any definite time. This rule is contained in Section 34 of the Indian Contract Act, which reads as under:

> *"If the future event on which the contract is contingent is the way in which a person will act at an unspecified time, the event shall be considered to become impossible when such person does anything which renders it impossible that he should so act within any definite time, or otherwise than under further contingencies."*

Thus, if the uncertain event is the future conduct of a third party, such event shall be considered impossible if that person does any act due to which the contract cannot be enforced in any definite time.

Example 9.17. *A* agreed to pay Rs. 5000 to *B* if he (*B*) married *C*. But subsequently, *C* married *D*. In this case, the marriage of *B* with *C* must now be considered impossible. Although it is possible in case *D* dies and *C* may afterwards marry *B*.

9.11. COMPARISON BETWEEN *A* CONTINGENT CONTRACT AND A WAGERING AGREEMENT

The following table gives the comparison between a contingent contract and a wagering agreement:

S. No.	*Contingent Contract*	*Wagering Agreement*
1.	It is perfectly valid and can be enforced in a Court of Law.	It is absolutely void and cannot be enforced in a Court of Law.
2.	In this case, the parties are interested in the happening or non-happening of the event. In other words, the parties are interested in the subject-matter of the contract.	In this case, neither party is interested in the happening or non-happening of the event other than the money he will win or lose. In other words, the parties have no other interest in the subject matter of the agreement except for the sum or stake they will win or lose.
3.	In this case, the future uncertain event is merely collateral or incidental.	In this case, the uncertain event is the only determining factor.
4.	In this case, there may not be reciprocal promises.	In this case, there are reciprocal promises.

5. All contingent contracts are not of a wagering nature, because all the contingent contracts are not void.	All wagering agreements are also contingent contracts because they are dependent on uncertain event.

LEGAL PROVISIONS (SECTIONS) DISCUSSED IN THE CHAPTER

Impartant legal provisions (sections) of the Indian Contract Act, 1872, discussed in this chapter, are reproduced hereunder:

1. *Section 31: Contingent contract Defined.*

   A "contingent contract" is contract to do or not to do something, if some event, collateral to such contract, does or does not happen.

2. *Section 32: Enforcement of Contingent Contract Dependent on the Happening of Event*

   Contingent contracts to do or not to do anything if an uncertain future event happens, cannot be enforced by law unless and until that event has happened. If the event becomes impossible, such contracts become void.

3. *Section 33: Enforcement of Contingent Contract Dependent on Non-Happening of Event*

   Contingent contracts to do or not to do anything if an uncertain future event does not happen, can be enforces when the happening of that event becomes impossible and not before.

4. *Section 36: Agreements Contingent on Impossible Events Void.*

   Contingent agreements to do or not to do anything, if an impossible event happens, are void, whether the impossibility of the event is known or not ot the parties to the agreement at the time when it is made.

TEST QUESTIONS

1. What do you understand by a contingent contract? What are the essentials and legal rules for a valid contingent contract?
2. Discuss the law relating to the enforcement of contingent contracts.
3. What is the validity of a contingent contract dependent (*a*) on an impossible event, and (*b*) on the future conduct of a person?
4. State the comparison between a contingent contract and a wagering agreement.

MULTIPLE CHOICE QUESTIONS

1. A contract dependent on the happening or non-happening of future uncertain event, is a

   (*a*) Contingent contract. (*b*) Uncertain contract.
   (*c*) Void contract. (*d*) Voidable contract.

2. A contingent contract is

   (*a*) void (*b*) voidable
   (*c*) valid (*d*) illegal.

3. A contingent contract dependent on the happening of future uncertain event can be enforced when the event

   (*a*) happens (*b*) becomes impossible
   (*c*) does not happen (*d*) all of these.

4. *A* contingent contract dependent on the non-happening of a future uncertain event becomes void when such event

   (*a*) happens (*b*) does not become impossible
   (*c*) does not happen (*d*) both (*a*) and (*b*).

5. *A* agrees to pay Rs. 1000 to *B* if a certain ship returns within a year. However, the ship sinks within the year. In this case, the contract becomes

(*a*) valid (*b*) void
(*c*) voidable (*d*) illegal.

6. *A* contingent contract dependent on the non-happening of specified uncertain event within fixed time can be enforced if the event
(*a*) does not happen within fixed time (*b*) becomes impossible before the expiry of fixed time
(*c*) happens within the fixed time (*d*) both (*a*) and (*b*)
7. *A* agrees to pay Rs. one lakh to *B* if he brings on earth a star from sky. This is a contingent contract and
(*a*) void (*b*) valid
(*c*) voidable (*d*) illegal.

ANSWERS

1. (*a*)	2. (*c*)	3. (*a*)	4. (*d*)	5. (*b*)	6. (*d*)
7. (*a*)					

OBJECTIVE TYPE QUESTIONS WITH REASONING

State with reasons whether the following statements are correct or incorrect

1. *A* contract dependent on the happening or non-happening of a future uncertain event, is an uncertain contract and thus void.
2. *A* contingent contract is a contract to do or not to do something if some event, collateral to such contract, does or does not happen.
3. *A* contract for the sale of goods to be delivered on arrival is a contingent contract as the delivery of goods is dependent on their arrival.
4. *A* agrees to pay Rs. 1,000 to *B*, if it rains, on next Monday. It is a contingent contract.
5. Where the goods are sent on approval, the contract is a contingent contract.
6. The contracts of insurance, indemnity and guarantee all fall in the category of contingent contracts.
7. A contingent contract is void due to uncertainty as its performance depends upon the happening or non-happening of a future uncertain event.
8. All wagering contracts are contingent contracts but all contingent contracts are not necessarily wagering agreements.
9. A contract is contingent if the happening or non-happening of an event collateral to the contract depends on the mere will or discretion of the promisor.
10. A contingent contract dependent on the happening of an impossible event is valid and can be enforced in a court of law.

ANSWERS

1. *Incorrect.* Such a contract is legally known as a contingent contract and is perfectly valid [Section 31].
2. *Correct.* It is the legal definition of the contingent contract as given in Section 31. In simple words, a contingent contract is a conditional contract.
3. *Incorrect.* The delivery of goods on arrival is a part of the main contract of sale of goods, not a condition upon which the contract is dependent.
4. *Correct.* The main contract between *A* and *B* is dependent upon future uncertain event (*i.e.*, rain). And this event is collateral to the main contract.
5. *Correct.* The performance of this contract depends upon an uncertain event *i.e.*, on the act of the buyer to accept (approve) or reject the goods.

6. *Correct.* The performance of all these contracts depend upon some contingency.
7. *Incorrect.* Contingent contracts have been recognised by the Indian Contract Act.
8. *Correct.* The wagering agreements are dependent on uncertain event, they are necessarily the contingent contracts. But all contingent contracts are not of wagering nature because all the contingent contracts are not void.
9. *Incorrect.* The collateral event, on which the performance of the contract depends, should not be the mere will or discretion of the promisor.
10. *Incorrect.* Such a contract is void and cannot be enforced by law. Since the impossible event can never happen, the contract is void *ab initio*.

PRACTICAL PROBLEMS

1. *A* agrees to sell his car to *B* at a price which shall be determined by *C*, a car dealer. Afterwords, *A* refused to sell the car stating that he is not bound by the agreement as it is void due to uncertainty. Can *B* enforce the agreement?

   Hint : Yes, *B* can enforce the agreement in a court of law. In this case, the agreement between *A* and *B* is a contingent contract which is perfectly valid and enforceable.
2. *A* agrees to pay Rs. 5,000 to *B* if a certain ship returns within a year. However, the ship sinks after two months. Can *B* recover the amount from *A*? Give reasons.

   Hint : No, *B* cannot recover the amount from *A*. It is a contingent contract which has become void as the happening of event (i.e. return of ship) has become impossible.
3. *A* agrees to pay Rs. 10,000 to *B* if a certain ship does not return within a year. Can *B* enforce this agreement? Give reasons.

   Hint : Yes, *B* can enforce this agreement when it becomes enforceable. It can be enforced in two cases, namely (a) if the ship does not return within one year, and also (b) if the ship sinks within one year.
4. *A* agrees to pay Rs.1,000 to *B* if he discovers a treasure by magic within one month. Can this contingent contract be enforced? Give reasons.

   Hint: No, it cannot be enforced in a court of law. A contingent contract dependent on the happening of impossible event is void.

10

CHAPTER

QUASI CONTRACTS

10.1. INTRODUCTION

We have already discussed that a contract can be enforced only when it has the essential elements of a valid contract namely, offer and acceptance, free consent, lawful object and consideration, and capacity of the parties to contract. However, in certain circumstances, the legal rights and obligations can be enforced in the Courts of Law even if there is no essential of a valid contract. The law as well as justice requires that such legal rights and obligations must be enforced, even if no real contract exists. For example, a person, in whose house certain goods were left by some other person by mistake, is bound to return them to the owner. Such kinds of contractual relations are known as 'quasi contracts'. In this chapter, we shall discuss the legal definition of the term quasi contracts, and the different circumstances in which such contracts arise.

10.2. DEFINITION OF A QUASI CONTRACT

The term 'quasi contract' may be defined as 'a relation which resembles that created by a contract.' As a matter of fact, 'quasi contract' is not a contract in the strict sense of the term, because there is no real contract in existence. Moreover, there is no intention of the parties to enter into a contract. It is an obligation, which the law creates in the absence of any agreement. Such obligations imposed by the law are generally described as 'quasi-contractual obligations'. It is to be noted that the Indian Contract Act does not use the term 'quasi contract' for such obligations. It describes the quasi-contracts as "certain relations resembling those created by contract". It is thus, obvious that the essential elements for the formation of a contract are not there. These are called quasi-contracts because the result of these obligations resembles those of a contract. The parties under such relations are put in the same position as if there was a contract between them.

10.3. BASIS OF QUASI CONTRACTS

The quasi contracts are based on the maxim of *'nemo debet locuplatari ex liena justua'*, *i.e.*, no man must grow rich out of another person's costs. In other words, these are based on the equitable principle that a person shall not be allowed to enrich himself at the expense of another. Lord Mansfield explained the quasi-contracts on the principle that 'Law as well as justice should try to prevent unjust enrichment'. The term 'unjust enrichment' means the enrichment of one person at the cost of another. In *Mahabir Kishore v. State of M.P.* AIR 1990 SC 313, the Supreme Court has observed that the principle of 'unjust enrichment' requires, that

1. the defendent (against whom the case is filed) has been enriched by the receipt of a benefit.
2. the enrichment is at the expense of the plaintiff (*i.e.*, who files the case).
3. the retention of the enrichment is unjust.

10.4. CIRCUMSTANCES (OR KINDS) OF QUASI CONTRACTS

Following are the circumstances in which the quasi contractual obligations arise. These are contained in Sections 68 to 72 of the Indian Contract Act.

1. Supply of necessaries to person who are incompetent to contract (Section 68).
2. Payment by an interested person (Section 69).
3. Non-gratuitous acts (Section 70).
4. Finder of goods (Section 71).
5. Payment of money or delivery of goods by mistake or under coercion (Section 72).

10.5. SUPPLY OF NECESSARIES TO PERSONS INCOMPETENT TO CONTRACT

Sometimes, a person supplies the necessaries to a person who is not competent to contract (*i.e.*, minor, persons of unsound mind such as lunatics, etc.), or to another person to whom the incompetent person is bound to support. In such cases, the person supplying the necessaries is entitled to recover the cost of necessaries from the property of such incompetent person. The term 'necessaries'[1] means the necessary items suitable to one's condition in life. This provision is contained in Section 68 of the Indian Contract Act, which reads as under:

"If a person incapable of entering into contract or any one whom he is legally bound to support, is supplied by another person with necessaries suited to his condition in life, the person who has furnished such supplies is entitled to be reimbursed from the property of such incapable person."

Thus, a person who supplies the necessaries to an incompetent person, is entitled to be reimbursed from the property of such incompetent person even if there is no contract between them.

Example 10.1. *A* supplied to *B*, a lunatic, the necessaries suitable to his condition in life. In this case, *A* is entitled to be reimbursed from *B*'s property.

Example 10.2. *A* supplied to the wife and children of *B*, a lunatic, the necessaries suitable to their condition in life. In this case, *A* is entitled to be reimbursed from *B*'s property.

Note: The point in both the above two examples has already been discussed in detail in Chapter 4.

10.6. PAYMENT BY AN INTERESTED PERSON

Sometimes, a person makes the payment which is the legal duty of another person.

---

1. The term 'necessaries' has already been discussed in detail in Chapter 4.

In such cases, the person who made the payment can recover such money from the person who is legally bound to pay. Such type of cases, usually, arise when a person does not pay the legal charges due on his property, and the payment is made by some interested person to protect the property from going into the hands of some third persons, *e.g.*, protecting the property from being auctioned. This provision is contained in Section 69 of the Indian Contract Act, which reads as under:

"A person who is interested in the payment of money which another is bound by law to pay, and who, therefore, pays it, is entitled to be reimbursed by the other."

Thus, an interested person who makes the payment is entitled to recover the money from the person who was legally bound to make the payment.

Example 10.3 *A* held land in Bengal on a lease granted by *B*, a Zamindar. The revenue payable by *B* fell in arrears. As such, his land was advertised for sale by the government. Under the revenue Law, the consequences of such sale was the annulment of *A*'s lease. In order to prevent the consequent annualment of his lease, *A* paid to the government the amount due from *B*. In this case, *A* is entitled to recover the amount from *B*. And *B* is bound to pay the same to *A*.

10.7. CONDITIONS FOR THE RECOVERY OF PAYMENT MADE BY AN INTERESTED PERSON

1. ***The person making the payment must be interested in paying the amount***
2. ***The person making the payment must not be legally bound to pay the amount***
3. ***The other person must be legally bound to make the payment***
4. ***The payment must not be made to self***

The following conditions must be satisfied for the recovery of payment made by an interested person:

1. ***The person making the payment must be interested in paying the amount:*** The first requirement for the application of this provision is that the person making the payment must have some interest in paying the amount. Moreover, the interest which such person seeks to protect must be legally recognised.

Example 10.4 *A*'s goods were wrongfully attached to realise the arrears of government revenue due from *B*. In order to save his property, *A* paid the government dues. It was held that *A* was entitled to recover the amount from *B* as he was interested in paying the dues.

[*Tulsa Kunwar* v. *Jageshwar*, (1906) 28 Allahabad 563]

2. ***The person making the payment must not be legally bound to pay the amount:*** The second requirement is that the person making the payment must not be bound by law to pay the amount. He should only be interested in making the payment in order to protect his own interest. If he himself is bound to make the payment, he cannot recover the same from another person.

Example 10.5. *A* held some land on a lease granted by *B*, a Zamindar. Under the Revenue Law, the tenant was liable to pay the revenue charges on the land. The land revenues fell in arrears and the land was advertised for sale by the government. Under the Revenue Law, the consequence of such sale was the termination of the lease. In order to prevent the termination of the lease, *A* paid the arrears of revenue charges. In this case, *A* cannot recover the revenue charges from *B* as the payment of the same was his own duty.

3. ***The other person must be legally bound to make the payment:*** The third requirement is that the concerned person from whom the money is sought to be recovered must be legally bound to pay the money.

Example 10.6. *A* was the owner of a warehouse. *B* imported certain goods and kept them in *A*'s warehouse without paying the customs duties for the goods imported. The goods were stolen without any negligence on the part of *A*. The custom authorities made a demand on *A* for the payment of custom duties which *A* paid. It was held that *A* was entitled to recover the amount from *B*, as *B* was bound by law to pay the custom duties.

[*Brook's Wharf* v. *Goodman Bros.*, (1937) 1 K.B. 534]

4. *The payment must not be made to self:* Lastly, the person making the payment must pay it to some other person and not to himself. Such cases may arise where the government makes the payment from one department to some other department.

Example 10.7. *A*, a zamindar, gave his land on lease to the Forest Department of Madras Government. *A* failed to pay the land revenue to the government. As such his land was advertised for sale. In order to save the property from being sold, the Forest Department made payment of the land revenues. It was held that the government was not entitled to recover the money from *A*. It was merely a transfer of money from one 'head' to 'another' within the government, and not the actual 'payment to some other person'. Though it was done to save the property from being sold. [*Secy. of State for India* v. *Fernandes*, (1907) 30 Madras 375]

10.8. 'NON-GRATUITOUS' ACTS

The term 'non-gratuitous acts' may be defined as the acts which are not done free. In other words, the acts which are done with the intention of being paid are the non-gratuitous acts. Sometimes, a person does some act or delivers something to another person with the intention of receiving payments for the same. In such cases, the other person is bound to make the payment if he accepts such services or goods, or enjoys their benefits. This provision is contained in Section 70 of the Indian Contract Act, which reads as under:

"Where a person lawfully does anything for another person, or delivers anything to him not intending to do so gratuitously and such other person enjoys the benefits thereof, the latter is bound to make compensation to the former in respect of, or to restore, the things so done or delivered."

Thus, a person who does some non-gratuitous acts for another, is entitled to recover the compensation for such acts.

Example 10.8. *A*, a tradesman, left certain goods at *B*'s house by mistake. *B* treated the goods as his own and used them. In this case, *B* is bound to pay for the goods to *A*.

Example 10.9. *A* saved *B*'s property from fire. The circumstances showed that he intended to act gratuitously. Here, *A* is not entitled to receive the compensation from *B*. But if *A* shows that from the very beginning his intention was of being paid, then he can recover the compensation from *B*.

10.9. CONDITIONS FOR THE RECOVERY OF COMPENSATION FOR NON-GRATUITOUS ACTS

1. *The person must lawfully do something for another person or deliver something to him*
2. *The person must not intend to act gratuitously*
3. *The other person must voluntarily accept the acts or goods and he must have enjoyed the benefits thereof*

The following conditions must be satisfied for the recovery of compensation for non-gratuitous acts.

1. *The person must lawfully do something for another person or deliver something to him:* The first requirement for the application of this provision is that the person must lawfully do something for another person or deliver something to him. The implication of the word 'lawfully' is that there must subsist some lawful relationship between the person claiming compensation and the person against whom it is claimed.

Example 10.10. *A* entered into a contract with the Municipality to construct a market. *A* constructed the market and the Municipality took over the possession and enjoyed the benefits of the market. However, the Municipality refused to pay *A* the agreed amount on the ground that the contract was not binding on the Municipality as it did not bear its seal as required by the Municipality Act. It was held that *A* was entitled to recover his dues under Section 70 of the Indian Contract Act though there was no binding contract between them. In this case, the lawful relationship arises between the two as the work done by *A* has been accepted and enjoyed by the Municipality [*Pallonge & Sons* v. *Lonavala Municipality*, 1969 BLR 835].

2. *The person must not intend to act gratuitously:* The second requirement is that the person doing some act or delivering something must not act gratuitously. In other words, he must have the intention that he will be paid for his services or goods, *i.e.*, he must contemplate payment from the very beginning. And if his intention is not to receive any money for his acts or services, then he cannot recover.

Example 10.11 *A* was managing the estate of his uncle *B*. He was under the impression that he will receive remuneration for his services. In this case, *A* is entitled to receive the compensation from *B* as he renders the services with the intention of getting remunerations.

3. *The other person must voluntarily accept the acts or goods and he must have enjoyed the benefits thereof:* Lastly, the person to whom the goods or services have been rendered, must have accepted them voluntarily and enjoyed their benefits.

[*Union of India* v. *Sita Ram*, AIR 1977 SC 329]

Example 10.12. A number of villages were drawing irrigation waters from a tank. Some of the villages were under direct State Tenancy, and the other under Zamindars. The government carried out the repairs of the tank for its preservation, and it had no intention to do so gratuitously for the zamindars. The zamindars also enjoyed the benefit of the repairs. The zamindars were held liable to make proportionate contribution towards the expenses of repair.

[*Damodar Mudaliar* v. *Secy of State*, (1894) 18 Madras 88]

10.10. FINDER OF GOODS

Sometimes, a person finds certain goods, belonging to some other person. In such cases, the goods do not become the property of the finder. The law imposes certain obligations on the finder of goods. It becomes his duty to keep the goods with care and take some steps to trace the true owner and return the goods to him. He is bound to take as much care of the goods as a man of ordinary prudence would take for his own goods under the similar circumstances. He also gets some rights in respect of the goods in certain circumstances, *e.g.*, when the true owner cannot be found, he can sell the goods which are of perishing nature. Under the law, the responsibility of finder of goods is the same as that of a bailee [Section 71].

A 'bailee' is a person to whom the goods have been delivered for some specific purpose upon a condition that on the fulfilment of the purpose, the goods shall be returned to the actual owner. The bailee should keep the goods with proper care. It is to be noted that the finder is entitled to retain the goods against everyone except the true owner of the goods.

Example 10.13. *A* found a diamond on the floor of *B*'s shop and handed it over to *B* to keep it till the true owner is found. Best efforts were made to trace the true owner and advertisement to this effect was given in the newspaper. But the true owner could not be traced. After sometime, *A* tendered to *B* the expenses incurred by him for tracing the true owner and requested him to return the diamond. *B* refused to return the diamond to *A*. It was held that, *B* must return the diamond to *A* as he alone was entitled to retain it against every other person except the true owner. [*Hollins* v. *Fowler* L.R. 7 H.L. 757]

Note: The rights and duties of a bailee shall be discussed in detail in chapter 15 on 'Bailment and Pledge'.

10.11. PAYMENT OF MONEY OR DELIVERY OF GOODS BY MISTAKE OR UNDER COERCION

Sometimes, a certain amount of money is paid or something is delivered to a person by mistake or under coercion. In such cases the person receiving the money or goods must repay or return the same to the person who has paid or delivered by mistake or under coercion. This provision is contained in Section 72 of the Indian Contract Act, which reads as under:

"A person to whom money has been paid or anything delivered by mistake or under coercion, must repay or return it."

Thus, a person paying the money or delivering the goods by mistake or under coercion is entitled to recover the same from the person to whom it has been so paid or delivered.

Example 10.14. *A* and *B* jointly owed Rs. 100 to *C*.*A* alone paid the amount to *C*. And *B* not knowing this fact, also paid Rs. 100 to *C*. In this case, *C* is bound to repay the amount to *B* who has paid it by mistake.

Similarly, the money paid to a wrong person due to a bonafide mistake can be recovered back. A debtor can also recover the amount of overpayment to a creditor paid by mistake.

Example 10.15. A paid some money to B by mistake which was in fact due to C. In this case, B must repay the money to C as it had been paid under a bonafide mistake.

Example 10.16. A, a lessee in a mining lease, paid, the royalties at a higher rate though he was bound to pay at a lower rate. In fact, the money was paid under the belief that it was legally due. It was held that the money paid under mistake of law can be recovered under Section 72.

[*Sir Shiba Prasad* v. *Maharaja Sarish Chandra*, AIR 1949 PC 297]

The money paid under coercion can also be recovered. The word 'coercion' is used in Section 72 in its general sense and not as defined in Section 15 of the Indian Contract Act[2].

Example 10.17. Certain goods belonging to A, a consignee, were lying with a railway company. The railway company refused to deliver the goods to the consignee, unless some illegal charges for carriage are paid. The consignee paid the charges, in order to obtain the goods. Here he (*A*) was entitled to recover from the railway company the charges which were illegally excessive. In this case the consignee (*A*) was forced to pay the charges (*i.e.*, under coercion).

10.12 COMPENSATION FOR FAILURE TO DISCHARGE OBLIGATIONS CREATED BY QUASI CONTRACTS

We have already discussed that a person is bound to discharge the obligations created by a quasi contract. If a person fails to disharge these obligations then it is treated as a breach of contract, and he shall be liable to pay the compensation in the same way as would have been payable in case of breach of contract.

Thus, if an obligation created by a quasi contract has not been discharged, the injured party is entitled to receive the same compensation from the party in default as he would have received from a person who had actually entered into a valid contract and failed to perform it [Section 73, para 3]

Example 10.18. *A* supplied certain goods to *B* by mistake. In fact, the goods were to be supplied to *C*. Moreover *B* used the goods as his own. In this case *A* is entitled to recover the compensation from *B* and the compensation shall the determined keeping in view the market rates of the goods at the dote of delivery of goods to *B*.

The compensation, which the injured party is entitled to receive, will be discussed in detail in chapter 12 on 'Discharge of Contract'.

---

2. *Seth Kanhayalal* v. *National Bank of India*, (1913) 40 IA 56.

LEGAL PROVISIONS (SECTIONS) DISCUSSED IN THE CHAPTER

Important legal provisions (sections) of the Indian contract Act, 1872, discussed in this chapter, are reproduced hereunder for ready reference.

1. ***Section 68: Claim of necessaries supplied to person incapable of contracting, or on his account***

   If a person, incapable of entering into a contract, or any one whom he is legally bound to support, is supplied by another person with necessaries suited to his condition in life, the person who has furnished such supplies is entitled to be reimbursed form the property of such incapable person.

2. ***Section 69: Reimbursement of person paying money due by another, in payment of which he is interested***

   A person who is interested in the payment of monay which another is bound by law to pay, and who therefore pays it, is entitled to be reimbursed by the other.

3. ***Section 70: Obiligation of person enjoying benefit of non-gratuitous act***

   Where a person lawfully does anything for another person, or delivers anything to him, not intending to do so gratuitously, and such other person enjoys the benefit thereof, the latter is bound to make compensation to the former in respect of, or to restore, the thing so done or delivered.

4. ***Section 71: Responsibility of finder of goods***

   A person wno finds goods belonging to another and takes them into his custody, is subject to the same responsibility as a bailee.

5. ***Section 72: Liability of person to whom money is paid, or thing delivered, by mistake or under coercion.***

   A person to whom money has been paid, or anything delivered, by mistake or under coercion, must repay or return it.

TEST QUESTIONS

1. Define quasi contracts. State the circumstances in which quasi contractual obligations arise.
2. What are the quasi contracts? Discuss the provisions of Indian contract Act 1872, relating to quasi contract.
3. State the relations resembling those created by contract. What is the legal name given to such relations? Is there any legal provision which recognises these relations? If yes, enumerate the same with examples.
4. Quasi contracts are based on the maxim *"nemo debet locuplatari ex liena justua"*. Explain the same with suitable examples.
5. "Quasi contracts are not contracts in the strict sense of the term. These are only the obligations created by law". Explain stating the provisions of Indian Contract Act.
6. Does a person liable for compensation if he fails to discharge quasi contractual obligations? If yes, state the rules in brief which govern the payment of compensation.
7. State the legal position of a finder of goods.

MULTIPLE CHOICE QUESTIONS

1. A person who supplies 'necessaries' to a minor is entitled to be reimbursed from the property of the minor on the basis of a
   (*a*) valid contract. (*b*) voidable contracts.
   (*c*) quasi contract. (*d*) contingent contract.
2. The basis of 'quasi contractual relations' is the
   (*a*) existence of a valid contract between the parties.
   (*b*) prevention of unjust enrichment at the expense of others.
   (*c*) provisions contained in Section 10 of the Contract Act.
   (*d*) existence of a voidable contract between the parties.
3. *A* left certain goods at *B's* house by mistake and *B* used the goods as his own. here, *A* can recover the price of goods brom *B*
   (*a*) True, on the basis of quasi contract (*b*) No, there is no valid contract between them.
4. Sometimes, a person finds certain goods belonging to some other persons. In such a case, the finder

(*a*) becomes the owner of the goods and can use them.
(*b*) is under a duty to trace the true owner and return the goods.
(*c*) can sell the perishable goods if true owner cannot be found.
(*d*) both (*b*) and (*c*).

5. If an obligation created by quasi contract has not been discharged, then the unjured party becomes entitled to receive compensation from a party in default.
(*a*) True, as Section 73 makes a provision in this regard.
(*b*) False, as Section 73 simply makes it enforceable without compensation.

ANSWERS

1. (*c*)	2. (*b*)	3. (a)	4. (*d*)	5. (*a*)

OBJECTIVE TYPE QUESTIONS WITH REASONING

State with reasons whether the following statements are correct or incorrect

1. In quasi-contracts, the promise to pay is always an implication of law not of facts.
2. A quasi-contracts is not at all an enforceable contract.
3. In a quasi-contract, though there is no real contract between the parties but intention to enter into a contract is definitely there.
4. The Indian Contract Act expressly uses the words 'quasi-contracts' to give legal recognition to these contracts.
5. A quasi-contract is enforceable because it possesses all the essential elements of a valid contract.
6. A minor is personally liable to pay for the necessaries supplied to him.
7. A person supplying necessaries to the dependents of a person of unsound mind is entitled to be reimbursed from the property of the person of unsound mind
8. A person who is interested in the payment of money which another is bound by law to pay, and who, therefore, pays it, is entitled to be reimbursed, by the other.
9. *A*, a tradesman, leaves certain goods at *B*' s house by mistake who treats the goods as his own. *B* is bound to pay for the goods to *A*.
10. The liability of the finder of goods is the same as of a bailee.

ANSWERS

1. ***Correct.*** A quasi-contract is created by law without any agreement between the parties. In the quasi-contract, the legal obligations are implied in law and imposed upon the parties.
2. ***Incorrect.*** The quasi-contractual obligations are enforceable as per rules contained in Sections 68 to 72.
3. ***Incorrect.*** In quasi-contract, there is neither a real contract nor the intention of the parties to enter into a contract. The contractual relations arise only by implication of law.
4. ***Incorrect.*** The Indian Contract Act uses the words 'certain relations resembling those created by contract' for quasi-contractual obligations.
5. ***Incorrect.*** A quasi-contract is enforceable not because of the fact that it possesses the essentials of valid contract, but because the law regards certain relations as those created by a contract.
6. ***Incorrect.*** A minor is not personally liable to pay for the necessaries supplied to him. It is the minor's property out of which the supplier is entitled to be rimbursed for the necessaries [Section 68]
7. ***Correct.*** It is the legal position on the point. In such cases, the quasi-contractual obligations arise which have been recognised by Section 68.

8. *Correct.* It is the legal position on the point. In such cases, the quasi-contractual obligations arise which have been recognised by Section 69.
9. *Correct. A's* act is non-gratuitous in this case and quasi-contractual obligations arise between *A* and *B* [Section 70]
10. *Correct.* It is the law on the point [Section 71].

PRACTICAL PROBLEMS

1. *A* supplied to the wife and children of *B*, a lunatic the necessaries suitable to the conditions in life. Can *A* recover the amount from *B*, personally? Give reasons.

   Hint : No, *A* cannot recover anything from *B* personally? Since *B* is an incompetent person, he is not personally liable. However, *A* is entitled to be reimbursed from *B*'s properly under Section 68 of the Indian Contract Act.
2. *A*, a minor, was facing a criminal prosecution in a court of law. He borrowed Rs.10,000 from *B*, a money-lender to defend himself. Can *B* recover the amount from *A*? Give reasons.

   Hint : No, *B* cannot recover the amount from *A* personally. Since a minor, being an incompetent person, is not personally liable. However, *B* can recover amount of loan from *A*'s property, if there is any.
3. *A* agreed to purchase a certain mill from *B* and certain municipal taxes were due on the mill. In order to save the mill from being sold in execution of a decree, *A* paid the due municipal taxes which were otherwise the liability of *B*, the mill owner. Can *A* recover the amount of taxes from *B*? Give reasons.

   Hint : Yes, *A* is entitled to recover the amount of municipal taxes from *B*. Here, by agreeing to purchase the mill, *A* had acquired sufficient interest in the mill, and he is entitled to recover the taxes on the basis of quasi-contract under section 69 of the Indian contract Act.
4. *A*, a tradesman, visited his friend *B* and stayed there for a night. Next day, while leaving, *A* left a box containing certain goods at *B*'s house by mistake. *B* treated the goods as his own and used them. Can *A* recover the price of goods from *B*? Give reasons.

   Hint : Yes, *A* is entitled to recover the price from *B*. Here, *A*'s act of leaving the goods at *B*'s house is a non-gratuitous act and he is entitled to recover the price on the basis of quasi-contract under section 70 of the Indian contract Act.
5. *A* and *B* jointly owed Rs. 50,000 to *C*. On due date, *A* alone paid the entire amount of Rs. 50,000 to *C*, and *B* not knowing about this fact, also paid Rs. 25,000 to *C*. Can *B* recover the amount from *C*? Give reasons.

   Hint : Yes, *B* is entitled to recover the amount from *C*. Here, *B* had paid the amount under mistake and he is entitled to recover the same on the basis of quasi-contract under section 72 of the Indian Contract Act.
6. *A* insured his goods with an insurance company against the risk of fire only. After sometimes, the goods were stolen from the godown and *A* recovered the amount form the insurance company. On becoming aware that the amount has been paid under mistake as the goods had not been destroyed by a peril insured against, the insurance company claimed the refund from *A*. Will it succeed? Give reasons.

   Hint : Yes, the insurance company will succeed in taking the refund from *A*. Here, the insurance company has paid the claim amount under mistake and it is entitled to recover the same on the basis of quasi-contract under section 72 of the Indian contract Act.

PERFORMANCE OF CONTRACTS

11.1. INTRODUCTION

We have already discussed that a valid contract creates the legal obligations on both the contracting parties. After the formation of a valid contract, the next step is the fulfillment of the object that the parties had agreed to do. For the fulfillment of the object, the parties become liable to perform their respective obligations. Performance of a contract means the carrying out of these obligation. After the performance, the contract is said to be discharged. In this chapter we shall discuss the legal provisions relating to the performance of a contract.

The obligation of the parties regarding the performance is contained in first part of Section 37 of the Indian Contract Act, which reads as under:

> *"The parties to a contract must either perform or offer to perform, their respective promises, unless the performance is dispensed with or excused under the provisions of this Act, or any other law"*

Thus, each party is bound to perform his obligation under the contract unless the performance is excused under the provisions of the Indian Contract Act or any other law. It is, therefore, the legal duty of each party to perform his obligation under the contract. Both the parties may discharge their respective duties either by actually performing the contract, or by making an offer to perform it. This is clear from the words used in Section 37 which reads "the party must either perform or offer to perform". Thus, the performance of contract can be discussed under the following two heads:

1. Performance of the promise.
2. Offer of performance of the promise (tender of performance).

11.2. PERFORMANCE OF THE PROMISE

Sometimes, a party fulfils all his obligations under the contract. In such cases, the party is said to have performed his promise. In other words, when a party has done, what he had undertaken to do, and nothing is left, the promise is said to be performed. Such party is discharged from his liability under the contract. This is known as the actual performance of the contract .

In case, any party fails to perform his obligations, there occurs a breach of the contract. The breach of contract discharges the other party from performing his obligations. This point will be discussed in detail in the next chapter under the heading "Discharge by Breach of Contract".

11.3. TENDER OF PERFORMANCE

A contract need not be actually performed. The party who is bound to perform his obligation under the contract, may make an offer to the other party to perform his obligation. An offer to perform obligation is called 'tender of performance'. And a valid tender of performance is equivalent to the performance of the promise.

11.4. EFFECT OF REFUSAL TO ACCEPT TENDER OF PERFORMANCE

On making a valid tender of performance by the promisor, it becomes the duty of the promisee to accept the performance. If the promisee does not accept the tender of performance, the promisor is discharged from his liability. Moreover, the promisor shall not be responsible for non-performance of the contract [Section 38].

Example 11.1. *A* entered into a contract with *B* to deliver certain goods at a certain price to *B*. *A* offered the goods to *B* at a proper time and place. But *B* refused to accept the goods. In this case, *A* is discharged from further liability.

It may, however, be noted that in case of payment of a debt, the rejection of a valid tender of money by the creditor will not discharge the debtor from the liability for the repayment of the debt.

11.5. ESSENTIALS OF A VALID TENDER OF PERFORMANCE

1. *The tender must be unconditional*
2. *The tender must be made at a proper time and place*
3. *The tender must provide a reasonable opportunity to the other party*
4. *The tender must be of the whole obligation*
5. *The tender must be made to a proper person*
6. *The tender must be made in the proper from*
7. *The person making a tender must be able and willing to perform his obligation*
8. *The tender may be made to any one of the joint promisees*

A valid tender of performance discharges a party from further liability. The tender of performance is valid, if it satisfies the following conditions:

1. ***The tender must be unconditional:*** The first requirement of a valid tender of performance is that it must be unconditional [Section 38 (1). An unconditional tender is one which is in accordance with the terms of the contract.

Example 11.2. *A*, adebtor, offered to pay *B*, his creditor, the amount due to him if *B* sells certain goods to him . It is a conditional tender, and therefore invalid.

2. ***The tender must be made at a proper time and place:*** The second requirement is that a tender of performance must be made at a proper time

and place [Section 38 (2)]. Generally, the time and place of performance are fixed by the parties in their contract. And the tender of performance must be made within the time and at the place so fixed.

Example 11.3. *A* contracted to deliver to *B* at his warehouse, 100 bales of cotton of a particular quality on 1st March, 1998. In order to make a valid tender of performance, *A* must bring the cotton to *B's* warehouse on 1st March, 1998 .

The rules regarding the time and place of performance are contained in Section 46 to 50 of the Indian Contract Act which will be discussed in Art. 11.9

3. ***The tender must provide a reasonable opportunity to the other party:*** The third requirement is that a valid tender of performance must provide the following types of reasonable opportunities to the party to whom the tender is made:

(a) ***The reasonable opportunity of ascertaining that the party making the tender is able and willing to perform the contract:*** The tender must be made under such circumstances that the person to whom it is made may have a reasonable opportunity of ascertaining that the person by whom it is made is able and willing to perform the whole promise [Section 38(2)].

(b) ***The reasonable opportunity of inspection of goods:*** If the offer is to deliver anything to the promise, he must have a reasonable opportunity to see that the things offered are the same as agreed [Section 38(3)]. And a tender of goods when the other party cannot inspect the goods, is not a valid tender.

Example 11.4. *A* contracted to deliver to *B* at his business house 100 bags of rice of particular quality on 31st March, 1998. In order to make a valid tender. *A* must bring the rice to *B's* Business house on the appointed day and under such circumstances the *B* may have a reasonable opportunity of satisfying himself that the rice offered is of the agreed quality and there are 100 bags of rice.

4. ***The tender must be of the whole obligation :*** A valid tender of performance must be of the whole obligation. An offer to perform a promise in part is not a valid tender. Moreover, a tender by instalment is not a valid tender unless the contract so provides.

However, a minor derivation from the terms of a contract may not render a tender unvalid.

Example 11.5. *A* contrated to deliver 4950 tonnes of wheat to *B*. But *A* delivered 4950 tonnes and 55 labs of wheat. The contract was held to be duly performed.

[*Shirten Anderson & Co.* v. *Weil Bros & Co.* (1972) 1 KB 574].

5. ***The tender must be made to a proper person:*** A valid tender of performance must be made to a proper person. The proper person is the promisee or his duly authorized agent. Thus, a tender of performance made to a stranger (*i.e.*, third party) is not a valid tender.

Example 11.6. *A* contracted to deliver certain goods to *B* on 1st June. One 1st June, *A* offered goods to *C*, the friend of *B*. It is not a valid tender of performance and thus *A* is not discharged from his obligations.

6. ***The tender must be made in the proper from:*** A valid tender of performance must also be made in a proper form, e.g., a tender of money must be in the legal tender money and not in any foreign currency or exchange or cheque. A payment by a cheque is a valid tender if the person to whom it is made is ready and willing to accept it.

7. ***The person making a tender must be able and willing to perform his obligation:*** The party making a tender must be in a position and willing to perform his promise. A party cannot be said to be able and willing if he has neither possession or nor control over the goods which he has promised to deliver.

---

1. *Jagat* v. *Naligopal*, 34 Calcutta 305.

8. ***The tender may be made to any one of the joint promisees:*** Sometimes, there are several joint promisees. In such cases, it is not necessary for the promisor to offer performance to everyone of them. *A* tender may be made to anyone of the joint promisees. And an offer to one of several joint promisees has the same legal consequences as an offer to all of them [Section 38, last para)].

11.6. PERSONS WHO SHOULD PERFORM THE CONTRACT

1. *The promisor himself*
2. *The legal representatives*
3. *The agent*
4. *The third person*

As matter of fact, the contract should be performed by the promisor himself. However, in certain cases, the contract may also be performed by his representatives or agents, etc. Whether a contract should be performed by the promisor himself or his agent etc. depends upon the intention of the parties. If the intention is that the contract must be performed by the promisor himself then he has to perform it. And if the intention is otherwise, the contract may be performed by the representatives, or agents. Thus, the intention of the parties is the deciding factor. Depending upon the intention of the parties the contract may be performed by the following persons:

1. ***The promisor himself:*** Generally, the contract should be performed by the promisor himself or by his legal representatives, or by any other competent person employed by him . But where it appears from the nature of the contract that it was the intention of the parties that the contract must be performed by the promisor himself, such contract must be performed by the promisor himself [section 40]. The contract involving personal skill or personal consideration of the promisor, must be performed by the promisor himself, e.g., a contract to paint, sing or marry, and the contracts of technical nature.

Example 11.7. *A* promised to paint a picture for *B*. As this promise involves personal skill of *A*, it must be performed by *A* himself. If *A* dies before painting the picture, the contract comes to an end and it cannot be enforced either by *A's* representatives or by *B*.

2. ***The legal representatives:*** The contracts which do not involve any personal skill or consideration may be performed by the legal representatives of the promisor if he dies before performance of the contract. Thus, if the promisor dies before performance, his legal representatives become liable to perform the contract [Section 37 (second para)]. But the contracts, which involve the use of personal skill or are founded on personal considerations cannot be performed by the legal representatives because such contracts come to an end on the death of the promisor.

Example 11.8. *A* contracted to sing a song in *B's* Theatre on 1st Jan. 1989 for Rs. 5000. *A* died before this date. This contract cannot be performed by *A's* representatives as it involves the personal consideration of the promisor (*A*). Moreover *B* cannot compel ***A's*** representatives to sing a song, because on the death of the promisor, such contracts come to an end.

3. ***The agent:*** The contracts which do no involve any personal skill or consideration may also be performed by an agent appointed by the promisor [Section 40]. For example, a contract to sell the goods may be performed by the agent appointed by the seller. Similarly a contract to pay the money may also be performed by the agent.

4. ***The third person:*** The general rule is that the contract must either be performed by the promisor himself or his legal representatives or an agent employed by the promisor or by his legal representatives. However, the performance by a third person is also effective if the promisee accepts the same. Once the promisee accepts the performance from a third person, then he cannot compel the promisor to perform the contract again [Section 41].

Example 11.9. *A* owed a large sum of money to *B*. *C*, a friend of *A*. offered to pay *B* a lesser sum in full satisfaction and settlement of *B's* claim on *A*. This was accepted by *B* in full settlement of his claim. It was held that since *B* has accepted the lesser payment from *C* in full settlement, he could not sue *A* for the balance. [*Kapurchand Godha* v. *Nawab Himyat Ali*. AIR 1963 SC 250]

11.7. PERSONS ENTITLED TO DEMAND PERFORMANCE

As a matter of fact, the performance can be demanded only by a person to whom the promise is made. Thus, the promisee is the only person who can demand performance of the promise under a contract. It may be noted that even if the promise is made for the benefit of the third person, the right to demand performance rests with the promisee only.

Example 11.10. *A* promised *B* to give Rs. 100 to *C*. In this case, the person who can demand performance is *B* (*i.e.*, the promisee) and not *C*.

However, in case of death of the promisee, the legal representatives of the deceased promisee can demand performance. But where the contract involves a personal skill or consideration, the legal representatives of the deceased promisee cannot demand performance. It may, however, be noted that in certain exceptional cases, the third party can also enforce the contract even though he is not a party to it. This has been discussed in detail in Chapter 3 on 'Consideration'.

11.8. PERFORMANCE OF JOINT PROMISES

1. ***The joint promisors or their representatives must jointly perform the promise***
2. ***The promisee may compel anyone of the joint promisors to perform the promise***
3. ***Rights and liabilities of the joint promisors among themselves***
4. ***The promisee may release one of the joint promisors***
5. ***Devolution of joint rights***

Sometimes, two or more persons enter into a joint agreement with one or more persons. In such cases the promise is known as a joint promise.

Example 11.11. *A*, *B* and *C* jointly borrowed a sum of Rs. 15,000 from *X* and *Y*, and jointly promised to repay the amount. It is a joint promise.

In case of joint promises, the question arises who is liable to pay and who can ask for payment. *i.e.*, who is liable to perform the promise and who can demand performance. The rules relating to the performance of joint promises are contained in Sections 42 to 45 of the Indian Contract Act, and may be discussed under the following heads:

1. *The joint promisors or their representatives must jointly perform the promise:* Sometimes, two or more persons make a joint promise. In such cases, the joint promisors must jointly fulfil the promise during their joint life time. And if anyone of them dies, his legal representatives must jointly with the surviving promisers fulfil the promise. On the death of all the promisors, the representatives of all of them must jointly fulfill the promise. This is however, subject to an agreement between the parties, *i.e.*, if the parties expressly or impliedly prescribe a different rule then the above rule will not apply. This rule is called the '***devolution of joint liabilities***' and is contained in Section 42 of the Indian Contract Act.

Example 11.12. *A*, *B* and *C* jointly promised to pay Rs. 6000 to *D*. Here *A*, *B* and *C* must jointly perform the promise. If *A* dies before performance, then his legal representatives must jointly with *B* and *C* perform the promise, and so on. And if all the three (*i.e. A*, *B* and *C*) die before performance, then the legal representatives of all must jointly perform the promise.

Note: The position under the English Law is different. If one of the several joint promisors dies, the rights and liabilities under the contract devolve upon the surviving joint promisors,. The legal representatives of the deceased promisor are not liable. However, the representatives of the last surviving promisor are liable.

2. ***The promisee may compel anyone of the joint promisors to perform the promise:*** Sometimes, two or more persons make a joint promise. In such cases, the promisee may compel anyone or more of the joint promisors to perform the whole of the promise. In other words, the liability of the joint promisors is joint and several. And the promisee may recover the entire amount from all of them jointly or form any one of them. This is, however , subject to an agreement between the parties [Section 43].

Example 11.13. *A*, *B* and *C* jointly promised to pay Rs, 30,000 to *D*. In this case *D* may compel either *A*, or *B* or *C* to pay him the entire sum of Rs. 30,000.

Sometimes, the promisee files a suit against one of the joint promisors only, and obtains a judgement (decree) of court which remains unsatisfied. In such cases, he can subsequently file a second suit against the other joint promisors.

Example 11.14. *A*, *B* and *C* jointly promised to pay Rs. 15,000 to *D*. And *D* filed a suit against *A* only and obtained judgement (decree) from the court. But only Rs. 10,000 were recovered from *A* as he had no otehr assets or money to satisfy the judgement. In this case, *D* can subsequently fill a suit against *B* or *C* or both of them for the recovery of the balance of Rs, 5000.

Note. The English Law on the point is different. Under the English Law, the liability of the joint promisors is joint. And thus, all must be sued jointly to make all of them liable. If suit is filed against one only, later on the suit against the other cannot be filed.

3. ***Rights and liabilities of the joint promisors among themselves:*** We have discussed above that only one of the joint promisors may be compelled to perform the whole of the promise. In such cases, the rights and liabilities of the joint promisors among themselves may be discussed under the following sub-heads:

(*a*) ***Joint promisors are liable to contribute equally:*** A joint promisor, who has been compelled to perform the whole of the promise, may require the other joint promisors to make an equal contribution towards the performance of the promise. This is however, subject to any different agreement between the joint promisors. [Section 43 (second para)].

Example 11.15. *A*, *B*, *C* and *D* jointly promised to pay Rs. 20,000 to *E*. *E* field a suit against *A* only and recovered the entire amount form him. In this case, *A* can recover Rs. 5,000 each from *B*, *C* and *D*.

A partner in a firm is a joint promisor with other partners. In case he is required to pay the debt of the firm, he is entitled to claim contribution from other partners.

(b) Joint promisors liable to share losses equally: Sometimes, any one of the joint promisors does not make any contribution. In such cases, the remaining joint promisors should bear the loss in equal shares [Section 43 (third para)].

Example 11.16. *A*, *B* and *C* jointly promised to pay Rs. 3000 to *D*. *A* was compelled to pay the entire sum of Rs. 3000 . In this case, *A* is entitled to recover Rs. 1000 each from *B* and *C*. But *C* is unable to pay anything. *A* is entitled to recover Rs. 1500 from *B*.

Example 11.17. *A*, *B* and *C* jointly promised to pay Rs. 12,000 to *D*. *A* was compelled to pay the entire sum of Rs. 12,000 . But *B* was insolvent, and his assets were sufficient to pay only one half of his share of contribution. In this case, *A* is entitled to receive Rs. 2000 from *B's* estate and Rs. 5000 from *C*. Here due to *B's* insolvency, the total loss is of Rs. 2000 because Rs. 2000 have been realised from *B's* estate. This loss of Rs. 2,000 is to be shared by *A* and *C* equally, and thus *C* becomes liable to pay Rs. 5000 instead of Rs. 4000.

(c) The contribution rule does not apply to principal debtor and surety: Sometimes, a creditor asks the principal debtor to furnish a surety for the repayment of the loan. In such cases, the principal debtor and the surety are considered as joint promisors to the creditor. However, the above rule of contribution does not apply between principal

2. *Bakshi Harhatt v. State of J&K* (1977) NOC 270 (J&K)

debtor and his surety even though they are the joint promisors. The creditor can recover the entire amount of loan either from principal debtor or the surety. If the surety is compelled to pay the entire amount then he can recover from the principal debtor the entire sum paid by him. However, the principal debtor cannot ask for any contribution if the creditor recovers the entire amount from him. Because by paying the creditor, the principal debtor is discharging his own liability [Section 43 (explanation)].

Example 11.18. *A* promised to pay Rs, 6000 to *D*. *B* and *C* were the sureties for the repayment of the amount by *A*. *A* failed to repay the amount, and *B* and *C* were compelled to repay the entire sum of money. In this case, *B* and *C* are entitled to recover the amount from *A*.

If in the above example, if *A* himself pays the entire sum of Rs. 6000 to *D*, then he cannot recover anything from *B* and *C*.

4. *The promisee may release one of the joint promisors.* Sometimes, a promisee releases one of the joint promisors. In such cases, the release of one promisor does not discharge the other joint promisor or promisors. Thus, the remaining joint promisors continue to be liable to pay the amount. It may also be noted that the released promisor remains liable to contribute to the other joint promisors [Section 44].

Example 11.19. *A*, *B* and *C* jointly promised to pay Rs. 9000 to *D*. *D* released *A* from liability. In this case, the release of *A* does not discharge *B* and *C* from their liability. They remain liable to pay the entire amount of Rs. 9000 to *D*. And though *A* is not liable to pay to *D* but he remains liable to pay to *B* and *C*. *i.e.*, he is liable to make the contribution to the other joint promisors.

Note: The English Law on this point is different. Under the English Law, the release of one of the joint promisors, is release of all other promisors.

5. *Devolution of joint rights:* We have already discussed the rules relating to the performance of joint promises by the joint promisors. However, there may be joint promisees also, *i.e.*, one person may make a promise to more than one persons jointly. In such cases, the rules relating to the performance of such joint promises are almost the same as discussed above. The only difference is that in case of joint promisors, they have the joint liability to perform the promise. But in case of joint promisees, they have the joint right to ask for the performance of the promise. Thus, where one person has made a joint promise to more than one person, then all the promisees must jointly claim performance so long as all are alive. And if anyone of them dies, his legal representatives must jointly with the surviving promisees claims the performance. On the death of all the joint promisees, the legal representatives of all of them must jointly claim the performance. This is, however , subject to an agreement between the parties, *i.e.*, if the parties expressly or impliedly prescribe a different rule, then the above rule will not apply. This rule is called the **'devolution of joint rights'** and is contained in Section 45 of the Indian Contract Act.

Example 11.20. *A* and *B* jointly lent Rs. 10,000 to *C*. And *C* promised *A* and *B* jointly to repay them that amount on a specified day. Here, *A* and *B* must jointly claim the performance. If *A* dies before performance, the right to claim performance rests with *A's* representative jointly with *B*, and if both *A* and *B* die, the rights to claim performance rests with the representatives of both of them.

11.9. TIME AND PLACE FOR PERFORMANCE

The rules regarding the time and place for performance are contained in Section 46 to 50 of the Indian Contract Act, which may be discussed under the following heads:

1. *Performance of the promise where no time is specified and also no application to be made :* Sometimes, the time for performance is not specified in the contract, and the promisor himself has to perform the promise without being asked (*i.e.*, without any demand) by the promisee. In such cases, the promise must be performed within a reasonable time [section46]. The term 'reasonable time' in each particular case is a question of fact . It depends upon the customs of the trade, special circumstances of the case or the intention of the parties at the time of making the contract.

2. *Performance of the promise where the time is specified but no application is to be made :* Sometimes, the day for performance is specified in the contract, and the promisor himself has to perform the promise without being asked (*i.e.* without any demand) by the promisee. In such cases, the promise may be performed at any time during the usual hours of business on the specified day. But the promise should be performed at the place where it was required to be performed [Section 47].

Example 11.21. *A* promised with *B* to deliver goods at *B's* warehouse, on the 1st January. On that day, *A* brought the goods to *B's* warehouse, but after the usual working hours. And the goods were not received at the warehouse. In this case, *A* has not performed his promise as the goods were not delivered during the usual hours of business.

3. *Performance of the promise where the time is specified and also the application is to be made:* Sometimes, the day for the performance is specified in the contract, and the promisor has to perform it only on being asked (*i.e.*, on demand) by the promisee. In such cases, the promisee must first apply to the promisor (*i.e.*, make a demand on the promisor) for the performance of the promise. Such demand for performance should be made at a proper time and place, and within the usual hours of business. The term 'proper time and place' is a question of fact in each particular case [Section 48].

Example 11.22. *A* promised to deliver 100 tins of ghee to *B* on a fixed day. *B* agreed to specify the place later on where the delivery was to be made. In this case, it is the duty of *B* to make a demand on *A* for the delivery of the tins and inform him the place where they are to be delivered.

4. *Performance of the promise where no place is specified and also no application is to be made:* Sometimes, the place for performance is not specified in the contract, and the promisor himself has to perform the promise without being asked by the promisee. In such case, the promisor, must first apply to the promisee to appoint a reasonable place for the performance of the promise. And thereafter, he should perform the promise at the place appointed by the promisee [Section 49]. However, the promisor is required to apply only where the promise is to be performed without any application by the promisee.

Example 11.23. *A* promised to deliver 100 bags of rice to *B* on a fixed day. In this case, *A* must apply to *B* to appoint a reasonable place for the purpose of receiving the rice. And then he should deliver the rice to *B* at the place appointed by him (*B*) .

5. *Performance of the promise where the manner and time for performance is prescribed by the promisee:* Sometimes, the manner and time for performance is prescribed by the promisee himself. In such case, the promise should be performed in the manner and at the time prescribed by the promisee [Section 50].

Example 11.24. *A* owed Rs 2000 to *B*. *B* desired *A* to pay the amount to *B's* account with United Bank. *A* also had his account in the United Bank, and as such gave instructions to the bank to transfer Rs. 2000 from his account to *B's* account, this was done by the Bank. Afterwards, and before *B* knew of the transfer of the amount to his account, the Bank failed. In this case, there has been a good payment by *A*. And thus, *B* cannot demand the payment again.

11.10. TIME AS THE ESSENCE OF THE CONTRACT

The term 'time as the essence of the contract' means that the time is an essential element, and the concerned parties must preform their respective promise within the specified time. The parties, to the contract, may specify the time for its performance,. In such cases, the time agreed for the performance of the contract must be strictly observed. As a matter of fact, whether the time was the essence of the contract or not, can be gathered from the intention of the parties, and from the terms of the contract.

[*Municipal Corpn. of Delhi* v. *Jagan Nath Ashok Kumar* (1987) 4 SCC 497].

In commercial transactions, the time is generally considered to be the essence of the contract. Thus, in a contract for the sale or purchase of goods, the prices of which fluctuate rapidly in the market, the time of delivery and payment are considered to be of the essence of the contract. However, in a contract for the sale of land or immovable property, the time is not considered to be of the essence of the contract[3].

In the following three cases, the time is generally considered to be of the essence of the contract:

1. Where the parties have expressly agreed to treat the time as of the essence of the contract.
2. Where the delay in performing the contract operates as an injury to the party.
3. Where the nature and necessity of the contract requires the time to be the essence of the contract, e.g., where a party asks for the extension of the time for performance.[4]

In cases, other than the commercial contracts, the ordinary presumption is that the time is not of the essence of the contract. In construction contracts, the time is likely to be the essence of the contract because construction is a commercial service

Example 11.25: *A* builder's commitment with a bank was that he would make their building ready within six months, he could not do so. In this case, the bank was allowed to terminate the contract. [*United Commercial Bank* v *Jawahar Lal Mills* (1989) 2 Cal LJ 246].

11.11. EFFECTS OF NON-PERFORMANCE OF CONTRACT WITHIN THE FIXED TIME

The effects of non-performance of the contract within the fixed time depend upon the fact whether or not the time was the essence of the contract, and thus, may be discussed under the following two heads:

1. *Where the time is of the essence of the contract:* Sometimes, the intention of the parties is that the time should be of the essence of the contract. In such cases, the contract must be performed within the fixed time. And if the party, who is bound to perform his promise within the fixed time, fails to do so then the contract becomes voidable at the option of the other party. Thus, the innocent party may put an end to the contract if he so chooses [Section 55 (first para)].

However, the promisee may accept the performance at any time other than the agreed time. It may be noted that if he does so, he cannot afterwards recover the compensation for the delay. But if at the time of such acceptance he gives notice to the promisor of his intention to recover the compensation, then he can recover it [Section 55 (third para)].

2. *Where the time is not of the essence of the contract:* Sometimes, the intention of the parties is that the time should not be of the essence of the contract, In such cases, the contract may or may not be performed within the fixed time. And the failure to perform the contract within the fixed time does not make the contract voidable. Thus, the innocent party does not have the right to put an end to the contract. However., he has the right to recover the compensation from the other defaulting party for any loss caused to him by the delayed performance [section 55 (second para)].

11.12. PERFORMANCE OF RECIPROCAL PROMISES

Sometimes, a party gives a promise in consideration of other party's promise. In

3. *Gomathninayatam Pilla* v. *Palaniswani Nadan*, (1967) 1 SCR 227; *Indira Kaur* v. *Sheolal kapoor*, AIR 1988 SC 1074.
4. *Orissa Textile Mill ltd. v. Ganewsh Das, AIR* 1961 Patna 107

such cases, both the promises are called the reciprocal promises. The term 'reciprocal promise' is defined in Section 2 (*f*) of the Indian Contract Act, which reads as under:

"Promises which form the consideration or part of consideration for each other are called reciprocal promises"

Thus, when a contract consists of exchange of promises, the promises are called reciprocal promises.

Example 11.26. *A* and *B* promised to marry each other. These are reciprocal promises. In this case, *A's* promise is the consideration for *B's* promise. And *B's* promise is the consideration for *A's* promise.

11.13. KINDS OF RECIPROCAL PROMISES

1. *Mutual and concurrent*
2. *Conditional and dependent*
3. *Mutual and independent*

The reciprocal promises may be classified[5] into the following three categories namely:

1. ***Mutual and concurrent:*** These are the promises which are to be performed simultaneously, *i.e.*, at the same time.

Example 11.27. *A* and *B* entered into a contract for the sale of 100 tins of refined oil. They contracted that *A* shall deliver oil tins to *B* to be paid for by *B* on delivery. In this case, the promises are mutual and concurrent as both the delivery of the oil tins and the payment of the price are to be made simultaneously.

2. ***Conditional and dependent:*** These are the promises where the performance of the promise by one party depends on the prior performance of the promise by the other party.

Example 11.28. A agreed to construct a house for *B*. And *B* agreed to supply the necessary material required for construction of the house. In this case, the promises are conditional and dependent as the performance of *A's* promises., (construction of the house) depends on the prior performance of *B's* promise (*i.e.*, the supply of necessary material) . Thus. *B* must first supply the necessary material to *A*.

3. ***Mutual and independent:*** these are the promises where each party must perform his promise independently without waiting for the other party to perform his promise., or without waiting whether or not the other party is willing to perform his promise.

Example 11.29. *A* and *B* entered into a contract for the sale of goods. *A* agreed to deliver the goods on 15th May, and *B* agreed to pay the price on 20th May. In this case, the promise are mutual and independent as *A* has to deliver the goods without waiting for the payment of the price by *B*.

11.14. RULES FOR THE PERFORMANCE OF RECIPROCAL PROMISES

1. *Rules for the performance of mutual and concurrent reciprocal promises*
2. *Rules for the performance of conditional and dependent reciprocal promises*
3. *Rules for the performance of mutual and independent reciprocal promises*

The rules for the performance of reciprocal promises are contained in section 51 to 54,57 and 58 of the Indian Contract Act, which may be discussed under the following heads:

1. ***Rules for the performance of mutual and concurrent reciprocal promises:*** We have already discussed that the mutual and concurrent promises are to be performed simultaneously. Thus, the promisor is not bound to perform his promise unless the promisee is ready and willing to perform his own promise {Section 51].

2. ***Rules for the performance of conditional and dependent reciprocal promises:*** In

5. This classification is according to Lord Mansfield as stated in *Jones* v. *Barkely*, 4 Dough 659,

conditional and dependent reciprocal promises, the performance of promise by one party depends upon the prior performance of the promise by the other party. If the party who is bound to perform his promise first, fails to perform it, then he cannot claim performance from the other party Moreover, the defaulting party becomes liable to pay the compensation to the other party for the loss suffered by the other on account of the non-performance of the contract. [Section 54].

Example 11.30. *A*, a furniture maker, contracted with *B* to make certain furniture for him. and *B* agreed to supply *A* the necessary timber. *B* failed to supply the necessary timber as such the furniture could not be made. In this case. *A* need not make the furniture and B cannot claim the performance from him. Moreover, *B* is bound to make compensation to *A* for any loss caused to him by the non performance of the contract.

3. *Rules for the performance of mutual and independent reciprocal promises:* The mutual and independent promises are to be performed by each party independently without waiting for the other party to perform his promise. And if either party fails to perform his promise, the other party may proceed against him for the damages. Though a party can recover damages from the defaulting party, but he cannot excuse himself from the performance by reason of the non-performance by the defaulting party.[6]

Example 11.31. *A* and *B* contracted for the sale of desert cooler. A agreed to pay the price on 21st April, and *B* agreed to deliver the cooler on 15th may. *A* failed to pay the price on 21st April. In this case, *B* cannot refuse to delivery the cooler on 15th May. However, he can file suit against *A* for the recovery of the price and damages.

Note: The other rules relating to the performance of reciprocal promises are discussed in the following Arts. 11.15 to 11.17

11.15. ORDER OF PERFORMANCE OF RECIPROCAL PROMISES

The order of performance of reciprocal promises may be fixed in the contract itself. But if the order of performance is not fixed in the contract, then the promises should be performed in the order which the nature of the contract requires [Section 52].

Example 11.32. *A* and *B* contracted that *A* shall construct a house for *B* at a fixed price. In this case, the nature of the contract requires that *A's* promise to construct the house must be performed before *B's* promise to pay for it. Thus, *A* must first construct the house, only then he can claim the price from *B*.

Example 11.33. *A* and *B* contracted that A shall sell his stock -in-trade to *B*. And *B* promised to give security for the payment of the price. In this case, *A* need not perform his promise until *B* gives security before he delivers up his stock-in-trade to *B*.

11.16. EFFECTS OF PREVENTING THE PERFORMANCE OF RECIPROCAL PROMISES

1. ***Promises to do legal things and other illegal things***
2. ***Promises in which one part is legal and the other illegal***

Sometimes, one party to a reciprocal promise prevents the other party from performing his promise. In such cases, the contract becomes voidable at the option of the party who is so prevented . And the party so prevented may also recover compensation from the other party for any loss suffered due to non-performance of the contract [Section 53].

Example 11.34. *A* and *B* contracted that *B* shall execute certain work for *A* for Rs. 1000. And *B* was ready and willing to execute the work accordingly. But *A* prevented him from doing so. In this case, the contract is voidable at the option of *B*. And if he decides to put an end to it, he is entitled to recover from *A* the compensation for any loss which he has sustained by its non-performance.

6. *Mackay* v. *Dick* (1881) 6. AC, 251.

Similarly, a contract will also become voidable where the obstruction to performance is caused by the inadequacy of the machinery or material supplied by one of the parties.

Example 11.35. *A* contracted with *B* to clear his (*B's*) mine and remove a rock from there. The crusher for the purpose was to be supplied by *B*. The crusher supplied was not suitable for the job. In this case, *A* has the right to recover his expenses and loss of profit.

11.17. LEGAL AND ILLEGAL RECIPROCAL PROMISES

1. ***Where the debt to be discharged is indicated by the debtor***
2. ***Where the debt to be discharged is not indicated***
3. ***Where neither party makes any appropriation***
4. ***Appropriation towards interest***

The rules regarding the enforcement of legal and illegal reciprocal promises may be discussed under the following heads:

1. ***Promises to do legal things and other illegal things:*** Sometimes, the persons enter into reciprocal promise, firstly to do certain things which are legal, and secondly to do certain other things which are illegal. In such cases, the first set of promises is a valid contract and can be enforced in a Court of Law. But the second set is a void agreement and thus, cannot be enforced in a court of Law. [Section 57].

Example 11.36. *A* and *B* agreed that *A* shall sell his house to *B* for Rs. 40.000. And that if *B* used it as gambling house, the price shall be Rs. 100,000 . In this case, the first set of reciprocal promises, namely to sell the house and to pay Rs. 40,000 for it, is a valid contract and can be enforced but the second set, namely, to sell the house and to pay Rs. 100,000 for it if the house is used as a gambling house, is a void agreement and cannot be enforced. In the second set of promiser, the object is unlawful.

2. ***Promises in which one part is legal and the other illegal:*** Sometimes, the persons enter into promise to do certain things which are legal, and alternatively to do certain other things which are illegal. In such cases, the legal part alone can be enforced in a Court of Law. [Section 58].

Example 11.37. *A* and *B* agreed that *A* shall pay to *B* Rs. 10,000. And in consideration, *B* shall afterwards deliver to *A* either 10 bags of rice or 2 kg smuggled opium. In this case, the agreement to deliver rice is valid. Whereas, the agreement to deliver opium is void.

11.18. APPROPRIATION OF PAYMENTS

Sometimes, a debtor owes several debts to the same creditor and makes payment which is not sufficient to discharge all the debts. In such cases, the payment is appropriated (*i.e.*, adjusted against the debts) as per Sections 59 to 61 of the Indian Contract Act. These Sections contain the rules as to against which debt the payment is to be appropriated, and may be discussed under the following heads:

1. ***Where the debt to be discharged is indicated by the debtor:*** As a matter of fact, the appropriation is the right given to the debtor for his benefit. He has the right to instruct his creditor to which particular debt the money paid is to be adjusted. And if the creditor accepts the payment. He is bound by the instructions of the debtor [Section 59]. If there is no express intimation by the debtor, the law will gather his intention from the circumstances regarding the payment, *e.g.*, if the amount paid by the debtor is the exact amount of one of the debts, it must be used to discharge that particular debt.

Example 11.38. *A* owed to *B* Rs. 1000, upon a promissory note which falls due on 1st June, *A* also owed to *B* two other debts of Rs. 2000 and Rs. 5000. On 1st June, *A* paid to *B* Rs. 1000. In this case the payment is to be adjusted against the debt due on promissory note only.

2. ***Where the debt to be discharged is not indicated:*** Sometimes, the debtor makes payment without any indication about the appropriation of the payment. In such cases, the creditor may adjust the payment according to his discrertion. The creditor would like to adjust the payment against a debt which is not likely to be recovered. But he may adjust the payment only against the legal debts and not against the illegal or disputed debts. However , the creditor may also adjust the payment against the debts which are time barred [Section 60].

Example 11.39. *A owed* several debts to *B*. Among these debts, one debt of Rs. 5000 is time barred (*i.e.*, the time limit for its recovery has expired). *A* paid Rs. 10,000 to *B* without indicating against which debt the amount is to be adjusted. In this case, *B* may adjust Rs. 5000 against the time barred debt of Rs. 5,000, and the balance against any other debt which he likes.

It may, however, be noted that the appropriation once made and communicated to the debtor is binding on the creditor, and cannot be subsequently altered by him to suit his convenience.

3. *Where neither party makes any appropriation:* Sometimes, the debtor does not expressly intimate anything about the appropriation of the payment, and the creditor also fails to make any appropriation. In such cases, the law prefers to wipe out the earlier debt in order of time irrespective of the fact that some of them are time barred And if there are several debts of the same date, the payment shall be adjusted against each debt proportionately [Section 61].

Example 11.40. *A* owed three debts of Rs. 2000, Rs 4000 and Rs 6000 to *B*, which were due on 31st March 1981, 31st December 1983 and 15th January of 1984 respectively. On 1st January 1984. *A* paid Rs 5000 to *B*. In this case Rs. 2000 shall be adjusted against the debt of Rs. 2000, which was due on 31st march 1981, and the balance of Rs, 3,000 shall be adjusted against the debt of Rs. 4000 which was due on 31 st. December 1983. And thus, the debt of Rs. 4000 will be discharged to the extent of Rs. 3000 and the balance of Rs. 1000 shall remain outstanding.

4. *Appropriation towards interest:* Sometimes, the debtor makes part payment without stating whether it is towards interest of principal. In such cases, the general rule is that the payment should first be adjusted towards interest and the balance towards the principal amount.[7]

From the above discussion, the rule of appropriation of payments may be summed up as under :

(*a*) Where the debtor has indicated the debt against which the payment is to be appropriated, the creditor is bound by such instructions if he accepts the payment.

(*b*) Where the debtor does not make any indication about appropriation of payment, the creditor may adjust the payment according to his own discretion.

(*c*) Where neither party makes any appropriation, the law allows the appropriation of debt in order of time.

LEGAL PROVISIONS (SECTIONS) DISCUSSED IN THE CHAPTER

Important legal provisions (sections) of the Indian Contract Act, 1872, discussed in this chapter are reproduced hereunder for ready reference:

1. ***Section 2 (f) Reciprocal Promises***

   Promises which form the consideration or part of the consideration for each other, are called reciprocal promises.

2. ***Section 37: Obilgation of Parties to Contract***

   The parties to a contranct must either perform, or offer to perform, their respective promises, unless

7. *Megh Raj* v. *Mst. Bayabat*, 1970 SC 161: *Rulia Devi* v. *Raghunath Prasad*, AIR 1979, Patna 115.

such performance is dispensed with or excused under the provisions of this Act, of any other law.

Promises bind the representatives of the promisors in case of the death of such promisors before performance, unless a contrary intention appears form the contract.

3. *Section 38: Effect of refusal to accept offer of performance*

Where a promisor has made an offer of performance to the promisee, and the offer has not been accepted, the promisor is not responsible for non-performance, nor does he thereby lose his right under the contract.

4. *Section 39. Effect of refusal of party to perform promise wholly*

When a party to contract has refused to perform, or disabled himself from performing, his promise in its entirety, the promisee may put an end to the contract, unless he has signified, by words or conduct, his acquiescence in its continuance.

5. *Section 40: Person by whom Promise should be performed*

If it appears form the nature of the case that it was the intention of the parties to any contract that any promise contained in it should be performed by the promisor himself, such promise must be performed by the promisor. In other case, the promisor or his representative may employ a competent person to perform it.

6. *Section 41: Effect of accepting performance from third person*

When a promisee accepts performance of the promise form a third person, he cannot afterwards enforce it against the promisor.

7. *Section 42: Devolution of joint liablities*

When two or more persons have made a joint promise, then, unless a contrary intention appears by the contract, all such persons during their joint lives, and after the death of any of them, his representatitive jointly with the survivor or surviours, and after the death of the last survivor, the representatives of all jointly, must fulfil the promise.

8. *Section 43: Any one of of joint promisors may be compelled to perform*

When two or more persons make a joint promise, the promisee may, in the absence of express agreement to the contrary, compel any One or more of such joint promisors to perform the whole of the promise.

Each promisor may compel contribution.—Each of two or more joint promisors may compel every other joint promisor to contribute equally with himself to the performance of the promise, unless a contracry intention appears form the contract.

Sharing of loss by default in contribution.—If any one of two or more joint promisors makes default in such contribution, the remaining joint promisors must bear the loss arising form such default in equal shares.

Explanation.—Nothing in the section shall prevent a surety form recovering, from his prinicpal, payments made by the surety on behalf of the principal, or entitle the principal to recover anything form the surety on account of payment made by the principal.

9. *Section 44: Effect of release of one joint promisor*

Where two or more persons have made a jont promise, a release of one of such joint promisors by the promisee does not discharge the other joint promisor or joint promisors, neither does it free the joint promissors so released form responsibility to the other joint promisor or joint promisors.

10. *Section 45: Develution of joint rights*

When a person has made a promise to two or more persons jointly, then, unless a contrary intention appears form the contract, the right to claim performace rests, as between him and them, with them during their joint lives, and after the death of any of them, with the representative of such deceased person jointly with the survivor or survivors and after the death of the last surviór, with the representatives of all jointly.

11. *Section 51: Promisor not bound to perform, unless reciprocal promisee ready and willing to perform*

When a contract consists of reciprocal promises to be simultaneously performed, no promisor need perform his promise unless the promisee is ready and willing to perform his reciprocal promise.

12. *Section 52: Order of performance of reciprocal promises*

Where the order in which reciprocal promises are to be performed is expressly fixed by the contract, they shall be performed in that order; and where the order is not expressly fixed by the contract, they shall be performed in that order which the nature of the transaction requires.

13. *Section 53: Liability of party preventing event on which the contract is to take effect*

When a contract contains reciprocal promises, and one party to the contract prevents the other form performing his promise, the contract becomes voidable at the option of the party so prevented: and he is entitled to compensation from the other party for any loss which he may sustain in consequence of the non-performace of the contract.

14. ***Sector 54: Effect of default as to that promise which should be performed, in contract consisting of reciprocal promises***

When a contract consists of reciprocal promises, such that one of them cannot be performed, or that its performiance cnanot be claimed till the other has been performed, and the promisor of the promise last mentioned fails to perform it, such prmisor cannot calim the performance of the reciporcal promise, and must make compensation to the other party to the contract for any loss which such other party may sustain by the non-performance of the contract.

15. ***Section 57: Reciprocal promise to do things legal, and also other things illegal***

Where persons reciprocally promise, firstly to do certian things which are legal, and secondly, under specified circumstances, to do certain other thigns which are illegal, the first set of promises is a contract, but the second is a void agreement.

16. ***Section 59: Application of payment where debt to be discharged is indicated***

Where a debtor, owing several distinct debts to one person, makes a payment to him, either with express intimation, or under circumstances implying, that the payment is to be applied to the discharge of some particular debt, the payment, if accepted must be applied accordingly.

17. ***Section 60: Application of payment where debt to be discharged is not indicated***

Where the debtor has omitted to intimate, and there are no other circumstances indicating to which debt the payment is to be applied, the creditor may apply it at his descretion to any lawful debt actually due and payable to him from the debtor, whether its recovery is or is not barred by the law in force for the time being as to the limitations of sutis.

18. ***Section 61: Application of payment where neither party appropriates***

Where neither party makes any appropriation, the payment shall be applied in discharge of the debts in order of time, whether they are or are not barred by the law in force for the time being as to the limitation of suits. If the debts are of equal standing, the payment shall be applied in discharge of each proportionably.

TEST QUESTIONS

1. What do you understand by the term 'performance of a contract'? What are the two important parts in which the performance of a contract may be studied? Discuss in detail with suitable examples.
2. What do you understand by the term 'tender of performance'? State the essentials of a valid tender of performance along with the effect of refusal to accept a tender of performance.
3. State the persons by whom the contract should be performed. In what circumstances the performance by a third party is effective?
4. State the persons who are entitled to perform the contract. In what circumstances a third party can enforce the contract?.
5. Define the term 'Joint promises'. State the provisions of the Indian Contract Act which govern the performance of joint promises. Support your answer with suitable examples.
6. What do you understand by the terms *'devolution of joint rights'* and *'devolution of joint liabilities'*?.
7. What are the liabilities of a joint promisor under a contract?.
8. Discuss in detail the rules relating to the time and place for performance of a contract.
9. What do you understand by the terms' time as the essence of contract'? What are the effects of non-performance of a contract within the specified time?
10. Define the term 'reciprocal promise'. What are the various kinds of reciprocal promises. State the rules for the performance of reciprocal promises along with their order of performance.
11. State the rules for the performance of legal and illegal reciprocal promises.
12. What rules govern the appropriation of payment by a debtor who makes payment of one of several debts owed by him to a creditor?

13. What do you understand by appropriations of payment? State the provision of Indian Contract Act which govern the appropriation of payments made by a debtor. Support your answer with suitable examples.

MULTIPLE CHOICE QUESTIONS

1. On the valid performance of the contractual obligations by the parties, the contract
(*a*) is discharged (*b*) becomes enforceable
(*c*) becomes void (*d*) none of these

2. Which of the following statements is not true?
(*a*) A valid tender of performance is equivalent to performance.
(*b*) On rejection of such tender, the promisor is discharged from his liability.
(*c*) On rejection of such tender, the promisor can also sue the promisee for breach of contract.
(*d*) On rejection of tender of money by the creditor, the debtor is discharged from liability to pay.

3. Which of the following persons can perform the contract?
(*a*) promisor alone (*b*) legal representatives of promisor
(*c*) agent of the promisor (*d*) all of these

4. *A*, *B* and *C* jointly promised to pay Rs. 60,000 to *D*. Before performance of the contract, *C* dies. Here, the contract
(*a*) becomes void on *C's* death
(*b*) should be performed by *A* and *B* along with *C's* legal representatives.
(*c*) should be performed by *A* and *B* alone.
(*d*) should be renewed between *A*, *B* and *D*.

5. *A*, *B* and *C* jointly promised to pay Rs 30,000 to *D*. For recovery of this amount, *D* filed a suit against *A* only. Is he justified?
(*a*) Yes, as the liability of joint promisors is joint and several.
(*b*) No, as the liability of joint promisors is joint only.

6. *A*, *B* and *C* jointly promised to pay Rs. 60,000 to *D*. *A* was compelled by *D* to pay the entire amount of Rs. 60,000. Here
(*a*) *A* can file a suit against *D* for recovery of amount exceeding his share.
(*b*) *A* is entitled to recover Rs. 20,000 each from *B* and *C*.
(*c*) On payment by *A*, the contract is discharged and *B* and *C* are also not liable to *A*.
(*d*) *D* is not justified here and is liable to refund the entire amount to *A*.

7. In commercial transactions, time is considered to be of the essence of the contract, and if the party fails to perform the contract within specified time, the contract becomes:
(*a*) Voidable at the option of the other party. (*b*) void and cannot be enforced.
(*c*) enforceable in higher court only. (*d*) illegal for non-compliance of legal terms.

8. Where the performance of a promise by one party depends on the prior performance of promise by the other party, such reciprocal promises fall under the category of
(*a*) Mutual and concurrent (*b*) Conditional and dependent
(*c*) Mutual and independent (*d*) both (*a*) and (*b*)

9. Can a time barred debt be adjusted by a creditor, where the debtor makes the payment without indicating the debt to be adjusted?
(*a*) Yes, in such a case the creditor is at liberty to do this.
(*b*) No, as a time-barred debt cannot be recovered.

ANSWERS

1. (*a*) 2. (*d*) 3. (*d*) 4. (*b*) 5. (*a*) 6. (*b*)
7. (*a*) 8. (*b*) 9. (*a*).

OBJECTIVE TYPE QUESTIONS WITH REASONING

State with reason whether the following statements are correct or incorrect.

1. The performance is one of the various modes of discharge of the contract and the contract is discharged as soon as one of the parties perform his part of obligation.
2. In case a valid tender of performance by the promisor is rejected by the promisee, then the promisor is excused from further performance.
3. Performance of the contract may be made only by the parties to the contract.
4. Performance by a third party is also effective if the promisee accepts the same.
5. When the promisee does not accept the offer of performance, the promisor is not responsible for non-performance.
6. If the promisors are joint, the promisee may compel any one or more of the joint promisors to perform the whole promise.
7. A tender of performance in instalment is a valid tender even if the contract stipulates the payment in full.
8. It is a mixed question of law and fact whether time was the essence of the contract.
9. In commercial transactions, the presumption is that the time is of the essence of the contract.
10. In construction related contracted the time is likely to be the essence of the contract.

ANSWERS

1. ***Incorrect.*** Though the performance is one of the modes of discharge of the contract, but the contract is discharged only when both the parties perform their respective obligations.
2. ***Correct.*** There is specific provision in section 38 to this effect.
3. ***Incorrect.*** Performance can also be made by the legal representatives or authorised agent of the parties [Section 37,40]. Performance by a third party is also effective if the promisee accepts the same [section 41].
4. ***Correct.*** The performance by a third party is recognised by section 41.
5. ***Correct.*** *A* valid tender of performance is equivalent to performance [Section 38].
6. ***Correct.*** The liability of joint promisors is joint and several [Section 43].
7. ***Incorrect.*** One of the requirements of a valid tender is that it must be unconditional and of the whole obligation.
8. ***Correct.*** It the judicially recognised rule of law.
9. ***Correct*** . However, in non-commercial transactions there is no such presumption.
10. ***Correct.*** The construction is a commercial service.

PRACTICAL PROBLEMS

1. *A* promised to deliver some goods to *B* on a certain day on the payment of Rs.2,000. However, *A* died before that date. Can *B* claim performance from *A*'s legal representatives? Give reasons.

   Hint : Yes, *B* can claim performance from *A*'s legal representatives. If the promisor dies before performance, his legal representatives are liable to perform the contract [Section 37 (second para)]

2. *A* contracted to sing a song in *B*'s theatre on 15th August, 2009 for the payment of Rs. 50,000. However, *A* died before this date. Can this contract be performed by *A*'s brother, who is also a singer? Give reasons.

   Hint : No, this contract cannot be performed by *A*'s brother The contracts involving personal skills come to an end on the death of the promisor.

3. *A, B* and *C* jointly promised to pay Rs. 1,20,000 to *D* which they owned to him (*D*). *A* alone was compelled by *D* to pay the entire amount of Rs. 1,20,000. *B* was declared insolvent and his assets were sufficient to pay only 50% of his share of contribution. Discuss the contribution which *A* is entitled to recover from other Joint promisors.

   Hint : *A* is entitled to receive Rs. 20,000 from *B*'s estate and Rs. 50,000 from C. Here, due to *B's* insolvency, the total loss is of Rs. 20,000 because only Rs. 20,000 (50%) have been realised from *B*'s estate. This loss is shared by *A* and *C* jointly and thus C is liable to contribute Rs. 50,000 instead of Rs. 40,000.

4. *A* owed Rs. 20,000 to *B* and *B* desired that *A* should pay the amount in *B*'s account in the Global Trust Bank. *A* also had his account in the Global Trust Bank and thus instructed the bank to transfer Rs. 20,000 from *A*'s account to *B*'s account which was accordingly done by the bank. Afterwards, the bank failed before *B* knew about the transfer of funds to his account. Can *B* again demand the money from *A*? Give reasons.

   Hint: No, *B* cannot demand the money again from *A*. Here, by acting as per the instructions of *B*, there has been a good performance of the contract.

5. *A* agreed to construct a house for *B* and *B* agreed to supply the necessary material for construction of the house. However, *B* refused to supply the necessary material, but insisted that *A* should perform the contract by himself buying the material from the market. Is *B* justified in doing so? Give reasons.

   Hint: *B* is not justified in doing so. Here, the propises are conditional and dependent and performance of *A*'s promise to construct the house depends upon the prior performance of *B*'s promise to supply necessary material for construction.

6. *A* contracted with *B* to execute certain repair work at his (*B*'s) house for a certain amount and *B* agreed to supply the scaffolding required for doing the job. *A* was ready with the material and labour at the site, but the scaffolding proveded by *B* was inadequate and of very poor quality and it was risky to execute the work by using that scaffolding. As such the work could not be executed and *A* claimed compensation for loss due to non-performance. Will he succeed ? Give reasons.

   Hint: Yes, *A* will succeed in his action. Here, *A* was ready and willing to perform the contract but could not do so due in adequate and inferior scaffolding provided by B. [Section 54]

7. *A* and *B* agreed that *A* shall pay Rs. 50,000 to *B* and in consideration *B* shall deliver to *A* either his maruti car or 50 bottles of smuggled liquor. Afterwards, *B* refused to deliver his car and *A* sued *B* for delivery of 50 bottles of liquor. Will he succeed? Give reasons.

   Hint: No, *A* will not succeed. In case of such alternative promises, only the legal part of promise is enforceable and the illegal part of promise is illegal and void. [Section 58]

8. *A* owned two debts to *B* one was of Rs. 40,000 and the other of Rs. 17,000. *B* wrote to *A* that he was in immediate need of Rs.15,000 approximately and at least this amount should be paid. *A* sent a demand draft of Rs. 17,000 to *B*. However, *B* appropriated this amount to the debt of Rs.40,000 which had already become time-barred. Is *B* justified in doing so? Give reasons.

   Hint: No, *B* is not justified in doing so. Here, the circumstances suggest that the intention of *A* in sending draft of Rs. 17,000 was clear to appropriated the same towards the debt of the like amount of Rs. 17,000. Also, by demanding the amount closed to the small debt of Rs. 17,000, the circumstances further suggest that he was also interested in appropriation towards the debt of Rs. 17,000.

12

CHAPTER

DISCHARGE OF CONTRACTS

1. Introduction.
2. Modes of Discharge of a Contract.
3. Discharge by Performance.
4. Discharge by Impossibility of Performance.
5. Doctrine of Frustration or Subsequent Impossibility.
6. English Law Regarding Doctrine of Frustration.
7. Difference Between Indian Law and English Law Regarding Frustration.
8. Specific Grounds of Frustra-tion of Subsequent Impossibility.
9. Non-applicability of the Doc-trine of Frustration.
10. Effect of Frustration.
11. Adjustment of Rights of the Parties.
12. Discharge by Agreement.
13. Novation.
14. Rescission.
15. Alteration.
16. Remission.
17. Waiver.
18. Acceptance of any other Satisfaction.
19. Accord and Satisfaction.
20. Discharge by Operation of Law.
21. Discharge by Lapse of Time.
22. Discharge by Breach of Contract.
23. Actual Breach of Contract.
24. Anticipatory Breach of Contract.
25. Measure of Damages in Anticipatory Breach of Contract.

12.1. INTRODUCTION

We have already discussed that a valid contract creates certain obligations on the contracting parties, and the parties become liable to fulfil their respective obligations. When the parties fulfil their respective obligations, their liability under the contract, comes to an end and the contract is said to be discharged. Thus, the discharge of a contract means that the parties are no more liable under the contract. In other words, when the rights and obligations created by the contract come to an end, the contract is said to be discharged. The discharge of a contract may, therefore, be defined as the termination of contractual relationship between the parties, In this chapter, we shall discuss the various modes of discharge of contract, and other legal provisions relating thereto.

12.2. MODES OF DISCHARGE OF A CONTRACT

Following are the various modes in which a contract may be discharged:

1. By performance.
2. By impossibility of performance.
3. By agreement.
4. By operation of law.
5. By lapse of time.
6. By breach.

26. Remedies for Breach of Contract.
27. Suit for Rescission.
28. Suit for Damages.
29. Suit for Quantum Meruit.
30. Case for Claim on Quantume Meruit.
31. Suit for Specific Performance.
32. Suit for Injunction.

12.3. DISCHARGE BY PERFORMANCE

The contract is said to be discharged when parties to a contract, perform their respective obligations which they have agreed to do. This point has already been discussed in detail in the previous chapter on 'Performance of Contract'

12.4. DISCHARGE BY IMPOSSIBILITY OF PERFORMANCE

1. *Initial impossibility*
2. *Subsequent or supervening impossibility*

Sometimes, the performance of a contract is impossible. In such cases, the contract is discharged because the parties cannot perform their respective obligations. This is based on the principle that the law does not recognise what is impossible. And what is impossible does not create any obligations. The impossibility of performance may be of the two types, namely (*a*) initial impossibility and (*b*) subsequent impossibility.

1. *Initial impossibility:* It is the impossibility which exists at the time of formation of a contract. It makes the contract *void ab initio, i.e.,* void from the very beginning. And thus, the contract does not create any rights and obligations on the contracting parties. This provision is contained in para 1st of Section 56 of the Indian Contract Act, which reads as under:

"An agreement to do an act impossible in itself, is void"

Example 12.1. *A* agreed with *B* to discover a treasure by magic. And *B* agreed to pay Rs. 500 to *A* for this act. This agreement is void due to initial impossibility.

Example 12.2. *A* promised to enclose a space between two straight lines. And *B* agreed to pay Rs. 1000 to *A* for this act. This agreement is void due to initial impossibility.

It is to be noted that the initial impossibility may be known or unknown to the parties at the time of agreement. In both the cases, the agreement is void and the parties are discharged as the void agreement does not create any rights and obligations on the contracting parties.

Example 12.3. A agreed to sell his horse to *B*. But unknown to both the parties, the horse had already died at the time of making the contract. In this case, the contract is void on the ground of initial impossibility.

However , if the initial impossibility is known to the promisor alone, he must pay compensation to the promisee for any loss which the promisee may suffer on account of non-performance of the contract. [Section 56, Para 3].

Example 12.4. *A*, a Hindu, who was already married, contracted to marry *B*, a Hindu Girl, According to law *A* being married, could not marry *B*. In this case, *A* must make compensation to *B* for the loss caused to her by the non-performance of the contract.

2. *Subsequent or supervening impossibility:* Sometimes, the performance of a contract is quite possible when it is made, But subsequently, some event happens which renders the performance impossible or unlawful. Such impossibility is called the subsequent or supervening. In other words, it is the impossibility which arises subsequent to the formation of the contract. It is also called the post contractual impossibility. The effect of such impossibility is that it makes the contract void, and the parties are discharged from further performance of the contract. And thus, the contract is discharged. This provision is contained in para 2 of Section 56 of the Indian Contract Act, which reads as under:

"A contract to do an act which after the contract is made, becomes impossible, or by reason of some event which the promisor could not prevent, unlawful, becomes void when the act becomes impossible or unlawful."

Thus, a subsequent impossibility renders the contract void. The contract is discharged in such cases.

Example 12.5. *A* and *B* contracted to marry each other. Before the time fixed for the marriage, *A* became mad. In this case, the contract becomes void due to subsequent impossibility, and thus discharged.

Example 12.6. *A*, an Indian citizen, contracted to supply certain goods to *B*, a foreigner, at his port. Afterwards, a war was declared between the two countries. In this case, the contract becomes void when the war is declared, and the parties are discharged from performing the contract. And thus, the contract is discharged.

It may, however, be noted that the contract becomes void on the ground of subsequent impossibility only if the following conditions are satisfied:

1. The act should have become impossible.
2. The impossibility should have been caused by the circumstances which were beyond the control of the concerned parties.
3. The impossibility should not be self induced *i.e.*, the impossibility should not be the result of the act of the parties.[1]

There are various circumstances which render the contract void on the ground of subsequent impossibility. These are discussed in the following pages under the headings 'Doctrine of Frustration', and 'Specific Grounds of Frustration.'

12.5. DOCTRINE OF FRUSTRATION OR SUBSEQUENT IMPOSSIBILITY

The term 'frustration' is the concept used in English law, which is the parallel concept of 'supervening impossibility'. The expression 'doctrine of frustration' means that in case of subsequent impossibility, the courts may declare the contract as void. It may be noted that the Indian Law regarding doctrine of frustration is codified and is contained in Section 56 of the Indian Contract Act, which has been discussed in Art. 15.4 above. On the ground of frustration (*i.e.*, subsequent impossibility) the contract becomes void in following circumstances:

1. Where the performance of the contract becomes physically impossible.
2. Where the basic purpose or object of the contract has failed, and it can no longer be carried out.

The Supreme Court has held that Section 56 applies to both kinds of frustrations. And the following observations of the Supreme Court are worth nothing in this regard:

"This much is clear that the word 'impossible' has not been used here in the sense of physical or literal impossibility. The performance of an act may not be literally impossible but it may be impracticable and useless from the point of view of the object and purpose which the parties had in view; and if an untoward event or change of circumstances totally upsets the very foundation upon which the parties rested in their bargain, it can very well be said that the promisor find it impossible to do the act which he promised to do".

[*Satyabrata* v. *Magneeram*, AIR 1954 SC 44].

From the above observations and the language of Section 56 of the Indian Contract Act, it becomes clear that the doctrine of frustration means the impossibility of performance due to subsequent un-expected event or change of circumstances.

1. *Boothlinga Agencies* v. *V.T.C. Pariaswami Nadar*, AIR 1969 SC 110.

Example 12.7. *A* contracted to sell to *B* certain quantity of potatoes to be grown in his farm. Subsequently, the crop of potatoes was destroyd by a disease. And *A* failed to supply the contracted quantity of potatoes to *B*. It was held that the contract was discharged as the performance had become impossible due to the destruction of potatoes. [*Howell* v. *Coupland* (1876) QBD 258 (CA)].

12.6. ENGLISH LAW REGARDING DOCTRINE OF FRUSTRATION

We have already discussed that the term' frustration' as used in English Law is the parallel concept of the term 'supervening impossibility' as used in Indian Law. It important to mention that in olden days, the English Common Law was very hard. And the impossibility of performance was no defence to an action for breach of contract unless the parties expressly provided for the same. Thus, earlier a person was bound to perform his promise even if the performance might have become subsequently impossible. But later on, the English Courts realised the hardships of this doctrine and laid down that *there is an implied term in every contract that it will become void when the performance becomes impossible due to certain subsequent events or change of circumstances.* However, the contract will become void only when such event or changed circumstances were beyond the knowledge and control of the concerned parties, and defeated the basic purpose of the contract. It may be noted that under the English Law also, the contract shall become void on the ground of frustration in the following two circumstances:

1. Where the performance of the contract becomes physically impossible.
2. Where the basic object or the contract has failed to materialise.

Example 12.8. *A* agreed to let a music hall to *B* for holding a music show on certain dates. But before the first day of the show, the music hall was destroyed by fire without the fault of either party. It was held that on the destruction of the music hall the contract become void as its performance depended upon the continued existence of the music hall. In this case, the performance of the contract had become physically impossible because of the destruction of the subject matter (*i.e.*, music hall) of contract. [*Taylor* v. *Coldwell Q.B.* (1863) 3 B & S 826 122 ER 309]

It may be noted that the contract will also beocme void where though the physical performance is possible, but the object which the parties had in mind, has failed to materialise.

Example 12.9. *A* hired a flat from *B* for June 26 and 27 for witnessing a coronation procession of King Edward VII. The purpose for which *A* hired the flat was known to *B*, though there was no reference to this in the contract. The coronation procession was cancelled due to the illness of the king. It was held that on the cancellation of the coronation procession, the contract became void as the real object of the contract has failed to materialise.

[*Krell* v. *Henri* (1903) 2 KB 740, C.A.]

12.7. DIFFERENCE BETWEEN INDIAN LAW AND ENGLISH LAW REGARDING DOCTRINE OF FRUSTRATION

We have discussed above, the Indian as well as the English law regarding frustration . It is clear that the effect of the doctrine under both the laws is same ,*i.e.*, the contract becomes void. However , as regards the application of the doctrine, the Indian Law differs from that of the English law. The Indian law lays down a rule of positive law and does not leave the matter to be determined according to the intention of the parties . And the contract becomes void when the whole purpose or basis of contract is frustrated by subsequent impossibility. The provision for subsequent impossibility has been specifically made in section 56 of the Indian contract Act. Whereas, the English law is based on the implied terms of the contract *i.e* the English law is applied on the ground that the parties impliedly agreed that in case of frustration , the contract shall become void.

12.8. SPECIFIC GROUNDS OF FRUSTRATION OR SUBSEQUENT IMPOSSIBILITY

1. *Destruction of the subject-matter*
2 *Failure of object due to non -occurence of contemplated event*
3. *Death or incapacity of the promisor*
4. *Change of circumstances*
5. *Change of law or change of government policy*
6. *Outbreak of war*

The following grounds of frustation (*i.e.*, impossibility of performance) have become well established, and the contract is discharged in these circumstances:

1. *Destruction of the subject-matter :* Sometimes, the subject-matter of the contract is destroyed after the formation of the contract. In such cases , the contract is discharged .And the partis are no more liable to perform their respective obligations. It may, however ,be noted that the destruction of subject -matter should be without any fault of the parties to the contract.

Example 12.10. *A* agreed to let out his truck to B on certain dates. Before these dates, the truck is totally damaged in accident without any fault of the partis . In this case the contract is discharged as the subject-matter (*i.e.*, truck) of the contract has destroyed.

Tailor's case discussed in Example 12.8 , is also relevant on this point.

Sometimes, the subject -matter is not destroyed , but it ceases to be available to the parties. In such cases also , the contract will become void , and thus discharged. However, where the parties can still perform their main obligation , despite the fact that the subject is discharged as the subject-matter has gone out of their hands , the contract may not be discharged on the ground of frustration.

Example 12.11. *A* was the authorised agent of *B* for dealing with the goods "manufactured or sold" by *B. B's* factory was destroyed . It was held that the agency between the agent (*A*) and principal (*B*) was not frustrated because the agent could still deal with the goods 'sold' by the principal. [*Turner* v. *Goldsmith*, (1891) 1 QB 544].

2 *Failure of object due to non -occurence of contemplated event:* Sometimes, the performance of a contract remains possible, but due to the non-occurrence of a contemplated event, the object or purpose of the contract is defeated. In such cases, the contract becomes void , and thus discharged . It may, however, be noted that the contract is discharged only when the happening of the event was the basis of the contract .In other words, the whole contract should be based on the event which has ceased to exist.

Example 12.12. *A* hired a taxi from *B* for January 1st and 2nd for the purpose of attending a conference at Shimla. The purpose for hiring the taxi was known to *B* .The conference was cancelled due to heavy snowfall in Shimla. In this case, the basic purpose of the contract was to attend a conference at Shimla .As the basic purpose has been defeated due to the cancellation of the conference, the contract is discharged.

Krell's case discussed in Example 12.9 is also relevant on this point.

3. *Death or incapacity of the promisor :* Sometimes , the nature or terms of a contract require personal performance by the promisor himself . In such cases, the death or incapacity of the promisor puts an end to the contract and it is discharged. The contracts involving personal skill of the promisor , *e.g.*, a contact to paint a picture , or sing a song. etc are the contracts of such nature.

Example 12.13. *A*, a circus motor cyclist contracted with *B*, the owner of circus, to perform particular action on his motor cycle. Before the performance, *A* died. In this case, the contract is discharged.

Example 12.14. *A*, a model girl, contracted with *B*, an advertising agency, to act in their fashion parade on a particular day. On the fixed date, *A* was hospitalised due to serious illness. In this case, the contract to act in the fashion parade is discharged.

4. *Change of circumstances:* Sometimes, the change of circumstances renders the performance impossible. In such cases, the contract may be discharged on the ground of frustration. It may, however be noted that the contract is discharged only when the change of circumstances has affected the performance of the contract to such an extent that the performance becomes virtually impossible. In other words, the contract is discharged only where the performance becomes extremely difficult or hazardous.

However, a normal change of circumstances does not frustrate the contract. In *Continental Construction Co. Ltd.* v. *State of M.P.* AIR 1988 SC 1166, the Supreme Court has stated that a normal change of circumstances such as normal price rise, does not frustrate the contract.

5. *Change of law or change of government policy:* Sometimes, the contracts are valid and lawful when they are made. But they become unlawful due to subsequent change in the law or change in the government policy. In such cases, the contract are discharged as their performance becomes impossible.

Example 12.15. *A*, a dealer of imported goods, entered into an agreement to sell certain imported goods to *B*. Subsequently, a law was made which banned the sale of imported goods. It was held that the contract is discharged as its performance had become impossible due to change in law. [*Bothalinga Agencies'case*, AIR 1969 SC 110]

Example 12.16. *A* agreed to sell his land to *B*. Subsequently, that land was acquired by the government. And A could not execute the sale deed as he ceased to be the owner by operation of law. It was held that the contract was discharged as its performance had become impossible.

[*Shiam sunder* v. *Durga*, AIR 1966 All. 185].

6. *Outbreak of war :* On the declaration of a war, the performance of the pending contracts with the citizens of other country, becomes impossible. Such contracts with the citizens of other country, becomes impossible. Such contracts are either suspended or declared as void by the government. The suspended contracts may be performed after the war is over. However, all the contracts entered into with aliend enemy during the war, are unlawful and void ab-initio.

Example 12.17. *A*, an Indian citizen, contracted to supply 100 pieces of a particular machine to *B*. a foreigner, at his port. Afterwards, a war was declared between the two countries. In this case, the contract becomes void on the declaration of the war. And thus, the contract between *A* and *B* is discharged.

12.9. NON-APPLICABILITY OF THE DOCTRINE OF FRUSTRATION

1. *Difficulty in performance*
2. *Commercial hardships*
3. *Impossibility due to the conduct of a third person*
4. *Impossibility induced by the party himself*
5. *Strikes, lock-outs and civil disrurbances*
6. *Failure of one of the several objects*

In the following circumstances, the doctrine of frustration is not applicable. And thus, the contract is not discharged on the ground of impossibility of performance:

1. *Difficulty in performance :* Sometimes, the performance of the contract does not become impossible, but becomes difficult only due to some subsequent event. In such cases, the parties remain bound to perform the contract.

Example 12.18. *A* agreed to sell to *B* 300 tons of Sudan groundnuts at Hamburg. The usual and normal sea route, at the time of contract, was via Suez Canal. The shipment was to be made in November\December 1956. On 2nd November 1956, the Suez canal was closed to traffic, and it was not reopened until April 1957. *A* refused to supply the goods on the ground that the performance has become impossible due to the closing of the Suez Canal. *B* stated that the goods could have been shipped via Cape Town (Cape of Goods Hope), the other route. However, *A* refused to ship the goods via Cape Town. In this case, the question arose, whether by reason of the closing of the Suez canal, the contract has been ended by frustration. It was held that the customary and usual route via Suez Canal being closed, *A* was bound to ship the goods by a reasonable and practicable route. The second route might be expensive but that did not render the contract fundamentally or radically different. And thus, there was no frustration of the contract. [*Tsakir Oglu & Co.* v. *Nablee & Thorl* (1962) AC 93]

2. *Commercial hardships:* Sometimes, a party to the contract is faced with commercial hardships. In such cases, the party is not discharged from the performance of his obligations simple on the ground that it will be non-profitable for him to perform the contract. As a matter of fact, Section 56 of the Indian Contract Act does not provide for the commercial hardship (*i.e.*, commercial impossibility).

Example 12.19. *A* agreed to supply certain goods to *B*, Due to the outbreak of war, there was a sharp increase in the price of the goods. In this case. *A* is not discharged form his liability to supply the goods to *B* on the ground of increase in price.

Thus, a party is not discharged from the liability to perform his part of the contract merely because on account of uncontemplated turn of events, the performance of the contract has become onerous (*i.e.*, burdensome).

3. *Impossibility due to the conduct of a third person:* Sometimes, the performance of a contract depends upon the behaviour of a third person. In such cases, the contract is not discharged if the performance becomes impossible due to the conduct (default, etc.) of the third person. In other words, the parties remain bound to perform their respective obligations.

Example 12.20. *A* agreed to supply certain goods to *B* which were to be imported by *C*. But *C* failed to import the goods. In this case, the contract between *A* and *B* is not discharged. And *A* is liable to pay damages to *B* for the non-performance of the contract.

In fact, a person supplying the goods cannot take the plea of impossibility of performance if he does not receive the requisite quantity from his own supplier.

[*Standard Chemical Co.* v *Palakol Coop Sugar Co.* (1988) 25 Reports 60]

4. *Impossibility induced by the party himself:* Sometimes, the performance of the contract becomes impossible due to the act or omission of the contracting party. In such cases, the contract is not discharged on the ground of frustration. In other words, the contract is not discharged in case of self-induced impossibility.[2]

5. *Strikes, lock-outs and civil disrurbances:* All such events do not discharge the contract unless specifically provided by the parties.

Example 12.21. *A* agreed to supply certain goods to *B*, which were to be procured from Algeria. Due to riots and civil disturbances in Algeria, the goods could not be procured, it was held that there was no excuse for the non-performance of the contract.

[*Jacob* v. *Credit Lyonnais* (1884) 12 QBD 589]

6. *Failure of one of the several objects:* Sometimes, a contract is entered into for several objects. In such cases, the contract is not discharged if only one of the objects fails. Thus, if the parties can still perform their main obligations despite the fact that one of the object has failed, the contract is not discharged on the ground of frustration.

Example 12.22. *A* agreed to give his boat on hire to *B* for the purpose of (*a*) viewing a naval review on the occasion of the coronation of King Edward VII, and (*b*) sailing round the fleet. Due to King's illness, the coronation was cancelled, but the fleet was assembled. It was held that the contract is not discharged as the boat could have been used to sale round the fleet.

[*Henri Bay Steam boot Co.* v. *Hutton,* (1903) K.B.683]

2. *Boothinga Agencies v. Parisawami Nadar,* AIR 1969 SC 110.

7. *Completed transfer of leasehold property:* The doctrine of frustration is not applicable to completed transfers of leasehold property. Sometimes, a person gives his property on lease to another person . And the transaction is completed by the lessor and the payment of rent by the lessee. In such cases, the validity of the lease shall not be affected by subsequent events.

Example 12.23. Before the partition of India. *A* gave lease of his agricultural land to *B* for one year. The rent was paid by *B* and he was also given the possession of the land. But before the land could be used for agricultural purpose, the partition took place. On the partition, the land of lease remained in Pakistan and the parties migrated to India. *B* filed a suit against *A* for the recovery of the rent already paid on the ground of frustration. It was held that he was not entitled to recover the rent. The Supreme Court observed that completed transfers are outside the scope of Section 56 of the Indian Contract Act.

[*Raja Dhruv Dev Chand* v. *Raja Har Mohinder Singh,* AER 1968 SC 1024].

But an agreement to lease was ended by frustration where before completing it the parties had to run away and could not go back to Pakistan to give or take possession of the land. [*Sushila Devi* v. *Hari Singh,* AIR 1971 SC 1956]

12.10. EFFECT OF FRUSTRATION OR SUBSEQUENT IMPOSSIBILITY

The effect of frustration (*i.e.,* subsequent impossibility) is that the contract becomes void. This provision is contained in Para 2 of Section 56 of the Indian Contract Act, which reads as under :

"A contract to do an act which after the contract is made, become impossible, or by reason of some event which the promisor could not prevent, unlawful, becomes void when the act becomes impossible or unlawful."

Thus, when subsequent to the formation of the contract, its performance becomes impossible or unlawful, the contract becomes void. And the contract is discharged. It may be noted that in case of frustration, the contract is discharged automatically, *i.e.,* frustration operates automatically. However, the contract becomes void on the ground of subsequent impossibility only if the following conditions are satisfied:

1. The act should have become impossible
2. The impossibility should have been caused by the circumstances which are beyond the control of the concerned parties.
3. The impossibility should not be self-induced, *i.e.,* the alleged impossibility should not be the result of the act of the parties.[3]

12.11. ADJUSTMENT OF RIGHTS OF THE PARTIES

Sometimes, a contract is apparently valid when it is made, but subsequently it becomes void. In such cases, if the party has received some benefit under the contract, then he must restore it to the other party [Section 65].

Example 12.24. *A* , a house owner, paid Rs 2000 to *B*, a contractor, in consideration of *B's* promise to paint *A's* house . At that time, none of the parties knew that the said house had already been destroyed due to floods. In this case, the agreement between *A* and *B* is void . And *B* must repay Rs. 2,000 to *A*

Example 12.25. *A* contracted to sing for *B* at a concert for Rs. 1000 which were paid in advance. *A* fell ill on the day of the concert and could not sing . In this case, *A* must refund to *B* Rs. 1000 paid in advance. However. *A* is not liable for the loss of profits which *B* would have made if A had been able to sing at the concert.

3. Boothlinga's case, AIR 1969 SC 110.

12.12. DISCHARGE BY AGREEMENT

A contract may be discharged by mutual agreement of the concerned parties. The parties may enter into a fresh agreement which provides for the extinguishment of their rights and obligations created by the original contract. In such cases, the original contract is discharged as the parties are not required to perform the original contract due to the fresh agreement. Section 62 and 63 of the Indian Contract Act contain the various methods of discharge by agreement, which respectively read as under:

"If the parties to a contract agree to substitute a new contract for it , or to rescind or alter it, the original contract need not be performed."

"Every promisee may dispense with or remit, wholly or in part, the performance of the promise made to him, or may extend the time of such performance, or may accept instead of it any satisfaction which he thinks fit"

The analysis of these sections reveal that the original contract is discharged when the parties enter into a fresh contract in place of original contract. Following important methods for the discharge of a contract by a fresh contract are recognised by these sections:

1 Novation.
2 Rescission.
3. Alternation.
4. Remission.
5. Waiver
6. Acceptance of any other satisfaction.

12.13. NOVATION

The term 'novation' may be defined as the substitution of existing contract for a new contract. In other words, when the parties to a contract agree to substitute the existing contract by a new contract, it is known as novation. It may be noted that the novation must be with the mutual consent of all the parties. The novation may be of the following two types:

1. *Novation involving change of parties, but the contract remaining the same:* Sometimes, the parties to the contract are changed. But the contract remains the same. In such cases, the contract between the original parties is discharged and need not be performed. However, the concurrence of all the parties is necessary, *i.e.*, all the parties must give their consent to the new contract.

Example 12.26. *A* owed certain money to *B* under a contract. It was agreed between *A*, *B* and *C* that *B* would thenceforth accept *C* as his debtor instead of *A*. In this case, *A* is discharged from his liability to pay the debt to *B*.

2. *Novation involving substitution of a new contract, but parties remaining the same:* Sometimes, the concerned parties to a contract agree to substitute the existing contract for a new one. In such cases, the original contract is discharged and need not be performed.

Example 12.27. *A* owed Rs. 10,000 to *B*. A entered into an agreement with *B* and gave *B* a mortgage of his land for Rs. 5000 in place of the debt of Rs. 10,000. It is a new contract and dis charges the original contract to pay Rs. 10,000.

The novation, as discussed above, will be valid only if the following conditions are satisfied:

(*a*) The new contract must be consented by all the parties, *i.e.*, all the parties must give their consent to novation.
(*b*) The new contract must be made before the breach of the original contract.
(*c*) The new contract must be valid and enforceable.

12.14. RESCISSION

The term 'rescission' may be defined as the cancellation of the contract. A contract may be rescinded by agreement between the parties at any time before it is discharged by performance or in some other way.

Example 12.28. *A* promised to deliver certain goods to *B* on a certain date. Before the due date of performance, *A* and *B* mutually agreed that the contract would not be performed. In this case, the parties have rescinded the contract. And thus, the contract is discharged.

12.15. ALTERATION

The term 'alteration' maybe defined as change in one or more terms of the contract. The alteration is valid when it is made with the consent of all the parties. And the valid alteration discharges the original contract, and the parties become bound by the new contract (*i.e.*, contract with altered terms).

Example 12.29. *A* agreed to supply to *B* 50 bags of rice at the rate of Rs. 100 per bag. The delivery was to be made in five equal instalments, the first supply was to commence from 1st June. Subsequently, *A* and *B* entered into an agreement that the delivery would be made in two equal instalments and the price would be Rs. 105 per bag. In this case, the old contract is discharged and the parties become bound by the contract with changed terms.

It is important to note here that in case of a written contract, the material alteration by one party without the consent of the other, also discharges the contract. In such a case, both the parties will be discharged from preforming their respective obligations.

12.16. REMISSION

The term remission' may be defined as the acceptance of lesser fulfilment of the terms of the promise, *e.g.*, acceptance of a less sum of money where more is due. In other words, the remission is the lesser fulfilment of the promise made. The remission is the valid discharge of the whole of the liability under the contract. Section 63 of the Indian contract Act contains this provision which provides that the party who has the right to demand performance of the contract may

(*a*) remit or dispense with it, wholly or in part.

(*b*) extend the time of performance.

(*c*) accept any other satisfaction instead of performance.

Example 12.30. *A* owed Rs 5000 to *B*. *A* paid Rs. 2000 to *B*, and *B* accepted it in full satisfication. In this case, *A* is discharged from his liability of Rs. 5000.

Example 12.31. *A* owed Rs. 10,000 to *B*. *A's* friend *C* paid Rs. 8000 to *B*, and *B* accepted it in full satisfaction of his claim over *A*. In this case, *A* is discharged from his liability of Rs. 10,000 to *B*.

Note: The English Law on this point is different. According to English Law, the remission must be supported by fresh consideration. Whereas in India, under Section 63, the remission is valid and binding even though there is no consideration for it.

[*Hari Chand Madan Gopal* v. *State of Punjab*, AIR 1973 SC 381].

12.17. WAIVER

The term 'waiver' may be defined as the abandonment (*i.e.*, giving up) of the rights by the party who is entitled to claim performance of the contract. On waiver, the other party to the contract is discharged from the performance of his liabilities under the contract. Section 63 of the Indian Contract Act contains this provision which provides that the party who has the right to demand performance may 'dispense with it', *i.e.*, may waive it.

Example 12.32. A promised to paint a picture for *B* . Afterwards, *B* forbade him to do so. In this case, *B* has waived his right to claim the performance. And thus, *A* is no longer liable to perform the promise.

However, the party who has waived the compliance with a particular condition, may also withdraw his waiver by giving reasonable notice.

12.18. ACCEPTANCE OF ANY OTHER SATISFACTION

Sometimes, the party entitled to claim performance accepts any other satisfaction instead of the performance of the contract. In such cases, the other party is discharged from the performance of his liability under the contract. Section 63 of the Indian Contract Act contains this provision which provides that the party who has the right to demand performance, may accept any other satisfaction, which he thinks fit, instead of the performance of the promise made to him. And such acceptance, discharges the whole obligations under the contract.

Example 12.33. *A* owed *B*, under a contract, a sum of money, the amount of which had not been ascertained. Without ascertaining the amount, *A* gave Rs. 2000 to *B*. And *B* accepted this amount in satisfaction of the sum due under the contract. In this case, *A* is discharged of the whole debt due under the contract, whatever may be its amount.

Example 12.34. *A* owed *B* Rs. 2000, and was also indebted to other creditors. *A* made an arrangement with all his creditors (including *B*) and offered to pay them 50 per cent of the amount due to them and the same was accepted by the creditors. According to this arrangement, *A* paid Rs. 1000 to *B*. In this case, *A* is discharged of his liability of Rs. 2000 to *B*.

12.19. ACCORD AND SATISFACTION

These two terms are used in English Law. The term 'accord' may be defined as the promise to accept less amount than what is due under the contract. And the term 'satisfaction' may be defined as the fulfilment of lesser obligation. Under the English Law, the old contract is discharged when the accord is followed by satisfaction. In other words, the accord and satisfaction discharge the original contract only if the promise to accept less sum has been actually carried out. Thus, a mere promise to accept less sum than what is due under the contract, does not discharge the old contract. The old contract is discharged only when the less sum is actually paid and accepted by the promisee. *i.e.*, there must be actual performance of the new promise and its acceptance by the other party.

Example 12.35. *A* owed *B* Rs. 2000. *B* agreed to accept Rs. 1500 in full satisfaction of his claim. Under the English law, the original debt of Rs. 2000 is not discharged. But when Rs. 1500 is actually paid by *A* and accepted by *B*, there is accord and satisfaction, and the original debt of Rs, 2000 is discharged. In this case, the agreement to accept Rs. 1500 is an accord, and the actual payment of this amount is the satisfaction.

12.20. DISCHARGE BY OPERATION OF LAW

1. *Material alteration*
2. *Insolvency*
3. *Death of a promisor*
4. *Merger of rights*

In certain circumstances, the contract is discharged by the operation of law, *i.e.*, the law regards the contract as discharged. Following are the circumstances under which the law regards the contract as discharges.

1. ***Material alteration :*** Sometimes, a contract is contained in a written document. And one party alters it in material particulars without the consent of the other party. In such cases, the effect of alteration would be the same as that of cancellation of the document. Thus, the material alteration discharges the parties from the performance of their respective obligations under the contract.

Example 12.36. *A* contracted to sell his plot of 500 sq. yards to *B* for Rs. 100,000. The sale deed was executed which was in possession of *A*. Before the registration of the sale deed, *A* altered the deed and made it a deed for the sale of 300 sq yards plot for Rs. 100,000. In this case, the contract is discharged and *B* is not bound to purchase the plot.

2. ***Insolvency*** : Sometimes, a person is declared insolvent by the Court of Law. In such cases, he is discharged from all liabilities and debts incurred prior to the court orders.

3. ***Death of a promisor :*** Sometimes, the contract involves personal skills or qualifications of the promisor himself. In such cases, the contract is discharged on the death of the promisor.

Example 12 37. A, an expert, agreed with *B* to translate some part of book from French to English. *A* died before the translation work started. In this case, the contract is of personal nature as it involves the personal qualification of the promisor (*A*) . And thus, the contract is discharged on the death of *A*.

4. ***Merger of rights :*** Sometimes, the inferior rights and the superior rights coincide and meet in one and the same person. In such cases, the inferior rights merge into the superior rights. On merger, the inferior rights vanish and are not required to be enforced.

Example 12.37. *A* gave his land on lease to *B*. Subsequently, B bought the land which he was holding under the lease. In this case, *B* becomes the owner of the property and his rights as a lessee merge into his rights as the owner. And thus, his rights as a lessee vanish, and are not to be enforced.

12.21. DISCHARGE BY LAPSE OF TIME

As a matter of fact, the contracts must be performed within the period of limitation, *i.e.*, the period specified by the Limitation Act. The Limitation Act lays down different limitation period for different kinds of contracts. If the contract is not performed and the aggrieved party does not enforce his rights within the limitation period, then he is debarred from enforcing the contract. In other words, after the expiry of limitation period, the courts will not enforce the contract. And thus, the contract is discharged as the parties cannot enforce their respective obligations through the Courts of Law.

Example 12.39. *A* borrowed Rs. 5000 from *B*, a money-lender, and agreed to repay the loan on 31st march 1983. On 31st March, 1983, A failed to repay the loan. But *B* did not take any legal action against *A* till 31st March, 1986. In this case, *B* cannot recover the amount of loan from *A* as the limitation period for the recover of loan is three years from the date of default, which has expired. And thus, *A* is discharged from his liability to pay the loan.

12.22. DISCHARGE BY BREACH OF CONTRACT

We have already discussed that in case of valid contract, the parties are bound to perform their respective obligations. If any party fails to perform his obligations, there occurs a breach of the contract. The 'breach of contract' means the failure of a party to perform his obligations.

The party who fails to perform his obligations, is said to have committed a breach of contract. And a breach of contract discharges the aggrieved party from performing his obligations. The breach of contract is of the following two types:

1. Actual Breach. 2. Anticipatory Breach.

12.23. ACTUAL BREACH OF CONTRACT

It occurs when on the due date of performance or during the performance, a party fails to perform his obligations. Thus, the actual breach of contract may be discussed under the following two heads.

1. ***Actual breach of contract on the due date of performance:*** Sometimes, on the due date of performance, one party fails to perform his obligations. In such cases, the other party is discharged from the performance of his obligations, and can hold the guilty party liable for the breach of contract.

Example 12.40. *A* agreed to sell his car to *B* on 1st June. But on 1st June, *A* refused to sell the car to *B*. On *A's* refusal to sell the car, there occurred a breach of the contract. And *B* can hold *A* liable for the breach of contract.

2. ***Actual breach of contract during its performance:*** Sometimes, one party performs his obligations under the contract and the other party fails or refuses to perform this obligations. It is an actual beach of contract *during* its performance. And sometimes, one party, no doubt, performs his obligations but not strictly according to the contract. It is also as an actual breach of contract. This type of breach of contract occurs when the party, performing the contract, commits a breach of the essential conditions to contract. However, the breach of non-essential terms does not discharge the contract. It only entitles the aggrieved party to claim damages from the defaulting party.

Example 12.41. *A* contracted to sell to *B* certain goods of particular description to be delivered on 15th March. On the due date of delivery, *A* delivered the goods to *B*. But the goods did not conform to the description. In this case, the breach of contract is committed during the performance of the contract as *A* has not performed the contract according to its terms. And thus, *B* is not bound to take delivery of the goods and pay for them.

12.24. ANTICIPATORY BREACH OF CONTRACT

It occurs when, prior to the due date of performance, the promisor absolutely refuses or disables himself from the performance of his obligations. In other words, it is a declaration by one party of his intention not to perform his obligations under the contract. Thus, the anticipatory breach is the premature destruction of the contract. *i.e.*, the repudiation of the contract before due date of performance.

Example 12.42. *A* contracted to supply to *B* 100 pieces of spark plugs on 15th December 1997. But before the due date of performance (*i.e.*, 15th December 1997), *A* informed *B* that he is not going to supply the spark plugs at all. On *A's* refusal to supply the goods, the anticipatory breach of the contract occurs. And *B* may put an end to the contract.

This doctrine of anticipatory breach is contained in Section 39 of the Indian Contract Act, which provides that when the promisor, prior to the due date of performance, altogether refuses to perform his obligations under the contract or disables himself from doing so there occurs a breach of contract. And the promisee may put an end to the contract.

Example 12.43. *A*. a tutor, entered into a contract with *B* to teach his son for three days in a week for six months. *B* agreed to pay Rs. 50 for each day of tution. After ten days of tution, *A* refused to teach *B's* son in future. On *A's* refusal to teach *B's* son in future, there occurs a breach of contract. And *B* is at liberty to put an end to the contract. In this case, *A* has refused to perform the contract in its entirety.

It may be noted that the anticipatory breach may take place either by express refusal to perform the contract, or by some act of the promisor which makes the performance impossible.

Example 12.44. *A* agreed to marry *B*. But before the agreed date of marriage, *A* married C. This is anticipatory breach of contract by *A*'s conduct which has made the performance impossible.

The important point in the anticipatory breach is that the party in default must have refused altogether to perform all his obligations under the contract. If it is not so, the other party would not be justified in putting an end to the contract.

Example 12.45. *A*, agreed to purchase from *B*, under two contracts, 300 tons of sugar to be delivered at different dates. *A* failed to take delivery under the first contract. And *B* claimed to put an end to both the contracts on the ground of anticipatory breach. It was held that *B* was not entitled to put an end to the contract as *A* did not refuse to perform the contract in its entirety.

[*R.B. Shah* v. *N. Gopal* (1906) 3 CWN. 477].

In case of an anticipatory breach of the contract, the aggrieved party may exercise either of the following two options:

1. He may treat the contract as discharged and bring an immediate action for damages.

2. He may treat the contract as operative and wait till the time of performance arrives.

12.25. MEASURE OF DAMAGES IN ANTICIPATORY BREACH OF CONTRACT

In case of anticipatory breach of contract, the damages are measured as follows:

1. Sometimes, the anticipatory breach is accepted by the aggrieved party and the contract is immediately put to an end. In such cases the damages would be assessed at the time when breach of the contract takes place. And the amount of damages will be measured by the difference between the price prevailing on the date of breach of contract and the contract price.

2. Sometimes, the anticipatory breach is not accepted by the aggrieved party and the contract is kept alive till the time of performance arrives. In such cases, the damages would be assessed at the time fixed for performance of the contract. And the amount of damages will be measured by the difference between the price prevailing on the date fixed for performance and the contract price.

Example 12.46. *A* agreed to supply to *B* 10 bags of wheat at the rate of Rs. 300 per bag. According to the terms of the contract, the supply of bags was to be made on 1st January, 2003. Before this date, *A* informed B that he would not supply any wheat to him. On *A's* refusal, *B* put an end to the contract, and purchased 10 bags of wheat from C at the rate for Rs. 320 per bag (the prevailing price at the time of breach). In this case, the loss suffered by *B* is Rs. 20(320-300) per bag. And thus, *B* is entitled to recover Rs. 200 (10 × 20) from *A* by way of damages.

Now supppose, *B* keeps the contract alive and waits till 1st January, 2003. On this date also, *A* fails to supply the wheat bags to *B*, and the price prevailing on 1st January, 2003 is Rs. 310 per bag. In this case, the damages will be calculated at the rate of Rs. 10 (310 – 300) per bag and *B* is entitled to recover Rs. 100 (10 × 10) from *A* by way of damages.

12.26. REMEDIES FOR BREACH OF CONTRACT

Following types of remedies are available to the aggrieved party (*i.e.*, the party who is not at fault):

1. Suit for rescission.
2. Suit for damages.
3. Suit for quantum meruit.
4. Suit for specific performance.
5. Suit for injunction.

12.27. SUIT FOR RESCISSION

The term 'rescission' may be defined as the cancellation of the contract. In other words, putting an end to the contract. Where a party commits a breach (*i.e.*, refuses to perform his obligations in the contract), the other party becomes entitled to put an end to the contract. He may bring an action for the rescission of the contract. On the rescission of the contract, the aggrieved or injured party (*i.e.*, party not in default) is discharged from all the obligations under the contract.

It is important to note that if the party rightfully rescinds the contract, he is also entitled to receive compensation for the damages sustained due to the non-fulfilment of the contract. [Section 75].

Example 12.47. *A*, a singer, contracted with *B*, the manager of a theatre, to sing at his theatre for two nights every week during the next two months. And *B* contracted to pay *A* Rs. 500 for each night's performance. On the sixth night, *A* wilfully absented herself from the theatre, and in consequence *B* rescinded the contract. In this case, *B* is also entitled to claim from *A* the compensation for damages which he has sustained through the non-fulfilment of the contract by *A*.

12.28. SUIT FOR DAMAGES

The term 'damages' may be defined as the monetary compensation payable by the defaulting party to the aggrieved party for the loss suffered by him. The aggrieved party may, bring an action for damages against the party who is guilty of the breach of the contract. And the party, guilty of breach, is liable to pay damages to the aggrieved party. The primary aim of damages is to compensate the aggrieved party, and to place him in the same position which he would have occupied had the breach of contract not occurred. It may, therefore, be noted that the damages are given by way of compensation for the loss suffered by the aggrieved party, and not for the purpose of punishing the defaulting party. The legal rules regarding the payment of damages will be discussed in detail in the next chapter.

12.29. SUIT FOR QUANTUM MERUIT

Literally, the expression 'quantum meruit' means 'as much as earned' . In legal sense, it means the 'payment in proportion to the work done' , *i.e.*, a person can recover compensation in proportion to the work done by him, This doctrine is applied where there is no express promise to pay definite remuneration to a person. And the person claims reasonable remuneration for the services rendered by him. The general rule, in this connection, is that where a party to a contract has not fully performed what the contract demands, he can bring no action for payment for the which he has done. However, in certain circumstances, a person may recover compensation on the basis of 'quantum meruit'. He can recover compensation where he has performed some work under a contract, and is prevented by the act of the other party from completing the full contract. He may also recover the value of the work done where the further performance of the contract becomes impossible. The claim on quantum meruit must be brought by a party who is not in default, However, in certain cases, the party in default may also sue on the basis of 'quantum meruit' for the work done if the contract is divisible.

12.30. CASES FOR CLAIM ON QUANTUM MERUIT

1. *Where the work has been done and accepted under a contract which is subsequently discovered to be void*
2. *Where one party abandons or refuses to perform the whole contract*
3. *Where something is done without any intention to do gratuitously*
4. *Where the contract is divisible and the party has enjoyed the benefits of the work done*

Following are the cases in which a claim on quantum meruit may arise:

1. ***Where the work has been done and accepted under a contract which is subsequently discovered to be void:*** Sometimes, some work is done and accepted under a contract which is subsequently discovered to be void. In such cases, the person who has performed the part of the contract is entitled to recover the amount for the work done. And the party, who receives and accepts the benefit under such contract, must make compensation to the other party [Section 65].

Example 12.48. *A*, a singer, contracted with *B*, the manager of a theatre, to sing at his theatre for two evening in every week during the next two months. And *B* agreed to pay her Rs. 100 for each performance. On the day of sixth performance, *A* wilfully absented herself from the theatre, and in consequence, *B* rescinded the contract. In this case, *B* must pay to *A* for five performances on which she had sung. Here though A is guilty, but she can recover for the five performances as the contract is divisible one.

2. *Where one party abandons or refuses to perform the whole contract:* Sometimes, a party performs a part of the contract, but abandons it without completing, or refuses to perform the remaining part. In such cases, the compensation for the work done may be recovered on the basis of quantum meruit.

Example 12.49. *A* was engaged by *B* to write a book to be published in instalments in a weekly magazine. After a few issues of the magazine had appeared, the magazine was discontinued. It was held that *A* could recover on quantum meruit for the work done under the contract.

[*Planche* v. *Colburn* (1831) 8 Bing. 14].

3. *Where something is done without any intention to do gratuitously:* Sometimes, a person does some act or delivers something to another person with the intention of receiving payments for the same. In such cases, the other person is bound to make the payment if he accepts such services or goods, or enjoys their benefit. This point has already been discussed in detail in Chapter 10.

4. *Where the contract is divisible and the party has enjoyed the benefits of the work done:* Sometimes, the contract is divisible and a party performs a part of the contract and refuses to perform the remaining part. In such cases, the party in default may sue on quantum meruit if the other party has enjoyed the benefits of the part performance.

Example 12.50. *A* contracted with *B* to deliver him 250 quintals of rice before the 1st May 1988. But *A* actually delivered 130 quintals of rice only before that date, and none after. However, *B* retained 130 quintals of rice. In this case, though *A* is guilty for the non-performance of the contract, but he is entitled to receive the price of 130 quintals of rice as the same has been accepted by *B*.

But if the contract is not divisible, *i.e.*, where it requires complete performance as a condition for payment, the party in default cannot claim payments for the work done on the basis of quantum meruit.

Example 12.51. *A*, a building contractor, agreed to construct a house for *B* for Rs. 2 lakhs. *A* did the work to the value of Rs. 40,000, and then abandoned the contract. Afterwards, *B* got the work completed from another contractor. It was held that *A* could not recover any thing for the work done because he was entitled to payments only on the completion of the work. In this case, the acceptance of part work by *B* was no ground for awarding remuneration as *B* had no option but to accept the part work, and no fresh contract to pay could be implied for *B's* acceptance.

[*Based on Sumpter* v. *Hedges* (1898) Q.B.673].

Sometimes, an individible contract for a lump sum is completely performed but of poor quality. In such cases, the person who has performed the contract is entitled to claim the lump sum less a deduction for the work of poor quality.

Example 12.52. *A* agreed to repair *B's* house for Rs. 5000. The payment was to be made on completion of the work according to the specifications. *A* did the work of repair, but there were some defects. It cost Rs. 1000 to *B* to remove those defects. It was held that *A* was entitled to recover Rs. 4000 (5000 – 1000) from *B*. [*Based on Dakin & Co.* v. *Lee* (1961)1 KB 566].

12.31. SUIT FOR SPECIFIC PERFORMANCE

The term 'specific performance' may be defined as the actual carrying out the respective obligations of both the parties. Sometimes, the damages are not an adequate remedy for breach of the contract. In such cases, the party aggrieved by the breach may bring an action for specific performance of the contract. And the court may direct the defaulting party to carry out his obligations according to the terms of the contract. It may be noted that the specific performance of the contract cannot be claimed as a matter of right. The courts are always at discretion to grant the relief by specific performance. The courts may, at their discretion, order specific performance of contracts in the following cases [Section 10, Specific Relief Act, 1963]:

1. Where there exists no standard for ascertaining the actual damages caused by the nonperformance of the contract.
2. Where the act agreed to be done is such that compensation in money, for its non-performance, would not afford adequat relief.

Thus, the specific performance of contract may be allowed by the courts where the subject matter of contract is not an ordinary article of commerce, or is of special value or interest, or consists of goods which are not easily available in the market. In such cases, the compensation in money would not be an adequate relief, *e.g.*, sale and purchase of unique and precious articles such as antiques, art paintings, old furniture, etc, It is also generally presumed that unless and until contrary is proved, the breach of a contract to transfer immovable property cannot be adequately relieved by compensation in terms of money.[4] And thus such contracts may also be specifically enforced.

There are certain cases, as listed below, in which the specific performance of the contract shall not be allowed by the courts [Section 14, Specific Relief Act, 1963]:

1. Where the compensation in terms of money is an adequate relief for the non-performance of the contract.
2. Where the contract is of personal nature, *i.e.*, depends upon the personal qualifications or volition of the parties, *e.g.*, a contract to sing a song, or paint a picture, etc.
3. Where the contract is in its nature determinable, *i.e.*, can be put to an end at any time by the parties. In such cases, the specific performance, will be of no help as the parties may put an end to the contract afterwards. *e.g.*, a contract to enter into a partnership at will, *i.e.*, where the duration of firm is not specified.
4. Where the performance of a contract involves the performance of a continuous duty which the courts cannot supervise.
5. Where the contract is inequitable to either party, *i.e.*, where the contract is not fair and just.

12.32. SUIT FOR INJUNCTION

The term 'injunction' may be defined as an order of the courts restraining a person from doing something which he promised not to do. In this case also the courts are at discretion to issue an injunction order. It is, usually, issued in cases where the compensation in terms of money is not an adequate relief. The injunction is a mode of securing the performance of the negative terms in the contract. Sometimes, a party to a contract does something which he had promised not to do. In such cases, the aggrieved party may file a suit for injunction. And the courts may at their discretion, issue an order restraining such person from doing what he promised not to do.

Example 12.53. *A*, a singer, agreed to sing at *B's* theatre for certain period. She further agreed that during the prescribed period she will not sing at any other theatre. Afterwards, *A* made a contract with *C* to sing at his theatre. And refused to sing at *B's* theatre. *B* filed a suit restraining A from singing at *C's* theatre. It was held that although *A* could not be compelled to sing at *B's* theatre, but she could be restrained by injunction from singing at *C's* theatre.

[*Lumely* v. *Wagner* (1852) S. De G.M & G. 604].

4. *Explanation* to Section 10 of the Specific Relief Act, 1963.

LEGAL PROVISIONS (SECTIONS) DISCUSSED IN THE CHAPTER

Impartant legal provisions (sections) of the Indian Contract Act, 1872 discussed in this chapter, are reproduced herunder for ready reference

1. ***Section 56: Agreement to do Impossible Act, Void***

   An agreement to do an act impossible in itself is void.

   Contract to do act afterwards becoming impossible or unlawful becomes void: A contract to do an act which, after the contract in made, becomes imposible or by reason of some event which the promisor could not prevent, unlawful, becomes void when the act becomes impossible or unlawful.

   Compensation for loss through non-performance of act known to be impossible or unalwful: Where one person has promised to do something which he knew, or with reasonable diligence, might have known, and which the promisee did not know, to be impossible or unlawful, such promisor must make compensation to such promisee for any loss which such promisee sustains through the non-performance of the promise.

2. ***Section 62: Effect of Novation, Rescission, and Alteration of Contract.***

   If the parties to a contract agree to substitute a new contract for it, or to rescind or alter it, the original contract need not be performed.

3. ***Section 63: Promisee May Dispense with or Remit Performace of Promise***

   Every promisee may dispense with or remit, wholly or in part the performance of the promise made to him, or may extend the time for such performance, or may accept instead of it any satisfaction which he thinks fit.

4. ***Section 75: Party Rightfully Rescinding Contract, Entitled to Compencation***

   A person who rightfully rescinds the contract is entilled to compensation for any damage which be has sustaimed through the non-performance of the contract.

TEST QUESTIONS

1. What do you mean by discharge of contract ? Discuss the various modes by which a contract may be discharged.
2. Discuss the impossibility of performance as a mode of discharge of contract, stating differently the effect of 'initial' and 'supervening' impossibility.
3. "The law does not compel the impossible" — comment.
4. "Impossibility of performance is, as a rule, not an excuse for non-performance of a contract"— discuss.
5. Discuss the doctrine of frustration with suitable examples. Is there any difference between Indian and English Law on the point ? The relevant provisions of Indian Contract Act on the point be also explained.
6. Does the frustration discharge the contract in all cases ? If not, then specify the circumstances in which the contract is not discharged on the ground of frustration.
7. Discuss the 'novation' and 'rescission' as a mode of discharge of contract giving suitable examples. What is the main point of difference between the two ?
8. What do you understand by breach of contract ? Discuss in detail giving suitable examples.
9. What do you understand by an anticipatory breach of contract ? State the different courses open to the aggrieved party in case of such a breach.
10. "An anticipatory breach gives an immediate right of action to the aggrieved party"— discuss with the help of examples.
11. Explain the position of aggrieved party in case of anticipartory breach of contract.
12. What remedies are available to an aggrieved party for the breach of a contract ?
13. "Where one party commits a breach of contract, the other party has the right to rescind it"—Discuss and state the circumstances in which the court may refuse the rescission.
14. What do you understand by the doctrine of quantum meruit ? State the cases in which a claim for quantum meruit arises.
15. "Where one party commits a breach, the other party is entitled to the specific performance

of the contract"—Discuss and state the circumstances in which the court shal refuse the specific performance.

16. When will a court refuse specific performance of a contract ?
17. Write short notes on the following ?
    (*a*) discharge of contract by alteration.
    (*b*) Discharge of contract by remission.
    (*c*) Discharge of contract by Operation of Law.
    (*d*) Discharge of contract by tender.
    (*e*) Accord and satisfaction.

MULTIPLE CHOICE QUESTIONS

1. When after the formation of a valid contract, an event happens which makes the performance of contract impossible, then the contract becomes:
   (*a*) void (*b*) voidable
   (*c*) valid (*d*) illegal
2. In which of the following cases, a contract is not discharged on the ground of subsequent impossibility?
   (*a*) Destruction of subject-matter (*b*) Death of the promisor
   (*c*) Commercial hardships (*d*) Change of Law.
3. A contract is discharged by novation which means the
   (*a*) substitution of existing contract for a new one.
   (*b*) Cancellation of the existing contract
   (c) Change in one or more terms of a contract
   (*d*) none of these.
4. A contract is discharged by rescisson which means the
   (*a*) Acceptance of lesser performance
   (*b*) cancellation of the existing contract.
   (*c*) change in one or more terms of a contract.
   (*d*) abandonment of rights by a party.
5. A contract is discharged if it is not performed within the limitation period prescribed by law. The limitation period for recover of money is
   (*a*) 2 years (b) 3 years
   (*c*) 4 years (*d*) 5 years.
6. When prior to the due date of performance, the promisor absolutely refuses to perform the contract. It is known as
   (*a*) abandonment of contract. (*b*) remission of contract.
   (*c*) actual breach of contract. (*d*) anticipatory breach of contract.
7. In case of anticipatory breach of contract, the aggrieved party may treat the contract
   (*a*) as discharged and bring an immediate action for damages.
   (*b*) as operative and wait till the time for performance arrives.
   (*c*) exercise option either (*a*) or (*b*) (*d*) only option (a) is available
8. An anticipatory breach does not give any right to claim compensation.
   (*a*) True (*b*) False
9. In case of breach of contract, which of the following remedy is available to the aggrieved party?
   (*a*) Suit for rescission. (*b*) Suit for damages.
   (*c*) Suit for specific performance. (*d*) all of these.
10. A party who rightfully rescinds the contract is also entitled to receive compensation from defaulting party.

(*a*) True. (*b*) False.

11. A party entitled to rescind the contract, loses the remedy where
    (*a*) he has ratified the contract.
    (*b*) third party has acquired right in good faith.
    (*c*) contract is not separable and rescission is sought of a part only.
    (*d*) all of these.
12. The relief by way of specific performance of contract is
    (*a*) with the discretion of the court. (*b*) right of a person and court must give it.
    (*c*) provided in the contract Act. (*d*) both (*b*) and (*c*)
13. Sometimes, a party is entitled to claim compensation in proportion to the work done by him. It is possible by a suit for
    (*a*) damages (*b*) injunction
    (*c*) quantum meruit (*d*) none of these

ANSWERS

1. (*a*)	**2.** (*c*)	**3.** (*a*)	**4.** (*b*)	**5.** (*b*)	**6.** (*d*)
7. (*c*)	**8.** (*b*)	**9.** (*d*)	**10.** (*a*)	**11.** (*d*)	**12.** (*a*)
13. (*c*)					

OBJECTIVE TYPE QUESTIONS WITH REASONING

State with reason whether the following statement are correct or incorrect

1. After the expiry of period of limitation, the parties can enforce their right by depositing penalty in the court.
2. Commercial impossibility is not a valid excuse for the non-performance of a contract.
3. In case of novation, if the new contract cannot be enforced for any reason, the parties remain bound by the old contract.
4. Strikes, lockout and civil disobediences discharge a contract on the ground of impossibility of performance.
5. Outbreak of war is not an excuse for nonperformance of contract.
6. Actual breach of contract takes place on the due date of performance and not during the performance.
7. Anticipatory breach of contract takes place during the performance of the contract.
8. In case of actual breach of contract, the contract becomes void if time is the essence of the contract.
9. In case of anticipatory breach of contract, the aggrieved party can put an end to the contract and bring an immediate action for damages without waiting for the due date of performance.
10. In case of anticipatory breach of contract, if the aggrieved party does not take any action till the due date of performance , then the party liable for breach may perform his promise on due date which will be binding on the aggrieved party.
11. The party rightfully rescinding the contract is also entitled to receive compensation for damages sustained due to non fulfillment of the contract
12. The party rightfully rescinding the contract can retain the benefits, if any received under the contract.
13. The damage for breach of contract are awarded by courts for the purpose of punishing the defaulting party.
14. The suit for claim on quantum meruit can be filed where the work done is complete but the contract is divisible.
15. The aggrieved party has the right to refuse monetary compensation and can insist upon the specific performance of the contract.

ANSWERS

1. *Incorrect.* On the expiry of limitation period, the contract is discharged. In fact, in such cases the parties are debarred from enforcing the contract, i.e., legally they cannot enforce the contract.
2. *Correct.* The difficulty in performance and commercial impossibility are not covered by the doctrine of supervening impossibility.
3. *Correct.* For the discharge of a contract by way of novation, the new contract must be valid and enforceable. If it is not so, then the parties remain bound by the original contract..
4. *Incorrect.* All such events do not fall under the category of supervening impossibility.
5. *Incorrect.* The law on the point is that on the declaration of war, the performance of pending contracts with the citizens of other country, become impossible. Such contracts are either suspended or declared void by the government.
6. *Incorrect.* It can also take place during the performance of the contract.
7. *Incorrect.* It takes place before the due date of performance. It is infact the repudiation of contract before the due date of performance.
8. *Incorrect.* In such a case, the contract becomes voidable not void [Section 55, para1].
9. *Correct.* The anticipatory breach of contract gives an immediate cause of action to the aggrieved party [Section 39].
10. *Correct.* It is the legal position on the point. By not taking immediate action, the aggreived party has in fact kept the contract operative for performance.
11. *Correct.* It is the legal position on the party's right of rescission [Section 75.]
12. *Incorrect.* On rescinding a contract, the party is bound to restore the benefit he has received under the contract
13. *Incorrect.* The damages are awarded by way of compensation for loss suffered by the aggreived party.
14. *Correct.* In case of indivisible contract, the claim on the quantum meruit is not maintainable
15. *Incorrect.* The specific performance cannot be claimed by a party as a matter of right.

PRACTICAL PROBLEMS

1. *A*, a Hindu boy, who was already married, contracted to marry *B*, a Hindu girl. Can this agreement be enforced? What right is available to *B*?

   Hint : No, this agreement is not enforceable in a court of law. It is void due to impossibility of performance as according to Hindu law a married person having a living wife, cannot marry again. *B* is entitled to recover compensation from *A* due to the loss suffered on account of non-performance as the impossibility of performance was known to the promisor *i.e. A*. [Section 56, para 3]
2. *A* contracted to sell to *B* certain quantity of potatoes to be grown in his farm. Subsequently, the whole crop of potatoes was destroyed by a disease and thus *A* failed to supply the contracted quantity of potatoes. *B* sued *A* for the performance of contract and *A* took the plea that he is not liable to perform the contract as the crop of potato has been destroyed. Is *A* justified in his defence? Give reasons.

   Hint : Yes, *A* is justified in his defence. Here, the contract was discharged as the performance had become impossible due to destruction of subject-matter *i.e.* potatoes.
3. *A* enters into a contract with *B* for supplying 800 tonnes of iron ore within four months. *A* fails to make delivery in time owing to difficulty in transport, but he admitted the availability of iron ore in the market at a higher price. Can *A* take the plea of impossibility of performance? Give reasons.

Hint : No, *A* cannot take the plea of impossibility of performance. It is a case of commercial impossibility and the contract is not discharged on this ground under section 56 of the Indian Contract Act. The cases of commercial hardships such a increase in prices are not covered by Section 56.

4. *A* agreed to give his taxi on hire to *B* for the purpose of (a) attending a singing programme in Shimla and (b) enjoying summer vacations at Kufri. Due to illness of main singer, the programme was cancelled and *B* refused to hire the taxi taking the plea of frustration. Is he justified? Give reasons.

Hint: No, *B* is not justified in taking the plea of frustration. Where only one of the several objects failed, the contract is not discharged on the ground of frustration.

5. *A* agreed to sell his horse to *B* for Rs.12,000 but unknow to both the parties, the horse was dead at the time of agreement. Discuss the right and liabilities of *A* and *B* regarding performance of contract. Would it make any difference to your answer, if the horse was seriously ill at the time of agreement and died within a few hours after having been delivered to *B* and price remaining unpaid.

Hint: The horse being dead at the time of agreement, the parties are discharged from performing their obligation as the case is covered under initial impossibility. But on the horse being seriously ill at the time of agreement, the parties are not discharged from performing their obligation. The horse having been delivered to *B* in terms of the agreement, he is liable to pay the price to *A* as he is bound to perform his part of obligation.

6. *A* owed Rs.10,000 to *B* under a contract and *B* owed Rs.10,000 to another person *C*. Afterwards, *B* ordered *A* to credit *C* with Rs.10,000 in his book, but *C* did not give his consent to this arrangement. Does *A* still owe Rs.10,000 to *B*? Give reasons.

Hint : Yes, *A* still owe Rs.10,000 to *B*. Since, *C* did not give his consent to the new arrangement, the parties remain bound by their original obligations.

7. *A* owed Rs.10,000 to *B* and *A*'s friend *C* paid Rs. 8,000 to *B* in full and final settlement of his claim over *A*, which *B* accepted. Can *B* recover the balance from *A*? Give reasons.

Hint : No, *B* cannot recover the balance from *A*. Here, the acceptance of lesser amount in full and final settlement by *B*, discharged the contract and *B* cannot ask for performance again.

8. *A* agreed to sell his horse to *B* for Rs. 5,000 on 1st December, 2007. But before this date, *A* repudiated the contract by informing *B* that he would not sell his horse at all. However, *B* did not accept the refusal and kept the contract alive till 1st December, 2007 The horse died before this date, but on 1st Dec. 2007, *B* filed a suit against *A* for damages for breach of contract. Will he succeed? Give reasons. Would your answer change had the horse died on 5th December, 2007.

Hint : No, *B* will not succeed in his action. In this case, since *B*, kept the contract alive, the contract would be treated as discharged by death of horse on the ground of impossibility of performance. However, in case, the horse dying on 5th December, 2007, *B* would be entitled to recover from *A*, the damages for breach of contract. In that event, *A* would be guilty of breach and the plea of impossibility of performance would not be available to him as the horse had died after the due date of performance.

9. *A*, a singer contracted with *B*, the manager of a theatre, to sing at his theatre for two nights every week during next two months. And *B* contracted to pay Rs.10,000/- for each night performance. On the 6th night, *A* wilfully absented herself from theatre. Can *B* repudiate the contract? What would be your answer if *A* with the consent of *B* sings on the 7 the night?

Hint : Yes, *B* can repudiate the contract and can also claim compensation for damages sustained due to non-performance on the 6th night. If *B* allows *A* to perform on the 7th night, then he cannot repudiate the contract though *B* can claim damages for 6th night's non-performance.

13

CHAPTER

DAMAGES FOR BREACH OF CONTRACT

1. Introduction.
2. Kinds of Damages.
3. Law Governing Damages.
4. English Law Governing Damages.
5. Legal Rules for the Payment of Damages.
6. Duty to Mitigate Damages.
7. Liquidated Damages and Penalty.
8. Legal Rules Governing the Distinction Between Liquidated Damages and Penalty.
9. Forfeiture of Earnest Money or Security Deposit.

13.1. INTRODUCTION

We have discussed, in the last chapter, the remedies for breach of contract. To file a suit for the recovery of damages for breach of contract, is one of the remedies available to the aggrieved party. The term 'damage' may be defined as the monetary compensation payable by the defaulting party to the aggrieved party for the loss suffered by him. On the breach of the contract, the aggrieved party may file a suit for damages against the party who is guilty of the breach of the contract. And the guilty party is liable to pay damages to the aggrieved party. In this chapter. We shall discuss the legal provisions regarding the damages for breach of contract.

13.2. KINDS OF DAMAGES

1. *Ordinary damages*
2. *Special damage*
3. *Remote or indirect damages*
4. *Nominal damages*
5. *Exemplary or vindictive damages*

Following are the various kinds of damages, and rules for the payment of these damages will be discussed in detail in Arts. 13.3 to 13.5.

1. ***Ordinary damages:*** These are the damages which are payable for the loss arising naturally and directly, in the usual course, from the breach of contract. In other words, the ordinary damages are due to natural and probable consequence of the breach of the contract.

Example 13.1. *A* hired *B's* ship for Rs. 20,000 for the purpose of carrying his goods from Bombay to Goa. On the due date, *B* refused to make his ship available for the purpose. A made an alternative arrangement for transporting his goods by road for Rs. 30,000, as no other ship was available on that day. In this case, the excess expenses of Rs. 10,000 incurred by *A* are the ordinary damages as they arise naturally and directly from the breach of the contract, and thus, *A* is entitled to receive a compensation of Rs. 10,000 from *B*.

2. ***Special damage:*** These are the damage which are payable for the loss arising due to some special or unusual circumstances. In other words, the special damages are not due to the natural and probable consequences of the breach of the contract.

Example 13.2. *A* contracted with *B* to supply him a certain piece of machinery at Rs. 1,000 to be delivered at a fixed day. *A* did not deliver the piece of machinery at the time specified. And in consequence, *B* had to purchase the same from another dealer at Rs. 1,200. Moreover, *B* was also prevented from performing a contract with *C* which he had already made on the basis of his contract with *A* and was compelled to make compensation to *C* for the non-performance of the contract. In this case, the amount of compensation paid by *B* to *C* are the special damages as they arise due to the special circumstances (*i.e., B*'s contract with *C*). These damages can be recovered only if at the time of the contract, *A* was informed of the contract between *B* and *C*. However, Rs. 200 (*i.e.,* the difference between the contract price and the price paid by *B* to another dealer) are the ordinary damages and can be recovered from *A*.

3. *Remote or indirect damages:* These are the damages which are payable for the loss arising due to some remote or indirect causes. These are also not due to the natural and probable consequences of the breach of the contract. Moreover, at the time of contract, such damages are not in the contemplation of the parties. Generally, the remote damages are not recoverable.

Example 13.3. *A* contracted to sell and deliver to *A* certain cloth on 1st of January. *B* intended to make cloth caps of particular kind for which there was demand only for the season. But this fact was not brought to the notice of *A*. The cloth was delivered only after the season for the caps was over. In consequence, *B* suffered the loss which he would have earned by selling the caps during the season. In this case, this loss of profits suffered by *B* are the remote damages as they arise due to indirect cause. (*i.e.,* the particular season for caps).

4. *Nominal damages:* These are the damages which are very small in amount. Such damages are awarded simply to establish the right of the party to claim damages for the breach of contract even though the party has suffered no loss.

Example 13.4. *A* contracted to buy a 'Hillman' car from *B*, a car dealer. But later on. *A* refused to buy the car. Within a week, *B* sold the car to another customer and suffered no loss on account of *A*'s refusal to buy the car. Even so, *B* wanted to recover damages. The court held that he was entitled to nominal damages only. [*Based on Charter* v. *Sullivan,* (1957)1 AUER 809]

5. *Exemplary or vindictive damages:* These are the damages which are claimed with the intention of punishing the party in default. As a general rule, such damages are not awarded as they are punitive in nature.

13.3. LAW GOVERNING DAMAGES

The law governing the payment of damages is based on the leading English case of **Hadley v. Baxandale (1854) 9 Ex. 341,** and is incorporated in Section 73 of the Indian Contract Act, which reads as under:

"When a contract has been broken, the party who suffers by such breach is entitled to receive, from the party who has broken the contract, compensation for any loss or damage caused to him thereby, which naturally arose in the usual course of things from such breach or which the parties knew, when they made the contract to be likely to result from the breach of it. Such compensation is not to be given for any remote and indirect loss or damage sustained by reason of the breach"

The analysis of this section shows that on breach of the contract, the party who suffers by such breach is entitled to receive the compensation according to the following principles:

1. The damages which arise naturally in the usual course from the breach , are recoverable In other words, the ordinary damages are recoverable.
2. The damages which the parties knew at the time of the contract as likely to result from the breach, are also recoverable. In other words, the special damages are also recoverable only if the parties had the knowledge about them at the time of contract.
3. The damages which arise due to remote or indirect cause, are not recoverable. In other words, the remote or indirect damages are not recoverable. These principles will be discussed in detail in Art. 13.5.

13.4. ENGLISH LAW GOVERNING DAMAGES

In the last article, we have discussed the Indian Law governing the payment of damages. The Indian Law as incorporated in Section 73 of the Indian Contract Act is the same as English Law on the point. And it is based on the leading English case of **Hadley v. Baxandale (1854) 9 Ex. 341.** The principles laid down in this case are discussed in the following example.

Example 13.5. *A* was carrying on extensive business as miller. His mill was stopped by breakdown of the crankshaft by which the mill was working. A delivered the crankshaft to *B*, a carrier, to be taken to a manufacture to copy it and make a new one. *A*'s servant told *B* that the mill was stopped, and that the crankshaft must be sent immediately. By some neglect on the part of *B*, the delivery of the shaft was delayed, and *A* received the crankshaft several days later than he would have otherwise received. *A* brought an action against *B* for the loss of profit which would have been earned during the period of delay. It was held, that *B* was not liable for the loss of profit during the period of delay, as *B* was not told of the special circumstances, that the delay would result in loss of profits. In this case, the fact that the whole mill was out of action for want of the crankshaft, was a special circumstance and it should have been pointed out in clear terms that the delay would result in the loss of profits.

In the light of the decision of this case, the following two rules were laid down:

1. *General damages:* The general damages, *i.e.*, the damages which arise naturally in the usual course from the breach itself, are recoverable. Thus, the person in default is liable for all the reasonable forceable consequences of his breach.
2. *Special damages:* The special damages, *i.e.*, which arise due to unusual circumstames are recoverable only if special circumstanes are brought to the knowledge of defaulting party.

Thus, the substance of these rules is that only such damages are recoverable as were, at the time of contract, reasonably foreseable as liable to result from the breach. Both these rules are, therefore, based on the principle of foreseeability . And the foreseeability depends upon the knowledge.[1]

13.5. LEGAL RULES FOR THE PAYMENT OF DAMAGES

1. *The ordinary damages are recoverable*
2. *The special damages are recoverable only if the parties knew about them*
3. *The remote of indirect damages are not recoverable*
4. *The nominal damages are awarded at the discretion of the courts*
5. *The exemplary or vindictive damages are not allowed*
6. *The party is not entitleld to recover damages unless he has actually suffered some loss*
7. *The damages for mental pain and sufferings are not recoverable*
8. *The damages are determined on the date of breach*
9. *The damages are compensatory and not penal*

The analysis of section 73 and the judicial decision reveal the following rules for the payment of damages:

1. *The ordinary damages are recoverable:* The ordinary damages are due to the natural and probable consequences of the breach, and are recoverable from the party in default. These damages are assessed on the basis of actual loss suffered by the aggrieved party. Thus, the ordinary damages are recoverable on the basis of the difference between the contract price and the market price of the goods on the date of the breach.

Example 13.6. *A* contracted to give his ship to *B* on hire for one year from 1st of January, for Rs. 50,000. Subsequently, *A* broke his promise. And on 1st of January, *B* hired another similar ship for one year for Rs. 60,000 as no other ship was available for Rs. 50,000 In this

1. *Victoria Laundry Ltd.* v. *Newman industries Ltd.*(1949) 2 K.B. 528.

case, *A* is liable to pay *B*, by way of compensation, Rs. 10,000 (*i.e.*, the difference between the contract price and the price for which *B* could hire another similar ship for one year from 1st of January).

2. *The special damages are recoverable only if the parties knew about them:* The special damages are due to some special or unusual circumstance. These damages are recoverable only if the special circumstances were in the knowledge of the parties at the time of making the contract, or if these special circumstances were brought to the notice of the defaulting party. If the defaulting party had no knowledge of the special circumstances, he will not be liable for the special damages, The leading case of Hadley v. Baxandale (discussed in Example 13.5) is good illustration on the point.

3. *The remote of indirect damages are not recoverable:* The remote or indirect damages are not due to natural and probable consequences of the breach of the contract, *i.e.*, these are the damages which arise indirectly from the breach. These damages are not in contemplation of the parties.

Example 13.7. *A*, a ship-owner, contracted with *B* to carry him from Calcutta to Sydney in *A's* ship sailing on the 1st of March. And *B* paid to *A* one half of his passage money by way of deposit. *A's* ship, did not sail on 1st of March, in consequence *B* was detained in Calcutta for sometime, and thereby put to some expenses. *B* proceeded to Sydney in another vessel and reached too late in Sydney. Due to delay in arriving in Sydney, *B* also lost some money which he would have earned if reached in time. In this case, *B* is entitled to recover from *A*, the deposit with interest, the expenses to which he is put up by his detention in Calcutta, and also the excess of the passage money paid for the second ship over the agreed amount for the first ship. But *B* is not entitled to recover the sum of money which he lost by arriving too late in Sydney.

However, under exceptional circumstances, the courts may allow such damages if at the time of contract, both the parties reasonably knew about the demages. It may also be noted that though the remote damages are not allowed, but the courts may, sometime, take into account the inconvenience caused by the breach of the contract.

Example 13.8. *A* and his wife travelled from Hampden to Wimbeldon. The train went in wrong direction, and consequently *A* and his wife had to get down at a place where there was no conveyance and no place to stay. They had to walk home at midnight, and Mrs. *A* got ill due to cold. *A* brought an action against the Railways for damages for inconvenience, and also damages for wife's illness. It was held that *A* was entitled to recover the damages for inconvenience. But the damages for wife's illness were not allowed as they were too remote. The court observed that, the inconvenience for walking back must be taken to have been within the reasonable contemplation of the parties. But the wife' cold was not necessary or even the probable consequence of the breach.

[*Hobbs* v. *London & South Western Railway Co.* (1857) LR to QB. 111].

4. *The nominal damages are awarded at the discretion of the courts:* The nominal damages are those which are very small in nature. These damages are awarded simply to establish the party's right to claim damages for the breach of contract. It may, however, be noted that the party cannot claim these damages as a matter of right. It is always at the discretion of the court whether or not to award the nominal damages, e.g., where a party suffers no loss, the court may allow nominal damages simply to establish that the party has proved his case and won.

Example 13.9. *A* contracted to buy a Maruti Car from *B*, a car dealer, But consequently, *A* refused to buy the car. Within a week, the car was sold to another customer without loss of profits. In fact, the demand for the Maruti Car far exceeded the supply, and the dealer was able to sell as many cars as he wanted. *B* wanted to recover from *A* the damages for breach of contract. In this case, *B* is entitled only to nominal damages as he has not suffered any loss on account of the breach of the contract. [*Based on Charter* v. *Sullivan* (1957) 1 All ER 809]

5. *The exemplary or vindictive damages are not allowed:* The exemplary damages are claimed with the intention of punishing the party in default. As a general rule, the exemplary damages are not awarded for the breach of contract as they are punitive in nature. However, in the following two case, the court may award exemplary damages:

(*a*) Where there is a breach of a promise to marry. In such cases, the damages will include compensation for loss to the feelings and reputation of the aggrieved party.

(*b*) Where a banker wrongfully dishnours customer's cheque, e.g., dishonour of customer's cheque when the banker has sufficient bunds to the credit of the cutomer. In such the damages are awarded taking into consideration the loss to the prestige and goodwill of the customer. The general rule, in this connection is, the smaller the amount of cheque the greater is the insult, and thus greater the amount of damages.

6. *The party is not entitleld to recover damages unless he has actually suffered some loss:* Sometimes, the party does not suffer any loss on account of the breach of the contract. In such cases, he cannot claim damages as a matter of right. This has been clearly pointed out by the Delhi high Court that Section 73 does not give any cause of action unless and until the damage is actually suffered.

Example 13.10. *A*, a contractor, agreed to supply sleepers to the Railway Administration. One of the terms of the contract was that on account of *A's* failure to supply the sleepers, he will have to pay damages to the Railway administration whether or not the Railways suffered any loss. *A* failed to supply the sleepeers. But the Railway did not suffer any loss. Even so a suit for damages was filed against A. The court disallowed the suit.

[*Union of India v. Tribhuwan Das Lalji Pate*, AIR 1971 Delhi 120][2]

7. *The damages for mental pain and sufferings are not recoverable:* Ordinarily, the damages for mental pain and sufferings caused by the breach are not allowed. However, such damages may be allowed in special cases, e.g., where the breach was reckless and caused bodily harm, and where the defaulting party had reasons to know that the breach would cause mental suffering. [American Restatement, Section 341]

Example 13.11. *A*, a banking corporation agreed to give loan to *B* for a trip to California. It was agreed that *B's* account would be credited with such sum as he may need on reaching his destination. *B* reached California, but *A* refused to give him the promised credit. *B* filed a suit against *A* for damages for humiliation and mental suffering. It was held that *B* was entitled to recover these damages. In this case, A could have foreseen that *B*, having gone away from home and among strangers, would naturally suffer humiliation and mental pain if his cheque was not honored. [*Western* v. *Olathe State Bank*, (1925) 78 Colorado 217].

8. *The damages are determined on the date of breach:* The damages are paid for the loss suffered by the aggrieved party on the date of breach. In a contract for the sale of goods, the measure of damages in the difference between the contract price and the market price of such goods on the date of breach.

9. *The damages are compensatory and not penal:* The damages are given by way of compensation for the loss suffered by the injured party, and not for the purpose of punishing the defaulting party. As a matter of fact, the primary object of awarding damages is to place the aggrieved party in the same position which he would have occupied had the breach of contract not occurred.

13.6. DUTY TO MITIGATE DAMAGES

We have alreaady discussed that the injured party is entitled to receive compensation for the loss suffered due to the breach of the contract. However, the injured party has to take all reasonable steps to minimise the loss caused by the breach. This is known as the duty to mitigate damages, and is cast upon the injured party. The purpose of imposing this duty is to minimise the loss. If he fails to take steps to minimise the loss, he cannot

2. *See also, Maula Bux* v. *Union of India* (1969) 2 SCC 544, AIR 1970 SC 1955: *Union of India* v. *Rampur Distillery and Chemicals Co. Ltd.* AIR 1973 SC 1998.

recover damages which result from such failure, *i.e.*, the damages, which result due to the negligence of the aggrieved party, are not recoverable [Sectioin 73, Explanation].

The duty to mitigate is, usually, expected in contracts for sale or purchase of goods. Where the buyer refuses to take delivery of the goods, the seller should resell the goods at the prevailing market price. And he may then recover from the defaulting buyer, as damages, the difference between the price he realised and the price he would have received from the defaulting buyer. Thus, in such cases, the seller's duty is to resell the goods at the prevailing market price. If he does not resell the goods and his loss is increased by the fall in market price, then he cannot recover the increased loss. It may be noted here that the steps to mitigate the loss should be taken at the time of breach of the contract. Similarly, where a seller refuses to deliver the goods, the buyer should buy the goods from any alternative source, if the goods are available.

13.7. LIQUIDATED DAMAGE AND PENALTY

Sometimes, at the time of the formation of the contract, the parties fix the amount of compensation that will be payable in case of breach of the contract. The amount so specified may be (*a*) liquidated damages, or (*b*) penalty.

1. ***Liquidated damages:*** Sometimes, the amount of compensation fixed for the breach of the contract is fair and genuine pre-estimate of the probable damages. Such an amount is known as liquidated damages.
2. ***Penalty:*** Sometimes, the amount of compensation fixed for the breach of the contract is not fair and genuine pre-estimate of the probable damages, but is disproportionate to the damages which may result in case of the breach of the contract. Such an amount is known as penalty.

Thus, the liquidated damages are the fair assessment of the amount which will compensate the aggrieved party for the loss suffered due to breach of the contract. Whereas, the penalty is not the fair assessment of the loss for breach. It is fixed with a view to prevent the party from committing the breach of the contract, *i.e.*, to compel the other party to perform the contract. The parties may use the expression either liquidated damages or penalty, but as regards the payment of liquidated damages and penalty, there is no difference between the two . In both the cases, only the 'reasonable compensation' is allowed by the court. The sum so named determines only the maximum liability, and the courts cannot allow damages beyond that limit, i.e., the courts cannot increase the amount of damages beyond the amount specified in the contract itself.

Example 13.12. *A* borrowed Rs. 500 from *B* and contracted to pay him Rs. 800 as damages, if he (*A*) failed to repay Rs. 500 on a given day. *A* failed to repay Rs. 500 on that day. In this case, *B* is entitled to recover from *A* such compensation (but not exceeding Rs. 800) as the court considers reasonable.

Example 13.13. *A* contracted with *B* that if *A* practised as a surgeon in Calcutta, he would pay B Rs. 5000 as penalty. *A* practised as a surgeon in Calcutta. In this case, *B* is entitled to recover from *A* such compensation (But not exeeding Rs. 5000) as the court considers reasonable.

However, the distinction between them cannot be altogether ignored. Generally, the courts reduce the amount if it appears to be by way of penalty. And if it does not appear to be penalty, the whole of the amount is allowd by the courts.

13.8. LEGAL RULES GOVERNING THE DISTINCTION BETWEEN LIQUIDATED DAMAGES AND PENALTY

Whether a sum specified in the contract is liquidated damages or penalty, is a question of construction, and is to be decided upon the terms and circumstances of each particular contract. However, the following legal rules afford some guidance to distinguish between the two:

1. The stipulation is considered as penalty if it provides that an increased interest will be paid from the date of default. [Section 74. Explanation 1].

Example 13.14. *A* borrowed Rs. 1000 from *B* and agreed to repay the amount with interest at 12 percent at the end of six months. The contract further provided that in case of default in repayment, the interest would be payable at the rate of 75 per cent from the date of default. This as a stipulation by way of penalty, and *B* is entitled only to recover from *A* such compensation as the court considers reasonable.

2. The stipulation is considered as penalty if it provides that in case of default, the money repaid shall be double of the money borrowed.

Example 13.15. *A* borrowed Rs. 100 from *B* and gave him a bond for Rs. 200 payable by five yearly instalments of Rs. 40 each. The contract further provided that in default of payment of any instalment, the whole amount of Rs. 200 becomes due. This is a stipulation by way of penalty.

However, a stipulation is not considered as penalty if it only provides that in case of default, the whole of the borrowed money shall become due

Example 13.16. *A* borrowed Rs. 1000 from *B* and undertook to repay the loan by five equal monthly instalments. The contract further provided that in default of payment of any instalment, the whole amount would become due. This stipulation is not by way of penalty and the contract may be enforced according to its terms.

3. The sum stipulated is considered as penalty if it is unreasonably large as compared with the loss likely to result from the breach of the contract.

Example 13.17. *A* contracted to buy certain goods from *B* for Rs. 1000. The contract further provided that if *A* refused to accept the goods, he would pay Rs. 5000 to *B* as damages. In this case, the amount fixed as damages is unreasonable, and thus is penalty.

4. The sum stipulated is considered as penalty if it is greater than the borrowed sum to be repaid.

Example 13.18. *A* borrowed Rs. 500 from *B* and agreed to repay the same on a particular date. The contract further provided that if *A* failed to make the payment on the fixed date, he would pay Rs. 1000 to *B* as damages. In this case, the amount fixed as damages is to be considered as penalty.

13.9. FORFEITURE OF EARNEST MONEY OR SECURITY DEPOSIT

Sometimes, a party to contract is required to deposit some money with the other party. This is generally done with a view to ensure performance of the contract,. The money so deposited may be either 'earnest money' or' security deposit'. The earnest money is part of the purchase price and is paid in advance. After the contract is completed, the earnest money is adjusted towards the purchase price. And if the party paying the earnest money fails to perform the contract, the other party can rescind (i.e., put an end to) the contract and retain he earnest money. Thus, the earnest money is liable to be forfeited. On the other hand, the security deposit is not part of the purchase price. It is deposited only as a security for the performance of the contract. After the contract is completed, the security deposit is not adjusted towards the purchase price. And if the party fails to perform the contract, it cannot be forfeited, as its forfeiture will amount to penalty[3] Thus, the security deposit is not liable to be forfeited.

Example 13.19. *A* contracted with *B* to purchase from him aeroscrap for Rs. 100,000 and paid Rs. 25,000 being 25 per cent of the purchase price. One of the conditions of the contract was that if *A* failed to pay the balance of purchase price, the deposit would be forfeited and the contract

3. *Chiranjit Singh* v. *Har Swarup,* AIR 1926 PC 1

cancelled. *A* defaulted in paying the balance and in consequence, *B* forfeited the deposit. A filed a suit against *B* for the recovery of the deposit. It was held that the deposit in question was intended as earnest money. It was part of the price and the seller was entitled to forfeit it.

[*Shree Hanuman Cotton Mills v. Tata Air Craft Ltd*. AIR 1970 SC 1986].

Example 13.20. *A* contracted to supply potatoes, eggs and fish etc to military headquarters. He also deposited Rs. 18,500 for due performance of the contract. *A* committed defaults in making regular and full supplies. And as per the terms of the contact, the government rescinded the contract and forfeited the deposit of Rs 18,500. It was held that the amount was a security deposit and the government was not entitled to forfeit the same. The court observed that the amount was not by way of earnest money because it was not to be appropriated towards the payment of price.

[*Maula Bux* v. *Union of India*, AIR 1970 SC 1955].

LEGAL PROVISIONS (SECTIONS) DISCUSSED IN THE CHAPTER

Important legal provisions (sections) of the Indian Contract Act 1872, discussed in this chapter, are reproduced herender for ready reference:

1. ***Section 73: Compensation for Loss or Damage Caused by Breach of Contract***

When a contract has been broken, the party who suffers by such preach is enlited to receive, form the party who has broken the contract, compensation for any loss or damage cuased to him theraby, which naturally arose in the usual conrse of things form such breach, or which the parties knew, when they made the contract, to be likely to result form the breach of it.

Such compensation is not be given for any remote and indirect loss or damage sustained by reason of the breach.

Compensation for failure to discharge obigation resembling those created by contract.—When an obligation resembling those created by contract has been incurred and has not been discharged, any person injured by the failure to discharge it is intiled to receive the same compensation form the party in default, as if such person had contracted to dischagre it and had broken his contract.

Explanation.—In estimating the loss or damage arising from a breach of contract, the means which existed of remedying the inconvenience cuased by the non-performance of the contract must be taken into account.

2. ***Section 74: Compensation for Breach of Contract Where Penalty Stipulated for***

When a contract has been broken, if a sum is named in the contract as the amount to be paid in case of such breach, or if the contract contains any other stipulation by way of penalty, the party complaining of the breach is entitled, whether or not actual damage or loss is proved to have been caused thereby, to receive form the party who has broken the contract, reasonable compensation not exceeding the amount so named or, as the case may be, the penalty stipulated for.

Explanation.—A stipulation for increased interest form the date of default may be a stipulation by way of penalty.

Exception.—When any person enters into any bail-bond, recognizance or other instrument of the same nature or, under the provisions of any law, or under the orders of the Central Government or of any State government, gives any bond for the performance of any public duty or act in which the public are interested, he shall be liable, upon breach of the condition of any such instrument, to pay the whole sum mentioned therein.

Explanation.—A person who enters into a contract with government does not necessarily thereby undertake any public duty, or promise to do an act in which the public are interested.

3. ***Section 75. Party Rightfully Rescinding the Contract is Entitled the Compensation***

A person who rightfully rescindes a contract, is entited to compensation for any damage which he has sutained through the non-fulfilment of the contract.

TEST QUESTIONS

1. State the law governing the payment of damages for breach of contract with reference to Indian as well as English Law. The legal rules for the payment of damage be explained with suitable examples.

2. Explain the principles governing the assessment of damages for breach of contract.
3. Discuss the legal position regarding award of damages for breach of contract.
4. State briefly the principles on which the damages are awarded for breach of contract.
5. Discuss the rule as laid down in *Hadley* v. *Baxendle* and its applicability in India. State the relevant provision of Indian Contract Act on the point.
6. "If a contract is broken, the law will endeavour so far as money can do it, to place the injured party in the same positions as if the contract has been performed"-Discuss.
7. Define (*a*) special damages, (*b*) exemplary damages, (*c*) nominal damages, (*d*) remote damages, (*e*) liquidated damages, and the circumstances in which such damages can be claimed.
8. Explain the terms 'penalty' and' liquidated damages' clearly indicating the legal rules governing the distinction between the two. What bearing has this distinction in India upon the question of compensation on the breach of contract?
9. If the parties to a contract have agreed on the amount of damages payable in case the contract is broken, can the court increase or decrease that amount? If yes, state the circumstances.

MULTIPLE CHOICE QUESTIONS

1. Generally, the following damages are not recoverable?
   (*a*) Ordinary damages (*b*) Special damages.
   (c) Remote damage (*d*) Nominal damages.
2. The special damages. *i.e.*, the damages which arise due to some special or unnual circumstances
   (*a*) are not recoverable altogether. (*b*) are illegal being punitive in nature
   (c) cannot be claimed as a matter of right. (*d*) can be claimed as a matter of right
3. The law governing the payment of damages is based on the leading English case of
   (*a*) *Hadley* v. *Baxandale* (*b*) *Hobbs* v. *London Rail Co.*
   (c) *Hadley* v. *Sulllivan* (*d*) *none of these*
4. Which of the following statements is incorrect?
   (*a*) Ordinary damages are recoverable.
   (*b*) Special damage are recoverable only if the parties knew about them.
   (*c*) Remote or indirect damages are not recoverable.
   (*d*) none of these statements is incorrect.
5. The fixed amount of compensation payable in case of breach and which is fair and genuine pre estimate of probable damages, is known as
   (*a*) Liquidated damages (*b*) Nominal damages
   (*c*) Special damages. (*d*) Penalty.
6. A stipulation which provides that an increased rate of interest will be paid from the date of default is regarded as
   (*a*) Remote damages (*b*) Liquidated damages
   (c) Penalty (*d*) None of these .
7. The 'earnest money' is a part of the purchase price paid in advance and is liable to be forfeited. Whereas, the security deposit is refundable and not liable to be forfeited
   (*a*) True, as it is the legal position. (*b*) No, as both can be forfeited.

ANSWERS

1. (*c*)	2. (*c*)	3. (*a*)	4. (*d*)	5. (*a*)
6. (*c*)	7. (*a*)			

OBJECTIVE TYPE QUESTIONS WITH REASONING

State with reasons whether the following statements are correct or incorrect.

1. Damages for breach of contract are awarded by courts to punish the party liable for breach of contract.
2. Ordinary damages are recoverable only if the parties had the knowledge about them at the time of contract.
3. Special damages are recoverable only if the special circumstance resulting in such damages are known to the parties.
4. If the special damages are to be claimed the special circumstances must be brought to the notice of the other party.
5. The Indian Law governing the payment of damages is based on the leading English case of Hadley v. Baxandale (1854) 9 Ex. 341 as there is no provision in the Indian contract Act.
6. Ordinarily, the damages for loss of reputation are not recoverable.
7. Since the nominal damages are awarded simply to establish party's right to claim damages, these can be claimed from the court as a matter of right.
8. Nominal damages are very small in amount and are generally awarded if there is no breach of contract.
9. On the breach of contract, the injured party has to take all reasonable steps to minimise the loss caused by the breach.
10. Liquidated damages means the amount of compensation, fixed in the contract, which is disproportionate to the damages likely to result from the breach.
11. Penalty is the fair and genuine pre-estimate of probable damages likely result from the breach.
12. The injured party is entitled to claim the exact amount of liquidated damages but not that of the penalty.

ANSWERS

1. *Incorrect.* The purpose of awarding damages is to compensate the aggrieved party and not to punish the defaulting party.
2. *Incorrect.* The ordinary damages are those which arise naturally in the ordinary course of breach. These are recoverable even if the parties had no knowledge about them.
3. *Correct.* These damages arise due to some special or unusual circumstances, these can be recovered only if the parties had the knowledge about them at the time of contract.
4. *Correct.* Reason as stated above in point 3
5. *Incorrect.* Section 73 of the Indian Contract Act incorporates the law governing payment of damages.
6. *Correct.* These are not due to natural and probable consequences of the breach. However, where a banker wrongfully dishonours customer's cheque, such damages may be recovered.
7. *Incorrect.* It is at the discretion of the court whether or not to award such damages.
8. *Incorrect.* All the damages, irrespective of their amount, are awarded in case of breach only.
9. *Correct.* The duty to mitigate damages is cast upon the injured party. The purpose of this duty is to avoid further loss [Section 73, explanation].
10. *Incorrect.* Liquidated damages means the amount of compensation, fixed in the contract, which is fair and genuine pre-estimate of probable damages.
11. *Incorrect.*It is not the fair assessment of the loss of breach. It is in fact disproportionate to the amount of probable (*i.e.*, expected) damages.
12. *Incorrect.* In both the case, only the 'reasonable amount of compensation' is allowed by the courts.

PRACTICAL PROBLEMS

1. *A* delivered a machine to *B*, a common carrier, to be conveyed to *A*'s mill without delay and also informed him that *A*'s mill was stopped for want of this machine. *B* unreasonable delayed the machine and in consequence *A* lost a profitable contract with the government. *A* sued *B* for the recovery of damages sustained due to loss of contract with the government. Will he succeed? Give reasons.

   Hint : No, *A* will not succeed as these are the special damages. However, *A* is entitled to recover the ordinary damages *i.e.* the average amount of profits which he would have earned by running the mill during the period of delay.

2. A contracted to buy a Maruti car form *B*, a car dealer. Afterwards, *A* refused to buy the car and within a week the car was sold to another customer without any loss of profit as the demand for Maruty car for exceeded the supply. Is *B* entitled to recover any damages from *A*? If yes, then what type of damages?

   Hint : Yes, *B* is entitled to the damages for breach of contract. He is entitled to nominal damages which are awarded simply to establish party's right to claim damages for breach. However, the awarding of nominal damages depends upon the discretion of the courts.

3. *A* borrowed Rs. 50,000 from *B* and agreed to repay the same with interest @12% p.a. at the end of one year. The contract further provided that in case of default in repayment, the interest would be paid @ 50% from the date of default til payment. *A* could not pay the loan amount in time. Can *B* recover the amount of interest as per the agreed terms? Give reasons.

   Hint : No, *B* cannot recover interest at the agreed rate of 50%. This stipulation is by way of penalty and *B* is entitled to such compensation as the court considers reasonable.

4. *A* contracted with *B* to purchase from him a plot of land for Rs. 25 Lakh and paid him Rs. 2.5 lakh being ten percent of the purchase price. It was also agreed that if *A* failed to pay the balance purchase price within three months, the deposit would be forfeited and contract cancelled. *A* defaulted in paying the balance in time and accordingly B forfeited the deposit. *A* sued *B* for recovery of the deposit amount. Will he succeed? Give reasons.

   Hint : No, *A* will not succeed in his action. Here, the amount deposited by *A* was earnest money which is liable to be forfeited in case of default by the party.

14

CHAPTER

INDEMNITY AND GUARANTEE

1. Introduction.
2. Contract of Indemnity.
3. English Law on Contract of Indemnity.
4. Essentials and Legal Rules for a Valid Contract of Indemnity.
5. Right of Indemnity-holder.
6. Rights of Indemnifier.
7. Commencement of Indemnifier's Liability.
8. Contract of Guarantee.
9. Essentials and Legal Rules for a Valid Contract of Guarantee.
10. Kinds of Guarantee.
11. Revocation of Continuing Guarantee.
12. Nature and Extent of Surety's Liability.
13. Rights of the Surety.
14. Rights Against the Principal Debtor.
15. Rights Against the Creditor.
16. Rights Against the Co-sureties.
17. Dischdrage of Surety from Lability.
18. Comparison Between Contract of Indemnity and Contract of Guarantee.

14.1. INTRODUCTION

In the preceding chapters, we have discussed the principles of general Law of Contract. The contracts of indemnity and guarantee are the special kinds of contracts. It may be noted that these contracts form the part of the General Law of Contracts. And therefore, they must have all the essentials of a valid contract, e.g., consideration, competency of the parties, free consent, lawful object etc. The special legal provisions relating to these contracts are contained in Sections 124 to 147 of the Indian Contract Act, which will be discussed in this chapter.

14.2. CONTRACT OF INDEMNITY

The term 'indemnity' may be defined as an act to compensate or protect against loss. In other words, to make good the loss. And a contract to indemnify or compensate a person from loss is known as contract of indemnity. The term' contract of indemnity' is defined in Section 124 of the Indian Contract Act, which reads as under:

> *"A contract by which one party promises to save the other from loss caused to him by the conduct of the promisor himself or by the conduct of any other person, is called a contract of indemnity."*

The analysis of this section shows that a contract of indemnity is a contract in which one person promises to protect or compensate the other for the loss suffered by him due to the conduct of the promisor or any other person. The following two parties are involved in a contract of indemnity:

1. ***Indemnifier:*** The party who gives the indemnity, *i.e.*, who promises to compensate for the loss, is know as indeminifier.
2. ***Indemnity-holder***: The party, for whose protection the indemnity is given, *i.e.*, who is protected against loss, is know as indemnity- holder or indemnified.

Example 14.1. *A* owed Rs. 1000 to *B*, however he disputed the claim. *A's* friend *C*, contracted to indemnify *A* against the consequences of any proceedings which *B* may take against him (*A*). It is contract of indemnity. And if under the proceedings, *A* is ordered to pay the amount to *B*, then he can recover the same from C. In this case, C is the indemnifier, and *A* the indemnity-holder.

It may be noted that the definition of the contract of indemnity as given in Section 124 of the Indian Contract Act, is not exhaustive. By this definition, the scope of indemnity is restricted to the cases where there is express promise to indemnify against the loss caused by

(*a*) the promiser himself, or (*b*) any other person.

It therefore, follows that the express promise to indemnify must be to indemnify against the loss caused by human acts. This definition of contract of indemnity excludes the following, namely:

(*a*) implied promise to indemnify, and

(*b*) cases of loss arising from accidents and events not dependent on conduct of human beings, *e.g.*, accidental fires, perils of the seas, etc.

Thus, the expression 'contract of indemnity' in Section 124 has been used in a narrow sense. And the general law about contract of indemnity is much wider than the contract of indemnity as defined in Section 124. According to the general law about contract of indemnity, the losses arising from accidents or events, which do not depend on the conduct of human beings, are also covered by the contract of indemnity.

In India, the courts have taken the view that the definition of contract of indemnity as given in Section 124, is not exhaustive, and the courts would apply the same equitable principles that the courts in England do.

[*Gajanan Moreshwar* v. *Moreshwar madan*, AIR 1942 Bombay 302].

14.3. ENGLISH LAW ON CONTRACT OF INDEMNITY

The English law defines the contract of indemnity in a wider sense. According to the English Law, a contract of indemnity means "a promise to save another harmless from loss caused as a result of a transaction entered into at the instance of the promisor". This definition includes a promise of indemnity against loss arising from any cause whatsoever, *e.g.*, fire, perils of sea, accidents, etc. Thus, it is not necessary that the loss must be caused by human beings. Keeping in view the wider concept of contract of indemnity, the English law in respect of indemnity is followed by the Indian Court, and the contracts of fire insurance and marine insurance are always regarded as the contract of indemnity.[1]

14.4. ESSENTIALS AND LEGAL RULES FOR A VALID CONTRACT OR INDEMNITY

1. *The contract of indemnity must satisfy the requirements of a valid contract*
2. *There must be promise to save the other party from some loss*
3. *The loss may be due to the conduct of the promisor himself or any other person*
4. *The contract of indemnity may be express or implied*

The essential elements of a contract of indemnity are discussed in points 1 and 2 in the following discussion, and the rests are its legal rules.

1. *The contract of indemnity must satisfy the requirements of a valid contract.* A contract of indemnity is a special kind of contract. As such, it must have all the essential elements of a valid contract, such as consideration, free consent, competency of the parties, legality of object and consideration. Thus, where the object of the contract of indemnity is opposed to public policy, it will not be a valid contract of indemnity.

1. AIR 1941 Lahore 68

Example 14.2. *A* requested *B*, a journalist, to publish a libel (defamatory statement) against *C*. And *A* promised to indemnify *B* for any loss which he may suffer by way of damages payable to *C*. It is not a valid contract of indemnity as its object is opposed to public policy.

2. *There must be promise to save the other party from some loss:* This is the most important element of a contract of indemnity. One party must promise to save the other party from any loss which he may suffer.

Example 14.3. *A* is appointed cashier in *B's* firm, at the request of *C.C* promised to indemnify *B* of any loss that he may suffer due to the dishonesty of *A*. In this case, the contract between *B* and *C* is the contract of indemnity.

3. *The loss may be due to the conduct of the promisor himself or any other person:* According to Section 124 of the Indian Contract Act, the indemnity may be for the loss which a party may sustain due to the conduct of the promisor himself or of any other person. As stated earlier, this provision restricts the scope of contracts of indemnity as it covers the loss caused by human agency only, *i.e.*, by the conduct of the promisor or of any other person. However, the general definition of the contract of indemnity is much wider and it also covers the losses arising from accidents or events which do not depend on the conduct of human beings, *e.g.*, the losses arising from accidental fire, perils of the seas, etc. Thus, the contracts of fire insurance, and marine insurance also fall in the category of contract of indemnity.

Example 14.4. *A* insured his house with *B*, an insurance company, against the risk of fire. *B* undertook to indemnify *A* for any loss which he may suffer due to the destruction of his house by fire, its a contract of indemnity

4. *The contract of indemnity may be express or implied:* The promise to indemnify a person against the loss suffered by him, may be express or implied. The express promise is one where a person promises in express terms to compensate the other from the loss. And the implied promise is one where the conduct of the promisor shows that he promised to indemnify the other party against the loss suffered by him.

Example 14.5. *A* and *B* claimed certain goods from *C* a godown keeper, as rival owners. *A* took the delivery of the goods from *C* and agreed to compensate him against any loss in case *B* turns out to be the true owner. It is an express contract of indemnity between *A* and *C*, as *A* has agreed in express terms to compensate *C* for any loss which he (*C*) may suffer.

Example 14.6. *A* , an auctioneer, sold certain goods on the instructions of *B*. Subsequently, it turned out that the goods did not belong to *B* but to another person *C*. And *C* recovered damages from *A* for selling the goods belonging to him. *A* brought an action against *B* for compensation of the loss which he had suffered by auction on *B's* directions. It was held that *A* was entitled to recover the compensation from *B*. The court observed that there was an implied promise by *B* to compensate *A* for any loss that he may suffer on account of any defect in *B's* authority to sell the goods . [*Adamson* v. *Jarvis* (1827) 4 Bing. 66]

14.5. RIGHTS OF INDEMNITY-HOLDER

1. *All damages which the indemnity-holder was compelled to pay*
2. *All costs which the indemnity-holder was compelled to pay in bringing or defending the suit*
3. *All sum which he paid in compromise of any such suit*

The rights of an indemnity-holder are contained in the various paragraphs of Section 125 of the Indian Contract Act. When the indemnity - holder is held liable to pay damages, then he becomes entitled to recover the compensation from the indemnifier. The indemnity -holder has the right to recover the following from the indemnifier, by way of compensation:

1. *All damages which the indemnity-holder was compelled to pay:* The indemnity-holder has the right to recover from the indemnifier all damages which he had paid in any suit in respect of the contract of indemnity. It may, however, be noted that the indemnity-holder must act within the scope of his authority [Section 125 (1)].

2. *All costs which the indemnity-holder was compelled to pay in bringing or defending the suit:* The indemnity-holder has the right to recover from the indemnifier all costs which he had paid in bringing or defending any suit in respect of contract of indemnity. It may, however, be noted that the indemnity-holder must act within the scope of his authority and not contrary to the orders of the indemnifier. Moreover, in bringing and defending the suit, he must act in the same way as a prudent man, *i.e.*, a person of ordinary intelligence would have acted under similar circumstances in his own case, The indemnity-holder may also recover all the costs of the suit where he was authorised by the indemnifier to bring or defend the suit [Section 125 (2)].

3. *All sum which he paid in compromise of any such suit:* The indemnity-holder has the right to recover from the indemnifier, all the amount which he had paid under the terms of the compromise of such suit. However, he must act within the scope of his authority, and the compromise must not be contrary to the orders of the indemnifier. Moreover, in compromising the suit, he must act as a prudent man. He may also recover such amount, where he was authorised by the indemnifier to compromise the suit [Section 125 (3)].

14.6. RIGHTS OF INDEMNIFIER

There is no provision in the Indian Contract Act about indemnifier's rights. The Act is silent on this point. It may, however, be said that indemnifier's rights are the same as those of a surety, which are the essential part of law. The following judical observations in *Simpson* v. *Thomson*, 3 AC 279. Are worth noting in this regard:

> *"It is well known principle of law that where one person has agreed to indemnify another, he will, on making goods the indemnity, be entitled to succeed to all the ways and means by which the person indemnified might have protected himself against or reimbursed himself for the loss."*

The rights of a surety will be discussed in Art 14.13.

14.7. COMMENCEMENT OF INDEMNIFIER'S LIABILITY

In the Indian Contract Act, there is no provision regarding the time of commencement of indemnifier's liability under the contract. Thus, for the purpose of knowing the time of commencement of indemnifier's liability, *i.e.*, when does the indemnifier become liable to pay, we have to look into the observations of the courts in various judicial decisions. There is difference of opinion among the different High Courts. Some High Courts have held that the indemnifier is not liable until the indemnified (*i.e.*, indemnity-holder) has incurred an actual loss[2]. In other words, the indemnifier becomes liable to pay only after the indemnity holder had suffered actual loss by paying off the claim. On the other hand, some High Courts have held that the indemnifier becomes liable to pay even before the indemnity-holder had incurred actual loss.[3] In other words, the indemnity holder can compel the indemnifier to make goods his loss even before he had suffered actual loss by paying off the claim. The latter view is generally accepted and it lays down the equitable principle that as soon as the liability of the indemnity-holder to pay becomes clear and certain, he should have the right to require the indemnifier to put him in a position to meet the claim. The following judicial observations are worth noting in this regard:

2. *Sham Sunder* v. *Chander Lal.*, AIR 1935. Lah. 974: *Ranganath* v. *Pachusao*, AIR 1935 Nag. 147.
3. *Kamnannath Bhattachajee* v. *Nobokumar* (1899) 26 Calcutta 241; *Ramadigathudayar* v. *Munamdai Achi* (1915) 38 Madras 791; *Abdul Majid* v. *Abdul Rashid* 1936 Allahabad 596; *Gajnan Mureshwar* v. *Mureshwar Madan* 1942 Bombay 302.

"Indemnity is not necessarily given by repayment after payment. Indemnity requires that the party to be indemnified shall never be called upon to pay."

[*Re Richardson, ex parte etc.* (1911) 2 K.B. 705].

Thus, if the indemnity-holder had incurred an absolute liability, he becomes entitled to call upon the indemnifier to save him from that liability and pay it off. In other words, the liability of the indemnifier commences as soon as the liability of the indemnity-holder becomes absolute, *i.e.*, clear and certain.

Example 18.7. *A & Co.* was acting as commission agents of *B* for the purpose of purchase of goods. In the capacity of the agent, *A & Co.* bought certain goods from *C* for its principal *B*. However, *B* refused to take the goods. *C* brought an action against *A & Co.* and became entitled to recover certain amount as damage from *A &Co.* Before paying the damages, *A & Co.* went into liquidation. The official liquidator of *A & Co.* filed a suit against *B* for the recovery of the amount of damages for which *A & co.* was held liable. It was held that the official liquidator of *A & Co* could recover the amount of damages from *B* even though *A & Co.* had not actually paid the amount to *C*.

[*Osman Jamal & Sons* v. *Gopal purshottm*, 1928 ILR 56 Cal 262]

14.8. CONTRACT OF GUARANTEE

The term 'guarantee' may be defined as an undertaking by one person to pay the amount due from another person. And a contract to pay the amount due from another person, in case the latter fails to pay, is known as contract of guarantee. The term 'contract of guarantee' is defined in Section 126 of the Indian Contract Act, which reads as under:

"A contract of guarantee is a contract to perform the promise, or discharge the liability of a third person in case of his default"

The analysis of this section shows that, a contract of guarantee is a contract in which a person promises to discharge the liability of a third person in case the third person fails to discharge his own liability. The following three parties are involved in a contract of guarantee:

1. ***Surety:*** The party who gives the guarantee is known as surety.
2. ***Principal debtor:*** The party on whose behalf the guarantee is given is known as a principal debtor, *i,e.*, the party in respect of whose default the guarantee is given.
3. ***Creditor.*** The party to whom the guarantee is given is known as creditor.

Thus, a contract of guarantee is a tripartite agreement between the surety, the principal debtor and the creditor in which the surety promises to pay the amount of debt to the creditor if the principal debtor fails to pay.

Example 14.8. *A* advanced a loan of Rs. 5000 to *B* at the request of *C*. And *C* promised to *A* that if *B* does not repay the amount then he (C) will pay. This is a contract of guarantee. In this case, *A* is the creditor, *B* is the principal debtor and *C* is the surety.

14.9. ESSENTIALS AND LEGAL RULES FOR A VALID CONTRACT OF GUARANTEE

1. ***The contract of guarantee must satisfy the requirements of a valid contract***
2. ***The contract of guarantee must be supported by consideration***
3. ***The contract of guarantee must be made by the parties competent to contract***
4. ***There must be someone primarily liable***
5. ***The promise to pay must be conditional***
6. ***There should be no misrepresentation***
7. ***There should be no concealment of facts***
8. ***The contract of guarantee may be oral or in writing***

The essential elements of contract of guarantee are discussed in points 1 to 7 below, and the rest are its legal rules:

1. *The contract of guarantee must satisfy the requirements of a valid contract:* A contract of guarantee is a special kind of contract. As such, it must have all the essential elements of a valid contract such as consideration, free consent, competence of the parties, legality of object and consideration.

Example 14.9. *A* requested *B* to give him a loan of Rs. 10,000. *B* agreed to give the loan if *C* guarantees the repayment of the loan. *C* refused to give the guarantee. However, the guarantee from C was obtained by practising coercion upon him. This is not a valid guarantee as surety's (*C's*) consent is not free.

As regards the consideration and capacity of the parties, a contract of guarantee has special features, which are discussed in the following two essentials:

2. *The contract of guarantee must be supported by consideration.* It is, however, not necessary that there should be direct consideration between the surety and creditor. The law presumes that the consideration received by the principal debtor is the sufficient consideration for the surety. Thus, something done for the benefit of the principal debtor is the sufficient consideration for a contract of guarantee. And it is not necessary that the surety himself must be benefitted (Section127).

Example 14.10. *A* requested *B* to sell and deliver to him a tape recorder on credit. *B* agreed to do so provided *C* will guarantee the payment of the price of the tape recorder. *C* promised to guarantee the payment of the price in consideration of *B's* promise to deliver the tape recorder to *A*. This is a sufficient consideration for *C's* promise of guarantee.

It may, however, be noted that there must be some consideration. If the consideration is totally absent then the contract of guarantee is invalid.

Example 14.11. *A* sold and delivered goods to *B*. Afterwards, *C without any consideration*, agreed to pay the price in default of *B*. The agreement is void as it is without any consideration.

Simultaneous tripartite contract between surety, creditor and principal debater is not necessary. When once a contract between principal debtor and creditor is formed, a contract by which the surety guarantees the debt, can also take place. And the consideration may move either from the creditor or the principal debtor. Thus a guarantee can be given after the loan has been advanced.

3. *The contract of guarantee must be made by the parties competent to contract:* The parties to a contract of guarantee, must also be competent to contract. However, the incapacity of the principal debtor does not affect the validity of a contract of guarantee. Thus, the requirement is that the creditor and the surety must be competent to enter into a valid contract. A principal debtor may be a minor. In such cases, the surety is regarded as principal debtor and is personally liable to pay the debt, though the principal debtor is not liable. In such cases, the contract between the creditor and surety is treated as a primary and independent, and not a collateral. The surety is also liable if the guarantee is given knowing the minority of the debtor. [*Kashiba* v. *Shripat* (1895)19 ILR Bom. 697][4]

Example 14.12. *A* requested *B* to lend Rs. 1000 to *C*, a minor. And *A* promised that if *C* failed to repay then he will pay the amount. In this case, though the principal debtor (*i.e.,C*) is a minor, but the contract between *A* and *B* is enforceable. And *B* can recover the amount from *A*.

4. *There must be someone primarily liable:* It is an essential requirement of a contract of guarantee that there must be some one primarily liable (*i.e.*, liable as principal debtor) other than the surety. As a matter of fact, a contract of guarantee presupposes the existence of a liability enforceable by law. If there is no such primary liability, there can be no valid contract of guarantee. However, as stated above, the guarantee given for minor's debt is enforceable.

Example 14.13. *A* owed Rs. 10,000 to *B*. After the debts became time -barred by the Law of Limitation. *C* gives a guarantee to *B* for the repayment of the amount. This is not a valid contract. of guarantee as the primary lability between *A* and *B* is not enforceable by law due to the expiry of limitation period.

5. *The promise to pay must be conditional:* It is another important essential element of a contract of guarantee. There must be a conditional promise to be liable on the default of the principal debtor. In other words, the liability of the surety should arise only when

4. For contrary view see *K.E. Nambiar* v. *M.K. Raman,* AIR 1957 Mad. 164

the principal debtor makes a default. Any liability, which is incurred independently of the 'default' of the principal debtor, is not within the definition of guarantee.

[*PN Bank* v. *Sri Vikram Cotton Mill*, AIR 1970 SC 1973].

Example 14.14. *A* and *B* two friends, went to *C's* shop. *A* bought some goods from the shop, and *B* said that if *A* fails to pay the price, then he (*B*) will pay. This is a contract of guarantee. In this case, the primary liability to pay the price is that of *A*. And *B's* liability arises only on the default of *A*, *i.e.*, if he fails to pay the price. [*Birkmyr* v. *Darnell* (1704) 91 Er 27, 1 Salk 27]

In the above example, if *A* says to the shopkeeper, "let *B* have the goods, I will be your paymaster, or I will see that you are paid". This is not contract of guarantee because *A* undertakes the primary liability which is independent of *B's*.

6. *There should be no misrepresentation:* It is also an essential element of a valid guarantee. The guarantee should not be obtained by misrepresenting the facts to the surety. The facts, which are likely to affect the degree of surety's responsibility, must be truly represented to him by the creditor. If the guarantee is obtained by the misrepresentation of such material facts, it will be invalid. The guarantee will also be invalid, if, with the knowledge and consent of the creditor, any material part of the transaction between the creditor and his debtor is misrepresented to the surety (Section 142).

Example. 14.15. *A* purchased, certain goods from *B*, a shopkeeper, on credit. After the expiry of credit period, *A* failed to pay the price of goods. In consequence of this, *B* refused to allow credit in future unless *A* furnishes guarantee for the payment of price. *C* gives guarantee for the payment of price by *A*. At the time of guarantee, *B* informed *C* that previously *A* was making all the payments on due date. In this case, the guarantee given by *C* is invalid as it is obtained by misrepresentation of the facts by *B* concerning the earlier dealings between *A* and *B*.

7. *There should be no concealment of facts:* The creditor should disclose to the surety the facts which are likely to affect the surety' liability. The guarantee obtained by concealment of such facts is invalid, Thus, the guarantee is invalid if it is obtained by the creditor by the concealment of material facts (Section143).

Example 14.16. *A* engaged *B* as a clerk to collect money from his (*A's*) creditors. *B* collected money from some creditors but failed to account for some of the money. In consequence of this, *A* called upon *B* to furnish security for his collections. *B's* friend, *C* gave a guarantee for *B's* collections. At the time of guarantee, *A* did not inform *C* about *B's* pervious conduct. After this guarantee, *B* collected some money but failed to account for all the collections. In this case, the guarantee given by *C*. is invalid as it was obtained by concealment of material facts by *A*. As such, *C* is not liable for *B's* default.

8. *The contract of guarantee may be oral or in writing:* A contract of guarantee may be either oral or in writing. [Section 126]. Whereas, as per English Law, the guarantee must be in writing and signed by the paraty who offers guarantee. [Section 4 of the Statute of Frauds].

14.10. KINDS OF GUARANTEE

1. *Specific or simple guarantee*
2. *Continuing guarantee*

Though there are many kinds of guarantee, yet the following two kinds are important from the subject point of view:

1. ***Specific or simple guarantee***: it is a guarantee which is given for a specific transaction. In other words, a guarantee which extends to a single transaction or debt, is known as a specific or simple guarantee. Such guarantee comes to an end as soon as the transaction is duly performed or the debt is duly discharged.

Example 14.17. *A* requested *B* to deliver five bags of wheat to *C*. The bags were to be delivered and paid for in a month. *A* promised that if *C* failed to pay the price within one month, then he will pay the same. *B* delivered five bags of wheat to *C* and *C* paid the price. Afterwards, *B* delivered four more bags of wheat to *C* which *C* did not pay for. In this case, the guarantee given by *A* was a specific guarantee which came to an end on the performance of the guaranteed transaction. And thus, *A* is not liable for four bags of rice delivered after the performance of the first promise.

2. *Continuing guarantee:* It is a guarantee which is given for a series of transactions of continuing nature. The term 'continuing guarantee' is defined in Section 129 of the Indian Contract Act , which provides that a guarantee which extends to series of transactions or debts, is known as a continuing guarantee. Such guarantee does not come to an end on the performance of a single transaction or discharge of a single debt. It remains enforceable even for the subsequent debts or transactions also. However, the surety can fix up a limit on his liability for time or amount of the guarantee. Thus, a continuing guarantee can be for a fixed period. The reason for the same is that, the continuing guarantee speaks of continuing transactions and not the period of such transactions.

[*Estern Bank Ltd.* v. *Parts Services of India*, AIR 1986 Cal. 61].

Example 14.18. At *A's* request, *B* employed *C* for collecting the rent of his (*B's*) zamindari. *A* promised *B* to be responsible up to Rs. 50,000 for the collection and payment by *C* of those rents. This is a continuing guarantee.

Example 14.19. *A* guaranteed payment to *B*, a tea dealer, to the amount of Rs. 5 lakh for any tea that he may supply to *C* from time to time. *B* supplied some tea to *C* to the value of Rs. 5 lakh, and *C* paid for it . Afterwards, *B* supplied some more tea to *C* to the value of Rs. 7 lakh. But *C* failed to pay for it. In this case, the guarantee given by *A* was a continuing guarantee as it extended to any tea that may be supplied by *B* to *C* from time to time. And thus, *A* is liable to *B* to the extent of Rs. 5 lakh .

Example 14.20. *A*, a fruit dealer, agreed to supply certain fruits to *B* on credit, at the request of C. And *C* gave a guarantee to *A* for the payment of the price for any fruits the he may supply to *B* from time to time within one year. *A* supplied some fruit to *B* to the value of Rs. 2 lakh and *B* paid for it. After the expiry of one year, *A* supplied some more fruits to *B* to the value of Rs. 50,000. But *B* failed to pay for it. In this case, the guarantee given by *C* was a continuing guarantee but it was valid for one year only. And thus, *C* is not liable to *A* for the price of the fruit supplied after the expiry of one year.

Note: A guarantee may be ***'retrospective guarantee'*** or ***'prospective'*** also. A guarantee given for a existing debt, is called a 'retrospective guarantee'. And the guarantee, given for a future debt, is called a 'prospective guarantee'. A guarantee given for the good conduct or honesty of a person employed in a particular office, is called a ***'fidelity guarantee'***. The guarantee may also be ***'absolute'*** or ***'conditional'***. An absolute guarantee means a guarantee where the surety unconditionally promises to pay in case of default of the principal debtor. A conditional guarantee mean a guarantee where the surety promises to pay in case some event, in addition to the default of the principal debtor, happens.

14.11. REVOCATION OF CONTINUING GUARANTEE

1. *By notice of revocation by the surety (Section 130)*
2. *By the death of the surety (Section 131)*

On the revocation *i.e.*, cancellation of a continuing guarantee, the liability of the surety comes to an end for the future transactions. However, the surety continues to be liable for the previous transactions. A continuing guarantee may be revoked in any of the following ways:

1. *By notice of revocation by the surety (Section 130):* A surety may revoke the continuing guarantee at any time, by giving a notice of revocation to the creditor. It may, however, be noted that a continuing guarantee can be revoked in respect of the future transactions only, and the surety remains liable for the transactions already entered into before the revocation.

Example 14.21. *A*, a shopkeeper, agreed to supply some goods to *B* on credit, at the request of *C*. And *C* gave a guarantee to *A* for the payment of the price up to Rs. 10,000. After three months, *C* revoked the guarantee by giving notice to *A*. But within these three months, *A* had already supplied goods to *B* worth Rs. 2,500. In this case, *C* is liable to pay Rs. 2,500 to *A* if *B* fails to pay the same. But he (*C*) will not be liable for the goods supplied after the revocation.

2. ***By the death of the surety (Section 131):*** A continuing guarantee is revoked on the death of the surety. However, the death of the surety revokes the continuing guarantee only if there is no contract to the contrary. It may be noted that the guarantee is automatically revoked on surety's death and no notice of death is required to be given to the creditor. In this case also, the revocation is effective for future transaction only, and surety's legal heir remains liable for the transactions already entered into before the death of the surety.

Example 14.22. At *A's* request, *B* employed *C* for collecting the rents of his (*B's*) house. *A* gave a guarantee to *B* to the extent of Rs. 5,000 for the due collections of rent by *C*. *A* collection of Rs. 1,000 was made by *C* and thereafter *A* died. On *A's* death, the guarantee gets revoked in respect of the collections made after *A's* death. However, *A's* legal representatives are liable up to Rs. 1,000 if *C* fails to give this amount to *B*.

Note: *A* continuing guarantee is also revoked when the surety is discharged from liability. The circumstances in which the surety is discharged from his liability will be discussed in Art. 14.17.

14.12. NATURE AND EXTENT OF SURETY'S LIABILITY

1. *Surety's liability is coextensive*
2. *Surety's liability may also be limited*
3. *Surety's liability arises immediately on default of the principal debtor*
4. *Surety's liability where the original contract between creditor and principal debtor is void or voidable*
5. *Surety's liability under continuing guarantee*

The nature and extent of surety's liability may be discussed under the following heads:

1. ***Surety's liability is coextensive:*** The liability of a surety is co-extensive with that of the principal debtor. This means that the surety is liable to the same extent to which the principal debtor is liable. In other words, the liability of the surety is the same as that of the principal debtor [Section 128]. Whatever amount of money a creditor can legally realise from the principal debtor, including interest, damages, cost, etc., the same amount can be recovered from the surty. The expression 'co-extensive with that of the principal debtor' shows the maximum extent of surety's liability. He is liable for whole of the amount for which the principal debtor is liable.

Example 14.23. *A* gave a guarantee to *B* for the repayment of the loan due from *C*. On due date, *C* failed to repay the loan. In this case, *A* is liable not only for the amount of the loan but also for any interest and other charges which may have become due.

2. ***Surety's liability may also be limited:*** The above principle is applicable where the surety undertakes to be liable for the whole debt. However, it is open to the surety to limit his liability. Thus the surety may, by an agreement, limit his liability to a fixed amount. In such cases, the surety's liability will not be more than the amount fixed by him.

Example 14.24. *A* gave a loan of Rs. 10,000 to *B* at *C's* request. And *C* gave a guarantee to *A* for the repayment loan by *B* up to Rs. 7,000. On the due date, *B* failed to pay the whole amount of loan,. In this case, *C* is liable only to the extent of .Rs. 7,000 as he has restricted his liability.

3. ***Surety's liability arises immediately on default of the principal debtor.*** The surety's liability arises immediately on the default of the principal debtor. In other words, the surety becomes liable to pay the amount of guarantee as soon as the default is committed by the principal debtor. However, the surety cannot be called upon to pay unless the principal debtor has committed the default.

Example 14.25. *A* gave a loan of Rs. 1500 to *B*. And *C* gave a guarantee to *A* for the repayment of the loan by *B*. Before the due date for the repayment of the loan, *B* was declared insolvent by the Court of Law. In this case, the surety (*C*) is not liable to pay the amount of loan because *B* has become insolvent without making any default in the repayment of the loan.

But in case default by the principal debtor, the creditor can immediately demand the amount from the surety, and the surety cannot ask the creditor to exhaust all the remedies open to him against the principal debtor first, and only then against the surety. He may sue the surety without suing the principal debtor. Moreover, he may also sue them jointly.

Example 14.26. *A* obtained a loan from a bank which was guaranteed by *B*. On due date, *A* made default in repaying the loan. And the Bank filed a suit against *B* (the surety) to recover the amount. The lower court ordered that the Bank should enforce the guarantee only after exhausting all its remedies against *A* (the principal debtor). This was confirmed by the Patna High Court. The matter then came in the Supreme Court. The supreme Court held that condition of such kind cannot be imposed upon the creditor. The creditor is not required to first exhaust his remedies against the principle debtor, he can sue the surety without suing the principal debtor. The Supreme Court observed that "the surety is a guarantor: and it is his business to see that the principal debtor pays, and not that of the creditor" [*Bank of Bihar* v. *Damodar Prasad*, AIR 1969 SC 297]

Thus, in case of default by the principal debtor, the creditor can immediately demand the amount from the surety. He is not required do give a notice of default to the surety. It may, however, be noted that where the contract of guarantee provides that the surety will not be liable unless some condition is fulfilled, then the surety is not liable until such condition is actually fulfilled *e.g.*, where it is provided in the guarantee that the surety shall be liable only after a notice of demand is served on him, then surety's liability will arise only after the notice of demand is served on him.

4. *Surety's liability where the original contract between creditor and principal debtor is void or voidable:* The liability of the surety is not necessarily, simultaneous with that of the principal debtor. Their liability is different arising from the different contracts. The contract between the surety and creditor is an independent contract and not a collateral one. Thus, it cannot be said that the surety will be liable only if the principal debtor is liable (though such restriction can be imposed by specific agreement to that effect). Therefore, when the original contract between the principal debtor and creditor is void, e.g., where the principal debtor is a minor, the surety will remain liable. In such a case, the surety is liable as if he was the principal debtor.[5] Similarly, where the original contract is voidable at the option of principal debtor who has exercised his option and revoked the contract, the surety may not be discharged from his liability. Moreover, the surety is also not discharged where the creditor fails to sue the principal debtor within the period of limitation, if the limitation period is otherwise available against the surety.

[*Mahant Singh* v. *U. Ba. Yi* (1939) 66 I.A.198].

Note: There is also a contrary view that the surety is not liable if the original contract between the principal debtor and the creditor is void. In *E.K. Nambiar* v. *V.K. Raman* (AIR 1957 Mad. 164) it was observed that "the liability of the surety is only ancillary and can rest only on a valid obligation on the part of the party whose debt or obligation is guaranteed". Thus, according to this view, the liability of the surety is secondary. If the original contract between principal debtor and creditor is void, the question of surety's liability does not arise. It is submitted, this view appears to be correct as in case of void contract between principal debtor and creditor there is no enforceable principal debt. However, it is for the courts to decide keeping in view the facts and circumstances of each particular case.

5. *Surety's liability under continuing guarantee:* This has already been discussed in detail in Art. 14.10

5. *Kashiba* v. *Shripat*. (1895) 19 ILR Bombay 697; *Tikki Lal* v. *Kamal Chand* (1940) Nagpur 1632.

14.13. RIGHTS OF THE SURETY

The rights of the surety may be discussed under the following three heads:

1. Rights against the principal debtor.
2. Rights against the creditor.
3. Rights against the co-sureties.

14.14. RIGHTS AGAINST THE PRINCIPAL DEBTOR

The surety has the following rights against the principal debtor:

1. *Right of subrogation*
2. *Right of indemnity*

1. *Right of subrogation:* The term 'subrogation' may be defined as the substitution of one person for another. According to the this right, when the surety has paid the debt or discharged the obligation of the principal debtor, he is invested with all the rights which the creditor had against the principal debtor, *i.e*, the surety steps into the shoes of the creditor (Section 140). Thus, upon payment of debt or discharge of the liability of the principal debtor, the surety becomes entitled to *all* the right which the creditor could have enforced against the principal debtor.

Example 14.27. *A* borrowed money from *B* and mortgaged his house as security. *C* was surety (guarantor) for the loan. *A* failed to repay the loan, and *B* recovered the amount from *C*. In this case, *C* steps into the shoes of *B* (the creditor), and can enforce the mortgage against *A*.

2. *Right of indemnity:* The term 'indemnity' means the compensation. When the surety has rightfully paid the loan or discharged the obligations of the principle debtor, he becomes entitled to recover from the principal debtor whatever amount (including interest and costs) he has paid under the guarantee. As a matter of fact, in every contract of guarantee there is an implied promise by the principal debtor to indemnify the surety (Section 145). However the amount wrongfully paid cannot be recovered. It may also be noted that the surety can recover the amount which has been actually paid to the creditor.

Example 14.28. *A* borrowed Rs. 10,000 from *B*, and *C* gave a guarantee to *B* for the repayment of the loan. On due date, *A* refused to repay the loan, *B* demanded the payment from *C*, who also refused to pay the money. *B* filed a suit for recovery against *C*, who defended the suit having reasonable grounds for doing so. However, *C* was compelled to pay the amount of the debt with costs. In this case, *C* can recover from B the amount of the principal debt along with the amount of costs paid by him. However if *C* had defended the suit without any reasonable ground, then he could not have been entitled to recover the amount of costs because it would then be the amount paid wrongfully.

14.15. RIGHTS AGAINST THE CREDITOR

1. *Right to claim securities*
2. *Right of set-off*
3. *Right to share reduction*

The surety has the following rights against the creditor:

1. *Right to claim securities:* On payment of the debt to the creditor, the surety becomes entitled to claim the securities which the creditor has against the principal debtor. However, he can claim only those securities which the creditor had at the time of the guarantee. This right is available to the surety whether or not he knows about the existence of such securities (Section 141). However , the surety can claim the securities from the creditor on the discharge of the full liability of the principal debtor which has been guaranteed by the surety. It may, however, be noted that the surety is not entitled to the securities which the creditor receives from the principal debtor *after* the contract of guarantee is entered into.

Example 14.29. *A* obtained a loan of Rs. 2,500 from *B*. *A* gave some jewellry as security. And

A's friend *C* also gave a guarantee for the repayment of the loan. After this contract of guarantee, due to fall in the price of jewellery, *B* obtained some goods from *A* as a further security for the same debt. In this case, *C* is entitled to claim only the jewellery from *B*. And he is not entitled to claim the goods from *B* as these were obtained by the creditor (*i.e., B*) after the guarantee was given.

It is important to note here that it is the duty of the creditor to keep the securities intact and not to give them up. If he gives up or returns the securities to the principal debtor without the consent of the surety, then the surety is discharged from liability *to the extent* of the value of such securities [Section 141, last para].

2. *Right of set-off* : The term 'set-off' may be defined as a counter claim or deductions from the amount of loan. Sometimes, the principal debtor is entitled to certain counter claim or deductions from the amount of loan taken from the creditor. In such case, if the creditor files a suit against the surety, then the surety is entitled to the benefit of any such counter claim or deductions which the principal debtor has against the creditor. In other words, the surety is entitled to use the defences of the debtor against the creditor.

Example 14.30. *A* borrowed Rs. 5,000 from *B*, and *C* gave a guarantee for the repayment of the loan. *A* also had a claim of Rs. 1,000 against *B* on some earlier transaction. On due date, *A* failed to repay the amount of loan, and *B* filed a suit against the surety (*C*) for the recovery of the loan. In this case, *C* is entitled to deduct Rs, 1,000 which *B* owed to *A*. And thus, *C's* liability is only for Rs. 4,000.

Sometimes, the surety has his own claim against the creditor. In such cases also, the surety can deduct the amount of his claims if the creditor files a suit against him on the basis of the guarantee.

3. *Right to share reduction:* Sometimes, after the recovery of the guaranteed amount from the surety, the debtor is declared insolvent and on debtor's insolvency, the creditor also receives some dividends (*i.e.,* share) out of the assets of insolvent. In such cases, the surity is entitled to claim the proportionate reduction of his liability by the amount of dividend claimed by the creditor.

Example 14.31. *A* agreed to supply certain goods to *B* on credit. And *A* 's friend *C* gave a guarantee for the payment of the price of the goods up to Rs. 2,000. *A* supplied goods to *B* to the amount of Rs. 10,000. But *B* failed to pay the price and *A* recovered the guaranteed amount of Rs. 2,000 from *C*. Subsequently, *B* became insolvent, and *A* proved the whole of his debt (*i.e.,* Rs.10,000) in insolvency of *B*. And *A* received 25 per cent of Rs. 10,000 as dividend in the insolvency. In this case, *C* can claim a refund of 25 per cent of Rs. 2,000, *i.e.,* Rs. 500 from *A* which he has already paid. [*Based on Hobson* v. *Bass* (1871) 6 Ch. A 792].

14.16. RIGHTS AGAINST THE CO-SURETIES

1. *Right to contribution*
2. *Right to share benefits of securities*

Sometimes, two or more persons give a guarantee for the same debt. In such cases, they are termed as co-sureties. All the co-sureties are equally liable to the creditor. The rights of co-sureties against each other may be discussed as under:

1. *Right to contribution-* On the payment of the guaranteed debt by one surety, he becomes entitled to claim contribution from the other co-sureties. And the co-sureties are liable to contribute equally (Section 146). Thus, when one co-surety discharges the entire obligation, he can obtain equal contributions from the other co-surety. This principle of equal contribution applies whether the sureties are liable jointly or seavearally, and whether their liability is under the same contract or different contract. However, if the co-sureties fix their liability by an agreement, then they are liable to contribute as agreed among themselves.

Example 14.32. *A* borrowed Rs. 10,000 from *B. C, D* and *E* gave a joint guarantee for the repayment of the loan. *C,D* and *E* have agreed among themselves that *C* will be liable for 25 per cent of the amount of loan, *D* also for 25 per cent, and E for 50 per cent. On the due date, *A* made default in the repayment of the loan. In this case *C* is liable to pay Rs. 2,500, D Rs 2,500 and *E* Rs. 5,000.

It is to be noted that where the co-sureties have agreed to guarantee different sums of one single debt to the principal debtor, even then they are liable to contribute equally subject to the maximum limit fixed by them (Section 147). Thus within the maximum limit fixed by the co-sureties, they are liable to contribute an equal amount.

Example 14.33. *A* borrowed Rs. 60,000 from *B. C, D* and *E* gave a joint guarantee for the repayment of the loan, However, *C* undertook to be liable up to Rs. 10,000, *D* up to Rs. 20,000 and *E* up to Rs. 30,000 On the due date, A made default to the extent of Rs. 30,000 In this case, *C, D* and *E* are liable to pay Rs. 10,000 each. (This is within the maximum limit of all of them). Now suppose, *A* had made default to the extent of Rs. 45,000. According to the principle of equal contribution, each surety should contribute Rs. 15,000. But in this case, *C's* liability is fixed up to Rs. 10,000. Therefore, *C* is liable to contribute Rs. 10,000 and the remaining Rs 35,000 will be contributed by *D* and *E* in equal shares, *i.e.,* Rs. 17,500 each. (This is within the maximum limit of *D* and *E*). And if *A* had made a default of the whole debt, *i.e.,* Rs. 60,000 then *C* , *D* and *E* are liable to pay Rs, 10,000 Rs. 20,000 and Rs. B 30,000 respectively.

Notes: 1. The right of contribution is available only when all the sureties guarantee one and the same debt. Moreover, the right of contribution arises when one co-surety has paid more than he is liable to pay.

2. Under the English law, the co-sureties are not liable to contribute equally. Their liability is to contribute in proportion to the amount guaranteed by each surety.

2. *Right to share benefits of securities:* Sometimes, at the time of guarantee, one of the co-sureties receives a security from the principal debtor, or on payment of the debt, he receives security from the creditor. In such cases, the co-sureties are entitled to share the benefit of the securities.

Example 14.34. *A, B* and *C* were sureties to *D* for the loan of Rs. 1,20,000 advanced to *E.* However, *A* had received a security of *E's* house. *E* made default in payment of the loan, and *D* recovered the amount from *A, B* and *C. A* obtained an order from the court for the sale of the house. In this case, *B* and *C* are also entitled to share the proceeds of the house realised by *A.*

14.17. DISCHARGE OF SURETY FROM LIABILITY

1. *By notice of revocation by the surety*
2. *By death of the surety*
3. *By variance in terms of contract*
4. *By release or discharge of the principal debtor*
5. *By composition with the principal debtor*
6. *By giving more time to the principal debtor*
7. *By promise not to sue the principal debtor*
8. *By impairing surety's remedy*
9. *By losing the security by the creditor*
10. *By invalidation of the contract of guarantee*

A surety is said to be discharged from liability when his liability under the contract comes to an end. The following are the various modes of discharge of surety:

1. *By notice of revocation by the surety:* A surety may revoke the guarantee, at any time, by giving notice of revocation to the creditor. On the revocation of the guarantee, the liability of the surety comes to an end. It may, however, be noted that only a continuing guarantee can be revoked by notice, and the surety is discharged from liability as to the future transactions. A specific guarantee cannot be revoked by the surety if his liability has already accrued under the contract.

2. *By death of the surety.* The death of the surety puts an end to surety's liability under the guarantee. However, the death of the surety operates as a revocation of the guarantee only in case of continuing guarantee. The revocation by death is effective only in respect of future transactions.

Note: Both the above points has already been discussed in detail in Art. 14.11.

3. *By variance in terms of contract (Section 133).* Once the contract of guarantee is entered into, it becomes the duty of the creditor not to make any change in the terms of the original contract between him and the principal debtor. If the creditor makes any variance (*i.e.*, change in terms) without the consent of the surety, then the surety is discharged as to the transactions subsequent to the change. In other words, if without the consent of the surety, the creditor makes any material change in the nature or terms of his contract with the principal debtor, the surety is discharged from liability. However, the surety is discharged in respect of the transactions which are subsequent to the change. If the change is with surety's consent, then he shall not be discharged from liability.

Example 14.35. *A*, a shopkeeper, agreed to appoint *B*, as his representative to sell goods on some salary. *C* gave a guarantee to *A* for *B's* due accounting for money received by him. Afterwards, without *C's* knowledge or consent, *A* and *B* agreed that *B* shall be paid by way of commission on the goods sold by him, and not by the fixed salary as agreed earlier. In this case. *C* is not liable for *B's* misconduct after the change in the terms of contract between *A* and *B*.

Example 14.36. *A*, a landlord, let out his house to *B* at a monthly rent of Rs. 11,000. And *C* gave a guarantee for the payment of the rent by *B*. Afterwards, without *C's* knowledge or consent, *A* and *B* entered in to another contract by which the rent was increased to Rs. 11,500 per month . In this case, the surety (*C*) was held to be discharged from his liability.

[*Based on Knatu Bibi* v. *Abdullah* (1880) 3 All 9]

The surety is also discharged from liability if the nature of the contract between the creditor and principal debtor is changed by some Act of the Legislature.

4. *By release or discharge of the principal debtor (Section 134):* Sometimes, the creditor releases or discharges the principal debtor from the liability. In such case, the surety is automatically discharged from his liability under the guarantee. The creditor may release the principal debtor by a fresh contract, or by some of his acts or omissions which has the effect of discharging the principal debtor. Thus, under this clause, the surety is discharged in the following two circumstances:

(*a*) If the creditor makes a fresh contract with the principal debtor by which the latter is released from his liability;

(*b*) If the creditor does any act of omission which has the effect of discharging the principal debtor from his liability.

Example 14.37. *A* borrowed Rs. 5,000. from *B*. The repayment of the loan was guaranteed by C. On due date, *A* was unable to repay the amount. However. *A* offered to *B* to pay Rs. 3,000 in full and final settlement of the amount borrowed by him. *B* accepted this offer, compromised and released *A* from the liability. In this case, C is also discharged from the liability as a release of a principal debtor is also the release of the surety.

Example 14.38. *A* contracted with *B* to grow a crop of rice in his (*A's*) land and deliver it to *B* at a fixed rate. And *C* gave a guarantee for *A's* performance of the contract. *B* diverted a stream of water which was necessary for the irrigations of *A*'s land and thereby prevented him from growing the rice crop. In this case, the creditor (*B*), by his act, has discharged the principal debtor (*A*). This also discharges the surety (*C*) from his liability under the guarantee.

Note: Where the principal debtor is discharged, by the operation of law, the surety is not discharged from liability. *e.g.,*, the discharge of principal debtor in insolvency, or by the expiry of limitation period, does not discharge the surety. However, where by the operation of law, the liability of the principal debtor is reduced, the surety's liability is also reduced proportionately e.g., where the liability of principal is reduced under some Debt Relief Act, the liability of surety will also be reduced.

5. *By composition with the principal debtor (Section 135) :* The term 'composition' may be defined as the amicable settlement of the accounts. Sometimes, the creditor enters into a composition agreement with the principal debtor, without the consent of the surety. In such case, the surety is discharged from his liability.

Example 14.39. *A* borrowed Rs. 5,000 from *B*. The repayment of the loan was guaranteed by C. Subsequently, *A* was unable to repay the loan. He entered into an agreement with *B* in which he agreed to transfer his furniture to *B* in full and final settlement of the loan. And *B* accepted the furniture under the terms of the agreement. This composition agreement between *A* and *B* discharges the surety (C) from liability.

6. ***By giving more time to the principal debtor (Section 135):*** Sometimes, without the consent of the surety, the creditor gives more time to the principal debtor for the repayment of the amount of loan or for the performance of the obligation. In such cases, the surety is also automatically discharged from liability if he does not give consent to the extension of time. However, if the surety gives his consent to the extension of time, then he is not discharged from his liability.

Example 14.40. *A* purchased a car from *B*. The price of the car was to be paid in installments. The payment of the installments was guaranteed by C. The amount of the instalments fell in arrears. *B* settled with *A* that he should pay certain sum immediately and the balance by the end of the month, It was held that the settlement amounted to giving time to the principal debtor (*A*) and the surety (*C*) was discharged from liability under the guarantee.

[*Midland Motors* v. *Newman* (1929)2 KB 256]

7. ***By promise not to sue the principal debtor (Section 135) :*** Sometimes, without the consent of the surety, the creditor enters into another agreement with the principal debtor and promises not to file a suit against him. In such cases, the surety is discharged from liability. However, if the surety gives his consent to such a contract, then he is not discharged from his liabilities. The main reason is that a surety is entitled, at any time, to require the creditor to call upon the principal debtor to pay the debt when it is due. And this right of the surety is affected when the creditor promises not to sue the principal debtor.

Example. 14.41. A owed a sum of Rs. 20,000 to *B*, which was guaranteed by *C*. The debt became payable. But *B* entered into an agreement with *A* and promised not to file a suit against him (*A*) for the recovery of the debt. In this case *C* is discharged from his liabilities under the guarantee.

It may, however, be noted that a mere 'forbearance to sue' the principal debtor, does not discharge the surety (Section 137). The term 'forbearance to sue' means to refrain from filling a suit, whereas the 'promise not to sue' binds the creditor and deprives him of the power of suing.

Example 14.42. *A* owed Rs. 10,000 to *B* which was guaranteed by C. The debt became payable. However, *B* did not sue *A*. for a year after the debt had become payable. In this case, *C* is not discharged from liability under the guarantee.

8. ***By impairing surety's remedy (Section 139):*** The term 'impairing surety's remedy' means damaging or diminishing the rights of the surety. As a matter of fact, it is the duty of the creditor not to do anything inconsistent with the right of the surety. Thus, if some act or omission of the creditor deprives the surety of his rights against the principal debtor, the surety is discharged from his liability.

Example 14.43. *A* contracted to build a ship for *B* for a given sum to be paid by instalments as the work reaches certain stages. C became surety to *B* for *A*'s due performance of the contract. *B*, without the knowledge of *C*, paid to *A* the last two instalments before the due date. In this case, *C* is discharged by the prepayment of the instalments.

Example 14.44. On *A's* request, *B* appointed C as a cashier in his firm. *A* gave a guarantee for the good conduct of *C* and the employer (*B*) undertook that he will check *C's* work at least once in a month. However, *B* omitted to check the work of *C*, and he (*B*) misappropriated a sum of money. In this case, the surety (B) is not liable.

9. ***By losing the security by the creditor*** **(Section 141, (last para):** Sometimes, at the time of guarantee, the creditor has some security against the principal debtor. If the creditor loses or parts with the security without the consent of the surety, the surety is discharged from his liabilities to the extent of the value of the security. However, the surety is not discharged if the creditor loses the security with his consent.

Example 14.45. *A* took a loan of Rs. 10,000 from a Bank. The loan was guaranateed by *B*. The bank also had a security by way of mortgage of *A*'s land. However, the Bank cancelled the mortgage. In this case, *B* is discharged from his liability to the extent of the value of the land.

This point has already been discussed in Art. 14.15.

10. ***By invalidation of the contract of guarantee:*** The surety is liable under the guarantee only if the contract of guarantee is valid. If the contract of guarantee is invalid then the surety will not be liable, *i.e.*, he will be discharged from his liabilities. Thus, where a guarantee is obtained by coercion, undue influence, fraud, etc., then it will not be valid and the surety is not liable under such a guarantee. Following circumstance have been specifically provided in the Indian Contract Act in which the contract of guarantee is invalid:

(*a*) Guarantee obtained by misrepresentation of facts.

(*b*) Guarantee obtained by concealment of facts.

(*c*) Guarantee obtained without any consideration.

These points have already been discussed in Art. 14.9.

(*d*) Guarantee on the contract that the creditor shall not act on it until co-surety joins.

Sometimes, a person gives a guarantee on the contract that he will be liable only if some other person also joins as co-surety. In such cases, the guarantee is invalid if the other co-surety does not join. And the surety is discharged from his liability (Section 144).

Example 14.46. *A* agreed with *B* to stand as surety for *C* for a loan of Rs. 5000, provided *D* also joins him as co-surety. *D* refused to join as co-surety. In this case, the guarantee is invalid, and *A* is not liable as surety.

14.18. COMPARISON BETWEEN CONTRACT OF INDEMNITY AND CONTRACT OF GUARANTEE

The following table gives the comparison between the contract of indemnity and the contract of guarantee:

S. No.	*Contract of Indemnity*	*Contract of Guarantee*
1.	There are two parties, namely the 'indemnifier' and the indemnity-holder.	There are three parties namely, the principal debtor, the creditor and the surety.
2.	The liability of the indemnifier is primary in nature.	The liability of the surety is secondary in nature.
3.	The liability of the indemnifier arise on the happening of some contingency, *i.e.*, when the indemnity-holder suffers some loss.	The liability of the surety arises on the default of the principal debtor.
4.	There is no existing debt or duty. The indemnity is given to make good the loss which the indemnified may suffer due to the act of the indemnifier or some other person.	There is always some existing debt or duty. The guarantee is given for the payment of the debt or the performance of the duty if the principal debtor makes defult.
5.	It is not necessary for the indemnifier to act at request of the indemnity-holder.	The surety generally gives the guarantee at the request of the principal debtor.
6.	The indemnifier cannot sue the third party for loss, in his own name, He can sue in the name of the indiminety- holder He can sue in the his own name only if there is an assignment in his favour.	On the discharge of debtor's liability, the surety can sue the principal debtor in his own name.

LEGAL PROVISIONS (SECTIONS) DISCUSSED IN THE CHAPTER

Important legal provisions (sections) of the Indian Contract Act, 1872, discussed in this chapter, are reproduced hereunder for ready reference:

1. *Section 124: "Contract of indemnity" defined*

A contract by which one party promises to save the other form loss caused to him by the conduct of the promisor himself, or by the conduct of any other person, is called a "contract of indemnity."

2. *Section 125: Rights of indemnity-holder when sued*

The promisee in contract of indmnity, acting within the scope of his authorlty, is entitled to recover from the promisor–

(1) all damages which he may be compelled to pay in any suit in respect of any matter to which the promise to indemnify applies;

(2) all costs which he may be compelled to pay in any suit if, in bringing or defending it, he did not contravene the orders of the promisor, and acted as it would have been prudent for him to act in the absence of any contract of indemnity, or if the promisor authorized him to bring or defend the suit;

(3) all sums which he may have paid under the terms of any compromise of any such suit, if the compromise was not contrary to the orders of the promisor, and was one which it would have been prudent for the promisee to make in the absence of any contract of indemnity, or if the promisor authorized him to compromise the suit.

3. *Section 126: 'Contract of guarantee', 'surety', 'principal debtor' and 'creditor'*

A contract of guarantee is a contract to perform the promise, or discharge the liability, of a third person in case of his default. The person who gives the guarantee is called the surety', the person in respect of whose default the guarantee is given is called the principal debotr', and the person to whom the guarantee is given is called the crditor'. A guarantee may be either oral or written.

4. *Section 127: Consideration for Guarantee*

Anything done or any promise made, for the benefit of the principal debtor, be a sufficient consideration to the surety for giving the guarantee.

5. *Section 128: Surety's Liability*

The liability of the surety is co-extensive with that of the principal debtor, unless it is otherwise provided by the contract.

6. *Section. 129: Continuing Guararntee*

A guarantee which extends to a series of transactions, is called a continuing guarantee.

7. *Section 130: Revocation of continuing Guarantee by Notice*

A continuing guarantee may at anytime be revoked by the surety, as to future transactions, by notice to the creadtor.

8. *Section 131: Revocation of Continuing Guarantee By surety Death*

The death of the surety operates in the absence of any contract to the contrary, as a revocation of a continuing guarantee, so far as regards future transactions.

9. *Section 133; Discharge of surety by variance in terms of contract*

Any variance, made without the surety's consent, in the terms of the contract between the principal debtor and the creditor, discharges the surety as to transactions subsequent to the variance.

10. *Section 134: Discharge of surety by release or discharge of principal debtor*

The surety is discharged by any contract between the creditor and the principal debtor, by which the principal debtor is released, or by any act or omission of the creditor, the legal consequence of which is the discharge of the principal debtor.

11. *Section 135: Discharge of surety when creditor compounds with, gives time to, or agrees not to sue, principal debtor*

A contract between the creditor and the principal debtor, by which the creditor makes a composition with, or promises to give time to, or not to sue, the principal debtor, discharges the surety, unless the surety assents to such contract.

12. *Section 136: Surety not discharged when agreement made with third person to give time to principal debtor*

Where a contract to give time to the principal debotr is made by the creditor with a third person, and not with the principal debotr, the surety is not discharged.

13. ***Section 137: Creditor's forbearance to sue does not discharge surety***

Mere forbearance on the part of the creditor to sue the principal debtor or to enforce any other remaedy against him does not, in the absence of any provision in the guarantee to the contracy, discharge the surety.

14. ***Section 138: Release of one co-surety does nto discharge others***

Where there are co-sureties, a release by the creditor of one of them does not discharge the others, neither does it free the surety so released form his responsibility to the other sureties.

15. ***Section 139: Discharge of surety by creditor's act or omission imparing surety's eventual remedy***

If the creditor does any act which is inconsistent with the rights of the surety, or omits to do any act which his duty to the surety requires him to do, and the eventual remedy of the surety himself against the principal debtor is therby impaired, the surety is discharged.

16. ***Section 146: Co-sureties liable to contribute equally***

Where two or more persons are co-sueties for the same debt or duty, either jointly or sevarally, and whether unde the same or different constract, and whether with or without the knowledge of each other, the co-sureties, in the absence of any contract to the contrary, are liable, as between themselves, to pay each an equal share of the whole debt, or of that part of it which remains unpaid by the principal debor.

17. ***Section 147: Liability of co-sureties bound in different sums***

Co-sureties who are bound in different sums are liable to pay equally as far as the limits of their respective obligations permit.

TEST QUESTIONS

1. Define a contract of indemnity. What are the essentials and legal rules for a valid contract of indemnity ?
2. State the rights of the indemnity-holder when sued. Does the law confer any right on the indemnifier ?
3. Define a contract of guarantee. What are the essentials and legal rules for a valid contract of guarantee?
4. "There can be no valid contract of guarantee unless there is someone primarily liable". In the light of this statement explain the essentials of a contract of guarantee. What will be the position of surety if the principal debtor is a minor?.
5. What are the various kinds of a guarantee?. Define a continuing guarantee and state how it can be revoked?
6. State the nature and extent of surety's liability. How and in what circumstances the surety is discharged from his liability?
7. "The liability of surety is secondary; it is coextensive with that of the principal debtor".- Comment.
8. Explain the circumstances under which a surety may be discharged from the liability by conduct of the creditor.
9. What is the liability of a surety when the creditor omits to sue the principal debtor within the period of limitation?
10. State the liability of a surety when the original contract between the creditor and a principal debtor is (*a*) voidable (*b*) void.
11. What are the surety's rights against the principal debtor and the creditor ? Does he has any right against the co-sureties? If yes, enumerate.
12. What are the rights of surety on the performance of his obligations?
13. "Between co-surities, there is equality of burden and benefit"- explain.
14. Explain the difference between a contract of indemnity and contract of guarantee.

MULTIPLE CHOICE QUESTIONS

1. A contract in which one person promises to compensate the other for the loss suffered by him due to conduct of the promisor or of any other person, is known as a

   (*a*) contract of indemnity. (*b*) contract of guarantee.

(c) quasi contract. (d) none of these.

2. The party who gives the indemnity is known as
   (a) indemnity-holder. (b) indemnifier.
   (c) surety. (d) principal debtor.
3. Section 124 defines the contract of indemnity in a wider sense as it also covers all contracts of insurance, whereas the English Law defines this term in a narrower sense as it does not cover insurance contracts.
   (a) True (b) False
4. One of the following is not an essential of a valid contract of indemnity, which states that it must
   (a) have requisites of a valid contract. (b) be to save a party from some loss.
   (c) be in writing and signed (d) be lawful in nature.
5. On making the payment of loss suffered by the indemnity-holder, the indemnifier's rights are not provided in any section of the Contract Act, thus he gets
   (a) right of surety. (b) moral right
   (c) fundamental rights (d) none of these.
6. The liability of the indemnifier to compensate the indemnity-holder commences when
   (a) indemnity-holder has sufferred actual loss.
   (b) liability of indemnity-holder becomes clear and certain.
   (c) he is called upon to pay.
   (d) he fixes the date for the same.
7. A contract in which a person promises to discharge liability of another person in case of default by such person, is known as a
   (a) quasi-contract. (b) contract of indemnity.
   (c) contract of guarantee. (d) none of these.
8. In a contract of guarantee, a person who promises to discharge another's liability, is know as
   (a) principal debtor (b) creditor.
   (c) indemnified (d) surety;.
9. A guarantee given for minor's debt. Is
   (a) valid (b) void.
   (c) voidable (d) illegal.
10. The liability of a surety is
    (a) more than that of principal debtor, (b) less than that of principal debtor
    (c) same as that of principal debtor. (d) dependent on court's discretion
11. The liability of a surety arises, when the
    (a) principal debtor commits default in payment.
    (b) creditor fails to recovery anything from principal debtor
    (c) surety is reimbursed by principal debtor
    (d) court directs him to pay.
12. On default of the principal debtor , the creditor cannot proceed against the surety until he exhausts all remedies against the principal debtor.
    (a) True (b) False
13. A surety is discharged from liability by
    (a) revocation notice by surety (b) material alteration in terms.
    (c) discharge of principal by creditor (d) all of these.
14. Two parties namely ''indemnifier' and 'indemnity-holder' are involved in a contract of indemnity. And the parties in a contract of guarantee are
    (a) Three, creditor, principal debtor and surety.
    (b) Two, creditor and principal debtor, as surety is simply a guarantor not a party.

ANSWERS

1. (*a*)	2. (*b*)	3. (*b*)	4. (*c*)	5. (*a*)	6. (*b*)
7. (*c*)	8. (*d*)	9. (*a*)	10. (*c*)	11. (*a*)	12. (*b*)
13. (*d*)	14. (*a*)				

OBJECTIVE TYPE QUESTIONS WITH REASONING

State with reasons whether the following statements are correct or incorrect.

1. The indemnifier's liability to pay commences only after the indemnity-holder has suffered actual loss by paying off the claim.
2. In a contract of guarantee, a surety is a person on whose behalf the guarantee is given.
3. There is no consideration in case of the contract of guarantee.
4. *A* says to a shopkeeper, "let *B* have the goods, I will be your pay master, or I will see that you are paid". It is not a contract of guarantee.
5. In a contract of guarantee, the primary liability is of surety.
6. A contract of guarantee need not be in writing. It may be oral or in writing.
7. A continuing guarantee is revoked by the death of the surety.
8. On surety's death, a continuing guarantee is revoked only if the notice of death is given to the creditor.
9. As per Indian Law, a contract of guarantee must be in writing.
10. The liability of surety is primary and independent.
11. The liability of surety is co-extensive with that of the principal debtor.
12. A continuing guarantee can never be recovered.
13. Co-sureties who have given guarantee for different amounts share the liability proportionately.
14. The death of the surety operates as a revocation of a continuing guarantee and not of the specific guarantee.

ANSWERS

1. *Incorrect.* The accepted judicial view is that indemnifier's liability to pay commences as soon as the liability of the indemnify-holder becomes absolute *i.e.,* clear and certain.
2. *Incorrect.* Surety is a person who gives the guarantee. On whose behalf guarantee is given is known as principal debtor.
3. *Incorrect.* The contract of guarantee must be supported by consideration However, it is not necessary that there should be direct consideration between the surety and creditor [Section127].
4. *Correct.* In this case A undertakes the primary liability which is independent of *B*'s liability. Whereas in a contract of guarantee, surety's liability should arise only when the principal debtor makes default.
5. *Incorrect.* In a contract of guarantee, the primary liability is of the principal debtor not that of the surety.
6. *Correct.* It is the legal rule on the point [Section 126].
7. *Correct.* It is the legal rule on the point [Section 131].
8. *Incorrect.* In case of surety's death, the continuing guarantee is automatically revoked and no notice of surety's death is required.
9. *Incorrect.* A contract of guarantee may be either oral or in writing.
10. *Incorrect.* In a contract of guarantee, the liability of surety is secondary and dependent on principal debtor's default to make the payment.

11. *Correct.* The liability of surety and principal debtor is just the same [Section 128].
12. *Incorrect.* A continuing guarantee is revocable [Section 130,131].
13. *Incorrect.* In such a case, the sureties are liable to contribute equally subject to the maximum limit fixed by them [Section 147].
14. *Correct.* It is the rule of law on the point [Section 131]. In case of a specific guarantee, surety's legal representatives remain liable for the guaranteed amount.

PRACTICAL PROBLEMS

1. '*T* and *Co*', *a* transport company was in possession of certain goods which were claimed by two persons *A* and *B*. *A* demanded the goods form '*T* and *Co*'.. '*T* and *Co*' delivered the goods to *A* and asked for and indemnity bond. *A* did not give any indemnity bond. Subsequently, *B* turned out to be the true owner and recovered compensation from '*T* and *Co*'. '*T* and *Co.*' sued *A* for compensation. Will it succeed ? Give reasons.

   Hint : Yes, '*T* and *Co*' will succeed in its action Here, there was an implied promise by *A* to indemnify '*T* and *Co*'. In this case, by demanding indemnity bond, '*T* and *Co*' made it clear that it had no intention to deliver the goods except on indemnity. Legally, the contract of indemnity may be express or implies.

2. *A* was enjoying overdraft facilities from a Bank and *B* guaranteed the repayment of the overdraft amount. However, the overdraft facility given to *A* was contrary to law and therefore void. *A* defaulted in repayment of overdraft amount and the bank sued the surety (*B*) for the recovery of the amount. Will the bank succeed? Give reasons.

   Hint : No, the bank cannot succeed in its action. Here, the overdraft being void, the bank had no claim against customer (*A*) and thus surety cannot be held liable for void claim.

3. *A* appointed *B* as a collection agent to recover money from his creditors. On several occasions, *B* failed to account for collections made by him and *A* called upon him to furnish security for his collections. *B*'s friend *C* gave guarantee for *B*'s collections, but *A* did not inform him about *B*'s previous conduct. Will the surety (*C*) be liable for *B*'s default to account for collections? Give reasons.

   Hint : No, the surety cannot be held liable. Here, the guarantee is invalid as it is obtained by concealment of facts. [Section 143]

4. *A*, *B* and *C* jointly agreed to stand surety for *D* for a bank loan of Rs.80,000. *A* and *B* signed the guarantee papers, but before *C*'s signatures could be obtained, he died in an accident. How the liability of *A* and *B* is affected?

   Hints : The guarantee is invalid and *A* and *B* are not liable for any amount. If one of the co-sureties does not join, other sureties are also discharged from liability. [Section 144]

5. *A* stands surety for *B* for any amount which *C* may lend to *B* from time to time during the next three months subject to a maximum of Rs. 50,000. One month later, *A* revokes the guarantee when *C* had already lent Rs. 5,000 to *B*. Referring to the provisions of the Indian Compact Act, 1872, decide whether *A* is discharged from all the liabilities to *C* for any subsequent loan. What would be your, answer in case *B* makes a default in paying back to *C* the money already borrowed *i.e.* Rs. 5000?

   Hints : *A* is discharged from all liabilities to *C* for any subsequent loan after the revocation of this continuing guarantee. However, for default in repaying Rs.5000, *A* is not discharged as revocation is effective for future transactions only. [Section 129]

6. *A* gave a guarantee to a bank for an overdraft facility up to Rs. 1,00,000 sanctiones to *B*. The overdraft facility of Rs. 50,000 was enjoyed by *B* and the surety (*A*) died. Does the bank had any remedy?

   Hints : Yes, the bank can recover the amount form *A*'s legal heirs. On surety's death, continuing guarantee is revoked for future transaction only but for the liability incurred before death, surety's legal heir are liable.

7. *A* gave a guarantee to *B* for the loan of Rs. 50,000 given by *B* to *C*. Before the due date of repayment of loan, *C* was declared insolvent by a court and *B* claimed the amount from surety (*A*). Will he succeed ? Give reasons.

Hints : No, *B* will not succeed. Surety's liability arise on default by the principal debtor. In this case, *C* has become insolvent without making any default in repayment.

8. *A* contracted with *B* to contruct a house, for fixed price, for *B* within stipulated time. The necessary building material was to be supplied by *B*, and *C* gave a guarantee for *A*'s performance of the contact. *B* omitted to supply the necessary material for the construction of the house. To what extend *C* is liable?

Hints : *C* is discharged from liability. Here *B*'s conduct has discharged *A* from performing the contract and consequently surety is automatically discharged. [Section 134]

9. *A* guaranteed the honesty of an accountant *C* employed by *B* who under took to keep informed *A* about *C*'s misconduct or dishonesty during the course of employment. On several occasions, *C* was guilty of dishonesty, but *B* did not inform *A* rather continued to employed him. Subsequently *C* again committed act of dishonesty and misappropriated *B*'s funds and *B* required *A* to make good the loss. Is *A* liable under the guarantee? Give reasons.

Hints : No, *A* is not liable. Creditor's act or omission, which deprives the surety of his rights against the principal debtor, discharges the surety. Here, *B*'s conduct of not informing *A* about *C*'s earlier misconduct discharges *A* from liability. [Section 139]

10. *A* owed a sum of Rs. 2,00,000 to *B* which was guaranteed by *C*. The debt became due, but without *C*'s consent, *B* entered into an agreement with *A* not to file any suit against him (*A*) for the recovery of this amount and to enforce his right against surety only. Accordingly, *B* sued *C*. Will he succeed?

Hints : No, *B* will not succeed in his action. Here, *B*'s agreement not to sue *A* has discharged the surety. [Section 135]

15
CHAPTER

BAILMENT AND PLEDGE

15.1. INTRODUCTION

The term 'bailment' is derived from a French word 'bailler' which means to deliver a thing under a contract for return at a specified time or under specified conditions. And the term 'pledge' means the delivery of goods as security for a loan or fulfillment of an obligation. The contract of 'bailment' and 'pledge' are also special types of contract. The legal provisions relating to these contracts are contained in Section 148 to 181 of the Indian Contract Act. It may be noted that the Indian Contract Act does not deal with all types of bailments and pledges. It only deals with the general principles relating to the contract of bailment and pledge. There are some other separate Acts which deal with the special types of bailment, e.g., The Carriage Act, 1865, The Railways Act, 1889, The Carriage of Goods by Sea Act, 1925. However, in this chapter we shall discuss the general principles of the contracts of bailment and pledge as contained in the Indian Contract Act.

15.2. BAILMENT

A bailment is a contract, which results from the delivery of goods. It implies a sort of relationship in which the personal property of one person, temporarily, goes into the possession of another person for some specific purpose. It may be noted that the ownership of the articles or goods remains with one person, while the possession is with another person. Thus, the bailment involves a change of possession only (not ownership) from one person to another, e.g., delivering a car, cycle, radio, TV., etc., for repair, or delivering garments to a drycleaner, leaving scooter, car at the parking, etc. The term 'bailment' is defined in Section 148 of the Indian Contract Act, which reads as under:

> *"A bailment is the delivery of goods by one person to another for some purpose, upon a contract that they shall, when the purpose is accomplished, be returned or otherwise disposed of according to the directions of the person delivering them."*

Thus, the delivery of goods by one person to another for some specific purpose, is known as bailment. The delivery of goods may also be for some specified period. The goods are delivered on the condition that they shall be returned back on the fulfillments of the specific purpose. The following are the two parties to a contract of bailment:

1. ***Bailor*** : The person who delivers the goods is known as the bailor.
2. ***Bailee*** : The person to whom the goods are delivered for specific purpose is known as the baliee.

Example 15.1. A deposited his luggage in a cloak room at railway station. This is a contract of bailment between *A* and the Railways.

Example 15.2. A gave his T.V. and V.C.R. to *B*, a mechanic, for repair. This is a contract of bailment between *A* and *B*.

Similarly, when a person delivers a piece of cloth to a tailor to be stitched into a shirt, or delivers some gold to a goldsmith for the purpose of making ornaments there arises a contract of bailment.

15.3. ESSENTIAL FEATURES OF A VALID BAILMENT

1. ***The delivery of possession***
2. ***The delivery should be on the basis of some contract***
3. ***The delivery should be for some purpose***
4. ***The delivery should be upon a condition to return***

The legal definition of bailment, discussed in the last article, reveals the essential features of bailment which are as under:

1. *The delivery of possession:* It is an essential and important element of the bailment that the possession of the goods must be delivered by the bailor to the bailee. If the possessions is not delivered to the bailee, then there will not arise any contract of bailment. It may be noted that only the possession of the goods passes from one person to the other, and not the ownership of the goods. If the ownership of the goods is transferred to the other person, then it will be a sale and not bailment.

Example 15.3. *A*, an old customer, went into a restaurant for the purpose of drinking water. When he entered the room, *B*, a waiter, took *A*'s coat, without being asked. And hung it on the hook behind him. When *A* rose to leave the restaurant, the coat was missing. It was held that the possession of the coat was delivered to the waiter and the restaurant keeper was held liable as bailee. In this case, the waiter by taking the coat into his possession had relieved *A* of its care, and thus, assumed the responsibility of bailee. However, had *A* instructed *B* where and how the coat should be put, perhaps the result would have been otherwise.

[*Based on Ultzen v. Nicolls* (1894) QB 92]

Example 15.4. *A*, a lady handed over to *B*, a goldsmith, her old jewellery for the purpose of melting it and making new one. Every evening as soon as *B*'s work for the day was over, *A* used to receive the semi-finished jewellery from *B* and put it into a box in *B*'s room. And she (*A*) kept the keys of the box in her possession. One night the jwellery was lost from the box. It was held that as the possession was not delivered to the bailee (*B*), therefore there was no contract of bailment, and *B* was not liable as bailee. The court observed that the delivery of possession is necessary to constitute bailment. And the delivery of possession to the bailee (*B*) came to an end as soon as the bailor (*A*) was put in possession of the melted gold.

[*Kaliaperumal* v. *Visolakshmi*, AIR 1938 Madras 32]

The delivery of the possession to the bailee may be of two kinds, namely:

(*a*) actual delivery, (*b*) constructive delivery.

The 'actual delivery' means the delivery when the bailer hands over the physical possession of the goods to the bailee. And the 'constructive delivery' means the delivery when there is no change of physical possession of the goods to the bailee. But some act on the part of bailor has the effect of putting the goods into the possession of the bailee (Section 149). For example, the delivery of a railway receipt amount to the delivery of goods. Sometimes, a person already in possession of the goods of another, contracts to hold them as bailee. In such cases, he becomes the bailee and the owner becomes the bailor of such goods although the goods may not have been actually delivered by way of bailment (Section 148 (explanation)). This also amount to constructive delivery.

Example 15.5. *A* purchased an air conditioner from *B*'s shop. *A* left the air conditioner at *B*'s shop and requested him to send it to his (A's) residence. In this case, *B* has taken the constructive delivery of *A*'s air conditioner. And thus, *B* has become the bailee.

2. *The delivery should be on the basis of some contract* : It is another essential element of the bailment. According to this element, the delivery of the goods to the bailee should be made on the basis of some contract. This is so because the bailment is always created by a contract between the bailor and the bailee. However, the contract may be express (i.e., oral or in writing) or implied (*i.e.*, inferred from the circumstances).

Example 15.6. *A*'s ornaments were stolen from his house. After sometime, the ornaments were recovered by the police. Subsequently, the ornaments were stolen from the police custody also. *A* brought an action against State (police deptt.) for damages. It was held that there was an implied contract of a bailment between *A* and the police deptt., and the police deptt. was bound to take reasonable care of the ornaments. And thus, the State was held liable for damages.

[*Basawa K.D. Patil* v. *State of Mysore* (1977) 4 SCC 358]

It may be noted that sometimes the bailment may arise even without a contract, e.g., the finder of the goods is treated as a bailee. The courts have also taken the view that there can be a valid bailment even without a contract.

3. *The delivery should be for some purpose:* It is also an essential element of bailment that the goods should be delivered by the bailor to the bailee for some specific purpose. It is, however, not necessary that the purpose should be expressly stated. It may be implied from the circumstances of each particular case, e.g., depositing the goods in a railway cloak room implies the delivery of the goods for the purpose of safe custody.

Example 15.7. *A* delivered some gold to *B*, a goldsmith, for the purpose of making ornaments. There is a contract of bailment between *A* and *B*.

4. *The delivery should be upon a condition to return:* It is a very important element of the contract of bailment. The goods must be delivered to the bailee for some purpose and subject to the condition that when the purpose is achieved, the goods should be returned to the bailor or disposed of according to his directions. If the bailee is not bound to return the goods or to dispose them according to bailor's direction, there is no bailment at all. However, goods may be returned in its original form or in its altered form, e.g., delivery of a piece of cloth to a tailor to be stitched into a coat, or delivery of gold to a goldsmith for making of ornaments.

Example 15.8. *A* delivered his furniture to *B*, a carpenter, for repair and polish. It is a contract of bailment and *B* is bound to return the furniture after the repair and polish work is over.

This element of bailment distinguishes it from many other contracts of the same kind, such as, sale, barter or exchange, In these transactions, the person, to whom the goods have been delivered, is under no obligation to return the same. Moreover, there is a transfer not only of the possession but also of the ownership of the goods.

Note. The bailment can be made only of movable goods. There can be no bailment of immovable property (e.g., land building, etc.).

15.4. CLASSIFICATION OF BAILMENT

1. *Bailment on the basis of charges*
2. *Bailment on the basis of benefits*

The bailment may be broadly classified on the basis of charges (i.e., reward) and benefits as discussed below:

1. ***Bailment on the basis of charges:*** On the basis of charges, the bailment may be classified into the following two types:

(*a*) ***Gratuitous bailment:*** It is a bailment without any charges or reward. In other words, when the goods are delivered by the bailor to the bailee without any charges, it is called a gratuitous bailment.

Example 15.9. *A* lent his scooter to his friend *B*, for two days without any charges. This is a gratuitous bailment.

(*b*) ***Non-gratuitous bailment:*** It is a bailment for some charges or reward. In other words. when the goods are delivered by the bailor to the bailee for some charges it is called a non-gratuitous bailment.

Example 15.10. A hired a taxi from *B* for Rs. 100 per day. This is a non-gratuitous bailment.

2. ***Bailment on the basis of benefits :*** On the basis of benefits, the bailment may be classified into the following three types:

(*a*) ***Bailment for the exclusive benefit of bailor:*** It is a bailment in which the goods are delivered by the bailor to the bailee only for the exclusive benefits of bailor himself.

Example 15.11. *A* while going out of station, delivered some ornaments to *B*, his neighbour, for safe custody without any charges. This is the bailment for the exclusive benefit or the bailor.

(*b*) ***Bailment for the exclusive benefit of bailee:*** It is a bailment in which the goods are delivered by the bailor to the bailee only for the exclusive benefits of bailee.

Example 15.12. *A* lent his cycle to *B*, his friend, for temporary use without any charges. This is the bailment for the exclusive benefit of the bailee (*i.e., B*).

(*c*) ***Bailment for the mutual benefit of both bailor and bailee:*** It is a bailment in which the goods are delivered by the bailor to the baliee for the mutual benefits of both of them.

Example 15.13. *A* delivered certain goods to *B*, a transporter, for the purpose of sending them at (*A*'s) business place. *B* agreed to carry the goods at his (*A*'s) business place for Rs. 1,000 as a transportation charges. This is the bailment for the mutual benefit of both the bailor (*i.e., A*) and the bailee (*i.e., B*) as both of them are to benefited. The bailor's benefit is that the goods are conveyed at his business place. And the bailee's benefit is that he gets charges for the transportation of goods.

15.5. DUTIES OF A BAILOR

1. *Duty to disclose faults in the goods bailed*
2. *Duty to bear extraordinary expenses*
3. *Duty of indemnifying the bailee*
4. *Duty to receive back the goods*

The duties of a bailor, in the bailment, are contained in various provisions of the Indian Contract Act. These may be broadly grouped under the following heads:

1. ***Duty to disclose faults in the goods bailed :*** It is the first and the foremost duty

of the bailor. As per the Indian Contract Act, the duties of a bailor to disclose faults in the goods bailed are different for gratuitous and non-gratuitous bailors. These are discussed in the following subheads:

(*a*) ***Duty of a gratuitous bailor:*** A 'gratuitous bailor' is the bailor who lends his goods or articles to the bailee without any charges. His duty is to disclose the faults which are known to him at the time of bailment, and which are material for the use of the goods and may put the bailee to extraordinary risks. If he does not disclose such faults, he is liable to pay damages to the bailee.

[Section 50, first para]

Example 15.14. *A* lent his horse to his friend *B* without any charges. *A* knew that the horse was vicious (mischievious), but he did not disclose this fault to *B*. While *B* was enjoying a ride, the horse suddenly ran away. As a result of this, *B* was thrown and injured. In this case, *A* is liable to *B* for the damages sustained by *B*.

(*b*) ***Duty of non-gratuitous bailor :*** A 'non-gratuitous bailor' is the bailor who lends his goods or articles to the bailee for some charges, *i.e.*, he is the bailor for reward. His duty is greater than that of the gratuitous bailor. It is his duty to see that the goods, which he delivers, are reasonably safe for the purpose of bailment. In case of fault in the goods, he will be liable for damages whether or not he was aware of the existence of the faults. [Section 150, second para].

Example 15.15. *A* hired from *B* a carriage alongwith a pair of horses and a driver for a specific journey. During the journey, a bolt in the under-part of the carriage broke away. As a result of this, the carriage became upset and *A* was injured. It was held that *B* was liable to pay damages to *A* for the injury sustained by him. The court observed that it was the bailor's duty to supply a carriage fit for the purpose for which it was hired. [*Hyman & wife* v. *Nye&Sons*, (1881) 6 QBD 685]

Note: Sometimes, the goods bailed are of dangerous nature (*e.g.*, explosives). In such cases, it is the duty of the bailor to disclose the nature of the goods.

[Great Northern Ry.' case (1932) 2 KB 742]

2. ***Duty to bear extraordinary expenses*** : It is the duty of the bailor to bear the extraordinary expenses incurred by the bailee for the purpose of bailment. However, the ordinary and reasonable expenses are to be borne by the bailee.

Example 15.16. *A* hired a taxi from *B* for the purpose of going to Delhi from Chandigarh. During the journey, a major defect occurred in the engine. And *A* had to pay Rs. 2,000 as repair charges,. These are the extraordinary expenses and it is the bailor's duty to bear such expenses. However, the usual and ordinary expenses such as the expenses for petrol and minor repairs, etc., are to be borne by the bailee himself.

It is to be noted that if the bailment is gratuitous, the bailor shall also repay the necessary expenses incurred by the bailee for the purpose of bailment {Section 158].

Example 15.17. *A* delivered his horse to his friend *B* for safe custody without any charges. *B* incurred some expenses for the feeding and medicine, etc., of the horse. In this case, these expenses are to be borne by the bailor (*i.e., A*) as the bailee has not to receive any charges for the bailment.

3. ***Duty of indemnifying the bailee:*** Sometimes, the bailor has no title to the goods bailed, and the bailee suffers some loss due to the defective title of the bailor. In such cases, it is the duty of the bailor to indemnify (*i.e.*, compensate) the bailee for the loss suffered by him. The bailor's title to the goods may be defective at the time of bailment, or at the time of receiving back the goods from the bailee, or at the time of giving directions in respect of the goods bailed. If the bailee suffers any loss due to any of such defects, the bailor must compensate him [Section 164].

Example 15.18. *A* found a gold ring and delivered it to *B* for safe custody. Subsequently *C*, the true owner, came to know that his ring is in *B*'s custody. *C* filed a suit against *B* and recovered the ring and compensation from him. In this case, *A* is bound to make good the loss suffered by the bailee (*B*).

In case of premature termination of gratuitous bailment, the bailors is also liable to indemnify the bailee if the loss of bailee due to such termination exceeds the benefit derived out of such bailment. [Section 159].

4. *Duty to receive back the goods:* It is the duty of the bailor to receive back the goods when they are returned by the bailee on the expiry of the term of bailment or on the fulfillment of the purpose of the bailment. If the bailor refuses to receive back the goods, then he becomes liable to pay the compensation to the bailee for the necessary expenses of custody.

Example 15.19. *A* delivered his cycle to *B*, a cycle-stand contractor, for two days. However, *A* did not take back the cycle for one month. In this case, *B* can claim the necessary expenses incurred by him for the safe custody of the cycle.

15.6. DUTIES OF A BAILEE

1. ***Duty to take reasonable care of the goods bailed***
2. ***Duty not to make unauthorised use of the goods bailed***
3. ***Duty not to mix the goods bailed with his own goods***
4. ***Duty to return the goods***
5. ***Duty to return the increase in the goods bailed***
6. ***Duty not to set up on adverse title against the bailor***

The duties of a bailee, in bailment, are contained in various provisions of the Indian Contract Act. These may broadly be grouped under the following heads:

1. *Duty to take reasonable care of the goods bailed :* It is the first and foremost duty of the bailee. According to this duty, the bailee is required to take reasonable care of the goods bailed to him. The degree of care required by the bailee is similar to that of a man of ordinary prudence. Thus, the bailee must take as much care as an ordinary sensible man would take under the similar circumstances, in respect of his own goods of the same type (Section 151). If he has taken the required degree of care, then he is not liable for any loss or destruction of the goods bailed (Section 152). But if the bailee is negligent in taking the care of the goods bailed, then he is liable to pay damages for loss or destruction of the goods.

Example 15.20. *A* was a passenger in one of *B*'s luxury coaches. *A* put her suit-case in the boot of the coach from where it was lost. It was held that *B* was liable for damages. In this case, it was *B*'s duty to take reasonable care for the safety of customer's luggage.

[*Houghland* v. *R.R. Luxury Coaches* (1962) 1 QB 694 CA)

Example 15.21. *A* bailed his ornaments to *B*. *B* kept the ornaments in a locked safe, and kept the keys of the safe in a cash box in the same room which was locked from outside. The room was situated on the ground floor and was easily accessible to burglars. The ornaments were stolen from the safe by using the keys from the cash box. *B* was held liable as he failed to take the care which the nature of the articles required. [*Rampal* v. *Gauri Shankar*, AIR 1952 Nagpur 8]

However, the bailee is not liable for damages if the goods are damaged or destroyed due to the events beyond the control of the bailee, e.g., riots, acts of God (such as war, heavy floods, fire), etc. Thus, where the bailed goods are burnt by mobs during the communal riots, the bailee may not be held liable.

2. *Duty not to make unauthorised use of the goods bailed:* It is another important duty of the bailee. He must use the goods bailed to him strictly according to the conditions of the contract of bailment, and also for the purpose for which they have been bailed to him. If the bailee makes any unauthorised use of the goods bailed to him, the contract of bailment becomes voidable at the bailor's option, and he may terminate it at any time, and ask for the return of the goods (Section 153). Moreover, the bailee is also liable to the bailor for any loss or damages caused to the goods due to the unauthorized use of the goods (Section 154). It may be noted that the bailee will be liable for such loss even if the bailee was not negligent, and even if the loss or damage is caused due to the act of God or other unavoidable incidents. Thus, it is the duty of the bailee not to make any unauthorised use of the goods bailed to him.

Example. 15.22. *A* lent a horse to *B* for his own riding only. *B* allowed *C*, a member of his family, to ride the horse. *C* rode with care. But the horse accidentally fell down and was injured. In this case, *B* is liable to pay the compensation to *A* for the injury done to the horse.

Example 15.23. *A* lent his car to *B* for his private use only. *B* used the car as taxi. In this case, the bailment is voidable at the option of *A*, and he can terminate it at any time. Moreover, *B* is also liable to pay compensation to *A* if any damage is caused to the car while using it as taxi.

3. *Duty not to mix the goods bailed with his own goods* : It is the duty of the bailee not to mix the bailor's goods with his own goods. He should maintain the separate entity of the bailor's goods This duty of the bailee may be discussed under the following three heads:

(*a*) ***Mixing the goods with bailor's consent* :** Sometimes, the bailee mixes the bailor's goods with his own goods with the consent of the bailor. In such cases, there is no liability of the bailee. Both the bailor and the bailee have a proportionate interest in such a mixture (Section 155).

(*b*) ***Mixing the goods without bailor's consent and the goods are separable:*** Sometimes, the bailee mixes the bailor's goods with his own goods without the consent of the bailor. However, the goods can be separated from each other. In such cases, the bailor and the bailee remain the owner of their respective goods. But the bailee is bound to bear the expenses of separation or division. He is also liable to pay damages which arise due to such mixing of the goods (Section 156).

(*c*) ***Mixing the goods without bailor's consent and goods are not separable:*** Sometimes, the bailee mixes the bailor's goods with his own goods without the consent of the bailor. And the goods cannot be separated from each other. In such cases, the bailee is bound to compensate the bailor for the loss of the goods (Section 157).

Note: Sometimes, accidentally or inadvertently, the bailor's goods get mixed up with the similar goods of the bailee. In such cases, both have a proportionate interest in the mixture. However, the cost of separation is to be borne by the bailee. The same result will follow if the goods are mixed up by an act of an unauthorised third party or by the 'act of God'

4. *Duty to return the goods:* The goods are bailed to the bailee for some specified time or specific purpose. It is the duty of the bailee to return the goods to the bailor on the expiry of the specified time of bailment. If the goods are bailed for some specific purpose, then the bailee should return the goods when the purpose of bailment is achieved . Sometimes, the bailor gives directions to the bailee for the return or delivery of the goods. In such cases, the bailee should return or deliver the goods according to the directions of the bailor. It may be noted that the bailee should return or deliver the goods without waiting for demand from the bailor (Section 160). If he fails to do so, he will keep the goods at his own risk, and will be liable for the loss or destruction of the goods (Section 161). The bailee will be liable for the loss even if it arises without his negligence, or due to 'act of God' of 'inevitable incidents'.

Example. 15.24. *A* delivered some books to *B*, a book binder, for the purpose of binding. *B* promised to return the bound books within a week. After one week, *A* demanded the delivery of the books bound. But *B* failed to return the books. Subsequently, the books were burnt in an accidental fire. In this case, *B* is liable for the loss of books. [*Shaw & Co.* v. *Symmons & Sons*(1917) KB 799]

5. *Duty to return the increase in the goods bailed:* Sometimes, there may be some increase in the goods bailed to the bailee, or some profit may arise from such goods. In such cases, the bailee is bound to return to the bailor such increase or profit. This is, however, subject to any contract to the contrary (Section 163).

Example 15.25. *A* left a cow in the custody of *B* to be taken care of. The cow gave birth to a calf. In this case, *B* is bound to deliver the cow and the calf to *A*.

6. *Duty not to set up on adverse title against the bailor:* The term 'adverse title' may be defined as the 'denial of title'. It is the duty of the bailee not to set up an adverse title against the bailor. This means that the bailee cannot say to the bailor that at the time of bailment he had no authority to bail the goods.

15.7. RIGHTS OF A BAILOR

1. ***Right to terminate the bailment***
2. ***Right to demand back the goods lent gratuitously at any time***
3. ***Right to file a suit against any wrong-doer***
4. ***Right to file a suit for the enforcement of the duties imposed upon a bailee***

As a matter of fact, the duties of the bailee are the rights of the bailor. And the bailor can seek the enforcement of these duties. In addition to this, the bailor has also the following rights:

1. *Right to terminate the bailment :* The bailor has a right to terminate the bailment if the bailee does any inconsistent act with regard to the goods bailed, e.g., where the bailee uses the goods in a manner inconsistent with the conditions of bailment. As a matter of fact, the contract of bailment becomes voidable at the option of the bailor if the bailee acts contrary to the terms and conditions of bailment. And in such circumstances, the bailor is entitled to terminate the contract (Section 153).

Example 15.26. *A* lent his tractor to *B* for the purpose of ploughing his field only. But *B* used the tractor in a trolly for the transportation of goods. In this case, the contract of bailment is voidable at the option of *A*, and he can terminate it.

2. *Right to demand back the goods lent gratuitously at any time :* In case of gratuitous bailment, the bailor has a right to demand the return of goods at any time. He may demand back the goods even if the bailment was for specified time or purpose. Thus, if the goods are bailed without any reward, the bailor is entitled to demand back the goods even before the expiry of the fixed time or the achievement of the purpose (Section 159).

Example 15.27. *A*, while going to Bombay, delivered his valuables to *B* for safe custody for one month However, *A* returned from Bombay after 10 days. He may demand the return of his valuables even though the time of one month has not expired.

3. *Right to file a suit against any wrong-doer :* A wrong-doer is a third person who does some wrongful act. If any wrong-doer does some injury to the goods bailed or deprives the bailee of the use of the goods, then the bailor may file a suit against the wrong-doer, and recover compensation from him (Section 180). Whatever is obtained by way of relief or compensation in any such suit, shall be divided between the bailor and the bailee according to their respective rights (Section 181).

Example 15.28. *A* bailed 100 bags of cement with *B*, a godownkeeper, for safe custody. *C* a fraudulent man, prepared a fake delivery order for 10 bags of cement and claimed the delivery from *B*, the godownkeeper. *B* believing in good faith, that 10 bags have been sold by *A* to *C*, delivered the same to *C*. In this case, *A* may file a suit against *C* for the recovery of the cement bags from him.

4. *Right to file a suit for the enforcement of the duties imposed upon a bailee :* We have already discussed the duties of a bailee such as duty to return the goods and increase, not to mix up the goods, to take care of the goods, etc. It may be noted that if the bailee neglects in his duties, the bailor has a right to enforce these duties by filing a suit against the bailee.

15.8. RIGHTS OF A BAILEE

1. *Right to compensation*
2. *Right to return the goods to anyone of the joint bailors*
3. *Right to recover agreed charges*
4. *Right to file a suit to decide the title of goods bailed*
5. *Right to file a suit against the wrong-doer*
6. *Right of lien*

As a matter of fact the duties of a bailor are the rights of the bailee. And thus, the bailee can seek the enforcement of these duties of bailor. In addition to this, the bailee also has the following rights:

1. *Right to compensation* : Sometimes, the bailor has no title to the goods bailed to the bailee. And due to this defective title of the bailor, the bailee suffers some loss. In s cases, the bailee is entitled to receive compensation from the bailor for the loss suffered due to the defective title of the bailor. (Section 164).

Example 15.29. *A* stole a bag containing some ornaments and delivered it to *B* for safe custody. Subsequently, *C*, the true owner of the bag, filed a suit against *B* and recovered the bag and compensation from him. In this case, *B* may recover the compensation from *A* for the loss suffered by him due to *A*'s defective title.

2. *Right to return the goods to anyone of the joint bailors* : Sometimes, several joint owners bail their goods to one bailee. In such case, the bailee may return the goods to anyone of the joint bailors, unless there is an agreement to the contrary. And he is not required to obtain the consent of the other joint owners. However, if there is some agreement that the goods should be returned or disposed of by the consent of all, then the consent of all the joint owners is necessary (Section 165).

3. *Right to recover agreed charges* : The bailee has the right to recover from the bailor the charges agreed for the bailment. But where there is no such agreement for any charges, the bailee has the right to ask the bailor for the payment of necessary expenses incurred by him for the purpose of bailment.

4. *Right to file a suit to decide the title of goods bailed:* Sometimes, a person other than the bailor, claims the goods from the bailee. In such cases, the bailee may apply to the court to decide the title of the goods so that he may deliver the goods to the right owner.

5. *Right to file a suit against the wrong-doer:* Sometimes, a third person deprives the bailee of the use of the goods bailed or does some injury to the goods bailed. In such cases, the bailee has a right to file a suit against such third person (known as wrong-doer) and recover compensation from him. As a matter of fact, the bailee's rights and remedies against the wrong-doer are just the same as those of the owner (Section 180).

Example 15.30. *A* delivered certain goods to the Railways for the purpose of carrying the goods from bombay to Delhi. When the goods reached Delhi, *B*, a third person, prepared forged railway receipts (the documents on the basis of which the delivery can be taken from Railways) and induced the Railways to deliver the goods to him. In this case, the bailee (*i.e.*, Railways) can file a suit against *B* for the recover of goods from him.[*Based on Purshottamdas* v. *Union of India*, AIR 1967 All 549]

6. *Right of lien:* The 'right of lien' may be defined as a right of a person to retain the possession of any property of some other person, until the charges due to the person in possession are paid. If the lawful charges of the bailee, in respect of the goods bailed, are not paid, he has a right to retain the possession of the goods until his lawful charges are repaid. The right of lien may be of 'particular lien 'or' of general lien'. These will be discussed in detail in Art. 15.10 and 15.11 respectively.

15.9. TERMINATION OF BAILMENT

1. *Expiry of the specified period*
2. *Achievement of the object*
3. *Inconsistent use of goods*
4. *Death of the bailor or bailee*
5. *Termination by a bailor*

The bailment is terminated in the following circumstances:

1. ***Expiry of the specified period :*** Sometimes, the contract of bailment is made for a specified period. In such cases, the bailment automatically terminates on the expiry of the specified period.

2. ***Achievement of the object :*** Sometimes, the contract of bailment is made for a specific purpose. In such cases, the bailment also terminates as soon as purpose of bailment is achieved.

3. ***Inconsistent use of goods :*** Sometimes, the bailee does some act with regard to the goods, which is inconsistent with the terms and conditions of bailment. In such cases, the contract of bailment becomes voidable at the option of the bailor, and he can terminate it if he so likes.

4. ***Death of the bailor or bailee :*** A gratuitous bailment is terminated on the death of a bailor or bailee [Section 162].

5. ***Termination by a bailor :*** A gratuitous bailment may be terminated by the bailor at any time. It may be noted that a bailor may terminate the gratuitous bailment even if it was for a specified time or specific purpose [Section 159, already discussed in detail].

15.10. PARTICULAR LIEN

We have already discussed that the lien is the right of a person to retain the possession of any property of some other person, until the charges due to the person in possession are paid. But in case of particular lien, the person has a right to retain the possession of only those particular goods in respect of which the charges are due, Generally, the bailee is entitled to this lien only. He has a right to retain only those goods in respect of which he has exercised some labour or skill in respect of the goods bailed. He can retain such goods until his remuneration for the services is paid. [Section 170].

Example 15.31. *A* delivered a rough diamond to *B* to be cut and polished. Accordingly, *B* cut and polished the diamond. In this case, *B* is entitled to retain the diamond till he is paid for the services he has rendered.

Example 15.32. *A* delivered a water geyser to *B* for repairs. *B* repaired the geyser. In this case, *B* can retain the geyser until the charges for repair are paid.

The bailee can exercise the right of particular lien only if the following conditions are fulfilled:

(*a*) The bailee must have rendered some services involving the exercise of labour or skill in respect of the goods bailed. And the labour or skill exercised by the bailee must be such which improves the goods.

(*b*) The labour or skill must have been exercised in accordance with the purpose of bailment.

(*c*) The bailee can retain only such goods in respect of which he has exercised his labour or skill.

(*d*) The bailee must be in lawful possession of the goods. And the right of lien is lost as soon as the possession is lost.

(*e*) The right of lien can be exercised only if the complete services have been rendered in respect of the goods bailed. If only a part of the work is done, bailee cannot claim lien for part payment.

(*f*) The bailee cannot exercise right of lien if he has agreed to perform the services on credit.

(g) The right of lien may be excluded by an agreement to the contrary. In other words, the bailee can exercise the right of particular lien only if there is no agreement to the contrary.

Example 15.33. *A*, the owner of car, delivered his car to B & Co.' to maintain it for three years on fixed annual charges. As per the terms of contract. *A* was entitled to take the car out of the company's garage as and when he liked. The amount of annual charges fell in arrear, and B & Co, claimed lien on the car. The court observed that what the company did was not to improve the car, but only to maintain it in its former condition. [*Hotton* v. *Car Maintenance Co.* (1915) 1 Ch. 621]

Example 15.34. *A* delivered some stock of sugar to *B* for the purpose of storage. *A* failed to pay the storage charges and *B* claimed lien on the sugar stock. It was held that such custody does not involve the exercise of labour or skill, therefore the bailee was not entitled to lien.

[*Chand mal* v. *Ganda Singh* (1885) Punj Rec. No. 60 P.. 126]

Example 15.35. *A* delivered his dog to *B*, a trainer, for the purpose of training the dog. Accordingly, *B* trained the dog. *A* failed to pay the training charges to *B*. In this case, *B* may retain the dog till his charges are paid. The training of the animal involves the use of skill and it also results in the improvement of the animal. However, if the animals are delivered only for safe custody or for grazing, etc., then the right of lien cannot be exercised.

Example 15.36. *A* gave a piece of cloth to *B*, a tailor, to make it into car seat covers. *B* promised to deliver the covers as soon as stitched. He further agreed to give a three months credit to *A* for the stitching charges. In this case, *B* cannot exercise his right of lien as he has given a credit for the price.

15.11. GENERAL LIEN

1. *Bankers*
2. *Factors*
3. *Wharfingers*
4. *Attorneys of a High Court*
4. *Attorneys of a High Court*
5. *Policy brokers*

It is the right of a person to retain possession of goods as security for a general balance of account. We have noted that the right of particular lien entitles the bailee to retain only those particular goods in respect of which charges are due. But the general lien entitles the bailee to retain any goods bailed to him for any amount due to him in respect of those goods or any other goods.

Example 15.37. *A* gave two securities to *B*, a banker, and took a loan against one security only. *A* failed to repay the amount of loan. In this case, *B* may retain both the securities until his dues are paid.

The right of general lien is a privilege and is given only to certain kinds of bailees namely, (*a*) bankers, (*b*) factors, (*c*) wharfingers, (*d*) attorneys of a High Court, (*e*) policy brokers. And no other person has this right of general lien. Thus, all other bailees except those mentioned above, have a right of particular lien only. However, the right of general lien can be given to other bailees by an express agreement to that effect (Section 171).

The right of general lien of bankers, brokers, etc., is discussed in the following pages:

1. *Bankers* : A'banker'[1] may be defined as an organisation or a person who estab-

1. "A banker is one who, in the ordinary course of his business, honours dcheques drawn upon him by person from and for whom he receives money on current accounts". — Hart, in his 'Law of Banking'

lishes the money business for profits, *i.e.*, who accepts the deposits and gives loans and earns profits by such transactions. A banker can exercise the general lien on all goods and securities deposited with him in *his capacity as a banker*. He may retain such goods and securities for any money due to him as a banker.

Example 15.38. *A* borrowed Rs. 10,000 from a bank and deposited some jewellery with the banks as security for the loan. *A* repaid this loan along with the interest. But he was still indebted to the bank for some other loan taken earlier. The bank may retain the jewellery for the repayment of earlier loan.

But where goods and securities are deposited with the banker for a specific purpose, e.g., for safe custody or for some other specific purpose, the banker has no general lien on such goods and securities. This is so because the acceptance of goods and securities for a special purpose excludes the general lien.

[*Cuthbert* v. *Robart Lubbock* (1909) 2 Ch. 226; *PNB v. Satya Pal, AIR.* 1956 Punjab 250]

Example 15.39. *A* deposited certain valuables in a bank for safe custody. *A* also took a loan from the bank and gave some other ornaments as security for the loan. *A* made default in the repayment of the loan. In this case, the bank cannot exercise lien on the valuables deposited for safe custody. But the bank may retain the jewellery which was bailed as security.

The following points based on the judicial decisions are important in connection with banker's lien:

(*i*) A bank cannot exercise lien, on the goods belonging to the firm, against partners' individual accounts. [*Gurbax Rai* v. *PNB*, AIR 1984 SC 1012].

(*ii*) A lending branch of a bank can exercise lien for the loans given by it, but not for the loans given by another branch of the same bank.

[*Syndicate Bank* v. *Davendra Karkera* AIR 1994 Kant.1; *see also SBI* v. *J. A. Hussian*, AIR 1993 Bom 67].

Note: for the purpose of bailment, the term 'goods' includes money also. Therefore, lien may be exercised on the 'money' with the banker. However, for the purpose of contract of sale, the term 'goods' does not include the money. Thus, 'money '(i.e., currency) is not the subject-matter of sale.

2. *Factors:* *A* 'factor' may be defined as an agent entrusted with the possession of goods for the purpose of selling on behalf of his principal . A factor can exercise general lien on the goods of his principal for his balance of account against the principal. Thus, if any money is due to the factor by his principal, he can retain the principal's goods until his dues are paid. It may, however, be noted that the goods must have been given to the factor in the ordinary course of business and in his capacity as a 'factor' only.

Example 15.40. *A* delivered a motor car to *B* for the purpose of selling it. But the car could not be sold due to higher price quoted by *A*. And *A* demanded back the car from *B*. But *B* refused to return the car until his service charges are paid. It was held that *B* was entitled to retain the car until his charges are paid by *A*. [*E.H. Parkash* v. *King Emperor,* AIR 1926 oudh 202].

It may be noted that like a banker, a factor cannot exercise the right of general lien on the goods which are delivered to him for a specific purpose.

3. *Wharfingers :* A'wharfinger' may be defined as a person who owns or keeps a wharf. The 'wharf' means a place, adjoining to water, which is used for the purpose of loading and unloading goods from the steamers. It may be noted that the wharf is not used for storing the goods. The goods remain only in transit over it at the time of loading and unloading. A wharfinger can exercise general lien on the goods bailed to him until his wharfage charges (i.e., charges for the use of his wharf) are paid.

4. *Attorneys of a High Court:* An 'attorney' may be defined as a person who acts legally for another, *i.e.*, A solicitor. An attorney of High Court can exercise the general lien on all the papers and documents of his client until his professional fee and other costs incurred by him are paid. It may, however, he noted that the documents or papers should have been delivered to him in his professional capacity. A solicitor who is discharged by his client, has the right to hold the papers entrusted to him until the expenses incurred by him are paid. However, if he himself decides not to act for the client, then he cannot retain the papers. In such cases, he must hand over the papers to his client.

5. ***Policy brokers :*** A 'policy broker' may be defined as an insurance agent who is employed to effect a policy of marine insurance. He can exercise general lien for any balance on any insurance amount due to him from the person who employed him to effect the insurance policy.

15.12. COMPARISON BETWEEN PARTICULAR LIEN AND GENERAL LIEN

The following table gives the comparison between particular lien and general lien:

S. No.	Particular lien	General lien
1.	This right can be exercised only against those goods in respect of which labour or skill has been exercised by the bailee.	This right can be exercised against all goods which are in the possession of the bailee. The exercise of labour or skill by the bailee is not essential.
2.	This right can be exercised only for the payment of bailee's charges for the use of his labour or skill.	This right can be exercised for the payment of any amount due to the bailee.
3.	This right is available to all the bailees who exercise some labour or skill in respect of the goods bailed to them.	This right is available only to limited number of bailees, namely, bankers, factors, wharfingers, attorneys of High Court, and policy brokers.

15.13. TERMINATION OF LIEN

1. *Surrender of possession*
2. *Payment of the amount due*
3. *Abandonment*

In the following circumstances, the right of lien can be terminated:

1. ***Surrender of possession:*** The right of lien is a personal right, which continues so long as the bailee is in possession of the goods. It is lost as soon as the possession of the goods is surrendered by the bailee.

2. ***Payment of the amount due:*** The right of lien is terminated as soon as the amount due to the bailee is paid to him. The tender (offer) of the amount also terminates the lien.

3. ***Abandonment:*** The bailee may give up his right of lien by entering into an agreement. In such cases, the lien is also terminated.

15.14. FINDER OF GOODS

The term 'finder of goods' may be defined as a person who finds the goods belonging to some other person and takes them in his possession, It may be noted that a person who finds the goods belonging to the other, is not bound to take them into his custody. He may or may not pick up the goods. But once he picks up the goods found and takes them into his possession, he becomes the bailee of such goods and his duties are the same as those of a bailee [Section 71].

15.15. DUTIES OF A FINDER OF GOODS

We have discussed above that a finder of goods becomes the bailee of the goods. Therefore, his duties are the same as those of a bailee. In brief, following are the duties of a finder of goods:

1. The finder of goods must take reasonable care of the goods found.
2. The finder of goods must return the goods to the real owner, who has paid the expenses incurred by the finder.
3. The finder of good must not use the goods for his own purpose.
4. The finder of goods must not mix up the goods with his own goods.
5. The finder of goods must also return the increase in the goods.
6. The finder of goods must make efforts to find the true owner.

Note: The duties of a bailee have already been discussed in Art. 15.6.

15.16. RIGHT OF A FINDER OF GOODS

1. *Right of lien*
2. *Right to file a suit for reward*
3. *Right of sale of goods*

The rights of a finder of goods are specifically stated in Section 168 and 169 of the Indian Contract Act. The following are the rights of a finder of goods.

1. ***Right of lien :*** The finder of goods has a right of particular lien. He may incur certain expenses in preserving the goods and in finding out the true owner. He can retain the goods found until he receives the compensation for such expenses. It may however, be noted that the finder has no right to file a suit against the true owner for such compensation [Section 168 (first para)].

2. ***Right to file a suit for reward :*** Sometimes, the true owner offers a reward for the return of the lost goods. In such cases, the finder of goods has a right to file a suit against the true owner for the recovery of the amount of reward. He may also exercise particular lien until he receives the reward [Section 168 (Second para)].

3. ***Right of sale of goods :*** In certain circumstances, the finder may sell the goods found . When the goods found can be sold in the market and the true owner cannot be found after reasonable search, or if the true owner is found, he refuses to pay the lawful charges of the finder, then the finder may sell the goods in the following circumstances [Section 169]:

(*a*) When the thing is in danger of perishing or of losing the greater part of its value, *i.e.,* when the goods are of perishable nature.

(*b*) When the lawful charges of the finder, in respect of the thing found, amount to two-third of its value.

15.17. PLEDGE

A pledge is a special kind of bailment. In this case, the goods are delivered as a security for a loan or for the fulfillment of an obligation. The term 'pledge' is defined in Section 172 of the Indian Contract Act, which reads as under :

"The bailment of goods as security for payment of a debt or for performance of a promise, is called pledge, The bailor in this case is called the 'pawnor' The bailee is called the 'pawnee'."

Thus, the pledge is a kind of bailment in which the goods are delivered by one person to another as a security for (*a*) the payment of a debt, or (*b*) the fulfillment of a promise. The following are the two parties to a pledge:

1. ***Pawnor or pledger:*** The person who delivers the goods, is known as pawnor or pledger.

2. *Pawnee or Pledgee:* The person to whom the goods are delivered as security, is known as the pawnee or pledgee.

Example 15.41. *A* borrowed Rs. 4,500 from *B* and delivered his diamond ring as security for the repayment of the loan. In this case, the bailment of diamond ring is a pledge. *A* is the pawnor, and *B* the pawnee.

15.18. ESSENTIAL FEATURES OF A VALID PLEDGE

1. *Delivery of possession*
2. *Delivery should be upon a contract*
3. *Delivery should be for the purpose of security*
4. *Delivery should be upon a condition to return*

The legal definition of pledge, discussed in the last article, reveals the essential features of pledge which are as under:

1. *Delivery of possession :* It is an essential and important element of a valid pledge that the possession of the goods must be delivered by the pawnor to the pawnee. It may be noted that only the possession of the goods passes from one person to the other and not the ownership. The ownership remains with the pawnor. If the possession is not delivered then there cannot be a valid pledge.

Example 15.42. *A*, a producer of a film borrowed a sum of money from *B*, a financial distributor. *A* agreed to deliver, as a security, the final prints of the film when it is ready. It was held that there was no valid pledge. In this case, there was only an agreement to deliver the possession, and not the actual transfer of possession.

[*Revenue Authority* v. *Sudarsanam Pictures*, AIR 1968 Madras 319].

The delivery of possession to the pawnee may be of two kinds (*a*) actual delivery, (*b*) constructive delivery. Actual delivery means the delivery of physical possession and constructive delivery means when there is no change of physical possession. The delivery of keys of a go down where the goods are stored is the constructive delivery. Similarly, the delivery of documents of titles which enables the pawnee to obtain the possession, is the constructive delivery of goods.

Example 15.43: *A* consigned certain goods with the Railways from Bombay for transit to Okhla. *A* took a loan of Rs. 23,000 from a Bank and endorsed the railway receipts in favour of the Bank as a security for the loan. The goods were lost in transit. The bank, as pledgee of the goods, filed a suit against the Railways for the loss of the goods. The trial court rejected the action of the Bank. But the High Court allowed the part recovery. The matter came before the supreme Court to decide the question whether the delivery of railway receipts amount to delivery of good. It was held that the delivery of the railway receipts was the same thing as the delivery of goods. The pledge was, therefore, valid and the pledgee (the bank) was entitled to sue for the loss. The bank was allowed to recover the full value of the goods and not merely the amount of loan.

[*Morvi mercantile Bank* v. *Union of India*. AIR 1965 SC 1954]

2. *Delivery should be upon a contract:* It is another essential element of a valid pledge that the delivery of possession should be made in pursuance of a contract of pledge. Thus, the delivery of goods should be made with an intention to create pledge. It is, however, not necessary that the delivery of the goods and the advance of money (*i.e.*, loan) should be simultaneous. Delivery may be made before or in contemplation of advance. In such cases, a valid pledge results as soon as the advance is made. The delivery may also be made after getting the advance. In such cases, a valid pledge results as soon as the goods are delivered.

Example 15.44. On November 1, *A* delivered his ring to *B* for the purpose of valuation and to know the loan that can be obtained on the security of the ring. On November 5, *B* advanced Rs. 500 to *A* on the security of the ring. It was held that the pledge was valid. The court observed that the delivery made on Novembers 1, was a good delivery for the purpose of creating a valid pledge, and the pledge was created from the moment when the money was advanced by way of loan.

[*Blundell Leigh* v. *Atten-borough* (1921) 3 KB 233].

3. *Delivery should be for the purpose of security :* The goods should be delivered by one person to another by way of a security. The pawnor should deliver the goods to the Pawnee as a security for the payment of a loan or for the fulfillments of an obligation. It may be noted that this particular essential element distinguishes the pledge from other similar transactions. If the delivery of goods is for some other purpose then it may be a bailment and not a pledge.

4. *Delivery should be upon a condition to return :* It is also an important element of a valid pledge. The goods should be delivered to the pawnee as a security for some loan or for the fulfillment of the promise. When such loan is repaid or promise is fulfilled, the security should be returned to the pawner.

Note: As pledge is a special kind of bailment, all the essential elements of bailment must also be present in the pledge. In fact, the essentials discussed above are the same as already discussed in case of bailment. Like bailment, the pledge can be made only of movable goods. There can be no pledge of immovable goods.

15.19. DUTIES OF A PAWNOR

1. *Duty to repay the loan*
2. *Duty to pay expenses in case of default*

The duties of the pawnor are almost similar to those of a bailor which have already been discussed in Art. 15.5 However, the following are some **additional duties** of the pawnor:

1. *Duty to repay the loan :* It is the duty of the pawnor to repay the loan taken from the pawnee. If he fails to repay the loan, as per the terms of the contract, the pawnee may bring a legal action against him for the recovery of the loan.

2. *Duty to pay expenses in case of default :* Sometimes, the pawnor makes default in payment of debt at the stipulated time However, he subsequently repays the loan and takes back the goods. In such cases, he must pay the expenses incurred by the pawnee due to default in repaying the loan at stipulated time.

15.20. DUTIES OF A PAWNEE

1. *Duty not to use of the pledged goods*
2. *Duty to return the goods*

The duties of the pawnee are almost similar to those of a bailor, which have already been discussed in Art. 15.6 However, the following are some **additional duties** of the pawnee:

1. *Duty not to use of the pledged goods :* The pawnee should not use the goods pledged by the pawnor. The reason for the same is that the goods, are pledged as a security and not for the use of the pawnee. If the pawnee uses the goods, he may be held liable for damages for any loss caused to the goods by such use.

2. *Duty to return the goods:* It is the duty of the pawnee to return the goods to the pawnor when the amount of debt has been paid by the pawnor.

15.21. RIGHT OF A PAWNOR

1. *Right to redeem the goods pledged*
2. *Right to receive the increase*

Like duties, the rights of the pawnor are also almost similar to those of a bailor as discussed in Art, 15.7. However, the following are some rights of the pawnor which need the special mention:

1. *Right to redeem the goods pledged* : The term 'redeem' may be defined as 'to clear by payment'. The right to redeem, therefore, means the right to recover back the goods by making the payment of the debt and other charges, if any. The pawnor has an absolute right to redeem the goods pledged, upon the satisfaction of the debt. When the time is fixed for the payment of the debt, the pawnor may redeem the goods even after the expiry of the fixed time. However, he can do so only before the goods are actually sold by the pawnee for the realisation of his debts (Section 177). In such cases, the pawnor becomes liable to pay the expenses incurred by the pawnee due to default in payment at the fixed time.

2. *Right to receive the increase:* Sometimes, during the period of pledge, there is some increase in the pledged goods. In such cases, the pawnor has the right to take back the increase along with the goods. However, the pawnor can receive the goods as well as the increase only upon the full payment of the amount of debt.

Example 15.45. *A* took some loan from *B* and pledged certain shares of a company. During the period of pledge, the company issued some bonus shares. It was held that these bonus shares also belonged to the pawnor.

[*M.R. Dhawan* v. *Madan Mohan*, AIR 1969 Delhi 313].

15.22. RIGHTS OF PAWNEE

1. *Right to retain the pledged goods*
2. *Right to extra-ordinary expenses*
3. *Right in case of default of the pawnor*
4. *Right to file a suit against the pawnor*
5. *Right to sell the goods*

The rights of the pawnee are also similar to those of a bailee as discussed in Art. 15.8. However, some of his rights are specifically mentioned in the Indian Contract Act, which are discussed in the following pages:

1. *Right to retain the pledged goods:* It is the first and important right of the pawnee. He has a right to retain the pledged goods until his all dues are paid. . He may also retain the goods if the interest due on the debt is not paid. Moreover, he may also retain the goods for the payment of all necessary expenses incurred by him in respect of the possession or for the preservation of the pledged goods [Section 173].

2. *Right to extra-ordinary expenses:* Sometimes, the pawnee incurs some extra-ordinary expenses for the preservation of the pledged goods. In such cases, he is entitled to receive these expenses from the pawnor. And he can file a suit against the pawnor for the recovery of such expenses [Section 175]. It may be noted that he can only file a suit against the pwnor for the recovery of such expenses, but he has no right to retain the goods for the payment of such expenses.

Example 15.46. A obtained some loan from *B* and pledged his horse with him. During the period of pledge, the horse developed some disease, and *B* incurred some expenses for curing the horse. In this case, *B* can file a suit against *A* for the recovery of these extra ordinary expenses incurred on curing the horse. But he cannot retain the horse for these expenses.

3. *Right in case of default of the pawnor:* Sometimes, the pawnor makes default in repayment of the debt, or in the performance of the promise at a stipulated time. In such cases, the pawnee may file a suit against the pawnor for the repayment of the debt or for the performance of the promise: or he may sell the pledged goods after giving a reasonable notice of sale to the pawnor [Section 176].

4. *Right to file a suit against the pawnor* . In case of default made by the pawnor, the pawnee may file a suit against the pawnor for the recovery of the debt or for the performance of the promise. At the same time, he may retain the pledged goods as a security for the payment of the debt or for the performance of the promise. When the amount is recovered, the goods are to be returned to the pawnor.

5. *Right to sell the goods:* In case of default made by the pawnor, the pawnee may also sell the goods pledged with him. However, he can do so only after giving a reasonable notice of sale. It may be noted that the requirement of giving reasonable notice is statutory requirement (i.e., legally compulsory) and cannot be excluded by a contract to the contrary. And any sale made without such notice is void.

Example 15.47. A borrowed some money from a bank and pledged some goods as security. One of the terms of the agreement was that the bank may sell the goods without any notice to the pawnor in case he fails to repay all the amount due. *A* made a default in repayment of the loan. The bank sent a reminder to *A*, to repay the loan. But *A* asked for some more time for repayment. The bank then sold the securities without giving any notice of sale. It was held that the sale was bad in law. The court observed that the pawnee should give a reasonable notice, of intended sale of security, to the pawnor. And such notice should be clear and specific in language.

[*Prabhat Bank* v. *Babu Ram*, AIR 1966 All. 134].

Sometimes, the proceeds of sale are less than the amount due from the pawnor. In such cases, the pawnor is still liable to pay the balance to the pawnee. And the pawnee can recover such balance by filing a suit . However, if the proceeds are greater than the amount due, the pawnee shall pay the surplus to the pawnor [Section 176 (second para)].

Note : The pawnee may sell the goods before filing the suit in a court of Law. If the suit is filed for the recovery of the amount, then the goods can be sold through court order only.

15.23. PLEDGE BY NON-OWNERS

1. ***Pledge by a mercantile agent***
2. ***Pledge by a person in possession under a voidable contract***
3. ***Pledge by a person having a limited interest in the goods***
4. ***Pledge by a seller in possession after sale***
5. ***Pledge by a buyer in possession before sale***

Generally ,it is the owner of the goods who can make a valid pledge. And a pledge, made by any other person, may not be valid. However, section 178, 178A and 179 of the Indian Contract Act provide certain circumstances in which the pledge made by non-owner is also valid. These are discussed in detail in the following pages:

1. *Pledge by a mercantile agent* : The 'mercantile agent' is an agent who has the authority either to sell the goods, or to consign the goods for the purpose of sale, or to buy the goods or to raise money on the security of the good.[2] A pledge made by a mercantile agent is valid [Section 178]. However, the pledge is valid only if the following conditions are satisfied:

(*a*) The mercantile agent must be in possession of the goods or documents of title to the goods.

(*b*) The possession of goods musts be with the consent of the owner of the goods.

2. Section 2(9) of the Sale of Goods Act, 1930.

(c) The goods must have been given to the mercantile agent in his capacity as mercantile agent.

(d) the mercantile agent must make the pledge in the ordinary course of his business as such agent.

(e) The pawnee must act in good faith. And he should not have any notice that the pawnor has no authority to pledge.

Example 15.48. *A* delivered his furniture to *B*, an auctioneer, for sale only. *B* pledged the furniture with *C* who acted in good faith and without any notice that *B* had no right to pledge, as *A* had delivered the furniture to *B* for sale only. In this case, the pledge made by *B* is valid.

Example 15.49. A let out his furnished house to *B*, an auctioneer. *B* pledge the furniture with C who acted in goods faith. In this case, the pledge made by *B* is not valid as he was possessing the furniture as a tenant of the house, and not in his capacity as an auctioneer.

2. *Pledge by a person in possession under a voidable contract:* Sometimes, a person obtains the possession of the goods by coercion, undue influence, fraud or misrepresentation. In such cases, the contract is voidable at the option of the true owner. However, the person in possession of the goods, under such a contract, can make a valid pledge of the goods even if the possession so obtained is not by free consent [Section 178-A]. But a person possessing the goods under a voidable contract can make a valid pledge only if the allowing conditions are satisfied:

(a) The possession must have been obtained under a voidable contract and not under a void contract.

(b) The voidable contract must not have been rescinded (*i.e.*, put to end) at the time of pledge. The contract can be rescinded by giving the notice to rescind the same.

(c) The pawnee must act in a good faith, *i.e.*, honestly. And he should not have any notice of pawnor's defective title.

Example 15.50. *A*, a fraudulent person, pretending himself to be a man of credit, induced *B* to give him a valuable ring. And *A* gave a cheque for the price of the ring, which proved to be worthless. Before the fraud could be discovered, *A* pledged the goods with *C*, who took it innocently. It was held that the pledge was valid. In this case, *A* was holding the ring under a voidable contract as he bought it by practising fraud upon *B*. And, the ring was pledged with C before the contract was put to an end. [*Phillips* v. *Brooks Ltd.* (1919) 2 KB 243].

3. *Pledge by a person having a limited interest in the goods :* Sometimes, a person pledges some goods in which he has only a limited interest. In such cases, the pledge is valid only to the extent of such limited interest i.e., to the extent of pawnor's interest in the goods [Section 179]. Thus, a pledgee (*i.e.*, pawnee) can further pledge the goods. However, the pledge will be valid to the extent of pawnee's interest only.

Example 15.51. *A* obtained Rs. 500 from *B* and pledged his goods with *B* as a security. *B* further pledged the goods with *C* for Rs. 1000. In this case, the pledge by *B* is valid to the extent of his interest in the goods. *B*'s interest in the goods is up to Rs. 500 (the amount advanced by him to (*A*). And the original pawnor (*A*) is entitled to obtain the goods from *C* on paving the amount of Rs. 500 and interest. For the balance amount (*i.e.*, Rs. 500 and interest, etc.) *C* has the right to file a suit against *B*. [*See Thakurdas* v. *Mathura Pd.* AIR 1958 All 66]

4. *Pledge by a seller in possession after sale :* Sometimes, the seller continues to be in possession of the goods even after the completion of sale. In such cases, he can make a valid pledge of the goods. However, the pledge is valid if the person receiving the goods (i.e., pawnee) acts in a good faith and without any notice of the previous sale.

[*Section 30 (1), Sale of Goods Act*, 1930].

Example 15.52. *A* purchased certain goods from *B* and paid the price. However, *A* left the goods in *B*'s possession Subsequently. *B* pledged the goods with *C* who obtained the goods in good faith and without any notice of the original sale. In this case the pledge by *B* is valid.

5. ***Pledge by a buyer in possession before sale :*** Sometimes, the buyer obtains the possession of the goods with the consent of the seller even before the completion of the sale, *i.e.*, the seller still has some rights over the goods. In such cases, he can make a valid pledge of the goods. However, the pledge is valid if the person receiving the goods (i.e., pawnee) acts in a good faith and without any notice that the seller has yet some right in the goods.

[*Section 30(2). Sale of goods Act*, 1930]

Example 15.53. *A* agreed to buy a fan from *B*. Before the payment of the price, *A* obtained the possession of the fan to try it for a few days. Later on, *A* pledged the fan to *C* who obtained it in good faith and without any notice of *B*'s rights over the fan. In this case, the pledge by *A* is valid.

15.24. COMPARISON BETWEEN BAILMENT AND PLEDGE

The following table gives the comparison between the bailment and the pledge:

S.No.	*Bailment*	*Pledge*
1.	It is created by an agreement between the parties.	It is also created by an agreement between the parties.
2.	In this case, the possession of goods is transferred from the bailor to the bailee. The ownership remains with the bailor.	In this case also, only the possession of goods is transferred from the pawnor to the pawnee. The ownership remains with the pawnor.
3.	It can be only of movable goods.	It can be only of movable goods.
4.	The goods are returned on the fulfilment of the object.	The goods are also returned on the fulfilment of the object.
5.	The delivery of goods may be for any purpose, e.g., safe custody, repair, carriage, etc.	The delivery of goods is for *specific purpose only i.e.*, as security for the repayment of a debt or for the performance of a promise.
6.	In case of default by the bailor, the bailee may retain the goods for the payment of his charges or may file a suit against the bailor for his charges. He has no right to sell the goods.	In case of default by the pawnor, the pawnee may retain the goods. He may also sell the goods after giving a reasonable notice of sale to the pawnor.
7.	The bailee may use the goods bailed if the contract of bailment so provides.	The pawnee cannot use the goods pledged to him.

15.25. HYPOTHECATION

The term 'hypothecation' may be defined as the creation of security on the movable goods of the borrower for securing the repayment of loan. In this case, the possession of the goods remains with the borrower. If the borrower makes default in the repayment of the amount of loan, the creditor may file a suit against the debtor for the recovery of the loan, and for sale of hypothecated goods.

Example 15.54. *A*, an auto parts dealer, obtained some loan from a bank. For repayment of the loan, *A* gave security of the material lying in his godown. It is a hypothecation, as security was allowed to remain in possession of the borrower.

Note: The term 'hypothecation' has been legally defined in section 2 (1)(n) of the Securitisation and Reconstruction of Financial Assets and Enforcement of Security Interest Act, 2002. Refer to Art. 20.19 in chapter 20.

The following table gives the comparison between pledge and hypothecation:

S. No	Pledge	Hypothecation
1.	It is created by an agreement between the parties.	It is also created by an agreement between the parties.
2.	It is created for the purpose of securing the repayment of loan.	It is also created for the purpose of securing the repayment of loan.
3.	It can be only of movable goods.	It can also be only of movable goods.
4.	The possession of the goods is transferred from the pawnor to the pawnee	The possession of the goods remains with the borrower (i.e., pawnor). Only a charges is created upon the goods by an agreement
5.	In case of default, the pledgee can sell the goods after giving notice of sale.	In case of default, the creaditor can file a suit for recovery of his debt and for the sale of hypothecated goods.

19.26. MORTGAGE

The term 'mortgage' may be defined as the creation of security on the immovable property of the borrower for securing the payment of loan. The mortgage is defined in Section 58 (*a*) of the Transfer of Property Act, 1882, which provides that the transfer of interest in the immovable property for the purpose of securing the payment of loan is called a mortgage. The transfer is called the 'mortgage', and the transferee, a 'mortgagee', The amount of money, together with interest the payment of which is secured, is called the 'mortgage-money'

The difference between hypothecation and mortgage is that, in the former only movable goods are hypothecated as surety for the repayment of the loan. Whereas in the latter only immovable property in mortagaged as surity for the repayment of the loan.

LEGAL PROVISIONS (SECTIONS) DISCUSSED IN THE CHAPTER

Important legal provisions (sections) of the Indian Contract Act, 1872, discussed in this chapter are reproduced hereuder for ready reference.

1. ***Secton 148: 'Bailment', bailor and 'bailee' defined.***

   A 'bailment' is the delivery of goods by one person to another for some purpose, upon a contract that they shall, when the purpose is accomplished, be returned or otherwise disposed of according to the directions of the person delivering them. The person delivering the goods is called the 'bailor'. The person to whom they are delivered is called the 'baliee'.

   Explanation.—If a person is already in possession of the goods of other contracts to hold them as a bailee, he therby becomes the bailee, and the owner becomes the bailor of such goods, although they may not have been delivered by way of bailment.

2. ***Section 150: Bailor's duty to disclose faults in goods bailed***

   The bailor is bound to disclose to the bailee faults in the goods bailed, of which the bailor is aware, and which materially interfere with the use of them, or expose the bailee to extraordinary risks; and if he does not make such disclosure, he is responsible for damage arising to the bailee directly from such faults.

   If such goods are bailed for hire, the bailor is responsible for such damage, whether he was or was not aware of the existence of such faults in the goods bailed.

3. ***Section: 153: Termination of bailment by bailee's act inconsistent with conditions***

   A contract of bailment is voidable at the option of the bailor, if the bailee does any act with regard to the goods bailed, inconsistent with the conditions of the bailment.

4. ***Section 154: Liability of bailee making unauthorised use of goods bailed***

If the bailee makes any use of the goods bailed which is not according to the conditions of bailment, he is liable to make compensation to the bailor for any damage arising to the goods from or during such use of them.

5. ***Section 168: Right of finder of goods, may use for specific reward offered***

The finder of goods has no right to sue the owner for compensation for trouble and expense voluntarily incurred by him to preseve the goods and to find out the owner; but he may retian the goods against the owner until he receives such compensation; and where the owner has offred a specific reward for the return of goods lost, the finder may sue for such reward, and may retian the goods until he receives it.

6. ***Section 169: When finder of thing commonly on sale may sell it***

When a thing which is commonly the subject of sale is lost, if the owner cannot with reasonable diligence be found, or if he refuses upon demand, to pay the lawful charges of the finder, the finder may sell it—

(1) when the thing is in danger of perishing or of losing the greater part of its value, or

(2) when the lawful charges of the finder, in respect of the thing found, amount to two-third of its value.

7. ***Section 172: 'Pledge', 'Pawnor' and 'pawnee' defined***

The bailment of goods as security for payment of a debt or performacne of a promise is called 'pledge'. The bailor is in this case called the pawnor'. The bailee is called 'pawnee'.

8. ***Section 173: Pawnee's right of retainer***

The pawnee may retain the goods pledged, not only for payment of the debt or the performance of the promise, but for the interests of the debt, and all necessary expenses incurred by him in respect of the possession or for the preservation of the goods pledged.

9. ***Section 174: Pawnee not to retain for debt or promise other than that for which goods pledged. Presumption in case of subsequent advances***

The pawnee shall not, in the absence of a contract to that effect, retain the goods pledged for any debt or promise other than the debt or promise for which they are pledged; but such contract, in the absence of anything to the contrary, shall be presumed in regard to subsequent advances made by the pawnee.

10. ***Section 175: Pawnee's right as to extraordinary expenses incureed***

The pawnee is entitled to receive from the pawnor extraordinary expenses incurred by him for the preservation of the goods pledged.

11. ***Section 176: Pawnee's right where pawnor makes default***

If the pawnor makes default in payment of the debt, or performance; at the stipulated time or the promise, in respect of which the goods were pledged, the pawnee may bring a suit against the pawnor upon the debt or promise, and retain the goods pledged as a collateral security; or he may sell the thing pledged, on giving the pawnor reasonable notice of the sale.

If the proceeds of such sale are less than the amount due in respect of the debt or promise, the pawnor is still liable to pay the balance. If the proceeds of the sale are greater than the amount so due, the pawnee shall pay over the surplus to the pawnor.

TEST QUESTIONS

1. Define bailment. Explain the essentials of a valid bailment with suitable examples.
2. Define bailment. Explain the duties of a bailee.
3. "Delivery of possession of goods is essential for the creation of valid bailment"-discuss, and state how the bailment can result without the actual delivery of goods.
4. What is bailment? How does it differ from sale? Discuss the rights and duties of a bailee.
5. "The position of a finder of goods is exactly that of a bailee' -comment.
6. Define pledge. What rights does a pawnee enjoy under the Indian Contract Act?
7. State the comparison between bailment and pledge. What are the rights of a pawnee when pawnor make default?
8. What are the rights of a bailor and a bailee?
9. What are the rights of a pawnor and pawnee?
10. The general lien is available to certain specified categories of bailees. What are those, and discuss their right of general lien?

11. "Goods can be pledged by the owner only except in certain circumstances"- discuss and state the cases in which the goods can be pledged by non-owners.
12. Distinguish between the pledge of movable property and hypothacation of movable property. Between a pledge and hypothecation which would you prefer as sucrity and why?
13. Write notes on the following :
    (*a*) Legal provisions when the bailee mixes the goods bailed to him with his own goods.
    (*b*) Distinction between a general lien and a particular lien.
    (*c*) Rights and obligations of a finder of goods.
    (*d*) Bailor's liability in case of defect in goods.

MULTIPLE CHOICE QUESTIONS

1. The transfer of ownership of goods by one person to another , for some specific purpose is known as
   (*a*) Bailment (*b*) Pledge
   (c) Hypothecation (*d*) None of these.
2. The delivery of goods by one person to another for some specific purpose, is known as
   (*a*) Bailment (*b*) Pledge
   (*c*) Hypothecation (*d*) Mortgage.
3. The bailmet of goods can be made by its owner of
   (*a*) Movable goods only (*b*) immovable goods only
   (c) both of these (*d*) none of these.
4. *A* lent his car to his friend *B* , for two days without any charges. It is a
   (*a*) non-gratuitous bailment (*b*) gratuitous bailment
   (*c*) hypothecation (*d*) beneficial bailment.
5. In which of the following ways, the bailment is not terminated ?
   (*a*) Expiry of specified period (*b*) Fulfillment of object
   (*c*) Bailor's insolvency (*d*) Death of bailor or bailee.
6. Which of the following persons does not have a right of general lien ?
   (*a*) Bankers (*b*) Wharfingers
   (*c*) Finder of goods (*d*) Factors and policy brokers.
7. Which of the following statements is true ?
   (*a*) The lien can be exercised for the realisation of time-barred debt.
   (*b*) The lien also gives a right to sell the goods for the recovery of lawful charges.
   (*c*) The bank cannot exercise lien , on goods belonging to firm , against partner's individual account.
   (*d*) The bank cannot exercise lien for loans given by another branch of the same bank.
8. The delivery of goods by one person to another as security for the repayment of a debt, is known as
   (*a*) Bailment (*b*) Hypothecation
   (*c*) Pledge (*d*) Mortgage.
9. In case of default made by the pawnor in repaying the loan , the pawnee may sell the goods after giving a notice of such sale.
   (*a*) True , as it is pawnee's right (*b*) False, as pawnee can only exercise lien.
10. Where the movable goods on which security is created for the repayment of loan , remains with the borrower , the transaction is known as
    (*a*) Bailment (*b*) Pledge
    (*c*) Hypothecation (*d*) Mortgage.

11. Creation of security on the immovable property for securing the repayment of the loans is known as
   (*a*) Bailment (*b*) Pledge
   (c) Hypothecation (*d*) Mortgage.

ANSWERS

1. (*d*)	2. (*a*)	3. (*a*)	4. (*b*)	5. (*c*)	6. (*c*)
7. (*b*)	8. (*c*)	9. (a)	10. (*c*)	11. (*d*)	

OBJECTIVE TYPE QUESTIONS WITH REASONING

State with reasons whether the following statements are correct or incorrect.

1. A bailment is the delivery of goods by one person to another for some purpose.
2. In a bailment there is transfer of possessory rights forever.
3. In a bailment, it is only the possession that passes from bailor to bailee and not the ownership.
4. A servant having the custody of his master's goods and using the same, becomes a bailee.
5. The bailment can be made of both movable as well as immovable goods.
6. Placing of ornaments in a bank locker is contract of bailment
7. When a person leaves some goods with his friend for being looked after, there results a contract of bailment.
8. A contract of bailment in which the bailee is not bound to return the goods to the bailor is valid and known as permanent bailment.
9. Bailment of goods, without any charges to be paid to the bailee, is invalid.
10. If the bailee fails to return the goods on the completion of the specific purpose, then he will keep the goods at his own risk.
11. A bailee is not required to return the accretion to the goods to the bailor on the completion of the contract of bailment .
12. If the goods are bailed for hire, the bailor is responsible for damages, whether he was or was not aware of the faults in the goods bailed.
13. Bailee can retain the goods bailed until he has been paid lawful charges.

ANSWERS

1. ***Correct***. It is the legal definition of the term bailment [Section 148].
2. ***Incorrect***. In case of bailment the possession of the goods is temporarily transferred to another person for some specific purpose.
3. ***Correct***. It is the requirement of bailment. If the ownership is transferred, then it will be sale not bailment.
4. ***Incorrect***. The mere custody of goods without possessory right does not create bailment.
5. ***Incorrect***. The bailment can be made only of movable goods.
6. ***Incorrect***. In this case, the ornaments are not delivered to the bank for any specific purpose to be performed by the bank. Moreover, the possessory rights remain with the owner of ornaments and not with the banker.
7. ***Correct***. The goods are delivered for some specific purpose i.e., being taken care of.

8. *Incorrect*. In valid contract of bailment, the goods must be delivered subject to the condition that on the fulfilment of the purpose, the goods should be returned back to the bailor.
9. *Incorrect*. Bailment without charge or reward is valid and is known as 'gratuitous bailment'
10. *Correct*. It is his duty to return the goods in time. In such a case, the bailee will be liable for the loss or destruction of goods even if the loss is without his negligence or due to 'act of God' [Section 161].
11. *Incorrect*. The bailee is under a duty to return any such accretion (i.e., increase) to the bailor [Section 163].
12. *Correct*. It is the duty of a bailor to disclose faults in the goods bailed. The duty of non-gratuitous bailor is comparatively greater [Section 150, second para].
13. *Correct*. The bailee has a particular lien. However , he has the right to retain only those goods in respect of which he has exercised some labour and skill and in respect of which his charges are due [Section 170].

PRACTICAL PROBLEMS

1. *A*'s ornaments were stolen form his house which were subsequently recovered by the police and kept in its custody. Thereafter, the ornaments were stolen from the police custody also. *A* sued the police department for damages. Will he succeed ? Give reasons.
   Hint : Yes, *A* will succeed. In this case, there was an implied contract of bailment and the police dept. was bound to take reasonable care of the ornaments.
2. *A* delivered 100 bags of food grains to *B*, an owner of a godown, for the purpose of storage. Some part of the bags were damaged due to very heavy floods which were first of its kind in the history of place. *A* sued *B* for damages. Will he succeed ? Give reasons.
   Hint : No, *A* will not succeed. In this case, the event which caused the loss was beyond the control of the bailee (*B*) and for losses on account of such acts of God the bailee is not liable.
3. *A* lent his car to *B* for a week to be used by him for the marriage function of his friend. However, *B* kept the car for a month and while going to return the car it was damaged by an attack by the mob. *A* claimed damages from *B* ? Will he succeed ? Give reasons.
   Hint : Yes, *A* will succeed in his action. In this case, the bailee (*B*) was bound to return the car in time and by not doing so he had kept the same at his own risk. [Section 161]
4. *A* purchased an old refrigerator from *B*, who agreed to repair it for fixed charge. After the repair work was ower, the refrigerator was returned to *A*, although the part of purchase money and repair charges were still unpaid. After sometime, the referigerator again broke down and out of grace *B* promised to repair the same without any charges and took its machine and another part for further repair. After repairing the same, *B* claimed lien on these parts until the earlier charges are paid. Is he justified ? Give reasons.
   Hint : No, *B* is not justified in claiming lien for earlier charges. In this case, the delivery of possession after carrying out the repairs earlier, had put an end to the lien which *B* had for the repair charges.
5. *A* borrowed Rs.2,00,000 from a bank and deposited some jewellery with the bank as security for the loan. *A* repaid this loan of Rs.2,00,000 alonjgwith interest in time, but he was still indebted to the bank for some loan taken earlier. The bank refused to return the jewellery unitl the earlier loan is also repaid. Is the bank Justified ? Give reasons.
   Hint : Yes, the bank is justified in doing so . The banker has a general lies on the goods and securities deposited with him in his capacity as a banker.
6. *A* found a diamond ring in market and took it in his possession. He gave advertisement in newspaper for finding the true owner, and *B* came with the proof of ownership and asked for the return of the ring. *A* refused to return the same until his lawful charges for tracing the owner are paid. Is he justified ? Give reasons.

Hints : Yes, *A* is justified in retaing the ring. *A* finder of goods has the right of lien for such lawful charges.

7. *A* borrowed some money from a bank and as security pledged with the bank certain shares allotted to him by a public limited company. Subsequently, the company declared dividend and also issued certain bonus shares. On the repayment of the loan alongwith interest, the bank claimed that it is entitled to the dividends and bonus shares which were declared and issued while the bank was keeping the shares as security. Is the claim of bank justified ? Give reasons.

Hints : No, the claim of bank is not justified. In the absence of any contract to the contrary, the bailee is bound to deliver to the bailor any increase or profits which may have accrued form the goods bailed [Section 163]. The pledge, being a form of bailment, the bank is not justified in its claim as there was no contract authorising the bank to retain increase or profit.

8. *A*, a film producer, borrowed a sum of money from *B* money-lender and agreed to deliver as security, the final prints of the film when ready. *A* failed to repay the loan in time and also did not deliver the final film prints to *B*. *B* claimed that he was entitled to the security for the realisation of his loan. Is he justified in his claim ? Give reasons.

Hints : No, *B* is not justified in his claim. In this case, there was only an agreement to deliver the possession and not the actual transfer of possession. If the possession is not delivered, there cannot be valid pledge.

9. *A*, a frandulent person, pretending himself to be a man of credit, induced *B*, a diamond-dealer, to give him a diamond ring and gave cheque for the price. The cheque proved to be worthless, but before the fraud could be discovered, *A* pledged the ring with *C* who took it innocently. Is the pledge valid ? Give reasons.

Hint : Yes, the pledge is valid. In this case, *A* was holding the ring under a voidable contract. In such a situation, the pledge of articles, before the voidable contract is put to and end, is valid. [Section 178-*A*]

10. *A* purchased certain goods from *B* and paid the price. However *A* left the goods in *B*'s possession. Subsequently, *B* pledged the goods with *C* who took the goods in good faith fouth and without any notice of original sale. Is it a valid pledge? Give reasons

Hint : Yes, it is a valid pledge. [Section 30 (1), of the Sale of Goods Act, 1930]

16

CHAPTER

NATURE AND KINDS OF AGENCY

16.1. INTRODUCTION

In the last chapters, our discussion was confined to the point that a person himself enters into all types of valid contracts. But due to the vast expansion of the modern business, it is not possible for a person to carry on all the business transactions himself (*i.e.*, personally). A person usually employs another person to act on his behalf. The person who acts on behalf of some other persons is known as an agent. And the person on whose behalf the agent acts, is known as the principal. The contract which creates the relationship of principal and agent is known as 'agency'. The legal provisions relating to agency are contained in Sections 182 to 238 of the Indian Contract Act, which will be discussed in chapters 16 to 19.

16.2. DEFINITION OF AGENT AND PRINCIPAL

The terms 'agent' and 'principal' are defined in Section 182 of the Indian Contract Act, which are as under:

1. ***Agent:*** A person, employed to do any act for another, or to represent another in dealing with third persons, is called an agent. In simple words, an agent is a person who acts on bahalf of some other person.
2. ***Principal:*** A person for whom such act is done or who is so represented, is called principal. In simple words, the principal is a person on whose behalf an agent acts.

The relationship between an agent and the principal is called agency, which may be created by an express or implied agreement.

Example 16.1. *A* appointed *B* to purchase 100 bags of rice on his behalf. In this case, *A* is the principal, and *B*, the agent. And the relationship between *A* and B is known as agency.

It may be noted that the definition given in Section 182 is very wide. According to this definition, a servant, a casual employee, and even a boy engaged to polish the shoes, appears to be the agents. But legally speaking, they are not agents. The main emphasis of the legal definition is on the powers of the agent to represent his principal in dealings with the third person. The agent brings his principal into legal relationship with the third person. Thus, an agent is the connecting link between his principal and the third person. His function is to bring his principal into contractual relations with third persons.

16.3. ESSENTIALS AND LEGAL RULES FOR A VALID AGENCY

1. *There should be an agreement between the principal and the agent*
2. *The agent must act in the representative capacity*
3. *The principal must be competent to contract*
4. *The agent need not be competent to contract*
5. *The consideration is not necessary*

The legal definition of the term 'agency', discussed in the last article, reveals the essential element of agency, and a valid agency must satisfy these essential requirements. The essential features of agency relationship are discussed in points 1 to 3 below, and the rest are its legal rules.

1. *There should be an agreement between the principal and the agent:* It is an essential element of a valid agency. According to this element, the agency must be created by an agreement between the principal and the agent. Thus, there must be an agreement by which a person is appointed as an agent by the other. The agreement may be express (*i.e.*, by words of mouth or in writing) or implied (*i.e.*, it may arise by the conduct of the parties, by necessity or circumstances of the cases). The 'express' and 'implied' agencies will be discussed in detail in Arts. 16.6 and 16.7

2. *The agent must act in the representative capacity:* It is the most important essential element of valid agency. The agent must act in the representative capacity, *i.e.*, he must represent his principal and act on his behalf, Moreover, the agent must have the power to create legal relationship of his principal with the third person.

Thus, the true nature of the relationship should be seen. If the agent acts in representative capacity and had the power to bind his principal with the third persons, the relationship is that of 'agency'.

Example 16.2. *A* appointed *B* as his agent and authorised him to purchase certain goods for him. *B* purchased the goods from *C* on credit on behalf of his principal. In this case, the principal (*A*) is bound by the purchase made by *B* on his behalf. And thus, he is liable to pay the price to *C*.

3. *The principal must be competent to contract:* It is another important essential element of a valid agency. The principal must be competent to enter into a valid contract, *i.e.*, he must be of sound mind, and have attained the age of majority (*i.e.*, he should have completed 18 years of age). Thus, a minor, or a person of unsound mind (*i.e.*, insane person) cannot appoint an agent to act on his behalf [Section 183]. It may be noted that an agent acting on behalf of an incompetent principal will be personally liable, for his acts, to third persons with whom be contracts.

Example 16.3. *A*, a minor, appointed *B* as his agent and authorised him to purchase 50 'Aristocrat' brief case for him. Accordingly, *A* purchased 50 'Aristocrat' brief cases, on credit from C on behalf of his principal *A*. But *A* refused to pay the price of the brief cases. In this case, the agent (*B*) is personally liable to C to pay the price of the brief cases.

4. *The agent need not be competent to contract:* Generally, an agent incurs no personal liability while contracting on behalf of his principal. Therefore, it is not necessary that he should be competent to contract. Thus, any person may become an agent and he need not be competent to contract [Section 184]. Even a minor can be appointed as an agent, and the principal shall be bound by the acts of such an agent. It may, however, be noted that such an incompetent agent shall not be liable to the principal. Thus, the principal cannot recover any compensation from an incompetent agent for losses caused by misconduct or unauthorised acts of such agent. It is, therefore, in the interest of the principal to appoint a competent person as his agent.

5. *The consideration is not necessary:* An agency is valid even without consideration. Thus, no consideration is required for the creation of a valid agency relationship [section 185]. Generally, an agent is remunerated by way of commission for the services rendered by him. However, no consideration is necessary for the validity of the appointment of the agent.

16.4. PRINCIPLES OF AGENCY

The agency relationship is based upon the following two established principles:

1. Whatever a person can lawfully do himself, he may also do the same through an agent. This is, however, subject to certain exceptions, *e.g.*, contracts involving personal services or skills such as painting, singing, marriage, etc.
2. He who acts through another is considered to have acted personally, *i.e.*, the acts of the agent are considered the acts of his principal.

16.5. CREATION OF AGENCY

The creation an agency, *i.e.*, creation of relationship of principal and an agent, may take place in any of the following ways:

1. Agency by express agreement.
2. Agency by implied agreement.
3. Agency by operation of law.
4. Agency by ratification.

These are also called the different kinds of agency and are discussed in the following pages.

16.6. AGENCY BY EXPRESS AGREEMENT

An agency may be created by an express agreement. In this case, an agent is appointed by an agreement in writing or by words of mouth. It may, however, be noted that no particular form or set of words is required for the appointment of an agent.

Example 16.4. *A* entered into an agreement with *B* authorising him to sell his (*A*'s) house for a particular amount. This is an express agency as *B* is appointed as an agent by an agreement between *A* and *B*.

The usual form of a written agreement is the 'power of attorney', executed on a stamped paper in favour of the agent. The power of attorney is a document which gives an authority to an agent to act, on behalf of the person who gives the authority, in accordance with the terms and conditions mentioned in it.

16.7. AGENCY BY IMPLIED AGREEMENT

An agency may also be created by an implied agreement. In this case, a person becomes an agent of the other due to the conduct of the parties or the course of dealing between the parties or the situation of a particular case, *e.g.*, when one person places another in such a situation in which the other person is understood to represent or act on his behalf, he becomes an implied agent.

Example 16.5. *A* and *B* were brothers. *A* lived in Delhi and *B* in Chandigarh. *B* had a flat in Delhi. *A* with *B*'s knowledge let out his flat. *A* used to realies the monthly rent and remit the amount to *B* who was accepting the same. In this case, *A* is the implied agent of *B* though he has not been expressly appointed.

The agency by an implied agreement includes the following agencies also:

1. Agency by estoppel.
2. Agency by holding out.
3. Agency by necessity.
4. Husband and wife relations.

16.8 AGENCY BY ESTOPPEL

The term 'estoppel' may be defined as prevention of a claim or assertion by law. In other words, when someone makes another person to believe that a particular thing or fact is true, then later on he cannot be allowed to deny the truth of that thing or fact. Thus, when a person, by his conduct or statement, wilfully leads another person to believe that a certain person is his agent, then he is estopped (*i.e.*, prevented) from denying the truth of the agency.

Example 16.6. *A* said to *B* in the presence and within the hearing range of *C*, the owner of the goods, that he (*A*) was *C*'s agent and was authorised to sell the goods. *C* listened this statement of *A* and remained silent. Subsequently, *A* sold the goods to *B*. This sale is binding on *C*, and afterwards he cannot deny *A*'s authority to sell the goods. In this case, *C* by remaining silent, has accepted *A* as his agent.

16.9. AGENCY BY HOLDING OUT

The agency by holding out is a kind of agency by estoppel. However, it is something more than estoppel. In this case, there is some prior positive or affirmative conduct of the principal, which indicates that a certain person was already his agent.

Example 16.7. *A* allowed his servant *B*, to purchase some goods on credit from *C*. *B* usually purchased goods from *C* on credit, and *A* used to pay the price. On one occasion, *A* gave cash to *B* to purchase the goods. But *B* misappropriated the money and purchased the goods on credit in *A*'s name. In this case, *A* is bound by his prior conduct in holding out that *B* was his agent. And thus, *C* can recover the price from *A*. This is due to the reason that *A* did not inform *C* about the termination of *B*'s services. [*Trueman* v. *Loder*, (1840) 9 LJ QB 165]

16.10. AGENCY BY NECESSITY

An agency may also be created by the necessity of a particular case. Sometimes, extraordinary circumstances may arise in which a person may be compelled to act as an agent of some person without requiring the consent or authority of the same person. Such an agency is called an agency by necessity, *e.g.*, a person entrusted with the goods may have to incur extraordinary expenses to preserve the goods. He may be allowed to recover it from the true owner on the basis of the agency. However, to constitute a valid agency by necessity the following conditions must be satisfied:

1. There must be real emergency and necessity to act on behalf of the principal.
2. The agent must not be in a position to communicate with the principal or to obtain his instructions.
3. The agent must act honestly and in the interest of the principal.
4. The agent must adopt reasonable and parcticable course under the circumstances of the case.

At one time, it was supposed that an agency by necessity is confined only to cases where there is existing relationship of principal and agent, and in certain emergencies, the agent exercises the unauthorised acts in a *good faith*. However, later on, the principle of agency by necessity is also extended to other exceptional cases, *i.e.*, in which there is no existing relationship of agency.

The circumstances in which an agency by necessity is created becomes clear from the following examples:

Example 16.8. *A* consigned certain quantity of butter with Railways. Due to strike, the butter was delayed in transit. The Railways sold the butter as it was of perishable nature. It was held that the sale was binding on the owner (*A*). In this case, the Railways became an agent by necessity.

[*Sims & Co.* v. *Midland Rly.* Co. (1913) 1KB 103].

Example 16.9. *A* consigned a horse with the Railway Company. When the horse reached the destination, nobody came to take its delivery. The Railway Company had no arrangement of its own to keep the animals. Therefore, it delivered the horse to a stable-keeper for its maintenance and safe custody. It was held that the Railway Company was an agent by necessity. And it was allowed to recover charges of the stable keeper.

[*Great Northern Rly Co.* v. *Swafield* (1874) LR Ex. 132]

Example 16.10. *A* consigned some goods with *B*, a master of a ship On its way to destination, the master of the ship (*B*) found that the goods were persishing rapidly. He took the ship to the nearest port and sold the goods for the best available price. It was held that *B* was an agent by necessity and the owner of the goods (*A*) was bound by the sale.

[*Couturier* v. *Hastie* (1856) 5 HLC 673]

Example 16.11. *A* stored some furniture in *B*'s house, free of charge. Thererafter, they lost contact with each other. After three years, *B* needed the space occupied by the furniture. He obtained *A*'s address from his bank and wrote two letters to him. But he received no reply. *B* then sold the furniture. Subsequently, *A* turned out and claimed the furniture from *B*. It was held that there was no agency by necessity as there was nothing in the nature of an emergency compelling *B* to sell the furniture. [*Sachs* v. *Milkos* (1948)2 KB 23]

16.11. HUSBAND AND WIFE RELATIONS

A wife, who lives with her husband, has an implied authority of her husband to buy articles of household necessity. This means that the wife is considered an implied agent of the husband for the purpose of buying household necessaries on credit, and the husband becomes bound to pay for the same. The agency relationship between husband and wife will be discussed in detail in Art.17.4 in the next chapter.

16.12. AGENCY BY OPERATION OF LAW

An agency may also come into existence by operation of law. In certain circumstances, the law treats one person as an agent of another. According to Partnership Act, every partner of the partnership firm is an agent of the firm for the purpose of the business of the firm. Moreover, he is also an agent of the other partners of the firm. And thus, the firm and the other partners are bound by the acts of a partner, which are don by him in the course of the business of the firm.

[*Section 18 and 19 of the Indian Partnership* Act,1932]

Example 16.12. *A*, *B* and *C* were the partners of a firm which was carrying on the business of shoe making. *A* bought some raw material from *D* on credit, for the purpose of the firm. And the raw material was bought in the name of he firm. In this case, the firm is bound by the purchases made by *A*, and is liable to pay the price to *D*.

16.13. AGENCY BY RATIFICATION

The term 'ratification' may be defined as the confirmation of the acts already done. Sometimes, a person does some acts on behalf of another person without his knowledge or authority. And such other person subsequently ratifies (*i.e.*, accepts or confirms) the acts done on his behalf. In such cases, a valid agency is created by the ratification [Section 196]. It is also known as *'ex-post facto agency'*, *i.e.*, agency arising after the event. Thus, when a person accepts or confirms the unauthorised acts done on his behalf, an agency by ratification is created. On ratification, the principal is bound by the acts already done on his behalf. The ratification may be express, or implied from the conduct of the person on whose behalf the acts are done. [Section197]

Example. 16.13. *A* insured *B*'s goods without his authority. Subsequently, *B* confirmed *A*'s act of insuring the goods, and accepted the insurance policy. In this case, the insurance policy is as valid as if *A* had been authorised by *B* to insure the goods.

[*Willims* v. *North China Ins. Co.* (1876) 1 CPD 757].

Example 16.14. *A* had some money which actually belonged to *B*. *A*, without *B*'s authority, gave this money to *C* as loan. Afterwards, *B* accepted interest on this money from *C*. In this case, *B*'s conduct (*i.e.*, acceptance of interest) implies a ratification of the loan given by *A*.

16.14. CONDITIONS FOR A VALID RATIFICATION

1. *The agent must act on behalf of the principal*
2. *The principal must be competent to contract and in existence at the time of contract by the agent*
3. *The principal must have the full knowledge of all material facts*
4. *The ratification must be of the whole transaction*
5. *The ratification should not cause any damage to third person*
6. *The ratification must be made within a reasonable time*
7. *The acts to be ratified should be valid and lawful*
8. *The act to be ratified must be existing at the time of ratification*

An agency by ratification is valid only if the following conditions are satisfied:

1. *The agent must act on behalf of the principal:* It is the essential condition of a valid ratification. According to this condition, one person (*i.e.*, agent) must have done some act on behalf of the ratifier (*i.e.*, principal), Moreover, the agent must act in such a way that his conduct shows that he is doing the act on behalf of his principal. However, if a person acts in his own name, which does not indicate any agency relationship, his act cannot be ratified.

Example 16.15. *A* authorised his agent *B* to buy 'Karachi Wheat' at a specified rate. As the wheat was not available at those rates, *B* bought the wheat from *C* at a higher rate. However, *B* bought the wheat in his own name and made no mention of his principal. *A* approved the purchase made by *B*. But when the price of wheat fell down, *A* refused to take delivery of the wheat. And *C* filed a suit against *A* for the breach of contract. It was held that *A* was not liable. The court observed that the agent (*B*) contracted in his own name, therefore his act was not open to anybody's ratification. And thus, the ratification made by *A* (the principal) was ineffective.

[*Keighley Maxted & Co. v. Durant* (1901) AC 240]

2. *The principal must be competent to contract and in existence at the time of contract by the agent:* It is another essential condition of a valid ratification. As a matter of fact, the ratification relates back to the date when the contract was made by the agent, *i.e.*, the ratification is effective from the back date when the act was done by the agent. It is, therefore, necessary that the principal who wants to ratify the act must be in existence at the time of contract made by the agent. Moreover, he must also be competent to contract at that time. Thus, an act done on behalf of a minor without his authority, cannot be ratified by him on his attaining majority. Similarly, a company, cannot ratify a contract made in its name before the company came into existence.

Example 16.16. *A*, a promoter, of an intended hotel company entered into a contract with *B* on behalf of the company. When the company was duly formed, it ratified the contract.After sometime, the company went into liquidation. And *B* filed a suit against *A*. *A* contended that he was not liable as the liability has passed to the company by ratification. It was held that the ratification was not effective, and *A* was personally liable. The court observed that the ratification can only be made by a person ascertained at the time of the act done and by a person in existence at that time.

[*Kelner* v. *Baxter* (1866) LR 2 CP 174].

3. *The principal must have the full knowledge of all material facts:* The ratification must be made with the full knowledge of all the material facts. If the ratifier does not have the full knowledge of the facts of the case, the ratification shall be ineffective and will not bind the parties to the contract.

Example 16.17. *A* authorised his agent *B* to purchase grains for him. *B* supplied his own grains to *A* at a higher price. *A* ratified the purchase without knowing that the grains belonged to *B* himself and he charged price higher than that in the market. It was held that the ratification made by *A* was not valid as it was made without the full knowledge of the facts of the case.

[*Damodharan* v. *Sheoram* (1907) 20 All 730]

4. *The ratification must be of the whole transaction:* The ratification must be made for the whole of the transaction done by the agent. A person cannot ratify a part of the transaction which is beneficial to him and reject the rest. Either the whole transaction should be ratified or rejected. It is to be noted that when a person ratifies a part of the transaction it is treated as the ratification of the whole transaction. [Section 199]

Example. 16.18. *A* without authority from *B*, purchased 100 ceiling fans for him. After this purchase, *B* discovered that 90 fans were good while 10 were defective. *B* accepted 90 good fans and rejected 10 defective ones. In this case, the acceptance of part of the fans amounts to ratification of the whole transaction. And thus, *B* is bound to take delivery of all the fans purchased on his behalf, including defective ones.

5. *The ratification should not cause any damage to third person:* A ratification is not valid if it causes some damage to a third person or terminates any right or interest of a third person. In other words, the acts which would become injurious to others by ratification, cannot be ratified. [Section 200]

Example 16.19. *A* was holding lease from *B*. The lease was terminable on three month's notice. *C*, an unauthorised person, gave notice of termination of lease to *A*. In this case, the notice cannot be ratified by *B* so as to be binding on *A*.

6. *The ratification must be made within a reasonable time:* The ratification becomes valid only if it is made within a reasonable time after the act to be ratified is done. And if any time is fixed for the performance of a contract, the ratification must be made before the expiry of that time.

Example 16.20. *A* without authority from *B*, insured his goods against fire. After the policy was taken, the goods were destroyed by fire. Subsequent to the fire, *B* ratified *A*'s act of insuring the goods, and accepted the insurance policy. In this case, the ratification made by *B* is not valid as *A*'s act should have been ratified before the loss of goods.

[Based on *Grover & Grover Ltd.* v. *Mathews* (1920) 2 KB 401]

However, in case of marine insurance (*i.e.*, insurance against perils of the seas), the insurance policy can be ratified even after the loss of the goods insured.

[*Williams* v. *North China Ins. Co.* (1876) 1 C.P.D. 757]

7. *The acts to be ratified should be valid and lawful:* The ratification can be made only of valid and lawful acts. Thus, an act which is void from the very beginning or which constitutes a criminal offence, cannot be ratified. However, a voidable contract may be ratified because it is not void from the very beginning.

Example 16.21. *A* forged *B*'s signature and withdrew some money from *B*'s account. Subsequently, *B* ratified *A*'s act of withdrawing the money on his behalf. The ratification is not valid as the forgery of signatures is an offence.

8. *The act to be ratified must be existing at the time of ratification:* A valid ratification can be made only of the acts which are existing at the time of ratification. If the act to be ratified (*i.e*, the transaction) is not existing at the time of ratification, it is invalid and without any effect, *e.g.*, a contract cannot be ratified after it is cancelled.

16.15. EFFECTS OF VALID RATIFICATION

A valid ratification establishes the relationship of principal and agnet between the ratifier. *i.e.,* the person ratifying the act and the person actually doing the act. However, the agency is created only for the purpose of the act ratified by the principal. And in so far as the ratified act is concerned, it also creates a binding contract between the principal and third party. It may be noted that a valid ratification relates back to the date on which the agent first contracted on behalf of the principal. In other words, a contract between the principal and the third party comes into existence not from the date of ratification, but from the date when the agent first contracted.Thus, ratification has the retrospective effect and is equivalent to previous authority.

Example 16.22. *A* made a certain offer to *B*, the managing director of a company. *B* accepted the offer on behalf of the company. However, *B* had no authority to do so.Subsequently, *A* withdrew the offer. But the company ratified *B'* s acceptance. It was held that *A* was bound by the contract. The court observed that company's 'ratification related back to the date on which the managing director first accepted the offer. Therefore, the withdrawal of offer by *A* was not effective. [*Bolton Partners* v. *Lambert* (1889) 41 Ch. D 295]

16.16. KINDS OF AGENTS

Though the agents are of several kinds, yet the important ones, from the subject point of view, may be discussed under the following heads:

1. Mercantile or commercial agents.
2. Non -mercantile or non-commercial agents.

16.17. MERCANTILE OR COMMERCIAL AGENTS

1. *Factor*
2. *Broker*
3. *Auctioneer*
4. *Commission agent*
5. *Del credere agent*
6. *Banker*

The term 'mercantile agent' may be defined as an agent who has the authority either to sell the goods, or to consign the goods for the purpose of sale, or to buy the goods or to raise the money on the security of the goods on behalf of his principal [Section 2 (9) of the Sale of Goods Act]. Thus, a mercantile agent is an agent who deals in the buying and selling of the goods. Following are some of the important mercantile agents:

1. *Factor:* A factor is a mercantile agent to whom the possession of the goods is given for the purpose of selling the same.A factor, usually, sells the goods in his own name. He has wide discretion regarding the selling of goods in his possession. He may sell the goods on credit,receive` payments of price and give valid receipts of discharges. A factor has general lien on the goods of his principal for all charges and expenses due from the principal.

2. *Broker:* A broker is a mercantile agent who is appointed to negotiate and make contracts for the sale or purchase of goods on behalf of his principal. He is not given the possession of the goods. His main function is to bring about a contractual relationship between his principal and the parties who wish to purchase or sell the goods. It may be noted that a broker makes contracts in the name of his principal and not in his own name.

3. *Auctioneer:* An auctioneer is a mercantile agent who is appointed to sell the goods at a public auction, *i.e.,* to sell the goods to highest bidder in public competition. He has the authority to receive the auctioned price and can sue for the same in his own name. He resembles with a factor in all respects. However, an auctioneer has only a particular lien over the goods of his principal, and not a general lien.

4. *Commission agent:* A commission agent is a mercantile agent who buys and sells the goods on behalf of his principal and receives commission for his charges. His only interest in the transaction is the commission which he received from his principal. The duties and responsibilities of a commission agent depends upon his agreement with his principal.

5. *Del credere agent:* A 'del credere agent' is a mercantile agent who, in addition to his work of bringing a contract between his principal and third parties, also undertakes to be liable to the principal for the default of the third party to perform the contract. In other words, he also guarantees to his principal the performance of the contract by the third party. He gets extra commission for this extra risk taken by him. Such commission is called the '*del credere commission*'. Thus, the del credere agent occupies the position of both an agent and a guarantor. However, his liability is secondary which arises only on the default of the third party.

6. *Banker:* Generally, the relationship between a banker and customer is that of a creditor and debtor. However, when the banker buys or sells securities, collects cheques, dividends, etc., on behalf of his customer, he also acts as an agent.

16.18. NON-MERCANTILE OR NON COMMERCIAL AGENTS

1. *Insurance agents*
2. *Counsels or advocates*

The term 'non-mercantile' or 'non-commercial' agent may be defined as an agent who does not usually deal in the buying or selling of the goods. As a matter of fact, he is the agent appointed by his principal to do some acts which are not done by mercantile agents. The following are some of the important non-mercantile agents:

1. *Insurance agents:* An insurance agent is an agent who is appointed to effect insurance policies on behalf of his principal. He receives commission for his services.

2. *Counsels or advocates*: A counsel or an advocate is a person who is engaged to conduct the legal proceedings on behalf of his principal (*i.e.,* client). He receives fees for his services.

16.19. CLASSIFICATION OF AGENTS

1. *Special agents*
2. *General agents*
3. *Universal agents*

The agents may be classified as under, on the basis of extent of the authority given by their respective principals:

1. *Special agents:* A special agent is an agent who is appointed to perform a special act. In other words, he is the agent who represents his principal in some particular transaction, *e.g.,* an agent employed to sell a piece of land or to buy a house. A special agent has limited authority which comes to an end as soon as the special act is performed. If he exceeds his authority, the principal is not liable for such unauthorised acts. Thus, the person dealing with such agent should make due enquiries from the principal as to the extent of his authority.

2. *General agents:* A general agent is an agent who is appointed to perform all acts relating to a particular trade or business for which he is appointed. A general agent can do all legal acts for the purpose of carrying on that trade or business, on behalf of his principal. It may be noted that the authority of a general agent is continuous until terminated. A person dealing with such agent may assume that he has the power to do all that is usual to do in the business for which he is the general laent. As a matter affect, a general agent has more powers than those enjoyed by special agents.

3. *Universal agents:* A universal agent is an agent who is appointed to do all the various trades or business of his principal. In other words, he is an agent who is authorised to do all the acts which his principal can lawfully do under the provisions of the law of the land. As a matter of fact, the universal agent has more powers than those enjoyed by special or general agents.

16.20. COMPARISON BETWEEN AN AGENT AND A SERVANT

The following table gives the comparison between an 'agent' and a 'servant':

S.No.	*Agent*	*Servant*
1.	He has the authority to do act on behalf of his principal and has the authority to create contractual relationship between his principal and third persons.	He has no such power to create contractual relationship between his employer and third persons. This term is generally used for domestic servants.
2.	He generally receives commission on the basis of the work done by him.	He is generally paid by way of salary or wages.
3.	He may work for serval principals at the same time.	He usually serves only one master at the same time.
4.	He is not subject to the direct control and supervision of his principal. He has often a discretion. However, he is bound to follow all the lawful instructions given by his principal.	He acts under the direct control and supervision of his master. And he is bound to follow all reasonable orders given to him by his master.
5.	The principal has the right to give directions as to what the agent has to do.	The master has not only this right, but also the right to give directions as to how the work is to be done.
6.	The principal is liable for the wrongful acts of his agent done within the 'scope of his authority'.	The master is liable for the wrongful acts of his servant done in the 'course of servant's employment'.

16.21. COMPARISON BETWEEN AN AGENT AND AN INDEPENDENT CONTRACTOR

The following table gives the comparison between an agent and an independent contractor:

S.No.	*Agent*	*Independent Contractor*
1.	He is under the control and supervision of his principal though such control and supervision is not direct.	He is not under the control and supervision of his employer.
2.	He is bound to follow all the lawful instructions given by his principal.	He is not bound to follow the instructions given by his employer. He is employed to do a specified work, the manner and the means of performance are purely at his discretion.
3.	He represents his principal and has the authority to create contractual relationship between his principal and third persons.	He does not represent his employer, and has no authority to create contractual relationship between his master and third persons.
4.	He is not personally liable for acts done by him within the scope of his authority.	He is personally liable for the acts done by him.

16.22. COMPARISON BETWEEN AN AGENT AND A BAILEE

The following table gives the comparison between an 'agent' and a 'bailee":

S.No.	Agent	Bailee
1.	He represents his principal and has the authority to create contractual relationship between his principal and third persons.	He does not represent the bailor, and has no authority to create contractual relationship between the bailor and third persons.
2.	He is not required to have the possession of his principal's goods.	He must have the possession of the goods belonging to the bailor. As a matter of fact the relationship of bailor and bailee subsists so long as the bailee holds the possession of bailor's goods.

In *United Commercial Bank* v. *Hem Chandra Sarkar*, AIR 1990 SC 1329, the Supreme Court has observed that one important distinguishing feature between bailee and an agent is that the bailee does not represent the bailor. Secondly, the bailee has no power to make contracts on bailors' behalf. Moreover, he can also not make the bailor liable for any of his acts.

LEGAL PROVISIONS (SECTIONS) DISCUSSED IN THE CHAPTER

Important legal provisions (sections) of the Indian Contract Act, 1872, discussed in this chapter are reproduced hereunder for ready reference:

1. ***Section 182: 'Agent'and 'principal' defined***

   An 'agent' is a person employed to do any act for another, or to represent another in dealings with third person. The person for whom such act is done, or who is so represented, is called the principal'.

2. ***Section 183: Who may employ agent***

   Any person who is of the age of majority according to the law to which he is subject, and who is of sound mind, may employ an agent.

3. ***Section 184: Who may be agent***

   As between the principal and third person any person may become an agent, but no person who is not of the age of majority and of sound mind can become an agent, so as to be responsible to his principle according to the provisions in that behalf herein contained.

4. ***Section 185: Consideration not necessary***

   No consideration is necessary to create an agency.

5. ***Section 198: Knowledge requisite for valid ratification***

   No valid ratification can be made by a person whose knowledge of the case is materially defective.

6. ***Section 199: Effect of ratifying unauthorized act forming part of a transaction***

   A person ratifying any unauthorized act done on his behalf ratifies the whole of the transaction of which such act formed a part.

7. ***Section 100: Ratification of unauthorized act cannot injure third person***

   An act done by one person on behalf of another, without such other person's authority, which, if done with authority would have the effect of subjecting a third person to damages, or of terminating any right or interest of a third person, cannot, by ratification, be made to have such effect.

TEST QUESTIONS

1. Define the term 'agency'. What are the essential and legal rules for a valid agency?
2. Define the terms 'principal', 'agent' and 'agency', and state the basic principles of agency. What is the effect of agency relationship when (*a*) the principal is minor, and (*b*) agent is minor.

3. "Agency in law connotes an authority or capacity in one person to create legal relationship between a person occupying the position of principal and third parties"--examine the concept of agency in the light of this statement.
4. Briefly explain the various modes by which an agency may be created.
5. What is agency by estoppel ? In what way does it differs from an agency by holding out?
6. Discuss agency by estoppel and agency by ratification.
7. "Ratification is tantamount to prior authority"--comment and explain the requisites of a valid ratification.
8. What are the different kinds of agents? How they can be classified?
9. State the comparison between the following:
   (*a*) Agent and servant. (*b*) Agent and independent contractor
   (*c*) Agent and bailee.
10. Write notes on the following:
   (*a*) Agency by estoppel. (*b*) Agency by holding out.
   (*c*) Agency by necessity. (*d*) Agency by ratification.

MULTIPLE CHOICE QUESTIONS

1. A person appointed to contract on behalf of another person, is known as
   (*a*) Principal (*b*) Agent
   (*c*) Independent contractor (*d*) Servant.
2. Which of the following is not an essential element of a valid agency?
   (*a*) Principal must be competent to contract.
   (*b*) Agent must be competent to contract.
   (*c*) Agent must act in representative capacity.
   (*d*) There must be express or implied agreement.
3. A single agent can be appointed by more than one persons by a power of attorney signed jointly by all principals.
   (*a*) True (*b*) False.
4. The wife is considered an implied agent of the husband for the purpose of buying household necessaries on credit.
   (*a*) True (*b*) False.
5. A mercantile agent to whom the possession of the goods is given for the purpose of selling the same, is know as
   (*a*) Broker (*b*) Factor
   (*c*) Commission agent (*d*) Insurance agent.
6. Which of the following agents cannot exercise a right of general lien?
   (*a*) Factor (*b*) Banker
   (*c*) Auctioneer (*d*) All of these.
7. Which of the following statements is not true?
   (*a*) An agent is not personally liable for acts done by him within the scope of his authority.
   (*b*) Principal is liable for wrongful acts of his agent done within the scope of his authority.
   (*c*) An independent contractor is personally liable for the acts done by him while working for his employer.
   (*d*) A bailor is personally liable for the acts of a bailee done during the period of bailment.

ANSWERS

1. (*b*)	**2.** (*b*)	**3.** (*a*)	**4.** (*a*)	**5.** (*b*)	**6.** (*c*)
7. (*d*)					

OBJECTIVE TYPE QUESTIONS WITH REASONING

State with reasons whether the following statements are correct or incorrect.

1. The agency relationship can be created only by an express agreement between the principal and agent.
2. Every person has a right to employ an agent lawfully.
3. A minor cannot be appointed as an agent, as he is not competent to contract.
4. No consideration is required to create an agency,
5. He who acts through another does it by himself.
6. A person can act as an agent of only one principal at a time.
7. A wife is an implied agent of the husband for the purpose of buying household necessaries on credit.
8. There may be a valid ratification by a person whose knowledge of the facts of the case is materially defective.
9. A valid ratification establishes the agency relationship not from the date of ratification but from the date when the agent first contracted.
10. In case an agent exceeds his authority and the acts done by him are subsequently ratified by the principal, the ratification relates back from the date when the agent had acted upon.
11. A person can ratify a part of the transaction which is beneficial to him and reject the rest.
12. A *del credere* agent occupies the position of both an agent and a guarantor.
13. A person may legally be treated as an agent even though he is actually not an agent.

ANSWERS

1. *Incorrect.* The agency may be created either by an express or implied agreement.
2. *Incorrect.* Only a person competent to contract can lawfully employ an agent [Section 183].
3. *Incorrect.* Any person can become an agent and he need not be competent to contract.
4. *Correct.* An agency without consideration is perfectly valid [Section 185].
5. *Correct.* The agency relationship is based upon this principle that 'he who does an act through another is considered to have acted personally'.
6. *Incorrect.* A single agent can be appointed by more than one principal by a power of attorney jointly signed by all the principals.
7. *Correct.* It is the legal position of the wife living with her husband.
8. *Incorrect.* The requirement of a valid ratification is that it must be made with the full knowledge of all material facts [Section198].
9. *Correct.* The ratification has the retrospective effective and is equivalent to previous authority.
10. *Correct.* The valid ratification has a retrospective effect.
11. *Incorrect.* The requirement of a valid reflation is that it must be made for the whole of the transaction done by the agent.
12. *Correct.* A del credere agent, in addition to his work as an agent, also guarantees to the principal the performance of the contract by the third party.
13. *Correct.* Such a situation arises in cases of 'agency by estoppel' and 'agency by holding out'.

PRACTICAL PROBLEMS

1. *A*, a minor, appointed *B* as his agent and authorised him to purchase 10 pairs of Reebock shoes for him. Accordingly, *B* purchased the shoes from *C*, on credit, on behalf of his principal. But *A* refused to pay the price, and *C* sued *B* for the price? Will *C* succeed ? Give reasons.

   Hint : Yes, *C* will succeed in his action. An appointment of an agent by an incompetent person is void and thus the principal is not liable. But in such a situation, an agent acting on behalf of incompetent principal, is personally liable for his acts.

2. *A* appointed *B*, a minor, as his agent to purchase certain goods from *C*, a shopkeeper, on credit. *B* purchased certain goods on credit on behalf of *A* and *A* paid the price to *C*. On one occasion, *A* gave ready cash to *B* for purchase of certain goods form *C*, but *B* purchased the goods on credit and misappropriated the cash given by *A*. *C* claimed the price from *A*. Is he liable to pay the price? Can *A* recover back the money from *B* given to him in cash on earlier occasion ? Give reasons

   Hint : Yes, *A* is liable to pay the price to *C*. An agency is valid even if the agent is incompetent to contract and the principal will be bound by the acts of his agent [Section 184] .However, *A* will not be in a position to recover back cash money from *B*, the minor agent, as contract with minor is *void ab-initio.*

3. *A* enters into a contract with *B*, a master of a ship. On its way to destination, *B* found that the goods were perishing rapidly as such he took the ship to nearest port and sold the goods for best available price. Is the owner of the goods bound by the sale ? Give reasons.

   Hint: Yes, the owner is bound by the sale. In this case, an 'agency by necessity' was created between *B* and the owner of goods.

4. *A* enters into a contract with *B* for the purchase of *B*'s motor-cycle for his (*A*'s) friend *C* although he is having no authority from *C* in this regard. However, *B* refuses to sell the motor-cycle. Subsequently, *C* ratifies the contract and sues *B* for breach of contract. *B* takes the plea that since he has cancelled the contract before ratification, he is not liable for breach. Is *B*'s plea justified ? Give reasons.

   Hint : No, *B*'s plea is not justified. Ratification dates back to the date on which the contract was entered into. In this case, an 'agency by ratification' was created between *A* and *C* on the date when the contract was originally made.

5. *A* without any authority from *B*, a 17 years minor, purchases a car from *C* for and on behalf of *B*. On attaining majority, B ratifies this transaction. Is it a valid ratification?

   Hint : No, it is not a valid ratification. In this case, the original contract between *A* and *C* is *void ab-initio* due to *B*'s minority, and ratification of a void act is not valid.

17 CHAPTER

RELATIONS OF PRINCIPAL WITH HIS AGENT

17.1. INTRODUCTION

We have already discussed that the relations of a principle and his agent are governed by an agreement between them. Thus, the principal and his agent may expressly enter into an agreement providing for their mutual duties and rights which govern their relations with one another. However , certain duties are imposed, by law, on every agent unless they are modified or excluded by an express agreement. These are discussed in the following pages.

17.2. DUTIES OF AN AGENT

The duties[1] of an agent, towards his principal, are contained in the various provisions of the Indian Contract Act. These may be boradly grouped under the following heads:

1. *Duty to follow the instructions of the principal*
2. *Duty to carry out the work with care and skill*
3. *Duty to render accounts to the principal*
4. *Duty to communication with principal*
5. *Duty not to deal on his own account*

1. *Duty to follow the instructions of the principal:* The first and the foremost duty of every agent is to conduct the business of his principal according to the instructions (directions) given by his principal in the agreement. And if no directions are given by the principal, then the agent should act according to the cuustoms of trade. If he fails to act according to such directions or customs, then he is liable to the principal for any loss suffered by the principal due to such an act of the agent. And if there is some profit, then he must account for the same to his principal. [Section 211]

1. The duties of an agent, towards his principal, are the rights of the principal. And by exercising his rights, the principal can seek the enforcement of agent's duties if he fails to perform them.

6. ***Duty not to make secret profits from agency***
7. ***Duty to pay the amount received for the principal***
8. ***Duty not to set up an adverse title***
9. ***Duty not to use the information, received in the course of agency, against the principal***
10. ***Duty to protect the interest of the principal in case of his death or insanity.***
11. ***Duty not to delegate authority.***

Example. 17.1. *A* instructed his agent *B* to store his (*A*'s) goods at particular place. *B* stored a part of the goods at a different warehouse which was equally safe. These goods were destroyed by fire without any negligence on the part of *B*. In this case, *B* was held liable to *A* for the loss of the goods destroyed as he did not act according to the instructions given by *A*.

[*Lilley* v. *Double day* (1881) 7 QBD 510]

Example 17.2. *A* appointed *B* as his agent for the purpose of carrying on a business for him (*A*). There was a custom in the business that the agent should invest at interest, from time to time, the money which was in his hands. *B* omitted to make such investments. In this case, *B* is liable to compensate *A* for the loss of interest suffered due to the non-investment of the money from time to time. Here, the agent has failed to act according to the customs of business.

2. *Duty to carry out the work with care and skill :* It is another important duty of an agent to carry on the business of agency with reasonable care and skill. The standard of reasonable care required from the agent depends upon the nature of his business and circumstances of each case. If the principal suffers any loss due to agent's neglect, want of skill, or misconduct, then the agent must compensate his principal for such loss [Section 212]. However, the agent is liable for direct damages and not for indirect or remote damages.

Example. 17.3. *A*, was an agent of *B*. *A* had the authority to sell the goods of his principal on credit. *A* sold the goods to C on credit without making proper and usual enquires as to the solvency (*i.e.*, creditworthiness) of C. At the time of sale, C was insolvent, In this case, *A* must make compensation to his principal for any loss suffered due to C's insolvency.

Example 17.4. *A*, an insurance broker, was employed by *B* to effect an insurance on a ship. *A* insured the ship but omitted to see that 'usual clauss' are inserted in the policy. The ship was, afterwards, lost in storm. Due to omission of the usual clauses in the policy, nothing could be recovered from the insurance company. In this case, *A* is bound to make good the loss suffered by *B*.

3. *Duty to render accounts to the principal:* It is the duty of an agent to keep true and correct account of all his transactions. And to explain the same to the principal whenever he asks for the same [Section 213].

4. *Duty to communication with principal:* Sometimes, an agent is involved in certain difficulties. In such cases, it is the duty of the agent to make reasonable efforts to communicate with his principal and obtain his instructions [Section 214]. However, in cases of emergency where there is no time to communicate with the principal, the agent may act in good faith without consulting the principal.

Example. 17.5. *A* consigned certain goods to *B*, his agent at Calcutta, and directd him to sent the goods immediately to C at Cuttack. On receiving the goods, *B* found that the goods could not bear the journey to Cuttack without spoiling. And thus, *B* sold the goods in Calcutta itself. In this case, the agent is justified in selling the goods at Calcutta as he has acted in good faith and for the benefit of his principal.

5. *Duty not to deal on his own account:* The relationship of a principal and his agent is of fiduciary nature, *i.e.*, of mutual trust and confidence. It requires that the agent must conduct his business of agency in absolute good faith. Thus, an agent should not deal on his own account and should not do anything which brings his personal interest and his duty to the principal, in conflict with each other. In other words, an agent must not become a principal party to the transaction as against his principal, *e.g.*, an agent appointed to sell the property should not buy himself, or an agent appointed to buy goods should not deliver his own goods. He may however, do so after obtaining the consent of his principal and after disclosing to the principal all the material facts in respect of the transaction. If the agent deals on his own account without principal's consent and without disclosing the full facts to him, the principal may repudiate (*i.e.*, cancel) the transaction if he can prove that:

(*a*) A material fact has been dishonestly concealed from him by the agent;

(*b*) The dealing of the agent has been disadvantageous to him [Section 215].

Example. 17.6. *A* directed *B*, his agent, to sell his (*A*'s) estate. *B* while surveying the estate thoroughly before selling, found a mine on the estate which was unknown to *A*. *B* informed *A* that he wished to buy the estate for himself. But conealed the discovery of the mine. *A* allowed *B* to buy the estate in ignorance of the mine *A*, on discovering that *B* knew of the mine at the time he bought the estate, may either cancel the sale, or he may also adopt) (*i.e.*, accept) the transaction at his option.

Example 17.7. *A* employed *B*, a stock broker, to purchase some shares for him. *B* sold his own shares to *A* without disclosing that the shares belonged to him. It was held that *A* could put an end to the contract and reject the shares. [*Armstrong* v. *Jackson* (1977) KB 822]

6. *Duty not to make secret profits from agency:* The term 'secret profits' means the advantages obtained by the agent over and above his agreed remuneration or commission, and which he would not have been otherwise able to make, except for his position as an agent. If the agent makes any secret profit, without the knowledge of his principal, then the principal can claim from the agent any such benefit which has resulted to him from the transaction [Section 216].

Example 17.8. *A* directed *B* an auctioneer, to sell certain goods belonging to him (*A*). *B* sold the goods to *C*, and received some secret commission from *C* also in addition to the normal commission from *A*. It was held that *B* was bound to hand over to *A* the secret commission received from *C*. [*Anderson* v. *Ramsay & Co.* (1903) 2 KB 635]

Note: The acceptance of bribe by an agent is also secret profits. As such the agent is liable to account for the same to his principal.

7. *Duty to pay the amount received for the principal:* It is the duty of an agent to pay to his principal all moneys received on his behalf. However, the agent is entitled to deduct his lawful charges from the money received on account of his principal, *e.g.*, the expenses properly incurred in conducting the business, and his own remunerations, etc. [Section 217, 218]

8. *Duty not to set up an adverse title:* The term 'adverse title' may be defined as the opposing or contrary title. It is the duty of an agent not to set upon adverse title against his principal. In other words, when the agent has obtained the goods belonging to his principal, then he should not say that the goods belong to himself or some third person, *i.e.*, he should not dispute the ownership of the principal.

9. *Duty not to use the information, received in the course of agency, against the principal:* Sometimes, an agent receives some information in the course of his agency. In such case, it is his duty to pass on the information to his principal, and not to use it against the interest of the principal. If the agent uses any such information against the interest of the principal, then he may recover compensation for the loss suffered by him due to such an act of the agent. The principal may also obtain a court order restraining the agent from using such information against him.

10. *Duty to protect the interest of the principal in case of his death or insanity:* On the death or insanity of the principal, the agency relationship is terminated. However, in such cases, it becomes the duty of the agent to take all reasonable steps to protect the interest assigned to him by his late principal [Section 209].

11. *Duty not to delegate authority :* As a matter of fact, a principal always appoints an agent in whom he has full trust and confidence about his integrity and competence. Thus, the agent must do personally, the work delegated to him by his principal. And it is his duty not to further delegate the work which has been delegated to him by his principal. Ordinarily, an agent cannot further delegate his authority. There are, however, certain execptions to this rule, which shall be discussed in Art. 17.5

17.3. RIGHTS OF AN AGENT

1. *Rights to retain money due from the principal*
2. *Right to receive remuneration*
3. *Right of lien*
4. *Right to be indemnified*
5. *Right to compensation*

The rights[2] of an agent are contained in various provisions of the Indian Contract Act. These may be broadly grouped under the following heads:

1. *Rights to retain money due from the principal:* The agent has the right to retain his principal's money until his claims in respect of his remuneration or expenses, etc., are satisfied. Thus when an agent receives the money on behalf of his principal, he has the right to retain money (out of the total money received) due to him from the principal in respect of the following [Section 217].

(*a*) advances made by the agent on behalf of his principle.
(*b*) expenses incurred by the agent in conducting the agency business.
(*c*) remunerations payable to the agent.

It may, however, be noted that the agent can retain the money due to him only out of such money which has been received by him on account of his principal and in respect of the business of agency. Thus, if the agent receives some money, on behalf of his principal, independently of the agency business, then the agent cannot retain his dues out of such money.

2. *Right to receive remuneration:* The agent has the right to receive the agreed remuneration from his principal. If no remuneration is fixed, the agent is entitled to receive reasonable remuneration. It may, however, be noted that the agent is entitled to receive the remuneration only when it becomes due. And the remuneration becomes due when the following conditions are fulfilled:

(*a*) When the act undertaken by the agent is completed [Setion 219], and
(*b*) When the transaction that has resulted, is the result of agent's services and efforts.

The fulfilment of the above conditions depends upon the terms of a particular contract, *i.e.,* whether or not the agent's remuneration has become due, depends on terms of each particular contract.

Example 17.9. *A* appointed *B*, as his agent, to introduce a customer who is willing to purchase his property. Accordingly, *B* introduced one customer *C* who was willing to purchase *A*'s property. The sale was settled between *A* and *C* and the earnest money was also paid to *A*. But the sale could not be completed due to *C*'s inability to arrange the full money. It was held that *B* was entitled to receive his agreed remuneration. [*Sheikh Farid Baksh* v. *Hargulal*, AIR 1937 Al 46]

Example 17.10. *A* appointed *B*, as his agent, to sell his house by auction. Accordingly, *B* held the auction. But he could not find a suitable purchaser. *C*, a person who attended the auction, obtained from *B* the address of *A* and contacted him. And *C* purchased the house from *A* without the intervention of his agent (*B*). It was held that *B* was entitled to receive his remuneration as the transaction (*i.e.,* sale) was the result of his efforts.[*Green* v. *Bartlett* (1863) 14 CB (Ns) 681]

In *Sarswati Devi v. Moti Lal*, AIR 1982 Raj 108, the court held that where the commission was payable to an estate agent as and when he introduced a ready and willing

2. The rights of an agent are the duties of the principal. And by exercising his rights, the agent can seek the enforcement of principal's duties, if he fails to perform them.

customer, the agent becomes entitled to his commission when such customer was introduced even if the principal refused to sign the agreement.

But when, it is expressly provided in the agreement of agency that the agent will get commission only on the *completion of the contract* between the principal and third party, the agent becomes entitled to receive his commission *only* on the completion of such contract and not before.

Note: If an agent is guilty of misconduct in the business of the agency, then he is not entitled to receive any remuneration in respect of that part of the business which he has misconducted [Section 220]. Moreover, an agent who misconducts, is also liable to compensate his principal.

3. *Right of lien:* The 'right of lien' is the right of a person to retain the possession of the property of another until the charges due to the person in possession of the goods, are paid. The agent has a right to retain the possession of the goods, belonging to his principal for the payment of his commission or other charges in respect of the goods [Section 221]. Thus, the agent has the right to retain the goods, papers and other property of the principal until his dues are paid. He may exercise his right of lien over the movable or immovable property of his principal. However, he has only a particular lien, *i.e.*, he can retain only those goods in respect of which his charges are due. The following conditions must be satisfied for the exercise of his right:

(*a*) The agent must have the possession of the goods belonging to his principal. However, the possession may be actual or constructive.

(*b*) The agent must have received such possession of the goods in his capacity as an agent and in the ordinary course of his duties. Moreover, the possession must be lawful.

(*c*) The agent must be lawfully entitled to receive his dues from the principal.

(*d*) There must not be any contrary agreement.

Example 17.11. *A* appointed *B*, as his agent, for the purpose of buying some goods on his behalf. *B* purchased those goods on behalf of his principal, and the principal paid the purchase price. The goods were, however, in the possession of *B*. Afterwards, *A* failed to pay the agreed amount of *B*'s commission. In this case, *B* may retain the possession of the goods until his dues for commission are paid by *A*.

4. *Right to be indemnified:* We know that the term 'indemnity' means the 'compensation' or 'protection against loss'. The agent has the right to be indemnified against all losses and expenses incurred by him in the course of the agency business. It may, however, be noted that the agent may recover the compensation only in the following two cases:

(*a*) Where the losses or expenses are incurred by the agent in doing the lawful authorised acts [Section 222], or

(*b*) Where the losses or expenses are incurred by the agent in doing some acts which are apparently lawful but turn out to be unlawful, However, such acts must be done in *good faith* and at the instructions of the principal [Section 223].

Example. 17.12. *A* appointed *B*, as his agent, for the purpose of buying 10 drums of oil for him. *B* entered into a contract with *C*, an oil dealer, for the purchase of 10 drums of oil for *A*. Accordingly, *C* delivered 10 drums of oil to *A*, but he refused to take the delivery of the oil . In consequence, *C* filed a suit against *B* for the breach of contract. *B* informed *A* of the suit. But *A* cancelled the contract altogether. *B* defended the suit and was compelled to pay damages and costs. He also incurred some expenses for the same. In this case, *B* is entitled to claim from *A* such damages, costs and expenses.

It may, however, be noted that the agent's right to indemnity does not extend to the acts which are apparently unlawful or criminal. Thus, where a person employs an agent to do an act which is criminal, the principal is not liable to the agent to indemnify him against the consequences of that act.

5. *Right to compensation:* The agent has also the right to receive compensation for the losses suffered due to the principal's negligence or want of skill [Section 225].

Example 17.13. *A*, a contractor, employed, *B*, a brick-layer, for the construction of a house. *A* put up the scaffolding (temporary structure for making or repairing a building). But the scaffolding was unskillfully put up which broke down and *B* was injured. In this case, *A* must makes compensation to *B* for the injuries sustained by him.

17.4. AGENCY RELATIONSHIP BETWEEN HUSBAND AND WIFE

The relationship between a husband and his wife is also that of a principal and agent. The husband is treated as a principal and the wife as his agent. But there is some difference in their relationship as a principal and agent. The agency relationship between them may be discussed under the following two heads:

1. *Wife living with her husband*
2. *Wife living apart from her husband*

(*a*) Wife living with her husband.

(*b*) Wife living apart from her husband.

1. *Wife living with her husband:* A wife living with her husband has the implied authority to buy the articles of household necessity. In other words, where the husband and his wife are living together, the wife is presumed to be the agent of her husband for the purpose of buying household necessaries. Thus, the husband is bound to pay the bills for the household credit purchases made by his wife. However, the husband is bound to pay for the credit purchases made by his wife only if the following conditions are satisfied:

(*a*) The husband and the wife must be living together.

(*b*) The husband and the wife must be living together in a domestic establishment of their own. And the wife should be the incharge of the domestic establishment.

(*c*) The wife must purchase the articles suited to the style in which the husband chooses to live.

When all the above conditions are satisfied, the wife is presumed to be the agent of his husband. And the husband is bound by the acts of his wife. However, the husband can escape the liability by proving any of the following, that:

(*a*) He has expressly forbidden his wife to buy goods on credit. And the tradesman was also expressly forbidden to supply the goods on credit to his wife:

(*b*) The wife was already supplied with sufficiency of the articles in question;

(*c*) The wife was supplied with sufficient funds to purchase the necessaries;

(*d*) The goods purchased were not necessaries.

Example 17.14. *A* was the manager of a hotel where his wife *B* was working as *manageress.* They were living together in the same hotel but they did not have any domestic establishment of their own. The wife purchased some clothes from *C* on credit. *C* demanded the payment from *A*, the husband of *B*. It was held that *A* was not liable to pay as there was no domestic establishment of their own. [*Debenham* v. *Mellon* (1880) AC 24]

2. *Wife living apart from her husband:* Sometimes, the husband and the wife are living separately. The wife may be living apart without any fault on her part. Or she may be living apart of her own will and without any justification. Where the wife is living apart, without any fault on her part, then she is legally entitled to receive maintenance from her husband. If the husband does not provide her the maintenance, the wife has an implied authority to purchase the necessaries of her life, and the husband will be bound to pay for the same. In such cases, the husband cannot escape liability by forbidding his wife from purchasing the goods on credit. Moreover, the husband will also be liable even if he had told the tradesman not to supply the goods on credit.

However, if the wife is living apart of her own will and without any justification, then she is not legally entitled to receive maintenance from her husband. In such case, the wife is not the agent of her husband and the husband is not liable even for the necessaries.

Note: In England, the implied agency of the wife has been abolished by the English Matrimonial Proceeding and Property Act, 1970.

17.5. DELEGATION OF AUTHORITY BY AN AGENT

Ordinarily, the agent is expected to perform his duties personally. And generally, he cannot further delegate the work which has been delegated to him by his principal. This is based on the general rule '*delegatus non-potest delegare*', which means that 'a delegate cannot further delegate'. Thus, an agent being a delegate of his principal, cannot pass on that delegated authority to someone else. This rule is incorporated in Section 190 of the Indian Contract Act, which reads as under:

"An agent cannot lawfully employ another to perform acts which he has expressly or impliedly undertaken to perform personally."

Thus, an agent cannot pass on his power to another person. The reason for this rule is that, the principal appoints a person to act on his behalf in whom he has full faith and confidence. Moreover, the principal relies upon the qualifications, skill and competence of the agent. It would, therefore, be unfair for the agent to pass on his powers to someone else. However, under *exceptional circumstances*, an agent may appoint another person as his sub-agent, and delegate all his power to the sub-agent. An agent may also appoint a sub-agent to assist him in some of his day-to-day acts, and may delegate some of his powers to the sub-agent

A person who is appointed by the agent and to whom the principal's work is delegated is known as 'sub-agent'

17.6. SUB-AGENT

The term 'sub-agent' is defined in Section 191 of the Indian Contract Act, which reads as under:

"A sub-agent is a person employed by and acting under the control of, the original agent in the business of the agency."

Thus, a sub-agent is a person appointed by the original agent to act in the business of agency. The sub-agent acts under the control of original agent and the relationship between the original agent and the sub-agent is that of principal and agent. It may be noted that the original agent has no general authority to appoint a sub-agent, in all circumstances. He can appoint a sub-agent only in the following exceptional circumstances:

1. Where the nature of work is such that the appointment of a sub-agent is necessary, *e.g.*, an agent appointed to sell the property may appoint an auctioneer.
2. Where the custom of a particular trade provided that a sub-agent can be appointed, *e.g.*, the architects generally appoint surveyors, estimators, draftsmen, etc.
3. Where the principal has expressly authorised the appointment of a sub-agent.
4. Where the appointment of a sub-agent becomes necessary due to some unforeseen emergencies.
5. Where the act to be done is purely ministerial in nature, *i.e.*, the acts which do not require personal or professional skill, *e.g.*, clerical or routine work.
6. Where the principal knows that the agent has an intention to appoint sub-agent, but he does not object to it.

17.7. RELATIONSHIP BETWEEN PRINCIPAL AND SUB-AGENT

> **1.** ***Where the sub-agent is properly appointed***
> **2.** ***Where the sub-agent is improperly appointed***

The relationship between the principal and the sub-agent may be discussed under two heads, namely:

(*a*) Where the sub-agent is properly appointed. [Section 192]

(*b*) Where the sub-agent is improperly appointed. [Section 193]

1. *Where the sub-agent is properly appointed:* In the circumstances stated above, the appointment of a sub-agent is proper and valid. Following are the effects of proper appointment of a sub-agent:

(*a*) The principal is represented by the sub-agent and is bound by his acts. Moreover, the principal is also liable to third parties for the acts of the sub-agent.

(*b*) The original agent is liable to the principal for the acts of the sub-agent, *e.g.* if the sub agent has misappropriated the principal's property or its sale proceeds, the original agent is responsible to the principal for the same.

(*c*) The sub-agent is responsible for his acts to the original agent. But he is not responsible to the principal except in cases of fraud or wilful wrong.

2. *Where the sub-agent is improperly appointed:* Sometimes, the appointment of a sub-agent is not within the exceptional circumstances discussed above. In such cases, the appointment of a sub-agent is unauthorised, and thus improper and invalid. Following are the effects of improper appointment:

(*a*) The principle is not represented by the sub-agent and is not bound by his acts, Moreover, the principal is not liable to third parties for the acts of the sub-agent.

(*b*) The original agent is liable to the principal and the third parties for the acts of sub-agent.

(*c*) The sub-agent is not responsible to the principal for any of his acts.

17.8. SUBSTITUTE AGENT

A 'substituted agent' is an agent named by the original agent to act on behalf of the principal. The term substituted agent is defined in Section 194 of the Indian Contract Act, which reads as under:

"Where an agent, holding an express or implied authority to name another person to act for the principal in the business of agency, has named another person accordingly, such person is not a sub-agent, but an agent of the principal for such part of the business of the agency as is entrusted to him."

Thus, a substituted agent is the agent appointed by the original agent to act for the principal. It may be noted that the original agent must have the authority to appoint such agent. The substituted agent is appointed to carry on the business of agency on behalf of the principal. It may also be noted that a substituted agent acts under the direct control of the principal and not under the original agent.

Example 17.15. *A* directed *B*, his solicitor, to sell his estate by auction. *A* also authorised *B* to employ an auctioneer for the purpose. *B* named *C*, an auctioneer, to conduct the sale. In this case, *C* is a substituted agent of *A*. He is *A*'s agent for the purpose of conducting the sale by auction.

Example 17.16. *A* authorised *B*, a merchant, to recover the money due to *A* from *C*. *B* instructed *D*, a solicitor, to take legal proceedings against *C* for the recovery of money due to *A*. In this case, *D* is a substituted agent of *A*. He is *A*'s agent for the purpose of acting as a solicitor on his behalf.

It may be noted that the original agent walks out of the scene after appointing the substituted agent. However, a duty is imposed upon the original agent to select a substituted agent with reasonable case.

17.9. COMPARISON BETWEEN SUB-AGENT AND SUBSTITUTED AGENT

The following table gives the comparison between a sub-agent and a substituted agent:

S.No.	Sub-Agent	Substituted agent
1.	A sub-agent is appointed by the agent, and also work under his control *i.e.*, a sub-agent is the agent of the original agent.	A substituted agent is also appointed by the agent, but he works under the control of the principal *i.e.*, the substituted agent is the agent of the principal.
2.	A sub-agent is responsible to the original agent alone, and not to the principal except for fraud or wilful wrong.	A substituted agent is responsible to the principal alone and not to the original agent.
3.	The original agent is responsible to the principal for the acts of the sub-agent.	The original agent is not responsible to the principal for the acts of the substituted agent if he has taken reasonable care in appointing him.
4.	There is no direct contract between the sub agent and the principal. Neither the principal can file a suit against the sub-agent for damages etc. nor the sub-agent against the principal for his remuneration etc.	There is a direct contract between the substituted agent and the principal. The principal can file a suit against the substituted agent for damages etc. The substituted agent can also file a suit against the principal for his remuneration etc.

LEGAL PROVISIONS (SECTIONS) DISCUSSED IN THE CHAPTER

Important legal provisions (sections) of the Indian Contract Act, 1872, discussed in this chapter are reproduced hereunder for ready reference:

1. ***Section 211: Agent's duty in conducting principal's business***

   An agent is bound to conduct the business of his principal according to the directions given by the principal, or in the absence of any such directions acording to the custom which prevails in doing business of the same kind at the place where the agent conducts such business. When the agent acts otherwise, if any loss be sustained, he must make it good to his principal, and if any profit accrues, he must account for it.

2. ***Section: 215: Right of principal when agent deals, on his own account, in business of agency without principal's consent***

   If an agent deals on his own account in the business of the agency, without first obtaining the consent of his principal and acquainting him with all material circumstances which have come to his own knowledge on the subject, the principal may repudiate the transaction, if the case shows, either that any material fact has been dishonestly concealed form him by the agent, or that the dealings of the agent have been disadvantageous to him.

3. ***Section 216: Principal's right to benefit gained by agent dealing on his own account in business of agency***

   If an agent, without the knowledge of his principal, deals in the business of the agency on his own account instead of on account of his principal, the principal is entitled to claim form the agent any benefit which may have resulted to him form the transaction.

4. ***Section 219: When agent's remuneration becomes due***

   In the absence of any special contract, payment for the performance of any act is not due to the agent until the completion of such act; but an agent may detain moneys recived by him on account of goods sold, although the whole of the goods consigned to him for sale may not have been sold, or although the sale may not be actually complete.

5. ***Section 220: Agent not entitled to remuneration for business misconducted***

   An agent who is guilty of misconduct in the business of the agency, is not entitled to any remuneration in respect of that part of the business which he has misconducted.

6. ***Section 221: Agent's lien on principal's property***

   In the absence of any contract to the contrary, an agent is entitled to retain goods, papers, and other property, whether movable or immovable of the principal recived by him, unitl the amount due to himself for commission, disbursements and services in respect of the same has been paid or accounted for to him.

TEST QUESTIONS

1. State briefly the duties and rights of an agent. What is the degree of skill required of an agent?
2. Discuss briefly the rights of an agent against his principal as provided in the Indian Contract Act.
3. Discuss the duties of an agent under the Indian Contract Act.
4. On what principle and to what extent can a wife pledge her husband's credit (*a*) while she lives with her husband (*b*) while she lives apart from husband.
5. "Delegatus non potest delegare"–comment.
6. Discuss the extent to which an agent can delegate his authority. What are the consequences of such delegation?
7. Define the term 'sub-agent'. When he can be appointed ? State the position of sub-agent in relation to the original agent, principal and third party.
8. What is the liability of an agent to his principal and third parties in the following cases:
   (*a*) When he properly appoints a sub-agent.
   (*b*) When he improperly appoints a sub-agent.
9. Define the term 'substitute agent'. State the comparison between sub-agent and substituted agent.
10. How do you distinguish between the liabilities of sub-agent and substituted agent to the principal?

MULTIPLE CHOICE QUESTIONS

1. Which of the following statements is not true?
   (*a*) An agent should conduct business according to his principals's instructions.
   (*b*) An agent is liable to account for any secret profit made by him.
   (*c*) An agent is not liable for any misinformation given to the principal.
   (*d*) An agent should not deal on his own account.
2. The agent becomes entitled to receive his remuneration on the fulfilment of which of the following conditions?
   (*a*) When the act undertaken by the agent is completed.
   (*b*) When the concluded transaction is the result of agent's services and efforts.
   (*c*) both (*a*) and (*b*) above
   (*d*) none of these as remuneration is payable without any condition.
3. Which of the following is not a right of the agent?
   (a) Right of lien (*b*) Right to be indemnified
   (*c*) Right to remuneration (*d*) Right to make secret profits.
4. A person appointed by the original agent to act in the business of agency, but under the control of original agent, is known as
   (*a*) Agent (*b*) Sub-agent
   (*c*) Substituted agent (*d*) Del credere agent.
5. A person appointed by the original agent to act for and under the control of the principal, is known as
   (*a*) Agent (*b*) Sub-agent
   (*c*) Substituted Agent (*d*) Del credere agent.

ANSWERS

1. (c)	2. (*c*)	3. (*d*)	4. (*b*)	5. (*c*)

OBJECTIVE TYPE QUESTIONS WITH REASONING

State with reasons whether the following statements are correct or incorrect.

1. If the agent fails to act according to principal's instructions, then he is liable to the principal for any loss suffered by him due to such failure to follow instructions.
2. The agency relationship entitles the agent to make and retain the secret profit out of the agency business.
3. Agent's duty to communicate with the principal is a legal duty and should be strictly followed even in cases of emergency, where there is no time to communicate with the principal.
4. An agent has the right to retain his principals's money until his claims in respect of his remuneration or expenses incurred in agency business are satisfied.
5. The agent can exercise general lien over the principal's goods in his possession until his commission charges are paid by the principal
6. An agent is entitled to receive compensation from the principal for the losses suffered due to principal's negligence or want of skill.
7. Where the husband and wife are living together, the husband is bound to pay the bills for the household credit purchases made by the wife.
8. Where a wife voluntarily leaves her husband and lives apart without any justification, then she is not an implied agent but merely an agent by necessity.
9. An agent can delegate all his powers to a sub-agent as the general principle in this regard is that *delegatus non-potest delegate* which means a delegate can further delegate his authority.
10. An agent cannot appoint a sub-agent.
11. A sub-agent is a person who is named by the agent to act for his principal.
12. A sub-agent is appointed by the original agent but he acts under the control and supervision of the principal.

ANSWERS

1. *Correct.* It is the duty of the agent to follow the instructions of his principal [Section 211].
2. *Incorrect.* It is the duty of the agent not to make any secret profit from agency [Section 216].
3. *Incorrect.* In cases of emergency, the agent may act in good faith without consulting the principal.
4. *Correct.* It is the agent's right to retain money for such expenses, etc. [Section 217]
5. *Incorrect.* An agent has only a particular lien *i.e.,* he can retain only those goods in respect of which his charges are due [Section 221].
6. *Correct.* It is agent's right to recover compensation in such cases [Section 225]. Every principal is under a duty of care not to expose his agent to unreasonable risks.
7. *Correct.* In such cases, the wife is presumed to be the agent of her husband for the purposes of buying household necessaries.
8. *Incorrect.* In such a case, the wife is neither an implied agent nor an agent by necessity.
9. *Incorrect.* The principal of *delegatus non-potest delegate* means that 'a delegate cannot further delegate'. However, a sub-agent can be appointed in certain exceptional circumstances [section 191].
10. *Incorrect.* A sub-agent can be appointed under certain circumstances.
11. *Incorrect.* A sub-agent is a person who is appointed by the original agent to act under his (original agent's) control.
12. *Incorrect.* A sub-agent acts under the control and supervision of the original agent.

PRACTICAL PROBLEMS

1. *A*, a commission agent, purchases certain goods for his principal *B* and stores the same in a godown. However, *A* does not insure the goods though he has specific instruction in this regard from his principal (*B*). Subsequently the goods are destroyed by fire and *B* sues *A* for damages. Will he succeed. Give reasons.

   Hint : Yes, *B* will succeed in his action. In this case, *A* has failed to follow the specific instruction given by his principal. [Section 211]

2. *A* engaged *B* as his agent to buy a second-hand Honda city car for him. *B* bought the car in the name of his nominee for Rs. 3.50 lakh and then purchased it himself for Rs. 4 lakh. Subsequently, *B* sold the same car to A for Rs. 4.50 lakh. Later on, *A* came to know about the modus operandi adopted by *B* and sues him for the recovery of secret profits made by *B*. Will he succeed ? If so, then how much amount he can recover ? Give reasons.

   Hint : Yes, *A* will succeed in his action and he is entitled to recover Rs. One lakh from *B*, being the secret profit earned by *B* over the original purchase price of Rs.3.5 lakh. [Section 216]

3. *A* directed his agent *B* to sell his (*A's*) estate. While surveying the estate thoroughly before selling, *A* found a mine on the estate which was unknown to *A* and *B* informed A that he wished to buy the estate for himself but conceated the discovery of mine. *A* allowed *B* to purchase the estate in ignorance of the mine. On discovering that B had concealed the mine information, *A* repudiated the contract. Is *A* justified in doing so ? Give reasons.

   Hint : Yes, *A* is justified in repudiating the contract. It is the duty of the agent not to deal in his own name without disclosing the full facts to his principal. If the agent does so, the principal is entitled to repudiate the contract. [Section 215]

4. *A* was appointed as an agent by '*B* and *Co*', a newspaper agency, for securing orders for advertisements and it was agreed that commission would be paid to *A* on the publication of advertisement. *A* obtained some order of certain advertisement, but his agency was terminated before these advertisements were published. However, after the termination of agency, *B* and *Co* published the advertisements secured by *A*. but refused to pay the commission to him. *A* claimed the commission. Is *A* justified in his claim? Give reasons.

   Hint : Yes, *A* is justified in his claim. In this case, the work undertaken by the agent was completed and the publication of the advertisements was the result of agent's, services and efforts. [Section 219]

5. *A* authorised his agent *B* to sell a mobile phone for him. Accordingly, *B* sold the mobile phone in good-faith and handed over the sale proceeds to him. Later on, it was discovered that the phone belonged to C who recovered the value of the phone and litigation charges from *B*. *B* claimed compensation for the same from *A*, but *A* refused to compensate. Is *A* justified in refusing to compensate *B* ? Given reasons.

   Hint : No, *A* is not justified. An agent is entitled to be compensated for losses and expenses incurred in the course of agency business. [Sections 222 and 223]

6. *A* instructed *B*, a merchant, to buy a ship for him. *B* employed *C*, a ship surveyor of good reputation, to choose a ship for *A*. The surveyer (*C*) made the choice negligently and the ship turned out to be unseaworthy and was sunk in the sea. *A* sued *B* for the loss caused to him and *B* defended on the ground that the loss should fall upon the surveyors (*C*) and not on *B*. Is *B*'s defence justified ? Give reasons.

   Hint : Yes, *B*'s defence is justified. In this case, *C* would be treated a substituted agent who is directly liable to the principal (*A*) Here, the nature of services expected from a merchant (*B*) showed that he had an implied authority to appoint a substituted agent and by employing a Surveyor of good reputation, *B* had exercised his discretion as a man of ordinary prudence would exercise in his own case. [Section 194 and 195]

RELATIONS OF PRINCIPAL WITH THIRD PARTIES

18.1. INTRODUCTION

We know that on the creation of a valid agency the agent becomes entitled to do certain acts on behalf of the principal, *i.e.*, the agent gets the authority to do certain acts. The agent also gets the authority to create a relationship between his principal and other persons (known as third party). The principal is bound by the acts of the agent which are done by him in the scope of his authority. In this chapter, we shall discuss the scope and extent of agent's authority, principal's relations with third parties, and the personal liability of the agent.

18.2. AGENT'S AUTHORITY

The term 'authority' of an agent may be defined as his power or capacity to bind the principal with the third party. The principal is bound by the acts of his agent done by him within the scope of his authority. The agent's authority to bind his principal, may be discussed under the following two heads:

1. Actual or real authority.
2. Ostensible or apparent authority.

18.3. ACTUAL OR REAL AUTHORITY

It is the authority which has been conferred upon the agent by his principal. It may be of two kinds, namely (*a*) express authority, or (*b*) implied authority.

1. *Express authority:* The 'express authority' is one which is given by the words, written or spoken. In other words, when the principal expressly authoritses the agent to do certain acts, the authority is known as express authority. And the principal is bound by agent's acts done within his express authority.

A 'power of attorney' is an example or express authority.

Example 18.1. *A* executed a power of attorney in favour of *B* authorising him to collect money from *C* on his (*A*'s) behalf. *B* received a sum of money from *C* due to *A*. Here *A* is bound by *B*'s act, and C is discharged from his obligation to pay the amount to *A*.

In *Syed Abdul Khader* v. *Rami Reddi* AIR 1979, SC 553, the Supreme Court has held that a power of attorney executed by several persons jointly in favour of one agent is also valid. This means that there can be more than one principal of one agent.

2. *Implied authority:* The 'implied authority' is one which is conferred upon the agent by the conduct of the principal. In other words, when the authority is not expressly given, but it is inferred from the conduct of the principal , the circumstances of the case or the course of dealing between the parties. Such an authority is known as implied authority. And the principal is bound by agent's acts done within his implied authority.

Example 18.2. *A* appointed *B*, an estate agent, to find a purchaser for certain property. *B* accepted deposits from *C*, a prospective customer, and misappropriated it. The principal (*A*) was held liable for *B*'s act, because an estate agent has an implied authority to accept deposits.

[*Ryan* v. *Pilkington* (1969) 1 WLR 403]

Example 18.3. *A* of Delhi owned a shop in Bombay and used to visit the shop occasionally. The shop was managed by *B*, his agent. *B* was in the habit of purchasing goods from *C* in *A*'s name for the purpose of the shop. *B* used to pay for the purchases out of *A*'s fund and *A* knew about it. In this case, *B* has an implied authority to purchase goods from *C* in the name of *A* for the purpose of the shop.

18.4. OSTENSIBLE OR APPARENT AUTHORITY

It is the authority which appears to be actual to others, though it is not so. It happens, when the principal creates an appearance which reasonably leads another to believe that his agent has some authority. In such cases, the principal is bound by the acts of the agent, and he cannot deny his agent's authority in dealing with third parties who assumed that the agent is authorised to deal on behalf of the principal. It is also known as *apparent authority* Generally, a title or a position of an agent, automatically gives him a measure of ostensible authority, *e.g.*, a general manager or managing director of a company has the ostensible authority to do all such things as fall within the usual scope of that office. Thus, the person dealing with him may assume that he has the usual authority of a general manager or managing director.

Example 18.4. *A* was acting as a manager in *B*'s hotel. *B* had forbidden *A* from buying cigars on credit. But *A* bought some cigars from *C* on credit. *C* trusted *A* as his name was appearing on the board. *A* failed to pay the price. *C* filed a suit against *B* for the recovery of the price. It was held that the principal (*B*) was liable to pay for the cigars The court observed that the cigars were such as would naturally be dealt in such establishment (*i.e.*, hotel l). *A*'s act was, therefore, within the ostensible authority.

[*Watteau* v. *Fenwick* (1893) 1 QB 346]

Thus, the ostensible authority is an appearance of authority. Whether or not there is appearance of authority in a particular case depends upon the facts of each case, *e.g.*, an appearance of authority may also arise from the course of dealing adopted in a particular case.

Example 18.5. *A* authorised his agent *B* to purchase iron for him on credit. *B* purchased some quantity of iron from *C* on credit and A paid for the same. At subsequent occasion, *A* gave the ready cash to *B* for the purchase of iron. But *B* again purchased the iron from *C* on credit, and misappropriated the money. It was held that A was liable to pay for the credit purchase, as the agent's act was within the ostensible authority. Here the dealings showed that *B* had the authority to purchase the iron on credit.

18.5. SCOPE AND EXTENT OF AGENT'S AUTHORITY

We know that the principal is bound by the acts of his agent. However , the agent's acts must be within the scope of his actual or apparent authority. The extent of agents's authority is stated in Section 188 of the Indian Contract Act , which reads as under:

"An agent, having an authority to do an act, has authority to do every lawful thing which is necessary in order to do such act.

An agent, having an authority to carry on a business, has authority to do every lawful thing necessary for the purpose, or usually done in the course, of conducting such business."

The analysis of this section shows that the agent's authority to do a particular act or business extends to all lawful things which are necessary for doing that act or business. Thus , the extent of agent's authority depends upon the following:

(*a*) The nature of the act or business the agent is appointed to do;

(*b*) The things which are usually done in carrying out such act or business;

(c) The usual customs and usages of trade which are lawful and reasonable.

Example: 18.6. *A* a resident of Bombay appointed an agent *B* in Calcutta to recover a debt due to him at Calcutta. In this case B has the authority to adopt any legal process necessary for the purpose of recovering the debt. And he may give a valid discharge for the same.

Example 18.7. *A* appointed *B* as his agent for the purpose of selling artificial manure. *B* had no authority to give any warranty about the goods. But *B* warranted to *C*, the buyer , that the manure contained 30 percent phosphate of lime. However, this warranty turned out to be false. *C* filed a suit against *A* for the breach of warranty. *A* was held liable to pay damages. In this case, the agent's act was within the scope of his authority as it was usual in the artificial manure trade to give a warranty of this kind. [*Dingle* v. *Hare* (1859)7 CB (NS) 145]

It may be noted that , where there is secret limitation on agent's authority, the third parties dealing with the agent are not affected, *i.e.*, the principal remains liable to third parties for the acts of the agent. But if the third party has the knowledge of any such limitation on agent's authority, the principal will not be liable for the restricted acts of the agent.

Example. 18.8. *A* executed a power of attorney in favour of *B* to operate his business. But *A* did not give any power to *B* to borrow the money. However, *B* borrowed money from *C* after showing him the power of attorney. It was held that *C* could not recover the loan from the principal (*A*) as he did not authorise *B* to borrow money. In this case, the power of attorney was shown to C and thus, he had the constructive notice that *B* had no power to borrow.

[*Jacobs* v. *Morris* (1902) 1 Ch. 168].

In *Timblo Irmaos Ltd. v. Jorge A.M. Sequeira*, (1977) 3 SCC 474, the Supreme Court has also held that the power to sell will not authorise the agent to borrow money or to pledge goods. Thus, an agent cannot borrow money on behalf of his principal unless he has clear authority to do so. But where the agent has been authorised to borrow money, then the principal is liable even if he has borrowed beyond authorised limits. This is so because the third party has no means of ascertaining that fact.

18.6. PRINCIPAL'S RELATIONS WITH THIRD PARTIES

We have already discussed that an agent enters into a contract with third party on behalf of his principal . And an agent acting within the scope of his authority , binds the principal. The position of the principal as regards the contracts made by the agent with the third parties , may be discussed under the following three heads:

1. Where the agent contracts for a named principal.
2. Where the agent contracts for an unnamed principal.
3. Where the agent contracts for an undisclosed principal.

18.7 PRINCIPAL'S RELATIONS WHERE THE AGENT CONTRACTS FOR A NAMED PRINCIPAL

1. *Acts of an agent within his authority*
2. *Act of an agent beyond his authority*
3. *Misrepresentation or fraud by an agent*
4. *Notice to the agent is the notice to the principal*
5. *Principal inducing belief that his agent's unauthorised acts are authorised*

Sometimes, the agent contracts with the third parties after disclosing the name and existence of his principal. In such cases , the rights and liabilities of a principal for his agent's acts may be discussed under the following sub-heads:

1. ***Acts of an agent within his authority:*** The principal is bound by the acts of his agent which are done in the scope of his authority (actual or apparent) . As a matter of fact, the acts of the agent are the acts of the principal , and have the same legal consequences as if the acts were done by the principal himself [Section 226]. Thus, the principal is bound by such acts of the agent. However, the acts should be lawful.

Example: 18.9. *A* athorised *B*, an agent to collect money on his behalf. *B* received from *C* a sum of money due to *A*. This receipt of money is binding on *A*, and *C* is discharged from his obligation to pay this amount to *A*.

2. ***Act of an agent beyond his authority:*** Ordinarily, the principal is not bound by the acts of an agent which are done by him beyond his actual or apparent authority. The principal's liability for the work done by an agent beyond his authority may be discussed under the following two heads:

(*a*) ***Where the work is separable:*** Sometimes, the agent does some work beyond his authority which is separable from the authorised work. In such cases, the principal is bound by the authorised work only [Section 227] .

Example 18.10. *A*, the owner of a ship and the goods in it, authorised *B*, his agent, to insure the ship for Rs. 40 lakhs. *B* procured an insurance policy for the ship for Rs. 40 lakhs. He also procured another policy for Rs. 40,000 for the goods lying in the ship. In this case, *A* is bound to pay the premium for the policy on the ship only. But he is not bound to pay the premium for the policy on the goods.

(*b*) ***Where the work is not separable:*** Sometimes, the agent does some work beyond his authority which is not separable from the authorised work. In such cases, the principal is not bound by the whole of the work. And he may repudiate the whole transaction [Section 288].

Example 18.11. *A* authorised *B* to buy 500 sheep for him. But *B* bought 500 sheep and 200 lambs for a total sum of Rs. 30,000. In this case, *A* may repudiate the whole transaction.

3. ***Misrepresentation or fraud by an agent:*** The principal is liable for the misrepresentation or fraud committed by his agent while acting in the course of his business. As a matter of fact, the misrepresentation made or fraud committed by an agent within the course of his business, has the same effect as if these have been committed by the principal himself. However, the principal is not liable for any fraud or misrepresentation of the agent which do not fall within agent's authority [Section 238].

Example 18.12. *A* offered to buy a block of flats from *B*. *A* enquired from *C*, the property manager of *B*, whether all the tenants were paying their rents regularly. *C* informed *A* that the tenants were paying rents regularly with immaterial enceptions. This statement turned out to be false. *B* was held liable in fraud because his agent (property manager) who knew the real facts had made a false statement.

[*Based on London County Freehold & Leasehold Properties Ltd.* v. *Bakerlay property & Insurance Co.* (1936) 2 All ER 1039]

4. *Notice to the agent is the notice to the principal:* The principal is bound by the notice given to his agent within the course of agency business. As a matter of fact, notice given to the agent in the course of the agency business has the same effect as if the notice has been given to the principal himself. *This means that the knowledge of the agent is the knowledge of the principal* [Section 229].

Example 18.13. *A* was the agent of an insurance company. *B* took out a policy with the insurance company against accidental injury. The proposal form contained a declaration that the proposer did not suffer from any physical infirmity. At the time of proposal, *B* was blind in one eye and this fact was known to *A*, the agent of the insurance company. *B* was illiterate and *A* filled in the form without disclosing *B*'s infirmity. It was held that the policy was valid and *B* could recover the full amount from the insurance company. In this case, the company was bound by the knowledge of the agent. [*Bawden* v. *London Ins. Co.* (1892) 2 QB 534].

5. *Principal inducing belief that his agent's unauthorised acts are authorised:* Sometimes, the principal induces the third party to believe that the agent has the authority to do certain acts, but in fact, the agent does not have any such authority. In such cases, the principal is bound by those acts of his agent[Section 237]. Thus, the principal is liable for the unauthorised acts of the agent, if the principal, by his conduct, has created an impression on the third party that the agent has the authority to do such acts. This, in fact, covers the case of 'estoppel' and 'ostensible authority'.

Note: Where the agent acts on behalf of a disclosed principal, his acts are treated as the acts of the principal. And the principal is bound by such acts of his agent. The agent can neither sue nor he sued upon a contract made by him on behalf of his principal. The reason for the same is that , such a contract is, in fact the contract of the principal and not that of the agent.

18.8. PRINCIPAL'S RELATIONS WHERE THE AGENT CONTRACTS FOR AN UNNAMED PRINCIPAL

Sometimes, the agent contracts with third parties after disclosing the fact, that he is an agent but without disclosing the name of his principal. In such cases also, the principal is bound by the contracts made on his behalf. And thus, the principal is liable to third parties for his agent's acts done on behalf of the principal. However, such acts must be within the scope of agent's authority, and the unnamed principal must be in existence at the time of contract. As a matter of fact, when the agent contracts after disclosing his representative character, the contract will be the contract of the principal, For all such acts, the agent is not personally liable unless there is something which shows that he intended to be personally liable.

Example 18.14. *A* appointed *B* as his agent for the purchase of some goods. *B* entered into an agreement with *C* for the purchase of those goods. *B* signed the agreement as a broker 'to my principal', but did not disclose the name of the principal, In this case, *B* is not personally liable as he contracted in the capacity of an agent.

However, the agent is personally liable if he declines to disclose the identity of the principal when asked by the third parties.

18.9. PRINCIPAL'S RELATIONS WHERE THE AGENT CONTRACTS FOR AN UNDISCLOSED PRINCIPAL

1. *Position of the agent*
2. *Position of the third party*
3. *Position of the principal*

Sometimes, the agent contracts with a third party without disclosing the name and existence of the principal. In such cases, the relationship between the principal, agent and the third party may be discussed as under:

1. ***Position of the agent:*** Since the agent has contracted in his own name, he is bound by the contract, and is personally liable to the third party. He my be sued, on the contract, by the third party. And he also has the right to sue the third party. In such cases, the relation between the principal and his agent are not affected, or in other words, they have their respective rights or duties against each other.

2. ***Position of the third party:*** On discovering the fact that there is a principal, the third party may file a suit either against the principal or his agent or both. If the third party decides to file a suit against the principal, he must allow the principal the benefit of all payments received by him (third party) from the agent.

Example 18.15. *A* an agent, without disclosing his principal, entered into an agreement with *B* to purchase 10 tins of ghee at the rate of Rs. 300 per tin. *A* paid Rs. 500 to *B* as advance money. On due date, *A* refused to take the delivery of the tins. Afterwards, *B* discovered that *A* was acting as an agent of *C*. In this case, *B* may file a suit against the principal (*C*) for the performance of the contract. But he must account for Rs. 500 which were received from his agent as the advance money.

Example 18.16. *A* sold 100 bales of cotton to *B* on credit. Afterwards, *A* discovered that *B* was acting as an agent of C., In this case, *A* may sue either *B* or C, or both for the performance of the contract.

Note: However, once the third party sues the agent alone, then he cannot sue the principal later on (Section 234).

3. ***Position of the principal:*** The principal also has the right to intervene and require the performance of the contract from the third party, However, the principal can obtain the performance only subject to the rights and obligations subsisting between the agent and the third party to the contract. In other words, the third party is entitled to be placed in the same situation as if the agent had been the contracting party. Thus, the third party is not put to any disadvantage by the intervention of the principal.

Example 18.17. *A* entered into a contract with *B*, a shopkeeper, for the purchase of furniture. *A* advanced a part payment of the price to *B*. Afterwards, *A* discovered that *B* is the agent of C. In this case C may ask, *A* to perform the contract. But he must account for the advance money received by his agent (*B*).

It may, however, be noted that if the principal discloses himself before the contract is completed, the third party may refuse to fulfil the contract. This is possible only if the third party can prove that if he had known about the principal or if he had known that the agent was not a principal, he would not have entered into the contract (Section 231). Moreover, the identity of the principal must be so material that the third party would not have entered into a contract had the identity of the principal been known to him.

Note: An undisclosed principal cannot intervene if some express or implied term or the contract excludes him from doing so.

18.10. PERSONAL LIABILITY OF AN AGENT

1. *The agent acting for a foreign principal*
2. *The agent acting for on undisclosed principal*
3. *The agent acting for an incompetent principal*
4. *The agent acting for a non-existing principal*
5. *The agent having an interest in the subject-matter of the contract*
6. *The agent receiving or paying money by mistake or fraud*
7. *Personal liability by agreement*
8. *Personal liability under some customs or usage of a trade*
9. *Exceeding authority*
10. *Pretended agent.*

We have already discussed that an agent is merely a connecting link between his principal and the third party. His main function is to establish contractual relationship between his principal and third parties. Thus, as a general rule, an agent cannot personally enforce the contract entered into by him on behalf of his principal, nor can he be personally held liable for such contracts [Section 230] However, if the agent undertakes personal liability, then he may be held liable for such contracts. Sometimes, an agent is also presumed to have contracted to be personally liable.

In the following circumstances, it is presumed that the agent undertook the personal liability:

1. *The agent acting for a foreign principal:* Sometimes, an agent contracts for the sale or purchase of goods for a principal residing abroad . In such cases, it is presumed that the agent undertakes personal liability. Thus, in such a case if there is a breach of contract, the third party can hold the agent personally liable. However, the agent can exclude his personal liability by contracting in a manner which shows his intention was not to incur personal liability.

2. *The agent acting for on undisclosed principal:* We know that sometimes the agent contract without disclosing the name of his principal. In such cases also , there is a presumption that the agent undertakes personal liability. Thus, where the agent acts in his own name, he is personally liable to the third party. But where the agent discloses his representative character, or the third party knows that he is acting as an agent of another, then the agent is not personally liable.

3. *The agent acting for an incompetent principal:* Sometimes, the agent contracts for a principal who is not competent to contract, such as minors or persons of unsound mind. In such cases, the agent is personally liable on the contract. It may be noted that, in such a case, the agent is personally liable even if he has disclosed the name of his principal.

4. *The agent acting for a non-existing principal:* Sometimes, the agent contracts for a principal who is fictitious or non-existent. In such cases, the agent is personally liable on the contracts, *e.g.*, the promoters, contracting on behalf of the company, which is yet to be incorporated, are personally liable.

5. *The agent having an interest in the subject-matter of the contract:* Sometimes, an agent has an interest in the subject matter of the contract. In such cases, the agent is personally liable to the extent of his interest in the contract. He can also enforce the contract to the extent of his own interest. As a matter of fact, the agent is the principal for his own interest in the subject matter of the contract. In such cases, his authority is said to be 'coupled with his interest.

6. *The agent receiving or paying money by mistake or fraud:* Sometimes, an agent receives some money from a third person by mistake or fraud. In such cases , he is personally liable to the third person for the refund of such money. Similarly, where an agent pays some money under a mistake or fraud, he has the right to recover it back from the persons to whom it has been paid.

7. *Personal liability by agreement:* Sometimes, at the time of entering into contract with a third party, it is expressly agreed that the agent shall be personally liable for the contract. In such cases, the agent incurs personal liability.

8. *Personal liability under some customs or usage of a trade:* Sometimes, the customs or usage of a particular trade provide that the agent shall also be personally liable for his acts. In such cases, the agent incurs a personal liability.

9. *Exceeding authority:* Sometimes, the agent contracts without having any authority or by exceeding his authority. In such cases, the agent is liable to the third party for any loss caused to him by reason of acting on false representation.

10. *Pretended agent:* The 'pretended agent' is an agent who pretends to act as the agent of another. In other words, he is a person who is falsely representing himself to be an authorised agent of another person. If the pretended agent induces third person to enter into a contract with him as such an agent, then he is personally liable to the third person for the loss of damage incurred due to such dealing [Section 235]. However, if the principal ratifies the act of the agent then he will not be personally liable. Moreover, if the third person already knew about the truth, then also the agent is not personally liable.

Sometimes, a person enters into a contract in the character of an agent. But in reality, he is acting on his own account and not as an agent. In such cases, he cannot enforce the other party for the performance of such contract [Section 236].

Example 18.18. *A* represented himself to be an agent of *B* and entered into an agreement with *C* for the purchase of his (*C*'s) house. In reality, *A* was not acting as *B*'s agent. But he was acting on his own account. In this case, *A* cannot enforce the performance of the contract, *i.e.*, he cannot compel *C* to sell the house to him.

Note: in case of personal liability of the agent, the third party may hold either agent or principal, or both liable. In other words, the third party has to choose between the liability of the agent, or the principal or both. But the choice once made in final.

LEGAL PROVISIONS (SECTIONS) DISCUSSED IN THE CHAPTER

Important legal provisions (section) of the Indian Contract Act 1872, discussed in this chapter are reproduced hereunder for ready reference.

1. ***Section 188: Extent of Agent,s Authority***

   An agent having an authority to do an act, has authority to do every lawful thing which is necessary in order to do such act.

   An agent having an authority to carry on a business, has authority to do every lawful thing necessary for the purpose, or usually done in the course of conducting such busines.

2. ***Section 189: Agent's Authority in Emergencey***

   An agent has authority, in an emargency, to do all such acts for the prupose of protecting his principal form loss as would be done by a person of ordinary produence, in his own case, under similar circumstances.

3. ***Section 226: Enforcement and consequences of agent's contracts.***

   Contracts entered into through an agent, and obligations arising from acts done by an agent, may be enforced in the same manner, and will have the same legal consequences as if the contracts had been entered into and the acts done by the principal in person.

4. ***Section 227: Principal how for bound, when agent exceeds authority***

   When an agent does more than he is authorised to do, and when the part of what he does, which is within authority, can be separated from the part which is beyond his authority, so much only of what he does as is within his authority is binding as between him and his principal.

5. ***Section 228: Principal not bound when excess of agent's authority is not separable.***

Where an agent does more than he is authroized to do, and what he does beyond the scope of his authority cannot be separated form what is within it, the principal is not bound to recognize the transaction.

6. ***Section 230: Agent cannot personally enforce, nor be bound by, contracts on behalf of principal.***

In the absence of any contract to that effect an agent cannot personally enforce contracts entered into by him on behalf of his principal, nor is he personally bound by them.

Presumption of contract to contrary.—Such a contract shall be presumed to exist in the following cases:

(1) where the contract is made by an agent for the sale or purchase of goods for a merchant resident abroad;

(2) where the agent does not disclose the name of his principal;

(3) where the principal, though disclosed, cannot be sued.

TEST QUESTIONS

1. What do you mean by agent's authority? What is the difference between 'actual authority' and ostensible authority? State the scope and extent of agent's authority.
2. State the legal relation between the principal, agent and third party, in the following cases, where the agent contracts for a named principal:
   (*a*) When the agent acts within the scope of his authority.
   (*b*) When the agent acts beyond his authority.
   (*c*) When the agent is guilty of fraud or misrepresentation.

   Is there any difference when the agent contracts without disclosing the name of his principal?
3. Discuss the liability of a principal when the agent exceeds his authority.
4. Explain the effects of a contract made by an agent with a third party (*a*) when the agent discloses the existence but not the name of the principal, (*b*) when the agent does not disclose even the name of the principal.
5. What do you mean by an 'undisclosed principal'? State the legal relationship between the principal, agent and third party when the agent contracts for an undisclosed principal.
6. "The agent is merely a connecting link between his principal and third party, and does not incur any personal liability"– comment stating the the circumstances in which an agent can be held personally liable.
7. State the rules relating to the personal liability for an agent for a contract entered into by him on behalf of his principal.
8. "The agent is personally liable only when he undertakes to be so liable"— comment stating the circumstances in which the agent is presumed to have made a contract to incur personal liability.

MULTIPLE CHOICE QUESTIONS

1. A power of attorney executed by several persons jointly in favour of one person, is valid.
   (*a*) True, as there can be more than one principals of one agent.
   (*b*) False, as there can be only one principal of one agent at a time.
2. Where one person allows another person to assume an appearance of authority to act on his behalf, such a position is known as
   (a) Express authority (*b*) Implied authority
   (*c*) Ostensible authority (*d*) None of these.
3. Which of the following statements is not true?
   (*a*) Principal is liable for fraud committed by his agent acting in the course of his business.
   (*b*) Principal is bound by agent's acts done in the scope of his authority.

(*c*) Authority given to sell goods also authorises the agent to borrow money and pledge the goods.
(*d*) Authority given to borrow money makes the principal liable even if agent borrows beyond authorised limits.

4. Where the agent contract with a third party without disclosing name and existence of his principal, in such a case on knowing about the principal, the third party may file a suit against the
(*a*) principal alone (*b*) agent alone
(*c*) both of them jointly (*d*) either agent or principal or both.
5. Where the agent contracts for a principal who is not competent to contract, in such a case the agent is
(*a*) personally liable (*b*) not personally liable
(*c*) exceeding authority (*d*) none of these.

ANSWERS

1. (*a*) 2. (*c*) 3. (*c*) 4. (*d*) 5. (*a*)

OBJECTIVE TYPE QUESTIONS WITH REASONING

State with reasons whether the following statements are correct or incorrect.

1. The principal is bound by the acts of his agent only when the agent has an express authority to do those acts.
2. An ostensible authority which appears to be actual to others is expressly given to the agent at the time of his appointment.
3. The principal is liable for frauds of his agent.
4. The principal is liable for the unauthorised acts of his agent, if the principal by his conduct, leads the third party to reasonably believe that the agent has that authority.
5. An ostensible authority denotes no authority at all.
6. The principal is not liable for the acts of his agent where the agent contracts with the third parties without disclosing the name of his principal.
7. Where the agent contracts with third party without disclosing the name and existence of the principal, the contract is without authority and void.
8. A principal is known as an unnamed principal where the agent contracts with third parties without disclosing the name as well as the existence of the principal.
9. As a general rule, the agent is not personally liable for the contracts entered into by him on behalf of his principal.
10. A pretended agent is personally liable to the third party for the losses incurred due to his dealings.

ANSWERS

1. *Incorrect.* The principal is also bound by his agent's act which are done in the scope of implied authority.
2. *Incorrect.* An ostensible authority is not expressly given to the agent. It is simply an appearance of authority.
3. *Correct.* A fraud committed by an agent within the course of his business has the same effect as if it has been committed by the principal himself [Section 238].
4. *Correct.* In such cases, agent's acts fall under the category of ostensihle authority which cannot be denied by the principal.
5. *Correct.* It is simply an appearance of authority.
6. *Incorrect.* The disclosure of principal's name is not the requirement for his liability. The

requirement in such a case is that the agent's act must be within the scope of his authority, and the principal must be in existence at the time of contract.

7. *Incorrect.* In such a case the contract is valid and it is the option of the third party either to file suit against the principal or his agent or both.
8. *Incorrect.* Such a principal is known as an undisclosed principal.
9. *Correct.* The main function of the agent is not to be personally liable but to establish contractual relationship between his principal and third parties [Section 230].
10. *Correct.* The pretended agent falsely represents himself to be the authorised agent where in fact, he is not so [Section 235].

PRACTICAL PROBLEM

1. *A* employed *B* as a manager of his business. It was incidental to such a business that the bills of exchange should be drawn and accepted from time to time by the manager. However, *B* was expressly told not to draw and accept any bill of exchange, but he accepted some bills of exchange drawn upon *A*. On the date of maturity of the bills of exchange, *A* was sued upon the bill. Is *A* liable to pay amount due upon the bills ? Give reasons.
   Hint : Yes, *A* will be held liable to pay the amount of bills accepted by his agent on his behalf. In this case, the circumstances shows that keeping in view the nature of business, *B* had an ostensible authority to accept bills on behalf of his principal.
2. *A*, an old lady, consulted *B*, the clerk of a solicitor firm, as to how to improve the income of her two cottages. *B* advised her to dispose of the cottage and asked her to bring the title deeds of the property. *B* obtained *A*'s signatures on certain blank papers and converted these documents as sale deed to himself. Subsequently, *B* sold the property and misappropriated the money. Can the firm be held liable ? Give reasons.
   Hint : Yes, the firm is liable for the frand committed by their representative in the course of his employment. [Section 238]
3. *A* sold 10 tins of refined oil to *B* on credit, afterwards *A* discovered that *B* was acting as agent of *C*. Can *A* recovery the price from *C* ? Give reasons.
   Hint: Yes, *A* can recover the price from *C*. In this case, the agent has acted without disclosing his principal. In such cases, the third party may either sue the agent or the principal for the price. [Section 234]
4. *A* represented himself to be the agent of *B* and entered into an agreement with *C* for the purchase of his truck. In fact, *A* was not acting as *B*'s agent but was acting on his own account. On coming to know about reality, *C* refused to sell the truck. Can *A* compel *C* to sell the truck to him ? Give reasons.
   Hint : No, *A* cannot compel *C* to sell the truck to him. In those cases, where a person pretends to be an agent when he is not, then he cannot compel a third party for the enforcement of the contract. [Section 236]

19

CHAPTER

TERMINATION OF AGENCY

1. Introduction.
2. Termination of Agency by Act of the Parties.
3. Termination of Agency by Operation of Law.
4. Effectiveness of Termination.
5. Irrevocable Agency.

19.1. INTRODUCTION

The term 'termination of agency' may be defined as the end of the relationship of a principal and his agent. The legal provisions relating to the termination of agency are contained in Sections 201 to 210 of the Indian Contract Act, and may broadly be grouped under the following two heads:

1. Termination of agency by act of the parties.
2. Termination of agency by operation of law.

19.2. TERMINATION OF AGENCY BY ACT OF THE PARTIES

1. Agreement between the principal and agent
2. Revocation by the principal
3. Renunciation of agency business by the agent

The agency relationship may be terminated by the act of the parties (*i.e.*, principal or his agent). Following are the cases in which an agency is terminated by the act of the parties:

1. ***Agreement between the principal and agent:*** The agency may be terminated by the mutual agreement between the principal and his agent. As the parties (*i.e*, the principal and agent) are free to make an agreement on agency, they are also at liberty to put an end to it. It may be noted that the parties may agree to terminated the agency relationship at any time and at any stage.

Example 19.1. *A* appointed *B*, as his agent, for the purpose of buying 50 chairs for him in five equal instalments. *B* bought 10 chairs for *A*. Subsequently, *A* and *B* entered into an agreement putting an end to the agency relationship between them. In this case, the agency is terminated.

2. ***Revocation by the principal:*** The term 'revocation' may be defined as the cancellation. The principal may revoke the authority of his agent, and the revocation puts an end to the agency relationship. However, the principal can revoke his agent's authority before it has been exercised by the agent so as to bind the principal. The revocation may be express or implied.

Example 19.2. *A* authorised *B* an auctioneer, to sell his (*A*) goods by auction. In this case, *A* may revoke *B*'s authority to sell the goods at any time before the auction is completed by knocking down in favour of highest bidder.

Example 19.3. *A* empowered *B* to let out his (*A*'s) house. Afterwards, *A* himself let out his house. In this case, there is an implied revocation of *B*'s authority to let out the house.

The revocation of agent's authority by his principal is subject to the following conditions:

(*a*) Where the agent has partly exercised his authority, the principal may revoke the agency for further acts only. He remains bound by the acts already done prior to the revocation.

(*b*) Where the agency is created for a fixed period, the principal may revoke the agency before the expiry of the fixed period only if there is some sufficient cause for the same. If the principal revokes the agency without any sufficient cause, then he must make compensation to the agent for its premature termination.

(*c*) Where the agency is continuous (*i.e.,* for a number of acts), or for a fixed period, the principal must give to the agent, a reasonable notice of revocation of the agency. If such a notice is not given, the principal will be liable to compensate the agent for any loss suffered by him.

(*d*) Where the agent himself has some interest in the subject-matter of agency, the agency cannot be revoked unless there is an express contract permitting the termination of agency. This point will be discussed in detail in Art. 19.5

3. ***Renunciation of agency business by the agent :*** The term 'renunciation' may be defined as the giving up. The agent may renounce the business of agency in the same manner in which the principal has the right of revocation. And the renunciation puts an end to the agency relationship. The agent has been given this right to renounce the agency business because a person cannot be compelled to continue as agent against his will. The renunciation may be express or implied.

Example 19.4. *A* appointed *B* as his agent, for the purpose of selling his (*A*'s) house. Subsequently, *B* renounced the business of agency by tendering his resignation to *A*. In this case, the agency is terminated by express renunciation by the agent.

Sometimes, the agency is created for a fixed period, and the agent renounces the business before the expiry of fixed period. In such cases, the agent must make compensation to the principal for its premature termination. It may be noted that just like revocation by the principal, the agent can renounce the agency business after giving a reasonable notice to the principal. Otherwise, the agent will be liable to the principal for any loss suffered by him.

19.3. TERMINATION OF AGENCY BY OPERATION OF LAW

1. *Completion of agency business*
2. *Death or insanity of the pincipal or the agent*
3. *Insolvency of the principal*
4. *Expiry of time*
5. *Destruction of subject-matter of the agency*
6. *Subsequent event rendering the agency unlawful*

The agency relationship may also be terminated by the operation of law. Following are the cases in which an agency is terminated by the operation of law:

1. ***Completion of agency business:*** The agency relationship is automatically teminated on the completion of agency business. Thus, where an agency is for a single transaction, the agency comes to an end on the completion of the transaction.

2. ***Death or insanity of the pincipal or the agent:*** The agency relationship is automatically terminated when either the principal or his agent dies. Moreover, the agency is also automatically terminated when either the principal or his agent becomes of unsound mind (*i.e.,* insane).

Example 19.5. *A* authorised *B*, his agent, to borrow some money on his behalf. Before *B* borrowed the money, *A* died. In this case, the agency is automatically terminated and *B* has no authority to borrow the money.

Example 19.6. *A* authorised *B*, his agent, for the purpose of selling his furniture. Before the furniture could be sold, *B* died. In this case, the agency is automatically terminated.

3. *Insolvency of the principal:* An insolvent is a person who has been declared by the court as unable to pay his debts. The agency is terminated when the principal is declared as an insolvent. The reason for the same is that on the insolvency of a person, the insolvent is disqualified from entering into contract in respect of his property. It is to be noted that as regards the insolvency of the agent, nothing is mentioned in the Indian Contract Act. It is submitted that as an agent is merely a connecting link between the principal and the third party, the insolving of the agent may not terminate the agency. However, this question is not finally decided.

Note: The bankruptcy, *i.e.*, insolvency of the agent, except in the cases where the act which the agent is asked to do is merely formal, also terminates the agency (*In Re.* (1893) 1 Q.B. 455).

4. *Expiry of time:* Sometimes, the agency is created for a fixed time. In such cases, the agency is automatically terminated on the expiry of that time. In this case, it is immaterial whether the purpose of agency is fulfilled or not within that period.

5. *Destruction of subject-matter of the agency:* The agency is also terminated when the subject matter of the contract of agency is destroyed.

Example 19.7. *A* appointed *B* as his agent, for the purpose of purchasing a particular car. Before the purchase, the car was completely destroyed in an accidental fire. In this case, the agency is terminated and *B*'s authority to buy the car comes to an end.

6. *Subsequent event rendering the agency unlawful:* Sometimes, the agency is valid when it is created. But it becomes unlawful by the happening of some subsequent event, *e.g.*, where the agent and the principal reside in different countries and a war is declared between these two countries, Similarly, the agency may also be declared as unlawful by some Act of Legislature.

Example 19.8. *A*, wine merchant, appointed *B* as his agent for the purchase of liquor for him for one year. Subsequently, the distillation of the liquor was prohibited by an Act of Parliament and its sale and purchase was also banned In this case, *B*'s authority to purchase liquor comes to an end.

Note: The termination of the authority of an agent automatically puts an end to the authority of the sub-agent appointed by the agent (Section 210). It may, however, be noted that the authority of a substituted agent will not be affected by the termination of an agent's authority.

19.4. EFFECTIVENESS OF TERMINATION

The termination of agent's authority takes effect from the time when it comes to the knowledge of the agent or third person [Section 210]. Thus, the termination may be effective at different times as regards the agent and as regards the third persons, *i.e.*,

(*a*) As regards the agent, the termination takes effect from the time when the agent comes to know of the termination, and

(*b*) As regards the third person, the termination takes effect from the time when the third person come to know of the termination.

Thus, if an agent knowing that his authority has been terminated, enters into a contract with a third party who deals with him without any knowledge of termination of his authority, the contract will be binding on the principal.

Example 19.9. *A* of Madras authorised *B*, an agent of Bombay, to sell some cotton lying in a warehouse in Bombay, Afterwards, *A* revoked, by a letter, *B*'s authority to sell the cotton and directed him to send the cotton to Madras. After receiving the letter of revocation, *B* entered into a contract with *C* for the sale of the cotton to him. *C* did not know anything about the letter of revocation. *C* paid the price to *B* who misappropriated it. In this case, the payment made by *C* is good, and *A* cannot demand again the price from *C*.

It may also be noted that even when the agency is terminated by the death of the principal, the termination is effective only when it comes to the knowledge of the agent.

Example 19.10. *A* directed *B*, his agent, to pay certain money to *C*. Afterwards, *A* died. After *A*'s death, but before hearing of it, *B* paid the money to *C*. In this case, the payment made by *B* is good as against the legal representative of *A*.

19.5. IRREVOCABLE AGENCY

1. *Where the agency is coupled with interest*
2. *Where the agent has partly exercised his authority*
3. *Where the agent has incurred a personal liability*

The term 'irrevocable agency' may be defined as the agency which cannot be revoked (*i.e.*, put to an end) by the principal. The agency is irrevocable in the following cases:

1. *Where the agency is coupled with interest:* The 'agency coupled with interest' is an agency which is created for the purpose of securing some benefit to the agent. And it is irrevocable. This provision is contained in Section 202 of the Indian Contract Act, which reads as under :

"Where the agent has himself an interest in the property which forms the subject matter of agency, the agency cannot, in the absence of an express contract, be terminated to the prejudice of such interest."

Thus, when an agent has some interest in the subject-matter of agency, the agency is irrevocable. It cannot be terminated during the subsistence of agent's interest. It may be noted that an agency coupled with interest is not terminated even on the death or insanity of the principal. However, if there is an express agreement providing for the termination of the agency, it can be terminated.

Example 19.11. *A* owed some money to *B*. And *A* authorised *B* to sell his (*A*'s) land and adjust the debts due to him (*B*) out of the sale proceeds of the land. It is an agency coupled with interest and *A* cannot revoke *B*'s authority. Moreover, this authority is also not terminated on the death or insanity of the principal (*A*).

Example 19.12. *A* consigned 100 bales of cotton to *B*, who had already made some advances to *A* on such cotton. *A* authorised *B* to sell the cotton an adjust the amount of his own advance out of the sale proceeds of the cotton. It is an agency coupled with interest , and *A* cannot revoke *B*'s authority . Moreover, this authority is also not terminated on the death of insanity or the principal (*A*).

The following conditions must be fulfilled for the creation of an agency coupled with interest:

(*a*) The interest of the agent must be existing at the creation of agency.

(*b*) The primary object of giving authority to the agent must be to secure the interest of the agent.

(*c*) The interest of the agent must be substantial and not an ordinary. It must be over and above his remunerations as an agent.

Example 19.13. *A* delivered certain goods to *B*, an agent, to be sold on *A*'s behalf. Subsequently, *B* advanced a sum of money to *A*. Before the sale of goods, *A* ordered *B* not to sell the goods. However *B* sold the goods in order to secure his advance. *A* filed a suit against *B* on the ground that the goods were sold without any authority. *B* contended that the agency was coupled with interest and his authority could not be revoked. It was held that the agency was not coupled with interest as the agent's interest arose *after* the creation of agency. And, thus, *B* had no authority to sell the goods. [*Smart* v. *Sandars* (1848) 5 CB 895]

2. *Where the agent has partly exercised his authority:* The agency is also irrevocable where the agent has partly exercised his authority. This provision is contained in Section

204 of the Indian Contract Act, which provides that when the agent has already exercised some authority, the principle cannot revoke the agent's authority for the acts already done. And the principal is bound by the acts already done on his behalf.

Example 19.14. *A* authorised *B*, his agent, to pay out of *A*'s funds lying with him a sum of Rs. 10,000 to *C* in four equal instalments. Subsequently, *A* revoked *B*'s authority by a letter. Before the receipt of the letter, *B* had already paid one instalment of Rs. 2,500 to *C*. In this case, *A* is bound by this payment.

3. *Where the agent has incurred a personal liability*: Sometimes, the agent contracts in his own name and makes himself personally liable for his acts. In such cases, the agency becomes irrevocable. And the principal cannot revoke the agent's authority leaving the agent exposed to the risk and liability already incurred by him.

Example 19.15. *A* authorised *B* to buy 100 bales of cotton on account of *A*, and to pay for it out of *A*'s funds, lying with him (*B*) . *B* bought 100 bales of cotton in his own name so as to make himself personally liable for the price. In this case, *A* cannot revoke *B*'s authority as regards the payment for the cotton.

TEST QUESTIONS

1. Discuss briefly the different modes in which the agency can be terminated. When does the termination take effect?
2. State the modes of termination of agency by the act of the parties.
3. State the effect of death, insanity and insolvency of the principal and agent on the agency.
4. State the circumstances in which the principal remains liable for agent's acts done even after revocation of agent's authority.
5. When is an agency irrevocable?
6. What is an agency coupled with interest? When it can be revoked?
7. Write notes on (*a*) Termination of agency by operation of law. (*b*) Effectiveness of termination of agency. (*c*) Irrevocable agency.

MULTIPLE CHOICE QUESTIONS

1. In which of the following cases, agency is not terminated?
   (*a*) completion of agency business (*b*) death of principal or agent
   (*c*) insolvency of principal (*d*) agent exceeding given authority.
2. In case the principal revokes the agency, he
   (*a*) remains bound by agent's acts done prior to revocation.
   (*b*) is not bound by agent's acts done prior to revocation.
   (*c*) is bound by agent's subsequent acts also.
   (*d*) liable to punishment as revocation is illegal.
3. The third party, who contracts with an agent without any knowledge of termination of agent's authority, can enforce the contract against the principal.
   (*a*) True (*b*) False.
4. Which of the following agency is irrevocable?
   (*a*) Agency for fixed period (*b*) Agency for single transaction
   (*c*) Agency coupled with interest (*d*) Continuing agency.

ANSWERS

1. (*d*) **2.** (*a*) **3.** (*a*) **4.** (*c*)

OBJECTIVE TYPE QUESTIONS WITH REASONING

State with reasons whether the following statements are correct or incorrect.

1. An agency once created cannot be terminated.
2. The principal along can revoke the authority given to the agent without obtaining the agent's consent.
3. Where the agent has partly exercised his authority, the principal cannot revoke the agency even for further acts.
4. Where the agency is for a fixed period, the principal cannot rveoke the agency before the expiry of the fixed period.
5. The agency can also be terminated by the agent alone by renunciation of the agency business.
6. An agency coupled with interest is irrevocable.
7. An agency coupled with interest is not terminated even on the death or insanity of the principal.
8. An agency for a single transaction is automatically terminated on the completion of the transaction.
9. Generally, an agency is terminated on the death of the principal or agent.
10. The termination of agency has an immediate effect and the principal incurs no liability to the third party from the date of termination.

ANSWERS

1. *Incorrect.* An agency is terminable by an act of the principal or agent, or by operation of law.
2. *Correct.* It is the principal's legal right to cancel agent's authority. However , he can revoked his agent's authority before it has been exercised by the agent so as to bind the principal, and after giving a reasonable notice to the agent.
3. *Incorrect.* In such a case, the principal can revoke the agency for further acts only[Section 204].
4. *Incorrect.* In such a case, principal can revoke the agency before the expiry of fixed period if there is some sufficient cause for the same [Section 205].
5. *Correct.* It is agent's right to terminate the agency by renunciation. A person cannot be compelled to continue as an agent against his will [Section 201].
6. *Correct.* In such an agency, the agent has some interest in the subject-matter, and the revocation will adversely affect his interest [Section 202].
7. *Correct.* It is the legal position on the point.
8. *Correct.* In such a case, the agency is terminated by the operation of law [Section 201].
9. *Correct.* In such a case, the agency is terminated by the operation of law [Section 201].
10. *Incorrect.* The termination is effective against the third party only from the time when the third party comes to know of the termination [Section 208].

PRACTICAL PROBLEMS

1. *A* authorised *B* to sell certain goods on his behalf. *B* started negotiations, for the sale of the goods, with *C* but before the transaction was concluded, *A* became insolvent. How the agency relationship is affected on A's insolvency ?

   Hint : The agency is terminated on the insolvency of principal (*A*) as an insolvent is disqualified from entering into contract in respect of his property.
2. *A* authorised *B*, an agent, to sell goods for him and agreed to pay 5% commission to *B* on

the price of the goods sold, Afterwards, *A* revoked *B*'s authority by writing a letter. After the letter was posted but before *B* received the same, *B* sold the goods to *C* for Rs. 20,000. Decide:

(a) Whether the sale is binding on *A*?

(b) Whether *B* is entitled to the commission ?

Hint : (a) Yes, the sale is binding on *A*. The termination is effective against the agent only when it comes to the knowledge of the agent.
[Section 208]

(b) Yes, *B* is entitled to his commission as transaction is valid, and is the result of agent's efforts.

3. *A* borrowed some money from *B*, a money lender, and authorised him to collect the rent of *A*'s commercial building and appropriate the same towards money due to him till the entire amount of loan is adjusted. Subsequently, *A* revoked the agency *i.e.* authority given to *B*. Is the revocation justified ? Give reasons and the legal provision applicable to the case.

Hint : No, the revocation is not justified. In this case, it is an agency coupled with interest and it is irrevocable under Section 202 of the Indian Contract Act.

4. *A* of Chandigarh authorised *B* of Delhi to sell 100 bales of cotton lying in his (*A*'s) godown at Delhi. Subsequently, *A* revoked *B*'s authority by a letter, but before the letter is received by *B*, he had already sold 10 bales of cotton to *C*. Is this sale binding on *A*? If yes, then does it also entitle *B* to receive commission for the 10 bales of cotton sold by him ?

Hint : Yes, the sale is binding on *A* as the agency is irrevocable as regards partly exercised authority [Section 204]. The agent in also entitled to the commission on the goods sold as per the terms of agency.

THE SALE OF GOODS ACT, 1930

- Nature of Contract of Sale
- Conditions and Warranties
- Transfer of Ownership (Passing of Property)
- Performance of Contract of Sale
- Rights of an Unpaid Seller
- Auction Sale

20

CHAPTER

NATURE OF CONTRACT OF SALE

20.1. INTRODUCTION

The sale of goods is a common transaction of all commercial contracts. Earlier the legal provisions relating to the contract of sale were contained in Sections 76 to 123 of the Indian Contract Act, 1872. However, as a result of the developments of modern commerce, certain amendments were required in these provisions. To suit these developments, in the modern commerce, Sections 76 to 123 of the Indian contract Act were repealed. And a new Act know as THE SALE OF GOODS ACT 1930 was passed in 1930 for the exclusive contracts dealing with the sale of only movable goods. This Act does not deal with the sale of immovable property. The transactions relating to immovable properties, *e.g.*, the sale, lease, gifts, etc., are governed by a separate Act known as 'Transfer of Property Act, 1882'. This Act is beyond the scope of this book.

The Sale of Goods Act came into force on 1st day of July 1930, and it extends to the whole of India except the state of Jammu and Kashmir. Now all the legal provisions relating to the sale of movable goods are contained in the Sale of Goods Act, 1930.

Note: In our discussion on the Law of Sale of Goods from chapters 20 to 25, unless otherwise stated, the Section mentioned are those of the Sale of Goods Act, 1930.

20.2. DEFINITION OF CONTRACT OF SALE

It is a contract by which the ownership of movable goods is transferred from the seller to the buyer. The term 'contract of sale' is defined in Section 4 (1) of the Sale of Goods Act, which reads as under:

"A contract of sale of goods is a contract whereby the seller transfers or agrees to transfer the

property in the goods to the buyer for a price."

The analysis of this section reveals that a contract to transfer property in the goods (*i.e.,* legal ownership of the goods) is know as a contract of sale. The ownership of the goods is transferred from the seller to the buyer for a price. Thus, the following parties are always involved in a contract of sale:

1. *Seller:* A person who sells or agrees to sell the goods, is known as seller [Section 2 (13)]

2. *Buyer:* A person who buys or agrees to by the goods is known as buyer [Section 2(1)].

It is to be noted that section 4(1) defined the contract of sale in a wider terms. It includes both 'sale' as well as an 'agreement to sell[1]'

20.3. SALE

In this case, the ownership of the goods is immediately transferred from a seller to a buyer. The term 'sale' is defined in Section 4(3) of the Sale of Goods Act, which reads as under :

"Were under a contract of sale the property in the goods is transferred from the seller to the buyer, the contract is called a sale."

The analysis of this section reveals that where the property in the goods (*i.e.,* legal ownership of the goods) is immediately transferred to the buyer, the contract of sale is called sale.

Example 20.1. *A* agreed to buy a haystake from *B* lying on *B*'s land. *A* was given the liberty to come on *B*'s land and to take away the haystake. This is a sale.

[*Wood* v. *Manley* (1839) 11 A & E 34,52 RR 271]

20.4. AGREEMENT TO SELL

In this case, the ownership of the goods is not immediately transferred from a seller to a buyer. But it transfers at some future date. The 'agreement to sell' is also defined in Section 4(3) of the Sale of Goods Act, which reads as under;

"Where under a contract of sale the transfer of property in the goods is to take place at a future time or subject to some condition thereafter to be fulfilled, the contract is called an agreement to sell."

The analysis of this section reveals that where the property in the goods (*i.e.,* legal ownership of the goods) is to be transferred to the buyer at some future date or on the fulfillment of a certain condition, the contract of sale is called an 'agreement to sell'.

Example 20.2. *A* agreed to buy from *B* a certain quantity of nitrate of soda. The ship, carrying the nitrate of soda, was yet to arrive. This is an 'agreement to sell'. In this case, the ownership of nitrate of soda is to be transferred to *A* on the arrival of the ship containing the specified goods (*i.e.* nitrate of soda). [*Johnson v. Mcdonald* (1842) 9 M & W 600, 60 RR 838]

Thus, the sale is different from an agreement to sell. An agreement to sell becomes a sale only when the ownership of the goods is transferred to the buyer. Section 4(4) of the Sale of Goods Act provides the time at which an agreement to sell becomes a sale. As per the section:

1. Where an agreement to sell provides that the ownership of the goods shall be transferred at some future date, it becomes sale when that date arrives, and
2. Where the ownership of the goods is to be transferred on the fulfillment of

1. Agreement to sell is also sometimes referred as an 'agreement to buy'.

some conditions, the agreement to sell becomes sale when those conditions are fulfilled.

Example 20.3. On 1st March 1998, *A* agreed to sell his car to *B* for Rs. 80,000. It was agreed between themselves that the ownership of the car will transfer to *B* on 31st March 1998 when the car is got registered in *B*'s name. It is an agreement to sell, and it will become sale on 31st March 1998 when the car is registered in the name of *B*.

20.5. DISTINCTION BETWEEN SALE AND AN AGREEMENT TO SELL

The following table gives the distinction between 'sale' and an 'agreement to sell':

S.No.	*Sale*	*Agreement to Sell*
1.	The ownership of the goods is transfered to the buyer immediately.	The ownership of the goods is transferred to the buyer at some future date.
2.	It is an executed contract as all the form alities of the contract are completed, and the buyer becomes the owner immediately.	It is an executory contract as all the formalities of the contract are not completed but something remains to be done, *e.g.*, the ownership passes to the buyer at a future date.
3.	The buyer is responsible for any loss or destruction of the goods even if the goods are in the possession of the seller. The seller is not responsible for such loss becausehe ceases to be the owner immediately on the completion of sale.	The seller is responsible for any loss or destruction of goods even if the goods are in the possession of the buyer. The buyer is not responsible for such loss because the seller remains the owner until the 'agreement to sell' becomes a sale.
4.	If the seller refuses to deliver the goods, the buyer may recover the goods from the seller by filing a suit in the Court of Law.	If the seller refuses to deliver the goods, the buyer cannot recover the goods from the seller. He can only recover damages from the seller by filing a suit in the Court of Law.
5.	If the buyer refuses to pay the price, the seller may recover it by filing a suit in the Court of Law.	If the buyer refuses to pay the price, the seller cannot recover it. He can only recover damages from the buyer by filling a suit in the Court of Law.
6.	Sometimes, the possession of the goods sold remains with the seller. In such cases, the seller cannot resell the goods to a third person. If he does so, he is guilty of breach of contract, and theoriginal buyer can claim damages from the seller. Moreover, the original buyer can also recover the goods from the new buyer if he (new buyer) does not act in *good faith* and knows about the original sale. However, if the new buyer acts in*good faith* and without the knowledge of original sale, the original buyer cannot recover the goods from him.	Generally, the possession of the goods sold remains with the seller. But in this case also, the seller cannot resell the goods to a third person. If he does so, he is guilty of breach of contract and the original buyer can claim damages from the seller. But the original buyer cannot recover the goods from the new buyer even if he (new buyer) does not act in good faith and knew about the original sale.
7.	Sometimes, the possession of the goods is still with the seller, and the buyerbecomes insolvent, before paying for the goods. In such cases, in the ab-	Sometimes, the possession of the goods is still with the seller, and the buyer becomes insolvent before paying for the goods. In such cases, the seller may refuse to deliver the

	sence of seller's right of lien, the seller must deliver the goods to the Receiver or Official Assignee.[2] The seller can claim only rateable dividend, in the insolvency, for the price of the goods.	goods to the Receiver or Official Assignee until he is paid the full price of the goods.
8.	Sometimes the seller, who is still in possession of goods, becomes insolvent and the goods are taken from him by the Receiver or Official Assignee. In such cases, the buyer, who has paid for the price, is entitled to recover the goods from the Receiver or Official Assignee, as he is the owner of the goods.	Sometimes, the seller, who is still in possession of the goods, become insolvent and the goods are taken from him by the Receiver or Official Assignee. In such cases, the buyer cannot recover the goods from the Receiver or Official Assignee even if the price has been paid by him, as he is not the price has been paid by him, as he is not the owner of the goods.
9.	It creates *jus in rem, i.e.,* right against the world at large. This means that the buyer gets the rights against anybody who disturbs his right to use the goods.	It creates *jus in personam, i.e.,* the right against the particular person. This means that the buyer gets the rights against the seller only.

20.6. ESSENTIALS OF A VALID CONTRACT OF SALE

1. *All the requirements of a valid contract must be fulfilled*
2. *There must be two parties to the contract of sale*
3. *There must be some goods as a subject-matter*
4. *The property in the goods must be transferred to the buyer*
5. *There must be some price for the goods*

The legal definition of the term 'contract of sale', as discussed above, reveals certain essential elements of a contract of sale. These are discussed as under, and are necessary for a valid contract of sale:

1. *All the requirements of a valid contract must be fulfilled:* It is an important and essential element of a contract of sale. According to this, a contract of sale must fulfil all the requirements of a valid contract, *e.g.,* free consent, consideration, competency of the parties, lawful object and consideration. If any of the essential elements of a valid contract is missing, then the contract of sale will not be vaild.

Example 20.4. *A* agreed to sell certain furniture to *B* without any consideration. This contract of sale is not valid as it is made without consideration. Similarly, an agreement to sell smuggled gold is not valid as its consideration is unlawful.

2. *There must be two parties to the contract of sale:* It is another essential element of a contract of sale that there must be two parties, one seller and the other buyer. The reason for the same is that in a contract of sale the ownership of the goods has to pass from one person to another. Thus, the seller and the buyer must be different person as one person cannot be both, the seller and the buyer.

Example 20.5. *A, B* and *C* were partners in a firm. After sometime, the firm was dissolved. And on the dissolution, the surplus assets including some goods were divided among all the three partners. It was held that the distribution of assets and goods among the partners was not a sale.

2. Receiver or official Assignee is an official appointed by the court in insolvency proceedings to take charge of insolvent's property.

The court observed that the partners were the joint owners of the goods, and they could not be both seller and buyer. [*State of Gujarat* v. *Raman Lal & Co.*, AIR 1965 Guj 60]

3. *There must be some goods as a subject-matter:* It is also an essential element of a contract of sale that the subject matter of the contract must be some goods. The term 'goods' is defined in Section 2(7) of the Sale of Goods Act. According to this section, goods means every kind of movable property and it includes (*a*) stock and share, (*b*) growing crops, grass, (*c*) the things attached to or forming a part of the land which can be severed from the land.

Example 20.6. *A* agreed to sell to *B* his wheat crop which is grown in his (*A*'s) field. They agreed that upon the payment of the price, *B* may cut the crop and take it away. It is a valid contract of sale as the growing crop is included in the term 'goods' and can be validly sold.

It may, however, be noted that the term 'goods' does not include 'immovable property'. And, thus, the Sale of Goods Act does not apply to immovable property, Moreover, the 'money' and 'actionable claims' are also not included in the term 'goods'.

Note: The 'actionable claims' means a claim which can be enforced through the Courts of Law, *e.g.*, a debt due from one person to another is an actionable claim. This also, cannot be the subject-matter of sale.

4. *The property in the goods must be transferred to the buyer:* The term 'property' in the goods means the ownership of the goods. In every contract of sale, the ownership of the goods must be transferred by the seller to the buyer, or there should be an agreement by the seller to transfer the ownership to the buyer. The term 'property' here means the general property, i.e., all ownership right of the goods, and not merely a special property, *i.e.*, limited right such as right of a pawnee. However, the physical delivery of the goods is not essential. If the title in the goods (*i.e.*, all the ownership rights) has been transferred to the buyer , it will be a valid contract of sale.

Example 20.7. *A* agreed to buy a new motor cycle from *B*, a dealer, for Rs. 20,000. *A* paid the price and the motor cycle was got registered in his name. *B* delivered the registration book (title of the motor cycle) to *A*. This is a valid contract of sale as the ownership of the motor cycle has been transferred to the buyer (*A*).

5. *There must be some price for the goods:* It is also an essential element of a contract of sale. According to this element, the goods must be sold for some price. The price is the money consideration for a contract of sale [Section 2(10)]. Where the ownership of the goods is transferred for any consideration other than the money, that will not be a sale but a 'barter' or 'exchange', *e.g.*, where the goods are exchanged for goods, it is not a sale but barter. It may, however, be noted that the consideration, may be partly in cash and partly in terms of *valued up goods* (*i.e.*, the goods, the price of which can be definitely measured in terms of money).

Example 20.8. *A* delivered to *B* 52 bullocks valued of Rs. 1,000 per bullock. In exchange of it, *B* delivered to *A* 100 quintals of barley valued as Rs. 300 per quintal an paid the difference in cash. This is a contract of sale. [Based on Aldridge v. *Johnson* (1857) 7 E & B 885]

Similarly, where an old car is returned to the dealer for a new one and the difference is paid in cash, that should also be a sale.

20.7. MODES AND FORM OF CONTRACT OF SALE

A contract of sale may be made in any way as provided in the Sales of Goods Act. The modes of making a contract of sale are provided in Section 5(1) of the Sales of Goods Act. According to this section, a contract of sale is made by an offer to buy or sell by one person, and the acceptance of such offer by another person. And it may be made in any one of the following modes:

1. There may be immediate delivery of goods, but the price to be paid at some future date.

2. There may be immediate payment of price, but the delivery to be made at some future date.
3. There may be immediate payment of price and the immediate delivery of goods.
4. The price and delivery of the goods may be postponed.
5. The price and delivery of the goods may be agreed to be made in instalments.

It may be noted that no particular form is necessary for the making of a contract of sale. It may be in any form, *e.g.*, a contract of sale may be made (*a*) in writing, or (*b*) by words of mouth, or (*c*) partly in writing and partly by words of mouth, or (*d*) may be implied from the conduct of the parties. However, if any particular mode is prescribed by any law, then the contract of sale must be made in that particular mode [Section 5(2)].

20.8. GOODS: THE SUBJECT–MATTER OF CONTRACT OF SALE

The term 'subject matter' means the things for which a contract of sale can be made. Only the goods can be the subject-matter of contract of sale. The term 'goods' means every kind of movable property, and includes (*a*) stock and shares, (*b*) growing crops, grass, (*c*) the things attached to or forming part of the land which can be severed (*i.e.*, separated) from the land. It may, however, be noted that the things attached to or forming part of the land may be the subject matter of the contract of sale only if it is agreed that they shall be removed from the earth,, *e.g.*, standing crops or trees may be sold if agreed to be removed from the earth. The Supreme Court has also held that standing trees may be sold as goods if they shall be removed within a reasonable time.

[*State of M.P.* v. *Oriental Paper Mills* (1977) 2 SCC 86]

However, the term 'goods' does not include the 'money' and 'actionable claims'. The term 'money' here means the legal tender (i.e, currency) and not old coins . And the term "actionable claim' means a claim which can be enforced through the Courts of Law, *e.g.*, debt due from one person to another is an actionable claim, and cannot be the subject-matter of contract of sale.

20.9. CLASSIFICATION OF GOODS

1. *Existing goods*
2. *Future goods*
3. *Contingent goods*

The goods forming subject-matter of the contract of sale may be classified as under: (1) Existing goods, (2) Future goods. (3) Contingent goods.

1. ***Existing goods:*** These are the goods which are in actual existence at the time of contract of sale, and the seller is either the owner of such goods or he has the possession of such goods. In case of sale by a mercantile agent or pledgee, the goods are in the possession of the seller (*i.e.*, mercantile agent or pledgee), but he is not the owner . The existing goods may be of the following three types:

(*a*) ***Specific goods:*** These are the goods which have been actually identified and agreed by the parties at the time of contract of sale [Section 2 (14)].

(*b*) ***Unascertained goods:*** The goods which are not specifically identified at the time of contract of sale, are known as unascertained goods. At the time of contract, such goods are described by description or sample only.

(*c*) ***Ascertained goods:*** The goods which are identified only after the formation of the contract of sale, are known as ascertained goods. As a matter of fact, when the 'unascertained goods' are identified and agreed upon by the parties, the goods are called the 'ascertained goods'.

Example 20.9. *A* had five cars of different make. He agreed to sell his 'fait' car to *B*, and *B* agreed to purchase the same car. In this case, the sale is for specific goods as the car has been identified and agreed at the time of the contract of sale.

Example 20.10. *A* had ten horses. He agreed to sell one horse to *B*. In this case, the contract is for the sale of unascertained goods as the horse has not been identified at the time of contract of sale.

Example 20. 11. *A* had 100 bales of cotton lying in his godown. He agreed to sell 50 bales of cotton to *B*, who agreed to purchase the same. After the making of the contract, the cotton bales to be delivered to *B* were identified and kept separate by *A*, and *B* agreed to take the delivery of the same. In this case, the contract is for the sale of ascertained goods, as the cotton bales to be sold are identified and agreed after the formation of the contract. It may be noted that before the ascertainment of the goods, the contract was for the sale of unascertained goods.

2. *Future goods:* These are the goods which are not in existence at the time of contract of sale. The seller acquires such goods after the making of the contract of sale. Thus, the future goods are those which are to be acquired or produce by the seller after the contract of sale is made [Section 2(6)]. A contract for the sale of future goods is an 'agreement to sell' and not 'sale' [Section 6(3)].

Example 20.12. *A*, a manufacturer of table fans, contracted to sell 100 fans to *B* at the rate of Rs. 400 per fan. *B* agreed to purchase the fans. However, the fans were yet to be manufactured by *A*. This is an agreement to sell and not sale.

3. *Contingent goods*: These are the goods which are also not in existence at the time of contract of sale. The contingent goods are a type of future goods. In this case, the acquisition of the goods by the seller depends upon the uncertain contingencies, *i.e.*, upon uncertain events which may or may not happen.

Example 20.13. *A* agreed to sell to B certain goods which are to be arrived by a ship. In this case, the contract is for the sale of contingent goods as the availability of the goods depends upon the arrival of the ship.

20.10. EFFECTS OF DESTRUCTION OF SUBJECT-MATTER

> 1. ***Goods perishing before making of the contract***
> 2. ***Goods perishing after an agreement to sell but before the sale is completed***

The effects of destruction of the subject-matter may be discussed under the following two heads:

(*a*) Goods perishing before making of the contract.

(*b*) Goods perishing after agreement to sell, but before the sale is completed.

1. *Goods perishing before making of the contract [Section 7]:* Sometimes, the goods have already been perished before making of the contract of sale. In such cases, the contract of sale is void if the contract is for the sale of *specific goods*, and the seller had no knowledge of the perishing of the goods. The result would be the same where the goods become so damaged as no longer to answer to their description in the contract. This principal is based on the rule of impossibility of performance of contract.

Under this provisions, a contract is void only if the following conditions are fulfilled:

(*a*) The contract must be for the sale of specific goods.

(*b*) The goods must have been perished before the contract is made.

(*c*) The seller must not have the knowledge of the destruction of goods.

The term 'perishing of goods' does not mean the physical destruction only. It also includes the cases in which the goods have lost their commercial value, *e.g.*, where sugar has been converted into *sharbat* by mixing of water, etc.

Example 20.14. *A* agreed to sell to *B* 100 bags of cement lying in his godown. In fact, that cement had already been destroyed by leakage of water and has been converted into stone. But this fact was not known to the seller (*A*) . In this case, the contract of sale is void.

Example 20.15. *A* sold to *B* a specific cargo of goods which was on its way from America to Bombay. The ship conveying the goods had been sunk before the day of the barging. The parties were not aware of this fact. In this case, the contract of sale is void.

2. *Goods perishing after an agreement to sell but before the sale is completed [Section 8]:* Sometimes, the goods perish after an agreement to sell is made but before the risk passes to the buyer, *i.e.*, before the completion of the sale. In such cases, the contract of sale becomes void if the contract is for the sale of *specific goods* and the goods are destroyed without any fault of the seller or buyer.

Under this provision, a contract of sale becomes void only if the following conditions are fulfilled :

(*a*) The contract of sale must be an 'agreement to sell' and not 'actual sale'.

(*b*) The agreement to sell must be for the sale of specific goods.

(*c*) The goods must have been perished before the agreement to sell becomes sale, *i.e.*, before the buyer becomes the owner of the goods sold, means before the risk passes to the buyer.

(*d*) The goods must have been perished without the fault of seller or buyer.

Example 20.16. *A* delivered a horse to *B* for trial for 8 days. It was agreed that the sale would be completed if the horse was found suitable for *B*'s purpose. The horse died on the third day without any fault of either party. It was held that the contract was void and *A* could not recover the price from *B*. [*Eliphic* v. *Barnes* (1880) CPD 321]

Example 20.17. *A* agreed to sell to *B*, 200 tonnes of potatoes to be grown on his (*A*'s) land. *A* sowed sufficient land to grow more than 200 tonnes of potatoes. But without any fault on *A*'s part, a diseases attacked the crop and only about eight tonnes of potatoes could be grown. It was held that the agreement had become void. [*Howell* v. *Coupland* (1876) 1 QBD 258]

It may be noted that both the Sections 7 and 8, discussed above, apply only to specific, goods. If the contract is for the sale of 'unascertained goods the contract shall not become void even if the entire stock of goods is destroyed.

Example 20.18. *A* agreed to sell to *B* 10 bales of Egyptian Cotton out of 100 bales lying in his godown. The goods were already destroyed by fire before the contract of sale. But both, *A* and *B* did not know about the fire. In this case, the contract is not void as it was not for the sale of specific goods, but for the sale of certain quantity of unascertained goods. And thus, *A* is liable to supply 10 bales of Egyptian Cotton to *B*, or to pay him the damages for breach of contract.

The provisions of both the above sections can be negatived or varied by an express agreement, between the parties. In other words, the parties may agree that the contract of sale shall not become void if the subject-matter of the contract is destroyed.

20.11. PRICE OF GOODS

The price of goods is the important element of a valid sale. There can be no valid sale of goods without the price. The term price is defined in Section 2(10) of the Sale of Goods Act, which reads as under:

"Price means the money consideration for a sale of goods."

In other words, the money paid for the purchase of goods is called the price. Thus, the price must be expressed in terms of money. The money here means the legal tender, *i.e.*, the money in circulation (currency of the country).

20.12. MODES OF FIXING THE PRICE

1. *The fixation of price by the contract of sale*
2. *The fixation of price in a manner provided in the contract of sale*
3. *The fixation of price by course of dealings*
4. *The fixation of proce by third party*
5. *The fixation of price by third party*

The price may be fixed in various ways. The different modes of fixing the price are contained in Section 9 of the Sale of Goods Act, which may be discussed under the following heads:

1. *The fixation of price by the contract of sale [Section 9(1)]:* The price may be expressly fixed by the contract of sale, The parties may fix any price they like.

2. *The fixation of price in a manner provided in the contract of sale [Section 9(1)]* : The contract of sale may provide for some manner in which price is to be fixed. In such cases, the price may be fixed in a manner provide in the contract.

3. *The fixation of price by course of dealings [Section 9(1)]:* Sometimes, the customs or usage of trade provide certain principles for the determination of the price. In such cases, the price may be determined from the course of dealings between the parties.

4. *The fixation of price by third party [Section 9(2)]:* Sometimes, none of the above principles is applicable. In such cases, the buyer shall pay to the seller a reasonable price. The term 'reasonable' price is a question of fact which depends on the circumstances of each particular case.

5. *The fixation of price by third party [Section 10]:* The parties may agree to sell and buy goods on the terms that the price shall be fixed by the valuation of a third party, It may, however, be noted that if such third party fails to make the valuation, the contract becomes void. But if the buyer has received the goods and has appropriated them, he becomes bound to pay reasonable price to the seller, Sometimes, the third party is influenced or prevented by the buyer or the seller from fixing the price. In such cases, the innocent party may recover damages from the defaulting party.

Example 20.19. *A* agreed to sell his 100 bags of rice to *B* at a price to be fixed by *C*. But *C* failed to fix the price. In this case, the agreement becomes void on *C*'s failure to fix the price.

Example 20.20. *A* agreed to sell his 100 quintals of wheat to *B* at a price to be fixed by *C*.*C* is willing to value wheat and fix the price. But, *A* by his wrongful acts, prevents *C* from making the valuation of the goods. In this case, *B* can claim damages from *A*.

20.13. HIRE PURCHASE AGREEMENT

A hire purchase agreement is an agreement under which the owner delivers his goods on hire basis to a person called 'hirer', for his use. And the hirer has the option to purchase the goods by paying the agreed amount in specified installments. The term 'hire purchase agreement' is defined in Section 2(*c*) of the Hire Purchase Act, 1972, which provides that in hire purchase agreement, the owner delivers his goods to a person (*i.e.*, hirer) for his use, and the hirer agrees to pay the fixed amount by specified periodical instalments. The parties also agree that after the payment of all the agreed instalments, the ownership of the goods will be transferred to the hirer. The hirer has the following two options:

1. He may purchase the goods after paying all the agreed instalments.
2. He may return the goods at any time and stop further payment of the instalments. The instalments already paid are treated as the hire charges for the use of goods hired.

Example. 20.21. *A* let a piano *B* on hire, on the following terms that:

(*a*) If *B* regularly pays 36 monthly instalments, the piano shall become his property.

(*b*) *B* can terminate the hire at any time and return the piano to *A*, and need not pay any more.

After paying a few instalments, *B* pledged the piano with *C*. *A* brought a legal action against *C* to recover the piano. It was held that *A* could recover piano from *C*. The court observed that *B* had no right to pledge the piano because he was not its owner. He had the possession only under a hire purchase agreement. In this case, *B* had the option to buy the piano by paying all the 36 instalments. And he was not under any legal obligation to purchase the piano.

[*Helby* v. *Malthews* (1893) AC 471]

However, if no option is given to the hirer, and he is bound to purchase the goods, then the agreement is not the hire -purchase agreement, *e.g.*, if in the above example, it is agreed that *B* must pay the 36 instalments and he cannot return the piano. Then it will not be a hire purchase agreement. But it will be an *'agreement to buy'*.

20.14. DISTINCTION BETWEEN SALE AND HIRE PURCHASE AGREEMENT

The following table gives the distinction between the sale and hire purchase agreement:

S.No.	*Sale*	*Hire Purchase Agreement*
1.	It may be made either orally or in writing.	It must be in writing.
2.	The ownership of the goods is transferred from the seller to the buyer as soon as the contract is made.	The ownership of the goods is transferred from the seller to the hirer only when all the agreed number of instalments are paid.
3.	The buyer has no option to return the goods. He is bound to take delivery of goods.	The hirer has an option to terminate the agreement at any stage. He may or may not buy the goods. On the termination of the agreement, the hirer cannot be compelled to pay the remaining instalments.
4.	The buyer becomes the owner and gets all the right of an owner , *e.g.*, right to pledge, resale, etc.	The hirer does not become the owner. His position is that of a bailee only. He becomes the owner, only when all the instalments are paid.
5.	In case of payment of price in instalments. each instalment is regarded as part payment of the price.	The instalment is regarded as the hire charges for the use of the goods. However, if the hirer exercises the option to purchase the goods, then each instalment is regarded as the part payment.
6.	It is governed by the Sale of Goods Act, 1930.	It is governed by the Hire Purchase Act, 1972.
7.	Sales tax is payable on the goods sold.	Sale tax is not payable on hire purchase until it becomes sale.

20.15. CONTRACT FOR WORK AND SKILL

The contract for work and skill means the contract which involves the exercise of skill and labour by one party on some goods or material supplied by the other. And the party, exercising the skill and labour, is paid for his work. Sometimes, the goods or material are also of the party who exercises the skill and labours and then delivers it to another for a price. In such cases, the contract is also for work and skill (sometimes called for work and material) if the principal object of the contract is to exercise work and skill and not the transfer of goods or material as it is. However, the test would seem to be whether the thing to be delivered has any individual existence before its delivery. If it has no such existence and the principal object of the contract is the exercise of skill and labour of the seller, the contract will be one for workd and skill. Whether a contract is for 'sale', or for 'work and skill' is a mixed question of fact and law, and depends upon the facts and circumstances of each particular case. And in each case, the courts will have to find out the principal object of the transaction and the intention of the parties[3] .Generally, a contract for work and skill is a 'contract for work' and not for the sale of specific goods, and thus, there is no transfer of ownership. But in certain circumstances, the ownership of the articles produced may pass to the party giving the order, *e.g.*, where an architect is employed to carry out alteration in a building and prepares plans for that purpose, the ownership of the plans passes to the employer on the payment of agreed remuneration.[4]

Example. 20.22. *A* delivered a block of marble to *B* for the purpose of carving it into a statue. *B* agreed to do so for Rs. 20,000. This is a contract of work and skill.

Example 20.23. *A* promised to paint a portrait of a lady for *B*. *A* also agreed to use his own paint and canvas for the purpose. And *B* promised to pay for the portrait as a work of art. It was held to be a contract for work and skill. In this case, the substance of the contract was that skill and labour should be exercised upon the production of the portrait. And the use of paint and canvas by *A*, which also passed to *B*, was only an ancillary to the main contract of painting the portrait.

[Based on *Robinson* v. *Graves* (1935) 1 KB 579]

Example 20.24. *A* entered into a contract with Railways for the construction of railway coaches on under-frame supplied by the Railways. The Sale Tax Officer treated the transaction as sale of the coaches by *A*, and accordingly levied sales tax on them. The case came before the Supreme Court which held that the contract was for work and labour, and not for sale. In this case, the contract was not for the sale of completed railway coaches, but for the construction of coaches on the under-frames supplied by the Railways.

[*State of Gujrat* v. *Variety Body Builders*, AIR 1976 SC 2108].

Example 20.25. *A* agreed to purchase a fur jacket from *B*. After inspecting several fur skins, *A* selected a colour and style of the jacket, and the price was also agreed. *B* agreed to make the jacket according to *A*'s requirement. It was also held to be a contract for the sale of goods.

[*Marcel Furriers Ltd.* v. *Tapper* (1953) All ER 15]

Note: The difference between the contract for sale, and for work and skill is that, in case of sale, the main object is to transfer the ownership and possession of the goods *as they are*. But in case of contract for work and skills, the main object is to exercise skill and labour upon the goods before transferring the ownership and possession. Thus, a contract for work an skill is mainly a contract for the sale of skill and labour. It may be noted that the Sale of Goods Act does not apply to contracts for skill and labour.

20.16. BARTER AND EXCHANGE

In case of 'barter', the goods are exchanged by one person for some goods with another person. And in case of 'exchange', the money is exchanged by one person for some different money with another person. Both these transactions are different from sales, as these do not contain essential elements of sale. In the former, the element of price is missing. And in the latter, the element of goods is missing. It may be noted that the Sale of Goods Act does not apply to barter and exchange.

3. *St. of Punjab* v. *Associated Hotels of India Ltd.* (1972) SCC 472
4. *Gibbon* v. *Pease* (1905) 1 K.B. 810 C.A.

20.17. GIFT OF GOODS

In case of gift of goods, the ownership of the goods is transferred by one person to another without any price of consideration. The gift of goods is different from a sale, as the element of price is missing. Thus, the main difference between the sale and gift of goods is that , in case of sale, the ownership of goods is transferred for some money consideration. But in case of gift, the ownership of goods is transferred without any money consideration. It may be noted that the Sale of Goods Act does not apply to gifts.

20.18. BAILMENT OF GOODS

In case of bailment, the goods are delivered by one person to another, known as bailee, for some purpose, and on the condition that the goods shall be returned back on the achievement of the purpose. It may be noted that only the possession of the goods is transferred to the bailee, and the ownership of the goods remains with the bailor (*i.e.*, the person delivering the goods). The bailment of goods is not a sale as it does no contain the essential elements of sale. The difference between the sale and bailment is that, in case of sale, the ownership of the goods is transferred for some money consideration, and the buyer is under no obligation to return the goods. But in case of bailment, the ownership of the goods is not transferred. Only the possession of the goods is transferred to the bailee and the possession may be transferred without and money consideration, as in case of gratuitous bailment. Moreover, the bailee is under legal obligation to return the goods as soon as the purpose is achieved or the time of bailment expires. It may be noted that the Sale of Goods Act doe not apply to bailment of goods.

20.19. PLEDGE AND HYPOTHECATION OF GOODS

In case of pledge, the goods are delivered by one person to another, known as pawnee, as security for the repayment of the loan taken from the pawnor. In this case, only the possession of the goods is transferred to the pawnee, and the ownership of the goods remains with the pawnor (*i.e.*, the person delivering the goods). On the repayment of the loan, the pawnee is bound to return the goods to the pawnor. However, if the pawnor makes default in repaying the loan, the pawnee may sell the goods after giving a notice to the pawnor. If the full amount of loan is not realised by the sale of the pledged goods, the pawnee may file a suit for the recovery of the balance.

In case of hypothecation, a charge is created on the goods of one person in favour of another person known as creditor, to secure the repayment of the loan taken from the creditor. In this case, both the possession as well as ownership of goods remain with the borrower. On the repayment of the loan, the goods are freed from the charge. However, if the borrower makes default in repaying the loan, the creditor may file a suit for the recovery of his dues, and for the sale of the hypothecated goods for the realisation of his dues.

The term 'hypothecation' has been legally defined in Section 2(1) (n) of the Securitisation and Reconstruction of Financial Assets and Enforcement of Security Interest Act, 2002, in the words reading as under:

"Hypothecation means a charge in or upon any movable property, existing or future, created by a borrower in favour of a secured creditor without delivery of possession of the movable property, to such creditor, as a security for financial assistance and includes floating charge and crystallization of such charge into fixed charge on movable property"

Note: Both the above transactions are different from sale. The main difference between 'sale and 'pledge' and 'hypothecation' is that in case of sale, the ownership of goods is transferred by one person to another. But in case of 'pledge' and hypothecation' the ownership of goods is not transferred by one person to another. It may be noted that the Sale of Goods Act does not apply to 'pledge' and 'hypothecation'.

20.20. MORTGAGE OF IMMOVABLE PROPERTY

In case of mortgage, a charge is created on the immovable property of one person in favour of another person, known as mortgagee, to secure the repayment of the loan taken from the mortgagee. In this case, only the special interest in the property is transferred to the mortgagee, and the ownership of the property remains with the mortgagor (*i.e.*, the person who mortgages his property). On the repayment of the loan, the mortgaged property is freed from charge. However, if the mortgagor makes default in paying the loan, the mortagagee may file a suit for the recovery of his dues. The mortgage is also different from sale of goods, as the ownership of the property is not transferred by the mortgagor to the mortagagee. The Sale of Goods Act deals with the movable goods only, whereas the mortgage is always of immovable property. It is governed by the Transfer of Property Act, 1882.

LEGAL PROVISIONS (SECTIONS) DISCUSSED IN THE CHAPTER

Important legal provisions (sections) of the Sale of Goods Act, 1930, discussed in this chapter, are reproduced hereunder for ready referance:

1. ***Section 2(b): Future Goods Defined***

   Future goods means the goods to be manfactured or produced by the seller after making of the contract of sale.

2. ***Section 2 (7): Goods Defined***

   Goods means every kind of movable property other than auctionable claims and money; and includes stock and share, growing crops, grass and things attached to or forming part of the land which are agreed to be severed before sale or under the contract of sale.

3. ***Section 2 (10): Price Defined***

   Price means the money consideration for a sale of goods.

4. ***Section 2 (11); Property Defined***

   Property means general property in goods, and not merely a special property.

5. ***Section 2 (14); Specific Goods Defined***

   Specific goods means goods identified and agreed upon at the time a contract of sale is made.

6. ***Section 4(1) (2): Contract of Sale***

   A contract of sale of goods is a contract wherby the seller transfers or agrrees to transfer the property in goods to the buyer for a price. There may be a contract of sale between one part-owner and another. A contract of sale may be absolute or conditional.

7. ***Section 4 (3): Sale and Agreement to sell***

   Where under a contract of sale the property in the goods is transferred from the seller to the buyer, the contract is called a sale, but where the transfer of the property in the goods is to take place at a future time or subject to some condition thereafter to be fulfilled, the contract is called an agreement to sell. An agreement to sell becomes a sale when the time elapses or the conditions are fulfilled subject to which the property in the goods is to be transferred [section 4 (4)].

8. ***Section 5: Contract of Sale How Mode***

   (1) A contract of sale is made by an offer to buy or sell goods for a price and the acceptance of such offer. The contract may provide for the immediate delivery of the goods or immediate payment of the price or both, or for the delivery or payment by instalments, or that the delivery or payment or both shall be postponed.

   (2) Subject to the provisions of any law for the time being in force, a contract of sale may be made in writing or by word of mouth, or partly in writing and partly by word of mouth or may be implied from the conduct of the parties.

9. ***Section. 7: Goods Perishing Before Making of Contract***

   Where there is a contract for the sale of specific goods, the contract is void if the goods without the knowledge of the seller have, at the time when the contract was made perished or become so damaged as no longer to answer to their description in the contract.

10. ***Section 8: Goods Perishing Before Sale but After Agreement to Sell.***
Where there is an agreement to sell specific goods, and subsequently the goods without any fault on the part of the seller or buyer perish or become so damaged as no longer to answer to their description in the agreement before the risk passes to the buyer, the agreement is thereby avoided.

11. ***Section 9: Ascertainment of Price.***
(1) The price in a contract of sale may be fixed by the contract or may be left to be fixed in manner thereby agreed or may be determined by the course of dealing between the parties.
(2) Where the price is not determined in accordance with the foregoing provisions, the buyer shall pay the seller a reasonable price. What is a reasonable price is a question of fact dependent on the circumstances of each particular case.

TEST QUESTIONS

1. Define the term 'contract of sale'. State the essentials of a valid contract of sale.
2. Define the term 'goods' as used in the Sale of Goods Act. Can a contract of sale be made of 'future goods'? If yes, what is the nature of such a contract?
3. Explain sale and distinguish it from an agreement to sell under Sale of Goods Act.
4. Explain the difference between a contract of sale and an agreement to sell. When does an agreement to sell ripen into sale?
5. What is the subject matter of contract of sale? What is the effect of a contract of sale if its subject-matter which is specific goods, (*a*) is already destroyed at the time of contract of sale, (*b*) destroyed after an agreement to sell but before it becomes sale? What difference will it make if the subject matter is unascertained goods ?
6. Define the term 'hire purchase agreement'. State the comparison between 'sale and 'hire purchase agreement'.
7. What is a 'contract for work and skill'? Distinguish it from sale.
8. Define the terms bailment, pledge and hypothecation. How do they differ from sale?
9. Define the term 'price'. What are the different modes of determination of price?
10. Write notes on (*a*) Barter and exchange. (*b*) Gift of goods an sale. (*c*) Mortgage of immovable property and sale.

MULTIPLE CHOICE QUESTIONS

1. The Sale of Goods Act, 1930 deals with the
(*a*) movable goods only (*b*) immovable goods only
(*c*) both movable and immovable goods (*d*) all goods except ornaments.
2. Legally , a contract of sale includes
(*a*) sale (*b*) agreement to sell
(*c*) barter (*d*) both (*a*) and (*b*)
3. A contract for the sale of goods which provides that the property would pass to the buyer on full payment of price and execution of sale deed, is known as
(*a*) Sale (*b*) Agreement to sell
(*c*) Hire-purchase Agreement (*d*) Sale of approval
4. The term 'goods', for the purpose of Sale of Goods Act, means every kind of movable property and it includes
(*a*) stoke and share (*b*) growing crops, grass
(*c*) both of these (*d*) none of these.
5. The term 'goods ' for the purpose of Sale of Goods Act, does not include
(*a*) money (*b*) actionable claims
(*c*) immovable property (*d*) all of these.

6. *A* agrees to deliver his old car valued at Rs. 80,000 to *B* , a car dealer, in exchange for a new car and agrees to pay the difference in cash, it is
   (*a*) Contract of Sale (*b*) Barter
   (*c*) Exchange (*d*) None of these.
7. A contract for the sale of 'future goods', is
   (*a*) Sale (*b*) Agreement to sell
   (*c*) Void (*d*) Voidable.
8. In a hire-purchase agreement, the hirer
   (*a*) has an option to buy the goods (*b*) Must buy the goods
   (*c*) Must return the goods (*d*) not given the possession of goods.

ANSWERS

1. (*a*)	**2.** (*d*)	**3.** (*b*)	**4.** (*c*)	**5.** (*d*)	**6.** (*a*)
7. (*b*)	**8.** (*a*)				

OBJECTIVE TYPE QUESTIONS WITH REASONING

State with reason whether the following statements are correct or in correct.

1. The contract of sale includes both 'sale' as well as an 'agreement to sell'
2. The term 'goods' means every kind of movable property other than actionable claims and money.
3. Actionable claims is a subject-matter of contract of sale.
4. Exchange of goods for goods between two parties amount to sale under the Sale of Goods Act, 1930.
5. Consideration in a contract of sale of goods can also be paid partly in money and partly in goods.
6. In an agreement to sell, the ownership of the goods passes to the buyer immediately.
7. A contract of sale can be validly made for the sale of future goods.
8. A contract for the sale of future goods in always an agreement to sell .
9. A hire -purchase agreement has two aspects namely, bailment and an agreement to sell.

ANSWERS

1. ***Correct.*** Section 4(1) of the Sale of Goods Act defines the term 'Contract of sale ' in wider term to include both sale and an agreement to sell.
2. ***Correct.*** Legal definition of the term goods given in section 2(7) makes a specific provision in this regard.
3. ***Incorrect.*** An actionable claim is not included in the term 'goods'
4. ***Incorrect.*** This type of exchange of goods amounts to barter. In fact, the price in terms of money is an essential element of sale.
5. ***Correct.*** In such a case, the price can be ascertained when the goods delivered alongwith money are the valued up goods [*Aldridge* v. *Johnson* (1857) 7 E & B 885].
6. ***Incorrect.*** In case of agreement to sell, the ownership passes to the buyer at some future date.
7. ***Correct.*** The goods forming subject-matter of contract of sale also includes the future goods.

8. *Correct.* The ownership of the future goods cannot be immediately transferred at the time of contract, it can only be transferred at some future date.
9. *Correct.* The hire's position is that of a bailee till he becomes the owner of goods by paying all the agreed instalments.

PRACTICAL PROBLEM

1. State the nature of transaction in the following cases:

   (*a*) *A* agreed to by a haystack from *B* laying on *B*'s land. *A* was given the liberty to come on *B*'s land and take away the haystack.

   (*b*) *A* contracted to sell his motor lorry to *B* for Rs. 200.000 and the ownership was agreed to be transferred to *B* on the full payment of price and execution of sale document.

   (*c*) *A* agreed to buy from *B* a certain quantity of electrical goods which were yet to arrive by ship.

   (*d*) *A* delivered a block of marble to *B* for the purpose of carving it into a statute, and *B* agreed to do so for Rs. 50,000.

   (*e*) *A*, a dentist makes a denture (false teeth) for his patient *B* by using his own material. *B* agreed to pay Rs. 10,000 for the same.

   (*f*) *A* agreed to give his two old cars to *B* in exchange for one new car.

   (*g*) *A* gives a suit length to *B*, a tailor to be stitched into a suit, the lining materials and buttons to be provided by *B*.

   (*h*) *A*, a member of a club takes home a supply of certain goods from the club retail counter and agrees to make the payment along with the monthly subscription.

   (*i*) *A*'s goods are sold in auction under an execution of a decree and he himself buys the goods at the highest bid.

   (*j*) *A* contracts to sell to *B* his wheat crop standing in his field and allows *B* to cut and take away the crop.

   Hints.

   (*a*) It is a sale [*wood* v *Manley* (1839) 11 A & E 34, 52 RR 271].

   (*b*) It is an agreement to sell. In this, case, ownership is to pass to the buyer on the fultilment of condition *i.e.* payment of price and execution of sale document.
   [*United India Ins. Com.* v. *Jameela Beavi*, AIR 1991 kerale, 380].

   (*c*) It is an agreement to sell. In this case, ownership is to be transferred on some future date i.e. on the arrival of the ship. [*Johnson* v. *Mecdonald*] (1842) 9 M&W 600,60 RR 838]

   (*d*) It is a contract of work and skill.

   (*e*) It is a contract of sale. [*Lee* v. *Griffin*]

   (*f*) It is a barter and not a sale.

   (*g*) It is a contract of work and material and not a sale.

   (*h*) It is a contract for sale of goods. In this case, the ownership is transferred to *A* as soon as he takes away the goods with him.

   (*i*) It is a valid contract of sale.

   (*j*) It is a sale. In this case, liberty is given to *B* to cut and take away the crop.

2. *A* agreed to sell to *B* 700 bags of groundnuts lying in his godown. Unknown to *A*, 100 bags of groundnuts had already been stolen at the time of contract. However, *A* delivered 600 bags to *B*, but *B* refused to take delivery of the same. Is *B* justified in doing so ? Give reasons.

   Hints. Yes *B*, is justified in refusing to take delivery of short quantity *i.e.* 600 bags. In this case, the buyer agreed to buy specific quantity, and to ask him to take less would be to compel him to do what he had not contracted to do. [*Barrow lane a Ballasd* v. *Phillips* (1929)1 KB 574]

3. *A* contracted to sell 1000 bottles of liquour to *B*. Before the liquor bottles could be delivered, the Government seized the whole quantity of liquor lying with *A* in public interest. *B* seeks your advice for filing a suit against *A* for breach of contract. Advise *B*.

   Hints. *B* will not succeed in the legal action. In this case, the contract becomes void under Section 8 as after seizure by the government, the subject matter of contract *i.e.* liquor bottles ceases to exist. The contract is also void under Section 56 of the Indian Contract Act, 1872, supervening impossibility.

4. *A* agreed to sell to *B* 100 bags of Egyptian cotton out of 1000 bales lying in his godown. But unknown to both the parties, the bales of cotton had already been destroyed by fire before the contract of sale. *B* wants to file a suit against *A* for the recovery of compensation. Is he justified ? Give reasons.

   Hints. Yes *B* is justified in his action. In this case, the contract has not become void under Section 8 which applies in cases on the sale of specific goods. Here, the contract was for the sale of certain quantity of unascertained goods.

5. *A* delivered his car to *B* for trial for 8 days. It was agreed that the sale would be completed if the car was found suitable for *B's* purpose. The car was destroyed on the third day in an accidental fire without any fault of either party. *A* seeks your advice for recovery of the car price from *B*. Advise him.

   Hints. In this case, the contract of sale has become void on the destruction of subject-matter *i.e.* car [Section 8]. Here, *A* will not succeed in his action for recovery of price from *B*.

6. *A* agrees to sell to *B* 100 bags of rice at a price to be fixed by his friend *C*. *B* takes the delivery of 100 rice bags immediately and uses them for his own business purpose. But *C* fails to fix the price. *B* offers to pay reasonable price to *A* but *A* asks for the return of rice bags.

   Hints. *A* is not justified in asking for the return of rice bags. In a case where third party fails to fix the price and the buyer receives and appropriates the goods, he becomes bound to pay a reasonable price to the seller. [Section 10]

7. In the above example, suppose *C* fails to fix the price and *B* has not yet taken the delivery of rice bags. *A* refuses to sell the rice bags to *B* since the price is not fixed *C*. In this situation, can *B* compel *A* to deliver the rice bags to him on the payment of reasonable price.

   Hints. No, *B* cannot do so. In such a situation, the contract becomes void. [Section 10]

8. *A*, a cycle dealer, delivered one 'Gold Star' cycle to *B*. It was agreed between them that *B* will pay Rs.1000 in ten monthly installments of Rs.100 each. After payment of five instalments, *B* defaulted in the payment of further instalments. Can *A* recover the balance instalments from *B*. Give reasons.

   Hints. The answer would depend upon the option given to *B*, which is as under:

   (*a*) If *B* was given the option to return the cycle at any time, then the transaction would be a hire-purchase agreement. In this case, *A* cannot recover the balance instalments and the instalments already paid will be treated as hire charges.

   (*b*) If *B* was not given any option to return the cycle but was bond to purchase the same, then it will not be a hire-purchase agreement and *B* will be bond to make the payment of balance instalments.

21

CHAPTER

CONDITIONS AND WARRANTIES

21.1. INTRODUCTION

In the last chapter, we have discussed that a contract of sale is made by an offer by the seller and its acceptance by the buyer. At the time of selling the goods, a seller usually makes certain statements or representations with a view to induce the intending buyer to purchase the goods. Such representations are generally about the nature and quality of goods, and about their fitness for buyer's purpose. It may be noted that these representations may be a mere expression of the opinion of the seller and may not form a part of the contract. But sometimes, these may also form a part of the contract and the intending buyer may rely upon such representaions. When these statements or representations do not form a part of the contract of sale, they are not relevant and have no legal effect on the contract. But when these form a part of the contract of sale and the buyer may rely upon them, they are relevant and have legal effect on the contract. A representation which forms a part of the contract of sale and affects the contract, is called a stipulation. How ever, every stipulation is not of equal importance. A stipulation which is most important for the formation of the contract of sale, is known as a 'condition'. But a stipulation which is of lesser importance for the formation of the contract of sale, is known as a 'warranty'. In this chapter, we shall discuss the legal provisions of conditions and warranties.

21.2. CONDITIONS[1]

The term 'condition' may be defined as a representation made by the seller which is

1. Some of the manufactures (*e.g.*, manufacturers of fans, motors, automobile, etc.) give guarantees for the proper working of their products in order to influence the buyers to buy their products. Such guarantees, in legal term are known as conditions.

so important that its non-fulfilment defeats the very purpose of the buyer. As a matter of fact, it is a stipulation which forms the basis of a contract of sale, *i.e.*, which is essential to the main purpose of the contract. The term condition is defined in Section 12(2) of the Sale of Goods Act, which reads as under:

"A condition is a stipulation essential to the main purpose of the contract, the breach of which gives rise to a right to treat the contract as repudiated."

Thus, a condition is an important representation by the seller which is essential to the main purpose of the contract. And if it proves to be false, the buyer has the right to terminate the contract, and to have the refund of the price.

Example 21.1. *A* consulted *B*, a car dealer, and told him that he wanted to purchase a car 'suitable for touring purpose'. *B*, suggested that a 'Bugatti'car would be fit for the purpose. Relying upon this statement, *A* bought or 'Bagatti' car. Later on, the car turned out to be unfit for the touring purpose. *A* wanted to reject the car and demanded the refund of the price. It was held that *A* was entitled to reject the car and to have the refund of the price. In this case, the suitability of the car, for touring purpose, was a condition of the contract. It was so important that its non-fulfilment defeated the very purpose for which *A* bought the car. [*Baldry* v. *Marshall*, (1925) 1. **KB** 260].

Example 21.2. *A* went to *B*, a horse dealer, and told him that he wanted a horse which could run at a speed of 45 m.p.h. *B* pointed out at a particular horse and said that this will suit his purpose. *A* bought that particular horse. Subsequently. it was discovered that the horse runs at a speed 20 m.p.h only. In this case, the representation made by the seller is a condition as it is essential to the main purpose of the contract. *A* may reject the horse and get back the price.

21.3. TYPES OF CONDITIONS

The conditions may be discussed under the following two heads:

(1) Express conditions. (2) Implied conditions.

21.4. EXPRESS CONDITIONS

It is a condition, which has been expressly agreed upon by both the parties at the time of the contract of sale. It may be noted that it is open to both the parties to include in their contract any number of express conditions.

21.5. IMPLIED CONDITIONS

1. *Condition as to title [Section 14 (a)]*
2. *Condition as to description [Section 15].*
3. *Condition as to sample [Section 17 (2)]*
4. *Condition as to sample as well as description [Section 15]*
5. *Condition as to quality or futness for buyer's purpose [Section 16 (1)]*
6. *Condition as to merchantability [Section 16 (2)]*

It is a condition, which the law implies into the contract of sale. In other words, it is the stipulation which has not been included in the contract of sale in express words. But the law presumes that the parties have incorporated it into their contract. It is to be noted that implied conditions are read into every contract of sale unless they are expressly excluded by the parties. Thus, both the parties are bound by the implied conditions unless they are excluded by the express agreement of the parties. These may also be excluded by the course of dealings between the parties or by usage of trade. [Section 62] In case of conflict between the express and implied conditions, the express term shall prevail and the implied terms shall not be considered. Following are the implied conditions which are contained in the Sale of Goods Act:

1. *Condition as to title* [*Section 14 (a)*]: It is an important implied condition in every contract of sale. According to this condition, it is presumed that the seller has a valid title to the goods, *i.e.*, he has the *right to sell* the goods. If later on, the buyer comes to know that the seller had no valid right to sell the goods, then he may reject the goods and claim the refund of the price. As a matter of fact, in every contract of sale there is an implied condition that the seller has a valid title to the goods, *i.e.*, he is entitled to sell the goods. This implied condition may be analysed as under:

(*a*) In case of sale, the implied condition is that the seller has the right to sell the goods, and

(*b*) In case of an agreement to sell, the implied condition is that the seller will have the right to sell the goods at the time when the ownership is to pass from the seller to the buyer.

Example 21.3. *A* bought a second hand car from *B*, a car dealer. After a few months, the car was taken by the police as it was a stolen one. And *A* was forced to return the car to the true owner. It was held that *A* could recover the full price from *B*. In this case, there was a breach of condition as to title as *B* had no *right to sell* the car. [*Rowland* V. *Divall* (1923) 2 KB 500]

The term *'right to sell'*is wider than the term *'right to pass property'*. The expression also means that the seller has a right to sell the goods in the same condition in which he is possessing them. Thus, when a person sells the goods by infringing the copyright or trade mark of the others, there is a breach of condition as to title.

Example 21.4. *A*, a businessman of England, bought 3000 tins of condensed milk from *B*, a dealer in **U.S.A**. When the tins reached England, it was found that 1000 tins contained the label of 'Nissly Brand'. *C* another manufacturer of the milk under the name of 'Nestle Brand', claimed that this was an infringement of his trademark. *A* had to remove the labels, in order to get clearance from custom authorities. Moreover, *A* had to sell the tins at loss. *A* brought an action against *B* for the breach of a condition. It was held that the seller had broken the implied condition that he had a right to sell. In this case, the seller had no right to sell the goods (tins) which contained the trade mark of another. [*Niblett* v. *Confectioners Material Co.* (1921) 3 KB 387]

2. *Condition as to description [Section 15].* Sometimes, the goods are sold by description. In such cases, the implied condition is that the goods shall correspond with the description. The term 'correspondence with description'means that the goods purchased by the buyer must be the same which were described by the seller. If subsequently, it is discovered that the goods do not correspond with the description, the buyer may reject the goods and claim the refund of the price, if already paid.

Example 21.5. *A* purchased from *B* a car, which he had never seen. *B* described the car as a 'brand new'. However, on delivery, *A* found that the car was used and repainted. And thus *A* returned the car to *B*. It was held that the sale was by description and the car did not correspond with the description. In this case, *A* was entitled to reject the car.

[Based on *Varley* v. *Whipp* (1900) 1 **Q. B.** 513]

The term 'sale by description' has not been defined in the Sale of Goods Act. However, it generally means the sale when the goods are described in the contract as of particular kind or class, *e.g., Basmati Rice, Long Staple Cotton, Desi Wheat, etc.* The sale will also be by description when the identity or quality of the thing is described, *e.g., Brand New Car, Maruti 85 Model, etc.* The term 'sale by description'includes the following situations:

(*a*) Sometimes, the buyer has never seen the goods but he buys on the basis of description given by the seller. In such cases the goods must correspond with the description given by the seller.

Example 21.5 (*a*). discussed above is relevant on the point.

(*b*) Sometimes, the buyer has seen the goods but he relies on the description given by the seller and not on what he has seen. In such cases also, the goods must answer to the description given by the seller.

Example 21.6 *A* advertises his car for sale as a "Herald Convertible, white 1961 Model". *B* examined the car and bought it. Subsequently, *B* discovered that the car was made of two parts which had been welded together. And only one part was of 1961 Model, whereas the other part was of old model. It was held that the sale was by description and *B* could reject the car as it did not correspond with the description. In this case, althouth *B* has examined the car, but he relied upon the description given by the seller (*A*). [*Beale* v. *Taylor* (1967) 1 WLR 1193]

(*c*) Sometimes, the packing of goods may be a part of the description.

Example 21.7. *A* sold to *B*, 3000 tins of Australian fruits which were agreed to be packed in cases each containing 30 tins. *A* delivered the substantial portion of the fruits in cases containing 24 tins. It was held that the method of packing was a part of the description. Therefore, *B* was entitled to reject all the goods. [*Moore & Co.* v. *Londover Co.* (1921) 2 KB 519 CA]

But where the goods correspond with the description, the buyer is bound to take the delivery for whatever worth they may be otherwise, *e.g.*, where the pigs were sold *'with all faults'*and they were what they stated to be. The buyer was without a remedy even when they turned out to be suffering from typhoid and infected other pigs of the buyer. [*Ward* v. *Hobbs* (1878)4 AC 13]

3. ***Condition as to sample*** **[*Section 17(2)*]**: Sometimes, the seller shows sample of the goods to the buyer. And the buyer, relying upon the quality of the goods from the sample, buys the goods. In such cases, there is an implied condition that the goods shall correspond with the sample in quality. And the goods shall be free from the defects which render them unmerchantable. It may be noted that in case of sale by sample there are the following three implied conditions :

(*a*) ***Correspondence of goods with the sample in quality*** **[*Section 17(2) (a)*].** It is first implied condition, which means that the goods delivered must correspond with the quality of the sample.

Example 21.8. *A* agreed to buy some rubber material from *B*. The sample of the rubber was shown to *A*. And the rubber was to be delivered in rolls of specific length and width. On receiving the goods (*i.e.*, rubber material), *A* found that the measurement of the material was different from that of the sample. It was held that the goods did not correspond with the sample in quality. The court observed that the measurements of rubber was part of its quality. [*E&S Ruben Ltd.* v. *Fair Bros* (1949) 1 KB 254]

(*b*) ***Reasonable opportunity of comparing the goods with the sample.*** **[*Section 17(2) (b)*]**: The second implied condition is that the buyer shall have a reasonable oppurtunity of comparing the bulk with the sample. If the seller refuses to allow such oppurtunity to the buyer, then the buyer may reject the goods and terminate the contract.

Example 21.19. *A* agreed to sell to *B* two parcels of wheat. The sample of wheat was shown to *B*. The buyer (*B*) went to *A*'s warehouse to examine the wheat. One parcel, which was lying in the seller's (*A*'s) warehouse, was shown to *B*. But *A* refused to show the other parcel to *B*, which was not in the warehouse. It was held that the buyer could put an end to the contract. [*Lorymere* v. *Smith* (1822) 1 B & C 1]

(*c*) ***Merchantability of the goods*** **[*Section 17(2) (c)*]:** The third implied condition is that the goods shall be free from latent defects (*i.e.*, the defects which are not discoverable on reasonable examination of the sample). When the goods delivered are defective, the buyer can reject the goods if the defect was not discoverable by reasonable examination of the sample. The condition as to merchantability will be discussed in detail as the 6th condition, in the following discussion.

Example 21.10. *A* sold some cloth of 'worsted coating'quality to *B*. The sample was also shown to *B*. Subsequently, it was discovered that the cloth was defective and unfit for stitching into coats, because the coats made out of it were not fit to stand ordinary wear. The same defect was in the sample but that was not discoverable on reasonable examination. It was held that goods (*i.e.*, cloth) were unmerchantable due to the latent defect. And the goods were not fit for purpose. [*Drummond & Sons v. Van Ingen* (1887) 12 AC 284]

4. *Condition as to sample as well as description* [*Section 15*]: Sometimes, the seller shows sample of the goods to the buyer and also gives him their description. In such cases, the implied condition is that the goods shall correspond with both, the sample as well as description. If the goods do not correspond either with the sample or the description, the buyer has the right to reject the goods.

Example 21.11. *A* agreed to sell to *B* some cotton which was described as 'Long Staple Cotton'. The sample was also shown to *B.A* delivered the cotton which was of the quality of sample. But subsequently, *B* found that the cotton was not 'Long Staple Cotton but Western Madras Cotton'. It was held that the buyer could reject the goods (*i.e.*, cotton) as they do not correspond with the description given by the seller, though they correspond with the sample.

[*Azemar v. Carella* (1867) 2 CP 431].

5. *Condition as to quality or fitness for buyer's purpose* [*Section 16* (1)]: Ordinarily, there is no implied condition that the goods shall be fit for the particular purpose of the buyer. But in certain circumstances, the seller is required to supply the goods which will be fit for the buyer's purpose, *e.g.*, where the buyer tells his purpose to the seller and buys the goods relying upon seller's skill and judgement. Thus, if the buyer makes his purpose clear to the seller and buys the goods relying upon his skill and judgement', then there is an implied condition that the goods shall be fit for the buyer's specific purpose. However, this implied condition will be there only if the following requirements are satisfied:

(*a*) The buyer requires the goods for a particular purpose

(*b*) The buyer should make known to the seller about that particular purpose.

(*c*) The buyer should rely on the seller's skill and judgment.

(*d*) The seller's business it to supply such goods whether he is the manufacturer or producer or not.

The case of *Baldry* v. *Marshal* discussed in Example 21.1 illustrates the point. It may be noted that though it is essential to make clear to the seller the purpose for which the buyer requires the good, but it is not necessary that the purpose should be expressed in words. The purpose can also be ascertained from the nature or description of goods. Similarly, the reliance on seller's skill may also arise by implication frorm the circumstances.

Example 21.12. *A*, a customer, had no knowledge about hot water bottles. He went to *B*, a chemist, and demanded a hot water bottle from him. *B* gave a bottle to him and stated that it was meant far hot water. After a few days, while using the bottle, it burst and injured *A*'s wife. It was found that the bottle was not fit for use as a hot water bottle, and the seller was held liable for damages. In this case, the buyer's purpose was clear from the nature of the bottle.

[*Priest* v. *Last* (1903) 2 K.B. 148]

Example 21.13. *A* bought a set of false teeth from *B*, a dentist. But the set was not fit for *A*'s mouth. *A* rejected the set of teeth and claimed the refund of price. it was held that *A* was entitled to do so as the only purpose for which he wanted the set of teeth was not fulfilled.

[*Dr. Baretto* v. *T. T. Pruce* AIR 1939 Nag. 19].

In connection with the condition as to quality or fitness for buyer's purpose, the following important points may be noted:

(*a*) Sometimes, the goods can be used for more than one purpose. In such cases, the buyer should inform his particular purpose to the seller. And if this is not done, the seller will not be liable if the goods do no suit buyer's particular purpose. However, in such cases, condition as to merchantability, must be satisfied.

Example 21.14. *A* bought 'hessian cloth' from *B*, a cloth merchant, Such cloth was generally used for paking purposes. It was found that due to unusual smell, the cloth was unfit for packing foodstuffs, though it was good as a packing cloth for other purposes. *A* wanted to reject the cloth on the ground that it was unfit for his purposes as he required it for packing foodstuffs. In this case, *A* was not allowed to reject the cloth as he never disclosed his particular purpose to the seller at the time of buying the "hessian cloth". [*Re Andrew Yule & Co.*, AIR 1932 Cal 879]

(*b*) Sometimes, there are special circumstances affecting the use of the goods for a particular purpose, and the seller is not aware of such circumstances. In such cases the implied condition as to fitness for buyer's purpose does not apply if these *special circumstances* have not been disclosed to the seller.

Example 21.15. *A* bought a tweed coat from *B*. After wearing the coat for sometime, *A* developed a termatitis (skin trouble). It was descovered that the coat was fit for the use of a normal man. And *A*'s skin trouble was due to his oversensitive skin. The court held that the implied condition as to fitness for buyer's purpose was not broken, as the coat was fit for the use of a normal man. In this case, it was *A*'s duty to disclose the fact of his oversensitivness to the seller at the time sale. [*Griffiths* v. *Peter Conway Ltd.* (1939) 1 AII ER 685]

(*c*) Sometimes, the goods are purchased under a patent or trade name. In such cases, there is no implied condition as to their fitness for any particular purpose. Thus where a buyer relies more on the trade name of a commodity than on the skill and judgment of the seller, the condition as to fitness for buyer's purpose does not apply [Section 16(1) (Second para)].

Example 21.16. *A* went to *B*'s shop and asked for a *'Merrit'* sewing machine. *B* gave *A* the *'Merrit'*sewing machine and *A* paid the price. *A* relied on the trade name of the machine rather than on the skill and judgement of the seller (*B*). In this case, there is no implied condition as to the fitness of the machine for buyer's particular purpose.

It is to be noted that a mere mention of the trade name or patent of the goods does not exclude the implied condition as to the fitness of goods for the buyer's particular purpose, if the buyer relies upon the skill and judgment of the seller. The case of *Baldry v. Marshall*, discussed in Example 21.1 is relevant on this point.

Note: It may be noted that in case of sale under trade name, the condition as to merchantability, discussed in the following pages, should be satisfied.

6. *Condition as to merchantability* [*Section 16* (2)]: The term 'merchantability'has not been defined in the Sale of Goods Act. However, it has been interpreted by the courts, and basically it means the two things, namely:

(*a*) If the goods are puchased for resale, then they should be immediately resaleable in the market under their description. Moreover, the goods should also be marketable at their full value, *e.g.*, the cement turned into stone by water, is not merchantable.

(*b*) if the goods are purchased for self use, then they should be reasonably fit for the purpose for which they are generally used, *e.g.*, a watch that will not keep proper time, a pen that will not write, and tobacco that will not smoke, etc., cannot be regarded as merchantable under such name.

In case of *sale by description*, there is an implied condition that the goods shall be of merchantable quality. Thus, the seller who sells the goods by description, is bound to deliver the goods of merchantable quality. However, this implied condition will be there only if the following requirements are satisfied:

(*a*) The goods must be sold by description.

(*b*) The seller's business is to supply the goods of that description whether he is the manufacturer or producear or not.

Example 21.17. *A & Co., a* firm of merchants, contracted to buy from *B*, a London Merchant, a number of bales of 'Manila Hemp'. This was to arrive from Singapore. The hemp arrived wetted by sea water, and it was so much damaged that it was not possible to sell it in the market as 'Manila Hemp.' It was held that the goods (*i.e.*, hemp) were not of merchantable quality. In this case, the hemp was not saleable under the description of 'Manila Hemp'.

[*Jones* v. *Just* (1868) LR 3 QB 197]

Example 21.18. *A* bought some cooking coal from *B*, a coal dealer, for domestic use. However, the coal contained an explosive substance which exploded and caused injury to *A*. It was held that the coal was not merchantable as it was not fit for using as cooking coal. And the buyer (*A*) was allowed to recover damages from the supplier (*B*).

[Based on *Wilson* v. *Rickett Cockerrel & Co.* (1954) 1 Q.B. 598]

The term *'merchantability'* also means that the goods must be properly packed.

Example 21.19: A purchased a bottle of 'Stone's Ginger Wine' from *B*. When *A* attemped to draw its cork with a cork screw, the neck of the bottle broke off and injured *A*'s hand. It was held that the bottle was not of merchantable quality, and *A* was entitled to recover damages from *B*.

[*Morelli* v. *Fitch & Gibbons* (1928) 2 K.B. 636]

It may be noted that where the goods are purchased for resale then the term 'merchantability'also includes that the goods should be such that their resale in the market does not violate any law (*i.e.*, their resale should not be prohibited by the law), *e.g.*, the confectionary must contain only permitted colours and a 'boiler'must satisfy the requirements of the Boilers Act.[2]

In connection with the condition as to mechantability, the following important points may be noted :

(*a*) ***Examination by the buyer***: Sometimes, the buyer purchases the goods after examination. in such cases, the implied condition as to merchantability shall not be applicable. Thus, the buyer is not entitled to the benefit of this condition if he has examined the goods. And the seller is not liable for defects which the examination 'ought to have revealed'[Section 16(2) (second para)].

(*b*) ***Comparison between the 'condition as to the fitness of goods for buyer's purpose, and 'condition as to merchantability':*** The following table gives the comparison between the two:

S. No.	*Condition as to fitness of Goods for Buyer's Purpose*	*Condition as to Merchantability*
1.	The buyer must rely on the skill and judgment of the seller.	The buyer is not required to rely on the skill and judgment of the seller.
2.	When the goods are sold under patent of trade name, then the condition as to fitness for buyer's purpose is not applicable. *i.e.*, it is not excluded.	When the goods are sold under patent or trade name, then the condition as to merchantability is applicable, *i.e.*, it is not excluded.
3.	There may be cases in which the goods are not fit for buyer's use but they may be merchantable.	There may not be such cases.

7. *Condition as to wholesomeness:* This condition is a part of the condition as to merchantability. It is applicable in cases of eatables, *i.e.*, foodstuffs and other goods which are used for human consumption. As per this condition, goods sold must be fit for human consumption. This condition will be explained in Art. 21.14.

Note. Conditions implied by customs are also discussed in Art. 21.14.

2. *Joseph Mayr* v. *Phani Bhusan Ghose*, Air 1939 Calcutta 210.

21.6. WARRANTIES

The term 'warranty' may be defined as a representation made by the seller which is not of that importance as a condition. And its non-fulfilment does not defeat the very purpose of the buyer. In fact, it is a stipulation which is not essential to the main purpose of the contract of sale, *i.e.*, it is only subsidiary or collateral to the main purpose. The term 'warranty'is defined in Section 12(3) of the Sale of Goods Act, which reads as under:

"A warranty is a stipulation collateral to the main purpose of the contract, the breach of which gives rise to a claim for damages but not a right to reject the goods and treat the contract as repudiated."

Thus, a warranty is a representation, by the seller, which is not very important factor in the sale of the goods. It is only collateral to the main purpose of the contract. And if it proves to be untrue, the buyer cannot put an end to the contract. He can only claim damages from the seller.

Example 21.20. *A*, a customer, went to *B*, a horse dealer, and told him that he wanted to buy a healthy horse. *B* pointed at a particular horse and said it to be healthy. Moerover, *B* informed *A* that the particular horse can also run at a speed of 40 k.m. per hour. *A* bought that particular horse. Subsequently, *A* found the horse to be healthy. But it could run only at a speed of 20 k.m. per hour. *A* wanted to reject the horse and to have the refund of the price. In this case, the representation made by the seller (*B*) is a warranty because it is only collateral to the main purpose. Thus, *A* cannot reject the horse on this ground.

Example 21.21. *A* bought two small ships from *B* relying upon the particulars furnished by *B* that the dead weight capacityof each ship was 460 tons. The capacity was in fact 360 tons. *A* wanted to reject the ships. It was held that the representation about the capacity of the ships was not a condition but a warranty only, and thus *A* could not reject the ships.

[*Harrison* v. *Knowles & Foster* (1917) 2 K.B. 606]

As a matter of fact, the importance of a stipulation should be seen in order to know whether it is a 'condition' or a 'warranty'. The terms used in the contract do not matter. Sometimes, a stipulation, called as a warranty in a contract, may be a condition if it is of great importance. Thus, in order to know whether a stipulation is a condition or a warranty, its relative importance in the contract of sale should be considered [Section 12(4)].

21.7. TYPES OF WARRANTIES

The warranties may be discussed under the following two heads:

(1) Express warranties (2) Implied warranties.

21.8. EXPRESS WARRANTIES

It is a warranty which has been expressly agreed upon by both the parties at the time of contract of sale. It may be noted that it is open to both the parties to include in their contract any number of express warranties.

21.9. IMPLIED WARRANTIES

1. *Warranty as to quiet possession* [*Section 14(b)*]
2. *Warranty as to quiet prossession [Sections 14 (b)]*
3. *Warranites impled by customs* [*Section 16 (3)*]

It is a warranty which the law implies into the contract of sale. In other words, it is the stipulation which has not been included in the contract of sale in express words, but the law presumes that the parties have incorporated it into their contract. It is to be noted that implied warranties are read into every contract of sale unless they are expressly excluded by the express agreement of the parties. These may also be excluded by the course of dealings between the paties or by usage of trade [Section 62]. In case of conflict between the express and implied warranties, the express terms shall prevail and the implied terms shall not be considered.

Following are the implied warranties which are contained in the Sale of Goods Act:

1. *Warranty as to quiet possession* [*Section 14(b)*]. It is an important implied warranty in every contract of sale. According to this warranty, it is presumed that the buyer shall have and enjoy the quiet possession of the goods. This means that where the buyer has obtained the possession of the goods, he has a right to enjoy them in a way he likes, *i.e.*, no one should interfere with the quiet enjoyment of the buyer. If buyer's right of possession and enjoyment is disturbed by anyone having a superior title to the goods, then the buyer can recover damages from the seller through Court of Law. However, this warranty is subject to an agreement to the contrary, *i.e.*, the warranty may be varied or restricted by an agreement between the parties.

Example 21.22. *A* purchased a second hand typewriter from *B*. *A* used it for sometime and also spent some money on its repairs. The typewriter turned out to be stolen one and as such *A* had to return it to the true owner. It was held that *A* could recover damages from *B* amounting to the price paid and the cost of repair. [*Mason* v. *Burmingham* (1949) 2 K.B. 545]

2. *Warranty as to free from encumbrance* [*Section 14(c)*]. It is the second implied warranty in every contract of sale. According to this warranty, it is presumed that the goods shall be free from any charge or encumbrance in favour of any third person. If the possession of the buyer is disturbed due to such charge in favour of third party, he can claim damages from the seller. However, there will not be any such warranty if the charge has been declared to the buyer at the time of sale or if he has notice of such charge.

Example 21.23. *A* obtained a loan of Rs. 200 from *B* and hypothecated his cycle with B as security for the repayment of the loan. Subsequently, *A* sold the same cycle to *C*, an innocent buyer, who had no knowledge about *B's* charge on the cycle. In this case, if *C's* possession is disturbed by *B* who is having charge on the cycle, then he (*C*) can claim damages from *A* for any loss which he may suffer due to such charge.

3. *Warranties implied by customs* [*Section 16(3)*]. Like implied conditions, implied warranties are also attached by custom or usage of trade. This is so because the parties enter into an agreement subject to the known customs or usages of trade.

21.10. CHANGE OF A CONDITION INTO A WARRANTY

> 1. ***Voluntary circumstances [Section 13(1)]***
> 2. ***Compulsory circumstances [Section 13 (23)]:***

Sometimes, a condition is changed to the status of a warranty, *i.e.*, it is reduced to a warranty, and the breach of condition is treated as the breach of a warranty. In such cases, the buyer loses the right to reject the goods on the ground of breach of condition. However, his right to recover damages continues. The circumstances in which a breach of condition is treated as a breach of warranty, may be discussed under the following two heads, namely:

(*a*) Voluntary circumstances, and (*b*) Compulsory circumstances.

1. *Voluntary circumstances* [*Section 13(1)*]. The express or implied conditions are for the benefit of the buyer. He may, at his option, treat them as warranties. The buyer may exercise his option in either of the following two ways:

(*a*) *Waiver of condition:* The buyer may waive off the condition, *i.e.*, if certain condition is not fulfilled, the buyer may give up the condition and accept the goods. The waiver, by the buyer, may be express or implied.

(*b*) *Option to treat the condition as a warranty*: The buyer may also, at his option, treat the breach of a condition as a breach of warranty. Thus, if certain condition is not fulfilled, the buyer may not put an end to the contract by rejecting the goods. He may accept the goods and recover damages from the seller for breach of warranty. Once the buyer exercises his option. *i.e.*, decides to treat the breach of condition as a breach of warranty, he cannot afterwards compel the seller for its fulfilment.

It may be noted that when the buyer waives off the condition or treats its breach as a breach of warranty, he does not lose his right to recover damages from the seller. He remains entitled to recover the damages as in case of breach of a warranty.

2. ***Compulsory circumstances [Section 13(2)]:*** Sometimes, the buyer is bound to treat the breach of condition as a breach of warranty. Such circumstances are contained in Section 13(2) of the Sale of Goods Act. This section provides that, if the contract is not divisible and buyer accepts all the goods or their part, then he cannot reject the goods on the ground that certain condition is not fulfilled. In such cases, he can only claim damages from the seller. This is, however, subject to an agreement to the contrary, *i.e.*, the agreement between the parties may give the right to the buyer to reject the goods. But where the contract is divisible and the buyer has accepted the part of the goods, he can exercise his right to reject the remaining goods.

It may be noted that in case the breach of contition is treated as a breach of warranty, then it does not mean that a condition has become a warranty. The condition remains a condition. Only the buyer's right changes, i.e., the buyer loses his right to reject the goods, he can only recover damages from the seller as in the case of breach of warranty.

21.11. COMPARISON BETWEEN CONDITIONS AND WARRANTIES

The following table gives the comparison between a condition and a warranty:

S. No.	*Condition*	*Warranty*
1.	It is a stipulation which is essential to the main purpose of the contract.	It is a stipulation which is only subsidiary or collateral to the main purpose of the contract.
2.	It is of vital importance. The main contract cannot be completed unless the condition is fulfilled.	It is not of vital importance. The main contract can be completed even if the warranty is not fulfilled.
3.	In case of breach of a condition, the buyer may put an end to the contract.	In case of breach of a warranty, the buyer cannot put an end to the contract. He can only claim damages from the seller.
4.	A breach of condition may be treate d as a breach of warranty.	A breach of warranty cannot be treated as a breach of condition.

21.12. EXCLUSION OF IMPLIED CONDITIONS AND WARANTIES

1. *By express agreement*
2. *By course of dealing*
3. *By customs or trade usages*

In certain circumstances, the liability for the breach of implied conditions and warranties may be excluded. The different modes, by which such liability can be excluded, are contained in Section 62 of the Sale of Goods Act. According to this section, the liability for implied conditions and warranties can be excluded in three way, namely (*a*) by express agreement, (*b*) by course of dealing between the partes, (c) by customs or trade usage.

1. ***By express agreement:*** The liability for implied conditions and warranties may be excluded by an express agreement between the parties. Thus, the seller can exclude his liability by expressly providing in the contract of sale, that he will not be liable for breach of any condition or warranty. It may, however, he noted that a party cannot exclude his liability to perform the contract in its *essential parts, e.g.*, where a contract is for the sale of a brand new thing, the seller cannot exclude his liability by delivering an old thing.

2. *By course of dealing:* The liability for implied conditions or warranties can also be excluded by the course of dealings between the parties. The term 'course of dealings' means the repeated occurrence of similar transactions between the parties. The parties may be dealing in such a way that the seller is not held liable for the breach of implied terms.

3. *By customs or trade usages*: Sometimes, the customs or usages of a particular trade are such that the parties are not held liable for the breach of implied conditions and warranties. Thus, these implied terms may be excluded by the customs or trade usages. This is so because the agreement between the parties are subject to established customs or trade usages. If such customs provide for the exclusion of the liability, then the parties are not liable for the breach of implied conditions and warranties.

21.13. DOCTRINE OF CAVEAT EMPTOR

The term *'caveat emptor'* is a Latin word which means *'let the buyer beware'*, *i.e.*, a buyer purchases the goods at his own risk. As a matter of fact, it is the buyer's duty to select goods of his requirement. And the seller is not bound to supply the goods which shall be fit for any particular purpose of the buyer or which should possess any particular quality. This rule is known as the 'doctrine of caveat emptor'. It is contained in the opening words of Section 16 of the Sale of Goods Act, which reads as under:

> *"Subject to the provisions of this Act and any other law for the time being in force, there is no implied warranty or condition as to the quality or fitness for any particular purpose of goods supplied under a contract of sale."*

In other words, it is not the seller's duty to give to the buyer the goods which are suitable for a particular purpose of the buyer. The buyer must take care of his own purpose while purchasing the goods, *i.e.*, it is his duty to purchase the goods of his requirement. And, if the buyer makes a wrong choice of the goods, he cannot blame the seller if the goods turn out to be defective or do not serve his purpose. The seller is not supposed to know the particular purpose for which the buyer is purchasing the goods.

Example 21.24. *A* sold certain pigs to *B* by auction. The pigs were sold "with all faults and errors of description" (*i.e.*, no warranty was given by the seller in respect of any fault or error of description). *B* paid the price for the pigs. The pigs were ill, and all, except one, died of typhoid fever. They also infected some of buyer's own pigs. It was held that there was no implied condition or warranty that the pigs were of good health. Thus, *B* could not recover damages from *A*. In this case, it was buyer's duty to see whether the pigs were healthy or not.

[*Ward v. Hobbs* (1878) 4 AC 13]

21.14. EXCEPTIONS TO THE DOCTRINE OF CAVEAT EMPTOR

1. *Condition as to quality or fitness for buyer's purpose*
2. *Condition as to merchantability*
3. *Condition as to wholesomeness*
4. *Conditions implied by custms*

As a matter of fact, the doctrine of caveat emptor originated during the time when almost all the sales took place in open market. And the buyer as well as seller used to come face to face, and the buyer had every opportunity to examine the goods or their fitness for a particular purpose. But as the trade expanded, it became difficult for the buyer to examine the goods beforehand due to the complex structure of modern goods. Moreover, some of the transactions are also being conducted by correspondence. Thus, it is only the seller, who can assure the quality of the goods and their fitness for buyer's purpose. Because of these reasons, it became necessary to restrict the application of the doctrine of caveat emptor by providing certain exceptions to it. These exceptions may be discussed under the following heads:

1. ***Condition as to quality or fitness for buyer's purpose:*** Ordinarily, there is no implied condition that the goods shall be fit for the particular purpose of the buyer. But in certain circumstances, the seller is required to supply the goods which shall be fit for buyer's purpose, *e.g.*, where the buyer tells his purpose to the seller and buys goods relying upon the seller's skill and judgment. Thus, if the buyer makes his purpose clear to the seller and buys the goods relying upon his skill and judgment, then there is an implied condition that the goods shall be fit for the buyer's specific purpose. And in such cases, the doctrine of caveat emptor does not apply.

2. ***Condition as to merchantability:*** Sometimes, the goods are sold by description. In such cases, there is an implied condition that the goods shall be of merchantable quality. Thus, in case of sale by description the seller is bound to deliver the goods of merchantable quality. And in such cases also, the doctrine of caveat emptor does not apply.

Note: The above two points have already been discussed in detail in Art. 21.5.

3. ***Condition as to wholesomeness:*** It is a part of the condition as to merchantability. This condition is applicable in cases of eatables, *i.e.*, foodstuffs and other goods which are used for human consumption. In such cases, in addition to the implied condition as to merchantability, another implied condition is that the goods must be wholesome, *i.e.*, sound, pure and fit for consumption at the time of sale. As a matter of fact, the goods shall not be merchantable if they are not fit for human consumption.

Example 21.25. *A* purchased some milk from *B*, a milk dealer. The milk contained some typhoid germs. After consuming the milk. *A's* wife got infection and died. It was held that *A* was entitled to recover damages from the milk dealer. In this case, the milk was not wholesome as it was not pure and fit for human consumption. [*Frost* v. *Aylesury Dairy Co.* (1905) 1 K.B. 608]

4. ***Conditions implied by customs:*** We have discussed above that the implied conditions as to 'fitness'and merchantability'are applicable only if certain requirements are fulfilled. However, the implied condition as to quality or fitness for a particular purpose may be attached by the custom or usage of trade [Section 16(3)]. This is so because the parties enter into an agreement with reference to those known usages. A custom may provide that a particular defect will amount to unfitness, and the buyer can reject the goods. But the customs must not be unreasonable and also not be inconsistent with the express terms of the contract.

Example 21.26. *A* sold certain drugs by auction, to *B*. In case of sale by auction, it was a trade usage to declare any 'sea damage' in the goods. In this case, the goods were sold without such declaration. Subsequently, the goods were found to be sea damaged. It was held that the sale without such declaration meant that the goods were free from any sea damage. And thus, *B* could reject the drugs and claim the refund of the price. [*Jones* v. *Bowden* (1813) 4 Taunt. 847]

LEGAL PROVISIONS (SECTIONS) DISCUSSED IN THE CHAPTER

Important legal provisions (sections) of the Sale of Goods Act, 1930, discussed in this chapter are reproduced hereunder for ready reference:

1. ***Section 12(2): Condition***

   A condition is a stipulation essential to the main purpose of the contract, the breach of the which gives right to treat the contract as repudiated.

2. ***Section 12 (3): Warranty***

   A warranty is a stipulation collateral to the main purpose of the contract, the breach of which gives rise to a claim for damages but not to a right to reject the goods and treat the contract as repudiated.

3. ***Section 14: Implied Conditions and warranties as to Title etc.***

In a contract of sale, unless the circumstances of the contract are such as to show a different intention, there is

(*a*) an implied condition on the part of the seller that, in the case of a sale, he has a right to sell the goods and that, in the case of an agreement to sell, he will have a right to sell the goods at the time when the property is to pass: _

(*b*) an implied warranty that the buyer shall have and enjoy quiet possession of the goods;

(*c*) an implied warranty that the goods shall be free from any charge or encumbrance in favour of any third party not declared or known to the buyer before or at the time when the contract is made.

4. ***Section 15: Implied Condition in Sale by Description***

Where there is a contract for the sale of goods by description, there is an implied condition that the goods shall correspond with the description; and, if the sale is by sample as well as by description, it is not sufficient that the bulk of the goods corresponds with the sample if the goods do not also correspond with the description,

5. ***Section 16: Implied Conditions as to Quality or Fitness***

Subject to the provisions of this Act and of any other law for the time being in force, there is no implied warranty or condition as to the quality or fitness for any particular purpose of goods supplied under a contract of sale, except as follows–

(1) Where the buyer, expressly or by implication, makes known to the seller the particular purpose for which the goods are required, so as to show that the buyer relies on the seller's skill or judgment, and the goods are of a description which it is in the course of the seller's business to supply (whether he is the manufacturer or producer or not), there is an implied condition that the goods shall be reasonably fit for such purpose:

Provided that, in the case of a contract for the sale of a specified article under its patent or other trade name, there is no implied condition as to its fitness for any particular purpose.

(2) Where goods are bought by description from a seller who deals in goods of that description (whether he is the manufacturer or producer or not), there is an implied condition that the goods shall be of merchantable quality:

Provided that if the buyer has examined the goods, there shall be no implied condition as regards defects which such examination ought to have revealed.

(3) An implied warranty or condition as to quality or fitness for a particular purpose may be annexded by the usage of trade.

(4) An express waranty or condition does not negative a warranty or condition implied by this Act unless inconsistent there with.

6. ***Section 17: Implied Conditions in a Sale by Sample***

(1) A contract of sale is a contract of sale by sample where there is a term in the contract, express or implied, to that effect.

(2) In the case of a contract for sale by sample, these is an implied condition:

(*a*) that the bulk shall correspond with the sample in quality;

(*b*) that the buyer shall have a reasonable oppportunity of comparing the bulk with the sample;

(*c*) that the goods shall be free form any defect, rendering them unmerchantable, which would not be apparent on reasonable examintion of the sample.

TEST QUESTIONS

1. Define the term 'condition'. Explain and illustrate the implied conditions in a contract of sale as provided in the Sale of Goods Act.
2. "A sale of goods implies certain conditions which are not subject to any contrary agreement between the contracting parties" –comment.
3. Discuss the provisions of the Sale of Goods Act relating to the implied conditions in a contract of sale by sample.
4. Does a conditions as to fitness for buyer's purpose apply in case of sale by trade name or patent? If not, why? What other condition is implied in such a case?
5. Define the term 'warranty'. Explain and illustrate the implied warranties in a contract of sale as provided in the Sale of Good Act. State the comparison between a condition and a warranty.
6. Explain the difference between a condition and a warranty.
7. "In a contract for the sale of goods, there is no implied condition or warranty as to the quality of the goods or their fitness for any purpose" — comment.

8. Comment on the following:
   (*a*) A vendor of goods need not point out patent defects.
   (*b*) Goods sold must be of merchantable quality.
9. "A contract of sale of goods is always subject to certain implied conditions, but they can be treated as warranties" – critically examine.
10. State the circumstances in which a condition is reduced to the status of a warranty. Can the implied conditions and warranties be also excluded? If yes, state the circumstances.
11. Explain the rule of caveat emptor. Discuss the cases in which the rule of caveat emptor does not apply.
12. "Let the buyer beware"— comment.

MULTIPLE CHOICE QUESTIONS

1. A stipulation which is essential to the main purpose of the contract, and if proves false, give the buyer a right to terminate the contract, is legally known as
   (*a*) condition (*b*) guarantee
   (*c*) warranty (*d*) none of these.
2. A stipulation which is collateral to the main purpose of the contract, and if proves false, gives the buyer only a right to claim damages, is known as
   (*a*) condition (*b*) guarantee
   (*c*) warranty (*d*) none of these.
3. Which of the following is not an implied condition in a contract of sale?
   (*a*) Condition as to title (*b*) Condition as to description
   (*c*) Condition as to free from encumbrance (*d*) Condition as to sample.
4. In case the goods, sold by sample as well as description, corresponds with the sample only, then the
   (*a*) buyer can reject the goods (*b*) buyer cannot reject the goods
   (*c*) contract is automatically terminated (*d*) seller is liable to punishment.
5. The implied condition that goods shall be fit for buyer's specific purpose, is applicable only where the buyer tells his purpose to the seller and relies upon seller's skill and judgment.
   (*a*) True, as it is the requirement of law.
   (*b*) False, as it is buyer's duty to select goods which serve his purpose.
6. The term 'merchantable'is defined is Section 14(2) of the
   (*a*) Sale of Goods Act, (*b*) Indian Contract Act
   (*c*) English Sale of Goods Act (*d*) None of these.
7. In case, a condition is changed to the status of a warranty, then the buyer
   (*a*) loses the right to reject goods (*b*) retains right to claim damages only
   (*c*) both (*a*) and (*b*) are true (*d*) both (*a*) and (*b*) are false.

ANSWERS

1. (*a*)	2. (*c*)	3. (*c*)	4. (*a*)	5. (*a*)	6. (*c*)
7. (*c*)					

OBJECTIVE TYPE QUESTIONS WITH REASONING

State with reasons whether the following statements are correct or incorrect.

1. A stipulation essential to the main purpose of the contract, the breach of which gives right to treat the contract as repudiated, is known as a warranty.
2. In every contract of sale, there is an implied condition that the seller has the right to sell the goods.

3. Where in case of sale by description the goods do not correspond with the description, the buyer is not entitled to reject the goods if the goods serve his purpose.
4. In a contract of sale by sample as well as by description, the bulk of the goods must correspond either to sample or to description.
5. In a contract of sale, the breach of implied condition gives right to repudiate the contract.
6. In a contract of sale, there is no implied condition as to quality or fitness of goods for a particular purpose.
7. In case of sale by description, there is no implied condition as to merchantability of goods.
8. In case of sale of goods under a patent or a trade name, there is no implied condition as to the fitness of goods for any particular pupose.
9. Where the buyer elects to treat the breach of condition as one of warranty, he may repudiate the contract.
10. The doctrine of 'caveat emptor'implies that the seller is under a duty to supply the goods suitable for buyer's purpose.

ANSWERS

1. *Incorrect.* Such a stipulation is known as a condition.
2. *Correct.* There can be no sale at all if the seller has no right to sell the goods. Such a condition is essential to protect the interest of innocent buyer.
3. *Incorrect.* In case of sale by description, the buyer has the right to reject the goods if they do not correspond with the description [Section 15].
4. *Incorrect.* In such a case, the implied condition is that the goods must correspond with *both* the sample as well as description
5. *Correct.* A condition is the stipulation which is essential to the main contract and must be strictly complied with.
6. *Correct.* It is the general rule on the point.
7. *Incorrect.* In such a case, the seller is bound to deliver the goods of merchantable quality.
8. *Correct.* In such a case, the buyer relies more on the trade name of a commodity than on skill and judgement of the seller [Section 16(1), second para].
9. *Incorrect.* Once the breach of condition is treated as a breach of warranty, the buyer loses the right to repudiate the contract though his right to recover damages continues.
10. *Incorrect.* This doctrine implies 'let the buyer beware' *i.e.*, a buyer purchases the goods at his own risk.

PRACTICAL PROBLEMS

1. *A* bought a second hand motor cycle from *B*. After a few months, the motor-cycle was taken by the police as it was a stolen one, and *A* had to return the motor cycle to the true owner. Can *A* recover the price from *B* ?

   Hints. Yes *A* can legally recover price paid to *B*. In this case, there is breach of condition as to title as *B* had no title to sell the motor cycle. [section 14 (a) *see Rowland* v *Divall* (1923) KB 500]
2. *A* contracted to sell to *B* the timbers of 15 mm thickness. But when *B* received the timber, it was discovered that the timbers varied in thickness from 15mm to 20mm. However, the timbers were fit for *B* purposes as he bought them to make cement barrels. *B* wants to reject the goods. Would he be justified in doing so ?

   Hints: Yes, *B* can reject the timber and he would be justified in doing so as there is a breach of condition as to description. In this case, the sale was by description and the goods did not correspond with the description given in the contract. [Section 15, *Across* v *Ranason* (1933) AC 470]
3. *A* advertised a vessel (*i.e.* ship) for sale describing as "Copper fastened vessel on the terms that it has to be taken with all faults, without allowance for any defects what so ever" On the basis of description, *B* purchased the ship, but it was discovered that the ship was partially copper fastened and would not be called in the trade as copper-fastened vessel'. Can *B* claim refund of price ? Give reasons.

Hints. Yes, *B* can claim refund of price. In this case, there is breach of condition as to description. [Section 15, *shepherd* v *Kain*]

4. *A* sold some cloth of 'worsted cotton quantity' to *B* after showing the sample. Lateron, it was discovered that the cloth was defective and unfit for stitching into coats as the coats made out of it were not fit to stand ordinary wear. The same defect was there in the sample. Can *A* be held liable to pay damages to *B* ? Give reasons.

   Hints. Yes, *A* is liable to pay damages to *B*. In the case, the goods *i.e.* cloth was not of merchantable quality. Here there was latent defect in the cloth which could not be discovered by ordinary examination. [Section 17 (2),(c), *Drummond sons* v *Van Ingen* (1887) 12 AC 284]

5. *A* sold to *B* certain quantities of 'Foreign' refined rape oil warranted only equal to samples'. The samples consisted of rape oil mixed with hemp oil. The oil tendered corresponded with the samples, but it was not such as is known in the market as "Foreign refined rape oil". Can *B* reject the goods ?

   Hints. Yes, *B* can reject the goods. In this case, the sale is by description and when the goods do not correspond with the description there is a breach of condition as to sale by description which entiles the buyer to repudiate the contract. [*Nichol* v *Dodts* (1854) 10 Ex. 191, 102, R.R. 523]

6. *A* contracts to sell Java Sugar according to the sample produced by him. On the delivery of the sample to *B*, the buyer, it transpires that the sugar agrees with sample but is not Java Sugar. Will *B* be entitled to any remedies ?

   Hints. Yes, *B* can repudiate the contract as the goods do not correspond with the description.

7. *A* enters into a chemists shop and asked for a hot water bottle. He is shown a bottle which the shop-keeper say, will not stand boiling water, but is meant for hot water. *A* buys the bottle, and one day while using it, it bursts and injures *A*. It is proved that the bottle was not fit for use as a hot water bottle. Can *A* recover damages from the shop-keeper ?

   Hints. Yes, *A* can be recover damages from the shop-keeper. In this case there is breach of condition as to fitness. Here, buyer's purpose was clear from the nature of the bottle. [Section 16, see also *Priest* v *Last*, (1903) 2, K, B, 148]

8. *A* sold certain quantity of pure ghee to *B* by showing the samples. The ghee was described as pure ghee. The ghee supplied correspond to the sample, but was adulterated with 25 % groundnut oil. Is the buyers bound to accept?

   Hints. No as there is breach of condition as to sample as well as description. [Section 15]

9. A lady buys synthetic pearls for a high price thinking that they are natural pearls. The seller does not correct her mistake. Has she any remedies against the seller ? Would your decision be different if the lady had told the seller: "I think they are natural pearls and therefore, agree to buy them at your price", and the seller was silent ?

   Hints. The lady has no remedy against the seller as the doctrine of caveat emptor applies in this case. In the second case, the decision will be different. Here, the lady can avoid the contract as there is a breach of condition as to quality. [Section 16 (1)]

10. A wholesale dealer in soaps agrees to sell and deliver two cases of NIRMA toilet soap to a sub-dealer but delivers that quantity of 'NIRMA' washing soap. What are the rights of the sub-dealer ?

    Hints. The sub-dealer can repudiate the contract on the ground of breach of condition as to description. [Section 15]

11. A lady who knew that she was allergic to a particular hair dye developed dermatitis as a result of having her hair dyed with that substance. She did not disclose her allergy to the shop-keeper while buying that hair dye. Is the shop-keeper liable for breach of implied condition ?

    Hints. No, the shop-keeper is not liable for breach of implied condition as to the fitness of the hair dye since that condition extends to the dyeing of the hair of a normal person.

    [Section 16 (1), *Ingham* v. *Emes* (1955) 2 Q.B.366, *Griffiths* v. *Peter Conway, Ltd*, (1939) ALL E.R. 683]

12. *A* sold to *B* a tin of disinfectant powder. He knew that it would be dangerous to open the tin without special care but he did not warn *B*. *B* without knowledge of the danger, opened the tin whereupon the powder flew into his eyes and injured him. *B* field a suit for damages for the injury. Will he succeed ?

    Hints. Yes, as the goods were not of merchantable quanlity. [Section 16 (2)]

13. *A* agreed to sell to *B* two parcels of rice of which the sample was shown to *B*. The buyer (*B*) went to *A's* warehouse to examine the parcel. One parcel lying in the warehouse was shown to *B*, but he was not allowed to see the other parcel which was lying at some other place. Can the buyer put an and to the entire contract ?

    Hints. Yes, as the buyer has not been given the opportunity to compare the goods with sample. [Section 17 (2) (b), see also *Lorymere* v *Smith* (1822) 1 B&C 1]

14. *A*, a housewife, ordered from *C*, a coal merchant, 'a ton of coalite' and it was duly delivered to her. When part of the consignment was put on fire in an open grate in *A*'s house, an explosion occurred which caused damage. *A* claims damages. Is she entitled to sue ?

Hints. Yes, as the goods are not of merchantable quality. [Section 16 (2)]

15. In a contract for the purchase of 3,000 tins of canned fruits packed in cases each containing 30 tins, a substantial part was tendered in cases containing 24 tins instead of 30. Can the buyer reject the cases?

Hints. Yes, as the goods do not correspond with the description of the goods ordered. [Section 15; *Moore & Co.* v. *Landaur & Co.*)]

16. *A* agreed to sell a second-hand reaping machine which *B*, the buyer, had not seen. The seller stated the machine was only one year old and had been used to cut 50 acres only. *B*, however, found that the machine, when it was delivered was very old and had even been repaired. Can *B* repudiate the contract ?

Hints. Yes, as there is a breach of the implied condition that the goods shall correspond with the description. [Section 15]

17. *A* sells a horse to *B*. When *B* goes with the horse he is arrested by the police on the charge of keeping stolen property as the horse belongs to *C*. Can *B* sue *A*, and if so, on what basis, and what damages can he recover ?

Hints. Yes, *B* can sue *A* and can also recover the loss suffered by him which is the direct and natural consequence of the breach of condition. [Section 14 (a), *Rowland* v. *Divall*]

18. *A* sold certain pigs to *B* by auction. The pigs were sold "with all faults and errors of description" (*i.e.* no warranty was given by the seller in respect of any fault or error of description). *B* paid the price for the pigs and took the delivery. The pigs were ill and all except one, died of fever. They also infected some of buyer's own pigs. Can *B* recover damages from *A* ? Give reasons.

Hints. No, as there was no implied condition or warranty that the pigs were of good health. In this case, it was buyer's duty to see whether the pigs were healthy or not. [*Ward* v. *Hobbs* (1878 4 AC 13]

22 CHAPTER

TRANSFER OF OWNERSHIP (PASSING OF PROPERTY)

22.1. INTRODUCTION

The term 'property in the goods' may be defined as the legal ownership of the goods. On the passing of the property to the buyer, he becomes the owner of the goods and acquires all the rights held by the seller in respect of the goods sold. The term 'property in the goods' must be distinguished from the term 'possession of the goods'. The term 'property in the goods' means the ownership of the goods, whereas the term 'possession of the goods' simply means the custody or physical control over the goods. A person may have the possession of the goods, but he may not be the owner of the same, *e.g.*, an agent, a servant or a bailee may have the possession of the goods. But he is not the owner, because the ownership of the goods lies with the principal, master or bailor. At the same time, a person may be the owner of the goods, but he may not have the possession of the goods. Thus, the transfer of possession is merely the delivery of the goods, and not the transfer of ownership.

It is to be noted that the ownership of the goods may pass with or without the transfer of possession.

The main purpose of a contract of sale is the transfer of ownership of the goods from a seller to a buyer. When the ownership of the goods is transferred to the buyer, he becomes the owner of the goods, and the seller ceases to be so. In this chapter, we shall discuss the legal provisions relating to the transfer of ownership of movable goods only as the Sale of Goods Act applies only to movable goods.

22.2. SIGNIFICANCE OF TRANSFER OF OWNERSHIP

1. *Risk passes with the ownership*
2. *Proprietary rights over the goods*
3. *Seller's right price*
4. *Insolvency of the seller or the buyer*

Many rights and liabilities of the parties are linked with the transfer of ownership. And thus, it is very necessary to determine the time at which the ownership of the goods passes form a seller to a buyer. The following points are significant for the transfer of ownership of the goods:

1. ***Risk passes with the ownership :*** Sometimes, the goods are lost or destroyed due to theft, fire, earthquakes, etc. In such cases, it is the owner who has to suffer the loss of the goods. Thus, before the ownership of the goods is transferred, it is the seller who has to bear the risk for the loss of the goods. And after the transfer of ownership, it is the buyer who has to bear the risk for the loss of the goods. In other words, the risk passes with the transfer of ownership.

Note: In this case, the possession of the goods is not relevant, *i.e.*, the loss is suffered by the party having the ownership of the goods and not by the party having the mere possession of the same.

2. ***Proprietary rights over the goods :*** The term 'proprietary rights' means the right relating to one's own property. As a matter of fact, after the transfer of ownership of the goods, the buyer becomes entitled to exercise all the proprietary rights over the goods, *i.e.*, he gets all the rights over the goods as their owner, *e.g.*, if the seller refuses to deliver the goods, the buyer can bring an action against him for the delivery of the goods. And if the seller has resold the same goods to another person, the original buyer can also recover the goods from such person in certain circumstances, Moreover, if the goods are damaged or destroyed due to some act of a third person, the buyer can take action against such person.

3. ***Seller's right for price :*** The seller becomes entitled to recover the price of the goods from the buyer only after the ownership of the goods has been transferred to the buyer.

4. ***Insolvency of the seller or the buyer :*** An 'insolvent' means a person who has been declared by the court to be unable to pay his debts. 'On the insolvency of a person, the Receiver or Official Assignee' takes the possession of the property belonging to the insolvent. In this connection, the ownership of the goods is very important because the Receiver or Official Assignee can take the possession only of those goods of which the insolvent is the owner. Thus, if the seller is declared insolvent, the Receiver cannot take over the possession of the goods from him, if the ownership had already been transferred to the buyer. Similarly, if the buyer is declared insolvent, the Receiver cannot take over the possession of the goods from him if the ownership is still with the seller.

22.3. RULES FOR THE TRANSFER OF OWNERSHIP

The rules for the transfer of ownership are contained in Sections 18 to 24 of the Sale of Goods Act. These rules determine the time at which the ownership of the goods is transferred from the seller to the buyer. However, the general rule is that the "transfer of ownership depends upon the intention of both the parties" As a matter of fact, the Sale of Goods Act leaves the whole question of 'transfer of ownership' upon the intention of the parties [Section 19]. The parties may fix any time for the transfer of ownership from the seller to the buyer. But sometimes, the intention of the parties is not clear from the contract itself. In such cases, their intention is ascertained in accordance with the rules laid down is Sections 18 to 24 of the Sale of Goods Act. These rules may be discussed under the following heads:

1. Transfer of ownership in case of sale of specific goods. [Section 20-22]
2. Transfer of ownership in case of sale of unascertained goods.[Section 18 and 23]
3. Transfer of ownership in case of sale on approval [Section 24]

22.4. TRANSFER OF OWNERSHIP IN CASE OF SALE OF SPECIFIC GOODS

1. *The ownership is transferred at the time of making the contract*
2. *The ownership may also be transferred at some other time*

In case of sale of specific goods, the rules relating to the transfer of ownership are contained in Sections 20 to 22 of the Sale of Goods Act. These may be discussed under the following subheads:

1. *The ownership is transferred at the time of making the contract:* The general rule, in case of specific goods, is that the ownership of the goods is transferred from the seller to the buyer at the time of making the contract. This rule is contained in Section 20 of the Sale of Goods Act. As per this section, the ownership is transferred at the time of the contract only if all the following conditions are fulfilled:

(*a*) The sale must be of specific goods.
(*b*) The goods must be in a deliverable state.
(*c*) The contract of sale must be unconditional.

On the fulfilment of all the above three conditions, the ownership of the goods is transferred from the seller to the buyer. It may be noted that it makes no difference if the payment of the price or the delivery of the goods or both are postponed.

Example 22.1. *A* sold to *B* 152 bales of yarn lying in his godown along with other bales. Before the bales could be identified and separated, all the bales were destroyed in a fire. It was held that the ownership of the bales had not transferred to the buyer as the bales were not identified and separated from the rest of the bales. Here, the contract was not for the sale of specific goods. [*L. Karn* v. *John & Co.* 1967 All 308].

2. *The ownership may also be transferred at some other time :* If any of the above discussed conditions is not satisfied, then the ownership will not be transferred at the time of contract of sale, *e.g.*, when the goods are not in a deliverable state, or the seller has to do some act in connection with the goods. In such cases, the rules contained in Section 21 and 22 of the Sale of Goods Act shall apply, which may be discussed under the following sub-heads :

(*a*) *Where the goods are to be put in a deliverable state by the seller :* Sometimes, the specific goods are not in a deliverable state at the time of contract, and the seller has to do some act to put them in a deliverable state. In such cases, the ownership is transferred to the buyer on the fulfilment of the following conditions [Section 21]:

(*i*) When the seller has done his act of putting the goods into a deliverable state, and
(*ii*) When the buyer came to know that the goods have been put into a deliverable state.

The seller may be required to do certain acts to put the goods into a deliverable state, *e.g.*, packing, filling the goods in containers, collecting the goods, separating or loading the goods etc.

Example 22.2. *A* sold to *B* some quantity of oil lying in cistern. As per the terms of the contract, *A* was required to fill the oil in drums and then the drums were to be taken away by *B*. *A* filled some of the drums in *B*'s presence. Before the remainder could be filled, a fire broke out and the whole quantity of oil was destroyed. It was held that the buyer must bear the loss of oil which was filled in drums, and the seller must bear the loss of remaining unfilled drums. [*Rugg* v. *Minett* (1809) 11 East 210].

(*b*) *Where the goods are to be weighed or measured by the seller to ascertain the price :* Sometimes the *specific goods* are in a deliverable state, but the seller has to do some act for the purpose of ascertaining their price. In such cases, the ownership is transferred to the buyer on the fulfillment of the following conditions [Section 22]:

(*i*) When the seller has done his act of ascertaining the price of the goods, and

(*ii*) When the buyer came to know that the price has been ascertained by seller's acts.

The seller may be required to do certain acts for the purpose of ascertaining the price of the goods, *e.g.*, to weigh the goods, measure the goods or to test the goods, etc.

Example 22.3. *A* sold some quantity of wheat to *B* at the rate of Rs. 10 per kg. However, *A* had to weight the wheat in order to know the price of the entire quantity of wheat sold to *B*. In this case, the ownership of the wheat shall transfer to *B* as soon as the *A* weighs the wheat and *B* comes to know about the same.

22.5. TRANSFER OF OWNERSHIP IN CASE OF SALE OF UNASCERTAINED GOODS

1. ***Ascertainment of goods***
2. ***Appropriation of goods to the contract***

The unascertained goods are the goods which are not specifically identified at the time of making the contract of sale. In case of sale of unascertained goods, the ownership is transferred to the buyer as soon as the goods are identified (*i.e.*, ascertained), and are set apart for the purpose of delivering to the buyer. This rule is contained in Sections 18 and 23 of the Sale of Goods Act. The analysis of these two sections reveals that in case of sale of unascertained goods, the ownership is transferred to the buyer on the fulfilment of both the following conditions :

(*a*) when the goods are ascertained, and

(*b*) When the goods are appropriated to the contract.

1. *Ascertainment of goods :* The term 'ascertainment' means the process by which the goods to be delivered under the contract are identified and set apart. It is a *unilateral act* of the seller alone to identify and set apart the goods. It may be noted that the ownership is not transferred merely by the ascertainment of the goods. After ascertaining the goods, these must also be appropriated to the contract.

2. *Appropriation of goods to the contract :* The term 'appropriation' means the process by which the goods to be delivered under the contract are identified and set apart with the *mutual consent* of the seller as well as buyer. It is a *bilateral act* of the seller and the buyer to identify and set apart the goods. The appropriation may be done either by the seller with the consent of the buyer, or by the buyer with the consent of the seller. Such consent may be express or implied [Section 23(1)]. Once the goods are appropriated with the mutual consent of the parties, they become the property of the buyer. And if they have not been delivered, they are in the custody of the seller as a bailee. However, the appropriation must be unconditional. Ordinarily, the act of appropriation is done by the seller, because the goods are generally in his possession. The seller may appropriate the goods in one of the following ways :

(*a*) By separating the contracted goods from the other with the consent of the buyer.

(*b*) By putting the contracted quantity in suitable receptacles, *i.e.*, by putting the goods into boxes, gunny bags, in case of liquids by putting them into bottles, etc., with the consent of the buyer.

(*c*) By delivering the contracted goods to the carrier or other bailee for the purpose of transmission to the buyer and without reserving the right of disposal.

Example 22.4. *A* agreed to sell to *B* the oil to be produced by him. The oil was filled by *A* into the bottles supplied by *B*. It is an effective appropriation and the ownership passes to the buyer when the oil is filled into the bottles. In this case, the buyer gave his consent to the appropriation by supplying the bottles. [*Langton* v. *Higginis* (1858) 4 H N 402]

22.6. TRANSFER OF OWNERSHIP IN CASE OF SALE ON APPROVAL

> 1. *Acceptance of goods*
> 2. *Adoption of transaction*
> 3. *Failure to returen the goods*

The term 'sale on approval' may be defined as the sale in which the buyer may return the goods within a reasonable time, if the goods do not serve his purpose. This is also known as **'sale on return'** basis. In case of sale on approval, the ownership is transferred to the buyer when he accepts the goods. It may be noted that the seller cannot ask for the return of the goods. He can only recover the price of the goods if the goods are not returned within a reasonable time. Section 24 provides that in case of sale on approval, the ownership is transferred to the buyer in any of the following three ways :

1. When he accepts the goods, or
2. When he adopt the transaction, or
3. When he fails to return the goods.

The above three points are discussed in detail in the following pages :

1. *Acceptance of goods :* The buyer may accept the goods and inform the seller accordingly. When the buyer gives his acceptance (*i.e.*, approval) to the seller, the ownership is transferred to the buyer. The acceptance of goods by the buyer may be express or implied. The cases discussed in next two points fall under the category of implied acceptance.

2. *Adoption of transaction :* The buyer may adopt the transaction by doing some act in respect of the goods. When the buyer does some act, which show that he has adopted the goods, the ownership is transferred to him on the act of adoption. It is known as the implied acceptance. It generally takes place when the buyer deals with the goods as his own, *e.g.*, sells or pledges the goods to the third persons.

Example 22.5. *A* delivered some diamonds to *B* on 'sale or return' basis, *B* delivered the diamonds to *C*, and *C* to *D* on similar terms. The diamonds were stolen while in the custody of *D*. In this case, *B* had adopted the transaction by delivering the diamonds to *C*. Thus, *B* is liable to pay the price to *A*. Similarly, *C* had also adopted the transaction by delivering the diamonds to *D*. And thus, *C* is also liable to pay the price to *B*. [*Genn* v. *Winkel* (1911) 28 TLR 483]

3. *Failure to return the goods :* The ownership is also transferred to the buyer when he fails to return the goods to the seller. As a matter of fact, this also amounts to implied acceptance of the goods. This point may be discussed under the following two sub-heads:

(*a*) ***When the time is fixed for the return of the goods :*** In such cases, if the buyer fails to return the goods within the fixed time, the ownership is transferred to the buyer on the expiry of such fixed time.

(*b*) ***When no time is fixed for the seturn of the goods :*** In such cases, if the buyer fits to seturn the goods within a *reasonable time*, the ownership is transferred to the buyer on the expiry of the reasonable time.

Example 22.6. *A* delievered a horse to *B* on 'sale or return' basis. It was agreed that *B* should try it for 8 days and then return if he did not like it. The horse die on the 3rd day without any fault of *B*. It was held that the horse was still the property of the seller. As such, the seller could not recover the price from the buyer.

22.7. DELIVERY TO A CARRIER

The term 'carrier' may be defined as a transportation agency to whom the goods are deli-vered for the purpose of transmission to the buyer. The delivery to the carrier means and includes the handing over the goods to such transportation agency, *e.g.*, a railways, a shipping corporation, a motor transport agency or post office, etc. The delivery of goods to the carrier is one of the modes of appropriation of goods. This mode of appropriation is recognised in Section 23 (2) of the Sale of goods Act. It may, therefore, be noted that where without reserving the right of disposal, the goods are delivered to the carrier for the purpose of transmission to the seller, the ownership passes to the buyer. However, the delivery to the carrier amounts to the delivery to the buyer only if the following requirements are satisfied :

1. The goods should agree with the contract, *i.e.*, the goods should be of contract quality.
2. The goods should be delivered to the carrier for the purpose of transmission to the buyer.
3. It must be made known to the carrier to which particular buyer the goods are appropriated. Moreover, the carrier must also know which particular goods belong to the buyer.
4. The seller should not reserve the right of disposal, *i.e.*, the seller should be ready and willing to part with the ownership of the goods.

Example 22.7. *A* bought 20 boxes of fish from *B*, a fish dealer. *B* consigned 190 boxes of fish with the Railway Deptt. of which 20 boxes were meant for *A* and the rest for some other buyer. But the boxes to be delivered to *A* were not sorted out and earnmarked. This was to be done by the Railway Deptt. itself. The consignment was delayed during the transportaion, and when ultimately the 20 boxes of fish were marked off for *A*, the fish had already deteriorated. *A* refused to take the delivery of the 20 boxes and *B* filed a suit against him for the recorery of the price. It was held that *A* was not liable to pay the price as at the time of deterioration, the ownership of the boxes of fish had not ransferred to him. In this case, the delivery of boxes to the carrier (*i.e.*, railway deptt.) did not amount to the delivery to the buyer (*A*) until the boxes were maked off for *A*. [*Healey* v. *Howlett & Sons* (1917) 1 KB 337]

22.8. RESERVATION OF RIGHT OF DISPOSAL

1. By taking the documents of title in his own name or his agent's name
2. By sending the bill of exchange for the price, to the buyer along with the doucument of title

Sometimes, the seller may like to retain the ownership of the goods until some later date, *e.g.*, until the price is paid or some conditions fulfilled. The seller may do so by reserving his right of disposal. The seller is said to have reserved his right of disposal where his action shows that he has an intention not to part with the ownership of the goods till the fulfilment of certain conditions. In such cases, the ownership of the goods is not transferred to the buyer until the conditions, imposed by the seller, are fulfilled. It may be noted that where the seller has reserved his right of disposal, the ownership of the goods is not transferred to the buyer even if the goods are delivered to the buyer or some carrier for the purpose of transmission to the buyer. The ownership is transferred to the buyer only when the conditions imposed by the seller are fulfilled [Section 25 (1)].

Example 22.8. *A* agreed to sell certain goods to *B*. One of the conditions of the contract of sale was that the buyer must pay the price before the delivery of the goods. In this case, by making th edelivery of goods conditional upon the payment of price, the seller has reserved his right of disposal. The ownership of the goods will not be transferred to *B* until this condition is fulfilled, *i.e.*, until the price is paid by him. [Based on *Loeschman* v. *Williams* (1815) 4 Camp. 181]

It may be noted that the seller may reserve his right of disposal by imposing any condition he likes. However, in the following two circumstances the seller is presumed to have reserved the right of disposal :

---

1. The bill of lading is the document on the basis of which the delivery of the goods can be taken from the shipping corporation or company.
2. The railway receipts is the document on the basis of which the delivery of the goods can be taken from the railways.

1. *By taking the documents of title in his own name or his agent's name* [*Section 25 (2)*] *:* Sometimes, the goods are shipped or delivered to the railways for carriage. But the document of title, *i.e.*, the bill of lading[1] (in case of carriage by sea) or the railway receipts[2] (in case of carriage by railways) are taken by the seller in his own name or in his agent's name. In such cases, the seller is presumed to have reserved the right of disposal.

2. *By sending the bill of exchange for the price, to the buyer along with the documents of title* [Section 25(3)] *:* Sometimes, the goods are delivered to a carrier (*i.e.*, the shipping corporation or railways) and the bill of lading or the railway receipts are taken in the name of the buyer. But the seller draws a bill of exchange on the buyer for the price of the goods, and sends the same to the buyer along with the bill of lading or railway receipts to secure the payment of the price. In such cases also, the seller is presumed to have reserved the right of disposal. And the ownership of the goods is not transferred to the buyer until he accepts the bill of exchange or pays the price of the goods.

22.9. PASSING OF RISK

The general rule in the contract of sale is that *'the risk prima facie passes with the ownership'*, *i.e.*, the risk and the ownership of the goods go together. In other words, the goods are at the risk of the party who has the ownership of the goods. This means that in case of loss of the goods, the loss shall be borne by the party who has the ownership of the goods at the time of loss. Thus, the actual delivery of goods is immaterial for the passing of the risk. It is only the ownership, which is relevant for the purpose. This provision is contained in Section 26 of the Sale of Goods Act. The analysis of this section reveals the following two rules :

1. The goods are at the risk of the seller if the ownership has not been transferred to the buyer. And in case of loss of the goods, he shall bear the loss.
2. The goods are at the risk of the buyer, if the ownership has been transferred to the buyer. And in case of loss of the goods, he shall bear the loss.

22.10. EXCEPTIONS TO THE RULE THAT RISK PASSES WITH THE OWNERSHIP

1. ***Agreement between the parties***
2. ***Goods are at the risk of the party in default***
3. ***Trade customs***

In the following exceptional circumstances, the goods may be at the risk of one party and their ownership may be with the other.

1. *Agreement between the parties :* The risk and the ownership may be separated by an agreement between the seller and the buyer. In other words, the terms of agreement between the parties may provides as to when the ownership shall be transferred and who shall suffer the loss.

Example 22.9. *A* sold some goods to *B* to be delivered to him at his place. The agreement specifically provided that during the transportation, the goods shall be the property of the seller but at the risk of the buyer. During the transportation, the goods were destroyed by an accident. In this case, the risk shall pass according to the terms of the agreement between the parties. Thus, the buyer will suffer the loss of the goods though the ownership of the goods is with the seller.

[Based on *M. Champalal* v. *C.P. Shah*, AIR 1970 Mysore 106].

2. *Goods are at the risk of the party in default :* Sometimes, the delivery of the goods is delayed due to the fault of either seller or buyer. In such cases, the goods shall be at the risk of the party in default though their ownership is with the other party [Section 26 (second Para)]. Thus, the defaulting party shall suffer the loss which has occurred due to such delayed delivery of the goods.

Example 22.10. *A* sold some quantity of apple juice to *B*. But *B* did not take the delivery of the goods for a long time. And the juice deteriorated due to this delayed delivery. It was held that the loss of deterioration should be suffered by *B*.

[*Demby Hamilton & Co.* v. *Baden (E. Wines) Ltd.* 1949 All ER 435].

3. *Trade customs* : The risk and the ownership may also be separated by the trade customs, *e.g.*, the trade custom may provide that the goods shall be at the risk of the buyer whether or not the ownership has been transferred to him.

22.11. TRANSFER OF TITLE BY NON-OWNERS

1. *Title by estoppel.*
2. *Sale by a mercantile agent*
3. *Sale by a joint owner*
4. *Sale by a person in possession under a voidable contract*
5. *Sale by a seller in possession of goods after their sale*
6. *Sale by a buyer in possession of goods after their sale*
7. *Sale by a finder of goods*
8. *Sale by a pawnee or pledgee*
9. *Sale by an official appointed by the court*

Sometimes, the goods are sold by a person who is not their absolute owner. In such cases, the buyer will not become the absolute owner of the goods, *i.e.*, he will not get a valid title to the goods. This is based on the following important Latin maxim;

"Nemo dat quod non habet"

This means that 'no one can transfer a better title than he himself has'. Thus, the buyer cannot get a better title than that of the seller. If the seller's own title is defective, the buyer's title will also be defective, *e.g.*, where a thief sells the goods, the buyer from such a thief gets no title to the goods. This rule is contained in Section 27 of the Sale of Goods Act, which reads as under :

> *"Where goods are sold by a person who is not the owner thereof and who does not sell them under the authority or with the consent of the owner, the buyer acquires no better title to the goods than that the seller had."*

Thus, where the goods are sold by a non-owner, the buyer does not get a better title to the goods than that of the seller, *i.e.*, the sale by a non-owner does not make the buyer an absolute owner of the goods.

Example 22.11. *A* stole a horse and delivered it to *B*, an auctioneer, for the purpose of selling it. *B* sold the horse to *C* at public auction. It was held that *C* obtained no title to the horse as the seller (*B*) had no title to it. [*Leo* v. *Bayes* (1856) 8 CB 599]

Example 22.12. *A* was a hirer of some goods under the hire purchase agreement. He sold the goods to *B* who bought them in a good faith. In this case, *B* will not become the owner of the goods because *A* was only a hirer and not the owner.

However, in the following exceptional circumstances, the buyer gets a valid title even if the seller is not the absolute owner of the goods. As a matter of fact, these exceptions are necessary to protect the *bona fide* commercial transactions, and the interest of the innocent buyers.

1. *Title by estoppel* : An estoppel is the prevention of a claim or assertion of law. In other words, when someone makes another person to believe that a particular thing or fact is true, then afterwards he cannot be allowed to deny the truth of that thing or fact. Thus, when the owner of goods, by his conduct or by statement, wilfully leads the buyer to believe that the seller has the authority to sell, then he is estopped (*i.e.*, prevented) from denying the seller's authority to sell. It is known as estoppel against the seller. If the buyer buys the goods in such belief, later on the owner cannot say that the seller had no authority to sell. And the buyer, who buys the goods in *good faith*, gets a valid title to the goods.

Example 22.13. *A* said to *B*, a buyer, in the presence of *C* that he (*A*) is the owner of the horse. But *C* remained silent though the horse belonged to him. *B* bought the horse from *A*. Here, the buyer (*B*) will get a valid title to the horse even though the seller (*A*) had no title to the horse. In this case, *C*, by his own conduct, is prevented from denying *A*'s authority to sell the horse.

2. *Sale by a mercantile agent* : A 'mercantile agent' is an agent who deals in the buying and selling of the goods on behalf of his principal, *e.g.*, an auctioneer. Where a mercantile agent sells goods in the ordinary course of his business, the buyer gets a valid title to the goods even if he (the mercantile agent) is not the owner of the goods [Section 27 (second para)]. This exception is necessary to protect the innocent buyers. However, the buyer will get a valid title only if the following conditions are a satisfied :

(*a*) The mercantile agent must be in possession of the goods or of the documents of title[3] to the goods.

(*b*) The mercantile agent must obtain the possession of the goods with the consent of the owner. Moreover, he must have the possession in his capacity as a mercantile agent.

(*c*) The mercantile agent must sell the goods in his capacity as such agent.

(*d*) The mercantile agent must sell the goods while acting in the ordinary course of business of such an agent.

(*e*) The buyer must act in a *good faith.* And he should presume that the mercantile agent has full authority to sell the goods.

Example 22.14. *A* delivered his car to *B*, a mercantile agent, for sale. *A* instructed *B* that the car should be sold at a stated price and not below that. But *B* sold the car to *C* below the stated price and misappropriate the money. However, *C* had bought the car in a *good faith.* In this case, *C* will get a valid title to the car and *A* cannot recover it back from him. However, he can claim the price of the car from *B*. [*Folkes* v. *King* (1923) 1 K.B. 282 CA]

Example 22.15. '*A & Co.*', a firm, purchased certain goods from *B*, a mercantile agent. But at the time of purchase, one of the partners of the firm knew that *B* had obtained the possession of the goods by practising fraud upon the owner. It was held that the firm did not get a valid title to the goods as the requirement of *good faith* was not satisfied. In this case, the partner knew that the seller's title was defective. [*Oppenheimer* v. *Frazer & Wyatt* (1907) 2 KB 50 CA].

3. *Sale by a joint owner* : A 'joint owner' means a person who owns the goods jointly with some other persons. When the joint owner is in the sole possession of the goods, and he sells them to a person who buys in a *goods faith,* the buyer gets a valid title to the goods [Section 28]. However, the buyer will get a valid title only if all the following conditions are satisfied :

(*a*) The joint owner must be in the sole possession of the goods.

(*b*) The joint owner must be in possession of the goods with the consent of other joint owners.

(*c*) The buyer must buy the goods in a *good faith.* And he should presume that the seller (*i.e.*, the joint owner) has the full authority to sell the goods.

Example 22.16. *A* and *B* were the joint owner of a truck. *A* had the possession of the truck with the consent of *B*. *A* sold the truck to *C* who bought it in a *good faith.* In this case, *A* will get a valid title to truck.

3. The document of title is the document which is used in the ordinary course of business as a proof of possession of the goods, or which authorises the holder of the document to transfer or receive the goods represented by the document, *e.g.*, bill of lading, railway receipts, etc.

4. *Sale by a person in possession under a voidable contract* : Sometimes, a person obtains the possession of the goods by coercion, undue influence, fraud or misrepresentation. In such cases, the contract is voidable at the option of the true owner, *i.e.*, true owner can put an end to the contract. However, the person in possession of the goods under such a contract can make a valid sale even if the possession so obtained is not by free consent. And the buyer, from such a person, gets a valid title to the goods [Section 29]. However, the buyer gets a valid title only if the following conditions are satisfied :

(*a*) The seller must have obtained the possession of the goods under a *voidable* contract and not under a *void* contract.

(*b*) The contract must not have been rescinded (*i.e.*, put to an end) at the time of sale, *i.e.*, at the time of sale the voidable contract should be in existence.

(*c*) The buyer must act in a *good faith*. And he should not have any knowledge about seller's defective title.

Example 22.17. *A* purchased a refrigerator from *B* by fraud. Here, *A* is holding the possession under a voidable contract. Before the contract is put to an end, *A* sold the refrigerator to *C* who bought it in *good faith* and without any notice of *A*'s defective title. In this case, *C* gets a valid title to the refrigerator even if *A* was holding it under a voidable contract.

5. *Sale by a seller in possession of goods after their sale* : Sometimes, the seller continues to have the possessions of the goods even after their sale. And he resells the same goods to a new buyer. In such cases, the second buyer gets a valid title to the goods if he buys them in a *good faith* and without any notice of the prior sale [Section 30 (1)]. The new buyer must have obtained the possession of the goods, or the documents of title to the goods.

Example 22.18. *A* sold two cows to *B*. *B* for his own convenience, let the cows in *A*'s possession. *A* resold both the cows to *C* who bought them in a good faith and without any notice of the prior sale. In this case, *C* will get a valid title to the cows. And *B* cannot recover the cows from *C*. He can only claim damages from *A*.

It may, however, be noted that the above rule is applicable only where the original sale has not been completed by the delivery of the goods, and the seller continues to have the possession of the goods after their sale. Sometimes, a seller, after completing all the formalities of sale, gets the same goods back for some specific purpose (*i.e.*, repairs, etc.). If such a seller resells those goods to a new buyer, then the second buyer will not get a valid title to the goods even though he buys in a *good faith*.

6. *Sale by a buyer in possession of goods after their sale* : Sometimes, with the consent of the seller, the buyer obtains the possession of the goods which he has bought or agreed to buy from the seller. But the seller still has some lien or other rights over the goods. And the buyer resells the same goods to a new person. In such cases, the second buyer gets a valid title free from seller's right if he buys them in a *good faith* and without any knowledge about the original seller's rights over the goods. [Section 30(2)] The resale by the first buyer may be made by actually transferring the goods or by transferring the documents of title to the goods. Moreover, it may also be made by the buyer himself or by his authorised agent.

Example 22.19. *A* agreed to buy some furniture from *B*. The payment of the price was to be made in two installments. The furniture was, however, delivered to *A*. But the ownership of the same was to be transferred to him on the payment of the second instalment. *A* sold the furniture to *C* who bought it in a *good faith*. In this case, *A* had the possession of the furniture under an *'agreement to buy'*, and thus *C* got a valid title to the furniture. [*Lee* v. *Butler (1897) Q.B. 318*]

7. *Sale by a finder of goods* : Sometimes, the finder of lost goods sells the goods to a buyer. In such cases, the buyer gets a valid title to the goods if the finder sells the goods under the permitted circumstances. It may be noted that the finder may sell the goods only when the owner cannot be found with reasonable diligence on the part of the finder, or where the owner is found but he refuses to pay the lawful charges of the finder. Moreover, the finder can sell the goods found only in anyone of the following two circumstances :

(a) If the goods are in danger of perishing or of losing the greater part of their value.

(b) If the lawful charges of the finder, in respect of the goods, amounts to a minimum of two third of their value.

8. *Sale by a pawnee or pledgee :* Sometimes, the pawnor makes default in the repayment of the amount of loan borrowed from the pawnee. In such cases, the pawnee may sell the goods after giving a reasonable notice to the pawnor. And the buyer from such a pawnor gets a valid title to the goods. This point has already been discussed in detail in Chapter on Bailment and Pledge.

9. *Sale by an official appointed by the court :* Sometimes, the courts appoint a person (known as Receiver, Official Receiver or Official assigner or Liquidator) to take the possession of the goods and authorise him to sell the same though he is not the owner of the goods. If any person buys these goods from such a person (*i.e.,* Receiver, etc.), he gets a valid title.

LEGAL PROVISIONS (SECTIONS) DISCUSSED IN THE CHAPTER

Important legal provisions (sections) of the Sale of Goods Act, 1930 discussed in this chapter, are reproduced hereunder for ready reference:

1. ***Section 2 (11): Property Defined***
   Property means general property in goods, and not merely a special property.
2. ***Section 18: Goods must be ascertained***
   Where there is a contract for the sale of unascertained goods, no property in the goods is transferred to the buyer unless and untilthe goods are ascertained.
3. ***Section 19: Property passes when intended to pass***
   (1) Where there is a contract for the sale of specific or ascertained goods, the property in them is transferred to the buyer at such time as the parties to the contract intend it to be transferred.
   (2) For the purpose of ascertaining the intention of the parties, regard shall be had to the terms of the contract, the conduct of the parties and the circumstances of the case.
   (3) Unless a different intention appears, the rules contained in sections 20 to 24 are rules for ascertaining the intention of the parties as to the time at which the property in the goods is to pass to the buyer.
4. ***Section 20: Specific goods in deliverable state***
   Where there is an unconditional contract for the sale of specific goods in a deliverable state, the property in the goods passes to the buyer when the contract is made, and it is immaterial whether the time of payment of the price or the time of delivery of the goods, or both, is postponed.
5. ***Section 21: Specific goods to be put into a deliverable state***
   Where there is a contract for the sale of specific goods and the seller is bound to do something to the goods for the purpose of putting them into a deliverable state, the property does not pass until such thing is done and the buyer has notice thereof.
6. ***Section 22: Specific goods in deliverable state, when the seller has to do anything thereto in order to ascetain price***
   Where there is a contract for the sale of specific goods in a deliverable state but the seller is bound to weigh, measure, test or do some other act or thing with reference to the goods for the purpose of ascertaining the price, the property does not pass until such act or thing is done and the buyer has notice thereof.
7. ***Section 23: Sale of unascertined goods and appropriation***
   (1) Where there is a ontract for the sale of unascertained or future goods by description and goods of that description and in a deliverable state are unconditionally appropriated to the contract, either by the seller with the assent of the buyer or by the buyer with the assent of the seller, the property in the goods thereupon passes to the buyer. Such assent may be express or implied, and may be given either before or after the appropriation is made.
   (2) **Delivery to carrier.**—Where, in pursuance of the contract, the seller delivers the goods to the buyer or to a carrier or other bailee (whether named by the buyer or not) for the purpose of transmission to the buyer, and does not reserve the right of disposal, he is deemed to have unconditionally appropriated the goods to the contract.

8. *Section 24: Goods sent on Approval or an Sale or Return*
Where the goods are delivered to the buyer on approval or on 'sale or return' or other similar terms, the property, therein passes to the buyer–
(*a*) When he signifies his approval or accpetance to the seller or does any other act adopting the transaction.
(*b*) if he does not signify his approval or acceptance to the seller but retains the goods without giving notice of rejection, then, if a time has been fixed for the return of the goods, on the expiration of such time, and if no time has been fixed, on the expiration of a reasonable time.

9. *Section 26: Risk Prima facie passes with property*
Unless otherwise agreed, the goods remain at the seller's risk until the property therein is transferred to the buyer, but when the property therein is transferred to the buyer, the goods are at the buyer's risk whether delivery has been made or not:
Provided that, where delivery has been delayed through the fault of either buyer or seller, the goods are at the risk of the party in fault as regards any loss which might not have occurred but for such fault:
Provided also that nothing in this section shall affect the duties or liabilities of either seller or buyer as a bailee of the goods of the other party.

TEST QUESTIONS

1. What do you mean by property in the goods ? State the significance of transfer of property, and the legal rules relating thereto.
2. What is meant by specific and unascertained goods ? In a contract for the sale of goods, state when the property in the goods passes to the buyer.
3. State the legal provisions relating to the passing of property in case of (*a*) sale of specific good, (*b*) sale of unascertained goods, and (*c*) sale on approval or sale on return.
4. State the circumstances in which the ownership of unascertained goods passes from the seller to the buyer under the Sale of Goods Act.
5. What are the rules governing the passing of title to the goods from the seller to the purchaser ?
6. Why is it important to know the exact time when the property in the goods passes from a seller to a buyer ? Explain with examples the rules governing the transfer of ownership from seller to buyer.
7. Comment on (*a*) delivery to a carrier, and (*b*) reservation of right of disposal.
8. "Risk prima facie passes with ownership"—comment. State the exceptions to this rule, if any.
9. Explain "no one can give a better title than he himself possesses"—Willes J. Also state the exceptions to this rule, if any.

MULTIPLE CHOICE QUESTIONS

1. The property in the goods means the
   (*a*) Possession of goods (*b*) Custody of goods
   (*c*) Ownership of goods (*d*) both (*a*) and (*b*)
2. The goods are at the risk of a party who has the
   (*a*) Ownership of goods (*b*) Possession of goods
   (*c*) custody of goods (*d*) both (*b*) and (*c*)
3. In case of unconditional contract of sale, the property passes to the buyer at the time of making the contract. For this rule to apply, the goods must be
   (*a*) specific (*b*) in a deliverable state
   (*c*) physically transferred to buyer (*d*) both (*a*) and (*b*)
4. In case of sale of standing trees, the property passes to the buyer when trees are
   (*a*) felled and ascertained (*b*) not felled but earmarked
   (*c*) counted and ascertained (*d*) both (*b*) and (*c*)
5. In case of sale of unascertained goods, the ownership is transfered to the buyer when the goods are

(a) ascertained (b) appropriated to the contract
(c) weighed and measured (d) both (a) and (b)

6. In case on sale of approval, the ownership is transferred to the buyer when he
   (a) accepts the goods (b) adopts the transaction
   (c) fails to return goods (d) in all the above cases.
7. A clause in a contract of sale which provides that the ownership will pass to the buyer only on the payment of full price, and in the meantime good would remain with seller but at the risk of buyer, is
   (a) valid and effective (b) void and ineffective
   (c) voidable (d) against law.
8. In case the delivery of goods is delayed due to the fault of party, then goods shall be at the risk of defaulting party even though the ownership is with the other party.
   (a) True, as there is a provision to this effect.
   (b) False, as it is against the general rule.

ANSWERS

1. (c)	2. (a)	3. (d)	4. (a)	5. (d)	6. (d)
7. (a)	8. (a)				

OBJECTIVE TYPE QUESTIONS WITH REASONING

State with reasons whether the following statements are correct or incorrect.

1. The expression 'property in the goods' means the possession of the goods.
2. Risk always passes with the ownership.
3. In a contract for sale of specific goods in a deliverable state, the property in the goods passes to the buyer on the payment of the price.
4. In a contract for the sale of specific goods not in a deliverable state, the ownership passes as soon as the goods are put in deliverable state whether or not the buyer has notice of the same.
5. In a contract for the sale of unascertained goods, no property in the goods in transferred unless and until the goods are ascertained.
6. In case of sale on approval, the ownership passes to the buyer immediately at the time of making the contract.
7. The risk and ownership go together. In no case they can be separated.
8. Ordinarily, no one can transfer a better title than he himself has.
9. A buyer buying goods from a mercantile agent does not get a valid title to the goods as the mercantile agent in not the owner.
10. A person in possession of goods under a voidable contract cannot transfer a valid title.

ANSWERS

1. ***Incorrect.*** This expression is not linked with the possession of goods. It means the legal ownership of the goods.
2. ***Correct.*** It is always the owner who has to bear the risk for loss of the goods.
3. ***Incorrect.*** In such cases, the property (*i.e.*, ownership) passes to the buyer immediately at the time of making the contract.
4. ***Correct.*** In such cases, the ownership of goods passes to the buyer when he comes to know of the fact that goods have been put in a deliverable state.
5. ***Correct.*** It is the legal rule on the point that in case of unascertainment goods, the property passes by the ascertainment and appropriation of goods.

6. *Incorrect.* In such cases, the ownership passes to the buyer when be accepts the goods or when he fails to return the goods within reasonable time [Section 24].
7. *Incorrect.* They can be separated by mutual agreement between the parties or also by trade customs.
8. *Correct.* It is the general rule based upon the latin maxim *Nemo dat guod non habet.*
9. *Incorrect.* The sale of goods by mercantile agent, in the ordinary course of his business, is valid even if he is not the over [Section 27, second para].
10. *Incorrect.* The buyer from such a person gets a valid title if he acts in *good faith* and buys the goods before recession of the voidable contract [Section 29].

PRACTICAL PROBLEMS

1. *A*, a car dealer, had many cars in his show room. Out of these cars, he sold one car to *B*. But the car sold to *B* was not identified and separated at the time of making the contract of sale. Before the car could be identified and separated, all cars were destroyed in an accidental fire in the show room. Who has to bear the loss of the car sold to *B* ?

   Hints. *A* has to bear the loss of car as he remained the owner of the car. In this case, the ownership of the car is not transferred to *B* at the time of contract of sale as the contract was not for the sale of specific goods. [Section 20 see *Provincial Auto co.* v.. *State* (1952) STC 147]
2. Suppose in the above problem, the car sold by *A* to *B* is identified and kept separate for delivery at the time of making the contract, Then who has to bear the loss, if that car is destroyed in an accidental fire befor delivery to *B*.

   Hints. *B* has to the bear the loss as in that case the property would have transferred to the buyer at the time of making the contract. [section 20]
3. *A* sells to *B* a horse which is to be delivered to *B* the next week. *B* is to pay the price on delivery. *A* asks his servant to keep the horse separate from the other horses. The horse, however, dies before it is delivered and paid for. Who shall suffer the loss ?

   Hints. *B*, shall suffer the loss. In this case, the contract is for the sale of specific goods in a deliverable state. Also the horse is kept separate for delivery to the buyer i.e. the goods are appropriated to the contract with the consent of buyer.
4. *A* sold to *B* the whole quantity of oil lying in cistern. As per the terms of contract, *A* was required to fill the oil in drums and then the drums were to be taken away by *B*. Some of the drums were filled in *B*'s presence. Before the remaining drums could be filled, the whole quantity of oil was destroyed in fire. Who shall bear the loss of oil ?

   Hints. *B* shall bear the loss of oil which were filled in drums, and the seller *i.e. A* shall bear the loss of remaining oil which could not be filled in drums. [Section 21; *Rugg* v. *Minett* (1809) 1 East 210]
5. *A* contracted to sell to *B* the whole quantity of rice lying at his farm at the rate of Rs. 30per kg. However, *A* had to weigh the rice in order to know the price of entire quantity of rice sold to *B*. *A* part of rice was weighed and taken away by *B*. But before the remaining quantity could be weighed, the remainder was carried away by floods. Who shall bear the loss of remaining quantity carried away by floods ?

   Hints. *A* shall bear the loss of remainder as the property of the same has not been passed to the buyer. [Section 22]
6. *A* sold to *B* 20 bags of sugar out of larges quantity. Four bags of sugar were filled in and taken away by *B*. Later on, *A* filled 16 more bags and informed *B* who promised to take the delivery of the same. Before *B* could take the delivery, the sugar bags were stolen. Who shall bear the loss of 16 bags ?

   Hints. *B*, the buyer, shall bear the loss. In this case, the goods have been appropriated with mutual consent and thus the ownership had passed to the buyer.

   [Section 23, *Rhode* v. *The waites* (1827) 6 B&C 388]
7. *A* delivered some jewellery to *B* on sale or return basis. *B* pledged the jewellery with *C*. Can *A* recover back the jewellery from *C* ?

   Hints. *A* cannot recover the jewellery from *C*. However *A* can recover the price of the same from the buyer *i.e. B*. In this case, the ownership of the jewellery had passed to *B* as he had adopted the transation by further pledging the jewellery. [Section 24, *Kirkhan* v. *Attenborough* (1897) 1QB 201]
8. *A* delivered some diamonds to *B* on "sale or return" basis. *B* delivered the diamonds to *C* and *C* to *D*

on similar terms. The diamonds were stolen while in the custody of *D*. Who shall suffer the loss ?

Hints. *C* shall suffer the loss of diamonds. In this case, *B* has adopted the transation by delivering the diamonds to *C* and thus is liable to pay the price to *A*. Similarly *C* has adopted the transation by further delivery to *D* and thus is liable to pay the price to *B*. As between *C* and *D*, the transation was still of sale or return which was not adopted by *D*, either expressly on impliedly, and thus the ownership had not passed to *D* at the time of loss. [Section 24, *Genn* v. *Winkel* (1911)28 TLR 483]

9. *A* delivered his jewellery to *B* on 'sale for cash only or return' basis. It was expressly provided in the contract that the jewellery shall remain *A*'s property until the price is paid. Before the payment of the price, *B* pledged the jewellery with C. Can *A* recover the jewellery from *C* ?

Hints. Yes, *A* can recover the jewellery from C. In this case, the pledge was not valid as at the time of pledge to *C*, the ownership was not transferred to *B*. [*Weiner* v. *Smith* (1905)2 KB 172]

10. *A* delivers his horse to *B* on sale or return within a week, The horse dies three days after it had been delivered while in the possession of *B*. Can *A* recover the price ? If so, under what circumstances ?

Hints. No, *A* cannot recover the price (Section 24, *Elphick* v. *Barnes*). He can recover the price only if *B* had expressly or by conduct signified his approval or acceptance to *A* within those three days.

11. There is a contract for the sale of a machine, weighing 30 tons. The machine is embedded in a concrete floor and the seller has to remove it from the floor. A part of the machine is damaged while being removed. The buyer refuses to take the machine. Is the buyer justified in doing so?

Hints. The buyer is justified in refusing to take the machine as it is not in a deliverable state. [Section 21]

12. *A* delivers some jewellery to *B* on 'sale or return' without specifying any time for its return in case of non-acceptance. *B* allows the jewellery to remain with himself without signifying his approval or refusal. After a month, a burglary takes place in *B*'s house and the jewellery is stolen. Can *A* sue *B* for the price of the jewellery?

Hints. Yes, *A* can sue *B* for the price of the jewellery as *B* retains the jewellery without giving notice of rejection within a reasonable time. As such, the property in the jewellery had passed to *B*. [Section 24]

13. In a contract of sale of goods, 200 specified bales of goat-skin containing 60 pieces in each bale were sold. In order to determine the price, it was necessary for the seller to count them before delivery. Before counting was completed, the bales were destroyed by fire. Who should bear the loss, the buyer or the seller ?

Hints. The seller as he has not done his act of ascertaing the price of goods. [Section 22]

14. There was a contract for the sale of goods to be of a stated specifications. The contract provided that the property in the goods was to be deemed to have passed to the buyer when the goods were put on board, and if any disputes arose the buyer was not to reject the goods but the dispute was to be referred to arbitration. The goods were not according to specification. The buyer rejected the goods and the seller sued him of damages for breach of contract. Decide.

Hints. The buyer is entitled to reject the goods as the seller has not delivered the goods according to specification.

15. *A* orders 140 bags of rice from *B*, pays for them and asks for delivery. *B* sends him a delivery order for 125 bags and writes saying that the remaining 15 bags are ready for delivery at his place of business. *A* waits for a month before sending for the 15 bags and in the meantime they are stolen. On whom will the loss fall ?

Hints. The loss will fall on *A* because *B* had appropriated the 15 bags to the contract and *A*'s assent to the appropriation was to be inferred from his conduct in not objecting. The property in the 15 bags had therefore passed to *A*. [Section 18 and 23 (1) *Pignataro* v. *Gilory*, (1919), 1KB. 459]

16. *A* entered into a contract with *B* for the sale of 814 tins of oil which were in transit for delivery to *A*. *A* had received the railway seceipts which he endorsed in facour of *B*, the buyer. Six days after the contract of sale, the kerosene tins were destroyed in fire while still in transit. Who shall bear the loss ? Give reasons.

Hints. *B* shall bear the loss. In this case, the ownership had transferred to the buyer on the date of sale when the railway receipts were endorsed in favour of *B*. [*Shankar Das J.Pd.* v. *Bhanna Ram*]

17. *A* placed an order with *B* requesting him to send the goods by sea. *B* took a bill of lading in the name of *A* and sent it to his own agent. The goods were, however, destroyed in the course of the voyage. Who shall bear the loss ?

Hints. *B* shall bear the loss. In the case, *B* did not intend the property in the goods to pass to *A* as he sends the bill of lading to his agent. The property in the goods, therefore, does not pass to *A* and as such *B* must bear the loss. [Section 25 (2)]

18. *A* entered the shop of *B* and selected certain ready-made garments for purchase. It was agreed that *B* shall deliver the garments to *A* next morning by *B*'s servant and the price shall be paid after 15 days. However, the garments were destroyed in fire the same night. Who shall bear the loss ?

Hints. *A*, the buyer, shall bear the loss. In this case, there was contract of sale for specific goods in deliverable state, and thus the ownership had transferred to the buyer at the time of making the contract. [Section 20]

19. *A* agrees to sell 100 quintals of rice to *B* out of a larger quantity lying in his godown. According to agreement, *B* sends gunny bags for the rice and *A* puts 100 quintals of rice in them and informs *B* of the same. But before *B* could take delivery, the godown catches fire and the bags are damaged. Who is to suffer the loss ?

Hints. *B* the buyer, shall suffer the loss. In this case, the ownership has transferred to the buyer and the risk passes with the ownership. [Section 26]

20. *A* agreed to buy a heavy machine from *B* for Rs.200'000. It was agreed that *B* shall immediately deliver the machine to him (A) but the price would be paid if *A*'s solicitor approve the transation. After taking possession *A* immediately further sold the machine to *C* who bought it in good-faith. However, *A*'s solicitors subsequently disapproved the transation. Can *B* recover back the machine from *C* ?

Hints. No, *B* cannot recover back the machine from C. He can only recover the price of the machine from *A*. In this case, *A* had the possession under an agreement to buy and thus he could pass a valid title to the second buyer *i.e.C.* [Section 30 (2), see also *lee* v. *Butler* (1897) Q.B. 318]

21. *A* entered into a hire-purchase agreement with *B* in relation to a piano on the condition that on paying 12 instalments of Rs. 1000 each the piano would be his property. After paying 6 instalments, *B* pledged the piano with *C* who took it in good faith. Can *A* take back the piano from *C*.

Hints. Yes, *A* can take back the piano from *C*. In case of hire-purchase agreement, the hirer only has the option to buy which does not entitle him to further pass on the title to third party till he becomes the owner. [see *Bolsize motor supply co*.v. *Cox* (1914) K.B. 244]

22. *A* entrusted a motor car to a mercantile agent for sale, stipulating that the car should not be sold below a certain price. To this, the agent professed to agree but he sold it to *B* who bought it in good faith for less than the stipulated price and absconded. Subsequently, *B* sold the car to *C*. *A* sues *C* to recover the car from him. Will he succeed ?

Hints. No, *A* will not succeed. In this case, the sale is by a merchantable agent who can pass a valid title to a bonafide purchaser by acting in the ordinary courses of business.

[Section 27, *Folkes* v *King* (1923) 1K.B. 282 C.A]

23. *A*, a jeweller, was entrusted with a diamond by *B* with the instructions that *A* should obtain offer for it. And if any such offer was approved by *B*, *A* should sell it to the offerer. Acting contrary to *B*'s instructions *A* sold the diamond to *C* who bought it in good faith. Thereafter, *A* absconded with the price money. Can *B* recover the diamond from *C* ?

Hints. No, *B* cannot recover the diamond from *C* who bought it in good faith from *A* who is a mercantile agent. [Section 27]

24. *B* buys from *A*, a furniture-maker, a sofa-set for Rs. 25,000 pays the whole amount of price and informs *A* that he will take the sofa-set away in a fortnight. *A*, thereafter sells the sofa-set to *C* and receives payment in cash. Examine the nature of *C*'s title to the sofa-set ?

Hints. *C* gets a good title to the sofa-set if he buys in good faith and without notice of the previous sale. [Section 30 (1)]

25. *A* delivers a gold necklace to *B* on "sale or return" basis. It is agreed between *A* and *B* that property is not to pass to *B* till he has paid price of the necklace. Without paying the price, *B* sells the necklace to C. Does C get a good title to the necklace ?

Hints. No, *C* does not get a good title to the necklace as *B* himself has no title to the necklace till he pays its price. Here, it has been specifically agreed that the property is not to pass to *B* till he has paid the price.

26. *A* finds a diamond ring. After making reasonable efforts to find the true owner, *A* sells the ring to *B*, who buys without any knowledge that *A* was merely a finder. Is the sale by *A* to *B* valid?

Hints. The finder of goods can sell the goods only in the circumstances permitted under section 169 of the Indian Contract Act, 1872 which are as under:

(*a*) If the goods are in danger of perishing or losing the greater part of their value, the finder can sell the goods.

(*b*) If the lawful charges of the finder in respect of the goods amount to a minimum of two-third of the value, then the finder can sell the goods.

In the present case, the sale by the finder will not be valid as it does not seem to fall in any of the above stated circumstances.

23

CHAPTER

PERFORMANCE OF CONTRACT OF SALE

23.1. INTRODUCTION

After the formation of a valid contract of sale, the next stage is its performance. The term 'performance of the contract of sale' may be defined as the performance of the respective duties of the seller and the buyer as per the terms of the contract. Thus, the performance of the contract of sale comprises the two parts, namely:

1. Seller's duty to deliver the goods.
2. Buyer's duty to accept the goods and pay the price.

It may be noted that the delivery of the goods and the payment of their price are the concurrent conditions, *i.e.*, both these conditions should be performed simultaneously (*i.e.*, at the same time). This provision is contained in Section 32 of the Sale of Goods Act, which provides that the delivery of the goods and the payment of the price are concurrent conditions, *i.e.*, the seller should be ready and willing to deliver the goods to the buyer, in exchange for the price. And the buyer should be ready and willing to pay the price to the seller in exchange for the possession of the goods. However, the parties may also agree otherwise, *i.e.*, they may enter into an agreement as to when the goods are to be delivered, and as to when the price is to be paid.

Example 23.1: *A* agreed to deliver certain goods to *B*. The price was to be paid by *B* on the delivery of the goods. In this case, *A* need not deliver the goods, unless *B* is ready and willing to pay the price of the goods on delivery. And *B* need not pay for goods, unless *A* is ready and willing to deliver them on the payment of the price.

Thus, each party should be ready and willing to perform his respective promise before he can call upon the other to perform his promise.

23.2. SELLER'S DUTY TO DELIVER THE GOODS

We have discussed, in the last article, that the seller should be ready and willing to deliver the goods to the buyer as per the terms of the contract. The term 'delivery of goods' may be defined as the voluntary and lawful transfer of the possession of goods from one person to another. In the case of sale of goods, the delivery should be *voluntary* and it should have the effect of putting the goods in the possession of the buyer. Thus, where a person steals the goods of another or takes the goods by force or fraud, there is no delivery of goods to such person.

23.3 MODES OF EFFECTIVE DELIVERY OF GOODS

1. *Actual delivery.*
2. *Sybmolic delivery*
3. *Constructive delivery or delivery by attornment*

The delivery of the goods may be made by doing anything which has the effect of putting the goods in the possession of the buyer or his authorised agent. It may be noted that the parties (*i.e.*, the seller and the buyer) may agree to treat any act as amounting to delivery. The different modes of effective delivery may be discussed under the following heads :

1. *Actual delivery*. The term 'actual delivery' may be defined as the delivery where the goods are handed over by the seller to the buyer or his authorised agent. In other words, when the goods are physically put in possession of the buyer, the delivery is said to be actual.

Example 23.2. *A* sold to *B* 10 tins of oil and delivered the same to him. In this case, there is actual delivery of oil from *A* to *B*.

2. *Symbolic delivery:* The term 'symbolic delivery' may be defined as the delivery by doing some act which has the effect of putting the goods in possession of the buyer. In other words, when the goods are not physically delivered to the buyer but are delivered by indicating or giving a symbol, the delivery is said to be symbolic, *e.g.*, the delivery of the keys of the godown in which the goods are lying, the transfer of documents of title to the goods (*e.g.*, railway receipts, bill of lading, delivery orders, title deeds, etc.) are the instances of symbolic delivery. Such type of delivery is made when the goods are bulky or incapable of actual delivery.

Example 23.3: *A* sold to *B* all the table fans lying in his godown. And *A* delivered the keys of his godown to *B* in order that he may get the fans from the godown. In this case, there is a symbolic delivery of table fans from *A* to *B*.

3. *Constructive delivery or delivery by attornment:* The term 'onstructive deliver' may be defined as the delivery when a third person, in possession of the goods, acknowledges to hold the goods on behalf of the buyers. *e.g*, where a warehouseman or a carrier, who holds the goods as bailee for the seller, agrees and acknowledges to hold the goods on behalf of the buyer, or when the seller himself agrees to hold the goods as a bailee for the buyer. It is also called a delivery by attornment.

Example 23.4. *A* sold to *B* 50 bags of rice which were in possession of *C*, a warehouseman. And *A* ordered *C* to transfer the rice to *B* accordingly, *C* transferred the rice, in his books, in *B's* name. In this case, there is a constructive delivery of goods from *A* to *B*.

23.4. RULES REGARDING EFFECTIVE DELIVERY OF GOODS

The rules regarding the delivery of goods are contained in Sections 33 to 38 of the Sale of Goods Act, which may be grouped as under:

1. *Possession of goods:* The delivery of the goods may be made in any of the modes discussed above. But it must have the effect of putting the goods in the possession of the buyer or his authorised agent. [Section 33]. Thus, the delivery of goods should be such

1. *Possession of goods*
2. *Demand for delivery of goods*
3. *Place for the delivery of goods*
4. *Time for the delivery of goods*
5. *Time for the demand or tender of delivery*
6. *Goods in the possession of a third person*
7. *Expebses for the delivery of goods*
8. *Part delivery of goods*
9. *Delivery of wrong quantity*
10. *Delivery of goods by instalment*
11. *Delivery to a carrier or wharfinger*
12. *Deterioration of goods during transit*

which enables the buyer to exercise his control over the goods.

2. ***Demand for delivery of goods:*** We have already discussed that it is seller's duty to be ready and willing to deliver the goods to the buyer. But he is not bound to deliver the goods unless the buyer makes a demand for the delivery of the goods [Section 35]. In other words, in the first place, the buyer must make a demand to the seller for the delivery of the goods to him. Only then the seller becomes liable to deliver the goods to the buyer. The parties may, however, agree otherwise, *i.e.*, it may be agreed that the seller shall deliver the goods without any demand by the buyer.

3. ***Place for the delivery of goods:*** The place for the delivery of goods may be specified in the contract itself. And where the place is so specified, the goods must be delivered at such place during the business hours and on a working day. But where no place is specified in the contract, then the following rules, contained in Section 36(1), shall apply:

(*a*) In case of sale, goods sold are to be delivered at the place where they are, at the time of sale;

(*b*) In case of an agreement to sell, the goods are to be delivered at the place where they are, at the time of agreement to sell;

(*c*) If at the time of agreement to sell, the goods are not in existence they are to be delivered at a place where they are manufactured or produced.

4. ***Time for the delivery of goods***: The time for the delivery of goods may also be specified in the contract itself. And when the time is so specified, the delivery is to be made by the seller within the specified time. Where no time is specified in the contract then the delivery of goods must be made within a reasonable time [Section 36 (2)]. The term *'reasonable time'* is a question of fact. It is different for different cases depending upon the facts and circumstances of each particular case.

5. ***Time for the demand or tender of delivery.*** The buyer must demand the delivery of goods at a reasonable hour. And the seller should also deliver them at a reasonable hour. Thus, the demand or tender of delivery must be made at a reasonable hour. The term *'reasonable hour'* is a question of fact [Section 36 (4)]. It is different for different cases depending upon the working hours of a particular business.

6. ***Goods in the possession of a third person.*** Sometimes, at the time of sale, the goods are in the possession of a third person. In such cases, the effective delivery takes place when such person acknowldeges to the buyer; that he holds the goods on his (buyer's) behalf [Section 36 (3)]. It may be noted that the requirement of the effective delivery is that, the third person must inform the buyer that be holds the goods on his behalf.

However, where the goods are sold by the transfer of documents of title, *e.g.*, railway receipts, bill of landing, etc., then the acknowledgement of the third person having the possession of the goods (*e.g.*, carrier, etc.) is not required. In such cases, the effective delivery of goods takes place on the transfer of documents of title.

7. *Expenses for the delivery of goods.* The expenses of putting the goods into a deliverable state are borne by the seller. And the expenses of receiving the goods are borne by the buyer. Howeve, the seller and the buyer may also agree otherwise, *i.e.*, they may agree that the expesnses of delivery shall be borne by the buyer [Section 36(5)].

8. *Part delivery of goods*. Sometimes, during the process of delivering the whole lot of goods, a part of the delivery is made by the seller. This is generally done when a huge quantity of goods is to be delivered. In such cases, the following rules, as contained in Section 34, shall apply:

(*a*) Where the part delivery is made in progress of the whole delivery, then it is treated as a delivery of the whole. And the ownership of the whole quantity is transferred to the buyer.

(*b*) Where the part delivery is made with the intention of separating it from the whole, then it is not treated as a delivery of the whole. And the ownership of the whole quantity is not transferred to the buyer.

Example 23.5. *A* sold certain goods to *B* which were lying in his (*A's*) warehouse. *A* ordered his warehouse-keeper to deliver those goods to *B*. *B* weighed all the goods and took away a part of them. It was held that this amounted to a delivery of the whole of the goods. In this case, *A's* act of ordering his warehouseman to deliver the goods to the buyer, and buyer's act of weighing all the goods shows that the delivery of the whole of the goods was contemplated by the parties.

[Based on *Hammond* v. *Anderson* (1803) 1 BR & P.N.R. 69; R.R. 763].

Example 23.6. *A* sold a stake of hay, grown on his land, to *B.B* asked the permission of *A* to cut and remove a part of the stake, which was granted by *A*. Afterwards, *B* cut that part of the stake and took away the same. It was held that this did not amount to the delivery of the whole stake of hay as the intention of the parties was to separate the part from the residue.

[*Bunney* v. *Poyntz* (1833) 4 B. & Ad. 568; R.R. 309].

9. *Delivery of wrong quantity.* The term 'wrong quantity' may include short delivery or excess delivery of goods than the agreed quantity. It also includes the delivery of agreed quality goods mixed with another quality. The rules dealing with the effect of delivery of wrong quantity may be discussed under the following heads:

(a) *Short delivery*. Sometimes, the seller delivers a less quantity of goods than be contracted to sell. In such cases, the buyer may reject the goods. However the buyer may also accept the short quantity, and pay at the contract price for the goods actually delivered to him [Section 37(1)].

(b) *Excess delivery*. Sometimes, the seller delivers a larger (*i.e.*, excess) quantity of goods than he contracted to sell. In such cases, the buyer may accept the contracted quantity of goods, or accept or reject the whole quantity. Thus, the buyer may exercise any of the following options [Section 37 (2)].

(*i*) He may accept the contract quantity and reject the excess.

(*ii*) He may accept the whole of the goods. If he does so then he shall have to pay for all the goods at the contract rate.

(*iii*) He may reject the whole quantity of goods.

It may be noted that in case of excess delivery, the buyer is free to exercise any of the above options. And he cannot be compelled to accept the contract quantity and reject the excess. However, if the excess is so small as to be negligible, the buyer may not reject the goods. This is based on the maximum *'de minimum non curatlex'*, *i.e.*, the law does not take account of trifles. On the same principle, the buyer may also not be allowed to reject the goods in case of negligible deficiency.

(c) *Mixed delivery.* Sometimes, the seller delivers the goods mixed with the goods of a different description. In such cases, the buyer may accept the contracted goods or reject the whole quantity of goods. Thus, the buyer may exercise any of the following options [Section 37 (3)]:

(*i*) He may accepted the goods which are in accordance with the contract and reject the rest.

(*ii*) He may reject the whole.

The above rules, regarding the delivery of wrong quantity of goods, are subject to any usage of trade, special agreement, or course of dealing between the parties [Section 37 (4)]. Thus, where such usage or special agreement, etc. provides that the goods shall be accepted or rejected in whole, then the above rules shall not apply.

10. *Delivery of goods by instalments:* As a matter of fact, the delivery of goods by instalments is not considered as a good delivery. And the buyer is not bound to accept the goods delivered to him by instalments, unless otherwise agreed [Section 38 (1)].

However, the parties may agree that the goods shall be delivered and accepted by instalments. Thus, the delivery of goods by instalments may be made and demanded only if the contract of sale provides for the same. The contract to make delivery by instalments may be express or implied. Where the seller starts delivering the goods by instalments and then buyer accepts the same without any objection, then he should accept the remaining instalments also as he has impliedly consented to delivery by instalments.

Example 23.7. *A* contracted to sell *B* 200-300 tons of coal. *A* shipped only 152 tons, and informed *B* about the same. But *B* made no reply. It was held that the buyer (*B*) merely consented to delivery of coal by instalments. [*Richardson* v. *Dunn* (1841) 2 Q.B. 218].

11. *Delivery to a carrier or wharfinger:* Sometimes, the sold goods are delivered to a carrier for the purpose of transmission to the buyer. In such cases, the delivery of goods to the carrier is treated as a delivery to the buyer. Similarly, where the sold goods are delivered to a wharfinger[1] for the purpose of safe custody, the delivery of goods to the wharfinger is also treated as delivery to the buyer [Section 39 (1)]. But, where it is agreed that the goods are to be delivered at a particular place (*e.g.*, at the buyer's mill) then the delivery of goods to a carrier does not amount to a delivery to the buyer.

[*Jagdish Pd.* v. *Produce Exchange Corpn.* AIR 1946 Cal. 245].[2]

12. *Dterioration of goods during transit:* Sometimes, the seller agrees to deliver the goods, at his own risk, at a place other than that where the goods are lying at the time of contract of sale. In such cases, the buyer shall bear the loss of deterioration of goods which is incidental *i.e.* natural in transit. [Section 40].

23.5. BUYER'S DUTY TO ACCEPT THE GOODS AND PAY THE PRICE

We have already discussed that the duty of a buyer, in the performance of the contract of sale, is to accept the goods and pay the price. When the seller delivers the goods, according to the contract, then it becomes the buyer's duty to accept them and pay the price. And when the goods are accepted and paid, the contract of sale is duly performed, *i.e.*, the contract is completed.

The term 'acceptance of goods' may be defined as the final assent of the byer that he has accepted the goods. It is to be noted that when the buyer receives the goods and takes

1. A person who takes care of the wharf, is called a wharfinger. A *wharf* is a place where the goods are stored before shipment or after unloading from the ship.
2. See also *Fertilezers Corp. of India* v. *Tata Iron & Steel Co.* Ltd. AIR 1965 Punjab 148.

possession of them, it does not mean that he has accepted the goods. Acceptance is something more than this. The reason for the same is that after receiving the goods, the buyer should have sufficient opportunity of examining the goods [Section 41]. The circumstances, in which the buyer is considered to have accepted the goods, are contained in Section 42 and are as under:

1. When the buyer informs the seller that he has accepted the goods.
2. When the buyer does any act to the goods which is inconsistent with the ownership of the seller, *i.e.*, when the buyer uses the goods in the capacity of an owner, *e.g.*, where he pledges or resells the goods, or makes some changes in the goods. However, dealing with the documents of title does not amount to acceptance.
[*Chao* v. *British Traders & Shippers Ltd*. (1954) 1 All ER 779]
3. When after the expiry of a reasonable time, the buyer retains the goods without informing the seller that he has rejected the goods. In other words, when he fails to return the goods within a reasonable time.

Example 23.8. *A* sold certain quantity of wheat to *B*, and shipped the same for the purpose of transmission to *B*. On the arrival of the ship, *B* took delivery of the wheat, and on the same day resold a part of the wheat to *C*. After three days, *B* discovered that the wheat was not in accordance with the contract, and he gave a notice to the seller *A* that he has rejected the wheat. And this notice of rejection was given within a reasonable time. It was held that the buyer *B* had accepted the wheat and the notice of rejection was ineffective. In this case, the buyer has accepted the goods (wheat) by reselling the part of the same.

[*Hardy & Co. v. Hillerns & Fowlers* (1923) 2 K.B. 409, C.A.]

23.6. BUYER'S RIGHT OF EXAMINATION

As a matter of fact, before accepting the goods, the buyer has a right to properly examine them, if it is not already done by him. The opportunity of examining the goods is given to the buyer to enable him to ascertain that the goods are in accordance with the contract. It may be noted that the buyer is not considered to have accepted the goods unless and until such an opportunity is given to him. Sometimes, the buyer requests for such an opportunity of examining the goods. In such cases, the seller is bound to give such an opportunity. If the seller refuses to allow this opportunity, the buyer may reject the goods [Section 41]. Where the buyer *rightfully* rejects the goods, it becomes his duty to inform the seller that he has rejected the goods. However, the buyer is not bound to return the goods to the seller. It is the duty of the seller to take back the goods at his own expenses [Section 43]. But If the buyer fails to inform the seller about the rejection of the goods, he may be deemed to have accepted the goods if he fails to return them within a reasonable time.

23.7. LIABILITY OF THE BUYER FOR REFUSING TO TAKE DELIVERY OF THE GOODS

Sometimes, the seller is ready and willing to deliver the goods, and requests the buyer to take the delivery. But the buyer does not take the delivery of the goods within a *reasonable time*. In such cases, the buyer is liable to the seller for the following [Section 44]:

1. Any loss which arises due to buyer's negbet or sefusal to take blivery of the goods, and
2. Reasonable charges for the care and custody of the goods.

Where the neglect or refusal of the buyer amounts to the repudiation (*i.e.*, cancellation) of the contract, the seller may exercise his other rights also, *e.g.*, he can claim damage for breach of contract.

23.8. CONTRACTS INVOLVING SEA TRANSIT

Sometimes, the goods are to be delivered to the buyer through sea routes. In all such cases, the parties may enter into certain contracts, which govern the delivery of the goods through sea routes. Following are the three important and usual forms of contracts of sale which involve the carriage of goods by sea :

1. C.I.F 2. F.O.B. 3. Ex-Ship.

The main features of these contracts are discussed in the following pages. It may, however, be noted that the parties may vary or add some other terms in the usual terms of such contracts. Moreover, they may also incorporate the terms of one form of contract in another form of contract. [*The Parchim* (1918) A.C. 157 PC]

23.9. C.I.F. CONTRACTS

1. Transfer of ownership
2. Protection of parties interest

The terms 'C.I.F.' means 'cost, insurance and freight'. And a 'C.I.F. contract is a contract for the sale of goods at a price which includes the cost of goods, insurance and freight charges. 'Thus, in such contracts, the charges of insurance during tranist and the freight charges are paid by the buyer. Where the buyer orders the goods from a seller, residing abroad, under a C.I.F. contract, the seller will insure the goods and deliver them to a shipping company for transmission to the buyer. And the insurance policy on the goods and the bill of lading shall be delivered to the buyer along with the invoice of the goods. It may be noted that in C.I.F. contracts, the seller is bound to perform the following duties:

1. To make out an invoice of the goods sold.
2. To ship the goods at the port of shipment.
3. To procure a contract of affreightment under which the goods will be delivered at a destination contemplated by the contract, *i.e.*, to enter into a contract with the shipping company for the transportation of the goods and obtain a bill of lading.
4. To insure the goods, obtain an insurance policy. The insurance should be arranged on such current terms as will be available for the benefit of the buyer.
5. To deliver all these shipping documents (*i.e.*, the invoice, bill of lading and the policy of insurance) to the buyer within a reasonable time.

If the sellers fails to deliver the shipping documents within a reasonable time, then he is guilty of breach of contract.[3] On the other hand, when the documents complete in all respects, are delivered to the buyer, it is his duty to take them and pay the price according to the terms of the contract. It may be noted that the buyer is under legal obligation to take the documents and pay the price without waiting for the arrival of the goods. And it is no defence for him to say that he has not examined the goods, or that the goods have been lost[4]. However, the buyer may refuse to take the shipping documents by proving any of the following:

(*a*) That the documents are invalid, *e.g.*, that the bill of lading is not correctly dated.[5]
(*b*) That the goods shipped are of different quality.[6]
(*c*) That the goods shipped are less in quantity.[7]

Sometimes, the buyer accepts the documents and pays the price of the goods. But on the arrival of the goods, he finds that the goods are not in accordance with the contract. In

3. *N Swami Chetti v. Soundarajan* AIR 1958 Madras 43.
4. *Mohanlal Kashinath v.k. Premji & Co.* (1928) 30 Bom. L.R. 415; AIR Bombay 170.
5. *Finaly & Co. v. K.H. Tong* (1929) 1 K.B. 400 C.A.
6. *Canada A.G. Exprots Co. v. Eilers* (1929) 35 Com. Cas. 90.
7. *Re Keighley Maxeted & Co.* (1894) 70 LT 155.

such cases, the buyer is entitled to reject the goods and recover back the price.[8]

The important points in connection with the C.I.F. contracts, may be summed up as under:

1. ***Transfer of ownership***: In case of C.I.F. contracts, the ownership of the goods is transferred to the buyer when the shipping documents are delivered to the buyer and he receives them by paying price of the goods.[9]

2. ***Protection of parties interest:*** The C.I.F. contract protects the interest of both, the seller and the buyer. It protects the seller in a way that the goods continue to be in his ownership until the buyer pays for them and gets the documents. And it protects the buyer in a way that he is required to pay the price only when the documents are delivered to him. These documents enable the buyer to obtain the goods as soon as they arrive at the destination. If in the meantime, the goods are lost during sea transit, neither party will be put to loss. The reason for the same is that the good being insured, the owner of the goods (whether the seller or the buyer as the case may be) can claim the loss from the insurance company.

23.10. F.O.B. CONTRACTS

The term 'F.O.B.' means 'free on board'. And a F.O.B. contract is a contract for the sale of goods where, for the purpose of transmission to the buyer, the seller has to put the goods on board a ship at his own expesnses. It may be ntoed that the seller has to bear only the expenses of loading the goods. Once the goods are loaded on board the ship, they are at buyer's risk, and he is responsible for freight, insurance and subsequent expenses.

1. *Transfer of ownership*
2. *Insurance of goods*

In F.O.B. contract, the seller has to perform the following duties:

1. To load the sold goods safely on the ship named by the buyer.
2. To meet the expenses of loading the goods.
3. To enter into a contract with the shipping company or ship owners for the transportation of goods and obtain a bill of lading. Such a contract should be upon reasonable terms.
4. To deliver the bill of lading to the buyer.
5. To give notice of shipment to the buyer to enable him to insure the goods during sea transit.

On the performance of the above duties, the contractual liability of the seller ceases, and the delivery of goods to the buyer is complete as far as he (*i.e.*, seller) is concerned. And therefore, the buyer is boud to pay the price of the goods when the shiping documents are presented to him even if the goods have been lost by that time[10].

The important points in connection with F.O.B. contracts, may be summed up as under:

1. ***Transfer of ownership***: In case F.O.B. Contracts the ownership of the good is transferred to the buyer as soon as the goods are loaded on board the ship. The ownership is so transferred even if the goods are not specific or ascertained. However, the

8. Hardy & Co. v Hillerns & Fowlers (1923) 2 KB 400 CA; see also AIR 1974 Karnatka. 200; Biddell Bros. v.E.C. Horst Co. (1911) 1 K.B. p. 960.
9. *The meramichi* (1915) p. 71; *T.R. Smith & Co. v. T.D.B. & Co.* (1940) 3 All England Reporter 60.
10. *Stock v. Inglis* (1889) QBD 564; affirmed 10 App Cas 263.

ownership of the goods will not be transferred to the buyer, if, by the shipping documents, the seller has reserved his rights of disposal. Thus, if the seller does not reserve his right of disposal, the goods are at buyer's risk after they are loaded on the ship.

2. *Insurance of goods:* In, certain circumstances, the insurance of the goods is usual. In such cases, the seller should give to the buyer such notice as will enable him to insure the goods. If the seller fails to give such notice, the goods shall be at his risk during the transit [Section 25 (3)]. But sometimes, the buyer has sufficient information about the shipment of the goods so as to enable him to insure them, then he cannot insist on a particular notice from the seller, *i.e.*, in such a case, the goods shall be at the risk of the buyer, even if no notice is given by the seller.

23.11. EX-SHIP CONTRACTS

1. ***Transfer of ownership***
2. ***Insurace of goods***
3. ***The Contract, whether C.I.F. or Ex-ship***

An ex-ship contracts is a contracts for the sale of goods in which the seller has to deliver the goods to the buyer at the port of destination. The freight charges are to be borne by the seller. It may be noted that during the voyage (sea route) the goods are at the risk of the seller. Thus, to protect his own interest, the seller may insure the goods, if he so wishes, at his own expenses. In an ex-ship contract, the seller has to perform the following duties:

1. To deliver the goods to the buyer at the port of destination, *i.e.*, to make the goods physically available at the port of destination to enable the buyer to take their delivery.
2. To pay the freight charges.
3. To hand over the proper delivery orders to the buyer to enable him to obtain the delivery of the goods from the ship owner.

On the performance of the above duties, the contractual liability of the seller ceases. Thereafter, the buyer becomes bound to pay the price of the goods.

The important points in connection with Ex-ship contracts may be summed up as under:

1. *Transfer of ownership:* In case of Ex-ship contracts, the ownership of the goods is transferred to the buyer only when the goods are actually delivered at the port of destination to enable the buyer to take their delivery.

2. *Insurance of goods*: In Ex-ship contracts, the seller is not bound to insure the goods on behalf of the buyer. Since the goods are at seller's risk during sea transit, he may insure the goods for his own benefit.

3. *The Contract, whether C.I.F. or Ex-ship:* In case of sea transit, whether a particular contract is C.I.F. contract or an Ex-ship contract, does not depend merely upon the word (*i.e.*, C.I.F. or Ex-ship) used by the parties in their contract. But it depends upon the essence of the contract, *i.e.*, upon the effect of the contract, *e.g.*, a contract referred as C.I.F. contract may not be so if by the other terms of the contract the goods are actually to be delivered at the port of destination. [*The Prachim* (1918) AC 157 PC]

23.12. COMPARISON BETWEEN C.I.F., F.O.B. AND EX-SHIP CONTRACTS

The following table gives the comparison between C.I.F., F.O.B. and Ex-Ship contracts:

S. No.	C.I.F. Contract	F.O.B. Contract	Ex-ship Contract
1.	In this case, the price of the goods includes the cost of the goods, insurance and freight charges.	In this case, the price of the goods does not inclue the insurance and freight charges.	In this case also, the price of the goods does not include the insurance and freight charges.
2.	In this case, the ownership of the goods is transferred to the buyer when the shipping documents are delivered to the buyer, and he receives them by paying the price of the goods.	In this case, the ownership of the goods is transferred to the buyer as soon as the goods are loaded on the ship named by the buyer.	In this case, the ownership of the goods is transferred to the buyer only when the goods are actually delivered at the port of destination to enable the buyer to take their delivery.
3.	In this case, the insurance of the goods sold is compulsory. And the seller is bound to insure the goods.	In this case, the insurance of the goods sold is not compulsory. The buyer may insure the goods to protect his interest as during the sea transit the goods are at his risk.	In this case also, the insurance of the goods sold is not compulsory. The seller may issure the goods to protect his interest as during the sea transit the goods are the his risk.
4.	In this case, the seller's duty is to insure the goods and deliver them to a shipping company for the purpose of transmission to the part of destination.	In this case, the seller's duty is to load the goods in a ship named	In this case, the seller's duty is to deliver the goods at the port of destination to enable the buyer to take their delivery.

LEGAL PROVISIONS (SECTIONS) DISCUSSED IN THE CHAPTER

Important legal provisions (sections) of the Sale of Goods Act, 1930, discussed in this chapter are reproduced herunder for ready reference:

1. ***Section 31: Duties of seller and buyer***

   It is the duty of the seller to deliver the goods and of the buyer to accept and pay for them, in accordance with the terms of the contract of sale.

2. ***Section. 32. Payment and delivery are concurret conditions***

   Unless otherwise agreed, delivery of the goods and payment of the price are concurrent conditions, that is to say, the seller shall be ready and willing to give possession of the goods to the buyer in exchange for the price, and the buyer shall be ready and willing to pay the price in exchange for possession of the goods.

3. ***Section 34: Effect of part delivery***

   A delivery of part of goods, in progress of the delelivery of the whole, has the same effect, for the purpose of passing the property in such goods, as a delivery of the whole; but a delivery of part of the goods, with an intention of severing it from the whole, does not operate as a delivery of the remainder.

4. ***Section 36: Rules as to delivery***

   (1) Whether it is for the buyer to take possession of the goods or for the seller to send them to the buyer is a question depending in each case on the contract, express or implied, between the parties. Apart from any such contract, goods sold are to be delivered at the place at which they are at the time of the sale, and goods agreed to be sold are to be delivered at the place at which they are at the time of the agreement to sell, or, if not then in existence, at the place at which they are manufactured or produced.

(2) Where under the contract of sale, the seller is bound to send the goods to the buyer, but no time for sending them is fixed, the seller is bound to send them within a reasonable time.

(3) Where the goods at the time of sale are in the possession of a third person, there is no delivery by seller to buyer unless and until such third person acknowledges to the buyer that he holds the goods on his behalf:

Provided that nothing in this section shall affect the operation of the issue or transfer of any document of title to goods.

(4) Demand or tender of delivery may be treated as ineffectual unless made at a reasonable hour. What is a reasonable hour is a question of fact.

(5) Unless otherwise agreed, the expenses of and incidental to putting the goods into a deliverable state shall be borne by the seller.

5. ***Section 40: Risk where goods are delivered at distant place***

Where the seller of goods agrees to deliver them at his own risk at a place other than that where they are when sold, the buyer shall, nevertheless, unless otherwise agreed, take any risk of deterioration in the goods necessary incident to the course of transit.

6. ***Section 42: Acceptance***

The buyer is deemed to have accepted the goods wnen he intimates to the seller that he has accepted them, or when the goods have been delivered to him and he does any act in relation to them which is inconsistent with the ownership of the seller, or when, after the lapse of a reasonable time, he retains the goods without intimating to the seller that he has rejected them.

TEST QUESTIONS

1. State the respective duties of the seller and the buyer in the performance of contract of sale.
2. What do you mean by the term 'delivery of goods' in a contract of sale? State the modes of effective delivery of goods and the legal rules relating thereto.
3. "Delivery of goods and payment of their price are the concurrent conditions" —Explain with examples.
4. "It is the duty of the seller to deliver the goods and of the buyer to accept and pay for them"— elucidate
5. State the buyer's duty to accept the goods and pay the price. What is the liability of the buyer if he refuses to take delivery of the goods?
6. What course is open to the buyer if the seller makes (*a*) part delivery, (*b*) short delivery, (*c*) excess delivery, and (*d*) mixed delivery, of goods.
7. State the legal provisions relating to delivery to the carrier or wharfinger.
8. Explain with examples the C.I.F., F.O.B. and Ex-ship contracts, and state the comparison between the three.
9. "C.I.F. contract is not a contract for sale of goods, but a contract for the sale of documents relating to the goods"—comment and state the duties of a seller and a buyer in such a contract.
10. Write short notes on legal provisions relating to (*a*) part delivery, (*b*) short delivery, (*c*) excess delivery, and (*d*) acceptance of goods.

MULTIPLE CHOICE QUESTIONS

1. Which of the following modes of delivery of goods is considered effective for a valid contract of sale?

   (*a*) Actual delivery (*b*) Symbolic delivery
   (*c*) Constructive delivery (*d*) all of these.

2. Delivering the keys of a godown in which goods sold are stored, amounts to

   (*a*) Actual delivery (*b*) Symbolic delivery
   (*c*) Delivery by attornment (*d*) None of these

3. In case the buyer rejects the whole quantity of goods due to short delivery or excess delivery, the contract is treated as

   (*a*) subsisting (*b*) cancelled
   (*c*) void (*d*) invalid

4. Where the goods are delivered to a carrier or wharfinger for the purpose of transmission to the buyer, the delivery is
   (*a*) invalid delivery
   (*b*) valid and effective
   (*c*) conditional
   (*d*) none of these
5. In a contract through sea, where the seller has to put the goods on board a ship at his expenses, the contract is known as
   (*a*) F.O.B. Contract
   (*b*) C.I.F. Contract
   (*c*) Ex-Ship contract
   (*d*) None of these
6. In a contract through sea, where the seller has to deliver the goods to the buyer at the port of destination, the contract in known as
   (*a*) F.O.B. Contract
   (*b*) C.I.F. Contract
   (*c*) Ex-Ship contract
   (*d*) None of these
7. In case of Ex-ship contract, during voyage the goods are at the risk of
   (*a*) sller
   (*b*) buyer
   (*c*) captain of the ship
   (*d*) none of these
8. In which of the following contracts, the seller is under an obligation to insure the goods?
   (*a*) Ex-ship Contract
   (*b*) F.O.B. Contract
   (*c*) C.I.F. Conrtact
   (*d*) all of these.

ANSWERS

1. (*d*)	2. (*b*)	3. (*a*)	4. (*b*)	5. (*a*)	6. (*c*)
7. (*a*)	8. (*c*)				

OBJECTIVE TYPE QUESTIONS WITH REASONING

State with reasons whether the following statements are correct or incorrect:

1. In the absence of any contract to the contrary, the delivery of goods and payment of price are the concurrent conditions.
2. A thief or a person who takes the goods by force is also deemed to be in possession of goods for the purposes of the Sale of Goods Act.
3. The delivery of keys of the godown, in which the goods are lying, to the owner amount to actual delivery.
4. The seller is not bound to deliver the goods unless the buyer makes a demand for the delivery of goods.
5. The delivery of part of the goods with the intention of separating it from the whole lot does not amount to the delivery of the whole.
6. The delivery of short quantity entitiles the buyer to reject the goods, but the delivery of excess quantity does not give such a right to the buyer.
7. When the goods are delivered to the buyers and he refuses to accept them, he is not bound to return the goods to the seller.
8. In C.I.F. contracts, the insurance and freight charges are paid by the seller.
9. In F.O.B. contracts, the seller has to bear the charges of loading the goods.
10. In ex-spit contracts, the goods are at seller's risk during voyage (sea route).

ANSWERS

1. ***Correct.*** For due performance of the contract of sale, both the seller and the buyer should perform their respective duties of delivery of goods and payments of price simultaneously [Section 32].
2. ***Incorrect.*** There is no vlontary and lawful delivery of goods to such persons.

3. *Incorrect.* Such a delivery amounts to symbolic delivery.
4. *Correct.* In the first place, it is buyer's duty to make a demand for delivery of goods [Section 35].
5. *Correct.* In such cases, the delivery is treated only of that part of goods which are delivered [Section 34].
6. *Incorrect.* The delivery of wrong quantity, whether short or excess, entitles the buyer to reject the whole lot [Section 37].
7. *Correct.* It is the law on the point. In such a case, the intimation of refusal to accept be goods is sufficient [Section 43].
8. *Incorrect.* In such contract, the insurance and freight charges are included in the price, and thus paid by the buyer.
9. *Correct.* F. O. B. refers to 'free on board' which required that the seller has to put the goods on board a ship at his own expenses.
10. *Correct.* In ex-ship contracts, it is seller's duty to deliver the goods, at his own risk, to the buyer at the port of destination.

PRACTICAL PROBLEMS

1. State the nature of delivery of goods in the following cases:

   (*a*) *A* sold to *B* 10 bags of rice and delivered the same to him.

   (*b*) *A* sold to *B* all the coolers lying in his godown and delivered the keys of godown to *B* so that he may take the coolers from the godown.

   (*c*) *A* sold to *B* 40 tins of ghee which was in possession of *C* a warehouseman and ordered *C* to transfer the tins to *B*. According *C* transferred 40 tins of ghee in his book in *B*'s name.

   Hints. (a) actual delivery, (b) symbolic delivery, (c) constructive delivery.

2. *A* sold 100 bags of wheat to *B* and delivered the same to railways for the purpose of transmission to the buyer (*B*). *A* also took the railway receipts in *B's* name and sent the same to him enabling him to take delivery of wheat on its arrival at the destination. Does it amount to effective delivery ? Give reasons.

   Hints. Yes, it amounts to effective delivery. In this case, by taking railway receipts in buyer's name, the seller has enabled the buyer to exercise control over the goods. [Section 33]

3. *A* sold to *B* some quantity of spirit made from molasses. One-Third of the quantity sold was delivered to *B*, and *A* pressed for the delivery of remainder spirit also. But the seller delayed it. In the meantime, the government barred the distillation of spirit from molasses and cancelled all the contracts for the sale of such spirit. Can the buyer (*B*) claim damages from the seller (*A*) ? Give reasons.

   Hints. Yes, *B* can claim damages from *A*. In this case, *A* had failed to deliver the goods sold within a reasonable time despite the buyer pressing for the delivery.

   [*Phillips* v. *Blair Martin* (1801) 4 Paton, scotch AC 256]

4. *A* sold 100 quintals of wheat to *B* lying in his (*A's*) warehouse. Afterwards, *B* sold to *C* 50 quintals of wheat out of the quantity purchased from *A* and requested, *A* to delivered these 50 quintals of wheat to *C*. Accordingly *A* delivered 50 quintals of wheat to *C*. Can this part delivery be reaganded as the delivery of whole quantity to *B* ? Give reasons.

   Hints. No, it cannot be regarded as the delivery of whole quantity. In this case, *B's* act of asking *A* to deliver only 50 quintals to *C* shows that the intention was not to treat the part delivery as the delivery of whole quantity.

5. *A* agreed to sell and deliver to *B* 100 bags of rice at the rate of Rs. 800 per bag. However, *A* delivered only 80 bags of rice to *B* and refused to deliver remaining 20 bags unless price of 80 bags is paid. What options are available to *B* ?

   Hints. *B* may reject the 80 bags supplied and need not to pay any amount. In such a case, *A* cannot force *B* to pay the price of 80 bags supplied to him. *B* may also accept the goods already supplied and pay the price as agreed between them [Section 37 (1)].

6. *A* contracted to supply 4950 tons of wheat to *B*. But *A* delivered 4950 tons and 55 lbs. However *A* made no attempt to charge *B* with excess quantity. *B* rejected the whole quantity of wheat. Is he justified ? Give reasons.

   Hints. *B* is not justified in rejecting the whole quantity. In this case, the excess delivery of 55 lbs. was so trivial as to be wholy insignificant. [*Shipton Anderson Co.* v. *Weil Bross. Co.* (1912) 106 LT 372]

7. *A* contracted to sell to *B* 200 tons of meat, 2 percent more or less. *A* delivered 300 tons of meat to *B* which he refused to accept. Is *B* justified in rejecting whole quantity ? Give reasons.

Hints. Yes, *B* is justified in rejecting the whole quantity. In case of excess delivery, the buyer has the right to reject the whole quantity. [Section 37 (2)]

8. *A* agreed to sell and deliver to *B* 100 tins of **Dalda** ghee at the rate of Rs. 750 per tin. *A* delivered 80 tins of Dalda ghee and 20 tins of Rath ghee. *B* rejected the whole quantity. *A* insisted that *B* is bound to accept at least the 80 tins of Dalda ghee and pay for the same. Is *A*'s claim justified ? Give reasons.

Hints. No, *A* is not justified in his claim. In this case, the option lies with the buyer (*B*). He may either accept the 80 tins of Dalda ghee and pay for the same and reject the Rath ghee. Or in the alternative, he may reject the whole quantity of ghee. [Section 37 (3)]

9. *A* contracted to sell to *B* 100 tons of flock by 20 instalments. The first 15 instalments were satisfactorily delivered, but the sixteenth instalments was defective However, the subsequent four instalments were also satisfactory. *B* wanted to repudiating the whole contract. Is he justified ? Give reasons.

Hints. No, *B* is not justified in repudiating the whole contract. In this case, the circumstance showed that there was no chance of the fault being repeated.

[Section 38 (2), *Mople flock Co. Ltd.* v. *Universal Furniture Pdts.. (Wembley) Ltd.*] (1943) 1 K.B. 148]

10. *A* agrees to sell to *B* five tons of oil at Rs. 50,000 per ton to be paid for at the time of delivery. *A* gives to *C*, a wharfinger, at whose wharf he had twenty tons of oil, an order to transfer five of them into the name of *B*. *C* marks the transfer in his books and gives *A's* clerk a notice of the transfer to *B*. *A's* clerk takes the transfer notice to *B* and offers to give it to him on payment of the price of oil. *B* refuses to pay, and consequently *C* refuses to deliver the oil to *B*. What are the rights of *A* and *B* ?

Hints. The transfer of contracted quantity of oil in *B's* name in wharfinger's book will be regarded as effective delivery of goods from seller to the buyer. *B* can therefore, claim delivery of the five tons of oil from the wharfinger even if he refuses to pay the price to him. However, the seller (*A*) will be entitled to recover the price of oil from *B*. [Section 39 (1)]

11. *A* contracts with B to purchase 30 tons of apple juice. *B* crushes the apples, puts the juice in casks and keeps it ready for delivery. *A* delays to take the delivery and the juice goes putrid and has to be thrown away. Is *A* liable to pay the price ?

Hints. Yes, *A* is liable to pay the price. In this case, the buyer should bear the loss as the delivery has been delayed because of his own fault. [Section 44, *Demby Hamilton Co.* v. *Borden*]

12. *A* sold certain quantity of wheat to *B* and shipped the same for the purpose of transmission to *B*. On arrival of the shipment, *B* took delivery of the wheat and on the same day resold a part of wheat to *C*. After three days, *B* discovered that wheat was not in accordance with contract quanlity and gave a notice to the seller about the rejection of the wheat. Is *B* justified in rejecting the wheat ?

Hints. No, *B* is not justified in rejecting the wheat. In this case, the buyer has accepted the goods by reselling the part of the same. [Section 42, *Hardy Co.* v. *Hillerns & Fowlers* (1923) 2 K.B. 409 C.A]

13. *A* sold to *B* a certain quantity of barley by sample. The delivery agreed to be made at a specified railway station. Accordingly, the barley was delivered at the specified railway station and after inspecting the sample, *B* further sold and delivered the barley to *C*. However, *C* rejected it as not being in accordance with sample. Thereupon, *B* also rejected the barley on the same ground and refused to make payment to *A*. Is *B* justified in his action ? Give reasons.

Hints. No, *B* is not justified in his action. In this case, *B* has accepted the goods by further reselling the same to *C*. [Section 42]

RIGHTS OF AN UNPAID SELLER

24.1 INTRODUCTION

The term 'unpaid seller' may be defined as the seller to whom the full price of the goods sold has not been paid. The legal definition of 'unpaid seller' is given in Section 45 of the Sale of Goods Act, which reads as under:

"The seller of the goods deemed to be an unpaid seller within the meaning of this Act–

(*a*) *When the whole of the price has not been paid or tendered;*

(*b*) *When a bill of exchange or other negotiable instrument has been received as conditional payment and the condition on which it was received had not been fulfilled by reason of the dishonour of the instrument or otherwise."*

The analysis of this section shows that a seller is considered to be an unpaid seller, when

1. The full price has not been paid or tendered to the seller.

2. The conditional payment is made by a bill of exchange or other negotiable instrument which has been dishonoured, *i.e.*, the buyer failed to pay the amount on maturity of the instrument.

Thus, a seller who has received a part of the price is also an unpaid seller. However, a seller is not an unpaid seller if the buyer has tendered (*i.e.*, offered to pay) the price, and the seller has refused to accept it. In such a case, the seller loses all rights of an unpaid seller.

The payment made by a negotiable instrument is always presumed to be a conditional payment, the condition being that it shall be duly honoured on maturity. Thus, where the price has been paid to the seller by a bill of exchange, cheque or a promissory note, the seller becomes an unpaid seller only when such bill of exchange, cheque, etc., is dishonoured.

Example 24.1. *A* sold certain quantity of jute to *B* for Rs. 1,000 *B* paid Rs. 500 and failed to pay the balance. In this case, *A* is in the position of an unpaid seller.

Example 24.2. *A* sold certain goods to *B* for Rs. 2,500. *B* made the payment by a cheque. *A* presented the cheque to the banker for payment, but the cheque was dishonoured. In this case, *A* is in the position of an unpaid seller.

24.2. RIGHTS OF AN UNPAID SELLER

The rights of an unpaid seller may be discussed under the following two heads:

1. Rights against the goods.
2. Rights against the buyer.

24.3. RIGHTS OF AN UNPAID SELLER AGAINST THE GOODS

Sometimes, after the sale of the goods, the seller still has the possession of the sold goods. In such cases, an unpaid seller has certain rights against the goods. These rights may be discussed under the following two heads:

1. Where the ownership of the goods is transferred to the buyer.
2. Where the ownership of the goods is not transferred to the buyer.

24.4. RIGHTS OF AN UNPAID SELLER WHERE THE OWNERSHIP OF THE GOODS IS TRANSFERRED TO THE BUYER

On the transfer of the ownership of the goods to the buyer, an unpaid seller has the following rights against the goods:

1. Right of Lien. 2. Right of stoppage in transit. 3. Right of resale.

24.5. RIGHT OF LIEN

The 'right of lien' is the right to retain the possession of the goods until certain charges due in respect of the goods are paid. An unpaid seller has the right to retain the goods in his possession and refuse to deliver them to the buyer until the full payment of the price is made to him, or the price is offered to him. This right is contained in Section 47(1) of the Sale of Goods Act. According to this section, an unpaid seller can exercise the right of lien over the goods if the price has not been paid or tendered (*i.e.*, offered) to him. This right can be exercised by the unpaid seller if the following conditions are satisfied:

(*a*) The unpaid seller must be in actual possession of the goods sold.

(*b*) The unpaid seller can retain the goods only for the payment of the price of the goods.

As a matter of fact, the right of lien is linked with the possession of the goods and not with the title of the goods. Thus, the goods must be in *actual possession* of the seller. It is, however, not necessary that he should possess the goods as an owner. He can exercise the righ of lien, even if he is possessing the goods as an agent or bailee for the buyer [Section 47(2)].

The seller, can retain the goods *only* for the price of the goods. He cannot retain the goods for any other charges, *e.g.*, maintenance, charges for storage of goods during the exercise of lien etc.

Example 24.3. *A* sold some specific goods to *B* for Rs. 500. The price was to be paid within fifteen days of sale. *B*, the buyer, became insolvent before the expiry of this credit period of fifteen days. In this case, *A* may retain the possession of the goods until the price is paid by *B*.

Example 24.4. *A* sold his jeep to *B* for Rs. 50,000. The price was to be paid within one month of sale. *B* did not pay the price within the agreed credit period of one month. A may refuse to deliver the jeep to *B* until the price is paid.

The important legal provisions relating to the unpaid seller's right of lien may be stated as under:

1. Where goods are sold without any stipulation as to credit (*i.e.*, in case of cash sale), unpaid seller may retain the goods if the buyer fails to pay the whole price. [Section 47(1)(*a*)].
2. Where the goods are sold on credit, the unpaid seller may reitan the goods if the buyer fails to pay the whole price after the expiry of credit period. [Section 47(1)(*b*)].
3. Where the buyer becomes insolvent, the unpaid seller may retain the possession of the goods until the whole price is paid. It is so because, the law does not compel a person to deliver the goods to an insolvent. [Section 47(1)(c)].
4. Where the unpaid seller has delivered a part of the goods, he may exercise his lien on the remaining part of the goods. But where the part delivery is made under the circumstances which show an agreement to waive a lien, the seller cannot retain the goods [Section 48]. In other words, where delivery of part goods is intended as delivery of the whole, the right of lien is lost.
5. The right of lien is indivisible in nature. And, the seller cannot be compelled to deliver a part of the goods on payment of proportionate price of the goods.

24.6. TERMINATION OF LIEN OR LOSS OF LIEN

1. *By delivery of goods to the carrier*
2. *By delivery of goods to the buyer*
3. *By waiver of the lien*
4. *By tender of price by the buyer*

Since the right of lien depends only upon the possession of the goods, it is lost as soon as the possession of the goods is lost. The circumstances, in which the unpaid seller's lien is lost, may be discussed under the following sub-heads:

1. *By delivery of goods to the carrier:* The unpaid seller loses his right of lien over the goods when the goods are delivered to some person (a carrier or other bailee) *for the purpose of transmission to the buyer* [Section 49(1)(*a*)].

Example 24.5. *A* sold 100 bags of cement to *B* and delivered them to the Railways for the purpose of transmission to the buyer *B*. *A* obtained the railway receipt in *B's* name and sent the same to *B* to enable him to obtain the delivery of the goods from the Railways. While the bags of cement were in transit, the buyer (*B*) became insolvent, and the seller (*A*) was still unpaid. In this case, the seller's right of lien is lost as the goods are delivered to the carrier (Railways). However, he still has the right of stoppage in transit.

2. *By delivery of goods to the buyer :* The unpaid seller also loses his right of lien when he delivers the goods to the buyer or his agent [Section 49(1)(*b*)].

Example 24.6. *A* sold certain goods to *B* and delivered them to him. *B* took the goods to the Railways for the purpose of carrying them to his place of business. However, due to loose packing, the goods were returned to A for repacking. While the goods were with the seller (*A*) for this purpose, the buyer (*B*) became insolvent. The seller still being unpaid, claimed to retain the goods in the exercise of his right of lien. In this case, the seller had lost his right of lien by delivering the goods to the buyer. And thus, he was not justified in retaining the goods when the goods were delivered to him for specific purpose (*i.e.*, repacking). [Based on *Valpy v. Gibson*]

3. *By waiver of the lien:* The right of lien is for the benefit of the seller. If he like, he may waive (give up) his right. And by waiver, the lien is lost [Section 49(1)(*c*)]. The waiver may be express or implied.

4. *By tender of price by the buyer:* When the buyer tenders the price or pays the price, the seller loses his right of lien as he ceases to be an unpaid seller. It may be noted that the seller cannot convert himself into an unpaid seller by voluntarily refusing to accept the price.

Note: The unpaid seller's lien is *not lost* by the mere fact that he has obtained from the court a decree (*e.g.*, final order of the court) for the payment of the price [Section 49(2)]. But the unpaid seller loses his right of lien after receiving the payment of the price from the buyer as per the decree.

24.7. RIGHT OF STOPPAGE IN TRANSIT

The term transit may be defined as the state of transmission of goods (*i.e.*, after the delivery of goods to the carrier and before taking over the possession by the buyer or his authorised agent). Thus, the term 'stoppage in transit' means the stopping of the goods while they are in the course of transit, *i.e.*, in the course of transmission to the buyer. We have already discussed that where the unpaid seller has parted with the possession of the goods, then his lien is lost. But in certain circumstances, he can stop the goods in transit and prevent them from reaching into the buyer's possession until the price is paid. This right is contained in Section 50 of the Sale of Goods Act, which provides that where the buyer becomes insolvent, and the unpaid seller has parted with the possession of the goods, he can stop the goods in transit until the price is paid or tendered (*i.e.*, offered) to him. The analysis of this section reveals that the right of stoppage in transit can be exercised if the following conditions are satisfied:

(*a*) The buyer has become insolvent.

(*b*) The goods are in the course of transit, *i.e.*, the goods have gone out of the actual possession of the seller. But they have not reached in the possession of the buyer.

(*c*) The unpaid seller can stop the goods in transit only for payment of the price of the goods.

Thus, the seller can exercise his right of stoppage in transit only when the buyer has become insolvent before the payment of the price. In such cases, it it necessary to protect the unpaid seller against the risk of his goods going to the possession of an insolvent. It is based on the principle that one man's goods shall not be applied to the payment of other man's debt.

Example 24.7. *A* of Bombay sold certain goods to *B* of Calcutta. *A* delivered the goods to the railways for the purpose of transmission to *B*. However, *B* became insolvent before the goods reached him. In this case, *A* may give notice to the railways and stop the goods from reaching *B* until the price is paid.

24.8. DURATION OF TRANSIT

The duration of transit is the period between the commencement and end of transit. The transit commences (*i.e.*, starts) from the time when the goods are delivered to the middleman (*i.e.*, carrier or other bailee), and it continues till the buyer or his agent takes the delivery of the goods [Section 51(1)]. The important legal provisions relating to the duration of transit may be summed up as under :

1. Sometimes, the goods are rejected by the buyer and the carrier continues to have the possession of the goods. In such cases, the transit does not come to an end [Section 51(4)].
2. Sometimes, the goods are delivered to a ship chartered by the buyer. In such cases, if the circumstances show that the carrier is acting as an agent of the buyer, then the transit comes to an end as soon as the goods are loaded on board the ship [Section 51(5)].

3. Sometimes the goods are delivered in parts. In such cases, the seller may stop the remainder of goods unless the delivery of part of the goods shows an intention to giving up the possession of the whole of the goods [Section 51(7)]

24.9. TERMINATION OF STOPPAGE IN TRANSIT OR LOSS OF RIGHT OF STOPPAGE IN TRANSIT

> 1. *Interception by the buyer*
> 2. *Carrier's acknowlegement to the buyer*
> 3. *Carrier's wrongful refusal to deliver*

The right of stoppage in transit depends upon the fact that the goods must be in transit. This right is lost when the transit comes to an end. The following are the circumstances in which the transit comes to an end, and the right of stoppage in transit is lost.

1. *Interception by the buyer:* Sometimes, the buyer or his agent takes the delivery of the goods from the carrier (middleman) before the goods arrive at the appointed destination. In such cases, the transit comes to an end. Although it may be wrongful for the carrier to deliver the goods to the buyer before they reach at the appointed destination, but so far as seller's right of stoppage is concerned that comes to an end. However, the seller may bring an action against the carrier for the recovery of damages [Section 51(2)]. But sometimes the buyer takes a seat as a passenger in the ship which is carrying the goods. In such cases the buyer's taking of seat does not amount to delivery of goods to him before their arrival at the appointed destination.

Example 24.8. *A*, at Sydney, purchased certain goods from *B*. The goods were to be shipped to Kimberley (in Western Australia). When the goods were shipped, the buyer (*A*) also took a seat in the ship for the purpose of going to Kimberley. The buyer became insolvent after the goods left Sydney and before they arrived at Kimberley. The seller stopped the goods in transit. It was held that the transit did not end as buyer's mere going with the ship did not amount to the taking delivery of the goods.

[*Lyons* v. *Hoffnung* 15 A.C. 391 PC]

2. *Carrier's acknowledgement to the buyer:* Sometimes, after the arrival of the goods at the appointed destination, the carrier acknowledges (*i.e.*, informs) to the buyer or his agent that now he is holding the goods on buyer's behalf. In such cases, the transit comes to an end. It is so because after the acknowledgement, the carrier holds the goods as an agent of the buyer. It is immaterial if any further destination is indicated by the buyer [Section 51(3)].

3. *Carrier's wrongful refusal to deliver the goods to the buyer:* Sometimes, the carrier wrongfully refuses to deliver the goods to the buyer or his agent. In such cases also, the transit comes to an end [Section 51(6)]. It may be noted that carrier's refusal must be wrongful, *i.e., without any just cause.*

Example 24.9: *A* sold certain timber to *B* and consigned them by ship. On arrival of the ship at the appointed destination, the agent of the buyer went to take possession of the timber. The captain said that he would deliver the timber on the payment of his freight charges. In the meantime, the buyer became insolvent, and the seller gave notice of stoppage to the captain of ship who was in charge of the ship and goods. And the timber was delivered back to the seller. It was held that the transit was not at an end as the captain's refusal to deliver the timber to the buyer's agent was justified. Moreover, buyer's agent has not taken the actual possession of the timber from the captain, though he went to take the possession.

[*Whitehead* v. *Anderson* 9 W & M 518]

24.10 MODES OF EXERCISING THE STOPPAGE IN TRANSIT

Section 52 (1) of the Sale of Goods Act provides that, an unpaid seller may exercise the right of stoppage in transit in any of the following two ways:

(*a*) By taking actual possession of the goods.

(b) By giving notice to the carrier to stop the goods and redeliver them to the seller or according to his directions.

It may be noted that where the notice is given to the carrier, then it becomes the duty of the carrier to redeliver the goods to the unpaid seller. However, the seller has to bear the expenses of redelivery.

24.11. COMPARISON BETWEEN RIGHT OF LIEN AND RIGHT OF STOPPAGE IN TRANSIT

The following table gives the comparison between the right of lien and right of stoppage in transit.

S.No.	*Lien*	*Stoppage in Transit*
1.	This right can be exercised only when the goods are in the actual possession of the seller.	This right can be exercised when the seller has parted with the goods, but they are in the possession of a middle man.
2.	This right can be exercised when the buyer fails to pay the price.	This right can also be exercised when the buyer fails to pay the price. But *only* when the buyer becomes insolvent before payment of the price.
3.	This right comes to an end as soon as goods go out of the possession of the the seller.	This right comes to an end as soon as the goods are delivered to the buyer.
4.	This right remains in force till the right of stoppage in transit starts.	This right starts when the right of lien comes to an end, and remains in force till the delivery of goods to the buyer.
5.	This right is to retain the possession of the goods.	This right is to regain (take back) the possession of the goods.

24.12. EFFECT OF SUB-SALE ON UNPAID SELLER'S RIGHTS OF LIEN AND STOPPAGE IN TRANSIT

Sometimes, the seller is unpaid and the buyer further sells the goods to some other person. In this case, unpaid seller's right of lien or stoppage in transit is not affected by such sale. And the unpaid seller can exercise these rights irrespective of any further sale by the buyer. In other words, the unpaid seller's right of lien or stoppage in transit is not affected by any further sale or other disposition (*e.g.*, pledge, etc.) of goods by the buyer [Section 53(1)). However, he can exercise these rights only if the legal requirements for exercising the right of lien and stoppage in transit are fulfilled.

Example 24.10. *A* sold 100 tons of oil to *B*. Out of this, *B* further sold 50 tons of the oil to *C*. And *B* gave *C* the delivery orders addressed to *A* requiring him (*A*) to deliver 50 tons oil to *C* out of the 100 tons sold to him (*B*). *A* delivered 25 tons of oil to *C*. Later on, *B* fell in arrears of price. *A* exercised his right of lien and refused to make further deliveries to *C*. It was held that *A* was justified in refusing further delivery of oil to *C*.

[*Mordaunt Bros.* v. *British Oil & Cake Mill* (1910) 2 KB 502].

If in the above example, *B* becomes insolvent, then also *A* can refuse to deliver the oil to *C*. However, in the following circumstances, the unpaid seller's rights against the goods are defeated by further sale or pledge of the goods by the buyer:

1. *Seller's consent:* Sometimes, the buyer further sells or pledges the goods with the consent of the seller. In such cases, the unpaid seller cannot exercise his right of lien or stoppage in transit.

2. *Transfer of documents of title:* Sometimes, the seller issues documents of title (*i.e.,* delivery orders, bills of lading, railway receipts, etc.) to the goods to the buyer. And the buyer further sells or pledges the goods by transferring the documents of title. In such cases, the unpaid seller's rights of lien and stoppage in transit are affected if the transferee acts in good faith *i.e.,* he does not have the knowledge of the fact that the original seller is unpaid and has rights against the goods.

Where the documents of title are transferred by way of sale, the above two rights of the original seller are completely defeated. And in case of pledge, these rights become subject to the right of the pledgee.

Example 24.11. *A* sold 3,000 bags of seeds to *B* and gave him 'delivery orders'. *B* sent a cheque for the price. *B* further sold the goods to *C* by endorsing the delivery orders in his favour. *B's* cheque was dishonoured, and consequently *A* became unpaid seller and claimed lien on the goods. It was held that *A's* lien was lost as *B* further sold the goods to a *bona fide* purchaser for value. [Based on *Jurgens Margarine v. Lous dreyfus Co.* (1914) 111 LT 248].

Example 24.12. *A* sold 400 tons of iron to *B*. *A* consigned the iron to a shipping company, and sent the bills of lading to *B*. And he (*B*) obtained a loan of Rs. 50,000 from *C* and pledged with him the bills of lading as security for the repayment of loan. While the goods were in transit, *B* became insolvent, and consequently *A* became an unpaid seller. In this case *A's* right of stoppage in transit is subject to the right of the pledgee, *i.e., C* will continue to have charge over the goods for the repayment his loan.

24.13. RIGHT OF RESALE

1. ***Where the goods are perishable***
2. ***Where the unpaid seller has excrcised his right of lien or of stoppage in transit and gives notice to the buyer of his intention to resell the goods***
3. ***Where the seller expressly reserve his right of resale***

An unpaid seller can resell the goods to someone else in certain circumstance. This right of unpaid seller is contained in Section 54(2) of the Sale of Goods Act, which provides that if the buyer fails to pay or offer the price within a reasonable time, the unpaid seller has the right to resell the goods in the following circumstances:

(*a*) Where the goods are of perishable nature, or

(*b*) Where the unpaid seller has exercised his right of lien or stoppage in transit and gives a notice to the buyer of his intention to resell the goods. And also,

(*c*) Where the unpaid seller has expressly reserved his right of resale.

These circumstances, in which the unpaid seller may resell the goods to some other person, are discussed in the following pages:

1. *Where the goods are perishable:* Sometime, the goods are of perishable nature and the buyer fails to pay the price within a reasonable time. In such cases, the seller may resell the goods to another person within a reasonable time. The term 'reasonable time' is a question of fact in each case.

2. *Where the unpaid seller has exercised his right of lien or of stoppage in transit and gives notice to the buyer of his intention to resell the good:* The unpaid seller may also resell the goods to some other person, if he has exercised his right of lien or stoppage in transit. In this case, he should give a notice to the buyer of his intention to resell the goods. And if after the receipt of such notice, the buyer does not pay or tender the price within a reasonable time, the seller may resell the goods. It may be noted that in such cases, on the resale of the goods the seller is also entitled to:

(*a*) Recover the difference between the contract price and resale price, from the original buyer, as damages.

(*b*) Retain the profit if the resale price is higher than the contract price.

It may also be noted that the seller can recover damages and retain the profits only when the goods are resold after giving the notice of resale to the buyer. But if the goods are resold by the seller *without* giving any notice to the buyer, the seller cannot recover the loss suffered on resale, Moreover, if there is any profit on resale he must return it to the original buyer, *i.e.*, he cannot keep such surplus with him [Section 54(2)].

3. ***Where the seller expressly reserve his right of resale:*** Sometimes, it is expressly agreed between the seller and the buyer that in case the buyer makes default in payment of the price, the seller will resell the goods to some other person. In such cases, the seller is said to have reserved his right of resale, and he may resell the goods on buyer's default. It may be noted that in such cases, the seller is not required to give notice of resale. He is entitled to recover damages from the original buyer even if no notice of resale is given.

Note: The right of resale can be exercised by the seller only when the buyer is in default.

24.14. RIGHT OF AN UNPAID SELLER WHERE THE OWNERSHIP OF THE GOODS IS NOT TRANSFERRED TO THE BUYER

Sometimes, the ownership of the goods sold is not tranferred to the buyer. In such cases, the unpaid seller has the **right of withholding the delivery of the goods sold,** if the buyer fails to pay the price, *i.e.*, the unpaid seller may refuse to deliver the goods to the buyer. Thus, where the contract is executory, there is no obligation on the part of the seller to complete it in the event the buyer fails to pay the price or becomes insolvent. And the seller will not be liable for damages for non-delivery until the price is tendered or paid. It may be noted that this right is in addition to other remedies available to the seller. This right is similar to and co-extensive with the right of lien and stoppage in transit [Section 46(2)].

24.15 RIGHTS AGAINST THE BUYER OR SELLER'S REMEDIES AGAINST THE BUYER

1. *Suit for price*
2. *Suit for damages for non-acceptances of goods*
3. *Suit for damage for repudiation of the contract before the due date of delivery of goods*
4. *Suit for interest*

The unpaid seller also has certain rights against the buyer. These rights may be discussed under the following heads:

(*a*) Suit for price.

(*b*) Suit for damages for non-acceptance of goods.

(*c*) Suit for damages for repudiation of the contract before the due date of delivery of goods.

(*d*) Suit for interest.

These are in fact seller's remedies against the buyer for breach of contracts of sale, and are explained as under.

1. *Suit for price:* The payment of price is the legal obligation of the buyer, and on transfer of the ownership of the goods to the buyer, he becomes bound to pay the price to the seller. If he does not pay the price in terms of the contract, the seller may bring a legal action against the buyer for the payment of the price [Section 55(1)]. Generally, the seller can sue for price of the goods sold only when the ownership of the goods is transferred to the buyer. But sometimes, the contract of sale provides that the price shall be paid on a certain day whether the goods are delivered or not. In such cases, if the buyer fails to pay the price on that day, the seller may file a suit against the buyer for the recovery of the price. It may be noted that in such a case, the transfer of ownership of the goods to the buyer is immaterial for seller's action for price [Section 55(2)].

2. ***Suit for damages for non-acceptances of goods:*** Sometimes, the seller is ready and willing to deliver the goods to the buyer. But the buyer wrongfully neglects or refuses to accept the goods and pay for them. In such cases, the seller may bring a legal action against the buyer for the recovery of damages suffered due to non-acceptance of the goods [Section 56].

3. ***Suit for damage for repudiation of the contract before the due date of delivery of goods:*** Sometimes, the buyer repudiates (*i.e.*, puts an end to) the contract before the due date of delivery of goods. In such cases, the seller has the following options [Section 60]:

(*a*) He may not immediately take any action against the buyer, and treat the contract as subsisting and wait till the date of delivery of goods.

(*b*) He may immediately treat the contract as repudiated and bring a legal action against the buyer for the recovery of damages.

Thus, the option of bringing the action lies with the seller. He may either wait till the date of delivery of goods arrives, or bring an immediate action for damages.

4. ***Suit for interest:*** We know that when the seller tenders the goods, but the buyer fails to accept and pay for them, then the seller may file a suit for the recovery of the price. *In such a suit*, the seller may also claim the interest on the amount of price payable by the buyer. The court may award the interest from the date of tender of the goods or from the date when the price is payable. The rate of interest to be awarded is at the discretion of the court. It may however, be noted that the interest can be recovered by the seller *only when* he is entitled to recover the price. Thus, when the seller's only remedy is for damages, he cannot file a suit for interest [Section 61].

24.16. BUYER'S REMEDIES AGAINST THE SELLER

1. *Suit for damages for non-delivery of goods*
2. *Suit for damages for repudiation of the contract before the due date of delivery*
3. *Suit for specific performance of contract*
4. *Suit for breach of warranty*

On breach of the contract of sale due to seller's default, the buyer has the following remedies (*i.e.*, rights) against the seller:

1. ***Suit for damages for non-delivery of goods:*** Sometimes, the buyer is ready and willing to take delivery of the goods. But the seller wrongfully neglects or refuses to deliver the goods to him. In such cases, the buyer may bring a legal action against the seller for the recovery of damages suffered by him due to non-delivery of the goods [Section 57].

2. ***Suit for damages for repudiation of the contract before the due date of delivery:*** Sometimes, the seller repudiates the contract before the due date of delivery of goods. In such cases, the buyer has the following options [Section 60]:

(*a*) He may not immediately take any action against the seller, and treat the contract as subsisting and wait till the date of delivery of goods.

(*b*) He may immediately treat the contract as repudiated and bring a legal action against the seller for the recovery of damages.

Thus, the option of bringing the action lies with the buyer. He may either wait till the date of delivery of goods arrives, or bring an immediate action for damages.

3. ***Suit for specific performance of contract:*** On the seller's failure to deliver the goods, buyer may file a suit for specific performance of contract against the seller. By such a suit, the buyer may obtain an order from the court compelling the seller to deliver the goods sold to the buyer. It may be noted that this remedy is available to the buyer only in the following cases:

1. When the contract is for the sale of specific or ascertained goods, and
2. The damages would not be an adequate remedy.

The courts generally allows the specific performance when the damages would not be an adequate remedy or where it would not be possible to ascertain the actual loss, *eg.*, where the goods are of unique or of special value such as a rare painting which may not be available in the market.

4. *Suit for breach of warranty:* In case of breach of warranty, the buyer has the following remedies [Section 59]:

(*a*) If the price has not been paid by the buyer, he may deduct from the price the loss suffered by him and pay the balance; or

(*b*) If the loss suffered is more than the price, the buyer may file a suit for damages. However, where the price has already been paid, the only remedy of the buyer is to bring a legal action for the recovery of damages suffered by him due to the breach of warranty.

5. *Suit for interest:* Sometimes, the buyer has already paid the price but the seller fails to deliver the goods. In such cases, the buyer may file a suit for the refund of the price. *In such a suit,* he may also claim interest on the amount of price paid by him. The court may award the interest from the date on which the payment of the price was made. It may, however, be noted that the interest can be recovered *only when* the buyer is entitled to the refund of the price. Thus, when the buyer's only remedy is for damages, he cannot file a suit for interest.

LEGAL PROVISIONS (SECTIONS) DISCUSSED IN THE CHAPTER

Important legal provisions (sections) of the Sale of Goods Act, 1930 disucssed in this chapter are reproduced herunder for ready reference:

1. ***Section 45: Unpaid seller defined***

(1) The seller of goods is deemed to be an "unpaid seller" within the meaning of this Act–

(*a*) when the whole of the price has not been paid or tendered;

(*b*) when a bill of exchange or other negotiable instrument has been received as conditional payment, and the condition on which it was received has not been fulfilled by reason of the dishonour of the instrument or otherwise.

(2) In this Chapter, the term "seller" includes any person who is in the position of a seller, as, for instance, an agent of the seller to whom the bill of lading has been endorsed, or a consignor or agent who has himself paid, or is directly responsible for, the price.

2. ***Section 47: Seller's lien***

(1) Subject to the provisions of this Act, the unpaid seller of goods who is in possession of them is entitled to retain possession of them until payment or tender of the price in the following cases, namely:—

(*a*) where the goods have been sold without any stipulation as to credit;

(*b*) where the goods have been sold on credit, but the term of credit has expired;

(*c*) where the buyer becomes insolvent.

(2) The seller may exercise his right of lien notwithstanding that he is in possession of the goods as agent or bailee for the buyer.

3. ***Section 48: Part delivery***

Where an unpaid seller has made part delivery of the goods, he may exercise his right of lien on the remainder, unless such part delivery has been made under such circumstances as to show an agreemnt to waive the lien.

4. ***Section 49: Termination of Lien***

(1) The unpaid seller of goods loses his lien thereon-

(*a*) when he delivers the goods to a carrier or other bailee for the purpose of trnasmission to the buyer without reserving the right of disposal of the goods;

(b) when the buyer or his agent lawfully obtains possession of the goods;

(c) by waiver thereof.

(2) The unpaid seller of goods, having a lien thereon, does not lose his lien by reason only that he has obtained a decrese for the price of the goods.

5. ***Section 50: Right of stoppage in transit***

Subject to the provisions of this Act, when the buyer of goods becomes insolvent, the unpaid seller who has parted with the prosession of the goods has the right of stopping them in tranist, that is to say, he may resume possession of the goods as long as they are in the course of tranist, and may retain them unitl payment or tender of the price.

6. ***Section 51 (1): Duration of transit***

Goods are deemed to be in course of transit form the time when they are delivered to a carrier or other baliee for the purpose of transmission to buyer, until the buyer or his agent in that behalf takes delivery of them form such carrier or other bailee.

7. ***Section 53: Effect of sub-sale or pledge by buyer***

(1) Subject to the provisions of this Act, the unpaid seller's right of lien or stoppage in transit is not affected by any sale or other disposition of the goods which the buyer may have made, unless the seller has assented thereto:

Provided that where a document of title to goods has been issued or lawfully transferred to any person as buyer or owner of the goods, and that person transfers the document to a person who takes the document in good faith and for consideration, then, if such last mentioned transfer was by way of sale, the unpaid seller's right of lien or stoppage in transit is defeated, and, if such last mentioned transfer was by way of pledge or other disposition for value, the unpaid seller's right of lien or stoppage in transit can only be exercised subject to the rights of the transferee.

(2) Where the transfer is by way of pledge, the unpaid seller may require the pledgee to have the amount secured by the pledge satisfied in the first instance, as far as possible, out of any other goods or securities of the buyer in the hands of the pledgee and available against the buyer. .

TEST QUESTIONS

1. Who is an unpaid seller? What are his rights against the buyer personally, and against the goods?
2. What are the rights of an unpaid seller?
3. Under the Sale of Goods Act, when is a seller of goods deemed to be an 'unpaid seller'? Explain the unpaid seller's right of lien over the goods. When does this right of an unpaid seller terminates?
4. In what circumstances can the right of stopping the goods in transit be exercised?
5. "The right of stoppage is transit is an extension of the right of lien"—comment.
6. "Right of stoppage in transit begins when the right of lien ends"—comment.
7. State the comparison between unpaid seller's right of lien and of stoppage in transit. When can the unpaid seller resell the goods?
8. What is the effect of sub-sale or pledge on unpaid seller's right of lien and stoppage in transit?
9. Write brief note on unpaid seller's right against the goods when the ownership of the goods has transferred to the buyer. Does he possess any right when the ownership of the goods has not transferred to the buyer?
10. Write notes on (a) Duration of transit. (b) Termination of transit. (c) Modes of exercising stoppage in transit. (d) Unpaid seller's remedies against the buyer personally.
11. Discuss briefly the remedies available to the aggrieved party (seller or buyer) in the event of breach of contract of sale.
12. State seller's remedies against the buyer is case of breach of contract of sale.
13. When is a seller entitled to sue the buyer for the price of goods? Can such a suit be brought before the property in the goods passed to the buyer?
14. What course of action is available to the seller when the buyer repudiates the contract before due date? Is there any case in which the buyer may perform the contract on due date notwithstanding the earlier repudiation by him? If yes, discuss.

15. State buyer's remedies against the seller in case of breach of contract of sale.

16. Write notes on (*a*) Suit for interest by the seller and buyer. (*b*) Suit for breach of warranty by the buyer.

MULTIPLE CHOICE QUESTIONS

1. The unpaid seller can exercise his right of lien over the goods for
(*a*) price of goods (*b*) storage charges
(*c*) any lawful charges (*d*) all of these.

2. The unpaid seller can exercise his right of lien over the goods, where he is in possession of the goods as a
(*a*) owner of goods (*b*) agent of buyer
(*c*) bailee for buyer (*d*) any of these.

3. In which of the following cases, the unpaid seller loses his right of lien?
(*a*) delivery of goods to buyer (*b*) delivery of goods to carrier
(*c*) tender of price by buyer (*d*) all the these.

4. The unpaid seller can exercise his right of stoppage of goods in transit where the buyer.
(*a*) becomes insolvent (*b*) refuses to pay price
(*c*) acts fraudulently (*d*) all the these.

5. Where by exercising the right of stoppage in transit the unpaid seller regains the posession of goods, then
(*a*) contract of sale in terminated (*b*) unpaid's seller lien revives
(*c*) unpaid's seller lien does not revive (*d*) seller's possession is unlawful.

6. On buyer's failure to pay the price within reasonable time, the unpaid seller can sell the goods to someone else, where
(*a*) goods are perishable (*b*) seller has reserved such right
(*c*) both of these (*d*) none of these.

7. Which of the following rights are available to the unpaid seller against the buyer?
(*a*) suit for price (*b*) suit for interest
(*c*) suit for the repudiation (*d*) all of these

8. Before the transfer of ownership, if the buyer wrongfully fails to accept the goods delivered by the seller, then the seller can file a suit for recovery of
(*a*) damages (*b*) price
(*c*) both (*a*) and (*b*) (*d*) none of these.

9. On the transfer of ownership, if the buyer fails to accept the goods and pay for them, then the seller can file a suit for recovery of
(*a*) price (*b*) interest
(*c*) none of these (*d*) both (*a*) and (*b*).

10. On seller's wrongful refusal to deliver the unascertained goods to the buyer, the buyer can file a suit for recovery of
(*a*) goods (*b*) damages
(*c*) both (*a*) and (*b*) (*d*) none of these.

11. On seller's refusal to deliver the goods, the buyer can file a suit for specific performance of contract on the fulfilment of following condition
(*a*) sale is for specific goods (*b*) damages not adequate remedy
(*c*) both (*a*) and (*b*) (*d*) buyer has no such right.

12. On the payment of price by the buyer, if the seller fails to deliver the goods, then the buyer can file a suit for
(*a*) refund of price (*b*) interest
(*c*) none of these (*d*) both (*a*) and (*b*).

ANSWERS

1. (*a*)	**2.** (*d*)	**3.** (*d*)	**4.** (*a*)	**5.** (*b*)	**6.** (*c*)
7. (*d*)	**8.** (*a*)	**9.** (*d*)	**10.** (*b*)	**11.** (*c*)	**12.** (*d*)

OBJECTIVE TYPE QUESTIONS WITH REASONING

State with reasons whether the following statements are correct or incorrect:

1. A seller to whom the part of price has been paid is not an unpaid seller.
2. A seller is not an unpaid seller if the buyer has tendered the price, and the seller has fused to accept it.
3. A seller who has received a cheque for the price of the goods, becomes an unpaid seller when such cheque is dishonoured.
4. The right of lien by an unpaid seller can be exercised for non-payment of price of goods and other charges.
5. An unpaid seller loses his right of lien when the documents of title to the goods have been delivered to the buyer.
6. An unpaid seller can exercise the right of stoppage of goods in transit if the buyer becomes insolvent.
7. 'Right of lien' and 'right to stoppage the goods in transit' may be exercised simultnaeously by an unpaid seller.
8. Where the goods are of perishable nature, the unpaid seller cannot re-sell the goods without any notice to the buyer.
9. A breach of contract of sale occurs only on buyer's default to pay the price.
10. Where the seller repudiate the contract before the due date of delivery of goods, he must immediately file a suit for recovery of damages.

ANSWERS

1. ***Incorrect.*** A seller to whom the whole of the price has not been paid is an unpaid seller [Section 45].
2. ***Correct.*** In such a case, the seller is not legally an unpaid seller. The price remains to be unpaid because of his own fault [Section 45].
3. ***Correct.*** On the dishonour of a cheque for the price, the price remains unpaid and the seller becomes an unpaid seller [Section 45(*b*)]
4. ***Incorrect.*** The right of lien can be exercised by an unpaid seller only for the price of goods, not for any other charges.
5. ***Incorrect.*** An unpaid seller's right of lien remains intact so long as he is having the actual possession of the goods.
6. ***Correct.*** Buyers's insolveney is an essential condition for the exercise of this right by an unpaid seller [Section 50].
7. ***Incorrect.*** The right to stoppage the goods in transit begins only when the unpaid seller loses the possession of the goods. With the loss of possession, the lien is lost. Thus, both cannot be exercised simultaneously.
8. ***Incorrect.*** In case of perishable goods, the seller has the right to re-sell the goods without giving any notice to the buyer [Section 54(2)].
9. ***Incorrect.*** The breach of contract of sale may also occur due to seller's default in the performance of his part of promise.
10. ***Incorrect.*** In such a case, the buyer has the option to treat the contract as subsisting and wait till the date of delivery of goods.

PRACTICAL PROBLEMS

1. *A*, a London merchant, places an order with *B*, a Bombay merchant, for 100 bales of cotton. *A* sends his ship to Bombay for cotton. *B* delivers the cotton on board the ship, and takes bill of lading from the master, making the cotton deliverable to *B*'s order or assigns. The cotton arrived at London, but before coming into *A*'s possession, *A* becomes insolvent. The cotton has not been paid for. Can *A* stop the cotton ? Give reasons.

   Hints. Yes, *B* can stop the cotton from going into *A*'s possession until the whole price of the cotton is paid to him. In this case, *B* is an unpaid seller and he can validly exercise his right of stoppage in transit in such circumstances. [section 51]

2. *A* sells to *B* a quantity of sugar lying in *A*'s warehouse. It is agreed that *B* shall get three months credit. *B* allows the sugar to remain in *A*'s warehouse. In the meantime, *B* becomes insolvent before the expiry of the three months, and the official Receiver demands delivery of the sugar from *A* without offering to pay. Is *A* bound to deliver the sugar to official Receiver ?

   Hints. *A* can exercise right of lien and he is not bound to deliver the goods to the Official Receiver till he is paid the total price of sugar. [Section 47 (1) (c)]

3. *A* sold to B 100 bales of cotton on credit and kept them in his warehouse on rent charged to the buyer. Before the period of credit expired, *B* sold away 25 bales and became insolvent. *A* seeks to exercise his lien on the remaining bales in the warehouse for the price of 100 bales and the rent in arreares. Decide giving. reasons.

   Hints. *A* can exercise right of lien on 75 bales for the price of 100 bales of cotton. However, he has no right of lien for the arrears of rent as the right of lien can be exercised for the payment of price only [section 47 (1)]. However, for the arrears of rent, he has the remedy of recovering the same through court of law.

4. *A* sold certain goods to *B* and delivered them to him. *B* took the goods to railways for the purpose of transmission to his place of business. However, due to lose packing, the goods were returned back to *A* for repacking. While the goods were with *A* for this purpose, the buyer (*B*) become insolvent. The seller (*A*), still being unpaid, wanted to retain the goods in the exercise of his right of lien. Can he do so ? Give reasons.

   Hints. *A*, cannot exercise his right of lien. In this case, *A* has lost his right of lien by delivering the goods to the buyer. He would not be justified in retaing the goods which were delivered back to him for specific purpose *i. e.* packing. [Section 49 (1) (b), *Valpy* v. *Gibson* (1847) 4 CB 837]

5. *A*, a merchant of Bombay, sold certain goods to *B* of Delhi. *A* delivered the goods to the Railways for the purpose of transmission to *B* at Delhi. On arrival of the goods at Delhi, *B* made the payment of transportation charges to the Railways and promised to take the goods after a week. The Railways agreed to hold the goods on *B*'s behalf during this period. In the meantime *B* became insolvent and *A* in the exercise of stoppage in transit right sent a notice to the Railways not to deliver the goods to *B* ? Can the Railway refuse to deliver the goods to *B* ? Give reasons.

   Hints. No, Railways cannot refuse to deliver the goods to *B*. In this case, the stoppage comes to an and on railways acknowledgemant to hold good on buyer's behalf. [Section 51 (3)]

6. *A* sells to *B* 80 quintals of grain out of a larger quantity lying in his granary. *B* sells 60 quintals out of those, the goods not yet being ascertained, to *C*, Then *C* having a delivery order from *B* forwards it to *A*, who informs *C* that he will send the grain in due course. *B* then becomes insolvent. Can *A* refuse to deliver the 60 quintals of grain to *C* ?

   Hints. *A* cannot refuse to deliver the 60 quintals of grain to C, but as to the reminder 20 quintals, he can exercise right of lien. [Section 53]

7. *A* sells and consigns certain goods to *B*, and sends him the bill of lading. *A* being still unpaid, *B* becomes insolvent and while the goods are still in transit, assigns the bill of lading for cash to *C*, who is aware of *B*'s insolvency. Can A stop the goods in transit ?

   Hints. Yes, A can stop the goods in transit as the assignment of the bill of lading to C is not in good faith. [Section 53]

8. A sells and consigns to *B* goods of the value of Rs 50,000. *B* assigns the railway receipt to *C* to secure a specific advance of Rs. 10,000 on the railway receipt. Before the goods reach destination, *B* becomes insolvent. *B* is indebted to C for Rs. 10,000. Can *A* stop the goods in transit ?

   Hints. Yes, *A* can stop the goods in transit. However, his right would be subject to *C*'s right over the goods to the extent of Rs. 10,000. [Section 53]

9. *A* sold certain goods to *B* and on *B*'s instruction delivered them to C, a forwarding agent, whom *B* had already instructed to ship them to a foreign country. C does so and while the goods are in transit, *A*

wants to exercise his right of stoppage in transit as *B* had been declared insolvent. Can he do so ? Give reasons.

Hints. No, *A* cannot exercise his right of stoppage in transit. In this case, the transit comes to an and as soon as the goods are deliver to *C*, the forwarding agent acting on behalf of the buyer. [Section 51]

10. A railway company is in possession of goods as a carrier when an unpaid seller gives notice of stoppage in transit to the railway company. The buyer of the goods owes money to the railway company also. Can the railway company exercise the right of lien over the goods in violation of the right of stoppage in transit of the seller ?

Hints. No, the railway company cannot exercise the right of lien over the goods in violation of the right of stoppage in transit of the seller. In this case, the unpaid seller has validly exercised his right of stoppage in transit by giving a noice to the carrier *i.e.* tailway company. [Section 52]

11. *A* of Delhi orders *B* of Mumbai to deliver certain goods to him at Delhi. *B* supplies the goods, but *A* delays to take the delivery. The station Master of Delhi railway Station informs *A* that the goods are lying at the Station at "*A*'s risk". Before taking delivery, *A* becomes insolvent, Can *B* recover the goods by stopping the goods in transit ?

Hints. No, *B* cannot recover the goods by stopping them in transit as transit comes to an end when the Station Master informs *A* that the goods are lying at his risk. [section 51]

12. *A* sells 100 bales of cotten to *B* and sends 50 bales by road transport and 50 bales by railway. *B* receives delivery of the bales sent by road transport, but before he receives the delivery of the bales sent by railway, he becomes insolvent. *A* being still unpaid, stops the goods in transit. Can *A* do so? Give reasons.

Hints. *A*, being still unpaid, can stop the 50 bales sent by railway as they are still in transit [Section 50].

13. *A* sold 400 tons of iron to *B*. *A* consigned the iron to a shipping company and sent the bill of lading to *B*. *B* obtained a loan Rs. 50,000 from *C* and pledged with him the bill of lading as security for the repayment of the loan. While the goods were in transit, *B* became insolvent. Since, the bill of lading is pledged with *C*, Can *A* exercise his right of stoppage in transit ?

Hints. Yes, *A* can exercise his right of stoppage in transit but his right would be subject to *C*'s charge over the goods for the repayment of the loan. [Section 53]

14. *A* is the owner of specific goods lying in *N*'s warehouse. He sells those goods to *B* and takes from *B* a bill of exchange for the price and hands over to *B* delivery order addressed to *N*. *B* resells the goods to *C* and gives *C* a delivery order but before *C* can obtain possession of the goods, *B* becomes insolvent and *A* warns *N* not to deliver the goods to anyone without his (*A*'s) order. Is *A* entitled to retain the goods against *C* ?

Hints. No, *A* is not entitled to retain the goods against C. In this case, seller's right of stoppage in transit is defeated by further sale by the buyer to a banafide purchase.[section 53]. Here, C is entitled to receive the goods as he is a banafide purchaser for consideration.

15. *A* sold certain goods to *B* and consigned them to *B* through Railways. In the meantime, *B* becomes insolvent and *A* sent a telegram to Railway authorities not to deliver the goods to *B*, *B* went to the parcel office of Railway Yard and by presenting Railway receipt took delivery of the goods and start putting them in the cart. Meanwhile, the Station Master came running with the telegram in hand and took possession of the goods from *B*. Discuss the rights of *A* and *B* to the goods in possession of Railway authorities.

Hints. *B* shall have the right to claim goods from railway authorities. In this case, seller's rights of stoppage in transit comes to end on delivery of the goods to the buyer by the Railways.

16. *A* sells and consigns certain goods to *B* for cash and sends the Railway Receipt to him. *B* becomes insolvent and while the goods are in transit, he assigns the railway receipt to *C*, who does not know that *B* is insolvent. *A* being an unpaid seller, wants to exercise his right to stoppage of goods in transit. Advise:

(*a*) whether *A* can do so.

(*b*) Would your answer be different if *C* was aware of *B*'s insolvency before the assignment of the railway receipt in favour of *C* ?

Hints. (*a*) *A* cannot exercise the right of stoppage in transit as the goods have been taken by *C* in good faith and for considerations.

(*b*)Yes, in such a case, *A* can validly exercise the right of stoppage in transit as *C* has not acted in good faith. [Section 53]

25

CHAPTER

AUCTION SALE

25.1. INTRODUCTION

We have already discussed that a contract of sale in made by an offer by one party and its acceptance by the other. And the sale of the goods may take place in various modes. One of the modes of sale is, the sale in public where different buyers come to purchase the goods, and the goods are sold to the person who is ready to pay the highest price. Such a sale is known as '*auction sale*'. Thus, the term 'auction sale' may be defined as a public sale. A person may himself sell his own goods by auction, or he may appoint an agent, known as auctioneer, to sell the goods by auction on his behalf. Normally, in an auction sale, the goods are sold on behalf of the owner by an *auctioneer*, and the agency relationship between the auctioneer and the owner is disclosed to the public.

In this chapter, we shall discuss the procedure of auction sale, and other legal provisions relating thereto.

25.2. PROCEDURE OF AUCTION SALE

The auction sale is usually organised by giving advertisements about the goods to be sold along with other terms and conditions of the sale by auction. The auctioneer gives wide publicity for the sale of the goods by auction, and fixes the time and place for it. The intending buyers, known as *bidders*, can inspect the goods, during the time fixed by the auctioneer, before or at the time of sale. On the time and place fixed for auction, the bidders are invited to compete for the purchase of the goods. The bidders offer their respective prices for which they are willing to purchase the goods. The auctioneer loudly speaks the prices offered by the bidders so that the other bidders may have an opportunity to offer higher price, if they want, and purchase the goods. In this way, the bidders go on offering more and more prices, and goods are *generally* sold to the highest bidder, *i.e.*, to the person who pays or is ready to pay the highest price.

The highest bid constitutes an offer to buy, and the fall of hammer or any other customary announcement constitutes an acceptance of the offer by the auctioneer. It may, however, be noted that the auctioneer is not bound to accept the highest bid. He may reserve his right to refuse any bid or to accept a lower bid in preference to a higher one.

[*M. Lachia Satty* v. *Coffee Board* (1980) 4 SCC 636]

25.3. LEGAL RULES REGARDING AUCTION SALE

The legal rules regarding the auction sale are contained in various provisions of Section 64 of the Sale of Goods Act, which may be discussed under the following heads: 1. Completion of auction sale. 2. Retraction of bid. 3. Transfer of ownership. 4. Seller's right to bid 5. Fraudulent sale. 6. Auction sale with reserve or upset price.

25.4. COMPLETION OF AUCTION SALE

We know that, in an auction sale, at an appointed time and place, the auctioneer puts up the goods for sale to the intending buyers (bidders) by inviting bidding from them. The bidders offer to pay the price by showing their willingness to pay the price. The auctioneer then accepts the highest bid by a tap with his hammer, or by any other customary manner. On such acceptance, the auction sale is complete. This rule is contained in Section 64(2) of the Sale of Goods Act, which provides that, the sale by auction is complete as soon as the auctioneer announces its completion (*i.e.*, the acceptance of the bid) by the fall of the hammer, or in any other customary manner, *e.g.*, by shouting one, two, three; or by shouting going, going, gone, etc.

On the fall of then hammer or any other customary manner of acceptance, the contract of sale comes into existence. It may however be noted that on the fall of the hammer, etc., the ownership does not transfer to the buyer. Only the contract of sale is completed. [*Consolidated Coffee Ltd.* v. *Coffee Board,* AIR 1981 SC 162]

The rule as to transfer of ownership will be discussed in detail in Art. 25.6.

25.5. RETRACTION OF BID

We have already discussed that the sale is complete as soon as the bid is accepted by the auctioneer. Before the completion of the sale, the bidder has the right to retract (*i.e.*, withdraw) his bid. This rule is also contained in Section 64(2) of the Sales of Goods Act, which provides that, before the sale is completed by the fall of the hammer, any bidder may withdraw his bid, *i.e.*, he has the right to say that he is not ready and willing to purchase the goods. This is based on the principle that a bid is an offer, and it can be revoked before it is accepted by the fall of the hammer.

Example 25.1. *A*, an auctioneer, held a public auction for the sale of certain goods. *B* attended the auction and made a highest bid for goods. But *B* withdrew his bid before the fall of the hammer. The auctioneer (*A*) contended that there was a completed sale when *B* offered to purchase the goods by giving his bid, and thus he (*B*) was bound to take the goods. It was held that *B*'s bid was an offer, and it could be revoked before the fall of the hammer.

[*Pyne* v. *Cave* (1789) 3 T. R. 148, 1 R. R. 679].

It may be noted that the withdrawal of the bid is valid even if one of the conditions of the sale is that 'a bid once made shall not be withdrawn'. The reason for the same is that such a condition in an auction sale is inoperative as being against the provisions of the law.

Example 25.2. *A*, an auctioneer hold a public auction for the sale of a air conditioner. *B* attended the auction and made a highest bid of Rs. 8,000. But he immediately withdrew his bid before the fall of the hammer. One of the conditions of the sale was that "a bid once made shall not be withdrawn". It was held that such a condition in an auction sale was inoperative, and the withdrawal of the bid was effective. [Based on *Campalal* v. *Jaigopal* 45, Mad 799].

Where the bidder withdraws his bid before the acceptance of his bid, his security amount cannot be forfeited. However, if the bidder withdraws his bid after the fall of the hammer, that amounts to a breach of contact and his security deposit will be liable to be forfeited.

25.6. TRANSFER OF OWNERSHIP

On the completion of sale by the fall of hammer, the ownership of the goods is immediately transferred to the buyer (*i.e.*, highest bidder) if the auction is of specific goods in a deliverable state. Thus, once the hammer falls for the sale of *specific goods in a deliverable state,* the highest bidder becomes the owner of the goods, and he can deal with the goods as his own.

Example 25.3. The public auction was held for the sale of sugar bags of specified lot and number which were in a deliverable state also. It was held by the court, that the ownership passed to the highest bidder when the papers were completed after knocking down.

[*Gangasagar Sugar Mills* v. *Rameshwar Das*, AIR 1992 Raj 14]

It may also be noted that after the fall of the hammer, the auctioneer cannot modify the terms of auction to prevent the ownership being passed to the buyer.

Example 25.4. At an auction for the sale of a car, *A*, the auctioneer, accepted *B*'s highest bid by the fall of the hummer. *B* was allowed to take away the car by giving a cheaque for the price. However, to protect his interest, *A* inserted a clause in the agreement that the ownership would not pass to *B* until the cheaque was cleared. The cheque was not cleared but in the meantime, *B* sold the car to *C*. It was held that the ownership of the car passed to *B* on the fall of the hammer, and thus sale to *C* was valid. [Based on *Dennant* v. *Skiner* (1948) 2 K.B. 164].

Example 25.5. At an auction for the sale of a silver flower vase (flower pot), *A*, the auctioneer accepted the highest bid of Rs. 500 of *B*. The auctioneer (*A*) purported to accept this bid by striking his hammer. But accidentally, he stroke the flower vase on the table. Immediately, *C*, another bidder, made a bid of Rs. 525 for the same flower vase before the auctioneer could strike the hammer. And *A* accepted *C*'s bid by striking his hammer. In this case, *C* is entitled to have the flower vase as the ownership is transferred to him by striking the hammer for his bid. And *B* cannot claim the flower vase as in his case, the striking of flower vase does not amount to the striking of hammer. Now suppose that the flower vase was of glass which is broken into pieces while being struck on the table. In that case, the loss would fall upon the seller, as the sale would not be considered complete in *B*'s favor by striking the vase which was broken to pieces.

Where the goods sold by auction are not specific and also not in deliverable state, then the ownership will not pass to the buyer even if the goods have been knocked down to him. Thus where the goods knocked down where neither weighed nor set apart for delivery, the court held that the ownership could not pass on the fall of the hammer.

[*Consolidated Coffee Ltd.* v. *Coffee Board*, AIR 1981 SC 162]

25.7. SELLER'S RIGHT TO BID

Sometimes, in an auction sale, the seller apprehends that the bidders may enter into a *knockout agreement*. (It is an agreement between the bidders not to bid against each other, with a view to prevent competition among themselves). In such cases, the seller has the right to bid in the auction, or to appoint a person to bid on his behalf. However, the seller can do so only if he has expressly reserved his right to do so, and the sale has been notified subject to such a right of the seller. This rule is contained in Section 64(3) of the Sale of Goods Act, which provides that, the seller or any one person of his behalf may bid at the auction if seller's right to bid is expressly reserved. It may, however, be noted that the seller can appoint *only one* bidder to bid on his behalf. If he appoints more than one bidder the sale is voidable, because in such cases the intention of the seller is not to protect his interest, but to enhance the price. [*Thornett* v. *Haines* (1846) 15 M & W 367]

As a matter of fact, if the seller makes use of pretended bidding to raise the price, the sale is voidable at the option of the buyer, and he can put an end to the contract of sale if he so chooses. [Section 64(6)].

Example 25.6. *A*, an auctioneer, held a public auction for the sale of a horse. It was notified that the seller or any one person on his behalf may also bid at the auction. *B* attended the auction and made a highest bid of Rs. 2,000 which was accepted by *A* by the fall of his hammer. Subsequently, *B* came to know that the seller had appointed three persons to bid on his behalf with the intention of enhancing the price. In this case, the sale is voidable at the option of *B*, and he may refuse to take the horse if he so chooses.

25.8. FRAUDULENT SALE

We have discussed in the last article, that the seller or any one person on his behalf may bid at the auction if the sale is notified to be subject to such a right of the seller. If the seller has not reserved his right to bid at the auction, he cannot bid at the auction. Moreover, then he cannot appoint *any* person to bid on his behalf. If he does so, the buyer may treat the sale as fraudulent. This rule is contained in Section 64(4) of the Sale of Goods Act, which provides that, where the seller's right to bid at the auction is not notified, the buyer may treat the sale as fraudulent if the seller or any person on his behalf bids at the auction. And the buyer may refuse to take the goods sold to him. In such cases, the sale is also fraudulent if the auctioneer knowingly takes any bid from the seller or any person on his behalf.

Example 25.7. *A*, an auctioneer, held a public auction for the sale of certain carpets, and it was not notified that the seller had the right to bid at the auctions. *B* attended the auction and made a highest bid, which was accepted by *A* by shouting one, two, three (the customary mode of accepting the bid). Subsequently, *B* came to know that one person was bidding on behalf of the seller with a view to enhance the price. In this case, the buyer (*B*) may treat the sale as fraudulent and refuse to accept the carpets sold to him.

25.9. AUCTION SALE WITH 'RESERVE OF UPSET' PRICE

The term 'reserve' or 'upset' price may be defined as the minimum price below which the auctioneer will not sell the goods put up for auction sale. In an auction sale, the seller has the right to make the sale subject to a reserve or upset price. And the sale may be notified subject to such price [Section64 (5)]. Normally, the reserve price is fixed by the seller to protect himself against the knockout agreements. Where the reserve price is fixed, the auction is known as 'with reserve'. In such cases, the auctioneer is not bound to accept the highest bid if it is below the reserve price. Even when, by mistake, the auctioneer knocks down (*i.e.*, completes the sale by striking of hammer or any other customary manner) the goods for less than the reserve price, he can refuse to deliver the goods to the buyer (*i.e.*, the bidder whose bid was accepted). And the buyer will have no remedy against the auctioneer. [*Rainbow* v. *Howkins* (1904) 2 K.B. 322].

Example 25.8. *A*, an auctioneer, held a public auction for the sale of certain goods. It was notified that the auction was subject to a reserve price. *B* attended the auction and made a bid which was lower than the reserve price. However, *A*, by mistake, accepted the bid by striking the hammer. On finding that the bid was below the reserve price, the auctioneer refused to deliver the goods to *B*. And *B* filed a suit against *A* for the recovery of the goods sold to him., It was held that the sale was not valid and *B* was not entitled to the goods. [*Manus* v. *Fortesque* (1900) 2 K.B. 1]

It may also be noted that where a reserve price has been fixed then, even if the goods are specific, the ownership will not pass if the highest bid falls short of the reserve price. [*Consolidated Coffee Ltd.* v. *Coffee Board* AIR 1981 SC 162]

Sometimes, no minimum price is fixed by the seller, and the auction is notified without any reserve price. In such cases, the auction is known as 'without reserve'. In case of auction 'without reserve' the auctioneer is bound to deliver the goods to a bidder *whose bid is accepted by* him. And he cannot refuse to deliver the goods on the ground that the real value of the goods is more that the amount of the bid accepted by him. It may, however, be noted that a valid contract of sale results only when the highest bid is accepted. But the auctioneer *in not bound* to accept the highest bid. And the refusal of the auctioneer to accept the highest bid gives no cause of action to the bidder at all. As the bidder is free to withdraw his bid before acceptance, the auctioneer is also free to refuse to accept the highest bid. [*Fenwick* v. *Macdonald* (1904) 6 F. (Court of Section) 850].

The auctioneer also has the right to make the auction subject to any conditions he likes.

Example 25.9. In an auction sale of coffee, one of the conditions was that, "The seller does not bind himself to accept the highest bid or any bid; he is not bound to assign any reason for his decision and his decision shall be final." This condition was held valid. The court observed that it gave a right to the seller to accept any bid, highest or the lowest. It conferred upon the seller the right to accept a lower bid in preference to a higher one.

[*Coffee Board* v. *Famous Coffee & Tea Works,* AIR 1965 Madras 14]

25.10. IMPORTANT TERMS IN AUCTION SALE

1. *Knock-out agreement*
2. *Damping*
3. *Puffers*
4. *Sale of goods in lots*

The following terms are important in an auction sale:

1. *Knock-out agreement:* The term 'knock-out agreement' may be defined as an agreement between the bidders not to bid against each other at an auction ale. Such agreements are made by the bidders with a view to prevent competition among themselves. By a knockout agreement, the various bidders agree that only one of them shall bid, and anything obtained by him shall afterwards be shared privately among themselves. It may be noted that knock-out agreements are not illegal. [*Jai Bhagwani Timber* v. *State,* AIR 1992 MP 250]

The seller may protect his interest against such agreements by reserving his right to bid at the auction or by fixing a reserve price. However, if a knock-out agreement is made with the *intention of defrauding* the seller, the auction sale is voidable at the option of the seller.

2. *Damping:* The term 'damping' may be defined as an unlawful act by which an intending purchaser is prevented from bidding or raising the price at an auction sale. The damping is usually done in any of the following ways :

(*a*) By pointing out defects in the goods put up for auction sale.

(*b*) By taking the intending buyers away from the place of auction by some other device.

It may be noted that the damping is illegal and the auctioneer can withdraw the goods from auction.

3. *Puffers:* The term 'puffer' may be defined as a person who is employed by the seller to raise the price by ficticious bids. A puffer has no intention to purchase the goods. Such persons are also known as *'by-bidders'*, *'white bonnets'*, or *'decoy ducks'*.

4. *Sale of goods in lots:* Sometimes, the goods are put up in lots for sale by auction. In such cases, each lot is, *prima facie* considered to be a separate subject for sale.

25.11. IMPLIED WARRANTIES IN AUCTION SALE

In an auction sale, the auctioneer impliedly gives the following warranties:

1. He warrants his authority to sell the goods on behalf of his principal.
   [*Anderson* v. *Croall & Sons* (1904) 6 F. 153 C S].
2. He warrants that he knows of no defects in his principal's title.
   [*Benton* v. *Campbell Parker & Co.* (1925) 2 K.B.410]
3. He warrants that possession of the goods would be given to purchaser against the payment of price. [*Benton's case*]
4. He warrants the quiet possession of goods by the purchaser. [*Benton's case*]

25.12. LIABILITIES OF AN AUCTIONEER

The Sale of Goods Act does not deal with the liabilities of an auctioneer in case of sale by auction. However, it has been held by courts that in an auction sale, the auctioneer incurs certain liabilities, though the extent of those liabilities depends upon the facts of each particular case. The liabilities of an auctioneer may be summer up as under:

1. The auctioneer warrants his authority to sell the goods on behalf of his principal. And if it is discovered that the auctioneer had no authority to sell the goods, he may be held liable for damages.
2. The auctioneer warrants that he knows of no defects in his principal's title. And in case of defect in principal's title, he may be held liable for damages.
3. The auctioneer warrants that the possession of the goods would be given to the purchaser on the payment of the price to him. And if the auctioneer refuses to give the possession on the payment of the price, he may be held liable for damages.
4. The auctioneer also warrants that the possession of the purchaser shall not be disturbed by his principal or himself. And if subsequently, purchaser's possession is so disturbed, the auctioneer may be held liable for damages.

LEGAL PROVISIONS (SECTIONS) DISCUSSED IN THE CHAPTER

Important legal provisions (sections) of the Sale of Good Act, 1930 discussed in this chapter are reproduced hereunder for ready reference:

1. ***Section 64: Auctiion Sale***

In case of sale be auction-

(1) where goods are put up for sale in lots, each lot is *prima facie* deemed to be the subject of a separate contract of sale;

(2) the sale is complete when the auctioneer announces its completion by the fall of the hammer or in other customary manner; and, until such announcement is made, any bidder may retract his bid;

(3) a right to bid may be reserved expressly by or on behalf of the seller and, where such right is expressly so reserved, but not otherwise, the seller or any one person on his behalf may, subject to the provisions hereinafter contained, bid at the auction;

(4) where the sale is not notified to be subject to a right to bid on behalf of the seller, it shall not be lawful for the seller to bid himself or to employ any person to bid at such sale, or for the auctioneer knowingly to take any bid from the seller or any such person; and any sale contravening this rule may be treated as fraudulent by the buyer;

(5) the sale may be notified to be subject to a reserved or upset price;

(6) if the seller makes use of pretended bidding to raise the price, the sale is voidable at the option of the buyer.

TEST QUESTIONS

1. Define the term 'auction sale' and state the legal rules regarding the auction sale.
2. Stete briefly the law which governs the sale of goods by auction.

3. State the circumstances, if any, in which the seller may bid at the auction. When does the auction sale become fraudulent?
4. Write notes on (*a*) Auction sale with reserve or upset price. (*b*) Knock-out agreement. (*c*) Damping. (*d*) Liabitities of an auctioneer.

MULTIPLE CHOICE QUESTIONS

1. An auction sale is complete on the
   (*a*) fall of hammer (*b*) delivery of goods
   (*c*) payment of price (*d*) both (*b*) and (*c*).
2. The bidder at an auction sale can withdraw his bid
   (*a*) any time during auction (*b*) before fall of hammer
   (*c*) before payment of price (*d*) none of these.
3. In an auction for the sale of specific goods in a deliverable state, the ownership passes to the buyer immediately on the
   (*a*) delivery of goods (*b*) payment of price
   (*c*) fall of hammer (*d*) both (*a*) and (*b*).
4. Where the seller has expressly reserved his right to bid in the auction, to bid on his behalf, the seller can appoint
   (*a*) one bidder only (*b*) two bidders
   (*c*) any number of bidders (*d*) none, seller has no such right.
5. Where in an auction sale, the seller appoints more than one bidder, the sale is
   (*a*) void (*b*) illegal
   (*c*) conditional (*d*) voidable.
6. Where in an auction sale notified with reserve price, the auctioneer mistakenly knocks down the goods for less than the reserve price, then the auctioneer is
   (*a*) bound by auction (*b*) not bound by auction
   (*c*) liable for damages (*d*) both (*a*) and (*c*).
7. An agreement between the bidders not to bid against each other at an auction sale, is known as
   (*a*) knock-out agreement (*b*) damping agreement
   (*c*) puffers' agreement (*d*) fraudulent agreement.
8. An unlawful act by which an intending purchaser is prevented from bidding or raising the price at an auction sale is known as
   (*a*) decoy ducking (*b*) puffering
   (*c*) damping (*d*) none of these.

ANSWERS

1. (*a*)	2. (*b*)	3. (*c*)	4. (*a*)	5. (*d*)	6. (*b*)
7. (*a*)	8. (*c*)				

OBJECTIVE TYPE QUESTIONS WITH REASONING

State with reasons whether the following statements are correct or incorrect:

1. In an auction sale, the auctioneer is bound to accept the highest bid.
2. In an auction sale, the contract of sale is complete only on the delivery of goods, and not on the fall of hammer.
3. After completion of sale in an auction, the property in the goods and the risk of loss caused in an accident to the auctioned property therein, is transferred to the bidder.
4. In an auction sale, a bid once given cannot be withdrawn.

5. On the completion of auction sale by the fall of hammer, the ownership of the goods in not immediately transferred to the buyer if the goods auctioned are neither specific nor in a deliverable state.
6. In an auction sale, the seller or any other person on his behalf may bid at the auction.
7. An auction sale is fraudulent if the seller bids at auction without reserving and notifying his right to bid.
8. In an auction sale, goods to be auctioned can be put for sale in lots.
9. In an auction sale, the bidders can enter into an agreement to skeep the bid low by eliminating competition among them.
10. Where the seller reserves his right to bid at auction, he can appoint maximum two persons to bid on his behalf.

ANSWERS

1. *Incorrect.* The auctioneer may reserve his right to refuse any bid or to accept a lower bid in preference to higher one. [*M. lachla Setty* v. *Coffee Board,* (1980) 4 SC 636]
2. *Incorrect.* In an auction sale, the contract of sale is complete on the fall of the hammer or any other customary mode of acceptance.
3. *Correct.* On the completion of auction sale, the bidder becomes the owner of the goods sold.
4. *Incorrect.* A bidder has the right to withdraw the bid before the sale is completed by the fall of the hammer.
5. *Correct.* In such a case, the ownership will tranfer only when the goods are ascertained and put in a deliverable state. [*Consolidated Coffee Ltd.* v. *Coffee Board,* AIR 1981 SC 162]
6. *Correct.* The law provides that the seller can do so if he has expressly reserved his right to bid at the auction [Section 64(3)].
7. *Correct.* There is a specific provision to this effect. In such case, the buyer may refuse to take delivery of good auctioned to him [Section 64(4)].
8. *Correct.* However in such a case, each lot is *prime facie* considered to be the subject matter of a separate contract of sale [Section 64(1)].
9. *Correct.* Such an agreement is known as knock-out agreement and it is not illegal.
10. *Incorrect.* The seller can appoint only one person to bid on his behalf.

PRACTICAL PROBLEMS

1. *A*, an auctioneer, hold an auction for the sale of a truck. *B* attended the auction and made the highest bid of Rs 80,000, but he immediately withdrew the bid before the fall of the hammer. One of the condition of the auction was that **'a bid once made shall not be withdrawn'**, which *B* also knew. Is *B* justified in doing so ? Give reasons.

   Hints: *B* is justified in withdrawing his bid. A bid is an offer which can be withdrawn before it is accepted by the fall of hammer. Any condition which restrict bidder's right to withdraw the bid is inoperative. [Section 64(2); Also see *Champalal V. Jaigpoal* 45, Mad 799]
2. At an auction for the sale of a glass flower vase, *A* made the highest bid of Rs. 5000, And the auctioneer purporting to accept the bid, strok the flower vase on the table and the vase was broken into pieces. Who shall bear the loss ? Give reasons.

   Hints: The loss would fall upon the seller. In this case, the sale would not be considered complete in *A*'s favour by striking the vase which was broken into pieces.
3. Suppose in the above problem the vase was of silver and purporting to accept *A*'s highest bid of Rs. 5000, the auunctioneer strok the silver vase on the table. Immediately, *B* another bidder, made a bid of 5500 for the same vase before the auctioneer could strike the hammer. The auctioneer accepted *B*'s bid of Rs. 5500 by striking the hammer on the table. Who is entitled to the flower vase, *A* or *B* ? Give reasons.

Hints : *B*, is entitled to the flower vase as ownership is transferred to him by striking the hammer for his bid. *A* cannot claim the flower vase as the striking of flower vase does not amount to acceptance of bid.

4. *A*, an auctioneer held a public auction for the sale of ten air conditioners. It was notified that the seller or any person on his behalf can also bid at the auction. *B* attended the auction and made the highest bid of Rs. 30,000 which was accepted by *A* by the fall of hammer. Subsequently, *B* came to know that the seller had appointed three persons to bid on his behalf with the intention of enhancing the price, and *B* refused to take delivery of the airconditioners. Is he justified in doing so? Give reasons.

Hints: *B* is justified in refusing to take delivery. The seller can appoint only one person to bid on his behalf. Where he appoints more than one bidder, the sale is voidable at the option of the buyer.

[Section 64(3)]

5. At a sale by auction without reserve, the auctioneer is instructed not to sell for less than a certain price. The auctioneer accepts the highest *bone fide* bid which, however, is lower than the instructed prices. (*a*) Is the sale valid ? (*b*) What are the rights of the principal against the auctioneer ?

Hints: (*a*) The sale is valid as the auction has been notified ' without reserve price'.

(*b*) The principal is entitled to claim from the auctioneer the difference between the instructed price and the price for which the goods are sold.

6. *A*, an auctioneer held a public auction, for the sale of certain goods. *B* attended the auction and made the highest bid. However, *A* refused to accept the bid. Is *A* justified in doing so? Give reasons.

Hints : yes, *A* is justified in refusing to accept the bid. The auctioneer is not bound to accept the highest bid, and such refusal does not give any cause of action to the bidder.

[*Fenwick* v. *Mcdonald* (1904) 6 F. (Court of Session) 850]

The Indian Partnership Act, 1932

- Nature of Partnership
- Registration of Firms
- Relations of Partners with One Another
- Relations of Partners with Third Parties
- Reconstitution of Firms
- Dissolution of Firms

26 CHAPTER

NATURE OF PARTNERSHIP

1. Introduction.
2. Essential Features of a Valid Partnership.
3. Test of Partnership.
4. Non-Partnership Interests.
5. Partners, Firm and Firm Name.
6. Legal Status of a Firm.
7. Classification of Partners and Their Liability.
8. Classification of Partnership.
9. Partnership on the Basis of Duration.
10. Partnership on the Basis of Extent of Business.
11. Partnership Deed.
12. Comparison Between Partnership and Co-ownership.
13. Comparison Between Partnership and Hindu Undivided Family.
14. Comparison Between Partnership and Company.

26.1. INTRODUCTION

Sometimes, two or more persons enter into an agreement to carry on a joint business and share the profits thereof. Such business relation is called 'partnership'. The legal provisions relating to the partnership are contained in THE INDIAN PARTNERSHIP ACT, 1932.[1] The term 'partnership' is defined in Section 4 of the Indian Partnership Act, which reads as under:

"Partnership is the relation between persons who have agreed to share the profits of a business carried on by all or any of them acting for all."

The analysis of this section reveals that the partnership is the business relationship between two or more persons who agreed to share the profits of their joint business. The persons who have entered into partnership, with one another are individually called 'partners'. And collectively they are called a 'firm'.

Example 26.1. *A* and *B* bought 100 bales of cotton. They agreed to sell the cotton for their joint account and share the profits. In this case, *A* and *B* are partners in respect of such cotton.

[*Birdichand* v. *Harakchand,* AIR 1940 Nagpur 211].

The above definition clearly highlights the following essential features of partnership; that it is

1. Results of an agreement.
2. Organised to carry on a business.
3. Carried to share the profits of a business.

---

1. Prior to the passing of this Act, the legal provisions relating to partnership were contained in Chapter XI of the Indian Contract Act, 1872.

4. Carried on by all or any of them acting for all.

These essential features have been restated by the Supreme Court in *Helper* v. *Syed Mohd*. (1987) 3 SCC 538.

Note. In our discussion on Law of Partnership from chapters 26 to 31, unless otherwise stated, the sections mentioned are those of the Indian Partnership Act, 1932.

26.2. ESSENTIAL FEATURES OF A VALID PARTNERSHIP

1. *There must be an association of two or more persons*
2. *There must be an agreement*
3. *There must be some business.*
4. *There must be sharing of profits*
5. *There must be mutual agency between the partners*

The legal definition of the 'partnership' as discussed in the last article, reveals the essential features of a valid partnership. These are discussed in detail in the following pages:

1. *There must be an association of two or more persons.* It is an important and essential element of a valid partnership. According to this element, there must be an association of two or more persons. In other words, there must be at least two persons to form a partnership. Moreover, the persons must be competent to enter into a contract. It may be noted that one person cannot be a partner with himself. Thus, when in the existing partnership firm, the number of partners is reduced to one, the firm is compulsorily dissolved.

Example 26.2. *A*, *B* and *C* were three partners carrying on spare partners business in partnership. Subsequently, *A* and *B* retired from the firm, and *C* continued the business. In this case, there is no partnership as C alone is carrying on the business.

It is to be noted that the Indian Partnership Act does not contain any provision about the maximum number of partners. However, Section 11 of the Companies Act, 1956 fixes the maximum limit of partners as under:

(*a*) Where the firm is carrying on the banking business, the number of partners should not exceed 10, and

(*b*) Where the firm is carrying on any other business, the number of partners should not exceed 20.

If the number of maximum partners exceed the above limit, the partnership becomes an illegal association. However, the association of persons more than this limit may be registered as company under the Companies Act, 1956.

Notes. 1. A company can become a partner in a firm as it is a person in legal terms.

[*M.M. Pulimoad* v. *Registrar of Firms,* (1987) 61 Comp. Cas. 209 (Kerala)].

2. A firm is not a person in legal terms. As such, two partnership firms cannot enter into partnership.

2. *There must be an agreement*. It is another important element of partnership. The partnership comes into existence only by an agreement between all the partners, and not by status or operation of law [Section 5]. This important feature distinguishes the partnership from other business relations such as co-ownership, or a Joint Hindu Family carrying on business. Because such business relations are created by operation of law and not by an agreement.

However, the agreement to constitute partnership may be express or implied. An express agreement is one which is made by words, spoken or written. And an implied agreement is one which is inferred from the course of dealings or from the conduct of the parties.

Example 26.3. *A* and *B*, two brothers, were living together with their father *C*. On the death of their father, they inherited certain properties which they did not divide. They sold a garden and invested this amount in a separate timber business. There was no partnership agreement, but it appeared that they intended to share the profits of this timber business. The business failed and the question arose about the distribution of liabilities. It was held that there was partnership and they must bear the liabilities as partners. In this case, there was an implied agreement of partnership which arose from the conduct of the partners.

[*Abdul* v. *Century whood Inds.* AIR 1954 Mysore 33]

Note. Like any other agreement, the agreement of partnership must satisfy all the essentials of a valid contract. An agreement of partnership may be for a fixed time, or for an unspecified period, or to carry on a particular adventure.

3. *There must be some business.* A partnership can be formed only to carry on a business. Thus, it can exist in business and business alone. And where there is no business, there is no partnership. The term 'business' is used in the widest sense, and it must be taken in a practical sense. It is taken to refer to any lawful activity which if successful would result in profits. And it includes every trade, occupation and profession [Section 2(*b*)]. It is not necessary that the business should consist of a long and permanent undertaking. A partnership may exist in a single business venture or undertaking.

Example 26.4. *A* and *B* agreed to produce a film and share the profits of hiring it out. It was held to be a partnership.

Similarly, a single road-building contract was held to be sufficient for a partnership as the construction of road is a business activity. However, if no business activity is involved, there cannot be any partnership. [*K. Juggiaha* v. *Venkatanant*, AIR 1984 A.P. 149]

Example 26.5. *A* and *B* bought 100 bags of rice and agreed to share the same between them. In this case, *A* and *B* are not partners as there is no business between them.

4. *There must be sharing of profits.* The sharing of the profit of a business is another essential element for the existence of a partnership. The term 'profits' means the net profits *i.e.*, the surplus money left after providing for all expenses. There must be an agreement among all the partners to share the profits of a business. However, they may share it in any way they like *i.e.*, either equally or in any other ratio. Where only one partner is entitled to the whole profits, there can be no partnership.

Example 26.6. *A* and *B* agreed to work together as partners. But they agreed that *A* shall receive all profits and shall pay wages to *B*. In this case, *A* and *B* are not partners as there is no sharing of profits.

It may be noted that the sharing of profits also includes the sharing of losses. However, it is not necessary that all partners may agree to share losses. The partners may agree that one or more of them shall not be liable for losses.

5. *There must be mutual agency between the partners.* The agency relations means that the business of partnership must be carried on by all the partners or by any partner acting for all other partners. In other words, in a partnership, a person must not act for himself alone, but for other partners also. Thus, each partner is a representative of all other partners. And he acts in both capacities, *i.e.* as an agent as well as principal. A partner is an agent of the other partner in the sense that by his acts he can bind the other partners. He is principal in the sense that he can be held liable for the acts of the other partners. The mutual relationship of agency is emphasised in Section 18 of the Indian partnership act, which read as under:

"Subject to the provision of this Act, a partner is the agent of the firm for the business of the firm".

As a matter of fact, the agency is the foundation of partnership and the law of partnership is the branch of the general law of agency. The agency relationship of partners is governed by the general law of agency.

Note. This essential element of partnership distinguishes it from the other business relations such as co-ownership etc.

26.3. TEST OF PARTNERSHIP

1. *Real relation of mutual agency*
2. *Sharing of profits is not a conclusive test of partnership*

We have discussed, in the last article, the essential elements of the partnership. In order to consider whether a group of persons is a partnership or not, these essential elements should be kept in view. And the test of valid partnership is that all these elements must be present in a group of persons to be called as partnership. If there is specific agreement of partnership between the persons, then there is no difficulty in knowing whether the group is partnership or not. In such cases, the agreement between the partners should be looked into keeping in view the legal definition of partnership as given in Section 4 of the Indian Partnership Act. If the agreement is regarding the sharing of profits of business, and the business is carried on by all or any of them acting for all, there is valid partnership. But in the absence of specific agreement, it becomes difficult to determine whether a partnership exists or not. In such cases, the rule laid down in Section 6 of the Indian Partnership Act should be kept in view. This section reads as under:

> *"In determining whether a group of persons is or is not a firm, or whether a person is or is not a partner in a firm, regard shall be had to the real relation between the parties, as shown by all relevant facts taken together."*

The analysis of this section reveals that the real relation between the partners is the deciding factor. And this relation is that of principal and agent. The true test of partnership may, therefore, be stated as under:

(*a*) The partnership is determined from the real relation between partners. And such relation should be that of agency; and

(*b*) The sharing of profit is not a conclusive test of partnership. And every person who receives a share of profits is not a partner.

These two points are discussed in detail in the following pages:

1. *Real relation of mutual agency:* In order to know whether a group of persons is a partnership or not, the real relation between the persons must be taken into account. And the real relation between the parties is to be determined from all the facts and surrounding circumstances at the time when the contract was entered into. Thus, while determining real relations between the parties, all the facts such as written or oral agreement, real intention and conduct of the parties, other relevant facts *e.g.*, book of account, correspondence, evidence of the employees etc., must be taken into account. Where the relations between the persons is that of agency, there is a partnership among such persons.

2. *Sharing of profits is not a conclusive test of partnership.* A person, who receives the profits of a business, is not necessarily a partner. *Explanation* II of Section 6 of the Indian Partnership Act gives a list of persons who might be interested in the profits of a business but are not partners. All such persons are mentioned below under the next heading.

In *Devji* v. *Magan Lal*, AIR 1965 SC 139, the Supreme Court has also observed that the true test of partnership is the agency relationship and not the sharing of profits.

26.4. NON-PARTNERSHIP INTERESTS

1. *Joint-owners sharing profits or gross returns*
2. *Money-lenders receiving profits*
3. *Servant or agent receiving profits*
4. *Widow or child of a deceased partner*
5. *Seller of goodwill*

The term 'non-partnership interests' may be defined as the persons who receive the profits but are not the partners. Such persons are mentioned in *Explanations I and* II of Section 6, and may be enumerated as under:

1. *Joint-owners sharing profits or gross returns.* The joint owners of a property who share the profits or gross returns arising from the property, are not the partners.

Example 26.7. *A* and *B* jointly purchased a tea shop. They incurred additional expenses for purchasing pottery and utensils for the job. Each one of them contributed half of the total expenses. The shop was then leased out on rent, and they shared the rent in equal proportions. It was held that they were co-owners and not partners. Joint co-ownership is not a business. In this case, the court observed that "nothing more is done by the parties than utilising the common property and obtain a return for such use by leasing the property for rent". Thus, *A* and *B* were simply co-owners as they never carried on any business.

[*Govind Nair* v. *Maga* (1948) 1 Madras 343].

2. *Money-lenders receiving profits.* A money-lender is a person who lends money on interest. Sometimes, a money-lender receives, in addition to or in place of his interest, a portion of the profits of a business. In such cases, he cannot be said to be a partner only on the ground that he receives the profits of the business.

Example 26.8. *A* advanced some money to *B* and *C*, two merchants. The merchants agreed to carry on the business subject to the control of *A* in several respects. *A* was to receive a commission of 20% on all the profits. It was held that there was no partnership between *A* and the merchants. The object of the agreement was to give *A* the maximum security for the repayment of his loan.

[*Mollow M. & Co.* v. *Court of Wards* (1872) LR 2 CP 419]

3. *Servant or agent receiving profits.* Sometimes, a servant or an agent of a business agrees to receive, in addition to or in place of his regular remuneration a portion of the profits of the business. In such cases, he cannot be said to be a partner only on the ground that he receives the profits of the business.

Example 26.9. *A*, a contractor, undertook a contract of loading and unloading railway wagons. He appointed *B* as his servant to manage the work. It was agreed that the servant would receive 75% of the profits as his remuneration and would bear all the losses, if any. It was held that *B* was the agent of *A* and not his partner. [*Munshi Abdul* v. *Chatterjee*, AIR 1963 Cal 204]

4. *Widow or child of a deceased partner.* Sometimes, the widow or a child of deceased partner receives a portion of profits as annuity. In such cases, they cannot be said to be the partners of the firm only on the ground that they receive the profits of the business. [*I.T. Commr.* v. *Kesharmal*, AIR 1968 A & N 68]

Example 26.10. *A*, *B* and *C* were carrying on a business of ready made garments in partnership. Afterwards, *A* died. But *B* and *C* continued the business and also agreed to give 10% of the profits of the firm to *D*, the widow of *A* every year. In this case *D* is not a partner in the firm.

5. *Seller of goodwill.* Sometimes, a person who sells his business alongwith its goodwill, is given a share in the profits of the business he has sold. In such cases, that person does not become a partner in the business only on the ground that he receives the profits of the business.

Example 26.11. *A*, a surgeon and druggist, sold his practice to *B* along with the name and style under which *A* was carrying on his practice. It was agreed that *A* would continue to attend his old profession and to the best efforts introduce *B* to his patients, and to do every reasonable act for promoting *B*'s profession. And *B* allowed a portion of the profits to *A*. It was held that *A* and *B* were not partners in the profession. [*Rawilson* v. *Clarke* (1846) 153 ER 860]

26.5. PARTNERS, FIRM AND FIRM NAME

The term 'partners', 'firm' and 'firm name' are defined in second para of Section 4 of the Indian Partnership Act, which reads as under:

"Persons who have entered into partnership with one another are called individually 'partners' and collectively 'a firm' and the name under which their business is carried on is called the 'firm name."

The analysis of this section reveals that legally the meaning of the terms 'partners', 'firm', and 'firm name' is as below:

1. Partners. The persons who form the partnership are individually known as partners.

2. Firm. The partners collectively known as a firm.

3. Firm name. The name under which partnership business is carried on is known as the firm name.

Example 26.12. *A, B* and *C* entered into a partnership with each other. They were carrying on the printing business under the name and style of 'A & Co.'. In this case, *A, B* and *C* are individually the partners, and collectively a firm. And 'A & Co.' is the firm name.

Thus, a firm is a collection of partners. It may be noted that a firm is *not a legal person* and has no separate legal entity, *i.e.*, a firm has no independence existente apart from its partners. As a matter of fact, the firm is nothing but partners bracketed together under one name.

The partners of a firm may carry on business under any name and style which they please to adopt. But certain names can be used only with the approval of the State Government. This restriction is contained in Section 58(3) of the Indian Partnership Act, which reads as under:

"A firm name shall not contain any of the following words, namely: 'Crown', 'Emperor', 'Empire', Imperial', 'King', 'Queen', 'Royal', or words expressing or implying the sanction, approval or patronage of Government or the Crown Representative, except when the State Government signifies its consent to the use of such words as part of the firm name by order in writing."

Thus, the above words, *i.e.*, crown, emperor etc. can be used as part of the firm name only with the written approval of the State Government.

26.6. LEGAL STATUS OF A FIRM

We have already discussed that a firm is merely a collection of partners. It has no separate legal entity apart from its partners. As a matter of fact, the assets of the firm are the joint property of the partners. Moreover, the partners are also personally liable for all the business obligations of the firm. Thus, the legal position of a firm is that it has no independent existence apart from its partners.

[*Malabar Fisheries* v. *C.I.T., Kerala, AIR 1980 SC 176*]

In *Keshavji Ravji & Co.* v. *C.I.T.* (1990) 2 SCC 246, the Supreme Court has restated that the firm is not a full person. Since, the firm has no separate legal entity, it is not recognised as a person for making partnership with another person or firm, or for subscribing to the memorandum of a company. It may also be noted that the partners of a firm are not considered its employees even if they are drawing remuneration for their services.

[*Regional Director of ESIC* v. *Ramnuja Match Industries*, AIR 1985 SC 278]

However, in mercantile or commercial usage, a firm is considered to have an existence separate from its partners. The business generally talks of the assets, liabilities and goodwill of the firm as if it were something separate from its partners. Under the Income-tax Act, also, the position is somewhat different. The firm is assessable as a separate unit. And the partners are also assessed separately. In some systems of law, for example, the Law of Scotland, the firm is recognised as a legal person separate from its partners.

26.7. CLASSIFICATION OF PARTNERS AND THEIR LIABILITY

1. *Actual partner*
2. *Dormant or sleeping partner*
3. *Nominal partner*
4. *Partner in profits only*
5. *Sub-partner*
6. *Incoming partner*
7. *Outgoing partner*
8. *Minor partner*
9. *Partner by estoppel or holding out*

Following are the different classes of partners:

1. *Actual partner.* Actual partner is one who takes active part in the conduct of the partnership business. He is also called an *ostensible partner*. An active partner and all other partners are liable to third parties for all the acts done by him in the ordinary course of business. In case of retirement from the firm, an actual partner must give a public notice of his retirement. If he fails to do so, he continues to be liable for the acts of other partners, even after retirement.

Note. An active partner's insanity or permanent incapacity to perform his duties is the ground for the dissolution of the firm. And the other partners may apply to the court for the dissolution of the firm on this ground.

2. *Dormant or sleeping partner.* A dormant partner is one who is neither active nor known to the outsiders. He is also called a sleeping partner. In reality he is partner in the firm and also contributes his share in the business. But he does not take active part in the conduct of the partnership business. Like an active partner, a dormant partner is also liable to the third parties for all the acts of the firm whether or not his existence is known to the third parties at the time of making the contract. However, there is some difference between an active and dormant partner. In the first place, the liability of a dormant partner comes to an end at the time of his retirement, and he is not required to give a public notice of the same. Secondly, a dormant partner's insanity or permanent incapacity to perform his duties is no ground for the dissolution of the firm. The reason of the same is that as a rule the dormant partner has no duties to perform.

3. *Nominal partner.* A nominal partner is one who has no real interest in the business. And he is not entitled to share the profits of the business. As a matter of fact, a nominal partner only lends his name to the firm. And his name is used in the firm as if he is an actual partner. It may be noted that a nominal partner does not contribute any capital and also does not take part in the conduct of the partnership business. However, a nominal partner is liable for all acts of the firm as if he was its actual partner.

4. *Partner in profits only.* A 'partner in profits only' is one who is entitled to share only the profits of the firm and is not liable for losses. Generally, such partners have no interest in the management of the business. However, they are liable to the third parties for all the acts of the firm.

5. *Sub-partner.* A sub-partner is one who shares the profits of another partner. Sometimes, a partner of a firm agrees to share his own share of profits with an outsider. In such cases, a sub partnership comes into existence between the contracting partner and the outsider. And such an outsider is called a sub-partner. In fact, a sub-partner is not a partner in the original firm. He has no right against the original firm. Moreover, he is also not liable for the debts of the original firm However, he can claim agreed share of profits from the contracting partner only.

6. ***Incoming partner.*** An incoming partner is one who is admitted as a partner into an already existing firm.

7. ***Outgoing partner.*** An outgoing partner is one who goes out of an existing firm (*i.e.*, retires from a firm) in which the remaining partners continue to carry on the business.

8. ***Minor partner.*** A minor partner is one who is below the age of 18 years. It may, however, be noted that a minor cannot be a full-fledged partner in a firm. He can only be admitted to the benefits of an already existing firm.

9. ***Partner by estoppel or holding out.*** A partner by estoppel is one who represents himself to be a partner in the firm, but in reality he is not so. Sometimes, a person, who is not really a partner, represents himself to be a partner and the persons dealing with the firm believe him to be a partner. In such cases, he is stopped (*i.e.*, prevented) from denying that he is not a partner. Such a person is called a partner by estoppel or by holding out.

26.8. CLASSIFICATION OF PARTNERSHIP

A partnership may be classified on the following two basis namely:

1. On the basis of duration.
2. On the basis of extent of business.

26.9. PARTNERSHIP ON THE BASIS OF DURATION

1. *Partnership at will*
2. *Partnership for a fixed period*

As a matter of fact, the partners are at liberty to fix the duration of the partnership. They may fix any duration of the partnership, or may remain silent about the same. On this basis, the partnership may be of the following two kinds:

1. ***Partnership at will.*** It is a partnership in which its duration is not fixed and can be dissolved by any one partner at his will at any time. Thus, a partnership is at will in the following two cases, as provided in Section 7:

(*a*) Where the partnership is not for a fixed period of time, or

(*b*) Where no provision is made as to when and how the partnership will come to an end.

Such a partnership is called a partnership at will because it is carried on at the willingness and desire of the partners, and can be put to an end at the will of any one of the partners. As there is no provision regarding the dissolution of the firm, it may be dissolved by any partner at anytime by giving, in writing, a notice of his intention to dissolve the firm. However, the notice should be given to all the partners. Where a date of dissolution is mentioned in the notice, the firm is dissolved from that date. And where no date of dissolution is mentioned, the firm is dissolved from the date of communication of notice.

2. ***Partnership for a fixed period.*** It is a partnership in which its duration is fixed and cannot be dissolved by any partner at his will. Such a partnership is dissolved on the expiry of the fixed period. However, a partnership for a fixed period can also be dissolved before the fixed period by adopting the modes of dissolution, as discussed in

chapter 31. It is to be noted that if a partnership continues to carry on the business even after the expiry of fixed period, the partnership becomes a partnership at will. And the rights and liabilities of the partners remain the same as they were before the expiry of the fixed period.

26.10. PARTNERSHIP ON THE BASIS OF EXTENT OF BUSINESS

> 1. *Particular partnership*
> 2. *General partnership*

The partners are also at liberty to carry on one or more adventures or undertakings in a business. On this basis, the partnership may be of the following two kinds:

1. ***Particular partnership.*** It is a partnership which is formed for the purpose of carrying on the particular adventure or understanding, *e.g.*, a partnership for the construction of a particular building, bridge, etc. Such a partnership comes to an end on the completion of the particular adventure or undertaking. If after the completion of that particular adventure or undertaking, the firm continues and proceeds to carry on other undertaking, then it becomes a partnership at will.

2. ***General partnership.*** It is a partnership which is formed for the purpose of carrying on business in general.

26.11. PARTNERSHIP DEED

We know that a partnership can be created only by an agreement. And such agreement may be oral or in writing. However, to avoid future disputes, it is always better to have the agreement in writing. Such an agreement in writing is called a 'partnership deed'. In other words, a partnership deed is the document which contains the terms and conditions of the partnership. The partnership deed should be carefully drafted and should be stamped according to the provisions of the Indian Stamp Act, 1899. The partnership deed usually contains the following particulars:

1. Name of the firm. 2. Name of the partners. 3. Nature and place of business of the firm. 4. Date of commencement of partnership firm. 5. Duration of the firm. 6. Amount of capital to be contributed by the partners. 7. Rules regarding the operation of accounts. 8. Ratio in which profits and losses are to be shared. 9. Rules relating to the admission, retirement or expulsion of partners. 10. Salaries of partners, if any. 11. Mode of dissolution of the firm. 12. Settlement of accounts on the dissolution of the firm, etc.

It is important to note that partnership deed is not necessary even for getting the firm registered under the Indian Partnership Act, with the Registrar of Firms. However, the written document, known as 'instrument of partnership', is necessary under the Income Tax Act, 1961 if the partners desire their firm to be assessed as such firm.

26.12. COMPARISON BETWEEN PARTNERSHIP AND CO-OWNERSHIP

The term 'co-ownership' or 'joint-ownership' means that a number of persons are having the ownerships of some property jointly. The co-owners are the joint owners of the property. But they are not partners as per the legal sense of the term. A group of persons merely collecting rent of joint properties gifted to them, is co-ownership and not a partnership. [*Ibrahim Shah Mohd.* v. *Noor Ahmad,* AIR 1984 Gujarat 126].

If a partnership firm has some property, it is the joint property of all the partners. To this extent the partners are co-owners also. The following Table gives the comparison between partnership and co-ownership:

S. No. Partnership	Co-ownership
1. It can arise only by an agreement of the partners.	It can arise by an agreement of the co-owners or in any other way.
2. The business is necessary for the existence of partnership. It cannot exist without business.	The business is not necessary for the existence of co-ownership. It can exist without business also.
3. There is relationship of agency between the partners, *i.e.*, the partners are the mutual agents.	There is no such agency relationship. The co-owners are not the mutual agents.
4. There is a statutory limit on maximum number of partners, *i.e.*, 10 in case of a firm carrying on banking business and 20 in any other business.	There is no statutory limit on maximum number of co-owners.
5. A partners cannot transfer his share to a third party without the consent of the other partners.	A co-owner can transfer (*i.e.*, sell) his share without the consent of other co-owners.
6. A partner cannot sue for the partition of the partnership property. However, he can sue his co-partners for the dissolution of the firm and for accounts.	A co-owner can sue for the partition of the joint property.
7. A partner has a right to retain the partnership property for the expenses incurred by him on such property on behalf of the firm. It is called a right of lien.	A co-owner has no such right to retain the co-ownership property.

26.13. COMPARISON BETWEEN PARTNERSHIP AND HINDU UNDIVIDED FAMILY

A Hindu undivided family carrying on a joint family business has some features common with the partnership. But the members of a Hindu undivided family carrying on a family business, as such are not partners in such business [Section 5, para 2]. The following Table gives the comparison between the partnership and Hindu undivided family.

S. No. Partnership	Hindu Undivided Family
1. It can arise only by an agreement of the partners.	It arises by operation of law. It cannot be created by an agreement of the members.
2. A new partner can be admitted in the partnership only with the consent of all the partners.	A person becomes a member only by birth in the family.
3. A partner acquires interest in the business only by an agreement.	A person acquires interest in the business by birth in the family.
4. There is a statutory limit on maximum number of partners, *i.e.*, 10 in case of a firm carrying on banking business and 20 in any other business.	There is no statutory limit on maximum number of members.
5. A minor cannot become a full-fledged partner. He can only be admitted to the benefits of partnership with the consent of all the partners.	A male minor is the full-fledged member. He becomes member merely by birth in the family.

6. There is a relationship of agency between the partner, *i.e.*, all the partners are mutual agents.	There is no such agency relationship between all the members of the family. The *karta* (*i.e.*, manager) of the family is the only representative of the family.
7. Every partner has an implied authority to bind the firm by his acts done in the ordinary course of the business.	Only the karta has an implied authority to bind the family by his acts. Other members of the family do not have such authority.
8. A partner is personally liable for the business obligations of the firm. The share of each partner in the partnership property and profits alongwith his private property is liable for the discharge of debts of the partnership.	A member is not personally liable for the business obligations of the family. Only his share of property and profits in the family is liable for the discharge of the debts of the family. However, the karta is personally liable for the business obligations of the family.
9. It is dissolved on the death or insolvency of any one partner.	It is not dissolved on the death or insolvency of any member.
10. The share of each partner is defined by virtue of an agreement between the partners.	The share of the members is not defined. It is fluctuating because of deaths and births of male members in the family.
11. A partner has a right to demand, inspect and copy any accounts of the firm. Moreover, he also has the right to demand the dissolution of the firm.	A member has no right to ask for any accounts of the past dealings of the family. There is no concept of dissolution of the family.
12. A partner has no right to demand the partition of the property of the firm.	A member has a right to demand the partition of the joint family property.
13. The partnership is usually registered as an unregistered firm suffers from certain disabilities.	There is no concept of registration of Hindu undivided family. And thus, no disabilities on account of non-registration.

26.14. COMPARISON BETWEEN PARTNERSHIP AND COMPANY

A company is an association of persons formed by registration under the Companies Act, 1956. The companies are of various types. However, the following two types may be noted for the purpose of comparison between a partnership and a company.

1. Public company 2. Private company.

Both these companies may be either limited companies or unlimited companies. A partnership and a company formed for the purpose of business have certain common features. However, both differ in many respects. The following Table gives the comparison between a partnership and a company:

S. No. *Partnership*	*Company*
1. It comes into existence by an agreement between the partners. And its registration is not compulsory.	It comes into existence only after registration under the Companies Act.
2. It has no separate legal existence apart from its members. It is merely the collection of persons.	It has separate legal entity apart from its members. It is a legal person in the eyes of law.
3. The number of members should not exceed 10 in case of a firm carrying on banking business, and 20 in case of any other business.	There is difference between the public and private company regarding the number of members. In a public company (limited or unlimited), the minimum number of members must

	be 7. And, there is no limit as to maximum number of members. In a private company (limited or unlimited) the minimum number of members must be 2 and maximum should not exceed 50.
4. The liability of partners is unlimited, *i.e.*, they are also personally liable.	The liability of members of a limited company is limited *i.e.*, they are liable to the extent of their share capital only and are not personally liable.
5. A partner cannot transfer his share without the consent of all the partners.	A member (shareholder) can transfer his share without the consent of other members.
6. It is dissolved on the death or insolvency of any one partner, *i.e.*, the death or insolvency of any one partner puts an end to the partnership.	It is not dissolved on the death or insolvency of any member. A company has a perpetual succession, *i.e.*, it continues unless put to an end by winding-up proceedings.
7. There is a relationship of an agency between the partners, *i.e.*, the partners are mutual agents.	There is not such relationship. The members are not the mutual agents.
8. Every partner has a right to take part in the management of the affairs of the firm.	Every member cannot take part in the management. The management of company is placed in the hands of elected members known as 'directors'.
9. It is not required to comply with certain legal requirements, *e.g.*, audit of accounts, filing of balance sheet, maintaining of prescribed register etc., is not compulsory.	It is required to comply with all these legal requirements.
10. A partner cannot contract with his own firm.	A member of a company can enter into contract with the same company.
11. The partners are the joint owners of the property of the firm.	The members are not the joint owners of the property. Its ownership belongs to the company.

LEGAL PROVISIONS (SECTIONS) DISCUSSED IN THE CHAPTER

Important legal provisions (sections) of the Indian Partnership Act, 1932, discussed in this chapter are reprouduced hereunder for ready reference :

1. ***Section 2 (b): Business Defined***

   Business includes every trade, occupation and profession.

2. ***Section 4 (First para): Defintion of Partnership***

   Partnership is the relation between persons who have agred to share the profits of a business carried on by all or any of them acting for all.

3. ***Section 4 (second para): Definition of Partner, Firm and Firm Name***

   Persons who have entered into partneship with one another are called individually partners and collectively a 'firm', and the name under which their business is carried on is called the 'Firm name'.

4. ***Section 5: Partnership Created by Contract***

   The relationship of partnership arises form contract and not form status.

5. ***Section 6: Modes of Determining Existence of Partneship***

   In determining whether a group of persons is or is not a firm, or whether a person is or is not a parther in firm, regard shall be had to the real relation between the parties, as shown by all relevant facts taken together.

   Explanation 1.—The sharing of profits or of gross returns arising form property by person holding a joint or common interest in that property does not of itself make such persons partners.

   Explanation 2.—The receipt by a person of a share of the profits of a business, or of a payment contingent upon the earning of profits or varying with the profits earned by a business, does not of iteself make him a partner with the persons carrying on the business;

and in particular, the receipt of such share or payment–

(*a*) by a lender of money to persons engaged or about to engage in any business,

(*b*) by a servant or agent as remuneration,

(*c*) by the widow or child of a deceased partner, as annuity or

(*d*) by a previous owner or part owner of the business, as consideration for the sale of the goodwill or share thereof,

does not of itself make the receiver a partner with the persons carrying on the business.

6. ***Section 7: Partnership at Will:***

Where no provision is made by contract between the partners for the duration of their parthership, or for the determination of their partnership, the partnership is "partnership at will".

7. ***Section 8: Particular Partnership***

A person may become a partner with another person in particular adventure or undertaking.

TEST QUESTIONS

1. Define partnership. What are the essential elements necessary in order to constitute a partnership between two or more persons?
2. "A partnership comes into existence by virtue of an agreement and not by status"–comment.
3. State the test of partnership. What are the legal rules for a valid partnership?
4. "The sharing of profits is only a *prime facie* evidence of partnership"—comment.
5. "The law of partnership is but an extension of the law of principal and agent"—comment.
6. State classification of partners and partnership.
7. Distinguish between co-ownership and partnership.
8. Explain the difference between a partnership firm and a Joint Hindu Family business.
9. State the comparison between partnership and (*a*) co-ownership, (*b*) Hindu Undivided Family, and (*c*) company.
10. Write notes on: (*a*) Partners, Firm and Firm name, (*b*) Legal status of a firm, (*c*) Partnership at will. (*d*) Partnership deed. (*e*) Non-partnership interests.

MULTIPLE CHOICE QUESTIONS

1. Prior to the enactment of the Indian Partnership Act, 1932 the legal provisions of partnership were contained in

   (a) The Indian Partnership Act, 1872 (*b*) The Indian Contract Act, 1872
   (*c*) Code of Civil Procedure (*d*) The Companies Act.
2. Which of the following is not an essential feature of partnership?

   (*a*) Result of an agreement (*b*) Organised to carry on business
   (*c*) Carried on by all or any of them acting for all
   (*d*) Separate legal entity.
3. Can a company become a partner in the partnership firm?

   (*a*) Yes, as the company is a legal person and has an independent existence.
   (*b*) No, as partnership is recognised among human beings only
4. As a company can become a partner in the firm, there can also be a partnership between two firms.

   (*a*) Yes, as the partnership firm is a legal person for this purpose.
   (*b*) No, as the partnership firm is not a legal person.
5. Which of the following persons, though receive profits, are not partners in a firm as per Section 6 of the Partnership Act.

(*a*) Joint-owners sharing profits (*b*) Money-lenders receiving profits
(*c*) Seller of goodwill receiving profits (*d*) All of these.

6. Which of the following statements is true?
(*a*) Partners of a firm are considered its employees
(*b*) Firm has no separate legal entity
(*c*) Same partners may constitute different firms
(*d*) Firm cannot enter into partnership with another firm.

7. A dormant partner is one who is
(*a*) entitled to share profits only (*b*) neither active nor known to outsiders
(*c*) not interested in the business of firm (*d*) not liable to outsiders.

8. A partnership is known as a partnership at will where
(*a*) its duration is not fixed (*b*) it can be dissolved at any time
(*c*) its duration is fixed (*d*) in both cases (*a*) and (*b*).

9. A partnership deed is necessary for getting the firm registered under the Indian Partnership Act, with the Registrar of Firms.
(*a*) True, as it is the requirement of law
(*b*) False, as it is not the requirement of law.

10. The statutory limit on maximum number of partners is ten in case of firm carrying on banking business, and in any other business it is
(*a*) ten (*b*) fiteen
(*c*) twenty (*d*) twenty-five.

ANSWERS

1. (*b*)	**2.** (*d*)	**3.** (*a*)	**4.** (*b*)	**5.** (*d*)	**6.** (*c*)
7. (*b*)	**8.** (*d*)	**9.** (*b*)	**10.** (*c*)		

OBJECTIVE TYPE QUESTIONS WITH REASONING

State with reasons whether the following statements are correct or incorrect.

1. The partnership arises by operation of law.
2. There must be at least two persons to form the partnership.
3. A major and a minor can create partnership.
4. A partnership may be formed with two partnership firms as partners.
5. A company can become a partner in a firm.
6. Sharing of profits is a conclusive evidence of partnership.
7. The test of existence of partnership is the element of 'sharing of profits' rather than mutual agency.
8. A sub-partner is not a partner in the original firm.
9. A partnership in which no provision in made for the duration of the firm, is known as a 'partnership at will'
10. All member of a Hindu Undivided Family are personally liable for the business obligation of the family.

ANSWERS

1. ***Incorrect.*** The relation of partnership arises from a contract between the partners and not from status or by operation of law.

2. ***Correct.*** Minimum number of two persons is the essential requirement of law for the formation of partnership.

3. *Incorrect.* The requirement of law is that the partners must be competent to contract. Legally, a minor is not competent to contract.
4. *Incorrect.* A firm is not a legal entity or legal person and cannot enter into valid partnership with another firm or person.
5. *Correct.* A company is a legal person in the eyes of law.
6. *Incorrect.* It not the conclusive test of partnership, though it is the *prime facie* evidence of the existence of partnership.
7. *Incorrect.* Mutual agency is the true test of the existence of partnership. Sharing of profits is only a *prima facie* evidence of partnership and the test of partnership.
8. *Correct.* A sub-partner has a profit sharing relationship only with a partner of the firm and not with the original firm.
9. *Correct.* As such a partnership can be dissolved by any partner at his will at any time.
10. *Incorrect.* Only the *karta* is personally liable for business obligations of the family.

PRACTICAL PROBLEMS

1. *A* and *B* were two partners carrying on a trading business in partnership under the name and style of Fortune Traders. After sometime, *B* retired from the business, but *A* continued to carry on the same business under the same name. Whether the business carried on by *A* alone is said to be carried on in partnership as the same name is being used ? Give reasons.

   Hints: No. In this case, there is no partnership as *A* alone is carrying on the business. There must be at least two partners to form a partnership.

2. Two firms carrying on banking business, each firm having six partners, amalgamated their business and started working as one business firm under the name and style of 'Easy Finance Group' (EFG).
   (*a*) What is the legal status of EFG?
   (*b*) What alternative is available to EFG to give itself a legal status ?
   (*c*) Would your answer differ if the firms are carrying on a trading business and the new business carried on by the amalgamated firm is also a trading one ?

   Hints: (*a*) It is an illegal association because in a firm carrying on banking business, the total number of partners must not exceed ten. [Section 11, the Companies Act, 1956]

   (*b*) The amalgamated firm can get itself registered under the Companies Act, 1956 and start the business as a company.

   (*c*) Yes, in that case, the new firm will not be an illegal association because in a firm carrying on any business other than a banking business, the maximums limit of partners is twenty.

   [Section 11, the Companies Act, 1956]

3. *A*, a lady, entrusted her **stridhan** (personal property) to her husband *B* who was making the business use of the property. The husband claimed that he has become joint owner of the property entrusted to him as it resulted in partnership. Is *B* justified? Give reasons.

   Hints: *B* is not justified in his claims. *A* partnership results from an agreement, in this case the entrustment of property by *A* to *B* for his business use was not an agreement of partnership, and thus the husband has not become the joint owner of the property

   [***Pratibha Rani*** v. ***Suraj kumar***, AIR 1985 SC 628]

4. State whether *A* and *B* are partners in the following circumstances:
   (*a*) *A* and *B* agreed to produce a film and share the profit by hiring it out.
   (*b*) *A* and *B* bought 100 bags of wheat and agreed to share the same between them.
   (*c*) *A* agreed with *B*, a goldsmith to buy and deliver gold to him (*B*). They further agreed that *B* shall make ornaments and resulting profits and loses shall be shared equally.
   (*d*) *A* and *B* are co-owners of a house which they let out to a tenant and share the rent equally.
   (*e*) *A* and *B* are the co-owners of a house which they are using as a hotel. After meeting the expenses, resulting profits are shared by them is equal ratio.
   (*f*) *A* and *B* agree to work together as fabricators, but *A* shall receive all profits and *B* shall get fixed monthly wages.

(*g*) *A*, a publisher, agreed to publish at his own expense, a book written by *B* and to pay *B* 20% of the net profits.

(*h*) *A*, a contractor, undertook a contract of loading and unloading railway wagons, and appointed *B* as his agent to manage the work. It was agreed that *B* would receive 75% of the profits as his remuneration and would bear all the losses, if any.

Hints: (*a*) Yes, it is a partnership as *A* and *B* agreed to carry on a business and to share profits.

(*b*) No, it is not a partnership as there is no business activity being carried on by *A* and *B*.

(*c*) Yes, it is a partnership as *A* and *B* agree to carry on a business activity and share the resulting profits and losses.

(*d*) No, it is not a partnership as joint owner are not partners if no business activity is carried on by them. [Section 6]

(*e*) Yes, it is a partnership as the co-owners are carrying on a business activity and sharing the resulting profits.

(*f*) No, it is not a partnership as servant receiving monthly wages is not a partner.

(*g*) No, it is not a partnership as there is no business activity being carried an by them jointly.

(*h*) No, it is not a partnership. *B* was merely an agent of *A* and not his partner.

[*Munshi Abdul* v. *Chatterjee*, AIR 1963 Cal. 204]

5. *A*, *B* and *C* were partners in a trading firm. Afterwards, *A* died, but *B* and *C* continued to carry on the business but agreed to give 10% of the profits of the firm to *D*, the widow of *A* **every** year. Is *D* a partner in the firm? Give reasons.

Hints: No, *D* will not be regarded as a partner. The widow or child of a deceased partner who receives a portion of profits as annuity, cannot be said to be a partner merely on the ground of receiving profits. [Section 6]

6. *A* and *B* enter into a partnership. However, in the partnership deed neither the duration of the firm is fixed nor any provision is made as to when and how the partnership will come to an end. Is it a legal partnership?

Hints: Yes, it is a legal partnership, and such a partnership is called a **partnership at will.**

[Section 7]

27
CHAPTER

REGISTRATION OF FIRMS

27.1. INTRODUCTION

The registration of a firm means the recording of firms's name, alongwith prescribed particulars, in the Register of firm kept in the office of the Registrar of Firms. The provisions, for the registration of firms, were introduced for the first time by the Indian Partnership Act, 1932. This Act provided for a separate Chapter No. VII on the 'Registration of Firms', containing 16 Sections (Sections 56 to 71) which deal with the registration of firms.

27.2. NEED FOR REGISTRATION OF A FIRM

As a matter of fact, the registration of a firm is not compulsory. It is optional for the firm either to get itself registered or not. It may be noted that there is no penalty for non-registration of a firm. Moreover, the non-registration does not affect the partnership agreement or any transaction between the partners and third party. In other words, the partnership agreements and other transactions remain valid even if the partnership firm is not registered. Yet indirectly, the registration of a firm becomes necessary at one time or the other. The reason for the same is that the Indian Partnership Act introduced certain disabilities which a registered firm has to suffer, *e.g.*, an unregistered firm cannot file a suit against any person for the price of the goods supplied by it. (The disabilities of an unregistered firm will be discussed in Art. 27.7). Thus, indirectly, the Indian Partnership Act has effectively ensured the registration of firms without making it compulsory.

27.3. PROCEDURE FOR REGISTRATION OF A FIRM

The registration of a firm is obtained by filing an application for registration with the Registrar of Firms[1]. This provision is contained in Section 58(1) of the Indian Partnership Act, which states that the registration of a firm is effected by sending, to the Registrar of Firms, an application for registration on the prescribed form along with the prescribed fee. The prescribed application form may be sent by post or deposited with the Registrar's

1. The State Government may appoint Registrars of Firms for the purpose of registration of firm, and may define the areas within which they shall exercise their powers and performs their duties (Section 57 of the Indian Partnership Act).

office. However, the prescribed application form should be sent or deposited with the Registrar of firms of that area in which any place of business of firm is situated or proposed to be situated.

It is to be noted that a firm may be got registered at any time, *e.g.*, at the time of its formation or at any time thereafter. Section 58 also requires that the application form to be filed with the Registrar of Firms, should state the following particulars:

1. The name of the firm.
2. The place or principal place of business of the firm.
3. The name of any other places where the firms carries on business.
4. The date when each partner joined the firm.
5. The name in full and permanent address of the partners.
6. The duration of the firm.

The application form containing the above particulars must be signed by *all* the partners or by their agents specially authorised in this behalf. Moreover, each person who has signed the application form must also verify it in the prescribed manner.

When the Registrar of Firms is satisfied that the requirements regarding the registration have been duly complied with, he registers the firm and enters its name in the Register of Firms [Section 59]. He then issues a certificate of registration.

Note: In the State Maharashtra Section 58 and 59 of the Indian Partnership Act, 1932 have been amended by The Indian Partnership (Maharashtra Amendment) Act, 1984 (Act 29 of 1984.) w.e.f. 1.1. 1985, which has the following effects:

1. The prescreibed application for registration mus be sent to the Registrar within a period of one year form the date of constitution of the firm.
2. On receipt of prescriped application, the Registrar shall record an entry in the Register of Firms and shall file the statement, and the firm shall be deemed to be registered on the date such entry is recorded and such statement is filed.

27.4. COMPLETION OF REGISTRATION

As regards the completion and effectiveness of registration of firm, there are different views based on judicial decisions. Both the viewpoints are stated below:

1. The registration is complete and effective as soon as the complete application form, alongwith prescribed fee under Section 58, is deposited in the office of the Registrar of Firms. The act of Registrar in recording an entry in Register of Firms, is only a routine duty. Thus, filing of application for registration makes an effective registration even if the Registrar delays his work. [*J.R. & O.M. Contractors* v. *I.T. Commissioner*, AIR 1967 AP 99]

2. The registration is complete and effective form the date when the Registrar files statement and makes entries in the Register of Firms. Thus, the firm becomes registered only when the entries are made in the Register of Firms.

[*CIT* v. *Jayalakshmi Rice and Oil Mill*, AIR 1971 SC 1015]

Following the latter view, the Bombay High Court has also held that where the name of a partner, filing the suit, was not on the Register of Firms on the date of filing the suit, such a suit was not maintainable.

[*Shivraj Fine Art Litho Works* v. *Purushottam*, AIR 1993 Bombay 32]

On this point, section 69(2) of the Indian Partnership Act, is also relevant. This section expressly states that an unregistered firm cannot file a suit against a third party for the enforcement of any right until (*a*) the firm is registered, and (*b*) the name of a person filling the suit *appears as partner in the Register of Firms*. From this provision, it is clear that the disability, imposed due to non-registration is removed only when partners' names appear in the Register of Firm. The partners names appear in the register only when the Registrar registers the firm and makes entries in the Register of Firm. Keeping this in view, the second view stated above should be followed.

27.5. CHANGE OF PARTICULARS AFTER REGISTRATION OF A FIRM

Sometimes, after the registration of a firm, certain changes may take place, *e.g.*, change of a firm name, change of place of business, change of partner's name etc. There are certain changes which require almost a new registration, and certain others in which only an information is required to be sent to the Registrar of Firms. All these changes may be summed up as under:

1. *Change in the firm name and principal place of business.* Sometimes, a registered firm changes its name or location of the principal place of business. In such cases, *A* new application form, containing changed particulars, is to be sent to the Registrar of Firms alongwith the prescribed fee. Such application form must also be signed and verified by all the partners in a manner required under Section 58 for the original registration. Thereafter, the Registrar shall record the change in the Register of Firms, and file the new application alongwith the original application for registration of the firm [Section 60]. *Thus, a change in the firm name, and principal place of business requires almost a new registration.*

2. *Other changes which do not require new registration:* Following are the changes which do not require the above procedure. In these cases, only the information of the change is to be sent to the Registrar of Firms who shall record the change:

(*a*) Change regarding the closing and opening of branches [Section 61].

(*b*) Change in the name or permanent address of any partner [Section 62].

(*c*) Change in the constitution of the firm and its dissolution [Section 63 (1)].

(*d*) Change regarding minor partner's decision on becoming a major [Section 63(2)].

27.6. PENALTY FOR FALSE PARTICULARS

As a matter of fact, all the particulars required to be furnished to the Registrar of Firms such as application form for registration, application form for the change of particulars, intimations and notices, must be true and complete. If any person, knowingly or without any belief in its truth, signs a false or incomplete statement, he shall be liable to be punishable with imprisonment upto three months, or with fine, or with both [Section 70].

27.7. EFFECTS OF NON-REGISTRATION OF A FIRM

We have already discussed that the registration of a firm is not compulsory. However, indirectly it becomes compulsory because an unregistered firm faces certain disabilities which can be removed only be the registration of a firm. These disabilities (called effects of non-registration) are contained in various provisions of Section 69 of the Indian Partnership Act, which may be discussed under the following heads:

1. *The partners cannot file a suit against the firm or other partners* [Section 69(1)] *:* It is one of the main disabilities of an unregistered firm. A partner of a unregistered firm cannot file a suit against the firm or his other present or part partners, for the enforcement of any right arising from a contract or conferred by the Indian Partnership Act. A partner can file a suit for the enforcement of such right *only* if the firm is a registered firm *and* his name appears as a partner in the Register of Firms. It may, however, be noted that this disability may be removed by getting the firm registered before filing the suit.

2. *The firm cannot file a suit against third parties* [Section 69(2)] *:* It is another disability of a unregistered firm. An unregistered firm cannot file a suit against any third party for the enforcement of any right arising from some contract. A suit can be filed by or on behalf of the firm only if the firm is a registered firm, and the names of the persons, filing the suit on behalf of the firm, appear as partners in the Register of Firms.

Example 27.1. 'A & Co', an unregistered firm, sold certain goods to *B* on credit. But *B* failed to pay the price of the goods. In this case, the firm cannot enforce its right in a Court of Law by filing a suit for the recovery of the price.

[Based on *Ram Adhar* v. *R.K. Tiwari,* AIR 1981 All 405].

This difficulty of an unregistered firm can be removed by getting the firm registered *before* filing the suit. It may be noted that once a suit is filed by an unregistered firm, it is liable to be dismissed and cannot be rectified by subsequent registration.

[*Puran Mal* v. *Central Bank of India,* AIR 1939 Punjab 235]

Note. There have been differences of opinion on the question whether registration of a firm is a condition precedent to the filing of a suit or whether the defect can be removed by the registration of the firm subsequent to the filing of the suit. Some courts have held that a suit by an unregistered firm could be validated by the subsequent registration of the firm[2]. And some courts have held that a subsequent registration could not cure the defect which existed at the time of filing the suit[3]. The latter view appears to be correct and has been approved by the Supreme Court in *Commr of Income-tax, A.P. Hyderabad v. M/s Jayalakshmi Rice & Oil Mills Contractor Co.* A.I.R. 1971 S.C. 1015. Thus the firm must first get registered and file a *fresh suit* if the earlier suit is dismissed on the ground of non-registration.

3. *The partner of the firm cannot claim a set-off.* [Section 69(3)] : The term 'set-off' may be defined as the adjustment of debts by one party due to him from the other party who files a suit against him. It is another disability of the partners and of an unregistered firm that it cannot claim a set-off when a suit is filed against it.

Example 27.2. 'A & Co.', an unregistered firm, borrowed Rs. 10,000 from *B*, a money-lender. The firm has also supplied certain goods worth Rs. 1,000, to *B* on credit. On firm's refusal to repay the loan, *B* filed a suit against it for the recovery of amount of loan. In this case, the firm cannot say that Rs. 1,000 owed by *B* to the firm should be set-off against *B*'s claim of Rs. 10,000 against the firm.

However, as per Section 69(4) (*b*), this right of set-off is not affected if the claim for set-off does not exceed Rs. 100 in value.

The disability of the partners and the firm to file a suit also extends to the enforcement of *other proceedings.* The term *'other proceedings'* also includes the arbitration proceedings. Thus, where it is provided in the partnership agreement that in case of dispute the matter shall be referred to arbitration, then if the firm is unregistered, this arbitration clause cannot be enforced by filing a suit if one party does not agree to refer the dispute to arbitration.

Example 27.3. *A* and *B* were partners in an unregistered firm. A clause in the partnership deed provided that in case of any dispute between the partners, the matter will be referred to arbitration. After sometime, a dispute arose between the partners, and *A* appointed an arbitrator. But *B* did not give his consent and refused to refer the dispute to the arbitrator. *A* filed a suit against *B* that he (*B*) should be compelled to refer the dispute to the arbitration as there was an arbitration clause in the partnership deed. *B* contended that the firm was not registered, and, therefore, the suit should be dismissed. It was held that the suit was not maintainable as the firm was unregistered. [*Jagdish C. Gupta* v. *Kajaria Traders,* AIR 1964 SC 1882].

2. *J. Badrudin v. Jaganath Godali* AIR 1939 Nagpur 301.
3. Puran Mall's case AIR 1939 Punjab 235.

27.8. EXCEPTIONS TO NON-REGISTRATION OF A FIRM

We have discussed, in the last article, the disabilities of an unregistered firm and its partners. However, the non-registration of a firm does not affect the following:

1. The third party can file a suit against the firm whether the firm is registered or not. And the firm cannot take the plea of its non-registration.

2. The partners of an unregistered firm can file a suit for the enforcement of three things, namely, (*a*) for the dissolution of the firm, (*b*) for the accounts of the dissolved firm. (*c*) for realisation of the property of the dissolved firm. [Section 69(3)(*a*)].

Example 27.4. *A* and *B* purchased a taxi and they were plying it in partnership. The firm was, however, unregistered. The business continued for one year, and then *A* sold the taxi without the consent of *B*, and did not pay anything to him. *B* filed a suit against *A* to recover his share in the sale proceeds. *A* defended the suit on the ground that the firm was not registered. It was held that the business was closed on the sale of the taxi, and the suit was maintainable as it was for the realisation of assets of a dissolved firm.

[*S. Ahmed Khan* v. *Turup Mohd Hayat*, AIR 1953 Mysore 4]

3. The rights of an unregistered firm or of its partners are not affected if the firm has no place of business in India. The State Government may also exempt the firm of a particular area (within Indian territories) from the applicability of all the provisions of registration [Section 69(4)(*a*)].

4. The unregistered firm or its partners may sue or enforce a claim of set-off if the subject- matter of the suit or set-off does not exceed Rs. 100 in value [Section 69(4)(*b*)].

5. The official Assignee, Receiver or court may bring an action to realise the property of an insolvent partner [Section 69(3)(*b*)].

6. The right of an unregistered firm to enforce a right which arise otherwise than out of a contract. As a matter of fact, firm's disability is to enforce the contractual rights, and not the others.

LEGAL PROVISIONS (SECTIONS) DISCUSSED IN THE CHAPTER

Important legal provisions (sections) of the Indian Partnership Act, 1932, discussed in this chapter are reprduced hereunder for ready reference:

1. ***Section 58: Application for Registration***

(1) The registration of a firm may be effected at any time by sending by post or delivering to the Registrar of the area in which any place of business of the firm is situated or proposed to be situated, a statement in the prescribed form and accompanied by the prescribed fee, stating -

(*a*) the firm name,
(*b*) the place or principal place of business of the firm,
(*c*) the names of any other places where the firm carries on business,
(*d*) the date when each partner joined the firm,
(*e*) the names in full and permanent addresses of the partners, and
(*f*) the duration of the firm.

The statement shall be signed by all the partners, or by their agents specially authorised in this behalf.

(2) Each person signing the statement shall also verify it in the manner prescribed.

(3) A firm name shall not contain any of the following words namely -
"Crown", "Emperor", "empress", "Emprie", "Imperial", "King", "Queen", "Royal", or words expressing or implying the sanction, approval or patronage of Governmet except when the State Government signifies consent to the use of such words as part of the firm name by order in writing.

2. ***Section 59: Registration***

When the Register is satisfied that the provisions of section 58 have been duly complied with, he shall record an entry of the statement in a register called the Register of Firms, and shall file the statement.

3. *Section 69: Effects of Non-Registration*

(1) No suit to enforce a right arising from a contract or conferred by this Act shall be instituted in any Court by or on behalf of any person suing as a partner in a firm against the firm or any person alleged to be or to have been a partner in the firm unless the firm is registered and the person suing is or has been shown in the Register of Firms as a partner in the firm.

(2) No suit to enforce a right arising from a contract shall be instituted in any Court by or on behalf of a firm against any third party unless the firm is registered and the persons suing are or have been shown in the Register of Firms as partners in the firm.

(3) The provisions of sub-sections (1) and (2) shall apply also to a claim of set-off or other proceeding to enforce a right arising from a contract, but shall not affect,

(*a*) the enforcement of any right to sue for the dissolution of a firm or for accounts of a dissolved firm, or any right or power to realise the property of a dissolved firm, or

(*b*) the powers of an official assignee, receiver or Court under the Presidency. Towns Insolvency Act, 1909, or the Provincial Insolvency Act, 1920, to realise the property of an insolvent partner.

(4) This section shall not apply, —

(*a*) to firms or to partners in firms which have no place of business in the territories to which this Act extends, or whose places of business in the said territories are situated in areas to which, by notification under section 56 this Chapter does not apply, or

(*b*) to any suit or claim of set-off not exceeding one hundred rupees in value which, in the Presidency-towns, is not of a kind specified in section 19 of the Presidency Small Cause Courts Act, 1882, or outside the Presidency-towns, is not of a kind specified in the Second Schedule to the Provincial Small Cause Courts Act, 1887, or to any proceeding in execution or other proceeding incidental to or arising from any such suit or claim.

4. *Section 70: Penalty for furnishing false particulars.*

Any person who, signs any statement, amending statement, notice or intimaton under this Chapter containing any particular which he knows to be false or does not believe to be true or containing particulars which he knows to be incomplete or does not believe to be complete, shall be punishable with imprisonment which may extend to three months, or with fine, or with both.

TEST QUESTIONS

1. What is meant by registration of a firm ? State the procedure of registration of a firm, and the effects of non-registration.
2. "The Indian Partnership Act has effectively ensured the registration of firms without making it compulsory"—comment.
3. Explain the procedure for the registration of a partnership firm under the Indian Partnership Act. Are there any advantages of such registration?
4. State the need for registration of firm. What acts or proceedings are not affected by non-registration?
5. State the procedure for recording changes in the firm after it has been registered. Is there any penalty for false particulars given for registration of changes?
6. Write notes on the following :

(*a*) Penalty for giving false particulars about registration or changes.

(*b*) Exceptions to non-registration.

MULTIPLE CHOICE QUESTIONS

1. The registration of partnership firm with the Registrar of firms is

(*a*) compulsory (*b*) optional

(*c*) required under Section 54 (*d*) required under Section 55

2. Which of the following statements, about the registration of firm, is not true:

(*a*) It must be done at the time of its formation.

(*b*) It may be done at the time of formation.

(*c*) It may be done before filing a suit against third party.

(*d*) It may be done at any time after its formation.

3. As per the accepted view, the registration of the firm is considered complete when
   (*a*) complete application for registration is filed with the Registrar.
   (*b*) Registrar files the statement and makes entries in the Register of Firms.
   (*c*) Registrar gives notice of registration to all partners.
   (*d*) court records the statement and certifies the entries in Register of Firms.
4. After the registration of a firm, a change in the firm name and principal place of business requires almost a new registration.
   (*a*) True (*b*) False
5. After the registration of a firm, for closing of an old branch and opening of a new branch, only information is required to be given to the Registrar.
   (*a*) True (*b*) False
6. Any person who knowingly signs any statement containing false particulars about registration, shall be liable to punishment with imprisonment upto
   (*a*) one month (*b*) two months
   (*c*) three months (*d*) six months
7. Which of the following is not the disability of an unregistered firm?
   (*a*) It cannot file a suit against third parties
   (*b*) Its partners cannot file a suit against the firm
   (*c*) It cannot claim a set-off exceeding Rs. 100.
   (*d*) It cannot be sued by a third party.

ANSWERS

1. (*b*)	2. (*a*)	3. (*b*)	4. (*a*)	5. (*a*)	6. (*c*)
7. (*d*)					

OBJECTIVE TYPE QUESTIONS WITH REASONING

State with reasons whether the following statements are correct or incorrect.

1. The registration of a partnership firm is compulsory under the Indian Partnership Act, 1932.
2. Though the registration of a firm is not compulsory, but the firm has to pay penalty for non-registration.
3. The Indian Partnership Act has effectively ensured registration of firms without making it compulsory.
4. The registration is complete and effective as soon as the complete application form is deposited in the office of the Registrar of firms.
5. An unregistered firm cannot file a suit against any third party to enforce a right arising from a contract.
6. The third party cannot file a suit against an unregistered firm unless the firm is registered.
7. An unregistered firm can file a suit for set -off.
8. A third party cannot exercise any right against a non-registered firm.
9. An unregistered firm or its partners can enforce a claim of set-off if the amount does not exceed Rs. 100.
10. A partnership deed is a mandatory document required for the existence of a partnership.

ANSWERS

1. ***Incorrect.*** It is optional for the firm either to get itself registered or not.
2. ***Incorrect.*** The Partnership Act does not provide for any penalty for non-registration.
3. ***Correct.*** As an unregistered firm has to face certain disabilities.

4. ***Incorrect.*** The accepted view is that the registration is complete and effective when the Registrar makes entries in the Register of Firms.
5. ***Correct.*** It is the disability of an unregistered firm [Section 69(2)].
6. ***Incorrect.*** Third party's right to file a suit against the firm is not affected due to non-registration of the firm.
7. ***Incorrect.*** It is the disability of an unregistered firm [Section 69(3)].
8. ***Incorrect.*** Third party's right to enforce rights against a firm are not affected by its non-registration.
9. ***Correct.*** It is a recognised exception to the disabilities of non-registration [Section 69(4)(*b*)].
10. ***Incorrect***. It is not mandatory, *i.e.*, legally compulsory for the partners to have a partnership deed. Even an implied agreement is sufficient for the existence of a partnership.

PRACTICAL PROBLEMS

1. *A* and *B* are carrying on their trading business in partnership which has not yet been registered. Firm had supplied material worth Rs. 2,00,000 to *C* who failed to pay the amount to the firm. The firm files a suit against *C* for the recovery of this amount.

   (*a*) Will the firm succeed in its action ?

   (*b*) Will your answer be different if the firm gets itself registered immediately after filing the suit?

   Hints: (*a*) No, the firm will not succeed An unregistered firm cannot file a suit against any third party for the enforcement of any right arising from some contract [Section 69(2)].

   (*b*) No, in this case also the answer will not be different from the given above. A subsequent registration cannot cure the defect which existed at the time of filling the suit

   [***Commr. of Income Tax,* v. *M/S Jayalakshmi Rice, Oil Mills*** AIR 1971 SC 1015]
2. An unregistered Firm applied for registration on 15th September, 2009. The application was pending before the Registras of Firms but before the registration could be effected, the firm filed a suit against *A*, for the recovery of its does of Rs 100,000 on 20th September, 2009. The Registrar made entries in the Register of Firms on 25th September, 2009 and the registration certificate dated 25th September ,2009 was also delivered to the firm. Is the suit maintainable ? Give reasons.

   Hints: No, the suit is not maintainable on account of non-registration. On the date of filing the suit, the firm was not registered, and member's name did not appear in the Register of Firms [Section 69(2)]. On that date, the firm had simply applied for registration.
3. An unregistered firm had borrowed Rs.50,000 from *A*, a moneylender. The firm had also spplied goods worth Rs. 5000 to *A* on credit. Since, the firm could not repay the loan amount in time, *A* filed a suit against the firm for the recovery of loan amount. Can the firm claims the set-off of Rs. 5000? Give reasons

   Hints: No, the firm cannot claim the set-off as it is an unregistered firm [Section 69(3)]. However, the right of set-off is not affected if the claim for set-off does not exceed Rs.100 in value. [Section 69(4)(*b*)]
4. *A* and *B* purchased a taxi to ply in partnership. They plied the taxi for about a year when *A*, without the consent of *B*, disposed of the taxi. *B* brought an action to recover his share in the sale proceeds. *A* resisted *B*'s claim on the plea that the firm was not registered. Will *B* succeed in his claim ? Give reasons.

   Hints: Yes, *B* will succeed in his claim. A partner of an unregistered firm can file a suit for the realisation of the property of the dissolved firm.

   [Section 69(3)(*a*); *S. Ahmed Khan* v. *Turup Mohd. Hayat*, AIR 1953 Mysore 4].
5. An unregistered firm sold goods worth Rs. 20,000 to *B*, who gave a cheque for the amount, But the cheque was dishonoured or presentation. *A* who was a partner in the firm, demanded money from *B* who paid only Rs. 10,000. In the meantime, the firm was dissolved and the sum of Rs 10,000, the unpaid balance, was assigned to *A* for realisation. *A* sued *B* for the recovery of the amount. *B* pleads that *A*'s suit is not maintainable as the firm was unregistered. Is *B*'s contention correct ?

   Hints: No, *B*'s contention is not correct. A suit for recovery of debts of a dissolved firm is also maintainable. [section 69(3) (*a*); *Kantilal* v. *Ghanshyam*, AIR 1994 Gujrat 56].
6. *A* and *B* were partners in an unregistered firm carrying on the business of furniture manufacturing. *C* was advanced Rs. 10,000 by the firm in lieu of the promise to supply wood. There was short supply of wood and Rs. 2000 were due from *C* to the partnership firm. The partnership was afterwards dissolved and in a division of the assets of partnership, this debt of Rs 2000 was allotted to *A*. Can *A* sue *C* to recover the amount?

   Hints: Yes, *A* can sue *C* for the recovery of the debt due to the firm. [Section 69(3) (*a*)]

RELATIONS OF PARTNERS WITH ONE ANOTHER (MUTUAL RELATIONS OF PARTNERS)

28.1. INTRODUCTION

We know that the relations of partners are governed by the principle of mutual agency. In fact, every partner is an agent of his other partners for all matters connected with the firm business. Thus, a partner has the power to bind his other partners into any amount of liability. In this chapter, we shall discuss the fundamental principles that govern the relations of one partner with other, and the duties and rights of partners towards their other partners.

28.2. PRINCIPLES GOVERNING THE MUTUAL RELATIONS

The relations of partners to one another are governed by the following principles:

1. ***By the provisions of an agreement.*** Since, partnership is the creation of an agreement, the mutual rights and duties of the partners may be settled by an agreement between the partners. There may be express agreement stating the rights and duties of the partners or such an agreement may be inferred by the course of dealings of the partners. It may be noted that the agreement, specifying the rights and duties of the partners, may be varied by the consent of all the partners. Such consent may be express or implied by a course of dealing [Section 11 (1)].

2. ***By the principle of absolute good faith.*** The mutual trust and confidence is the basis of partnership. Therefore, the second important principle which governs the mutual relations of the partners, is the fundamental principle of absolute *good faith.* The partners are bound to be just and faithful to each other [Section 9]. The mutual confidence between the partners is the life blood of the furm, and the duty of good faith cannot be excluded by any agreement between the partners.

28.3. DUTIES OF PARTNERS TOWARDS ONE ANOTHER

1. *Duty of good faith*
2. *Duty to carry on the firm's business to the greatest common advantage*
3. *Duty to render true account*
4. *Duty to give full information*
5. *Duty to indemnify for loss caused by*

All the duties of the partners are based on this fundamental principle of *good faith.* Every partner must use his all efforts to secure maximum profits for the firm. **General duties** of the partners are contained in Section 9 of the Indian Partnership Act, which reads as under:

6. *Duty to attend diligently*
7. *Duty to share losses*
8. *Duty to account for personal profits.*
9. *Duty to account for profits of a competing business*
10. *Duty to use firm property exclusively for firm*
11. *Duty to act within authority*
12. *Duty not to transfer his rights and interest*

"Partners are bound to carry on the business of the firm to the greatest common advantage, to be just and faithful to each other, and to render true accounts and full information of all things affecting the firm to any partner or his legal representative."

The analysis of this section reveals the following **general duties** of the partners towards one another:

1. Duty of good faith.
2. Duty to carry on the firm business to the greatest common advantage.
3. Duty to render true accounts.
4. Duty to give full information.

These duties along with the other duties contained in various provisions of the Indian Partnership Act, are discussed in detail in the following pages:

1. *Duty of good faith.* It is the foremost and important general duty of the partners. Every partner should act in *good faith*, and he should be just and faithful in his dealings with the other partners. *Good faith* requires that a partner should not deceive the other partners by concealment of material facts, *e.g.*, a partner should not try to make secret profits, for himself, at the expense of the firm.

2. *Duty to carry on the firm's business to the greatest common advantage.* This duty is also based upon the principle of *good faith*. Every partner is bound to carry on the business of the firm to the greatest common advantage. He must use his knowledge and skill for the common benefit of the firm. And he should not make any personal or private profits.

Example 28.1. *A* and *B* were partners in a firm of sugar refiners. *A* had greater skill in buying the sugarcane and he was entrusted to buy the same for the firm. He supplied the sugarcane from his personal stocks which he had bought earlier at a lower price. He charged the prevailing market price and made considerable profits for himself. It was held that the firm was entitled to those profits and *A* must account to the firm for these private (personal) profits. In this case, A's act was not for the common benefit of the firm. As such, he had to account for the personal profits.

[*Bentley* v. *Craven* (1853) 18 Beav. 75].

3. *Duty to render true accounts.* It is another duty of every partner that he should keep proper accounts, and render correct and true accounts of partnership. In other words, he should explain all the accounts to the other partners and give true and correct picture of the same.

4. *Duty to give full information.* It is also the duty of every partner that he should give full information of all things affecting the firm, to his co-partners. This duty is also based on the fundamental principle of utmost *good faith*. It extends to all kinds of transactions and every partner is required to disclose all material facts relating to the partnership affairs. Thus, if a partner is in possession of more information about the affairs and assets of the firm, he should not conceal that from the other partners.

Besides the above general duties, there are **other duties** also which are contained in different sections of the Indian Partnership Act. These are discussed below:

5. *Duty to indemnify for loss caused by fraud.* The term 'indemnify' means 'to make good' or 'to compensate'. It is the duty of every partner to make good the loss suffered by the firm due to his fraud. Thus, if some loss is caused to the firm due to the fraud of a particular partner, the firm has the right to recover the loss from the same partner [Section 10]. The purpose of this provision is that every partner should deal honestly with the customers of the firm. It may, however, be noted that the firm and the innocent partners shall remain liable to the third parties for the fraud of the other partners, though they (the firm and innocent partners) can recover compensation from the partner who is guilty of fraud. It is to be noted that it is an *absolute duty*, and it cannot be excluded by any other agreement to the contrary.

Example 28.2. *A* and *B* were two partners in a firm of solicitors. *C* a lady, consulted *A* about the improvement of the income of her property. *A* advised her to dispose of this property, and asked her to bring the title deeds of this property. *A* obtained *C*'s signature on a plain paper and also took the title deeds from her. *A* converted this paper as sale deed to himself. Thereafter, he sold the property and misappropriated the money. In this case, the firm is liable to *C* for fraud committed by *A*. However, *A* is liable to compensate the firm for the loss suffered due to his fraud.

6. *Duty to attend diligently.* It is the duty of every partner that he should diligently (*i.e.* carefully) attend to the affairs of the business of the firm [Section 12(*b*)].

If the partner is not careful in conducting the firm's business, then he should compensate the firm for any loss suffered by it. In other words, if a partner does not attend diligently the business of the firm, and the firm suffers a loss due to his 'wilful neglect', then he is bound to make compensation to the firm [Section 13(*f*)]. However this duty can be excluded by an agreement between the partners.

It may be noted that a partner is not entitled to receive any remuneration, whether in the shape of salary, commission, etc., for conducting the business of the firm [Section 13(*a*)]. This is, however, subject to an agreement to the contrary, *i.e.*, there may be an agreement which may provide for remuneration to the partners.

7. *Duty to share losses.* It is the duty of every partner to share equally the losses suffered by the firm. However, this duty is subject to an agreement to the contrary, *i.e.*, the partners may agree to share the losses in different proportions.

8. *Duty to account for personal profits.* It is the duty of every partner not to make any personal profits. And if any partner makes any personal profits, then he is bound to account for such profits and pay the same to the firm. This duty is based on the principle of *good faith*, which requires that a partner shall not make personal profits at the expense of the firm. Thus, if a partner makes personal profits in any of the following ways, he must give account of those profits and pay back the same to the firm [Section 16(*a*)]:

(*a*) Personal profits from any transaction of the firm.
(*b*) Personal profits from the use of the property of the firm.
(*c*) Personal profits from the business connection of the firm.
(*d*) Personal profits from the use of the name of the firm.

Example 28.3. *A* and *B* were partners in a firm. They were carrying on the business of importing salt from foreign countries and reselling the same. *A* was authorised to buy the salt for the firm. While buying salt for the firm, *A* bought some quantity for himself and resold the same on his personal accounts. It was held that *A* was liable to account for these personal profits. The reason for the same is that the opportunity to make personal profits came in *A*'s way while he was carrying on the business of the firm. [*Pulin* v. *Mahendra (1921)* 34 Cal. L.J. 405].

However, the above duty is subject to a contract between the partners *i.e.*, by a contract, the partners may allow all or any of them to earn personal profits by using firm name, property etc.

9. *Duty to account for profits of a competing business.* It is the duty of every partner not to carry on any business similar to, or in competition with the business of the firm. If any partner carries on such a business and earns profits, he is bound to account for such profits and pay the same to the firm. [Section 16(*b*)].

Example 28.4. *A* and *B* were partners in a business. The firm was carrying on the business of supplying meat to the Government. Subsequently, it was found that *B* was also engaged with some other persons in supplying meat to the Government, and earned personal profits. It was held that *B* was bound to account to the firm for profits so made by him. In this case, *B* earned personal profits by carrying on a business competing with that of the business of the firm.

[*Loch* v. *Lynam* (1854) 4 Ir. Ch. 188]

However, the above duty is subject to a contract between the partners, *i.e.*, by a contract, the partners may allow all or any of them to carry on any business whether or not competing with the business of the firm.

10. *Duty to use firm property exclusively for firm.* Since the partnership property belongs to all the partners, it is therefore, the duty of every partner to use the partnership property exclusively for the business of the firm (Section 15.) If any partner makes personal profits by using the partnership property, then he must give account of such profits and pay back the same to the firm [Section 16(*a*)].

Example 28.5 *A* and *B* owned a ship under a partnership. *A* made considerable personal profits by making various contracts. It was held that *A* was liable to account for such profits as these were made from the use of partnership property. The reason for the same is that the partnership property belongs to all the partners. It is, therefore, the duty of every partner to use the partnership property strictly and solely for the business of the firm. He cannot use the same for his own use. [*Gardner v. Mccutcheon*, 4 Beas 534 (1842); 55 RR 154.]

The above duty is, however, subject to an agreement to the contrary, *i.e.*, the partners may agree to use the partnership property in any manner they decide.

11. *Duty to act within authority.* It is the duty of every partner that he should act within the scope of actual or implied authority. The scope of partner's implied authority will be discussed in the next chapter.

12. *Duty not to transfer his rights and interest.* Since the relation between the partners is of mutual trust and confidence. it is therefore, the duty of every partner that he should not transfer his rights and interest in the firm to an outsider so as to make him a partner in the firm. However, a partner can transfer his share of profits [Section 29].

28.4. RIGHTS OF PARTNERS TOWARDS ONE ANOTHER

1. *Right to take part in business*
2. *Right to be consulted*
3. *Right to have access to books*
4. *Right to share profit*
5. *Right to interest on capital and on advance*
6. *Right to indemnity*
7. *Right to use the partnership property*
8. *Right to be consulted at the time of admission of a new parter*
9. *Right to retire form the firm*
10. *Right of retiring partner*
11. *Right not to be expelled*
12. *Right ro remuneration*

The mutual rights of partners depend upon the provisions of the partnership agreement. However, subject to an agreement between the partnership, the law confers the following rights upon all the partners:

1. *Right to take part in business.* It is the right of every partner to take part in the management of the business. It may be noted that this right is available to all the partners. This is, however, subject to contract between the partners, *i.e.*, the partners may provide, by a contract, that this right shall not be available to some partners [Section 12(*a*)].

This right should be exercised by the partners for promoting the interest and reputation of the firm and not for damaging the same.

2. *Right to be consulted*. It is also the right of every partner to be consulted in all matters affecting the business of the firm. Moreover, every partner also has the right to express his opinion before any decision is taken by the other partners. In some cases, the difference of opinion may arise among the partners *i.e.*, all partners may not agree on a certain point. The difference of opinion may be either on (*a*) ordinary matters, or (*b*) on fundamental matters (*i.e.*, the matters affecting the nature of business). In such cases, the differences are resolved, *i.e.*, settled as per rules contained in Section 12(*c*) of the Indian Partnership Act, which may be summed up as under:

(*a*) Where the difference of opinion is over an *ordinary matter*, the same may be settled by a *majority* of the partners.

(*b*) Where the difference of opinion is over a *fundamental matter*, the same can be settled with the consent of all the partners.

3. *Right to have access to books.* It is the right of every partner to have access to the books of the firm. Thus, every partner has the right to examine all the records, books and accounts of the firm. Moreover, he can also have the copy of such accounts etc. It may be noted that a partner may exercise this right himself or by his agent. This right is, however, subject to a contract between the partners, *i.e.*, the partner may agree, by a contract that this right shall not be available to some of the partners [Section 12(*d*)].

4. *Right to share profits.* As a matter of fact, the partnership is formed to share the profits of a business. It is, therefore, the right of every partner to share equally the profits earned by the firm. Thus, every partner has the right to have equal share in the profits of the firm. However, the partners may also agree to share the profits in different proportions [Section 13(*b*)].

5. *Right to interest on capital and on advance.* Ordinarily, the partners have no right to receive any interest on their contribution towards the capital. However, the partnership agreement may provide that the partners shall be entitled to interest on capital at a certain rate. Where such interest is to be paid, it shall be paid only out of profits [Section 13(*c*)]. If the firm suffers loss, the partners are not entitled to any interest on the capital. However, the partners may provide, by a contract, that the interest on capital shall be paid event if the firm suffers loss.

Sometimes in addition to the contribution towards the capital, a partner also advance a sum of money for the purpose of the business of the firm. In such cases, he is entitled to interest on such advance at the rate of 6% per annum [Section 13(*d*)]. Such interest on advance is payable even if the firm suffers loss.

6. *Right to indemnity.* The right to indemnity means the right to recover from the firm the expenses incurred and payments made by a partner. The partner of a firm has a right to recover expenses incurred and payments made by him in the following two circumstances [Section 13(*e*)]:

(*a*) *Expenses incurred in the ordinary course of business*. In the first place, a partner has a right to recover from the firm any expenses incurred by him 'in the ordinary course of partnership business'.

(*b*) *Expenses incurred in an emergency.* In the second place, a partner has a right to recover from the firm any expenses incurred by him in order to protect the property of the firm from a loss threatened by an emergency.

7. *Right to use the partnership property.* The partnership property is the joint property of all the partners. It is, therefore, the right of every partner to use the partnership property. It may, however, be noted that the partnership property should be used exclusively for the purpose of the partnership business.

8. *Right to be consulted at the time of admission of a new partner.* It is the right of every partner to be consulted at the time of admitting a new partner in the firm. As a matter of fact, a new partner cannot be introduced, *i.e.*, admitted into the firm without the consent of all the partners. This is, however, subject to an agreement to the contrary.

9. *Right to retire from the firm.* A partner has the right to retire from the firm if he finds it difficult to adjust with the other partners. However, he can retire from the firm in any one of the following ways:

(*a*) with the consent of all other partners.

(*b*) in accordance with an express agreement by the partners.

(*c*) by giving a written notice of retirement to all other partners. This clause is applicable only where the partnership is at will.

10. *Right of retiring partner.* The following are the rights of retiring partner:

(*a*) *Right to carry on competing business:* A retiring partner has the right to carry on any business after his retirement. He may start a new business next door to the firm and may also advertise such business.

(*b*) *Right to share subsequent profits :* Sometimes, after the retirement of a partner the remaining partners do not return the share of retired partner's property, but use the same in the business of the firm. In such cases, the retiring partner has the right to claim the profits as earned by the use of his share of property.

11. *Right not to be expelled.* Every partner has the right to continue in the firm and he cannot be expelled from it by the other partners. However, the partners may enter into a contract providing for the expulsion of a partner by majority of the partners. But such a power must be exercised in *good faith*. This point will be discussed in detail in Chapter 30.

12. *Right to remuneration.* Generally, the partners are not entitled to receive any remuneration for taking part in the conduct of the business of the firm. However, the partnership agreement may expressly provide for the payment of remuneration to *working partners*. It may be noted that in the absence of a specific agreement, a partner is not entitled to any remuneration even if he renders extraordinary services.

[*Shelat Bros*. v. *Nandlal Harilal*, AIR 1973 Madras 78]

28.5. PARTNERSHIP PROPERTY

The term 'partnership property' means the joint property of all the partners as opposed to their personal property. For the following reasons it becomes necessary to determine the partnership property:

1. The 'partnership property can be used only for the purposes of the business of the firm.
2. The partners cannot deal with any portion of the partnership property as their own.
3. The partners cannot transfer to any one their interest in a specific item of partnership property.
4. The debts of the firm are paid firstly out of the partnership property, on the dissolution of the firm.

As a matter of fact, it is for the partners to determine by an agreement, among themselves, as to what shall be the partnership property and what shall be their separate property. And if there is no such agreement between the partners, the rules contained in Section 14 of the Indian Partnership Act, are applied in determining whether or not a particular property is the partnership property. The analysis of this section reveals that in the absence of any contract providing for the partnership property, the following shall be considered to be the partnership property:

(*a*) *Property originally brought in the firm.* Any property which is brought by the partners, at the commencement of the partnership, and put into the common stock of the firm for their common use is the partnership property alongwith all rights and interests in the same.

(*b*) *Property acquired afterwards.* Any property which is acquired by or for the firm, after the commencement of the partnership, is the partnership property alongwith all rights and interests in the same. Moreover, any property acquired for the purpose and in the course of business of the firm, also belongs to the firm.

(c) Property acquired with firm's money. Any property which is acquired in firm's name with the money belonging to the firm, is undoubtedly a partnership property. Moreover, the property acquired in partner's name but with the money belonging to the firm, is also presumed to the partnership property unless contrary intention appears.

[*Y.V. Chowdry* v. G. *Lakshmidevamma*, AIR 1994 Madras 140]

(d) Goodwill of the business of the firm. Any goodwill earned by the firm is also the partnership property. The term 'good will ' means the value of the reputation of the firm. It may be noted that the goodwill is very valuable asset of the firm even if one cannot touch or see it . It is an intangible asset which results in higher profits due to the good reputation of the firm.

(e) Trade marks, patents, copyrights etc. These are not specifically mentioned in Section 14, as property of the firm. However, these are also to be regarded as property of the firm.

Thus, in order to determine whether or not a particular property is partnership property, the regard shall be had to the sources from which the property was obtained, the purpose for which it was acquired and the mode in which it had been dealt with.

Example 28.6 *A*, *B* and *C* were partners in a printing business. At the commencement of the partnership, all of them purchased one printing machine each, for the common use of the firm business. In this case, the printing machines are the partnership property as they ase originally brought into the common stock of the firm.

Example 28.7 *A* and *B* were carrying on a 'tent house' business in partnership with each other. After sometime, they purchased 1,000 chairs and 400 tables for the expansion of their business. In this case, these chairs and tables are the partnership property as they are purchased by the firm for the purpose of partnership business.

Example 28.8 *A* and *B* were partners in a transport business. *A* bought two trucks in his own name but with the money of the partnership business. In this case, the trucks are the partnership property as they are purchased with the money belonging to the firm.

Sometimes, the personal property of a partner is being used in the business of the firm. In such cases, it does not become partnership property simply because it is being used in the business of the firm. It would require @ very clear agreement to convert personal property of a partner into the joint property of the firm. If the prersonal property is being used with the intention of making it the partnership property, then it will become the partnership property.

Example 28.9 *A* was the owner of a cotton mill . He entered into partnership with *B* and *C*. The business of the firm was carried on at *A*'s mill. However, the value of assets of the mill was credited to *A*'s capital account, and he was also allowed interest on it. Subsequently, the mill was enlarged and improved by the firm and also a new building was constructed on the land acquired by the firm. It was held that the mill had become the property of the firm.

[*Robinson v. Ashtan*, (1875) 20 Eq. 25; 44 LJC Ch. 542]

LEGAL PROVISIONS (SECTIONS) DISCUSSED IN THE CHAPTER

Important legal provisions (sections) of the Indian Partnership Act, 1932, disucussed in the this chapter are reprouced hereith for ready reference:

1. ***Section 13: Mutual Rights and Liabilities***

Subject to contract between the partners–

(*a*) a partner is not entitled to receive remuneration for taking part in the conduct of the business;

(*b*) the partners are entitled to share equally in the profits earned, and shall contribute equally to the losses sustained by the firm;

(*c*) where a partner is entitled to interest on the capital subscribed by him, such interest shall be payable only out of profits;

(*d*) a partner making, for the purposes of the business, any payment or advance beyond the amount of capital he has agreed to subscribe, is entitled to interest thereon at the rate of six per cent, per annum;

(*e*) the firm shall indemnify a partner in respect of payments made and liabilities incurred by him -

(*i*) in the ordinary and proper conduct of the business, and

(*ii*) in doing such act, in an emergency, for the purpose of protecting the firm from loss, as would be done by a person of ordinary prudence, in his own case, under similar circumstances; and

(*f*) a partner shall indemnify the firm for any loss caused to it by his wilful neglect in the conduct of the business of the firm.

2. **Section 16: Partnes' to Account for Personal Profits**

Subject to contract between the partners–

(a) if a partner derives any profit for himself from any transaction of the firm, or from the use of the property or business connection of the firm or the firm name, he shall account for that profit and pay it to the firm;

(*b*) if a partner carries on any business of the same nature as and competing with that of the firm, he shall account for and pay to the firm all profits made by him in that business.

TEST QUESTIONS

1. State the principles governing the mutual relations of partners. What are the duties of the partners towards one another?
2. In the absence of a contract to the contrary, how the mutual relations of partners are determined? Explain.
3. State the rights of partners towards one another.
4. What are the rights and liabilities of a partner under the Indian Partnership Act.
5. What is meant by partnership property? What things are included in it?
6. Write notes on (*a*) Partnership property. (*b*) Goodwill of business. (*c*) Partner's right to interest on advance and capital.

MULTIPLE CHOICE QUESTIONS

1. It is the duty of every partner to share in equal proportions the losses suffered by the firm.
   (*a*) True, as losses are always shared equally
   (*b*) False, as partners may agree to share losses in different proportions.
2. Which of the following is an absolute duty and cannot be excluded by an agreement to the contrary?
   (*a*) Duty to indemnify for loss caused by fraud.
   (*b*) Duty to indemnify for loss caused by negligence.
   (*c*) Duty to share losses equally.
   (*d*) Duty to account for profits of a competing business.
3. Which of the following is not the right of a partner, *i.e.*, which he cannot claim as a matter of right?
   (*a*) Right to take part in business. (*b*) Right to have access to account books.
   (*c*) Right to share profits. (*d*) Right to receive remuneration.
4. A partner who receives certain remuneration from the firm as per the express agreement, becomes an employee of the firm.
   (*a*) True (*b*) False.
5. Goodwill is the property of the firm, and like any other property it belongs proportionately to all the partners.
   (*a*) True (*b*) False.

ANSWERS

1. (*b*) 2. (*a*) 3. (*d*) 4. (*b*) 5. (*a*)

OBJECTIVE TYPE QUESTION WITH REASONING

State with reasons whether the following statements are correct on incorrect.

1. The partners are bound to be just and faithful to each other.
2. If a firm suffers some loss due to fraud of a partner, then the firm can recover the loss from that partner.
3. A partners duty to indemnify for the losses caused by his fraud can be excluded by an agreement between the partners.
4. A partner is under a duty to account for the personal profits earned from the use of the property of the firm and not the profits earned by using the firm's name.
5. A partner can transfer his share of profits to an outsider but not his rights and interest in the firm.
6. A partner has a right to examine the books and accounts of the firm, but he cannot have a copy of such accounts.
7. A partner, whether active or dormant, is entitled to have access to any of the books of the firm and take out a copy thereof.
8. A partner in a firm has a right to receive interest on advances given by him to the firm @12% per annum.
9. A partner in a firm has a right to receive interest on his contribution towards the capital @ 6% per annum.
10. All partners are not joint owners of the property of the firm unless otherwise provided in the agreement.

ANSWERS

1. ***Correct.*** This principle of good faith is the basis of partnership relationship [Section 9].
2. ***Correct.*** It is the duty of a partner to indemnify the firm for the loss caused by his fraud [Section 10].
3. ***Incorrect.*** It is an *absolute duty* of a partner and cannot be excluded by an agreement between the partners.
4. ***Incorrect .*** A partner is under a duty to account for both types of personal profits earned by him [Section 16(*a*)]
5. ***Correct.*** It is partners duty to maintain mutual trust and confidence, and not to transfer his rights and interest in the firm to an outside [Section 29].
6. ***Incorrect.*** A partners right to have access to the account books also includes the right to have a copy of the same [Section 12(*d*)]
7. ***Correct.*** It is the right of every partner [Section 12(*d*)]
8. ***Incorrect.*** A partner is entitled to receive intuest on advances @ 6% p.a. only [Section 13(*d*)]
9. ***Incorrect.*** A partner is not entitled to receive *any* interest on his contribution towards *capital* unless there is a specific agreement for the same [Section 13(*c*)].
10. ***Incorrect.*** All partners are jointly entitled to the partnership property.

PRACTICAL PROBLEM

1. *A*, *B*, and *C* were partners in a firm of sugar refiners. *A* was a wholesale grocer and had great skill in buying sugar at a right and proper time for the business. Accordingly the business of selecting and purchasing sugar was entrusted to *A*. According to his skill and knowledge, *A* bought sugar for himself at a time when he thought it likely to rise. The sugar rose in value and the firm was in want of same.

He sold his own sugar to the firm without letting the partners know that it was his sugar that was sold. Is he accountable to the firm for profit he makes? Give reasons.

Hints: Yes, *A* is accountable to the firm for personal profits made by him. In this case, *A*'s act was not for the common benefit of the firm. [Section 16 (*a*); *Bentley* v. *Craven* (1853) 18 Beav. 75]

2. *A* and *B* were partners in a firm carrying on the business of supplying meat to the government. Subsequently, it was found that *B* was also engaged with *C*, an outsider, for supplying the meat to the same government and earned personal profits. Can B retain for himself the personal profits so earned ? Give reasons.

Hints : No, *B* cannot retain personal profits made out of his arrangement with C. In this case, *B* earned personal profits by carrying on a business competing with that of the firm. [Section 16 (*b*); *Loch* v. *Lynam* (1854) 4 Ir. Ch. 188]

3. *A*, *B* and *C* are partners in a trade. *C* without the knowledge of *A* and *B*, obtains for his own benefit a lease of the house in which partnership business is carried on. Are *A* and *B* entitled to participate in the benefit of the lease?

Hints: Yes, *A* and *B* are entitled to participate in the benefit of the lease. *A* partner cannot make personal profits from any business transaction of the firm. [Section 16 (*a*)]

4. *A* and *B* were partners in a firm and their business was in dissolution. *B* was the managing partner and the conduct of dissolution was left to him. *A* advised *B* to dispose of certain bales of cotton immediately, but *B* said that these should be disposed of at the end of the dissolution. By that time, the prices came down and the goods realised much less than they could have realised otherwise. Can *B* be held liable for this loss suffered due to low prices ? Give reasons.

Hints: No, *B* cannot be held liable for this loss. In this case, the loss was not due to wilful 'neglect' of *B* as *B* had no reason to anticipate sudden fall in the prices. [*Cragg* v. *Ford* 1 y & C CC 280]

5. *A* and *B* were partners in a firm engaged in the business of importing electrical items from china and re-selling the same in India. *A* was authorised to make all purchases for the firm. While buying the goods for the firm, *A* also bough some quantity for himself and resold the same on his personal accounts. Is *A* liable to account for these personal profits? Give reasons.

Hints: Yes, *A* is liable to account for these personal profit. In this case, the opportunity to make personal profits came in *A*'s way while he was carrying on the business of the firm. [Section 16(*a*)]

6. *A* and *B* carry on partnership business as merchants trading between Bombay and London. *C*, a merchant in London, to whom they send their consignments, secretly allows *B* a share of the commission which he received upon such consignments in consideration of *B* using his influence to obtain consignments for him. Is *B* liable to account to the firm for the moneys so received by him ?

Hints: Yes, *B* is liable to the firm for the money so received by him.

7. *A* was the owner of a workshop building. He entered into partnership with *B* and *C* to carry on car repair and service business which was to be carried on at *A*'s workshop building. However, the value of the assets of workshop was credited to *A*'s capital account and he was also allowed interest on the same. Subsequently, the workshop was enlarged and improved by the firm and a new building was also constructed on the land acquired by the firm. Has *A*'s workshop become partnership property ? Give reasons.

Hints: Yes , *A*'s workshop has become partnership property. In this case, *A*'s personal property is used for firm's business and the circumstances suggest that it is so used with the intention of making it a partnership property. [See *Robinson* v. *Ashtan* (1875) 20 Eq. 25;44 LJC ch.542]

29

CHAPTER

RELATIONS OF PARTNERS WITH THIRD PARTIES

29.1. INTRODUCTION

The expression 'third party' means any person who is not a partner in the firm [Section 2(*d*)]. In the last chapter, we have discussed the mutual relations of partners, *i.e.*, the rights and duties of partners towards one another. It may be noted that the business of the firm is conducted by its partners and they deal with the third parties on behalf of the firm. And such dealings of a partner give rise to legal relationship which binds the firm and all its partners. In this Chapter, we shall discuss the relations of partners with third parties, *i.e.*, the liabilities of the firm and its partners towards third parties. It may, however, be noted that the partners are liable only for the acts of the firm.

29.2. PARTNERS'S LIABILITY FOR THE ACTS OF A FIRM

As a matter of fact, every partner is liable for the acts of the firm, which are done while he is a partner. This provision is contained in Section 25 of the Indian Partnership Act, which reads as under:

"Every partner is liable, jointly with all the other partners and also severally for all acts of the firm done while he is a partner."

Thus, each partner is liable, for the acts of the firm. And the liability of partners is joint and several. The term 'joint and several liability' means that a partner can be held liable individually, and also jointly with other partners. It may, however, be noted that the liability of a partner is only for the 'acts of the firm'. Moreover, he is liable for those acts only which are done while he is a partner in the firm. Thus, the term 'acts of the firm' is very important in connection with partner's liability towards third parties.

29.3. ACTS OF A FIRM

The term 'act of the firm' is defined in Section 2(*a*) of the Indian Partnership Act, which reads as under:

"An act of a firm means any act or omission by all the partners or by any partner or agent of the firm which gives rise to a right enforceable by or against the firm".

The analysis of this section reveals that, an act of the firm means an act of the partners or agents of the firm which gives rise to a right which can be enforced by and against the firm. However, only those acts of the partners are treated as the acts of the firm which are done by the partners in the usual course of business *i.e.*, within authority.

29.4. AUTHORITY OF A PARTNER

The authority of a partner means the capacity of a partner to bind the firm by his act. Every partner is both the principal and the agent. He is principal in the sense, that he is bound by the acts of the firm. And he is an agent in the sense, that the firm and other partners are bound by his acts. It may, however, be noted that a partner is an agent only for the business of firm [Section 18]. Thus, an act of a partner, done by him as an agent, in the usual course of business, is an act of the firm. In fact it is such act which is to be described as the authority of a partner, and the firm is bound by it. The authority of the partner may be express or implied. The *'express authority'* means the authority which is given to a partner by an agreement of all the partners. All acts of a partner within the scope of his express authority will bind the firm. However, it is not necessary that every power should be given to the partners by an agreement. A partner may also do certain acts without any express authority, and the firm is bound by all such acts. But, the firm is bound only if such acts are within the scope of his implied authority. The *'implied authority'* means the authority which is not given by an express agreement of the partners. The scope and concept of implied authority is contained in Section 19 of the Indian Partnership Act which is discussed in the following pages.

29.5. DOCTRINE OF IMPLIED AUTHORITY

The scope and concept of implied authority is contained in Section 19 of the Indian Partnership Act, which reads as under:

"Subject to the provisions of Section 22[1]*, the act of a partner which is done to carry on, in the usual way, business of the kind carried on by the firm, binds the firm. The authority of a partner to bind the firm conferred by this section is called his implied authority."*

The analysis of this section reveals that, the firm is bound by the acts of the partners, which are done in usual way, to carry on the business of the firm. And such authority to bind the firm is called the implied authority. However, the firm will be liable only if the following conditions are fulfilled:

(*a*) The act of a partner must be of such a nature which is common in the type of business carried on by the firm, *i.e.*, the act must relate to the normal business of the firm.

(*b*) The act must be done in the usual way.

(*c*) The act must be done in the name of the firm [Section 22]. If an act is done in personal name of a partner, then the firm cannot be held liable for such acts. In such cases, the partner will be personally liable to third parties.

---

1. Section 22 of the Indian Partnership Act provides that the firm is bound by partner's act only if it is done in the name of the firm.

Thus, the implied authority of a partner is linked with the nature of the business, and the usual manner of carrying it . Since the requirements of one business may be different from those of the others, therefore the nature of business and the practice, customs etc. of the businessmen engaged in that kind of business must be known before deciding the acts of a partner which can bind a firm. For this purpose, distinction should be made between 'trading business' and 'non-trading or professional business'. In case of trading business, the firm usually deals with the sale and purchase of goods, and an act of a partner to borrow money may be within his implied authority. But in case of 'non-trading or professional business' such an act of a partner may not be within his implied authority. [*Higgins* v. *Bean Camp* (1914-15) All ER 937]

It has been judicially established by the courts that in the partnership of a *general commercial nature,* the following acts fall within the implied authority of a partner:

(*a*) He may pledge or sell the partnership property.
(*b*) He may buy goods on account of partnership.
(*c*) He may borrow money, contract debts, and pay debts.
(*d*) He may make, draw or accept the negotiable instruments.

29.6. ACTS WITHIN THE IMPLIED AUTHORITY

We have discussed, in the last article, the scope and extent of the implied authority of a partner. From the discussion of the same, the following acts may be said to fall under the implied authority of a partner:

1. To engage a lawyer and defend the action brought against the firm.
2. To purchase goods of the kind that are used in the business of the firm,
3. To engage servants to perform the business of the firm,
4. To receive payment of the debts due to the firm and give receipts for the same,
5. To settle accounts with the persons dealing with the firm,
6. To sell the goods of the firm, and
7. In case of a trading firm (*a*) to borrow money for the purpose of the firm and pledge the goods of the firm as security for the repayment of same. (*b*) to make, draw, accept and endorse bills of exchange and other negotiable instruments in the name of the firm.

However, the nature of the business of a firm must be kept in view while determining whether or not a particular act is within the implied authority of a partner.

29.7. ACTS OUTSIDE THE IMPLIED AUTHORITY

1. *Statutory restrictions*
2. *Restrictions imposed by partnership deed*

Sometimes, certain restrictions are imposed on the implied authority of a partner. The implied authority of a partner is said to be restricted when a partner is prohibited from doing an act which would otherwise be within the scope of his implied authority. And such restricted acts fall outside the implied authority of a partner. These restrictions may be discussed under the following two sub-heads:

1. *Statutory restrictions.* The statutory restrictions are those which are imposed by the Indian Partnership Act itself. Section 19(2) of the Act provides that an implied authority of a partner does not empower him to do the following acts, namely:

(*a*) To submit a dispute, relating to the business of the firm, to arbitration.
(*b*) To open a banking account, on behalf of the firm, in his own name.
(*c*) To compromise or relinquish any claim or portion of claim by the firm.

(*d*) To withdraw a suit or proceedings filed on behalf or the firm.
(*e*) To admit any liability in a suit or proceedings against the firm.
(*f*) To acquire immovable property on behalf of the firm.
(*g*) To transfer immovable property on behalf of the firm.
(*h*) To enter into partnership on behalf of the firm.

However, the above restrictions are subject to any usage or custom of trades, *i.e.*, the authority to do any of the above acts may be established if it is shown that there is a usage or custom of trade which allows such acts. It may be noted that the firm will not be bound by these restricted acts of a partner whether or not the person dealing with the firm knew about the restrictions.

2. ***Restrictions imposed by partnership deed.*** The restrictions on the implied authority may also be imposed by a partnership deed (*i.e.*, an agreement between the partners). First para of Section 20 of the Indian Partnership Act, provides that, the implied authority of the partners may also be restricted by an agreement between them. However, the firm will be liable for such restricted acts, if the person dealing with the firm has no knowledge of such restrictions [Section 20, second para]

Note. The difference between the statutory restrictions and the restrictions imposed by partnership agreement is that in case of statutory restrictions the firm is not liable whether the person dealing with the firm has knowledge of restrictions or not. But in case of restrictions imposed by the partnership agreement, the firm is liable if the third party has no knowledge of the restrictions.

29.8. PARTNER'S AUTHORITY IN EMERGENCY

In an emergency, a partner can do certain acts even if he has no authority (express or implied) to do such acts. And the firm will be liable for such acts of the partner. However, the firm will be liable only if the following conditions are satisfied [Section 21]:

1. The act must be done in an emergency, *i.e.*, in a situation which requires such acts to be done.
2. The act must be done to protect the firm from the loss threatened by the emergency.
3. The act must be reasonable in the circumstances, *i.e.*, the partner must have taken such steps as would have been done by a person of ordinary prudence in his own case and under similar circumstances.

29.9. LIABILITY OF A FIRM AND ITS PARTNERS TO A THIRD PARTY

The liability of the firm and its partners to the third party may be discussed under the following heads.

1. Liability for wrongful acts of a partner [Section 26].
2. Liability for misapplication of money or property by a partner [Section 27].
3. Liability by holding out [Section 28].

29.10. LIABILITY FOR WRONGFUL ACTS OF A PARTNER

A firm is liable to third parties for all the wrongful acts of a partner. Where any third party dealing with the firm suffers a loss from the wrongful acts of any partner, the firm is liable for such loss. However, the firm will be liable only if the wrongful act is done either (*a*) in the ordinary course of business of the firm, or (*b*) with the authority of all other partners [section 26]. The term 'wrongful acts' includes fraud or negligence of the partners.

Example 29.1 *A* and *B* were partners in a firm. They were carrying on the business of buying and selling the wine. *C*, a wine merchant., employed the firm of *A* and *B* for buying and selling the wine for him on commission basis. *C* gave a sum of money to the firm, for this purpose. *A* the active partner of the firm, gave to C the false accounts of purchase and sale of wine and misappropriated the money. It was held that the firm was liable to pay the money to C.

[*Rapp* v. *Latham* 2 B & A 795; (1919) 21 RR 495].

29.11. LIABILITY FOR MISAPPLICATION OF MONEY OR PROPERTY BY A PARTNER

In the ordinary course of business of a firm, money or property belonging to third parties, is likely to be received by the firm or its partners. If a partner misapplies (*i.e.*, misappropriates) it to his own use, the firm is liable for the same. This provision is contained in Section 27 of the Indian Partnership Act which lays down the following two rules in this regard:

1. Where money or property is received by a partner and then misapplied by the *same partner*.
2. Where money or property is received by the firm and then misapplied by *any of the partners*.

In both these cases, the firm will be liable. It may be noted that in the first case, the money or property must have been received by a partner while acting under the apparent (or implied) authority. Moreover, it is also necessary that the money should have been misapplied by the same partner who has received it. In the second case, the money or property must have been received by the firm *in the course of its business*, and misapplied by any one of the partners.

Example 29.2. *A* and *B* were partners as solicitors. *C* a client of the firm, gave some money to *A* for investing in a *specific security*. *A* did not invest the money but misappropriated it to his own use. *C* filed a suit against the firm for the recovery of the money given to *A*. It was held that the firm was liable to make good the loss suffered by C as it was in the ordinary course of solicitors' business to receive money. [*Blair* v *Bromley* (1847) 2 Ph 354].

Example 29.3. *A*, *B* and *C* were partners in a firm of bankers. *D*, a customer of the firm, deposited his ornaments with the firm for safe custody. *A* and *B* sold these ornaments and misappropriated the money. *C*, being a sleeping partner, did not know anything about this act of *A* and *B*. *D* filed a suit against the firm including all the three partners. It was held that all the three partners were liable for full value of the ornaments. [*Devaynes* v. *Noble* (1816) 1 Mer 579]

But where the act of a partner is not within the ordinary course of business of the firm, then the firm cannot be held-liable for misappropriation by the partner. Similarly, the firm is also not liable where a third party deals only with one partner and not with the firm.

Note. Both the Sections 26 and 27 of the Indian Partnership Act, discussed above, provide for the liability of the firm for the wrongful act of its partners. However, the point of distinction is that Section 26 lays down the *general rule* regarding the liability of the firm for the wrongful acts of a partner. On the other hand, Section 27 deals with one particular wrong, *i.e.*, misapplication by a partner of money or property of the third party.

29.12. LIABILITY BY HOLDING OUT

Sometimes, a person is not a partner in the firm, but he knowingly permits himself to be represented as a partner. In such cases, he is held liable as if he was a partner in the firm. And such a person is known as a partner by holding out or by estoppel.

Example 29.4. *A* introduced *B* to *C* as his partner. And *B* remained silent. In fact *A* and *B* were not partners In this case, *B* becomes a partner by holding out. And he can be held liable to the third parties for the acts of the firm. [*Martyn* v. *Gray* (1863) 14 CB (NS) 824[.

However, a person can be held liable as a partner by holding out only if all the following conditions, as contained in Section 28(1), are satisfied:

1. There must be a representation by a person that he is a partner in the firm, *i.e.*, a person to be held liable must represent himself to be a partner of the firm. The representation may be express (*i.e.*, by words spoken or written) or implied (*i.e., by* conduct).
2. The third party who wants to hold another person liable by holding out must have the knowledge of the representation made by that person, and
3. The third party who want to hold another person liable by holding out must have acted on the faith of such representation and given credit to the firm, *i.e.*, the third party must have given credit to the firm on the faith of such representation. And it is immaterial whether the person representing himself to be a partner does or does not know that the representation has reached the third party giving credit to the firm.

Example 29.5 *A* was carrying on his business under the name of *'A. B* & Co.,'. In fact, *B* was a manager in *A*'s business, and not his partner. *C*, a trader, believing *B* to be the partner in the business, supplied certain goods to the firm on credit. But *A* failed to pay the price of the goods. *C* filed a suit against both *A* and *B* for the recovery of the price of the goods. It was held that *B* was also liable for the price. In this case, by permitting his name to be used in the title of the firm, *B* had made a representation that he was a partner in the firm. And thus, he was liable to those who gave credit to the firm on the faith of that he was a partner in the firm.

[*Bevan* v. *National Bank Ltd*. (1906) 27 TLR 65]

It may be noted that only that person (*i.e.*, third party) can enforce liability under this section to whom the representation has been made, and who has acted on it and given credit to the firm. In other words, a person representing himself to be a partner is liable only to the person who had acted on the faith of the representation.

Note. An important application of the principle of holding out takes place when a partner retires from the firm and public notice of his retirement is *not* given. In such cases, the retiring partner remains liable by holding out to those customers of the firm who give credit to the firm without the knowledge of his retirement. But if a public notice of partner's retirement is given, then he cannot be held liable by holding out.

29.13. EXCEPTIONS TO HOLDING OUT

1. *Sleeping partner*
2. *Deceased partner*
3. *Insolvent partner*

In the following cases, the principle of holding out does not apply, and a partner or his estate cannot be held liable to third parties:

1. *Sleeping partner.* A sleeping or dormant partner is liable so long as he remains a partner in the firm. But when he retires from the firm, then he cannot be held liable by holding out. And a public notice of his retirement is not necessary. The reason for the same is that his existence in the firm is not known ti the outsiders. However, if his existence in the firm was known to some customers, then a public notice of his retirement must be given at least to those customers.[2]

2. *Deceased partner.* Sometimes, a partner dies but the remaining partners continue the business of the firm. In such cases, the estate or legal representatives of a deceased partner cannot be held liable for any act of the firm done *after* his death. It does not matter that the business of the firm is continued by the surviving partners in the same style and place, and even if the name of the deceased partner appears in the name and affairs of the firm [Section 28(2)]. It may be noted that a public notice of partner's death is not necessary. As a matter of fact, the death is a notice by itself.

2. See Lindley on Partnership 93 (12th edn. By Scamell, 1962)

3. ***Insolvent partner.*** Sometimes, a partner becomes insolvent but the remaining partners continue the business of the firm. In such cases, the insolvent partner or his estate cannot be held to be liable for any act of the firm done *after* his insolvency. As a matter of fact, the insolvency of a partner terminates his liability from the date he is declared as an insolvent. It may be noted that a public notice of partner's insolvency is not required to terminate his liability [Section 45, second para].

29.14. POSITION OF A MINOR IN A FIRM

A minor cannot become a partner in a firm. However, a minor may be admitted to the benefits of an existing firm. This provision is contained in Section 30(1) of the Indian Partnership Act, which reads as under:

"A person who is a minor according to the law to which he is subject may not be a partner in a firm, but with the consent of all the partners for the time being, he may be admitted to the benefits of partnership."

The analysis of this section reveals that, a minor cannot be a full-fledged partner in a firm. He can only be admitted to the benefits of an existing firm, *i.e.*, he can share only the profits of the firm but will not be personally liable as a partner. A minor can be so admitted to the benefits of a firm only with the consent of all the partners of the firm. It may be noted that a partnership between two or more persons must be in existence before a minor can be admitted to the benefits of the firm. There cannot be a partnership consisting of all the minors, or of one major and all other minors:[3] The only concession in favour of a minor is that he can be admitted to the benefits of an *existing* firm. It must be noted that he cannot be a full-fledged partner even in an existing firm[4]. A partnership deed that attempts to make a minor a full-fledged partner, is void to that extent[5].

29.15. RIGHTS AND LIABILITIES OF A MINOR IN A FIRM

The rights and liabilities of a minor, admitted to the benefits of a firm, may be discussed under the following two heads:

1. Position of a Minor before Attaining the Age of Majority.
2. Position of a Minor on Attaining the Age of Majority.

29.16. POSITION OF A MINOR BEFORE ATTAINING THE AGE OF MAJORITY

Before attaining the age of majority, the right and liabilities of a minor, admitted to the benefits of a firm, may be summed up as under:

1. A minor has the right to receive the agreed share of property and of profits of the firm [Section 30(2)].
2. A minor has the right to access and to inspect the accounts of the firm. He may also have the copy of the accounts of the firm [Section 30(2)]. It may be noted that he has the right to access to the *accounts only*, and not to all the books of the firm.
3. A minor has a right to file a suit for his share of property or profits of the firm. However, he can file a suit only after leaving the firm [Section 30(4)].
4. A minor is not personally liable for any act of the firm. Only his share of property or profits is liable [Section 30(3)].

---

3. *Shivaram* v. *Gaurishankar* AIR 1961 Bombay 136.
4. *Commissioner of Income Tax* v. *Dawarkadas Khetan & Co.* AIR 1961. Supreme Court 680.
5. *Commissioner of Income Tax* v. *Shah Mohandas,* AIR 1966 Supreme Court 15.

29.17. POSITION OF A MINOR ON ATTAINNING THE AGE OF MAJORITY

1. *Rights and liabilities where he becomes a partner*
2. *Rights and liabilities where he does not become a partner*

On attaining the age of majority, the minor admitted to the benefits of a firm has to decide within six months whether he shall remain in the firm or leave it. This period of six months starts from the date on which he has attained the age of majority (*i.e.*, when he became a major), or from the date when he first comes to know that he has been admitted into the benefits of the firm, whichever is later . It may be noted that within this period of six months, he should give a public notice in respect of either of the following:

1. That he has decided to become a partner.
2. That he has decided not to become a partner.

If he fails to give such a notice, then he automatically becomes a partner on the expiry of said period of six months [Section 30(5)]. On attaining the age of majority, the rights and liabilities of a minor who was admitted to the benefits of the firm may be discussed under the following two sub-heads:

1. *Rights and liabilities where he becomes a partner.* When such a minor, on attaining the age of majority, becomes a partner in the firm, then

(*a*) His rights and liabilities will be similar to those of a full-fledged partner.

(*b*) He will be personally liable for all the acts or the firm from the date he was admitted, even as a minor, to the benefits of the firm.

(*c*) His share in the property and profits remains the same as was before becoming a partner.

2. *Rights and liabilities where he does not become a partner.* When such a minor, on attaining the age of majority, does not become a partner in the firm, then

(*a*) His rights and liabilities shall continue to be those of a minor upto the date of public notice.

(*b*) His share shall not be liable for any acts of the firm done after the date of public notice.

(*c*) He shall be entitled to sue the partners for his share of property and profits.

Note. A public notice is given by notice to the Registrar of Firms under Section 63 of the Indian Partnership Act, and by publication in the Official Gazette and in at least one vernacular newspaper circulating in the district where the firm to which it relates has its place or principal place of business [Section 72(*a*)].

LEGAL PROVISIONS (SECTIONS) DISCUSSED IN THE CHAPTER

Important legal provisions (sections) of the Indian Partership Act, 1932, discussed in this chapter, are repreduced hereunder for ready reference:

1. ***Section 2(a): Act of firm***

An act of the firm means any act or omision by all the partner or by any partner or agent of the firm which gives rise to right enforceable by or against the firm.

2. ***Section 18: Partner to be agent of the firm***

Subject to the provisions of this Act, a partner is the agent of the firm for the purpose of the business of the firm.

3. ***Sectins 19: Implied authority of partner as agnet of the firm***

(1) Subject ot the provisions of sections 22, the act of a partner which is done to carry on, in the usual way, business of the kind carried on by the firm, binds the firm. The authority of a partner to bind the firm conferred by this section is called "implied authority".

(2) In the absence of any usage or custom of trade to the contrary, the plied authority of a partner does not empower him to -
  (*a*) submit a dispute relating to the business of the firm to arbitration,
  (*b*) open a banking account on behalf of the firm in his own name,
  (*c*) compromise or relinquish any claim or portion of a claim by the firm,
  (*d*) withdraw a suit or proceeding filed on behalf of the firm,
  (*e*) admit any liability in a suit or proceeding against the firm,
  (*f*) acquire immovable property on behalf of the firm,
  (*g*) transfer immovable property belonging to the firm, or
  (*h*) enter into partnership on behalf of the firm.

4. ***Section 20: Extensions and restrication of partner's implied authority***

The partners in a firm may, by contract between the partners, extend or restrict the implied authority of any partner.

Notwithstanding any such restriction, any act done by a partner on behalf of the firm which falls within his implied authority binds the firm, unless the person with whom he is dealing knows of the restriction or does not know or believe that partner to be a partner.

5. ***Section 21: Partner's authority in an emergency***

A partner has authority, in an emergency, to do all such acts for the purpose of protecting the firm from loss as would be done by a person of ordinary prudence, in his own case, acting under similar circumstances, and such acts bind the firm.

6. ***Section 22: Mode of doing act to bind firm***

In order to bind a firm, an act or instrument done or executed by a partner or other person on behalf of the firm shall be done or executed in the firm name, or in any other manner expressing or implying an intention to bind the firm.

7. ***Section 26: Libility of the firm for wrongful acts of partner***

Where, by the wrongful act or omission of a partner acting in the ordinary course of the businsess of a firm, or with the authority of his partners, loss or injury is cuased to any third aprty, or any penalty is incurred, the firm is liable therefor to the same extent as the partner.

8. ***Section 27: Libility of firm for misapplication by partners***

Where—

(*a*) a partner acting within his apparent authority receives money or property from a third party and mispaplies it, or

(*b*) a firm in the course of its business receives money or property from a third party, and the money or property is misapplied by any of the partners while it is in the custody of the firm, the firm is liable to make good the loss.

9. ***Section 28: Holding out.***

(1) Any one who by words spoken or written or by conduct represents himself, or knowingly permits himself to be represented, to be a partner in a firm, is liables as a partner in that firm to any one who has on the fiath of any such representation given credit to the firm, whether the person representing himself or represented to be a partner does or does not know that the representation has reached the person so giving credit.

(2) Where after a partner's dath, the business is continued in the old firm name, the contined use of that name or of the deceased partner's name as part thereof shall not of itself make his legal representative or his estate liable for any act of the firm done after his death.

TEST QUESTIONS

1. Discuss the doctrine of implied authority of a partner. State the acts which are within the implied authority of a partner, and also the acts which are outside his implied authority.
2. What is implied authority of a partner, and what is its scope?
3. What do you understand by implied authority of a partner? What are the limitations on the exercise of such authority?
4. What are the statutory restrictions on the implied authority of a partner? Will third party be affected by restrictions placed on the implied authority of a partner? Explain.
5. What is an act of the firm? Is a partnership firm liable for fraud or negligence committed by its partner?

6. When can a person, even though he is not a partner, be made liable as a partner?
7. "A minor cannot be a partner but share the benefit of a partnership" —critically examine.
8. What are the rights and liabilities of a minor participating in a partnership firm?
9. Explain Partner's liability by holding out. What are the exceptions to the principle of holding out?
10. Write notes on the following:
    (*a*) Implied authority of a partner (*b*) Partnership by holding out.

MULTIPLE CHOICE QUESTIONS

1. Which of the following acts are not included in the implied authority of a partner?
   (*a*) To buy or sell goods on account of partnership
   (*b*) To borrow money for the purposes of the firm.
   (*c*) To enter into partnership on behalf of the firm.
   (*d*) To engage a lawyer to defend action against the firm.
2. A person, even if he is not a partner in the firm, may be held liable as partner if he knowingly permits himself to be represented as a partner.
   (*a*) True, as the principle of holding out applies in such a case.
   (*b*) False, as a person can become a partner only by agreement not otherwise.
3. After retirement from firm, which of the following partners is not liable by holding out, even if the public notice of retirement is not given?
   (*a*) Active partner (*b*) Sleeping partner
   (*c*) Representatives of deceased partner (*d*) both (*b*) and (*c*).
4. Which of the following statements is not true about minor's position as a partner?
   (*a*) He cannot become a full-fledged partner in a new firm.
   (*b*) He can become a full-fledged partner in an existing firm.
   (*c*) He can be admitted only to the benefits of any existing firm.
   (*d*) He can become partner on becoming a major.
5. A valid partnership can be formed with one major partner and other minors admitted only to the benefits of the firm.
   (*a*) True (*b*) False.

ANSWERS

1. (*c*)	2. (*a*)	3. (*d*)	4. (*b*)	5. (*b*)

OBJECTIVE TYPE QUESTIONS WITH REASONING

State with reasons whether the following statements are correct or incorrect.

1. An 'act of a firm' means an act of a partner which gives rise to a right enforceable by or against the firm.
2. The firm is bound by the acts of a partner only if the partner has the express authority to do the acts.
3. In case of a non-trading or professional firm, a partner has an implied authority to borrow money on behalf of the firm.
4. A partner has implied authority to engage a lawyer and defend the action brought against the firm.
5. The implied authority of a partner empowers him to transfer immovable property on behalf of the firm.
6. The implied authority of a partner empowers him to acquire immovable property on behalf of the firm.

7. The implied authority of a partner does not include entering into partnership on behalf of the firm.
8. The implied authority of a partner does not empower him to open a bank account, on behalf of the firm, in his own name.
9. *A* and *B* are not partners but *A* introduces *B* to *C* as his partner and *B* remains silent. In this case *B* becomes liable to third parties for the acts of the firm.
10. A minor admitted to the benefits of a firm can become a partner before majority by giving a public notice.
11. On attaining majority , if the minor partner fails to give the public notice of decision whether or not to become a partner, then he automatically becomes a partner on the expiry of six months.

ANSWERS

1. ***Correct.*** As the firm acts through its partner only [Section 2(*a*)].
2. ***Incorrect.*** The firm is also bound by the acts of a partner which are done by him within the scope of his implied authority.
3. ***Incorrect.*** Such a firm does not deal with the sale and purchase of goods, there is no presumption of implied authority to borrow money.
4. ***Correct.*** It is usual for a partner to engage a lawyer to protect the interest of the firm.
5. ***Incorrect.*** This power of a partner has been expressly excluded from implied authority by Section 19(2) of the Partnership Act.
6. ***Incorrect.*** Reasons as in point 5 above.
7. ***Correct.*** Reasons as in point 5 above.
8. ***Correct.*** Reasons as in point 5 above.
9. ***Correct.*** In this case, *B* becomes a partner by holding out who can be held liable as if he was a partner in the firm.
10. ***Incorrect.*** He can become a full-fledged partner only on attaining majority, not before.
11. ***Correct.*** It is the legal position on this point [Section 30(5)].

PRACTICAL PROBLEMS

1. *A* and *B* were carrying on a business of cinematographic theatre proprietors in partnership. The partnership deed provided that money can be borrowed by a partner only with the consent of the other partner or in the usual course of business. *A* borrowed a certain sum of money from *C*, a money-lender, without the consent of *B* and misappropriated the same to his own use. Can *B* also be held liable to repay the money borromed by *A*, the other partner? Give reasons.

   Hints: No, *B* cannot be held liable to repay the money borrowed by *A*. In this case, there was no implied authority to borrow money as the firm was a non-trading concern.

   [Section 19, 22; *Higgins* v. *Bean Camp* (1914-15) All ER 937]
2. *A* a partner in a firm of architects, borrowed Rs. 50,000 on behalf of the firm from *B*. *B* knew that *A* had no express authority from the partners to borrow any money but he lent the money on an assurance from *A* that the money would be applied for the payment of a debt of the firm. The money borrowed from *B* was, in fact, so applied, Can *B* recover the amount from the firm ? Give reasons.

   Hints: No, *B* cannot recover money from the firm. In case of non-trading firms, a partner has no impled authority to borrow money on behalf of the firm. [Section 19 and 22]
3. *A*, *B* and *C* are member of a banking firm. *D* who owes the firm Rs 20,000 pays it to *A*. *A*, without informing *B* and *C* about the payment by *D*, misappropriates the amount. Is *D* discharged of his debt to the firm by the payment he made to *A* ? Give reasons.

   Hints: Yes, *D* is discharged from his lability by making payments to *A*, one of the partners. In this case, the firm is a banking firm, and the money is received by a partner in the usual course of banking business of the firm. [Section 19]
4. *A*, *B* and *C* run a partnership business as paper merchants. *A* orders on credit a carton of cold drink

bottles to be delivered at his house for the use of the family. The order is made out on the firm's note paper and in the name of the firm.

(*a*) Is the firm liable for the price of the cartons supplied ?

(*b*) Would your decision be different if *A* had ordered the bottles to be delivered at the firm's business to be used at a party arranged in honour of an important customer visiting the firm ?

Hints: (*a*) No, the firm is not liable for the price of cartons supplied.

(*b*) Yes, in that case the firm may be held liable. [Section 19 and 22]

5. *A* and *B* were partners in a firm carrying on the business of garges and repairing of cars. The partnership agreement provided that the partners shall not buy or sell the cars on behalf of the firm. *A* sold a second hand car to which the firm had no title because the car was for repair job. On coming to know that the firm had no title to sell the car, the buyer claimed the amount from the firm including, the other partner. Can *B* be held liable for this amount ? Give reasons.

Hints: Yes, *B*, being a partner can also be held liable to the buyer. In this case, the buyer didn't know anything about the restrictions. Otherwise also, *A*'s act was with in the scope of implied authority because the garage owners usually sell second hand cars.

[*Mercantile Credit* co.v. *Garrod* (1969) All ER 1103]

6. *A & Co.* and *B & Co.* were two separate firms carrying on competing business. *A*, a partner of *A & Co* bribed a clerk of *B & Co.* and induced him to give secret information about the price and customers of *B & Co.* Due to supply of this information, *B & Co.* suffered a loss in the business which brought an action against *A & Co.* for the recovery of loss sufferes by them. Can *A & Co.* be so held lible for this loss? Give reasons.

Hints: Yes, *A & Co.* is liable for this loss. In this case, *A*'s act was done within implied authority, and the secret information was obtain by *A* by wrongful acts *i.e.* by giving bribe to the clerk of competitor.

[Section 26; *Hamilyn* v. *John Houston & Co.* (1902) 87 LT 500: (1903)1KB 81]

7. *A* and *B* were carrying on a trading business in partnership dealing in sale purchase of goods. *A* was a sleeping partner and had financed the business, and *B* was an active partner dealing in the sale purchase of goods. *B* purchased certain goods, which he knew that the goods were stolen one, and further sold them in the ordinary course of firms business. The true owner of the goods, claimed the goods from the firm. *A* wanted to avoid liability on the ground of misconduct by the other partner (*B*). Can *A* avoid the lability ? Give reasons.

Hints: No, *A* cannot avoid liability. In this case, the firm is liable to the true owner for the wrongful act of its partner. [Section 26; *Harruk Chand* v. *Govind Lal*, (1901) 10 Cal. W. No 1053]

8. *A*, *B* and *C* were partners in a firm carrying on banking business. *D*, a customer of the firm, deposited a box, containing securities, with the firm for safe custody. Afterwards, *D* authorised *A* only to take out some securities and to replace them with some other. While replacing securities, *A* misappropriated some of them. Can the firm be held liable for misappropriation of securities by *A* ? Give reasons.

Hints: No, the firm cannot be held liable. In this case, *D* elected to deal only with a particular partner and not with the firm. Moreover, the act of replacing the securities cannot be said to be in the ordinary course of a banking firm. [Exp.Eyre (1842) 2 CI & F 250]

9. *A* and *B* are partners. *A* with the intention of cheating *B*, goes to a shop and purchases such articles on behalf of the firm as might be used in the ordinary course of the partnership business, but converts them to his own separate use, there being no collusion between him and the seller, Is the firm liable for the price of goods?

Hints: Yes, the firm is liable. The firm is liable for the acts of a partner which are done in the ordinary course of business. [Section 19,22]

10. *A* and *B* are solicitors in partnership. *C*, a client of the firm, hands a sum of money to *A* to be invested in a specific security. *A* never invests it but applies it to his own use. *B* receives no part of the money and knows nothing of the transaction. Is *B* liable to make good the loss ?

Hints: Yes, *B* is liable. In fact the firm is liable for misapplication of money by any of its partners.

[Section 27; *Blair* v. *Bromley* (1847) 2 Ph. 354]

11. *A*, a money lender, gave a loan to *B* for establishing a cattle farm. *A* took very deep interest in the business and used his personal influence for obtaining the lease of the premises for the farm. Moreover, he also used to be present in the farm and was receiving parties and their demands. *C* supplied some building materials to the farm under the impression that *A* was also a partner. Can *A* be held liable as a partner for the materials supplied by *C* ? Give reasons.

Hints: Yes, *A* can be held liable to C as a partner. In this case, *A* is liable by the principle of 'holding out' as he had, by his conduct represented himself to be a partner of the firm. [Section 28(1)]

12. *A* and *B* are partners of a firm. After sometime, *C* a minor son of *B*, is admitted to the benefits of the partnership. Soon after the admission of *C*, *B* dies and the business of the firm is carried on by *A*. During this period, *A* speculates and suffers heavy losses. The creditors of the firm demand the losses from *A* and *C* on the ground that **C** is also liable up to his capital investment in the firm. Advise *C*.

Hints: *C* is not liable. In this case, on the death of *B*, the partnership between *A* and *B* comes to an end and there can be no partnership between *A* and *C* as *C* is minor. The losses arise after the end of partnership, as such *C* incurs no liability for the losses after *B*'s death.

30

CHAPTER

RECONSTITUTION OF FIRMS

1. Introduction.
2. Admission of a Partner.
3. Liability of an Incoming Partner.
4. Retirement of a Partner.
5. Liability of a Retiring Partner.
6. Rights of a Retiring Partner.
7. Expulsion of a Partner.
8. Liabilities and Rights of an Expelled Partner.
9. Insolvency of a Partner.
10. Death of a Partner.
11. Transfer of Partner's Interest.
12. Rights and Duties of Partners After Change in the Constitution of a Firm.

30.1. INTRODUCTION

The term 'reconstitution of a firm' may be defined as a change in the constitution (*i.e.*, composition) of the firm. The constitution of the firm may change by any one of the following events:

1. Admission of a partner [Section 31].
2. Retirement of a partner [Section 32].
3. Expulsion of a partner [Section 33].
4. Insolvency of a partner [Section 34].
5. Death of a partner [Section 35].

The firm, which is constituted after the occurrence of any one of these events, is called a reconstituted firm.

Note. The expulsion, insolvency or death of a partner is a sort of retirement. Because in all these cases, a partner is no more a partner in the firm.

30.2. ADMISSION OF A PARTNER

A new partner can be admitted in an existing firm only with the consent of *all* the partners. A newly admitted partner is known as 'incoming partner'. The provision relating to the admission of a partner is contained in Section 31(1) of the Indian Partnership Act, which reads as under:

"Subject to contract between the partners and to the provision of Section 30,[1] *no person shall be introduced as a partner into a firm without the consent of all the existing partners."*

The analysis of this section reveals that, a new partner can be admitted into an existing firm in any of the following ways:

1. With the consent of all the partners, or
2. In accordance with a contract already entered into between the partners for the admission of a new partner.

Thus, a new partner can be admitted into an existing firm either with the consent of all the partners or as per a clause in the partnership deed, regarding admission of a person.

1. Section 30 relates to the minor as a partner in the firm. This has already been discussed in previous chapter

Example 30.1. A partnership agreement between *A* and *B* contained a clause that *A* would have the right to bring his son *C* into partnership on attaining the age of 21 years. When *C* attained the age of 21 years, *B* refused to accept him as a partner. It was held that *B* could not do so, as the partnership agreement operated as a contract according to which new partner was admitted.

[*Byrne* v. *Reid* (1902) 2 Ch 735].

It may be noted that a partnership agreement may empower certain partners to nominate a new partner. But where such nominated partner is *not acceptable to other partners*, they cannot be forced to enter into partnership with him.

[*Satyanarayanamurthi v. Gopalan*, AIR 1939 Mad 891]

30.3. LIABILITY OF AN INCOMING PARTNER

The liability of an incoming partner may be discussed under the following two heads:

1. *Liability for the acts of the firm done before admission.* An incoming partner is not liable for the acts of the firm done before his admission into the firm [Section 31(2)]. Thus, he is not liable for the past debts of the firm.

However, by an agreement with the old partners, an incoming partner may also agree to be liable for the past debts of the firm. But such an agreement is binding only between the partners. This does not give the right to any creditor to sue an incoming partner for the past debts of the firm. However, an incoming partner is liable to the creditors for the past debts if the following two conditions are satisfied:

(*a*) The reconstituted firm has assumed the liability for past debts of the old firm, and

(*b*) The creditors have been informed of this new arrangement, and they have accepted the constituted firm as their debtor and discharged the old firm of its liability.

2. *Liability for the acts of the firm done after admission.* As a matter of fact, the liability of an incoming partner starts from the date of his admission into the firm. Thus, he is liable for all the acts of the firm done *after* he became a partner in the firm.

30.4. RETIREMENT OF A PARTNER

1. *By consent*
2. *By agreement*
3. *By notice*

A partner may retire from an existing firm. The partner who retires from an existing firm is known as a 'retiring partner' or an 'outgoing partner'. The provision relating to the retirement of a partner is contained in Section 32(1) of the Indian Partnership Act, which reads as under:

"A partner may retire—

(*a*) *with the consent of all other partners.*

(*b*) *in accordance with an express agreement by the partners, or*

(*c*) *where the partnership is at will, by giving notice in writing to all the other partners of his intention to retire."*

The analysis of this section reveals that, a partner may retire from the firm in any one of the following three modes:

1. *By consent:* A partner may retire, at any time with the consent of all other partners.

2. *By agreement* : The partners may enter into an express agreement about the retirement of a partner. In such cases, a partner may retire according to the terms of the agreement.

In *Vishnu Chandra v. Chandrika Pd. Agarwal*, AIR 1983 SC 523, the Supreme Court has held that an agreement, which permitted a partner to retire by one month's notice, was valid.

3. *By notice* : In case of partnership at will a partner may retire from the firm by giving in writing, a notice of his retirement to all the other partners. It may be noted that a partner can retire by notice only when the firm is 'at will' and not in case of a firm in which the duration is fixed or otherwise certain.

Note. In a two-member firm, there is no question of retirement either by agreement or by notice, the dissolution being inevitable in such a case. [*Srikishan Gupta* v. *R.B. Gupta*, AIR 1990 Allahabad 171].

30.5. LIABILITY OF A RETIRING PARTNER

The liability of a retiring partner may be discussed under the following two heads:

1. *Liability for the acts of the firm done before retirement.* A retiring partner continues to be liable to third parties for the acts of the firm done before his retirement. Moreover, he will also be liable for all transactions of the firm begun but unfinished at the time of his retirement. Thus, a retiring partner remains liable for all the acts of the firm done upto the date of his retirement.

However, a retiring partner may be discharged from his liability by means of an agreement between himself, the partners of the reconstituted firm (*i.e.*, remaining partners), and the third party [Section 32 (2)]. Such an agreement is called '*novation*'. The novation which discharges a retiring partner from liability requires the following two things:

(*a*) The remaining partners must have agreed with the retiring partner to release him from the existing debts and liabilities, and

(*b*) The creditors must be informed of the retirement and they must have accepted the reconstituted firm as their debtor.

Such an agreement may be express or implied. An implied agreement arises when a creditor continues to deal with the reconstituted firm after he has knowledge of retirement.

Example 30.2 *A*, *B* and *C* were partners in a firm. *D* was the creditor of the firm. After some time, *A* retired from the firm. But *B* and *C* carried on the business of the firm even after *A*'s retirement. *D* agreed with *A* and with the reconstituted firm of *B* and *C* that he will treat the reconstituted firm as his debtor. In this case, *A* is discharged from his liability to *D*.

2. *Liability for the acts of the firm done after retirement.* A retireing partner also continues to be liable to third parties for the acts of the firm done even after his retirement unitil a public notice of his retirement is given [Section 32 (3)]. This liability of a retiring partner is based on the principle of 'holding out'. However, a retiring partner will not be liable for the acts of the firm done after his retirement if a public notice of his retirement is given. The notice of retirement may be given either by the retiring partner or by any partners of the reconstituted firm [Section 32 (4)]. It may be noted that if a dormant (*i.e.* sleeping) partner retires from the firm, he will not be liable for the acts of the firm done after his retirement even if a public notice of his retirement is not given. The reason for the same is that such a partner is not known to the outsiders.

However, a retiring partner is not liable to any third party who deals with the firm without knowing that he was a partner, even if a public notice of his retirement is not given [Section 32(3), proviso]. As a matter of fact, a retiring partner is liable to those persons who deal with the firm under the assumption that he is still a partner.

30.6. RIGHTS OF A RETIRING PARTNER

1. ***Right to carry on competing business***
2. ***Right to share subsequent profits***

The rights of a retiring partner may be discussed under the following heads.

1. *Right to carry on competing business* : A retiring partner has the right to carry on *i.e.*, start any business after his retirement. He may even start a new business which is competing with that of the firm. Moreover, he may start such a business even next door to the reconstituted firm, and may also advertise for such business [Section 36(1)]. As a matter of fact, such a right is necessary to assure the freedom of trade to every individual. However, to safeguard the interest of the firm, the Indian Partnership Act imposes the following restrictions on this right of a retiring partner [Section 36 second para]:

(*a*) He cannot use the name of the firm.

(*b*) He cannot represent himself that he is carrying on the business of the firm.

(*c*) He cannot solicit the existing customers who were dealing with firm before he ceased to be a partner. In other words, he cannot break away the customers of the firm to his own benefit.

Sometimes, the partners of the reconstituted firm think that the above restrictions are not sufficient to protect the interest of the firm. In such cases, they may impose further restrictions and restrain the retiring partner from carrying on a similar business. However, the restriction on retiring partner's right to carry on a similar business should not be absolute. Such a restriction will be valid only if it satisfied the following conditions [Section 36(2)] :

(*a*) The restriction must specify the period or the local limit of restraint, and

(*b*) The restriction must be reasonable.

2. *Right to share subsequent profits:* On the retirement of a partner, it is the duty of remaining partners to settle the accounts with him *i.e.*, the remaining partners should pay to the retiring partner his share of property and profits in the firm. But sometimes, the remaining partners do not pay such share of the retiring partner but use the same in the firm business. In such cases, in the absence of a contract to the contrary, the retiring partner can exercise either of the following rights [Section 37]:

(*a*) He may receive interest at the rate of 6% per annum on the amount of his share in the property of the firm.

(*b*) He may demand such share of profits as may be attributable to the use of his share of property of the firm.

30.7. EXPULSION OF A PARTNER

Ordinarily a partner cannot be expelled from the firm. However, in certain exceptional cases, he can be expelled by following a prescribed procedure. The provision relating to the expulsion of a partner is contained in Section 33(1) of the Indian Partnership Act, which reads as under:

"A partner may not be expelled from a firm by any majority of the partners, save in the exercise in good faith of powers conferred by a contract between the partners."

The analysis of this section reveals that, generally a partner cannot be expelled from the firm. He can be expelled only if the following conditions are satisfied:

(*a*) The power of expulsion should be given to the partners by an *express contract* between them.

(*b*) The power of expulsion should be exercised by *majority of partners*.

(*c*) The power of expulsion should be exercised in absolute *good faith*.

All the above conditions must be satisfied before a partner is expelled from the firm. If these conditions are not satisfied, then the expulsion of a partner is not proper, and is without any legal effect.

Example 30.3. *A* was a partner in a firm of drapers. The partnership agreement authorised the expulsion of a partner when he was guilty of flagrant breach of duty. *A* was convicted of travelling without ticket. On this ground, he was expelled by the majority giving him a notice of expulsion. The expulsion was held to be justified. Doing an act which brings a partner within the penalties of criminal law is a flagrant breach of duty. [*Carmichael* v. *Evans*, (1904) 90 LT 573]

The power of expulsion can be exercised only by a majority, and not by a single partner. Thus, in a firm of three partners where two are guilty of misconduct, the third cannot be allowed to expel others as it would amount expulsion by a minority. In such a case, the better choice is the dissolution of firm.

30.8. LIABILITIES AND RIGHTS OF AN EXPELLED PARTNER

The liabilities and right of an expelled partner are the same as those of a retiring partner. The liabilities and rights of a retiring partner have already been discussed in Arts 30.5 and 30.6.

It may, however, be that in cases of improper or wrongful expulsion, the expelled partner does not cease to be a partner of the firm. But he is entitled to be reinstated in his position. However, he cannot recover damages for wrongful expulsion.

30.9. INSOLVENCY OF A PARTNER

Sometimes, one of the partners of a firm is declared as an insolvent by the court. In such cases, he ceases to be a partner from the date of the order of insolvency. He ceases to be a partner whether the firm is dissolved or not [Section 34 (1)]. Under ordinary circumstances, the firm is automatically dissolved as one of its members ceases to be a partner due to his insolvency [Section 42(*d*)]. However, the partners may specifically provide in their agreement that in such cases, the firm shall not be dissolved and the remaining partners may continue the firm's business. In cases, where the firm is not dissolved, the effects of insolvency are as under [Section 34(2)]:

1. The estate of the insolvent partner is not liable for the acts of the firm which are done *after* the order of insolvency. It may be noted that a public notice to the effect that a partner has become insolvent is also not necessary [Section 45, second para]. The fact of insolvency is a notice by itself.
2. The firm is also not liable for any act of the insolvent partner done after the date of the order of insolvency.

30.10. DEATH OF A PARTNER

On the death of a partner, a change occurs in the constitution of the firm if the remaining partners continue the firm. Under ordinary circumstances, the firm is automatically dissolved on the death of a partner [Section 42 (*c*)]. However, the partners may specifically provide in their agreement that in such cases, the firm shall not be dissolved, and the remaining partners shall continue the firm's business. Where the firm is not dissolved by the death of a partner, the estate of a deceased partner is not liable for any acts of the firm which are done after his death [Section 35]. In this case also, a public notice to the effect that a partner has died, is not necessary [Section 45, second para]. The death of a person is also a notice by itself.

30.11. TRANSFER OF PARTNER'S INTEREST

A partner may transfer his interest in the firm by way of absolute sale, by mortgage or by creation of charge on his interest. However, on the transfer of such interest, the transferee does not become a partner in the firm. Section 29 of the Indian Partnership Act expressly states that during the continuance of the firm, the transferee of a partner's interest *does not have the right*:

1. To interfere in the conduct of business, or
2. To require accounts of the firm, or
3. To inspect the books of the firm.

Thus, by the transfer of his interest in the firm, a partner cannot make the transferee a partner in the firm. The reason for the same is that a partner can be admitted into an existing firm *only* with the consent of all the partners. It may be noted that if any partner has any objection to the transfer of partner's interest, he can apply to the court for dissolution of the firm under Section 44(*e*).

However, the transferee of a partner's interest has the following two rights:

1. During the continuance of the firm, the transferee is entitled to receive the share of profits of the transferring partner. [Section 29(1)].
2. On the dissolution of the firm, the transferee is entitled to receive the transferring partner's share in the assets of the firm. He also has this right when the transferring partner ceases to be a partner in the firm.

30.12. RIGHTS AND DUTIES OF PARTNERS AFTER CHANGE IN THE CONSTITUTION OF A FIRM

On a change in the constitution of a firm, the rights and duties of the partners of the reconstituted firm remain the same as they were before the change in the firm [Section 17(*a*)]. However, after the change in the firm, the partners may enter into a fresh agreement which may provide different rights and duties of the partners. Section 17 of the Indian Partnership Act provides for the following two more types of changes in the firm:

(*a*) Where the firm continues after the expiry of the term of the firm [Section 17(*b*)].

(*b*) Where the firm carries on an additional undertaking [Section 17(*c*)].

In these cases also, the rights and duties of the partners of the reconstituted firm shall be the same as they were before the change in the firm.

Example 30.4. *A* and *B* were partners, in a firm having 60% and 40% share respectively. *A* died and his son *C* carried on the partnership business with *B*. There was no other express agreement as to their shares etc. It was held that C was entitled to 60% share.

[*Dawood Sahib* v. *Sheik Mohideen*, AIR 1938 Madras 5].

Example 30.5. *A* and *B* were partners for 7 years. And *A* was taking no active part in the business. After 7 years. *B* continued the firm in the same name on the same premises, and also with the property of the firm. Moreover, no accounts were settled between *A* and *B*. In this case, the firm is not dissolved and *A* is entitled to participate in the profits on the terms and conditions of the original agreement. [*Parsons* v. *Hayward*, (1862) 4 D.F. 474]

LEGAL PROVISIONS (SECTIONS) DISCUSSED IN THE CHAPTER

Important legal provisions (sections) of the Indian Partnership Act, 1932 discussed in this chpater are reproduced hereunder for ready reference:

1. *Section 31: Introduction of a partner*

(l) Subject to contract between the partners and to the provisions of section 30, no person shall be introduced as a partner into a firm without the consent of all the existing partners.

(2) Subject to the provisions of section 30, a person who is introduced as a partner into a firm does not thereby become liable for any act of the firm done before he became a partner.

2. *Section 32: Retirement of a partner*

A partner may retire,

(*a*) with the consent of all the other partners,

(*b*) in accordance with an express agreement by the partners, or

(*c*) where the partnership is at will, by giving notice in writing to all the other partners of his intention to retire.

(2) A retiring partner may be discharged from any liability to any third party for acts of the firm done before his retirement by an agreement made by him with such third party and the partners of the reconstituted firm,

3. *Section 33. Expulsion of a partner*

(1) A partner may not be expelled from a firm by any majority of the partners, save in the exercise in good faith of powers conferred by contract between the partners.

(2) The provisions of sub-sections (2), (3) and (4) of section 32 shall apply to an expelled partner as if he were a retired partner.

4. *Section 34: Insolvency of a partner*

(l) Where a partner in a firm is adjudicated an insolvent, he ceases to be a partner on the date on which the order of adjudication is made, whether or not the firm is thereby dissolved.

(2) Where under a contract between the partners the firm is not dissolved by the adjudication of a partner as an insolvent, the estate of a partner so adjudicated is not liable for any act of the firm and the firm is not liable for any act of the insolvent, done after the date on which the order of adjudication is made.

5. *Section 35: Liability of estate of deceased partner*

Where under a contract between the partners, the firm is not dissolved by the death of a partner, the estate of a deceased partner is not liable for any act of the firm done after his death.

TEST QUESTIONS

1. What are the provisions of the Indian Partnership Act with regard to the admission of a partner into the partnership? What will be the liability of an incoming partner?
2. What are the provisions of the Indian Partnership Act with regard to the retirement of a partner from the partnership? What will be the liability and rights of an outgoing partner?
3. What are the provisions of the Indian Partnership Act with regard to the expulsion of a partner from the partnership? What will be the liability and rights of an expelled partner?
4. Write notes on (*a*) Insolvency of a partner. (*b*) Death of a partner.

MULTIPLE CHOICE QUESTIONS

1. The reconstitution of the firm takes place in case of
   (*a*) Admission of a partner (*b*) Retirement of a partner
   (*c*) Expulsion or death of a partner (*d*) All of the above.
2. A new partner can be admitted in the firm with the consent of
   (*a*) all the partners (*b*) simple majority of partners
   (*c*) special majority of partners (*d*) new partner only.
3. A partner may retire from an existing firm
   (*a*) with consent of all partners (*b*) as per express agreement
   (*c*) by written notice in partnership at will (*d*) all of the above.
4. An accepted view is that where the existence of a retiring partner was not known he is not liable for debts incurred by the firm after his retirement even if public notice of his retirement was not given
   (*a*) True (*b*) False
5. A partner may be expelled from the firm on the fulfilment of the condition that the expulsion power is exercised.
   (*a*) as given by express contract (*b*) by majority of partners
   (*c*) in absolute good faith (d) all of the above.
6. On the insolvency of a partner, the insolvent ceases to be a partner in the firm whether the firm is dissolved or not
   (*a*) True (*b*) False

ANSWERS

1. (*d*)	2. (*a*)	3. (*d*)	4. (*a*)	5. (*d*)	6. (*a*)

OBJECTIVE TYPE QUESTIONS WITH REASONING

State with reasons whether the following statements are correct or incorrect.

1. A new partner can be admitted in an existing firm with the consent of majority of the partners.
2. An incoming partner is not liable for the acts of the firm done before his admission into the firm.
3. A new partner may be introduced in the firm by any existing partner of the firm.
4. A partner can retire from an existing firm only with the consent of all other partners.
5. A partner may retire from a 'partnership at will' simply by giving a written notice of retirement to all other partners of the firm.
6. A retiring partner continues to be liable to third parties for the acts of the firm done after his retirement until a public notice of his retirement is given.
7. A sleeping partner retiring from the firm is not liable for the acts of the firm done after his retirement even if a public notice of his retirement is not given.
8. A retiring partner cannot start a business competing with the business of the firm for a period of one year.
9. A partner can be expelled from the firm only if the power of expulsion is given to the partners by express contract.
10. The invalid expulsion of a partner does not give him a right to claim damages.

ANSWERS

1. *Incorrect.* A new partner can be admitted in an existing firm with the consent of all the partners [Section 31]
2. *Correct.* The liability of a new partner starts from the date of his admission into the firm.
3. *Incorrect.* Reasons as in point (1) above.
4. *Incorrect.* A partner may also retire in accordance with an express agreement between the partners [Section 32(1)(*b*)]
5. *Correct.* There is a specific provision in the regard [Section 32(1)(c)]
6. **Correct.** In such a case, a retiring partner remains liable by the principle of holding out.
7. **Correct.** In case of a sleeping partner, the public notice of his retirement is not required because such a partner is not known to the outsiders.
8. *Incorrect.* There is no such restriction in this regard. In fact he has the right to start any business [Section 36(1)].
9. **Correct.** It is the requirement of law for expulsion. Moreover, such power should be exercised by majority of the partners in good faith [Section 33(1)]
10. *Correct.* In such a case, he is entitled to be reinstated as a partner in the firm, but not entitled for any damages.

PRACTICAL PROBLEMS

1. *A* and *B* were partners in a trading firm. *C* was one of the creditors of the firm. After sometime, *D*, a new partner was admitted into the firm. Can *D* be held liable for the debts due to *C* which were prior to his admission ?

   Hints: No, *D* cannot be held liable for the past debts. [Section 31(2)]

2. *A*, *B* and *C* were partners in a firm. After sometime, *A* an active partner, retired from the firm. But no public notice of his retirement was given, and *B* and *C* continued to carry on the business of the firm. *D* a customer of the firm, supplied some goods to the reconstituted firm.

   (*a*) Can *A* also be held liable along with *B* and *C* for the price of goods supplied by *D*?

   (*b*) Would your answer differ, if *A* was a sleeping partner?

   Hints: (*a*) Yes, *A* is also liable as the public notice of his retirement was not given [Section 32(3)] (*b*) Yes, in that case, *A* would not be liable. In case of a sleeping partner retiring from the from, no public notice of retirement is required as such a partner is not know to the outsiders.

3. *A, B* and *C* were partner in a firm of drapers. The partnership deed authorised the expulsion of a partner when he was found guilty of flagrant breach of duty. *A* was convicted of travelling without ticket. On this ground, he was expelled by the other partners *B* and *C*. Is the expulsion justified ?

Hints: Yes, the expulsion is justified. In this case, the partnership deed authorised expulsion on the ground of flagrant breach of duty. Doing an act which brings a partner within the penalties of criminal law is a flagrant breach of duty. Also, the expulsion decision was takes by majority of partners.
[*Carmichael* v. *Evans*. (1904) 90 LT 573]

4. *A, B* and *C* were partners in a firm. By his wilful neglect and misconduct *C* caused serious loss to the business of the firm. After several warnings to *C, A* and *B* passed a resolution expelling *C* from the firm. By another resolution they admitted *D* as a partner in place of *C*. *C* objects to his expulsion as also to the admission of *D*. Is he justified in his objections ?

Hints: Yes, *C* is justified in his objections. In the absence of an express agreement authorising expulsion, the expulsion of a partner is not proper and is without any legal effect. [Section 33(1)]

C's objection to the admission of *D* is also justified as a new partner can be admitted only with the consent of all the partners. [Section 31 (1)]

5. *A* was a partner in a firm of *A, B* and *C* carrying on a trading business. The firm ordered some goods for the firm business. By the time, the goods were supplied, *A* had already expired. Is *A*'s estate liable for the price of goods supplied after *A*'s death ?

Hints: No, *A*'s estate cannot be held liable. The estate of a deceased partner is not liable for the acts of firm done after his death. [Section 35]

31

CHAPTER

DISSOLUTION OF FIRMS

1. Introduction.
2. Dissolution of Firm.
3. Dissolution of Partnership.
4. Modes of Dissolution of a Firm.
5. Dissolution Without the Intervention of the Court.
6. Dissolution With the Intervention of the Court.
7. Consequence of Dissolution of a Firm.
8. Liabilities of Partners After Dissolution of a Firm.
9. Rights of Partners After Dissolution of a Firm.
10. Mode of Settlement of Accounts.
11. Payment of Debts of Firm and Individual Debts of Partners.
12. Sale of Goodwill After Dissolution.

31.1. INTRODUCTION

In the preceding chapters, we have discussed the formation of the partnership firm, and the relations of partners with one another, and also with third parties. However, there are certain events which put an end to a partnership firm. Moreover, the partners may also like to put an end to the partnership firm for various reasons. Putting an end to the partnership firm is legally known as the dissolution of the firm. In this chapter we shall discuss the various modes of dissolution of the firm, rights and liabilities of partners after dissolution, and other legal provisions relating to dissolution of firms.

31.2. DISSOLUTION OF FIRM

The term 'dissolution of firm' may be defined as putting an end to partnership between all the partners *i.e.*, closing down the firm as a whole. It is defined in Section 39 of the Indian Partnership Act, which reads as under:

"The dissolution of partnership between all the partners of a firm is called the dissolution of the firm."

The analysis of this section reveals that, when the firm as a whole is closed down, it is called the dissolution of the firm. Thus, in case of dissolution of the firm, the business of the firm is stopped and the relations between *all* the partners come to an end.

Example 31.1. *A*, *B* and *C* were partners in a firm. After some time, *A* died and the firm was closed down. In this case, the firm is dissolved and the relations between all the partners come to an end. The death of a partner automatically dissolves the firm unless there is an agreement to the contrary.

31.3. DISSOLUTION OF PARTNERSHIP

The term 'dissolution of partnership' may be defined as a change in the relations of partners, and not the extinction of relationship. In this case, the firm as a whole is not closed down. But only the relations between some of the partners come to an end, and the remaining partners continue to carry on the business of the firm. Thus, the 'dissolution of firm' is different from 'dissolution of partnership'.

Example 31.2 *A*, *B* and *C* were partners in a firm. There was an agreement between them that the firm shall not be dissolved on the death or insolvency of a partner. After some time, *A* was declared as an insolvent by the court. In this case, the firm as a whole is not dissolved. Only the partnership between *A*, *B* and *C* is dissolved, and a new partnership between *B* and *C* comes into existence. The new firm is called the 'reconstituted firm'. Thus, only the relations between the partners are changed on *A*'s insolvency.

Example 31.3 *A* and *B* were partners in a firm. After some time, *C* was admitted as a new partner in the firm. In this case also, the partnership between *A* and *B* is dissolved, and a new partnership between *A*, *B* and *C* comes into existence which is called the 'reconstituted firm'.

In *Wajid Ali v. CIT*, AIR 1988 SC 757, the Supreme Court has also held that where on the death of a partner, his legal heirs joined the firm in accordance with the provisions of partnership deed, the firm would not stand dissolved. In such a case, the firm would continue with the changed relations between the partners.

It therefore, follows that the dissolution of partnership may or may not result in the dissolution of the firm. But the dissolution of firm necessarily means the dissolution of partnership.

31.4. MODES OF DISSOLUTION OF A FIRM

The modes of dissolution of a firm are contained in Section 40 to 44 of the Indian Partnership Act. These may be discussed under the following two heads:

1. Dissolution without the intervention of the court.
2. Dissolution with the intervention of the court (*i.e.*, dissolution by the court order).

31.5. DISSOLUTION WITHOUT THE INTERVENTION OF THE COURT

1. *Dissolution by consent of all the partners*
2. *Dissolution by contract between the partners*
3. *Compulsory dissolution*
4. *Dissolution on the happening of certain contingencies*
5. *Dissolution by notice*

A firm may be dissolved without the intervention of the court *i.e.*, without going to the court of Law. The dissolution without the intervention of the court may take place in any of the following ways.

1. *Dissolution by consent of all the partners [Section 40].* A partnership firm may be dissolved with the consent of all the partners. This principle applies to all cases whether the firm is for a fixed duration or for an uncertain duration (*i.e.*, at will).

2. *Dissolution by contract between the partners [Section 40].* A firm may also be dissolved in accordance with a contract between the partners in the same way as a firm is formed with the contract between the partners. There may be a separate contract for the dissolution of the firm, or it may also be contained in the partnership deed itself.

3. *Compulsory dissolution [Section 41].* In the following cases, the firm is compulsorily dissolved. In these cases, the firm is compulsorily dissolved even if there is a contrary contract between the partners *i.e.*, even if the partners agree that the firm shall not be dissolved in such cases.

(a) Insolvency of all the partners. Sometimes, all the partners of the firm become insolvent. In such cases, the firm is dissolved. The firm is also dissolved when all the partners except one have become insolvent. The reason for the same is that when a partner is declared as insolvent by the court, he ceases to be a partner from the date of the order of insolvency [Section 34(1)].

(b) Business of the firm becoming unlawful. Sometimes, an event happens which makes the business of the firm unlawful. In such cases, the firm is also dissolved. This includes the case where the business of the firm is rendered unlawful by the outbreak of war, or where the object for which the firm was formed becomes unlawful or illegal, or where the business remains lawful but it is forbidden to be carried on in partnership. It may be noted that this provision applies to the cases where a valid firm had come into existence, but it has become unlawful or illegal due to some subsequent event.

Example 31.4. *A* and *B* were carrying on the business of importing sugar from certain countries. Subsequently, the import of sugar was banned by the Government. In this case, the firm is dissolved as the business of the firm has become unlawful.

Note. Sometimes, a firm is carrying on several separate business. In such cases, the illegality of one or more business does not cause the dissolution of the firm in respect of its lawful business *i.e.*, the firm continues to exist so long as there is lawful business.

4. *Dissolution on the happening of certain contingencies* [*Section* 42]. On the happening of any one of the following contingencies (*i.e.* events), the firm is *automatically* dissolved. This is, however, subject to a contract, between the partners, to the contrary, *i.e.* the partners may agree that the firm shall not be dissolved in such cases.

(a) *Expiry of fixed term :* Sometimes, the firm is constituted for a fixed term. In such cases, the firm is dissolved on the expiry of that term. This is, however, subject to a contract to the contrary, *i.e.*, if the contract provides that the firm shall not be dissolved, then it will not be dissolved.

(b) *Completion of the adventure or undertaking :* Sometimes, the firm is constituted to carry out one or more adventure or undertakings. In such cases, the firm is dissolved on the completion of such adventure or undertaking. This is also subject to a contract to the contrary.

(c) *Death of a partner :* Sometimes, one of the partners of a firm dies during the continuance of the firm. In such cases, the firm is dissolved on the death of the partner. This is subject to a contract to the contrary. However, where there are only two partners, the death of one partner dissolves the firm even if the partnership agreement provides that the firm shall not be dissolved on the death of a partner. The reason for the same is that there must be at least two partners in a firm.

(d) *Insolvency of a partner :* Sometimes, one of the partners of a firm is declared as insolvent by the court. In such cases the firm is dissolved from the date of the order of insolvency. This is also subject to a contract to the contrary. However, where all the partners, or all except one, have been declared as insolvent, the firm shall be compulsorily dissolved even if the partnership agreement provided that the firm shall not be dissolved on the insolvency of any partner.

5. *Dissolution by notice* [*Section* 43]. A firm can also be dissolved by any partner by giving a notice of dissolution to the other partners. It may, however, be noted that the firm can be dissolved by notice only where the partnership firm is *'at will'*. If the firm is not at will, then it cannot be dissolved by notice of dissolution. The firm is to be at will where the duration of the firm is uncertain (*i.e.*, neither the duration is fixed nor there is any provision regarding the dissolution of the firm). The notice by a partner of his intention to dissolve the firm should be in writing and signed by him. Moreover, the notice should be clear, and served upon all the partners. The firm is dissolved from the date mentioned in the notice as the date of dissolution. If no such date is mentioned in the notice, then the firm is dissolved from the date when the notice is communicated to all the partners.

Example 31.5 *A* and *B* were partners in a firm. The partnership deed provided that the firm can be terminated (dissolved) 'by mutual agreement only'. After sometime, *A* gave a notice of dissolution to *B*. It was held that the firm cannot be dissolved by the notice of dissolution. The reason for the same is that in this case, firm is not *'at will'* as the mode of dissolution is provided in the partnership deed itself. [*Moss* v. *Elphic* (1910) 102 LT 639].

31.6. DISSOLUTION WITH THE INTERVENTION OF THE COURT

1. *Insanity of a partner*
2. *Permanent incapacity of a partner*
3. *Misconduct of a partner*
4. *Persistent breach of agreement*
5. *Transfer of interest*
6. *Perpetual losses in business*
7. *Other just and equitable grounds*

Sometimes, a partner wants that the firm should be dissolved. But the other partners may not agree to the dissolution. In such cases, he can go to Court of Law, and file a suit for dissolution of the firm. A partner may like to have the firm dissolved for various reasons. It may, however, be noted that the court has the discretion to pass an order of dissolution *i.e.*, the court may or may not allow the dissolution of the firm. A partner may file a suit for dissolution of the firm on any one of the following grounds, and the court may dissolve the firm if it is satisfied about the same.

1. *Insanity of a partner* [*Section 44(a)*]. Sometimes, a partner becomes insane *i.e.*, of unsound mind. In such cases, the court may allow the dissolution of the firm. The suit for dissolution of the firm may be filed by any one of the partners other than the partner who has become insane. The suit may also be filed by the next friend (*i.e.*, legal representative) of the insane partner. When the court is satisfied about the insanity of the partner, it may pass an order of dissolution of the firm. It may, however, be noted that the insanity does not itself dissolve the firm. The firm can be dissolved only by an order of the court.

2. *Permanent incapacity of a partner* [*Section 44(b)*]. Sometimes, a partner becomes permanently incapable of performing has duties. In such cases also, the court may allow the dissolution of the firm. The suit for dissolution of the firm may be filed by any one of the partners other than the partner who has become incapable. When the court is satisfied that the incapacity is of permanent nature, it may pass an order of dissolution of the firm. The incapacity may be due to various reasons e.g. mental or physical illness, blindness etc. However, the insanity must be of a permanent nature. In this case also, the firm is not automatically dissolved. It can be dissolved only by an order of the court.

Note. The above rule is not applicable to the incapacity of a sleeping partner. The reason for the same is that a sleeping partner does not take active part in the business of the firm. And thus, his incapacity is not likely to affect the business of the firm.

3. *Misconduct of a partner* [*Section 44 (c)*]. Sometimes, a partner is guilty of misconduct. In such cases also, the court may allow the dissolution of the firm. The suit for dissolution of the firm may be filed by any one of the partners other than the partner who is guilty of misconduct. When the court is satisfied that the misconduct adversely affects the partnership business, it may pass an order of dissolution of the firm. It may be noted that the firm can be dissolved only when the misconduct of a partner is such that it is likely to affect prejudicially (*i.e.*, adversely) the business of the firm. *i.e.*, when the misconduct is likely to damage the business of the firm. It is, however, not necessary that the misconduct should be directly connected with the firm. The only requirement is that the misconduct should be such which adversely affects the partnership business. The nature of business should be kept in view while determining the effect of misconduct on the partnership business. Gambling by a partner, conviction of a partner travelling without ticket, breach of trust, etc. have been held to be sufficient misconduct for the dissolution of the firm. Similarly, adultery by one partner with the wife of another partner was held to be sufficient misconduct for the dissolution as it destroys the mutual confidence[1]. But if the misconduct does not affect the business prospectus of a firm, the court may not dissolve it.

1. *Abbot* v. *Crump* (1870) BLR 109.

Example 31.6. *A* and *B* were carrying on a banking business in partnership. *A* had committed adultery with several women in the city, and his wife has left him on this ground. *B* applied to the court for the dissolution of the firm on this ground. But the court rejected *B*'s application and held that the firm cannot be dissolved on this ground. The reason for the same is that the misconduct of *A* does not have any adverse effect on their business as bankers.[*Snow* v. *Milform* (1868) 18 LT 142]

4. *Persistent breach of agreement* [*Section 44(d)*]. Sometimes, a partner wilfully or persistenitly (*i.e.* frequently) commits a breach of agreements relating to the management of the affairs of the firm, or conducts the partnership business in such a way that the other partners find it difficult to carry on the partnership business with him. In such cases, the court may allow the dissolution of the firm. The suit for dissolution of the firm may be filed by any one of the partners other than the partner who commits the breach of agreements. When the court is satisfied about such a conduct of the partner, it may pass an order of dissolution of the firm. As a matter of fact, the conduct of a partner, which destroys the mutual confidence between the partners is sufficient ground for dissolution of the firm. Thus, keeping erroneous accounts and not entering receipts, continuing quarrelling between the partners, refusal to meet on matters of business, taking away books of the firm, and misappropriations of income etc., are held to be sufficient ground for dissolution of a firm.

5. *Transfer of interest* [*Section 44(c)*]. Sometimes, a partner transfers the whole of his interest or share to a third party. In such cases, the court may allow the dissolution of the firm. The court may also allow the dissolution when the entire share of a partner is attached or sold by an order of the court. The suit for dissolution of the firm may be filed by any one of the partners other than the partner who has transferred his interest or share. When the court is satisfied about the transfer of partner's share, it may pass an order of dissolution of the firm.

6. *Perpetual losses in business* [*Section 44(f)*]. Where the business of a firm cannot be carried on, except at a loss, the court may allow the dissolution of the firm. The suit for dissolution of the firm may be filed by any one of the partner. When the court is satisfied that the business of a firm cannot be carried on, except at a loss, it may pass an order of dissolution of the firm. It may be noted that, under this clause, a firm can also be dissolved before the expiry of the fixed period.

7. *Other just and equitable grounds* [*Section 44(g)*]. A firm may also be dissolved by the court on any other just and equitable ground. A 'just and equitable ground', is a ground which is fair and reasonable according to the opinion of the court. This clause gives a very wide discretionary power to the court. It may be noted that under this clause, the court's power is not confined to the grounds of the like nature as discussed above. The court may dissolve the firm on any ground when the court thinks it to be just and equitable that the firm should be dissolved.

Note. The right of a partner to file a suit for dissolution on any of the above seven ground cannot be excluded by any agreement to the contrary.

[*Hardit Singh* v. *Mukha Singh* AIR 1973 & K 46.]

31.7. CONSEQUENCES OF DISSOLUTION OF A FIRM

The consequences of dissolution of a firm may be discussed under the following heads:

1. Liabilities of partners after dissolution of a firm. 2. Rights of partners after dissolution of a firm. 3. Mode of settlement of accounts. 4. Payment of debts of firm and individual debts of partners. 5. Sale of goodwill after dissolution.

31.8. LIABILITIES OF PARTNERS AFTER DISSOLUTION OF A FIRM

On the dissolution of a firm, the liabilities of its partners after the dissolution may be discusd under the following two heads:

1. ***Liabilities for the acts done after dissolution :*** On the dissolution of a firm, the first important step is to give a public notice of the dissolution. The public notice is necessary to terminate the liability of the partners. If it is not given, the partners shall remain liable to the third party for their acts done even after the dissolution of the firm [Section 45].

However, this principle does not apply to the case of a deceased partner, insolvent partner, and a retiring dormant (sleeping) partner. These partners are not liable for the acts done after the dissolution of the firm even if the public notice of dissolution is not given.

2. ***Liability to account for personal profits earned after dissolution :*** Sometimes, a firm is dissolved on account of the death of a partner. And before its affairs are completely wound-up, the surviving partners or the representative of the deceased partner carry on the business of the firm and earn personal profits at the expense of the firm *i.e.* by using firm's name or firm's property. In such cases, they are liable to account for the personal profits [Section 16(*a*)] and 50]. However, where a partner or his representative has bought the goodwill of the firm, he will not be liable to account for such profits [Section 50, second para].

31.9. RIGHTS OF PARTNERS AFTER DISSOLUTION OF A FIRM

1. *Rights to have business wound-up after dissolution*
2. *Right to earn personal profits by using firm's name*
3. *Right to have the premium returened on premature dissolution of a firm*
4. *Right where partnership contract is rescinded for fraud or misrepresentation*
5. *Right to restrain partners form the use of firm name or firm property*

On the dissolution of a firm, the rights of the partners after the dissolution may be discussed under the following heads:

1. ***Rights to have business wound-up after dissolution :*** The term 'winding up' may be defined as the putting an end to the affairs of the firm. It includes the realisation of the assets of the firm and payment of its debts and liabilities out of the assets so realised. On the dissolution of the firm, each partner is entitled to the following rights in connection with the winding-up of the firm [Section 46]:

(*a*) He is entitled to have the property of the firm utilised in payment of its debts and liabilities.

(*b*) He is entitled to have the surplus distributed among all the partners according to their rights. The surplus here means the surplus amount left after the payment of all the debts and liabilities of the firm.

2. ***Right to earn personal profits by using firm's name :*** Sometimes, on the dissolution of a firm, a partner buys the goodwill of the firm. In such cases, he has the right to use the firm's name and earn personal profits [Section 50, second para].

3. ***Right to have the premium returned on premature dissolution of a firm.*** Sometimes, at the time of joining an established firm, a partner is required to pay a sum of money to the old partners as a premium for his admission. It is paid under the hope that the firm shall continue to exist and he shall enjoy the fruits of the goodwill (business reputation) of the firm. But if the firm is dissolved before the expiry of the fixed term, the new partner has a right to get back the amount paid as a premium. It may, however, be noted that he is entitled to the premium if the firm is dissolved before the expiry of fixed

term and the dissolution is not due to the death of a partner [Section 51]. The amount of premium shall be determined keeping in view two factors, namely (*a*) the terms upon which he became a partner, and (*b*) the duration of the period for which he remained a partner. However, in the following cases, he shall not be entitled to the refund of premium [Section 51 second para]:

(*a*) Where the dissolution is due to the death of a partner.

(*b*) Where the dissolution is mainly due to the misconduct of the partner, who had paid the premium.

(*c*) Where the dissolution is in pursuance of an agreement which contains no provision for the refund of the premium.

(*d*) Where the firm was not for a fixed period.

4. *Right where partnership contract is rescinded for fraud or misrepresentation :* Sometimes, a partner is induced to join the firm by fraud or misrepresentation by other partners. In such cases, he is entitled to put an end to the partnership agreement on discovering such fraud or misrepresentation. In addition to other rights, he is also entitled to the following rights [Section 52]:

(*a*) *Right of lien or retention of surplus :* Sometimes, a surplus of firm's assets is left after paying its debts. In such cases, he is entitled to retain the surplus for any sum paid by him for the purchase of a share in the firm, and also for the amount of capital contributed by him.

(*b*) *Right of subrogation :* Sometimes, he makes a payment towards the debts of the firm. In such cases, he is entitled to rank as a creditor of the firm in respect of such payments. This means that if he pays off any creditor of the firm out of his own pocket, he steps into the shoes of that creditor, *i.e.*, he becomes the creditor of the firm for that amount.

(*c*) *Right to be indemnified :* He is entitled to recover indemnity (*i.e.*, compensation) from the partner who is guilty of fraud or misrepresentation. He can recover the indemnity against all the debts of the firm.

5. *Right to restrain partners from the use of firm name or firm property :* After the dissolution of a firm, every partner has a right to restrain the other partners from carrying on a similar business in the firm name [Section 53]. A partner can also be restrained from using the property of the firm for his own benefit.

Example 31.7. The affairs of a firm were being wound-up. One of its partners, attempted to lease out firm's property to a third person without the consent of other partners. The court restrained him from doing so at the instance of other partners. [*Rajendra K. Sharma* v. *Brijendra K. Sharma*, AIR 1994 Allahabad 62]

It may, however, be noted that a partner can be so restrained until the affairs of the firm are completely wound-up. However, a partner cannot be restrained from using the firm name for his own benefit, if he has bought the goodwill of the firm.

31.10. MODE OF SETTLEMENT OF ACCOUNTS

After the dissolution of a firm, the accounts of the firm are settled according to the terms of partnership. If there is no specific agreement then the accounts are settled according to the rules contained in Section 48 of the Indian Partnership Act. This section lays down the following two fundamental rules regarding the settlement of accounts:

1. *Payment of losses :* The losses of the firm, including the deficiencies of capitals shall be paid in the following manner and order:

(*a*) First of all, the losses shall be paid out of the profits.

(*b*) If the profits are not sufficient to pay the losses, then the balance of loss shall be paid out of capital, and (*c*) It still some balance of losses remains, it shall be paid by the partners individually in the proportion in which they where entitled to share profits.

2. *Utilisation of assets* : The assets of the firm, including any sums contributed by the partners to make up deficiencies of capital, shall be utilised in the following manner and order:

(*a*) First of all, the assets shall be utilised in paying the debts of the firm to the third parties.

(*b*) If there is any surplus, the same shall be utilised in paying each partner the amount of loan advanced to the firm other than the capital. This is done in proportion to the advances made by the partners.

(c) If there is still any surplus, the same shall be utilised in paying each partner towards the amount of his capital. This is done in proportion to the amount of capital contributed by the partners.

(*d*) If there is still any surplus, the same shall be divided among all the partners in proportion to their share in the profits of firm.

Sometimes, the assets of the firm are sufficient to pay the outside debts of the firm and the advances of the partners. But they are insufficient to repay the full amount of capital of each partner. In such cases, the deficiency in capital shall be regarded as the loss of the firm, and must be borne by the partners in the proportion in which they are entitled to share the profits. Thus, where the partners have agreed to share profits and losses equally, but have contributed unequal amount of capital, then if the assets are not sufficient to pay the full capital of the partners, the deficiency of capital (being the loss) must be made up by contribution by the partners in equal shares (*i.e.*, in profit sharing ratio). This is, however, subject to an agreement to the contrary *i.e.*, the partners may enter into an agreement regarding the share of such deficiencies.

Example 31.8. *A*, *B* and *C* were partners in a firm. They contributed the capital Rs. 40,000 Rs. 20,000 and Rs. 5,000 respectively making a total capital of Rs. 65,000. They agreed to share equally the profits and losses of the firm. On dissolution of the firm, it was found that after satisfying the outside debts and liabilities of the firm, the assets were only Rs. 20,000. In this case the deficiency of capital is Rs. 45,000 (65,000 – 20,000). This being the losses, each partner has to contribute to the losses equally (*i.e.*, in profit sharing ratio). Thus, each partner must contribute Rs. 15,000 to make up the deficiency. After this is done, the assets then available are Rs. 65,000 arrived at as Rs. 20,000 (assets after paying the outside liabilities) + Rs. 45,000 (the contribution made by the partners). This will be distributed among the partners according to their contributions towards the capital. So that each will suffer a total loss of Rs. 15,000. However, in actual practice, it will not be necessary for *A* and *B* to pay Rs. 15,000 each in cash. But the matter will be worked out on the basis of notional adjustment. In this adjustment, *C* whose capital was only Rs. 5,000, will have to pay Rs. 10,000. In this way *C*'s loss will come to Rs. 15,000. Now out of Rs. 30,000 (Rs. 20,000 of assets and Rs. 10,000 paid by *C*), *A* and *B* will get 25,000 and Rs. 5,000 respectively. In this way the total loss suffered by *A*, *B* and *C* will be Rs. 15,000 each.

Sometimes, a partner becomes insolvent and nothing can be recovered from him as his contribution to make up the deficiency. In such cases, the other solvent partners will not be liable to contribute for him. They will contribute only that amount which comes to be their share of deficiency. This rule was laid down in the leading case of ***Gurner v. Murrya***, (1904) 89 LT 665, which is discussed in the following example.

Example 31.9. *A*, *B* and *C* were partners in a firm. According to the terms and conditions of partnership agreement, the profits were to be shared in equal proportions. The capitals contributed by the partners were in unequal shares. The firm was dissolved, and after paying the outside creditors and paying back advances of the partners, the assets were not sufficient to pay back the capital of the partners. *A* and *B* paid their share of deficiency. But nothing could be recovered from *C* as he was insolvent. It was held that the solvent partners (*i.e. A* and *B*) were not liable to make contribution of insolvent's (*C*'s) share of deficiency. The court observed that the true principle of division was that each partner should contribute equal (*i.e.*, in profit sharing ratio) to make up the deficiency of capital. And if a partner failed to contribute the share of his deficiency, the other partners were not bound to make contribution in respect of that default. The effect of this decision may be stated as under.

(*a*) The solvent partners should bring their share of deficiency in cash; and

(*b*) The assets then available should be distributed among the solvent partners in proportion to their capital. The net effect of these rules will be that the deficiency of capital of the insolvent partner will be distributed among the solvent partners in the ratio of their respective capital.

Example 31.10. *A*, *B* and *C* were partners in a firm. They contributed to the capital Rs. 30,00, Rs. 10,000 and Rs. 5,000 respectively making a total capital of Rs. 45,000. They agreed to share equally the profits and losses of the firm. On dissolution of the firm, it was found that after paying the outside debts and liabilities of the firm, the assets were only Rs. 15,000. Thus, the deficiency of capital is Rs. 30,000 (Rs. 45,0000 – 15,000). This being the losses, each partner has to contribute to these losses equally (*i.e.*, in profit sharing ratio). However, *C* was insolvent and nothing could be recovered from him. In this case the assets will be distributed as under:

In the first place, *A* and *B* will have to bring their share of deficiency in cash *i.e.*, Rs. 10,000 each. The assets then available will be Rs. 35,000 (Rs. 15,000 + Rs. 10,000 + Rs. 10,000). These will be distributed between A and B in proportion of their contribution to the capital *i.e.*, in the ratio of 3 : 1. *A* will get Rs. 26,250, and *B* will get Rs. 8,750. The ultimate result will be that *A* on the whole will have lost Rs. 13,750 (Rs. 30,000 + Rs. 10,000 – Rs. 26,250), and *B* will have lost Rs. 11,250 (Rs. 10,000 + Rs. 10,000 – Rs. 8,750). This is in accordance with the rule laid down in *Garner. v. Murray*. The effect of this rule is that in case of insolvency of a partner, the partner who has contributed a greater part of the capital may lose more than his other partners even if they were sharing profits and losses in equal proportions. As a matter of fact, the deficiency of insolvent partner (*C*) alone amounting to Rs. 5000 (his share of contribution to the deficiency *i.e.*, Rs. 10,000 – his share of capital *i.e.*, Rs. 5,000) gets distributed among the solvent partners (*A* and *B*) in the ratio of their share of capital.

Note. The ordinary loss of the firm is shared by the partners in profit sharing ratio. But the loss due to the insolvency of a partner has to be shared by the solvent partners in the ratio of their capital.

31.11. PAYMENT OF DEBTS OF FIRM AND INDIVIDUAL DEBTS OF PARTNERS

On the dissolution of a firm, there may be instances when the individual (*i.e.*, private) debts of partners are also due alongwith the debts of the firm. The difficulty may arise when the assets of the firm are insufficient to pay its debts. In such cases, the debts are paid in accordance with the rules contained in Section 49 of the Indian Partnership Act which may be summed up as under:

1. First of all, the property of the firm is utilised in payment of debts of the firm. And if there is any surplus, then the share of each partner in such surplus, shall be utilised in payment of his individual debts.
2. The personal property of the partners is first utilised in payment of their individual debts. And if there is any surplus, the same shall be utilised in payment of debts of the firm.

It, therefore, follows that the creditors of the firm should be first paid out of the assets of the firm. And the individual creditors of the partners should be first paid out of the personal assets of the partners. Thus, where the assets of the firm are not sufficient to meet the debts of the firm, the creditors of the firm can resort to the personal property of the partners only if the individual debts of the partners have been paid out of it.

31.12. SALE OF GOODWILL AFTER DISSOLUTION

The term 'goodwill' may be defined as the value of the reputation of the business of a firm. It may be noted that the goodwill is very important and valuable asset of the firm, even if one cannot touch or see it. It is an intangible asset which results in higher profits due to the good reputation of the firm. On the dissolution of a firm, the goodwill is included in the assets of the firm. It may be sold either separately or alongwith the other properties of the firm. However, the partners may enter into an agreement whether to include it in the assets or to sell it separately [Section 55(1)]. The following two points are important in connection with the sale of goodwill:

1. ***Right of the seller of goodwill (i.e. partners) to carry on a competing business.*** This right of the seller of goodwill (*i.e.* partners of the firm whose goodwill is sold) is contained in Section 55(2) of the Indian Partnership Act. According to this section, after selling the goodwill of a dissolved firm, every partner is at liberty to start a business competing with that of the buyer. Moreover, he may also advertise for such business. However, the interest of the buyer of the goodwill should also be protected. To protect his interest, the Indian Partnership Act imposes following restrictions on the seller of goodwill [Section 55(2) second para]:

(*a*) He cannot use the firm name.

(*b*) He cannot represent himself that he is carrying on the business of the firm.

(*c*) He cannot solicit the customers who were dealing with the firm before dissolution. In other words, he cannot approach those customers for the purpose of diverting them to his new business.

2. ***Agreement in restraint of trade:*** On the sale of goodwill of a firm, it becomes necessary to protect the interest of the buyer of goodwill. Moreover, it is also necessary to maintain the value of the goodwill sold to a person for his benefit. This may be done by restricting the rights of seller of goodwill as stated above. But sometimes, the buyer of goodwill thinks that such restrictions are not sufficient to protect this interest. In such cases, further restrictions may be imposed and the seller of goodwill may be restrained altogether from carrying on a competing business. This provision is contained in Section 55(3) of the Indian Partnership Act. According to this section, on the sale of goodwill of a firm, any partner of the firm selling the goodwill may agree with the buyer of goodwill not to carry on any business similar to that of the firm. However, the restriction on partner's right to carry on a similar business should not be absolute. Such a restriction will be valid only if it satisfies the following conditions:

(*a*) The restriction must specify the period or the local limits of restraint, and

(*b*) The restriction must be reasonable.

As a matter of fact, such an agreement is necessary to protect the interest of the buyer of goodwill. The object of such agreement is to enable the buyer of goodwill to have sufficient time to establish himself in the business.

LEGAL PROVISIONS (SECTIONS) DISCUSSED IN THE CHAPTER

Important legal provisions (sections) of the Indian Partneship Act, 1932, discussed in this chapter are reproduced hereunder for ready reference:

1. *Section 39: Dissolution of Firm*

The dissolution of partnership between all the parters of a firm is called the dissolution of the firm.

2. *Section 40: Dissolution by Agreement*

A firm may be dissolved with the consent of all the partners or in accordance with contract between the partners.

3. *Section 41: Compulosry dissolution*

A firm is dissolved-

(*a*) by the adjudication of all the partners or of all the partners but one as insolvent, or

(*b*) by the happening of any event which makes it unlawful for the business of the firm to be carried on or for the partners to carry it on in partnership:

Provided that, where more than one separate adventure or undertaking is carried on by the firm, the illegality of one or more shall not of itself cause the dissolution of the firm in respect of its lawful adventures and undertakings.

4. *Section 42: Dissolution on the happening of certain contingencies*

Subject to contract between the partners, a firm is dissolved-

(a) if constituted for a fixed term, by the expiry of that term;

(*b*) if constituted to carry out one or more adventures or undertakings, by the completion thereof;

(*c*) by the death of a partner; and

(*d*) by the adjudication of a partner as an insolvent.

5. *Section 43: Dissolution by notice of partnership at will*

(1) Where the partnership is at will, the firm may be dissolved by any partner giving notice in writing to all the other partners of his intention to dissolve the firm.

(2) The firm is dissolved as from the date mentioned in the notice as the date of dissolution or, if no date is so mentioned, as from the date of the communication of the notice.

6. *Section 44: Dissolution by the Court*

At the suit of a partner, the Court may dissolve a firm on any of the following grounds, namely:

(*a*) that a partner has become of unsound mind, in which case the suit may be brought as well by the next friend of the partner who has become of unsound mind or by any other partner;

(*b*) that a partner, other than the partner suing, has become in any way permanently incapable of performing his duties as partner;

(*c*) that a partner, other than the partner suing, is guilty of conduct which is likely to affect prejudicially the carrying on of the business, regard being had to the nature of the business;

(*d*) that a partner, other than the partner suing, wilfully or persistently commits breach of agreements relating to the management of the affairs of the firm or the conduct of its business, or otherwise so conducts himself in matters relating to the business that it is not reasonably practicable for the other partners to carry on the business in partnership with him;

(*e*) that a partner, other than the partner suing, has in any way transferred the whole of his interest in the firm to a third party, or has allowed his share to be charged under the provisions of rule 49 of Order 21 of the First Schedule to the Code of Civil Procedure, 1908 (5 of 1908), or has allowed it to be sold in the recovery of arrears of land-revenue or of any dues recoverable as arrears of land-revenue due by the partner;

(*f*) that the business of the firm cannot be carried on save at a loss; or

(*g*) on any other ground which renders it just and equitable that the firm should be dissolved.

TEST QUESTIONS

1. Discuss the different modes of dissolution of a firm.
2. Distinguish between 'dissolution of a firm' and 'dissolution of partnership'. And state under what circumstances will a court dissolve the firm?
3. "The dissolution of partnership may or may not result in the dissolution of the firm, but the dissolution of the firm necessarily means the dissolution of partnership" — discuss, and state the consequences of dissolution of a firm.
4. Explain the grounds on which the partnership firm may be dissolved by the court.
5. State the circumstances in which the firm is automatically dissolved. Can a partnership at will also be dissolved?
6. What are the liabilities and rights of partners after the dissolution of the firm? Does the partner's authority continue after the dissolution? If yes, for what purpose?

7. What are the modes of settlement of accounts after the dissolution of the firm?
8. What rules shall apply for payment of debts when partners' individual debts are also outstanding alongwith the debts of the firm?
9. Write notes on the following:
   (*a*) Agreement in restraint of trade in the event of dissolution of the firm.
   (*b*) Sale of goodwill after the dissolution of the firm.

MULTIPLE CHOICE QUESTIONS

1. The expression 'dissolution of firm' and 'dissolution of partnership' have the same meaning and are used interchangeably.
   (*a*) True, as the firm as a whole is closed down in both the cases.
   (*b*) False, as the firm as a whole is not closed down in latter case.
2. A partnership firm is compulsorily dissolved where
   (*a*) all partners have become insolvent
   (*b*) firm's business has become unlawful
   (*c*) the fixed term has expired
   (*d*) in cases (*a*) and (*b*) only.
3. On which of the following grounds, a partner may apply to the court for dissolution of the firm?
   (*a*) Insanity of a partner
   (*b*) Misconduct of a partner
   (*c*) Perpetual losses in business
   (*d*) All of the above.
4. An accepted view is that where all the partners except one die or become insolvent, the firm is dissolved.
   (*a*) True, as there must be at least two partners to continue the firm.
   (*b*) False, as the firm is dissolved only where all the partners die or become insolvent.
5. On an application to the court for dissolution of the firm on the ground of insanity of a partner or misconduct of a partner, the court is bound to order dissolution of the firm.
   (*a*) True, as Section 44 makes it obligatory
   (*b*) False, as there is no such obligation.

ANSWERS

1. (*b*)	2. (*d*)	3. (*d*)	4. (*a*)	5. (*b*)

OBJECTIVE TYPE QUESTIONS WITH REASONING

State with reasons whether the following statements are correct or incorrect

1. The term 'dissolution of firm' and 'dissolution of partnership' are synonymous and are used interchangeably in the law of partnership.
2. The firm is compulsorily dissolve when all the partners except one have become insolvents.
3. The death of a partner automatically dissolves the firm.
4. The firm is automatically dissolved on the insanity of a partner.
5. Whether the partnership is at will or not, it can be dissolved by a partner by giving a notice in writing of his intention to dissolve the firm.
6. Permanent incapacity of partner is not a ground for dissolution of partnership firm.
7. Misconduct of a partner is not a ground for dissolution of the firm.
8. Where the business of the firm cannot be carried on except at losses, it can be dissolved even before the expiry of the fixed period.
9. On the dissolution of firm, the rule for the settlement of accounts is that first of all the assets shall be utilised in paying the amount of loan advanced by each partner.
10. A partner who has purchased the goodwill of the firm on the dissolution of the partnership firm, has a right to make use of the firm name for earning profits.

ANSWERS

1. *Incorrect.* In case of dissolution of firm, the business of the firm is stopped and the relations between all the partners come to amend. In case of dissolution of partnership, only the relations between some of the partners come to an end, and the remaining partners continue to carry on the business.
2. *Correct.* On becoming insolvent, a partner ceases to be the partner in the firm, and the remaining sole partner cannot constitute the partnership.
3. *Correct.* There is a specific legal provision in this regard. This is however, subject to a contrary agreement between the partner [Section 42].
4. *Incorrect.* In case of insanity of the partner, the firm can be dissolved only by an order of the court.
5. *Incorrect.* Only a 'partnership at will' can be dissolved by giving such a notice by the partner.
6. *Incorrect.* A suit for dissolution of firm can be filed in the court on this ground, and the court may allow the dissolution [Section 44 (*b*)].
7. *Incorrect.* The court may allow dissolution of the firm on this ground when the misconduct is likely to affect adversely the business of the firm [Section 44(*c*)].
8. *Correct.* There is no use of carrying on the business at losses. Any partner may apply to the court for the dissolution of the firm. [Section on 44(*f*)].
9. *Incorrect.* In the first place, the assets are utilised in paying the debts of the firm to the third party.
10. *Correct.* This right is necessary, to justify purchaser's interest in the firm's goodwill.

PRACTICAL PROBLEM

1. *A*, *B* and *C* are partners in a firm. The partnership agrement provides that the firm shall be dissolved on the insolvency of a partner. After sometime, all the three partners become insolvent.
   (*a*) Is the firm dissolved?
   (*b*) Will it make any difference to your answer if only *A* and *B* become insolvent ?

   Hints: (*a*) Yes, the firm is dissolved. A firm is compulsorily dissolved when all the partners become insolvent. [Section 41]

   (*b*) No, in that case also the firm will be compulsorily dissolved. The reason for the same is that when a partner is declared insolvent by the courts he ceases to be a partner from the date of order of the court [Section 34(1)]. Thus, when all partners, except one, have become insolvent, the firm is dissolved because there must be at least two partners to continue a firm.
2. *A* and *B* are carrying on the business of importing sugar from certain countries. Subsequently, the import of sugar is banned by the government.
   (*a*) Is the firm dissolved ?
   (*b*) Will it make any difference if the above firm of *A* and *B* is also carrying on another legal business alongwith that of importing sugar ?

   Hints: (*a*) Yes, the firm is dissolved. A firm is compulsorily dissolved as, after the ban on import of sugar, the business of the firm has become unlawful.

   (*b*) Yes, in that case the firm will not be compulsorily dissolved in respect of the second legal business.
3. *A* and *B* were partners in a firm. The partnership deed provided that the firm can be dissolved by mutual agreement only. After sometime, *A* alone wanted to dissolve the firm and gave a notice of dissolution to *B*. Can the firm be dissolved on *A*'s notice to *B* ? Give reasons.

   Hints: No, the firm is not dissolved by notice of dissolution. The reason for the same is that the firm is not *at will* as the mode of dissolution has been provided in the partnership deed itself. *A* firm can be dissolved by notice only where the partnership is at will. [Section 43]
4. *A* and *B* were partners in a firm and the partnership deed provided that any one of the partners can

retire with the consent of the other partner. After sometime, *A* wanted to dissolve the firm and gave a notice of dissolution to *B*. Can the firm be dissolved on *A*'s notice of dissolution ? Give reason.

Hints: No, the firm is not dissolved by notice of dissolution. The reason for the same is that the firm is not *at will* as the provision relating to retirement means the mode of dissolution. A firm can be dissolved by a notice of dissolution only where the partnership is at will when the mode of dissolution is prescribed, the firm cannot be said to be *at will*.

[Section 43; *Erach F.D. Mehta* v. *Minoo*, AIR 1971 SC 1653]

5. *A, B* and *C* were partners in a firm carrying on transport business and the duration of partnership was agreed to be ten years. After running the business for four years, it was found that during the last four years the business resulted in loss in each year. *A* insisted that the business should be continued for the full term of ten years, though *B* and *C* were not anxious to run the business. What course is open to the remaining partners *B* and *C* ?

   Hints: *B* and *C* has the option to apply to the court for dissolution of the firm under section 44 (f) on the ground of perpetual losses. Where the business of a firm cannot be carried on except at loss, the court may allow the dissolution of the firm even if the term of partnership has not expired.

6. *A* and *B* are partners in a firm constituted for a period of ten years. After two years, *A* is convicted of travelling in railway without ticket. *B* wants the dissolution of firm. Advise him.

   Hints: *B* can apply to the court for dissolution of the firm under section 44 (c) on the ground of misconduct of a partner. The court can dissolve the firm on this ground as travelling without ticket amounts misconduct by the partner. In this case, misconduct followed by conviction under criminal law will definitely affect the partnership business and thus dissolution on this ground be justified.

   [See *Carmichacl* v. *Evans* (1904) 90 LT 573]

7. *A* and *B* were partners carrying on a banking business. *A* had committed adultery on several women in the city and his wife had left him on this ground. *B* applied to the court for dissolution of the firm on this ground. Will he succeed ?

   Hints: No, *B* will not succeed. In this case, though *A* is quality of misconduct but his misconduct does not have any adverse affect on their business as bankers. [See *Snow* v. *Milform* (1868) 18 LT 142]. In this case, the court observed that how can it be said that a man's money is less safe because one of the partner commits adultery. It was further observed that in those cases where the moral conduct of a partner would affect the firm business, it can be a ground for dissolution of the firm *e.g.* where a medical man had entered into partnership with another and it was found that his conduct was very immoral towards some of his patients, the firm can be dissolved on the ground of misconduct by the partner.

8. *A* and *B* enter into partnership as solicitors for a term of five years. *A* pays a premium of Rs. 80,000 to *B* who knows before entering into the partnership that *A* is inexperienced and incompetent. After the expiration of two years, *B* complains that *A*'s incompetent is injurious to the business, and calls upon him to dissolve the partnership The firm is dissolved by mutual agreement and *A* seeks return of a proportionate part of the premium.

   (*a*) Is *A* entitled to return of proportionate part of premium ?

   (*b*) Would your answer differ if the firm is dissolved due to misconduct of *A* ?

   Hints: (*a*) Yes, *A* is entitled to return of proportionate part of premium paid. The amount of premium shall be determined keeping is view two factors namely.

   (*i*) The term upon which *A* became a partner, and

   (*ii*) The duration of period for which *A* remained partner.

   (*b*) Yes, in that case, *A* would not be entitled to the return of proportionate premium.

   [Section 51, second para]

The Negotiable Instruments Act, 1881

- Nature of Negotiable Instruments
- Promissory Notes, Bills of Exchange and Cheques
- Parties to a Negotiable Instrument and their Capacity
- Holder and Holder in Due Course
- Negotiation and Liability of Parties
- Presentment of Negotiable Instruments
- Dishonour of Negotiable Instruments
- Discharge from Liability
- Crossing of Cheques
- Miscellaneous Provisions
- Banker and Customer
- Hundis

32

CHAPTER

NATURE OF NEGOTIABLE INSTRUMENTS

32.1. INTRODUCTION

In business dealings, all the transactions do not take place in terms of money. With expanding commerce and trade, the growing demands for money could not be met merely with the exchange of money. Under certain circumstances, the businessman may not have ready cash with him. Moreover, he may not like to carry huge amount of money in his pocket. As such he needs certain facilities to enable him to facilitate the business dealings. Due to these reasons, businessmen adopted a new method of exchanging documents (such as bills of exchange, cheques, bank drafts etc) in place of actual currency for their day to day transactions. These documents which are used as substitute for money, are known as negotiable instruments.

These days, the negotiable instruments are the most common credit devices, and are freely used in commercial transactions and monetary dealings. These instruments are legally employed by merchants as an effective substitute for money. The legal provisions relating to the negotiable instruments are contained in the **Negotiable Instruments Act, 1881**. The object and purpose of this Act is to legalise the system under which claims upon certain mercantile instruments are treated like ordinary goods passing from one hand to another.

The Negotiable Instruments Act came into force on first day of March, 1882. It deals with promissory notes, bills of exchange and cheques.

Note. In our discussion, on Law of Negotiable Instruments, from chapters 32 to 43 unless otherwise stated, the sections mentioned are those of the Negotiable Instruments Act, 1881.

32.2. DEFINITION OF A NEGOTIABLE INSTRUMENT

The term 'negotiable instrument' may be defined as a *written* promise or order to pay money which may be transferred from one hand to another as a substitute for money. In simple words, it is a piece of paper which entitles a person to a sum of money mentioned in it, and which is freely transferable from person to person. It may be transferred by mere delivery or by endorsement and delivery. The terms 'endorsement' and 'delivery' will be discussed in Chapter 36.

It may be noted that the term negotiable instrument as such is not defined in the Negotiable Instruments Act. However, section 13 defines it by specifying three kinds of negotiable instrument. This section reads as under :

> *"A negotiable instrument means a promissory note, bill of exchange or cheque payable either to order or to bearer."*

Thus, section 13 speaks of only three kinds of instruments (*i.e.*, documents). However, it does not mean that there cannot be any other kind of negotiable instrument than these three. In fact every document which entitles a person to a sum of money and which is transferable by delivery or by endorsement and delivery, is entitled to be called a negotiable instrument. In *Smith's leading cases*, 535 (12th edn. 1915), it is said that where by the custom of a trade, an instrument is transferable like cash, by delivery, and is capable of being sued upon by the person holding it for the time being, it is entitled to the name negotiable instrument, and the property in it passes to a *bona fide* transferee for value.

The person to whom the negotiable instrument is transferred becomes entitled to get the money mentioned in it. He also has the right to further transfer it to any one he likes. As a matter of fact, a person who gets a negotiable instrument in *good faith* and for consideration, becomes its owner and has an unconditional right to receive the money mentioned in it. This is emphasised in Willis[1] definition of a negotiable instrument which reads as under:

> *"A negotiable instrument is one, the property in which is acquired by any one who takes it bona fide and for value notwithstanding any defect of title in the person from whom he took it."*

Thus, the free negotiability (*i.e.*, transferability) is an important characteristic of a negotiable instrument. Following are the two conditions for a negotiability:

1. The negotiable instrument should be freely transferable, and
2. The person who obtains a negotiable instrument in *good faith* and for value, becomes entitled to recover the money mentioned in it. And his title is not affected by any defect in the title of the person from whom he obtained the instrument.

32.3. CHARACTERISTICS OF A NEGOTIABLE INSTRUMENT

The characteristics of a negotiable instrument are as under:

1. A negotiable instrument must be in writing.
2. A negotiable instrument must be signed by its maker.
3. A negotiable instrument must contain an unconditional promise or order to pay some money, *i.e.*, the amount should not be made payable on some condition.
4. A negotiable instrument must contain a certain (*i.e.*, definite) amount of *money only*.
5. A negotiable instrument must be freely transferable from one person to another.
6. On the transfer of a negotiable instrument from one person to another, the transferee who receives it in *good faith* and for value, has the right to recover the amount mentioned in the instrument in his own name. Such a person is known as a *holder in due course*. His rights are not affected by any defect in the title of the transferee or any prior party. This point will be discussed in detail in Art. 35.4.

1. The Law of Negotiable Securities, 5-6 (4th Edn.)

32.4. PRESUMPTIONS ABOUT NEGOTIABLE INSTRUMENTS

1. *Consideration*
2. *Date*
3. *Time of acceptance*
4. *Time of transfer*
5. *Order of endorsements*
6. *Stamp*
7. *Holder in due course*
8. *Fact of dishonour*

Following are the important presumptions about all the negotiable instruments [Section 118 and 119]. It may be noted that in case of any dispute about these presumptions, these need not be proved by the person who holds the negotiable instrument until contrary is proved.

1. *Consideration* : It is presumed that every negotiable instrument has been made or drawn for the consideration. Moreover, when a negotiable instrument is accepted, endorsed, negotiated or transferred, it is also presumed that it was so accepted, endorsed etc. for a consideration.

2. *Date:* In case of a dated negotiable instrument, it is presumed that it has been made or drawn on the date that appears on it.

3. *Time of acceptance:* In case of an accepted bill of exchange, it is presumed that it has been accepted within a reasonable time after being made, and before its maturity (*i.e.*, the due date of payment).

4. *Time of transfer:* It is also presumed that every transfer of a negotiable instrument has been made before its maturity.

5. *Order of endorsements:* It is also presumed that the endorsements appearing on the negotiable instrument have been made in the same order in which they appear on the instrument.

6. *Stamp:* Sometimes, a negotiable instrument is lost or destroyed. In such cases it is presumed that it was duly stamped.

7. *Holder in due course:* A 'holder in due course' is a person who has obtained a negotiable instrument in *good faith* and for value. It is presumed that every holder of a negotiable instrument is a 'holder in due course'. In case of dispute, it is the duty of a party liable for payment to prove that the person holding the negotiable instrument is not the holder in due course. But if the party liable for payment shows that the negotiable instrument was obtained from its lawful owner by means of an offence or fraud, then it is the duty of the holder to prove that he is a holder indue course, *i.e.*, to prove that he obtained the negotiable instrument in *good faith* and for value.

8. *Fact of dishonour:* Sometimes, a negotiable instrument is dishonour *i.e.*, the party liable for payment fails to make the payment. In such cases, the holder has the right to file a suit for recovery of the amount, after giving a due notice of dishonour. However, before filing the suit, he may obtain a certificate from a Notary Public about the fact of dishonour. Such a certificate is known as 'protest'. On the proof of such a protest, the court shall presume the fact of dishonour. This point will be discussed in detail in Arts. 38.11 and 43.12.

Note. The above facts are presumed unless and until contrary is proved. In other words, these presumptions are rebuttable by evidence *i.e.*, the party liable for payment may prove by evidence that these facts do not exist.

32.5. KINDS OF NEGOTIABLE INSTRUMENTS

1. *Promissory note*
2. *Bill of exchange*
3. *Cheque*

There are many kinds of negotiable instruments. But the Negotiable Instruments Act mentions only three kinds of negotiable instruments. These are specified in Section 13 of the Act which reads as under:

"A negotiable instrument means a promissory note, bill of exchange or cheque payable either to order or to bearer."

The analysis of this section reveals that, the Negotiable Instruments Act recognises the following three kinds of negotiable instruments, namely:

1. ***Promissory note:*** It is a negotiable instrument, in writing which contains an unconditional *promise* by one person to pay a certain sum of money to a specified person.

2. ***Bill of exchange :*** It is negotiable instrument, in writing, which contains an conditional order directing a certain person to pay a certain sum of money to the bearer of the instrument or to a specified person.

3. ***Cheque :*** It is negotiable instrument, in writing which contains an unconditional *order* directing a specified *banker* to pay a certain sum of money to the bearer of the instrument or to a specified person.

All these three kinds of negotiable instruments will be discussed in detail in the next chapter. Though the Negotiable Instruments Act speaks of only above three kinds of negotiable instruments, but it does not mean that there cannot be any other negotiable instruments than these three. As a matter of fact, every other document which fulfils the requirements of a negotiable instrument, is recognised by the usage or customs as the negotiable instrument *e.g.*, hundis, treasury bills, bankers drafts, share warrants, dividend warrants, bearer debentures etc. are negotiable instruments recognised by the customs and other Acts (such as Companies Act). Thus, every document which entitles a person to a sum of money, and which is freely transferable from one hand to another, is entitled to be called a negotiable instrument.

Note. Money Orders, Postal Orders, Deposit Receipts, Bill of Lading, Railway Receipts, Dock Warrants etc. are not negotiable instruments. Though these documents are transferable by delivery and endorsement, yet they cannot give a better title to the transferee than that of the transferror.

32.6. CLASSIFICATION OF NEGOTIABLE INSTRUMENTS

1. *Inland instruments*
2. *Foreign instruments*
3. *Bearer instruments*
4. *Order instruments*
5. *Instruments payable on demand*
6. *Time instruments*

The negotiable instruments may broadly be classified under the following six heads:

1. ***Inland instruments:*** The term 'inland instrument' is defined in Section 11 of the Negotiable Instruments Act, which reads as under:

"A promissory note, bill of exchange or cheque drawn or made in India, and made payable in, or drawn upon any person resident in India, shall be deemed to be an inland instrument."

The analysis of this section reveals, that, in any of the following cases an instrument is an inland instrument:

(*a*) An instrument which is drawn in India and also payable in India.

(*b*) An instrument which is drawn in India on any person resident in India whether payable in India or outside India.

Example 32.1 *A*, a resident of Chandigarh, drew (*i.e.*, made) a bill of exchange in Chandigarh on *B*, a merchant in London. And *B* accepted the bill of exchange as payable in Delhi. It is an inland bill of exchange. In this case, the bill of exchange was drawn in India and also payable in India.

Example 32.2. *A*, a resident of Bombay, drew a bill of exchange in Bombay on *B*, a merchant in Delhi. And *B* accepted the bill of exchange as payable in New York. It is also an inland bill of exchange. In this case, the bill of exchange was drawn in India on a person resident in India. It is immaterial that the amount is payable in New York.

It is to be noted that the nature of an inland instrument is not changed by the fact of its being in circulation in a foreign country. Thus, an inland instrument remains inland even if it has been endorsed in a foreign country *e.g.*, if the bills of exchange mentioned in above two examples, are endorsed in France, they will remain inland bills.

2. *Foreign instruments:* The term 'foreign instrument' is defined in Section 12 of the Negotiable Instruments Act, which states that a foreign instrument is one which is not an inland instrument.

Example 32.3. *A* drew a bill of exchange in India on *B*, a merchant residing in London. It was also made payable in London. It is a foreign bill of exchange.

Example 32.4. *A* drew a bill of exchange in London on *B*, a merchant residing in London. But the bill of exchange was made payable in India. It is also a foreign bill.

Similarly, a bill of exchange drawn in London and payable in London is a foreign bill. And a bill of exchange drawn in London on a person residing in India, is also a foreign bill.

3. *Bearer instruments.* The term 'bearer' instrument ' may be defined as negotiable instrument the payment of which can be taken by a person who has the possession of the instrument. This term is defined *in Explanation II* to Section 13(1) of the Negotiable Instruments Act, which reads as under:

> *"A promissory note, bill of exchange or cheque is payable to bearer which is expressed to be so payable or on which the only or last endorsement is an endorsement in blank."*

The analysis of this section reveals that, a negotiable instrument is payable to bearer in any of the following cases:

(*a*) Where the instrument is expressed to be payable to bearer.

(*b*) Where the only endorsement or the last endorsement on the instrument is an endorsement in blank (*i.e.*, where the instrument is endorsed by the holder simply by signing his name and without writing transferer's name). Thus, where an instrument is originally payable to a particular person, but subsequently endorsed in blank, the instrument will become payable to bearer.

It may be noted that a bearer instrument can be negotiated (*i.e.*, transferred) by mere delivery *i.e.*, no further formality is required for transferring a bearer instrument.

Example 32.5. The negotiable instruments made in the following words are the bearer instruments:

(*a*) pay to *A* or bearer

(*b*) pay the bearer.

Example 32.6. *A* made a cheque payable to *B* and delivered the same to him. Afterwards, *B* put his signatures on the back of the cheque and delivered it to *C*. In this case, the cheque becomes a bearer one in the hands of *C* as *B* did not write the name of any person at the time of endorsement *i.e.*, the only endorsement on the cheque is an endorsement in blank.

4. *Order instruments.* The term order instrument may be defined as the instrument the payment of which can be taken by a particular person to whom it is made payable or if it is made payable to the order of that particular person. This term is defined in Explanation I to Section 13(1) of the Negotiable Instruments Act, which reads as under:

"A promissory note, bill of exchange or cheque is payable to order which is expressed to be so payable, or which is expressed to be payable to a particular person, and does not contain words prohibiting transfer or indicating an intention that it shall not be transferable."

The analysis of this section reveals that a negotiable instrument is payable to order in any of the following cases:

(*a*) Where the instrument is expressed to be payable to order.

(*b*) Where the instrument is expressed to be payable to a particular person and which does not contain any words restricting its further transfer.

An order instrument is also negotiable (*i.e.*, transferable). But it can be negotiated by an endorsement on it, and then its delivery.

Example 32.7. The negotiable instruments, made in the following words, are order instruments:

(*a*) Pay to *A* or order.

(*b*) Pay to the order of *A*.

(*c*) Pay to *A*.

Example 32.8. A negotiable instrument made in the words as 'Pay to *A* only', is not an order instrument because its transfer is restricted by using the word 'only'.

5. *Instruments payable on demand.* The 'instruments payable on demand' are defined in Section 19 of the Negotiable Instruments Act. In this connection first part of Section 21 of the Act is also relevant. Both these sections respectively read as under:

"A promissory note or bill of exchange in which no time for payment is specified, and a cheque, are payable on demand."

"In a promissory note or bill of exchange the expression 'at sight' and 'on presentment' means on demand."

The analysis of these sections reveal that, the following instruments are payable on demand:

(*a*) A promissory note or a bill of exchange in which no time for payment is specified.

(*b*) A promissory note or a bill of exchange which is expressed to be payable 'on demand', or 'at sight', or 'on presentment'.

(*c*) A cheque. As a matter of fact, the cheques are always payable on demand.

It may be noted that the instruments payable 'on demand' may be presented for payment at any time.

6. ***Time instruments :*** The term 'time instrument' may be defined as the instrument which is payable some time in future. Thus, the following instruments are time instruments.

(*a*) A promissory note or a bill of exchange which is payable after a fixed period *e.g.*, 60 days after sight.

(*b*) A promissory note or a bill of exchange which is payable on a specified day *e.g.*, on 31 March, 2004.

(*c*) A promissory note or a bill of exchange which is payable on the happening of an event which is certain to happen, *e.g.*, on the death of a person.

(*d*) A promissory note or a bill of exchange which is payable 'after sight'.

Notes 1. The expression 'after sight' in a promissory note means that the payment cannot be demanded on the promissory note till it has been shown to the maker. And in case of a bill of exchange the expression 'after sight' means after acceptance, or after noting for non-acceptance, or after protest for non-acceptance [Section 21].

2. A cheque cannot be a time instrument because the cheque is always payable on demand.

32.7. IMPORTANT TERMS

1. *Ambiguous instruments*
2. *Inchoate Instrument*

Following are the important terms in negotiable instruments:

1. *Ambiguous instruments* : The term 'ambiguous' instrument is defined in Section 17 of the Negotiable Instruments Act. As per this section, an ambiguous instrument is one which in form is such that it may either be treated as a promissory note or bill of exchange. In such cases, the holder may either treat it as a promissory note or bill of exchange. Once he exercises his option, he is bound by it, *i.e.*, he cannot fall back that it is the other kind of instrument.

Example 32.9. *A* firm was carrying on its business in Bombay and Delhi. Its Bombay branch drew a bill of exchange on the Delhi branch. In this case, the holder of the bill of exchange, may also treat it as a promissory note drawn by the Bombay branch payable in Delhi. The reason for the same is that the drawer and the drawee of the bill of exchange are the same person.

Example 32.10. *A* drew a bill of exchange on *B*, a fictitious person not in existence. And *A* endorsed the bill of exchange in favour of *C* and delivered the same to him. In this case also, *C* may treat the bill of exchange as a promissory note made by *A*. The reason for the same is that where the drawee is a fictitious person the instrument is ambiguous.

2. *Inchoate Instrument* : The term 'inchoate instrument' means an incomplete instrument in some respects *e.g.*, an instrument not mentioning the amount payable, or the name of the payee. Section 20 of the Negotiable Instruments Act contains the legal provision in this regard. As per this section, an inchoate instrument is a blank or an incomplete instrument. When a person signs and delivers to another a blank or incomplete stamped instrument, he authorises the other person to make or complete a negotiable instrument for any amount not exceeding the amount covered by the stamp. When the instrument is so filed up, the person signing the instrument becomes liable, in the capacity in which he has signed, to any *holder in due course* for such amount. The liability of the signer is restricted to the amount specified in the instrument which is covered by the stamp. It may be noted here that no person other than a *holder in due course* can recover from the person delivering the instrument anything in excess of the amount intended to be paid by him.

Example 32.11. *A* owed Rs. 500 to *B*. He gave a stamped and signed promissory note to *B* leaving blank the space for amount. And *B* filled Rs. 700, in the space left for amount. In this case, *B* cannot recover Rs. 700 from *A* as he *B* is not a holder in due course. He can recover Rs. 500 only which *A* intended to pay under the instrument.

If after completing the promissory note for Rs. 700, *B* transfers it to *C*, a holder in the due course, then *C* will be entitled to recover the full amount of Rs. 700 if the stamp affixed is sufficient to cover Rs. 700. And *A* will be bound to pay the full amount to *C*.

The following points are important in connection with an inchoate instrument:

(*a*) The liability of the person who signs and delivers an incomplete stamped instrument arises only when the blanks are filled in and the instrument is completed.

(*b*) The signer becomes liable only when the instrument is delivered to the transferee. Thus, where a person signs his name on a stamped promissory note, and keeps it in his table drawer, and someone steals and completes the instrument, then he cannot recover the amount from the signer. It may be noted that in such a case, even a holder in due course cannot recover the amount from the signer.

(*c*) The instrument must be stamped one, and the stamp affixed must be sufficient to cover the amount filled in the instrument.

32.8. LAW APPLICABLE TO NEGOTIABLE INSTRUMENTS

The law applicable to the negotiable instruments is contained in the Negotiable Instruments Act, 1881. It may, however, be noted that this Act does not affect Section 31 of the Reserve Bank of India Act, 1934 which reads as under:

(1) No person in India other than the Reserve Bank or as expressly authorised by this Act, the central Government shall draw accept, make or issue any bill of exchange, hundi, promissory note or engagement for the payment of money payable to bearer on demand, or borrow, owe or take up any sum or sums of money on the bills, hundis, or notes payable to bearer on demand of any such persons;

Provided that cheques or drafts, including hundis payable to bearer on demand or otherwise, may be drawn on person's account with a banker, shroff or agent.

(2) Notwithstanding anything contained in the Negotiable Instruments Act, 1881, no person in India other than the Bank, or as expressly authorised by this Act, the Central Government, shall make or issue nay promissory note expressed to be payable to the bearer of the instrument."

The effect of this section may be stated as under:

(*a*) A bill of exchange, promissory note or hundi cannot be made payable to 'bearer on demand'. However, a cheque payable to bearer on demand can be drawn on person's account with a banker.

(*b*) A promissory note cannot be made payable to the bearer. This makes the word "or to bearer' in the definition of a promissory note given in Section 4 of the Negotiable Instruments Act, as inoperative.

The object of the above provision of Reserve Bank of India Act is to protect the Government's power of issuing paper currency, *i.e.*, the notes payable to bearer on demand. It may be noted that this provision shall prevail over and above the provisions of the Negotiable Instruments Act.

Notes. The expression 'payable to *bearer on demand*' means that anybody without an endorsement from the holder of the negotiable instrument, can get the payment of the amount mentioned in the instrument. Whereas, in case of a negotiable instrument payable to a particular person or to his order, any body having its possession cannot get the payment. In such a case, the person entitled to the payment will be either the person in whose favour the instrument is drawn or the endorsee from him.

LEGAL PROVSIONS (SECTIONS) DISCUSSED IN THE CHAPTER

Important legal provisions (section) of the Negotiable Instrument Acts, 1881, discussed in this chapter, are reproduced hereunder for ready reference:

1. ***Section 11: Inland Instrument***

"A promissory note, bill of exchange or cheque drawn or made in India and made payable in, or drawn upon any person resident in India shall be deemed to be an inland instrument"

2. *Section 12: Foreign Instrument*

"Any such instrument not so drawn, made or made payable shall be deemed to be a foreign instrument"

3. *Section 13(1): Negotiable Instrument*

"A negotiable instrument means a promsssory note, bill of exchange or cheque payable either to order or to bearer".

4. *Section 13(1) Explanation 1: Order Instrument*

"A promissory note, bill of exchange or cheque is payable to order which is expressed to be so payable or which is expressed to be payable to a particular person and does not contain words prohibiting transfer or indicating an intention that it shall not be transferable.

5. *Section 13 (1): Explanation II: Bearer Instruments*

"A promissory note, bill of exchange or a cheque is payable to bear which is expressed to be so payable or on which the only or the last indorsement is an indorsement in blank".

6. *Section 17: Ambiguous Instruments*

"Where an instrument may be construed either as a promissory note or a bill of exchange, the holder may at his eletion treat it as either, and the instrument shall be thenceforward treated accordingly".

7. *Section 19: Instruments Payable on Demand*

"A promissory note or bill of exchange in which no time for payment is specified, and a cheque, are always payable on demand".

8. *Section 21: At sight, on presentation, After sight*

"In a promissory note or bill of exchange, the expression, at sight and 'on presentment' means on demand. the expressiion after sight means, in a promissory note, after presentment for sight, and in a bill of exchange after acceptance, or noting for non-acceptance, or protest for non-acceptance.

TEST QUESTIONS

1. What do you understand by the term negotiable instrument? What are its special characteristics? State the law applicable to negotiable instruments as modified by the Reserve Bank of India Act, 1934.
2. How will you classify the negotiable instruments? What are the kinds of a negotiable instrument as expressly dealt in the Negotiable Instruments Act, 1881?
3. What are the special presumptions as to negotiable instrument?
4. What are the special characteristics of negotiable instruments?
5. Write notes on the following :
   (*a*) Inland and Foreign Instrument.
   (*b*) The provision of the Reserve Bank of India Act, 1934 modifying the Negotiable Instruments Act, 1881.
   (*c*) Inchoate Instruments.
   (*d*) Bearer and Order Instruments.

MULTIPLE CHOICE QUESTIONS

1. The Negotiable Instruments Act makes specific mention of three instruments, namely cheque, bill of exchange and
   (*a*) promissory note, (*b*) hundi,
   (*c*) bank draft, (*d*) customary note.
2. Which one of the following is not the characteristic of a negotiable instrument?
   (*a*) It must be in writing (*b*) It must be freely transferable
   (*c*) It must be registered (*d*) It must contain definite amount of money.

3. In legal terms, a person who receives a negotiable instrument in good faith and for valuable consideration is known as
   (*a*) Holder (*b*) Holder for value
   (*c*) Holder in due course (*d*) Holder in rights.
4. A negotiable instrument drawn in India on a person residing in India, and payable outside India is known as
   (*a*) Inland instrument (*b*) Foreign instrument
   (*c*) Indo-foreign instrument (*d*) None of these.
5. An instrument originally payable to a particular person but subsequently endorsed in blank become a bearer instrument on such endorsement
   (*a*) True (*b*) False.
6. A negotiable instrument in which no time for payment is specified is payable
   (*a*) after acceptance (*b*) after sight
   (*c*) after one month (*d*) on demand.
7. A cheque is always payable on demand
   (*a*) True (*b*) False.

ANSWERS

1. (*a*) **2.** (*c*) **3.** (*c*) **4.** (*a*) **5.** (*a*) **6.** (*d*)
7. (*a*)

OBJECTIVE TYPE QUESTIONS WITH REASONING

State with reasons whether the following statements are correct or incorrect.

1. The term 'negotiable instrument' is defined in Section 13 of the Negotiable Instrument Act, 1881 in the wider sense so as to include every written and signed instrument.
2. It is presumed that every negotiable instrument has been made or drawn for consideration.
3. A bill of exchange contains an unconditional promise by one person to pay a certain sum of money to the bearer of the instrument or to a specified person.
4. An inland instrument endorsed in a foreign country becomes a foreign instrument.
5. An instrument on which the last endorsement is an endorsement in blank is a bearer instrument.
6. An instrument made in the words as 'pay to *A* only' is an order instrument.
7. A cheque is always payable on demand.
8. A promissory note cannot be made payable to bearer.

ANSWERS

1. *Incorrect.* Section 13 defines the term so as to include only three kinds of instruments namely promissory note, bill of exchange and cheque.
2. *Correct.* It is the legally recognised presumption about negotiable instruments.
3. *Incorrect.* A bill of exchange contains an unconditional *order* directing a certain person to pay a certain sum of money to the bearer or to a specified person.
4. *Incorrect.* The nature of inland instrument is not changed by the mere fact of its being circulation in a foreign country.
5. *Correct.* As such an instrument can be transferred by a mere delivery of the instrument.

6. *Incorrect.* It is not an order instrument as its further transfer is restricted by using the word 'only'.
7. *Correct.* As no time for payment is specified in the cheque, it may be presented for payment at any time.
8. *Correct.* In view of section 31 of the Reserve Bank of India Act, 1934, a promissory note cannot be made payable to bearer.

PRACTICAL PROBLEMS

1. *A*, a resident of Delhi, draws a bills of exchange in Delhi on *B*, a merchant in Chandigarh. *B* accepts the bill of exchange as payable in Singapore. State whether it is an inland instrument or foreign instrument ? Give reasons.

   Hint : It is an inland instrument. An instrument drawn in India on any person residing in india is an inland instrument whether payable in India or outside India. [Section 11]
2. *A* a resident of London draws a bills of exchange on *B*, a merchant in London. *B* accepts the bills of exchange as payable in India. State whether it is an inland or foreign instrument? Give reasons.

   Hint : It is a foreign instrument. An instrument which is not an inland instrument is a foreign instrument [Section 12]. In this case, the bill is drawn outside India on persons residing outside India, thus it is not an inland bill.
3. State which of the following are 'bearer' and 'order' instruments, if drawn in the following words?
   (*a*) Pay to *A*.
   (*b*) Pay to *A* or order.
   (*c*) Pay to *A* or bearer.
   (*d*) Pay the bearer.

   Hint : Instruments in points (a) and (b) are order instruments and those in points (c) and (d) are bearer instrument.
4. State which of the following instruments are payable on demand ?
   (*a*) A cheque
   (*b*) A promissory note or a bill of exchange in which no time for payment is specified.
   (*c*) A promissory note or a bill of exchange which is expressed to be payable 'at sight' or 'on presentation'.

   Hint : All the above instruments are payable on demand [Sections 19 and 22]. A cheque is always payable on demand.
5. A bill of exchange is drawn in words reading as "Pay to *A* the sum of rupees fifty thousand only". However, in , figure the amount was stated as Rs. 5000. Which of these amounts shall be taken as the amount of the instrument ? Give reasons stating the applicable legal provision.

   Hint : The bill the exchange will be treated for Rs. 50,000. In such a case, the amount stated in words in considered to be the amount of instrument. [Section 18]
6. *A* owed Rs. 50,000 to *B* and delivered a stamped and signed promissory note to *B* leaving blank the space for amount. *B* filled Rs. 60,000 in the space left blank for amount. Can he recover the entire amount of Rs. 60,000?

   Hint : No, *B* cannot recover Rs. 60,000. It is an inchoate instrument and *B* is entitled to recover Rs. 50,000 *i.e.* the amount which *A* intended to pay under the instrument. [Section 20]

33

CHAPTER

PROMISSORY NOTES, BILLS OF EXCHANGE AND CHEQUES

33.1. INTRODUCTION

In the last chapter, we have discussed the 'negotiable instruments' in general. But the Negotiable Instruments Act makes a specific mention of only three kinds of negotiable instruments namely, promissory notes, bills of exchange and cheques. In this chapter, we shall discuss in details these three negotiable instruments.

Note. The term 'negotiable instruments', 'Promissory note' and 'bill of exchange' are frequently used in this chapter as well as in subsequent chapters of Negotiable Instruments Act. At most of the places, we shall use the words 'instrument', 'note' and 'bill' for the words 'negotiable instruments', 'promissory note' and 'bill of exchange' respectively.

33.2. PROMISSORY NOTE

The term 'promissory note' may be defined as a promise in writing by a person to pay a certain sum of money to a specified person. The legal definition of this term is contained in Section 4 of the Negotiable Instruments Act, which reads as under:

> *"A promissory note is an instrument in writing containing an unconditional undertaking signed by the maker to pay a certain sum of money only to, or to the order of a certain person, or to the bearer of the instrument."*

The analysis of this section shows that, a promissory note is a written and signed promise to pay a certain sum of money to a specified person or his order.

Example 33.1. The following negotiable instruments signed by *A* are valid promissory notes as they fulfil the requirements of legal definition discussed above.

(*a*) I promise to pay *B* or order Rs. 500.

(*b*) I acknowledge myself to be indebted to *B* in Rs. 1000, to be paid on demand for value received.

Example 33.2. The following negotiable instruments signed by *A* are not valid promissory notes as they do not fulfil the requirements of legal definition discussed above:

(*a*) *B*, I.O.U. (I owe you) Rs. 500.

(*b*) I promise to pay *B* Rs. 500, and all other sums which shall be due to him.

(*c*) I promise to pay *B* Rs. 500, first deducting thereout any money which he may owe me.

(*d*) I promise to pay *B* Rs. 500 seven days after my marriage with C.

(*e*) I promise to pay *B* Rs. 500 on *D*'s death, provided *B* leaves enough to pay that sum.

(*f*) I promise to pay *B* Rs. 500 and to deliver him my black horse on 1st January.

It may be noted that the bank notes and currency notes are not to be treated as promissory notes. They are expressly excluded from the category of promissory notes. It may also be noted that the words *'or to the bearer'* in the last line of legal definition, are not operative. The reason for the same is that Section 31 of the Reserve Bank of India Act, 1934, specifically provides that a promissory note cannot be made payable to bearer. Thus, a valid promissory note is one which is payable to a specified person or his order.

33.3. PARTIES TO A PROMISSORY NOTE

Following are the two main parties in a promissory note:

1. ***Maker:*** It is a person who makes the promissory note and promises to pay the money stated therein.
2. ***Payee:*** It is a person to whom the amount of promissory note is payable *i.e.,* to whom the promise to pay is made.

33.4. SPECIMEN OF A PROMISSORY NOTE

Following is the *general specimen* of a promissory note :

Rs. 500 Bombay, April 14, 2003

Three months after date, I promise to you *B* or order the sum of rupees five hundred for value received.

To *B*

Bombay

Stamp

Sd/-*A*

In this specimen, *A* is the maker, and *B* is the payee as the amount of Rs. 500 is to be paid to him or any other person to whom he orders. In this specimen, the promissory note is made at Bombay.

33.5. ESSENTIALS OF A VALID PROMISSORY NOTE

1. *It must be in writing*
2. *It must contain an express promise to pay*
3. *The promise to pay must be unconditional*
4. *It must contain a promise to pay in terms of money only*
5. *It must contain promise to pay a definite (i.e., certain) amount of money*
6. *It must contain certain parties*
7. *It must be signed by the maker*
8. ***Intention to make a promissory note and its delivery***
9. ***Other formalities***

Following are the essential elements (requirements) of a valid promissory note.

1. *It must be in writing:* The first requirement of a valid promissory note is that it must be in writing. An oral promise to pay a sum of money is not a promissory note. However, the writing may be in ink or in pencil. It also includes printing and typewriting.

2. *It must contain an express promise to pay :* The second requirement of a valid promissory note is that it must contain an express promise to pay money. A mere implied promise to pay is not sufficient. It may be noted that a mere acknowledgment of a debt is not a promissory note. The reason for the same is that by the mere acknowledgment of a debt, a person does not promise to pay the debt. He simply acknowledges his liability to pay the same.

Example 33.3. The following negotiable instruments signed by *A* are valid promissory notes as they contain an express promise to pay:

(*a*) I promise to pay *B* the sum of Rs. 1,000.

(*b*) I acknowledge myself to be indebted to *B* in Rs. 1,000 to be paid on demand, for value received.

Example 33.4. The following negotiable instruments signed by *A* are not valid promissory notes as they contain a mere acknowledgment of debt:

(*a*) *B*, I.U.O. (I owe you) Rs. 1,000.

(*b*) *B*, I am liable to pay you Rs. 500.

3. *The promise to pay must be unconditional* : The third requirement is that, the promise to pay should not depend upon a condition or upon the happening of an *uncertain event*. It may be noted that a conditional or an uncertain promissory note is bad, and thus invalid.

Example 33.5. The following instruments signed by *A* are not valid promissory notes:

(*a*) I promise to pay *B* Rs. 500 seven days after my marriage with C. It is an uncertain promissory note because *A* may never marry *C*.

(*b*) I promise to pay *B* Rs. 500 on *C*'s death, provided *C* leaves me enough to pay that amount. In this case, though the death of C is certain at one time or the other. But the payment is conditional because the promise to pay depends upon the condition if C leaves the sufficient amount to pay. This is an uncertain event because C may not leave sufficient amount at the time of death.

(*c*) I promise to pay *B* Rs. 500 as soon as possible. It is an uncertain promissory note because it is difficult to ascertain *A*'s possibility of making payment.

But sometimes, an instrument is made payable on the happening of a *certain event* which is bound to happen. In such cases, the instrument is valid because there is no uncertainty regarding its payment.

Example 33.6. *A* signed an instrument in the words readings as "I promise to pay *B* Rs. 500 seven days after *C*'s death. It is a valid promissory note because the death is a certain event and is bound to happen.

Similarly, a promise to pay at a particular place or after a specified time, is not conditional. It is a valid promissory note.

Example 33.7. *A* signed an instrument in the words reading as "I promise to pay *B* Rs. 1,000 thirty days after date (*i.e.*, after the date the promissory note was prepared)". It is a valid promissory note.

4. *It must contain a promise to pay in terms of money only* : The fourth requirement of a valid promissory note is that it must be payable in terms of money and money only. If the instrument contains a promise to pay something other than money or something in addition to money, it will not be a valid promissory note.

Example 33.8. The following instruments signed by *A* are not valid promissory notes as they do not contain a promise to pay in terms of money only:

(*a*) I promise to pay *B* Rs. 500 and also to deliver him my black horse on 1st January next.

(*b*) I promise to pay *B* in 30 shares and 20 bonds of a company.

(*c*) I promise to deliver to *B* 100 bags of rice.

5. *It must contain promise to pay a definite (i.e., certain) amount of money:* The fifth requirement of a valid promissory note is that the amount of money payable must be definite. In other words, the promise must be to pay a certain amount of money. If the amount payable is not definite, then the promissory note will not be valid.

Example 33.9. The following instruments signed by *A* are not valid promissory notes as they do not contain the promise to pay a definite amount of money:

(*a*) I promise to pay *B* Rs. 1,000 and all other sums which shall be due to him.

(*b*) I promise to pay *B* Rs. 5000, first deducting thereout any money which he may owe to me.

(*c*) I promise to pay *B* Rs. 550 and the fine according to rules.

But sometimes, the language of a promissory note is such that the amount payable can be easily ascertained. In such cases, the promissory note is valid.

Example 33.10. The following instruments signed by *A* are valid promissory notes as there is no uncertainty regarding the amount payable:

(*a*) I promise to pay *B* Rs. 6,000 in 12 monthly instalments of Rs. 500 each on the first of every month. If I fail to pay any instalment on the due date, then the whole balance unpaid shall become due [Section 5, third para].

(*b*) I promise to pay *B* Rs. 2,000 alongwith simple interest at the rate of 15% per annum.

6. *It must contain certain parties:* The sixth requirements is that the parties to a promissory note must be certain. Thus, both the parties namely, (*a*) the maker, and (*b*) the payee must be indicated with certainty on the face of the instrument. However, the parties may be described by name or designation, *e.g.*, manager of a bank, the principal of a college etc. It may also be noted that it is not necessary that the payee should be specifically mentioned in the instrument. It is sufficient if on reading the documents, as a whole there is no doubt as to the person who is the payee, *e.g.*, where a name is written in the address only, and not in the instrument itself.

7. *It must be signed by the maker:* The last requirement of a valid promissory note is that it must be signed by the maker. The instrument will be complete only when it is signed by the maker. It may be noted that even if the instrument is written by the maker in his own hand and his name appears in the body of the instrument, his signature must be there. If the maker is illiterate, he may put his thumb mark. However, the signatures may be in any part of the instrument.

8. *Intention to make a promissory note and its delivery:* In addition to the requirements of Section 4 of the Negotiable Instruments Act (as discussed above), an instrument to be a promissory note must be such as to show the intention to make a promissory note[1], and must be delivered [Section 48]. A promissory note is inchoate, and incomplete until it is delivered to the payee [Section 46]. If a person signs a promissory note in his home and keeps it there, it is not a promissory note, and he does not become liable to any one even if somebody's name is written on it. The making of a note is only a preparation. It is not an offer at all, and therefore, it does not become any part of the contract. The contract arises only on the delivery of a properly signed promissory note and not before that. Thus, the promissory note is complete, and the maker becomes liable to pay only when the duly singed note is voluntarily delivered to the payee.

[*Bhagwan Das* v. *Girdharilal*, 1966 SC 543].

1. *Bahdurrinisa* v. *vasudev*, AIR 1967 AP 123.
2. *Bapanna Krishnayya* v. *Chaprala Baburao*, AIR 1977 AP (N) 42

9. *Other formalities:* As a matter of fact, the requirements mentioned above are essential for the validity of a promissory note. The lack of any one or more of these requirements will not make the document, a promissory note[2]. There are certain other formalities, such as *number, date, place, consideration, attestation* etc. which are *usually found* in a promissory note. But they are not essential in law. The omission to mention date and place where it is made or where it is payable, does not invalidate the instrument. However, the date should be mentioned where the amount is payable at a certain time after date. Similarly, the omission of words, *'for value received'* does not invalidate the promissory note . Because there is presumption as regards the consideration.

But a promissory note must be properly stamped as required by the Indian Stamp Act, 1899, and stamp must also be properly cancelled.

33.6. BILL OF EXCHANGE

The term 'bill of exchange' may be defined as an order, in writing, requiring certain person to pay a certain sum of money to a specified person. The legal definition of the term is given in Section 5 of the Negotiable Instruments Act which, reads as under:

"A bill of exchange is an instrument in writing containing an unconditional order, signed by the maker, directing a certain person to pay a certain sum of money only to, or to the order of a certain person or to the bearer of he instrument."

The analysis of this section shows that, a bill of exchange is a written and signed order directing a person to pay a certain sum of money to the bearer of the instrument or to a specified person or his order. Generally, a bill of exchange is drawn by a creditor, who directs his debtor to pay the money to the person specified in the instrument.

Example 33.11. *A* wrote and signed an instrument ordering *B* to pay Rs. 500 to *C*. This is a bill of exchange. In this instrument *B* has been ordered to pay Rs. 500 to C.

It may be noted that a bill of exchange cannot be made payable to the *bearer on demand*. Section 31 of the Reserve Bank of India Act, 1934, specifically prohibits the issue of such bills of exchange. Thus, a bill of exchange drawn as under is not a valid bill of exchange:

"On demand pay to the bearer the sum of rupees five hundred, for value received."

However, a bill of exchange payable on demand, in which name of the payee is mentioned, is valid. Thus, a bill of exchange drawn as under is a valid bill of exchange:

"On demand pay to A or order the sum of rupees five hundred for value received."

In this case, though the bill of exchange is payable on demand but it is payable to a specified person (*i.e., A*) or his order (*i.e.,* to a person to whom *A* requires to be paid). And thus, it is a valid bill of exchange.

33.7. PARTIES TO A BILL OF EXCHANGE

Following are the three main parties in a bill of exchange:

1. *Drawer:* It is a person who makes a bill of exchange. In other words, he is the maker of bill of exchange.

2. *Drawee:* It is a person who is ordered (*i.e.,* directed) to pay the amount of the bill of exchange *i.e.,* on whom the bill of exchange is drawn. When the drawee accepts the bill of exchange (*i.e.,* when he gives his consent to make the payment of the bill on due date), he is called the 'acceptor'.

3. *Payee:* It is a person to whom the amount of bill of exchange is payable.

In some cases, the drawer and the payee may be the same person *e.g.,* when a person signs a bill of exchange reading as "pay to me or my order". Thus, if *A* signs a bill of exchange ordering *B* to pay the amount to himself *A*, then the drawer and the payee will be the same person (*i.e., A*). Sometimes, the drawer and the drawee may also be the same person, *e.g.*, a bill of exchange drawn by one branch of a firm on its another branch. In such cases the holder of the bill, at his option, may treat it either a bill of exchange or a promissory note [Seciton 17].

33.8. SPECIMEN OF A BILL OF EXCHANGE

Following is the *general specimen* of a bill of exchange:

Rs 500

Delhi, April 14, 2003

Three months after date pay to C or order the sum of rupee five hundred, for value received

To B
11, Model Town
Delhi.

Stamp
Sd/- *A*

In this specimen , *A* is the drawer. *B* is the drawee as the bill of exchange is addressed to him and he has been ordered (*i.e.*, directed)) to pay the amount of Rs. 500. And C is the payee as the amount is to be paid to him or any other person to whom he orders. In this specimen, the bill is drawn at Delhi.

33.9. ESSENTIALS OF A VALID BILL OF EXCHANGE

1. *It must be in writing*
2. *In must contain an express order to pay*
3. *The order to pay must be unconditional*
4. ***It must contain an order to pay in terms of money only***
5. *It must contain an order to pay a definite (i.e., certain) amount of money*
6. *In must contain certain parities*
7. *It must be signed by the drawer*
8. *Intention to make a bill of exchange and its delivery*
9. *Other formalities*

The legal definition of the term 'bill of exchange' as discussed in the last article, is almost similar to that of a promissory note. Thus, the essential requirements are more or less the same. However, the bill of exchange differs from a promissory note in some particular respects, *e.g.*, a bill of exchange is an 'order to pay' money, whereas a promissory note is a 'promise to pay' money. The requirements of a bill of exchange, in brief, are as under.

1. *It must be in writing:* The first requirement of a valid bill of exchange is that it must be in writing. Like promissory note, a bill of exchange also cannot be oral.

2. *In must contain an express order to pay:* The second requirement of a valid bill of exchange is that it must contain an express order to pay money. This feature of a bill of exchange distinguishes it from a promissory note. Because, a promissory note contains a *promise* to pay and not an order to pay. It may be noted that a mere request to pay money, is not a bill of exchange. However, the order to pay may be in the form of a request, *i.e.*, an order to pay may be in a polite language. But, merely giving an authority to a person to pay money, is not an order.

Example 33.12. The following instruments signed by *A* are valid bills of exchange as they contain an order to pay, though the language used is vary polite:

(*a*) *B*, please pay Rs. 500 to C or order.

(*b*) *B* will much oblige me by paying to C Rs. 500.

Example 33.13. The following instruments signed by *A* are not valid bills of exchange as they contain only a request to pay and no order to pay:

(*a*) *B*, please let C have Rs. 500, and place it to my account and oblige.

(*b*) *B*, I shall be highly obliged if you make it convenient to pay Rs. 1,000 to *C*.

3. *The order to pay must be unconditional:* The third requirement of a valid bill of exchange is that the order to pay must be unconditional. In other words, the order to pay should not depend upon a condition or upon the happening of an uncertain event.

4. *It must contain an order to pay in terms of money only:* The fourth requirement of a valid bill of exchange is that it must be payable in terms of money and money only. If the instrument contains an order to pay something other than money or something in addition to money, it will not be valid bill of exchange.

5. *It must contain an order to pay a definite (i.e., certain) amount of money:* The fifth requirement of a valid bill of exchange is that the amount of money ordered to be paid must be definite . In other words, an order must be to pay a certain amount of money.

6. *In must contain certain parities:* The sixth requirement is that, the parties to a bill of exchange must be certain. Thus, all the three parties namely, (*a*) the drawer, (*b*) the drawee, and (*c*) the payee must be certain, *i.e.,* indicated in a bill of exchange with reasonable certainty.

7. *It must be signed by the drawer:* The last requirement of a valid bill of exchange is that, it must be signed by the drawer. The instrument will be complete only when it is signed by the drawer.

8. *Intention to make a bill of exchange and its delivery:* In addition to the requirements of Section 5 of the Negotiable Instruments Act (as discussed above), an instrument to be a bill of exchange must be such as to show the intention to make a bill of exchange and must be delivered. A bill of exchange is inchoate and incomplete until it is delivered to the payee. This point has already been discussed in detail in case of a promissory note.

9. *Other formalities:* As a matter of fact, the requirements mentioned above are essential for the validity of a bill of exchange. And the lack of any one or more of these requirements will not make the document, a bill of exchange. There are certain other formalities, such as number, date, place, consideration, attestation etc., which are usually found in a bill of exchange. But they are not essential in law. Thus, the omission to mention number, date single etc. does not invalidate the instrument. But a bill of exchange must be properly stampted as required by the Indian Stamp Act, 1899, and the stamp must also be properly cancelled.

33.10. CHEQUE

The term 'cheque' may be defined as a bill of exchange which is drawn upon a banker and is always payable on demand. The legal definition of the term as contained in Section 6 of the Negotiable Instruments Act, has been amended by the Negotiable Instruments (Amendments and Miscellaneous Provisions) Act, 2002 w.e.f., 6.2.2003 and the amended section reads as under:

> *"A cheque is a bill of exchange draw on a specified banker and not expressed to be payable otherwise than on demand and it inclues the electronic image of a truncated cheque and a cheque in electronic form."*

The analysis of this section shows that, a cheque is a bill of exchange with the following two additional requirements:

1. A cheque is always drawn on a specified bank, and
2. A cheque is always payable on demand.

A cheque, being a bill of exchange, must have all its essential requirements. Thus, a cheque must contain an unconditional order on a specified banker to pay a certain sum of money. Therefore, by a cheque, a banker is directed to pay a certain amount of money on demand.

The Negotiable Instruments (Amendment and Miscellaneous Provisions) Act, 2002 has also added an Explanation – I to section 6 defining the experssion *cheque in electronic form* and *truncated cheque* as under :

(*a*) A *"cheque in electronic form"* means as cheque which contains the exact mirror image of a paper cheque, and is generated, written and signed in a secure system ensuring the minimum safety standards with the use of digital signature (with or without biometric signatre) and asymmetric crypto system.

(*b*) A *"truncated cheque"* means a cheque which is truncated (*i.e.*, shortened) during the course of clearing cycle, either by the clearing house or by the bank whether paying or receiving payment, immediately on generation of an electronic image for transmission, substituting the further physical movement of the cheque in writing.

33.11. PARTIES TO A CHEQUE

Following are the three main parties in a cheque:

1. *Drawer:* It is a person who makes the cheque. In other words, he is the maker of a cheque.

2. *Drawee:* It is a banker who is directed to pay the amount of the cheque, *i.e.*, on whom the cheque is drawn. It may be noted that in case of a cheque, the drawee is *always a banker*.

3. *Payee:* It is a person to whom the amount of cheque is payable.

However in some cases, the drawer and the payee may be the same person, *e.g.*, where a person draws a cheque 'payable to self'.

33.12. SPECIMEN OF A CHEQUE

Following is the *general specimen* of a cheque:

Date. .... 20 ....

PUNJAB NATIONAL BANK

Sector 17, Chandigarh.

Pay. .... Mr. *B* or .... bearer

the sum of rupees five hundred only. Rs. 500/-

No. .... Sd/- *A*

In this specimen, *A* is the drawer. The Punjab National Bank, Sector 17, Chandigarh is the drawee bank as the cheque is drawn on this bank. And *B* is the payee as the amount of Rs. 500 is to be paid to him.

33.13. ESSENTIALS OF A VALID CHEQUE

1. *It must have all the essentials of a bill of exchange*
2. *It must be drawn on a specified banker*
3. *It must be payable on demand*

The legal definition of the term 'cheque', discussed in the last article, reveals that it is a special kind of a bill of exchange drawn upon a banker. The essential elements (*i.e.*, requirements) of a cheque are as under:

1. *It must have all the essentials of a bill of exchange:* The primary requirement of a valid cheque is that it must have all the essential elements of a bill of exchange. The reason for the same is that the cheque is primarily a bill of exchange drawn upon a banker. The essentials for a bill of exchange have already been discussed in detail in Art. 33.9 which may be summed up as under:

(*a*) It must be in writing. (*b*) It must contain an unconditional order to pay. (*c*) It must contain an order to pay in terms of money only. (*d*) It must contain an order to pay a definite amount of money. (*e*) It must contain certain parties. (*f*) It must be signed by the drawer.

In addition to these essentials of a bill of exchange, the cheque must also satisfy the following two requirements:

2. *It must be drawn on a specified banker:* The first additional requirement of a valid cheque is that it must be drawn on a specified banker. A cheque drawn on any person other than a banker, is not valid.

3. *It must be payable on demand:* The second additional requirement of a valid cheque is that it must be payable on demand. As a matter of fact, a cheque is *always* payable on demand.

It is to be noted that all cheques are bills of exchange. But all bills of exchange are not cheques. A bill of exchange becomes a cheque only when it satisfies the above two additional requirement.

Notes 1. No acceptance of a cheque is required. Moreover, a cheque is also not required to be stamped.

2. A cheque is equivalent to cash payment. The payment is deemed to be made on the date of issue. [*K. Saraswathy v. Samasundram Chettiar*, AIR 1989 SC 1553]

33.14. MARKING OF A CHEQUE

The term 'marking of a cheque' may be defined as the writing on a cheque by the drawee banker that it would be honoured when duly presented for payment. A cheque may be marked with words 'approved' or 'good'. The marking of a cheque may be made by the drawee banker at the instance of the drawer, or the holder or the collecting banker. The effect of marking is that the payee is certain to get the payment. In some places, there is custom among bankers to mark cheques as 'good for payment'. It may, however, be noted that the marking of a cheque does not amount to an acceptance. A cheque being intended for immediate payment, does not require any acceptance. It may be noted that in Negotiable Instruments Act, there is no provision about the marking of cheques such as 'approved', 'good' or 'good for payment'. Moreover, in India, there is no such recognised practice of marking of cheques.

33.15. COMPARISON BETWEEN A PROMISSORY NOTE AND A BILL OF EXCHANGE

The following Table gives the comparison between a promissory note and a bill of exchange:

S. No.	*Promissory Note*	*Bill of Exchange*
1.	In this case there are two parties, namely (*a*) the maker, and (*b*) the payee.	In this case, there are three parties, namely, (*a*) the drawer, (*b*) the drawee, and (*c*) the payee. However, in some cases, the drawer and the payee may be the same person. And sometimes, the drawer and the drawee may also be the same.
2.	It contains an unconditional *promise*, by the maker, to pay money, *i.e.*, the maker himself promises to pay, the amount.	It contains an unconditional order, by the drawer to another, to pay money, *i.e.*, the maker (drawer) orders someone else (*i.e.*, drawee) to pay the amount.

3. *Explanation* to Section 44 of the Negotiable Instruments Act.

3. It does not require any acceptance of the maker before it is presented for payment. The reason for the same is that, it is signed by the person who is liable to pay. It is presented for payment without any prior acceptance.	It generally, requires the acceptance of the drawee, before it is presented for payment. The drawee becomes liable to pay only when he accepts the bill of exchange. A bill of exchange which is payable 'after acceptance' or 'after a certain period' must be presented to drawee for his acceptance.
4. In this case, the liability of the maker of a promissory note is primary and absolute. Because the maker himself promises to pay the money.	In this case, the liability of the drawer (maker) of a bill of exchange is secondary and conditional. Because he becomes liable to pay only when the acceptor fails to pay the money.
5. In this case, the maker stands in an immediate relationship with the payee. And thus, the payee can demand payment from the maker.	In this case, on acceptance of the bill of exchange, drawer's immediate relationship is with the acceptor and not with the payee[3]. And thus, the payee cannot demand payment from the drawer directly. He should first demand the payment from acceptor.
6. It can never be made payable to bearer.	It can be made payable to bearer. But it cannot be made payable to a 'bearer on demand'.
7. In this case, the maker and the payee cannot be the same person, because A promise to pay money to self is not a promissory note.	In this case, the drawer and the payee may be the same person, because the drawee can be ordered to pay the money to drawer himself.
8. It is generally written by a debtor who himself promises to pay the money to his creditor.	It is generally written by a creditor who orders his debtor (drawee) to pay the money.
9. In case of dishonour of a promissory note, there is no need to give a notice of dishonour to the maker. He is liable to pay the amount due on the promissory note even if no notice of dishonour is given to him.	In case of dishonour of a bill of exchange, the notice of dishonour must be given by the holder to all the prior parties (including drawer and endorsers) who are liable to pay the money. If no notice of dishonour is given, such parties shall not be liable to pay the amount due on the bill of exchange.
10. It cannot be drawn is sets, *i.e.*, parts.	It can be drawn in sets also.
11. In this case, no protest is required. The term protest will be discussed in Art. 38.11.	In this case, foreign bills of exchange must be protested for dishonour when such protest is required by the law of the place where the bills are drawn.
12. In this case, there is no question of conditional acceptance, as promissory notes are not required to be accepted.	In this case, there can be a conditional acceptance of a bill of exchange.

33.16. COMPARISON BETWEEN A BILL OF EXCHANGE AND A CHEQUE

The following table gives the comparison between a bill of exchange and a cheque:

S. No. *Bill of Exchange*	*Cheque*
1. It is usually drawn on some person. However, it may also be drawn on a banker. Thus, the drawee in case of a bill of exchange can be any person including a banker.	It is always drawn on a banker. Thus, the drawee in case of a cheque is always a banker.

2. It may be payable on demand or after the expiry of a fixed period.	It is always payable on demand. As a matter of fact, a cheque is meant for immediate payment.
3. It generally, requires acceptance before the payment can be demanded from the drawee. Thus, in the first instance, the bill of exchange is presented for acceptance. The drawee becomes liable to pay the amount due on the bill of exchange only when he accepts the bill.	It does not require any acceptance. As the cheque is meant for immediate payment, it is presented for payment and not for acceptance. However, the banker is liable to pay the amount of cheque only if there is sufficient amount in drawer's account.
4. In this case, there is no provision regarding the crossing of bill of exchange.	In this case, there is a provision regarding the crossing of cheques. The payment of a crossed cheque can be obtained only through the bank account.
5. It cannot be made payable to bearer on demand.	It can be made payable to bearer on demand.
6. It must be stamped.	It does not require any stamp.
7. In case of dishonour of a bill of exchange, the notice of dishonour must be given to the drawer. If notice is not given to the drawer, he will not be liable for payment.	In case of dishonour of a cheque, the notice of dishonour is not required.
8. In this case, the drawer of a bill of exchange is discharged from liability if the bill is not presented to the acceptor for payment.	In this case, the drawer of a cheque is not discharged from liability if the cheque is not presented for payment.
9. In this case, three days of grace are allowed from the due date within which the payment can be made. However, in case of a bill of exchange payable on demand, no days of grace are allowed.	In this case, there is no question of days of grace. The reason for the same is that a cheque is alaways payable on demand, *i.e.*, immediately on presentation for payment.
10. In case of dishonour of a bill of exchange, it is generally 'noted' or 'protested' for dishonour.	In case of dishonour of a cheque, it is not required to be 'noted' or 'protested' for dishonour.
11. In this case, the payment of a bill of exchange cannot be countermanded, *i.e.*,. the drawer of a bill of exchange cannot stop the other parties from making payment.	In this case, the payment of a cheque can be countermanded, *i.e.*, on drawer's request, the banker can stop the payment of a cheque in certain circumstances.

33.17. SOME IMPORTANT KINDS OF BILLS OF EXCHANGE

Following are some important kinds of bills of exchange:

1. Accommodation bill.
2. Fictitious bill
3. Documentary bill and clean bill.
4. Bill in sets.

33.18. ACCOMMODATION BILL

It is a bill of exchange which is made only to provide financial help to some party. An accommodation bill is drawn accepted or endorsed, without any consideration, by some person with a view to lend the credit of his name on the bill so that the person taking the bill can get the money for the same. The person who signs (*i.e.*, accepts) the bill without any consideration, in order to accommodate some other person, is known as 'accommodating party' (or accommodation party), and the person who has been accommodated, is known as 'accommodated party.

Note. In form and in all other respects, an accommodation bill is similar to other (*i.e.*, ordinary) bill of exchange. There is nothing on the face of it to distinguish it from an ordinary trade bill of exchange.

Example 33.14. *A* was in need of Rs. 1,500. He approached his friend *B* for this purpose. But *B* was not in a position to lend money. However, he (*B*) suggested that *A* may draw a bill of exchange on him (*B*) which he would accept. Accordingly, *A* drew a bill of exchange on *B*, and *B* accepted the same. This is an accommodation bill. If the credit of *A* is good, he can get the bill discounted with his banker and can get the amount. And thus, *A* will be in a position to raise the money. In this case, *B* is the accommodating party, and *A* is the accommodated party.

Since an accommodation bill is drawn for the benefit of the 'accommodated party', there is an implied agreement between the 'accommodating party' and 'accommodated party' that either–

(*a*) The accommodated party will himself pay the bill on maturity, or

(*b*) The accommodated party will provide funds to the accommodating party to make the payment of the bill on maturity, or

(*c*) The accommodated party will indemnify the accommodating party for any payment which the accommodating party might make in respect of the bill.

33.19. FICTITIOUS BILL

It is a bill of exchange in which the name of the drawer, or payee or both is fictitious. The term 'fictitious person' means (*a*) a person who is not in existence or (*b*) a pretended person, *i.e.*, a person who is in existence but never intended by the parties to be the drawer or payee of the bill of exchange. It may be noted that when a fictitious bill is accepted by the drawee, then the *holder in due course* of the bill can recover the amount due on it from such a drawee if he can prove that the signature of the supposed drawer and that of the first endorser are in the same handwriting. This point will be discussed in detail in Art. 35.4.

33.20. DOCUMENTARY BILL AND CLEAN BILL

Sometimes, a seller of goods draws a bill of exchange on the buyer for the price of the goods. And the documents of title to the goods such as bill of lading, railways receipt, warehouse receipt etc., and some other documents such as invoice, shipping papers, marine insurance policy etc. are attached to the bill. In such cases, the bill of exchange is called a documentary bill. Such documents are delivered to the buyer only on the acceptance or payment of the bill. On the other hand, when no documents of title etc. are attached to a bill of exchange it is called a clean bill.

33.21. BILL IN SETS

A bill of exchange drawn in parts is known as a bill in sets. Sometimes, the drawer and the payee of a bill of exchange are at distant places or in different countries. In such cases, the bill of exchange, which is sent from one place to another may be lost or miscarried in transit. This causes a lot of inconvenience and delay to the person to whom the bill is sent. In order to avoid such delay and inconvenience, and to ensure the safe transmission of at least one part of the bill, it is drawn in parts (generally three). These parts together constitute one set. And the whole set is considered only one bill. Generally, each part is sent by a separate post. And if one or two parts are lost in transit, the payee can present the part which he has for acceptance or payment as the case may be. It may be noted that generally foreign bills are drawn in sets. Inland bills are rarely drawn in sets. Following are the rules regarding the bill in sets.

1. Each part of a bill in set must be numbered and contain a reference to other parts.
2. Each part must contain a provision that it shall continue to be payable so long as the other parts, remain unpaid. When payment is made on one of the parts, the entire bill comes to an end, *i.e.*, it is considered to be paid.

3. The drawer must sign all the parts of a set and deliver them to the payee. However, the stamp is affixed on one part only.
4. The drawee's acceptance is required only on one part [Section 7 (third para)], and may be given on any part. If an acceptor gives his acceptance on more than one part and they fall in the hands of different *holders in due course*, then the acceptor shall be liable on every such part as if it were a separate bill [Section 132 (exception)].

Specimen of a bill in set

No............... New Delhi, 1st March, 2010

Rs. 1,000

Two months after sight of this first part of the bill of exchange (second and Third of the same tenor and date being unpaid), pay to *C* or order the sum of rupees one thousand only, for value received.

To M/s B & Co. Stamp

London Sd/- *A*

In this set of a bill of exchange, the second part should contain a reference to first and third parts, and the third part should contain a reference to first and second parts.

LEGAL PROVISIONS (SECTIONS) DISCUSSED IN THE CHAPTER

Important legal provisions (section) of the Negotiable Instruments Act, 1881, discussed in this chapter, are reproduced hereunder for ready reference:

1. ***Section 4: Promissiory Note***

   "A promissory note is an instrument in writing (not being a bank-note or a currency note) containing an unconditional undertaking signed by the maker, to pay a certain sums of money only to, or to the order of a certain person or to the bearer of the instrument"

2. ***Section 5: Bill of Exchange***

   "A bill of exchange is an instrument in writing containing an uncorditional order, signed by the maker, directing a certain person to pay a certain sum of money only to, or to the order of, a certain person or to the bearer of the instrument".

3. ***Section 6: Cheque***

   "A cheque is bill of exchange drawn on a specified banker and not expressed to be payable otherwise than on demand and it includes the electronic image of a truncated cheque and a cheque in the electronic form".

4. ***Section 6, Explanation I (a): Cheque in Electronic Form***

   "A cheque in electronic form means a cheque which contains the exact mirror image of a paper cheque, and is generated, written and signed in a secure system ensuring the minimum safety standards with the use of digital signature (with or without biometries signature) and asymmetric crypto system".

5. ***Section 6, Explanation I (b): Truncated Cheque***

   "A truncated cheque means a cheque which is truncated during the course of clearing cycle, either by the clearing house or by the bank whether paying or receiving payment, immediately on generation of an electronic image for transmission, substituting the further physical movement of the cheque in writing".

6. ***Section 132: Bills in Sets***

   "Bills of exchange may be drawn in parts, each part being numbered and containing a provision that it shall continue payable only so long as other remain unpaid. All the parts together make a set; but the whole set constitute only one bill, and is extinguished when one of the parts, if a separate bill, would be extinguished".

TEST QUESTIONS

1. Define the term promissory note. What are the essentials of a valid promissory note? State the main parties to a promissory note.
2. What is a promissory note? How does it differ from a bill of exchange?
3. What is a bill of exchange? State its essential characteristics. In what way does it differ from a cheque?
4. "A cheque is a specimen of a bill of exchange with two additional qualifications"—explain stating these additional qualifications.
5. State the comparison between (*a*) promissory note and bill of exchange, (*b*) bill of exchange and cheque.
6. What are the main parties to a promissory note, bill of exchange, and a cheque? Give the specimen of these instruments.
7. Write notes on the following:
   (*a*) Marking of cheques. (*b*) Fictitious bill. (*c*) Bill in sets.

MULTIPLE CHOICE QUESTIONS

1. A promissory note cannot be made payable to bearer.
   (*a*) True, as the Reserve Bank of India Act, 1934 prohibits such promissory notes.
   (*b*) False, as the Negotiable Instruments Act authorises issue of such promissory notes.
2. Which of the following is a valid promissory note?
   (*a*) *A* I owe you some amount (*b*) *A* I owe you Rs. 1000
   (*c*) I promise to pay *A* or order Rs. 1000 (*d*) I promise to pay the bearer Rs. 1000.
3. Which of the following is not an essential of a valid promissory note?
   (*a*) It must be signed by maker (*b*) It must be stamped
   (*c*) It must be in writing (*d*) It must be registered.
4. A bill of exchange payable to bearer on demand is
   (*a*) valid (*b*) voidable
   (*c*) invalid (*d*) conditional.
5. A person who is directed to pay the amount of bill of exchange is known as
   (*a*) drawer (*b*) drawee
   (*c*) payee (*d*) creditor.
6. A bill of exchange dishonoured due to non-acceptance by the drawee, becomes
   (*a*) void (*b*) voidable
   (*c*) invalid (*d*) none of these.
7. An accepted view is that a cheque is equivalent to cash payment, and the payment is deemed to be made on the date of issue.
   (*a*) True (*b*) False.
8. All cheques are bills of exchange, but all bills of exchange are not cheques.
   (*a*) True (*b*) False.
9. Which of the following statement is incorrect?
   (*a*) A cheque in electronic form is included in the definition of cheque.
   (*b*) An electronic image of a truncated cheque is included in the legel definition of cheque.
   (*c*) The Negotiable Instruments Act, 1881 has been amended in 2002 by the Amendment Act No. 55 of 2002 to include the above two provisions.
   (*d*) The provisions, in points (*a*) and (*b*) above were already there in view of the Amendment Act of 1988.

ANSWERS

1. (*a*)	2. (*c*)	3. (*d*)	4. (*c*)	5. (*b*)	6. (*d*)
7. (*a*)	8. (*a*)	9. (*d*)			

OBJECTIVE TYPE QUESTIONS WITH REASONING

State with reasons whether the following statements are correct or incorrect

1. An instrument reading as " I promise to pay *B* Rs. 5,000 and all other sums which shall become due to him" is a valid promissory note.
2. A promissory note should contain the promise to pay in terms of money only.
3. A bill of exchange reading as "on demand pay to the bearer the sum of rupees one thousand, for value received" is a valid bill of exchange.
4. The acceptance of a bill of exchange is not necessary for its validity.
5. A bill of exchange cannot be made payable to "beare on demand".
6. The drawee of a cheque is the person to whom the payment is to be made, *i.e.*, to whom the cheque is payable.
7. No acceptance of a cheque is required.
8. A bill of exchange in which a drawer or payee is a non-existent person, is known as an accomodation bill.

ANSWERS

1. *Incorrect.* The amount payable to *B* is not certain in the instrument.
2. *Correct.* It is one of the important essentials of a promissory note.
3. *Incorrect.* In terms of Section 31 of the Reserve Bank of India Act, 1931, a bill of exchange cannot be made payable to bearer on demand.
4. *Correct.* A bill of exchange which is not accepted, does not become invalid. It only becomes dishonoured by non-acceptance.
5. *Correct.* Section 31 of the Reserve Bank of India Act, 1934 prohibits the issue of such bills.
6. *Incorrect.* In case of a cheque, the drawee is always a banker.
7. *Correct.* A cheque is intended for immediate payment as such it does not require any acceptance.
8. *Incorrect.* Such a bill is know as a fictitious bill.

PRACTICAL PROBLEMS

1. State whether the following instrument signed by *A* are valid promissory notes:
   (a) I acknowledge my self to be indebted to *B* in Rs.10,000 to be paid on demand for value received.
   (b) I promise to pay *B* Rs.5,000 seven day after *C*'s death.
   (c) I promise to pay *B* Rs.12,000 in 12 monthly instalments of Rs.1,000 each on the first of every month. If I fail to pay any instalment on due date, then the whole balance unpaid shall become due.
   (d) I am liable to pay *B* Rs.1,000.
   (e) I promise to pay *B* Rs.5,000 seven day after my marriage with *C*.
   (f) I promise to pay *B* Rs.5,000 on *C*'s death provided *C* leaves me enough to pay that amount.
   (g) I promise to pay *B* Rs.12,000 in regular monthly instalments.

Hint : Instruments mentioned in points (a) to (c) are valid promissory notes as they fulfil all the requirements of a promissory note as per section 4 of the Negotiable Instruments Act, 1881. Other instruments in points (d) to (g) are not valid as they do not fulfil the legal requirements. In instrument (d), there is no express promise to pay, in (e) and (f) promise to pay is conditional and in (g) the promise to pay is not of definite amount of money as the amount of regular monthly instalment is not specified.

2. State whether the following instrument signed by *A* are valid bills of exchange:

(a)*B*, please pay Rs.10,000 to *C* or order.

(b)*B*, I shall be highly obliged if you make it convenuent to pay Rs.10,000 to *C*.

Hint : Instrument in point (a) is a valid promissory note as there is an order to pay though it is in polite language. And the instrument in point (b) is not a valid promissory note as it contain only a request to pay and not an order to pay. [Section 5]

3. *A* draws a cheque in favour of *B* writing as "Pay Rs.50,000 to *B* thirty days after date". Is it a valid cheque ? Give reasons.

Hint : No, it is not a valid cheque. *A* cheque is always payable on demand, but in this case, the words "30 days after date" take away the characteristic of a demand instrument.

4. *A* was in need of Rs.70,000 and he approach his friend *B* for this purpose. Since *B* was not in a position to lend money, he suggested that *A* may draw a bill of exchange on him (*B*) which *B* will accept. Accordingly *A* drew a bill of exchange on *B* and he accepted the same. *A* further endorsed the bill to *C* a holder for value. Can *C* recover the amount of bill from *B* on maturity of the bill.

Hint : Yes, *C* can recover the amount of bill from *B* on maturity. In this case, the instrument is an 'accommodation bill' and the holder for value is entitled to recover the amount from acceptor (*i.e.* accommodating party) though the acceptor can afterwards claim the amount from accommodated party (*i.e.* drawer, (*A*) in this case).

34

CHAPTER

PARTIES TO A NEGOTIABLE INSTRUMENT AND THEIR CAPACITY

1. Introduction.
2. Parties to a Promissory Note.
3. Parties to a Bill of Exchange.
4. Parties to a Cheque.
5. Capacity of Parties.

34.1. INTRODUCTION

In the previous chapters, we have discussed the main parties with reference to each negotiable instrument, *i.e.*, promissory note, bill of exchange and cheque. However, there are certain other persons who also become the parties to a negotiable instrument. In this chapter, we shall discuss all the parties who are involved in each type of negotiable instrument. The capacity of the parties, *i.e.*, competency of the parties to make, draw, accept, etc. the negotiable instruments, shall also be discussed with reference to certain person such as minor, agents, corporations, legal representatives etc.

34.2. PARTIES TO A PROMISSORY NOTE

1. *Maker*
2. *Payee*
3. *Holder*
4. *Indorser*
5. *Indorsee*

Following are the parties who are involved in a promissory note:

1. ***Maker:*** It is a person who makes the promissory note and promises to pay the amount stated therein.

2. ***Payee:*** It is a person to whom the amount of promissory note is payable, *i.e.*, to whom the promise to pay is made.

3. ***Holder:*** It is a person who is either the payee or the indorsee of the promissory note. This will be discussed in detail in chapter 35 on 'Holder and Holder in Due Course'.

4. ***Indorser:*** It is a person who indorses (*i.e.*, transfers) the negotiable instrument (promissory note in this case) to another person. Sometimes, the holder of a promissory note indores the same to another person. In such cases, the holder is known as an indorser. In simple words, he is the transferor of the promissory note.

5. ***Indorsee:*** It is a person to whom the negotiable instrument (promissory note in this case) is indorsed (i.e., transferred). In simple words, he is the transferee of the promissory note.

34.3. PARTIES TO A BILL OF EXCHANGE

Following are the parties who are involved in a bill of cxchange:

1. ***Drawer:*** It is a person who draws the bill of exchange, *i.e.*, he is the maker of a bill of exchange.

2. ***Drawee:*** It is a person who is directed (*i.e.*, ordered) to pay the amount of the bill

1. *Drawer*
2. *Drawee*
3. *Acceptor*
4. *Acceptor for honour*
5. *Payee*
6. *Holder*
7. *Indorser*
8. *Indorsee*
9. *Drawee in case of need*

of exchange, *i.e.*, on whom a bill of exchange is drawn.

3. *Acceptor:* It is a person who accepts the bill of exchange. Generally, the drawee accepts the bill of exchange and on acceptance, he becomes the acceptor.

4. *Acceptor for honour:* Sometimes, the original drawee refuses to accept the bill of exchange, or refuses to furnish better security when demanded by the notary. In such cases, any person may accept the bill in order to safeguard the honour of the drawer or any indorser, and bind himself by the acceptance. Such person is called the 'acceptor for honour'. Thus, any person may voluntarily become a party to a bill of exchange as an 'acceptor for honour'.

5. *Payee:* It is a person to whom the amount of the bill of exchange is payable.

6. *Holder:* It is a person who is either the payee or the indorsee of the bill of exchange. This will be discussed in detail in chapter 35 on 'Holder and Holder in Due Course'.

7. *Indorser:* It is a person who indorses (*i.e*, transfers) the bill of exchange to another person.

8. *Indorsee:* It is a person to whom the bill of exchange is indorsed (*i.e.*, transferred). In simple words, he is the transferee of bill of exchange.

9. *Drawee in case of need:* Sometimes, in the bill of exchange, the name of another drawee is mentioned in addition to the original drawee. The purpose of such a drawee is that he should be approached for acceptence or payment of the bill of exchange when it is dishonoured, either by non-acceptance or by non-payment, by the original drawee. Such additional drawee is known as a 'drawee in case of need'.

When the original drawee refuses to accept the bill of exchange, then the holder must present the bill to the 'drawee in case of need' for his acceptance or payment. And the 'drawee in case of need' may either accept the bill of exchange or pay the amount mentioned in the same [Section 116]. The name of drawee in case of need may be inserted either in the bill by the drawer or in any indorsement by the indorser. Where a 'drawee in case of need' is named in the bill of exchange, the bill is not dishonoured till such drawee refuses to accept or pay the bill [Section 115].

34.4. PARTIES TO A CHEQUE

1. *Drawer*
2. *Drawee*

Following are the parties who are involved in a cheque:

1. *Drawer:* It is a person who draws a cheque.

2. *Drawee:* It is the banker on whom the cheque is drawn. In case of cheque, the drawee is always a banker.

Note. The parties such as payee, holder, indorser, indorsee, have the same meaning as in case of a promissory note or bill of exchange.

34.5. CAPACITY OF PARTIES

The 'capacity of the parties' means their competency (*i.e.*, capability) to enter into a valid contract. Every person who is capable of entering into a valid contract, can also become a party to a negotiable instrument and be bound by the same. The competency of

1. *Minors*
2. *Persons of unsound mind*
3. *Insolvents*
4. *Corporations or companies*
5. *Agents*
6. *Partners*
7. *Legal heirs*
8. *Joint Hindu Family*

the parties to enter into a valid contract is defined in Section 11 of the Indian Contract Act, 1872. According to this section, a person who is major, of sound mind, and is not disqualified from contracting by law, is competent to enter into a valid contract. These persons can become a party to a negotiable instrument and become liable thereon. This follows that the capacity of a person to draw, make, accept or indorse a negotiable instrument, is co-extensive with his capacity to enter into a contract. Thus, a person incapable of contracting, cannot bind himself by the negotiable instrument. But in certain circumstances, he may make the other parties liable. Sometimes, some of the parties to a negotiable instrument are competent to contract, but some are not. In such cases, only the competent parties are liable under the instrument and the incompetent are not. The legal provisions regarding the incapacity of certain person in connection with the negotiable instruments, are discussed in the following pages.

1. *Minors:* A minor is not competent to contract and cannot bind himself by becoming a party to any negotiable instrument. However, a minor may draw, indorse, deliver and negotiate a negotiable instrument so as to bind all other parties except himself [Section 26]. Thus, a minor whether he is drawer, maker, acceptor or indorser is not liable on the negotiable instrument. It may, however, be noted that the negotiable instrument does not become void merely because a minor is a party to it. The instrument remains binding on all other parties. But he may operate as a channel to convey title and liability.

Example 34.1. *A B* and *C* executed a promissory note in favour of *D. C* is the minor. In this case, *C* is not liable under the note. But *A* and *B* shall remain liable to pay the money to *D*.

[*Sulochna* v. *Pandiyan Bank Ltd.*, AIR 1975 Madras 70]

However, the minor's rights under the negotiable instrument are not affected, *e.g.*, if he is the payee, or indorsee, or holder, then he can enforce the payment.

[*Alagarsami* v. *Ramanathan*, 56 MLJ 399]

Example 34.2. *A* drew a cheque in favour of *B*, a minor. In this case, *B* can recover the money due on the cheque.

2. *Persons of unsound mind:* Like minors, the persons of unsound minds are also not competent to contract. And thus, they are not liable under the negotiable instruments. Lunatics, idiots and drunken persons are included in this category. The bills of exchange and promissory notes drawn or made by such persons are void as against them. But the other parties remain liable. However, such persons shall be liable under tha negotiable instrument, if the instrument is made or drawn during lucid intervals, *i.e.*, during the period when they were of sound and sober mind.

3. *Insolvents:* An insolvent is not competent to enter into a valid contract unless he is discharged by the court. Thus, an insolvent cannot draw, make, accept or indorse a negotiable instrument. But if he indorses an instrument, of which he is the payee, to a holder in due course, then the holder in due course can recover the amount from all prior parties except the insolvent. The insolvent cannot sue on a negotiable instrument. The reason for the same is that the property of the insolvent goes into the hands of Receiver or Official Assignee, appointed by the court of insolvency for the purpose. But if an instrument is executed in his favour after adjudication (*i.e.*, after he is declared insolvent by the court), he can bring an action on it unless the Receiver or Assignee intervenes, *i.e.*, unless the negotiable instrument is taken by Receiver or Assignee.

4. *Corporations or companies:* A corporation or a company is an artificial person created by law. It has separate legal entity independent of its members. It exists in the eyes of law, though it has no physical shape or form. Therefore, it can become a party to a negotiable instrument through human agents. A corporation comes into existense by a special Act of Legislature, and a company is formed by registration under the Companies Act, 1956. The contractual capacity of the corporation is expressly defined by the Special Act under which it is formed. Whereas, the contractual capacity of a company, registered under the Companies Act is regulated by the terms of its Memorandum of Association, Articles of Association, and the provisions of the Companies Act. Thus, whether a corporation or a company can draw, make or accept the negotiable instruments depends upon the provisions of the Special Act or the Memorandum or Article of Association, as the case may be. If the corporation or a company is expressly authorised to do so, it can become a party to a negotiable instrument. If it exceeds the powers and executes a negotiable instrument, the same is void. Even a holder in due course cannot make the corporation or company liable on such instrument.

Note. A trading company has implied powers to draw or accept negotiable instrument. But a non-trading company has no such powers unless it is expressly authorised by its Memorandum or Articles of Association.

5. *Agents:* The authority of an agent depends upon the terms and conditions of the agreement between the agent and his principal. It may be noted that a person, who is capable of contracting, may make or accept or otherwise become a party to a negotiable instrument either himself or through a duly authorised agent acting in his name. Thus, the negotiable instruments can be drawn or accepted by duly authorised agents on behalf of their principles. But the authority of an agent to draw, accept or indorse negotiable instruments must be expressed in clear terms. The general authority to transact business and to receive and discharge debts does not authorise an agent to accept or indorse the bills of exchange so as to bind his principal. The authority only to draw a negotiable instrument does not of itself empower the agent to indorse the same. Similarly, the authority only to indorse does not authorise the agent to accept the bills. It, therefore, follows that the agents's authority to draw, accept or indorse the negotiable instruments must be expressed in very clear terms. Thus, an agent can bind his principal by drawing, accepting or indorsing a negotiable instrument if the following conditions are satisfied:

(*i*) The principal must be competent to contract.

(*ii*) The agent must be authorised to draw, accept or indorse the negotiable instruments.

(*iii*) The agent's authority must be expressed in clear terms.

(*iv*) The agent must not exceed his authority.

(*v*) The agent must act in the name of the principal, *i.e.*, he should make it clear on the face of the instrument that he is signing as an agent *i.e.*, by using the words 'for and on behalf'.

An agent does not incur any personal liability for acts mentioned above if all these above conditions are satisfied. However, in the following cases, the agent becomes personally liable for his acts, and the principal will not incur any personal liability:

(*a*) If the agent puts his singatures on the negotiable instrument without making it clear that he is signing as an agent.

(*b*) If the agent executes the negotiable instrument without authority, or by exceeding his authority.

Note. The provisions relating to agent's capacity to execute negotiable instruments are contained in Sections 27 and 28.

6. *Partners:* The principle of agency relationship is also applicable in case of partnership. As a matter of fact, every partner is the agent of the firm, and the partners are agents and principals of each other. The firm and other partners are liable under the instrument, if a partner signs the instrument in the name of the firm and on behalf of the firm.

In a trading firm, each partner has the implied authority to bind the firm and his co-partners by drawing, signing, making accepting, endorsing the negotiable instruments in the name of the firm. But the partner of non-trading firm cannot do so unless he has an express authority for the same.

7. *Legal heirs:* After the death of the holder of a negotiable instrument, his legal heirs (*i.e.,* representatives) become entitled to the instruments. And the legal heirs of a deceased holder can sue on the negotiable instruments for the recovery of the amount. The legal heirs are also liable for any liability of the deceased. It may, however, be noted that a legal heir is liable on the negotiable instrument only to the extent of the assets of the deceased received by him. But if the legal heir signs his name on the negotiable instruments, he becomes personally liable unless by clear words he limits his liability to the extent of the assets of the deceased received by him as a legal heir [Section 29]. However, he may escape his personal liability by adding the words to his signature such as "without recourse to me personally" or "without recourse".

8. *Joint Hindu Family:* A 'Karta' (or manger) of a Joint Hindu Family represents the family in all transactions of the family with the outside world. He can draw a promissory note, a bill of exchange and cheque whenever necessary for carrying on the family business. He can also borrow money on promissory note or a bill of exchange for the purpose of carrying on the family business. Such a promissory note or a bill of exchange is binding on all the members of the joint family and can be enforced against them. In other words, all the members of the family are liable to pay the money. It may be noted that the minor members are equally liable to the extent of their shares.

TEST QUESTIONS

1. Who can be a party to a negotiable instrument? State all the parties to a promissory note, bill of exchange and a cheque.
2. What do you mean by the capacity of a party to a negotiable instrument? State the extent to which a minor can be a party to a negotiable instrument.
3. Whether a minor can be a party to a negotiable instrument? If yes, to what extent? How is the liability of other parties affected if minor is a party to a negotiable instrument?
4. Write notes on the capacity of following person to become a party to a negotiable instrument:

   (*a*) Persons of unsound mind. (*b*) Insolvents.

   (*c*) Corporation or companies. (*d*) Agents.

   (*e*) Partners. (*f*) Joint Hindu Family.

MULTIPLE CHOICE QUESTIONS

1. On acceptance of a bill of exchange by the drawee, he is legally known as

   (*a*) acceptor (*b*) acceptor for honour

   (*c*) drawee in case of need (*d*) none of these.

2. A person can became an acceptor for honour of a bill of exchange only if his name is mentioned in the bill.
   (*a*) True (*b*) False.
3. A person can become a 'drawee in case of need' only if his name is mentioned in the bill
   (*a*) True (*b*) False.
4. A negotiable instrument drawn in favour of a minor is
   (*a*) void (*b*) voidable
   (*c*) valid (*d*) invalid.
5. Which of the following is not competent to draw a valid negotiable instrument?
   (*a*) insolvent (*b*) company
   (*c*) agent (*d*) both (*b*) and (*c*).

ANSWERS

1. (*a*) 2. (*b*) 3. (*a*) 4. (*c*) 5. (*a*)

OBJECTIVE TYPE QUESTIONS WITH REASONING

State with reasons whether the following statements are correct or incorrect.

1. 'Acceptor for honour' is a person who accepts the promissory note to safeguard the honour of the drawer of the note and bind himself by such acceptance.
2. A 'drawee incase of need' is approached for acceptance or payment of a bill of exchange when the bill is dishonoured either due to non-acceptance or non-payment by the original drawee.
3. A cheque drawn is favour of a minor is not valid as the minor is not competent to contract.
4. A corporation or a company is not comptent to draw, make or accept a negotiable instrument as it is not a natural person.
5. A promissory note or a bill of exchange executed by the 'karta' of a Joint Hindu Family for carrying on joint family business is binding on all the family member including minors.

ANSWERS

1. ***Incorrect.*** Any person may voluntarily accepts a *bill of exchange* and bind himself. A promissory note is not required to be accepted.
2. ***Correct.*** The purpose of mentioning the name of a 'drawee in case of need' is to give an opportunity to the holder of the bill to present the same to the 'drawee is case of need' for his acceptance or payment, when the bill is dishonoured due to non-acceptance by the original drawee.
3. ***Incorrect.*** A minor can be a payee or indorsee of negotiable instrument.
4. ***Incorrect.*** A corporation or company being a legal person has the capacity to become a party to a negotiable instrument.
5. ***Correct.*** However, the minors are liable only to the extent of their shares in the family business.

PRACTICAL PROBLEMS

1. *A* draws a cheque in favour of *B*, a minor. *B* indorses the cheque in favour of *C*, who further indorses in favour of *D*. On presentation by *D*, the cheque is dishonoured by the bank. Is this cheque valid ? If yes, then discuss against whom, *C* and *D* can exercise their rights.

   Hint : Yes, the cheque is valid. As per section 26, a minor may draw, indorse, deliver and negotiate a negotiable instrument so as to bind all other parties except himself. In this case, *D* can claim the amount from *C*, and *C* can claim the same from drawer of the cheque i.e. *A*.

2. *A*, *B* and *C*, a minor, executed a promissory note in favour of *D*. State the liability of *A*, *B* and *C* to pay the amount.

   Hint : *C*, being minor, is not liable, but *A* and *B* shall remain liable to pay the money to *D*.

3. *A* owned Rs.20,000 to *B* and he drew a cheque for this amount in favour of *B* and delivered the same to him. However, *A* died before the encashment of cheque, and *B* claimed the amount from *A*'s legal representative. Can they be held liable for the amount payable by *A*?

   Hint : Yes, the legal representatives of deceased are liable on the negotiable instrument. However, they are liable only to the extent of the assets of deceased received by them. [Section 29]

4. *A* drew a cheque in favour of *B*, a minor. On presentation, the cheque was dishonoured. *B*, claimed the amount from *A'* but *A* refused to pay saying that the cheque was void due to *B*'s minority. Is *A* justified in taking this plea ?

   Hint : No, *A* is not justified in taking this plea. It is the settled law that a minor can be a beneficiary. In this case, the minor, being payee, is the beneficiary and thus entitled to recover the amount of cheque form *A*.

HOLDER AND HOLDER IN DUE COURSE

35.1. INTRODUCTION

We know that in commercial transactions, the negotiable instruments are used in substitution of money, and are easily transferable from one person to another. As a matter of fact, the negotiable instrument entitles its payee to receive the amount due on the instrument (*i.e.*, amount mentioned alongwith its interest, if mentioned). And the payee may validly transfer the negotiable instrument to any person for the payment of his own debts. On such a transfer, the transferee becomes entitled to receive the amount due on the negotiable instrument. There may also be cases where a person finds or steals a negotiable instrument and transfers the same for payment of his own debts. Whether such a transferee can recover the money due on the negotiable instrument, depends upon the fact whether he is the 'holder' or 'holder in due course'. The law requires that a person can recieve the money due on the negotiable instrument if he is a 'holder' or 'holder-in-due course'. In this chapter, we shall discuss the meaning of these terms, and the legal provisions relating thereto.

35.2. HOLDER

The terms 'holder' is defined in Section 8 of the Negotiable Instrument Act, which reads as under:

"The 'holder' of a promissory note, bill of exchange or cheque means any person, entitled in his own name, to the possession thereof and to receive or recover the amount due thereon from the parties thereto."

Thus, a holder is the person, who is entitled to the possession of the negotiable instrument in his own name and is also entitled to receive the money due on the same. The analysis of this section reveals that a person becomes a holder of the negotiable instrument if the following conditions are satisfied:

1. He must be entitled, in his own name, to the possession of the instrument; and
2. He must also be entitled, in his own name, to receive or recover the amount due on the instrument.

It may be noted that the words. *'entitled in his own name'* as used in Section 8, are of great significance. If the person is not entitled to the negotiable instrument in his own name, then he is not the holder of the instrument. The *'payee', bearer'* and the *'endorsee'* of the negotiable instrument are entitled to the instrument in their own name, and thus, are the holder of the same.

Example 35.1. *A* advanced Rs. 500 to *B*. and *B* executed a promissory note for the payment of the same. However, the promissory note was not executed in the name of *A* but in the name of *C*, a benamidar. On maturity (*i.e.*, when the payment became due), *B* failed to pay the amount due on the promissory note and *A* brought an action against *B* for recovery of the same. It was held that he could not recover the amount as he was not the holder of the promissory note. In this case, *A* was not entitled to the promissory note in his own name.

[*Sarjoo Prasad* v. *Rampayari*, AIR 1950 Patna 493]

It may also be noted that a person who has obtained the negotiable instrument by theft, is not a holder of the same. The reason for *the same is that he is not entitled to recover the amount* due on the instrument in his own name. For the same reason, an agent holding an instrument for his principal will also not be a holder of it, although he may receive its payment. Only a holder can bring a legal action to recover the amount due on the instrument. No other person can bring such an action.

35.3. HOLDER IN DUE COURSE

The term 'holder in due course' is defined in Section 9 of the Negotiable Instrument Act, which reads as under:

"Holder in due course means any person who for consideration become—

The possessor of a promissory note, bill of exchange or cheque, if payable to the bearer, or the payee or indorsee thereof, if payable to order, before the amount mentioned in it became payble, and without having sufficient cause to believe that any defect existed in the title of the person from whom he derived his title."

Thus, a holder in due course is a person who takes the possession of negotiable instrument in *good faith* and for value (*i.e.*, consideration). Moreover, he must also get the instrument before its maturity (*i.e.*, before it is due for payment). As a matter of fact, the holder in due course is the true owner of the instrument. The analysis of this section reveals that a person becomes a holder in due course of the negotiable instrument if all the following conditions are satisfied:

1. *He must be the holder of the negotiable instrument, i.e.*, in case of a *bearer* instrument, he must be the possessor of the same, and in case of an *order* instrument he must be the payee or indorsee of the same.
2. *He must have obtained the negotiable instrument before its maturity, i.e., before the amount mentioned in the instrument becomes payable*. In other words, the instrument should not be overdue.
3. *He must have obtained the negotiable instrument for valuable consideration.* A person who takes the instrument without consideration, does not become a holder in due course of the same.
4. *He must have obtained the negotiable instrument in good faith, i.e., without having sufficient cause to believe that any defect existed in the title of the person from whom he derived his title.*
5. *He must take the negotiable instrument which is complete and regular on the face of it*. If a negotiable instrument is incomplete, *e.g.* blank, undated, not properly stamped, without drawer's name, then the holder will not become the holder in due course of such instrument.

If *all* the above requirements are satisfied, the holder of the negotiable instrument becomes its 'holder in due course'. As a matter of fact, he becomes the owner of the instrument irrespective of any defects in the title of the person from whom he received the instrument. A holder in due course can recover the amount of the instrument from all the previous parties even if there were some defects in earlier transfers. It is important to note that *once the instrument passes through the hands of a holder in due course, it becomes free from all defects.* And any person who takes the instrument from a holder in the course, can recover the amount from any one of the parties prior to such holder.

35.4. RIGHTS AND PRIVILEGES OF A HOLDER IN DUE COURSE

1. *Rights in case of inchoate stamped instrument*
2. *Rights on fictitious bill*
3. *Rights in case of prior defects in the instrument*
4. *Rights against the prior parties*
5. *Right in case of conditional delivery of instrument*
6. *Title free from all defects*
7. *Presumption as to title*
8. *Estoppel against denying the original validity of the instrument*
9. *Estoppel against denying the capacity of the payee to endorse the instrument*
10. *Estoppel against denying the signatures or capacity of prior parties*

The 'holder indue course' enjoys certain special rights and privileges. These may be discussed under the following heads:

1. *Rights in case of inchoate stamped instrument:* An 'inchoate instrument' means an incomplete instrument. Sometimes, a person puts his signatures on a stamped paper and delivers it to another to fill it as a negotiable instrument for a certain amount. In such cases, the person signing the blank stamped paper becomes liable to pay the amount filled in the instrument, which is covered by the stamp on it. The person to whom such signed paper is delivered may fraudulently fill it up for a greater amount than authorised by the person signing the paper, and transfer the same to a person who takes it without any notice of such fraud. Such a transferee can recover the full amount of the instrument from the drawer or maker (*i.e.*, who signs and delivers the instrument) only if the following two conditions are satisfied namely [Section 20]:

(*a*) If he is the holder in due course of the instrument, and

(*b*) If the amount filled is sufficiently covered by the stamp on the instrument.

Example 35.2. *A* signed his name on a blank stamped paper and delivered the same to *B* with an authority to fill it up as a promissory note for Rs. 2,000. But *B* fraudulently filled it as a promissory note for Rs. 5,000. The stamp put on the paper was sufficient to cover the amount of Rs. 5,000. Subsequently, *B* indorsed the promissory note in favour of *C*, a holder in due course, who took it without any knowledge of the fraud. In this case, *C* is entitled to recover Rs. 5,000 from *A*, and he (*A*) cannot escape his liability on the ground that in filling the amount, his authority has been exceeded by B.

It may, however, be noted that if the amount filled is not sufficiently covered by the stamp on the instrument then the holder in due course can recover only that amount which is covered by the stamp.

2. *Rights on fictitious bill:* A 'fictitious bill' is a kind of a bill of exchange which is payable to a fictitious person, *i.e.*, a bill of exchange where payee is fictitious. The 'fictitious' payee means the payee who is not in existence, or if in existense he is never intended by the drawer to have the payment. Sometimes, a person draws a bill of exchange payable to a fictitious person, and the drawee accepts the same. After acceptance of the bill of exchange, the same may be endorsed by the drawer in the name of a ficititious person (*i.e.*, the drawer himself endorses the same as a fictitious payee). During the course of negotiation, such a bill of exchange may come in the hands of a holder in due course. In such cases, the right of the holder in due course is that he can recover the amount of the bill from the acceptor. And the acceptor cannot escape his liability on the ground that the payee was a fictitious person [Section 42].

However, the holder in due course must prove that the signature of the drawer and that of the first endorser (*i.e.*, fictitious payee) are in the handwriting of the same person.

Example 35.3. *A* drew a bill of exchange on *B* for Rs. 1,000 payble to *C*, a fictitious non-existent person. *B* accepted the bill of exchange and returned the same to *A*. Subsequently, *A* endorsed the bill of exchange to *D* by signing as the endorser (*i.e.*, as *C*). During the course of negotiations, the bill came in the hands of *E* a holder in due course. In this case, *E* can recover the amount of the bill from the acceptor (*B*) by showing that the signatures of the drawer (*A*) and the first endorsed (*C*) are in the same handwriting. And *B* cannot escape liability on the ground that the bill of exchange is fictitious and indorser's (*C*) signatures are forged by *A*. However, *D* cannot recover from *B*, as he (*D*) is not a holder in due course.

3. *Rights in case of prior defects in the instrument:* A holder in due course can recover the amount of the instrument irrespective of any defect in the title of the prior parties, *i.e.*, his rights to receive the amount due on the instrument are not affected even if there were some prior defects in the instrument [Section 58]. Thus, when any negotiable instrument is lost or obtained by means of an offence or fraud or for an unlawful consideration, no other person except a holder in due course is entitled to receive the amount due on it.

Example 35.4. *A* obtained, by fraud, a promissory note for Rs. 5,000 from *B*, and endorsed the same to *C* who received it in good faith and for value. In this case, *C* is the holder in due course and he can recover the amount from *B*. And *B* cannot avoid the liability on the ground that from him *A* obtained the note by fraud.

4. *Rights against the prior parties:* A holder in due course has a right to recover the amount due on the instrument from any one of the parties prior to himself. As a matter of fact, every prior party is liable to make payment to the holder in due course until the instrument is duly satisfied, *i.e.*, the payment due on the instrument is duly made [Section 36]. The term 'prior parties' includes the maker and acceptor of the instrument, and all the intervening endorsers.

5. *Right in case of conditional delivery of instrument*: Sometimes, a negotiable instrument is delivered to a person, upon some condition, *i.e.*, it will be effective on the happening of a certain event. In such cases, the negotiable instrument cannot be further negotiated unless such event happens. And if transferred before the event, the transferee will not get a good title to the instrument. However, if it is transferred to a holder in due course, his rights will not be affected by such condition [Section 47]. He can recover the amount due on the instrument from the parties liable to make payment, and the liable party cannot avoid liability on the ground that delivery of instrument was conditional only.

Example 35.5. *A* made a promissory note for Rs. 4,500 payable to *B*, and delivered the same to *B* on the condition that he (*B*) will demand payment only on the death of *C*. Before the death of *C*, *B* indorsed and delivered the promissory note to *D*, a holder in due course. In this case, *D* can recover the amount due on the promissory note from *A*. And *A* cannot avoid his liability on the ground that the payment was to be made on the death of *C*.

Similarly, where a negotiable instrument is delivered for some special purpose, *e.g.*, for discounting only. And the holder transfers the same to a holder in due course, instead of discounting. In such cases also, the holder in due course can recover the amount due on the instrument, and the liable party cannot avoid his liability on the ground, that the delivery of the instrument, was for special purpose only and not for transferring it to someone else [Section 46, para 3].

Note. Ordinarily, a negotiable instrument must contain an unconditional promise to pay. And if the promise to pay is dependent upon some condition, the negotiable instrument will not be valid. But when a negotiable instrument is dependent on such a condition, *which is bound to take* *place* (*e.g.* death), the instrument will be valid. Thus, in the above example, the promissory note is not bad though the amount is payable on the death of a person.

6. *Title free from all defects*: A holder in due course gets the negotiable instrument free from all defects in the title of the transferor or any of the previous holders of the instrument. In other words, his title to the instrument is better than all the prior parties. Thus, the general rule of transfer of property that "no one can transfer a better title than he himself has" (*nemo dat quod non-habet*), does not apply to negotiable instrument. Any holder who receives the instrument from a holder in due course gets same free from all defects even if he had knowledge of some prior defects. But he must not be a party to such defects [Section 53].

Thus, *once the instrument passes through the hands of a holder in due course, it is purged (i.e., cured) of all prior defects.* As a matter of fact, the holder in due course, serves as a channel to protect all the subsequent holders.

Example 35.6 *A* had a bill of exchange for Rs. 1,800 drawn upon *B*, the drawee. And he, (*A*) obtained *B's* acceptance to the bill of exchange by fraud. Thereafter, *A* indorsed and delivered the same to *C* who took it in good faith and for value. *C* further indorsed and delivered the bill of exchange to *D*. In this case, when the bill of exchange came in the hands of *C*, *i.e.*, the holder in due course, it became free from all defects. Now *D* also gets a good title to the bill of exchange, and can claim the amount from the acceptor (*B*). Now suppose that *D* endorses the bill to *A* for value. In such a case, *A* would not be entitled to recover the amount on the bill as he himself was a party to the fraud.

7. *Presumption as to title*: Every holder of a negotiable instrument is presumed to be a holder in due course. Thus, he is not required to prove that he is the holder in due course of the instrument, *i.e.*, he has received the negotiable instrument in good faith and for value. This presumption is, however, rebuttable, *i.e.*, the party liable for payment can prove that the holder is not the holder in due course [Section 118(*g*)].

8. *Estoppel against denying the original validity of the instrument:* Sometimes, the holder in due course files a suit for the recovery of the amount due on the instrument, against the maker of a promissory note, or the drawer of a bill of exchange or cheque, or an acceptor of a bill of exchange for the honour of the drawer. In such cases, the maker or the drawer cannot escape their liability on the ground that the instrument was invalid when it was made or drawn, *i.e.*, the maker or the drawer is estopped (*i.e.*, prevented) from denying the validity of the instrument [Section 120].

9. *Estoppel against denying the capacity of the payee to endorse the instrument:* Sometimes, a holder in due course files a suit, for the recovery of the amount due on the instrument, against the maker of a promissory note or the acceptor of an order bill of exchange. In such cases, the maker or the acceptor cannot escape their liability on the ground that the payee had no capacity (*i.e.*, not competent) to indorse the promissory note or the bill of exchange at the time of making it, *i.e.*, the maker or the acceptor is estopped from denying payee's capacity to indorse the the instrument [Section 121].

10. *Estoppel against denying the signatures or capacity of prior parties:* Sometimes, the holder in due course files a suit, for the recovery of the amount due on the instrument, against the indorsers. In such cases, the indorser cannot escape their liability on the ground that the signatures of any prior party were forged or that he (*i.e.*, prior party) was not competent to contract, *i.e.*, the indorser is estopped that from denying the signatures or capacity to contract of any prior party to the instrument [Section 122].

Note. It may be noted that this privilege is available to all the subsequent holders. The reason for the same is that by an indorsement, the indorser of the instrument guarantees that all previous indorsements are genuine, and that all prior parties had capacity to enter into valid contracts.

35.5. COMPARISON BETWEEN A HOLDER AND A HOLDER IN DUE COURSE

The following Table gives the comparison between a holder and a holder in due course:

S. No. *Holder*	*Holder in due course*
1. A holder means any person entitled in his own name to the possession of the instrument and to recover or receive the amount due thereon from the parties.	A holder in due course means a holder who has taken the instrument in good faith and for value, and also before its maturity.
2. In this case, the consideration is not necessary, *e.g.*, an instrument may be given in gift. As the gift is without any consideration, the donee becomes the holder, and not the holder in due course.	In this case, the consideration is must, *i.e.*, the holder gets the instrument for some consideration.
3. A holder does not get a good title if the title of any prior party is defective. In other words, he cannot have a better title than that of a person from whom he got the instrument.	A holder in due course gets a title free from any defect. In other words, he gets a better title than that of a person from whom he got the instrument.
4. A holder may acquire the instrument even if it has become due for payment, *i.e., even after maturity.*	A holder in due course must acquire the instruent before it has become due for payment, *i.e., before maturity.*
5. A holder of an instrument can recover the amount from a person who has signed it and also from the transferor from whom he obtained. In other words, the holder cannot enforce his right against all the prior parties.	A holder in due course can recover the amount from any of the prior parties until the instrument is duly discharged. In other words, he can enforce his rights against all the prior parties.
6. A holder does not enjoy any special privilege.	A holder in due course enjoys certain special privileges.

LEGAL PROVISIONS (SECTIONS) DISCUSSED IN THE CHAPTER

Important legal provisions (sections) of Negotiable Instruments Act, 1881, discussed in this chapter, are reproduced hereunder for ready reference:

1. ***Section 8: Holder***

   " The holder of a promissory note, bill of exchange or cheque means any person entitled in his own name to the possession thereof and to receive or recover the amount due thereon from the parties thereto.

   Where the note, bill or cheque is destroyed, its holder is the person so entitled at the time of such loss or destruction".

2. ***Section 9: Holder is Due Course***

   Holder in due course means any person who for a consideration became the possessor of a promissory note, bill of exchange or cheque if payable to bearer,

   Or the payee or indorsee thereof, if payable to order, before the amount mentioned in it became payable, and without having sufficient cause to believe that any defect existed in the title of the person from whom he derived his title".

3. ***Section 36: Liability of Prior Parties to Holder in Due Course***

   "Every prior party to a negotiable instrument is liable thereon to a holder in due course until the instrument is duly satisfied".

4. ***Section 53: Holder Deriving Title from Holder in Due Course***

   "A holder of a negotiable instrument who derives title from a holder in due course has the rights thereon of that holder in due course".

5. *Section 58: Instruments Obtained by Unlawful Means or for Unlawful Consideration*

"When a negotiable instrument has been lost, or has been obtained from any maker, acceptor or holder thereof by means of an offence or fraud, or for an unlawful consideration, no possessor or indorsee who claims through the person who found or so obtained the instrument is entitled to receive the amount due thereon form such maker, acceptor or holder, or from any party prior to such holder, unless such possessor or indorsee is, or some person through whom he claims was, a holder thereof in due course".

6. *Section 118 (g) : Holder is a Holder in Due Course*

This section contains the legal provision providing that a holder is **presumed** to be a holder in due course, which is as under:

"Until the contrary is proved, a presumption shall be made that the holder of a negotiable instrument is a holder in due course; **provided** that, where the instrument has been obtained from its lawful owner, or from any person in lawful custody thereof, **by means of an offence or fraud**, or has been obtained from the maker or acceptor thereof by means of an offence or fraud, or for unlawful consideration, **the burden of proving that the holder is a holder in due course lies upon him.**"

TEST QUESTIONS

1. Define the terms 'holder' and 'holder in due course' under the Negotiable Instrument Act. And distinguish between the two.
2. Define the term 'holder in due course'. What are the rights and special privileges of a holder in due course?
3. When a person becomes a holder in due course?
4. "A holder in due course gets a title free from all equities"—comment.
5. "Every holder in due course must be a holder but every holder may not be a holder in due course"—explain.
6. "A negotiable instrument once passes through the hands of a holder in due course it is purged of all prior defects"—explain.
7. To what extent it is true to say that "a holder in due course serves as a channel to protect all subsequent parties".
8. Can the following defences be taken against a holder in due course in a suit filed by him? If not, why?
   (*a*) That the instrument was invalid when made.
   (*b*) That the payee was not competent to indorse the instrument.
   (*c*) That the signature of the indorser was forged.

MULTIPLE CHOICE QUESTIONS

1. A holer is a person who is entitle to the instrument in his own name, and the term includes
   (*a*) payee of instrument (*b*) bearer of instrument
   (*c*) endorsee of instrument (*d*) all of these.
2. A person becomes a 'holder in due course' of a negotiable instrument if he receives it
   (*a*) in good faith (*b*) for value
   (*c*) before maturity (*d*) by satisfying all these.
3. A holder in due course can recover the amount of the instrument irrespective of any defect in the title of prior parties.
   (*a*) True, as it is his special privilege (*b*) False, defect in title makes the instrument void.
4. *A* found a negotiable instrument lying on the road, and transferred it to *B* who received it in good faith, and for consideration. Can *B* recover the amount due on the instrument?
   (*a*) Yes, as he is the holder in due course. (*b*) No, as *A* had no title to the instrument.

ANSWERS

1. (*d*) 2. (*d*) 3. (*a*) 4. (*a*)

OBJECTIVE TYPE QUESTIONS WITH REASONING

State with reasons whether the following statements are correct or incorrect.

1. A person, who obtains a negotiable instrument by theft, becomes its 'holder' and not the 'holder in due course'.
2. A person, who obtains a negotiable instrument is *good faith* and for value, becomes a holder in due course of the instrument.
3. A holder in due course can recover the amount of the instrument irrespective of any defect in the title of the prior parties.
4. A 'holder' who receives a negotiable instrument from a 'holder in due course' will get the same subject to the prior defects in the instrument.
5. Every holder of a negotiable instrument is presumed to be a holder in due course.

ANSWERS

1. *Incorrect.* Such a person is neither a 'holder' nor a 'holder in due course', as he is not entitled to the instrument in his own name.
2. *Correct.* As the requirements for becoming a holder is due course are fulfilled [Section 9].
3. *Correct.* A holder in due course becomes the owner to the instrument and his right to recover the amount due on the instrument are not affected by such defects [Section 58].
4. *Incorrect.* Such a holder will get the instrument free from all defects in the instrument. Once the instrument passes through the hands of a holder in due course, it is purged of all prior defects.
5. *Correct.* It is the recognised presumed about the holder of the instrument [Section 118(*g*)].

PRACTICAL PROBLEMS

1. *A* borrowed Rs.10,000 from *B*, a money lender and at *B*'s instance executed a promissory note for the payment of the same in favour of *C*, a benamidar. On the due date, *A* failed to pay the amount of promissory note to *B*. Can *B* recover the amount of loan from *A* on the basis of the promisory note executed for the repayment of the loan ? Give reasons.
   Hints : No, *B* cannot recover the amount on the basis of the promisory note as he is not the holder of the same. In this case, *B* is not entitled to the promissory note in his own name.
2. *A* signed, as a maker, a blank stamped paper and delivered the same to *B* with an authority to fill it as a promissory note for Rs. 2000. *B* fraudulently filled it as a promissory note for Rs.4,000 and then endorsed the same in favour of *C*, for consideration, who took it without any knowledge of fraud. Can *C* recover the amount of the instrument *i.e.* Rs.4,000 from *A*? Give reasons.
   Hints : Yes, *C* can recover the amount of the instrument. In this case, *C* is the holder in due course of the instrument and is entitled to enforce the same for full value if the stamp is sufficient to cover the amount of the instrument. [Section 20]
3. *A* obtained *B*'s acceptance on a bill of exchange by fraud and then indorsed the same to *C*, who took it in good faith and for value. *C* further indorsed the same to *D* who knew about the earlier fraud. Decide whether *D* gets a good title to the bill ?
   Hint : Yes, *D* gets a good title to the bill of exchange. Any holder who receives the instrument from a holder in due course gets the same free from all defects even if he had knowledge of some prior defects. [Section 53]
4. *A*, by a fraud, obtained a promissory note from *B* for Rs.5000 and indorsed the same in favour of *C* who took it in good faith and for value. Can *B* avoid his liability to make the payment of the promissory note to *C* on the ground that it was obtained from him by a fraud ? Give reasons.
   Hint : No, *B* cannot avoid his liability on the ground of fraud. In this case, *C* is the holder-in -due course and is entitled to enforce the instrument.

NEGOTIATION AND LIABILITY OF PARTIES

36.1. INTRODUCTION

We know that negotiable instruments are used as substitute of money. One of the essential features of negotiable instruments is that they are freely transferable from one person to another. Such a transfer of a negotiable instrument is known as negotiation. A negotiable instrument may be transferred in two ways, namely:

(1) By negotiation

(2) By assignment.

36.2. NEGOTIATION

The term 'negotiation' may be defined as the transfer of a negotiable instrument by one person to another so as to constitute the transferee the holder of the instrument. This term is defined in Section 14 of the Negotiable Instruments Act, which reads as under:

"When a promissory note, bill of exchange or cheque is transferred to any person so as to constitute that person the holder thereof, the instrument is said to be negotiated".

The analysis of this section reveals that the negotiation takes place when the following two conditions are satisfied:

1. The negotiable instrument is transferred from one person to another; and
2. The transfer is made in such a manner so as to make the transferee the holder of the negotiable instrument.

Thus, the essence of the negotiation is

that it must be made with the intention of transferring a title of the instrument to the transferee.

Example 36.1. *A* delivered a cheque for Rs. 7500 to *B* and requested him to keep it in safe custody. This is not a negotiation of the cheque to *B*. In this case, the transfer of the cheque to *B* makes him a bailee only, and not the holder of the cheque.

36.3 MODES OF NEGOTIATION

We know that the negotiable instruments are of two types, namely (a) bearer instruments, and (*b*) order instruments. Keeping in view these types of the instruments, the Negotiable Instruments Act provides for the following two modes of negotiation:

1. Negotiation by delivery.
2. Negotiation by indorsement and delivery.

36.4 NEGOTIATION BY DELIVERY

In case of *bearer instruments*, the negotiation can be made by simple delivery of the instrument. This provision is contained in Section 47 of the Negotiable Instruments Act, which reads as under:

"Subject to the provisions of Section 58, a promissory note, bill of exchange or cheque payable to bearer is negotiable by delivery thereof".*

The analysis of this section reveals that a negotiable instrument payable to bearer can be transferred by mere delivery, and the person to whom the instrument is delivered becomes the holder of the same. It may, however, be noted that the instrument must be actually delivered and the delivery must also be *voluntary*. Thus, a person who finds or steals a bearer instrument is not the holder of the same. The reason for the same is that the instrument has not been delivered to him voluntarily. However, if a finder of a thief delivers the bearer instrument to another person for some consideration, the latter will become the holder in due course of the instrument if he receives the same in *good faith* and before maturity.

Example 36.2. *A* was the holder of cheque for Rs. 1,200 payable to bearer. He kept the cheque in his table drawer. *B*, a miscreant, stole the cheque from *A*'a table drawer. In this case, there is no negotiation of the cheque from *A* to *B* as it was not voluntarily delivered to *B*.

36.5. NEGOTIATION BY INDORSEMENT AND DELIVERY

In case of an *order instrument*, the negotiation can be made only by indorsement on the instrument *and* its delivery. This provision is contained in Section 48 of the Negotiable Instruments Act, which reads as under:

"Subject to the provisions of Section 58, a promissory note, bill of exchange or cheque payable to order is negotiable by the holder by indorsement and delivery thereof."*

The analysis of this section reveals that a negotiable instrument payable to a particu-

* Section 58 provides that sometimes a person finds an instrument, or obtains it by some offence or fraud, or for an unlawful consideration. In such cases, any possessor or indorsee of the instrument, who claims through such a person, is not entitled to receive the amount of the instrument unless he is the holder in due course.

lar person or his order can be transferred by making an indorsement on it *and* then delivering the same. It may be noted that this mode of negotiation requires the following two formalities to be complied with:

1. The holder must indorse the negotiable instrument, *i.e.* he must sign his name on the instrument, and
2. The duly signed instrument must be delivered to the transferee (indorsee).

In this case, the transferee becomes the holder of the negotiable instrument only when the duly indorsed (*i.e.* signed by the transferor) instrument is delivered to him. Thus, a mere indorsement on the instrument does not amount to negotiation, unless there is delivery of the same.

Example 36.3. *A* drew a cheque for Rs. 10,000 payable to *B* and delivered it to him. *B* indorsed the cheque in favour of *C* but kept it in his table drawer. Subsequently, *B* died, and cheque was found by *C* in *B*'s table drawer. In this case, C does not become the holder of the cheque as the negotiation was not completed by delivery of the cheque to him.

36.6. DELIVERY AND ITS IMPORTANCE IN NEGOTIATION

The term 'delivery' means the voluntary transfer of the possession of the instrument from one person to another. The delivery should be with the intention of transferring the ownership of the instrument to the person to whom it is delivered *i.e.* the intention should be to make the transferee the holder of the instrument. Thus, the delivery of the instrument is a very important formality to complete the negotiation. The importance of delivery is emphasised in Section 46 of the Negotiable Instruments Act which states that, a negotiable instrument is said to be made accepted or indorsed when it is completed by delivery. Thus, a mere writing and signing of the instrument does not make it operative. [*Thrappa* v. *Umedmalji*, 1942, Bombay 205].

Example 36.4 *A* made a promissory note for Rs. 2000 payable to *B*. *A* died and the promissory note was found in *A*'s papers. *A*'s legal heirs delivered the promissory note to *B*. In this case, B cannot recover the amount of promissory note because it was not delivered to him by *A*. And the legal heirs were not authorised by *A* to deliver the promissory note. [*Bromage* v. *Lloyd* (1847) 1 Ex. 32].

36.7. KINDS OF DELIVERY

1. *Actual delivery*
2. *Constructive delivery*
3. *Conditional delivery*

The delivery of a negotiable instrument may be of the following kinds:

1. *Actual delivery.* It takes place when the instrument changes hands physically *i.e.* when the instrument is physically delivered by the transferor to the transferee.

2. *Constructive delivery.* It takes place when the instrument is delivered to an agent, clerk, or servant of the transferee who holds the instrument on behalf of the transferee.

Example 36.5. *A* was the holder of negotiable instrument for Rs. 800 payable to bearer. The instrument is in the hands of ***A's*** banker. The same banker is also the banker of ***B***. ***A*** directed the banker to transfer the instrument to ***B's*** credit in his books. The banker acted accordingly, and possessed the instrument as ***B***'s agent. In this case, there is a constructive delivery of the negotiable instrument, and the instrument in negotiated to ***B***.

3. *Conditional delivery.* The conditional delivery is the delivery which is effective on the fulfilment of certain condition. It may be noted that where an instrument is delivered conditionally, the netgotiation is not complete till the condition is fulfilled, and the transferee does not become the holder till that date. An instrument delivered conditionally is called an '*Escrow*'. Similarly, when an instrument is delivered for a special purpose, the transferee does not become the holder of the instrument.

Example 36.6. *A* was the holder of a cheque for Rs. 500 payable to bearer. He delivered it to his banker for collection. In this case, the cheque is delivered for special purpose and not to entitle the banker to further negotiate it.

36.8. INDORSEMENT

The term 'indorsement' may be defined as signing one's name on the negotiable instrument for the purpose of transferring it to another person. In other words, it means the signing of a negotiable instrument for the purpose of negotiation. Usually, the indorsement is made by signing one's name on the back of the instrument. However, it may also be made on the face of the instrument. Sometimes, the back is already full of indorsements. In such cases, the further indorsements may be signed on a slip of paper attached to the instrument. Such a slip is called *"allong"* and becomes part of the instrument. The following two parties are involved in an indorsement:

1. ***Indorser:*** The person who signs the instrument is called the 'indorser'
2. ***Indorsee:*** The person to whom the instrument is transferred by indorsement is called the 'indorsee'.

It may be noted that simply signing one's name on the back of the instrument is not sufficient to compelete the indorsement. The indorsement is complete by delivering the signed instrument to the 'indorsee'.

36.9. PERSONS ENTITLED TO INDORSE THE NEGOTIABLE INSTRUMENT

1. *Payee*
2. *Indorsee*
3. *Maker or drawer*
4. *Stranger*

The persons who may indorse and negotiate the negotiable instrument are specified in Section 51 of the negotiable Instruments Act. According to this section, every sole maker, drawer, payee or indorsee of a negoliable instrument may endorse the same. Thus, section 51 enables all parties to an instrument to entorse the same. The authority of these persons to indorse the negotiable instrument may be discussed as under:

1. ***Payee:*** As a matter of fact, the payee of an instrument is the rightful person to make the first indorsement. However, he may indorse the same only if he is the holder of the instrument. Thereafter, the instrument may be indorsed by any person who has become the holder of the instrument.

2. ***Indorsee:*** Any person who has become the holder of the negotiable instrument, may indorse the same. Thus, an indorsee may also indorses the instrument if he is the holder of the same.

3. ***Maker or drawer:*** Ordinarily, the maker of a promissory note and the drawer of a bill of exchange cannot endorse the same.

4. ***Stranger:*** An indorsement cannot be made by a stranger (i.e. a person other than those stated above or who is not a party to the instrument). If any person other than those mentioned above, indorse it, the indorsement is void and he cannot be made liable as indorser. [*Thakursey* v. *Kishandas,* AIR *1925 Sind 9*].

36.10. KINDS OF INDORSEMENT

An indorsement may be of the following kinds:

1. Blank or general indorsement. 2. Full or special indorsement. 3. Restrictive indorsement. 4. Partial indorsement. 5. Conditional indorsement. 6. Sans recourse indorsement. 7. Facultative indorsement. 8. Contingent indorsement.

36.11. BLANK OR GENERAL INDORSEMENT

Sometimes, the indorser signs his name on the instrument without mentioning the name of indorsee. In such cases, it is known as blank or general indorsement [Section 16(1)]. In other words, an indorsement in blank means simply putting of indorser's signature on the instrument (usually on the back of the instrument) without mentioning the name of the indorsee. The effect of a blank indorsement is that the instrument becomes a bearer, even if originally it was payable to order [Section 54]. Thus, an instrument indorsed in blank can be further negotiated by its simple delivery.

Example 36.7. A bill of exchange was payable to *A*. *A* signed only his name on the back of the bill. This is an indorsement in blank. And the bill becomes a bearer bill, and can be further transferred by mere delivery.

36.12. FULL OR SPECIAL INDORSEMENT

Sometimes, the indorser signs his name on the instrument and also writes the name of the indorsee (*i.e.,* the person to whom the payment is to be made) In such cases, the indorsement is known as full indorsement (or 'indorsement in full') [Section 16(1), second para].

In other words, indorsement in full means putting of indorser's signature on the instrument and also writing the name of a person to whom the amount is to be payable. In this case, an order instrument remains an order instrument. It can be futher negotiated only by an indorsement by the indorsee.

Example 36.8. A bill was payable to *A.A* wrote on its back "pay to *B* or order", and signed the bill. This is an indorsement in full. *A* may also simply write "pay to *B, and* sign *i.e.* the use of the words "or orders" is not necessary. In this case also, the indorsement is full indorsement.

36.13. CONVERSION OF BLANK INDORSEMENT INTO FULL INDORSEMENT

A blank indorsement may be converted into a full indorsement. The holder of an instrument indorsed in blank, may convert it into an indorsement in full by writing the name of some person (indorsee) above the indorser's signatures. The indorser may do so without signing his own name. The advantage of such indorsement is that the holder does not become liable as an indorser though he transfers the instrument. [Section 49]

Example 36.9. *A* was the holder of a bill of exchange. He indorsed it in blank by simply signing his name on the back of it, and delivered it to *B*. Above *A*'s signature *B* wrote the words, "pay to C or order". In this case, the writing by *B* will make it the indorsement in full from *A* to *C*. Here, *B* is not liable as an indorser of the bill because he has not signed it.

36.14. RESTRICTIVE INDORSEMENT

Sometimes, the indorser signs his name on the back of the instrument and adds some words by which the rights of the indorsee are restricted. In such cases, the indorsement is known as restrictive indorsement. In other words, when by express words the right or further negotiation is taken away or restricted, that is called a restrictive indorsement. An indorser can make the restrictive indorsement in any one of the following way. [Section 50]

1. He may altogether exclude the right of further negotiation, or
2. He may restrict the right of further negotiation, or
3. He may merely constitute the indorsee as an agent to indorse the instrument or to receive its contents for the indorser or for some other specified person.

The effect of restrictive indorsement is that the indorsee gets the rights to receive the payment when due, and he can sue the parties for it. But he cannot further negotiate the instrument except as authorised by indorser. Thus, in case of restrictive indorsement the indorsee does not become the owner of the instrument, as in case of other indorsement.

Example 36.10. *A* signed the following indorsements on different negotiable instruments:

(*a*) "Pay the amount to *B* only".

(*b*) "Pay *B* for my use"

(c) "Pay *B* or order for the account of *A*."

In this case, the indorsements are restrictive as they exclude the right of further negotiation by *B*.

Example 36.11. *A* signed the following indorsements on different negotiable instruments:

(a) "Pay *B*"

(b) "Pay *B* value in account with Oriental Bank"

In this case, these are not restrictive indorsements as they do not exclude the right of further negotiation by *B*.

36.15. PARTIAL INDORSEMENT

A partial indorsement is invalid and does not operate as a negotiation of the instrument. The partial indorsement is not allowed because it will cause inconvenience to prior parties. Moreover, it will subject them to plurality of action and interfere with the free circulation of the instruments.

Example 36.12. *A* was the holder of a bill for Rs. 1,000. He indorsed it as "pay Rs. 500 to *B* and Rs. 500 to *C*". This is a partial indorsement and is invalid. In this case, neither *B* nor *C* can recover the amount, or indorse it further.

But sometimes the amount due has already been partly paid. In such cases, a note to that effect may be made on the instrument and then it may be negotiated for the balance [Section 56].

Example 36.13. *A* was the maker of a promissory note for Rs. 1,000. He paid Rs. 500 to the holder and this fact was noted on the instrument. Now this promissory note can be indorsed for the balance of Rs. 500.

36.16. CONDITIONAL INDORSEMENT

Sometimes, the indorser limits or excludes his own liability by putting some condition in the instrument. In such cases, it is known as conditional or qualified indorsement. It differs from the restrictive indorsement. The restrictive indorsement prohibits further negotiability of the instrument. But the conditional indorsement does not prohibit the negotiability . It simply limits or excludes the liability of the indorser.

36.17. SANS RECOURSE INDORSEMENT

Sometimes, the indorsee does not want to incur any liability as indorser. In such cases, he may exclude his liability by express words in the indorsement. He can do so by adding certain words such as *"sans recourse"*, *'without recourse'* etc. Such an indorsement is called 'sans recourse' indorsement.

Example 36.14. A singed the following indorsements on different instruments:

(a) "Pay *B* or order sans recourse".

(b) "pay *B* or order without recourse to me".

(c) "Pay *B* or order at his own risk"

These are 'sans recourse' indorsements as the indorser (*A*) has excluded his own liability.

In such cases, if the instrument is dishonoured, the indorsee or the subsequent holder cannot ask the indorser for payment of the same.

Sometimes, an indorser who has excluded his own liability in this manner, afterwards becomes the holder of the instrument in the normal process of negotiation. In such cases, all the intermediate indorsers continue to be liable to him [Section 52].

Example 36.15. *A* was the payee and holder of a bill of exchange. He indorsed it 'sans recourse' to *B*. *B* further indorsed it to *C* and then *C* to *D*. *D* indorsed it to *A*. In this case, *A* can recover the amount of the bill from *B*, *C* or *D*.

36.18. FACULTATIVE INDORSEMENT

Sometimes, by express words the indorser abandons some right or increases his own liability. In such case the indorsement is called facultative indorsement. He may do so by giving up some rights to which he is entitled under the negotiable instrument.

Example 36.16. *A* was the holder of a bill of exchange for Rs. 1,900. He made an indorsement on it reading as "pay to *B* or order. Notice of dishonour waived". This is a facultative indorsement. In this case, *A* has given up his right to receive the notice in case of dishonour of bill. This increases his liability, because he is liable to pay the amount of the bill even though no notice of dishonour has been given to hum.

36.19. CONTINGENT INDORSEMENT

Sometimes, an indorser makes the indorsement in such a way that his liability depends upon the happening of a specified event which may or may not happen. In such cases, the indorser will not be liable until the happening of such an event. If the event becomes impossible or does not happen in specified time (if the time is specified), then the liability of the indorser comes to in end *i.e.* he is no more liable to pay the amount due on the instrument.

Example 36.17. *A* the holder of instruments signed the following indorsements on different negotiable instruments:

(*a*) "Pay *B* or order on the arrival of ship"

(*b*) "Pay *B* or order on his marriage with *C*"

In these cases, *A*'s liability will arise only on the arrival of the ship or on *B*'s marriage with *C* as the case may be. If these events do not happen at all, then *A*'s liability comes to an end.

36.20. EFFECT OF INDORSEMENT

An unconditional indorsement completed by delivery of the instrument has the following legal effects [Section 50]

1. The ownership of the instrument is transferred from the indorser to the indorsee.
2. The indorsee gets the rights of further negotiation.
3. The indorsee gets the rights to bring an action for recovery against all the parties whose names appear on the instrument.

36.21. EFFECT OF CANCELLATION OF INDORSEMENT

The effect of cancellation of indorsement is that the indorser, whose remedy is impaired, is discharged from liability to the holder who cancels the indorsement (Section 40). In other words, if a holder of the negotiable instrument cancels any indorsement on it, then he cannot recover the amount from the indorser whose remedy is impaired against the prior party.

Example 36.18. *A* was the holder of a bill of exchange payable to *B* or order. It contained the following indorsements, all in blank:

First indorsement by *B*.

Second indorsement by *C*.

Third indorsement by *D*

Fourth indorsement by *E*.

A cancelled the indorsement by *C* and *D* without the consent to *E*, and filed a suit against *E* for the recovery of the amount due on the bill of exchange. In this case, *A* cannot recover the amount from *E* because *E*'s remedy against *C* and *D* is destroyed by *A* by cancelling the indorsement.

36.22. NEGOTIATION BACK

Sometimes, during the course of negotiation, the negotiable instrument comes back to the original indorser. This is called negotiation back. Thus, where an indorser negotiates an instrument and again becomes its holder before its maturity, the instrument is said to be 'negotiated back' to that holder. In such cases, the intermediate indorsers are not liable to the holder to whom the instrument is negotiated back.

Example 36.19. *A*, the holder of bill of exchange, indorsed it to *B*. *B* indorsed it to *C*. *C* to *D*. *D* to *E*, and *E* indorsed it again to *A*. In this case, the indorsement by *E* to *A* is a 'negotiation back' And *B*, *C*, and *E* are not liable to *A*.

This rule is made to prevent the multiplicity of actions, and *it is an exception to the general rule that a holder in due course can sue all prior parties*. This process of multiplicity of actions is explained below on the basis of above example.

In the above example, *A* becomes the holder in due course by the second indorsement by *E* to *A*. Now *A* being a holder in due course, has the right to recover the amount from *B*, *C*, *D* and *E*. And he (*A*) being a prior party, is also liable to all of them. If *A* is allowed to sue *E*, then *E* could sue *D*, *D* could sue *C*, and *C* could sue *B*, and *B* could sue *A* and this will lead to circuity of legal actions without any purpose. The law prohibits such multiplicity of actions. Thus, *A* having been pushed to his original position of holder, cannot suit *B*, *C*, *D* and *E*.

But sometimes, the original indorser expressly excludes his liability at the time of indorsement and the instrument is again negotiated back to him. In such cases, he can sue all the intermediate indorsers *e.g.* where the first indorsement was 'sans recourse'.

Note. Sometimes, the original indorser, to whom the instrument is negotiated back cancels all the indorsements on it, and further indorses the same. Such a transaction is known as *'taking up of a bill'*.

36.23. ASSIGNMENT

The term 'assignment' may be defined as the transfer of one's right to recover the payment of a debt. It may be noted that the promissory notes, bills of exchange and cheques represent the debts. Thus, they are also assignable (transferable) without an indorsement. As a matter of fact, the assignment is the sale of 'person's right to receive the payment of a debt'. The assignment takes place by means of a written document signed by the person who transfers his rights, under the negotiable instrument, to the other. The following two parties are involved in an assignment:

1. *Assignor:* The person who transfers his right under the negotiable instrument, is called an assignor.
2. *Assignee:* The person to whom such rights are transferred, is called an assignee.

It may be noted that in both, 'negotiation' and 'assignment' there is the transfer of the right to receive the payment of a debt. However, the rights of a transferee by negotiation are substantially superior to those of an assignee. The assignee gets the right of the assignor only. He does not get the rights of a holder in due course.

Note. The Negotiable Instruments Act deals with the transfer of instrument by negotiation only, and not with the transfer by assignment.

36.24. COMPARISON BETWEEN NEGOTIATION AND ASSIGNMENT

The following Table gives the comparison between the negotiation and the assignment.

S. No.	*Negotiation*	*Assignment*
1.	In this case, the mode of transfer is simple. The negotiation can be made either by mere delivery of the instrument, or by indorsement on the instrument itself and its delivery.	In this case, the mode of transfer is not so simple. The assignment can be made only by a separate written document signed by the transferor.
2.	In this case, the consideration is always presumed. The indorsee is not required to prove that he has obtained the instrument for consideration.	In this case, the consideration is not presumed. The transferee must prove that he has obtained the instrument (by assignment) for consideration.

3. In this case, the transferee gets a better title than that of the transferor if he is the holder in due course. As a matter of fact, the holder in due course takes the instrument free from all defects in the title of the transferor.	In this case, the transferee gets the same title as that of the transferor, whether it is good or bad. As a matter of fact, the transferee takes the instrument (by assignment) subject to all defects in the title of the transferor.
4. In this case, there is no need to give a notice of transfer to the debtor (*i.e.*, the person liable to pay the amount of the instrument). The parties are liable to pay the amount even without such notice.	In this case, a notice of transfer must be given to the debtor by the transferee. Without such notice, the assignment is not complete and effective.

36.25. LIABILITY OF PARTIES

The liability of all the parties of a negotiable instrument may be discussed under the following heads:

1. Liability of maker of a promissory note and acceptor of a bill of exchange. 2. Liability of drawer of a bill of exchange or of a cheque . 3. Liability of drawee of a cheque 4. Liability of indorser. 5. Liability of prior parties.

36.26. LIABILITY OF MAKER OF A PROMISSORY NOTE AND ACCEPTOR OF A BILL

The liability of both, the maker of a promissory note and the acceptor of a bill of exchange, is the same. They are primarily liable to pay the amount due on the instrument. This means that they are bound to pay the amount of the instrument (i.e., note or bill) on its maturity according to its apparent tenor *i.e.* terms of the instrument [Section 32, para 1]. In default of such payment, they become liable to compensate any subsequent party for the loss caused to him by such default [Section 32, para 2].

36.27. LIABILITY OF DRAWER OF A BILL OF EXCHANGE OR OF A CHEQUE

The liability of the drawer of a bill or of a cheque is contained in Section 30 of the Negotiable Instruments Act, and may be discussed as under:

1. *Drawer of a bill of exchange.* On the dishonour of a bill of exchange by the drawee, either by non-acceptance or by non-payment, the drawer becomes liable to compensate the holder or any indorser who has been compelled to pay , for the loss suffered by him. But to make the drawer liable, the notice of dishonour must be given to or received by him. Thus, the liability of drawer of a bill is secondary because the primary liability is that of the acceptor., *i.e.* the drawer of a bill becomes liable to pay the amount only on the default of the acceptor. But until the bill is accepted, the drawer is primarily liable.

2. *Drawer of a cheque.* On the dishonour of a cheque, the drawer becomes liable to compensate the holder. In this case also, to make the drawer liable the notice of dishonour must be given to or received by him. There is also a criminal liability of the drawer. It will be discussed in detail in Art. 36.32.

Note. The point of difference between the liability of the drawer of a bill and that of a cheque is that the liability of the drawer of a cheque is primary and not secondary. The reason for the same is that the holder of a bill can recover the amount from the drawee (acceptor). But the holder of a cheque has no remedy against the drawee *i.e.* banker. His remedy is only against the drawer.

[*PNB* v. *Bank of Baroda*, AIR 1944 PC 58].

36.28. LIABILITY OF DRAWEE OF A CHEQUE

> 1. *Banker' s liability where the amount of cheque is increased by fraud*
> 2. *Banker's liability in case of forgery of customer's signature*
> 3. *Banker's liability in case of forgery in indorsement*

We know that the drawee of a cheque is always a banker (bank). When the bank has sufficient funds of the drawer, then it must make the payment of the cheque when required to do so When the bank refuses to make payment without any sufficient cause, then it must compensate the drawer for any loss or damage caused by such default (Section 31). Thus, the liability of the drawee of a cheque arises when it is having sufficient amount in drawer's account properly applicable to the cheque, but refuses, to pay the amount of the cheque. It may be noted that the banker is liable only to the drawer of a cheque and not to the holder. The reason for the same is that the relationship between banker and his customer (drawer) is contractual, and the holder is not a party to such contract. The holder's remedy is only against the drawer and not the banker.

However, there are certain circumstances in which the banker is justified in refusing the payment of a cheque. In such circumstance, the banker is not liable to the drawer in refusing payment, even if there is sufficient funds in his account. Following are the circumstances, in which the banker is justified in refusing payment:

(*a*) When the cheque is post-dated.

(*b*) When the cheque is out-dated. It is the custom of bankers in India not to pay a cheque if it is presented after 6 months from the date of issue.

(*c*) When the customer has countermanded (*i.e.*, stopped) payment of a particular cheque. In this case, the customer has to do so by a notice in writing not to pay a particular cheque.

(*d*) When the cheque is mutilated *i.e.*, torn etc.

(e) When the cheque is of doubtful validity *e.g.*, undated, amount differing in words and figures etc.

(*f*) When the customer has died.

(*g*) When the customer has become insolvent.

(*h*) When the customer has become insane (*i.e.*, of unsound mind)

(*i*) When the customer's signature does not agree with the specimen signature.

(*j*) When a garnishee order has been issued *i.e.*, when the banker has received a court order attaching the balance of the customer's account.

(*k*) Where the balance in customer's account is not sufficient to meet the cheque. In such a case, drawer is liable to be punished with imprisonment upto two years or with fine upto twice the amount of cheque or with both [Section 138 added by amendment in 1988. It will be discussed in detail in Art 36.32].

All the above points will be discussed in detail in chapter 42. Following three points are also important in connection with the liability of a banker:

1. *Banker' s liability where the amount of cheque is increased by fraud:* Sometimes, a dishonest person alters or increases the amount of a cheque by using some techniques, and the banker pays the increased amount. In such cases, whether the banker should suffer the loss of excess payment or it should be allowed to be recovered from the customer (*i.e.* the drawer of the cheque) depends upon the following:

(*a*) Where the customer has drawn a cheque with reasonable precautions and the amount is increased by some dishonest person and the banker pays the amount, then the banker must bear the loss *i.e.*, the banker cannot charge the customer with the increased amount. [*Hall* v. *Fuller* (1825) 5 B & C 750].

(*b*) Where the customer is negligent in drawing his cheque *e.g.,* leaves unusual spaces on the cheque and the amount is raised by adding some words or figures, then the banker is not liable for the raised amount. Such loss falls on the customer.

[*London Jt. Stock Bank* v. *Mcmillan* (1918) AC 777].

2. *Banker's liability in case of forgery of customer's signature:* As a matter of fact, it is the duty of the banker to be acquainted with the customer's signature. If the payment is made against a cheque on which the customer's signature is forged, then the banker must suffer the loss *i.e.,* the banker is liable to pay the amount again to his customer. The reason for the same is that the earlier payment by the banker is without authority.

[*Bhagwandas* v. *Creet* (1904) IlR 3 Cal. 249].

3. *Banker's liability in case of forgery in indorsement:* Though that it is banker's duty to be acquainted with the customer's signature, but it is not banker's duty to acquaint himself with the handwriting of several persons who may indorse a cheque. Thus, the banker is not liable if he makes the payment of a cheque on which the indorsement was forged (Section 85).

36.29. LIABILITY OF INDORSER

The liability of an indorser is conditional and arises only in case of dishonour of the instrument *i.e.,* his liability arises only if there is default by the party who is primarily liable to pay the amount due on the instrument on its maturity . It means that, in case of dishonour of the negotiable instrument, every indorser is liable to all the parties who are subsequent to him [Section 35]. As a matter of fact, by indorsing the instrument, the indorser gives a guarantee to the subsequent parties that the instrument shall be paid on its maturity, and that if it is dishonoured he shall be liable to any subsequent party for the loss caused to him by such dishonour. However, an indorser will be liable only if a notice of dishonour is given to him, or received by him *i.e.,* he himself comes to know of the dishonour.

It is to be noted that an indorser can exclude his liability by express words in the indorsement or can make his liability conditional *e.g.,* by 'sans recourse' or conditional indorsement.

36.30. LIABILITY OF PRIOR PARTIES

Any person who is a party to the negotiable instrument, prior to the holder in due course, is liable to him (the holder in due course) until the amount due on the instrument is paid [Section 36]. Thus, when an instrument is dishonoured, the holder in due course can hold all or any one of the prior parties liable for the amount due on the instrument. It may be noted that the liability of the intervening (*i.e.,* prior) parties is joint and several *i.e.,* the holder in due course may recover the amount from one party or from all of them jointly.

Example 36.20 *A* was a holder of a bill of exchange for Rs. 5,000. He took from *B,* the acceptor of the bill of exchange, Rs. 4,000 in full satisfaction of his claim against him (*B*) for the bill. In this case, all other parties (*i.e.,* the drawer and indorsers) are discharged from their liability. However, the holder may expressly reserve his right to sue the other parties.

36.31. BASIC PRINCIPLES OF LIABILITY OF PARTIES

We have already discussed the liability of the parties to a negotiable instrument. It may be noted that the liability of the parties is based on the principle of suretyship *i.e.,* certain parties are liable as principal debtors, and certain are liable as sureties (guarantors). This provision is contained in Section 37 of the Negotiable Instruments Act. According to this section, the following parties are liable as principal debtors *i.e.,* their liability is primary:

1. The maker of a promissory note.
2. The drawer of a cheque..
3. The drawer of a bill of exchange until acceptance.
4. The acceptor of a bill of exchange.

And all the other parties are liable as sureties (guarantors) i.e., their liability is secondary and arises only on default by a party who is primarily liable. This is , however, subject to a contract to the contrary.

Example 36.21. *A* made a promissory note for Rs. 1,000 payable to *B* and delivered the same to him. Afterwards, *B* indorsed the promissory note to *C*, *C* to *D* and *D* to *E*. In this case, the primary liability is that of *A* as he is the maker of the promissory note. And the liability of other parties (*B*, *C* and *D*) is secondary. Thus, *B*, *C* and *D* are liable to pay the amount due on the promissory note to *E* only if *A* fails to pay on due date.

36.32. CRIMINAL LIABILITY OF DRAWER FOR DISHONOUR OF CHEQUES

An amendment to this effect was made in 1988, when a New Chapter XVII comprising sections 138 to 142 was added to the Negotiable Instruments Act, 1881.

Sometimes, a cheque issued by a person (*i.e.*, drawer) is dishonoured *i.e.* returned unpaid due to insufficient funds in his bank account. In such cases, the drawer is deemed to have committed an offence. For this offence, he is punishable with imprisonment for a term which may extend to two* year, or with fine which may extend to double the amount of cheque or with both. However, this criminal liability of the drawer of a dishonoured cheque arises where the cheque was given by him for the payment of any *legally enforceable* debt or other liability [Section 138]. Moreover, to make the drawer criminally liable, the following conditions should also be satisfied:

1. The cheque has been presented to the bank for payment within a period of six months from the date on which it is drawn or within period of its validity, whichever is earlier [Section 138 (a)]
2. Within thirty** days of the receipt of information from the bank about dishonour, the payee or the holder in due course, as the case may be, gives a written notice to the drawer demanding payment of the said cheque [Section 138 (b)].
3. The drawer of the cheque fails to make payment within the next fifteen days after receiving such a demand notice [Section 138 (c)]. The cause of action starts from the 16th day onward.

On the fulfilment of these conditions, an offence against the drawer becomes complete, and the criminal action can be started against him after the expiry of fifteen days period mentioned in point (3) above. However, to make the drawer criminally liable, a written complaint must be filed against him within one month from the date of cause of action *i.e.*, within one month after the expiry of fifteen days period as mentioned in Section 138 (c) above [Section 142].

In may be noted that, till the cheque is returned by the bank as unpaid, no offence is made out against the drawer of the cheque under section 138 [*Anil K. Sawhney* v. *Gulshan Rai*, 1993 LW (Crl.) 641 (SC)]. Moreover, the dishonour of cheque by itself does not make the drawer criminally liable. It is only the failure to pay the amount within fifteen days of the receipt of demand notice that gives a cause of action against the drawer.

[*M/s Ancon Engg. Co.* v *Amitava Goswami*, (1994) 3 Crimes 769 (Cal.)].

The following points, in connection with drawer's criminal liability , are important to be noted here:

1. In pursuant to the demand notice by the payee, it is necessary for the drawer to

* Enhanced from one year by the Negotiable Instruments (Amendments) Act, 2002.

** Enhanced from *fifteen* days by the Negotiable Instruments (Amendments) Act, 2002.

make payment of the entire amount of the cheque. Any part payment is not sufficient to evade prosecution under this provision. [M/s Ancon Enggs.'s case].

2. The complaint for this offence should be made in writing by the payee or the holder in due course [Section 142 (*a*)].
3. The written complaint should be made before a Metropolitan Magistrate or a judicial Magistrate of first class [Section 142 (c)].
4. The payee cannot lodge a complaint after the completion of one month from the date on which the cause of action arose under Section 138 (c).

[*V.N Samant* v. *M/s K.G.N. Traders* (1994) 3 Crimes, 725 (Karnataka)].

In case, this offence is committed by a company, it is liable to be punished accordingly. Moreover, every person who was incharge of conducting company's business, shall also be liable to be punished under this provision [Section 141 (1)]. Further, the director, manager, secretary or other officer of the company will also be liable for this offence, if it can be shown that the offence has been committed with his consent or connvinance [Section 141 (2)].

Note. 1. The word 'company' for the purpose of this section, means any body corporate and includes a firm of other association of individuals [Section 141, *Explanation* (*a*)]. And the word 'director' in relation to a firm means a partner in the firm [Section 141, *Explanation* (*b*)].

2. Sometimes, a customer has an arrangement with a bank for the payment of his cheques upto certain amount *e.g.*, where he avails a loan facility upto specified amount. In such case also, the drawer is criminally liable if his cheque is dishonoured because of the fact that the cheque exceeds the amount arranged to be paid as per agreement with the bank [Section 138].

LEGAL PROVISIONS (SECTIONS) DISCUSSED IN THE CHAPTER

Important legal provisions (sections) of the Negotiable Instruments Act, 1881 discussed in this chapter, are reproduced hereunder for ready reference:

1. ***Section 14: Negatiation***

"When a promissory note, bill of exchange or cheque is transferred to any person, so as to constitute that person the holder thereof, the instrument is said to be negotated".

2. ***Section 15: Indorsement***

"When the maker or holder of a negotiable instrument signs the same, otherwise than as such make, for the purpose of negotiation, on the back or face thereof or on a slip of paper annexed thereto, or so signs for the same purpose a stamped paper intended to be completed as a negotiable instrument, he is said to indorse the same, and is called the "indorser"

3. ***Section 16: Indorsement in Blank, Indorsement in Full and Indorsee***

"(1) If the indorser signs his name only, the indorsement is said to be "in blank" and if he adds a direction to pay the amount mentioned in the instrument to, or to the order of , a specified person, the indorsement is said to be "in full", and the person so specified is called the "indorsee" of the instrument.

(2) The provisions of this Act relating to payee shall apply with the necessary modifications to an indorsee.

4. ***Section 30: Liability of Drawer***

"The drawer of a bill of exchange or cheque is bound in case of dishonour by the drawee or acceptor theref, to compensate the holder, provided due notice of dishonour has been given to, or received by, the drawer as hereinafter provided".

5. ***Section 31: Liability of Dramee of Cheque***

"The drawee of a cheque having sufficient funds of the drawer in his hands properly applicable to the payment of such cheque must pay the cheque when duly required so to do, and in default of such payment, must compensate the drawer for any loss or damage caused by such default".

6. *Section 32: Liability of Maker of Note and Accpetor of Bill*

"In the absence of a contract to the contrary, the maker of a promissory note and the acceptor before maturity of a bill of exchange are bound to pay the amount thereof at maturity according to the apparent tenor of the note or acceptance respectivley, and the acceptor of a bill of exchange at or after maturity is bound to pay the amount thereof to the holder on demand.

In default of such payment as aforesaid, such maker or acceptor is bound to compensate any party to the note or bill for any loss or damage sustained by him and caused by such default.

7. *Section 35: Liability of Indorser*

In the absence of a contract to the contrary, whoever indorses and delivers a negotiable instumen before maturity, without, in such indorsement, expressly excluding or making conditional his own liability, is bound thereby to every subsequent holder, in case of dishonour by the drawee, acceptor or maker, to compensate such holder for any loss or damage caused to him by such dishonour, provided due notice of dishonour has been given to, or received by, such indorser as hereinafter provided.

Every indorser after dishonour is liable as upon an instrument payable on demand.

8. *Section 36: Liability of Prior Parties to Holder in Due Course:*

"Every prior party to a negotiable instrument is liable thereon to a holder in due course until the instument is duly satisfied.

9. *Section 37: Maker, Drawer and Acceptor Liable as Principals*

The maker of a promissory note or cheque, the drawer of a bill of exchange unitl acceptance, and the acceptor are, in the absence of a contract to the contrary, respectively liable thereon as principal debtors, and the other parties thereto are liable thereon as sureties for the maker, drawer or acceptor, as the case may be.

10. *Section 40: Discharge of Indorser's Liability*

"Where the holder of a negotiable instrument, without the consent of the indorser, destroys or impairs the indorser's remedy against a prior party, the indorser is discharged form liability to the holder to the same extent as if the instrument had been paid at maturity.

11. *Section 46: Delivery*

"The making, acceptance or indorsement of promissory note, bill of exchange or cheque is completed by delivery, actual or constructive.

As between parties standing in immediate relation; delivery to be effectual must be made by the party making, accepting or indorsing the instrument, or by a person authorized by him in that behalf.

As between such parties and any holder of the instrument other than a holder in due course, it may be shown that the instrument was delivered conditionaily or for a special purpose only, and not for the purpose of transferring absolutely the property therein.

A promissory note, bill of exchange or cheque payable to bearer is negotiable by the delivery thereof.

A promissory note, bill of exchange or cheque payable to order is negotiable by the holder by indorsement and delivery thereof"

12. *Section 47: Negotiation by Delivery*

"Subject to the provisions of section 58, a promissory note, bill of exchange or cheque payable to bearer is negotiable by delivery thereof.

Exception.—A promissory note, bill of echange or cheque delivered on condition that it is not to take effect except in a certian event is not negotiable (except in the hands of a holder for value without notice of the condition) unless such event happens".

13. *Section 48: Negotiation by Indorsements*

"Subject to the provisions of section 58, a promissory note, bill of exchange or cheque payable to order, is negtotiable by the holder by indorsement and delivery thereof".

14. *Section 49: Conversion of Indorsement in Blank into Indorsement in Full*

The holder of negotiable instument indorsed in blanks may, without signig his own name, by writting above the indorser's signature a directions to pay to any other person as indorsee, convert the indorsement in blank into an indorsement in full, and the holder does not thereby incur the responsibility of an indorser.

15. *Section 50: Effect of Indorsement*

The indorsement of a negotiable instrument followed by delivery transters to the indorsee the property therien with the right of further negotiation; but the indorsement may by express words, restrict or exclude such right, or may merely constitute the indorsee an agent to indorse the instrument, or to receive its contents for the indorser, or for some other specified person.

16. *Section 52: Indorser who Excludes his own liability or Makes it Conditional*

The indorser of a negotiable instrument may, by express words in the indorsement, exclude his own liability thereon, or make such liability or the right of the indorsee to receive the amount due thereon depend upon the hppening of a sepcified event, although such event may never happen.

Where an indorser so excludes his liability and afterwards becomes the holder of the instrument, all intermediate indorsers are liable to him.

17. *Section 85: Cheques Payable to Order*

(1) Where a cheque payable to order purports to be indorsed by or on behalf of the payee, the drawee is discharged by payment in due course.

(2) Where a cheque is originally expressed to be payable to bearer, the drawee is discharged by payment in due course to the bearer thereof, notwithstanding any indorsement whether in full or in blank appearing thereon, and notwithstanding that any such indorsement purports to restrict or exclude further negotiation.

TEST QUESTIONS

1. Explain clearly the term 'negotiation'. What are the different modes of negotiation? State the importance of delivery in negotiation.

2. What is meant by negotiation? How is it effected? Distinguish between negotiation and assignment.

3. What do you mean by indorsement? What are its various kinds? Can a negotiable instrument be indorsed in parts? If yes, when?

4. Explain the meaning of 'special' and 'restrictive' indorsement. Who may indorse such an instrument?

5. "A partial indorsement does not operate as a negotiation of the instrument" — comment.

6. What is the liability of a maker of a promissory note? What is its nature? Does it differ from the liability of a drawer of a bill and cheque? If yes, in what way?

7. State the basic principles of liability of parties to a negotiable instrument. What is the liability of prior parties, and indorsers?

8. Write notes on the following:

(*a*) Sans recourse indorsement. (*b*) Facultative indorsement.
(c) Contingent indorsement. (*d*) Restrictive indorsement.
(*e*) Negotiation back.

9. Is there any criminal liability of the drawer of a cheque? If yes, in what circumstances?

MULTIPLE CHOICE QUESTIONS

1. A negotiable instrument payable to order can be transferred by

(*a*) Simple delivery (*b*) indorsement
(*c*) indorsement and delivery (*d*) registered post

2. In case, a finder or a thief of a bearer negotiable instrument transfers it to a person who receives the same in good faith and for valuable consideration, then such a transferee is

(*a*) entitled to receive the payment (*b*) not entitled to receive the payment
(*c*) punishable for helping a thief (*d*) conditional owner of the instrument

3. A negotiable instrument is complete and operative as soon as it is written and signed by the maker.
   (*a*) True, as the requirement as to writing and signing is complied with
   (*b*) False, as the requirement as to delivery of instrument is not complied with
4. In case, back of a negotiable instrument is full of indorsements, a slip of paper may be attached to the instrument for signing indorsements. Such a slip is legally known as
   (*a*) allonge (*b*) escrow
   (*c*) zickri chit (*d*) peth
5. An indorsement made by an indorser by signing his name and also by writing the name of the indorsee, is known as
   (*a*) general indorsement (*b*) special indorsement
   (*c*) restrictive indorsement (*d*) none of these
6. An indorsement by which the indorser excludes his liability by express words, is known as
   (*a*) facultative indorsement (*b*) restrictive indorsement
   (*c*) sans recourse indorsement (*d*) contingent indorsement
7. When during the course of negotiation, the negotiable instrument comes back to the original indorser, it is known as
   (*a*) negotiation back (*b*) reverse indorsement
   (*c*) facultative indorsement (*d*) back recourse indorsement
8. The liability of the maker of a promissory note and acceptor of a bill of exchange, is
   (*a*) primary (*b*) secondary
   (*c*) conditional (*d*) none of these
9. On the acceptance of the bill of exchange by the drawee, the liability of the drawer becomes
   (*a*) primary (*b*) secondary
   (*c*) extinct (*d*) none of these
10. On the dishonour of a cheque due to insufficient funds, the criminal liability of the drawer is the fine only which may extend to double the amount of cheque, and there is no imprisonment.
   (*a*) True (*b*) False

ANSWERS

1. (*c*)	2. (*a*)	3. (*b*)	4. (*a*)	5. (*b*)	6. (*c*)
7. (*a*)	8. (*a*)	9. (*b*)	10. (*b*)		

OBJECTIVE TYPE QUESTIONS WITH REASONING

State with reasons whether the following statement are correct or incorrect.

1. A negotiable instrument payable to bearer can be transferred by mere delivery without any indorsement on the instrument.
2. *A* drew a cheque for Rs. 5,000 payable to *B* and delivered the same to him who indrosed the cheque in favour of C and kept it in his table drawer. This act of *B* entitles C to the cheque as negotiation is proper by way of indorsement.
3. Only payee of an instrument in entitled indorse the same.
4. An instrument indorsed in blank can be further negotiated by simple delivery even if the instrument was originally payable to order.
5. An instrument becomes void if the indorser excludes him liability at the time of making the indorsement.

6. A drawer of a cheques is liable to be imprisoned if his cheque is dishonored due to insufficient funds.
7. On the dishonour of a cheque, the drawee is primarily liable to make the payment of the cheque.
8. The maker of a promissory note, drawer of a cheque, acceptor of bill are liable as principal debtors.

ANSWERS

1. *Correct.* Indorsement is required in case of order instrument only.
2. *Incorrect.* In this case , C does not become the holder of the cheque as negotiation is not completed by delivery of cheque to him.
3. *Incorrect.* An indorsee may also further indorse the instrument.
4. *Correct.* The effect of blank indorsement is that the instrument become a bearer instrument [Section 54]
5. *Incorrect* . Such an indorsement is known as 'sans recourse indorsement' and is legally recognised [Section 52]
6. *Correct* .The bouncing of cheques due to insufficiency of funds in an offence as per Section 138.
7. *Incorrect.* In such a case, it is the drawer of the cheque who is liable and not the drawee.
8. *Correct.* The liability of these parties is primary and not secondary [Section 37].

PRACTICAL PROBLEMS

1. *A* draw a cheque for Rs. 50,000 payable to *B* and delivered the same to him. *B* endorsed the cheque in favour of *C*, but kept the same in his table drawer. Subsequently, *B* died and the cheque was found by *C* in *B*'s table drawer. Does *C* become the holder of the cheque? Give reasons.

   Hint : No, *C* does not become the holder of the cheque. In this case, negotiation of the instrument was not completed by delivery. In case of an order instrument, the negotiation can be made only by endorsement and delivery of the instrument [Section 48].
2. *A* owed Rs. 10,000 to *B* and made a promissory note for this amount in favour of *B*. For safety reasons, *A* cuts the promissory note into two pieces and posted one half to *B*. Subsequently, *A* changed his mind and did not send the other half to *B*. Can *B* recover the amount on the basis of the half promissory note? Give reasons.

   Hint : No, *B* cannot recover the amount on the basis of half instrument. A per section 46, the making of an instrument is completed by its delivery, actual or constructive. The delivery of half instrument cannot be treated as the constructive delivery of the whole instrument.
3. *A*, a holder of a bill of exchange, indorsed it in blank by putting his signature on its back and delivered the same to *B*. *B* added the words "pay to C or order" above *A*'s signature on the back, but did not put his own signature. Is the endorsement valid ? Give reasons.

   Hint : Yes, the indorsement is valid and will be treated as an indorsement from *A* to *C*. Here *B* is not liable as and endorser of the bill as he has not signed the same [Section 49].
4. *A*, a holder of a bill for Rs.4,000 indorsed it as "pay Rs.2,000 to *B* and Rs.2,000 to *C*". Can *B* and *C* recover the respective amount ?

   Hint : No, neither *B* nor *C* can recover any amount. It is the case of partial indorsement, which is invalid and does not operate as negotiation of the instrument.
5. *A* was indebted to *B* for Rs.5,000 and gave a cheque of this amount drawn in favor of *B* to *B*'s agent. The agent indorsed the cheque in his favour by forging B's signature and misappropriated the amount. Is the bank discharged from its liability ? Give reason.

Hint : Yes, the bank is discharged as the payment has been made in due course. The banker is not liable if the payment of a cheque is made on which indorsement was forged [Section 85]

6. *A* cheque drawn in favour of *B* is stolen and the thief forged *B*'s signature and indorsed the same in favour of *C*. The banker made the payment to *C* in due course. Can *B* recover the amount of cheque from the banker ? Give reasons.

   Hint : No, as the banker is discharged by making the payment in due course. In this case, the signatures of an endorses are forged and the banker is protected under section 85 of the Negotiable Instruments Act, 1881.

37

CHAPTER

PRESENTMENT OF NEGOTIABLE INSTRUMENTS

37.1. INTRODUCTION

We have already discussed that negotiable instruments are used as substitute for money. However, the money due on the instruments can be received only after presenting the same to the parties liable for payment. The process of presenting or placing the instrument before the maker, acceptor or drawee is known as a 'presentment of a negotiable instrument'. As a matter of fact, the presentment of a negotiable instrument is required for the following purposes:

1. Presentment for acceptance. 2. Presentment for sight. 3. Presentment for payment.

Note. The presentment for acceptance is required in case of bills of exchange only, and the presentment for sight only in case of promissory notes. However, the presentment for payment is necessary in all kinds of negotiable instruments.

37.2. PRESENTMENT OF A BILL OF EXCHANGE FOR ACCEPTANCE

The presentment for acceptance is necessary only in case of bills of exchange [Section 61]. *If the bill is not presented for acceptance, no party is liable to the holder who makes default in its presentment*. The term 'acceptance of a bill' means the indication by the drawee of his assent to the drawer that he will pay the amount of the bill of exchange on due date. In other words, it is the consent of the drawee signed upon the bill of exchange. The bill is said to be accepted when the drawee writes the word 'accepted' on the bill and signs his name below it. And the drawee is then called the 'acceptor' of the bill of exchange. However, the writing of the word 'accepted' is not necessary. The acceptance may be given by the drawee by simply signing his name on the bill. It may, however, be noted that the acceptance must be in writhing An oral acceptance is not a valid acceptance. *The liability of the drawee arises only when the bill of exchange has been validy accepted by him*. The following are the essentials of a valid acceptance of a bill of exchange:

1. The acceptance must appear on the bill of exchange itself.
2. The acceptance must be in writing.
3. The acceptance must be signed by the drawee or his duly authorised agent.
4. The acceptance must be completed either by delivering the accepted bill of exchange to the holder, or by giving notice of acceptance to the holder or to some other person on holder's behalf.

However, it is not necessary that every bill of exchange should be presented for acceptance. There are certain bills which are not required to be presented for acceptance, and there are certain others which must be presented for acceptance. Following are the bills or exchange which *need not be presented* for acceptance:

(*a*) A bill of exchange payable on demand.

(*b*) A bill of exchange payable on fixed date, *e.g.*, on 31st March, 2003.

(*c*) A bill of exchange payable on fixed number of days after date, *e.g.*, 30 days after date.

Following are the bills of exchange which must be presented for acceptance in order to make the parties liable [Section 61]:

(*a*) A bill of exchange payable at a given time after acceptance or after sight. Here the term 'after sight' means that the bill is payable at a given time after it has been presented to the drawee for his knowledge.. In such cases, the presentement of a bill for acceptance is necessary in order to fix the date of maturity

(*b*) A bill of exchange in which there is an express term that it shall be presented for acceptance before it is presented for payment.

(*c*) A bill of exchange which is payable at a place other than the place of residence or business of the d rawee.

Though in certain cases, it is optional to present the bill of exchange for acceptance, yet it is always desirable to have the bill accepted due to the following reasons:

1. In order to obtain additional security of acceptor's name on the bill or exchange.
2. In order to have an immediate right of recourse against the drawer and other parties if the bill is dishonoured by non-acceptance. Because in such a case, the holder can immediately proceed against the drawer or other parties for the recovery of the amount due on the bill.

37.3. KINDS OF ACCEPTANCE

The acceptance of a bill of exchange may be of the following two kind, namely:

1. General acceptance. 2. Conditional acceptance.

37.4. GENERAL ACCEPTANCE

A general acceptance is one which is given without any condition regarding the payment of the amount due on the bill of exchange. It is also known as an '*absolute acceptance*' A general acceptance is according to the apparent tenor of the bill of exchange, *i.e.*, the drawee accepts the bill as originally drawn. In case of general acceptance, the drawee makes himself liable to pay the amount due on the bill of exchange without any condition. As a matter of fact, the acceptance must be general.

37.5. CONDITIONAL ACCEPTANCE

1. *Acceptance on the happening of an event*
2. *Acceptance of partial amount*
3. *Acceptance for payment at a specified place*
4. *Acceptance for payment at a different time*
5. *Acceptance by some of the drawees only*
6. *Acceptance for payment in instalments*

A conditional acceptance is one which is given upon some conditions regarding the payment of the amount due on the bill of exchange. It is also known as a '*qualified acceptance*'. In case of a conditional acceptance, the drawee makes himself liable to pay the amount due on the bill of exchange only if conditions of acceptance are fulfilled. It may be noted that the conditional acceptance varies the effect of the bill of exchange as originally drawn. The holder of a bill of exchange may refuse to take back the bill which has been accepted conditionally. And he may treat such a bill as dishonoured by non-acceptance. However, he may also take such a bill. But in this case, all parties prior to himself shall not be liable on the bill of exchange unless they give their consent to the conditional acceptance. Thus, the holder takes the conditionally accepted bill at his own risk, and can recover the amount due on the bill from the acceptor only as no other party will be liable to pay the amount. Following are the instances of conditional acceptance:

1. *Acceptance on the happening of an event:* It is the acceptance by which the drawee undertakes to pay the amount due on the bill of exchange on the happening of an event, *e.g.*, an acceptance reading as "accepted, payable only when the ship arrives at Bombay", or "accepted, payable when sufficient funds are available".

2. *Acceptance of partial amount:* It is the acceptance by which the drawee undertakes to pay only a part of the amount due on the bill of exchange, *e.g.*, a bill drawn for Rs. 1,000, and accepted in words reading as "accepted for Rs. 600 only".

3. *Acceptance for payment at a specified place:* It is the acceptance by which the drawee undertakes to pay the amount due on the bill of exchange only at a specified place and not elsewhere, or to pay at a place different from the place mentioned in the bill itself, *e.g.*, an acceptance reading as "accepted, payable at Punjab National Bank *only*" or "accepted, payable at Punjab National Bank and *not elsewhere*"

4. *Acceptance for payment at a different time:* It is the acceptance by which the drawee undertakes to pay the amount due on the bill of exchange at a time different from that mentioned in the bill itself. *e.g.*, a bill drawn payable 30 days after date and accepted in words reading as "accepted payable 60 days after date".

5. *Acceptance by some of the drawees only:* It is the acceptance by which only one of the several drawees undertakes to pay the amount due on the bill of exchange.

6. *Acceptance for payment in instalments:* It is the acceptance by which the drawee undertakes to pay the amount due on the bill of exchange in instalments. A bill drawn for Rs. 500 and accepted in words reading as "accepted payable in monthly instalments of Rs. 100".

37.6. RULES REGARDING THE PRESENTMENT OF A BILL FOR ACCEPTANCE

1. *Persons who should present the bill for acceptance*
2. *Persons to whom the bill should be presented for acceptance*
3. *Time for presentment for acceptance*
4. *Place for presentment for acceptance*

The rules regarding the presentment of a bill of exchange for acceptance may be discussed under the following heads:

1. *Persons who should present the bill for acceptance:* A bill of exchange should be presented for acceptance by any person who is entitled to demand the acceptance of the same. The *holder* of the bill or his duly authorsied agent is entitled to demand the acceptance of the bill. And thus, he can present the bill for acceptance.

2. *Persons to whom the bill should be presented for acceptance:* A bill of exchange should be presented for acceptance to the person who can accept the same. As per Sections 33 and 75 of the Negotiable Instruments Act following are the persons who can accept the bill of exchange:

(*a*) ***The drawee of a bill or his duly authorised agent:*** As a matter of fact, the drawee is the only person to whom the bill of exchange should be presented for acceptance at the first instance [Section 33].

(*b*) ***The joint drawees of a bill of exchange:*** If there are several drawees who are not partners of a firm, then the bill must be presented to all the drawees (Section 34).

(c) ***The legal representatives (i.e., heirs) of a drawee:*** After drawee's death, the bill of exchange should be presented to his legal representatives for acceptance [Section 75].

(*d*) ***The official receiver or assignee:*** After the insolvency of the drawee, the bill should be presented to his receiver or official assignee for acceptance [Section 75].

(*e*) ***The drawee in case of need:*** If the original drawee refuses to accept the bill of exchange, then the bill should be presented for acceptance to a 'drawee in case of need,' if there is any. He is the person whose name is mentioned in the bill (in addition to the name of the drawee) to whom the payee should approach in case the original drawee refuses to accept [Section 33].

(*f*) ***The acceptor for honour:*** If the bill of exchange is not accepted, and is noted or protested for non acceptance, then the bill may be accepted by the acceptor for honour, *i.e.*, the person who accepts the bill for the honour of any party liable on the bill of exchange [Section 33].

3. *Time for presentment for acceptance:* The rules regarding the time for presentment of a bill of exchange for acceptance may be stated as under:

(*a*) ***Where the time for presentment is specified:*** In such cases, the bill must be presented for acceptance within that time, *i.e.*, before the expiry of the specified time [Section 62].

(*b*) ***Where the time for presentment is not specified:*** In such cases, the bill must be presented for acceptance within a reasonable time of its being drawn [Section 62]. The term 'reasonable time' is a question of fact that depends upon the means of communication available and the usage of a particular trade.

It may, however, be noted that all the bills of exchange must be presented for acceptance before maturity. Moreover, the presentment must also be made on a business day and during the business hours only. The term 'business hours depends upon the custom and usage of particular trade.

4. *Place for presentment for acceptance:* The rules regarding the place for presentment of a bill of exchange for acceptance may be stated as under:

(*a*) ***Where the place for presentment is specified:*** In such cases, the bill must be presented for acceptance at that place only. If after reasonable search, the drawee cannot be found at that place, then the bill is deemed (*i.e.*, considered) to be dishonoured by non-acceptance [Section 61].

(*b*) ***Where the place for presentment is not specified:*** In such cases, the bill should be presented for acceptance at drawee's place of business or residence. If, after reasonable search, the drawee cannot be found there, then the bill is deemed (*i.e.*, considered) to be dishonoured by non-acceptance [Section 61].

Note. Where presentment by post is authorised by agreement or custom,then presentment for acceptance by registered letter is sufficient.

37.7. EFFECT OF NON-PRESENTMENT OF A BILL FOR ACCEPTANCE

We know that in certain cases, the presentment of a bill of exchange for acceptance is compulsory. In such case, the holder must present the bill for its acceptance. If he fails to do so, then no party on the bill shall be liable to such holder [Section 61 (first para last line)]. In other words, if the holder fails to present the bill for acceptance, the drawer, and all the indorsers, prior to the defaulting holder, shall be discharged from their liability to such holder. It may be noted that when the bill of exchange is presented to the drawee for his acceptance, he is entitled to 48 hours (exclusive of public holidays) to consider whether he will accept the bill or no. If the bill is not returned after acceptance, the proper approach for the holder is to treat the bill as dishonoured. It may also be noted that if the holder allows more time than the said 48 hours, then all the previous parties who do not give consent to the extended time, are discharged from their liability to such holder [Sections 63 and 83].

37.8. CASES IN WHICH PRESENTMENT OF A BILL FOR ACCEPTANCE IS EXCUSED

The holder of a bill of exchange becomes entitled to recover the amount only when the bill is duly presented for acceptance, and the same is dishonoured due to non-acceptance (*i.e.*, not accepted) However, there are certain cases in which the presentment for acceptance is excused (*i.e.*, the holder is not required to present the bill for acceptance). And the holder may treat the bill as dishonoured and proceed to recover the amount from the liable parties. Following are the case, in which presentment of a bill of exchange for acceptance is not essential:

1. When, after reasonable search, the drawee cannot be found [Section 61].
2. When the drawee is a fictitious person or one incapable of contracting [Section 91].
3. When although the presentment is irregular, but acceptance has been refused on some other ground.

But in all other cases, where presentment is compulsory, the bill of exchange must be presented for acceptance. Even if the drawee is dead or becomes insolvent, the bill should be presented to his legal heirs or the Receiver or Official Assignee as the case may be [Section 75].

37.9. ACCEPTANCE FOR HONOUR

As a general rule, a bill of exchange should be accepted only by the drawee, *i.e.*, the person on whom it is drawn. But in certain cases, a person who is in no way liable on the bill of exchange may come forward and accept it for the honour of the drawee or any other party liable on the bill of exchange. Such acceptance is known as 'acceptance for honour'. Sections 108 to 112 of the Negotiable Instruments Act contain the provisions relating to the "acceptance for honour". These will he discussed in detail in Chapter 41.

37.10. PRESENTMENT OF A PROMISSORY NOTE FOR SIGHT

The term 'presentment for sight' may be defined as the showing of a negotiable instrument (generally promissory note) to the maker for his knowledge. The presentment for sight is required *only in case of a note payable after sight*. In this case, there is no need of writing or signature of the maker on the promissory note to validate such presentment. It is, however, advisable for the holder to get an acknowledgment of presentment by the maker by writing the word 'seen' on the promissory note, or by initialling and dating the promissory note. It is not necessary that every promissory note should be presented for sight. There are certain promissory notes which are not required to be presented for sight, and there are certain others which must be presented for sight. Following are the promissory notes which need not be presented for sight:

(*a*) A promissory note payable 'at sight'.

(*b*) A promissory note payable on demand.

(*c*) A promissory note payable on fixed date, *e.g.*, 15th June, 2003.

(*d*) A promissory note payable on the expiry of fixed period, *e.g.*, 30 days after date.

Following are the promissory notes which must be presented for sight:

(*a*) A promissory note payable at a given time 'after sight' [Section 62].

(*b*) A promissory note in which there is an express term that it shall be presented for sight before it is presented for payment.

The above notes are required to be presented for sight in order to make the parties liable and fix the maturity of the instrument. In default of such presentment, no party is liable to the holder who makes such default [Section 62].

Note. A promissory note does not require acceptance. The reason for the same is that the maker of the promissory note is primarily liable to pay the amount due on it and there is no other person (like acceptor as in case of a bill of exchange) to be made primarily liable.

37.11. RULES REGARDING THE PRESENTMENT OF A NOTE FOR SIGHT

The rules regarding the presentment of a promissory note for sight may be summed up as under:

1. A promissory note should be presented for sight by its holder or his duly authorised agent.
2. A promissory note should be presented for sight to its maker.
3. The presentment for sight should be made within a reasonable time after the making of a promissory note.
4. The presentment for sight should be made on a business day and during the business hours only.
5. If after a reasonable search, the maker cannot be found, then the presentment is excused and the promissory note is treated as dishonoured.

37.12. EFFECT OF NON-PRESENTMENT OF A PROMISSORY NOTE FOR SIGHT

We know that in certain cases, the presentment of a promissory note for sight is compulsory. In such cases, the holder must present the promissory note for sight. If he fails to do so, it has the same effect as in case of non-presentment of a bill of exchange for acceptance. Thus, if the holder fails to present a promissory note for sight, no party on the promissory note shall be liable to such holder [Section 62]. As a matter of fact, there is no debt due and no cause of action arises until presentment for sight has been made.

37.13. PRESENTMENT OF NEGOTIABLE INSTRUMENTS FOR PAYMENT

After a negotiable instrument is made (completed by acceptance or sight, where required), the next stage is that it must be presented for payment to the parties who are primarily liable to pay the amount due on the instrument. Thus, a promissory note, a bill of exchange and a cheque must be presented for payment to the maker, acceptor or drawee thereof respectively. [Section 64].

37.14. RULES REGARDING THE PRESENTMENT OF NEGOTIABLE INSTRUMENTS FOR PAYMENT

1. *Persons who should present an instrument for payment*
2. *Persons to whom the instrument should be presented for payment*
3. *Time for presentment for payment*
4. *Place of presentment for payment*

The rules regarding the presentment of negotiable instruments for payment may be discussed under the following heads:

1. *Persons who should present an instrument for payment:* A negotiable instrument should be presented for payment by a person who can give a valid discharge to the debtor, *i.e.*, by payment to whom the debtor's liability to pay comes to an end. A holder or his duly authorised agent, can give a valid discharge to the debtor. And thus, he can present the instrument for payment.

2. *Persons to whom the instrument should be presented for payment:* A negotiable instrument should be presented for payment to the party who is primarily liable. According to Sections 64 and 75, following are the persons to whom an instrument should be presented for payment:

(*a*) ***The maker:*** In case of promissory note, a maker is primarily liable to make the payment. Thus, a promissory note should be presened to him for payment. It can also be presented to his duly authorised agent.

(*b*) ***The acceptor:*** In case of bill of exchange, the acceptor is primarily liable to make the payment. Thus, a bill or exchange should be presented to him for payment. It can also be presented to his duly authorised agent.

(*c*) ***The drawee:*** In case of a cheque, the payment is to be made by the drawee banker. Thus, a cheque should be presented to the banker for payment. It can also be presented to his duly authorised agent.

(*d*) ***The legal representative of the maker, acceptor, drawee:*** If the maker, acceptor or drawee is dead, the negotiable instrument should be presened to his legal representative for payment

(*e*) ***The Official Receiver or Assignee:*** If the maker, acceptor or drawee becomes insolvent the negotiable instrument should be presented to his official receiver or assignee for payment.

3. *Time for presentment for payment:* The rules regarding the time for presentment of payment may be stated as under:

(*a*) ***Where an instrument is payable after a fixed period of time, e.g., 30 days after date:*** In such cases, the instrument must be presented for payment on its maturity [Section 66] *i.e.*, on the date when its payment becomes due. It may be noted that an earlier presentment is premature and the party is not liable to pay the amount due on the instrument. It may also be noted that the delay, even of a brief period (say a day) discharges all parties other than the maker or acceptor of the instrument.

(*b*) ***Where an instrument is payable on demand:*** In such cases, instrument must be presented for payment within a *reasonable time* after it is received by the holder [Section 74]. It may be noted that the cheques are always payable on demand. Thus, the holder of a cheque must present it for payment within reasonable time after it is received by him. If he fails to do so, all parties except the drawer, will be discharged from liability to the holder [Section 73].

(*c*) ***Where a promissory note is payable by instalments:*** In such cases, the note must be presened for payment on the third day after the date fixed for payment of each instalment. If any instalment is not paid on such presentment, it has the same effect as non-payment of a promissory note at maturity [Section 67] *i.e.,* the instrument is treated as dishonoured.

It may, however, be noted that all the instruments must be presented for payment during the usual hours of business' . In case of a cheque, it must be presented for payment during the usual 'banking hours' [Section 65].

4. ***Place of presentment for payment:*** The rules regarding the place of presentment for payment may be stated as under:

(*a*) ***Where place of presentment is specified in the instrument itself:*** In such cases, the presentment for payment must be made at that place only. The place of payment may be specified by using certain phrases in the instrument such as "payable at 128, World Trade Centre, Connaught Place, New Delhi, and not elsewhere", or "payable at 213, Raheja Chambers, Nariman Point, Bombay".

(*b*) ***Where the place of presentment is not specified in the promissory note or bill of exchange:*** In such cases, it must be presented for payment at the place of business, if any, or at the usual residence of the maker, drawee, or the acceptor as the case may be [Section 70]. And if the maker, drawee, or acceptor has no known place of business or of fixed residence, then the presentment may be made to him in person (*i.e.,* personally) wherever he can be found [Section 71]. As regards the presentment of a cheque, it must be presented for payment at the banker upon which it is drawn [Section 72].

Note. Where the presentment for payment by post is authorised by agreement or custom, then presentment by registered letter is sufficient [Section 64].

37.15. EFFECT OF NON-PRESENTMENT OF NEGOTIABLE INSTRUMENTS FOR PAYMENT

In case an instrument is not presented for payment as per the rules discussed above, the parties, *other than those primarily liable*, are discharged from their liability to the holder [Section 64]. Thus, following are the parties who are discharged from their liability to the holder in case of non-presentment of various negotiable instruments for payment:

1. In case of a promissory note, all the parties other than the maker (such as indorsers).
2. In case of a bill of exchange, all the parties other than the acceptor (such as drawer and indorsers).
3. In case of a cheque, all the parties other than the drawer (such as indorsers).

The reason for the same is that the liability of these parties is conditional upon the presentment of the negotiable instruments for payment. And if this condition is not fulfilled, they are dicharged from making the payment. However, in case of a promissory note which is payable on demand, and is not payable at a specified place, no presentment is necessary to hold the maker liable for payment [Section 64 (Exception)].

37.16. CASES IN WHICH THE PRESENTMENT OF NEGOTIABLE INSTRUMENTS FOR PAYMENT IS EXCUSED

Section 76 of the Negotiable Instruments Act specifies certain cases, in which the presentment of a negotiable instrument for payment is excused (*i.e.,* the holder is not required to present the instrument for payment). And at the due date for presentment, the holder may treat the instrument as dishonoured and proceed to recover the amount from the other liable parties. Following are the cases, in which presentment of the instrument to the parties primarily liable is not essential.

1. When the maker, drawee or acceptor of a negotiable instrument intentionally prevents its presentment for payment.
2. When the negotiable instrument is payable at the place of business of the maker, drawer or acceptor, and he closes, such place on business day during the usual business hours.
3. When the negotiable instrument is payable at some other specified place, and the maker, drawer or acceptor or any other person authorised to pay the amount does not attend at such place during the usual business hours.
4. When the negotiable instrument is not payable at any specified place, and the marker, drawee or acceptor cannot be found after due search.
5. When the liable party undertakes to pay the amount due on the instrument inspite of its presentment for payment.
6. When, after the maturity of the instrument, the liable party makes the part payment against the total amount due on the instrument.
7. When the liable party promises to pay the amount, due on instrument, in whole or in part.
8. When the liable party waives off his right to take advantage of any default in presentment for payment.
9. When the drawer does not suffer any damage for want of presentment for payment, *e.g.*, when the drawer draws a bill of exchange on himself, or when the drawee is a fictitious person.
10. When the presentment of the negotiable instrument for payment becomes impossible, *e.g.*, declaration of war.
11. When the bill of exchange is dishonoured by the drawee for non-acceptance, then further presentment to him for payment is not necessary.
12. When the maker refuses to pay the money or puts forward certain defences.

[*Sevaram* v. *Jayaram*, AIR 1966 Madras 297].

But in all other cases, a negotiable instrument must be presented for payment to make the other parties liable on the instrument. Even if the party to whom the presentment has to be made is dead or becomes insolvent, the negotiable instrument must be presented for payment to his legal representatives (*i.e,* heirs) or the Receiver or Official Assignee, as the case may be.

37.17 PAYMENT FOR HONOUR

As a general rule, the payment due on the negotiable instrument can be made by the party who is liable to pay the same. But in case of a *bill of exchange*, any person, under certain circumstances, may pay the amount due on the bill of exchange for the honour of any party who is liable to pay the same. Such payment is known as 'payment for honour'. Sections 113 and 114 of the Negotiable Instruments Act contain the legal provisions relating to 'payment for honour'. These will be discussed in detail in Art . 41.7.

LEGAL PROVISIONS (SECTIONS) DISCUSSED IN THE CHAPTER

Important legal provisions (sections) of the Negotiable Instruments Act, 1881 discussed in this chapter, are reproduced hereunder for ready reference:

1. ***Section 33: Only drawee can be acceptor except in case of need or for honour.***
No person except the drawee of a bill of exchange, or all or some of several drawees, or a person named therein as a drawee in case of need, or an acceptor for honour, can bind himself by an acceptance.

2. ***Section 34: Acceptance by several drawees not partners.***
Where there are several drawees of a bill of exchange who are not partners, each of them can accept if for himself, but non of them can accept it for another without his authority.

3. ***Section 61: Presentment for acceptance***
A bill of exchange payable after sight must, if no time or place is specified therein for presentment, be presented to the drawee thereof for acceptance, if he can, after reasonable search, be found, by a person entitled to demand acceptance, within a reasonable time after it is drawn, and in business hours on a business day, in default of such presentment, no party thereto is liable thereon to the person making such default.
If the drawee cannot, after reasonable search, be found, the bill is dishonoured.
If the bill is directed to the drawee at a particular place, it must be presented at that place; and if at the due date for presentment he cannot, after reasonable search, be found thereon, the bill is dishonoured.
Where authorized by agreement or usage, a presentment through the post office by means of a registered letter is sufficient.

4. ***Section 62: Presentment of promissory note for sight***
A promissory note, payable a certain period after sight must be presented to the maker thereof for sight (if he can after reasonable search be found) by a person entitled to demand payment, within a reasonable time after it is made and in business hours on a business day. In default of such presentment, no party thereto is liable thereon to the person making such default.

5. ***Section 63: Drawee's time for deliberation***
The holder must, if so required by the drawee of a bill of exchange presented to him for acceptance, allow the drawee forty-eight hours (exclusive of public holidays) to consider whether he will accept it.

6. ***Section 64: Presentment for payment.***
(1) Promissory notes, bills of exchange and cheques must be presented for payment to the maker, acceptor or drawee thereof respectively, by or on behalf of the holder as hereinafter provided. In default of such presentment, the other parties thereto are not liable thereon to such holder.
Where authorized by agreement or usage, a presentment through the post office by means of a registered letter is sufficient.
Exception.– Where a promissory note is payable on demand and is not payable at a specified place, no presentment is necessary in order to charge the maker thereof.

7. ***Section 65: Hours of presentment.***
Presentment for payment must be made during the usual hours of business and, if at a banker's, within banking hours.

8. ***Section 66: Presentment for payment of instruments payable after date or sight***
A promissory note or bill of exchange, made payable at a specified period after date or sight thereof, must be presented for payment at maturity.

9. ***Section 67: Presentment for payment of promissory note payable by instalments***
A promissory note payable by instalments must be presented for payment on the third day after the date fixed for payment of each instalment: and non-payment on such presentment has the same effect as non-payment of a note at maturity.

10. ***Section 68: Presentment for payment of instrument payable at specified place and not elsewhere***
A promissory note, bill of exchange or cheque made, drawn or accepted payable at a specified place and not elsewhere must, in order to charge any party thereto, be presented for payment at that place.

TEST QUESTIONS

1. What is meant by 'presentment of negotiable instruments? State the instruments which are required to be presented for acceptance, for sight and for payment.
2. What is meant by acceptance of a bill or exchange? What are the essentials of a valid acceptance? State the rules relating to the presentment of a bill of exchange for acceptance.
3. What are the different kinds of acceptance? State the legal effect of a conditional (qualified) acceptance. Is the holder bound to take the conditional acceptance?

4. Is presentment of a negotiable instrument for acceptance necessary in all cases ? State the cases in which presentment for acceptance is excused.
5. State by whom and to whom the bill should be presented for acceptance. What is the effect of non-presentmentt of a bill of exchange for acceptance?
6. What steps should be taken by the holder on drawee's refusal to accept the bill?
7. Explain 'presentment for payment' of negotiable instruments. Under what circumstances the presentment for payment is not necessary?
8. State by whom and to whom a negotiable instrument should be presented for payment. State the cases in which the presentment for payment is excused.
9. Write notes on the following:
   (*a*) Acceptance for honour,
   (*b*) Payment for honour,
   (*c*) Presentment for sight,
   (*d*) Conditional or qualified acceptance, and
   (*e*) Time and place for presentment of negotiable instruments for acceptance and payment.

MULTIPLE CHOICE QUESTIONS

1. The presentment for acceptance is required in case of a
   (*a*) bill of exchange
   (*b*) promissory note
   (*c*) cheque
   (*d*) both (*a*) and (*b*).
2. The presentment for sight is required in case of a
   (*a*) bill of exchange
   (*b*) promissory note
   (*c*) cheque
   (*d*) both (*b*) and (*c*).
3. The presentment for payment is required in case of a
   (*a*) bill of exchange
   (*b*) promissory note
   (*c*) cheque
   (*d*) all of these.
4. Which of the following bill of exchange must be presented for acceptance of the drawee?
   (*a*) A bill payable on demand
   (*b*) A bill payable on fixed date
   (*c*) A bill payable 30 days after date
   (*d*) none of these.
5. Though the acceptance is required only in case of a bill of exchange but in certain cases it is optional to present the bill for acceptance
   (*a*) True
   (*b*) False.
6. The presentment for sight is required only in case of a promissory note. Which of the following note must be presented for sight?
   (*a*) a note payable at sight
   (*b*) a note payable after sight
   (*c*) a note payable on demand
   (*d*) all of the above.
7. A failure to present a negotiable instrument for payment as per the rules, discharges
   (*a*) all parties to the instrument
   (*b*) all parties except those secondarily liable
   (*c*) all parties except those primarily liable
   (*d*) none of the parties to the instrument.
8. A negotiable instrument should be presented for payment to the party who is
   (*a*) primarily liable
   (*b*) secondarily liable
   (*c*) willing to make payment
   (*d*) capable of making payment.

ANSWERS

1. (*a*)	2. (*b*)	3. (*d*)	4. (*d*)	5. (*a*)	6. (*b*)
7. (*c*)	8. (*a*)				

OBJECTIVE TYPE QUESTIONS WITH REASONING

State with reasons whether the following statements are correct or incorrect:

1. The presentment for acceptance in required in all the types of negotiable instruments.
2. A bill can be validly accepted by the drawer only as he is the person primarily liable on the bill.
3. A holder who makes default in presenting the bill for acceptance is not entitled to recover the amount of the bill.
4. On the death or insolvency of the drawee, the presentment of a bill of exchange for acceptance is excused.
5. On acceptance of a bill, it is not required to be presented for payment as then it becomes the duty of the acceptor to come forward and make the payment.
6. A cheque can be presented for payment at any time within a period of reasonable time.
7. When the maker, drawee or acceptor of a negotiable instrument intentionally prevent its presentment for payment, then the holder may treat the instrument an dishonoured and proceed to recover the amount from the liable parties.

ANSWERS

1. *Incorrect.* It is required is case of bill of exchange only.
2. *Incorrect.* A bill of exchange in accepted by the drawee and if the refuses, then by the drawee in case of need , if there is any.
3. *Correct.* On such a default, the drawer and all indorsers prior to the defaulting holder are discharged from their liability to holder [Section 61, first Para last line]
4. *Incorrect.* In such a case the bill should be presented for acceptance to drawee's legal heirs or Official Assignee an the case may be [Section 75].
5. *Incorrect.* All the negotiable instrument *i.e.,* a promissory note, a bill of exchange and cheque *must* be presented for payment to the maker, acceptor or the drawee thereof respectively [Section 64].
6. *Correct.* A cheque in always payable on demand. A demand instrument must be presented for payment within a reasonable time after it is received by the holder [Section 74].
7. *Correct.* In such a case, the presentment of a negotiable instrument for payment is excused [Section 76].

PRACTICAL PROBLEMS

1. *A*, the holder of a bill of exchange for Rs. 10,000 drawn upon *B*, indorses the same in favour of *C* in discharge of his liability. *C* Presents the bill for acceptance to *B*, who accepts by writing the words "accepted for Rs.8,000 only" *C* takes back the accepted bill from *B* without informing *A* about the conditional acceptance. Can *C* recover the balance of Rs.2,000 from *A* ? Give reasons.

   Hints : No, *C* cannot recover the balance of Rs.2,000 from *A*. In this case, there is conditional (partial) acceptance and the holder takes the partially accepted bill at his own risk as the prior parties are not liable unless they give their consent to the conditional acceptance.
2. *A*, the holder of a bill of exchange, indorses the bill to *B* who further indorses the same to *C*. However, *C* does not present the bill for acceptance to its drawee, but claims the amount from *B*. Is *B* liable to pay the amount of the bill?

   Hint : No, *B* is not liable to *C* for the amount of the bill. If the bill is not presented for acceptance by a holder, then no party on the bill is liable to such holder. [Section 61]

38

CHAPTER

DISHONOUR OF NEGOTIABLE INSTRUMENTS

38.1. INTRODUCTION

In the preceding chapter, we have noted that the liability of the parties arises, when the instrument is duly presented for acceptance or for payment, as the case may be. There may be cases when the party, who is liable to accept or to pay, refuses to accept or pay the instrument when duly presented for the acceptance or payment, as the case may be. When the acceptance or payment is refused, the instrument is said to be dishonoured. Thus, a negotiable instrument may be dishonoured in either of the following ways:

1. Due to non-acceptance.
2. Due to non-payment.

The instruments which are required to be presented for acceptance may be dishonoured either due to non-acceptance or due to non-payment after its acceptance. But the instruments, which are not required to be presented for acceptance, can only be dishonoured due to non-payment. Thus, a bill of exchange may be dishonoured due to non-acceptance or non-payment because acceptance is required only in case of a bill of exchange. And a cheque or a promissory note can only be dishonoured due to non-payment as these do not require any acceptance.

38.2. DISHONOUR OF A BILL OF EXCHANG DUE TO NON-ACCEPTANCE

Only a bill of exchange can be dishonoured due to its non-acceptance. According to Section 91, a *bill of exchange* is treated as dishonoured due to its non-acceptance in any of the following cases:

1. Where a bill is properly presented to the drawee for acceptance and he refuses to accept it, or he does not accept it within 48* hours from the time of presentment for acceptance.

2. Where presentment for acceptance is excused and the bill remains unaccepted.

3. Where there are more than one drawees who are not partners, and any one of them defaults in accepting the bill of exchange.

4. Where the drawee is incompetent to contract.

5. Where the drawee gives a conditional, *i.e.*, qualified acceptance.

6. Where the drawee cannot be found after a reasonable search.

7. Where the drawee is a fictitious person.

It may, however be noted that where, a *'drawee in case of need'*, is mentioned in the bill of exchange, then the bill is not dishonoured until it is dishonoured by such a drawee [Section 115].

38.3. DISHONOUR OF NEGOTIABLE INSTRUMENTS DUE TO NON-PAYMENT

Every negotiable instrument is required to be presented for payment. If the payment is not made on such presentment, the instrument is said to be dishonoured due to non-payment. According to Section 92, a promissory note, a bill of exchange or a cheque is dishonoured due to its non-payment in the following ways:

1. Where a *promissory note* is properly presented to its maker for payment and he fails to make the payment, the promissory note is dishonoured due to non-payment.
2. When a *bill of exchange,* after its acceptance, is properly presented to the acceptor for payment and he fails to make the payment, the is dishonoured due to non-payment.
3. Where a *cheque* is presented to the banker for payment and he fails to make payment, the cheque is dishonoured due to non-payment.

It may be noted that a negotiable instrument is also taken as dishonoured due to non-payment, where its presentment for payment is excused (*i.e.*, not required), and the instrument when overdue, remains unpaid [Section 76, already discussed in Art. 37.16.].

38.4. DISHONOUR OF CHEQUES DUE TO INSUFFICIENT FUNDS

Sometimes, a cheque is dishonoured due to insufficient funds in drawer's bank account. In such cases the drawer is also criminally liable for this offence. The punishment may extend upto imprisoment of two year*, or fine upto double the amount of cheque, or both [Section 138, added by amendment in 1988]. This point has already been discussed in detail in Art 36.32.

38.5. NOTICE OF DISHONOUR

We have already discussed that a negotiable instrument may be dishonoured either due to its non acceptance or non-payment. In both the cases of dishonour, a notice of dishonour must be given by the holder to all such parties to whom be wants to make liable on the instrument, *i.e.*, from whom he wants to recover the amount due on the instrument. The object of giving such a notice of dishonour is to inform the party liable on the instrument about their liability which accrues as a result of the dishonour of the instrument.

---

* The time of 48 hours is allowed under Section 63.

* Enhanced from one year by the Negotiable Instruments (Amendments) Act, 2002.

38.6. RULES REGARDING NOTICE OF DISHONOUR

1. *Persons by whom the notice of dishonour should be given*
2. *Persons to whom the notice of dishonour should be given*
3. *Form and mode of giving notice of dishonour*
4. *Time of giving notice of dishonour*

The rules regarding the notice of dishonour may be discussed under the following heads:

1. ***Persons by whom the notice of dishonour should be given:*** A notice of dishonour must be given by the holder of the negotiable instrument or by some other party who is liable on the instrument [Section 63]. It may be noted that a party who receives the notice of dishonour must also give the notice of dishonour to the prior parties to whom be wants to make liable [Section 95]. The authorised agent of any of the above parties may also give the notice of dishonour.

2. ***Persons to whom the notice of dishonour should be given:*** A notice of dishonour must be given to all such parties to whom the holder wants to make liable. The notice of dishonour may also be given to the duly authorised agent of the liable party. Where the liable party is dead, the notice should be given to his legal representatives (*i.e.*, legal heirs). And where the liable party has been declared insolvent, the notice of dishonour should be given to his Receiver or Official Assignee.

The notice of dishonour is not necessary to the parties who are primarily liable, because it is their duty to pay the instrument on due date.

3. ***Form and mode of giving notice of dishonour:*** A notice of dishonour may be in any form. But it must expressly inform the party to whom it is given that the instrument has been dishonoured, and that he will be held liable on it. Moreover, the party liable for payment must also be informed the way in which the instrument was dishonoured. The notice of dishonour may be oral or in writing. If it is in writing, it may be sent by post. It should be directed to the party's place of business, and where he has no such place, to his residence [Section 94].

4. ***Time of giving notice of dishonour:*** A notice of dishonour must be given within a 'reasonable time' of dishonour. The term 'reasonable time', will depend upon the nature of the negotiable instrument and the usual course of dealing between the parties with respect to similar instruments. In calculating the reasonable time, public holidays must be excluded [Section 105].

38.7. EFFECT OF DEFAULT IN GIVING NOTICE OF DISHONOUR

The consequence of not giving due notice of dishonour is that all parties who are entitled to require such notice are discharged from their liability. In fact, the liability of the drawer[1] and that of the indorser[2] arises only on notice of dishonour being given to them unless the notice is excused under Section 98.

Thus, the holder cannot sue the party to whom the notice of dishonour has not been given. However, the maker of a note, and the acceptor of a bill remain liable without notice because they are primarily liable on the instrument [Section 93].

38.8. CASES IN WHICH NOTICE OF DISHONOUR IS EXCUSED

As per Section 98, following are the cases in which the notice of dishonour is excused, *i.e.*, in these cases, the holder is not required to give a notice of dishonour:

1. When the notice of dishonour is dispensed with by the party entitled to the same.

1. Section 30 of the Negotiable Instruments Act.
2. Section 35 of the Negotiable Instrument Act.

2. When the drawer has countermanded payment, no notice of dishonour is necessary to charge the drawer. This is so because the drawer has made it impossible for the holder to obtain payment.
3. When the party charged could not suffer damages if no notice of dishonour is given to him, *e.g.*, if at the time when the cheque is drawn, the drawer did not have any funds in his account with the drawee banker.
4. When the party entitled to the notice of dishonour cannot be found after due search.
5. When the party who has to give notice is unable to do so without any fault of his own, *e.g.*, serious illness or any unavoidable accident.
6. When the acceptor is also the drawer no notice of dishonour is necessary to charge the drawer, *e.g.*, when a firm draws a bill of exchange on its branch.
7. When the promissory note is not negotiable, no notice of dishonour is necessary in case of its dishonour.
8. When the party entitled to notice of dishonour, unconditionally promises to pay the amount due on the instrument.

38.9. DUTIES OF A HOLDER ON DISHONOUR OF A NEGOTIABLE INSTRUMENT

The following are the duties of a holder on the dishonour of a negotiable instrument:

1. ***Notice of dishonour***: On the dishonour of a negotiable instrument, the holder must give notice of dishonour to such parties to whom he wants to make liable. After giving due notice of dishonour, the holder may bring an action against the liable parties for recovery of the amount due on the instrument.

2. ***Noting and protest:*** On the dishonour of a negotiable instrument, the holder may also get the instrument noted and protested for dishonour. However, noting and protesting is done only in case of promissory note and bill of exchange. This point will be discussed in detail in Arts. 38.11 and 38.12.

38.10. NEGOTIABLE INSTRUMENTS ACQUIRED AFTER THEIR DISHONOUR

Sometimes, a person acquires a negotiable instrument after its dishonour. In such cases, he gets the rights of his immediate transferor, if he takes it with the notice (*i.e.*, knowledge) of dishonour. Same is the case when the instrument is acquired after maturity [Section 59]. Thus, such a transferee cannot become a holder in due course of the instrument. It may be noted that this is an exception to the general rule that the holder in due course gets better title than that of his transferor.

38.11. NOTING OF A DISHONOURED NEGOTIABLE INSTRUMENT

The term 'noting' means the recording of the fact of dishonour by a Notary Public[3] upon the negotiable instrument. Where a promissory note or bill of exchange is dishonoured, the holder can, after giving due notice of dishonour, sue the liable parties for the recovery of amount due on the instrument. However, before suing, the holder may also get the fact of dishonour, authenticated by 'noting' by a Notary Public. In such cases, the Notary Public makes a formal demand for acceptance or payment upon the maker, drawee or acceptor. And on their refusal to accept or pay, the Notary Public records the fact of dishonour and makes noting on the instrument. The *recording of such a fact*, on the instrument, is called 'noting'. It may be noted that the noting is done in case of *promissory notes* and *bills of exchange only* [Section 99].

The noting should specify the following particulars [Section 99, para 2]:

3. Notary Public is a person who is appointed under the Notaries Act to attest certain documents.

(*a*) The fact of dishonour. (*b*) The date of dishonour. (*c*) The reason, if any, for dishonour. (*d*) If the instrumnet has not been expressly dishonoured, the notice should state why the holder treats it dishonoured. (*e*) The charges of Notary Public.

The noting must be made within a reasonable time[4] after the dishonour of the negotiable instrument. It may be noted that the noting is not compulsory under law. If the dishonoured instrument is not 'noted' it does not affect the rights of the holder of the instrument in any way. But it has certain advantage, *e.g.*, it provides an authentic evidence of dishonour.

38.12. PROTEST OF A DISHONOURED NEGOTIABLE INSTRUMENT

The term 'protest' means the formal certificate of dishonour issued by the Notary Public to the holder of a promissory note or bill of exchange. It may be noted that the protest is issued after noting the fact of dishonour. According to Section 100, if a promissory note or bill of exchange is dishonoured due to non-acceptance or non-payment, the holder may get the fact of dishonour noted and certified by a Notary Public. Such *certificate* of Notary Public is called the 'protest'. The protest must contain the following particulars (Section 101):

(*a*) The instrument itself or an exact copy of it. (*b*) The name of the person for whom and against whom the instrument has been protested. (*c*) The fact of and reasons for dishonour. (*d*) The place and time of dishonour. (*e*) The signature of the notary public. (*f*) In the event of an acceptance for honour or of a payment for honour, the name of the person for whose honour it is accepted or paid. Also the manner in which such acceptance or payment was offered and effected.

The holder must get the instrument protested within a reasonable time. It may be noted that protest is not compulsory in case of inland promissory note and bill of exchange. However, foreign bill of exchange must be protested for dishonour when such protest is required by the law of the place where they are drawn [Section 104].

Note. The difference between 'noting' and 'protest' is that the noting is *merely a record of fact of dishonour* on the instrument itself by a Notary Public. And a protest is a *formal certificate of dishonour* issued by the Notary Public to the holder of the instrument, *i.e.*, in this case the Notary Public certifies the fact of dishonour and issue a separate certificate to that effect.

38.13. PROTEST FOR BETTER SECURITY

Sometimes, before the maturity of a bill of exchange, its acceptor becomes insolvent or his credit is publicly impeached. In such cases, the holder of the bill of exchange may demand a better security from the acceptor through a Notary Public. If the acceptor refuses to give a better security, this fact may be noted and certified by the Notary Public. Such a certificate is a called a protest for better security [Section 100 (second para)]. The demand for better security should be made within a reasonable time after the acceptor has lost his credibility. And the protest should also be certified within a reasonable time after the acceptor refuses to give better security.

It may be noted that the acceptor is not bound to give better security. And on refusal by the acceptor to give a better security, the holder has no immediate right of action against th drawer and indorsers. He will have to wait till the date of maturity. The main advantage of protest for better security is that the bill of exchange may be accepted for honour after such protest has been made.

4. It is same as in case of notice of dishonour. See Sections 105 and 106 of the Negotiable Instruments Act.

38.14. ADVANTAGES OF PROTEST OF A DISHONOURED NEGOTIABLE INSTRUMENT

Following are the main advantages of protest of a dishonoured negotiable instrument:

1. It provides an authentic and satisfactory evidence of dishonour.
2. If a suit is filed on the basis of a dishonoured negotiable instrument, the court shall, on the proof of the protest, presume the fact of dishonour unless and until such fact is disproved.

38.15. NOTICE OF PROTEST OF DISHONOURED NEGOTIABLE INSTRUMENT

Sometimes, a promissory note or a bill of exchange is required by law to be protested. In such cases, the notice of protest should be given instead of notice of dishonour. It may be noted that a notice of protest is to be given in the same manner and subject to the same conditions as in case of a notice of dishonour. The notice of protest may be given by the Notary Public who makes the protest [Section 102].

38.16. COMPENSATION FOR DISHONOUR

In case of dishonour of a negotiable, the party, who is liable to pay the amount due on it, is also bound to pay the compensation to the holder or indorser of the instrument. The rules for determining the amount of compensation may be stated as under:

1. ***Compensation to the holder:*** The holder of a negotiable instrument is entitled to recover the amount due on the instrument alongwith the expenses properly incurred in presenting, noting and protesting the instrument [Section 117(*a*)].

2. ***Compensation to indorser:*** Sometimes the indorser, who is liable on the instrument, pays the amount due on it. In such cases, he is entitled to recover the amount so paid with interest at the rate of 18 per cent per annum from the date of payment until the tender or realisation of the amount. He is also entitled to recover all expenses incurred for dishonour and payment [Section 117(*c*)]. Priod to the amendment it 1988, this interest rate of 18 per cent was 6 per cent only.

3. ***Re-exchange:*** Sometimes, the holder or indorser entitled to claim the amount, resides in a country different from that in which the person sought to be made liable resides. In such cases, the holder or the indorser is entitled to receive the amount at the current rate of exchange between the two countries on the date of dishonour [Section 117(*b*)(*d*)].

4. ***Re-draft:*** The party entitled to compensation may draw a bill of exchange payable at sight or on demand on the party liable to compensate him, for the amount due to him together with all expenses properly incurred by him. Such a bill of exchange is known as 're-draft'. The re-draft must be accompanied by the original instrument dishonoured and the protest, if any. If the re-draft is dishonoured, the party dishonouring the same is liable to make compensation in the same manner as in the case of the original bill of exchange [Section 117(*e*)].

LEGAL PROVISIONS (SECTIONS) DISCUSSED IN THE CHAPTER

Important legal provisions (sections) of the Negotiable Instruments Act, 1881, discussed in this chapter, are reproduced hereunder for ready reference:

1. ***Section 59: Instrument Acquired After Dishonour or When Querdue.***
   The holder of a negotiable instrument, who has acquired it after dishonour, whether by non-acceptance or non-payment, with notice thereof, or after maturity, has only as against the other parties, the rights thereon of his transferor.
2. ***Section 63: Drawee's Time for Deliberation***
   " The holder must, if so required by the drawee of a bill of exchange presented to him for acceptance, allow the drawee forty-eight hours exclusive of public holidays, to consider whether he will accept it"

3. *Section 91: Dishonour by Non-acceptance*
A bill of exchange is said to be dishonoured by non-acceptance when the drawee, or one of the several drawees not being partners, makes default in acceptance upon being duly required to accept the bill, or where the presentment is excused and the bill is not accepted.

4. *Section 92: Dishonour by Non-payment.*
A promissory note, bill of exchange or cheque is said to be dishonoured by non-payment when the maker of the note, acceptor of the bill or drawee of the cheque makes default in payment upon being duly required to pay the same.

5. *Section 93: By and to whom notice of dishonour should be given.*
When a promissory note, bill of exchange or cheque is dishonoured by non-acceptance or non-payment, the holder thereof, or some party thereto who remains liable thereon, must give notice that the instrument has been so dishonoured to all other parties whom the holder seeks to make severally liable thereon, and to some one of several parties whom he seeks to make jointly liable thereon.
Nothing in this section renders it necessary to give notice to the maker of the dishonoured promissory note, or the drawee or acceptor of the dishonoured bill of exchange or cheque.

6. *Section 95: Party receiving must transmit notice of dishonour.*
Any party receiving notice of dishonour must, in order to render any prior party liable to himself, give notice of dishonour to such party within a reasonable time, unless such party otherwise receives due notice as provided by section 93.

7. *Section 97: When party to whom notice given is dead*
When the party to whom notice of dishonour is despatched is dead, but the party despatching the notice is ignorant of his death, the notice is sufficient.

8. *Section 98: When notice of dishonour is unnecessary*
No notice of dishonour is necessary–
(*a*) when it is dispensed with by the party entitled thereto;
(*b*) in order to charge the drawer, when he has countermanded payment'
(*c*) when the party charged could not suffer damage for want notice;
(*d*) when the party entitled to notice cannot after due search be found; or the party bound to give notice is, for any other reason, unable without any fault of his own to give it;
(*e*) to charge the drawers, when the acceptor is also a drawer;
(*f*) in the case of a promissory note which is not negotiable
(*g*) when the party entitled to notice, knowing the facts, promises unconditionally to pay the amount due on the instrument.

9. *Section 99; Noting*
When a promissory note or bill of exchange has been dishonoured by non-acceptance or non-payment, the holder may cause such dishonour to be noted by a notary public upon the instrument, or upon a paper attached thereto, or partly upon each.
Such note must be made within a reasonable time after dishonour, and must specify the date of dishonour, the reason, if any, assigned for such dishonour, or if the instrument has not been expressly dishonoured, the reason why the holder treats it as dishonoured, and the notary's charges.

10. *Section 100: Protest*
When a promissory note or bill of exchange has been dishonoured by non-acceptance or non-payment, the holder may, within a reasonable time, cause such dishonour to be noted and certified by a notary public. Such certificate is called protest.
Protest for better security
When the acceptor of a bill of exchange has become insolvent, or his credit has been publicly impeached, before the maturity of the bill, the holder may, within a reasonable time, cause a notary public to demand better security of the acceptor, and on its being refused may, with a reasonable time, cause such facts to be noted and certified as aforesaid. Such certificate is called a protest for better security.

11. *Section 115: Drawee in case of need.*
Where a drawee in case of need is named in a bill of exchange, or in any indorsement thereon, the bill is not dishonoured until it has been dishonoured by such drawee.

TEST QUESTIONS

1. A negotiable instrument may be dishonoured either due to 'non-acceptance' or due to 'non-payment' Explain both kinds of dishonour. State the instruments which are dishonoured due to non-acceptance, and those due to non-payment.
2. When does dishonour of a bill of exchange by non-acceptance take place? What are the circumstances under which presentment for acceptance, is excused?
3. What is meant by dishonour by non-acceptance, and dishonour by non-payment? What

steps should be taken by the holder on the dishnour of a negotiable instrument?

4. What is a notice of dishonour? Why it is required to be given? State by whom and to whom the notice of dishonour should be given.
5. What are the rules regarding the notice of dishonour? What is the effect of default in giving a notice of dishonour? State the cases in which the notice of dishonour is excused.
6. What is meant by 'noting' and 'protest' of a dishonoured negotiable instrument? Is the 'noting' and 'protest' obligatory under the Negotiable Instrument Act? What are the advantages of protest?
7. What are the rules for determining the amount of compensation payable in case of dishonour of a negotiable instrument?

MULTIPLE CHOICE QUESTIONS

1. A bill of exchange is treated as dishonoured due to non-acceptance, where the drawee
   (a) does not accpt within 48 hours of presentment (b) is incompetent to contract
   (c) gives a conditional acceptance (d) in all the above cases.
2. An accpted view is that a cheque is equivalent to cash payment, and the payment is deemed to be made on the date of issue
   (a) True (b) False.
3. On the dishonour of a cheque due to insufficient funds, the drawer is made criminally liable by an amendment passed in
   (a) 1986 (b) 1988
   (c) 1990 (d) 1992.
4. In case of dishonour of a cheque, the holder's remedy is against the
   (a) drawee of cheque (b) drawer of cheque
   (c) indorsee of cheque (d) both (a) and (c).
5. After the dishonour of a negotiable instrument, the holder may get the fact of dishonour authenticated by a Notary Public. The 'noting' may be done in case of
   (a) promissory note (b) bill of exchange
   (c) cheque (d) both (a) and (b).
6. In case of dishonour of a bill of exchange or a cheque, the 'noting' is compulsory to recover the amount from the liable parties.
   (a) True (b) False.

ANSWERS

1. (d)	2. (a)	3. (b)	4. (b)	5. (d)	6. (b)

OBJECTIVE TYPE QUESTIONS WITH REASONING

State with reasons whether the following statements are correct or incorrect.

1. A bill of exchange is treated as dishonoured if the drawee does not accept the same within 48 hours from the date of presentment for acceptance.
2. The notice of dishonour of a negotiable instrument due to non-payment is necessary to all the parties including those who are primarily liable.
3. In case of dishonour of a promissory note or a bill of exchange, it is obligatory to get the fact authenticated by 'noting' by a Notary Public.
4. Like 'noting', the 'protest' of a dishonoured promissory note or a bill of exchange is not compulsory under the law of Negotiable Instruments.
5. A holder of a bill of exchange may demand a 'protest for better security' from the acceptor if the acceptor refuses to accept the bill on maturity.

ANSWERS

1. *Correct.* Legally, it is treated as dishonoured [Section 91, and 63].
2. *Incorrect.* Such a notice of dishonour is not necessary to a party who is primarily liable because it is his duty to pay the instrument on due date.
3. *Incorrect.* The 'noting' in such a case is not obligatory though it is advantageous to get the same as it provides an authentic evidence of dishonour.
4. *Correct.* Reasons as in point 3 above. However, a foreign bill of exchange must be protested for dishonour where such protest is required by the law of the place where they are drawn [Section 104].
5. *Incorrect.* A protest for better security can be demanded if the acceptor becomes insolvent or his credit is impeached *before* the maturity of the bill of exchange.

PRACTICAL PROBLEMS

1. *A* draws a bill of exchange on *B*, payable 90 days after acceptance. The bill passes through several hands before *C* becomes its holder. On presentation by *C*, *B* refuses to accept the bill. Discuss the rights of *C*.

   Hint : In this case, the bill is dishonoured due to non-acceptance, Thus C may hold the indorsers and the drawer liable on the bills by giving them a notice of dishonour. However, the drawee (*B*) shall not be liable as the drawee can be held liable only in the event of non-payment of an accepted bill.
2. *A* owes Rs.50,000 to *B* and draws a cheque of Rs. 50,000 in favour of *B*. On presentation for payment, the cheque was dishonoured due to insufficient funds and *B* serves a notice in writing on *A* demanding the payment of the cheque. However, *A* expresses his inability to make payment and seeks two month's time for making the payment. Can *A* still be held criminally liable. Give reasons ?

   Hint : Yes, *A* can be held criminally liable under section 138 of the Negotiable Instruments Act. In case of dishonour of the cheque, the drawer has to make payment of the cheque amount within 15 days of the receipt of the notice demanding the payment of dishonoured cheque. If the payment is not made within this time, the drawer becomes criminally liable under section 138.
3. *A* draws a cheque of Rs.10,000 infavour of *B*, a minor. *B* indorses the cheque in favour of *C*. On presentation of the cheque for payment by *C*, the cheque is dishonoured due to insufficient funds. Can *C* proceed against *A* for the recovery of cheque amount ? Give reasons.

   Hint : Yes, *C* can proceed against *A* for the recovery of the cheque amount. *B*, being a minor, is not personally liable. However, as per section 26 of the Negotiable Instruments Act, a minor may draw, endorse, deliver and negotiate a negotiable instrument so as to bind all other parties except himself.
4. *A* draws a bill of exchange on *B*, payable three months after acceptances. The bill passes through several hands before *C* becomes its holder. On presentation of the bill by *C* for acceptance, *B* refuses to accept the bill. *C* further indorses the bill to *D* who takes it with the notice *i.e.* knowledge of dishonour. Can *D* enforce his rights in the capacity of a holder-in-due course? Give reasons.

   Hint : No, *D* cannot enforce his rights as a holder in due course. *A* person who acquires a dishonoured negotiable instrument with the notice of dishonour, gets the rights of his immediate transferor only and cannot become the holder in due course of the instrument. [Section 59]

39

CHAPTER

DISCHARGE FROM LIABILITY

39.1. INTRODUCTION

We have already discussed that when a valid negotiable instrument is made, the parties become liable to pay the amount due on the instrument. The liability of some parties is primary and of some others it is secondary. In this chapter we shall discuss, how the parties are discharged from their respective liability to pay the amount. The 'discharge from liability' means that party's liability, on instrument comes to an end. The term 'discharge' in relation to negotiable instrument has two meanings, namely:

1. Discharge of the negotiable instrument.
2. Discharge of one or more parties from their liability on the negotiable instrument.

39.2. DISCHARGE OF THE NEGOTIABLE INSTRUMENT

The negotiable instrument is said to be discharged when *all the rights* of the person involved in it are over, *i.e.*, no person related with the instrument has any further claim over others. This happens when the party who is primarily and ultimately liable on the instrument, is discharged form his liability. In other words, when the liability of primary party comes to an end, the instrument is said to be discharged. A negotiable instrument may be discharged in any one of the following ways:

1. By payment in due course. 2. By the primarily liable party becoming the holder of the instrument. 3. By renunciation of the rights by the holder. 4. By cancellation of the negotiable instrument. 5. By discharge as a simple contract.

39.3. BY PAYMENT IN DUE COURSE

1. *The payment should be made by the party who is primarily liable*
2. *The payment must be made to the rightful holder*
3. *The payment should be made in good faith and without negligence*

The payment in due course discharges a negotiable instrument and all the parties who are primarily liable to pay the amount due on the instrument. The term 'payment in due course' is defined in Section 10 of the Negotiable Instrument Act, which states that, payment in due course is the payment which is made in good faith and in accordance with the apparent tenor of the instrument, *i.e.*, according to what appears on the face of the instrument to be the intention of the parties. Thus, it is the payment made on maturity of the instrument and of the entire amount due on it. It may be noted that a payment before maturity does not discharge the instrument unless the instrument is cancelled or the fact of payment is recorded on the instrument. Such cancellation or recording of the fact of payment is necessary to prevent its further negotiation. Similarly, when an instrument is payable on demand, its payment will not be an effective discharge of the instrument unless the instrument is cancelled. As a rule, person making the payment should get back the instrument. In fact, he is entitled to have the instrument delivered to him on making the payment of the amount due on it [Section 81].

Example 39.1. *A*, the maker of a demand promissory note, paid the amount due on it to the payee. But *A* failed to obtain back and cancel the promissory note. Subsequently, the payee transferred the same promissory note to *B*, a holder in due course. And *B* claimed from *A* the amount due on the promissory note. On his refusal to pay, *B* filed a suit against *A* for the recovery of the amount due on the promissory note. It was held that *A* was liable to pay the amount to *B*. In this case the instrument was not discharged as it was not cancelled.

[*Srinivasa* v. *Gounder*, AIR 1966 Madras 176].

It may be noted that the following conditions must also be satisfied in order to discharge a negotiable instrument by payment in due course:

1. *The payment should be made by the party who is primarily liable:* The acceptor is primarily liable in case of a bill of exchange, the maker in case of promissory note, and the drawer in case of a cheque. It may be noted that the payment by a party who is not primarily liable, does not discharge the instrument.

2. *The payment must be made to the rightful holder*:* In case of a bearer instrument, the rightful holder is the person who is in possession of the instrument. Thus, payment to a finder or theif of a bearer instrument will discharge the parties liable to pay, if there is nothing to excite the suspicions of a prudent man, *i.e.*, there is nothing to show that he is not entitled to receive it. In case, where the instrument is payable to order, it is necessary that the payment be made to the genuine endorsee. If payment is made to a person whose title is made through a forged indorsement it will not discharge the payer, and he will remain liable to the true owner of the instrument. Thus, in case of order instruments, the payment to a finder or thief of the instrument is not valid discharge. However, a banker is discharged if the payment is made in due course even if the indorsement was forged [Section 85(1)].

3. *The payment should be made in good faith and without negligence* [*Section* 10]. This means that the circumstances should not afford reasonable ground for believing that the person to whom the payment is made is not entitled to receive the amount. If there is some suspicion, and the person making the payment does not make necessary inquiry, then the payment will not be a payment in due course.

* This follows from the combined reading of Section 10, 78 and 82(*e*).

39.4. BY THE PRIMARILY LIABLE PARTY BECOMING THE HOLDER OF THE INSTRUMENT

Sometimes, the acceptor of a bill of exchange becomes its holder in his own right *at or after* its maturity. In such cases, the bill of exchange is discharged (Section 90). This happens by 'negotiation back'. A bill of exchange when comes back to the acceptor after a number of negotiations and he becomes its holder, then the process is known as 'negotiation back'. If this happens at or after maturity, the bill of exchange is discharged, and no party is liable on such a bill of exchange. However, the following two conditions must be satisfied:

1. The acceptor must have taken the bill of exchange *at or after maturity.* If he takes it before maturity, then the bill is not discharged because he may again endorse the same; and
2. The acceptor must take the bill of exchange *in his own rights* and not in any other capacity such as agent, administrator etc.

[*Chalmer's Bill of Exchange* Act, 1882 (13th edn. 1964), 213]

39.5. BY RENUNCIATION OF THE RIGHTS BY THE HOLDER

Sometimes, the holder of a negotiable instrument renounces or gives up his rights against all the parties. In such cases, the instrument is discharged. The renunciation may be made by delivering the instrument to the party who is primarily liable, It may be noted that unless the instrument is so delivered to the primarily liable party, the renunciation must be made in writing.

39.6. BY CANCELLATION OF THE NEGOTIABLE INSTRUMENT

Sometimes, the holder of a negotiable instrument intentionally cancels it. In such cases, the instrument is discharged. It may be noted that the cancellation should be made with the intention of discharging all the parties. Moreover, the cancellation must be apparent, *i.e.,* clear from the instrument itself. The cancellation of the instrument may take place by the physical destruction of the instrument or by crossing out signatures on the instrument.

39.7. BY DISCHARGE AS A SIMPLE CONTRACT

A negotiable instrument may also be discharged in the same way as a simple contract for payment of money. Thus, like a simple contract, a negotiable instrument may be discharge by an agreement of the parties in the form of novation, or by rescission or by substitution of another negotiable instrument for the original instrument. However, it must be provided in a contract that all the parties shall be discharged from their liability under the negotiable instrument.

39.8. DISCHARGE OF ONE OR MORE PARTIES FROM THEIR LIABILITY ON THE NEGOTIABLE INSTRUMENT

We have discussed above that when all the parties to a negotiable instrument are discharged from liability, the instrument is said to be discharged. But sometimes, only some of the parties to a negotiable instrument are discharged from their liability, whereas other parties continue to be liable thereon. In such cases , it is only a discharge of some of the parties. The instrument in itself is not discharged and it continues to be negotiable. It may be noted that where only some of the parties are discharged from their liability, the amount due on the instrument can be recovered from the undischarged parties, *e.g.*, on the discharge of the drawer or an indorser of a bill or exchange from their liability, the acceptor remains liable to pay the amount due on the bill of exchange. A party may be discharged in any one of the following ways:

1. By cancellation of the name of a party. 2. By release of party. 3. By payment . 4. By allowing the drawee more than forty-eight hours to accept the bill of exchange. 5. By non-presentment of a bill of exchange for acceptance. 6. By delay in presenting a cheque for payment. 7. By conditional acceptance. 8. By operation of law. 9. By the drawee banker making the payment in due course. 10. By material alteration.

39.9. BY CANCELLATION OF THE NAME OF A PARTY

Sometimes, the holder of a negotiable instrument intentionally cancels one or more names of the parties to a negotiable instrument. In such cases, the party whose name has been so cancelled, is discharged from his liability to such a holder, *i.e.*, the holder cannot recover the amount due on the instrument from that party whose name has been cancelled. According to Section 82 (*a*), the maker, an acceptor and an indorser of a negotiable instrument is discharged from his liability to the holder, if his name is cancelled by the holder with the intention of discharging him from his liability. It may be noted that the parties subsequent to the party whose name has been cancelled are also discharged from their liability to the holder and to any person who gets the instrument form such a holder. However, the following two conditions must be satisfied to discharge a party from liability:

1. The cancellation of party's name must be with the intention of discharging that party from his liability.
2. The cancellation must be apparent (*i.e., clear*) on the face of the instrument.

It is to be noted that in case of a bill of exchange, when acceptor's name is cancelled, the effect is the same as that of cancellation of the instrument. The reason for the same is that all the parties are also discharged by cancellation of acceptor's name. This is based upon the principle of the law of guarantee that when a principal debtor is discharged, the sureties (*i.e.*, guarantors) are also discharged from their liability. Similarly, the cancellation of maker's name also operates as the discharge of the instrument. But the cancellation of indorser's name discharges only that indorser and the indorsers subsequent to him, the parties prior to such indorsers remain liable.

39.10. BY RELEASE OF A PARTY

Sometimes, the holder of a negotiable instrument himself releases (discharges) a party from his liability. In such cases, that party is not liable to pay the amount due on the instrument. According to Section 82(*b*), the maker acceptor and indorser of a negotiable instrument is discharged from his liability to the holder, if the holder himself discharges him by any method other than cancellation. The holder may discharge the parties by any method such as by agreement, by waiving his right etc. It may be noted that a person who gets the instrument from such a holder with the knowledge that a party is discharged, can also not recover the amount from the party who was discharged by the holder.

39.11. BY PAYMENT

The payment is the most common mode of discharging a party from his liability. Since a negotiable instrument is meant for payment of money, a payment in due course discharges both the instrument and the parties to it. According to Section 82(*c*), the maker, acceptor and indorser of a bearer instrument is discharged from his liability to all the parties by making a payment in due course. The term 'payment in due course' has already been discussed in detail in Art. 39.3.

39.12. BY ALLOWING THE DRAWEE MORE THAN FORTY-EIGHT HOURS TO ACCEPT THE BILL OF EXCHANGE

This rule is applicable to bills of exchange only. When the holder presents the bill of exchange to the drawee for his acceptance, the drawee whould be allowed only forty-eight hours to consider whether he will accept it or not [Section 63]. If the holder allows the drawee more than forty-eight hours (exclusive of public holidays), then all the previous parties who do not give their consent to such extended time are discharged from their liability to such holder [Section 83].

39.13. BY NON-PRESENTMENT OF A BILL OF EXCHANGE FOR ACCEPTANCE

A bill of exchange payable *after sight* must be presented to the drawee for his acceptance, within a reasonable time after it is drawn (*i.e.*, made). If the holder makes default in presentment, then no party to the instrument is liable to such a holder, *i.e.*, all the parties are discharged form their liability to the holder who makes a default in presentment [Section 61].

39.14. BY DELAY IN PRESENTING A CHEQUE FOR PAYMENT

A cheque must be presented for payment within a reasonable time of its issue. If the holder makes a delay in presenting the cheque, and in the meantime something happens (*e.g.*, the banker fails) which prevents the banker form making payment, then the drawer of the cheque is discharged from his liability to the holder [Section 84]. It may be noted that though the drawer is discharged from his liability, but the holder of the cheque becomes creditor of the drawee banker and can recover the amount from the insolvent banker [Section 84(3)], *i.e.*, the holder can prove his claim, in the insolvency proceedings, to the extent of damages suffered by the drawer.

It may also be noted that the drawer of a cheque is discharged to the extent of actual damages suffered by him due to delay in presenting the cheque.

Example 39.2. A drew a cheque for Rs. 2,000 in favour of *B* and delivered the same to him. When the cheque was ought to be presented, *A* had only Rs. 500 in his bank account. *B* did not present the cheque for unreasonable long time. And in the meantime, the banker failed. In this case, the drawer (*A*) is discharged from his liability up to Rs. 500 only. And thus, the holder (*B*) can recover Rs. 1500 from *A*, and for the balance Rs. 500 he can prove his claim in the insolvency proceedings of the banker.

39.15. BY CONDITIONAL ACCEPTANCE

Generally, a bill of exchange should be accepted without any condition or qualification. Thus, when the holder of a bill of exchange presents the bill to the drawee for his acceptance, then he should insist that it should be accepted without any condition. If the acceptance is conditional, then the holder has the right to treat the bill as dishonoured. But if the holder approves the conditional acceptance, all the previous parties, who do not consent the conditional acceptance, are discharged from their liability to such a holder who takes the conditional acceptance. However, if the prior parties also approve the conditional acceptance, then they will remain liable [Section 86].

39.16. BY OPERATION OF LAW

In certain cases, the parties are also discharged from their liability by operation of law, *e.g.*, when a debtor is declared an insolvent, he is discharged from his liability, or by the expiry of limitation period[1] (the time prescribed by law for the recovery of debts). Thus, if the amount due on a negotiable instrument is not recovered within the time prescribed by law, then the party liable for payment is discharged from his liability to make the payment.

39.17. BY THE DRAWEE BANKER MAKING THE PAYMENT IN DUE COURSE

The drawee banker is discharged from his liability by making the payment of a cheque in due course. The banker will be discharged from liability even if the payment was made to the wrong person. According to Section 85, in the following two cases, the

1. The limitation period for the recovery of debt is three years from the date of default.

banker is discharged by making payment in due course even if it is made to a wrong person:

1. *When in an order cheque the payee's indorsement is forged:* Sometimes, a cheque payable to order purports to be indorsed by or on behalf of the payee. In such cases, the banker's liability will be over if the payment is made in due course even though subsequently it may turn out that such indorsement was forged. The reason for the same is that the banker is not supposed to know the signatures of the indorsers.

Example 39.3. *A* drew a cheque for Rs. 2,000 payable to *B* or order. *C* stole the cheque and forged *B*'s indorsement upon it and received the payment from the banker, who made the payment in due course. In this case, the banker is discharged from his liability to pay the cheque again.

It may, however be noted that where the *drawer's signatures* are forged , and the banker makes the payment on forged signature, the banker will not be discharged from his liability. The reason for the same is that the banker is supposed to know the signature of his customer (drawer).

2. *When the payment of a bearer cheque is made ignoring the indorsement at the back of the cheque:* Sometimes, a cheque is originally payable to bearer. And the banker makes the payment, in due course, to the bearer ignoring the indorsement at the back of the cheque. In such cases, the banker is discharged from his liability to pay the cheque again. This is because of the rule that *"once a bearer cheque always a bearer cheque"*. The object of this rule is to provide protection to the banker who, per chance, may overlook the indorsements and makes the payment of the bearer cheque to the bearer thereof. Thus, for the purpose of discharge of liability of the drawee banker, once a bearer cheque always remains a bearer cheque.

Note. The above rule of payment in due course is also applicable to bank drafts [Section 85 A]

39.18. BY MATERIAL ALTERATION

The term 'material alteration' means the alteration in the material parts of the instrument. It is the alteration which destroys the identity of the original instruments, and affects the rights and liabilities of the parties to the instrument. As a matter of fact, any change in an instrument which causes it to speak a different language in legal effect from that which it originally spoke ,or which changes the legal identity of the instrument either in its terms or in the relation of the parties to it , is a material alteration[2]. Thus, in order to know whether an alteration is material of not, the nature of the alteation must be examined. If it affects the very purpose of the original instrument, *i.e.,* if it goes to the root of the instrument, it is a material alteration.

When a negotiable instrument is materially altered, it becomes void as against those parties who were liable prior to the alteration, and have not given consent to the alteration [Section 87]. In other words, material alteration of a negotiable instrument discharges those parties, who were liable prior to the alteration. But if such parties give their consent to the alteration, then their liability on the instrument is not affected by such alteration. Following are some of the **instances of material alteration:**

1. Alteration of the date 2. Alteration of the amount payable. 3. Alteration of the time of payment. 4. Alteration of the place of payment. 5. Alteration of the rate of interest. 6. Tearing an instrument in a material part. 7. Where a bill of exchange is accepted generally, the addition of a place of payment.

---

2. *Rampadarath* v. *Hari Narain*, AIR 1965 Patna 2241; *Kalianna Gowdner* v. *Palanj Gownder*, AIR 1970 Supreme Court 1942.

It may, however, be noted that the above list is not exhaustive. There may be other material alterations depending upon the nature and facts of each particular case. Following are the **instances of alterations which are not material.** In these cases, the instrument remains valid and the parties are not discharged from their liability.

1. An alteration which is made for the purpose of correcting a clerical error or mistake in an instrument, *e.g.*, correcting of mistake in a bill of exchange dated 1985 instead of 1958.
2. An alteration which is made to carry out the common intention of the parties [Section 87] *e.g.*, where the drawer of the instrument forgets to write the words 'or order' after the name of the payee, the subsequent insertion of these words will not affect the validity of the instrument.
3. An alteration which is made with the consent of the parties [Section 87].
4. An alteration which is made before the completion or issue of the negotiable instrument.
5. An alteration which is made to convert an incomplete name of a person into the complete name of the same person.
6. An alteration which has resulted from an unintentional act, *e.g.*, mutilation of the instrument by washing in a garment etc.

39.19. AUTHORISED ALTERATIONS

The authorised alterations are those which are permitted by the Negotiable Instruments Act. Even though these are material but they do not invalidate the negotiable instrument. Following alterations are permitted by Section 87 of the Negotiable Instruments Act:

1. Filling blanks in an incomplete stamped negotiable instrument [Section 20].
2. Conversion of an 'indorsement in blank' into an 'indorsement in full' [Section 49].
3. Making qualified (conditional) acceptance [Section 86].
4. Crossing of an uncrossed cheque [Section 125].

39.20. EFFECT OF MATERIAL ALTERATION

The effect of material alteration is stated in first part of Section 87 of the Negotiable Instruments Act. According to this section, any material alteration renders the negotiable instrument void, and discharges all those persons from their liability who have become parties *at the time of making the alteration*. However, the following conditions must be satisfied for the applicability of this section:

1. The alteration must be material. 2. The alteration must be intentional 3. The alteration must be without the consent of the parties. 4. The alteration must not be to carry out the common intention of the parties. 5. The alteration must be apparent on the face of the negotiable instrument. If the alteration is not apparent, then the instrument will remain a valid security in the hands of a holder in due course.

In, may however, be noted that a material alteration does not affect the liability of those parties who have become liable after the alteration is made. Thus, an acceptor or indorser of a negotiable instrument is bound by his acceptance and indorsement even if there was any previous alteration of the instrument [Section 88] *i.e.*, the acceptor or indorser is not discharged from liability even if some alteration in the negotiable instrument was made before its acceptance or indorsement.

Note. Sometimes, a negotiable instrument has been materially altered but it does not appear to have been so altered. In such cases, if the liable party makes the payment in due course, then he will be discharged from his liability in spite of the fact that the instrument was materially altered [Section 89].

LEGAL PROVISIONS (SECTIONS) DISCUSSED IN THE CHAPTER

Important legal provisions (sections) of the Negotiable Instruments Act, 1881 discussed in the chapter, are reproduced hereunder for ready reference :

1. *Section 10; Payment in due course*

"Payment in due course means payment in accordance with the apparent tenor of the instrument in good faith and without negligence to any person in possession thereof under circumstances which do not afford a reasonable ground for believing that he is not entitled to receive payment of the mount mentioned therein".

2. *Section 82: Discharge from liability*

The maker, acceptor or indorser respectively of a negotiable instrument is discharged from liability thereon–

(*a*) **By cancellation.**– to a holder thereof who cancels such acceptor's or indorser's name with intent to discharge him, and to all parties claiming under such holder;

(*b*) **By release.**– to a holder thereof who otherwise discharges such maker, acceptor or indorser, and to all parties deriving title under such holder after notice of such discharge;

(*c*) **By payment.**– to all parties thereto, if the instrument is payable to bearer, or has been indorsed in blank, and such maker, acceptor or indorser makes payment in due course of the amount due thereon.

3. *Section 83: Discharge by allowing drawee more than forty-eight hours to accept*

If the holder of a bill of exchange allows the drawee more than forty-eight hours, exclusive of public holidays, to consider whether he will accept the same, all previous parties not consenting to such allowance are thereby discharged from liability to such holder.

4. *Section 84: When cheque not duly presented and drawer damaged thereby*

(1) Where a cheque is not presented for payment within a reasonable time of its issue, and the drawer or person on whose account it is drawn had the right, at the time when presentment ought to have been made, as between himself and the banker, to have the cheque paid and suffers actual damage through the delay, he is discharged to the extent of such damage, that is to say to the extent to which such drawer or person is a creditor of the banker to a larger amount than he would have been if such cheque had been paid.

(2) In determining what is a reasonable time, regard shall be had to the nature of the instrument, the usage of trade and of bankers, and the facts of the particular case.

(3) The holder of the cheque as to which such drawer or person is so discharged shall be a creditor, in lieu of such drawer or person, of such banker to the extent of such discharge and entitled to recover the amount from him.

5. *Section 85: Cheque payable to order*

(1) Where a cheque payable to order purports to be indorsed by or on behalf of the payee, the drawee is discharged by payment in due course.

(2) Where a cheque is originally expressed to be payable to bearer, the drawee is discharged by the payment in due course to the bearer thereof, not with standing any indorsement whether in full or in blank appearing thereon, and notwithstanding that any such indorsement purports to restrict or exclude further negotiation."

6. *Section 87: Effect of material alteration.*

Any material alteration of a negotiable instrument render the same void as against any one who is a party thereto at the time of making such alteration and does not consent thereto, unless it was made in order to carry out the common intention of the original parties.

Alteration by indorsec: And any such alteration if made by an indorsec, discharges his indorser form all liability to him in respect of the consideration thereof."

7. *Section 88: Acceptor or indorser bound notwithstanding previous alteration*

An acceptor or indorser of a negotiable instrument is bound by the acceptance or indorsement notwithstanding any previous alteration of instrument.

8. *Section 89: Payment of instrument on which alteration is not apparent*

Where a promissory note, bill of exchange or cheque has been materially altered but does not appear to have been so altered, or where a cheque is presented for payment which does not at the time of presentation appear to be crossed or to have had a crossing which has been obliterated, payment thereof by a person or banker liable to pay and paying the same according to the apparent tenor thereof at the time of payment and otherwise in due course, shall discharge such person or banker from all liability thereon; and such payment shall not be questioned by the reason of the instrument having been altered, or the cheque crossed.

9. ***Section 90: Extinguishment of rights of action or bills in acceptor's hands***
If a bill of exchange which has been negotiated is, at or after maturity, held by the acceptor in his own right, all rights of action thereon are extinguished.

TEST QUESTIONS

1. What do you understand by the discharge of an instrument? State the different modes of discharge of an instrument.
2. State under what circumstances the liability in promissory note, bill of exchange and cheque is discharged.
3. What are the various modes of discharge from liability of parties to a negotiable instrument?
4. What is the difference between discharge of a negotiable instrument, and discharge of a party to a negotiable instrument? When a negotiable instrument is said to be discharged?
5. What do you mean by material alteration of a negotiable instrument? State the effect of material alteration. What alterations are authorised by the Negotiable Instruments Act?

MULTIPLE CHOICE QUESTIONS

1. A negotiable instrument is said to be discharged when the liability of which of the following parties comes to an end?
   (*a*) primarily liable party (*b*) secondarily liable party
   (*c*) subsequent liable party (*d*) none of the parties.
2. A bill of exchange is discharged when its acceptor by negotiation back, becomes its holder
   (*a*) at maturity (*b*) after maturity
   (*c*) before maturity (*d*) either (*a*) or (*b*).
3. In which of the following cases of forgery, a banker is discharged form liability by making a payment in due course
   (*a*) payee's indorsement (b) drawer's signatures
   (*c*) both (*a*) and (*b*) (*d*) none of these.
4. A banker is discharged from liability even if the payment of a bearer cheque is made ignoring the subsequent indorsements at the back of the cheque
   (*a*) True (*b*) False.
5. Material alteration of a negotiable instrument, without the consent of the parties, discharge the parties who have become liable
   (*a*) after such alteration (*b*) prior to such alteration
   (*c*) because of alteration (*d*) without such alteration.
6. Which of the following is not a material alteration?
   (*a*) alteration of date (*b*) alteration of amount
   (*c*) alteration of time of payment (*d*) alteration correcting clerical mistake.

ANSWERS

1. (*a*)	2. (*d*)	3. (*a*)	4. (*a*)	5. (*b*)	6. (*d*)

OBJECTIVE TYPE QUESTIONS WITH REASONING

State with reasons whether the following statements are correct or incorrect.

1. When the liability of a primary party comes to an end, the negotiable instrument is said to be discharged.
2. The 'payment in due course' discharges a negotiable instrument and all the parties who are primarily liable to pay the amount due on the instrument.
3. When the acceptor of a bill of exchange becomes its holder in his own right before maturity of the bill, the bill of exchange is discharged.
4. In case of a bill of exchange, the cancellation of acceptor's name with the intention of discharging him has the effect of cancellation of the instrument.

5. A banker making the payment of a bearer cheque over looking the indorsement at the back of the cheque, is liable to make the payment again to the endorsee of the cheque.

ANSWERS

1. ***Correct.*** In such a case, no other party remains liable on the instrument.
2. ***Correct.*** As payment in due course is the payment made in *good faith* and according to the apparent tenor of the instrument.
3. ***Incorrect.*** A bill of exchange is discharged only when the acceptor becomes its holder in his own right *at or after* maturity [Section 90].
4. ***Correct.*** By cancellation of acceptors's name, all the parties to the bill are discharged from liability.
5. ***Incorrect.*** The banker enjoys protection while making the payments of bearer cheques . For the purpose of discharge of liability of the drawee banker, *once a bearer cheque always a bearer cheque.*

PRACTICAL PROBLEMS

1. *A*, the maker of a demand promissory note, paid the amount due on it to the payee, *B*. However, *A* failed to obtain back and cancel the promissory note. Subsequently, *B* transferred the same promissory note to *C*, a holder in due course. Does *C* get any right on the basis to the promissory note ? Give reasons.

   Hint : Yes, *C* being a holder in due course is entitled to recover the amount due on the promissory note. In this case, the promissory note was not discharged as it was not cancelled after making the payment.
2. *A* draws a cheque of Rs. 10,000 in favour of *B* and delivers the same to him. When the cheque was ought to be presented for payment, *A* had only Rs.6,000 in his bank, but *B* did not present the cheque for unreasonable longtime. In the meantime , the banker failed. Can *B* recover the entire amount of the cheque from *A* ? Give reasons.

   Hint : No, *B* cannot recover the entire amount of Rs. 10,000 from *A*. In this case, *B* can recover only Rs.4,000 from *A* as he is discharged from his liability up to the amount Rs.6,000 *i.e.* the amount which he had in his account when the cheque ought to have been presented for payment. However, for the amount of Rs. 6,000, B can prove his claim in the insolvency proceedings of the banker.
3. *A* drew a cheque for Rs.5,000 payable to *B* or order. The cheque was stolen by *C*, a thief , who forged B's indorsement and indorsed the cheque to C. *C* received the payment from the bank, who made the payment in due course. Can the banker be held liable to make the payment to *B*? Give reasons.

   Hint: No, the bank cannot be held liable to make the payment again to *B*. In such cases, the bank is discharged by making the payment in due course even though subsequently the indorsement is discovered to be forged. [Section 85]
4. *A*, a thief, stole a blank cheque from *B*'s table drawer and filled it for Rs. 10,000 in his favour and forged B's signature on the cheque. On presentation for payment, the bank makes the payment to A. Is the bank discharged from liability to compensate B for the loss suffered due to payment on forged cheque? Give reasons.

   Hint: No, the banker is not discharged from its liability. The banker is supposed to know and verify the signature of his customer (drawer).

40

CHAPTER

CROSSING OF CHEQUES

40.1. INTRODUCTION

The cheques are of two types, namely, *open* (*or uncrossed*) cheques, and *crossed* cheques. The payment of the open cheque is made at the counter of the banker on its presentation. The open cheque is liable to a great risk in the course of its circulation. When an open cheque is stolen or lost, the wrong person (thief or finder) may go to the banker and take away the payment, unless it is stopped by the drawer. In such a case, it becomes difficult to trace the wrong person. In order to avoid such risks and to protect the interest of the original genuine holder, the system of crossing the cheque was introduced.

A cheque is said to be crossed when two parallel transverse lines are drawn across the face of a cheque. Usually, the parallel lines are drawn on the left hand top corner of the cheque as shown in the specimen given below.

Specimen of Crossing

Punjab National Bank
Parliament Street,
New Delhi

Dated.....

Pay to.. or Bearer

The Sum of Rupees .... Rs. [ ]

No.............

Sd/-

However, these parallel lines may also be drawn anywhere on the face of a cheque.

40.2. EFFECT OF CROSSING OF THE CHEQUE

The crossing of a cheque affects the mode of payment of the cheque. The holder of a crossed cheque cannot have the payment at the counter of the banker. The payment of such a cheque can be obtained only by opening an account with a banker. Thus, first the holder of a crossed cheque has to open an account with some banker, and then deposit the cheque into his account to enable the banker to collect its payment on his behalf and credit the same into his account. The holder can then withdraw the money from his account. Thus, in case of a crossed cheque generally, the following two bankers are involved for its payment:

1. ***Paying banker:*** It is the banker which makes the payment of a crossed cheque. In other words, the paying banker is the drawee of the crossed cheque, *i.e.,* the banker on whom the cheque is drawn.
2. ***Collecting banker***: It is the banker which collects the amount of the cheque, on behalf of its customer from the paying banker.

For example, *A* drew a cheque for Rs. 1,000 on Punjab National Bank in favour of *B*. And after crossing the cheque, *A* delivered the same to *B*. *B* had his account in Canara Bank and deposited the cheque in his account. The Canara Bank collected the amount of the cheque from Punjab National Bank on behalf of *B*. In this case, Punjab National Bank is the paying banker, and Canara Bank, the collecting banker.

40.3. OBJECTS OF CROSSING OF THE CHEQUE

The main object of crossing of cheque is to assure that only the rightful holder gets the payment of the cheque. It provides protection and security to the true owner of the cheque as it is payable only through a banker. If a wrongful person obtains the payment of a crossed cheque, then he can be traced because he has to operate through a banker by opening an account.

40.4. TYPES OF CROSSING OF THE CHEQUE

The crossing of a cheque is of the following four kinds:

1. General crossing. 2. Special crossing. 3. Not negotiable crossing. 4. Restrictive crossing.

Note. The first two types are the basic types of crossing. The remaining two types of crossing are made by adding certain specified words to either of the basic type of crossing. It may be noted that the reference of first three types of crossing is made in the Negotiable Instruments Act, whereas, the last type of crossing has been developed out of business usages.

40.5. GENERAL CROSSING

A cheque is said to contain a general crossing when two parallel lines are drawn across the face of the cheque [Section 123]. The lines may be without any word between them as shown below in specimen 1, or may contain some words such as & Co. or 'not negotiable' or 'not negotiable' alongwith '& Co.' as shown below in specimen 2, 3 and 4 respectively. It may, however, be noted that there should not be the name of any banker between the parallel lines.

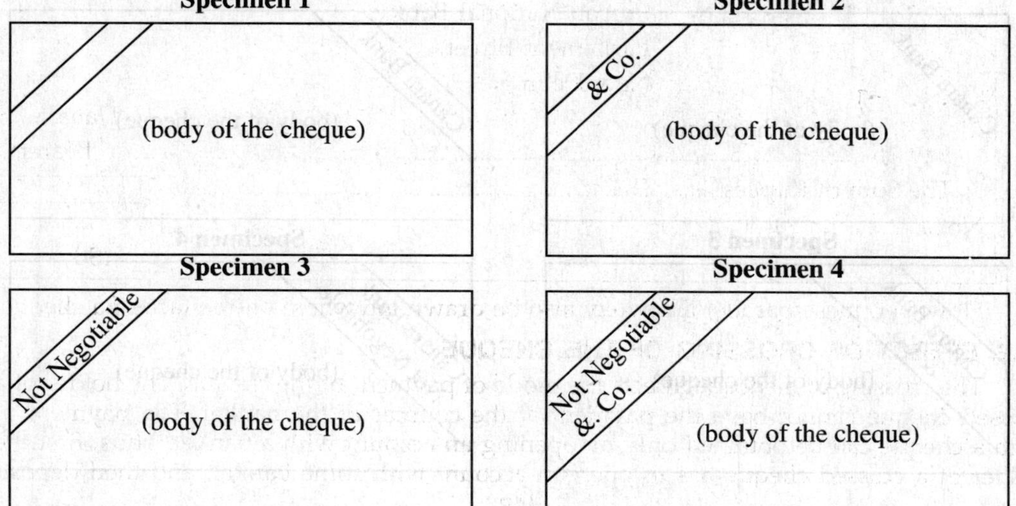

It may be noted that when a cheque contains a general crossing, the banker on whom it is drawn shall not pay it in any other way except to a collecting banker (*i.e.*, the banker which collects the amount of the cheque on behalf of the holder, from the drawee banker) [Section 126]. It means that the drawee banker is not to make the payment of the cheque at the counter. But the payment is to be made only to the collecting banker, which collects the cheque on behalf of the holder. Thus, the payee or holder of the cheque can get it collects only by opening an account with some banker (*i.e.*, the collecting banker). However, the collecting banker may be any banker of the choice of the holder. The effect of using different words in general crossing as shown in above specimens, is as below:

1. ***General crossing with two parallel lines***: It is a simple crossing which prohibits the banker to make cash payment at the counter. The payee in order to get the payment of the cheque, may deposit it with his banker. The payee also has the right to indorse the cheque. In this case the indorsee will get a better title, than that of the indorser if he (indorsee) is the holder is due course.

2. ***General crossing containing word '& Co.' within two parallel lines:*** The effect of such a crossing is same as stated above.

3. ***General crossing containing words 'not negotiable' within two parallel lines:*** The effects of such a crossing is also the same as stated above. The only difference in this case is that the indorsee cannot get a better title than that of the indorser. Thus, if the title of the indorser is defective, the title of indorsee will also be defective. This point will be discussed in detail in Art. 40.7.

4. ***General crossing containing the word 'not negotiable & Co.' within two parallel lines:*** The effect of such a crossing is the same as stated above in case of general crossing containing the words 'Not negotiable' within the two parallel lines.

40.6. SPECIAL CROSSING

A cheque is said to contain a special crossing when the name of some banker is written across the face of the cheque [Section 124]. For example, if a cheque is drawn on Punjab National Bank and across its face the holder writes the name of some other bank, *e.g.*, Canara Bank. This type of crossing is called a special crossing to Canara Bank. In this case, the name of the banker to whom the cheque is crossed, may be wirtten without any parallel lines as shown below in specimen 1. However, generally the name of the banker is written within the two parallel lines as shown below in specimen 2. The name of the banker may also be written alongwith certain words such as '& Co' or 'not negotiable as shown below in specimens 3 and 4 respectively.

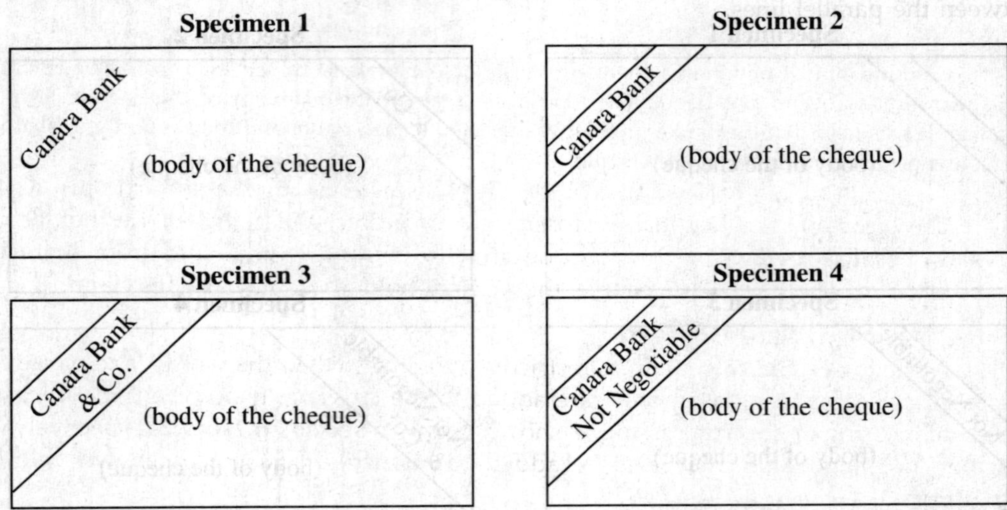

It may be noted that when a cheque contains a special crossing, the banker on whom it is drawn shall not pay it in any other way except to the banker to whom it is crossed, *i.e.*, whose name appears across the cheque [Section 126]. Thus, the payee or holder of the cheque can get it collected only by opening an account with the *specified banker* whose name appears across the cheque. The effect of using different words in special crossing as shown in above specimens, will be the same as discussed in Art. 28.5. The only difference in this case is that the payment of such a cheque can be obtained by depositing it only with the banker whose name appears across the cheque *i.e.*, to whom it is crossed.

40.7. NOT NEGOTIABLE CROSSING

A cheque is said to contain a 'not negotiable crossing' when the words 'not negotiable' are added to the crossing. It may be done in case of general crossing or special crossing as shown below in specimen 1 and 2 respectively.

The effect of the addition of the words not negotiable is that when such a cheque is indorsed, the indorsee cannot get a better title than that of the indorser. In other, words, a person who takes a crossed cheque containing the words 'not negotiable', cannot get a better title than that of his transferor (indorser) *i.e.* if the title of indorser is defective then the title of indorsee will also be defective. Moreover, the indorsee from such an indorsee can also not get a better title to the cheque [Section 130]. Thus, 'not negotiable crossing' materially diminishes the negotiable value of the cheque, in the sense, that the person taking it shall get only the rights of the transfer- or, but no better rights. And thus, he cannot become the holder in due course. However, if there is nothing wrong with the title of the prior parties, the holder may recover the amount of the cheque. But if something is wrong anywhere, he will be affected by the same, and may not recover the amount of the cheque. Thus, the cheque containing a 'not negotiable crossing' remains transferable. But any person who takes such a cheque, he takes it at his own risk.

Specimen 1

Not Negotiable

(body of the cheque)

Specimen 2

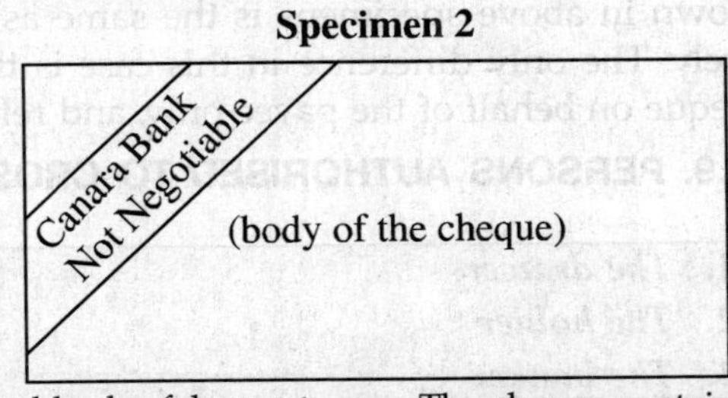

Example 40.1. *A* obtained a cheque from its holder by false pretences. The cheque contained the words "& Co and not negotiable". He also obtained the payment of the cheque form the banker. It was held that the banker 's title was affected by the fraud, and he was accountable to the true owner for the amount of the cheque.

[*Great Western Rly. Co.* v. *London & County Banking Co.* (1901) AC 414].

The *object* of 'not negotiable crossing' is to protect the rights of the holder of a cheque, because, even if such a cheque goes to wrong hands and from there it is transferred to a holder in due course, the original holder will not lose his claim.

40.8. RESTRICTIVE CROSSING

A cheque is said to contain a 'restrictive crossing', when the words 'a/c payee', *i.e.*, account payee or 'a/c payee only' are added to the crossing. It may be done in case of general crossing or special crossing as shown below in specimen 1 and 2 respectively. The words 'not negotiable' may also be added to restrictive crossing as shown below in specimen 3.

Specimen 1

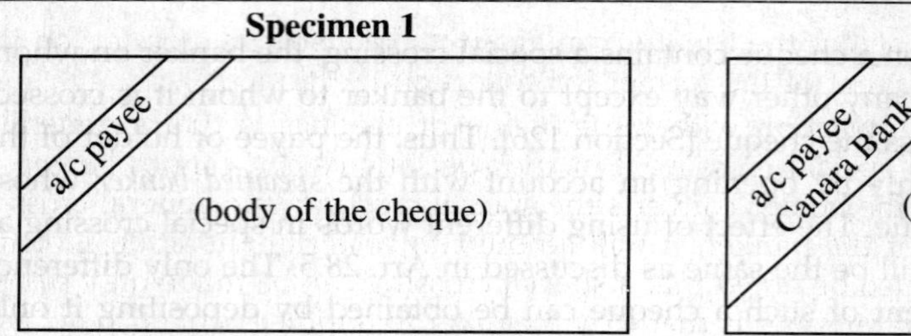

Specimen 2

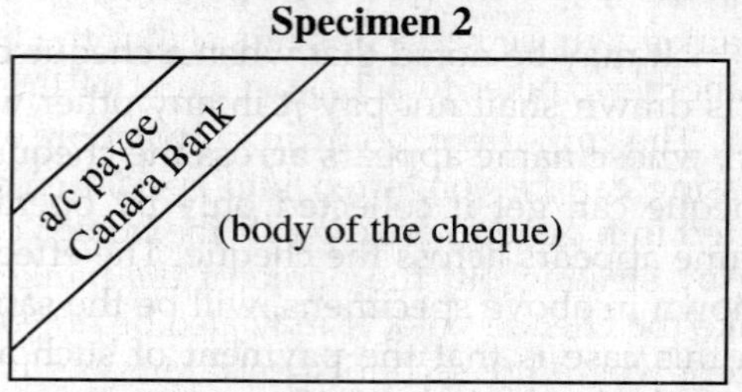

Specimen 3

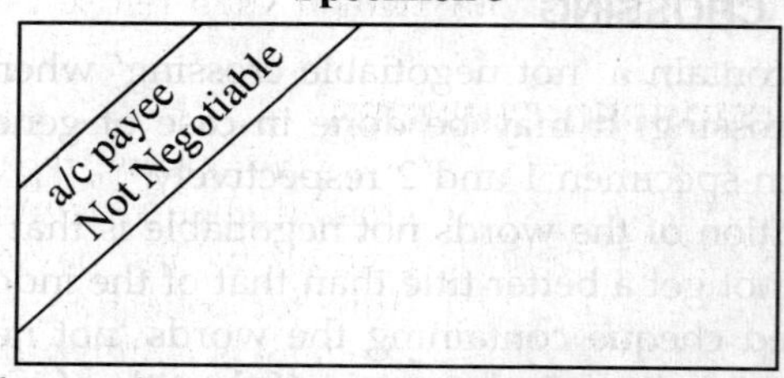

The effect of such words is that the collecting banker is supposed to collect the cheque only on behalf of the payee and credit the amount to his account only. It the collecting banker collects it on behalf of some other person, it can be held responsible for the same. The object of adding these words in a crossing is to give protection to the payee. Even if such a cheque is lost, no person other than the payee can get the payment of the same. It may be noted that merely by such crossing there is no prohibition on the indorsement of the cheque [*National Bank v. Silke* (1891) 1 QB 435]. However, in actual practice the restrictive crossing hinders negotiability of the cheque because no banker would like to collect it on behalf of any other person except the payee. The effect of using the words 'a/c payee' in the general or special crossing, or alongwith the words 'not negotiable' as shown in above specimens is the same as discussed in Arts. 28.5, 28.6 and 28.7. respectively. The only difference in this case is that the collecting banker generally collects the cheque on behalf of the payee only, and refuses to collect it on behalf of any other person.

40.9. PERSONS AUTHORISED TO CROSS THE CHEQUE

1. *The drawer*
2. *The holder*
3. *The banker*

The following persons are authorised to cross the cheque.

1. *The drawer:* The drawer is entitled to cross the cheque in any way he likes. He may make a general, special, not negotiable or restrictive crossing on the cheque before issuing it.

2. *The holder*: The holder is entitled to cross the cheque after receiving it. He may cross the cheque in any one of the following ways [Section 125]:

(*a*) Where the cheque is uncrossed, the holder, may make a general, special or not-negotiable crossing.

(*b*) Where the cheque contains a general crossing, the holder may convert it into a special crossing by adding the name of some banker.

(*c*) Where the cheque contains a general or special crossing (without the words 'not negotiable'), the holder may add the words 'not negotiable'.

3. The banker: The banker is entitled to cross the cheque after receiving it for collection of payment. It may make a special crossing on the cheque to another banker for the purpose of collection of payment from the drawee banker (*i.e.*, paying banker). Thus, a banker, whose name appears across the cheque, can again make a special crossing on it to another banker to act as an agent of the former for collection [Section 125].

The important point in connection with the crossing of cheques is that a general crossing can be converted into special crossing. But the special crossing cannot be converted into general crossing. If the holder converts the special crossing into general crossing by striking out the name of the banker, it will amount to material alteration which make the cheque void. It may also be noted that a special crossing can be made only once except where the second special crossing is made by a banker to another banker to act as an agent of the former, for collection of payment. Where a cheque contains special crossing to more than one banker, then the paying banker shall refuse to make the payment of the same [Section 127].

40.10. PAYMENT OF THE CROSSED CHEQUES

1. *Payment of a cheque containing general crossing:*
2. *Payment of a cheque containing special crossing:*

We know that the payment of a crossed cheque is not made in cash at the counter by the paying banker. The procedure for collection of payment of crossed cheques is different for the different types of basic crossing (*i.e.* general crossing, and special crossing) which may be discussed under the following heads:

1. ***Payment of a cheque containing general crossing***: The payment of a cheque containing general crossing is always collected by the payee through some banker. In such cases, it is the duty of the paying banker (*i.e.*, drawee banker) to pay such a cheque to any banker in which the holder opens the account for the purpose [Section 126 (first para)].

2. ***Payment of a cheque containing special crossing:*** The payment of a cheque containing special crossing is always collected by the payee through the banker to whom it is crossed (*i.e.*, the banker whose name is mentioned between the parallel lines by which the cheque is crossed). In such cases, it is also the duty of the paying banker to pay such a cheque only to the banker to whom it is crossed [Section 126 (second para)].

If a cheque contains special crossings in favour of more than one banker, then the paying banker should refuse to make its payment except when the second special crossing is made by the banker to whom it is crossed, to another banker to act as the agent of the former for the purpose of collection.

40.11. PROTECTION OF A PAYING BANKER

A paying banker is one which makes the payment of a crossed cheque. It is the bank on which the crossed cheque is drawn. It may be noted that when the payment is made in due course, *i.e.*, as per the principles stated above, the paying banker is discharged from his liability to the same extent as if the payment has been made to the true owner of the cheque. This will be so even if the amount of cheques does not reach the true owner. This special protection of the paying banker is contained in Section 128.

However, in the following two circumstances, the payment by the paying banker is considered to be irregular, and the paying banker becomes liable to the true owner of cheque for any loss suffered by him due to such irregular payment [Section 129].

1. If, in case of cheque containing general crossing, the paying banker makes its payment at the counter;
2. If, in case of a cheque containing special crossing, the paying banker makes its payment to a banker other than the banker to whom the cheque is crossed.

Another protection of the paying banker is that where at the time of presentment for payment, a cheque does not appear to be crossed or where the crossing is obliterated (*i.e.*, destroyed or erased), the banker making the payment in good faith and without negligence will be discharged from his liability on the cheque [Section 89].

40.12. PROTECTION OF A COLLECTING BANKER

1. *The cheque must be crossed*
2. *The payment must be collected for a customer*
3. *The banker must act as an agent of its customer*
4. *The banker must act in good faith and without negligence*

A collecting banker is one which collects the payment of a crossed cheque on behalf of its customer. In the collection of payment of a crossed cheque, there is also risk as the customer on whose behalf the payment of a cheque is collected may not be its true owner. In such cases, the collecting banker may become liable to the true owner of the cheque for helping a wrong person to receive money to which he was not entitled. But it is very difficult task for the collecting banker to examine the validity of title of its customers specially when the banker has to collect a large number of cheque daily. Therefore, the collecting banker deserves to be protected against such liability. The protection to the collecting banker is provided by Section 131 which states that the collecting banker is not liable if it collects payment of a crossed cheque for its customer, in *good faith* and without negligence. The analysis of this section reveals that the following condition must be fulfilled to afford protection to a collecting banker.

1. *The cheque must be crossed:* The first requirement is that the collecting banker must collect the payment of already crossed cheques only. If the cheque is uncrossed, the banker is not protected if the customer's title turns out to be defective. Banker cannot avail protection by subsequently crossing the cheque.

2. *The payment must be collected for a customer:* The second requirement is that the collecting banker must collect the payment of a crossed cheque on behalf of its customer. A customer means a person who keeps an account with the banker.

3. *The banker must act as an agent of its customer:* The third requirement is that the collecting banker must collect the payment of a crossed cheque as an agent of its customer. In other words, the banker should not collect the cheque for himself as a holder in due course. It is, however, immaterial that the banker credits the customer's account before the amount is actually collected from the paying banker [Section 131 (*Explanation*)].

4. *The banker must act in good faith and without negligence.* The last requirement is that in collecting the payment of crossed cheque, the collecting banker must have acted in good faith and without negligence. If there are circumstances which arouse a suspicion in the mind of a collecting banker regarding the title of a person who wants to get the cheque collected, then the banker is supposed to make proper inquiries before collecting the cheque. If the banker fails to make any such inquiry, he will not be acting in good faith.

LEGAL PROVISIONS (SECTIONS) DISCUSSED IN THE CHAPTER

Important legal provisions (sections) of the Negotiable Instruments Act, 1881, discussed in this chapter, are reproduced here under.

1. ***Section 123: Cheque crossed generally***
   Where a cheque bears across its face an addition of the words "and company" or any abbreviation thereof, between two parallel transverse lines, or of two parallel transverse lines simply, either with or without the words "not negotiable", that addition shall be deemed a crossing and the cheque shall be deemed to be crossed generally.
2. ***Section 124: cheque crossed specially***
   Where a cheque bears across its face an addition of the name of a banker either with or without the words "not negotiable", that addition shall be deemed a crossing, and the cheque shall be deemed to be crossed specially, and to be crossed to that banker.

3. ***Section 125: Crossing after issue***
Where a cheque is uncrossed, the holder may cross it generally or specially.
Where a cheque is crossed generally, the holder may cross it specially.
Where a cheque is crossed generally or specially, the holder may add the words "not negotiable".
Where a cheque is corossed specially, the banker to whom it in crossed may again cross it specially to another banker, his agent, for collection.

4. ***Section 126: Payment of cheques crossed generally***
Where a cheque is crossed generally, the banker on whom it is drawn shall not pay otherwise than to a banker.
Payment of cheques crossed specially : Where a cheque is crossed specially, the banker on whom it is drawn shall not pay it otherwise than to the banker to whom it is crossed, or his agent, for collection.

5. ***Section 127: Payment of cheque crossed specially more than once***
Where a cheque is crossed specially to more than one banker, except when crossed to an agent for the purpose of collection, the banker on whom it is drawn shall refuse payment thereof.

6. ***Section 128: Payment in due course of crossed cheque***
Where the banker on whom a crossed cheque is drawn has paid the same in due course, the banker paying the cheque, and (in case such cheque has come to the bands of the payee) the drawer thereof, shall respectively be entitled to the same rights, and be placed in the same position in all respects, as they would respectively be entitled to and placed in if the amount of the cheque had been paid to and received by the true owner thereof.

7. ***Section 129: Payment of crossed cheque out of due course***
Any banker paying a cheque crossed generally otherwise than to a banker, or a cheque crossed specially otherwise than to the banker to whom the same is crossed, or his agent for collection, being a banker, shall be liable to the true owner of the cheque for any loss he may sustain owing to the cheque having been so paid.

8. ***Section 130: Cheque bearing "not negotiable"***
A person taking a cheque crossed generally or specially, bearing in either case the words "not negotiable", shall not have and shall not be capable of giving, a better title to the cheque than that which the person from whom he took it had.

9. ***Section 131: Non-liability of banker receiving payment of cheque***
A banker who has in good faith and without negligence received payment for a customer of a chequue crossed generally or specially to himself shall not, in case the title to the cheque proves defective, incur any liability to the true owner of the cheque by reason only of having received such payment.
Explanation I. A banker receives payment of a crossed cheque for a customer within the meaning of this section notwithstanding that he credits his customer's account with the amount of the cheque before receiving payment thereof.
Explanations II. It shall be the duty of the banker who receives payment based on an electronic image of a truncated cheque held with him, to verify the *prima facie* genuineness of the cheque to be truncated and any fraud, forgery or tampering apparent on the face of the instrument that can be verified with due diligence and ordinary care.

10. ***Section 131A: Application Chapter to drafts***
The provisions of this Chapter shall apply to any draft, as defined in section 85A, as if the draft were a heque.

TEST QUESTIONS

1. What do you mean by crossing of a cheque? State the effect and object of crossing of a cheque. How the payment of a crossed cheque is made?
2. What are the different kinds of crossing? State the difference between a general and special crossing.
3. Define 'not negotiable' and 'restrictive crossing'. What is the difference between the two? State the legal effect of the words not negotiable written in the crossing of a cheque.
4. Discuss the legal implications of crossing of a cheque, with special reference to a cheque crossed (*a*) Generally, (*b*) Punjab National Bank, (*c*) Not negotiable, and (*d*) a/c payee.
5. Discuss the protection available to a paying banker and collecting banker in the matter of payment and collection of cheque.

MULTIPLE CHOICE QUESTIONS

1. A cheque is said to contain a general crossing when two parallel lines are drawn across the face of the cheque

(*a*) without any words (*b*) with words '& Co.'
(*c*) with words 'not negotiable' (*d*) in all the above cases.

2. A cheque is said to contain a special crossing when two parallel lines are drawn across the face of the cheque and by writing between the lines the
(*a*) name of some bank (*b*) name of some bank and '& Co.'
(*c*) a/c payee only (*d*) in (*a*) and (*b*) cases.

3. 'Account payee crossing' is always a special crossing.
(*a*) True, as it is the requirement of banking law.
(*b*) False, as it can be in general crossing also.

4. After receiving an uncrossed cheque, its holder can make on it
(*a*) general crossing (*b*) special crossing
(*c*) either (*a*) or (*b*) (*d*) neither (*a*) nor (*b*)

5. The payment of a crossed cheque can be obtained
(*a*) at the counter (*b*) by depositing in account
(*c*) by the payee only (*d*) both (*a*) and (*c*).

6. The payment of a cheque, containing special crossing can be obtained
(*a*) by depositing in any bank (*b*) by depositing in named bank
(*c*) at the counter of named bank (*d*) either (*a*) or (*c*).

ANSWERS

1. (*d*)	**2.** (*d*)	**3.** (*b*)	**4.** (*c*)	**5.** (*b*)	**6.** (*b*)

OBJECTIVE TYPE QUESTIONS WITH REASONING

State with reasons whether the following statements are correct or incorrect.

1. The crossing of cheques has been made obligatory by the Negotiable Instruments (Amendments) Act, 1988.
2. Only the cheques are compulsorily required to be crossed and there is no such compulsion in case of a promissory note or a bill of exchange.
3. The payment of a crossed cheque cannot be obtained at the counter of the bank.
4. When the words 'Not Negotiable' are written between the parallel lines of crossing of the cheque the crossing becomes the special crosing.
5. The payment of a cheque containing special crossing in always collected by the payee through the banker to whom it is crossed.

ANSWERS

1. ***Incorrect.*** No such clause in inserted by this Amendment Act.
2. ***Incorrect.*** No negotiable instrument is compulsorily required to be crossed.
3. ***Correct.*** The payment of a crossed cheque can be obtained only by opening an account with a banker.
4. ***Incorrect.*** A special crossing in one when the name of some banker is written between the lines of crossing.
5. ***Correct.*** No other banker can collect the payment of such a cheque . In fact the paying banker in under a duty to pay such a cheque only to the banker to whom it is crossed [Section 126]. Thus, only the specified banker can collect the payment of such a cheque and then pay to the customer, *i.e.*, account holder.

PRACTICAL PROBLEMS

1. *A* draws a cheque for Rs. 5,000 in favour of *B* and delivers the same to him after crossing the cheque. However, the words "a/c payee" are not added in the crossing. Can *B* obtain the payment of the cheque at the bank counter ?

   Hint: No, *B* cannot obtain the payment at bank counter. The payment of a crossed cheque can be obtained by deposing the cheque in one's bank account in some bank.

2. In the above example, the words "a/c payee" are added in the crossing. *B* further indorses the cheque in favour of *C*. How can *C* obtain the payment of this cheque ? Give reasons.

   Hint: *C* cannot obtain the payment of this cheque. The effect of "a/c payee" crossing is that the collecting banker is supposed to collect the cheque only on behalf of the payee and credit the amount to his account only.

3. *A* draws a cheque for Rs. 10,000 in favour of *B* and delivers the same to him after crossing the cheque and writing "canara bank" between the crossed lives. *B* has his account in Corporation bank and deposits the cheque in his account. The corporation bank refuses to collect the cheque in *B*'s account. Is the bank justified ? Give reasons.

   Hint: Yes, the corporation bank is justified in refusing to collect the cheque. In such cases of special crossing, the payee can get the cheque collected only by opening an account with the specified banker whose name appears across the cheque. In the present case, the payment of the cheque can be obtained by opening an account with the canara bank only.

41

CHAPTER

MISCELLANEOUS PROVISIONS

41.1. INTRODUCTION

In the previous chapters we have discussed, topic-wise, all the relevant provisions of the Negotiable Instruments Act. But there are certain provisions which are referred to in various chapters, but were not discussed in detail as their reference was sufficient at those places. Now in this chapter, we shall discuss all those miscellaneous provisions in detail. For the sake of convenience all such provisions are combined separately.

41.2. MATURITY OF NEGOTIABLE INSTRUMENTS

The payment of a negotiable instrument can be demanded only when its payment is due. When the payment becomes due, the instrument is said to be at maturity. Thus, maturity is the date on which the payment of an instrument falls due. For the purpose of knowing maturity, the negotiable instruments can be classified into the following three categories.

1. ***Negotiable instruments payable on demand:*** A negotiable instrument payable on demand is due for payment immediately after issue. It is payable when the demand is made *i.e.,* when its payment is demanded. As a matter of fact, such instruments are meant for immediate payment. And thus, no question of their maturity arises. They are due for payment from the date of their issue.

Note. The expressions 'at sight' and 'on presentment' also mean 'on demand' [Section 21].

2. ***Negotiable instruments payable on a specified date:*** A negotiable instrument payable on a specified date (*e.g.* 31st March, 1998) is due for payment on the third day after the specified date. Thus, such an instrument is at maturity on the third day after the specified date. The procedure for calculating the date of maturity will be discussed in Art. 41.4.

3. ***Negotiable instruments payable after certain period after its date:*** A negotiable instrument payable after certain period after its date (*e.g.* two months after the date of instrument) is due for payment on the third day after the specified period. Thus, such an instrument is at maturity on the third day after the specified period. The procedure for calculating the date of maturity will be discussed in Art. 41.4.

41.3. DAYS OF GRACE

The term 'days of grace' may be defined as the days which are added for calculating the date of maturity. Every promissory note or a bill of exchange, payable otherwise than on demand, is at maturity on the third day after the day on which it is payable. Thus, where a promissory note or a bill of exchange is payable on a specified date or after a specified date, the date of maturity is not the date on which the instrument is expressed to be so payable. But it is the third day after that date. These three days are called the days of grace.

The following negotiable instruments are *entitled* to the days of grace:

1. A bill of exchange or a promissory note payable on a specified date.
2. A bill of exchange or a promissory note payable 'after sight'.
3. A bill of exchange or a promissory note payable at a certain period after date.
4. A bill of exchange or a promissory note payable at a certain period after the happening of a certain event.

The following negotiable instruments are *not entitled* to the days of grace.

1. A bill of exchange or a promissory note in which no time for payment is specified *i.e.* a bill or a note payable on demand [Section 19].
2. A bill of exchange or a promissory note payable 'at sight' or 'on presentment'. As a matter of fact, such bills and notes are payable on demand [Section 21].
3. A cheque, as it is always payable on demand.

It may be noted that when the days of grace are allowed, the ascertainment of the date of maturity becomes important. The reason for the same is that such instruments are to be presented for payment on the last day of grace. And their payment cannot be demanded before that date. As a matter of fact, the presentment of the instrument for payment before that date is in valid and does not entitle a person to file a suit if the payment is refused by the party to whom the instrument was presented for payment.

Note. The difference between the terms 'after sight' and 'at sight' is that the term 'after sight', in a promissory note means 'after presentment for sight', and in a bill of exchange it means 'after acceptance' or 'after noting or protest for non-acceptance'. Whereas the term 'at sight' means 'on demand' in case of promissory note as well as bill of exchange.

41.4. CALCULATION OF DATE OF MATURITY

1. ***Where a bill of exchange or a promissory note is payable after a stated number of months***
2. ***Where a bill of exchange or a promissory note is payable after a stated number of days***
3. ***When the day of maturity is holiday***

The date of maturity is calculated in case of bills of exchange and promissory notes where the days of grace are allowed. The date of maturity is calculated in accordance with the following principles:

1. ***Where a bill of exchange or a promissory note is payable after a stated number of months*** [*Section 23*]. Sometimes, a bill of exchange or a promissory note is made payable after a stated number of months after date, or after sight, or after a certain event. In such cases, it is at maturity on the third day after the stated number of months *i.e.* it becomes payable three days after the stated number of months.

Example 41.1. A bill of exchange dt. 15th February, 1998 was made payable two months after date. The bill of exchange is at maturity on 3rd day after 15th April 1998 *i.e.* on 18th April, 1998.

Example 41.2. A promissory note dt. 31st December, 1998 was made payable one month after sight. The promissory note was presented for sight on 25th January, 1999. In this case, the promissory note is at maturity on 3rd day after 25th February, 1999 *i.e.* on 28th February, 1988. Here, one month is to be counted from 25th January, 1999 *i.e.* from the date of presentment for sight.

Sometimes, the months in which the stated period would terminate has no corresponding day. In such cases, the period shall terminate on the last day of such month.

Example 41.3. A promissory note dt. 29th January, 1997 was made payable one month after date. The promissory note is at maturity on 3rd day after 28th Feburary, 1997 *i.e.* on 3rd March 1997. As the month of February in this year has only 28 days. Similarly, the bill of exchange dt. 28th, 29th, 30th, 31st January, 1997 made payable on month after date will be at maturity on 3rd March. 1997.

2. *Where a bill of exchange or a promissory note is payable after a stated number of days* [*Section 24*]. Sometimes, a bill of exchange or a promissory note is made payable after a stated number of days after date, or after sight, or after a certain event. In such cases, it is at maturity on the third day after the stated number of days *i.e.* it becomes payable three days after the stated number of days. It may be noted that while counting the stated number of days, the day on which the instrument is drawn, or presented for sight, or the day on which the event happens shall be excluded.

Example 41.4. A bill of exchange dt. 10th January, 1998 was made payable 15 days after date. In this case, the 15 days will be counted from 11th January, 1998. The 15th day from 11th January, 1998 is 25th January, 1998. Thus, the bill of exchange is at maturity on the 3rd day after 25th January, 1998 *i.e.* on 28th January 1998.

Example 41.5. A promissory noted dt. 28th January, 1997 was made payable 60 days after sight. The promissory note was presented for sight on 15th February, 1997. In this case 60 days will be counted from 16th February, 1997. The 60th day from 16th February, 1997 is 16th April, 1997. Thus, the promissory note is at maturity on 3rd day after 16th April, 1997 *i.e.* on 19th April, 1997.

3. *When the day of maturity is holiday* [*Section 25*]. Sometimes the day of maturity happens to be a public holiday. In such cases, instrument shall be at maturity on the previous business day. It may be noted that the expression 'public holiday' includes Sunday and any other day declared by the Central Government by notification in the Official Gazette, to be a holiday. Thus, if the maturity of a bill of exchange or a promissory note falls on Sunday, it shall be due for payment on Saturday and not on Monday.

Note. In case of a cheque, there is no question of calculation of date of maturity as it is always payable on demand.

41.5. ACCEPTANCE FOR HONOUR

We know that a bill exchange is generally accepted only by the drawee *i.e.* a person on whom it is drawn. But in certain cases, a person who is in no way liable on the bill of exchange, may come forward and accept it for the honour of the drawer or any other party liable on the bill. Such acceptance is known as "acceptance for honour". This is a peculiar kind of acceptance which is allowed when the original drawee of a bill of exchange refuses to accept it or refuses to give better security when demanded. When a bill of exchange is dishonoured by non-acceptance, the credit and honour of the parties, particularly of the drawee, is adversely affected. Similarly, when the acceptor of a bill of exchange has become insolvent, the holder would feel insecure. In order to save the honour of such parties, the bill of exchange can also be accepted for honour by any person with the consent of the holder of the bill. In this connection Sections 108 and 109, provide that when a bill of exchange has been noted or protested for non-acceptance or for better security, any persons may accept the bill for the honour of any one party liable on the bill of exchange. The analysis of these sections reveals that the following conditions must be satisfied for a valid acceptance for honour:

1. The acceptance for honour can be made only in case of a bill of exchange which has been noted or protested for non-acceptance or for better security. Thus, before

the acceptance for honour, the bill must have been noted or protested for non-acceptance, or for better security.

2. The acceptance for honour must be made with the consent of the holder.
3. The acceptance for honour can be made by any person who is not a party already liable on the bill of exchange.
4. The acceptance for honour should be made in writing on the bill of exchange itself.
5. The acceptance for honour must be made for the honour of any one party liable on the bill of exchange. A person desiring to accept for honour must declare in writing that he accepts the bill for the honour of the drawer or of a particular person named therein. And when the acceptance does not express for whose honour it is made, it shall be deemed to be made for the honour of the drawer [Section 110].
6. The acceptance for honour must be signed by the 'acceptor for honour'.
7. The acceptance for honour must be made before the bill of exchange is over due. And it should be for the full amount of the bill.

41.6. LIABILITIES AND RIGHTS OF AN ACCEPTOR FOR HONOUR

An acceptor for honour takes the place of the person for whose honour he has accepted the bill of exchange. Thus, his liabilities and rights are the same as those of a person, for whose honour the acceptance was given. These may be discussed as under:

1. *Liabilities:* On a valid acceptance for honour, the acceptor for honour binds himself to all parties, subsequent to the party for whose honour he accepts to pay the amount of the bill of exchange [Section 111]. Thus, he is liable to pay the amount of the bill to the party who is subsequent to the party for whose honour the bill was accepted.

Example 41.6. A bill of exchange was negotiated through *A*, *B*, *C* and *D*, and was accepted by *E* for the honour of *B*. In this case, *E* is liable to *C* and *D* only and not to *A* as he (*A*) is a prior party to *B*.

It may also be noted that the liability of an acceptor for honour is conditional and arises only if the original drawee, after being approached again on the date of maturity, does not pay the amount due on the bill. In this way, the position of an acceptor for honour is slightly better than that of the ordinary acceptor, because an ordinary acceptor is primarily liable. It is to be noted that an acceptor for honour is liable only if the following conditions are satisfied;

(*a*) The bill of exchange must be presented *again* to the original drawee for payment on the date of maturity.

(*b*) The bill of exchange must be noted or protested for non-payment if the original drawee still refuses to pay the amount due on the bill [Section 112], and

(*c*) The bill of exchange must be presented to its 'acceptor for honour' for payment on the next date after the day of its maturity [Section 111].

2. *Rights.* After making the payment of the bill of exchange, an acceptor for honour is entitled to recover the amount from the party for whose honour he had accepted the bill of exchange, and also from all parties prior to such a party. And such party including the prior parties is liable to compensate the 'acceptor for honour' for all loss or damage sustained by him in consequence of such acceptance [Section 111].

41.7. PAYMENT FOR HONOUR

As a general rule of law, one cannot make any payment voluntarily on behalf of somebody else and then claim the amount from the person on whose behalf the payment had been made. But in certain cases of a bill of exchange, any person may pay the amount due on the bill for the honour of any party liable to pay the same. Such payment is known as 'payment for honour'. The payment for honour may be made by any person whether or not he is liable as a party to the bill. A payment for honour can be made in case of a bill of exchange which has been accepted by the drawee, and later on it is dishonoured by non-payment. It may be noted that the payment for honour can be made *only in case of a bill of exchange.* In this connection Section 113 provides that where a bill of exchange has been noted or protested for non-payment, any person may pay the same for the honour of any party. The analysis of this section reveals that the following conditions must be satisfied for a valid payment for honour.

1. The bill of exchange must have been dishonoured by non-payment.
2. The bill of exchange must have been noted or protested for non-payment after its dishonour by non-payment.
3. Before making the payment, the person, who desires to pay, must have previously declared before a Notary Public, the party for whose honour he makes the payment. And such declaration must have been recorded by the Notary Public.
4. The payment for honour must be made for the honour of any party liable to pay the amount due on the bill of exchange.

After making the payment of a bill of exchange, the 'payer for honour' is entitled to the same rights as the holder of a bill of exchange to whom the payment has been made, has against all the parties. It may be noted that he can also recover all sums so paid, with interest thereon, and all expenses properly incurred in making such payment, from the party for whose honour he has paid the amount [Section 114].

Thus, the payer for honour can recover from the party for whose honour he has paid, and from all parties prior to such a party. However, the parties subsequent to the party for whose honour the payment has been made, are discharged from their liability.

41.8. EFFECT OF ABSENCE OR FAILURE OF CONSIDERATION

Consideration is presumed to be there in every negotiable instrument. However, it does not mean that the consideration is always there. Because the party liable for payment may prove that there is no consideration at all, or that there is only a partial consideration. When total or partial absence of consideration is proved, the liability of the parties is affected. Sections 43 to 45 of the Negotiable Instruments Act, contain the provisions which state the effect of such absence or failure of the consideration, which may be discussed under the following two heads:

1. Effect of total absence or failure of consideration.
2. Effect of partial absence or failure of consideration.

41.9. EFFECT OF TOTAL ABSENCE OR FAILURE OF CONSIDERATION

The effect of total absence or failure of consideration may be discussed under the following two heads:

1. ***Effect between immediate parties.*** Sometimes, a negotiable instrument is made, drawn, accepted, indorsed or transferred without any consideration or sometimes the consideration fails subsequently. In such cases, the instrument is void as between the immediate parties and they are not liable to pay the amount of the instrument [Section 43 (first part)]. The following are the parties who are in immediate relation with one another:

(*a*) The drawer of a bill stands in immediate relation with acceptor.

(*b*) The maker of a promissory note, bill of exchange or cheque stands in immediate relations with the payee.

(*c*) The indorser stands in immediate relation with his indorsee.

(*d*) Other parties who sign the instrument may also by agreement, stand in immediate relations with a holder [Section 44 (Explanation)].

Thus, if a promissory note or a bill of exchange is drawn without any consideration, the maker of note or bill is not liable to pay. Similarly where the instrument is indorsed without any consideration, the indorsee who receives it without consideration cannot recover the amount from his indorser.

Example 41.7. *A* made a promissory note in favour of *B*, and delivered the same to *B* without any consideration. Thereafter, *B* transferred the same to *C* without consideration. And *C* transferred it to *D* without consideration. In this case, the immediate parties are *A* and *B*, B and *C*, and *D*. Thus, *B* cannot recover anything from *A*, as there was no consideration between *A* and *B*. Similarly, *C* cannot recover from *B*, and *D* from *C* as they also got the promissory note without consideration.

2. *Effect between remote parties.* Sometimes, a person receives a negotiable instrument without any consideration but transfers the instrument to a holder for some consideration. In such cases, the holder for consideration and every subsequent holder deriving title from him, with or without consideration, may recover the amount due on such instrument from the transferor for consideration or from any prior party to such transferor [Section 43 (second part)]. Thus, a holder for consideration is not affected by the prior absence of consideration, and he can recover the amount from the transferor for consideration, and also from all the parties prior to such transferor. Moreover, any subsequent holder who got the instrument from a holder for value can also recover the amount from the transferor for consideration and from all the prior parties. Thus, once the instrument gets into the hands of a 'holder in due course', he or any subsequent holder deriving title from him, can recover the amount from transferor for consideration or from any prior party to such transferor.

Example 41.8. *A* made a promissory note in favour of *B* and delivered it to *B* without any consideration. Thereafter, *B* transferred the same to *C* without consideration. And *C* transferred it to *D* for consideration *D* further transferred it to E without any consideration. In this case *D* is the holder for value. He can recover, the amount from *C* who transferred it to *D* for consideration. Moreover, *D* can also recover the amount from *B* and *A* because a person who takes a negotiable instrument for consideration can claim the amount from transferor for consideration or from any prior party thereto. Here, *E* can also recover the amount from *A*, *B* and *C* because any person who derives a title from holder for value can also recover the amount from prior parties. Here *E* derived his title from *D* who was a holder for value. However, *E* cannot recover anything from *D* because *E* and *D* are immediate parties to the transaction and there was no consideration.

41.10. EFFECT OF PARTIAL ABSENCE OR FAILURE OF CONSIDERATION

1. *Partial absence of money consideration*
2. *Partial absence of consideration not consisting of money*

The effect of partial absence or failure of consideration may be discussed under the following two heads.

1. *Partial absence of money consideration.* Sometimes, there is a partial absence or failure of money consideration. In such cases, parties standing in immediate relations to each other cannot recover more than the actual consideration (*i.e.* only reduced consideration can be recovered). In other words, the partial absence or failure of money consideration in a negotiable instrument affects the rights of the holder against the immediate parties who signed the instrument. Such holder is entitled to recover only the amount of reduced consideration [Section 44].

Example 41.9. *A* drew a bill of exchange on *B* for Rs. 5,000 payable to the order of *A*. *B* accepted this bill of exchange, but refused to make the payment on the due date. And A filed a suit against *B* for recovery of the amount due on the bill of exchange. *B* proved that the bill was accepted for value as to Rs. 4,000, and the balance of Rs. 1,000 as an accommodation to *A*. In this case, *A* can recover only Rs. 4,000 from *B*.

It may be noted that the above rule applies only where the holder stands in immediate relation with the signer of the instrument. The right of a transferee from such holder who may be a holder for value or a holder in due course is not affected by such partial absence of money consideration.

Example 41.10. *A* drew a bill of exchange on B for Rs. 4,000 payable to the order of *A*. And this bill of exchange was duly accepted by *B*. Thereafter, *A* indorsed and delivered the bill of exchange to *C* for Rs. 4,000. In this case *C*, becomes the holder for value and can recover the full amount (*i.e.* Rs. 4,000) either from *A* or from *B* even if *B* proves that the bill was accepted for value as to Rs. 2,000, and the balance of Rs, 2,000 as an accommodation to *A*.

2. *Partial absence of consideration not consisting of money.* Sometimes, there is a partial failure or absence of consideration other than the money. In such cases also, the rights of the holder against the immediate parties who signed the negotiable instruments, are affected in the same way as there is a failure of money consideration. Thus, such holder is entitled to recover only the amount of reduced consideration. It may, however, be noted that this rule is applicable if the consideration which has failed can be ascertained in terms of money without any collateral enquiry [Section 45].

Example 41.11. *A* promissed to supply 100 tins of ghee to *B* at the rate of Rs. 350 per tin. And *B* signed a promissory note for Rs. 35,000 in favour of *A* for the price of ghee. A supplied only 60 tins of ghee. In this case, there is a failure of consideration to the extent of 40 tins of ghee. The price of these tins of ghee comes out to be Rs. 14,000 which can be determined without any collateral enquiry. Here, although *B* signed a promissory note for Rs. 35,000, but he is liable to pay only Rs. 21,000 as the part consideration has failed due to short supply of 40 tins of ghee.

It may be noted that the above rule applies only where the holder stands in immediate relation with the signer of the instrument. The right of a transferee from such holder, who may be holder for value or holder in due course is not affected by such partial failure of consideration even if it could be ascertained without any collateral enquiry.

41.11. NEGOTIABLE INSTRUMENTS OBTAINED BY UNLAWFUL MEANS

1. ***Stolen instruments***
2. ***Forged instruments***
3. ***Instrument obtained by fraud***
4. ***Instruments obtained for an unlawful consideration***

Section 58 provides that any person who obtains a negotiable instrument by unlawful means (such as offence, by fraud or for unlawful consideration), cannot recover the amount due on the instrument. However, if such instrument comes into the hands of a holder in due course, he gets a good title to it, and can recover the amount due on the instrument. Moreover, any person who gets the instrument through the holder in due course, can also recover the amount due on the instrument. Following are the instruments which are referred to in Section 58 of the Negotiable Instruments Act, and no person except a holder in due course gets a good title to such instruments.

1. *Stolen instruments.* A stolen instrument is one which has been lost and found by a person, or which has been stolen from the custody of its rightful holder. It may be noted that a finder or a person, who obtains a negotiable instrument by theft, does not acquire a good title to it. And thus, he cannot recover the amount due on the instrument. But if the found or stolen instrument is payable to bearer and the finder or the thief transfers it to any person, who receives it in good faith and for value, such a transferee, being a holder in due course will get a good title to the instrument and can recover the amount due on it from the parties liable for payment. It may, however, be noted that where a found or stolen negotiable instrument is payable to order, and the finder or the thief forges the indorsement of the rightful owner and transfers it to a *bona fide* transferee for value, then such a transferee acquires no legal title to the instrument. The reason for the same is that a forgery does not confer any title.

Example 41.12. A drew a bill of exchange for Rs. 1,000 payable to *B* or order. It was stolen from *B*'s custody, and the thief forged *B*'s signature and indorsed it to *C* who took it in good faith and for value. In this case, *C* does not get any title to the bill of exchange.

2. *Forged instruments.* A forged instrument is one on which the signature of a drawer, maker or acceptor is forged. A forged instrument is totally ineffective and its holder cannot recover the amount due on it. As a matter of fact, the forgery is not a case of defective title, but there is a complete absence of title from the very beginning. Even if a forged instrument comes into the hands of a holder in due course, he also cannot recover the amount due on it, because there was no title to the instrument.

Example 41.13. A drew a bill of exchange for Rs. 1,500 on *B* payable 60 days after acceptance and indorsed the same to *C*. *C* forged *B*'s acceptance and negotiated it to *D*, a *bona fide* holder for value. In this case, *D* does not get any title to the bill of exchange.

3. *Instrument obtained by fraud.* A negotiable instrument must be made, accepted, indorsed or transferred with the free consent of all the parties. If any person obtains the negotiable instrument by fraud or coercion he does not get a good title to the instrument and cannot enforce its payment. Any possessor or indorsee who gets the instrument from the person, who acquired it by fraud or coercion, can also not claim its payment from any party to the instrument.

However, if such instrument is transferred to a person who becomes a holder in due course, then he gets a good title and can recover the amount due on the instrument. Moreover, any person who derives his title through the holder in due course can also recover the amount due on the instrument.

4. *Instruments obtained for an unlawful consideration.* A negotiable instrument must be made accepted, indorsed or transferred for a lawful consideration. If the consideration for a negotiable instrument is unlawful, then the instrument is void and creates no obligation between the parties to the instrument. But it may be noted that if such instrument comes into the hands of a holder in due course, he gets good title to it and can recover the amount due on it. Moreover, any person, who derivers his title through the holder in due course, can also recover the amount due on the instrument.

41.12. FORGED INDORSEMENT

Sometimes, a negotiable instrument is negotiated by means of forged indorsement. In such cases, the indorsee does not a get a good title to the instrument even if he is a *bona fide* holder for value. It may be noted that when a party primarily liable on a negotiable instrument pays the amount due on it to a wrong person (*i.e.* the person who holds the instrument under a forged indorsement), he remains liable to the true owner of the instrument. However, in case of cheques the paying banker is given statutory protection against the payment of cheques having forged indorsement. And the banker cannot be held liable if it makes payment in good faith and without any negligence [Section 85]. But the banker will not be protected where the payment of a cheque is made on which the drawer's signature was forged. The reason for the same is that the banker is protected only in case of forgery of indorser's signature and not in case of forgery of drawer's signature.

TEST QUESTIONS

1. What do you understand by maturity of negotiable instrument? State the rules relating to the calculation of date of maturity.
2. What do you understand by 'acceptance for honour'? State the liabilities and rights of an acceptor for honour.
3. What are the provisions of the Negotiable Instruments Act dealing with the effect of partial absence or partial failure of consideration on a negotiable instrument on the rights of the parties thereto?
   (*a*) Where the consideration consists of money.
   (*b*) Where the consideration does not consist of money.
4. "The defence of absence of consideration in case of a negotiable instrument is available only between parties in immediate relationship"–comment.
5. What is the presumption as to consideration for a negotiable instrument? State the effect of total absence or failure of consideration.
6. Discuss the instruments obtained by unlawful means giving reference of the appropriate Sections of the Negotiable Instruments Act.
7. Write notes on the following:
   (*a*) Days of grace. (*b*) Payment for honour.
   (*c*) Stolen instruments. (*d*) Instrument obtained by fraud
   (*e*) Forged instruments (*f*) Forged indorsement.

MULTIPLE CHOICE QUESTIONS

1. The payment of a negotiable instrument becomes due
   (*a*) at maturity (*b*) before maturity
   (*c*) after maturity (*d*) on 3rd day of maturity
2. The negotiable instruments payable on demand are due for payment
   (*a*) from 3rd day of date of issue (*b*) from the date of issue
   (*c*) after 15 days of date of issue (*d*) after 30 days of date of issue
3. The negotiable instruments payable on a specified date, are due for payment
   (*a*) from the specified date (*b*) from the date of issue
   (*c*) from 3rd day after specified date (*d*) after presentment for sight
4. Which of the following negotiable instrument is not entitled to days of grace?
   (*a*) a bill of exchange payable on specified date (*b*) a promissory note payable on specified date
   (*c*) a promissory note payable 'after sight' (*d*) a cheque
5. A negotiable instrument made without any consideration at all, is
   (*a*) void between all parties (*b*) voidable between all parties
   (*c*) void between immediate parties (*d*) voidable between immediate parties
6. In case, the finder or thief of an order instrument transfer the same, by forging rightful owner's signatures, to a *bona fide* transferee for value, such a transferee acquires a good title to the instrument.
   (*a*) True, as he becomes a holder in due course.
   (*b*) False, as forgery does not confer any title.

ANSWERS

1. (*a*) 2. (*b*) 3. (*c*) 4. (*d*) 5. (*c*) 6. (*b*)

OBJECTIVE TYPE QUESTIONS WITH REASONING

State with reasons whether the following statements are correct or incorrect.

1. A negotiable instrument payable on demand is due for payment immediately after issue.
2. A negotiable instrument payable on a specified date is due for payment on the next day after specified date.
3. A negotiable instrument can be presented for payment on any day during the three days of grace and the liable party refusing to make the payment will be guilty of default.
4. A person who receives a stolen instrument payable to bearer in *good faith* and for value gets a good title to the instrument.
5. A 'holder in due course' who receives a forged instrument in good faith and for value is entitled to recover the amount due on it as he gets the instrument free from all defects.

ANSWERS

1. *Correct.* Such an instrument is meant for immediate payment as such it is due for payment from the date of its issue.
2. *Incorrect.* Such an instrument is due for payment on the third day after the specified date.
3. *Incorrect.* A negotiable instrument entitled to days of grace is to be presented for payment on the last day of the grace. Presentment for payment before that date is not valid.
4. *Correct.* Such a person is the 'holder in due course' of the instrument.
5. *Incorrect.* A forged instrument is invalid from the very beginning as there was no title to the instrument.

PRACTICAL PROBLEMS

1. Ascertain the date of maturity of the following negotiable instrument:
   (a) A bill of the exchange dated 10th February, 2008 payable two month after date.
   (b) A promissory note dated 31st December, 2007 payable one month after sight ,which was presented for sight on 16th January, 2008.
   (c) A promissory note dated 29th , January 2007 payable one month after date.
   Hint: A bill of exchange or a promissory note payable after a stated number of months after date or after sight is at maturity on the third day after the stated number of months [Section 23]. The date of maturity in these cases is as under:
   (a) 13th April , 2008 (b) 19th February, 2008 (c) 3rd March, 2007.
2. *A* bill of exchange date 12th July, 2007 is made payable one month after date. Calculate the date of maturity of the bill.
   Hint: 14th August, 2007. In case the date of maturity of a bill of exchange or a promissory note falls on a public holiday or on Sunday, it shall be due for payment (*i.e.* at maturity) on the previous business day and not on the next day. [Section 25]
3. *A* draws a bill of exchange for Rs.10,000 on *B* payable to *C* or order. It is stolen from *C*'s custody and the thief forges *C*'s signature and indorses the same to *D* who takes the bill in good faith and for value. Does *D* get a valid title to the bill ? Give reasons.
   Hint: No, *D* does not get any title to the bill . In case of forged indorsement on stolen instruments, the holder or the holder in due course does not get any title to the instrument. [Section 58]

42

CHAPTER

BANKER AND CUSTOMER

42.1. INTRODUCTION

The banker and customer relations are governed by a contract between them. Certain obligations and rights of a banker arise out of the relationship between the banker and his customer. In this chapter we shall discuss the legal relationship between a banker and a customer alongwith the obligations and rights of a banker, and other legal provisions relating thereto.

42.2. BANKER

The term 'banker' is defined in Section 3 of the Negotiable Instruments Act, which reads as under:

"Banker includes any person acting as a banker and any post office saving bank"

The analysis of this section reveals that, a banker means any person who acts as a banker, and it also includes a post office saving bank. It may be noted that this section does not clearly define the term banker. It simply states who is included in the term 'banker'. As a matter of fact, there is no statutory definitionof the term 'banker' in any Act. However, Sections 5 (*b*) and 5 (*c*) of the Banking Regulation Act, 1949, which respectively define the term 'banking' and 'banking company' helf us in knowing who is a banker. These sections respectively read as under:

"Banking means the accepting, for the purpose of lending or investment, of deposits of money from the public, repayable on demand or otherwise, and withdrawal by cheque, draft, order or otherwise".

"Banking company means any company which transacts the business of banking in India"

The analysis of these two provisions reveals that a banker is one who accepts money form the public for the purpose of lending or investment, and repays the same by cheque or otherwise. The accepted definition of the term 'banker' is given by ***Dr. Herbert L. Hart,*** the author of the well-know treatise, *Law of Banking* in the following words:

"A banker is one, who in the ordinary course of his business, honours cheques drawn upon him by persons from and for whom he receives money on current account".

The definition given by *Dr. Hart* is further supported by ***Sir John Paget,*** another great author who states that "no person or body corporate or otherwise can be a banker who does not (1) take deposit accounts, (2) take current accounts, (3) issue and pay cheques, and (4) collect cheques crossed and uncrossed for his customers"[1]. It may, however, be noted that every person who receives the money of another, and pays it according to his orders cannot be regarded as a banker, unless he establishes that business for profit.[2] *Sir John Paget* has also stressed that a banker's main business must be that of banking from which, generally, he should be able to earn his living.

42.3. CUSTOMER

There is no statutory definition of the term 'customer' also. But it is defined in judicial decisions which is commonly accepted in England as well as in India. A customer means a person who keeps an account with a banker. It may be a current account or a deposit account. It is, however, not necessary that the account should be of long standing. So far as the banking dealings are concerned, the term 'customer' signifies a relationship in which duration is not material. Thus, a customer is a person whose money has been accepted by the banker on the footing that the banker will honour cheques upto the amount standing to his credit irrespective of the fact whether his connection is of short or long standing[3]. *Dr. Hart*, an author of Law of Banking defines the term customer in the following words:

> *"A customer is one who has an account with a banker or for whom a banker habitually undertakes to act as such".*

Thus, a person is a customer who has some sort of bank account in his name and for whom the banker undertakes to provide the facilities as a banker.

It may, however, be noted that mere casual acts of service do not create the relationship of banker and customer. The dealing must be of a banking nature. Thus, if a person occasionally goes to the bank to buy a draft or to get the cheque encashed without opening the account or to deposit valuables in a locker, he does not become a customer of the banker, because such transactions are not regarded in the nature of real banking business.

42.4. LEGAL RELATIONSHIP BETWEEN A BANKER AND A CUSTOMER

The legal relationship between a banker and his customer is based on the contract between them. Primarily, their relationship is that of a debtor and creditor. When a customer deposits money with a banker, the banker becomes the debtor and the customer becomes the creditor. And when the banker lends money to his customer, the banker becomes the creditor and the customer, the debtor.

It is to be noted that the money deposited with the banker is at his disposal, and he can deal with it as he wants. The banker is, however, under an obligation to honour the cheques of his customer *i.e.* the banker is under obligation to repay the money when the customer demands payment.

42.5. OBLIGATIONS OF A BANKER

1. ***Obligation to honour cheques of his customer***
2. ***Obligation not to disclose information concerning his customer's account or affair***
3. ***Obligation to maintain proper and accurate account***

The obligations of a banker, arising out of his relationship with the customer, may be discussed under the following heads:

1. *Obligation to honour cheques of his customer.* The banker is under statutory obligations to honour the cheques of his customer. This provision is contained in Section 31 of the Negotiable Instruments Act, which reads as under:

1. *The Law of Banking* by sir John Paget, 4th Edn., p. 5.
2. *R. Pillai* v. *S. Ayyar,* (1920) 43 Madras 816. In this case, it was held that a Government Treasury is not a banker as it does not carry the business for profit.
3. *Taxation Commissioner* v. *English, Scottish & Australian Bank,* (1920) AC 683, p. 687.

4. Obligation to abide by the directions given by the customer
5. Obligation to collect cheques and drafts on behalf of the customer

"The drawee of a cheque having sufficient funds of the drawer in his hands, properly applicable to the payment of such cheques, must pay the cheque when duly required so to do, and in default of such payment, must compensate the drawer for any loss or damage caused by such default".

The analysis of this section reveals that, the banker is legally bound to honour the cheques of his customer so long as there are *sufficient funds* to the credit of his customer properly applicable to the payment of the cheque. If the banker wrongfully refuses to honour these cheques, he is liable to the customer for damages. The damages which the customer can recover for unjustified dishonour of cheque is not limited to actual pecuniary loss, but also extends to loss of credit or injury to his reputation. Thus, the customer can recover very substantial damages.

It may, however, be noted that the banker is liable to the customer (drawer of a cheque) only. The payee or the holder of a cheque has no cause of action against the banker as there is no privity of contract between the banker and the payee or the holder. In certain circumstances, the banker is justified in refusing the payment of a cheque. In such cases, he is not liable for damages. These circumstances will be discussed in Arts. 42.7, 42.8 and 42.9.

2. ***Obligation not to disclose information concerning his customer's account or affair.*** The relationship between the banker and his customer is confidential. And thus, the banker should not disclose the information concerning the account and affair of his customer. This is to protect the credit and reputation of the customer. If the banker fails in this duty, he may be held liable for damages for loss of credit or reputation.

3. ***Obligation to maintain proper and accurate account.*** The banker is also under obligation to maintain proper and accurate account of all credits and debits of his customer. If the banker makes some wrong credit in his customer's account and relying upon the accuracy of the entry, the customer acts in *good faith* and alters his position to his prejudice, then the banker may not recover the amount from the customer which was wrongly credited to his customer's account. The customer's position is altered to his prejudice when on the basis of the amount to his credit, he issues cheques which are duly paid by the banker. It may, however, be noted here that customer should also act in good faith and without negligence.

Moreover, if the banker wishes to close the account of his customer, he must give a reasonable notice to his customer. This enables the customer to make other arrangements, and the customer may not issue any more cheques.

4. ***Obligation to abide by the directions given by the customer.*** Since the relationship of banker and customer is governed by terms of the contract between them, the banker must abide by the specific and clear instructions which are expressly given by the customer. However, the banker is under obligation to abide by the instructions only if they are within the scope of their relationship.

5. ***Obligation to collect cheques and drafts on behalf of the customer.*** A banker is also under obligation to collect the cheques and drafts on behalf of his customer. In such a case, the banker needs special protection because it is difficult to verify the title of each and every holder of a cheque. The protection of a 'paying' and 'collecting' banker has already been discussed in Chapter 40.

42.6. RIGHTS OF A BANKER

1. *Right of general lien*
2. *Right to interest and incidental charges*
3. *Right of set off*

The banker also has certain rights against his customer which may be discussed under the following heads.

1. ***Right of general lien.*** This right of banker is contained in Section 171 of the Indian Contract Act, which reads as under:

"Bankers may, in the absence of a contract to the contrary, retain as a security for a general balance of account, any goods bailed to him".

The analysis of this section reveals that, a banker can exercise his right of lien on all goods and securities deposited with the banker. It is, however, necessary that the goods should have been given to the banker only as a bailee because the lien extends only to the goods which have been bailed to the banker. This point has already been discussed in chapter 15.

2. ***Right to interest and incidental charges.*** The banker is entitled to charge interest on the money lent to his customer, and also to claim incidental charges *e.g.* commission for collection etc. However, the banker can claim the interest and incidental charges as per the rules communicated to the customer.

3. ***Right of set off.*** Sometimes the customer has two accounts with the same bank. And there is credit balance in one and debit balance in the other. In such cases the banker has the right to combine the two accounts, and set off the debit balance of one against the other showing the credit balance.

42.7. BANKER JUSTIFIED IN REFUSING THE PAYMENT OF CHEQUES

We have discussed in Art. 42.5 that the banker is under legal obligation to pay the cheques of his customers. However, in certain circumstances the banker is justified in refusing payment. In such cases, the customer cannot claim damages from the banker for refusing payment of his cheques. These circumstances may be discussed under the following two heads:

1. Circumstances when the banker *may* refuse the payment.
2. Circumstances when the banker *must* refuse the payment.

42.8. CIRCUMSTANCES WHEN THE BANKER MAY REFUSE THE PAYMENT

1. *When the cheque is post-dated*
2. *When the cheque is out-dated i.e. stale*
3. *When the cheque is ambiguous or of doubtful validity*
4. *When the cheque is mutilated*
5. *When a cheque is not duly presented for payment*
6. *When the funds in customer's account are insufficient*
7. *When the customer's signature does not agree*
8. *When the funds in customer's account are not applicable to the payment of the cheque*
9. *When the account is in joint names*
10. *When the banker has a claim for set-off*

Following are the circumstances in which the banker *may refuse* to make the payment of his customer's cheque:

1. ***When the cheque is post-dated.*** As a matter of fact, the banker is required to pay a cheque on the date it bears, and not before that date *e.g.* where a cheque is dated 15th March, 2003 and it is presented for payment on 10th March 2003 the banker may refuse the payment, and it will not amount to dishonour of a cheque. It may be noted that if the banker pays a post-dated cheque, he can be held liable for damages if by reason of the premature payment of the post dated cheque, the banker is not able to meet the customer's other cheques presented within time.

2. *When the cheque is out-dated i.e. stale.* Sometimes, a cheque is out-dated. In such cases, the banker may refuse the payment. In India, it is a custom of the banker not to pay a cheque if it is presented after six months from the date of its issue. After six months, the cheque is known as a stale cheque.

3. *When the cheque is ambiguous or of doubtful validity.* Sometimes, the validity of a cheque is doubtful. In such cases, the banker may refuse the payment. The validity of a cheque may be in doubt where it is not properly drawn *e.g.* the amount in words and in figures differs, or not dated, or its indorsements are not proper and regular. Thus, when some confusion about the validity of a cheque arises, the banker may refuse the payment. Irregular and materially altered cheques create such confusion.

4. *When the cheque is mutilated.* Sometimes, the cheque is mutilated *e.g.* torn into two pieces. In such cases, the banker may refuse the payment. As a matter of fact, a mutilated cheque creates suspicion about the validity of a cheque.

5. *When a cheque is not duly presented for payment.* Sometimes, the cheque is not duly presented for payment *e.g.* where a cheque is presented after banking hours. In such cases, the banker may refuse the payment. Moreover, when a cheque is presented at a branch where the customer has no account, the banker may also refuse to honour the cheque.

6. *When the funds in customer's account are insufficient.* Sometimes, the balance in customer's account is not sufficient to meet the payment of the cheque. In such cases, the banker may refuse the payment. It may be noted that the banker is under no obligation to make the part payment of a cheque.

In case of bank's refusal to honour customer's cheque due to insufficient funds in his account, the drawer of the cheque may be held criminally liable for this offence. The provisions relating to criminal liability are contained in Sections 138 to 142 which were added to the Negotiable Instruments Act by an amendment in 1988. These have already been discussed in Chapter 36.

7. *When the customer's signature does not agree.* Sometimes the customer's signature on the cheque does not agree with his signature in the bank record. In such cases, the banker may refuse the payment of his cheque.

8. *When the funds in customer's account are not applicable to the payment of the cheque.* Sometimes, a customer has money in the bank in the form of fixed deposit, recurring deposit, or any other funds over which the bank has marked or signed lien. If such a customer issues a cheque against these deposits, the banker may refuse the payment of such a cheque as these funds are not applicable to the payment of the cheques.

9. *When the account is in joint names.* Sometimes, the bank account is in the joint name of two or more persons, and the cheque is required to be signed by all the joint account holders. In such cases, if the cheque is not signed by all of them, the banker may refuse the payment of such a cheque.

Note. In case of a joint account in the nature of 'either or survivor' the banker is not justified in refusing the payment of a cheque if it is signed by any of the account holders.

10. *When the banker has a claim for set-off.* Sometimes, a banker has certain claims against his customer (*e.g.* claim for loan given to the customer). And at the same time, the customer has some funds in his account with the same banker. In certain circumstances, the banker can set off the amount of his claim against his customer's funds. In such cases, the banker may refuse the payment of a cheque issued against such funds.

42.9. CIRCUMSTANCES WHEN THE BANKER MUST REFUSE THE PAYMENT

1. *When the customer has countermanded payment*
2. *When the customer has died*
3. *When the customer has become insolvent*
4. *When the customer has become a person of unsound mind (i.e. insane)*
5. *When a garnishee order has been received by the banker*
6. *When the cheque is lost*
7. *When the account is closed*
8. *When holder's title is defective*

Following are the circumstances in which the banker is *bound to refuse* the payment of a cheque:

1. *When the customer has countermanded payment.* The term 'countermand' means the issue of instruction to the banker not to pay a particular cheque. Thus, where a customer issues instructions to the banker not to make the payment of a particular cheque, the banker must not make the payment. A cheque, the payment of which is stopped by the customer is known as a 'stopped cheque'. And a stopped cheque is a piece of waste paper in the hands of payee. It is, however, necessary that a countermand to be effective must reach the banker before he had paid the cheque in the ordinary course. It may also be noted that the countermand notice must be duly signed by the customer and give correct particulars of the cheque.

2. *When the customer has died.* Sometimes, the banker receives notice of customer's death. In such cases, he must refuse the payment of the cheque presented after the notice of death. However, if the payment is made before the banker receives the notice of death, the payment is valid and banker is justified in making such payment.

3. *When the customer has become insolvent.* Sometimes, the banker receives the notice of customer's insolvency. In such cases also, he must refuse the payment of the cheques presented after the notice.

4. *When the customer has become a person of unsound mind (i.e. insane).* Sometimes, the banker receives the notice that his customer has become insane. In such cases also, he must refuse payment of the cheque presented after the notice.

5. *When a garnishee order has been received by the banker.* The term 'garnishee order' may be defined as a court order attaching the balance in customer's account. When the banker receives such order, then he is bound to refuse the payment of the customer's cheque.

6. *When the cheque is lost.* Sometimes, the drawer informs the banker that a particular cheque is lost. In such cases, banker must refuse the payment of that cheque.

7. *When the account is closed.* Sometimes, the customer closes his account and gives notice to the banker. In such cases, the banker must not pay any cheque of the customer after the closure of the account.

8. *When holder's title is defective.* Sometimes, the banker comes to know of any defect in the title of the person presenting the cheque. In such cases, he must refuse the payment of the cheque.

Note. Other provisions relating to the Banker and Customer relationship such as liability of the drawer (*i.e.* customer) of a cheque, liability of the drawee (*i.e.* banker) of a cheque, discharge of banker from liability, protection of a paying banker and protection of a collecting banker have already been discussed in chapters 36, 39 and 40.

TEST QUESTIONS

1. Define the terms 'banker' and 'customer'. State the special features of legal relationship between a banker and his customer.
2. "A banker is bound to honour his customer's cheque". Discuss fully, and state to what extent this statement is true.

3. Are there any circumstances in which the banker is justified in refusing the payment of his customer's cheque? If yes, discuss separately the circumstances when the banker may refuse the payment, and the circumstances in which the banker must refuse the payment.
4. State the circumstances under which a banker would be justified in dishonouring a cheque.
5. Write notes on the following:
   (a) Banker's obligation to honour cheques of his customer.
   (b) Banker's liability to the payee of a cheque if the banker refuses payment.

MULTIPLE CHOICE QUESTIONS

1. The term 'banker' as defined in Section 3 of the Negotiable Instruments Act, also includes any post office saving bank.
   (a) True (b) False
2. The term 'customer', in relation to a banker, means a person who keeps with a banker
   (a) current account for six months (b) deposit account for six months
   (c) both accounts for six months (d) either account irrespective of duration.
3. In case of banker's refusal to honour the cheque inspite of sufficient funds in customer's account, the banker is
   (a) liable to compensate the drawer (b) not liable to compensate drawer
   (c) criminally liable under section 138 (d) liable to be delisted.
4. In case of dishonour of a cheque due to insufficient funds in drawer's account, the drawer is liable to imprisonment which may extend upto
   (a) three months (b) six months
   (c) one year (d) two years.
5. In which of the following circumstances, a banker may refuse to make the payment of his customer's cheque?
   (a) where cheque is post dated (b) where cheque is stale
   (c) where funds are insufficient (d) in all the above cases
6. The banker must refuse to make the payment of a cheque where the customer has countermanded payment or where a garnishee order has been received by the banker.
   (a) True (b) False

ANSWERS

1. (a)	2. (d)	3. (a)	4. (c)	5. (d)	6. (a)

OBJECTIVE TYPE QUESTIONS WITH REASONING

State with reasons whether the following statements are correct or incorrect.

1. A person who goes to the bank to buy a draft becomes the customer of the bank for the legal purpose.
2. A banker is under no obligation to honour the cheques of his customer even if there are sufficient funds in customer's account.
3. A banker has the right to retain, as security, any goods bailed to him by his customer.
4. A banker who refuses the payment of a post-dated cheque is liable to compensate his customer on account of dishonour of the cheque.
5. The banker must refuse to make the payment of a cheque where the customer has countermanded payment.

ANSWERS

1. *Incorrect.* A casual act of service does not create the relationship of banker and customer.
2. *Incorrect.* In case of sufficient funds in customer's account, the banker is legally bound to honour the cheques of his customer.
3. *Correct.* A banker has a right of general lien [Section 171, the Indian contract act, 1872].
4. *Incorrect.* A banker is justified in refusing the payment of a post-dated cheque.
5. *Correct.* By countermanding payment, the customer issues specific instructions to stop the payment of a particular cheque.

43
CHAPTER

HUNDIS

43.1. INTRODUCTION

We have already discussed that the Negotiable Instruments Act deals only with three kinds of negotiable instruments, namely, promissory notes, bills of exchange and cheque. However, there are many other negotiable instruments recognised by the local usages and customs. A hundi is one of those instruments. The term 'hundi' is derived from the Sanskrit word *'hund'* which means *'to collect*. Thus, hundi is an instrument which enables a person to collect the money mentioned in it.

The hundis are negotiable instruments written in vernacular language *i.e.* in an ordinary everyday language of the people of the particular place. In other words, a hundi is an indigenous negotiable instrument written in local language of the people. The hundis may be in the form of promissory note or bill of exchange. But more often, they are in the form of bill of exchange. It will be interesting to know that the hundis have been in circulation in India even before the Negotiable Instruments Act, 1881 came into existence, and have been recognised by the customary law as valid and effective negotiable instruments. It may, however, be noted that the provisions of Negotiable Instruments Act do not apply to hundis. They are governed by the local usages and customs of the trade where they are intended to be used. Thus, an oral acceptance of hundis is valid. Moreover, a notice of dishonour may not be required to be given if there is a custom to that effect. But if there is no customary rule on a particular point, the courts may apply the provisions of the Negotiable Instruments Act. Moreover, the provisions of this Act may also apply if the parties have expressly excluded any customary rule by their agreement.

43.2. CLASSIFICATION OF HUNDIS

1. *Darshani hundi*
2. *Muddati or miadi hundi*

The hundis may broadly be classified into the following two categories, namely:

1. ***Darshani hundi.*** The term *'darshani'* means *'at sight'*. Thus, a darshani hundi is one which is payable at sight. It is just like a demand bill of exchange *i.e.* which is payable on demand. A darshani hundi should be presented for payment within a reasonable time by the holder.

2. ***Muddati or miadi hundi.*** The term *'muddat'* or *miad'* means a specified time.

Thus, *muddati* or *miadi* hundi is one which is payable after a specified period of time *e.g.* sixty days after sight etc. It is just like a time bill of exchange *i.e.* which is payable at a certain time in future.

43.3. KINDS OF HUNDIS

We have discussed, in the last article, the two main categories of hundis. There are several kinds of hundis prevalent in the country which may belong to any of the two main categories. Following are some of the commonly known and important kinds of hundi which may be either darshani or muddati:

1. Shah jog hundi. 2. Nam jog hundi. 3. Firman hundi. 4. Dhani jog hundi.

5. Jawabi hundi. 6. Jokhami hundi.

43.4. SHAH JOG HUNDI

The term *'shah'* means a respectable person. Thus, a shah jog hundi is one which is payable only to a shah. It is freely transferable from one person to another by mere delivery, and no indorsement is required for the same. However, the shah jog hundi is transferable till it reaches the hands of the shah. Once the hundi reaches the shah, he should, after making due enquiries to secure himself, present it to the drawee for acceptance or for payment. The drawee of the hundi (*i.e.* the person on whom the hundi is drawn), must make sure that he makes the payment on it only to a shah. However, he is not bound to pay the amount unless he is satisfied as to the respectability and creditworthiness of the shah presenting the hundi. If he makes payment to a person other than the shah, he will not be entitled to recover the money so paid, from the drawer (*i.e.* the maker of the hundi). It may be noted that the name of the shah must be indorsed on the hundi when it is presented (*i.e.* the last indorsee must be the shah presenting the hundi). If shah's name is not indorsed on the hundi, the drawee may refuse the payment. If after acceptance, the shah indorses the hundi to some other person, the drawee can refuse to make the payment, as the payment can be made only to the shah.

A shah jog hundi is payable on the responsibility of the shah. As a matter of fact, the shah guarantees the genuineness of the hundi. And thus if the hundi turns out to be false or stolen one, the money paid by the drawee can be recovered by him from the shah by filing a separate suit against him. It may, however, be noted that the shah does not guarantee the solvency of the drawer of hundi.

Notes. 1. A shah jog hundi differs from a bill of exchange in two respects, namely (*a*) the acceptance of the drawee is not generally written across the hundi, but the particulars are entered in drawer's book. (*b*) usually, it is not presented for acceptance before the due date for payment.

2. Although, a shah jog hundi is transferable by delivery. But it is not similar to a bearer bill of exchange, because its transferability is restricted when it is indorsed to a shah.

3. In case of fraud or forgery, the holder is relieved from liability if he produces the person who has committed the fraud or forgery.

43.5. NAM JOG HUNDI

The term *'nam'* means the name of a person. Thus, a nam jog hundi is one which is payable to the person named in the hundi or according to his order. It is similar to a shah jog hundi, except that in place of the word 'shah' the name of the payee is mentioned in the hundi. It can be negotiated like a bill of exchange payable to order.

43.6. FIRMAN HUNDI

The term *'firman'* means order. Thus, a firman hundis one which is payable to order. It can be negotiated like instruments payable to order *i.e.* by indorsement and delivery.

43.7. DHANI JOG HUNDI

The term *'dhani'* means holder. Thus, a dhani jog hundi is one which is payable to the holder or bearer. It can be negotiated like instruments payable to bearer *i.e.* by mere delivery. It is also known a *'dekhandar hundi'*.

43.8. JAWABI HUNDI

The term *'jawabi'* means the answer. Thus, a jawabi hundi is one which is used for remittance of money from one place to another. On receipt of the money, the payee has to send an answer (*i.e.* jawab), to the person remitting the money, that he has received the money. In this case, the money is remitted through a banker. The person desirous of sending the money, writes a jawabi hundi and delivers the same to his banker alongwith the remittance (*i.e.* money). And the banker either indorses the hundi on any of its branch near the payee's place or negotiates its transfer.

On making the payment to the payee, his receipt is obtained on the letter, and the same is sent to the drawer in the same order. It, thus, resembles money order.

43.9. JOKHAMI HUNDI

The term *'jokham'* means the risk. Thus, a jokhami hundi is one which is drawn, by the seller on the buyer for the price of the goods sold, and which also covers the risk of loss of goods till they reach the buyer. It implies a condition that the money shall be payable by the drawee (who is the buyer) only in the event of safe arrival of the goods against which the hundi is drawn. It may be noted that the custom of drawing jokhami hundi is prevalent when the goods sold are to be sent through ships.

A jokhami hundi is drawn by the consignor of goods on the consignee for the price of the goods shipped on the ship mentioned in the hundi. The hundi is then negotiated by the drawer (consignor) to a third person (generally an insurer) who charges some commission for the risk involved, and pays the price to the drawer after deducting his commission. If the goods arrive safely, the insurer may recover the goods or the full amount of the hundi from the consignee, (drawee) as stated in the hundi. And if the goods are lost in transit the loss falls on the insurer.[1] Thus, a jokhami hundi is the combination of a bill of exchange and an insurance policy because it is drawn with two-fold objects, namely:

1. To put the drawer of the hundi in funds. As by indorsing the hundi to the insurer, he immediately gets the purchase price of the goods less commission charges.
2. To protect the buyer who is liable to pay the price only when he receives the goods. As the hundi is negotiated to the insurer, the loss falls on him (insurer) if the goods are lost in transit.

Note. The jokhami hundi is in the nature of an insurance policy with the difference that the money is paid by the insurer beforehand *i.e.* before the loss of the goods, and can be recovered back by him if the ship carrying the goods arrive, safely. Whereas, in case of insurance policy, the insurer pays the money only when the loss is suffered by the insured person.

43.10. IMPORTANT TERMS

1. ***Zickri chit***
2. ***Peth***
3. ***Perpeth***
4. ***Purja***
5. ***Khoka***

Following are some of the important terms in connection with the hundis:

1. *Zickri chit.* The term 'zickri chit' may be defined as the letter of protection given to the holder of a hundi by the drawer or any prior party (*i.e.* party prior to holder). It is addressed to some respectable person residing in the town where the hundi is payable, requesting him to pay the amount of the hundi in case of its dishonour (*i.e.* in

1. As regards the loss of goods during sea transit, the rule of marine insurance shall apply.

case the drawee refuses to accept or pay the amount of the hundi). And in case of dishonour of hundis, such person accepts the hundi and pays its amount on maturity. The position of such a person is just like an 'acceptor for honour'.

2. *Peth.* The term 'peth' may be defined as the duplicate of a hundi. Sometimes, the original hundi is lost. In such cases, the holder may demand from the drawer a duplicate one. Such a duplicate hundi is called a 'peth'.

3. *Perpeth.* The term 'perpeth' may be defined as the duplicate of the duplicate hundi. Sometimes, a peth is lost. In such cases, the holder may demand from the holder another duplicate and so on. And each of the subsequent duplicates is called a 'perpeth'.

4. *Purja.* The term 'purja' may be defined as a request in writing by the borrower to the lender to pay the amount mentioned therein. It bears a ten paise stamp. It may be noted that 'purja' is not a negotiable instrument. These are commonly used for temporary loans.

5. *Khoka.* A hundi when paid up and cancelled is then called a 'khoka'.

TEST QUESTIONS

1. Define the term hundi. State the various classes and kinds of a hundi.
2. State the law which governs the hundis. Does the Negotiable Instruments Act apply to hundis?
3. Write notes on: (*a*) Shah jog hundi. (*b*) Jokhami hundi. (*c*) Zickri chit.

MULTIPLE CHOICE QUESTIONS

1. A hundi is an indigeneous negotiable instrument written in local language of people, which may be in the form of either a bill of exchange or a promissory note.
   (*a*) True, as it is the accepted definition
   (*b*) False, as hundi is always in the form of a bill of exchange
2. A hundi which is payable 'at sight' is known as
   (*a*) miadi hundi (*b*) zikri hundi
   (*c*) darshani hundi (*d*) none of these
3. A hundi which is payable to the holder or bearer is known as
   (*a*) nam jog hundi (*b*) firman hundi
   (*c*) jawabi hundi (*d*) dhani jog hundi
4. A letter of protection given by a drawer to the holder of a hundi which enables him to receive payment in case of dishonour, is known as
   (*a*) Zickri chit (*b*) Perpeth
   (*c*) Khoka (*d*) Purja
5. The duplicate of a hundi is known as
   (*a*) Perpeth (*b*) Peth
   (*c*) Khoka (*d*) Purja
6. A hundi when paid up and cancelled, is then called
   (*a*) Perpeth (*b*) Purja
   (*c*) Khoka (*d*) none of these

ANSWERS

1. (*a*)	2. (*c*)	3. (*d*)	4. (*a*)	5. (*b*)	6. (*c*)

OBJECTIVE TYPE QUESTIONS WITH REASONING

State with reasons whether the following statements are correct or incorrect.

1. A *darshani hundi* means the hundi which is payable after a specified period of time.
2. A *firman hundi* can be negotiated by indorsement and delivery.
3. A duplicate of a hundi is known as perpeth.
4. A 'purja' is a kind of a hundi and thus a negotiable instrument.

ANSWERS

1. ***Incorrect.*** A darshani hundi is one which is payable at sight.
2. ***Correct.*** A *firman hundi* is one which is payable to order.
3. ***Incorrect.*** A duplicate of a hundi is known as peth. A perpeth is the duplicate of the duplicate hundi.
4. ***Incorrect.*** A purja is not a negotiable instrument.

The Payment of Bonus Act, 1965

- Introduction and Application of the Act
- Legal Provisions Relating to Payment of Bonus
- Miscellaneous Provisions and Schedules.

INTRODUCTION AND APPLICATION OF THE ACT

1. Introduction
2. Definition of Bonus
3. Objects of the Payment of Bonus Act.
4. Application of the Act.
5. Class of Employees to which the Act Does not Apply.
6. Definitions.

44.1. INTRODUCTION

A commission known as the Bonus Commission was appointed by the Central Government by its resolution dated 6th December, 1961. The commission submitted its report to the Government on 18th January, 1964. The Government accepted the report with slight modifications and in order to give legal effect to the recommendation of the Bonus Commission, the Government promulgated the payment of bonus ordinance in May 1965 which was subsequently replaced by the Payment of Bonus Act, 1965 in September 1965.

The Payment of Bonus Act, 1965 came into force on 25th September, 1965 and its extends to the whole of India. The Act is the comprehensive and exhaustive law dealing with bonus in all its aspects. This Act has been recently amended by the Payment of Bonus (Ammendment) Act, 2007 (45 of 2007).

In this chapter, we shall discuss the objects of the Act, application of the Act and the definitions of the important terms as used and defined in the Act.

Note. In chapters 44 to 46, unless otherwise stated, the sections mentioned are those of the Payment of Bonus Act, 1965.

44.2. DEFINITION OF BONUS

The term 'bonus' in ordinary sense means extra payment or extra benefit. Legally, this term is neither defined in the Payment of Bonus Act, 1965 nor in any other enactment. Though, there is no legal definition of the term 'bonus', but after the enactment of the Payment of Bonus Act, 1965, it is amply clear that *"bonus is the annual statutory payment made by the employer to his employees under the provisions of this Act."* In other words, bonus is the annual payment which the employer is *legally bound to pay* to his employees as per the provisions of the Payment of Bonus Act, 1965. In view of the legal sanction accorded to the payment of bonus, the earlier interpretations treating the bonus as an *ex gratia payment* (*i.e.*, payment as an act of grace) made by an employer to his workers to provide a stimulus for extra effort by them in the production process, have lost their validity and are no more relevant.

44.3. OBJECTS OF THE PAYMENT OF BONUS ACT

The object of the Act as stated in the Act, is to provide for the payment of bonus to persons employed in certain establishments and for matters connected therewith.

In *Jalan Trading Co. (P) Ltd.* v. *Mills Mazdoor Union*, AIR 1967 SC 691, the Supreme Court has observed that the object of the Payment of Bonus Act is to maintain peace and harmony between labour and capital (*i.e.* management) by allowing the employees to share the prosperity of the establishment.

Thus, keeping in view the preamble of the Act and the judicial pronouncements, the objects of the Act may be summed up as under:

1. To provide for the payment of bonus to persons employed in establishments to which the Act applies and to impose statutory liability on an employer of such establishments to pay bonus to the employees.
2. To maintain peace and harmony between labour and management.
3. To define the principles of payment of bonus according to the prescribed formula.
4. To provide for payment of minimum and maximum bonus and linking the payment of bonus with the scheme of 'set-off and set on' to ensure a reasonable degree of uniformity.
5. To provide machinery for enforcement of the liability for payment of bonus.

44.4. APPLICATION OF THE ACT

The payment of Bonus Act, 1965 extends to the whole of India [Section 1 (2)]. Regarding applicability of the Act, Section 1(3) provides that unless otherwise provided in the Act, it shall apply to the following:

1. Every factory* [Section 1(3) (a)].
2. Every other establishment in which 20 or more present are employed *on any day* during an accounting year [Section 1 (3) (*b*)].

It may, however, be noted that the appropriate government may by notification in the official gazette, apply the provisions of this act to any establishment employing less than 20 but not less than 10 persons. The appropriate Government can do so after giving a notice of not less than two months of its intention to do so [Section 1 (3), proviso]. This provision has been introduced for the benefit of the employees of smaller concerns which were not earlier covered by the Act.

Following some of the important points regarding the applicability of the Act:

(*a*) The employment of 20 or more persons even for one day in a year is sufficient to attract the provisions of the Act. The requirement of Section 1 (3) (*b*) is the employment of 20 or more persons *on any day* during an accounting year.

(*b*) An establishment to which this Act applies shall continue to be governed by the Act even if the number of persons employed therein falls below 20, or as the case may be, below the number specified in the notification applying the Act to other establishment employing less than 20 persons [Section 1 (5)].

(*c*) The appropriate Government may, by Gazette notification, exempt any establishment or class of establishments from the application of all or any of the provisions of the Payment of Bonus Act, 1965. The appropriate Government may do so if, after considering the financial position and other relevant circumstances of such establishment, it is of the opinion that it will not be in public interest to apply all or any of the provisions of this Act to the establishment. The exemption may be for a period specified in the notification and subject to such conditions as the government may think it to impose [Section 36].

* Factory means the factory as defined in Section 2 (*m*) of the Factories Act, 1948 [Section 2(17), the payment of Bonus Act, 1965].

44.5. CLASSES OF EMPLOYEES TO WHICH THE ACT DOES NOT APPLY

Section 32 specifies certain classes of employees to which the Payment of Bonus Act, 1965 does not apply. As per this section, following categories of employees are excluded from the operation of this Act:

1. Employees employed by the Life Insurance Corporation of India;
2. Seamen as defined in clause (42) of section 3 of the Merchant Shipping Act, 1958.
3. Employees registered or listed under any scheme made under the Dock Workers (Regulation of Employment) Act, 1948, and employed by registered or listed employers;
4. Employees employed by an establishment engaged in any industry carried on by or under the authority of any department of the Central Government or a State Government or a local authority;
5. Employees employed by,
   (*a*) the Indian Red Cross Society or any other institution of a like nature (including its branches);
   (*b*) universities and other educational institutions;
   (*c*) institutions (including hospitals, chambers of commerce and social welfare institutions) established not for purposes of profit;
6. *Employees employed through contractors on building operations;*
   Note : *The clause 6 stated above has been omitted by the Payment of Bonus (Amendment) Act, 2007 (45 of 2007) w.e.f., 1-4-2006. Now the Act would be applicable to the employees employed through contractors on building operations.*
7. Employees employed by the Reserve Bank of India;
8. Employees employed by,
   (*a*) the Industrial Finance Corporation of India;
   (*b*) any financial corporation established under section 3, or any joint financial corporation established under Section 3A, of the State Financial Corporations Act, 1951;
   (*c*) the Deposit Insurance Corporation;
   (*d*) The National Bank of Agriculture and Rural Development;
   (*e*) the Unit Trust of India;
   (*f*) the Industrial Development Bank of India;
   (*g*) the Small Industries Development Bank of India established under Section 3 of the Small Industries Development Bank of India Act, 1989;
   (*h*) the National Housing Bank;
   (*i*) any other financial institution other than a banking company being an establishment in public sector, which the Central Government may, by notification in the Official Gazette, specify, having regard to
      (*i*) its capital structure;
      (*ii*) its objectives and the nature of its activities;
      (*iii*) the nature and extent of financial assistance or any concession given to it by the government; and
      (*iv*) any other relevant factor;
9. Employees employed by inland water transport establishments operating on routes passing through any other country.

44.6. DEFINITIONS

The terms and expressions used in the Payment of Bonus Act, 1965 are defined in various sub-sections of section 2 of the Act and are discussed in the following pages. It is important to note here that the words and expressions used but not defined in this Act and defined in the Industrial Disputes Act, 1947, shall have the same meaning respectively assigned to them in that Act [Section 2 (22)].

1. Accounting year

The term 'accounting year' is defined in Section 2 (1) of the Act. The period which constitute accounting year has been defined differently in relation to different kind of establishment *i.e.* whether it is a corporation or a company or any other establishment:

(*a*) *In relation to a corporation,* the accounting year means the year ending on the day on which the books and accounts of the corporation are to be closed and balanced;

(*b*) *In relation to a company,* the accounting year means the period in respect of which any profit and loss account of the company laid before it in annual general meeting is made up, whether that period is a year or not;

(*c*) *In any other case,* the accounting year means

(*i*) the year commencing on the 1st day of April; or

(*ii*) if the accounts of an establishment maintained by the employer thereof are closed and balanced on any day other than the 31st day of March, then, at the option of the employer, the year ending on the day on which its accounts are so closed and balanced:

It may, however be noted that once an option is exercised by the employer under clause (*ii*), above, it shall not again be changed except with the previous written permission of the prescribed authority and upon such conditions as that authority may think fit.

2. Allocable surplus

The term 'allocable surplus' is defined in section 2 (4) of the Act. It is the workers' share in available surplus. The percentage which constitutes 'allocable surplus' differs in relation to an employer being a company, and in other cases.

(*a*) *In relation to an employer, being a company* (other than a banking company) which has not made the arrangements prescribed under the Income Tax Act for the declaration and payment within India of the dividends payable out of its profits in accordance with the provisions of section 194 of that Act, the 'allocable surplus' means 67% of the available surplus in an accounting year.

(*b*) *In relation to any other employer*, the 'allocable surplus' means 60% of the available surplus in an accounting year.

3. Appropriate Government

The term 'appropriate government' is defined in section 2(5) of the Act, as under:

(*a*) In relation to an establishment in respect of which the appropriate government under the Industrial Disputes Act, 1947 is the Central Government, the appropriate government for the purposes of this Act is the Central Government.

(*b*) In relation to any other establishment, the appropriate government for the purpose of this Act is the Government of the State in which such establishment is situated.

4. Available surplus

The term 'available surplus' is defined in section 2(6) of the Act, and it means the available surplus computed under Section 5 of the Act.

According to Section 5, the available surplus in respect of any accounting year shall be the *gross profits* for that year after deducting from it certain prior charges as mentioned in section 6. To arrive at the available surplus, the following sums, as specified in section 6, are deductible from the gross profits:

(*a*) Any amount of depreciation admissible under the Income Tax Act.

(*b*) Any amount of development rebate, development allowance or investment allowance which is allowed as deduction under the Income Tax Act.

(*c*) Any direct tax which the employer is liable to pay on his income, profits and gains during the accounting year.

(*d*) Such sums as are specified in the Third schedule. This schedule specifies certain sums to be deductible in respect of different categories of employers.

Note. Computation of available surplus will be discussed in detail in Chapter 46.

5. Award

The term award is defined in Section 2 (7) of the Act, and for the purposes of this Act, it means an interim or a final determination of any industrial dispute or of any question relating thereto by any Labour Court, Industrial Tribunal, or National Tribunal constituted under the Industrial Disputes Act, 1947, or by any other authority constituted under any corresponding law relating to investigation and settlement of industrial disputes in force in a State and includes an arbitration award made under section 10A of that Act or under that law.

6. Banking company

The term 'banking company' is defined in section 2 (8) of the Act, and for the purposes of this Act, it means a banking company as defined in section 5 of the Banking Companies Act, 1949, and includes the State Bank of India, any subsidiary bank as defined in the State Bank of India (Subsidiary Banks) Act, 1959, any corresponding new bank specified in the First Schedule to the Banking Companies (Acquisition and Transfer of Undertakings) Act, 1970, any corresponding new bank constituted under section 3 of the Banking Companies (Acquisition and Transfer of Undertakings) Act, 1980, any co-operative bank as defined in clause (bii) of section 2 of the Reserve Bank of India Act, 1934 and any other banking institution which may be notified in this behalf by the Central Government.

7. Company

The term 'company' is defined in Section 2 (9) of the Act, and for the purposes of this Act, it means any company as defined in Section 3 of the companies Act, 1956 and also includes a foreign company as defined in the Companies Act.

8. Co-operative society

The term 'co-operative society' is defined in Section 2 (10) of the Act, and for the purposes of this Act, it means a society registered or deemed to be registered under the Co-operative Societies Act, 1912, or any other law for the time being in force in any State relating to co-operative societies.

9. Corporation

The term 'corporation' is defined in Section 2 (11) of the Act, and for the purposes of this Act, it means any body corporate established by or under any Central, Provincial or State Act but does not include a company or a co-operative society.

10. Direct Tax

The term 'direct tax' is defined in Section 2 (12) of the Act, and for the purposes of this Act, it means the following taxes:

(*a*) Any tax chargeable under the following Acts:

- (*i*) The Income Tax Act.
- (*ii*) The Super Profits Tax Act, 1963
- (*iii*) The companies (Profits) Surtax Act, 1964.
- (*iv*) The Agricultural Income Tax Laws, and;

(*b*) Any other tax which the central government may by notification declare to be a direct tax for the purposes of this Act.

11. Employee

The term 'employee' is defined in Section 2 (13) of the Act, and for the purposes of this Act, it means any person (other than an apprentice) employed on a salary or wages not exceeding Rs. 10,000* per month in any industry to do any skilled or unskilled, mannal, supervisory, managerial, administrative, technical or clerical work for hire or reward. It makes no difference whether the terms of employment of such person are express or implied.

12. Employer

The term 'employer' is defined in Section 2(14) of the Act, and for the purposes of this Act, it is defined separately in relation to an establishment which is a factory and in relation to any other establishment:

1. ***In relation to an establishment which is a factory:*** In this case, the employer means the following persons:
   (*a*) The owner or occupier of the factory.
   (*b*) The agent of such owner or occupier.
   (*c*) The legal representatives of a deceased owner or occupier of the factory.
   (*d*) The person named as a manager of the factory under Section 7 (1)(f) of the Factories Act, 1948.
2. ***In relation to any other establishment:*** In this case, the employer means the following persons:
   (*a*) The person who has the ultimate control over the affairs of the establishment.
   (*b*) The authority which has the ultimate control over the affairs of the establishment.
   (*c*) The manager, managing director or managing agent of the establishment where the affairs of the such establishment are entrusted to such manager, managing director or managing agent.

13. Establishment in Public Sector

The term 'establishment in public sector' is defined in section 2 (16) of the Act, and for the purposes of this Act, it means an establishment owned, controlled or managed by:

(*a*) a government company as defined in section 617 of the Companies Act, 1956;
(*b*) a corporation in which not less than 40% of its capital is held (whether singly or taken together) by,
   (*i*) the government; or
   (*ii*) the Reserve Bank of India; or
   (*iii*) a corporation owned by the government or the Reserve Bank of India;

14. Establishment in Private Sector

It mean any establishment other than an establishment in public sector [Section 2 (15)].

15. Gross Profits

The term 'gross profits' is defined in section 2 (18) of the Act, and it means the gross profits calculated under Section 4 of the Act. Section 4 provides that the gross profits derived by an employer from an establishment in respect of the accounting year shall,

* This limit has been increased from Rs. 3,500 by the Payment of Bonus (Amendment) Act, 2007 w.e.f., of 1-4-2006. Earlier the limit of Rs. 3500 was applicable which was increased from Rs. 2500 by the Payment of Bonus (Amendment Act, 1995.

(*a*) in the case of a banking company, be calculated in the manner specified in the First Schedule;

(*b*) in any other case, be calculated in the manner specified in the Second Schedule.

The First Schedule and the Second Schedule of the Payment of Bonus Act, 1965 specifies the items which are to be added and deducted for the computation of gross profits of the respective companies. These schedules have been reproduced as Annexures I and Annexures II at the end of Chapter No. 46

16. Salary or Wages

The terms 'salary or wages' is defined in Section 2 (21) of the Act stating therein what is included in the salary or wages and what is excluded from it.

As per this section, the salary or wages means all remuneration capable of being expressed in terms of money which would, on the fulfilment of the express or implied terms of employment, be payable to an employee in respect of his employment or work done in such employment. It will also **include** dearness allowance (*i.e.,* all cash payments by whatever name called, paid to an employee on account of rise in the cost of living). However, the following items/allowances are **not included** in the salary or wages.

(*a*) Any remuneration in respect of over-time work.

(*b*) Any other allowance which the employee is for the time being entitled to;

(*c*) The value of any house accommodation or of supply of light, water, medical attendance or other amenity or of any service or of any concessional supply of foodgrains or other articles;

(*d*) Any travelling concession.

(*e*) Any bonus (including incentive, production and attendance bonus);

(*f*) Any contribution paid or payable by the employer to any pension fund or provident fund or for the benefit of the employee under any law for the time being in force;

(*g*) Any retrenchment compensation or any gratuity or other retirement benefit payable to the employee or any ex gratia payment made to him;

(*h*) Any commission payable to the employee.

It is important to note here that where an employee is given in lieu of the whole or part of the salary or wage payable to him, free food allowance or free food by his employer, such food allowance or the value of such food shall, for the purpose of this clause, be deemed to form part of the salary or wage of such employee. [Section 2 (21), Explanation].

TEST QUESTIONS

1. State the objects of the Payment of Bonus Act and explain how the term 'bonus' can be defined? Explain clearly the legal provisions relating to the applicability of the Act.
2. Giving the relevant section, state the classes of employees to which the payment of Bonus Act does not apply.
3. Explain the following terms as defined in the payment of Bonus Act, 1965

   (*a*) Accounting year (*b*) Employee

   (*c*) Employer (*d*) Establishment in public sector
4. Define the terms 'allocable surplus' and 'available surplus' stating clearly the prior charges which are to be deducted from the gross profit to arrive at the available surplus.

5. Define the term employee as used in the payment of Bonus Act. State the items/allowances which are not included in the salary to wages payable to an employee.

MULTIPLE CHOICE QUESTIONS

1. The Payment of Bonus Act, 1965 came into force on 25th September, 1965 and it extends to the
   (*a*) whole of India
   (*b*) Whole of India except the state of Jammu and Kashmir
   (*c*) States notified by the government from time to time
   (*d*) all the states except the union territories.
2. The Payment of Bonus Act, 1965 applies to
   (*a*) every factory as defined in Section 2 (*m*) of the Industrial Disputes Act, 1947.
   (*b*) every other establishment in which 20 or more persons are employed on any day during an accounting year.
   (*c*) both (*a*) and (*b*)
   (*d*) none of these.
3. For the applicability of the payment of Bonus Act, 1965 to an establishment, it is obligatory that 20 or more person must have been employed and working in an establishment through out the accounting year.
   (*a*) True (*b*) False
4. The Payment of Bonus Act, 1965 does not apply to the employees employed by the
   (*a*) Industrial Finance Corporation of India
   (*b*) Reserve Bank of India
   (*c*) Universities and other educational institutions.
   (*d*) All of the above
5. In which of the following sections of the payment of Bonus Act, 1965, the term 'bonus' is defined?
   (*a*) Section 2 (4) (*b*) Section 2 (13)
   (*c*) Section 2 (21) (*d*) none of these

ANSWERS

1. (*a*)	2. (*c*)	3. (*b*)	4. (*d*)	5. (*d*)

OBJECTIVE TYPE QUESTIONS WITH REASONING

State with reasons whether the following statements are correct or incorrect.

1. The payment of Bonus Act, 1965 applies to an establishment in which 20 or more persons have been employeed through out the year.
2. The expressions used but not defined in the payment of Bonus Act, 1965 shall have the same meaning as assigned to them in the Industrial Disputes Act, 1947.
3. The expression 'employee' for the purposes of the Payment of Bonus Act, 1965 means a person employed in any industry on a monthly salary or wages not exceeding Rs. 10,000.
4. The expression 'salary or wages' includes the amount of bonus payable to an employee.

ANSWERS

1. ***Incorrect.*** The requirement of law is that the employment of 20 or more persons *on any day* during an accounting year is sufficient for the applicability of the Act [Section 1(3) (*b*)].

2. ***Correct.*** Section 2(22) of the Act makes a specific provision in the regard.
3. ***Correct.*** Earlier the limit of monthly salary was Rs. 3500 which has been raised to Rs. 10,000 by the Payment of Bonus (Amendment) Act, 2007.
4. ***Incorrect.*** The 'bonus' has been expressly excluded from the term 'salary or wages' as defined in section 2 (21).

PRACTICAL PROBLEMS

1. State with reasons whether the following persons are entitled to receive bonus under the Payment of Bonus Act, 1965:
   (*a*) An apprentice under the Apprentice Act.
   (*b*) An employee employed through contractors on building operations.

   Hint : (*a*) An apprentice is not entitled to receive bonus under the Payment of Bonus Act, 1965 as he is excluded from the definition of employee under section 2 (13).

   (*b*) In view of the Payment of Bonus (Amendment) Act, 2007, such an employee has become entitled to receive bonus. Prior to this amendment, such an employee was excluded from entitlement for bonus under Section 32, claus (vi). Now this clause has been omittled by this Amendment Act of 2007.
2. A workshop is employing 50 workmen. A shop-supervisor is drawing a monthly wages of Rs. 9000. HRD paid bonus to all employees except the supervisor. The supervisor contends that he is also entitled to bonus. Refering to the provisions of Payment of Bonus Act, 1965, decide whether HRD's action is correct ?

   Hints: No, HRD's action is not correct. The upper limit of salary fixed in section 2 (13) has been increased from Rs.3500 to Rs 10,000 p.m. by the Payment of Bonus (Amendment) Act, 2007. In view of this, the supervisor drawing monthly salary of Rs. 9000 is entitled to receive bonus from the company.

45

CHAPTER

LEGAL PROVISIONS RELATING TO PAYMENT OF BONUS

45.1. INTRODUCTION

The payment of bonus to the employees is the statutory liability of an employer. It is calculated and paid as per the provisions of the Payment of Bonus Act, 1965. The different legal provisions of the Act relating to the eligibility for bonus, disqualification for bonus, calculation of bonus, payment of minimum and maximum bonus etc. specify the rules regarding the payment of bonus. In this chapter we shall explain and discuss all the legal provisions relating to the payment of bonus.

The amount of bonus payable to an employee under the Payment of Bonus Act, 1965, shall be paid in cash [Section 19]. The bonus is payable even if there are losses in an accounting year. This ensures the regular payment of bonus to the employees.

45.2. RULES REGARDING THE PAYMENT OF BONUS

The rules regarding the payment of bonus as contained in various sections of the Act may be discussed under the following heads:

1. Eligibility for bonus [section 8]
2. Disqualification for bonus [section 9]
3. Payment of minimum bonus [section 10]
4. Payment of maximum bonus [section 11]
5. Calculation of bonus with respect to certain employees [section 12]
6. Proportionate reduction of bonus in certain cases [Section 13]
7. Computation of number of working days [Section 14]
8. Adjustment of customary or interim bonus against bonus payable under the Act [Section 17]

9. Time limit for payment of bonus [Section 19]
10. Recovery of bonus due from an employer [Section 21]
11. Payment of bonus linked with production or productivity [Section 31 A].

45.3. ELIGIBILITY FOR BONUS

The eligibility for bonus is provided in Section 8 of the Act. As per this section *every employee* shall be entitled to be paid bonus by his employer in an accounting year in accordance with the provisions of this Act provided he has *worked* in the establishment for not less 30 working days in that year.

The words 'worked' is section 8 should mean "ready and willing to work". Thus, when an employee is *suspended* by the employer but is subsequently reinstated in service, then it cannot be said that such an employee did not work for the establishment. In such a case, the employee is ready and willing to work but he is prevented from working by an overt act on the part of the employer[1].

An employee in the following cases is held to be entitled to bonus under the Act.

1. A probationer is an employee and as such is entitled to bonus.
[*Bank of Madura Ltd.* v. *Employee's union*, 1970 (2) LLJ 21]
2. A retrenched employee is eligible to get bonus provided he has worked for minimum qualifying period.
[*East Asiatic Co. (P) Ltd.* v. *Industrial Tribunal*, (1961) 1 LLJ 720].
3. A dismissed employee reinstated with back wages is entitled to bonus.
[*Gannon India Ltd.* v. *Niranjan Das* (1984) 2 LLJ 223]
4. A piece-rated worker is entitled to bonus.
[*Mathuradas Kani* v. *L.A. Tribunal*, AIR 1958 SC 899]
5. A part-time employee as a sweeper engaged on regular basis is entitled to bonus.
[*Automobile Karamchari Sangh* v. *Industrial Tribunal*, (1970) 38 FJR 268]
6. A temporary employee is entitled to bonus on the basis of total number of days worked by him.

Note. An employee is covered under the definition of employee as given in Section 2 (13) if his salary per month does not exceed Rs. 10,000. If an employee's is salary exceeds this limit, then he will not be covered by the definition of employee and thus would not be eligible for bonus under the Act. The maximum limit of monthly salary has been increased from Rs. 3500 by the Payment of Bonus (Amendment) Act, 2007 w.e.f. 1. 4. 2006.

45.4. DISQUALIFICATION FOR BONUS

The disqualification for bonus is provided in section 9. As per this section, an employee shall be disqualified from receiving bonus under the Act, if he is *dismissed* from service on account of the following reasons:

(*a*) Fraud, or
(*b*) Riotous or violent behaviour while on the premises of the establishment, or
(*c*) Theft, misappropriation or sabotage of any property of the establishment.

The important question on the point of disqualification of bonus is that whether an employee dismissed from service is disqualified from receiving *any bonus* under the Act or only the bonus of the accounting year in which the said act of misconduct (fraud, theft etc). was committed? The different High Courts have taken different view on this point which is explained by the following example.

Example. 45.1. An employee working in an establishment commits fraud during the accounting year 2000-2001but continues to work during the subsequent accounting years 2001-2002 and 2002-2003, and has clean record during these subsequent years. On the basis of the fraud commit-

1. *Project Manager, Ahemdabad Project, ONGC. Sabramati* v. *Sharm K. Sehgal (expired) by his Legal Representative,* (1995) 1 LLJ 863 (Guj).

ted in 2000-2001, the employee is dismissed from service at the end of the accounting year 2002-2003. In this case, does he lose the bonus for the accounting year of misconduct *i.e.* 2000-2001 or for all the three accounting years ending with 2002-2003.

On the point involved in the above example, the views expressed by the Karnatka and Patna High Courts are as under:

1. The employee does not lose the bonus for the subsequent accounting years 2001-2002 and 2002-2003 as the right of the management to forfeit bonus would be only with reference to the accounting years in which the said misconduct was committed and not with reference to any years preceding or succeeding the accounting year in question. [*Himalaya Drug Co. Makali* v. *II Addl. Labour Court, Bangalore,* (1986) 2 Lab. LJ 45 (Karnataka)].
2. The employee loses the bonus for the subsequent accounting years also as in case of dismissal, the employee stands disqualified from receiving *any bonus* under the Act and not only the bonus of the accounting year in question. [*M/s Sriram Bearings Ltd.* v. *The Presiding Officer, Labour Court, Ranchi,* (1986)2 Lab LJ 459 (Patna)].

In *Pandian Roadways Corpn. Ltd.* v. *Presiding Officer,* (1996) 2 CLR 1175 (Madras), the Madras High Court has also taken the view that an employee who is dismissed from service on the ground of misconduct as mentioned in Section 9, is disqualified from *any bonus* and not merely for the bonus of the accounting year in which he is dismissed.

An employee in the following cases, is not entitled to any bonus:

1. An employee employed through contractors on building operation is not entitled to bonus [Section 32 (vi)].
2. An employee employed by inland water transport establishments operating on routers passing through any other country [Section 32 (*xi*)].
3. An apprentice is not entitled to bonus.

[*Wheel & RIM Co.* v. *Govt. of T.N.* (1971) 2 LLJ 299]

45.5. PAYMENT OF MINIMUM BONUS

The legal provisions relating to the payment of minimum bonus are contained in Section 10, which was amended in 1980, and may be stated as under:

1. Every employer is bound to pay bonus to every employee in respect of the accounting year commencing on any day in the year 1979 and in respect of every subsequent accounting year.
2. The minimum limit of bonus payable by the employer is 8.33% of the salary or wages earned by the employee during the accounting year or one hundred rupees, whichever is higher. However, where an employee has not completed 15 years of age at the beginning of the accounting year, the minimum amount of bonus payable to such an employee is 8.33% of the salary or wages, or Rs. 60 whichever is higher [Section 10, provision].

   Note: Where an employee has not worked for all the working days in an accounting year, the minimum bonus of Rs. 100 or Rs. 60, as the case may be, if such bonus is higher than 8.33% of his salary or wages for the days he has worked in that accounting year, shall be proportionately reduced [Section 13].
3. The employer is bound to pay minimum bonus to the employees whether or not there is any allocable surplus in the accounting year. In fact, the statutory minimum bonus is payable whether or not there are any profits in the accounting year, and even if, the employer suffers losses during the accounting year.

[*State* v. *Sardar Dalip Singh,* (1979) Lab IL 913]

It is important to note that the Payment of Bonus Act creates a statutory right in the employees and imposes a statutory liability upon the employers covered by the Act to pay a minimum bonus.[2] In fact, after coming into force of this Act, bonus has become an implied term of employment not dependent upon the profits[3].

As regards the payment of festival bonus, if has been held by Karnataka High Court that if a custom as a practice prevails in an establishment and festival bonus is paid continuously for a longer period, a right accruses to the workmen to demand such customary right or festival bonus [*Management of Cipla Ltd. v. Ciple Karmikara Sangha*, 2001 II LLJ 476 (Karn)]; see also AIR 1972 SC 70]

Note: Though section 10 requires the payment of minimum bonus by the establishments to which the Act apples, but the appropriate Government may exercise its powers under Section 36 and exempt any establishment from the operation of Section 10 having regard to the financial position and other relevant circumstances of any establishment which is unable to pay minimum bonus [AIR 1969 273 (Madras)]

45.6. PAYMENT OF MAXIMUM BONUS

The legal provision relating to the payment of maximum bonus is contained in Section 11 of the Act as inserted by the Amendment Act of 1980, and may be stated as under:

1. The bonus at a higher rate than the minimum rate is payable only when the allocable surplus in a particular accounting year exceeds the amount of minimum bonus payable to the employees. Thus, the question of the applicability of this provision arises only when the allocable surplus in an accounting year exceeds the amount of minimum bonus payable to the employees during that year.
2. The maximum limit of bonus payable to an employee is 20% of the salary or wages earned by the employee during the accounting year.
3. In a situation as stated in point 1 above, *in lieu of the minimum bonus*, the amount of bonus payable to every employee shall be in proportion to the salary or wages earned by the employee during the accounting year subject to a maximum of 20% of such salary or wages. It may be noted that where in any accounting year, the allocable surplus exceeds the amount of minimum bonus payable, then the employer is bound to pay the bonus at a higher rate as stated above.
4. In computing the allocable surplus under the above mentioned provision, the amount set on or the amount set off under the provision of Section 15 shall be taken into account in accordance with the provisions of that section. The provision of Section 15 shall be discussed in Art. 34.6.

45.7. CALCULATION OF BONUS WITH RESPECT TO CERTAIN EMPLOYEES

An employee for the purposes of the Payment of Bonus Act, 1965, means any person (other than an apprentice) employed in any industry on a salary or wage not exceeding Rs. 10,000/ per month[4]. The effect of this amended provision is that an employee drawing a monthly salary upto Rs. 10,000/ is eligible for bonus. However, the calculation of bonus

2. *Anand Oil Industries* v. *Labour Court, Hyderabad,* AIR 1979 AP 182.
3. *Gopalan* v. *Angamali Chit Fund*, AIR 1977 Ker 120. The Supreme Court has also observed that the restriction imposed by the Bonus Act in compelling the employer to pay a minimum bonus even in years where there has been loss is reasonable or in public interest [AIR 1979 SC, 233].
4. Section 2 (13), Payment of Bonus Act, 1965. The limit is raised from Rs. 3,500 p.m. to Rs. 10,000 p.m. by the Payment of Bonus (Amendment) Act, 2007 (45 of 2007) w.e.f. 14.2.2006. A person drawing salary more than Rs. 10000. p.m. is not an employee for the purposes of this Act, and thus not eligible for bonus.

is made as per section 12.

Section 12 as amended by the Payment of Bonus (Amendment) Act, 2007 provides that where the salary or wage of an employee exceeds Rs. 3,500 pm, the bonus (minimum or the maximum) payable to such an employee shall be calculated as if his salary or wage were Rs. 3500 p.m. This means that though the wage ceiling of an employee entitling him to bonus has been raised to Rs. 10,000 p.m. but the amount of bonus payable to those employees drawing salary between Rs. 3500 and Rs. 10,000 p.m. will be calculated as if his salary or wages were Rs. 3500 per month.[5]

Example. 45.2. *A* is an employee of an establishment to which the payment of Bonus Act applies drawing a monthly salary of Rs. 5200. The employer has declared a 9% bonus for the accounting year. In this case, *A*'s bonus for the year will be Rs. 3,780 calculated as under:

$$\text{Rs. } 3500 \times \frac{9}{100} \times 12 = \text{Rs. } 3{,}780.$$

Note : Section 12 has been amended by the Amendment Act of 2007 (45 of 2007) w.r.e.f. 1–4–2006). By this Amendment, the limit of monthly salary for the purpose of calculation of the bonus under this section has been raised to Rs. 3,500 from Rs. 2,500.

45.8. PROPORTIONATE REDUCTION IN BONUS IN CERTAIN CASES

Section 13 makes a provision under which the bonus can be reduced proportionately in certain cases. As per this section, where an employee has not worked for all the working days in an accounting year, then the minimum bonus of Rs. 100 or Rs. 60, as the case may be, if such bonus is higher than 8.33% of his salary or wages for the days he has worked in that accounting year, shall be proportionately reduced. Section 14 discussed in the next article provides how to compute the number of working days for the purposes of proportionate reduction in bonus.

45.9. COMPUTATION OF NUMBER OF WORKING DAYS

Section 14 provides that the following days shall be deemed to be the working days of an employee and shall be counted while calculating the total working days on which he has been on work for the purpose of bonus:

1. Days when he has been laid off under an agreement or as permitted by standing orders under the Industrial Employment (Standing Orders) Act. 1946, or under the Industrial Disputes Act. 1947, or under any other law applicable to the establishment [Section 14(*a*)].
2. Days on which he has been on leave with salary or wages [Section 14 (*b*)].
3. Days on which he has been absent due to temporary disablement caused by accident arising out of and in the course of his employment [Section 14 (*c*)].
4. Days on which the employee has been on maternity leave with salary or wage, during the accounting year [Section 14 (d)].

45.10. ADJUSTMENT OF CUSTOMARY OR INTERIM BONUS AGAINST BONUS PAYABLE UNDER THE ACT

Sometimes, the employer pays some puja bonus or other customary bonus to his employees. In such cases, the employer is entitled to deduct the amount of such bonus from the amount of bonus payable to the employee under the Act in respect of that accounting year and the *employee shall be entitled to receive only the balance* [Section 17 (*a*)].

5. In *Indian cable Co.* v. *Workmen*, AIR 1972 SC 2195, the Supreme Court has also upheld this view point.

Similarly, where a part of bonus payable under the Act has been paid by the employer before the date on which such bonus becomes payable, the same is also to be deducted from the amount of bonus payable, as stated above [Section 17 (*b*)].

It is also important to note here, that where the employer suffers any financial loss in any accounting year due to the misconduct of an employee, then the employer shall be entitled to deduct the amount of such loss from the amount of bonus payable to the employee under the Act in respect of that accounting year only and the employee shall be entitled to receive the balance, if any [Section 18].

45.11. TIME LIMIT FOR PAYMENT OF BONUS

All amounts payable to an employee by way of bonus under the payment of Bonus Act shall be paid in *cash.* The time limit for the payment of bonus differs in cases where any dispute regarding the payment of bonus is pending, and in other cases where no such dispute is pending, which is as under:

1. ***Where a dispute regarding the payment of bonus is pending before any competent authority*** **[Section 19 (*a*)]:** In such cases, the bonus shall be paid within a month from the date on which the award given in the dispute become enforceable or the settlement of the dispute comes into operation.

2. ***Where no such dispute is pending i.e. in any other case*** **[Section 19 (*b*)].** In such cases, the bonus shall be payable within a period of 8 months from the close of the accounting year. However, this period of 8 months may be extended by Appropriate Government upto maximum of 2 years if the employer makes an application for extension and shows that there are sufficient reasons for the extension.

It is important to note here that the claim for bonus under point 2 stated above, can be made *only after the close of the accounting year.* The reason for the same is that the gross profits can be calculated only at the end of the accounting year, and the available and allocable surplus can also be worked out only at the end of the accounting year. It may be noted that even the directions given by a tribunal to make it obligatory for the management of a mill to make half-yearly payment of bonus is contrary to the spirit of Section 19. However, an employer may *voluntarily* pay amount during the accounting year by way of part bonus which he is entitled to adjust while making formal payment at the close of the accounting year.

45.12. RECOVERY OF BONUS DUE FROM AN EMPLOYER

In those cases where any money by way of bonus is due to an employee from his employer under a settlement or an award or agreement, the employee is entitled to recover the same by following the procedure prescribed in Section 21 of the Act. It is important to note here that the mode of recovery of bonus prescribed under this section shall be available only if the bonus sought to be recovered is due *under a settlement or an award or an agreement*. It will not apply to recovery of bonus which is payable under the Act.[7]

The provisions relating to the recovery of bonus, as contained in Section 21, are as under:

1. The bonus due to an employee from his employer under a settlement or an award or agreement, can be recovered by him by making an application to the appropriate government for the recovery of the same.
2. The application may be made by the employee himself or by any person authorised by him in writing. In case of death of the employee, such an application may be made by his assignee or heirs.

---

6. *Binny Ltd.* v. *Workmen*, AIR 1973 SC 353
7. *Labour Inspector* v. *Authority P.W. Act*, (1976) 1 LLJ 551 (M.P.)

3. On receipt of the application, if the appropriate government is satisfied that any money is so due to the employee, it shall issue a certificate for that amount to the collector, and the collector shall proceed to recover the same in the same manner as an arrear of land revenue.
4. The application to the appropriate government should be made within one year from the date on which the money became due to the employee from the employer. However, the Government may entertain such application even after the expiry of said period of one year, if it is satisfied that the applicant had *sufficient cause* for not making the application within the prescribed period of one year.

Note. For the purpose of this section an 'employee' incudes a person who is entitled to the payment of bonus under the payment of bonus act but who is no longer in employment [Section 21, explanation].

45.13. PAYMENT OF BONUS LINKED WITH PRODUCTION OR PRODUCTIVITY

The employer and his employees may enter into an agreement or settlement for payment of an annual bonus linked with production or productivity in lieu of bonus, based on profits payable under the Bonus Act. Such an agreement or settlement is valid and in that case, the employees shall be entitled to receive bonus due to them under such agreement or settlement. This special provision is contained in Section 31A which was insered by the Payment of Bonus (Amendment) Act, 1976.

The following points are important to note in connection with the payment of production or productivity based bonus under an agreement or settlement:

1. Any such agreement or settlement by which the employees relinguish their right to receive the minimum bonus under section 10 of the Bonus Act shall be null and void in so far as it purports to deprive them of such right [Section 31 A (proviso 1)]. This provision seeks to guarantee the minimum bonus to the employees. Thus, employees' right to minimum bonus under the Act cannot be taken away by any agreement or settlement between the employer and his employees.
2. The production or productivity based bonus payable under an agreement or settlement shall in no case exceed 20% of the salary or wages earned by them during the relevant accounting year [Section 31A, second proviso].

TEST QUESTIONS

1. Explain briefly the rules regarding payment of bonus as contained in the relevant provisions of the Act.
2. State the conditions for eligibility for bonus. When is an employee disqualified from receiving bonus?
3. Explain clearly the legal provisions relating to the payment of minimum and maximum bonus under the Act. Is there any situation in which the employer is not required to pay the minimum bonus? If yes, mention the provision.
4. Does the Payment of Bonus Act, 1965 impose any obligation on the employer to pay minimum bonus? Give the relevant provision. What is the quantum of minimum and maximum bonus?
5. Who is eligible to receive bonus? How is the bonus calculated in respect of an employee whose monthly salary exceeds Rs. 3,500 but does not exceed Rs. 10,000?
6. State the maximum amount of bonus payable to an employee. Is there any ceiling to this maximum amount? What rules exist in the Act relating to the time limit for payment of bonus by an employer?
7. Who is liable to pay the bonus and who is eligible to receive it? How are the number of working days computed for eligibility of bonus?

8. Can the bonus payable to an employee be reduced? If yes, explain the provision. Which days are deemed to be the working days of an employee and are counted while calculating total number of working days for the purpose of bonus?
9. State the procedure for calculation of working days and proportionate reduction of bonus under the Payment of Bonus Act, 1965.
10. What procedure shall an employee adopt for the recovery of the amount of bonus due to him from his employer under the Payment of Bonus Act, 1965.
11. Can the employer adjust the customary or interim bonus, paid to an employee, against the bonus payable under the Act? Also explain the provisions relating to the payment of bonus linked with production or productivity.
12. "The employer and his employees can enter into an agreement or settlement for the payment of annual bonus linked with production or productivity in lien of bonus payable under the Act"— Explain giving the relevant provision.
13. Examine the entitlement of following persons to receive bonus under the Payment of Bonus Act:
    (*a*) A dismissed employee
    (*b*) A retrenched employee
    (*c*) A piece-rated worker
    (*d*) A part-time employee
    (*e*) A probationer
    (*f*) An apprentice
14. Write a short notes on: (*a*) "Loss of an employee's right to bonus" and (*b*) Employee's entitlement to received bonus linked with productivity.

MULTIPLE CHOICE QUESTIONS

1. An employee is entitled to be paid bonus by his employer in an accounting year if he has worked in the establishment for a minimum period of
    (*a*) 28 working days
    (*b*) 30 working days
    (*c*) 42 working days
    (*d*) none of these
2. Which of the following person is not entitled to receive bonus under the Act?
    (*a*) A probationer
    (*b*) A retrenched employee
    (*c*) A part-time employee
    (*d*) An apprentice
3. An employee dismissed from service is disqualified from receiving bonus if dismissal from service is on account of
    (*a*) Fraud
    (*b*) Theft
    (*c*) Riotous behaviour
    (*d*) In all the cases
4. The minimum limit of bonus payable under the Act is 8.33% of the salary or wages earned by the employee during the accounting year or Rs. 100, whichever is higher.
    (*a*) True
    (*b*) False
5. The maximum limit of bonus payable to an employee is fixed by way percentage of salary or wages earned by the employee during the accounting year, and the percentage is:
    (*a*) 10%
    (*b*) 15%
    (*c*) 20%
    (*d*) 25%
6. Which of the following days are counted while calculating the total working days for the purpose of bonus?
    (*a*) Days on which employee has been on leave with salary.
    (*b*) Days on which employee has been on maternity leave with salary.
    (*c*) Days on which employee has been absent due to temporary disablement arising in the course of employment.
    (*d*) All of the above.
7. Where no dispute regarding the payment of bonus is pending, then from the close of the accounting year the bonus must be paid within a period of:
    (*a*) 8 months
    (*b*) 10 months
    (*c*) 12 months
    (*d*) none of these

ANSWERS

1. (*b*) 2. (*d*) 3. (*d*) 4. (*a*) 5. (*c*) 6. (*d*)
7. (*a*)

OBJECTIVE TYPE QUESTIONS WITH REASONING

State with reasons whether the following statements are correct or incorrect.

1. The amount of bonus payable to an employee under the Payment of Bonus Act, 1965 may be paid either in cash or in kind.
2. The period of suspension of an employee is considered to calculate the number of working days where such an employee is reinstated in service.
3. The employer is bound to pay the minimum bonus to the employees whether or not there is any allocable surplus in the accounting year.
4. An employee drawing a monthly salary of Rs. 3800 per month is to be paid bonus considering his salary to be Rs. 3500 per month.
5. The bonus payable to an employee cannot be reduced proportionately even if the employee has not worked for all the working days in an accounting year.
6. The employer is entitled to deduct the customary bonus paid to the employee, from the amount of bonus payable under the Act.

ANSWERS

1. ***Incorrect.*** The bonus under the Act is payable only in cash [Section 19].
2. ***Correct.*** In such a case, the employee is ready and willing to work for the establishment but is prevented from working by an overt act on the part of the employer.
3. ***Correct.*** The payment of minimum bonus by the employer is his statutory liability irrespective of the allocable surplus.
4. ***Correct.*** The bonus payable to the employees drawing salary between Rs. 3500 and Rs. 10,000 per month will be calculated as if his salary or wages were Rs. 3500 per month [Section 12 as amended by the Amendment Act of 2007.]
5. ***Incorrect.*** In such a case, the bonus payable can be reduced proportionately [Section 13]
6. ***Correct.*** In this regard, there is specific provision in the payment of Bonus Act, 1965 [Section 17 (*a*)].

PRACTICAL PROBLEMS

1. *A* worked in an establishment for 25 days in an accounting year. Is he entitled for bonus for that accounting year?
   Hint: No, *A* is not entitled for bonus for that accounting year. An employee is entitled for bonus in an accounting year if he has worked in the establishment for not less than 30 working days in that year. [Section 8]
2. *A* a temporary employee drawing a salary of Rs.3,000 per month, in an establishment to which the Payment of Bonus Act, 1965 applies was prevented by the employers from working in the establishment for two months during the financial year 2007-2008 pending certain inquiry. Since there were no adverse findings, '*A*' was re-instated in service. Later, when the bonus was to be paid to other employees, the employer refused to pay bonus to '*A*' even though he has worked for the remaining ten months in the year. Referring to the provisions of the Payment of Bonus Act, 1965, examine the validity of employer's refusal to pay bonus to '*A*'.
   Hint: The employer is not justified in refusing to pay the bonus. An employee's right to receive bonus is lost only if the employee is dismissed from services on the grounds of fraud, violence, theft misappropriation etc. In this case, *A* is not dismissed from services. [Section 9]

3. An employer had been paying to his employees every year at the time of Deepawali one month's basic wages as Deepawali bonus for the last 10 years in addition to the bonus payable under the Payment of Bonus Act, 1965. The bonus had been paid even in those years when there were losses. The employer now wants to adjust Deepawali bonus paid by him for the current accounting year against the bonus payable by him under the Act, for the current accounting year. State with reference to the provisions of the Payment of Bonus Act, 1965. whether it is possible for the employer to make the above adjustments.

   Hints: Yes, the employer is entitled to adjust Deepawali bonus against the bonus payable under the Act. [Section 17]

4. An employee working in an establishment commits fraud during the accounting year 20004-2005, but continues to work during the subsequent accounting year 2005-2006 and has clean record during this year. On the basis of fraud committed in 2004-2005, the employee is dismissed from service at the end of the accounting years ending with 2005-20006. Does the employee lose the bonus for 2004-2005 only or for both accounting years ending with 2005-2006.

   Hint: The employee loses his right to bonus for both the accounting years. In *Pandian Roadways Corpn. Ltd.* v. *Presiding officer*, (1996) 2 CLR 1175 (Madras), the Madras High court has held that an employee who is dismissed from service on the ground of misconduct as mentioned in Section 9, is disqualified from any bonus and not merely the bonus of the accounting year in which he is dismissed.

5. Mr. E joined as supervisor on monthly salary of Rs. 3400 on 1. 02. 2007 and resigned from his job on 28. 02. 2007. The company declared a bonus of 20% to all eligible employees and paid it on time. Mr E knowing the facts made a claim to HRD, which rejected the claim. Is Mr. E entitled to bonus ?

   Hint : No, Mr. E is not entitled to bonus as he has not worked for 30 days in that accounting year as required by section 8.

6. Sate with reasons whether the following persons are entitled to receive bonus under the Payment of Bonus Act, 1965.

   (*a*) A probationer

   (*b*) A retrenched employee

   (*c*) A dismissed employee reinstated with back wages.

   Hints : (*a*) A brobationer is entitled to bonus if the conditions of eligibility for bonus are fulfilled *i.e.,* he has worked for not less than 30 days in that accounting year.

   (*b*) A retrenched employee is entitled to bonus if he had worked for a period of not less than 30 days in that accounting year.

   (*c*) A dismissed employee is entitled to receive bonus. An employee includes a person who is entitled to the payment of bonus, but who is no longer in employment. [Section 21, Explanation]

7. Advise Sky Park Wooden Toys Ltd. on the following issues:

   (*a*) The company wants to adjust the puja bonus already paid to the workmen while calculating the amount of bonus payable to them during accounting year.

   (*b*) The company wants to give wooden toys as bonus instead in cash.

   Hints : (*a*) The company can adjust the puja bonus already paid to the workmen as Section 17 of the Payment of Bonus Act, 1965 makes a provision for such adjustment.

   (*b*)The company cannot give wooden toys as bonus instead in cash as bonus under the Act is payable only in cash. [Section 19]

46
CHAPTER

MISCELLANEOUS PROVISIONS AND SCHEDULES

1. Introduction
2. Computation of Gross Profits.
3. Computation of Avoidable Surplus.
4. Sums Deductible From Gross Profits.
5. Calculation of Direct Tax Payable by the Employer.
6. Set on and Set off of Allocable Surplus.
7. Special Provisions with Respect to New Establishments.
8. Application of the Act to the Establishment in Public Sector
9. Reference of Disputes under the Act.
10. Presumption About Accuracy of Balance Sheet and Profit and Loss Account of Corporations and companies.
11. Finality of the Audited Accounts of Banking Companies.
12. Presumption About Accuracy of Audited Accounts and Audit of Accounts of Employers who are not Corporations or Companies.
13. Inspectors.
14. Penalty and Offences.
15. Central Government's Powers to Make Rules.
16. Application of Certain Laws not Barred
17. Annexures:Schedules of the Act.

46.1. INTRODUCTION

In the previous chapter, we have discussed the legal provisions relating to the payment of bonus. There are many other legal provisions contained in the Payment of Bonus Act which are equally important from the subject point of view. All these have been clubbed together and discussed in detail in this chapter. The Schedules of the Act have also been reproduced as Annexures at the end of this chapter for ready reference and convenience of the students.

Following important provisions are discussed in detail in this chapter:

1. Computation of gross profits [Section 4].
2. Computation of available surplus [Section 5]
3. Sums deductible from gross profits [Section 6].
4. Calculation of direct tax payable by the employer [Section 7] .
5. Set on and set off of allocable surplus [Section 15].
6. Special provisions with respect to new establishments [Section 16].
7. Application of the Act to certain establishments in public sector in certain cases [Section 20].
8. Reference of disputes under the Act [Section 22]

   OR

   Application of the Industrial Disputes Act, 1947 to the disputes under the Bonus Act.

9. Presumption about accuracy of balance sheet and profit and loss account of corporations and companies [Section 23].
10. Finality of the Audited accounts of banking companies [Section 24].
11. Audit of accounts of employers other than corporations or companies [Section 25].
12. Inspectors [Section 27].
13. Penalty and offences [Section 28, 29, 30].
14. Central Government's powers to make rules [Section 38].
15. Application of certain laws [Section 39].

46.2. COMPUTATION OF GROSS PROFITS

The computation of gross profits of an establishment in respect of an accounting year is the first important step for the purposes of bonus formula under the Act. It is calculated according to the provisions of section 4 which is as under:

1. In case of a banking company, the gross profits shall be calculated in the manner specified in the First Schedule.
2. In case of a non-banking company, the gross profit shall be calculated in the manner Specified in the Second Schedule.

The First Schedule and the Second Schedule specify certain items which are to be added and deducted while calculating the gross profits. These schedules have been reproduced at the end of this chapter.

46.3. COMPUTATION OF AVAILABLE SURPLUS

After the determination of gross profits as stated above, the next step is the computation of the available surplus. It is calculated according to the provisions of section 5. As per this section, 'available surplus' in respect of an accounting year is the aggregate of the following items:

1. Gross profits for the accounting year after deducting certain prior charges as specified in Section 6.
2. The amount equal to the tax saved, on the amount of bonus payable under the Act, in respect of the immediately preceding accounting year.

46.4. SUMS DEDUCTIBLE FROM GROSS PROFITS

Available surplus, as discussed in the previous article, comprises the gross profits after deduction of certain prior charges. The following sums as specified in Section 6, are to be deducted from the gross profits as prior charges:

1. Any amount by way of depreciation admissible in accordance with the provisions of sub-section (1) of section 32 of the Income Tax Act, or in accordance with the provisions of the agricultural income-tax law, as the case may be;
2. Any amount by way of development rebate or investiment allowance or development allowance which the employer is entitled to deduct from his income under the Income Tax Act.
3. Any direct tax which the employer is liable to pay for the accounting year in respect of his income, profits and gains during that year. This deduction is subject to the provisions of section 7 which deals with the calculation of direct tax payable by the employer. This section 7 will be discussed in detail in the next article.
4. Any other sums as are specified in respect of the employer in the Third Schedule. This schedule specifies the deductible sums in respect of different categories of employer, and is reproduced at the end of this chapter.

46.5. CALCULATION OF DIRECT TAX PAYABLE BY THE EMPLOYER

As per Section 7 of the Act, any direct tax payable by the employer for any accounting year shall, subject to the following provisions, be calculated at the rates applicable to the income of the employer for that year, namely,

1. In calculating such tax no account shall be taken of the following:
   (*a*) any loss incurred by the employer in respect of any previous accounting year and carried forward under any law for the time being in force relating to direct taxes.
   (*b*) any arrears of depreciation which the employer is entitled to add to the amount of the allowance for depreciation for any following accounting year or years under sub-section (2) of section 32 of the Income Tax Act.
   (c) any exemption conferred on the employer under section 84 of the Income Tax Act or of any deduction to which he is entitled under sub-section (1) of section 101 of that Act, as in force immediately before the commencement of the Finance Act, 1965.
2. Where the employer is a religious or a charitable institution to which the provisions of section 32 do not apply and the whole or any part of its income is exempt from tax under the Income Tax Act, then, with respect to the income so exempted, such institution shall be treated as if it were a company in which the public are substantially interested within the meaning of that Act.
3. Where the employer is an individual or a Hindu Undivided Family, the tax payable by such employer under the Income Tax Act shall be calculated on the basis that the income derived by him from the establishment is his only income.
4. Where the income of any employer includes any profits and gains derived from the export of any goods or merchandise out of India and any rebate on such income is allowed under any law for the time being in force relating to direct taxes, then, no account shall be taken of such rebate.
5. No account shall be taken of any rebate other than development rebate or investment allowance or development allowance or credit or relief or deduction (not hereinbefore mentioned in this section) in the payment of any direct tax allowed under any law for the time being in force relating to direct taxes or under the relevant annual Finance Act, for the development of any industry.

46.6. SET ON AND SET-OFF OF ALLOCABLE SURPLUS

We have discussed in the previous chapter that the bonus at a higher rate than the minimum rate is payable when the allocable surplus in an accounting year exceeds the amount of minimum bonus payable to the employees. The allocable surplus for the payment of bonus for the relevant accounting year is computed after taking into account the figures of *set on* and *set off* in the previous year. The legal provisions relating to the 'set on' and 'set off' of allocable surplus are contained in Section 15 and may be stated as under:

1. ***Set on of allocable surplus*** **[Section 15 (1)]:** In a case where the allocable surplus for any accounting year exceeds the amount of maximum bonus payable to the employees under section 11, then the excess amount, subject to a limit of 20% of the total wages or salary of the employees in that accounting year, shall be carried forward for being set on in the succeeding accounting year. This excess will be so carried forward upto and inclusive of the fourth accounting year.

The excess amount carried forward as stated above, shall be utilised for the purpose of payment of bonus in the manner illustrated in Fourth Schedule*. This schedule has been reproduced as Annexure IV at the end of this chapter.

2. ***Set off of allocable surplus*** **[Section 15(2)]:** In a case where there is no allocable surplus for any accounting year or the allocable surplus for that year falls short of the amount of minimum bonus payable under Section 10, then such minimum amount or the deficiency as the case may be, shall be carried forward for being set off in the succeeding accounting year upto and inclusive of the fourth accounting year in the manner illustrated in the Fourth Schedule. It may be noted that the deficiency shall be carried forward for being set off only if there is no amount or sufficient amount carried forward and set on under section 15 (1) discussed above which could be utilised for the purpose of payment of the maximum bonus.

3. ***Utilisation of carried forward amount*** **[Section 15 (4)]:** In a case, where in any accounting year any amount has been carried forward and set on and set off under section 15 as discussed above, then in calculating bonus for the succeeding accounting year, the amount set on and set off carried forward from the earlier accounting year shall first be taken into account [Section 15 (4)]

Note. The principle of set on and set off as illustrated in the Fourth Schedule shall, for the purpose of payment of bonus under this Act, apply to all other cases not covered under Section 15 (1) or 15 (2) as discussed above [Section 15 (3)].

46.7. SPECIAL PROVISIONS WITH RESPECT TO NEW ESTABLISHMENTS

In case of new establishments, Section 16 of the Act makes special provisions with regard to the payment of bonus. As per this section, new establishment is exempted from the liability to pay bonus for the initial five accounting years. However, if the employer earns profits in any accounting year during this period of five years, then the bonus shall be payable in respect of that accounting year in which the employer earns profits from the establishment. Thus, so long as the employer does not start deriving profits from the new establishment, he is exempted from liability to pay bonus for the first five accounting years. It may be noted that an establishment exempted under this section from liability to pay bonus, is not liable to pay even the minimum bonus as required by section 10 of the Act.[1] Section 16 is, therefore, an exception to section 10 of the Act.

Before explaining the legal provision of Section 16, it is important to know the meaning of 'new establishment' and 'profits' for the purposes of the exemption under this section.

(*a*) ***New establishment:*** It means a newly set up establishment, whether set up before or after the commencement of this Act. But an establishment shall not be deemed to be newly set up merely by reason of a change in its location, management, name or ownership [Section 16, Explanation I].

(*b*) ***Profits:*** The word 'profits' should be construed according to its ordinary sense *i.e.,* in a sense in which it is used in trade and industry. Infact, the rationale behind section 16 (1) is that it is only when the employer starts making profits in the commercial sense, he should become liable to pay bonus to the employees[2].

1. *Workmen of Hindustan Machine Tools* v. *Presiding Officer, National Tribunal, Calcutta,* AIR 1973, SC 2300.
2. *Central Coal Washery* v. *Workmen,* AIR 1978 SC 1424.

* Fourth Schedule explains with example how the amount 'set on' and 'set off' is to be carried forward and utilised for payment of bonus.

The employer can be said to have earned profits only when the profits remain after adjusting the depreciation as per the provisions of Income Tax Act. Explanation II to Section 16, specifically provides that an employer shall not be deemed to have derived profit in any accounting year unless :

(*i*) he has made provision for that year's depreciation to which he is entitled under the Income Tax Act or, as the case may be under the agricultural income-tax law, and

(*ii*) the arrears of such depreciation and losses incurred by him in respect of the establishment for the previous accounting years have been fully set off against his profits.

As per section 16, the liability for the payment of bonus by a new establishment is to be judged with reference to different accounting years, which is as under:

1. *First five accounting years:* In the first five accounting years following the accounting year in which the employer sells the goods produced or manufactured by him or renders services, as the case may be, from such establishment, bonus shall be payable only in respect of the accounting year in which the employer derives profits from such establishment. And such bonus shall be calculated in accordance with the provisions of this Act in relation to that year, but without applying the 'set on' and 'set off' provisions of section 15 [Section 16 (1A)].

2. *Sixth and seventh accounting years :* For the sixth and seventh accounting years following the accounting year in which the employer sells the goods produced or manufactured by him or renders services, as the case may be, from such establishment, the bonus shall be payable under the provisions of the Act. However the provisions of 'set on' and 'set off' of section 15 shall apply subject to the following modifications [Section 16 (1B)]:

(*a*) For the sixth accounting year, set on or set off, as the case may be, shall be made in the manner illustrated in the Fourth Schedule taking into account the excess or deficiency, if any, as the case may be, of the allocable surplus set on or set off in respect of the fifth and sixth accounting years.

(*b*) For the seventh accounting year, set on or set off, as the case may be, shall be made in the manner illustrated in the Fourth Schedule taking into account the excess or deficiency, if any, as the case may be, of the allocable surplus set on or set off in respect of the fifth, sixth and seventh accounting years.

3. *From the eight accounting year onward :* From the eighth accounting year following the accounting year in which the employer sells the goods produced or manufactured by him or renders services, as the case may be, from such establishment, the provisions of section 15 shall apply in relation to such establishment as they apply in relation to any other establishment. [Section 16 (1C)]

46.8. APPLICATION OF THE ACT TO THE ESTABLISHMENT IN PUBLIC SECTOR

The provisions of the Payment of Bonus Act shall also apply to the establishments in public sector if the following conditions as contained in section 20 are satisfied:

1. The establishment in public sector sells any goods produced or manufactured by it or renders any services in competition with an establishment in private sector, and
2. The income from such sale or service or both is not less than 20% of the gross income of the establishment in public sector.

46.9. REFERENCE OF DISPUTES UNDER THE ACT OR APPLICATION OF THE INDUSTRIAL DISPUTES ACT, 1947 TO THE DISPUTES UNDER THE BONUS ACT

The payment of Bonus Act does not provide for any machinery to resolve the disputes relating to bonus. However, it is not to be construed as that there is no machinery to resolves the bonus disputes. Solution to such disputes is there but under the Industrial Disputes Act, 1947 and not under the payment of Bonus Act. Section 22 of the Bonus Act makes a specific provision in this regard.

The legal position, as provided in Section 22, to resolve the disputes relating to bonus is as under :

1. A dispute between an employer and his employees relating to the bonus *shall be deemed (i.e., considered) to be an industrial dispute* within the meaning of the Industrial Disputes Act, 1947 or within the meaning of any corresponding law relating to investigation and settlement of industrial disputes in force in a State.

2. A dispute between an employer and his employees would be considered as an industrial dispute by virtue of Section 22, only if it is one of the following two types of dispute:

(*a*) A dispute with respect to the bonus payable under the Payment of Bonus Act, 1965.

(*b*) A dispute with respect to the application of the Payment of Bonus Act to an establishment in public sector.

Thus, it is not every dispute between an employer and employees which would be covered by Section 22. This section would be attracted only if the dispute falls in any one of two categories stated above[3].

3. The dispute falling in either of the above two categories shall be decided according to the provisions of the Industrial Disputes Act, or any other corresponding law relating to investigation and settlement of industrial dispute in force in a State. However, if the parties *i.e.* employer and the employees have expressly provided any mode for settlement of the dispute, it shall be resolved accordingly.

46.10. PRESUMPTION ABOUT ACCURACY OF BALANCE SHEET AND PROFIT AND LOSS ACCOUNT OF CORPORATIONS AND COMPANIES

The disputes[4] may arise between an employer, being a corporation or a company (other than a banking company), and employees with respect to the bonus payable under the Act or with respect to the application of the Act to an establishment in public sector. Where such dispute arises and is pending before the concerned arbitrator or Tribunal (*i.e.* competent authority) and during the course of proceedings, the audited Balance Sheet and the Profit and Loss Account of the employer (*i.e.* corporation or company) are produced before the competent authority, then such competent authority may presume that the statements and particulars contained in the Balance Sheet and Profit and Loss Account are accurate. However, the presumption of such accuracy is there if in case of a corporation its accounts are audited by the Comptroller and Auditor General of India, and in case of a company its accounts are audited by auditors duly qualified to act as auditors of the company under Section 226 (1) of the Companies Act, 1956.

---

3. *Sanghvi Jivraj G. Chand 2. Ors* v. *Secretary, Madras Chillis Grain Kirana Merchante Workers Union*, (1969) 1 LLJ 719 (SC).
4. Such disputes are referred in section 22.

It may be noted that in view of this presumption of accuracy, it is not necessary for the corporation or the company to prove the accuracy of such statements and particulars by filing of an affidavit or by any other mode [Section 23].

Following points are important to note regarding the presumption of accuracy:

1. If the competent authority is satisfied that those statements and particulars are not accurate, then it may take such steps as it thinks necessary to find out the accuracy of such statements and particulars [Section 23 (1), proviso].
2. If the accuracy of the particulars contained in the Balance Sheet, and Profit and Loss Account have not been challenged (*i.e.,* no objection is taken) in the case, then it will have to be relied upon[5].
3. Any trade union or the employees who are *a party to the dispute* may make an application to the competent authority (arbitrator or Tribunal) requiring any clarification relating to any items in the Balance Sheet or the Profit and Loss Account. If the competent authority is satisfied that the so required clarification is necessary, it shall direct the employer (corporation or company) to furnish the clarification to the trade union or the employees within the time specified in the direction. The corporation or the company is bound to comply with the such directions [Section 23 (2)].

46.11. FINALITY OF THE AUDITED ACCOUNTS OF BANKING COMPANIES

The disputes of the nature as discussed in the last article, may also arise between an employer, being a banking company, and its employees. Where such dispute arises and is pending before the competent authority and during the course of proceedings, duly audited accounts of the banking company are produced before the competent authority, then the said authority shall not permit any trade union or employees to question the correctness of such accounts. However, the trade union or the employees may be permitted to obtain from the banking company such information as is necessary for verifying the amount of bonus due under the Act [Section 24 (1)].

It is important to note here that the trade union or the employees shall not be entitled to obtain any information from the banking company which it is not compelled to furnish under Section 34 A of the Banking Regulation Act, 1949 [Section 24 (2)].

46.12. PRESUMPTION ABOUT ACCURACY OF AUDITED ACCOUNTS AND AUDIT OF ACCOUNTS OF EMPLOYERS WHO ARE NOT CORPORATIONS OR COMPANIES

The presumption about the accuracy of duly audited accounts of employers, not being corporations or companies, is provided for in Section 25 of the Act. This section also makes a provision regarding the audit of accounts of such employer if the same have not been audited. These provisions may be stated as under:

1. Where a dispute, with respect to the bonus payable under the Act or with respect to the application of this Act to an establishment in the public sector, between an employer (not being a corporation or company) and his employees has been referred to the arbitrator or Tribunal (*i.e.,* competent authority), and the *duly audited accounts*[6] of such employer are placed before such authority, then the competent authority may pressume that the audited accounts are accurate [Section 25 (1)].

---

5. *ILC Manufacturers* v. *Workmen* AIR 1972 SC 343.
6. It means the accounts audited by auditors duly qualified to act as auditors under Section 226 (1) of the companies Act, 1956.

2. When the competent authority finds that the accounts of such employer have not been duly audited, and it is of the opinion that the audit of accounts is necessary for deciding the question referred to it, then it may direct the employer to get his account audited within specified time. The employer is bound to comply with such directions [Section 25 (2)].
3. Where the employer fails to get the accounts audited as per directions, then the said authority may get the accounts audited by such auditor or auditors as it thinks fit [Section 25 (3)].
4. When the accounts are so audited either under clause (2) or clause (3) as stated above, then the presumption of accuracy would apply to the accounts so audited [Section 25 (4)].

46.13. INSPECTORS

The inspectors are appointed by the Appropriate Government by a notification in the Official Gazette. The Government may appoint inspectors for *the purposes of this Act* and may define the limits within which they shall exercise jurisdiction [Section 27 (1)]. It is important to note that the inspector shall be deemed to be a public servant within the meaning of the Indian Penal Code, 1860 [Section 27 (3)].

Powers of inspectors have been specified in Section 27 (2) of the Act. For the purposes of ascertaining whether any of the provisions of this Act has been complied with, the inspectors shall have the following powers:

1. He may require an employer to furnish such information as he may consider necessary [Section 27 (2) (*a*)].
2. He may at any reasonable time and with such assistance, if any, as he thinks fit, enter any establishment or premises connected therewith. He may also require anyone found in charge of such establishment or premises to produce before him for examination any accounts, books, registers and other documents relating to the employment of persons or the payment of salary or wage or bonus in the establishment [Section 27 (2) (*b*)].
3. He may, examine, with respect to any matter relevant to any of the purposes aforesaid, the employer, his agent or servant or any other person found in charge of the establishment or any premises connected therewith. He may also examine any person whom the Inspector has reasonable cause to believe to be or to have been an employee in the establishment [Section 27 (2) (*c*)].
4. He may make copies of, or take extracts from, any book, register or other document maintained in relation to the establishment [Section 27 (2) (*d*)].
5. He may exercise such other powers as may be prescribed [Section 27 (2) (*e*)].

It may be noted that any person required by the inspector to produce any accounts, books, register or other documents or to give any information as stated above, shall be legally bound to do so [Section 27 (4)]

Note: The above powers given to an inspector under section 27 shall not enable him to require a banking company to furnish or disclose any statement or information or to produce, or give inspection of any of its books of account or other documents, which a banking company cannot be compelled to furnish, disclose, produce or give inspection of, under the provisions of section 34A of the Banking Regulation Act, 1949 [Section 27 (5)].

46.14. PENALTY AND OFFENCES

1. *Penalties* [Section 28]
2. *Offences by companies* [Section 29]
3. *Cognizance of offences* [Section 30]

The provisions relating to penalties and offences under the payment of Bonus Act, 1965, are under:

1. *Penalties* [Section 28] : Any person committing an offence under this Act shall be punishable for punishable with imprisonment upto six months or with five up to Rs. 1,000, or with both. A person shall be liable to this punishment in the following cases :

(*a*) If he contravenes any of the provisions of the Payment of Bonus Act or any rule made thereunder, or

(*b*) If he fails to comply with any direction given to him or any requisition made to him under the provisions of this Act.

2. *Offences by companies* [Section 29] : In case of offences by a company, the company, as well as its officers, shall be liable for punishment under the Act. The provisions in this regard are made in section 29, and may be stated as under:

(*a*) If the person committing an offence under this Act is a company, then the company as well as every person who, at the time the offence was committed, was in charge of, and was responsible to the company for the conduct of business of the company, shall be deemed to be guilty of the offence and shall be liable to be proceeded against and punished accordingly [Section 29 (1). However, such a person shall not be liable to any punishment if he proves that the offence was committed without his knowledge or that he exercised all due diligence to prevent the commission of such offence [Section 29 (1), proviso].

(*b*) Irrespective of anything contained in the above mentioned provision, where an offence under this Act has been committed by a company and it is proved that the offence has been committed with the consent or connivance of, or is attributable to any neglect on the part of, any director, manager, secretary or other officer of the company, such director, manager, secretary or other officer shall also be deemed to be guilty of that offence and shall be liable to be proceeded against and punished accordingly [Section 29 (2)].

Note. For the purposes of this section,

(*a*) "company" means any body corporate and includes a firm or other association of individuals; and

(*b*) "director", in relation to a firm, means a partner in the firm [Section 29, Explanation].

3. *Cognizance of offences* [Section 30]: A court shall take cognizance of any offence punishable under this Act, only on complaint made by or under the authority of the appropriate government or an officer of that government (not below the rank of a Regional Labour Commissioner in the case of an officer of the Central Government, and not below the rank of a Labour Commissioner in the case of an officer of the State Government) specially authorised in this behalf by the government. [Section 30 (1)].

No court inferior to that of a Presidency Magistrate or a Magistrate of the First Class shall try any offence punishable under this Act [Section 30 (2)].

46.15. CENTRAL GOVERNMENT'S POWERS TO MAKE RULES

The legal provisions in this regard are contained in Section 38, and may be stated as under:

1. The Central Government may make rules for the purpose of carrying into effect the provisions of this Act.

2. In particular, and without prejudice to the generality of the foregoing power, such rules may provide for,

(*a*) the authority for granting permission under the proviso to sub-clause (iii) of clause (1) of section 2;

(*b*) the preparation of registers, records and other documents and the form and manner in which such registers, records and documents may be maintained under section 26;

(*c*) the powers which may be exercised by an Inspector under clause (*e*) of sub-section (2) of section 27;

(*d*) any other matter which is to be, or may be, prescribed.

3. Every rule made under this section shall be laid as soon as may be after it is made, before each House of Parliament, while it is in session for a total period of thirty days, which may be comprised in one session or in two or more successive sessions and if before the expire of the session immediately following the session or the successive sessions aforesaid both Houses agree in making any modification in the rule or both Houses agree that the rule should not be made, the rule shall thereafter have effect only in such modified form or be of no effect, as the case may be; so, however, that any such modification or annulment shall be without prejudice to the validity of anything previously done under that rule.

46.16. APPLICATION OF CERTAIN LAWS NOT BARRED

Section 39 of the payment of Bonus Act, 1995 provides that except as otherwise expressly provided, the provisions of this Act shall be in addition to and not in derogation of the Industrial Disputes Act, 1947, or any corresponding law relating to investigation and settlement of industrial disputes in force in a State.

46.17. ANNEXURES:SCHEDULES OF THE ACT

The First, Second, Third and Fourth Schedules of the Payment of Bonus Act, 1965 have been reproduced hereunder:

1. ANNEXURE-I: FIRST SCHEDULE

This schedule prescribes the manner of computation of gross profits of a banking company. To arrive at the gross profits for the purposes of bonus, certain items are to be added back to the Net Profit and certain other items are be deducted from the Net profit. These items are specified in the First Schedule which is reproduced hereunder:

THE FIRST SCHEDULE

[See clause (*a*) of section 4]

COMPUTATION OF GROSS PROFITS

Accounting year ending ______

Item No.	*Particulars*	*Amount of sub-item Rs.*	*Amount of main items Rs*	*Remarks*
*1.	Net profit as shown in the profit and loss account after making usual and necessary provisions.			
2.	**Add back provision for:**			
	(*a*) Bonus to employees			
	(*b*) Depreciation			
	(*c*) Development Rebate Reserve			Refer Foot Note (1)
	(*d*) Any other reserves			
	Total of Item No. 2.....	Rs......		Refer Foot Note (1)

* *Where the profit subject to taxation is shown in the profit and loss account and the provisions made for taxes on income is shown, the actual provisions for taxes on income shall be deducted from the profit.*

3. **Add back also:**
   (*a*) Bonus paid to employees in respect of previous accounting year. — Refer Foot Note (1)
   (*b*) The amount debited in respect of gratuity paid or payable to employees in excess of the aggregate of
   (*i*) the amount, if any, paid to, or provided for payment to, an approved gratuity fund; and
   (*ii*) the amount actually paid to employees on their retirement or on termination of their employment for any reason.
   (*c*) Donations in excess of the amount admissible for income-tax.
   (*d*) Capital expenditure (other than capital expenditure on scientific research which is allowed as a deduction under any law for the time being in force relating to direct taxes) and cap ital losses (other than losses on sale of capital assets on which depreciation) has been allowed for income tax). — Refer Foot Note (1)
   (*e*) Any amount certified by the Reserve Bank of India in terms of subsection (2) of section 34A of the Banking Regulation Act, 1949.
   (*f*) Losses of, or expenditure relating to, any busi ness situated outside India.

   Total of Item No. 3 .... Rs ....

4. **Add also** income, profits or gains (if any) credited directly to published or disclosed reserves, other than
   (*i*) capital receipts and capital profits (including profits on the sale of capital assets on which depreciation has not been allowed for income-tax);
   (*ii*) profits of, and receipts relating to, any business situated outside India;
   (*iii*) income of foreign banking companies from investment outside India.

   Net total of Item No. 4 .... Rs. ......

5. Total of Item Nos. 1, 2, 3 and 4 .... Rs.............

6. **Deduct:**
   (*a*) Capital receipts and capital profits (other than profits on the sale of assets on which depreciation has been allowed for income tax). — Refer Foot Note (2)
   (*b*) Profits of, and receipts relating to, any business situated outside India. — Refer Foot Note (2)
   (*c*) Income of foreign banking companies from investments outside India. — Refer Foot Note (2)
   (*d*) Expenditure or losses (if any) debited directly to published or disclosed reserves, other than
   (*i*) capital expenditure and capital losses (other than losses on sale of capital

assets on which depreciation has not been allowed for income-tax);

(ii) losses of any business situated outside India.

(e) In the case of foreign banking companies proportionate administrative (overhead) expenses of head-office allocable to Indian business. — Refer Foot Note (3)

(f) Refund of any excess direct tax paid for previous accounting years and excess provision, if any, of previous accounting years, relating to bonus, depreciation, or development rebate, if written back. — Refer Foot Note (2)

(g) Cash subsidy, if any, given by the government or by any body corporate established by any law for the time being in force or by any other agency through budgetary grants, whether given directly or through any agency for specified purposes and the proceeds of which are reserved for such purposes.

Total of Item No. 6 .... Rs. ....

7. Gross profits for purposes of bonus (Item No. 5 minus Item No. 6) Rs ....

Explanation.— In sub-item (*b*) of Item 3, "approved gratuity fund" has the same meaning assigned to it in clause (5) of section 2 of the Income Tax Act.

Foot Notes: (1) If, and to the extent, charged to Profit and Loss Account.

(2) If, and to the extent, credited to Profit and Loss Account.

(3) In the proportion of Indian Gross Profit (Item No. 7) to total world gross profit (as per consolidated profit and loss account, adjusted as in Item No. 2 above only).

2. ANNEXURE II. SECOND SCHEDULE

This schedule prescribes the manner of computation of gross profits of a non-banking company. To arrive at the gross profits for the purposes of bonus, certain items are to be added back to the Net Profits as per Profit and Loss Account and certain others are to be deducted from it. These items are specified in the Second Schedule which is reproduced as under:

THE SECOND SCHEDULE

[Refer section 4 (b)]

COMPUTATION OF GROSS PROFITS

Accounting year ending

Item No.	*Particulars*	*Amount of sub-items Rs.*	*Amount of main items Rs*	*Remarks*
1.	Net profit as per P & L Account			
2.	**Add back provision for :**			
	(*a*) Bonus to employees			
	(*b*) Depreciation			
	(*c*) Direct taxes, including the provision (if any), for previous accounting years			
	(*d*) Development rebate/investment			Refer

allowance/development allowance reserve. Foot Note (1)

(e) Any other reserves Refer Foot Note (1)

Total of Item No. 2. .... Rs. .....

3. **Add back also:**

(a) Bonus paid to employees in respect of previous accounting years. Refer Foot Note (1)

(b) The amount debited in respect of gratuity paid or payable to employees in excess of the aggregate of

(i) the amount, if any, paid to, or provided for payment to, an approved gratuity fund; and

(ii) the amount actually paid to employees on their retirement or on termination of their employment for any reason.

(b) Donations in excess of the amount admissible for income-tax.

(c) Any annuity due, or commuted value of any annuity paid, under the provisions of section 280D of the Income Tax Act during the accounting year.

(d) Capital expenditure (other than capital expenditure on scientific research which is allowed as a deduction under any law for the time being in force relating to direct taxes) and capital losses (other than losses on sale of capital assets on which depreciation has been allowed for income-tax or agricultural income tax). Refer Foot Note (1)

(e) Losses of, or expenditure relating to, any business situated outside India.

Total of Item No. 3. .... Rs.. ......

4. **Add also** income, profits or gains (if any) credited directly to reserves, other than

(i) capital receipts and capital profits (including profits on the sale of capital assets on which depreciation has not been allowed for income-tax or agricultural income-tax);

(ii) profits of, and receipts relating to, any business situated outside India;

(iii) income of foreign concerns from investments outside India.

Net total of Item No. 4. .... Rs. ....

5. **Total of Item Nos. 1, 2, 3 and 4** .... Rs. ....

6. **Deduct:**

(a) Capital receipts and capital profits (other than profits on the sale of assets on which depreciation has been allowed for income-tax or agricultural income-tax). Refer Foot Note (2) Refer Foot Note (2)

(b) Profits of, and receipts relating to, any business situated outside India.

(c) Income of foreign concerns from investment outside India. Refer Foot Note (2)

(d) Expenditure or losses (if any) debited directly to reserves, other than (*i*) capital expenditure and capital losses (other than losses on sale of capital assets on which depreciation has not been allowed for income-tax or agricultural income-tax);

(*ii*) losses of any business situated outside India.

(*e*) In the case of foreign concerns proportionate administrative (overhead) expenses of head office allocable to Indian business. — Refer Foot Note (3)

(*f*) Refund of any direct tax paid for previous accounting years and excess provision, if any, of previous accounting years relating to bonus, deprecia tion, taxation or development rebate or development allowance, if written back. — Refer Foot Note (2)

(*g*) Cash subsidy, if any, given by the government or by any body corporate established by any law for the time being inforce or by any other agency through budgetary grants, whether given directly or through any agency for specified purposes and the proceeds of which are reserved for such purposes.

Total of Item No. 6 .... Rs. ....

7. Gross Profit for purposes of bonus Rs .... (Item No. 5 minus Item No. 6)

Expalantion.— In sub-item (aa) of Item 3, "approved gratuity fund" has the same meaning assigned to it in clause (5) of section 2 of the Income Tax Act.

Foot Notes (1) If, and to the extent, charged to Profit and Loss Account.

(2) If, and to the extent, credited to Profit and Loss Account.

(3) In the proportion of Indian Gross Profit (Item No. 7) to Total World Gross Profit (as per consolidated profit and loss account, adjusted as in Item No. 2 above only).

3. ANNEXURE III. THIRD SCHEDULE

This schedule specifies the items (*i.e.,* sums) which are to be deducted from the gross profits to arrive at the available surplus. These deductible sums depend upon the category of the employer *i.e.,* whether the employer is a company other than a banking company, or a banking company, or a corporation, or a co-operative society or any other employer not falling under any of these categories. This schedule is reproduced as under:

THE THIRD SCHEDULE

[Refer clause (*d*) of section 6]

Item No.	*Category of employer*	*Further sums to be deducted*
1.	Company, other than a banking company	(*i*) The dividends payable on its preference share capital for the accounting year calculated at the actual rate at which such dividends are payable; (*ii*) 8.5% of its paid up equity share capital as at the commencement of the accounting year; (*iii*) 6% of its reserves shown in its balance sheet as at the commencement of the accounting year, including any profits carried forward from the previous accounting year:

Provided that where the employer is a foreign company within the meaning of section 591 of the Companies Act, 1956, the total amount to be deducted under this item shall be 8.5% on the aggregate of the value of the net fixed assets and the current assets of the company in India after deducting the amount of its current liabilities (other than any amount shown as payable by the company to its Head Office whether towards any advance made by the Head Office or otherwise or any interest paid by the company to its Head Office) in India.

2. Banking company

(*i*) The dividends payable on its preference share capital for the accounting year calculated at the rate at which such dividends are payable;

(*ii*) 7.5% of its paid up equity share capital as at the commencement of the accounting year;

(*iii*) 5% of its reserves shown in its balance sheet as at the commencement of the accounting year, including any profits carried forward from the previous accounting year;

(*iv*) any sum which, in respect of the accounting year, is transferred by it

(*a*) to a reserve fund under sub-section (1) of section 17 of the Banking Regulation Act, 1949; or

(*b*) to any reserves in India in pursuance of any direction or advice given by the Reserve Bank of India, whichever is higher:

Provided that where the banking company is a foreign company within the meaning of section 591 of the Companies Act, 1956, the amount to be deducted under this item shall be the aggregate of

(*i*) the dividends payable to its preference shareholders for the accounting year at the rate at which such dividends are payable on such amount as bears the same proportion to its total preference share capital as its total working funds in India bear to its total world working funds;

(*ii*) 7.5% of such amount as bears the same proportion to its total paid up equity share capital as its total working funds in India bear to its total world working funds.

(*iii*) 5% of such amount as bears the same proportion to its total disclosed reserves as its total working funds in India bear to its total world working funds;

(*iv*) any sum which, in respect of the accounting year, is deposited by it with the Reserve Bank of India under sub-clause (*ii*) of clause (*b*) of sub-section (2) of section 11 of the Banking Regulation Act, 1949, not exceeding the amount required under the aforesaid provision to be so deposited.

3. Corporation

(*i*) 8.5% of its paid up capital as at the commencement of the accounting year;

(*ii*) 6% of its reserves, if any, shown in its balance sheet as at the commencement of the accounting year, including any profits carried forward from the previous accounting year.

4. Co-operative society

(*i*) 8.5% of the capital invested by such society in its establishment as evidenced from its books of accounts at the commencement of the accounting year;

	(*ii*) such sum as has been carried forward in respect of the accounting year to a reserve fund under any law relating to co-operative societies for the time being in force.
5. Any other employer not falling under any of the aforesaid categories	8.5% of the capital invested by him in his establishment as evidenced from his books of accounts at the commencement of the accounting year: Provided that where such employer is a person to whom Chapter XXII-A of the Income Tax Act applies, the annuity deposit payable by him under the provisions of that Chapter during the accounting year shall also be deducted: Provided further that where such employer is a firm, an amount equal to 25% of the gross profits derived by it from the establishment in respect of the accounting year after deducting depreciation in accordance with the provisions of clause (*a*) of section 6 by way of remuneration to all the partners taking part in the conduct of business of the establishment shall also be deducted, but where the partnership agreement, whether oral or written, provides for the payment of remuneration to any such partner, and (*i*) the total remuneration payable to all such partners is less than the said 25% of the amount payable, subject to a maximum of forty-eight thousand rupees to each such partner; or (*ii*) the total reumuneration payable to all such partners is higher than the said 25%, such percentage, or a sum calculated at the rate of forty-eight thousand rupees to each such partner, whichever is less, shall be deducted under this proviso: Provided also that where such employer is an individual or a Hindu Undivided Family (*i*) an amount equal to 25% of the gross profits derived by such employer from the establishment in respect of the accounting year after deducting depreciation in accordance with the provisions of clause (*a*) of section 6; or (*ii*) forty-eight thousand rupees, whichever is less, by way of remuneration to such employer, shall also be deducted.
6. Any employer falling under Item No. 1 or Item No. 3 or Item No. 4 or Item No. 5 and being a licensee within the meaning of the Electricity (Supply) Act, 1948	In addition to the sums deductible under any of the aforesaid Items, such sums as are required to be appropriated by the licensee in respect of the accounting year to a reserve under the Sixth Schedule to that Act shall also be deducted.

Explanation— The expression "reserves" occurring in column (3) against Item Nos. 1(*iii*), 2 (*iii*) and 3(*ii*) shall not include any amount set apart for the purpose of,

(*i*) payment of any direct tax which, according to the balance-sheet, would be payable;

(*ii*) meeting any depreciation admissible in accordance with the provisions of clause (*a*) of section 6;

(*iii*) payment of dividends which have been declared, but shall include,

(*a*) any amount, over and above the amount referred to in clause(*i*) of this Explanation, set apart as specific reserve for the purpose of payment of any direct tax; and

(*b*) any amount set apart for meeting any depreciation in excess of the amount admissible in accordance with the provisions of clause (*a*) of section 6.

4. ANNEXURE IV: FOURTH SCHEDULE

This schedule explains, with example as to how the amount 'set on' and 'set off' is to be carried forward and utilised for the payment of bonus. The Fourth Schedule is reproduced as under:

THE FOURTH SCHEDULE

[Refer sections 15 and 16]

In this Schedule, the total amount of bonus equal to 8.33% of the annual salary or wage payable to all the employees is assumed to be Rs. 1,04,167. Accordingly, the maximum bonus to which all the employees are entitled to be paid (20% of the annual salary or wage of all the employees) would be Rs. 2,50,000.

Year	*Amount equal to 60% or 67% as the case may be, of available surplus allocable as bonus*	*Amount payable as bonus*	*Set on or set off of the year carried forward*	*Total set on or set off carried forward*	
	Rs.	Rs.	Rs.	Rs.	of (year)
1.	1,04,167	1,04,167*	Nil	Nil	
2.	6,35,000	2,50,000**	Set on 2,50,000**	Set on 2,50,000**	(2)
3.	2,20,000	2,50,000** (inclusive of 30,000 from year-2)	Nil	Set on 2,20,000	(2)
4.	3,75,000	2,50,000**	Set on 1,25,000	Set on 2,20,000 1,25,000	(2) (4)
5.	1,40,000	2,50,000** (inclusive of 1,10,000 from year-2)	Nil	Set on 1,10,000 1,25,000	(2) (4)
6.	3,10,000	2,50,000**	Set on 60,000	Set on Nil* 1,25,000 60,000	(2) (4) (6)
7.	1,00,000	2,50,000** (inclusive of 1,25,000 from year-4 and 25,000 from year-6)	Nil	Set on 35,000	(6)
8.	Nil (due to loss)	1,04,167* (inclusive of 35,000 from year-6)	Set off 69,167	Set off 69,167	(8)
9.	10,000	1,04,167*	Set off 94,167	Set off 69,167 94,167	(8) (9)
10.	2,15,000	1,04,167* (after setting off 69,167 from year-8 and 41,666 from year-9)	Nil	Set off 52,501	(9)

* Minimum
** Maximum
# The Balance of Rs. 1,10,000 Set on from year-2 lapses.

TEST QUESTIONS

1. What is gross profit? How it is computed (*a*) in case of a banking company, and (*b*) in case of a non-banking company?
2. What is available surplus? How it is computed? Explain clearly specifying the sums deductible from the gross profit as prior charges.
3. Explain the provisions relating to deduction of prior charges from gross profits for arriving at the available surplus under the Payment of Bonus Act, 1965.
4. Explain and illustrate the rules relating to 'set on' and 'set off' of allocable surplus under the Payment of Bonus Act.
5. What deductions are allowed under the Third Schedule in determining the available surplus in case of:
   (*a*) A banking company (*b*) A non-banking company
6. How will you determine the direct tax payable by the employer for the purpose of computation of available surplus for an accounting year under the Payment of Bonus Act, 1965.
7. State special provisions of the Payment of Bonus Act, 1965 with regard to newly set up establishments.
8. Explain the circumstances under which the provisions of the Payment of Bonus Act, 1965 apply to the 'establishments in public sector'.
9. Comment on the following with reference to the provisions of the Payment of Bonus Act, 1965:
   (*a*) The excess of allocable surplus over the amount of maximum bonus can be set on and carried forward.
   (*b*) A financial loss to the employer due to employee's misconduct is deductible from the amount of bonus payable to the employee
   (*c*) The maximum amount of surplus that can be set on.
10. "A dispute between an employer and his employees relating to bonus shall be deemed to be an industrial dispute within the meaning of the Industrial Disputes Act, 1947"– Explain with regard to the reference of disputes under the Payment of Bonus Act, 1965.
11. Examine with reference to the provisions of the Payment of Bonus Act 1965, the possibility of a non-banking company relying on its Balance Sheet and Profit and Loss Account in case of a dispute with its employees relating to bonus payable under the Act and the limitations, if any, in this regard.
12. "Audited accounts of banking companies not to be questioned"— comment with reference to the provisions of the Payment of Bonus Act.
13. Discuss the provisions of the Payment of Bonus Act, 1965 relating to the appointment, powers and functions of an inspector appointed under the Act.
14. Explain the provisions of the Payment of Bonus Act, 1965 relating to 'penalties' with special reference to offences by companies.

MULTIPLE CHOICE QUESTIONS

1. In case of a non-banking company, the gross profits shall be calculated in the manner specified in the
   (*a*) First Schedule (*b*) Second Schedule
   (*c*) Third Schedule (*d*) Fourth Schedule
2. Which of the following items comprise the 'available surplus' in respect of an accounting year?

(*a*) Gross profits for the accounting year after deducting certain prior charges as specified in Section 6.
(*b*) The amount equal to the tax saved, on the amount of bonus payable under the Act, in respect of the immediately preceding accounting year.
(*c*) The item mentioned in both (*a*) and (*b*)
(*d*) The item mentioned in (*a*) only

3. The maximum limit of surplus which can be carried forward for being 'set on' in the succeeding year is
(*a*) 20% of the total wages or salary of the employee in the accounting years.
(*b*) 20% of the gross profits in the accounting year.
(*c*) 20% of the maximum amount payable as bonus in an accounting year.
(*d*) Rs. 50,000 in an accounting year.

4. The principle of set on and set off is illustrated in which of the following schedule of the Payment of Bonus Act:
(*a*) First Schedule (*b*) Second Schedule
(*c*) Third Schedule (*d*) Fourth Schedule

5. A new establishment though exempted from the liability to pay bonus for initial 5 accounting years, but remains liable to pay bonus if it earns profits in any accounting year during this period of five years.
(*a*) True (*b*) False

6. Which of the following statements is *not* correct?
(*a*) From the sixth accounting year a new establishment becomes liable to pay bonus but the provisions of 'set on' and set off apply with certain modifications for the 6th and 7th year.
(*b*) Section 16 is an exception to section 10 as the new establishment is not liable to pay minimum bonus for the initial five years.
(*c*) The Payment of Bonus Act shall apply to an establishment in public sector when its sells it goods in competition with an establishment in private sector and income from such sale is not less than 20% of its gross income.
(*d*) The disputes between an employer and his employee relating to bonus are settled by the Tribunal established under section 22 of the Payment of Bonus Act, 1965.

7. An inspector under the payment of Bonus Act, 1965, is appointed by
(*a*) Tribunal (*b*) Arbitrator
(*c*) Appropriate Government (*d*) Management of the Employer

ANSWERS

1. (*b*) **2.** (*c*) **3.** (*a*) **4.** (*d*) **5.** (*a*) **6.** (*d*)
7. (*c*)

OBJECTIVE TYPE QUESTIONS WITH REASONING

State with reasons whether the following statements are correct or incorrect

1. The amount carried forward for being set on and set off in the succeeding accounting year cannot be carried forward beyond fourth year inclusive of the accounting years.

2. A new establishment is exempted from the liability to pay bonus for the initial five accounting years.

3. A new establishment exempted from liability to pay bonus under Section 16 is required to pay only the minimum bonus under section 10, for the initial five years.

4. The expression 'profits' in section 16 is to be construed in its ordinary sense and the employer can be said to have earned profits only when the profits remain after adjusting the depreciation as per the Income Tax Act.

5. A dispute between an employer and his employees with respect to the bonus payable under the Payment of Bonus Act, 1965 is to be decided according to the provisions of the Industrial Disputes Act, 1947.
6. Where during the course of proceeding relating to a bonus dispute, the audited Balance Sheet and Profit and Loss Account of the company (employer) are produced before the arbitrator, then the company is required to prove the accuracy of these statements by filing an affidavit.

ANSWERS

1. *Correct.* Section 15 of the Act makes a specific provision in this regard.
2. *Correct.* Section 16 of the Act gives this special benefit to the new establishments.
3. *Incorrect.* A new establishment is exempted for five years even from the liability to pay minimum bonus.
4. *Correct.* The rationale behind section 16(1) is that it is only when the employer starts making profits in commercial sense, he should become liable to pay bonus to the employees.
5. *Correct.* Such a dispute is deemed to be an industrial dispute by virtue of Section 22 of the Payment of Bonus Act, 1965.
6. *Incorrect.* In such a case, there is a presumption about the accuracy of these statements [Section 23].

The Payment of Wages Act, 1936

- Introduction and Application of the Act
- Payment of Wages
- Deductions from Wages
- Miscellaneous Provisions and Penalties

47

CHAPTER

INTRODUCTION AND APPLICATION OF THE ACT

47.1. INTRODUCTION

With the growth of industries in India, problems relating to payment of wages to persons employed in industry took an ugly turn. The industrial units were not making payment of wages to their workers at regular intervals and wages were not uniform. The industrial workers were forced to raise their heads against their exploitation.

In 1926, Government of India wrote to local governments to ascertain the position with regard to the delays which occurred in the payment of wages to the persons employed in Industry. Material so collected was placed before the Royal Commission on Labour which was appointed in 1929. The Royal Commission made some valuable recommendations and on the report of the Commission, Government of India re-examined the subject and in February, 1933 the Payment of Wages Bill, 1933, was introduced in the Legislative Assembly but could not take shape of the Act because of dissolution of the Assembly. In 1935 the Payment of Wages Bill, based upon the same principles as the earlier Bill of 1933 but thoroughly revised was introduced in the Legislative Assembly on 15th February, 1935. The Bill was referred to the Select Committee. Select Committee presented its report on 2nd September, 1935. Incorporating the recommendations of the Select Committee, the Payment of Wages Bill, 1935 was again introduced in the Legislative Assembly, and having been passed by the Legislative Assembly, the Bill received Assembly's assent on 23rd April, 1936, and became the Payment of Wages Act, 1936 (4 of 1936). It came into force on 28-3-1937.

The Payment of Wages Act, 1936 has recently been amended in 2005 by the Payment of Wages (Amendment) Act, 2005.

In this chapter we shall discuss the objects and application of the Act, the definitions of important terms used and defined in the Act, and the changes introduced by the Payment of Wages (Amendment) Act, 2005.

Note: In this part of the book, unless otherwise stated, the sections mentioned are those of the Payment of Wages Act, 1936.

47.2 OBJECTS AND APPLICATION OF THE ACT

The object of the Payment of Wages Act, 1936 as provided in the Preamble of the Act is "to regulate the payment of wages of certain classes of employed persons".

The use of the expression "certain classes of employed persons" is important for the Act as the Act applies to employed persons drawing on an average wages less than Rs. 6,500/- per month [Section 1 (6)]. In order to ensure the payment of wages to the persons covered by the Act, various provisions have been made in the Act.

The Payment of Wages Act, 1936 extends to the whole of India [Section 1 (2)]. It came into force on 28th March, 1937. The provisions relating to the applicability of the Act, have been made in Sections 1 (4) to 1(6) of the Act.

Section 1(4) provides that in the first instance, the Act applies to the payment of wages to the following:

1. Persons employed in any factory.
2. Persons employed (otherwise than in a factory) upon any railway by a railway administration either directly or through a sub-contractor.
3. Persons employed in an industrial or other establishment as specified in Section 2 (ii) (*a*) to 2 (ii) (*g*). These have been discussed in Art. **47.5**
4. Any class of persons employed in any establishment or class of establishment specified by the appropriate government [Section 5].

In respect of point 4 mentioned above, it may be noted that the Appropriate Government may, by notification in the Official Gazette, extend the provisions of this Act to any establishment specified by the appropriate government exercising the power to specify under Section 2 (ii) (h). However for doing so, the appropriate government should give three month's prior notice of its intention to do so [Section 1 (5)]. This provision has been introduced for the protection of persons employed in the establishments to which the government intends to extend the application of the Act.

47.3. WAGE CEILING FOR APPLICATION OF THE ACT

The wage ceiling (*i.e.,* maximum wage limit) for the applicability of the Act, is Rs. 6,500 per month. The wage-ceiling has been enhanced from Rs. 1,600 per month to Rs. 6,500 per month by the Payment of Wages (Amendment) Act, 2005.

Section 1(6) contains this provision which states that the Act applies to wages payable to an employed person in respect of a wages period *if such wages for that wage period do not exceed six thousand five hundred rupees per month* or such other higher sum which, on the basis of figures of the Consumer Expenditure Survey published by the National Sample Survey Organisation, the Central Government may, after every five years, by notification in the Official Gazette, specify.

47.4. DEFINITIONS

The terms and expressions used in the Payment of Wages Act, 1936 are defined in various sub-sections of Section 2 of the Act and are discussed in the following pages:

1. Appropriate Government

The term 'appropriate government' is defined in Section 2 (i) of the Act as under:

(*a*) In relation to railways, air transport service, mines and oil fields, the appropriate government is the Central Government.

(*b*) In relation to all other cases, the appropriate government is the State Government.

2. Employed person

The term 'employed person' is defined in Section 2 (*ia*) of the Act and for the purposes of this Act, it includes the legal representatives of a deceased employed person.

3. Employer

The term 'employer' is defined in Section 2 (*ib*) of the Act, and for the purposes of this Act, it includes the legal representatives of a deceased employer.

4. Factory

The term 'factory' is defined in Section 2 (*ic*) of the Act and for the purposes of this Act, it means a factory as defined in Section 2 (*m*) of the Factories Act, 1948 and includes any place to which the provision of that Act applies.

5. Mine

The term 'mine' is defined in Section 2 (*iia*) of the Act and for the purposes of this Act, it has the same meaning as assigned to it in Section 2 (1) (*j*) of the Mines Act, 1952.

6. Plantation

The term 'plantation' is defined in Section 2 (*iii*) of the Act and for the purposes of this Act it has the same meaning as assigned to it in Section 2 (*f*) of the Plantation Labour Act, 1951.

7. Railway Administration

The term 'railway administration' is defined in Section 2 (*v*) of the Act and for the purposes of this Act it has the same meaning as assigned to it in Section 2 (32) of the Railways Act, 1989.

8. Industrial or Other Establishments

9. Wages

The above two terms have been discussed in detail in the next two articles.

47.5. INDUSTRIAL OR OTHER ESTABLISHMENT

The term 'industrial or other establishment' is defined in Section 2 (*ii*) of the Payment of Wages Act, 1936 and for the purposes of this Act it means the following:

(*a*) Tramway service, or motor transport service engaged in carrying passengers or goods or both by road for hire or reward;

(*b*) Air transport service other than such service belonging to, or exclusively employed in the military, naval or air forces of the Union or the Civil Aviation Department of the Government of India;

(*c*) Dock, wharf or jetty;

(*d*) Inland vessel, mechanically propelled;

(*e*) Mine, quarry or oil-field;

(*f*) Plantation;

(*g*) Workshop or other establishment in which articles are produced, adapted or manufactured, with a view to their use, transport or sale;

(*h*) Establishment in which any work relating to the construction, development or maintenance of buildings, roads, bridges or canals, or relating to operations connected with navigation, irrigation or the supply of water or relating to the generation, transmission and distribution of electricity or any other form of power is being carried on;

(*i*) Any other establishment or class of establishments which *[the appropriate Government] may, having regard to the nature thereof, the need for protection of persons employed therein and other relevant circumstances, specify, by notification in the Official Gazette;

In the *Tamil Nadu Water Supply and Drainage Board* v. *M.D. Vijayakumar & Ors,* (1991) 1 LLJ 260 (Madras), the Tamil Nadu Water Supply and Drainage Board was created for regulation and development of drinking water and drainage in the State of Tamil Nadu. It was held that the Board is an establishment falling in clause (*g*) of Section 2 (*ii*) stated in point '*h*' above. The court held that it is clear that this Board is an establishment in which work relating to operations connected with supply of water is being carried on.

In *K.L.Garg* v. *New India Assurance Co. & Ors,* (1992) 1 LLJ 190 (P&H), it was held that the New India Assurance Co. does not fall within the definition of 'industrial or other establishment' under clause (h) of Section 2 (*ii*) stated in point (*i*) above as no notification specifying the insurance company to be an establishment, has been issued by the government. In the absence of such notification, the insurance companies do not fall in the *definition of 'industrial or other establishment'*.

47.6. WAGES

The term 'wages' is defined in Section 2 (*vi*) of the Act stating therein what is included in the 'wages' and what is excluded from it.

As per this section. **"wages"** means all remuneration (whether by way of salary, allowances, or otherwise) expressed in terms of money or capable of being so expressed which would, if the terms of employment, express or implied, were fulfilled, be payable to a person employed in respect of his employment or of work done in such employment, and **includes** – the following remuneration/sums:

(*a*) Any remuneration payable under any award or settlement between the parties or order of a Court;

(*b*) Any remuneration to which the person employed is entitled in respect of overtime work or holidays or any period;

(*c*) Any additional remuneration *payable under the terms of employment* whether called a bonus or by any other name.

(*d*) Any sum which by reason of the termination of employment of the person employed is payable under any law, contract or instrument which provides for the payment of such sum, whether with or without deductions, but does not provide for the time within which the payment is to be made;

(*e*) Any sum to which the person employed is entitled under any scheme framed under any law for the time being in force,

However, the following allowances/items are **not included** in the 'wages':

(*i*) Any bonus (whether under a scheme of profit sharing or otherwise) *which does not form part of the remuneration payable under the term of employment* or which is not payable under any award or settlement between the parties or order of a Court;

(*ii*) The value of any house-accommodation, or of the supply of light, water, medical attendance or other amenity or of any service excluded from the computation of wages by a general or special order of **[the appropriate Government];

* Substituted by the Payment of Wages (Amendment) Act, 2005 for the words "Central Government or a State Government".

** Substituted by the Payment of Wages (Amendment) Act, 2005 for the word "State Government".

(iii) Any contribution paid by the employer to any pension or provident fund, and the interest which may have accrued thereon;

(iv) Any travelling allowance or the value of any travelling concession;

(v) Any sum paid to the employed person to defray special expenses entailed on him by the nature of his employment.

(vi) Any gratuity payable on the termination of employment in cases other than those specified in sub-clause(d) stated above.

Following points based upon the judicial decisions are important to note in connection with the definition of the term wages:

1. The bonus payable under the Payment of Bonus Act, 1965 amounts to wages with-in the definition of wages.[1] After coming into force of the Payment of Bonus Act, bonus has become an *implied term of employment* not dependent upon the profits and therefore comes under the category of remuneration.

   [*Gopalan* v. *Augmati Chit Fund*, AIR 1977 Kerala 120]

2. The amount of retrenchment compensation payable to employees under Section 25-F (b) of the Industrial Disputes Act, 1947, are sums payable to the employee on termination of the services and therefore 'wages' as defined by clause 'd' above.

   [*D.A. Divekar* v. *A.K. Shah*, (1955) 2 LLJ 501]

3. A workman whose service is terminated in consequence of transfer of an undertaking, whether by agreement or by operation of law, has a statutory right under Section 25-F of the Industrial Disputes Act, 1947, to compensation unless such right is defeated under the proviso of that section. The same is the position in the case of closure under Section 25-FFF of that Act. Such compensation would be wages as defined in clause(d) of Section 2 (VI) of the Payment of Wages Act, as it is the sum which by reason of the termination of employment of the person employed is payable under any law.

   [*Payment of Wages Inspector* v. *B.E.S. & Co., AIR 1969 SC 590*]

4. The amount of lay-off compensation under Section 25-C of the Industrial Disputes Act, 1947 does not come within the definition of 'wages' as given in the Payment of Wages Act.

   [*Trichinopoly Mills Ltd.* v. *Swaminathan & Ors.* ((1956) 1 LLJ 269, Madras]

47.7. THE PAYMENT OF WAGES (AMENDMENT) ACT, 2005

1. *Enhancing the wage ceiling of Rs. 1600 per month to Rs. 6500 per month*
2. *To substitute the expressions "the Government" a State Government" by the expression " appropriate Government"*
3. *Removing the ambiguities/weakness form the existant provisions of the Act and prescribing more effective grievance redressal*
4. *Strengthening compesnation and penal provisions of Act.*

The Payment of Wages Act, 1936 was enacted with a view of ensuring that wages payable to employed persons covered by the Act were disbursed by the employers within the prescribed time limit and that no deductions other than those authorised by law were made by them. The last amendment was made in 1982 and several provisions of the Act have become obsolete over the years. Many proposals have been received by the Government for amending various provisions which are creating practical difficulties in enforcement of this Act. In order to bring this law in uniformty with other labour laws as also to make it more effective and practicable, the following changes, *inter alia*, have been made in the Act:

1. *D.P. Kelkar* v. *Ambadas*, AIR 1971 Bombay 124

1. ***Enhancing the wage ceiling of Rs. 1600 per month to Rs. 6500 per month***: The then existing ceiling of Rs. 1000 per month was last revised to Rs. 1600 per month in 1982. Since then a large number of employed persons have gone out of the purview of the Act due to successive rise in wages levels resulting from rise in the cost of living. Thus, with a view to covering more employed persons, the wage ceiling has been enhanced from Rs. 1600 per month to Rs. 6500 per month.
2. ***To substitute the expressions "the Central Government" or "a State Government" by the expression "appropriate Government"***: In Parliamentary enactments relating to labour, other than the Payment of Wages Act, 1936, the enforcing authorities are either the Central Government or the State Governments depending upon the nature of industry. However, for implementing the Payment of Wages Act, 1936, matters are referred to the State Governments and quite often action required to be taken by them is delayed. In order that this law is in conformity with the other labour laws, the concepts of "appropriate Government" is introduced by this Amendment Act of 2005.
3. ***Removing the ambiguities/weakness from the existant provisions of the Act and prescribing more effective grievance redressal***: Over the years, it has been noticed that certain provisions of the Act have been differently interpreted thus leading to administrative difficulties in implementing the same. In order to remove ambiguities, appropriate changes have been made in sections 3, 7, 8 and 15 of the Act which respectively deal with responsibility for payment of wages, deductions from wages, fines and claims in certain cases.
4. ***Strengthening compensation and penal provisions of the Act***: The penal provisions of the Act have become almost insignificant due to passage of time as well as decrease in money value since these provisions were last amended in 1982. The penal provisions have been made more stringent by enhancing the quantum of penalties by amending section 20 of the Act.

TEST QUESTIONS

1. Explain the legal provisions relating to the applicability of the Payment of Wages Act, 1936. What is the wage-ceiling for application of the Act?
2. Write a note on the changes introduced by the Payment of Wages (Amendment) Act, 2005.
3. Define the term 'wages' as defined in the Payment of Wages Act, 1936 stating clearly the items included in and excluded from 'wages'.
4. Explain the following terms as defined in the Payment of Wages Act, 1936.
   (*a*) Appropriate Government (*b*) Wages
   (*c*) Employer and Employed person (*d*) Industrial or Other Establishment
5. Write a note on objects and application of the Payment of Wages Act, 1936. State the items which are not included in 'wages' payable to employed persons.
6. Define the term 'industrial or other establishment' as used in the Payment of Wages Act, 1936. State the items which are included in 'wages' payable to employed persons.

MULTIPLE CHOICE QUESTIONS

1. The Payment of Wages Act, 1936 came into force on 28th March, 1937 and it extends to
   (*a*) whole of India (*b*) whole of India except Jammu & Kashmir
   (*c*) states notified from time to time (*d*) all states except union territories

2. The Payment of Wages Act, 1936 applies to persons employed in
   (*a*) any factory
   (*b*) industrial or other establishment
   (*c*) railway
   (*d*) all of these
3. For the applicability of the Payment of Wages Act, 1936, the wage ceiling has been enhanced from Rs. 1600 per month to
   (*a*) Rs. 4500 per month
   (*b*) Rs. 5500 per month
   (*c*) Rs. 6500 per month
   (*d*) Rs. 7500 per month
4. The term 'industrial or other establishment' as defined in section 2 (ii) of the Payment of Wages Act, 1936 means:
   (*a*) Dock, wharf or jetty
   (*b*) Mine, quarry or oil field
   (*c*) Inland vessel, plantation
   (*d*) all of these
5. In which of the following section of Payment of Wages Act, the term 'wages' is defined?
   (*a*) 2 (ii)
   (*b*) 2 (vi)
   (*c*) 2 (iia)
   (*d*) 2 (via)

ANSWERS

1. (*a*) **2.** (*d*) **3.** (*c*) **4.** (*d*) **5.** (*b*)

OBJECTIVE TYPE QUESTIONS WITH REASONING

State with reasons whether the following statements are correct or incorrect.

1. The term 'appropriate government' under the Payment of Wages Act, 1936 includes only the Central Government.
2. The expressions 'employer' and 'employed person', for the purposes of the Payment of Wages Act, 1936 also include the legal representatives of deceased employer and deceased employed person.
3. The expression 'wages' include the amount of bonus payable to an employed person.
4. Any travelling allowance or the value of any travelling concession is included in 'wages' as defined in the Payment of Wages Act.

ANSWERS

1. ***Incorrect.*** Both the Central and the State Governments are included in the definition of appropriate government [Section 2 (*i*)].
2. ***Correct.*** The sections 2 (*ib*) and 2 (*ia*) defining these terms make express provision in this regard.
3. ***Correct.*** The payment of bonus has become an implied term of employment not dependent upon the profits and thus comes under the category of remuneration.
4. ***Incorrect.*** These expressions have been expressly excluded under Section 2 (*vi*) defining the term 'wages'.

48

CHAPTER

PAYMENT OF WAGES

48.1 INTRODUCTION

The term 'wages*' means all remuneration (whether by way of salary, allowance or otherwise) expressed in terms of money or capable of being so expressed which would, if the terms of employment, express or implied, were fulfilled, be payable to a person employed in respect of his employment or work done in such employment.

The main object of the Payment of Wages Act, 1936 is to regulate the payment of wages of certain classes of employed persons. In this chapter we shall discuss the legal provisions relating to payment of wages which may be grouped under the following heads:

1. Responsibility for payment of wages [Section 3]
2. Fixation of wage-period [Section 4]
3. Time of payment of wages [Section 5]
4. Mode of payment of wages [Section 6]

48.2. RESPONSIBILITY FOR PAYMENT OF WAGES

The responsibility for the payment of wages is that of the employer. He is legally responsible to pay wages to the persons employed by him.

It is important to note that for the purposes of the payment of wages, the 'employer' includes the legal representatives of the deceased employer [Section 2 (*ib*)]. Thus, where the employer dies, it shall be the responsibility of his legal representatives to make the payment of wages to the employed person. Likewise, the expression 'employed person' also includes the legal representatives of the deceased employed person. This means that in case of death of the 'employed person', his legal representatives shall be entitled to receive the wages to which the deceased employed person had become entitled to receive.

The legal provisions relating to employer's responsibility for payment of wages are contained in Section 3 of the Act which has recently been amended by the Payment of Wages (Amendment) Act, 2005. These provisions are as under:

* This term has been discussed in detail in the previous chapter.

1. Responsibility of employer [Section 3 (1)]

Every employer shall be responsible for the payment of all wages required to be paid under this Act to persons employed by him.

2. Responsibility of certain named, nominated or designated persons [Section 3 (1) a to e]

The clauses (a) to (e) of Section 3 (1) specifies the following cases in which the responsibility for payment of wages shall be of the certain named, nominated or designated persons:

(*a*) ***In case of persons employed in factories*** : In this case, if a person has been named as the manager of the factory under Section 7 (1) (f) of the Factories Act, 1948, such manager shall be responsible for the payment of wages to the employed persons.

(*b*) ***In case of persons employed in industrial or other establishments*** : In this case, if there is a person responsible to the employer for the supervision and control of industrial or other establishment, then such person shall be responsible for the payment of wages to the employed persons.

(*c*) ***In case of persons employed upon railways (other than in factories)*** : In this case, if the employer is the railway administration and the railway administration has nominated some person in this behalf for the local area concerned, then such nominated person shall be responsible for payment of wages to the employed persons.

(*d*) ***In case of persons employed in the case of contractord*** : In this case, a person designated by such contractor who is directly under his charge, shall be responsible for the payment of wages to the employed persons.

(*e*) ***In case of persons employed in any other case*** : In this case, a person designated by the employer as a person responsible for complying with the provisions of this Act, shall be responsible for payment of wages to the employed persons.

3. Ultimate responsibility of employer [Section 3 (2)]

It shall be the responsibility of the employer to make payment of all wages required to be made under this Act in case the *contractor* or the *person designated by the employer* fails to make such payments.

The provisions of clauses 3 (1) (d), 3 (1) (e) and 3 (2) discussed in points (d), (e) and 3 above, have been inserted by the Payment of Wages (Amendment) Act, 2005. The object was to remove the ambiguities and weaknesses from the existing provisions. The amended Section 3 has removed the doubts regarding responsibility for payment of wages in case the contractor or the person designated by the employer fails to make the payment. Now it has been specifically made clear that in case of such failure on the part of the contractor or designated person, it shall be the responsibility of the employer himself to make the payment of wages.

48.3. FIXATION OF WAGE-PERIOD

The expression 'wage-period' means the period in respect of which the wages shall be payable. The persons who are responsible for the payment of wages to the employed persons, shall fix the wage-period in respect of which the wages shall be payable by them. It may, however, be noted that the wages period shall not in any case exceed one month [Section 4].

48.4. TIME OF PAYMENT OF WAGES

1. *Cases where less than one thousand persons are employed*
2. *Other cases whwe more persons are employed*
3. *Cases where employment is terminated*
4. *Payment of wages on working day*

The legal provisions relating to the time of payment of wages are contained in Section 5 and may be discussed as under :

1. ***Cases where less than one thousand persons are employed* [Section 5 (1) (*a*)]** : If the number of persons employed in any railway, factory or industrial or other establishment is less than one thousand persons, wages shall be paid before the expiry of the seventh day after the last day of the wage period in respect of which wages are payable.
2. ***Other cases where more persons are employed* [Section 5 (1) (*b*)]** : The wages of every person employed in *any other* railway, factory or industrial or other establishment, shall be paid before the expiry of the tenth day after the last day of the wage period in respect of which wages are payable.
   However, in the case of persons employed on a dock, wharf or jetty or in a mine, the balance of wages found due on completion of the final tonnage account of the ship or wagons loaded or unloaded, as the case may be, shall be paid before the expiry of the seventh day from the day of such completion [Section 5, proviso].
3. ***Cases where employment is terminated* [Section 5 (2)]** : In case of the termination of the employment of an employee, the wages earned by such employee shall be paid before the expiry of the *second working day* from the day on which his employment is terminated.
   However, where the employment of any person in an establishment is terminated due to the closure of the establishment for any reason other than a weekly or other recognised holiday, the wages earned by him shall be paid before the expiry of the *second day* from the day on which his employment is so terminated [Section 5 (2), proviso]. In this case, the second day may or may not be the working day.
4. ***Payment of wages on working day* [Section 5 (4)]** : All payment of wages shall be made on a working day. However as discussed above, in case of termination of employment due to closure of establishment, the wages shall be paid before the expiry of second day from the day of termination even if it is not the working days.
   The appropriate government may exempt the persons responsible for payment of wages from the operation of the above provisions relating to the time of payment of wages as discussed in points (1) to (3). The appropriate government may make an order of exemption in the following cases [Section 5 (3)] :
   (*a*) Where wages are payable to persons employed upon any railway otherwise than in a factory, or
   (*b*) Where wages are payable to persons employed as daily rated workers in Public Works Department of the Central or State Government. However, in this case no exemption order shall be made except in consultation with the Central Government.

48.5. MODE OF PAYMENT OF WAGES

All wages shall be paid in current coin or currency notes or in both.

However, the employer may, after obtaining the written authorisation of the employed person, pay him the wages either by cheque or by crediting the wages in his bank account [Section 6].

TEST QUESTIONS

1. "The responsibility for payment of wages is that of employer"- explain.
2. Discuss the legal provisions, relating to payment of wages, as contained in the Payment of Wages Act, 1936.
3. Discuss the legal provisions relating to employer's responsibility for payment of wages as contained in the Payment of Wages Act, 1936.
4. What is wage-period? Explain the legal provisions relating to time of payment of wages as contained in the Payment of Wages Act, 1936.
5. Write short notes on the following :
   (*a*) Time of payment of wages (*b*) Mode of payment of wages.

MULTIPLE CHOICE QUESTIONS

1. In case of person employed in factories, the person responsible to make payment of wages under the Payment of Wages Act, 1936, is
   (*a*) The person named as manager of the factory under the Factories Act, 1948.
   (*b*) The person named as incharge of the factory under the Payment of Wages Act, 1936.
   (*c*) The person responsible for the supervision and control of the factory.
   (*d*) The person nominated by the Trade Union of which the employed person is the member.
2. The provisions relating to the responsibility for payment of wages are contained in which of the following Section of Payment of Wages Act, 1936 ?
   (*a*) Section 2 (*b*) Section 3
   (*c*) Section 4 (*d*) None of these
3. In case the contractor or the person designated by the employer fails to make the payment of wages under the Payment of Wages Act, then under Section 3 (2) it shall be the responsibility of the
   (*a*) contractor (*b*) Appropriate Government
   (*c*) employer (*d*) contractor and employer jointly
4. The 'wage-period' under section 4 of the Payment of Wages Act, 1936 shall not in any case exceed
   (*a*) one month (*b*) 30 days
   (*c*) two months (*d*) 60 days
5. Under the Payment of Wages Act, 1936, all the payment of wages should be made on
   (*a*) 1st day of the month (*b*) 5th day of the month
   (*c*) wage-day (*d*) working day

ANSWERS

1. (*a*)	2. (*b*)	3. (*c*)	4. (*a*)	5. (*d*)

OBJECTIVE TYPE QUESTIONS WITH REASONING

State with reasons whether the following statements are correct or incorrect

1. Other than the employer, certain named, nominated or designated persons are also responsible for payment of wages under the Payment of Wages Act, 1936.
2. Where the number of persons employed in any railway, factory or industrial or other establishment is less than one thousands persons, the wages shall be paid before the expiry of the 10th day after the last day of the wage-period.

3. Where the employment of any person is terminated due to closure of the establishment for any reason other than a weekly or other recognised holiday, the wages earned by the employee shall be paid before the expiry of the second working day from termination.
4. All the wages shall be paid in current coins or currency notes or in both.

ANSWERS

1. *Correct.* Section 3 (1) clauses (a) to (e) expressly make legal provisions in this regard.
2. *Incorrect.* In such cases, the wages shall be paid on the expiry of the 7th day after the last day of wage-period [Section 5 (1) (a)]. The wages on the expiry of 10th day are paid in cases other than those mentioned here [Section 5 (1) (b)].
3. *Incorrect.* In such cases, the wages shall be paid before the expiry of *second day* from termination and this day may or may not be the working day [Section 5 (2), proviso]
4. *Correct.* Section 6 makes a specific provision in this regard.

49

CHAPTER

DEDUCTIONS FROM WAGES

49.1. INTRODUCTION

Ordinarily, the wages of an employed person should be paid to him without making any deductions. Sections 7 (1) of the Payment of Wages Act lays down a general prohibition against any deduction from the wages of an employed person. This section provides that the wages of an employed person shall be paid to him without deductions of any kind except those authorised by or under this Act. Thus, only the permissible or authorised deductions are allowed to be made from the wages of an employed person.

The legal provisions relating to the deductions from wages may be discussed under the following heads:

1 Deemed deductions [Section 7 (1), Explanation I & II]
2. Authorised or permissible deductions [Section 7 (2)]
3. Extent of authorised deductions [Sections 7 (3)]
4. Legal provisions relating to authorised deductions [Section 8 to 13]

49.2. DEEMED DEDUCTIONS

Every payment made by the employed person to the employer or his agent shall, for the purposes of this Act, be deemed to be a deduction from wages [Section 7 (1), Explanation I].

Any loss of wages resulting from the imposition, upon a person, of the following penalties shall not be deemed to be a deduction from wages :

(*i*) the withholding of increment or promotion (including the stoppage of increment at an efficiency bar):

(*ii*) the reduction to a lower post or time scale or to a lower stage in a time scale : or (*iii*) suspension;

However, the above stated penalties shall not be deemed to be a deduction from wages only if the rules framed by the employer for the imposition of any such penalty are in conformity with the requirements, if any, specified by the State Government by Gazette Notification [Section 7 (1), Explanation II].

49.3. AUTHORISED OR PERMISSIBLE DEDUCTIONS

Authorised or permissible deductions are those which are specified in this Act and can be made only in accordance with the provisions of this Act. Any deductions from the wages of employed person governed by the Payment of Wages Act, unless authorised by the Act, shall be considered to be illegal. Section 7(2) specifies the list of authorised deductions. The circumstances and manner in which the authorised deductions can be made are provided in Sections 8 to 13 which will be discussed later in this chapter.

In view of Section 7 (2), deductions from wages of an employed person shall be made only in accordance with the provisions of this Act, and may be of the following kinds only, namely:

1. Deductions for fines [Section 7 (2) (*a*)].
2. Deductions for absence from duty [Section 7 (2) (*b*)].
3. Deductions for damage or loss of goods or money [Section 7 (2) (*c*)].
4. Deductions for house-accommodation supplied by employer [Section 7 (2) (*d*)].
5. Deductions for amenities and services supplied by employer [Section 7 (2) (*e*)].
6. Deductions for recovery of advances [Section 7 (2) (*f*)].
7. Deductions for recovery of loan from labour welfare fund [Section 7 (2) (*ff*)].
8. Deductions for recovery of loan for house building [Section 7 (2) (*fff*)].
9. Deductions for income-tax payable by the employed person [Section 7 (2) (*g*)].
10. Deductions under the order made by court or competent authority [Section 7 (2) (*h*)].
11. Deductions for subscriptions to a recognised or approved provident fund [Section 7 (2) (*i*)].
12. Deductions for repayment of advances from any recognised or approved provident fund [Section 7 (2) (*i*)].
13. Deductions for payments to cooperative societies [Section 7 (2) (*j*)].
14. Deductions for payment of insurance premium to Life Insurance Corporation of India [Section 7 (2) (*k*)].
15. Deductions for payment of contribution to a welfare fund [Section 7 (2) (*kk*)].
16. Deductions for payment of membership fee to any registered trade union [Section 7 (2) (*kkk*)].
17. Deductions for payment of insurance premium on Fidelity Guarantee Bonds [Section 7 (2) (*l*)].
18. Deductions for recovery of losses sustained by railway administration [Section 7 (2) (*m*), (n), (*o*)].
19. Deductions for contribution to Prime Minister's National Relief Fund or to any other notified Fund [Section 7 (2) (*p*)].
20. Deductions for contribution to any insurance scheme framed by the Central Government for the benefit of its employees [Section 7 (2) (*q*)].

In *Balmer Lawrie Workers' Union, Bombay* v. *Balmer Lawrie & Co. Ltd.*, (1985) 1 LLJ 314, the Supreme Court has observed that any deduction from the wages of the workmen, under a settlement between representative of workers union and the employer would be a permissible deduction as it is the outcome of an understanding between the parties even though such deduction may not be authorised or permissible under the Act.

Above deductions alongwith the legal provisions as contained in Sections 8 to 13 providing for the circumstances and manner in which such deductions can be made will be discussed in detail in the following pages.

49.4. EXTENT OF AUTHORISED DEDUCTIONS

The extent (*i.e.*, the total amount) of the authorised deductions is prescribed in Section 7 (3) of the Act. As per this section, the total amount of deductions which may be made in respect of all the above authorised deductions in any wage period from the wages of any employed person shall not exceed the percentage as stated below:

1. ***In case of deductions for payment to cooperative societies* [*Sections 3 (i)*]:** In case where deductions are wholly or partly made for payments to co-operative societies under Section 7 (2) (j), the total amount of deductions shall not exceed 75% of the wages payable to the employed person in the wage-period.
2. ***In other cases* [*Section 3 (ii)*]:** In case of all authorised deductions other than the deduction for payment to co-operative societies, the total amount of such deductions shall not exceed 50% of the wages payable to the employed person in the wage-period.

If the total deductions authorised under the Act exceeds the above stated percentage of 75% or 50%, the excess may be recovered in such manner as may be prescribed [Section 7 (3) Explanation].

However any amount payable by an employed person under any law is recoverable by the employer from the wages of such person. Section 7 (4) makes a specific provision in this regard which lays down that nothing contained in Section 7 shall preclude the employer from recovering from the wages of the employed person or otherwise any amount payable by such person under any law for the time being in force other than the Railways Act, 1989.

49.5. LEGAL PROVISIONS RELATING TO AUTHORISED DEDUCTIONS

The legal provisions relating to authorised deductions listed in the previous article are contained in Section 8 to 13 of the Act which provide the circumstances and manner in which such deductions can be made. These provisions are discussed below under separate heads in Articles 49.6 to 49.13.

49.6. DEDUCTIONS FOR FINE

Sections 7 (2) (a) provides that deductions by way of fine from the wages of an employed person shall be made only in accordance with the provisions of this.

The general requirements and conditions for the imposition and deduction of fine are provided in Section 8, which may be stated as under :

1. The fine can be imposed on an employed person only in respect of such acts or omissions on his part as the employer, with the previous approval of appropriate Government or prescribed authority, may have specified by notice [Section 8 (1)]. Thus, the fine can be imposed only in respect of specified acts or omissions on the part of the employed person.
2. A notice specifying such acts and omissions shall be exhibited in the prescribed manner on the premises in which the employment is carried on or in the case of

persons employed upon a railway (otherwise than in a factory), at the prescribed place or places [Section 8 (2)].

3. No fine shall be imposed on any employed person until he has been given an opportunity of showing cause against the fine, or otherwise, than in accordance with such procedure as may be prescribed for the imposition of fines [Section 8 (3)].
4. The total amount of fine which may be imposed in any one wage-period on any employed person shall not exceed an amount equal to three per cent of the wages payable to him in respect of that wage-period [Section 8 (4)].
5. No fine shall be imposed on any employed person who is under the age of fifteen years [Sections 8 (5)].
6. No fine imposed on any employed person shall be recovered from him by instalments or after the expiry of ninety* days from the day on which it was imposed [Section 8 (6)].
7. Every fine shall be deemed to have been imposed on the day of the act or omission in respect of which it was imposed [Section 8 (7)].
8. All fines and all realisations thereof shall be recorded in a register to be kept by the person responsible for the payment of wages under section 3 in such form as may be prescribed; and all such realisations shall be applied only for such purposes which are beneficial to the persons employed in the factory or establishment as are approved by the prescribed authority [Section 8 (8)].

When the persons employed upon or in any railway, factory or [3] industrial or other establishment are part only of a staff employed under the same management, all such realisations may be credited to a common fund maintained for the staff as a whole, provided that the fund shall be applied only for such purposes as are approved by the prescribed authority [Section 8, Explanation].

49.7. DEDUCTIONS FOR ABSENCE FROM DUTY

Section 7 (2) (b) provides that deductions, for absence from duty, from the wages of an employed person shall be made only in accordance with provisions of this Act.

The general requirements and conditions for such deductions are provided in Section 9, which may be stated as under:

1. The deductions for absence from duty may be made only on account of the absence of an employed person from the place of work. The 'place of work' means the place or places where by the terms of employment, an employed person is required to work. The absence from duty may be for the whole or any part of the period during which an employer person is required to work [Section 9 (1)]
2. An employed person shall be deemed to be absent from the place where he is required to work if, although present in such place, he refuses, in pursuance of a stay-in strike or for any other cause which is not reasonable in the circumstances, to carry out his work [Section 9, Explanation].
3. The amount of such deductions, should bear to his wages the same proportion as his absence bears to the total wage-period during which he was by the terms of his employment required to work [Section 9 (2)]
4. If ten or more employed persons, acting in concert, absent themselves *without due notice* required under the terms of their contracts of employment and *without reasonable cause,* such deduction from any such person may include such amount

* Substituted by the Payment of Wages (Amendment) Act, 2005 for the "sixty days"

not exceeding his wages for eight days as may by any such terms be due to the employer in lieu of due notice. These provisions are subject to any rule made by the appropriate government [Section 9 (2), proviso].

49.8. DEDUCTIONS FOR DAMAGES OR LOSS OF GOODS OR MONEY

Section 7 (2) (c), provides that deductions for damages or loss of goods or money from the wages of an employed person shall be made only in accordance with the provisions of this Act.

The general requirements and conditions for such deductions are provided in Section 7 (2) (c) and Section 10, which may be stated as under :

1. The deductions for damage to or loss of goods are allowed only when the goods were expressly entrusted to the employed person for custody. And the deduction for loss of money is allowed only in respect of that money for which the employed person is required to give account. In addition to this, such deductions will be allowed only where such damage or loss is *directly attributable to the neglect or default of the employed person* [Section 7 (2) (*c*)].
2. Such deductions shall not exceed the amount of damage or loss caused to the employer by the neglect or default of the employed person [Section 10 (1)].
3. Such deductions shall not be made until the employed person has been given an opportunity of showing cause (*i.e.*, reasons) against the deductions. Or such deductions can be made only in accordance with such procedure as may be prescribed for making such deductions [Section 10 (1A)].
4. All such deductions and all realisations thereof shall be recorded in a register to be kept by the person responsible for making payment of wages [Section 10 (2)].

49.9. DEDUCTIONS FOR SERVICES RENDERED TO EMPLOYED PERSONS

The following two types of services rendered to the employed person are covered under this clause:

(*a*) ***House-accommodation supplied to the employed person*** **[Section 7 (2) (*d*)]:** The house-accommodation may be supplied by the employer or by the government or any housing board whether or not the government or the housing board is the employer.

(*b*) ***Amenities and services supplied to the employed person*** **[Section 7 (2) (*e*)]:** The amenities and services should be supplied by the employer. Deductions for such amenities or services are allowed as the State Government or the specified officer may, by general or special order authorise.

The word 'services' in this clause does not include the supply of tools and raw material required for the purposes of employment [Section 7 (2) (*e*), Explanation].

The general requirements and conditions for both the above deductions are provided in Section 11, which may be stated as under :

1. The deductions for 'house-accommodation' and for 'amenities and services' supplied to the employed person shall not be made from the wages of an employed person unless these services have been accepted by him as terms of employment or otherwise [Section 11].

2. The deductions for 'house-accommodation' and for 'amenities and services', as the case may be, shall not exceed an amount equivalent, to the value of 'house-accommodation' or 'amenities and services' supplied to the employed person [Section 11].

3. The deductions for amenities and services shall be subject to such conditions as the appropriate government may impose [Section 11].

49.10. DEDUCTIONS FOR RECOVERY OF ADVANCES

Sections 7 (2) (f) provides that the deductions for recovery of advances from the wages of an employed person shall be made only in accordance with the provisions of this Act. Every type of advance, including advances for travelling allowance or conveyance allowance, is covered under this clause. The deductions for interest due in respect of the advance and for adjustment of over-payment of wages are also allowed under this section.

The general requirements for such deductions are provided in Section 12 which provides that these deductions shall be made subject to the following conditions :

1. Recovery of an advance of money given before employment began, shall be made from the first payment of wages in respect of a complete wage-period, but no recovery shall be made of such advances given for travelling expenses [Section 12 (*a*)].
2. Recovery of an advance of money given after employment began, shall be subject to such conditions as the appropriate Government may impose [Section 12 (*aa*)]
3. Recovery of advances of wages not already earned, shall be subject to any rules made by the appropriate Government regulating the extent to which such advances may be given and the instalments by which they may be recovered [Section 12 (*b*)].

49.11. DEDUCTIONS FOR RECOVERY OF LOANS

Section 7 (2) (*fff*) provides that deductions for recovery of loans from the wages of an employed person shall be made only in accordance with the provisions of this Act. The loan granted for house-building or for any other purpose approved by the State Government is covered under this clause. The deductions for interest due on such loan is also allowed under this section.

The general requirements for such deductions are provided in Section 12-A which lays down that these deductions shall be subject to any rules made by the Appropriate Government regulating the extent to which such loans may be granted and the rate of interest payable thereon.

The deduction for recovery of loans made from any fund constituted for the welfare of labour in accordance with rule approved by the State Government and the interest due in respect thereof, is also allowed [Section 7 (2) (*ff*)].

49.12. DEDUCTIONS MADE WITH WRITTEN AUTHORISATION OF EMPLOYED PERSON

1. *Deductions for payment of insurance premium on Life*
2. *Deductions for purchase of goverment securities*
3. *Deductions for contribution to a welfare funad*
4. *Deductions for payment of membership fee to registered trade union*
5. *Deductions for contribution to PM's Relif Fund*

Following deductions are allowed from the wages of an employed person if these are made with the *written authorisation* of the employed person:

1. ***Deductions for payment of insurance premium on life*** **[*Section 7 (2k)*]** : The deduction for payment of any premium to the Life Insurance Corporation of India on the life insurance policy of the employed person is authorised deduction. However, these deductions shall be made subject to such conditions as the Appropriate Government may impose [Section 13].

2. ***Deductions for purchase of government securities*** **[*Sections 7 (2) (k)*]:** The deductions for the purpose of securities of the Central Government or State Government, or for any amount being deposited in any Post Office Saving Bank in furtherance of any savings scheme of any such government are authorised deductions. However, these deductions shall be made subject to such conditions as the Appropriate Government may impose [Section 13]:

3. *Deductions for contribution to a welfare fund* [*Section 7* (2) (*kk*)]: The deduction for payment of employed person's contribution to any fund constituted by the employer or by the trade union registered under the Trade Union Act, 1926, for the welfare of the employed persons or their family members or both are authorised deductions. However, such fund must be approved by the appropriate government or any officer specified in this behalf, and the payments should be made during the continuance of such approval.

4. *Deductions for payment of membership fee to registered trade union* [*Section 7* (2) (*kkk*)]: : The deductions for payment of the fees payable by an employed person for the membership of any trade union registered under the Trade Unions Act, 1926 are authorised deductions.

5. *Deductions for contribution to PM's Relief Fund* [*Section 7* (2) (*p*)] : The deductions for contribution to Prime Minister's National Relief Fund or to a specified fund notified by the Central Government are authorised deductions.

49.13. DEDUCTIONS FOR RECOVERY OF LOSSES SUSTAINED BY RAILWAY ADMINISTRATION

The deductions for recovery following types of losses sustained by railway administration are allowed if made in accordance with the provisions of this Act :

1. Losses sustained on account of acceptance, by the employed person, of counterfeit or base coins or mutilated or forged currency notes [Section 7 (2) (*m*)].
2. Losses sustained on account of the failure of the employed person to invoice, to bill, to collect or to account for appropriate charges due to the railway administration in respect of fares, freight, demurrage, wharfage and carnage or in respect of sale of goods in catering establishments or in respect of sale of commodities in grain shops [Section 7 (2) (*n*)].
3. Losses sustained on account of any rebate or refund incorrectly granted by the employed person where such loss is directly attributable to his neglect or default [Section 7 (2) (*o*)].

The general requirements for deductions of above stated losses are provided in Section 10 (1 *A*) which lays down that such deductions shall not be made unless the employed person has been given an opportunity of showing cause (*i.e.*, reasons) against the deductions. Or such deductions can be made only in accordance with such procedure as may be prescribed for making such deductions.

49.14. OTHER AUTHORISED DEDUCTIONS

We have discussed above the deductions in respect of which separate provisions have been made in Sections 8 to 13 in addition to the requirements of Section 7 (2) specifying these deductions.

Following are the deductions in respect of which no such separate provisions have been made, but these have been duly authorised under Section 7 (2) of the Act.

1. Deductions for income-tax payable by the employed person [Section 7 (2) (*g*)].
2. Deductions required to be made by order of the court or other authority competent to make such order [Section 7 (2) (*h*)].
3. Deductions for subscription to any provident fund to which the Provident Fund

Act, 1925 applies. A recognised provident fund and any provident fund approved by the appropriate government is also covered under this clause. The deductions for repayment of advances from such provident funds are also allowed [Section 7 (2) (i)].

4. Deductions for payments to co-operative societies as approved by the appropriate government* or by any officer specified in this behalf [Section 7 (2) (*j*)]. These deductions shall be made subject to such conditions as the appropriate government* may impose [Section 13].
5. Deductions for payments to a scheme of insurance maintained by the Indian Post Office [Section 7 (2) (*j*)]. These deductions shall be made subject to such conditions as the appropriate government* may impose [Section 13].
6. Deductions for payment of insurance premiad on Fidelity Guarantee Bonds [Section 7 (2) (l)].
7. Deductions for contribution to any insurance scheme framed by the Central Government for the benefit of its employees [Section 7 (2) (*q*)].

TEST QUESTIONS

1. Discuss the legal provisions, relating to deductions from wages, as contained in the Payment of Wages Act, 1936.
2. "Deductions from wages of an employed person shall be made only in accordance with the provisions of the Payment of Wages Act" — Comment.
3. What do you mean by authorised deductions? Enumerate the deductions authorised under the Payment of Wages Act, 1936.
4. Explain the requirements and conditions under which deductions by way of fine be made from the wages of an employed person. What is the extent of authorised deductions under the Payment of Wages Act, 1936 ?
5. "Deductions from the wages can also be made with written authorisation of employed person"–comment stating the relevant provisions of the Payment of Wages Act, 1936.
6. State the losses sustained by Railway Administration for which deductions can be made from the wages of an employed person. Is there any provision in the Payment of Wages Act for giving an opportunity of showing cause against such deductions ?
7. Write short notes on the following specifying the legal provisions as contained in the Payment of Wages Act, 1936 ;
   (*a*) Deductions for absence from duty.
   (*b*) Deductions for damages or loss of money or goods.
   (*c*) Deductions for services rendered to employed person.
   (*d*) Deductions for recovery of loans and advances.

MULTIPLE CHOICE QUESTIONS

1. Which of the following deductions from wages of an employed person are allowed under Section 7 (2) of the Payment of Wages Act, 1936 ?
   (*a*) deduction for fine
   (*b*) deductions for absence from duty
   (*c*) deductions for income tax payable by the employed person.
   (*d*) all of the above.
2. Where deductions are made for payments to a co-operative society under Section 7 (2) (j) of the Payment of Wages Act, the total amount of deductions shall not exceed :

* Substituted by the Payment of Wages (Amendment) Act, 2005 for "State Government"

(*a*) 25% of the wages payable in the wage-period
(*b*) 50% of the wages payable in the wage-period
(*c*) 75% of the wages payable in the wage-period
(*d*) 85% of the wages payable in the wage-period.

3. The fine for which deduction is allowed under the Payment of Wages Act, shall not be imposed on any employed person who is under the age of
   (*a*) 15 years (*b*) 18 years
   (*c*) 21 years (*d*) none of these
4. Deductions for which of the following services rendered to the employed person are allowed under Section 7 (2) of the Payment of Wages Act ?
   (*a*) House accommodation (*b*) Amenities and services
   (*c*) both (*a*) and (*b*) (*d*) none of the above
5. Which of the following statements is incorrect in respect of Section 7 (2) of the Payment of Wages Act, 1936 ?
   (*a*) deductions for contribution to Prime Minister's National Relief Fund is authorised one.
   (*b*) deductions for payment of insurance premia on Fidelity Guarantee Bond is authorised one.
   (*c*) deductions for contribution to any insurance scheme formed by Central Government for the benefits of its employee is authorised one.
   (*d*) None of these

ANSWERS

1. (*d*)	2. (*c*)	3. (*a*)	4. (*c*)	5. (*d*)

OBJECTIVE TYPE QUESTIONS WITH REASONING

State with reasons whether the following statements are correct or incorrect.

1. As a general rule the wages of an employed person shall be paid to him without deductions of any kind except those authorised under the Payment of Wages Act, 1926.
2. Every payment made by the employed person to the employer or his agent shall be deemed to be as deduction from wages under the Payment of Wages Act.
3. The fine imposed on any employed person can be recovered from him by instalments not exceeding four instalments.
4. The deduction for damage or loss to the goods entrusted to the employed person for custody is allowed under Section 7 (2) (*c*) of the Payment of Wages Act, 1936 irrespective of the reason for such damage or loss.
5. The deductions for losses sustained by the Railway Administration, on account of acceptance by the employed person of counterfeit or base coins or mutilated or forged currency notes are allowed under the Payment of Wages Act, 1936.

ANSWERS

1. ***Correct.*** Only the deductions authorised under Section 7 (2) of the Act are permissible.
2. ***Correct.*** Section 7 (1), Explanation, makes the express provision in the regard.
3. ***Incorrect.*** The fine imposed cannot be recovered by instalments. Also, the fine cannot be recovered after the expiry of 90 days from the date on which it was imposed [Section 8 (6)].
4. ***Incorrect.*** The deduction for such loss or damage is allowed only when the same is directly attributable to the neglect or default of the employed person.
5. ***Correct.*** Section 7 (2) (m) makes the express provision in this regard.

50

CHAPTER

MISCELLANEOUS PROVISIONS AND PENALTIES

1. Introduction.
2. Authorities to Hear and Decide Claims.
3. Application for Directions.
4. Procedure on Receipts of Application for Directions.
5. Payment of Undistributed Wages in cases of Death of Employed Person.
6. Penalty for Offences.

50.1 INTRODUCTION

In the previous chapters we have discussed the legal provisions relating to the payment of wages and deductions from wages. There are many other provisions in the Payment of Wages Act, 1936, which are equally important from the subject point of view. All these provisions alongwith the provisions for penalties have been clubbed together and explained in this chapter.

Following important provisions are explained in this chapter:

1. Authorities to hear and decide claims [Section 15 (1)].
2. Application for Directions [Section 15 (2)].
3. Procedure on Receipt of Application for Directions [Section 15 (3)].
4. Payment of Undistributed Wages in cases of Death of Employed Person [Section 25 A].
5. Penalty for Offences [Section 20].

50.2. AUTHORITIES TO HEAR AND DECIDE CLAIMS

The Appropriate Government has the power under Section 15 (1) to appoint the Authority to hear and decide all claims arising out of, (*a*) deductions from wages, or (*b*) delay in payment of wages, and (*c*) all matters incidental to such claims. The appointment shall be made by a notification in the Official Gazette and the area within which such authority shall exercise its jurisdiction shall also be specified by the Appropriate Government. The following officers may be appointed as authorities under this section :

1. Any Commissioner for Workmen's Compensation; or
2. Any officer of the Central Government exercising functions as,—
   (*i*) Regional Labour Commissioner; or
   (*ii*) Assistant Labour Commissioner with at least two years' experience; or
3. Any officer of the State Government not below the rank of Assistant Labour Commissioner with at least two years' experience; or

4. A presiding officer of any Labour Court or Industrial Tribunal, constituted under the Industrial Disputes Act, 1947, or under any corresponding law relating to the investigation and settlement of industrial disputes in force in the State; or
5. Any other officer with experience as a Judge of a Civil Court or a Judicial Magistrate.

The Appropriate Government may, if it considers necessary to do so, appoint more than one authority for any specified area.

50.3 APPLICATION FOR DIRECTIONS

An application for seeking directions from the above mentioned authority can be made in the following cases [Section 15 (2)] :

(1.) Where contrary to the provisions of this Act, any deduction has been made from the wages of an employed person, or
(2.) Where contrary to the provisions of this Act, any payment of wages has been delayed.

The applications for these directions may by made be any of the following persons:

(*a*) Employed person himself.
(*b*) Any legal practitioner.
(*c*) Any official of a registered trade union authorised in writing.
(*d*) Any inspector under this Act.
(*e*) Any other person acting with the permission of the authority.

It is important to note that every such application shall be presented within twelve months from the date on which the deduction from the wages was made or from the date on which the payment of the wages was due to be made, as the case may be. However, such application may be admitted after the said period of twelve months when the applicant satisfies the authority that he had sufficient cause for not making the application within such period.

50.4. PROCEDURE ON RECEIPT OF APPLICATION FOR DIRECTION

The procedure to be followed by the authority to entertain the application, is laid down in Section 15 (3) to 15 (4) and may be stated as under :

1. The Authority shall hear the applicant and the employer or other person responsible for payment of wages [Section 15 (3)].
2. After giving them an opportunity of being heard and after such further inquiry as may be necessary, the Authority may pass the necessary directions, that is to say :
   (*a*) *In case of application for refund of deducted amount*, the Authority may direct the refund of the deducted amount, or
   (*b*) *In case of application for delayed wages*, the Authority may direct the payment the delayed wages.

   Such a direction may be made together with the payment of such compensation as the authority may think fit. However, the amount of compensation shall not exceed ten times the amount deducted in the former case, and not exceeding Rs. 3000 but not less than Rs. 1,500 in the latter case [Section 15 (3)].
3. In cases, where the amount deducted or delayed wages are paid before the disposal of the application, the Authority may direct the payment of such compensation as the authority thinks fit but not exceeding Rs. 2,000 [Section 15 (3)].
4. The provisions stated above are without prejudice to any other penalty to which such employer or other person is liable under this Act (Section 15 (3)].
5. The application for claim shall be disposed of (*i.e.*, decided) as far as practicable

within three months from the date of registration of claim by the authority. However, this period may be extended if *both the parties* to the dispute agree for any *bona fide* reason [Section 15 (3), provisos].

6. In the case of delayed payment, no direction for the payment of compensation shall be made if the authority is satisfied that the delay was due to :
   (*a*) a *bona fide* error or *bona fide* dispute as to the amount payable to the employed person; or
   (*b*) the occurrence of an emergency, or the existence of exceptional circumstances, the person responsible for the payment of the wages was unable, in spite of exercising reasonable diligence; or
   (*c*) the failure of the employed person to apply for or accept payment.
7. If the authority hearing an application under this section is satisfied—
   (*a*) that the application was either malicious or vexatious, the authority may direct that a penalty not exceeding three hundred seventy five rupees be paid to the employer or other person responsible for the payment of wages by the person presenting the application; or
   (*b*) that in any case in which compensation is directed to be paid by the employer but the applicant ought not to have been compelled to seek redress under this section, the authority may direct that a penalty not exceeding three hundred seventy five rupees be paid to the appropriate Government by the employer or other person responsible for the payment of wage [Section 15 (4)].

50.5. PAYMENT OF UNDISTRIBUTED WAGES IN CASES OF DEATH OF EMPLOYED PERSON

The legal provisions relating to the payment of undistributed wages in case of death of employed person are contained in Section 25 A of the Act, which makes the following rules in this regard :

1. Subject to the other provisions of the Act, all amounts payable to an employed person as wages shall, if such amounts could not or cannot be paid on account of his death before payment or on account of his whereabouts not being known—
   (*a*) be paid to the person nominated by him in this behalf in accordance with the rules made under this Act; or
   (*b*) where no such nomination has been made or where for any reasons such amounts cannot be paid to the person so nominated, be deposited with the prescribed authority who shall deal with the amounts so deposited in such manner as may be prescribed.
2. Where, in accordance with the above provisions, all amounts payable to an employed person as wages—
   (*a*) are paid by the employer to the person nominated by the employed person, or
   (*b*) are deposited by the employer with the prescribed authority,
   the employer shall be discharged of his liability to pay those wages

50.6. PENALTY FOR OFFENCES

The provisions relating penalty for offences under the Act are contained in Section 20 of the Act, which are as under :

1. Whoever being responsible for the payment of wages to an employed person shall be punishable with fine which shall not be less than Rs. 1500 but which may extend to

Rs. 7,500, if he contravenes any of the provisions relating to the following [Section 20 (1)]:

(*a*) Time of payment of wages [Section 5]
(*b*) Authorised deductions [Sections 7]
(*c*) Fines [Section 8]
(*d*) Deductions for absence from duty [Section 9]
(*e*) Deductions for damage or loss [Section 10]
(*f*) Deductions for services rendered [Section 11]
(*g*) Deductions for recovery of advances [Section 12]
(*h*) Deductions for recovery of loans [Section 12 A]
(*i*) Deductions for payment to co-operative societies and insurance scheme [Section 13]

2. Whoever being required under this Act to maintain any records or registers or to furnish any information or return—

(*a*) fails to maintain such register or record; or
(*b*) wilfully refuses or without lawful excuse neglects to furnish such information or return; or
(*c*) wilfully furnishes or causes to be furnished any information or return which he knows to be false; or
(*d*) refuses to answer or wilfully gives a false answer to any question necessary for obtaining any information required to be furnished under this Act,

shall, for each such offence, be punishable with fine which shall not be less than one thousand five hundred rupees but which may extend to seven thousand five hundred rupees [Section 20 (3)].

3. If any person fails or wilfully neglects to pay the wages of any employed person by the date fixed by the authority in this behalf, he shall, without prejudice to any other action that may be taken against him, be punishable with an additional fine which may extend to seven hundred fifty rupees for each day for which such failure or neglect continues [Section 20 (6)].

TEST QUESTIONS

1. What authorities can be appointed to hear and decide the claims arising under the Payment of Wages Act, 1936 ?
2. When and by whom an application for seeking directions from the authorities under the Payment of Wages Act be made ? State the applicable legal provisions.
3. Explain the legal provisions relating to the procedure followed by the authorities under the Payment of Wages Act, 1936.
4. Write short note on the following :
   (*a*) Payment of undistributed wages in cases of death of employed person.
   (*b*) Penalty for offences.

MULTIPLE CHOICE QUESTIONS

1. An authority, under the Payment of Wages Act, 1936, to hear and decide the claim is appointed by
   (*a*) Appropriate Government (*b*) State Government
   (*c*) President of India (*d*) Labour Commissioner
2. Which of the following officer can be appointed as an authority under the Payment of Wages Act ?

(a) Any Commissioner for Workmen's Compensation
(b) Any Labour Commissioner with at least two years experience
(c) A presiding officer of any Labour Court
(d) All of the above.

3. Which of the following persons can make an application for relief to the authority under the Payment of Wages Act ?
(a) Employed person himself (b) Any legal practitioner
(c) both (a) and (b) (d) none of the above

4. Which of the following statements is not correct under the Payment of Wages Act, 1936 ?
(a) The authority may pass an order directing the employer to make the payment of delayed wages.
(b) The authority cannot pass an order directing the refund of deducted amount.
(c) The authority may also direct the payment of compensation in addition to the other relief.
(d) The authority shall dispose of the claim application as far as possible within three months from the date of registration of claim with the authority.

5. The provisions relating to penalty for offences under the Payment of Wages Act are contained in
(a) Section 18 (b) Section 19 (c) Section 20 (d) Both Section 18 & 19

ANSWERS

1. (a)	2. (d)	3. (c)	4. (b)	5. (c)

The Payment of Gratuity Act, 1972

- Introduction and Application of the Act.
- Payment, Forfeiture and Recovery of Gratuity.
- Miscellaneous Provisions and Penalties.

INTRODUCTION AND APPLICATION OF THE ACT

51.1. INTRODUCTION

The 'gratuity' is a sort of retiring benefit to the workmen who have rendered long and unblemished service to the employer and thereby contributed to the prosperity of the employer.

Although the right of industrial workers had long been recognised by Tribunals, yet the law relating to payment of gratuity was very vague and uncertain before the passing of this Act. There was a good deal of disparity in the various schemes for the payment of gratuity. It was thus felt necessary to have Central Law on the subject so as to ensure a uniform pattern of payment of gratuity to the employees through out the country. Ultimately all controversies were set at rest by passing the Payment of Gratuity Act, 1972 (39 of 1972).

The Payment of Gratuity Act, 1972 came into force on 16th September, 1972 and it extends to the whole of India.

In this chapter we shall discuss the object of the Act, application of the Act and the definition of important terms, including employer, employee and continuous service, as used and defined in the Act.

Note : In this part of the book, unless otherwise stated, the sections mentioned are those of the Payment of Gratuity Act, 1972.

51.2. OBJECT OF THE PAYMENT OF GRATUITY ACT

The object of Payment of Gratuity Act as provided in the Preamble of the Act is to provide for a scheme for the payment of gratuity to employees engaged in factories, mines, oil fields plantations, ports, railway companies, shops or other establishments and for matters connected therewith or incidental thereto.

In *Delhi Cloth and General Mills Co. Ltd.* v. *Workmen*, (1968) 36 FJR 247, it was observed that the object of providing a gratuity scheme is to provide a retiring benefit to the workmen who have rendered long and unblemished service to the employer and thereby contributed to the prosperity of the employer.

Thus, keeping in view the preamble of the Act and judicial observations, the objects of the Act may be stated as under :

1. To provide for a scheme for the payment of gratuity to employees.
2. To provide for matters connected or incidental to the scheme for payment of gratuity.
3. To provide retiring benefits to employees who have rendered continuous services to his employer and thereby contributed to his prosperity.
4. To define the principles of payment of gratuity according to the prescribed formula.
5. To provide machinery for the enforcement of liability for payment of gratuity.

51.3. APPLICATION OF THE ACT

The Payment of Gratuity Act, 1972 extends to the whole of India. However, in so far as it relates to plantations or ports, it shall not extend to the State of Jammu and Kashmir [Section 1(2)]. Regarding applicability of the Act, Section 1(3) provides that it shall apply to the following :

1. Every factory, mine, oilfield, plantation, port and railway company;
2. Every shop or establishment within the meaning of any law for the time being in force in relation to shops and establishments in a State in which ten or more persons are employed, or were employed, *on any day* of the preceding twelve months;
3. Such other establishments or class of establishments, in which ten or more employees are employed, or were employed, on any day of the preceding twelve months, as the Central Government may, by notification, specify in this behalf.

It is important to note that a shop or establishment to which this Act has become applicable shall continue to be governed by the Act even if the number of persons employed therein at any time after the applicability of the Act, falls below ten [Section 1 (3A)].

It is also important to note that this Act has an overriding effect, which means that the provisions or rule of this Act shall have effect inspite of the fact that there is anything inconsistent in any other Act regarding the payment of gratuity [Section 14].

In *C. Kuppuswami* v. *E.I.D. Parny (India) Ltd.*, (1989) 1 LLN 85 (Madras), it was held that a pension scheme cannot defeat the benefit of gratuity.

51.4. EXEMPTION FROM APPLICATION OF THE ACT

1. ***Exemption of any establishment etc.***
2. ***Exemption of employees.***

The power to exempt any establishment or employees from the provisions of the Payment of Gratuity are vested in the Appropriate Government under Section 5, which may be stated as under :

1. Exemption of any establishment etc. [Section 5 (1)] : The appropriate government may exempt any establishment, factory, mine, oil field, plantation, port, railway company or shop to which this Act applies, from the provisions of operations of this Act if in the opinion of the appropriate government, the employees in such establishment, factory etc. are entitled to received the gratuity or pension benefits not less favourable than the benefits given under this Act.

The appropriate government may do so by issuing notification of exemption and subject to such terms and conditions as may be specified in the notification.

2. Exemption of employees [Section 5 (2)]: The appropriate government may exempt any employee or class of employees employed in any establishment, factory, mine, oilfield, plantation, port, railway company or shop to which this Act applies from the operation of the provisions of this Act, if in the opinion of appropriate government such employees are entitled to receive the gratuity or pension benefits not less favourable than the benefits given under this Act.

The appropriate government may do so by issuing notification and subject to such terms and conditions as may be specified in the notification.

51.5. DEFINITIONS

The terms and expressions used in the Payment of Gratuity Act, 1972 are defined in various sub-section of Section 2 of the Act and are discussed in the following pages :

1. Appropriate Government

The term 'Appropriate Government' is defined in Section 2 (a) of the Act as under :

(*a*) In relation to the following establishments, the appropriate government for the purposes of this Act is the Central Government :

(*i*) An establishment belonging to or under the control of Central Government.

(*ii*) An establishment having branches in more than one State.

(*iii*) An establishment of a factory belonging to or under the control of Central Government.

(*iv*) An establishment of a major port, mine, oil field or railway company.

(*b*) In relation to any other establishment, the appropriate government for the purpose of this Act is the State Government.

2. Employee

The term 'employee' is defined in Section 2 (e) of the Act and for the purposes of this Act it means any person (other than an apprentice) employed on wages in any establishment, factory, mine, oilfield, plantation, port, railway company or shop to do any skilled, semi-skilled, unskilled, manual supervisory, technical or clerical work.

Following important points in relation to the definition of the term 'employee' have been specifically made clear in Section 2 (e) itself :

(*a*) The terms of employment of such a person may be express or implied.

(*b*) The capacity in which such a person is employed is not relevant. He may or may not be employed in a managerial or administrative capacity.

(*c*) Any person who holds a post under the Central Government or a State Government and is governed by any other Act or by any rules providing for payment of gratuity, shall not be included in the definition of employee.

The following judicial decisions are important to note in connection with the definition of employee:

(*i*) A workman who rolls *beedies* for his employer but at his own house is an 'employee' within the meaning of Section 2 (e) of the Act. Home worker is considered to be working in the establishment for the purposes of this Act.

[*Bagi Beedi Factory* v. *Appellate Authority*, 1998 LLR 23
P.H. Ramlal & Co. v. *Chand Bibi*, (1981) 1 LIC 790 (Guj)].

(*ii*) An employee, whose main duties are only supervisory in nature but for a short period is required to discharge additional or incidental functions falls in the category of employee and cannot be deprived of the benefits of this Act.

[*Vishwanath* v. *M.P.S.R.T. Corpn.*, (1987) 55 FLR 1 (MP)].

(*iii*) A worker engaged for work on temporary basis according to availability of work, is not an employee.

[*K. Velukutty Acharya* v. *Harrison Malayalam Ltd*. (1993) 66 FLR 423 (Ker) (DB)].

3. Employer

The term 'employer' is defined in Section 2 (f) of the Act, and for the purposes of this Act, it is defined separately in relation to government owned and non-governments owned establishment, factory, mine, oilfield, plantation, port, railway company or shop:

(a) *In relation to any establishment, factory, mine, oilfield, plantation, port, railway company or shop belonging to or under the control of the Government or State Government* : In this case, an employer means a person or authority appointed by the appropriate Government for the supervision and control of employees. And where no person or authority has been so appointed the Head of the Ministry or Department concerned will be the 'employer'.

(b) *In relation to any establishment, factory etc. belonging to or under the control of any local authority* : In this case, an 'employer' means a person appointed by such authority for the supervision or control of employees. And where no person has been so appointed the chief executive officer of the local authority will be the 'employer'.

(c) *In relation to any establishment, factory etc. not falling under the above categories* : In this case an 'employer' means a person or authority having the ultimate control over the affairs of the establishment, factory, mine, oil field, plantation, port, railway company or shop. And where the affairs of such establishment etc. are entrusted to any person, such a person shall be the 'employer' whether called a manager, managing director or by any other name.

4. Controlling Authority

The term 'controlling authority' is defined in Section 2 (*d*) of the Act and for the purposes of this Act it means any officer appointed by the appropriate government for the administration of this Act.

The appropriate government may, by notification, appoint any officer to be the controlling authority, who shall be responsible for the administration of this Act. And different authorities may be appointed for different areas [Section 3].

5. Family

The term 'family' is defined in Section 2 (*h*) of the Act and for the purposes of this Act, it is defined separately in case of a male employee and female employee :

(a) *In the case of a male employee* : In this case, the family of an employee shall be deemed to consist of the employee, himself, his wife, his children, whether married or unmarried, his dependent parents and the dependent parents of his wife and the widow and children of his predeceased son, if any.

(b) *In the case of female employee* : In this case, the family of an employee shall be deemed to consist of the employee, herself, her husband, her children, whether married or unmarried, her dependent parents and the dependent parents of her husband and the widow and children of her predeceased son, if any.

In relation to the family of an employee it is important to note that where the personal law of an employee permits the adoption by him of a child, any child lawfully adopted by him shall be deemed to be included in his family, and where a child of an employee has been adopted by another person and such adoption is, under the personal law of the person making such adoption, lawful, such child shall be deemed to be excluded from the family of the employee [Section 3, Explanation].

51.6. CONTINUOUS SERVICE

The concept of 'continuous service' is relevant under the Payment of Gratuity Act,

1972 as the gratuity to an employee is payable on his termination only if he has rendered *continuous service* for not less than five years.

The term 'continuous service' is defined in Section 2 A of the Act, and for the purposes of this Act, Section 2 A (1) makes the following provisions in this regard :

An employee shall be considered to be in 'continuous services' for a specified period if he has been in *uninterrupted service* for that period. It may be noted that the service which may be interrupted on account of the following reasons shall be considered to be uninterrupted service :

(*a*) sickness (*b*) accident (*c*) leave (*d*) absence from duty without leave (*e*) lay-off, (*f*) strike or a lock-out (*g*) cessation of work not due to any fault of the employee.

However the absence from duty, in respect of which an order treating the absence as break in service has been passed in accordance with standing orders, rules or regulations governing the employees, shall not be considered as uninterrupted service [Section 2 A(1)].

The continuous services for a period of one year or six months is also relevant under the Act, as this period is considered while calculating the period for which the gratuity is payable. Section 2A further specifies the circumstances in which an employee is considered to be in continuous service of one year or six months even if he has not been in uninterrupted service for this period. Section 2A (2) makes the following provisions in this regard :

1. Employees of non-seasonal establishment [Section 2A (2)] : Such employees are considered in continuous service of one year or six months on the following basis :

(*a*) *Deemed continuous service of one year* : Where an employee of a non-seasonal establishment is not in continuous service (uninterrupted service) of one year, he shall be deemed to be in continuous service under the employer for the said period of one year, if the employee during the period of twelve calender months preceding the date with reference to which calculation is to be made, had *actually* worked under the employer for not less than—

(*i*) one hundred and ninety days, in the case of any employee employed below the ground in a mine or in an establishment which works for less than six days in a week; and

(*ii*) two hundred and forty days, in any other case;

(*b*) *Deemed continuous service of six months* : Where an employee of a non-seasonal establishment is not in continuous service (uninterrupted service) of six months, he shall be deemed to be in continuous service under the employer for the said period of six months, if the employee during the period of six calendar months preceding the date with reference to which the calculation is to be made, had *actually* worked under the employer for not less than—

(*i*) ninety-five days, in the case of an employee employed below the ground in a mine or in an establishment which works for less than six days in a week; and

(*ii*) one hundred and twenty days, in any other case.

It is important to note that for the purposes of above two provisions, the number of days on which an employee has actually worked under an employer shall include the days on which—

(*i*) he has been laid-off under an agreement or as permitted by standing orders made under the Industrial Employment (Standing Orders) Act, 1946, or under the Industrial Disputes Act, 1947, or under any other law applicable to the establishment;

(*ii*) he has been on leave with full wages, earned in the previous year;

(*iii*) he has been absent due to temporary disablement caused by accident arising out of and in the course of his employment; and

(*iv*) in the case of a female, she has been on maternity leave; so, however, that the total period of such maternity leave does not exceed twelve weeks. [Section 2 A(2), Explanation].

2. ***Employees of seasonal establishment [Section 2 A (3)]*** : Where an employee of a seasonal establishment is not in continuous service (uninterrupted service) for any period of one year or six months, he shall be deemed to be in continuous services under the employer for such period if he has *actually* worked for not less than seventy-five per cent of the number of days on which the establishment was in operation during such period.

TEST QUESTIONS

1. State the objects of the Payment of Gratuity Act, 1972. Explain clearly the legal provisions relating to the applicability of the Act.
2. Define the expression 'appropriate government' as used in the Payment of Gratuity Act, 1972. State the establishment and the employees who may be exempted by the appropriate government from the provisions of the Act.
3. Explain clearly the terms 'employee' and 'employer' as used in the Payment of Gratuity Act, 1972.
4. Giving the relevant sections, explain the legal provisions relating to the expression 'continuous service' as used in the Payment of Gratuity Act, 1972.
5. Write short notes on the following :

   (*a*) Controlling authority (*b*) Family

   (*c*) Continuous Service (*d*) Application of the Act

MULTIPLE CHOICE QUESTIONS

1. The Payment of Gratuity Act, 1972 came into force on 16th September, 1972 and it extends to the

   (*a*) whole of India

   (*b*) all states except union territories

   (*c*) States notified by government from time to time

   (*d*) Jammu and Kashmir and Union territories
2. The Payment of Gratuity Act, 1972 applies to

   (*a*) Every factory, mine, oil field, plantation, port and railway company

   (*b*) Every shop or establishment within the meaning of any law in which ten or more persons are employed or were employed on any day of the preceding twelve months

   (*c*) both (*a*) and (*b*)

   (*d*) none of these
3. For the applicability of the Payment of Gratuity Act, 1972 to an establishment, it is obligatory that 10 or more persons must have been continued to be employed once the Act became applicable to that establishment

   (*a*) True (*b*) False

4. The term 'employee' under the Payment of Gratuity Act is defined in
   (*a*) Section 2 (a) (*b*) Section 2 (f)
   (*c*) Section 2 (e) (*d*) Section 2 (d)
5. Under the Payment of Gratuity Act, 1972, gratuity to an employee in payable on his termination only if he has rendered continuous service for not less than
   (*a*) 3 years (*b*) 5 years
   (*c*) 7 years (*d*) 10 years.

ANSWERS

1. (*a*)	2. (*c*)	3. (*b*)	4. (*c*)	5. (*b*)

OBJECTIVE TYPE QUESTIONS WITH REASONING

State with reasons whether the following statements are correct or incorrect :

1. The Payment of Gratuity Act, 1972 may also apply to *any* establishment in which 10 or more persons were employed on any day of the preceding twelve months.
2. The employees of an establishment to which the Payment of Gratuity Act applies may be exempted from the application of the Act.
3. An apprentice is also included in the category of 'employee' as defined in the Payment of Gratuity Act.
4. For the application of the Payment of Gratuity, 1972 the terms of employment of the employee must be express *i.e.* in writing.
5. An employee shall be considered to be in continuous service for a specified period if he has been in uninterrupted service for that period even if the service is interrupted due to absence from duty without leave.

ANSWERS

1. ***Correct.*** Section 1 (3) makes a specific provision in this regard which authorises the Central Government to specify such establishment for the applicability of the Act.
2. ***Correct.*** Appropriate government may by notification, give this exemption if in its opinion such employees are entitled to receive the gratuity or pension benefit not less favourable than the benefits given under the Act [Section 5 (2)].
3. ***Incorrect.*** Section 2 (e) expressly excludes the apprentice from the category of 'employee'.
4. ***Incorrect.*** The terms of employment of such persons may be express or implied.
5. ***Correct.*** Section 2A(1) makes specific provision in this regard.

PAYMENT, FORFEITURE AND RECOVERY OF GRATUITY

1. Introduction.
2. Payment of Gratuity.
3. Forfeiture of Gratuity.
4. Recovery of Gratuity.

52.1. INTRODUCTION

The payment of gratuity is the statutory (*i.e.*, legal) duty of the employer and to receive the same is the statutory right of the employee. It is calculated and paid as per the provisions of the Payment of Gratuity Act, 1972. The different legal provisions of the Act relating to the eligibility for payment of gratuity, forfeiture of gratuity, duty to pay gratuity, recovery of gratuity etc. specify the rules regarding the payment of gratuity. The Payment of Gratuity (Central) Rules, 1972 contains the rules which are applicable in relation to the provisions contained in the Payment of Gratuity Act, 1972.

The maximum amount of gratuity payable to an employee shall not exceed rupees three lakh and fifty thousand [Section 4 (3)]. The gratuity shall be paid in cash or if so desired by the payee, The Payment of Gratuity (Central) Rules, 1972].

In this Chapter we shall discuss the legal provisions of the Payment of Gratuity Act, 1972 as well as the Rules of the Payment of Gratuity (Central) Rules, 1972 relating to the following topics :

1. Payment of gratuity [Section 4].
2. Forfeiture of gratuity [Section 4 (6)].
3. Recovery of gratuity [Section 8].

In this chapter, unless otherwise specified, the sections and the rules mentioned are those of the Payment of Gratuity Act, 1972 and the Payment of Gratuity (Central) Rules, 1972 respectively.

52.2. PAYMENT OF GRATUITY

1. *Eligibility for gratuity* [*Section 4 (1)*].
2. *Payment to nominee or heir in case of death of the employee [Section 4 (1), (proviso second)]*.
3. *Application for payment of gratuity [Section 7 (1)]*.
4. *Employer's duty to pay gratuity* [*Section 7 (2) (3) (3A)*].
5. *Computation of gratuity* [*Section 4 (2) (4)*].
6. *Maximum limit of gratuity amount and mode of payment* [*Section 4(3), Rule 9*].

The payment of gratuity is the statutory duty of the employer. Even if there is change of ownership of establishment, the new employer cannot escape from the liability of the payment of gratuity to the employees.*

The legal provisions relating to the payment of gratuity are contained in Section 4 and 7 of the Act, and may be discussed under the following heads :

* P.K. Damodaram V.M. Kasim Kanju, (1993) I, LLJ 1211 (Ker.)

1. *Eligibility for gratuity* [*Section 4 (1)*]. The gratuity under the Act is payable to a person who is an 'employee' as defined in the Act.

The gratuity shall be payable to an employee on the termination of his employment after he has rendered continuous service of not less than five years. In other words, an employee shall be eligible for gratuity on the termination of his employment if he has rendered continuous services for a minimum period of five years.

The gratuity to an employee is payable on his termination (*i.e.*, on the cessation of service) in the following cases :

(*a*) on his superannuation, or

(*b*) on his retirement or resignation, or

(*c*) on his death or disablement due to accident or disease.

It is important to note here that the completion of continuous service of five years shall not be necessary where the termination of the employment of any employee is due to death or disablement. The 'disablement' here means such disablement as incapacitates an employee for the work which he was capable of performing before the accident or disease resulting in such disablement [Section 4 (1), Explanation].

2. Payment to nominee or heir in case of death of the employee [Section 4 (1), (proviso second)]. In the case of death of the employee, gratuity payable to him shall be paid to his nominee or, if no nomination has been made, to his heirs, and where any such nominees or heirs is a minor, the share of such minor shall be deposited with the controlling authority who shall invest the same for the benefit of such minor in such bank or other financial institution, as may be prescribed, until such minor attains majority.

Each employee who has completed one year of service, shall make nominaion in favour of one or more members of his family. If the employee has no family, nomination may be made in favour of any person [Section 6].

The legal provisions relating to nomination will be discussed in Art. 53.3 later in this part of the book.

3. Application for payment of gratuity [Section 7 (1)]. Any person who is eligible for payment of gratuity under this Act shall send a written application to the employer for the payment of such gratuity. An application may also be made by any person authorised in writing by the eligible person. The application for payment of gratuity should be made within the following time as prescribed in Rule 7 of the Payment of Gratuity (Central) Rules, 1972:

(*a*) An application by an eligible employee should ordinarily be made in the prescribed Form 'I' within 30 days from the date the gratuity become payable [Rule 7 (1)]

(*b*) An application by the nominee of an eligible employee should ordinarily be made in the prescribed Form 'J' within 30 days from the date the gratuity became payable [Rule 7 (2)]

(*c*) An application by the legal heir of an eligible employee should ordinarily be made in the prescribed Form 'k' within one year from the date the gratuity become payable [Rule 7 (3)].

However, an application after the expiry of above specified period shall also be entertained by the employer if the applicant shows sufficient cause (*i.e.*, reason) for the delay in filing the application for payment of gratuity [Rule 7 (5)].

* *P.K. Damodaram* v. *M.Kasim Kanju*, (1993) I LLJ 1211 (ker.)

An application for payment of gratuity shall be presented to the employer either by personal service or by registered post acknowledgement due [Rule 7 (6)].

4. *Employer's duty to pay gratuity* [*Section* 7 (2) (3) (3A)] : It is employer's duty to pay gratuity to an eligible employee when the gratuity becomes so payable. The Act has cast the following duties on the employer :

(*a*) *Duty to determine the amount of gratuity* [*Section* 7(2)] : As soon as the gratuity becomes payable, the employer shall determine the amount of gratuity. The employer is under legal duty to determine the amount whether or not any application for the payment of such gratuity has been made to the employers. On determining the amount of gratuity, the employer should give a notice in writing to the person to whom the gratuity in payable and also to the controlling authority specifying the amount of gratuity so determined.

(*b*) *Duty to arrange to pay the amount* [Section 7 (3)] : The employer shall arrange to pay the amount of gratuity within 30 days from the date it becomes payable to the person to whom the gratuity is payable. It means that it is the employer's duty to pay the gratuity amount within 30 days from the date the gratuity becomes payable.

If the employer fails to pay the gratuity amount within this period of thirty days, then he is liable to pay it alongwith simple interest at a rate notified by the Central Government till the payment is made. However, no such interest is payable if the delay in payment is due to the fault of the employee [Section 7 (3A)].

(*c*) *Duty to give notice for payment of gratuity when application for payment is made to employer* [*Rule* 8] : When an application for payment is made to the employer as stated in point (3) above, then within 15 days of the receipt of such application, the employer should issue the following notice, in the prescribed form, to the applicant :

(*i*) If the claim for gratuity is found admissible (*i.e.*, justified), the notice to the applicant should specify the amount of gratuity payable and the date for the payment. The date so fixed for payment should not be the date later than the thirtieth day after the date of receipt of application.

(*ii*) If the claim for gratuity is not found admissible, the notice to the applicant should specify the reasons why the claim for gratuity is not considered admissible.

In both the above cases, the copy of the notice should also be endorsed to the controlling authority.

5. *Computation of gratuity* [*Section* 4 (2) (4)]. The provisions relating to the computation of gratuity as contained in Section 4 (2) (4) of the Act may be summed up as under :

(*a*) For every completed year of service or part thereof in excess of six months, the employer shall pay gratuity to an employee at the rate of fifteen days' wages based on the rate of wages last drawn by the employee concerned [Section 4 (2)].

(*b*) In the case of a piece-rated employee, daily wages shall be computed on the average of the total wages received by him for a period of three months immediately preceding the termination of his employment, and, for this purpose, the wages paid for any overtime work shall not be taken into account [Section 4 (2), proviso].

(*c*) In the case of an employee who is employed in a seasonal establishment and who is not so employed throughout the year, the employer shall pay the gratuity at the rate of seven days wages for each season. [Section 4(2), second proviso].

(*d*) In the case of a monthly rated employee, the fifteen days wages shall be calculated by dividing the monthly rate of wages last drawn by him by twenty-six and multiplying the quotient by fifteen [Section 4(2), Explanation].

(e) For the purpose of computing the gratuity payable to an employee who is employed, after his disablement, on reduced wages, his wages for the period preceding his disablement shall be taken to be the wages received by him during that period, and his wages for the period subsequent to his disablement shall be taken to be the wages as so reduced [Section 4 (4)].

6. *Maximum limit of gratuity amount and mode of payment* [*Section 4(3), Rule 9*]. Legal provisions in this regard are as under :

(a) *Maximum limit of gratuity* : The maximum amount of gratuity payable to an employee shall not exceed rupees three lakh and fifty thousand [Section 4(3)].

The employee may enter into an agreement or contract with the employer for receiving better gratuity than provided under the Act [Section 4(5)]. This means that if for the purposes of computation of the amount of gratuity, the terms of agreement or settlement are better than the Act, the employee is entitled for that benefit. However, the maximum statutory ceiling of rupees three lakh and fifty thousand cannot be reduced by mutual agreement or settlement. [*Bharat Commerce & Industries* v. *Ramprasad* 2001 LLR, 918 (MP)]

(b) *Mode of payment of gratuity* : The gratuity payable under the Act shall be paid in cash, or if so desired by the payee, in demand draft or bank cheque to the eligible employee or to his nominee or legal heir as the case may be.

[Rule 9, the Payment of Gratuity (Central) Rule, 1972]

52.3. FORFEITURE OF GRATUITY

The legal provisions relating to the forfeiture of gratuity are contained in Section 4(6) of the Payment of Gratuity Act, 1972 and may be summed up as under :

1. The gratuity payable to an employee shall be forfeited where the services of an employee have been terminated due to any act, wilful omission or negligence on the part of the employee and employee's such act etc. has caused :

(a) damage or loss to the property belonging to the employer, or

(b) destruction of the property belonging to the employer.

In this case, the gratuity payable to the employee shall be forfeited to the extent of the damage or loss caused to employer's property due to employees act, omission or negligence [Section 4(6) (a)].

2. The gratuity payable to an employee *may* be forfeited :

(a) If the services of such employee have been terminated for his riotous or disorderly conduct or any other act of violence on his part, or

(b) If the services of such employee have been terminated for any act which constitutes an offence involving moral turpitude, provided that such offence is committed by him in the course of his employment.

In the above stated cases, the gratuity payable to an employee *may* be forfeited wholly or partially [Section 4(6) (b)].

Following judicial decisions are important to note in connection with the forfeiture of gratuity by the employer :

(i) The right of the employer to forfeit the amount of gratuity of an employee whose services were terminated due to any act, wilful omission or negligence causing any damage to the employer's property is *limited* to the extent of damage and the proof of such damage.

[*Permali Wallance Ltd.* v. *State of M.P.* (1996) II LLJ 515 (MP)].

(ii) The right of the employer to forfeit the gratuity is available only in the circumstances enumerated in Section 4 (6), as stated in points (1) and (2) above, and is not available in any other circumstances as employee's right to gratuity is the statutory right.[*K.C.Mathew* v. *Plantation Corpn. of Kerala Ltd.* (2001) LLR 123 (Ker.)].

(*iii*) The refusal by the employees to surrender land belonging to the employer is not a ground for forfeiture of gratuity.

[*Travancore Plywood Industries Ltd.* v *Regional Joint Labour Commr.*, (1996) II LLJ 85 (Ker.)].

(*iv*) In case of termination of services on account of offence involving moral turpitude, the gratuity may be wholly or partially forfeited. In this regard, the Karnataka High Court has held that when an offence of theft under law involves moral turpitude, gratuity stands wholly forfeited in view of Section 4 (6) of the Act.

[*Bharat Gas Mines Ltd.* v. *Regional Labour Commr.* (*Central*), (1987) 70 FJR 11 (Karn.)].

52.4. RECOVERY OF GRATUITY

We know that it is the statutory (legal) right of the eligible employee to receive gratuity from his employer. And the employer is under the legal duty to pay the gratuity to the employee or his nominee or legal heirs as the case may be. If the gratuity is not paid by the employer within the prescribed time, then the employee or the other person entitled to the gratuity has the legal right to recover the same from the employer.

The right of the persons entitled to recover the gratuity has been recognised under Section 8 of the Payment of Gratuity Act, 1972. The legal provisions as contained in this section may be summed up as under :

1. If the amount of gratuity payable under the Act is not paid by the employer, within the prescribed time, to the person entitled to the gratuity, then such person has the right to make an application to the Controlling Authority for recovery of the same.
2. On receipt of the application for recovery of gratuity, the controlling authority shall issue a recovery certificate for the amount of gratuity, to the collector who shall start the recovery process. However, before issuing such recovery certificate, the controlling authority shall give a reasonable opportunity to the employer for showing reasons against the issue of such certificate.
3. The collector shall recover from the employer the amount of gratuity alongwith the compound interest at such rate as the Central Government may specify by notification. However, the amount of interest payable under this section shall in no case exceed the amount of gratuity payable under the Act.
4. The collector shall recover the amount of gratuity as arrears of land revenue and shall pay the same to the entitled person.

TEST QUESTIONS

1. Discuss in detail the legal provisions relating to the payment of gratuity.
2. "Payment of gratuity is the statutory duty of the employer and to receive the same the statutory right of the employee" — comment.
3. What is the maximum limit and mode of payment of gratuity ? Discuss the legal provisions relating to computation of gratuity.
4. Under what circumstances the gratuity payable to an employee be forfeited ?

5. Write notes on the following :
   (*a*) Eligibility for gratuity
   (*b*) Computation of gratuity
   (*c*) Employer's duty to pay gratuity
   (*d*) Recovery of gratuity

MULTIPLE CHOICE QUESTIONS

1. Which of the following statements is correct ?
   (*a*) Payment of gratuity is the statutory duty of the employer.
   (*b*) To receive the gratuity is the statutory right of the employee.
   (*c*) The gratuity shall be payable to an employee on the termination of his employment after he has rendered continuous services of not less than five years.
   (*d*) all of these

2. The gratuity to an employee is payable on his termination on his :
   (*a*) superannuation
   (*b*) retirement or resignation
   (*c*) death or disablement
   (*d*) all of these

3. The correct statement regarding nomination by an employee, for the purpose of receiving gratuity on his death is that it can be made in favour of :
   (*a*) one or more members of his family
   (*b*) any other person where employee has no family
   (*c*) both of these
   (*d*) none of these

4. It is employer's duty to pay the gratuity within the specified time from the date it becomes payable. The time specified in the Act is :
   (*a*) 30 days
   (*b*) 45 days
   (*c*) 60 days
   (*d*) 90 days

5. The maximum amount of gratuity payable to an employee under the Payment of Gratuity Act, 1972, is :
   (*a*) Rs. 1.50 lakh
   (*b*) Rs. 3.50 lakh
   (*c*) Rs. 5 lakh
   (*d*) Rs. 5.5 lakh

6. The gratuity payable to an employee under the Payment of Gratuity Act, 1972, be paid in :
   (*a*) cash only
   (*b*) bank draft only
   (*c*) instalments
   (*d*) either cash or bank draft

ANSWERS

1. (*d*)	**2.** (*d*)	**3.** (*c*)	**4.** (*a*)	**5.** (*b*)	**6.** (*d*)

OBJECTIVE TYPE QUESTIONS WITH REASONING

State with reasons whether the following statements are correct or incorrect.

1. If the death or disablement of an employee takes place before the completion of continuous service of five years, no gratuity shall be paid as the necessary condition of five years service is not fulfilled.

2. In case of death of the employee who has not made any nomination, the gratuity shall be deposited with the controlling authority irrespective of the fact whether or not the employee has left any legal heir.

3. An application by an eligible employee or by his nominee for the payment of gratuity should be made within 30 days from the date the gratuity became payable. In case of application by legal heirs, it may be made within one year from the date the gratuity become payable.
4. The employee may enter into an agreement or contract with the employer for receiving better gratuity than provided under the Payment of Gratuity Act, 1972.
5. The gratuity payable to an employee cannot be forfeited as it is the statutory (legal) right of the employee to receive gratuity.

ANSWERS

1. *Incorrect.* In case of death or disablement of the employee, the condition for continuous service of five years is not applicable [Section 4(1), Explanation].
2. *Incorrect.* In case of no nomination by the employee, the gratuity on his death is payable to his legal heir. The gratuity is deposited with the controlling authority where the nominee or the heir is a minor [Section 4(1), second proviso].
3. *Correct.* Rules 7(1), (2) & (3) of the Payment of Gratuity (Central) Rules, 1972 makes express provision in this regard.
4. *Correct.* Section 4(5) authorises such agreement. However, the maximum statutory ceiling of Rs. 3.5 lakh cannot be reduced by mutual agreement [*Bharat Commerce Industries* v. *Ramprasad*, 2001 LLR, 918 (MP)].
5. *Incorrect.* The gratuity can be forfeited in the circumstances provided under Section 4(6) of the Act.

PRACTICAL PROBLEMS

1. *A* was an employee of Tea Estate Ltd. The whole of the undertaking of Tea Estate Ltd. was taken over by a new company. Asia Tea Estate Ltd. The services of *A* remained continued in the new company. After serving for one year, *A* met with an accident and became permanently disabled. *A* applied to the new company for the payment of gratuity. The company refused to pay gratuity on the ground that *A* has served only for a year in the company. Examine the validity of the refusal of directors in the light of the provisions of the Payment of Gratuity Act, 1972. [*CA - PCC, Group – I, Nov. 2008*]

   Hints: The refusal of directors in not justified. As per section 4(1) of the payment of Gratuity Act, 1972, the gratuity shall be payable to an employee on the termination of this employment after he has rendered continuous services of not less than five years. However, this requirement of five years continuous services shall not be necessary where the termination of an employee is due to death or permanent disablement of the employee [Section 4(1) Explanation].

   In the present case, *A* is entitled to recover grathuity after becoming permanently disabled, and the requirement of continuous service of five years would not be applicable in his case.

2. National Steels Ltd. decided to forfeit the amount of gratuity of its employees *A*, *B* and *C* on account of disorderly conduct and other acts which caused loss to the property belonging to the company. *A*, *B* and *C* committed the following acts:

   (*i*) *A* refused to surrender the occupied land belonging to the company.

   (*ii*) *B* committed theft under law involves offence of moral turpitude.

   (*iii*) *C*, after superannuation, continued to occupy the quarter of the company for six months.

   Against the decision of the company, *A*, *B* and *C* applied to the court for relief. The company contended that the right to gratuity is not a stahutory right and the forfeited amount of gratuity was within the law. Examine the contention of the company and the decision taken by the company to forfeit the amount of gratuity in the light of the Payment of Gratuity Act, 1972.
   [*CA – PCC, Group – I June, 2009*]

Hints: The right to gratuity is the statutory right of the employees, and the gratuity can be forfeited only in the circumstances permitted under section 4(6) of the Payment of Gratuity Act, 1972.

In this case, the company has forfeited the entire gratuity payable to *A*, *B* and *C*, the legality of forfeiture is as under.

(*i*) It is not a valid ground for forfeiture of gratuity. The company is, therefore, not justified to forfeit A's gratuity on this ground.

[*Travancore Plywood Ind. Ltd.* V. Regional Jt. Commr. (1996) II LLJ 85 (Ker.)]

(*ii*) It is valid ground for forfeiture, and the company is justified in forfeiting *B*'s gratuity. On this ground, the whole of gratuity may be forfeited.

(*iii*) It is not a valid ground for forfeiture of entire gratuity. In such a case, the company is entitled to charge the quarter rent as per rules and after adjustment of such charges, *C* is entitled to receive the balance gratuity.

53

CHAPTER

MISCELLANEOUS PROVISIONS AND PENALTIES

53.1. INTRODUCTION

In the previous chapter, we have discussed the legal provisions relating to the payment of gratuity. There are many other legal provisions contained in the Payment of Gratuity Act, 1972 which are equally important from the subject point of view. All these provision alongwith the provision for penalties have been clubbed together and discussed in detail in this chapter.

Following important provisions are explained in this chapter.

1. Compulsory insurance [Section 4A]
2. Nomination [Section 6]
3. Inspectors [Section 7A and 7B]
4. Penalties [Section 9, 10, 11]
5. Appropriate Government's power to make rules [Section 15]

53.2. COMPULSORY INSURANCE

The provision for compulsory insurance has been introduced in the Act with a view to provide an insurance cover to the employer who are under legal duty to pay gratuity to employees.

The provisions relating to compulsory insurance are contained in Section 4A of the Act and may be summed up as under :

1. Every employer, other than an employer or an establishment belonging to, or under the control of, the Central Government or a State Government, *shall*, obtain an insurance in the manner prescribed, for his liability for payment towards the gratuity under this Act, from the Life Insurance Corporation of India established under the Life Insurance Corporation of India Act, 1956 or any other prescribed insurer. The employer shall obtain such insurance with effect from such date as may be notified by the Appropriate Government [Section 4A(1)].

2. The appropriate Government may, subject to such conditions as may be prescribed, exempt every employer who had already established an approved gratuity fund in respect of his employees and who desires to continue such arrangement, and every employer employing five hundred or more persons who establishes an approved gratuity fund in the manner prescribed, from the liability to obtain compulsory insurance [Section 4A(2)].

3. Where an employer fails to make any payment by way of premium to the insurance referred to in sub-section (1) or by way of contribution to an approved gratuity fund referred to in sub-section (2), he shall be liable to pay the amount of gratuity due under this Act (including interest, if any, for delayed payments) *forthwith* to the controlling authority [Section 4A(5)].

4. Whoever contravenes the provisions of point 3 above, shall be punishable with fine which may extend to ten thousand rupees and in the case of a continuing offence with a further fine which may extend to one thousand rupees for each day during which the offence continues [Section 4A (6)].

53.3. NOMINATION

The employee has the right to appoint a nominee who can legally recover the amount of gratuity in the event of death of the employee. Section 6 contains the legal provisions in this regard which may be stated as under :

1. Each employee, who has completed one year of service, shall make, within such time, in such form and in such manner, as may be prescribed, nomination for the purpose of receiving gratuity in the event of death of the employee [Section 6(1)].
2. An employee may, in his nomination, distribute the amount of gratuity payable to him under this Act amongst more than one nominee [Section 6(2)].
3. If an employee has a family at the time of making a nomination, the nomination shall be made in favour of one or more members of his family, and any nomination made by such employee in favour of a person who is not a member of his family shall be void [Section 6(3)].
4. If at the time of making a nomination the employee has no family, the nomination may be made in favour of any person or person but if the employee subsequently acquires a family, such nomination shall forthwith become invalid and the employee shall make within such time as may be prescribed, a fresh nomination in favour of one or more members of his family [Section 6(4)].
5. A nomination may, subject to the provisions of sub-section (3) and (4), be modified by an employee at any time, after giving to his employer a written notice in such form and in such manner as may be prescribed, of his intention to do so [Section 6(5)].
6. If a nominee predeceases the employee, the interest of the nominee shall revert to the employee who shall make a fresh nomination, in the prescribed form, in respect of such interest [Section 6(6)].
7. Every nomination, fresh nomination or alteration of nomination, as the case may be, shall be sent by the employee to his employer, who shall keep the same in his safe custody [Section 6(7)].

53.4. INSPECTORS

The appropriate Government may, by notification, appoint as many Inspectors, as it deems fit, for the purposes of this Act.

The appropriate Government may, by general or special order, define the area to which the authority of an Inspector so appointed shall extend and where two or more Inspectors are appointed for the same area, also provide, by such order, for the distribution or allocation of work to be performed by them under this Act [Section 7A].

For the purposes of ascertaining whether provisions or conditions of this Act are duly complied with, the inspectors have the following powers [Sections 7 B]:

1. Power to require an employer to furnish such information as may be considered necessary.
2. Power to enter and inspect any place in any factory, mine etc. for the purposes of examining records.
3. Power to examine employer or employee with respect to relevant matter.
4. Power to make copies or take extracts from the relevant register or record etc.
5. Power to exercise such powers as may be specifically prescribed by the Appropriate Government.

53.5 PENALTIES

The provisions relating to penalties and cognizance of offences under the Payment of Gratuity Act, 1972 are as under :

1. ***Penalties* [*Section 9*]**: This section makes the following provisions :

(*a*) *Any person* who knowingly makes or causes to be made any false statement or false representation, for the purpose of avoiding any payment to be made by himself under this Act, shall be punishable with imprisonment upto six months or with fine upto Rs. 10,000 or with both.

A person who knowingly makes such false statement with a view to enable any other person to avoid such payment shall also be punishable with punishment as stated above [Section 9(1)].

(*b*) *An employer* who contravenes, or make default in complying with, any of the provisions of this Act or any rule or order made thereunder shall be punishable with imprisonment for a term which shall not be less than three months but which may extend to one year, or with fine which shall not be less than ten thousand rupees but which may extend to twenty thousand rupees, or with both [Section 9(2)].

However, where the offence relates to non-payment of any gratuity payable under this Act, the employer shall be punishable with imprisonment for a term which shall not be less than six months but which may extend to two years unless the court trying the offence, for reasons to be recorded by it in writing, is of opinion that a lesser term of imprisonment or the imposition of a fine would meet the ends of justice [Section 9(2), proviso].

2. ***Exemption of employer from liability* [*Section 10*]** : The employer charged with an offence punishable under this Act can avoid his liability if he proves to the satisfaction of the court that :

(*a*) He has used his due diligence to exforce the execution of this Act, and

(*b*) Some other person has committed the offence without his knowledge, consent or connivance.

3. ***Cognizance of offences* [*Section 11*]** : A court shall take cognizance of any offence punishable under this Act only on a complaint made by or under the authority of appropriate Government [Section 11(1)].

In those cases, where the amount of gratuity has not been paid, or recovered, within six months from the expiry of the pescribed time, the appropriate Government shall authorise the controlling authority to make a complaint against the employer, where upon the controlling authority shall within fifteen days from the date of such authorisation, make such complaint to a magistrate having jurisdiction to try the offence [Section 11, proviso].

No court inferior to that of a Metropolitan Magistrate or a Judicial Magistrate of the first class shall try any offence punishable under this Act [Section 11 (2)].

53.6. APPROPRIATE GOVERNMENT'S POWERS TO MAKE RULES

The legal provisions in this regard are contained in Section 15, and may be stated as under :

1. The appropriate Government may, by notification, make rules for the purpose of carrying out the provisions of this Act.
2. Every rule made by the Central Government under this Act shall be laid, as soon as may be after it is made, before each House of Parliament while it is in session, for a total period of thirty days which may be comprised in one session or in two or more successive sessions, and if, before the expiry of the session immediately following the session or the successive sessions aforesaid, both Houses agree in making any modification in the rule or both Houses agree that the rule should not be made, the rule shall, thereafter, have effect only in such modified form or be of no effect, as the case may be; so, however, that any such modification or annulment shall be without prejudice to the validity of anything previously done under that rule.

TEST QUESTIONS

1. Discuss the provisions relating to 'compulsory insurance' and 'nominations' under the Payment of Gratuity Act, 1972.
2. Who can appoint inspectors under the Payment of Gratuity Act, 1972 ? Enumerate the powers of the inspectors.
3. Under what circumstances an employer can be held guilty of an offence under the Payment of Gratuity Act, 1972 ? How the employer can avoid his liability for an offence ?
4. Write short notes on :

   (*a*) Cognizance of offences under the Payment of Gratuity Act.

   (*b*) Appropriate Government's powers to make rules.

MULTIPLE CHOICE QUESTIONS

1. Which of the following statements is incorrect regarding nomination under the Payment of Gratuity Act ?

   (*a*) An employee may, in his nomination, distribute the amount of gratuity payable to him amongst more than one nominee.

   (*b*) If an employee has a family at the time of making nomination, the nomination must be made in favour of his family members only.

   (*c*) If an employee, having his family, makes nomination in favour of a person other than family member, the nomination shall be void.

   (*d*) If the nominee dies before the employee, the nominee's interest shall revert back to the employee who shall make a fresh nomination.
2. A nomination once made by an employee is final and cannot be modified later on.

   (*a*) True, as Section 6 of the Payment of Gratuity Act is clear on this point.

   (*b*) False, as the nomination can be modified by the employee at any time after giving a written notice to his employer of his intention to do so.
3. Any person who knowingly makes a false statement for the purpose of avoiding any payment to be made by himself under the Payment of Gratuity Act, 1972, shall be punishable with

(a) imprisonment upto six months or with fine upto Rs. 10,000 or with both.
(b) imprisonment upto six months and with fine upto Rs. 10,000.
(c) imprisonment upto one year or with fine upto Rs. 5,000 or with both.
(d) imprisonment upto one year and with fine upto Rs. 5,000.

4. An employer who is guilty of non-payment of any gratuity under the Payment of gratuity Act shall be punishable with minimum imprisonment of
(a) 3 months but not exceeding 6 months
(b) 6 months but not exceeding one year.
(c) 6 months but not exceeding two years
(d) one year but not exceeding two years.

5. An employer charged with an offence punishable under the Payment of Gratuity Act cannot avoid his liability.
(a) True, as the liability to pay gratuity being statutory, no relaxation is given under the Act.
(b) False, as Section 10 provides that if the employer proves to the satisfaction of the court that he has used his due diligence to enforce the Act and some other person has committed the offence.

ANSWERS

1. (c)	2. (b)	3. (a)	4. (d)	5. (b)

The Information Technology Act, 2000

- Introduction and Electronic Governance.
- Digital Signature and Digital Signature Certificate.
- Authorities Under the Act.
- Penalties, Adjudication and Offences.

54

CHAPTER

INTRODUCTION AND ELECTRONIC GOVERNANCE

54.1. INTRODUCTION

Now-a-days the information technology has assumed an important role in the business transactions all over the world. Business transactions are being made with the help of computer. Businessmen as well as individuals are increasingly using computers to create, transmit and store information in the electronic form instead of traditional paper documents. Information technology comprises of application of computers to create, store, process and use of information particularly in the field of commerce. Information stored in electronic form in cheaper. Also it is easier to store, retrieve and speedier to communicate the information. The information technology enables the corporate management to have access to timely, accurate and relevant data with the use of computers, communication, telephone, internet etc. which help better co-ordination and quick decision-making.

The 'statement of objects and reasons' appended to the Information Technology Bill, 2000 set out the following objects :

New communication systems and digital technology have made dramatic changes in the way we live. A revolution is occurring in the way people transact business. Business and consumers are increasingly using computers to create, transmit and store information in the electronic form instead of traditional paper documents. Information stored in electronic form has many advantages. It is cheaper, easier to store, retrieve and speedier to communicate. Although people are aware of these advantages, they are reluctant to conduct business or conclude any transaction in the electronic form due to lack of appropriate legal framework. The two principal hurdles which stand in the way of facilitating electronic commerce and electronic governance are the requirements as to writing and signature for legal recognition. At present many legal provisions assume the existence of paper based records and documents and records which should bear signatures. The Law of Evidence is traditionally based upon paper based records and oral testimony. Since electronic commerce eliminates the need for paper based transactions, hence to facilitate e-commerce, the need for legal changes have become an urgent necessity. International trade through the medium of e-commerce is growing rapidly in the past few years and many countries have switched over from traditional paper based commerce to e-commerce.

There is a need for bringing in suitable amendments in the existing laws in our country to facilitate e-commerce. It is, therefore, proposed to provide for legal recognition of electronic records and digital signatures. This will enable the conclusion of contracts and the creation of rights and obligations through the electronic medium. It is also proposed to provide for a regulatory regime to supervise the Certifying Authorities issuing Digital Signature Certificates. To prevent the possible misuse arising out of transactions and other dealings concluded over the electronic medium, it is also proposed to create civil and criminal liabilities for contravention of the provisions of the proposed legislation.

With a view to facilitate Electronic Governance, it is proposed to provide for the use and acceptance of electronic records and digital signatures in the Government offices and its agencies. This will make the citizens interaction with the Governmental offices hassle free.

The Information Technology Bill was passed by both Houses of Parliament and it received the assent of the President on 9th June, 2000 and became **The Information Technology Act, 2000 (21 of 2000).** The Act came into force on 17th October, 2000 vide G.S.R. 788 (E) dated 17th October, 2000.

The Information Technology Act, 2000 is based on the Model Law on Electronic Commerce which were adopted by the United Nations Commission on International Trade and Law (UNCITRAL) in 1996. The Model Laws provide for equal legal treatment of users of electronic communication and paper based communication.

In this chapter we shall discuss the objects and application of the Act, definitions of various terms used in the Act and other related provisions.

In this part of the book, unless otherwise specified, the Sections mentioned are those of the Information Technology Act, 2000.

54.2. OBJECTS OF THE ACT

The objects of the Information Technology Act, 2000 as provided in the preamble of the Act may be stated as under :

1. To provide legal recognition for transactions carried out by means of electronic data interchange and other means of electronic communications, commonly referred to as 'electronic commerce' which involves the use of alternative to paper based methods of communication and storage of information.
2. To facilitate electronic filing of documents with government agencies.
3. To provide the matters connected therewith or incidental thereto.

Thus, the Act has been enacted with a view of give boost to electronic commerce (e-commerce), e-transactions and similar activities associated with commerce and trade and also to facilitate electronic governance (e-governance) by means of reliable electronic records.

54.3 APPLICATION OF THE ACT

The Information Technology Act, 2000 extends to whole of India [Section 1(2)]. The provisions of the Act shall also apply to any offence or contravention committed outside India by any person irrespective of his nationality if the act or conduct constituting the offence or contravention involves a computer, computer system or computer network located in India [Sections 1(2) and 75]

The Act shall come into force on 17th October, 2000. Regarding applicability, Section 1(4) provides that the Act shall **not** apply to the following :

(*a*) A negotiable instrument (other than a cheque) as defined in section 13 of the Negotiable Instruments Act, 1881.

(*b*) A power-of-attorney as defined in section 1A of the Powers of Attorney Act, 1882.

(*c*) A trust as defined in section 3 of the Indian Trust Act, 1882.

(*d*) A Will as defined in clause (h) of section (2) of the Indian Succession Act, 1925, including any other testamentary disposition by whatever name called;

(*e*) Any contract for the sale or conveyance of immovable property or any interest in such property;

(*f*) Any such class of documents or transactions as may be notified by the Central Government in the Official Gazette.

54.4. DEFINITIONS OF THE TERMS USED IN THE ACT

The terms and expressions used in the Information Technology Act, 2000 are defined in various sub-sections of Section 2 of the Act and are discussed in the following pages :

1. Computer

The term 'computer' is defined in Section 2(1) (i) of the Act and for the purposes of this Act, it means any electronic, magnetic, optical or other high-speed data processing device or system which performs logical, arithmetic and memory functions by manipulations of electronic, magnetic or optical impulses, and includes all input, output, processing, storage, computer software or communication facilities which are connected or related to the computer in a computer system or computer network.

2. Computer network

The term 'computer network' is defined in Section 2(1) (j) of the Act and for the purposes of this Act, it means the interconnection of one or more computers through:

(*i*) the use of satellite, microwave, terrestrial line or other communication media; and

(*ii*) terminals or a complex consisting of two or more interconnected computers whether or not the interconnection is continuously maintained.

3. Computer resource

The term 'computer resource' is defined in Section 2(1) (k) of the Act and for the purposes of this Act, it means computer, computer system, computer network, data, computer data base or software.

4. Computer system

The term 'computer system' is defined in Section 2(1) (l) of the Act and for the purposes of this Act, it means a device or collection of devices, including input and output support devices and excluding calculators which are not programmable and capable of being used in conjunction with external files which contain computer programmes, electronic instructions, input data and output data that perform logic, arithmetic, data storage and retrieval, communication control and other functions.

5. Data

The term 'data' is defined in Section 2(1) (o) of the Act and for the purposes of this Act, it means a representation of information, knowledge, facts, concepts or instruction which are being prepared or have been prepared in a formalised manner, and is intended to be processed, is being processed or has been processed in a computer system or computer network, and may be in any form (including computer printouts magnetic or optical storage media, punched cards, punched tapes) or stored internally in the memory of the computer.

6. Electronic form

The term 'electronic form' is defined in Section 2(1) (r) of the Act and with reference to information it means any information generated, sent, received or stored in media, magnetic, optical, computer memory, micro film, computer generated micro fiche or similar device.

7. Electronic gazette

The term 'electronic gazette' is defined in Section 2(1) (*s*) of the Act and for the purposes of this Act it means the Official Gazette published in electronic form.

8. Electronic record

The term 'electronic record' is defined in Section 2(1) (*t*) of the Act and for the purposes of this Act, it means data, record or data generated, image or sound stored, received or sent in an electronic form or micro film or computer generated micro fiche.

9. Function

The term 'function' is defined in Section 2(1) (*u*) of the Act and in relation to a computer, it includes logic, control, arithmetical process, deletion, storage and retrieval and communication or telecommunication from or within a computer.

10. Information

The term 'information' is defined in Section 2(1) (*v*) of the Act and it includes data, text, images, sound, voice, codes, computer programmes, software and data bases or micro film or computer generated micro fiche.

11. Digital signature

The term 'digital signature' is defined in Section 2(1) (*p*) of the Act and for the purpose of this Act. it means authentication of any electronic record by a subscriber by means of an electronic method or procedure in accordance with the provisions of section 3.

12. Affixing digital signature

The expression 'affixing digital signature' is defined in Section 2(1) (*d*) of the Act and for the purposes of this Act, it means adoption of any methodology or procedure by a person for the purposes of authenticating an electronic record by means of digital signature.

13. Digital signature certificate

The expression 'digital signature certificate' is defined in Section 2(1) (*g*) of the Act and it means a Digital Signature Certificate issued under Section 35 (4) of this Act.

14. Access

The term 'access' is defined in Section 2(1) (*a*) of the Act and for the purposes of this Act, it means gaining entry into, instructing or communicating with the logical, arithmetical or memory function resources of a computer, computer system or computer network.

15. Originator

The term 'originator' is defined in Section 2(1) (*za*) of the Act, and for the purposes of this Act, it means a person who sends, generates, stores or transmits any electronic message; or causes any electronic message to be sent, generated, stored or transmitted to any other person but does not include an intermediary.

16. Intermediary

The term 'intermediary' is defined in Section 2(1) (*w*) of the Act, and with respect to any particular electronic message, it means any person who on behalf of another person receives, stores or transmits that message or provides any service with respect to that message.

17. Addressee

The term 'addressee' is defined in Section 2(1) (*b*) of the Act and for the purpose of this Act, it means a person who is intended by the originator to receive the electronic record but does not include any intermediary.

18. Private key

The term 'private key' is defined in Section 2(1) (*zc*) of the Act and it means the key of a key pair used to create a digital signature.

19. Public key

The term 'public key' is defined in Section 2(1) (*zd*) of the Act and it means the key of a key pair used to verify a digital signature and listed in the Digital Signature Certificate.

20. Key pair

The term 'key pair' is defined in Section 2(1) (*x*) of the Act and, in an asymmetric crypto system it means a private key and its mathematically related public key, which are so related that the public key can verify a digital signature created by the private key.

21. Asymmetric crypto system

The expression 'asymmetric crypto system' is defined in Section 2(1) (*d*) of the Act and it means a system of a secure key pair consisting of a private key for creating a digital signature and a public key to verify the digital signature.

22. Secure system

The term 'secure system' is defined in Section 2(1) (*ze*) of the Act and for the purposes of this Act, it means computer hardware, software, and procedure that—

(*a*) are reasonably secure from unathorised access and misuse;
(*b*) provide a reasonable level of reliability and correct operation;
(*c*) are reasonably suited to performing the intended function; and
(*d*) adhere to generally accepted security procedures.

23. Verify

The term 'verify' is defined in Section 2(1) (*zh*) of the Act and in relation to a digital signature, electronic record or public key, with its grammatical variations and cognate expressions, it means to determine whether—

(*a*) the initial electronic record was affixed with the digital signature by the use of private key corresponding to the public key of the subscriber;

(*b*) the initial electronic record is retained intact or has been altered since such electronic record was so affixed with the digital signature.

24. Subscriber

The term 'subscriber' is defined in Section 2(1) (*zg*) of the Act and it means a person in whose name the Digital Signature Certificate is issued.

25. Security procedure

The term 'security procedure' is defined in Section 2(1) (*zf*) of the Act and it means the security procedure prescribed under Section 16 of this Act by the Central Government.

26. Licence

The term 'licence as defined in Section 2(1) (*z*) means a licence granted to a Certifying Authority under Section 24 of this Act.

27. Prescribed

The term 'prescribed as per Section 2(1) (*zb*) means prescribed by the rules made under this Act.

28. Controller

As per Section 2(1) (*m*) it means the Controller of Certifying Authorities appointed under Section 17(1) of this Act.

29. Cyber Appellate Tribunal

As per Section 2(1) (*n*), it means The Cyber Regulations Appellate Tribunal established under Section 48(1) of this Act.

30. Certifying Authority

As per Section 2(1) (*g*), it means a person who has been granted a licence to issue a Digital Signature Certificate under Section 24 of this Act.

31. Adjudicating Officer

As per Section 2(1) (*c*), it means an Adjudicating Officer appointed under Section 46(1) of this Act.

32. Certification practice statement

The expression 'certification practice statement' is defined in Section 2(1) (h) of the Act, and it means a statement issued by a Certifying Authority to specify the practice that the Certifying Authority employs in issuing Digital Signature Certificate.

54.5 ELECTRONIC GOVERNANCE

1. *Legal recognition of electronic records [Section 4]*
2. *Legal recognition of digital signature [Section 5]*
3. *Use of electronic records and digital signatures in government and its agencies [Section 6]*
4. *Retention of electronic records [Section 7]*
5. *Publication of rules, regulation etc. in electronci Gazette [Section 8]*
6. *No right to insist that the document should be accepted in electronic form [Section 9]*
7. *Central Government's powers to make rules in respect of digital signature [Section 10]*

The object of the Information Technology Act, 2000 is to provide legal recognition for transactions carried out by means of electronic data interchange and other means of electronic communication commonly referred to as 'electronic commerce'.

The Act facilitates electronic governance to accord legal recognition to electronic record, digital signatures, and electronic form of dealing with government offices and its agencies.

Following legal provisions relating to the electronic governance are provided in the Act:

1. *Legal recognition of electronic records* **[Section 4]:** Where any law provides that information or any other matter shall be in writing or in the typewritten or printed form, then, inspite of anything contained in

such law, such requirement shall be deemed to have been satisfied if such information or matter is —

(*a*) rendered or made available in an electronic form; and

(*b*) accessible so as to be usable for a subsequent reference.

2. ***Legal recognition of digital signature*** **[Section 5]:** Where any law provides that information or any other matter shall be authenticated by affixing the signature or any document shall be signed or bear the signature of any person, then, inspite of anything contained in such law, such requirement shall be deemed to have been satisfied, if such information or matter is authenticated by means of *digital signature* affixed in such manner as may be prescribed by the Central Government.

For the purposes of this section, "signed", with its grammatical variations and cognate expressions, shall, with reference to a person, mean affixing of his hand written signature or any mark on any document and the expression "signature" shall be construed accordingly [Section 5, Explanation]

The 'digital signature' and legal provisions thereto will be discussed in the next chapter.

3. ***Use of electronic records and digital signatures in government and its agencies*** **[*Section 6*]:** Where any law provides for the following requirements *i.e.*,

(*a*) the filing of any form, application or any other document with any office, authority, body or agency owned or controlled by the appropriate Government in a particular manner;

(*b*) the issue or grant of any licence, permit, sanction or approval by whatever name called in a particular manner;

(*c*) the receipt or payment of money in a particular manner,

then, inspite of anything contained in any other law for the time being in force, such requirement shall be deemed to have been satisfied if such filing, issue, grant, receipt or payment, as the case may be, is effected by means of such electronic form as may be prescribed by the appropriate Government [Section 6(1)].

The appropriate Government, may, by rules prescribe—

(*a*) the manner and format in which such electronic records shall be filed, created or issued;

(*b*) the manner or method of payment of any fee or charges for filing, creation or issue any electronic record under.

4. ***Retention of electronic records*** **[*Section 7*]:** Where any law provides that documents, records or information shall be retained for any specific period, then, that requirement shall be deemed to have been satisfied if such documents, records or information are retained in the electronic form, if—

(*a*) the information contained therein remains accessible so as to be usable for a subsequent reference;

(*b*) the electronic record is retained in the format in which it was originally generated, sent or received or in a format which can be demonstrated to represent accurately the information originally generated, sent or received;

(*c*) the details which will facilitate the identification of the origin, destination, date and time of despatch or receipt of such electronic record are available in the electronic record:

However, the above provision does not apply to any information which is automatically generated solely for the purpose of enabling an electronic record to be despatched or received [Section 7(1)]

This section shall also not apply to any law that expressly provides for the retention of documents, records or information in the form of electronic records [Section 7(2)].

5. ***Publication of rules, regulation etc. in electronic Gazette*** [*Section 8*] : Where any law provides that any rule, regulation, order, bye-law, notification or any other matter shall be published in the Official Gazette, then, such requirement shall be deemed to have been satisfied if such rule, regulation, order, bye-law, notification or any other matter is published in the Official Gazette or Electronic Gazette:

However, where any rule, regulation, order, by-law, notification or any other matter is published in the Official Gazette or Electronic Gazette, the date of publication shall be deemed to be the date of the Gazette which was first published in any form.

6. ***No right to insist that the document should be accepted in electronic form*** [*Section 9*]: The provisions of Sections 6, 7 and 8 discussed in points 3, 4 and 5 above shall not confer a right upon any person to insist that any Ministry or Department of the Central Government or the State Government or any authority or body established by or under any law or controlled or funded by the Central or State Government should accept, issue, create, retain and preserve any document in the form of electronic records or effect any monetary transaction in the electronic form.

7. ***Central Government's powers to make rules in respect of digital signature*** [*Section 10*] : In respect of the digital signature, the Central Government may, by rule, prescribe:

(*a*) the type of digital signature;

(*b*) the manner and format in which the digital signature shall be affixed;

(*c*) the manner or procedure which facilitates identification of the person affixing the digital signature;

(*d*) control processes and procedures to ensures adequate integrity, security and confidentiality of electronic records or payments; and

(*e*) any other matter which is necessary to give legal effect to digital signatures.

54.6. ATTRIBUTION, ACKNOWLEDGEMENT AND DISPATCH OF ELECTRONIC RECORDS

1. *Attribution of electronic records*
2. *Acknowledgement of receipt*
3. *Time and place of dispatch and receipt of electronic record*

Under the Information Technology Act, 2000 it is important to know, (a) when the electronic record is considered to be attributed to the originator? (*b*) how the acknowledgement of receipt of electronic record is given and when such acknowledgement is required? and (*c*) how to determine the time and place of dispatch and receipt of electronic record?

The legal provisions in this regard are contained in Section 11, 12 and 13 of the Act and may be discussed as under :

1. ***Attribution of electronic records*** [*Section 11*] : An electronic record shall be attributed to the originator, if it was sent:

(*a*) by the originator himself

(*b*) by a person who had the authority to act on behalf of the originator in respect of that electronic record; or (*c*) by an information system programmed by or on behalf of the originator to operate automatically.

For the definition of 'originator' refer to Art 54.4 on Definitions.

2. ***Acknowledgement of receipt* [*Section 12*]:** Section 12 makes the following provision regarding the form of acknowledgement and the circumstances when the electronic record is considered to have been sent by the originator:

(*a*) *Form and method of acknowledgement receipt* [*Section 12 (1)*]: Where the originator has not agreed with the addressee that the acknowledgement of receipt of electronic record be given in a particular form or by a particular method, an acknowledgement may be given by—

(*i*) any communication by the addressee, automated or otherwise; or

(*ii*) any conduct of the addressee, sufficient to indicate to the originator that the electronic record has been received.

(*b*) Stipulation by originator binding himself [*Section 12*(2)]: Where the originator has stipulated that the electronic record shall be binding only on receipt of an acknowledgement of such electronic record by him, then, unless acknowledgement has been so received, the electronic record shall be deemed to have been never sent by the originator.

(*c*) No stipulation by originator binding himself [*Section 12*(3)] : Where the originator has not stipulated that the electronic record shall be binding only on receipt of such acknowledgement, and the acknowledgement has not been received by the originator within the time specified or agreed or, if no time has been specified or agreed to within a reasonable time, then, the originator may give notice to the addressee stating that no acknowledgement has been received by him and specifying a reasonable time by which the acknowledgement must be received by him and if no acknowledgement is received within the aforesaid time limit he may after giving notice to the addressee, treat the electronic record as though it has never been sent.

3. ***Time and place of dispatch and receipt of electronic record* [*Section 13*] :** The originator and the addressee may themselves agree about the time and place of dispatch and receipt of electronic record. If there is no such agreement, then it is governed by the following rules as provided in Section 13 of the Act.

(*a*) *Dispatch of electronic record* [*Section 13*(1)]: Save as otherwise agreed to between the originator and the addressee, the despatch of an electronic record occurs when it enters a computer resource outside the control of the originator.

(*b*) Time of receipt of electronic record [*Section 13*(2)] :

Save as otherwise agreed between the originator and the addressee, the time of receipt of an electronic record shall be determined as follows, namely:—

(*i*) if the addressee has designated a computer resource for the purpose of receiving electronic records,—

(*a*) receipt occurs at the time when the electronic record enters the designated computer resource; or

(*b*) if the electronic record is sent to a computer resource of the addressee that is not the designated computer resource, receipt occurs at the time when the electronic record is retrieved by the addressee;

(*ii*) if the addressee has not designated a computer resource along with specified timings, if any, receipt occurs when the electronic record enters the computer resource of the addressee.

(*iii*) ***Place of dispatch and receipt of electronic record*** **[*Section 13* (3)]:** Save as otherwise agreed to between the originator and the addressee, an electronic record is deemed to be dispatched at the place where the originator has his place of business, and is deemed to be received at the place where the addressee has his place of business.

Notes : 1. The provisions of sub-section (2) discussed in point (b) above shall apply inspite of that the place where the computer resource is located may be different from the place where the electronic record is deemed to have been received under Section 13(3) [Section 13 (4)].

2. For the purposes of section 13 discussed above

(*a*) if the originator or the addressee has more than one place of business, the principal place of business, shall be the place of business;

(*b*) if the originator or the addressee does not have a place of business, his usual place of residence shall be deemed to be the place of business;

(*c*) "usual place of residence", in relation to a body corporate, means the place where it is registered. [Section 13 (5)].

TEST QUESTIONS

1. State the objects of the Information Technology Act and explain the provisions relating to applicability of the Act.

2. Define the terms 'computer resource' and 'computer system' Enumerate the documents to which the Information Technology Act does not apply.

3. What do you mean by 'electronic form' and 'electronic record' ? Also explain the expression 'data' as defined in Section 2(1) (o) of the Information Technology Act, 2000.

4. What do you mean by electronic governance ? Explain the provisions of the Information Technology Act relating to electronic governance.

5. Write short note on the following as used in the Information Technology Act, 2000:

(*a*) Attribution of electronic record (*b*) Acknowledgement of receipt

(*c*) Dispatch of electronic record (*d*) Originator and intermediary

MULTIPLE CHOICE QUESTIONS

1. The Information Technology Act, 2000 come into force on :

(*a*) 9th June, 2000 (*b*) 17th October, 2000

(*c*) 15th December, 2000 (*d*) none of these

2. The Information Technology Act, 2000 extends to whole of India and it shall also apply to any offence or contravention committed outside India.

(*a*) True, if the act or conduct constituting offence involves a computer, computer system or computer network located in India [Section 75].

(*b*) False, as Section 1(2) specifically states that it extends to the whole of India and not outside India.

3. The Information Technology Act shall not apply to

(*a*) a negotiable instrument other than a cheque.

(*b*) a power of attorney

(*c*) any contract for the sale of immovable property

(*d*) all of the above

4. A person who is intended by the originator to receive the electronic record is, under the IT Act, known as
   (*a*) intermediary (*b*) originator's agent
   (*c*) addressee (*d*) keyholder
5. Any person who on behalf of another person receives, stores or transmits a message is, under the IT Act, 2000, known as
   (*a*) intermediary (*b*) originator
   (*c*) addressee (*d*) none of these
6. The key of a key pair used to create a digital signature is known as
   (*a*) public key (*b*) private key
   (*c*) creator key (*d*) secret key
7. The key of a key pair used to verify a digital signature is known as
   (*a*) public key (*b*) private key
   (*c*) verifying key (*d*) secret key

ANSWERS

1. (*b*) **2.** (*a*) **3.** (*d*) **4.** (*c*) **5.** (*a*)
6. (*b*) **7.** (*a*)

55
CHAPTER

DIGITAL SIGNATURE AND DIGITAL SIGNATURE CERTIFICATE

55.1. INTRODUCTION

The digital signature are the electronic equivalent of the handwritten signatures used for authentication of electronic records. Since in an electronic message or transaction affixing of handwritten signature is not possible, authentication has to be achieved by some electronic or digital method. The digital signature facilitates such authentication.

In this chapter, we shall discuss the meaning of 'digital signature', legal provisions relating to the issue of 'digital signature certificate' and the duties of subscribers.

55.2. DIGITAL SIGNATURE

The term 'digital signature' means authentication of any electronic record by a *subscriber* by means of an electronic method or procedure in accordance with the provisions of Section 3 of the Act [Section 2 (1) (*p*)].

Subscriber is a person in whose name the Digital Signature Certificate is issued by the Certifying Authority [Section 2(1) (*zg*).

Following points are important to note in connection with digital signature:

1. *Affixing digital signature* [*Section 2*(*1*) (*d*)]: It means the adoption of any methodology or procedure by a person for the purposes of authenticating an electronic record by means of digital signature.

2. *Authentication of electronic records by subscribers* [*Section 3*]: A subscriber is a person in whose name the Digital Signature Certificate is issued [Section 2(1) (*zg*)]. Any subscriber may authenticate an electronic record by affixing his digital signature [Section 3(1)]. Section 3 makes the following provisions regarding authentication of electronic records:

***(a) 'Asymmetric crypto system' and 'hash function'* [*Section 3*(*2*)]:** In case of electronic transmission of business or legal message and documents, it is necessary to ensure that these are authentic and have not been tempered with by any person during transmission. Keeping this in view, Section 3(2) provides that the authentication of the electronic record shall be effected by the use of '*asymmetric crypto system*' and '*hash function*' which develop and transform the initial electronic record into another electronic record. These two terms are explained below :

(*i*) **Asymmetric crypto system:** It means a system of a secure key pair consisting of a private key for creating a digital signature and a public key to verify the digital signature [Section 2(1) (f)]. It is the system of 'encryption' (coding) and 'decryption' (decoding) methodologies and software tools.

In 'asymmetric crypto system' each person will have two corresponding and matched keys, one called the 'private key' which is always kept secure with such person, and the other called the 'public key' which the person shares with others and makes available to others on specialised databases called 'repositories' or through Certification Authorities.

The public and private keys are used for encryption (coding) and decryption (decoding) of the messages respectively. The sender uses the intended receiver's public key (which he can freely obtain from the receiver or download from a public repository) to encrypt the message. The receiver on receiving the message uses his corresponding key (which is available only with him) to decrypt the encrypted message. The public key and the private key of any person or entity would be so mathematically linked that a message encrypted using one key can only be decrypted by using the other corresponding key.

(*ii*) **Hash function:** It is defined in Section 3(2), Explanation, and it means an algorithm mapping or translation of one sequence of bits into another, generally smaller, set known as "hash result" such that an electronic record yields the same hash result every time the algorithm is executed with the same electronic record as its input making it computationally infeasible—

(*a*) to derive or reconstruct the original electronic record from the hash result produced by the algorithm;

(*b*) that two electronic records can produce the same hash result using the algorithm.

(*b*) **Verification:** Any person by the use of a public key of the subscriber can verify the electronic record [Section 3(3)]. The private key and the public key are unique to the subscriber and constitute a functioning key pair [Section 3(4)].

55.3. DIGITAL SIGNATURE CERTIFICATE

The Digital Signatures Certificate is issued by the Certifying Authority under Section 35 of the Act. The purpose of this certificate is to authenticate the identity of an individual. It ensures that the purported send is in fact the person who sent the message. It is signed digitally by the Certifying Authority.

55.4. LEGAL PROVISIONS RELATING TO ISSUE OF DIGITAL SIGNATURE CERTIFICATE

1. ***Application to Certifying Authority [Section 35 (1) (2) (3)]***
2. ***Grant of Digital Signatures Certificate [Section 35 (4)]***
3. ***Representations by the Certifying Authority upon the issue of certificate [Section 36]***
4. ***Suspension of Digital Signature Certificate [Section 37]***
5. ***Revocation of Digital Signature Certificate [Section 38]***
6. ***Notice of suspension or revocation [Section 39]***

The legal provisions relating to the issue of such certificate and other related matters, as contained in different sections, may be discussed as under :

1. *Application to Certifying Authority* [*Section 35* (*1*) (*2*) (*3*)] : Any person may make an application to the Certifying Authority for the issue of a Digital Signature Certificate in such form as may be prescribed by the Central Government [Section 35 (1)]. The following points are important in connection with the application :

(*a*) Every such application shall be accompanied by such fee not exceeding twentyfive thousand rupees as may be prescribed by the Central Government, to be paid to the Certifying Authority. However, different fees may be prescribed for different classes of applicants [Section 35(2)].

(*b*) Every such application shall be accompanied by a certification practice statement or where there is no such statement, a statement containing such particulars, as may be specified by regulations [Section 35(3)].

Note: For 'certification practice statement' refer to Art. 54.4 on 'Definition'.

2. ***Grant of Digital Signatures Certificate*** **[*Section 35(4)*] :** On receipt of an application for issue of Digital Signature Certificate, the Certifying Authority may, after consideration of the certification practice statement or the other statement referred above and after making such enquiries as it may deem fit, grant the Digital Signature Certificate or for reasons to be recorded in writing, reject the application.

However, no Digital Signature Certificate shall be granted unless the Certifying Authority is satisfied that—

(*a*) the applicant holds the private key corresponding to the public key to be listed in the Digital Signature Certificate;

(*b*) the applicant holds a private key, which is capable of creating a digital signature;

(*c*) the public key to be listed in the certificate can be used to verify a digital signature affixed by the private key held by the applicant:

It may also be noted that no application shall be rejected unless the applicant has been given a reasonable opportunity of showing cause against the proposed rejection.

3. ***Representations by the Certifying Authority upon the issue of certificate*** **[*Section 36*] :** A Certifying Authority while issuing a Digital Signature Certificate shall certify that—

(*a*) it has complied with the provisions of this Act and the rules and regulations made thereunder;

(*b*) it has published the Digital Signature Certificate or otherwise made it available to such person relying on it and the subscriber has accepted it;

(*c*) the subscriber holds the private key corresponding to the public key, listed in the Digital Signature Certificate;

(*d*) the subscriber's public key and private key constitute a functioning key pair;

(*e*) the information contained in the Digital Signature Certificate is accurate; and

(*f*) it has no knowledge of any material fact, which if it had been included in the Digital Signature Certificate would adversely affect the reliability of the representations in clauses (*a*) to (*d*).

4. ***Suspension of Digital Signature Certificate*** **[*Section 37*] :** The Certifying Authority which has issued a Digital Signature Certificate may suspend such Digital Signature Certificate, in the following cases:

(*a*) on receipt of a request to that effect from—

(*i*) the subscriber listed in the Digital Signature Certificate; or

(*ii*) any person duly authorised to act on behalf of that subscriber;

(*b*) if it is of opinion that the Digital Signature Certificate should be suspended in public interest.

A Digital Signature Certificate shall not be suspended for a period exceeding fifteen days unless the subscriber has been given an opportunity of being heard in the matter [Section 37(2)]. On suspension of a Digital Signature Certificate under this section, the Certifying Authority shall communicate the same to the subscriber [Section 37(3)].

5. *Revocation of Digital Signature Certificate* [*Section 38*] : A Certifying Authority may revoke a Digital Signature Certificate, issued by it, in the following cases [Section 38(1)] :

(*a*) where the subscriber or any other person authorised by him makes a request to that effect; or

(*b*) upon the death of the subscriber; or

(*c*) upon the dissolution of the firm or winding up of the company where the subscriber is a firm or a company.

A Certifying Authority may also revoke a Digital Signature Certificate which has been issued by it **at any time,** if it is of opinion that—

(*a*) a material fact represented in the Digital Signature Certificate is false or has been concealed;

(*b*) a requirement for issuance of the Digital Signature Certificate was not satisfied;

(*c*) the Certifying Authority's private key or security system was compromised in a manner materially affecting the Digital Signature Certificate's reliability;

(*d*) the subscriber has been declared insolvent or dead or where a subscriber is a firm or a company, which has been dissolved, wound-up or otherwise ceased to exist [Section 38(2)].

A Digital Signature Certificate shall not be revoked unless the subscriber has been given an opportunity of being heard in the matter [Section 38 (3)]. On revocation of a Digital Signature Certificate under this section, the Certifying Authority shall communicate the same to the subscriber [Section 38(4)].

6. *Notice of suspension or revocation* [*Section 39*] : Where a Digital Signature Certificate is suspended or revoked under section 37 or section 38, the Certifying Authority shall publish a notice of such suspension or revocation, as the case may be, in the repository specified in the Digital Signature Certificate for publication of such notice [Section 39(1)].

Where one or more repositories are specified, the Certifying Authority shall published notices of such suspension or revocation, as the case may be, in all such repositories [Section 39(2)].

55.5. DUTIES OF SUBSCRIBERS

1. *Generating key pair [Section 40]*
2. *Acceptance of Digital Signature Certificate [Section 42 (1)]*
3. *Certification of facts [Section 41 (1)]*
4. *Control of Private key. [Section 42]*

A 'subscriber' means a person in whose name the Digital Signature Certificate is issued [Section 2(1)zg].

The duties of the subscribers who have obtained the Digital Signature Certificate from some Certifying Authority, are contained in different sections of the Act, and may be discussed under the following heads:

1. *Generating key pair* [*Section 40*]: Where any Digital Signature Certificate, the public key of which corresponds to the private key of that subscriber which is to be listed in the Digital Signature Certificate has been accepted by a subscriber, the subscriber shall generate that key pair by applying the security procedure.

2. *Acceptance of Digital Signature Certificate* [*Section 41* (*1*)] : A subscriber shall be deemed to have accepted a Digital Signature Certificate in the following cases:

(*i*) If he publishes or authorise the publication of a Digital Signature Certificate:

(*a*) to one or more persons,

(*b*) in a repository, or

(*ii*) If he otherwise demonstrate his approval of the Digital Signature Certificate in any manner.

3. *Certification of facts* [*Section 41(2)*]: By accepting a Digital Signature Certificate, the subscriber certifies to all who reasonably rely on the information contained in the Digital Signature Certificate that—

(*a*) the subscriber holds the private key corresponding to the public key listed in the Digital Signature Certificate and is entitled to hold the same;

(*b*) all representations made by the subscriber to the Certifying Authority and all material relevant to the information contained in the Digital Signature Certificate are true;

(*c*) all information in the Digital Signature Certificate that is within the knowledge of the subscriber is true.

4. *Control of private key.* [*Section 42*] : Every subscriber shall exercise reasonable care to retain control of the private key corresponding to the public key listed in his Digital Signature Certificate and take all steps to prevent its disclosure.

If the private key corresponding to the public key listed in the Digital Signature Certificate has been compromised, then, the subscriber shall communicate the same without any delay to the Certifying Authority in such manner as may be specified by the regulations. It may be noted that the subscriber shall be liable till he has informed the Certifying Authority that the private key has been compromised.

TEST QUESTIONS

1. What do you mean by 'digital signature'? How can electronic record be authenticated under the Information Technology Act, 2000 ?
2. Define the 'Digital Signature Certificate'. Explain the provisions of the Information Technology Act, 2000 relating to the issue of such certificate.
3. What do you mean by 'subscriber' ? What are the duties of subscriber under the Information Technology Act, 2000 ?
4. Write short notes on the following:

   (*a*) Grant of Digital Signature Certificate

   (*b*) Suspension of Digital Signature Certificate

   (*c*) 'Asymmetric Crypto System' and 'Hash Function'.

   (*d*) Subscribers' duty of control of private key

MULTIPLE CHOICE QUESTIONS

1. An electronic record, under the IT Act, 2000, can be authenticated by the subscriber by:

   (*a*) affixing his digital signature (*b*) preserving private key

   (*c*) verification (*d*) both (*b*) and (*c*)

2. A 'subscriber' is a person in whose name the 'digital signature certificate' is issued under the IT Act, 2000.

   (*a*) True, as Section 2(1) (zg) of the Act defines so.

   (*b*) False, as subscriber is a person who issues such certificate.

3. The Digital Signature Certificate under the IT Act, 2000 is issued by the :

(*a*) Controller (*b*) Certifying Authority

(*c*) Appellate Tribunal (*d*) Cyber Authority

4. An application for the issue of Digital Signature Certificate should be accompanied by the prescribed fee not exceeding :

(*a*) Rs. 15,000 (*b*) Rs. 20,000

(*c*) Rs. 25,000 (*d*) Rs. 30,000

5. Which of the following statements is incorrect?

(*a*) The Certifying Authority issuing the Digital Signature Certificate may suspend it on receipt of a request to that effect from the subscriber.

(*b*) The Certifying Authority issuing the Digital Signature Certificate certifies that subscriber's public key and private key constitute a functioning key pair.

(*c*) The Certifying Authority issuing the Digital Signature Certificate may revoke it upon the death of the subscriber.

(*d*) The Digital Signature Certificate once issued cannot be revoked by the Certifying Authority as the power of revocation is vested in the Cyber Appellate Tribunal.

ANSWERS

1. (*a*)	**2.** (*a*)	**3.** (*b*)	**4.** (*c*)	**5.** (*d*)

56 CHAPTER

AUTHORITIES UNDER THE ACT

1. Introduction.
2. Regulation of Certifying Authorities.
3. Controller of Certifying Authorities.
4. Powers of Controller.
5. Certifying Authority.
6. Licence to Act a Certifying Authority.
7. Duties of Certifying Authority.
8. Adjudicating Officer.
9. Cyber Appellate Tribunal.
10. Appeal to Cyber Appellate Tribunal.
11. Procedure and Powers of Cyber Appellate Tribunal.
12. Appeal to High Court.

56.1. INTRODUCTION

The 'Authorities' are required for the effective implementation and enforcement of the provisions of any Act. The Information Technology Act, 2000 provides for the appointment of following authorities:

1. Controller of Certifying Authorities
2. Certifying Authority
3. Adjudicating Officer
4. Cyber Appellate Authority

The provisions relating to appointment, functions, powers and duties of these authorities will be discussed in detail in this chapter.

56.2 REGULATION OF CERTIFYING AUTHORITIES

Sections 17 to 34 contained in Chapter VI of the Information Technology Act, 2000 make provisions relating to regulation of certifying authorities. These provisions may be grouped under the following heads:

1. Controller of Certifying Authorities : Appointment, Functions, Powers and Duties.
2. Certifying Authority : Licence to act as certifying authority, procedure, duties.

These provisions are discussed in detail in the following pages.

56.3 CONTROLLER OF CERTIFYING AUTHORITIES

1. *Appointment of Controller*
2. *Functions of Controller*
3. *Controller to act as repository*

The provisions of the Act relating to Controller may be discussed under the following heads:

1. *Appointment of Controller* : The Controller of Certifying Authorities is appointed by the Central Government. Section 17(1) of the Act provides that the Central Government may, by notification in the Official Gazette, appoint a Controller of Certifying Authorities for the purposes of this Act and may also by the same or subsequent notification, appoint such number of Deputy Controllers and Assistant Controllers as it deems fit.

Other provisions relating to controller, as contained in Section 17, are as under :

(*a*) The controller shall discharge his functions under this Act subject to general control and directions of the Central Government [Section 17(2)].

(*b*) The Deputy Controllers and Assistant Controllers shall perform the functions assigned to them by the Controller under the general superintendence and control of the Controller [Section 17(3)].

(*c*) The qualifications, experience and terms and conditions of service of Controller, Deputy Controllers and Assistant Controllers shall be such as may be prescribed by the Central Government [Section 17(4)].

(*d*) The Head Office and Branch Office of the office, of the Controller shall be at such places as the Central Government may specify, and these may be established at such places as the Central Government may think fit. [Section 17(5)].

(*e*) There shall be a seal of the Office of the Controller [Section 17(6)].

2. *Functions of Controller* [*Section 18*]: Functions of the Controller are provided in Section 18 of the Act. The Controller may perform all or any of the following functions, namely:—

(*a*) exercising supervision over the activities of the Certifying Authorities;

(*b*) certifying public keys of the Certifying Authorities;

(*c*) laying down the standards to be maintained by the Certifying Authorities;

(*d*) specifying the qualifications and experience which employees of the Certifying Authority should possess;

(*e*) specifying the conditions subject to which the Certifying Authorities shall conduct their business;

(*f*) specifying the contents of written, printed or visual materials and advertisements that may be distributed or used in respect of a Digital Signature Certificate and the public key;

(*g*) specifying the form and content of a Digital Signature Certificate and the key;

(*h*) specifying the form and manner in which account shall be maintained by the Certifying Authorities;

(*i*) specifying the terms and conditions subject to which auditors may be appointed and the remuneration to be paid to them;

(*j*) facilitating the establishment of any electronic system by a Certifying Authority either solely or jointly with other Certifying Authorities and regulation of such systems;

(*k*) specifying the manner in which the Certifying Authorities shall conduct their dealings with the subscribers;

(*l*) resolving any conflict of interests between the Certifying Authorities and the subscribers;

(*m*) laying down the duties of the Certifying Authorities;

(*n*) maintaining a database containing the disclosure record of every Certifying Authority containing such particulars as may be specified by regulations, which shall be accessible to public.

3. *Controller to act as repository* [*Section 20*] : A 'repository' is an online database of Digital Signature Certificate and other related information useful for those who conduct their business operations through the medium of computer internet or e-commerce. Section 20 makes the following provisions in this regard:

(*a*) The Controllers shall be the repository of all Digital Signature Certificate issued under this Act [Section 20(1)].

(*b*) In order to ensure that the secrecy and security of the digital signatures are assured, the controller shall

(*i*) make use of hardware, software and procedures that are secure from intrusion and misuse;

(*ii*) observe such other standards as may be prescribed by the Central Government [Section 20(2)].

(*c*) The Controller shall maintain a computerised data base of all public keys in such a manner that such data base and the public keys are available to any member of the public [Section 20(3)].

56.4. POWERS OF CONTROLLER

1. *Power to recognise a foreign Certifying Authority*
2. *Power to delegate*
3. *Power to investigate contraventions*
4. *Power to have access to computers and data*
5. *Power to give directions so Certifying Authority*
6. *Power to give directions to a government agency*
7. *Power to grant licence to issue Digital Signature Certificate*
8. *Power to revoke or suspend licence of a Certifying Authority*

The powers of Controller of Certifying Authorities, as contained in various sections of the Act, may be discussed under the following sub-heads:

1. ***Power to recognise a foreign Certifying Authority*** **[*Section 19*]** : The Controller may, with the previous approval of the Central Government, and by notification in the Official Gazette, recognise any foreign Certifying Authority as a Certifying Authority for the purposes of this Act. The Controller may specify the restrictions for recognition [Section 19(1)].

On such recognition, the Digital Signature Certificate issued by such Certifying Authority shall be valid for the purposes of this Act [Section 19(2)].

The Controller may, if he is satisfied that any Certifying Authority has contravened any of the conditions and restrictions subject to which it was granted recognition as stated above, he may, for reasons to be recorded in writing, by notification in the Official Gazette, revoke such recognition [Section 19(3)].

2. ***Power to delegate*** **[*Section 27*]** : The Controller may, in writing, authorise the Deputy Controller, Assistant Controller or any officer to exercise any of his powers.

3. ***Power to investigate contraventions*** **[*Section 28*]** : The Controller or any officer authorised by him in this behalf has the power to take up for investigation any contravention of the provisions of this Act, rules or regulations made thereunder [Section 28(1)].

The Controller or any officer authorised by him in this behalf shall exercise the like powers which are conferred on Income-tax authorities under Chapter XIII of the Income-tax Act, 1961, and shall exercise such powers, subject to such limitations laid down under that Act [Section 28(2)].

4. ***Power to have access to computers and data*** **[*Section 29*]** : The Controller or any person authorised by him shall, if he has reasonable cause to suspect that any contravention of the provisions of this Act, rules or regulations made thereunder has been committed, have access to any computer system, any apparatus, data or any other material connected with such system, for the purpose of searching or causing a search to be made for obtaining any information or data contained in or available to such computer system [Section 29(1)].

The Controller or any person authorised by him may also, by order, direct any person incharge of, or otherwise concerned with the operation of, the computer system, data apparatus or material, to provide him with such reasonable technical and other assistance as he may consider necessary [Section 29(2)].

5. ***Power to give directions to Certifying Authority*** **[*Section 68(1)*]**: The Controller may by order, give directions to a Certifying Authority or any employee of such Authority to take such measures or to stop carrying such activities as specified in the order if those are necessary to ensure compliance with the provisions of this Act, rules or any regulation made thereunder.

6. ***Power to give directions to a government agency*** **[*Section 69(1)*]**: The Controller may, by order, give directions to any agency of the government to intercept any information transmitted through any computer resource (*i.e.*, computer system or computer network etc.) if it is necessary or expedient in the interest of the sovereignity or integrity of India, the security of the State, friendly relations with foreign State or public order or for preventing incitement to the commission of any cognizable offence.

7. ***Power to grant licence to issue Digital Signature Certificate*** **[*Section 24*]** : The Controller has the power to grant a licence to a person to issue Digital Signature Certificate. A person to whom such a licence is granted is called the Certifying Authority. The legal provisions relating to grant of such licence will be discussed in detail in Art 56.6.

8. ***Power to revoke or suspend licence of a Certifying Authority*** **[*Section 25*]** : The Controller also has the power to revoke or suspend the licence granted to a person to act as a Certifying Authority. For detail on the point refer to Art. 56.6.

56.5. CERTIFYING AUTHORITY

The 'Certifying Authority' means a person to whom a licence has been granted by the Controller to issue Digital Signature Certificate [Section 2(1) (g)].

Thus, a person becomes a Certifying Authority when a licence is granted to him by the Controller of Certifying Authorities. The grant of such licence and the duties of a Certifying Authority are discussed in detail in the following pages.

56.6. LICENCE TO ACT AS CERTIFYING AUTHORITY

1. *Application for grant of licence to act as Certifying Authority*
2. *Procedure for grant or rejection of licence*
3. *Renewal of licence*
4. *Revocation or suspension of licence*
5. *Notice of suspencsion or revocation of licence*

The legal provisions relating to the grant of such licence and other related matters, as contained in different sections, may be discussed as under :

1. *Application for grant of licence to act as Certifying Authority* **[*Section 21 & 22*]** : Any person may make an application to the Controller for grant of a licence to issue Digital Signature Certificate [Section 21(1)]. The applicant should fulfill such requirements with respect to qualification, expertise, manpower, financial resources and other infrastructure facilities which are necessary to issue Digital Signature Certificate as may be prescribed by the Central Government [Section 21(2)].

Following points are important to note in connection with application for licence:

(*i*) Every application for issue of a licence shall be in such form as may be prescribed by the Central Government [Section 22(1)].

(*ii*) Every application for issue of a licence shall be accompanied by—

(*i*) a certification practice statement;

(*ii*) a statement including the procedures with respect to identification of the applicant;

(*iii*) payment of such fees, not exceeding twenty-five thousand rupees as may be prescribed by the Central Government;

(*iv*) such other documents, as may be prescribed by the Central Government [Section 22(2)].

Note : For definition of certification practice statement refer to Art 54.4 on Definitions.

2. *Procedure for grant or rejection of licence* [*Section 24*]: On receipt of an application for grant of licence, the Controller may after considering the documents accompanying the application and such other factors, as he deems fit, grant the licence or reject the application. However, no application shall be rejected under this section unless the applicant has been given a reasonable opportunity of presenting his case.

A licence granted by the Controller shall:

(*a*) be valid for such period as may be prescribed by the Central Government;

(*b*) not be transferable or heritable;

(*c*) be subject to such terms and conditions as may be specified by the regulations [Section 21(3)].

3. *Renewal of licence* [*Section* 23] : An application for renewal of a licence shall be—

(*a*) in such form;

(*b*) accompanied by such fees, not exceeding five thousand rupees,

as may be prescribed by the Central Government and shall be made not less than forty-five days before the date of expiry of the period of validity of the licence.

4. *Revocation or suspension of licence* [Section 25]: Legal provisions in this regard are as under :

(*a*) ***Revocation of a licence* [Section 25(1)]:** The Controller may revoke the licence if, after making an inquiry, he is satisfied that a Certifying Authority has—

(*i*) made a statement in, or in relation to, the application for the issue or renewal of the licence, which is incorrect or false in material particulars;

(*ii*) failed to comply with the terms and conditions subject to which the licence was granted;

(*iii*) failed to maintain the procedures and standards specified in* section 30;

(*iv*) contravened any provisions of this Act, rule, regulation or order made thereunder;

However, no licence shall be revoked unless the Certifying Authority has been given a reasonable opportunity of showing cause (*i.e.*, reasons) against the proposed revocation.

(b) *Suspension of a licence* [Section 25(2)]: The Controller may, if he has reasonable cause to believe that there is any ground for revoking a licence under sub-section (1), by order, suspend such licence pending the completion of any enquiry ordered

* The procedure specified in Section 30 will be discussed in Art 56.7

by him [Section 25(2)]. However, no licence shall be suspended for a period exceeding ten days unless the Certifying Authority has been given a reasonable opportunity of showing cause against the proposed suspension.

No Certifying Authority whose licence has been suspended shall issue any Digital Signature Certificate during such suspension [Section 25(3)].

5. *Notice of suspension or revocation of licence* [Section 26]: This section makes the following provisions regarding notice of suspension or revocation:

(*a*) Where the licence of the Certifying Authority is suspended or revoked, the Controller shall publish notice of such suspension or revocation, as the case may be, in the data base maintained by him [Section 26 (1)].

(*b*) Where one or more repositories are specified, the Controller shall published notices of such suspension or revocation, as the case may be, in all such repositories [Section 26(2)].

(*c*) The data base containing the notice of such suspension or revocation, as the case may be, shall be made available through a web site which shall be accessible round the clock [Section 26, proviso first].

(*d*) The Controller may, if he considers necessary, publicise the contents of data base in such electronic or other media, as he may consider appropriate [Section 26, proviso second]

56.7. DUTIES OF THE CERTIFYING AUTHORITY

1. ***Duty to follow certain procedures***
2. ***Duty to ensure compliane of the Act***
3. ***Duty to display licence***
4. ***Duty to surrender licence***
5. ***Duty to disclose***
6. ***Duty to notify occurrence of an adverse event***

The duties of a Certifying Authority, as contained in different sections of the Act, may be discussed under the following heads:

1. *Duty to follow certain procedures* [Section 30] : In performance of its job, every Certifying Authority shall follow certain procedures relating to security of system. Section 30 provides that every Certifying Authority shall:

(*a*) make use of hardware, software, and procedures that are secure from intrusion and misuse;

(*b*) provide a reasonable level of reliability in its services which are reasonably suited to the performance of intended functions;

(*c*) adhere to security procedures to ensures that the secrecy and privacy of the digital signatures are assured; and

(*d*) observe such other standards as may be specified by regulations.

2. *Duty to ensure compliance of the Act* [*Section 31*]: Every certifying Authority shall ensure that every person employed or otherwise engaged by it complies, in the course of his employment or engagement, with the provisions of this Act, rules, regulations or orders made thereunder.

3. *Duty to display licence* [*Section 32*]: Every Certifying Authority shall display its licence at a conspicuous place of the premises in which it carries on its business.

4. *Duty to surrender licence* [*Section 33(1)*]: Every Certifying Authority shall surrender its licence to the controller immediately after its suspension or revocation.

5. *Duty to disclose* [*Section 34(1)*]: In a manner specified by the regulations, every Certifying Authority shall disclose the following:

(a) its Digital Signature Certificate which contains the public key corresponding to the private key used by that Certifying Authority to digitally sign another Digital Signature Certificate;

(b) any certification practice statement relevant thereto;

(c) notice of the revocation or suspension of its Certifying Authority certificate, if any; and

(d) any other fact that materially and adversely affects either the reliability of a Digital Signature Certificate, which that Authority has issued or the Authority's ability to perform its services.

6. Duty to notify occurrence of an adverse event [*Section 34*(2)] : The Certifying Authority shall make reasonable efforts to notify any person who is likely to be affected by the occurrence of any event which in its opinion, may materially and adversely affect the integrity of its computer system or the conditions subjects to which a Digital Signature Certificate was granted.

The Certifying Authority may also act in accordance with the procedure specified in its certification practice statement to deal with such event or situation.

56.8. ADJUDICATING OFFICER

An 'Adjudicating Officer' is appointed by the Central Government for the purposes of adjudging whether any person has committed a contravention of any of the provisions of this Act or any rule, regulation, direction or order made thereunder.

The Adjudicating Officer is appointed for holding inquiry in the manner prescribed by the Central Government and for imposing penalty or award compensation in accordance with the provisions of the Act [Section 46]

Other provisions relating to Adjudication Officers will be discussed in detail in Chapter 57.

56.9. CYBER APPELLATE TRIBUNAL

1. *Establishment of Cyber Appellate Tribunal*
2. *Compsotion of Cyber Appellate Tribunal*
3. *Qualifications for appointment as Presiding Officer of the Cyber Appellate Tribunal*
4. *Term of office*
5. *Salary, allowances and other terms and conditions of service of Presiding Officer*
6. *Filling up of vacancies*
7. *Resignation and removal*
8. *Orders constituting Appllate Tribunal to be final and not be invalidate its proceedings*
9. *Staff of the Cyber Appellate Tribunal*
10. *Civil court not to have jurisdication*

The Cyber Appellate Tribunal is an appellate authority established under the Information Technology Act, 2000 for the purposes of hearing appeals against the orders passed by the Controller or an Adjudicating Officer. An appeal against the order of the Cyber Appellate Tribunal lies to the High Court.

The provisions relating to establishment constitution, staff, procedure, powers etc. of the Cyber Appellate Provisions are contained in Chapter X (Section 48 to 64) of the Act and may be discussed as under:

1. *Establishment of Cyber Appellate Tribunal* [*Section 48*] : The Central Government shall, by notification, establish one or more appellate tribunals to be known as the Cyber Regulations Appellate Tribunal [Section 48(1)].

The Central Government shall also

specify, in the notification, the matters and places in relation to which the Cyber Appellate Tribunal may exercise jurisdiction [Section 48(2)].

2. ***Composition of Cyber Appellate Tribunal* [*Section 49*]:** A Cyber Appellate Tribunal shall consist of one person only (hereinafter referred to as the Presiding Officer of the Cyber Appellate Tribunal) to be appointed, by notification, by the Central Government.

3. ***Qualifications for appointment as Presiding Officer of the Cyber Appellate Tribunal* [*Section 50*]:** A person shall not be qualified for appointment as the Presiding Officer of a Cyber Appellate Tribunal unless he—

(*a*) is, or has been, or is qualified to be, a Judge of a High Court; or

(*b*) is, or has been, a member of the Indian Legal Service and is holding or has held a post in Grade I of that Service for at least three years.

4. ***Term of office* [*Section 51*]:** The Presiding Officer of a Cyber Appellate Tribunal shall hold office for a term of five years from the date on which he enters upon his office or until he attains the age of sixty-five years whichever is earlier.

5. ***Salary, allowances and other terms and conditions of services of Presiding Officer* [*Section 52*]:** The salary and allowances payable to, and the other terms and conditions of service including pension, gratuity and other retirement benefits of, the Presiding Officer of a Cyber Appellate Tribunal shall be such as may be prescribed:

Provided that neither the salary and allowances nor the other terms and conditions of service of the Presiding Officers shall be varied to his disadvantage after appointment.

6. ***Filling up of vacancies* [*Section 53*]:** If, for reason other than temporary absence, any vacancy occurs in the office of the Presiding Officer of a Cyber Appellate Tribunal, then the Central Government shall appoint another person in accordance with the provisions of this Act to fill the vacancy and the proceedings may be continued before the Cyber Appellate Tribunal from the stage at which the vacancy is filled.

7. ***Resignation and removal* [*Section 54*]:** The Presiding Officer of a Cyber Appellate Tribunal may, by notice in writing under his hand addressed to the Central Government, resign his office [Section 54(1)]. However the said Presiding Officer shall, unless he is permitted by the Central Government to relinquish his office sooner, continue to hold office until the expiry of three months from the date of receipt of such notice or until a person duly appointed as his successor enters upon his office or until the expiry of his term of office, whichever is the earliest [Section 54(1), proviso].

The Presiding Officer of a Cyber Appellate Tribunal shall not be removed from his office except by an order by the Central Government on the ground of proved misbehaviour or incapacity after an inquiry made by a Judge of the Supreme Court in which the Presiding Officer concerned has been informed of the charges against him and given a reasonable opportunity of being heard in respect of these charges [Section 54(2)].

The Central Government may, by rules, regulate the procedure for the investigation of misbehaviour or incapacity of the aforesaid Presiding Officer [Section 54(3)].

8. ***Orders constituting Appellate Tribunal to be final and not to invalidate its proceedings* [*Section 55*]:** No order of the Central Government appointing any person as the Presiding Officer of a Cyber Appellate Tribunal shall be called in question in any manner and no act or proceeding before a Cyber Appellate Tribunal shall be called in question in any manner on the ground merely of any defect in the constitution of a Cyber Appellate Tribunal.

9. ***Staff of the Cyber Appellate Tribunal* [*Section 56*]:** The Central Government shall provide the Cyber Appellate Tribunal with such officers and employees as that Government

may think fit. [Section 56(1)]. The officers and employees of the Cyber Appellate Tribunal shall discharge their functions under general superintendence of the Presiding Officer [Section 56(2)].

The salaries, allowances and other conditions of service of the officers and employees of the Cyber Appellate Tribunal shall be such as may be prescribed by the Central Government. [Section 56(3)].

10. *Civil court not to have jurisdiction* [*Section 61*]: No court shall have jurisdiction to entertain any suit or proceeding in respect of any matter which an adjudicating officer appointed under this Act or the Cyber Appellate Tribunal constituted under this Act is empowered by or under this Act to determine and no injunction shall be granted by any court or other authority in respect of any action taken or to be taken in pursuance of any power conferred by or under this Act.

56.10. APPEAL TO CYBER APPELLATE TRIBUNAL

Any person aggrieved by an order made by controller or an adjudicating officer under this Act may prefer an appeal to a Cyber Appellate Tribunal having jurisdiction in the matter [Section 57(1)].

Other important provisions relating to the appeals to the Appellate Tribunal may be stated as under:

1. No appeal shall lie to the Cyber Appellate Tribunal from an order made by an adjudicating officer with the consent of the parties [Section 57(2)].
2. Every appeal shall be filed within a period of forty-five days from the date on which a copy of the order made by the Controller or the adjudicating officer is received by the person aggrieved and it shall be in such form and be accompanied by such fee as may be prescribed [Section 57(3)].

   However, the Cyber Appellate Tribunal may entertain an appeal after the expiry of the said period of forty-five days if it is satisfied that there was sufficient cause for not filing it within that period [Section 57(3), proviso].
3. On receipt of an appeal, the Cyber Appellate Tribunal may, after giving the parties to the appeal, an opportunity of being heard, pass such orders thereon as it thinks fit, confirming, modifying or setting aside the order appealed against [Section 57(4)].
4. The Cyber Appellate Tribunal shall sent a copy of every order made by it to the parties to the appeal and to the concerned Controller or adjudicating officer [Section 57(5)].
5. The appeal filed before the Cyber Appellate Tribunal shall be dealt with by it as expeditiously as possible and endeavour shall be made by it to dispose of the appeal finally within six months from the date of receipt of the appeal [Section 57(6)].

56.11. PROCEDURE AND POWERS OF CYBER APPELLATE TRIBUNAL

The provisions relating to procedure and powers of the Cyber Appellate Tribunal are laid down in Section 58 of the Act and may be discussed as under :

1. *Procedure* [*Section 58(1)*]: The Cyber Appellate Tribunal shall not be bound by the procedure laid down by the Code of Civil Procedure, 1908, but shall be guided by the principles of natural justice. And, subject to the other provisions of this Act and of any rules, the Cyber Appellate Tribunal shall have powers to regulate its own procedure including the place at which it shall have its sittings.

2. ***Powers*** **[*Section 58*(2)]**: The Cyber Appellate Tribunal shall have, for the purposes of discharging its functions under this Act, the same powers as are vested in a civil court under the Code of Civil Procedure, 1908, while trying a suit, in respect of the following matters, namely:—

(*a*) summoning and enforcing the attendance of any person and examining him on oath;

(*b*) requiring the discovery and production of documents or other electronic records;

(*c*) receiving evidence on affidavits;

(*d*) issuing commissions for the examination of witnesses or documents;

(*e*) reviewing its decisions;

(*f*) dismissing an application for default or deciding it *ex parte*;

(*g*) any other matter which may be prescribed.

Every proceeding before the Cyber Appellate Tribunal shall be deemed to be a judicial proceeding within the meaning of sections 193 and 228, and for the purposes of section 196 of the Indian Penal Code (45 of 1860) and the Cyber Appellate Tribunal shall be deemed to be a civil court for the purposes of section 195 and Chapter XXVI of the Code of Criminal Procedure, 1973 [Section 58(3)].

56.12. APPEAL TO HIGH COURT

Any person aggrieved by any decision or order of the Cyber Appellate Tribunal may file an appeal to the High Court within sixty days from the date of communication of the decision or order of the Cyber Appellate Tribunal to him on any question of fact or law arising out of such order [Section 62].

However, the High Court may, if it is satisfied that the appellant was prevented by sufficient cause from filing the appeal within the said period, allow it to be filed within a further period not exceeding sixty days [Section 62, proviso].

TEST QUESTIONS

1. State the authorities appointed under the Information Technology Act, 2000. Briefly explain the provisions relating to their appointments.

2. How and by whom the Controller of Certifying Authorities is appointed under the Information Technology Act ? State the functions of the Controller.

3. Explain the powers conferred on the Controller under the Information Technology Act, 2000.

4. What do you mean by 'Certifying Authority'? Discuss the provisions relating to the grant of licence to act as Certifying Authority.

5. Cyber Appellate Tribunal is an appellate authority — Discuss in detail specifying the provisions of the Information Technology Act, 2000.

6. Write notes on the following under the Information Technology Act, 2000.

(*a*) Duties of Certifying Authority

(*b*) Appeal to Cyber Appellate Tribunal

(*c*) Procedure and Powers of Cyber Appellate Tribunal

(*d*) Appeal to High Court

MULTIPLE CHOICE QUESTIONS

1. Which of the following statements, under the IT Act, 2000, is incorrect?

(*a*) Controller of Certifying Authorities is appointed by the Central Government.

(*b*) Certifying authority is appointed by the Controller.
(*c*) Adjudicating Officer is appointed by the Controller.
(*d*) Cyber Appellate Tribunal is established by the Central Government.

2. Which of the following powers is not vested in the Controller of Certifying Authorities?
(*a*) Power to recognise a Foreign Certifying Authority.
(*b*) Power to investigate contraventions. (*c*) Power to impose penalty for offences.
(*d*) Power to grant licence to issue Digital Signature Certificate.

3. The Certifying Authority under the IT Act, 2000 means a person
(*a*) to whom a licence has been granted by the Controller to issue Digital Signature Certificate.
(*b*) appointed by the Central Government to act as such authority.
(*c*) appointed by the Cyber Appellate Tribunal to certify the appeals filed before it.
(*d*) who is appointed for holding inquiry in case of contravention of the provisions of the Act.

4. An appeal against the order made by Controller or an adjudicating officer should be filed before the Cyber Appellate Tribunal within how many days of the receipt of copy of such order?
(*a*) 30 days (*b*) 45 days (*c*) 60 days (*d*)90 days

5. An appeal against the decision or order of the Cyber Appellate Tribunal, under the IT Act, 2000, lies to
(*a*) Cyber Regulations Appellate Tribunal (*b*) Super Cyber Appellate Tribunal
(*c*) Commissioner of Appeals (*d*) High Court

ANSWERS

1. (*c*)	**2.** (*c*)	**3.** (*a*)	**4.** (*b*)	**5.** (*d*)

PENALTIES, ADJUDICATION AND OFFENCES

57.1. INTRODUCTION

The penalties are imposed upon persons who contravene the provisions of the Act. A duly appointed officer is required for adjudication and imposing penalties. Contravention of certain provisions amounts to criminal offence for which punishment by way of imprisonment and fine is imposed.

In this chapter we shall discuss the legal provisions relating to penalties, adjudication and offences as provided in different provisions of the Information Technology Act, 2000.

57.2. PENALTIES

1. *Penalty for damage to computer, computer system etc.*
2. *Penalty for failure to furnish information, return etc.*
3. *Penalty for residuary contraventions.*

The legal provisions relating to penalties are contained in Section 43 to 45 of the Act and may be discussed under the following heads:

1. ***Penalty for damage to computer, computer system etc.*** [*Section* 43]: Any person who, without permission of the owner or any other person who is incharge of a computer system or computer network, indulges in any of the following acts, shall be liable to pay damages by way of compensation not exceeding one crore rupees to the person so affected:

(*a*) accesses or secures access to such computer, computer system or computer network;

(*b*) downloads, copies or extracts any data, computer data base or information from such computer, computer system or computer network including information or data held or stored in any removable storage medium;

(*c*) introduces or causes to be introduced any computer contaminant or computer virus into any computer, computer system or computer network;

(*d*) damages or causes to be damaged any computer, computer system or computer network, data, computer data base or any other programmes residing in such computer, computer system or computer network;

(*e*) disrupts or causes disruption of any computer, computer system or computer network;

(*f*) denies or causes the denial of access to any person authorised to access any computer, computer system or computer network by any means;

(*g*) provides any assistance to any person to facilitate access to a computer, computer system or computer network in contravention of the provisions of this Act, rules or regulations made thereunder ;

(*h*) charges the services availed of by a person to the account of another person by tempering with or manipulating any computer, computer system, or computer network.

For the purposes of this section the expressions 'computer contaminant' 'computer database', 'computer virus' and 'damage' have been defined as under in the Explanation of Section 43:

(*i*) "computer contaminant" means any set of computer instructions that are designed—

(*a*) to modify, destroy, record, transmit data or programme residing within a computer, computer system or computer network; or

(*b*) by any means to usurp the normal operation of the computer, computer system, or computer network;

(*ii*) "computer database" means a representation of information, knowledge, facts, concepts or instructions in text, image, audio, video that are being prepared or have been prepared in a formalised manner or have been produced by a computer, computer system or computer network and are intended for use in a computer, computer system or computer network;

(*iii*) "computer virus" means any computer instruction, information, data or programme that destroys, damages, degrades or adversely affects the performance of a computer resource or attaches itself to another computer resource and operates when a programme, data or instruction is executed or some other event takes place in that computer resource;

(*iv*) "damage" means to destroy, alter, delete, add, modify or rearrange any computer resource by any means.

2. ***Penalty for failure to furnish information, return etc.*** **[*Section 44*]:** If any person who is required under this Act or any rules or regulations made thereunder to—

(*a*) furnish any document, return or report to the Controller or the Certifying Authority fails to furnish the same, he shall be liable to a penalty not exceeding one lakh and fifty thousand rupees for each such failure;

(*b*) file any return or furnish any information, books or other documents within the time specified therefor in the regulations fails to file return or furnish the same within the time specified therefor in the regulations, he shall be liable to a penalty not exceeding five thousand rupees for every day during which such failure continues;

(*c*) maintain books of account or records, fails to maintain the same, he shall be liable to a penalty not exceeding ten thousand rupees for every day during which the failure continues.

3. *Penalty for residuary contraventions* [*Sections 45*]: Whoever contravenes any rules or regulations made under this Act, for the contravention of which no penalty has been separately provided, shall be liable to pay a compensation not exceeding twenty-five thousand rupees to the person affected by such contravention or a penalty not exceeding twenty-five thousand rupees.

57.3. ADJUDICATION

1. *Power to adjudicate*
2. *Appointment of adjudicating officers*
3. *Decision by adjudicating officer*
4. *Adjudicating officer to have powers of a civil court*
5. *Factors to be taken into account by the adjudicating officer*

The legal provisions relating to adjudication are contained in Sections 46 and 47 of the Act and may be discussed under the following heads :

1. *Power to adjudicate* [*Section 46(1)*] : The power of adjudication has been vested in the adjudicating officer appointed by the Central Government.

2. *Appointment of adjudicating officers* [*Sections 46(1) (3)*]: For the purposes of adjudging whether any person has committed a contravention of any of the provisions of this Act or of any rule, regulation, direction or order made thereunder, the Central Government shall appoint an officer to be an adjudicating officer for holding an inquiry. Following points are important to note in connection with the adjudicating officer:

(*a*) An officer to be appointed as adjudicating officer should not be below the rank of a Director to the Government of India or an equivalent officer of a State Government [Section 46(1)].

(*b*) An adjudicating officer shall hold an inquiry in the manner prescribed by the Central Government.

(*c*) No person shall be appointed as an adjudicating officer unless he possesses such experience in the field of Information Technology and legal or judicial experience as may be prescribed by the Central Government [Section 46(3)].

(*d*) Where more than one adjudicating officers are appointed, the Central Government shall specify by order the matters and places with respect to which such officers shall exercise their jurisdiction [Section 46(4)].

3. *Decision by adjudicating officer* [*Section 46(2)*]: The adjudicating officer shall, after giving the concerned person a reasonable opportunity for making representation in the matter and if on such inquiry, he is satisfied that the person has committed the contravention, he may impose such penalty or award such compensation as he thinks fit in accordance with the provisions of that section.

4. *Adjudicating officer to have powers of a civil court* [*Section 46(5)*]: Every adjudicating officers shall have the powers of a civil court which are conferred on the Cyber Appellate Tribunal under sub-section (2) of section 58, and—

(*a*) all proceedings before it shall be deemed to be *judicial proceedings* within the meaning of sections 193 and 228 of the Indian Penal Code, 1860.

(*b*) shall be deemed to be a *civil court* for the purposes of sections 345 and 346 of the Code of Criminal Procedure, 1973.

Powers of Cyber Appellate Tribunal have already been discussed in Art. 56.11

5. *Factors to be taken into account by the adjudicating officer* [*Section 47*]: While adjudging the quantum of compensation under this Chapter, the adjudicating officer shall have due regard to the following factors, namely:—

(*a*) the amount of gain of unfair advantage, wherever quantifiable, made as a result of the default;

(*b*) the amount of loss caused to any person as a result of the default;

(*c*) the repetitive nature of the default.

57.4. OFFENCES

1. *Tampering with computer source document*
2. *Heacking with computer system*
3. *Publishing of information which is obscene in electronic form*
4. *Securing access to protected system*
5. *Penalty for misrepresentation*
6. *Penalty for breach of confidentiality and privacy*
7. *Pendlty for publishing Digital Signature Certificate false in certain particulars*
8. *Pendalty for publishing for fraudulent purposes*
9. *Confiscation of articles*

Certain acts which are considered offences under the Information Technology Act, 2000 are detailed in Chapter XI (Sections 65 to 76) of the Act. These offences alongwith the penalty for the same are discussed hereunder :

1. ***Tampering with computer source document* [*Section 65*]:** Any person who knowingly or intentionally conceals, destroys or alters or intentionally or knowingly causes another to conceal, destroy, or alter any computer source code used for a computer, computer programme, computer system or computer network, when the computer source code is required to be kept or maintained by law for the time being in force, shall be punishable with imprisonment up to three years, or with fine which may extend up to two lakh rupees, or with both.

The expression, "computer source code" means the listing of programmes, computer commands, design and layout and programme analysis of computer resource in any form [*Section 65, Explanation*].

2. ***Hacking with computer system* [*Section 66*] :** Any person who with the intent to cause or knowing that he is likely to cause wrongful loss or damage to the public or any person, destroys or deletes or alters any information residing in a computer resource or diminishes its value or utility or affects it injuriously by any means, commits hacking [Section 66(1)].

The person who commits hacking shall be punished with imprisonment upto three years or with fine upto two lakh rupees or with both [Section 66(2)].

3. Publishing of information which is obscene in electronic form. [Section 67]: Any person who publishes or transmits or causes to be published in the electronic form, any material which is lascivious or appeals to the prurient interest or if its effect is such as to tend to deprave and corrupt persons who are likely, having regard to all relevant circumstance, to read, see or hear the matter contained or embodied in it, shall be punished as under:

(*a*) On first conviction with imprisonment of either description for a term which may extend to five years and with fine which may extend to one lakh rupees, and

(*b*) In the event of a second or subsequent conviction with imprisonment of either description for a term which may extend to ten years and also with fine which may extend to two lakh rupees.

4. ***Securing access to protected system*** **[*Section 70*]:** The appropriate Government may, by notification in the Official Gazette, declare that any computer, computer system or computer network to be a protected system. The appropriate Government may also by order in writing, authorise the persons who are authorised to: have access to such notified protected system [Section 70(1) (2)].

Any person who secures access or attempts to secure access to a protected system in contravention of the provisions of this section shall be punished with imprisonment of either description for a term which may extend to ten years and shall also be liable to fine [Section 70(3)].

5. ***Penalty for misrepresentation*** **[*Section 71*]:** Any person who makes any misrepresentation to, or suppresses any material fact from the Controller or the Certifying Authority for obtaining any licence or Digital Signature Certificate, as the case may be, shall be punished with imprisonment for a term which may extend to two years, or with fine which may extend to one lakh rupees, or with both.

6. ***Penalty for breach of confidentiality and privacy*** **[*Section 72*]:** Any person who, in pursuance of any of the powers conferred under this Act, rules or regulations made thereunder, has secured access to any electronic record, book, register, correspondence, information, document or other material without the consent of the person concerned, discloses such electronic record, book, register, correspondence, information, document or other material to any other person, shall be punished with imprisonment for a term which may extend to two years, or with fine which may extend to one lakh rupees, or with both.

7. ***Penalty for publishing Digital Signature Certificate false in certain particulars*** **[*Section 73*]:** No person shall publish a Digital Signature Certificate or otherwise make it available to any other person with the knowledge that—

(*a*) the Certifying Authority listed in the certificate has not issued it; or

(*b*) the subscriber listed in the certificate has not accepted it; or

(*c*) the certificate has been revoked or suspended,

unless such publication is for the purpose of verifying a digital signature created prior to such suspension or revocation [Section 73(1)]

Any person who contravenes the above provisions shall be punished with imprisonment for a terms which may extend to two years, or with fine which may extend to one lakh rupees, or with both [Section 73(2)].

8. ***Penalty for publication for fraudulent purposes*** **[*Section 74*]:** Any person who knowingly creates, publishes or otherwise makes available a Digital Signature Certificate for any fraudulent or unlawful purpose shall be punished with imprisonment for a term which may extend to two years, or with fine which may extend to one lakh rupees, or with both.

9. ***Confiscation of articles*** **[*Section 76*]:** Any computer, computer system, floppies, compact disks, tape drives or any other accessories related thereto, in respect of which any provision of this Act, rules, orders or regulations made thereunder has been or is being contravened, shall be liable to confiscation:

However, where it is established to the satisfaction of the court adjudicating the confiscation that the person in whose possession, power or control these articles are found, is not responsible for the contravention, the court may, instead of making an order for confiscation, make such other order as it may think fit.

Any penalty imposed or confiscation made under this Act shall not prevent the imposition of any other punishment to which the person affected thereby is liable under any other law for the time being in force [Section 77].

57.5. NETWORK SERVICE PROVIDER NOT TO BE LIABLE

Section 79 of the Act specifically declares that any person providing any service as a network service provider shall not be liable under this Act, rules or regulations made thereunder for any third party information or data made available by him if he proves that the offence or contravention was committed without his knowledge or that he had exercised all due diligence to prevent the commission of such offence or contravention.

Explanation. —For the purposes of this section,—

(*a*) "network service provider" means an intermediary;

(*b*) "third party information" means any information dealt with by a network service provider in his capacity as an intermediary.

57.6. OFFENCES BY COMPANIES

Sections 85 of the Act makes the following provisions regarding offences by companies:

1. Where a person committing a contravention of any of the provisions of this Act or of any rule, direction or order made thereunder is a company, every person who, at the time the contravention was committed, was in charge of, and was responsible to, the company for the conduct of business of the company as well as the company, shall be guilty of the contravention and shall be liable to be proceeded against and punished accordingly [Section 85(1)].

2. Nothing contained in above provision shall render any such person liable to punishment if he proves that the contravention took place without his knowledge or that he exercised all the due diligence to prevent such contravention [Section 85(1), proviso].

3. Where a contravention of any of the provisions of this Act or of any rule, direction or order made thereunder has been committed by a company and it is proved that the contravention has taken place with the consent or connivance of, or is attributable to any neglect on the part of, any director, manager, secretary or other officer of the company, such director, manager, secretary or other officer shall also be deemed to be guilty of the contravention and shall be liable to be proceeded against and punished accordingly [Section 85(2)].

4. *Explanation.*—For the purposes of this section,—

(*i*) "company" means any body corporate and includes a firm or other association of individuals; and

(*ii*) "director", in relation to a firm, means a partner in the firm.

TEST QUESTIONS

1. Explain the provisions of Section 43, 44 and 45 of the IT Act, 2000 relating to penalties for contravention.
2. How and by whom an adjudicating officer is appointed ? Discuss the provisions of the IT Act, 2000 relating to adjudication.
3. Discuss the provisions of the IT Act, 2000 relating to the (*a*) tampering with computer source document, (*b*) hacking with computer system and (*c*) publishing of obscene information in electronic form.
4. Write short notes on the following under the IT Act, 2000

(*a*) Confiscation of articles (*b*) Liability of Network Service Provider

(*c*) Offences by companies

MULTIPLE CHOICE QUESTIONS

1. Any person who, without the permission of the owner, damages any computer, computer system or computer network shall be liable to pay damages by way of compensation under the IT Act, 2000 upto:

(*a*) one lakh rupees (*b*) Ten lakh rupees
(*c*) one crore rupees (*d*) none of these

2. For the purpose of penalty due to damage under the IT Act, 2000, the term damage means:

(*a*) to destroy any computer resource
(*b*) to alter or delete any computer resource
(*c*) to modify or rearrange any computer resource
(*d*) all of the above

3. An adjudicating officer, under the IT Act, 2000, for holding inquiry and imposing penalty is appointed by the

(*a*) Controller (*b*) Central Government
(*c*) Cyber Appellate Tribunal (*d*) High Court

4. The tampering with computer source document is punishable under the IT Act, 2000, with

(*a*) imprisonment upto 3 years or fine upto two lakh rupees or both.
(*b*) imprisonment upto 2 years or fine upto one lakh rupees or both.
(*c*) imprisonment upto one year or fine upto Rs. 50,000 or both
(*d*) with fine only upto Rs. 50,000.

5. The person who commits 'hacking' under the IT Act, 2000 shall be punished with imprisonment upto three years or with fine upto two lakh rupees or with both.

(*a*) True, as this punishment is provided under Section 66 for the offence of hacking.
(*b*) False, as for the contravention of hacking only penalty upto Rs. 10,000 is imposed by the adjudicating officer.

ANSWERS

1. (*c*)	**2.** (*d*)	**3.** (*b*)	**4.** (*a*)	**5.** (*a*)